ROGET'S SUPER THESAURUS

Marc McCutcheon

WRITER'S DIGEST BOOKS
Cincinnati, Ohio

Roget's Superthesaurus. Copyright © 1995 by Marc McCutcheon. Printed and bound in the United States of America. All rights reserved. No part of this book may be reproduced in any form or by any electronic or mechanical means including information storage and retrieval systems without permission in writing from the publisher, except by a reviewer, who may quote brief passages in a review. Published by Writer's Digest Books, an imprint of F&W Publications, Inc., 1507 Dana Avenue, Cincinnati, Ohio, 45207. (800) 289-0963. First edition.

Other fine Writer's Digest Books are available from your local bookstore or direct from the publisher.

99 98 97 96   6 5 4 3

Library of Congress Cataloging-in-Publication Data

McCutcheon, Marc.
    Roget's superthesaurus / by Marc McCutcheon.—1st ed.
        p.   cm.
    ISBN 0-89879-658-X
    1. English language—Terms and phrases. I. Title.
PE1591.M416   1995
823'.1—dc20   94-34221
                                                                    CIP

Edited by William Brohaugh
Designed by Angela Lennert
Jacket design by Angela Lennert

DEDICATION

To my wonderful parents,

Mary and Errol McCutcheon

ABOUT THE AUTHOR

Marc McCutcheon is a writer and lexicographer

who lives in South Portland, Maine with his wife,

Deanna, and two children, Kara and Matthew.

His most recent books include

Descriptionary,

Writer's Guide to Everyday Life in the 1800s,

and

The Compass in Your Nose & Other

Astonishing Facts About Humans.

INTRODUCTION

You now hold in your hands what we feel is the most innovative and useful thesaurus on the market. It has been carefully crafted to provide:

. . . **a comprehensive bank of synonyms** to help you avoid repetitiveness and improve word accuracy. For example, did the man *walk*, *squelch* or *slog* through the mud? As every professional writer knows, the right synonym choice is crucial in adding power, depth and pizzaz to compositions.

. . . **a reverse dictionary component** to show you the exact word when you know what a thing is but not what the thing is called.

Beyond the need to locate synonyms for, say, CAT (kitty, feline, tabby, etc.) you'll sometimes need to know words used to accurately *describe* a cat. For instance, what do you call that white patch under a cat's neck? (Locket.) The white patches on the feet? (Mittens, gloves.) The reflective eye layer that glows in the dark? (Tapetum.) A mating cry? (Caterwaul.) One who loves cats? (Ailurophile.) This exclusive reverse dictionary component will, once and for all, stop you from calling something a "whatchmacallit," a "doohickey" or a "thingamajig." Astonishingly, it's the one extremely useful component that other thesauri have overlooked over the years, and only *Superthesaurus* has it.

. . . **a built-in vocabulary book.** Throughout the thesaurus, vocabulary words are CAPITALIZED, given a pronunciation key, and sampled in a sentence. No need to buy a separate vocabulary builder. *Superthesaurus* highlights hundreds of sharp words to help you bushwack your way out of the wilderness of Tarzan-like communication and into the vernacular of the world's greatest wordsmiths. Once again, no other thesaurus has this component. It's a *Superthesaurus* exclusive.

. . . **quotations that double as synonyms.** Many entries throughout *Superthesaurus* have them. For example, you may want to call MOUNTAINS hills or peaks, but if you really want to impress, why not quote Lord Byron and call them "The Palaces of Nature"? You'll find such quotes immediately following the normal list of synonyms.

. . . **antonyms.** For when you need the opposite of a synonym. For example, an antonym of ATTRACTIVE would be *Repulsive.* Antonyms are always listed at the very end of an entry.

Superthesaurus is arranged alphabetically. It has no space-wasting index to make itself look bigger than it really is. To find the word you want, simply turn to its order in the alphabet. Typically, you'll make just *one* reference stop instead of two or three, as is necessary in indexed formats.

Unlike most other thesauri, *Superthesaurus* includes many "minor" words as head entries. That way annoying cross references are greatly reduced. When you encounter a "minor" word, at least two or three synonyms are given in the hope that one of those words will be the one you need. That way you again sidestep the need for a time-consuming cross-reference.

Usages are divided by separate entries for adjective [*a.*], adverb [*adv.*], noun [*n.*], pronoun [*pron.*], verb [*v.*], and preposition [*prep.*] Separate senses within each part of speech are clearly delineated by number, by brief definition or definitive word or, occasionally, when meanings are closely-related, by a simple semi-colon between word lists. Slang or informal words are delineated by a simple [*] asterisk.

Use *Superthesaurus* to sharpen your writing in letters, reports, articles, novels and poetry. Use it to beef up your vocabulary, locate a quotation, or help you fill out that challenging crossword puzzle. The longer you use *Superthesaurus* the more you'll appreciate its extra features.

If you need synonyms, any old thesaurus will do. If you want to become a word master, turn to the one source that puts it all together: *Superthesaurus.*

A

aback TAKEN *a.* startled, taken unawares, surprised, confused, *thrown off guard.

abaft *a.* aft, astearn, rearward, behind, back.

abandon *n.* unrestraint, carelessness, free-spiritedness, spontaneity, wildness, wantonness, intemperance, impulsiveness, devil-may-care attitude. ANT. *restraint, reserve, restriction, self-consciousness.*

abandon *v.* leave, desert, discard, forsake, quit, dump, *turn one's back on, cast off, reject, relinquish, discontinue, renounce, lay aside, *leave in the lurch, *cut one's losses, *throw in the towel, strand, drop, give up, *wash one's hands of, *deep six, ditch. ANT. *stick with, take up, continue, adopt.*

abandoned *a.* **1.** DESERTED given up, forgotten, left behind, rejected, stranded, forsaken, cast off, cast aside, discarded, destitute, forgotten, scorned, desolate, friendless. **2.** UNRESTRAINED unreserved, uncontrolled, dissolute, wild, loose, immoral, wicked, shameless, licentious, lewd, wanton. ANT. *1. used, adopted, taken up, befriended. 2. restrained, reserved, moral, seemly.*

abase *v.* humble, humiliate, degrade, *prostrate oneself, deflate, *put down, debase, vitiate, devalue. ANT. *honor, *puff up.*

ABASHED *a.* [uh BASHED] embarrassed, ill at ease. *Mary spoke unabashedly about contraceptives.* SYN. embarrassed, ashamed, humiliated, red-faced, disconcerted, discomfitted, mortified, chagrined, disgraced. ANT. *reassured, relaxed, cool.*

ABATE *v.* [uh BATE] to subside, lessen, reduce. *The pain from a stubbed toe gradually abates.* SYN. subside, lessen, reduce, weaken, slacken, diminish, decrease, wane, dwindle, decline, let up, taper off. ANT. *grow, expand, intensify, surge.*

abattoir *n.* slaughterhouse, butchery.

abbey *n.* monastery, cloister, friary, convent, nunnery, ministry.

WORD FIND

area restricted to members: cloister
governed by prior or prioress: priory
orders: Benedictine, Dominican, Franciscan, Jesuit, Paulist, Trappist
resident: monk, friar, nun
superior or head: abbot, abbess

abbreviate *v.* shorten, abridge, condense, cut, reduce, contract, curtail, clip, compress, synopsize. ANT. *expand, broaden, enlarge.*

abbreviation *n.* shortening, condensation, abridgement, contraction, reduction, summary, synopsis, brief, abstract, short version, short form.

WORD FIND

ABCs: fundamentals, rudiments, basics, simple elements
AC: alternating current; air conditioning
A.D.: anno Domini; in the year of the Lord
aka: also known as
anon: anonymous
ASAP: as soon as possible
aux.: auxiliary
AWOL: absent without leave
B.A.: Bachelor of Arts
B.C.: before Christ
blvd.: boulevard
B.S.: Bachelor of Science
BTU: British thermal unit
BYOB: bring your own booze
CB: Citizens Band
C: Celsius, centigrade
c: copyright
Cdr.: Commander
CEO: chief executive officer
chm.: chairman
cl.: centiliter
cm.: centimeter
c/o: care of
co.: company
COD: cash on delivery
Col.: Colonel
corp.: corporation
CPA: certified public accountant
CPR: cardiopulmonary resuscitation
cu.: cubic
DA: district attorney
DC: direct current
D.D.: Doctor of Divinity
D.D.S.: Doctor of Dental Science
DOA: dead on arrival
Dr.: Doctor
DST: daylight-saving time
dt's: delerium tremens
EEG: electroencephalogram
e.g.: exempli gratia; for example
EKG: electrocardiogram
ERA: earned run average
ESP: extrasensory perception
Esq.: Esquire
et al: et alia; and others
etc.: etcetera; and so forth

F: Fahrenheit
FM: frequency modulation
f.o.b.: freight on board
FYI: for your information
g: gram
GIGO: garbage in, garbage out
GOP: Grand Old Party
HMS: His/Her Majesty's Ship
Hon.: Honorable
hq.: headquarters
ibid: ibidem; in the same place
i.e.: id est; that is
IQ: intelligence quotient
ISBN: International Standard Book Number
kg: kilogram
km: kilometer
l: liter
lb.: pound
LPN: licensed practical nurse
Ltd.: limited
M.A.: Master of Arts
MC: master of ceremonies
M.D.: Doctor of Medicine
mg: milligram
ml: milliliter
mm: millimeter
MO: modus operandi; method of operation
MP: Military Police
mph: miles per hour
ms.: manuscript
M.S.: Master of Science
M.S.W.: Master of Social Work
N/A: not applicable
oz.: ounce
PA: public address (system)
PC: personal computer
Ph.D.: Doctor of Philosophy
p.m.: post meridiem; afternoon
pp.: pages
pro tem: pro tempore, for the time being
P.S.: postscript
PX: post exchange
RBI: runs batted in
RFD: Rural Free Delivery
RIP: rest in peace
R.N.: registered nurse
rpm: revolutions per minute
RSVP: respondez s'il vous plait, please answer
Rx: pharmaceutical prescription
SASE: self-addressed stamped envelope
SOS: save our ship/souls
TBA: to be announced
TGIF: thank God it's Friday
TKO: technical knockout

UFO: unidentified flying object
VIP: very important person
viz.: videlicet, that is to say, namely
VP: vice president

ABDICATE v. [AB duh KATE] to relinquish, surrender or give up one's power, office or responsibilities. *The king abdicated in 1452.* SYN. relinquish, step down, retire, resign, renounce, yield, surrender, quit, abandon, repudiate, give up, withdraw. ANT. *usurp, assume power, take charge.*

abdomen n. stomach, belly, gut, midsection, paunch, tummy, *breadbasket, *spare tire, *middle-aged spread.

abdominal a. intestinal, visceral, duodenal.

abduct v. kidnap, steal away, seize, grab, spirit away, snatch, *shanghai.

aberrant a. abnormal, deviant, unusual, anomolous, irregular, unconventional, odd, freakish, weird, errant, peculiar. ANT. *normal, usual, typical, *par for the course.*

ABERRATION n. [AB uh RAY shun] something untypical, unusual or unexpected; a deviation from the norm. *A blizzard in Texas is an aberration of local weather patterns.* SYN. deviation, abnormality, irregularity, quirk, freak, nonconformity, departure, oddity, eccentricity. ANT. *norm, average, mean.*

ABET v. [uh BET] to incite, encourage or support, especially in the performance of a wrongdoing. *She was arrested for aiding and abetting a drug smuggler.* SYN. incite, encourage, support, sanction, conspire, goad, spur, endorse, promote, help. ANT. *discourage, prevent, prohibit, undermine.*

abettor n. assistant, co-conspirator, inciter, instigator, confederate, accomplice, accessory, *partner in crime.

abeyance n. suspension, cessation, inaction, intermission, pause, latency, remission, dormancy, quiescence. ANT. *continuance, continuation, prolongation.*

ABHOR v. [ab HOR] to hate, detest or be disgusted by. *We abhor bigots.* SYN. hate, detest, loathe, despise, view with horror, scorn, shrink from, be sickened by, feel disgust for. ANT. *love, cherish, embrace.*

abhorrent a. loathsome, detestable, despicable, disgusting, abominable, horrible, sickening, nauseating, hateful, repulsive, offensive, repugnant, heinous. ANT. *nice, attractive, good, commendable, admirable.*

abide v. **1.** TO WAIT FOR await, stand fast, stay, remain, bide. **2.** TOLERATE put up with, withstand, *hang in there, bear, accept, submit to, stomach. **3.** RESIDE dwell, stay, live, lodge.

abide by *v.* comply, obey, observe, respect, conform to, adhere to.

abiding *a.* enduring, lasting, everlasting, eternal, unchanging, permanent, indestructible, durable. ANT. *short-lived, impermanent, transient.*

ability *n.* capability, faculty, facility, power, skill, talent, prowess, flair, competence, aptitude, capacity, knack, know-how, expertise, dexterity, proficiency, finesse, mind for, eye for, native ability, eye-hand coordination. ANT. *inability, incompetence, ineptitude, inadequacy.*

ABJECT *a.* [AB ject] the absolute worst or most miserable. *They live in abject poverty.* SYN. miserable, wretched, stark, hopeless, pitiful, pathetic, degrading, squalid, humbling, destitute.

abjure *v.* give up, renounce, forswear, recant, retract, disclaim, take back, renege, disavow, withdraw. ANT. *uphold, swear by, maintain.*

ablaze *a.* blazing, flaming, on fire, aflame, burning, *going up in smoke, consumed by flames, roaring, crackling.

able *a.* capable, habile, skillful, talented, competent, qualified, practiced, expert, deft, adroit, masterful. ANT. *incompetent, ineffectual, weak, unskilled, unable.*

able-bodied *a.* healthy, fit, strong, robust, capable, sound, in fine fettle, strapping.

abloom *a.* flowering, in flower, blooming.

ablution *n.* washing, cleansing, bath, purification.

ably *a.* capably, competently, deftly, expertly, adroitly

abnegate *v.* give up, forgo, abstain, renounce, abdicate, refrain, forbear. ANT. *indulge, binge, imbibe.*

abnegation *n.* self-denial, renunciation, abstinence, abdication, relinquishment.

abnormal *a.* atypical, irregular, odd, unusual, aberrant, deviant, unnatural, unexpected, unconventional, weird, eccentric, queer, anomalous, strange. "Not conforming to standard. In matters of thought and conduct, to be independent is to be abnormal." — Ambrose Bierce. ANT. *normal, usual, standard.* SEE ECCENTRIC, NEUROTIC, PSYCHOTIC

abnormality *n.* aberration, anomaly, deviation, peculiarity, oddity, freak, deformity, malformation, irregularity, eccentricity.

aboard *a.* on board, on deck, topside, in, boarded, consigned.

abode *n.* residence, home, living quarters, habitation, habitat, dwelling, domicile, lodging, roof over one's head, *pad, *digs, nest.

WORD FIND
animal: den, lair, hutch, warren, sty, burrow, diggings.
bird: nest, roost, aerie, aviary, cote.

abolish *v.* end, destroy, eliminate, eradicate, stop, annul, quash, extinguish, defeat, terminate, repeal, stamp out, uproot, abrogate. ANT. *institute, establish, adopt.*

abolition *n.* ending, annulment, moratorium, abrogation, repeal, elimination, eradication, termination, dissolution.

abolitionist *n.* opponent, subversive, activist, advocate, propagator.

A-bomb *n.* atomic bomb, thermonuclear bomb, *physics package. SEE NUCLEAR BOMB

ABOMINABLE *a.* [uh BOM un uh bul] loathsome, nasty. *The crossbow was an abominable invention.* SYN. nasty, vile, loathsome, abhorrent, heinous, despicable, atrocious, hateful, execrable, awful, horrible, deplorable, repulsive, disgusting. ANT. *admirable, nice, commendable.*

Abominable Snowman *n.* yeti, beast, creature. SEE MONSTER

abominate *v.* loathe, despise, hate.

abomination *n.* **1.** SOURCE OF LOATHING anathema, bete noir. **2.** LOATHING aversion, abhorrence, hatred, disgust, repugnance, detestation.

aboriginal *a.* indigenous, native, endemic, first, original, primitive.

aborigine *n.* native, first inhabitant, indigene, primitive, *bushman.

WORD FIND
AUSTRALIAN ABORIGINE
weapon: boomerang, waddy, nulla, woomera, blowpipe
wilderness: outback

abort *v.* **1.** MISCARRY expel. **2.** FAIL fall short, miss, go awry. **3.** CANCEL cut short, terminate, *scrub, *axe, *ditch, *can, *shit-can, *deep-six.

abortion *n.* **1.** MISCARRIAGE feticide, termination, aborticide, expulsion, infanticide. "The direct murder of the innocent." — Pope Pius XI. "If men could get pregnant, abortion would be a sacrament." — Florynce R. Kennedy. **2.** FAILURE incompletion, defeat, disaster, blunder.

abortive *a.* unsuccessful, fruitless, futile, useless, vain, unproductive, ineffectual. ANT. *successful, fruitful, effective.*

abound *v.* teem, overflow, flood, *be knee-deep

in, jam with, pack with, be abundant with, proliferate, swell, swarm.

about *prep.* ENCIRCLING on every side, all around, enveloping, encompassing, surrounding. **2.** APPROXIMATELY almost, nearly, close to, more or less, roughly. **3.** REFERRING TO concerning, in reference to, regarding, relative to, as respects, dealing with, touching on.

about *a.* **1.** IN THE REVERSE DIRECTION backwards, around, opposite direction. **2.** HERE AND THERE hither and thither, helter-skelter, far and wide.

about-face *n.* reversal, turnaround, volte-face, change of heart, *flip-flop, *backpedaling, *a 180, recantation.

above *a.* **1.** OVERHEAD up, skyward, higher up, over, atop, heavenward. **2.** GREATER more, larger, over and above. **3.** SUPERIOR higher, greater, outranking, surpassing.

aboveboard *a.* open, forthright, honest, in plain view, *on the table, straightforward, frank, candid, plain, direct, square, *on the up and up. ANT. *underhand, under the table, dishonest, sneaky.*

above suspicion *a.* irreproachable, inculpable, scrupulous, chaste, *having clean hands, innocent, pure.

abracadabra *n.* hocus-pocus, spell, incantation, charm, chant, invocation, mumbo jumbo, gibberish.

abrade *v.* scrape, chafe, grate, rub, erode, scuff, grind, scour.

abrasion *n.* **1.** SCRATCH scrape, chafe, excoriation. **2.** FRICTION scratching, scraping, wearing away, erosion, chafing.

abrasive *a.* **1.** ANNOYING irritating, cutting, nasty, saber-tongued, acid-tongued, galling, hurtful, biting, sarcastic. **2.** SCRAPING scratching, chafing, grating, eroding, grinding, grating, scouring, wearing, rough, coarse, rasping.

abrasive *n.* abradent, scourer, scraper, polisher, burnisher, buffer.

WORD FIND

course corundum: emery

dark, granular mineral used in grinding, polishing: aluminum oxide, corundum

jewelry and metal polisher made of ferric oxide: rouge

knife-sharpening stone: whetstone

manicuring stick: emery board

metal-polishing limestone: rottenstone

polishing powder made of chert or limestone: tripoli

rough carpenter's paper: sandpaper

rough file used on wood: rasp

volcanic rock used for scouring, smoothing: pumice

abreast *a.* beside, side by side, aside, *cheek to jowel.

ABRIDGE *v.* [uh BRIJ] to shorten, reduce or lessen. *To bring down costs, the new dictionary will be abridged and printed in paperback.* SYN. contract, shorten, condense, decrease, reduce, cut, abbreviate, diminish, *boil down, curtail. ANT. *expand, broaden, enlarge.*

abridgement *n.* condensation, reduction, summary, digest, abstract, brief, synopsis, outline. ANT. *enlargement, expansion.*

abroach *a.* opened, broached, let out.

abroad *a.* overseas, out of the country, away, traveling, touring.

abrogate *v.* abolish, cancel, repeal, annul, revoke, rescind, terminate, eliminate, quash, *scrub.

abrupt *a.* **1.** SUDDEN unexpected, surprising, unforeseen, swift, precipitate, unanticipated. **2.** CURT gruff, brusque, brisk, discourteous, rude. **3.** STEEP sheer, precipitous. ANT. **1.** *anticipated, expected.* **2.** *courteous, polite, gracious.*

abscess *a.* swelling, fester, boil, pimple, carbuncle, ulcer, pustule.

abscission *n.* cutting, separation, removal. SEE OPERATION, SURGERY

abscond *v.* flee, escape, go in hiding, *vamoose, *skedaddle, clear out, skip town, *make tracks, *scram, *fly the coop, *cut and run, *split, *beat feet, *duck out, *make oneself scarce, *give the slip.

absence *n.* **1.** NONATTENDANCE AWOL, nonappearance, truancy. **2.** LACKING dearth, need, want, privation, void, vacuum. ANT. **1.** *attendance, presence.* **2.** *fulfillment, abundance.*

absent *a.* **1.** AWAY elsewhere, gone, out, truant, AWOL, on leave, *playing hooky. **2.** PREOCCUPIED absent-minded, *out to lunch, abstracted, daydreaming, *off in space, *out of it. ANT. **1.** *present, here, attending.* **2.** *attentive, alert, on one's toes.*

absentee *n.* *no-show, truant, malingerer.

absenteeism *n.* absence, truancy, desertion, malingering, shirking.

absently *a.* inattentively, absent-mindedly.

absent-minded *a.* inattentive, scatterbrained, *out to lunch, dreamy, oblivious, daydreaming, lost, forgetful, abstracted, preoccupied, absorbed, remote, *spacey, *head in the clouds, distrait. ANT. *attentive, alert, sharp, fo-*

cused.

absolute *a.* **1.** TOTAL utter, complete, perfect, pure, unadulterated, consummate, outright, entire, undiluted, unmitigated. **2.** DEFINITE positive, unquestionable, certain, actual, exact, undeniable, unequivocal, indisputable. **3.** AUTHORITARIAN dictatorial, tyrannical, despotic, autocratic, totalitarian, ironhanded. ANT. *1. incomplete, imperfect. 2. indefinite, questionable, uncertain. 3. democratic.*

absolutely *a.* **1.** TOTALLY utterly, completely, perfectly, entirely. **2.** DEFINITELY positively, unquestionably, certainly, undeniably, *no ifs, ands or buts, *no two ways about it, surely, precisely, conclusively.

absolution *n.* forgiveness, remission, pardon, clearance, acquittal, amnesty.

ABSOLVE *v.* [ab ZOLV] to free from blame, guilt or responsibility. *They have been absolved of their sins.* SYN. acquit, exonerate, forgive, pardon, vindicate, remit, free, clear, exculpate, excuse. ANT. *charge, accuse, blame, condemn.*

absorb *v.* **1.** DRINK UP suck, assimilate, blot, sop up, sponge, osmose, consume. **2.** ENGROSS fascinate, interest, mesmerize, grip, rivet, enthrall, spellbind, comprehend, assimilate, understand. ANT. *1. spit out, spew, discharge, repel. 2. bore, confuse, tire.*

absorbed *a.* **1.** ASSIMILATED blotted, consumed. **2.** ENGROSSED interested, fascinated, riveted, mesmerized, captivated, spellbound, rapt. ANT. *bored, restless, unfocused.*

absorbent *a.* bibulous, pervious, permeable, porous, spongelike, retentive, *thirsty.

absorbing *a.* engrossing, arresting, enthralling, riveting, spellbinding, fascinating, interesting, mesmerizing.

absorption *n.* **1.** ASSIMILATION consumption, osmosis, retention, digestion, soaking up. **2.** ENGROSSMENT fascination, interest, captivation, riveting, enthrallment, spellbinding.

ABSTAIN *v.* [ub STANE] to voluntarily hold back, to refrain from or go without. *Everyone is trying to abstain from smoking.* SYN. refrain, desist, eschew, go without, forebear, *swear off, shun, spurn, *stay on the wagon, deny oneself. ANT. *indulge, imbibe.*

abstainer *n.* teetotaler, *health nut, ascetic, "A weak person who yields to the temptation of denying himself a pleasure." — Ambrose Bierce.

ABSTEMIOUS *a.* [ab STEEM ee us] eating and drinking in moderation, abstaining from

drink, practicing restraint. *Sylvester Graham of Graham Cracker fame was noted for his clean-living, abstemious lifestyle.* SYN. temperate, moderate, self-restraining, teetotaling, sober, abstinent, ascetic, self-denying.

abstention *n.* abstaining, abstinence, refraining.

ABSTINENCE *n.* [AB stuh nunce] abstaining, voluntary self-denial, the swearing off of unhealthy food and drink. *Longevity and abstinence often go hand in hand.* SYN. abstaining, self-restraint, teetotalism, sobriety, chastity, temperance, forbearing, self-denial, self-abnegation, asceticism, celibacy, moderation. "The virtue of those too ill or too old to enjoy life." — ANON. "The beginning of saintliness." — Moses Luzzato. ANT. *indulgence, extravagance, *pigging out.*

ABSTRACT *a.* [AB STRACT] not easily identified or defined, not based on the concrete, abstruse, theoretical, nonrepresentational. *His notions of the universe were wildly abstract and difficult to envision.* SYN. nonrepresentational, theoretical, conceptual, abstruse, indefinite, incomprehensible, general, nonspecific, amorphous, symbolic, recondite. ANT. *specific, clear, concrete.*

abstract *n.* **1.** CONDENSATION brief, abridgement, synopsis, summary. **2.** ART nonrepresentational art form, amorphous art form, geometrical art form. "A product of the untalented, sold by the unprincipled to the utterly bewildered." — Al Capp. SEE ART

abstract *v.* **1.** TAKE AWAY remove, extract, detach, separate. **2.** SUMMARIZE synopsize, abbreviate, condense, abridge.

abstracted *a.* LOST IN THOUGHT lost in reverie, preoccupied, daydreaming, brooding, absent-minded, withdrawn, in a trance, *off in space, remote, inattentive, *out to lunch. ANT. *alert, attentive, sharp.*

abstraction *n.* absent-mindedness, preoccupation, reverie, daydreaming, withdrawal, brooding, reflecting, mulling.

ABSTRUSE *a.* [ab STROOS] difficult to understand. *Einstein's abstruse theories.* SYN. recondite, deep, incomprehensible, complex, inscrutable, undecipherable, profound, unfathomable, *clear as mud, arcane, esoteric, cerebral. ANT. *clear, simple, obvious, *child's play.*

absurd *a.* ridiculous, ludicrous, laughable, silly, preposterous, foolish, outrageous, asinine, idiotic, loony, stupid, crazy, nonsense.

absurdity *n.* joke, foolishness, nonsense, idiocy,

*bullshit, *crock of shit, *bunk, *fiddle faddle, *hogwash, piffle, *rubbish, *tripe, drivel, twiddle-twaddle.

abundance n. lots, plenty, loads, piles, slew, *scads, *tons, *oodles, plethora, surplus, bounty, *miser's hoarde, profusion, enough, bountiful, overflowing, wealth. ANT. *scarcity, dearth, paucity.*

abundant a. plentiful, bountiful, copious, profuse, abounding, more than enough, immeasurable, inexaustible, teeming, overflowing. ANT. *scarce, scant, rare, sparse.*

abuse n. **1.** MISTREATMENT maltreatment, ill-treatment, injury, harm, assault, cruelty, torment, brutality, molestation, exploitation, terrorizing, *stepping on, torturing, beating, thrashing, battery. **2.** INSULTING OR HARSH LANGUAGE belittlement, degradation, denigration, deprecation, tongue-lashing, defamation, maligning, invective, criticism, upbraiding, dressing-down, ridicule, vilification, put-downs, verbal abuse. ANT. *1. care, kindness. 2. sweet talk, compliments, flattery.*

abuse v. **1.** MISTREAT maltreat, ill-treat, injure, exploit, harm, assault, disrespect, terrorize, molest, brutalize, manhandle, *step on, strong-arm, torture, beat, thrash, rape. **2.** VERBALLY ABUSE OR USE HARSH LANGUAGE belittle, degrade, denigrate, deprecate, tongue-lash, defame, malign, criticize, upbraid, dress down, ridicule, vilify, put down, insult, *dis, *dig, *dump on, *bad-mouth, *trash, *shit on. ANT. *1. coddle, respect, nurture, pamper, dote on. 2. sweet talk, flatter, compliment.*

abusive a. **1.** HARMFUL injurious, cruel, brutal, hurtful, exploitive, dominating, ruthless, rough, disrespectful. **2.** VERBALLY ABUSIVE offensive, insulting, vile, nasty, denigrating, gross, obscene, disparaging, critical, ridiculing, maligning, upbraiding, cutting. ANT. *1. helpful, kind, nurturing. 2. sweet, *honey-tongued, flattering.*

abut v. border on, lean on, adjoin, end on, conjoin, juxtapose.

abutment n. junction, juxtaposition, connection, conjunction.

abutter n. neighbor

abuzz a. buzzing, chattering, babbling, busy, jumping, hopping, active, animated, spirited, astir, kinetic, restless, bustling.

abysmal a. **1.** UNFATHOMABLE immeasurable, deep, bottomless, vast, abyssal, immense. **2.** DESPAIRINGLY BAD wretched, awful, pitiful, the lowest, depressing, miserable.

abyss n. depth, chasm, void, fissure, the deep, gulf, hole, bottomless pit.

AC n. **1.** air conditioning. **2.** alternating current.

academia n. academe, scholarly world, school, college, groves of academe, ivy halls.

academic a. **1.** SCHOLARLY scholastic, collegiate, university, professorial, studious, bookish, erudite, learned, cultured. **2.** THEORETICAL hypothetical, conjectural, speculative, suppositional, immaterial, moot. SEE COLLEGE, SCHOOL, TEACHER

academic n. scholar, student, teacher, professor, pupil, educator, tutor, doctor.

academy n. **1.** SCHOOL private school, institute, institution, secondary school, prep school, finishing school. **2.** ASSOCIATION fellowship, institution, atheneum, club.

Academy Award n. Oscar.

a capella a./adv. choral, voices only, without instruments.

accede v. **1.** CONSENT agree, submit to, give in, give assent, yield, acquiesce. **2.** ATTAIN assume, enter upon, inherit.

accelerant n. catalyst.

accelerate v. speed up, race, hasten, step up; *put the pedal to the metal, *floor it, *gun it, *squeal out, *burn rubber, *red line, *peel out. ANT. *decelerate, slow down, wind down, brake, stop.*

acceleration n. speeding up, increasing velocity, *stepping on it, quickening. ANT. *decelerating, slowing, braking.*

accelerator n. throttle, gas pedal.

accent n. **1.** EMPHASIS stress, significance. **2.** EMPHASIS OF PRONUNCIATION stress, accentuation, delivery, attack, inflection, articulation, enunciation, rhythm, tone. **3.** REGIONAL SPEAKING MANNER brogue, burr, drawl, twang, dialect. **4.** EMBELLISHMENT ornament, dressing, touch.

accent v. accentuate, highlight, underscore, underline, spotlight, emphasize, point up, punctuate. ANT. *downplay, ignore, hide.*

accentuate v. SEE ACCENT

accept v. **1.** TAKE receive, get, welcome, acquire, obtain. **2.** SUBMIT TO allow, tolerate, take in stride, endure, capitulate, stand for. **3.** BELIEVE IN adopt, acknowledge, agree, concur, confirm, *swallow, *buy, recognize, affirm, *take as gospel. ANT. *1. reject, give, refuse. 2. reject, refuse, oppose. 3. disbelieve, reject.*

acceptable a. adequate, good enough, worthy, satisfactory, suitable, respectable, fair, passable, tolerable, okay, *up to snuff, *passes muster. ANT. *unacceptable, subpar, objectionable, poor.*

acceptance a. acknowledgement, approval, adoption, assent, recognition, agreement, *the okay, *the green light, *the go-ahead. ANT. *rejection, refusal, disagreement.*

accepted a. **1.** RECEIVED taken, acquired, welcomed. **2.** AGREED UPON acknowledged, approved, recognized, endorsed, believed in, affirmed, sanctioned, upheld, authorized, accredited, conventional, normal, standard. ANT. *2. rejected, refused, unconventional.*

access n. entry, entree, admission, passage, pathway, approach, ingress, admittance, doorway. SEE ENTRANCE

accessible a. **1.** OBTAINABLE reachable, attainable, available, at hand, handy, approachable. **2.** FRIENDLY AND OPEN approachable, available, obliging, familiar, sociable, genial, gracious, *having an open door policy. **3.** EASY TO UNDERSTAND comprehensible, simple, lucid, uncomplicated, unsophisticated. ANT. *1. unobtainable, out of reach, unavailable. 2. closed, unfriendly, unapproachable. 3. abstruse, cerebral, complex, difficult.*

accession n. succession, assumption, inauguration, attaining, assuming office, ascending the throne, coming to power.

accessorize v. supplement, add on, ornament, adorn, attach, equip, accent, trim, accent.

accessory n. **1.** EXTRA add-on, attachment, adornment, peripheral, accent, supplement, trimming, equipment, gear, appendage, trapping. **2.** ACCOMPLICE confederate, confidante, cohort, associate, *partner in crime, co-conspirator, helper, assistant.

accident n. **1.** CHANCE fluke, serendipity, luck, fortuity, circumstance, happenstance, twist of fate, *shit luck. "An inevitable occurrence due to the action of immutable natural laws." — Ambrose Bierce. **2.** MISHAP mistake, blunder, misfortune, calamity, casualty, misadventure, disaster, catastrophe, wreck, *crack-up, *pile-up, *fender-bender, collision, *rear-ender, *T-bone, *sideswiping, crash, rollover. "A condition in which presence of mind is good, but absence of body better." — Foolish Dictionary.

accidental a. chance, fortuitous, serendipitous, random, freak, unforeseen, unintentional, haphazard, unwitting, *fluky, inadvertent, unpremeditated. ANT. *planned, intended, premeditated.*

accidentally a. fortuitously, randomly, unwittingly, haphazardly, by chance, unintentionally, by some fluke. ANT. *intentionally, planned, by design.*

accident-prone a. clumsy, *klutzy, inept, *two left feet, bungling, bumbling, attention-seeking, neurotic, having a death wish, *all thumbs.

acclaim n. applause, acclamation, ovation, cheers, praise, bravos, kudos, approval, adulation, honor, plaudits. ANT. *boos, hisses, jeers, heckles, catcalls, *razzing, *Bronx cheers.*

acclaim v. applaud, cheer, approve, *give thumbs up to, extol, praise, *sing the praises of, laud, hail, shout, bravo. ANT. *razz, *give a Bronx cheer, boo, hiss, reject, disapprove.*

acclaimed a. applauded, cheered, praised, approved, extolled, hailed, lauded. ANT. *rejected, jeered, booed, *razzed.*

acclamation n. applause, ovation, cheers, whistles, plaudits, bravos. SEE ACCLAIM

ACCLIMATE v. [ACK luh mate] to adapt, adjust or accustom (oneself) to a different environment or situation. *Lowlanders have a difficult time acclimating themselves to the thinner air supply found at high altitudes.* SYN. accustom, adapt, adjust, habituate, get used to, inure, naturalize, familiarize, fit in, condition, harden.

acclimatize v. SEE ACCLIMATE

ACCOLADE n. [AK uh LADE] an award or honor. *The dance troupe is winning accolades from critics nationwide.* SYN. honor, recognition, tribute, praise, acclaim, applause, exaltation, kudos, credit, award, prize.

accommodate v. **1.** OBLIGE aid, assist, help, perform a kindness, serve, furnish, do a favor, grant, indulge, lend a hand. **2.** HOUSE lodge, quarter, put up, board, furnish a room, shelter, entertain, take in. **3.** ADAPT accustom, adjust, bend, conform, acclimate, reconcile, modify, fit, tailor.

accommodating a. obliging, helpful, pleasing, gracious, considerate, hospitable, benevolent, charitable, cooperative, sympathetic. ANT. *disobliging, unsympathetic, cold-hearted, ungracious.*

accommodation n. **1.** ASSISTANCE aid, favor, service, grant, kindness, nicety, courtesy, help. **2.** LODGING room, quarters, housing, *digs, bed and breakfast, boarding, furnishing, suite, berth, bed, shelter, flat, arrangements. **3.** ADAPTATION adjustment, habituation, acclimatization, modification, change, fitting, conformation, reconciliation. ANT. *1. rejection, turning away, hindrance. 3. malad-*

justment, rigidity.

accompanied a. escorted, paired, tended, chaperoned, shown around, guarded, protected.

accompaniment n. backup, harmony, background, instrument, rhythm player, *sidekick.

accompany v. go with, escort, pair, tend, chaperone, show around, protect, guide, usher, be one's sidekick, *hang out with, consort, keep company, *shadow, *tag along, join.

ACCOMPLICE n. [uh COM pliss] one who accompanies or assists another in a wrongful act; a partner in crime. *Machine Gun Willy and two accomplices robbed the bank.* SYN. associate, colleague, ally, confederate, accessory, abettor, co-conspirator, henchman, partner in crime, consort, *gun moll. "One associated with another in crime, having guilty knowledge and complicity, as an attorney who defends a criminal, knowing him guilty."—Ambrose Bierce. SEE CRIME, CRIMINAL

accomplish v. achieve, effect, bring to fruition, fulfill, complete, consummate, attain, bring about, perform, *pull it off, effectuate, produce, execute, score, realize, engineer, make happen, *cut the mustard, *nail it. ANT. *fail, fall short, *blow, *choke.*

accomplished a. **1.** ACHIEVED completed, fulfilled, consummated, attained, brought about, finished, performed, executed, realized, *pulled off, *nailed, brought to fruition, produced. **2.** SKILLED proficient, talented, expert, practiced, adept, perfected, masterly, *crack, *crackerjack, deft, experienced, learned, polished. ANT. *1. uncompleted, unfulfilled, failed, *blown, fallen short. 2. unskilled, unseasoned, amateur, *green, *rough around the edges.*

accomplishment n. achievement, fulfillment, realization, deed, fait accompli, execution, attainment, completion, consummation, feat, coup, effort, performance, success. ANT. *failure, defeat, *flop, *washout, debacle.*

ACCORD n. [uh CORD] harmony, mutual understanding. *They ended their hostilities and reached accord.* SYN. harmony, agreement, concurrence, concert, unison, unity, accordance, rapport, mutual understanding, concordance, *a meeting of the minds, consensus. ANT. *discord, friction, disagreement, dissidence.*

accord v. **1.** CONCEDE grant, bestow, accede, allow, give, acquiesce. **2.** HARMONIZE agree,

concur, correspond, match up, *see eye to eye, *sing from the same hymnal, jibe.

accordant a. in agreement, agreeing, congruous, harmonious, matching.

accordingly a. **1.** FITTINGLY properly, correspondingly. **2.** THEREFORE hence, consequently, thus, so, subsequently, whereupon, as a result.

according to prep. **1.** IN ACCORDANCE WITH in line with. **2.** PER alla, as stated by, on the authority of, as reported by.

according to Hoyle sl. according to rule, *by the book, *by the numbers, correct, indisputable, according to the highest authority.

accordion n. concertina, *squeezebox, melodeon, *groanbox, *windbox, *stomach Steinway.

ACCOST v. [uh COST] approach or greet aggressively. *Sally was accosted by an ambitious salesman.* SYN. assail, greet, approach, *hit on, confront, assault, annoy, hail, intrude, address, call, buttonhole, solicit.

account n. **1.** CHRONICLE explanation, report, story, description, narrative, statement, detailing, *blow by blow, *play by play, run down, version. **2.** FINANCIAL RECORD balance, ledger, books, credits and debits, computation, reckoning, accrual, profit and loss statement, register, invoice, tab, calculation. **3.** WORTH importance, value, weight, consequence, significance, merit.

account v. **1.** RECKON add up, calculate, balance the books. **2.** ANSWER FOR explain, give a reason for, justify, rationalize. **3.** CONSIDER hold, regard, deem, estimate, judge, believe, rate, view.

account of, on prep. because, since, for the sake of, by virtue of.

account, on no prep. under no circumstances, for no reason, never.

account, take into prep. consider, allow for, think about.

accountability n. responsibility. SEE ACCOUNTABLE

accountable a. responsible, liable, beholden, answerable, obligated, duty-bound, culpable, held to blame. ANT. *excused, exempt, *let off the hook.*

accountant n. bookkeeper, auditor, CPA, certified public accountant, controller, comptroller, bank examiner, clerk, *number cruncher, *bean counter, *pencil pusher, *desk jockey, actuary. SEE ACCOUNTING

accounting n. **1.** RECORDING AND INTERPRETING FINANCIAL ACCOUNTS bookkeeping, balancing the books, reckoning, crediting and debiting, auditing, computing, calculating, recording. **2.** FINANCIAL STATEMENT account, balance sheet, ledger, spreadsheet, accrual, budget, invoice.

WORD FIND

account book: ledger, daybook, journal

annual accounting period: calendar year, fiscal year

cheating on records to hide profits: cooking the books

collection of assets after business closes: liquidation

computer program organizing financial data into rows and columns: spreadsheet

decreasing value of asset over time: depreciation

discrepancy corrections: reconciling

ease of converting assets to cash: liquidity

employee pay: payroll

enter a transaction: log

entry of earnings not yet received or of expenses not yet paid: accrual

examination of accounts: audit

examiner of accounts: auditor

expenses greater than income: negative cash flow

expenses less than income: positive cash flow

head accountant of business or government: controller, comptroller

increasing value of asset over time: appreciation

items and property of value: assets

losing money: in the red

making money or realizing net profit: in the black

money owed to creditors: accounts payable, liabilities, outstanding accounts

money to be received: accounts receivable

month by month budget: rolling budget

net profit or loss: bottom line

payout: disbursement

profit and loss statement: P & L

project income and expenses for the year: annualize

pure profit: net

record-keeping method having equal credit for each debit: double-entry accounting

records: books

revenues before costs are deducted: gross

state-licensed accountant: CPA, certified public accountant

total assets minus liabilities: net worth

uncollectable debt: write-off

value of assets beyond what is owed on them: equity

withdrawal of funds by business owner: draw

accoutre v. dress, equip, outfit, gear up.

accoutrement n. trappings, outfit, clothes, dress, equipment, gear, attire, habiliment.

accredit v. **1.** AUTHORIZE certify, sanction, recognize, license, qualify, approve, legitimize, endorse, validate, warrant, vouch for. **2.** ATTRIBUTE credit, ascribe, assign, charge.

accretion n. growth, accumulation, augmentation, addition, enlargement, expansion, increase. ANT. *shrinkage, dispersement, scattering.*

accrual n. growth, accumulation, amassing, increase.

accrue v. accumulate, add up, grow, amass, increase, collect, expand, pile up, compound.

acculturation n. naturalization, assimilation, nationalization, culture shock.

accumulate v. heap, collect, pile up, gather, accrete, expand, aggregate, stack up, grow, accrue, swell, amass, assemble. ANT. *throw off, shed, shuck, disperse, scatter.*

accumulation n. collection, heap, pile, gathering, accretion, assembly, aggregation, agglomeration, mass, growth, accrual, swelling, hoarde, stockpile. ANT. *dispersal, disbursement, shedding, scattering.*

accuracy n. precision, correctness, exactness, fidelity, factualness, veracity, truth, meticulousness, perfection. ANT. *inaccuracy, imprecision, slackness.*

accurate a. correct, precise, right, error-free, unerring, perfect, exact, actual, factual, *on the button, *on target, *on the money, *on the mark, flawless, veracious, faultless, meticulous, faithful. ANT. *incorrect, wrong, flawed, imperfect, inaccurate.*

accurately a. correctly, precisely, rightly, perfectly, flawlessly, exactly, actually, factually, meticulously. ANT. *inaccurately, incorrectly, wrongly.*

accursed a. cursed, condemned, damned, ill-fated, doomed, bedeviled, hexed, ruined, undone, stricken, *done for. ANT. *blessed.*

accusation n. charge, *rap, blame, implication, indictment, insinuation, allegation, complaint, citation, smear, inculpation, recrimination.

accusatory a. accusing, finger-pointing, blaming.

accuse v. charge, blame, indict, implicate, cite, finger-point, prosecute, inculpate, impeach, recriminate, impute, *hang on, *finger for,

*pin on.

accuser *n.* incriminator, prosecutor, *fink, *stool pigeon, *tattletale, *rat, informer, plaintiff, adversary.

accustom *v.* familiarize, habituate, acquaint, adapt, get used to.

accustomed *a.* **1.** USUAL customary, characteristic, conventional, established, familiar, fixed, set, everyday, general, routine, traditional. **2.** USED TO habituated, familiarized, acclimated, acquainted with, naturalized, adapted, in the habit of, toughened, seasoned. ANT. *1. unusual, uncharacteristic, unconventional. 2. unaccustomed, unfamiliar with, unseasoned, green.*

AC-DC *a. Sl.* bisexual, *bi, swinging both ways, *ambidextrous.

ace *n.* expert, champion, master, star, hero, *crack hand, *crackerjack, *hotshot, *pistol, *whiz, *whiz kid. ANT. *loser, benchwarmer, second-stringer.*

ace *v.* hit it, nail it, score, execute, succeed, hit the bullseye, defeat, *smoke the competition. ANT. **blow it, *choke, lose.*

acedia *n.* apathy, despair.

ace in the hole hold out, card up one's sleeve, *secret weapon, reserve.*

acephalous *a.* **1.** headless. **2.** leaderless

acerbate *v.* **1.** EMBITTER sour, poison, gall. **2.** EXASPERATE aggravate, ruffle, annoy, disturb, *rattle one's cage, perturb, provoke.

ACERBIC *a.* [uh SUR bick] anything sour, bitter or sharp. *She was an insulting, acerbic-tongued witch.* SYN. sour, bitter, harsh, sharp, astringent, acidic, acrid, tart, caustic. ANT. *sweet, honeyed, nectarous, saccharine.*

acerbity *a.* **1.** SOURNESS bitterness, astringency, sharpness, harshness, tartness, acidity, acridity, pungency. **2.** NASTINESS irritability, annoyance, sharpness, sourness, bitterness, brusqueness, rancor, sarcasm, venom, acrimony, ill humor, grouchiness. ANT. *1. sweetness, nectarous. 2. sweetness, friendliness, good humor.*

aces *a.* great, excellent, wonderful, top-notch, fabulous.

ache *n.* pain, twinge, pang, soreness, stitch, spasm, throb, discomfort, hurt, pounding, stabbing, smarting, burning, pinching.

ache *v.* **1.** HURT throb, pound, pang, twinge, pain, spasm, stab, sear, smart, suffer, agonize. **2.** SYMPATHIZE pity. **3.** YEARN FOR long for, hunger, crave, need, pine for.

achievable *a.* doable, attainable, reachable, obtainable, feasible.

achieve *v.* accomplish, realize, do, attain, complete, bring about, effect, produce, carry off, succeed, consummate, actualize, follow through, engineer, *pull off, *swing, score, win one. ANT. *fail, fall short, *blow it, *choke, quit.*

achievement *n.* accomplishment, attainment, production, success, score, exploit, feat, fulfillment, realization, acquirement, consummation, *master stroke, coup, masterpiece, creation, triumph, conquest, *feather in one's cap.

ACHILLES' HEEL *n.* [uh KILL eez HEEL] a metaphor used to illustrate a vulnerability or a mortal weakness, from the myth of Achilles, whose body was immunized from harm everywhere but on his heel. *Nobody is all-powerful; even dictators have at least one Achilles' heel.* SYN. weakness, vulnerability, *soft underbelly, susceptibility, frailty, fragility, chink in the armour, deficiency, failing, handicap. ANT. *omnipotence, strength, immortality.*

acid *n.* corrosive, astringent, chemical.

WORD FIND

ant irritant: formic acid

aspirin: acetylsalicylic acid

corrosive used in explosives: sulfuric acid, oil of vitriol

mild antiseptic: boric acid

milk-derived: lactic acid

odoriferous corrosive poison used in explosives, antiseptics: phenol

protein-forming: amino acids

stomach acid: hydrochloric acid

urine-derived: uric acid

vinegar ingredient: acetic acid

vitamin C: ascorbic acid

white poison in insecticides: arsenic acid

ANT. *alkali*

acid *n. Sl.* LSD, *blotter, *blue cheer, *blue heaven, *California sunshine, *D, *dot, *electric Kool Aid, *flash, *green dragon, *orange sunshine, *purple haze, *travel agent, *wedding bells, *yellows.

acid *a.* **1.** OF TASTE sour, bitter, tart, astringent, harsh, sharp, biting, acerbic, vinegary. **2.** ILL-TEMPERED OR SHARP-TONGUED sarcastic, caustic, *saber-tongued, venomous, nasty, cutting, vitriolic, biting, stinging, snide, sardonic, acerbic, scathing. ANT. *1. sweet, sugary, honey. 2. good-humored, sweet, kind, warm, flattering.*

acidhead *n. Sl.* *junkie. SEE ADDICT

acidity *n.* sourness, bitterness, acerbity, sharpness, harshness, astringency, causticity.

ACID TEST n. [ASS id test] a test of value, quality or genuineness, a metaphor evolved from the jeweler's nitric acid test to determine the authenticity of gold. *The voluntary adoption of expensive, double-hulled tankers has long served as an acid test of the oil industry's sincerity concerning environmentalism.* SYN. trial, proving ground, analysis.

acidulous a. sour, tart, harsh, citric. SEE ACID

acknowledge v. 1. ADMIT recognize, own up to, accept, grant, concede, acquiesce, declare, profess. 2. THANK recompense, reward, repay, requite. 3. RESPOND TO notice, address, respond, nod at, recognize, greet, salute, hail. ANT. 1. *deny, refuse, refute.* 3. *ignore, overlook, pass over, snub.*

acknowledgement n. 1. ADMISSION avowal, recognition, acceptance, granting, concession, acquiescence, declaration, profession, confession. 2. THANK YOU recompense, reward, repayment, remittance, expression of gratitude. 3. RESPONSE TO notice, address, nod, recognition, greeting, salute, hailing, bow, curtsy, reply. ANT. 1. *denial, refusal, refutation.* 3. *ignoring, oversight, snub.*

ACME n. [ACK me] the very highest; the peak. *The acme of his career.* SYN. summit, pinnacle, peak, high point, zenith, crown, apex, top, apogee; greatest, best, supremacy. ANT. *lowest, valley, pit, bottom.*

acne n. pimples, *zits, blackheads, pustules, facial eruption, skin inflammation, blemishes, pockmarks, *pizza face.

acolyte n. altar boy, assistant, attendant, helper, aid.

acorn n. oak nut

acoustic a. sound, sound properties, hearing, auditory, phonic, audio, aural.

acoustics n. sound qualities, echoes, noise properties, sound transmission, sound frequencies.

WORD FIND
absorbs all sound, produces no echoes: anechoic
boom produced by object moving faster than sound: sonic boom
harmonious sound: consonance
hearing tester: audiometer
high frequency sound above human hearing: ultrasound
inharmonious sound: dissonance
less than speed of sound: subsonic
lowest sound audible to ear: threshold frequency

noise made from blend of all audible frequencies: white noise
prolonged sound caused by vibration or reflection: resonance
quality of sound: timbre
rebounding sound wave: echo
speed of sound: sonic, 741 mph
unit of noise intensity level: decibel

acquaint v. 1. MAKE AWARE inform, advise, enlighten, familiarize, let know, notify, apprise, divulge, clue in. 2. MEET introduce, make conversant, familiarize.

acquaintance n. 1. ACQUIRED KNOWLEDGE familiarity, understanding, experience, awareness, conversance, enlightenment, cognizance. 2. ASSOCIATE colleague, neighbor, peer, co-worker. "A person whom we know well enough to borrow from, but not well enough to lend to." — Ambrose Bierce. ANT. 1. *ignorance, inexperience.* 2. *complete stranger.*

acquainted a. 1. AWARE informed, advised, enlightened, familiarized, apprised of, familiar with, aware of, clued in, versed in.

ACQUIESCE v. [AK we ESS] to yield, give in or assent without enthusiasm. *The dictator acquiesced only after the Bush administration rattled its saber.* SYN. consent, defer, yield, assent, comply, accede, accept, *buckle under, *cave in, give in, agree, capitulate, concur, abide by, come around, submit, *fall in line. ANT. *resist, fight, challenge, rebuff, make a stand.*

acquiescence n. yielding, compliance, acceptance, consenting, *buckling under, capitulation, submission, concurring, *caving in, deferring, assenting, subservience, servility. ANT. *resistance, making a stand, rebellion.*

acquire v. get, obtain, gain, procure, buy, purchase, acquisition, earn, catch, *get one's hands on, *get hold of, *land, net, *snag, *scare up, secure. ANT. *give away, sell, lose, relinquish.*

acquired immune deficiency syndrome n. AIDS, sexually transmitted disease (STD), HIV.

acquirement n. skill, ability, education, capability, knowledge, accomplishment.

acquisition n. attainment, procurement, acquirement, securing, purchase, gain, takeover, gift, proceed, grant, obtainment.

acquisitive a. greedy, materialistic, grasping, avaricious, grabby, hoarding, rapacious, *gold-digging.

ACQUIT v. [uh KWIT] 1. TO RELEASE free or

clear one from a responsibility or charge. *Lizzie Borden was acquitted of murder charges against her father and stepmother, but a cloud of suspicion continues to hang over her name.* SYN. release, clear, free, excuse, exonerate, absolve, pardon, forgive, relieve, exempt, let off, exculpate. **2.** BEHAVE conduct, act, comport, bear. ANT. *1. convict, condemn, damn.*

acquittal *n.* discharge, release, clearance, exoneration, pardon, reprieve, exculpation, absolution, liberation.

acre *n.* 160 square rods, 43,560 square feet, 405 hectare, acreage, parcel, plot, real estate.

acreage *n.* parcel, plot, holding, land, real estate, property, expanse.

acrid *a.* **1.** SHARP TO TASTE OR SMELL bitter, irritating, harsh, pungent, sour, acid, acerbic, stinging, caustic, stinking, foul-smelling, biting. **2.** BITTER IN SPEECH sarcastic, sardonic, caustic, biting, acid, saber-tongued, venomous, snide. ANT. *1. sweet, mild. 2. sweet, flattering, good-humored.*

ACRIMONIOUS *a.* [AK ri MO nee us] bitter, nasty, spiteful. *The divorcing couple testified against each other acrimoniously.* SYN. bitter, biting, caustic, nasty, spiteful, sarcastic, sardonic, sharp, vitriolic, venomous, acerbic, snarling, snide. ANT. *sweet, kind, civil.*

acrimony *n.* bitterness, nastiness, causticity, vitriol, spite, sarcasm, asperity, harshness. ANT. *sweetness, civility, kindness.*

acrobat *n.* gymnast, tumbler, aerialist, tightrope walker, stuntman, stunt woman, circus performer, trapeze artist, contortionist.

acrobatics *n.* gymnastics, tumbling, somersaulting, flipping, balancing.

acronym *n.* abbreviation.

acrophobia *n.* fear of heights. SEE PHOBIA

across *a.* crosswise, crossways, transversely, crisscross, astride.

across *prep.* **1.** OVER opposite to, to the other side, beyond, in front of. **2.** INTO CONTACT WITH upon, into.

across-the-board *a.* **1.** WIN, PLACE AND SHOW **2.** ALL everything, comprehensive, sweeping, all-inclusive, blanket, total, complete. ANT. *limited, partial.*

acrostic *n.* word puzzle, word play, word game.

act *n.* **1.** DEED action, execution, performance, task, turn, endeavor, undertaking, measure, accomplishment, step, exploit, feat. **2.** DECREE enactment, ruling, bill, edict, measure, law, ordinance, amendment, mandate, proclamation, judgment, resolution. **3.** FALSE BEHAVIOR affectation, pose, *false front, pre-

tense, make-believe, put-on, posturing, sham, performance, *Oscar performance, airs, feigning. **4.** STAGE ROUTINE bit, *schtick, sketch. **5.** PART OF A PLAY scene, act one, act two, epilogue, prologue.

act *v.* **1.** DO perform, execute, get involved, spring into action, carry out, achieve, begin, *jump in, undertake, function, move, proceed. "Genius is the ability to act wisely without precedent—the power to do the right thing the first time."—Elbert Hubbard. **2.** BEHAVE conduct onself, comport, deport, carry oneself, perform, be like. **3.** PERFORM IN AN ENTERTAINMENT portray, personify, impersonate, mimic, role-play, characterize, enact, *ham it up, play a part, star, burlesque.

acting *n.* PERFORMANCE IN AN ENTERTAINMENT depiction, method acting, characterization, impersonation, mimicry, dramatization, portrayal, rendition, *hamming it up, mime, pantomime, theatrics. "Acting is honesty. If you can fake that, you've got it made."—George Burns. "To seem natural rather than to be natural."—Alan Milne.

acting *v.* PRETENDING bluffing, faking, feigning, putting up a false front, playing make-believe, posing, putting up a facade, affecting.

acting *a.* SUBSTITUTING surrogate, functioning, operating, alternate, temporary, deputy, interim, provisional, pro tem, adjutant.

action *n.* **1.** ACTIVITY motion, movement, functioning, performance, working, energy, commotion. **2.** ACT deed, move, effort, enterprise, exercise, exploit. "Deeds are better things than words are, Actions mightier than boastings."—Longfellow. "Well done is better than well said."—Ben Franklin. **3.** EFFECT influence. **4.** LEGAL ACTION lawsuit, suit, claim, case. **5.** COMBAT battle, hostilities, gunfire, enemy fire, fighting. **6.** EXCITEMENT movement, slam-bang entertainment.

activate *v.* start, begin, initiate, stimulate, spark, actuate, prompt, goad, prod, set in motion, ignite, impel, *flip the switch, energize, motivate. ANT. *stop, turn off, extinguish, paralyze.*

active *a.* **1.** BUSY moving, functioning, working, industrious, on the go, commotive, kinetic, stirring, astir, restless, bustling. **2.** ENERGETIC lively, agile, quick, spry, vital, spirited, hearty, nimble, vigorous, sprightly, alert, frisky, animated. **3.** PARTICIPATING functional, acting, operative. ANT. *1. inactive, static, stationary. 2. dead, slow, tired, paralyzed. 3. inactive.*

ACTIVISM n. [AKT uh vizm] taking direct action to bring about political or social change. *Voting is activism in its simplest form.* SYN. involvement, action, acting, commitment, militancy, advocacy, taking responsibility, influencing, effecting change. ANT. *apathy, passivity, ignoring.*

activist n. doer, *a mover and shaker, *lightning rod, *spark, champion, advocate, *influence peddler, logroller.

activity n. **1.** ACTION movement, commotion, motion, bustle, hustle. **2.** LIVELINESS energy, vivacity, vigor, alertness, briskness. **3.** PASTIME pursuit, recreation, venture, game, hobby. ANT. *1. inactivity, stillness, inertia. 2. sloth, tiredness, exhaustion.*

act of God n. natural disaster, unforeseen event, accident, freak accident.

actor n. **1.** DOER perpetrator, participant, activist, executor, mover, agent, operative. **2.** THESPIAN performer, player, actress, star, character, entertainer, mimic, mime, movie idol, matinee idol, impersonator, artist, leading man, leading lady. "A musician who plays on a home-made instrument — himself." — Helen Hayes. "A person who makes faces for a living." — Anon.

WORD FIND

group: cast, company (stock company), ensemble, repertory, troupe
improvisation: ad lib
main role: lead
minor role: bit player, cameo, extra, spear carrier, walk on
monologue performer: monologist
natural, realistic: method actor
negotiates contracts, finds work: agent
overacting or bad acting: ham, mugger
publicizes: press agent, publicist
secondary role: supporting actor
silent performer: mime, pantomime
substitute: stand-in, understudy
traveling: barnstormer
typecast: character actor
veteran: trouper
SEE ACTRESS, MOVIE

actress n. leading lady, starlet, diva, prima donna, ingenue. SEE ACTOR, MOVIE

actual a. real, authentic, factual, true, bona fide, existing, concrete, genuine, tangible, certain, veritable, de facto. ANT. *false, imaginary, fictitious, unreal, nonexistent.*

actuality n. reality, fact, truth, verity, materiality.

actualize v. make real, bring about, realize, effectualize, produce, engineer, accomplish, reach.

actually a. really, in fact, in reality, truthfully, truly, genuinely, literally, in actuality, de facto, as a matter of fact.

actuary n. statistician, accountant, insurance professional.

actuate v. put into motion, activate, start, ignite, effectuate, motivate, impel, goad, prompt, stimulate, initiate, *put into gear, *get rolling, spur, rouse. ANT. *stop, extinguish, deter, *throw a wrench in the works.*

act up v. misbehave, act out, raise hell, *sow one's wild oats, rebel, *kick, *throw a tantrum, carry on.

acuity n. acuteness, sharpness, keenness, shrewdness.

ACUMEN n. [AK yuh mun] mental sharpness, accurate and quick judgment. *Frank lacks the acumen needed to succeed in the stock market.* SYN. sharpness, shrewdness, quickness, intelligence, perceptiveness, keenness, insight, judgment, astuteness, discernment, acuity, smarts, sagacity, wisdom. ANT. *ignorance, dullness, stupidity, naivete.*

acute a. **1.** SHARP pointed, needle-like. **2.** KEEN sharp, shrewd, quick, smart, astute, perceptive, bright, discerning. **3.** SENSITIVE receptive, responsive, perceptive. **4.** SEVERE serious, critical, crucial, vital, important, grave, momentous, urgent, dangerous, intense. **5.** SHRILL high, piercing. ANT. *1. dull, blunt. 2. dull, obtuse, slow, stupid. 3. insensitive, imperceptive. 4. mild, unimportant, insignificant. 5. low, bass.*

A.D. adv. anno Domini, in the year of the Lord.

ADAGE n. [ADD ij] an old saying illustrating some universal truth. *"Charity begins at home" and "Honesty is the best policy" are popular adages.* SYN. saying, proverb, aphorism, axiom, folk wisdom, motto, maxim, platitude, precept, truism, cliche.

ADAMANT a. [AD uh mant] not giving in or yielding, stubborn. *LBJ was adamant about not being typed as a Southerner, because that meant political handicaps.* SYN. unyielding, unrelenting, stubborn, inflexible, unbending, rigid, intractable, obdurate, immovable, firm, resolute, fixed, uncompromising, determined. ANT. *flexible, yielding, acquiescing.*

adapt v. adjust, modify, assimilate, conform, suit, reform, acculturate, fit, alter, change, accommodate, orient, bend, acclimate, attune, convert, harden, temper, habituate, evolve, reinvent, retrofit, *change one's spots.

adaptable *a.* adjustable, modifiable, convertible, alterable, changeable, transformable, variable, flexible, pliable.

adaptation *n.* adjustment, modification, alteration, change, transformation, variation, assimilation, conformation, accommodation, hardening, retrofit, tempering, acclimation, evolution, metamorphosis.

adapter *n.* connector, plug, fitting.

adaptive *a.* adjusting, modifying, altering, flexible, hearty, robust.

add *v.* **1.** ADD ON affix, attach, append, tack on, adjoin, suffix, annex. **2.** INCREASE augment, supplement, enlarge, lengthen, amplify, boost, raise, heighten, *beef up, build on. **3.** TOTAL sum up, calculate, compute, figure, tally, reckon, enumerate, count. ANT. *1. subtract, remove. 2. subtract, decrease, reduce.*

addendum *n.* addition, appendix, supplement, attachment, adjunct, codicil, extension, augmentation.

addict *n.* *junkie, *fiend, *dopehead, *head, *freak, *acid head, *meth head, *coke head, user, *mainliner, *speed freak, *pothead, *space cadet, enthusiast, devotee, nut, -phile, adherent, buff, hound, zealot.

addicted *a.* hooked, dependent, devoted, attached, obsessed, disposed to, in the habit, *stuck on, zealous about, *nuts about.

addiction *n.* habit, dependency, *monkey, *monkey on one's back, craving, enslavement, obsession, habituation, alcoholism.

addictive *a.* habit-forming, enslaving, hooking.

add insult to injury *v.* aggravate, exacerbate, worsen, *add fuel to the fire, heighten, provoke.

addition *n.* **1.** TALLYING summation, calculation, tabulation, reckoning, computation, counting. **2.** AUGMENTATION addendum, add-on, attachment, extension, increase, supplement, adjunct, annex.

additional *a.* more, extra, added, supplementary, further, over and above, increased.

additive *n.* agent, enhancing agent, preservative.

addled *a.* muddled, befuddled, confused, *numb, mixed up, *out to lunch, *foggy, *dim, *out of it, bewildered, disoriented.

add-on *n.* supplement, accessory, peripheral, augmentation.

address *n.* **1.** SPEECH oration, lecture, talk, salutation, letter. **2.** MAILING ADDRESS R.F.D., route, street number, P.O. box, destination. **3.** LOCATION residence, place, home, quarters, domicile.

address *v.* **1.** DIRECT speak to, greet, approach, salute, acknowledge, write to. **2.** HANDLE consider, deal with, confront, undertake, focus on, take up, engage in.

adduce *v.* cite, prove, provide, illustrate, point out, show, affirm, name.

adept *a.* skilled, deft, adroit, expert, masterful, proficient, capable, practiced, dexterous, sharp, competent, *crack, *crackerjack, savvy, talented. ANT. *unskilled, incompetent, fumbling, bumbling.*

adequacy *n.* enough, sufficiency, capability, competence.

adequate *a.* sufficient, enough, suitable, acceptable, satisfactory, respectable, ample, tolerable, okay, admissible, not bad, fair, able. ANT. *inadequate, unsatisfactory, intolerable, insufficient, lacking.*

adequately *a.* sufficiently, acceptably, satisfactorily, suitably, capably, amply. ANT. *inadequately, insufficiently.*

adhere *v.* **1.** STICK affix, cling, stay, attach, hold fast, cement, fasten, cleave, cohere. **2.** STAY WITH OR BE DEVOTED TO support, observe, follow, abide by, respect, maintain, practice, be attached, keep to, be faithful. ANT. *1. separate, come unglued, repel. 2. stray, condemn, ignore, detract.*

ADHERENT *n.* [ad HEER ent] a supporter or follower of a cause or belief. *An adherent of conservative politics.* SYN. follower, supporter, disciple, believer, advocate, backer, fan, devotee, observer, ally, *card-carrying member. ANT. *detractor, opponent, enemy of, critic of.*

adhesion *n.* sticking, stickiness, adherence, attachment, cling, holding fast, hold.

adhesive *n.* glue, tape, velcro, cement, paste, *stickum, binder, gum, mortar, resin, plaster.

AD HOC *a.* [ADD HOK] for a specific purpose, as a committee, impromptu. *An emergency ad hoc committee was formed.* SYN. specified, specific, provisional, special, impromptu.

adieu *interj.* goodbye, farewell, au revoir, adios, sayonara, arrivederci, auf Wiedersehen, *toodleloo, *toodles. SEE GOODBYE

AD INFINITUM *adv.* [add in fuh NITE um] forever, endlessly. *The Congressman said taxes would continue to rise ad infinitum.* SYN. forever, endlessly, continuously, on and on, neverending, perpetually, relentlessly, unlimitedly.

adios *interj.* farewell, adieu, au revoir. SEE GOODBYE

adipose n. fat.

adjacent a. abutting, juxtaposed, near, close, adjoining, next to, aside, beside, neighboring, contiguous, alongside, bordering, proximate, meeting. ANT. *distant, remote.*

adjoin v. 1. ABUT touch, be contiguous to, unite, contact, connect, impinge on, border, verge. 2. JOIN affix, unite, connect, link.

adjoining a. abutting, adjacent, touching, contacting, neighboring, connecting, bordering, contiguous, verging. ANT. *separate, apart.*

adjourn v. 1. RECESS rest, pause, close, delay, suspend, put off, hold. 2. MOVE transfer.

adjournment n. recess, rest, pause, break, delay, intermission, suspension, postponement.

ADJUDICATE v. [uh JOO di KATE] to judge and settle a case. *A "kangaroo court" is a court in which a case is adjudicated dishonestly or incompetently.* SYN. judge, adjudge, try, hear, decide, process, arbitrate, mediate, determine, settle, sit in judgment, referee.

adjudication n. judgment, decision, determination, settlement.

adjunct n. supplement, auxiliary, subordinate, addition, extra, associate, aid, assistant.

adjure v. command, charge, entreat, order, require, obligate.

adjust v. conform, fit, alter, change, accommodate, bend, suit, accustom, *doctor, adapt, modify, straighten, tune, fine-tune, *fiddle with, calibrate, square, rectify, tweak, service, balance.

adjustable a. adaptable, alterable, pliable, conformable, accommodating, modifiable, changeable, serviceable, flexible, tractable.

adjustment n. 1. COMFORMATION fitting, alteration, change, accommodation, adaption, bending, retrofit, *doctoring, modification, calibration, tune up, sizing, rectification, squaring. 2. SETTLEMENT claim, liability, compensation, reimbursement, remuneration.

adjutant n. assistant, aid, helper.

ad lib n. improvisation, extemporization, invention, *offhand remark, impulse.

ad lib v. improvise, extemporize, *wing it, *take it, invent, *play it by ear, speak impromptu, speak off the top of one's head, fabricate, vamp.

AD LIB a. [ADD LIB] improvised, unrehearsed. *The act was performed completely ad lib.* SYN. improvisational, unrehearsed, *off the cuff, *on the spur of the moment, extemporaneously, impulsively.

ad man n. copywriter, huckster, *b.s. artist.

admeasure v. apportion.

administer v. 1. GOVERN manage, administrate, head, direct, oversee, officiate, superintend, supervise, conduct, regulate, rule, operate, control. 2. GIVE OUT dispense, mete out, deliver, apply, distribute, provide, give. 3. HELP serve, lend a hand.

administration n. 1. GOVERNING overseeing, commanding, policy-making, application, execution, legislation, regulation, superintendence, supervision, management. 2. MANAGEMENT leadership, government, bureaucracy, bureau, cabinet, headquarters, governing body, executive branch, board, command, *front office, legislature, establishment, ministry, board of directors, department, *brass, *the powers that be. 3. DISPENSATION delivery, application, giving. 4. TERM OF POWER reign, dynasty, *run, incumbency, tenure.

administrator n. manager, supervisor, superintendent, executive, executor, CEO (chief executive officer), bureaucrat, official, director, overseer, governor, head, chair, leader, *paper shuffler.

admirable a. model, praiseworthy, enviable, excellent, honorable, respectable, commendable, wonderful, ideal, great, exceptional, revered, laudable, superior. ANT. *despicable, low, rotten.*

admiral n. commander. "That part of the warship which does the talking while the figurehead does the thinking." —Ambrose Bierce. SEE NAVAL OFFICER

admiration n. esteem, adoration, reverence, approval, regard, idolizing, applause, awe, respect, veneration, glorification, fondness, *foot-kissing, worship. "A very short-lived passion, that immediately decays upon growing familiar with its object."—Joseph Addison. "The daughter of ignorance."—Benjamen Franklin. ANT. *disgust, despising, loathing, disrespect.*

admire v. regard, esteem, look up to, respect, revere, idolize, praise, worship, model after, honor, put on a pedestal, hail. ANT. *loathe, despise, look down on, disrespect.*

admirer n. fan, devotee, follower, disciple, supporter.

admissible a. acceptable, permissible, allowed, passable, legitimate, legal, lawful, okay, tolerable, proper, suitable. ANT. *inadmissible, illegal, intolerable.*

admission n. 1. ENTRANCE entry, passage, access. **2.** DOOR CHARGE cover charge, ticket, entrance fee, gate. **3.** ACKNOWLEDGEMENT OR CONFESSION admitting, granting, profession, *owning up, *fessing up, revelation, affirmation, disclosure, divulgence, testimony, deposition. ANT. *1. blockage, barring, impediment. 3. concealment, cover-up, secret, confidentiality.*

admit *v.* LET IN accept, let pass, grant access, check, grant, okay, permit, *give the nod to. **2.** CONFESS acknowledge, concede, grant, *own up, *fess up, *come clean, reveal, disclose, divulge, confide, *sing, *spill the beans, *bare one's soul, testify. ANT. *1. block, bar, refuse. 2. withhold, keep secret, hide, deny.*

admittance *n.* entrance, entry, permission, pass, passage.

admittedly *a.* confessedly, honestly, truthfully, frankly.

admix *v.* intermix, blend, combine, mingle.

admixture *n.* blend, combination, mixture, compound, melange.

ADMONISH *v.* [ad MON ish] to caution or advise, often scoldingly. *He was admonished for drinking and driving.* SYN. **1.** CAUTION warn, forewarn, advise, exhort. **2.** REPROVE rebuke, berate, scold, *tell off, *come down on, *call on the carpet, *take to task, chastise, reproach. **3.** REMIND apprise, inform, warn. ANT. *2. commend, compliment, reward.*

admonition *n.* **1.** CAUTION warning, forewarning, advice, apprisal, counsel. **2.** REPROVAL scolding, *dressing down, *talking to, reprimand, upbraiding, *slap on the wrist, remonstrance, rebuke, reproach. ANT. *2. commendation, reward, compliment.*

AD NAUSEUM *a.* [AD NAWZ e um] to the point of illness or disgust. *He went on about his accomplishments ad nauseum.* SYN. to a sickening degree, to nauseating extremes, to the point of queasiness, too much, more than one can stomach.

ado *n.* trouble, fuss, excitement, running around, *to-do, bother, travail, hubbub, confusion.

adobe *n.* clay, brick.

adolescence *n.* puberty, pubescence, youth, teen years, *awkward years, minor, immaturity, junior high years, high school age. "A kind of emotional seasickness. Both are funny, but only in retrospect." — Arthur Koestler. "That period in life when a boy refuses to believe that someday he'll be as stupid as his parents." — Anon. "That period when the young feel their parents should be told the facts of life." — Anon.

adolescent *n.* teenager, teen, *teenybopper, youth, sophomore, junior, minor, youngster, *bobbysoxer, *sweet sixteen, juvenile. "One who has reached the age of dissent." — Harold Leslie. "The awkward age when a child is too old to say something cute and too young to say something sensible." — Anon.

Adonis *n.* *hunk, *beefcake, *dreamboat, *stud, Greek god, *God's gift to women, *heartbreaker, *lady-killer.

adopt *v.* **1.** TAKE IN ANOTHER'S CHILD take under one's wing, take in, foster, surrogate, mother, father, raise. **2.** SELECT OR TAKE UP choose, appropriate, employ, take, espouse, assume, take on, opt, use. **3.** VOTE IN select, approve, back, support, sanction, ratify. ANT. *1. orphan, disown, shun. 2. reject, shun, refuse.*

adorable *a.* charming, cunning, cute, appealing, captivating, cuddly, lovely, lovable, sweet, precious, darling, irresistible, *huggable. ANT. *gross, disgusting, repulsive, monstrous.*

adoration *n.* love, devotion, worship, veneration, affection, exaltation, reverence, hero worship, idolization, adulation, admiration, infatuation. ANT. *revulsion, repulsion, despising, disgust.*

adore *v.* admire, love, worship, hero-worship, idolize, respect, venerate, honor, look up to, praise, revere, glorify, esteem, *carry a torch for, be taken with, deify, *put on a pedestal, *dig, *groove on, adulate, cherish. ANT. *loathe, disrespect, despise, *spit on.*

adorn *v.* ornament, don, bedeck, dress, decorate, embellish, beautify, trim, festoon, garnish, spruce up, emblazon.

adornment *n.* ornament, decoration, dressing, embellishment, bauble, trinket, trimming, spangle, garnish, trapping, frills, finery, frippery, doodad.

adrenalin *n.* epinephrine, stress hormone, *fight or flight hormone.

adrift *a.* drifting, free-floating, directionless, wandering, unanchored, at the wind's will, astray, aimless, afloat, derelict, loose.

ADROIT *a.* [uh DROYT] mentally or physically skilled. *Sculpting with an adroit hand.* SYN. skillful, deft, dexterous, expert, clever, *crack, sharp, talented, experienced, masterful, practiced, proficient, nimble, astute. ANT. *maladroit, bumbling, fumbling, *dim.*

adulate *v.* flatter, *apple polish, gush, admire, worship, *kiss feet, *brown-nose, fawn, *fall all over. ANT. *disrespect, ignore, insult.*

adulation n. flattery, *feet-kissing, *apple-polishing, *brown-nosing, worshipping, fawning, exaltation, sycophancy, blarney, toadying, blandishment, slavishness, adoration.

adult a. grown-up, mature, aged, seasoned, of age, developed, ripe.

adult n. grown-up, mature person, *big person, man, woman, lady, gentleman. "An obsolete child." — Theodore Geisel.

ADULTERATE v. [uh DULL tuh RATE] to make impure, to spoil or contaminate. *The once pristine waters off Alaska have been adulterated with spilled oil.* SYN. spoil, debase, corrupt, defile, contaminate, ruin, devalue, poison, denature, pollute, degrade, taint, water down, depreciate. ANT. *purify, concentrate.*

adulterer n. adulteress, *cheat, philanderer, fornicator; whore, slut, *Casanova, *skirtchaser, *wolf, *womanizer.

adultery n. infidelity, unfaithfulness, sex, *sleeping around, promiscuity, affair, fornication, *cheating, *stepping out, *swinging, *fooling around on the side, *playing around, *musical beds, *two-timing, *getting a little on the side, philandering, *cheating, *womanizing. "The application of democracy to love." — H.L. Mencken.

advance n. **1.** FORWARD MOVEMENT progression, progress, headway. **2.** PROGRESSION progress, improvement, innovation, breakthrough, development, discovery. **3.** FLIRTATION overture, *move, offer, proposal, invitation. **4.** PAYMENT loan, wages, prepayment, front, retainer, deposit.

advance v. **1.** BRING FORWARD progress, move ahead, propel, push, come, go, make headway, proceed, forge ahead, continue, gain ground, promote. **2.** ASCEND IN RANK promote, step up, *climb up the corporate ladder, move up. **3.** HELP hasten, quicken, aid, assist, further, forward, facilitate, back. **4.** PROPOSE suggest, put forward, submit, proffer, recommend. **5.** PREPAY deposit, retain, loan, front. ANT. *1. stop, reverse, go back. 2. demote, step down. 3. impede, detract, block.*

advanced a. **1.** AHEAD, SUPERIOR forward, beyond, higher, cutting edge, leading edge, progressive, ahead of the times, liberal, avant-garde, precocious, *light years ahead, developed. **2.** GETTING ON IN YEARS aged, venerable, seasoned, experienced. SEE OLD ANT. *1. behind, backwards, slow, obsolete. 2. young, green.*

advance man n. publicist, press agent.

advancement n. **1.** PROMOTION move up, graduation, rise. **2.** PROGRESS breakthrough, innovation, development.

advantage n. **1.** SUPERIORITY edge, *leg up, *upper hand, head start, help, assistance, aid, favor, leverage, *ace in the hole, odds. **2.** BENEFIT gain, profit, blessing, boon, asset. ANT. *1. disadvantage, liability, handicap, weakness.*

advantage, take v. use, impose upon, *step on.

advantageous a. favorable, opportune, profitable, beneficial, auspicious, expedient, propitious, fortunate, for the best. ANT. *unfavorable, inopportune, harmful.*

advection n. transference.

ADVENT n. [ADD vent] the coming or arrival of. *The advent of television in the 1920s was met with skepticism, even by its inventor.* SYN. coming, arrival, appearance, forthcoming, onset, beginning. ANT. *end, demise, death.*

adventure n. thrill-seeking, venture, escapade, expedition, quest, enterprise, geste, dare, risk, danger, hazard, peril, exploration, outing, exploit, undertaking, mission, safari, trek, hunt, odyssey, voyage, *armchair adventure, *cliffhanger. "Something you seek for pleasure, or even for profit, like a gold rush or invading a country . . . the thing you will to occur." — Katherine Anne Porter.

adventurer n. **1.** THRILL-SEEKER explorer, soldier of fortune, hero, heroine, risk-taker, *hired gun, daredevil, voyager, wanderer, swashbuckler, pioneer, knight, trailblazer, pirate, Don Quixote, romantic, *armchair adventurer. "An outlaw . . . Adventure must start with running away from home." — William Bolitho. **2.** SPECULATOR gold-digger, investor, opportunist, fortune hunter, gambler, entrepreneur, *wide-eyed dreamer. ANT. *1. homebody, stick-in-the-mud, *killjoy, milquetoast, Nervous Nellie.*

adventuresome a. venturesome, risk-taking, thrill-seeking, adventurous, daring, foolhardy, opportunistic, bold, enterprising.

adverb n. modifier

ADVERSARY n. [ADD ver ser ee] an opponent or enemy. *The two adversaries squared off in the ring.* SYN. opponent, enemy, foe, rival, protagonist, contestant, antagonist, competitor. ANT. *friend, partner, ally.*

ADVERSE a. [ad VURS] unfavorable or harmful. *The game was cancelled due to adverse weather conditions.* SYN. unfavorable, harmful, bad, negative, unpropitious, opposing, unfortunate, hostile, injurious, conflicting, detrimental. ANT. *favorable, positive, propitious, beneficial.*

ADVERSITY n. [ad VUR sit ee] hardship, unfavorable conditions. *He overcame great adversity to succeed in his profession.* SYN. hardship, misfortune, trouble, ill-fortune, bad luck, calamity, difficulty, distress, suffering, setbacks, disaster, hard times. ANT. *good fortune, ease.*

advertise v. publicize, promote, sell, pitch, plug, ballyhoo, hype, tout, push, puff, herald, proclaim, publish, broadcast.

advertisement n. ad, advert, commercial, plug, blurb, spot, broadside, flier, handbill, classified ad, placard, circular. "Legalized lying." — H.G. Wells. "The rattling of a stick inside a swill bucket." — George Orwell.

advertising n. promotion, publicity, pitching, ballyhoo, selling, heralding, puffery, touting, drumming up, hyping, pushing, proclaiming. "The science of arresting the human intelligence long enough to get money from it." — Stephen Leacock. "The art of making whole lies out of half truths." — Edgar Shoaff.

WORD FIND

accounts, handles advertising: account executive

ad company: agency

addresses of potential customers: mailing list

ad run in selected locale: spot ad

aggressive style of selling: hard sell

ambitious presentation: dog and pony show

award for radio and TV advertising excellence: Clio

catchy phrase or lyric: hook, jingle, slogan

consumer group serving as guinea pigs: test market

editorial-like newspaper ad: advertorial

dishonest touting of high-priced item after advertising low-priced item: bait and switch

expansion of ad campaign beyond test market: rollout

free item, inducement to buy: premium

good word in: plug

graphic design, art head: art director

hand-distributed ad: handbill

hidden "buy" messages in advertising: subliminal advertising

hinged ad boards worn over shoulders: sandwich board

hyperbole: hype, puffery, ballyhoo

illustrated ad in paper or magazine: display ad

mail advertising: direct mail

multimedia sales effort: campaign

New York cluster of large ad agencies: Madison Avenue

plant in audiences to help sell: shill

pre-ad that arouses interest in upcoming product: teaser

posting ads on public structures without permission: sniping

presentation: pitch

print publicity: ink

promotional material given to media: press kit

public relations: PR

recommendation, affirmation of product's quality by consumer: testimonial

royalty paid to performer each time ad runs: residual

telephone advertising: telemarketing

trademark design: logo

writer of ads: copywriter

SEE RADIO, TELEVISION

advice n. counsel, tip, direction, opinion, word to the wise, schooling, guidance, admonition, recommendation, suggestion, hint. "Like snow; the softer it falls, the longer it dwells upon, and the deeper it sinks into, the mind." — Coleridge. "Always a confession." — Emile Herzog.

advisable a. recommended, wise, good advice, good counsel.

advise v. **1.** COUNSEL recommend, tip, direct, guide, admonish, suggest, hint, give a word to the wise, exhort, point out, forewarn, advocate. **2.** NOTIFY inform, let know, educate, fill in, clue in.

advisement n. consideration.

advisory n. report, warning, notice, forewarning, caution.

ADVOCATE n. [ADD vuh ket] one who speaks for or supports a cause or another person. *An advocate for senior citizens' welfare.* SYN. supporter, proponent, pleader, defender, abettor, espouser, champion, activist, propagator, backer, ally, activist, lawyer. ANT. *detractor, opponent, critic.*

ADVOCATE v. [ADD vuh kate] To support a cause or a person. *She advocates equal rights.* SYN. support, propagate, defend, back, plead for, promote, champion, espouse, speak for, uphold, endorse, stand up for. ANT. *fight against, criticize, oppose.*

aegis n. sponsorship, auspices, protection, patronage.

aerial a. **1.** AIRBORNE airy, atmospheric, by air, by aircraft, skyward, heavenward, aloft, up, up and away, supernal. **2.** UNREAL imaginary, ethereal, intangible, fanciful, visionary. **3.** ANTENNA

aerobics *n.* cardiovascular exercise, wind exercises, calisthenics, *dancercise, gymnastics.

aesthete *n.* dilettante, connoisseur, art lover.

AESTHETIC *a.* [es THET ik] pertaining to beauty and that which is pleasing to the eye. *The architecture is aesthetically pleasing.* SYN. beauty, beautiful, artistic, pleasing to the eye, gorgeous. ANT. *ugly, unattractive.*

affable *a.* friendly, amiable, sociable, good-natured, warm, approachable, easy, *chummy, *buddy-buddy, benign.

affair *n.* **1.** MATTER happening, activity, doing, business, thing, operation, concern. **2.** SOCIAL FUNCTION *to-do, gala, black-tie affair, function, party, dinner, celebration. **3.** LOVE AFFAIR affaire d' amour, liaison, tryst, *fling, romance, rendezvous, intimacy.

affect *v.* **1.** INFLUENCE sway, change, act on, evoke, impress, stir, impact upon. **2.** TOUCH THE EMOTIONS move, melt one's heart, warm one's heart, pluck at the heartstrings, disturb, perturb, touch a nerve, stir, *cut to the quick, *hit home. **3.** ASSUME make a pretense, feign, fake, put on, *B.S., adopt, *sham, pose, posture.

affectation *n.* pretense, fraud, airs, show, performance, *going Hollywood, act, pose, posture, mannerism.

affected *a.* **1.** INFLUENCED impressed, swayed, changed, acted upon, stirred, impacted upon. **2.** TOUCHED perturbed, moved, stirred, impressed, distressed, heartened, warmed, agitated. **3.** ARTIFICIAL phony, fake, assumed, contrived, show-off, counterfeit, pretentious, studied, unnatural, feigned, precious, mannered, *full of it, *Hollywood. ANT. *1. unchanged, untouched. 2. unmoved, unaffected. 3. real, authentic, true, down to earth, sincere.*

affection *n.* love, warmth, tenderness, friendship, feeling, devotion, *soft spot, solicitude, fondness, regard, attachment, close feelings. ANT. *hatred, loathing, disgust, coldness.*

affectionate *a.* warm, loving, tender, giving, solicitous, devoted, friendly, *touchy-feely, *lovey-dovey, sensuous, doting, fond, feeling, demonstrative. ANT. *cold, cool, undemonstrative, aloof.*

affidavit *n.* sworn statement, testimony.

affiliate *n.* member, associate, relation, ally, fellow, peer, brother, sister, counterpart, subsidiary, subdivision, branch, part.

affiliate *v.* ASSOCIATE connect, network, join, unite, incorporate, connect, band, *team up with. ANT. *disband, break up, scatter.*

affiliation *n.* association, connection, alliance, network, membership, relationship, union, incorporation, partnership.

AFFINITY *n.* [uh FIN uh tee] attraction, liking. Also, a close relationship or similarity between things. *Children have a natural affinity for junk food. There was a peculiar affinity between Adolph Hitler and Eva Braun.* SYN. **1.** RELATIONSHIP connection, resemblance, likeness, kinship, compatibility, similarity. **2.** LIKING, ATTRACTION fondness, inclination, bent, predilection, affection, leaning, partiality, fancy, penchant. ANT. *1. dissimilarity. 2. repulsion, aversion.*

affirm *v.* assert, declare, firm up, confirm, validate, uphold, proclaim, attest, profess, insist, *swear to, vouch.

affirmation *n.* assertion, declaration, confirmation, validation, avowal, word, swearing, oath, profession.

affix *v.* **1.** ATTACH stick, fasten, bind, fix, connect, staple. **2.** ADD append, annex, tack on. ANT. *1. detach, unfasten, remove. 2. subtract.*

afflict *v.* plague, distress, trouble, bother, prey on, hurt, harm, pester, beset, burden, molest, agitate, torment, torture, injure, weaken. ANT. *relieve.*

affliction *n.* hardship, pain, trouble, illness, suffering, burden, plague, curse, handicap, scourge, *cross to bear, torment, torture, misfortune, adversity, calamity. ANT. *blessing, godsend, gift.*

affluence *n.* riches, abundance, wealth, opulence, plenty, prosperity, luxury, fortune. ANT. *poverty, destitution, lack.*

AFFLUENT *a.* [AFF loo unt] wealthy, opulent. *The affluent residents of Beverly Hills.* SYN. rich, wealthy, prosperous, opulent, well-to-do, well-off, moneyed, *loaded, *well-heeled, *flush, *fat, *filthy rich, *rolling in dough, abundant, plentiful, bountiful. ANT. *impoverished, destitute, *poor as Job's turkey.*

affront *n.* insult, offense, slight, put-down, dig, disrespect, *crack, *shot, *swipe, injury, denigration, barb, slur. ANT. *compliment, flattery.*

AFFRONT *v.* [uh FRUNT] to insult or offend. *He was sorely affronted.* SYN. insult, offend, injure, hurt, irritate, annoy, gall, rile, displease, provoke, pique, slight. ANT. *compliment, flatter, adulate.*

aficionado *n.* devotee, connoisseur. SEE FAN

afoot *a*. about, up and about, astir.

afraid *a*. scared, frightened, fearful, terrified, panic-stricken, alarmed, apprehensive, anxious, shocked, frozen, rattled, startled, leery, jumpy, *wide-eyed with fear, shaky, quivering, *chicken, *chickenshit, *sweating bullets, *scared shitless, *spooked, *scared stiff, faint-hearted, paralyzed, *saucer-eyed, horrified. ANT. *courageous, cool, calm, fearless*. SEE FEAR

afresh *a*. anew, again, once more.

African *a*. Negro, Negroid, black, Nigerian, Egyptian, Algerian, Libyan, Sudanese, Ethiopian, Ugandan, Kenyan, Tanzanian, Angolan, Zambian, Botswanian, South African, Namibian, Bantu, Gabunese, Moroccan, Tunisian, Senegalese, Ghanaian, Bushman, Pygmy, Masai, Zulu.

WORD FIND

bushman: Qung

dance: juba

desert: Sahara, Kalahari, Libyan

garment: tobe, kaross, haik

gold region: Rand

grassland: veldt

house: tembe

hut: kraal, tembe

language: Bantu, Hamite, Swahili, Hausa

tableland: karoo

tree: cola, baobab, baku, sassy, moli, kola, bumbo, gamdeboo

village: dorp, stad, kraal

wind: simoom, simoon

wood: ebony, teak

aft *a*. astearn, abaft, back.

after *a*. **1.** LATER afterward, thereafter, following, subsequent. **2.** BEHIND preceded by, in back of, following.

after *prep*. in pursuit of, looking for, in search of.

afterlife *n*. heaven, hereafter, eternity, bliss.

aftermath *n*. consequence, aftereffect, result, outcome, effect, fallout, repercussions.

again *a*. once more, repeatedly, anew.

agape *a*. or *adv*. **1.** OPEN gaping, wide open. **2.** STATE OF AMAZEMENT dumbstruck, flabbergasted, astonished, saucer-eyed, goggle-eyed, bug-eyed, wonderstruck.

age *n*. **1.** PERIOD OF TIME generation, duration, lifetime, era, epoch, period, century, millenium, cycle, span. **2.** STAGE season, phase, point, year, maturity, majority, minority, adulthood, declining years, youth, adolescence, infancy, middle age. "It takes about ten years to get used to how old you are."—

Unknown. "[Something that] doesn't matter unless you're a cheese."—Billie Burke.

age *v*. mature, ripen, develop, grow older, season, weather, mellow, slow down, waste away. "To take in sail."—Emerson. SEE OLD, OLD AGE, OLD-FACED

aged *a*. elderly, old, venerable, advanced, matured, past one's prime, vintage, seasoned, weathered, ripened, ageless, *long in the tooth, *one foot in the grave, old as Methuselah, worn, decrepit, decayed, deteriorated. ANT. *fresh, green, unseasoned*. SEE ANTIQUE, OLD, OLD-FACED

ageless *a*. eternal, infinite, perpetual, timeless.

agency *n*. **1.** ORGANIZATION department, office, bureau, company, corporation, firm, concern, operation. **2.** POWER auspices, action, operation, means, influence, work, activity, medium.

AGENDA *n*. [uh JEN da] a list of things to be done. *What's on your agenda today?* SYN. schedule, list, program, itinerary, calendar, docket, planning, lineup.

agent *n*. **1.** DOER actor, executor, functionary, mover. **2.** REPRESENTATIVE assignee, delegate, deputy, advocate, proxy, middleman, broker, go-between, proctor, salesman, envoy, handler. **3.** FORCE power, instrument, cause, mechanism, means.

agglomeration *n*. heap, jumble, mass, pile, gathering, collection, cluster.

agglutinate *v*. join, attach, adhere, glue, stick.

aggrandize *v*. enlarge, extend, expand, blow up, exaggerate, increase, inflate, puff up. ANT. *minimalize, shrink, deflate*.

aggravate *v*. **1.** MAKE WORSE worsen, exacerbate, intensify, heighten, deepen, *add fuel to the fire, *fan the flames, *rub it in. **2.** ANNOY irritate, *bug, exasperate, vex, provoke, inflame, rile, irk, ruffle, *rub the wrong way, *miff, *yank one's chain, *rattle one's cage, *piss off. ANT. *1. lessen, relieve, mitigate. 2. calm, humor, pacify*.

aggravation *n*. **1.** WORSENING exacerbation, intensification, deepening, inflammation, magnifying, deepening. **2.** ANNOYANCE irritation, vexation, exasperation, inflammation, *pain, *pain in the ass, hassle, nuisance, *headache, *thorn in one's side, bother. ANT. *1. improvement, lessening, relieving. 2. pleasure, delight*.

aggregate *n*. composite, total, mass, cluster, mix, blend, assembly, sum total, whole.

aggress *v*. attack, *jump on, initiate.

aggression *n*. **1.** ASSAULT attack, offensive, raid,

invasion, blitzkrieg. **2.** HOSTILITY offensiveness, violence, belligerence, combativeness, pugnaciousness, fight. "An innate, independent, instinctual disposition in man … it constitutes the most powerful obstacle to culture." — Sigmund Freud.

aggressive *a.* **1.** HOSTILE belligerent, combative, offensive, violent, pugnacious, nasty, quarrelsome, militant. **2.** BOLD OR COMPETITIVE enterprising, *go-getting, *high octane, ambitious, assertive, persistent, pushy, vigorous, obnoxious, domineering, forceful, *ballsy. ANT. *1. passive, peaceful, mild. 2. passive, lazy, ineffectual, laid-back, timid.*

aggressor *n.* attacker, initiator, invader, raider, trespasser, assailant, provoker, offender, instigator.

aggrieve *v.* distress, wrong, disturb, hurt, injure, offend, slight, trouble, wound.

aggrieved *a.* wronged, offended, distressed, disturbed, injured, hurt, afflicted, wounded, depressed, troubled.

aghast *a.* terrified, horrified, horror-struck, dismayed, appalled, stunned, shocked, agape. ANT. *unperturbed, undisturbed.*

agile *a.* nimble, quick, spry, deft, keen, brisk, light-footed, dexterous, sprightly, active, lithe, lively, supple. ANT. *clumsy, ponderous, oafish.*

agility *n.* nimbleness, quickness, keenness, sharpness, light-footedness, dexterity, sprightliness, suppleness, liveliness, adroitness. ANT. *clumsiness, slowness, oafishness.*

aging *n.* maturing, growing, seasoning, senescent, declining, mellowing, getting old, wearing out, wilting. SEE AGE

agitate *v.* **1.** SHAKE OR MIX stir, move, churn, make turbulent, bounce, disturb, toss. **2.** DISTURB EMOTIONALLY shake up, stir, arouse, inflame, ignite, wind up, jolt, fluster, excite, incite. ANT. *2. becalm, quiet, pacify.*

agitation *n.* **1.** SHAKING OR MIXING stirring, churning, turbulence, bouncing, disturbance, tossing, turning. **2.** EMOTIONAL DISTURBANCE arousal, excitement, inflammation, stirring, jolt, turmoil, upheaval, commotion, provocation, rabble rousing. ANT. *2. becalming, quieting, pacifying.*

agitator *n.* rabble-rouser, firebrand, *mover and shaker, rebel, provocateur, incendiary, anarchist, inciter, troublemaker, instigator, spark.

aglow *a.* radiant, shining.

agnate *a.* akin. SEE RELATED

agnomen *n.* SEE NICKNAME

AGNOSTIC *n.* [ag NOS tik] one who believes that it is impossible to know whether or not God exists. *Agnostics believe nothing beyond the material world can be known by the human mind.* SYN. disbeliever, freethinker, skeptic, cynic, doubter, doubting Thomas, philosopher, thinker, atheist. "One who doesn't know whether God exists, but is afraid to say so loudly in case God might hear him." — Eugene Brussell. ANT. *believer, faithful one.*

agnosticism *n.* freethinking, disbelief, faithlessness, doubting, closed-mindedness, skepticism, atheism. "Simply means that a man shall not say he knows or believes that for which he has no grounds for professing to believe." — Thomas Huxley. ANT. *faith, belief, devoutness.*

agog *a.* eager, excited, anxious, enthusiastic, expectant.

agonize *v.* suffer, bleed, struggle, worry, fret, torture oneself, stew, lose sleep over, brood over, *sweat bullets, writhe, stay awake nights, grapple.

agony *n.* suffering, pain, torture, distress, torment, misery, struggle, affliction, sorrow, discomfort, dolor. ANT. *bliss, euphoria, pleasure.*

agrarian *a.* agricultural, pastoral, rural, rustic. SEE AGRICULTURE, FARM, FARMING

agree *v.* concur, accord, accede, be of one mind, come to terms, consent, grant, fall in line, side with, *see eye to eye, *square with, harmonize, correspond, coincide, jibe. ANT. *disagree, differ, oppose.*

agreeable *a.* **1.** CONSENTING conforming, complying, amenable, in accord, accepting. **2.** PLEASING acceptable, good, likable, to one's liking, unobjectionable, appealing, felicitous, pleasurable. ANT. *disagreeable, unacceptable.*

agreement *n.* **1.** WRITTEN OR ORAL CONTRACT understanding, contract, bargain, deal, covenant, pact, arrangement. **2.** HARMONY, ACCORD conformity, compromise, correspondence, accordance, consensus, accession, understanding, compatibility, uniformity, *meeting of the minds.

agriculture *n.* farming, crop-raising, husbandry, cultivation, agronomy. SEE FARM, FARMING

aground *a.* ashore, beached, stuck fast, stranded.

ahead *a.* in front, foremost, before, forward, advanced, leading, fronting, preceding, outdistancing. ANT. *behind, rearward, back.*

aid *n.* assistance, help, service, support, benefit,

helping hand, contribution, benevolence, kindness, welfare.

aid *v.* assist, help, serve, support, benefit, contribute, pitch in, lend a hand, oblige, abet.

aide *n.* assistant, adjutant, *right-hand man, aide-de-camp.

AIDS SEE ACQUIRED IMMUNE DEFICIENCY SYNDROME

ail *v.* trouble, pain, distress, bother, upset, afflict, hurt.

ailing *a.* ill, aching, afflicted. SEE SICK

ailment *n.* illness, malady, affliction. SEE SICKNESS

aim *n.* intention, target, goal, object, purpose.

aim *v.* **1.** POINT direct, draw a bead on, level, train, zero in on, measure, eye. **2.** DIRECT ONE'S EFFORTS shoot for, go for, try for, plan, intend, aspire.

aimless *a.* purposeless, pointless, drifting, straying, wandering, desultory, haphazard.

air *n.* **1.** gas, atmosphere, oxygen, nitrogen, ozone, sky, aerospace. **2.** BEARING manner, attitude, deportment, appearance, aura. **3.** AFFECTATION pose, posture, pretense, manner, haughtiness. SEE ATMOSPHERE, WIND

air *v.* **1.** AERATE ventilate, let out, expose, dry, cool, freshen. **2.** ANNOUNCE PUBLICLY publicize, confess, profess. **3.** BROADCAST transmit, televise.

aircraft *n.* airplane, jet, balloon, helicopter, dirigible, blimp, lighter-than-air craft, airship, airliner, zeppelin, *chopper, *egg beater, flying machine, *whirlibird, flying saucer, UFO, ultralight, Learjet, Cessna Citation, Rockwell Sabreliner, Grumman Gulfstream, Concorde, SST, Airbus, Boeing 707-757, Douglas DC-10.

WORD FIND

air hole causing sudden drop: air pocket

air traffic jam: stack

air washed behind: backwash, prop wash, slipstream

altitude measuring device: altimeter

approach to airport: approach, glidepath

automatic flying system: autopilot

boom after exceeding speed of sound: sonic boom

broadside wind hazard: crosswind

cargo, baggage and passengers: payload

climbing stunt turn of 180 degrees: chandelle

cockpit: cabin

course: flight path

cover over motor: cowling

crash-land in water: ditch

dangerous wind condition: wind shear

detracted landing gear and flaps: flying clean

distance required for safe landing: rollout

disturbed air: turbulence

double-winged craft: biplane

drive on ground: taxi

exhaust trail in sky: contrail

falling out of sky due to low air speed: stall

faster than speed of sound: supersonic, hypersonic

flap on trailing edge of wing: aileron, airfoil

flap that slows aircraft or increases rate of descent: spoiler

flashing white lights on wingtips: strobes

flight data recorder: black box

fluid-based controls: hydraulics

green identification light on right side: starboard light

high-speed wind stream: jet stream

ice accumulation: icing

international flight route: corridor

late-night flight: redeye

light, single-seat aircraft: ultralight

long body portion: fuselage

loss of engine combustion during flight: flameout

lowest possible speed before stalling: critical speed

maximum altitude according to weather conditions: ceiling

motorless plane: glider

navigation computer system: inertial navigation system, loran

nose forced up or down by wind: pitching

opposing wind during flight: headwind

oxygen deprivation over 12,500 feet: hypoxia

perfect landing: three-point landing

physics behind flight: aerodynamics

pitch and roll display: artificial horizon

radio landing aid: microwave landing system

raise air pressure: pressurize

rapid, uncontrolled descent: dive, spin

red light on left side of craft: port light

roll and yaw caused by wind gust: Dutch roll

rollover stunt: barrel roll

sideways motion caused by wind: crabbing

speedometer: air speed indicator

stunt flying exhibition: barnstorming

tail flap controlling up and down movement of craft: elevator

tail flap that turns craft: rudder

triangular wing: delta wing

turn: bank

UFO: bogey

unmanned, radio-controlled craft: drone
vertical stabilizer at tail: fin
workshop, shelter: hangar
SEE AIR FORCE, AIRPORT, BALLOON, DIRIGIBLE, ROCKET, SATELLITE, SPACESHIP

Air Force n. air defense. A-4 Skyhawk, A-6 Intruder, A-7 Corsair, A-10 Thunderbolt, AC-130 Hercules, B-52 Stratofortress, C-5A Galaxy, C-141 Starlifter, F-4 Phantom, F-14 Tomcat, F-15 Eagle, F-16 air combat fighter, F-101 Voodoo, F-105 Thunderchief, KC-135 Stratotanker, B-2 Stealth Bomber, F-117A Stealth Fighter, P-3 Orion, Harrier.
WORD FIND

air attack: air strike, bombing run, dog fight, strafing
airborne early warning system: AWACS
altitude code for thousands of feet: angels
bombing over large area: carpet bombing
bombs: eggs
distress call: mayday
electronic jamming: music
emergency takeoff: scramble
enemy shot down, code: splashed
fire upon enemy aircraft: engage
gravity suit: anti-g suit
group: echelon, escadrille, squadron, wing
information gathering: reconnaissance
landing, wish to land, code: pancake
missile fired, code: fox away
one aircraft flight: sortie
over land, code: feet dry
over water, code: feet wet
radar confusers comprised of metal foil, strips dropped from air: chaff
reduced visibility, code: popeye
suspected carrier of nuclear weapons, code: purple
target position in relation to aircraft: clock code position
UFO assumed to be enemy: bogey
unmanned reconnaissance craft: drone
SEE AIRCRAFT, AIRPORT, ROCKET, MISSILE, NAVY

airhead n. Sl. idiot, dolt. SEE MORON

airplane SEE AIRCRAFT

airport n. airfield, airstrip, jetport, air base, aerodrome, landing strip, runway.
WORD FIND

ascent area beyond runway: clearway
baggage conveyor: baggage carousel
barrier, wall that shields passengers from jet exhaust: blast fence
centerline landing, takeoff strip: runway
control center: control tower
driveway leading on or off runway: taxiway

glassed-in enclosure in control tower: cab
ground traffic directors: marshallers
guide lights leading to airport: approach lights, sequence flashers; barrette
loading and refueling area: apron
luggage carrier, assistant: skycap
maintenance and aircraft shelter: hangar
maintenance crew: ground crew
off-runway waiting area: holding bay
overseeing agency: FAA, Federal Aviation Administration
pilot's weather and route info center: flight service center
radio-guided landing system: microwave landing system
tower personnel: air traffic controller
turnoff lanes off runway: rollout lanes
wind direction indicator: wind sock
SEE AIRCRAFT, AIR FORCE, DIRIGIBLE

airs SEE AIR

airtight a. **1.** SEALED TIGHT hermetic. **2.** Invulnerable, impregnable, flawless.

aisle n. walkway, lane, corridor, passageway, nave.

akin a. **1.** RELATED kin, kindred, agnate. **2.** SIMILAR like, resembling, analogous, identical, germane.

ALACRITY n. [uh LAK ri tee] eager willingness. *He accepted his nomination for beauty contest judge with great alacrity.* SYN. eagerness, willingness, enthusiasm, readiness, fervor, quickness. ANT. *hesitance, reservation, reluctance.*

alarm n. **1.** FEAR shock, terror, horror, astonishment, anxiety, panic, trepidation, fight or flight response, apprehension, distress. **2.** ALERT siren, bell, horn, whistle, tocsin, call to arms, alarum, blast. ANT. **1.** *calm, nonchalance, reassurance.*

alarm v. **1.** FRIGHTEN shock, scare, terrify, horrify, astonish, panic, distress, startle. **2.** ALERT warn, arouse, caution, signal. ANT. *calm, reassure, soothe.*

ALARMIST n. [uh LARM ist] one who overreacts to a situation and spreads alarm needlessly. *Those who believe the world will end soon are generally brushed off as alarmists.* SYN. prophet/voice of doom, scaremonger, Chicken Little, Cassandra.

ALBATROSS (around one's neck) n. [AL ba tross] used metaphorically to symbolize a burden of guilt or disgrace; from the albatross that brought bad luck after it was shot and hung around the Mariner's neck in "The Rime of the Ancient Mariner." *Watergate* *was Richard Nixon's albatross.* SYN. burden, disgrace, cross to bear, millstone, misery, woe, load.

album *n.* anthology, folder, scrapbook, notebook, miscellany.

alcohol *n.* liquor, spirits, *booze, *firewater, *joy juice, *the sauce, *hard stuff, intoxicant. SEE BEER, DRINK, MOONSHINE, WINE

alcoholic *a.* fermented, intoxicating, spiritous, distilled, inebriative, hard.

alcoholic *n.* *lush, drunk, *boozer, *rummy, *souse, *sot, *wino.

alcove *n.* recess, nook, niche, bower, bay.

ale *n.* beer, lager, stout.

alert *a.* on guard, watchful, ready, vigilant, on one's toes, keen, wide-awake, wary, attentive, *on the ball, *with it, sharp, active, lively. ANT. *asleep, *out to lunch, comatose.*

alert *n.* alarm, signal, warning, tocsin.

alert *v.* warn, signal, inform, notify.

alias *n.* a.k.a. (also known as), assumed name. SEE PEN NAME

alibi *n.* explanation, defense, plea, excuse, *cover story, pretext.

alien *a.* **1.** FOREIGN strange, odd, unfamiliar, exotic, outlandish.

alien *n.* **1.** FOREIGNER immigrant, illegal alien, outsider, refugee, stranger, noncitizen. **2.** EXTRATERRESTRIAL spaceman, space creature. ANT. *native, citizen, local.*

alienate *v.* estrange, distance, separate, come between, disengage, shut out, ignore.

alight *v.* settle, land, light.

align *v.* true, aline, line up, level, make flush.

alike *a.* like, similar, identical, comparable, kindred, corresponding, mirror images.

alimony *n.* support payment, child support, allowance. "Disinterest, compounded annually." — Walter McDonald. "Buying oats for a dead horse." — Arthur Baer.

alive *a.* **1.** LIVING vital, animate, existing, *alive and kicking, organic. **2.** LIVELY alert, vigorous, vivacious, animated, spirited, bubbly, energetic, vibrant, bustling. ANT. *1. dead, inanimate, nonfunctioning. 2. sluggish, lethargic, slothlike.*

all *n.* total, totality, whole, entirety, everything, *bag and baggage.

all *a.* whole, entire, complete, every, each, each and every.

all-around *a.* versatile, multifaceted, complete.

ALLAY *v.* [uh LAY] to quiet, lessen or relieve. *A reassuring word to allay your fears.* SYN. reduce, quiet, lessen, abate, alleviate, mitigate, ease, slake, put to rest, sooth, assuage. ANT.

magnify, intensify, heighten.

allegation *n.* assertion, accusation, charge, incrimination, claim, statement, complaint, indictment, insinuation.

ALLEGE *v.* [uh LEJ] to make an assertion, particularly without proof. *We allege that Ralph took the last cookie.* SYN. assert, accuse, charge, incriminate, claim, state, complain, indict, declare, insinuate, affirm, attest, purport.

allegiance *n.* loyalty, devotion, support, obedience, fidelity. ANT. *disloyalty, disobedience, betrayal.*

allegory *n.* parable, fable, moral, myth, story, tale.

allergen *n.* irritant, ragweed, pollen, dust mite, dander.

allergic *a.* sensitive, susceptible.

allergy *n.* sensitivity, susceptibility, hypersensitivity, immune defense, hay fever.

alleviate *v.* lighten, lessen, reduce, relieve, ease, mitigate, allay, soften, diminish, slake, assuage. ANT. *exacerbate, intensify, aggravate.*

alley *n.* passage, lane, cul-de-sac, deadend, walkway.

alliance *n.* **1.** UNION joining, association, affiliation, partnership, coalition, confederacy, league, federation, consortium. **2.** AGREEMENT pact, friendship, treaty, covenant, understanding, deal, contract.

allied *a.* joined, associated, affiliated, federated, confederate, cooperative, unionized, united, amalgamated. ANT. *independent, sole.*

all-nighter *n.* *redeye, *graveyard shift/duty.

ALLOCATE *v.* [AL uh KATE] to allot or distribute. *Allocate funds to meet the budget.* SYN. allot, distribute, mete, dole out, assign, designate, earmark, ration, appropriate, set aside.

allocation *n.* distribution, ration, allotment.

allot *v.* assign, apportion, mete. SEE ALLOCATE

allotment *n.* portion, distribution, share, part, cut, parcel, measure, allocation, ration.

all-out *a.* total, maximum. SEE THOROUGH

allow *v.* **1.** PERMIT let, tolerate, put up with, grant, approve of, *give the green light to, authorize, *give the go-ahead. **2.** ADMIT acknowledge, concede, acquiesce. **3.** ALLOT allocate, give, set aside, plan for. ANT. *1. forbid, prohibit, refuse. 2. deny, reject.*

allowance *n.* share, allotment, pay, support, ration, appropriation, subsidy, stipend, recompense, contribution, percentage, earnings.

all-purpose *a.* multitalented, multifaceted. SEE VERSATILE

all right *a.* **1.** SEE OKAY **2.** SEE INTACT, WELL

allude *v.* refer to, hint, suggest, imply, mention in a roundabout way, make an allusion to, *dance around.

allure *n.* attraction, magnetism, charm, appeal, sex appeal, fascination, temptation.

allure *v.* attract, entice, fascinate, bait, charm, seduce, tempt, captivate, beguile, lure, tantalize.

alluring *a.* attractive, charming, seductive, enticing, fascinating, tempting, bewitching, captivating, beguiling, irresistible, tantalizing, magnetic. ANT. *repulsive, repelling, nauseating.*

ALLUSION *n.* [a LOO zhun] an indirect reference, an implication, not to be confused with *delusion* or *illusion*. *He made an allusion to Dickens when he said, "It was the best of times, it was the worst of times."* SYN. reference, mention, implication, hint, suggestion, casual remark, inference.

ally *n.* associate, partner, confederate, helper, collaborator, colleague, affiliate, friend. ANT. *enemy, foe, adversary.*

almighty *a.* omnipotent, invincible, invulnerable, all-powerful, supreme.

almost *a.* nearly, just about, approaching, close to, well-nigh, virtually, verging, practically.

alms *n.* charity, handout, assistance, contribution, donation, benefaction, welfare, dole, aid.

aloft *a.* airborne, flying, skyward.

alone *a.* **1.** LONE solitary, isolated, friendless, separate, unaccompanied, abandoned, alienated, solo, desolate, lonesome, *solitary as an oyster. SEE SOLITUDE **2.** PEERLESS unique, without equal, unparalleled, unsurpassed, incomparable, singular. ANT. *1. mobbed, crowded, grouped. 2. ordinary, common, *dime a dozen.*

along *prep.* BESIDE over the length of, alongside, parallel with.

ALOOF *a.* [uh LOOF] distant or remote. *He was strangely quiet and aloof, like a lone wolf.* SYN. distant, remote, reserved, *at arm's length, cool, standoffish, chilly, *stuck up, unapproachable, closed, unfriendly, unsociable. ANT. *friendly, warm, open.*

aloud *a.* audible, loudly, intelligibly, distinctly. ANT. *inaudibly, silently.*

alpine *a.* lofty, alpestrine, high. SEE MOUNTAINOUS

already *a.* by now, before now, previously, beforehand.

also *a.* in addition, and, furthermore, plus, as well, *to boot, moreover.

altar *n.* platform, table, shrine.

alter *v.* change, modify, fit, adjust, reform, shift, adapt, revise, correct, amend. ANT. *maintain, keep.*

alteration *n.* change, modification, fitting, adjustment, shift, adaptation, revision, correction, amendment.

altercation *n.* quarrel, fight, argument, dispute, wrangle, *row, bickering, *tiff, squabble, *run-in, *words, falling out. SEE FIGHT ANT. *peace, harmony.*

ALTER EGO *n.* [ALL ter EE go] another side of one's personality. Also, a close friend or companion. *Everyone has an alter ego; Hitler liked dogs.* SYN. **1.** dark side, private side, id, counterpart, doppelgänger. **2.** sidekick, *buddy, pal, companion, comrade, chum, confidante, soul mate.

alternate *n.* backup, second, stand-in, double, substitute, surrogate.

alternate *v.* take turns, rotate, switch off, change, reciprocate, vacillate.

alternative *n.* choice, option, backup, pick, selection, replacement, substitute.

although *conj.* albeit, in spite of, notwithstanding, granting that.

altitude *n.* height. SEE ELEVATION

altogether *a.* completely, wholly, totally, all told, in toto, utterly, entirely, absolutely.

ALTRUISM *n.* [AL troo IZ um] unselfish concern for others, humanitarianism without selfish gain. *Anonymous donations and other forms of altruism.* SYN. selflessness, humanitarianism, benevolence, kindness, philanthropy, charity, big-heartedness, magnanimity, humaneness. *"Disregarding one's own cause."* — Eugene Brussell. ANT. *selfishness, greediness, piggishness.*

altruistic *a.* selfless, unselfish, humanitarian, benevolent, kind, giving, philanthropic, charitable, big-hearted, magnanimous, humane. ANT. *selfish, self-centered, greedy, cold-hearted.*

always *a.* forever, everlasting, perpetually, relentlessly, unremittingly, infinitely, eternally, unceasingly, constantly. ANT. *never, temporarily.*

amalgam *n.* mixture, blend, combination, amalgamation, alloy, compound.

amalgamate *v.* mix, blend, combine, compound, consolidate, fuse, merge, integrate, unite. ANT. *separate, divide, diffuse, disperse.*

amalgamation *n.* SEE AMALGAM

amass *v.* lump, pile, heap, accumulate, gather,

assemble, collect, compile, save, acquire, *squirrel away, stockpile, hoard. ANT. *disperse, scatter.*

amateur n. nonprofessional, dabbler, dilettante, neophyte, tyro, novice, rookie, layman, *bush-leaguer, *lightweight. "A public nuisance who confounds his ambition with his ability." — Ambrose Bierce. ANT. *professional, master, virtuoso.*

amateurish a. unprofessional, unskilled, inexperienced, bumbling, fumbling, incompetent, inept, unpolished, rough, *bushleague, second-rate, insipid, hackneyed. ANT. *professional, skilled, polished.*

amatory a. sexual, loving, passionate, lustful, amorous, erotic, romantic, sensual, ardent, rapturous.

amaze v. astonish, stun, fascinate, flabbergast, dumbfound, shock, *blow one away, jolt, electrify, *curl one's hair, surprise, *bowl one over, *wow.

amazement n. astonishment, fascination, shock, wonder, surprise, bewilderment, disbelief, awe, wide-eyed wonderment.

amazing a. astonishing, fascinating, stunning, shocking, wonderful, surprising, bewildering, prodigious, awesome, unbelievable, astounding, incredible, marvelous. ANT. *ho-hum, boring, nothing special.*

ambassador n. diplomat, representative, emissary, delegate, consul, goodwill ambassador, envoy, agent. "A paid political tourist." — Anon. "A politician who is given a job abroad in order to get him out of the country." — Anon.

amber a. gold. SEE YELLOW

ambience n. atmosphere, air, milieu, environment, climate, setting, surroundings, aura.

AMBIGUOUS a. [am BIG yoo us] having two or more meanings or interpretations, unclear, confusing. *Politicians often make ambiguous statements in order not to offend anyone.* SYN. unclear, vague, equivocal, hazy, *clear as mud, indefinite, uncertain, obscure, duplicitous, dubious, questionable, lefthanded. ANT. *clear, unequivocal, certain.*

ambition n. **1.** DRIVE determination, striving, spirit, initiative, enterprise, will, motivation, *get up and go, hunger. "The wings of great actions." — Johann Goethe. "Nets to catch the wind." — John Webster. "A mental condition which compels one to work one's self to death in order to live." — Anon. **2.** GOAL aspiration, aim, target, dream, desire, wish. ANT. *laziness, apathy, sloth.*

ambitious a. **1.** ENTERPRISING aspiring, determined, hard-driving, *go-getting, aggressive, hungry, motivated, hard-working, striving, eager, avid, zealous, emulous, goal-oriented, *high octane, industrious. **2.** DEMANDING formidable, difficult, lofty, taxing, prodigious. ANT. **1.** *lazy, slothful, inert.* **2.** *undemanding, simple, humble.*

AMBIVALENT a. [am BIV uh lent] having mixed or contrasting attitudes. *Many people have ambivalent feelings about abortion.* SYN. mixed, conflicting, contradictory, wavering, vacillating, undecided, confused, of two minds, indecisive. ANT. *certain, concrete, *no two ways about it, settled.*

amble v. stroll, saunter, shuffle, ramble, *mosey, *sashay. SEE WALK

ambrosial a. fit for the gods, delectable, mouthwatering. SEE DELICIOUS

ambush n. ambuscade, surprise attack, *booby trap, assault, mugging, hiding place, cover, blind.

ambush v. attack, jump, assault, surprise, *bushwack, waylay.

AMELIORATE v. [uh MEEL yuh RATE] improve, make better, mend, amend, correct, upgrade, fix, relieve. *We could ameliorate environmental degradation by limiting population.* ANT. *exacerbate, aggravate, worsen.*

AMENABLE a. [uh MEN uh bul] willing, responsive or agreeable. *He was amenable to change.* SYN. open, acquiescent, cooperative, obedient, tractable, pliable. ANT. *unwilling, closed-minded, disagreeable.*

amend v. **1.** IMPROVE better, correct, fix, mend, ameliorate. **2.** CHANGE revise, correct, edit, alter, revise, transform. ANT. *worsen, damage, corrupt.*

amendment n. **1.** IMPROVEMENT betterment, amelioration, upgrade, correction, reform, revision. **2.** ADDITION modification, attachment, addendum, supplement, adjunct, rider.

amends n. apology, redress, recompense, atonement, restitution, reparation.

amenity n. **1.** PLEASANTNESS agreeableness, civility, courtesy, geniality, politeness, manners. **2.** COMFORT nicety, extra, frill, luxury, convenience, pleasantry, refinement, creature comfort, facility. ANT. **1.** *unpleasantness, rudeness, nastiness.* **2.** *discomfort, bare necessity.*

AMIABLE a. [AY mee uh bul] friendly, good-natured. *The dolphin has always been seen as a fun-loving, amiable sort.* SYN. friendly, good-natured, congenial, sociable, agreeable, outgoing, amicable, affable, approachable, good-humored, cordial, warm. ANT. *cold, unfriendly, antisocial.*

amicable *a.* friendly, peaceable, affable, easygoing, gracious, congenial, neighborly, benign, amiable, harmonious. ANT. *unfriendly, nasty, aggressive.*

amid *prep.* amidst, among.

amiss *a.* wrong, improper, awry, incorrect, mistaken, out of place, *screwy, faulty, askew, inappropriate. ANT. *right, correct, okay.*

amity *n.* friendship, goodwill, peace, harmony, accord, brotherhood, fellowship, understanding, concord. ANT. *hostility, antagonism, discord.*

ammunition *n.* *ammo, ordnance, shot, bullets, shells, munitions, arms, materiel, explosives, grenades, canisters.

WORD FIND

bullet-holding belt worn over shoulder: bandolier, cartridge belt
cartridge with no projectile: blank
case of projectiles fired from cannon: canister
cast-iron balls: grapeshot
dangerous fragments of: shrapnel
glowing trail across sky, produces: tracer
gun's bullet-storage receptacle: clip, magazine
one shot: round
stockpile of ammo: munitions dump
wagon that carries ammunition: caisson
SEE BOMB, BULLET, GUN, MISSILE, NUCLEAR BOMB, WAR, WEAPON

amnesia *n.* memory loss, fugue.

AMNESTY *n.* [AM nes tee] a pardon, often of a political nature. *The war resistors were granted amnesty.* SYN. pardon, forgiveness, absolution, exemption, excusing, clemency, lenience, immunity. "The state's magnanimity to those offenders whom it would be too expensive to punish." —Ambrose Bierce. ANT. *damnation, sentencing, condemnation.*

among *prep.* amidst, amid, in, between, in the middle of.

amorous *a.* loving, sexual, erotic, seductive, ardent, *horny, *hot, romantic, *turned on, in love, sensual, passionate, lustful, smitten, *spoony, *in the mood.

AMORPHOUS *a.* [uh MOR fus] shapeless, without form. *Abstract art is sometimes completely amorphous.* SYN. shapeless, vague, formless, undefined, nondescript, characterless, nebulous. ANT. *defined, outlined, specific.*

amount *n.* **1.** AGGREGATE total, sum, bottom line, *whole shebang. **2.** QUANTITY number, total, count, mass, volume, measure.

amour *n.* affair, fling, tryst, relationship, dalliance, romance, liaison.

ampitheater *n.* theater, coliseum. SEE ARENA

ample *a.* **1.** LARGE spacious, capacious, commodious, huge, immense, extensive, roomy. **2.** ABUNDANT sufficient, plenty, enough, copious, lavish, bountiful, more than adequate. ANT. **1.** *tiny, cramped, restricted.* **2.** *inadequate, insufficient, small.*

amplify *v.* increase, heighten, intensify, enlarge, magnify, strengthen, augment, *crank, *beef up, turn up, boost. ANT. *decrease, diminish, turn down.*

amputate *v.* cut off, remove, sever, dismember, excise, lop off. SEE OPERATION

amuck *a.* berserk, wild, violent.

amulet *n.* charm, talisman, good luck piece, fetish.

amuse *v.* occupy, entertain, interest, divert, beguile, distract, regale, engross, tickle, cheer. ANT. *bore, put to sleep, weary, cloy, depress.*

amusement *n.* entertainment, diversion, pleasure, pastime, distraction, enjoyment, fun, sport, game, play, merriment, *laughs, *jollies. "A metaphysical trick to deceive our anguish." —Jean De Menasce.

amusing *a.* **1.** OCCUPYING absorbing, engrossing, entertaining, diverting, distracting, beguiling, cheering. **2.** FUNNY hilarious, tickling, comical, silly, foolish, ludicrous, zany, sidesplitting, whimsical, droll, jocular, *a scream. ANT. **1.** *boring, somnolent, dull.* **2.** *depressing, grim, sad.*

anachronism *n.* misfit, incongruity.

analgesic *n.* pain reliever, anesthetic, numbing agent, painkiller, opiate.

analogous *a.* comparable, similar, corresponding, like, congruous, equivalent, akin, cognate, homologous. ANT. *dissimilar, different, opposite.*

ANALOGY *n.* [uh NAL uh jee] A comparison between two similar or dissimilar things. *An analogy between self-confidence and speaking ability.* SYN. comparison, similarity, resemblance, semblance, likeness, relationship, kinship, correlation, correspondence. ANT. *difference, dissimilarity.*

analysis *n.* examination, dissection, investigation, study, breakdown, test, assay, evaluation, review, interpretation.

analytical *a.* investigative, inquisitive, evaluating, critical.

analyze v. examine, dissect, investigate, study, break down, test, assay, evaluate, review, interpret.

anarchist n. rebel, revolutionary, radical, rabble-rouser, nihilist, insurrectionist, terrorist, agitator, *red. "[One who] may want his neighbor to be governed, but he himself doesn't want to be governed." — George Bernard Shaw.

ANARCHY n. [AN ar kee] chaos, disorder; absence of government. *The riots brought widespread looting and anarchy.* SYN. chaos, disorder, confusion, lawlessness, rioting, turmoil, mayhem, bedlam, revolution, violence, collapse of authority. ANT. *order, law and order, organization.*

anathema n. **1.** THE DAMNED the accursed, the condemned, pariah, outcast, heretic, villain. **2.** CURSE ban, excommunication, denunciation, proscription, imprecation, damnation, condemnation. ANT. *1. the blessed. 2. blessing.*

anatomy n. structure, skeleton, framework, composition. "Something everybody has but it looks better on a girl." — Bruce Raeburn.

ancestor n. **1.** FOREBEAR forefather, father, progenitor, elder, procreator. **2.** PREDECESSOR precursor, forerunner, originator, prototype, antecedent, ascendant. ANT. *1. offspring, descendant, progeny. 2. successor.*

ancestry n. lineage, heredity, background, family tree, stock, pedigree, parentage, heritage, history, blood, roots, progenitors, forefathers. "If famous, something we all take credit for as if we had something to do with it." — Anon. "A lamp to posterity." — Sallust.

anchor n. mooring, grapnel, hook, support, security, stability, hold, safeguard.

WORD FIND

heaviest, released from the bow: bower
hoist: cat, weigh
hoisting rig: capstan, windlass
light anchor used to free ship run aground: kedge
prongs: flukes
round, flukeless type: mushroom anchor
small: kedge, grapnel, killick
stone: killick
SEE SHIP

anchor v. moor, secure, fix, cat. ANT. *weigh anchor, release.*

ancient a. old, aged, venerable, primitive, primordial, antiquated, prehistoric, antediluvian, primeval, timeworn, immemorial, outmoded, fossilized, archaic, *old as the hills, early. ANT. *new, fresh, young, contemporary.*

ancillary a. subordinate, auxiliary, helper, servant, adjunct, accessory, supplementary. ANT. *principal, main, prime.*

ANDROGYNOUS a. [an DRAW juh nus] having male and female characteristics. *Many rock stars like to dress androgynously.* SYN. unisexual, bisexual, hermaphrodite, epicene, cross-sexual.

android n. robot, automaton.

anecdote n. vignette, story, tale, character sketch, narrative, illustration, account, incident.

anemia n. iron deficiency, chlorosis, iron-poor blood.

anemic a. weak, pale, pallid, wan, colorless, feeble.

anesthesia n. numbness, insentience, analgesia, loss of feeling.

anesthetic n. analgesic, painkiller, opiate, ether, Procaine, soporific.

anew a. again, once more, afresh.

angel n. **1.** HEAVENLY BEING cherub, guardian angel, spirit, archangel, seraph, divine messenger, fallen angel, spirit. "The dispensers and administrators of the Divine beneficence toward us...." — John Calvin. **2.** WONDERFUL PERSON sweetheart, saint, dear, darling, honey, doll. **3.** FINANCIER backer, supporter, *sugar daddy, underwriter, benefactor, patron. ANT. *1. devil, demon. 2. jerk, devil, bastard.*

angelic a. saintly, heavenly, spiritual, righteous, seraphic, cherubic, virtuous, chaste, divine, beautiful, lovely, holy, ethereal, radiant. ANT. *devilish, demonic, dark.*

anger n. rage, fury, irritation, annoyance, outrage, indignation, ire, wrath, resentment, temper, venom, *dander, huff, petulance, vexation, passion, animosity, rankling, spitting rage, murderous rage, *slow burn, pique, snarling rage, bitterness, gall, spleen, virulence, ill feelings, infuriation, *piss and vinegar, *burning, *stew, *piss hemorrhage, *conniption fit, soreness, umbrage. "[Anger] boils at different degrees." — Ralph Waldo Emerson. "Momentary insanity." — Horace. "A wind which blows out the lamp of the mind." — Robert Ingersoll. ANT. *glee, calm, affection, goodwill.* SEE ANGRY

anger v. enrage, infuriate, irritate, annoy, outrage, incense, *get one's dander up, rankle, *rattle one's cage, *yank one's chain, embitter, chafe, *burn one up, rile, bristle, antagonize, *raise one's hackles, blow up, *stir up, gall, *piss off, *bend out of shape, *get a rise out of, madden, *make blood boil, inflame, *make one hot under the collar, *miff, *steam, *tee off, *tick off, displease, irk, *get on one's nerves, nettle, provoke. ANT. *please, tickle, pacify, placate.*

angle n. **1.** BEND curve, crook, knee, vertex, elbow, acute angle, obtuse angle, right angle, reflex angle. **2.** POINT OF VIEW perspective, viewpoint, position, standpoint, slant.

angler n. SEE FISHERMAN

angry a. mad, enraged, infuriated, *pissed, irritated, annoyed, incensed, *spitting mad, bitter, *boiling, *stewing, burning, bristling, *gone ballistic, raging, *bent out of shape, enflamed, *hot under the collar, *miffed, *steamed, *teed off, *ticked off, displeased, provoked, *hot, irked, indignant, irate, galled, nettled, cross, vexed, wrathful, fuming, *mad as a hornet, *mad as a wet hen, *having a fit, *having a hissy fit, *having a conniption fit, *having a piss hemorrhage, livid, *blowing a gasket, *blowing a fuse, *in a snit, *apeshit, *having a cow, *spitting tacks, *seeing red, *popping one's cork, rabid, venomous, volcanic, fiery, explosive, peeved, *hot and bothered, *huffy, *in a lather, *sore, *in a tizzy, *bellowing fire and brimstone, *full of piss and vinegar, berserk, frenzied, snarling mad, *throwing a nutty. ANT. *pleased, gleeful, euphoric, placated.*

WORD FIND

Facial expressions and body language: scorching look; piercing look; keep-your-mouth-shut look; eyes narrowed with contempt; level stare; glower; scowl; withering glare; warning look; eyes blazing murderously; eyes sharpening; sneer; frown; snarl; smouldering eyes; lips curling with disgust; spasm of irritation crossing one's face; stony expression; face flushing with indignation; eyes bulging from their sockets; face turning red, then purple; veins in neck standing out in livid ridges; crazed look; unyielding jaw; sticking out chin defiantly; looking about wildly; eyes raking the room; predatory expression; lips contorted grotesquely; smiling maliciously; face lit with bitter triumph; teeth gritted; lips pursed with suppressed fury; face pinched, tight; arrogantly impassive; rolling one's eyes; knitted brow; gesticulating furiously; nostrils flaring; vein throbbing at temple; veins in neck swelling dangerously; stomach knotting; throwing up hands with disgusted resignation; bunch fists; stalk out; storm out.

Speech, voice tone: grind out the words between clenched teeth; stammer with rage; spit out the words with contempt; spew out the words with malicious glee; mutter peevishly under one's breath; speak with grave deliberation; speak with brutal detachment; speak with bitter resentment; taunt; sputter; splutter; scream in exasperation; mock in a sniveling singsong; sibilate; sniff; snort; speak in ragged bursts; speak in strangled tones; gibber; croak; clip one's words; maunder into one's shirt; speak in stentorian bellows; jeer; hoot; speak in grudging tones; voice rising hysterically; voice thick with insinuation; voice tinged with menace; voice rising an octave; voice degenerating to a guttural rasp; voice ascending to a murderous falsetto; voice growing husky/hoarse; voice dripping with spite; snap, hiss, fume, bark, boom, cry, growl, grumble, huff, pant, roar, shriek, thunder, wail, yammer, blurt.

angst n. tension, depression. SEE ANXIETY

anguish n. distress, suffering, agony, pain, grief, misery, torment, woe, dolor, sorrow. ANT. *joy, euphoria, pleasure.*

angular a. **1.** BENT crooked, bending, elbowed, doglegged, cornered. **2.** RAWBONED gaunt, bony, lean, spindly, lanky, spare, scrawny, anorexic, skeletonlike. ANT. *1. straight, flat. 2. fat, fleshy, beefy, plump.*

animal n. **1.** LIVING ORGANISM beast, creature, mammal, critter, varmint, pet, beast of burden, game, stock, denizen of the forest, vertebrate, invertebrate, quadruped, herbivore, carnivore, ungulate, vermin, scavenger. "Agreeable friends—they ask no questions, they pass no criticisms."—George Eliot. "Man in a stage of arrested development."—Christian Morgenstern. SEE INDIVIDUAL ANIMALS **2.** BRUTISH HUMAN pig, *Neanderthal, hoodlum, beast. See Chart, page 30.

animate a. **1.** ALIVE living, breathing, vital. **2.** ACTIVE animated, dynamic, vigorous, lively.

animate v. enliven, breath life into, vitalize, activate, invigorate, stimulate, quicken.

animated a. lively, lifelike, gay, energetic, spirited, active, vivacious, energized, dynamic. ANT. *lifeless, dull, dead.*

animal (continued)
WORD FIND

Animal	Group	Male	Female	Young
antelope	herd	buck	doe	kid
ass	herd/drove	jack	jenny	colt/foal
badger	cete	boar	sow	cub
bear	sloth	boar	sow	cub
bee	swarm/hive	drone	queen	
buffalo	herd	bull	cow	calf
camel	herd/flock	bull	cow	foal/calf
cattle	herd/drove	bull	cow	calf/heifer
deer	herd	buck/stag	doe	fawn
dog	pack	hound	bitch	puppy/whelp
elephant	herd	bull	cow	calf
elk	gang	bull	cow	calf
ferret	business	dog	bitch	
fish	school/shoal			
fox	skulk	vix	vixen	cub
frog	army/colony			tadpole
goat	herd/tribe	billy	nanny	kid
goose	gaggle/skein	gander	goose	gosling
horse	herd/stable	stallion	mare	colt/foal/filly
kangaroo	troop			joey
leopard	leap	leopard	leopardess	cub
lion	pride	lion	lioness	cub
monkey	troop/tribe			
moose		bull	cow	calf
mouse	nest			
mule	span/barren/rake			
otter		dog	bitch	
ox	herd/drove/yoke			
pheasant	bouquet/covey			
pig	litter/herd	boar	sow	piglet/farrow/shote
rabbit	nest	buck	doe	bunny
rhino	crash			
seal	herd/pod			cub
sheep	drove/flock	ram	ewe	lamb
sparrow	host			
squirrel	dray			
tiger		tiger	tigress	cub
toad	knot			
turtle	bale			
whale	gam/pod	bull	cow	calf
wolf	pack/rout	dog	bitch	cub/pup/whelp

animation SEE SPIRIT, MOTION PICTURE

ANIMOSITY n. [AN uh MOSS ih tee] feelings of hatred or hostility. *It's normal to feel a certain amount of animosity toward the tax collector.* SYN. hatred, hostility, enmity, antagonism, bitterness, ill will, dislike, hard feelings, animus, resentment. ANT. *love, affection.*

animus n. hatred, ill will. SEE ANIMOSITY

annals n. chronicles, history, accounts, annuals, history, records, archives, registers.

annex n. addition, new wing, addendum, attachment.

annex v. add, attach, append, join, incorporate, connect, merge, unite. ANT. *detach, disconnect.*

annihilate v. destroy, demolish, obliterate, crush, kill, wipe out, decimate, exterminate, liquidate, nullify.

annihilation n. demolition. SEE DESTRUCTION

anniversary n. commemoration. SEE HOLIDAY

annotate v. commentate, notate, intepret, footnote, expound, elucidate.

annotation n. note, footnote, commentary, explanation, elucidation.

announce v. proclaim, declare, broadcast, herald, voice, trumpet, state, publish, notify, annunciate.

announcement n. proclamation, declaration, broadcast, heralding, voicing, trumpeting, statement, notification.

announcer n. emcee, broadcaster, reporter, *deejay, newscaster, anchor man/woman, *voice-over, herald, trumpeter, crier.

annoy v. irritate, pester, bother, disturb, *bug, *get under one's skin, *get on one's nerves, vex, chafe, nettle, ruffle, gall, irk.

annual a. yearly, perennial.

annuity n. payment, allowance.

annul v. abolish, cancel, eliminate, void, nullify, invalidate, rescind.

annulment n. invalidation, nullification, cancellation, voiding, elimination, abolishment, repeal.

anoint v. consecrate, bless, make holy, rub oil on, smear with oil.

ANOMALOUS a. [uh NOM uh lus] strange, out of place. An anomalous July snowstorm. SYN. deviating, abnormal, irregular, inconsistent, strange, odd, out of place, unexpected, atypical, quirky. ANT. normal, typical, usual.

ANOMALY n. [uh NOM uh lee] an abnormality or irregularity. A snowstorm in Florida is an anomaly. SYN. abnormality, irregularity, exception to the rule, quirk, oddity, deviation, rarity, departure from the norm. ANT. the norm, regularity, same old thing.

anonymous a. nameless, unknown, unsigned, unidentified, incognito, secret, pseudonymous, uncredited. ANT. named, showcased, spotlighted.

answer n. 1. REPLY acknowledgement, response, counter, rejoinder, *comeback, retort, reaction, feedback. 2. SOLUTION explanation, resolution.

answer v. 1. REPLY acknowledge, respond, counter, rejoinder, *come back, retort, reaction, give feedback. 2. SOLUTION explanation, resolution. 3. BE ACCOUNTABLE own up to, be held responsible, pay for, atone for, rectify. 4. SERVE measure up, suffice, qualify,

satisfy, pass muster.

answerable a. liable, responsible, accountable. ANT. unaccountable.

antagonism n. hostility, enmity, opposition, friction, animosity, discord, rancor, clashing, ill will, rivalry. ANT. friendliness, agreement, harmony.

antagonist n. opponent, adversary, foe, enemy, rival, disputant. ANT. friend, colleague, advocate.

antagonize v. offend, rile, repel, alienate, oppose. ANT. befriend, sooth. SEE ANGER

ante n. wager, stake, bet.

ANTECEDENT n. [AN ti SEED unt] what came before or previously. The buckboard was an antecedent of the Model T. SYN. forerunner, precursor, predecessor, ancestor. ANT. descendant, successor.

antecedent a. previous, prior, precursory, preceding, former, first. ANT. posterior, subsequent, later.

antechamber n. hall, foyer, lobby.

antedate v. precede, predate, antecede.

antediluvian a. primitive, primordial, pre-Flood, ancient, prehistoric, antique, archaic.

antenna n. 1. INSECT APPENDAGE feeler, sense organ. 2. SIGNAL RECEIVER aerial, *rabbit ears.

anterior a. 1. FORE front, forward. 2. PREVIOUS before, prior, antecedent.

anthology n. collection, treasury, compilation, miscellany, omnibus.

antic(s) n. foolishness, tricks, pranks, jokes, shenanigans, stunts, tomfoolery, romps.

anticipate v. expect, look forward to, foresee, predict, forecast, envision, apprehend.

anticipation n. expectation, apprehension, preconception, foresight, dread, prospect, contemplation.

anticlimax n. letdown, disappointment, much ado about nothing, *dud, *bomb, disillusionment, bathos, *comedown, fizzle.

antidote n. 1. ANTIVENIN antitoxin, neutralizer, counteracting agent. 2. CURE remedy, neutralizer, medicine, vaccine, curative, corrective.

ANTIPATHY n. [an TIP uh thee] an acute dislike, aversion. He feels a certain antipathy toward telephone solicitors. SYN. aversion, dislike, hatred, antagonism, animosity, revulsion, loathing, distaste, abhorrence, enmity, repugnance. ANT. liking, attraction, appeal, affection.

antiquated a. obsolete, old-fashioned, outmoded, outdated, demode, dated, archaic, passé, bygone, fossilized, venerable, old world, seasoned, primordial. ANT. *new, modern, cutting edge, fresh.*

antique *n.* relic, curio, collectible, heirloom, artifact, antiquity, *hand-me-down, museum piece. "Remnants of history which have casually escaped the shipwrecks of time." — Francis Bacon. "Glorified scrap." — Max Gralnick.

antique *a.* SEE ANTIQUATED

antiquity *n.* **1.** PREHISTORY yore, olden days, dark ages. **2.** SEE ANTIQUE

antiseptic *n.* germicide, disinfectant, sterilizing agent, alcohol, iodine, chlorine.

antiseptic *a.* sterile, disinfected, clean, sanitary. ANT. *septic, contaminated, infected.*

antisocial *a.* **1.** UNSOCIABLE aloof, misanthropic, unfriendly, reclusive, withdrawn, uncommunicative, hermitic, solitary. **2.** HOSTILE antagonistic, depraved, indifferent, rebellious, destructive, troublesome, cruel. ANT. *1. friendly, warm, gregarious, outgoing. 2. friendly, kind, caring, benevolent.*

ANTITHESIS *n.* [an TITH uh sis] opposite, in contrast. *Love is the antithesis of hate.* SYN. opposite, contrast, reverse, converse, inverse, contradiction, contrary.

antithetical *a.* reverse, converse. SEE OPPOSITE

antitoxin *n.* antivenin, remedy. SEE ANTIDOTE

anxiety *n.* nervousness, tension, angst, apprehension, jitters, *shakes, *pins and needles, uneasiness, *butterflies, foreboding, misgiving, *heebie-jeebies, free-floating anxiety. ANT. *calm, relaxation, tranquility, ease.* "The *essence of conscience.*" — Freud. SEE FEAR

anxious *a.* **1.** NERVOUS tense, apprehensive, jittery, shaky, *on pins and needles, uneasy, *sweating bullets, disquieted, fearful, edgy, *uptight, jumpy, *strung out, overwrought, *unglued, *wired, *worked up, ill at ease.

WORD FIND

Facial expressions and body language: wide-eyed, blinking nervously, smiling spastically, forcing a smile, lip-twitching, pacing, throat-clearing, gulping, swallowing a lump in the throat, face paling, nails dug into palms, palms sweating, stomach knotting, stomach clenching and fluttering, fidgeting, finger-drumming, sweating, hyperventilating, spasms crossing the face, swallowing dryly, teeth-grinding/gnashing/clamping, toes curling tightly in one's shoes, hand-wringing, clasping and unclasping hands, struggling to control one's voice, voice strained/constricted/quavering/strangled/rising an octave, ad-

renalin coursing through arteries, butterflies in stomach, nausea, jitters, heart palpitations.

SEE FRIGHTENED

2. EAGER *itching, impatient, *raring to go, intent, fervent, desirous. ANT. *1. relaxed, calm, cool, at ease. 2. apathetic, indifferent.*

anyhow *a.* anyway, nonetheless, in any case, regardless.

anyone *pron.* anybody, one, everybody.

apace *a.* swiftly, quickly, rapidly. SEE FAST

apart *a.* **1.** IN PIECES OR TO PIECES disassembled, dismantled, piecemeal, asunder, disassociated, scattered. **2.** SEPARATE by itself, alone, independent, individual, singly, isolated. **3.** APART FROM besides, with the exception of, save for, excluding. ANT. *1. together. 2. among, amidst, together.*

apartheid *n.* segregation, separation, discrimination, racism.

apartment *n.* flat, room, duplex, rental unit, walk-up, efficiency apartment, place, *pad, *digs, tenement, suite.

apathetic *a.* uninterested, indifferent, uncaring, unmoved, listless, unconcerned, impassive, cool, dispassionate, phlegmatic, unsympathetic, removed. ANT. *passionate, caring, interested.*

APATHY *n.* [AP uh thee] disinterest, indifference. *To bring about change is to first overcome voter apathy.* SYN. indifference, disinterest, uninvolvement, dispassion, impassivity, languor, unconcern, detachment, coolness. "The worst sin toward our fellow creatures . . . ." — George Bernard Shaw. ANT. *passion, interest, concern, involvement.*

ape *n.* primate, simian, gorilla, chimpanzee, orangutan, gibbon, monkey. "An animal with the effrontery to resemble man." — Anon. "What an ugly beast . . . and how like us." — Cicero.

ape *v.* mimic, imitate, mock, parody, copy.

aperture *n.* opening, hole, gap, slot, orifice, stoma, crack.

apex *n.* top, peak, tip, zenith, summit, pinnacle, vertex, acme, crown, height. ANT. *bottom, trough, rock-bottom, depth, nadir.*

aphorism *n.* saying, proverb, maxim, axiom, adage, epigram, dictum. "Portable wisdom." — William Alger.

aphrodisiac *a.* seductive, titillating, arousing, erotic, sexy.

aphrodisiac *n.* *love potion, eyringo, *Spanish fly, oysters.

APLOMB *n.* [uh PLOM] confidence, poise.

She addressed the audience with great aplomb. SYN. confidence, poise, self-assurance, composure, savoir faire, equanimity, sangfroid, air. ANT. *anxiety, self-consciousness, insecurity.*

apocalyptic *a.* prophetic, revelatory, oracular, prescient.

apocryphal *a.* fictitious, doubtful, dubious, questionable, counterfeit, spurious, unsubstantiated. ANT. *true, authentic, genuine.*

apologetic *a.* sorry, regretful, remorseful, contrite, *on one's knees, conciliatory, prostrate, penitent, sheepish. ANT. *stubborn, self-righteous, defensive.*

apologize *v.* beg one's pardon, express regrets, retract, make amends, *crawl back on one's hands and knees, atone, beg for forgiveness, *eat crow, *eat humble pie, humble oneself.

apology *n.* regrets, remorse, plea, prostration, retraction, amends, atonement, *eating crow, *eating humble pie, repentance, acknowledgement, defense. "[T]he foundation for a future offense." — Ambrose Bierce.

apostate *n.* renegade, defector, deserter, heretic.

apostle *n.* missionary, advocate, champion, evangelist, proponent, preacher, witness, messenger, follower, disciple.

apothecary *n.* druggist, pharmacist, chemist BRIT.

apotheosis *n.* glorification, deification, immortalization.

apotheosize *v.* glorify.

appall *v.* dismay, horrify, shock, stun, disconcert, astound, frighten, take aback, harrow, disgust, sicken.

appalling *a.* dismaying, horrifying, shocking, stunning, disconcerting, astounding, frightening, ghastly, dreadful, harrowing, disgusting, sickening.

apparatus *n.* device, equipment, appliance, machine, tackle, mechanism, gadget, contraption, tool, *doohickey, *gizmo, outfit, instruments, contrivance, *thingamajig, *whatsis.

apparel *n.* clothing, attire, garments, dress, outfit, garb, costume, accoutrement, raiment, *duds, *threads, *getup. SEE CLOTHING

apparent *a.* **1.** EVIDENT visible, manifest, clear, obvious, plain, conspicuous, out front, open, unconcealed. **2.** SEEMING ostensible, probable, evident, possible, presumable, outward. ANT. *1. unclear, vague, hidden. 2. doubtful, certain.*

apparition *n.* ghost, specter, spirit, phantom, spook, manifestation, poltergeist, wraith, presence, hallucination, mirage. SEE GHOST

appeal *n.* **1.** PETITION entreaty, plea, request, imploration, supplication, application, call. **2.** ATTRACTION charm, allure, charisma, sex appeal, glamour, *je ne sais quoi, *it.

appeal *v.* **1.** REQUEST plead, entreat, implore, ask, beseech, request, solicit, beg, petition. **2.** ATTRACT interest, tempt, entice, fascinate. ANT. *2. repel, repulse, disgust.*

appear *v.* **1.** COME INTO VIEW show, emerge, loom, materialize, issue, surface, present, arrive, turn up, *meet the light of day. **2.** SEEM look, be obvious. ANT. *1. disappear, vanish.*

appearance *n.* **1.** SHOWING presentation, emerging, arrival, materialization, manifestation, coming. **2.** OUTWARD APPEARANCE facade, image, impression, illusion, semblance, exterior, guise. **3.** LOOK form, shape, demeanor, countenance, air, character, mien, features, bearing, aspect.

APPEASE *v.* [uh PEEZ] to pacify or placate. *We tried to appease the angry bear with a bucket of blueberries.* SYN. pacify, placate, quiet, satisfy, assuage, relieve, alleviate, soothe, mollify, subdue, smooth over, defuse, conciliate. ANT. *aggravate, exacerbate, antagonize.*

appellation *n.* name, title, designation, label, *moniker, *handle.

append *v.* add, affix, attach, adjoin, annex, tack on. ANT. *subtract, remove.*

appendage *n.* adjunct, attachment, limb, member, extremity, offshoot, branch, tail, arm, tentacle.

appendix *n.* addition, supplement, addendum, codicil, postscript, epilogue, index, outgrowth.

appertain *v.* belong. SEE PERTAIN

appetite *n.* hunger, craving, desire, taste, ravenousness, sweet tooth, thirst, hankering, penchant, yen, passion, yearning. ANT. *revulsion, repulsion, distaste.*

appetizer *n.* tidbit, snack, starter, hors d'oeuvre, finger food, dip, cold cuts, kickshaw, olives, anchovies.

WORD FIND

bread, toast or cracker with spread: canape

dough casing filled with minced meat or vegetables: dim sum

drink, alcoholic: aperitif

herring fillet rolled up on pickle or onion: rollmops

Italian marinated vegetables, sliced meats: antipasto

raw vegetables served with dip: crudites

appetizing *a.* appealing, mouth-watering, delectable, savory, delicious, palatable, inviting, tantalizing, toothsome, luscious, tempting, ambrosian. ANT. *nauseating, sickening, repulsive.*

applaud *v.* **1.** CLAP cheer, give a hand, give a standing ovation, hurrah, whistle. **2.** ACCLAIM laud, hail, praise, sing the praises of, commend, cheer, extol, compliment, give a pat on the back. ANT. *1. boo, hiss, *give a Bronx cheer. 2. pan, *give thumbs down, knock.*

applause *n.* clapping, ovation, cheers, hurrahs, bravos, whistles, encores, praise, acclaim, plaudits, kudos, tribute, approval. "Often less a blessing than a snare." — Edward Young. ANT. *boos, hisses, rejection, denigration, disapproval.*

apple *n.* pome, pippin, fruit, codling.

WORD FIND

apple of one's eye: sweetheart, angel, honey, love, cherished one.

apple-pie order: shipshape, neat, good, orderly, just so.

bright green and crisp: Granny Smith

dark red winter apple: Winesap

late fall variety: Jonathan

red: McIntosh, Red Delicious, Rome (Beauty)

red winter: Baldwin

rough-skinned and mottled winter apple: russet

Russian: Astrachan

wild: crab

yellowish red winter variety: Northern Spy

yellow, large, with red streaks: Gravenstein

apple-polisher *n. Sl.* *brownnose, toady. SEE FLATTERER

applesauce *n. Sl.* hokum, baloney. SEE NONSENSE

appliance *n.* mechanism, apparatus, machine, instrument, contrivance, gadget, *gizmo, modern convenience, contraption.

applicable *a.* pertinent, relevant, germane, fitting, suited, apposite, appropriate, usable. ANT. *inapplicable, irrelevant, impertinent.*

applicant *n.* candidate, job seeker.

application *n.* **1.** UTILIZATION employment, use. **2.** REMEDY dressing, ointment, poultice, salve, balm, lotion, medication. **3.** REQUEST solicitation, inquiry, petition, appeal, form, resume. **4.** DILIGENCE attention, *stick-to-itiveness, zeal, devotion. **5.** RELEVANCE pertinence, aptness, suitability.

apply *v.* **1.** UTILIZE use, employ, implement. **2.** DRESS spread on, put on, administer, smear. **3.** DEVOTE dedicate, concentrate, *buckle down, *put one's nose to the grindstone, persevere, *give one's all, be diligent, *focus one's energies. **4.** REQUEST petition, appeal, solicit, requisition. **5.** PERTAIN fit, suit, relate, refer.

appoint *v.* **1.** DESIGNATE name, nominate, select, choose, assign, install, commission, fix, set. **2.** FURNISH equip, accoutre, outfit, arrange.

appointment *n.* **1.** DESIGNATION naming, nomination, selection, assignment, installation, placement, job, office, position, *gig. **2.** ENGAGEMENT assignment, rendezvous, meeting, date, tryst. **3.** FURNISHING equipment, accoutrement, outfit, accessory, fitting, trapping.

apportion *v.* allot, divide, distribute, dole out, allocate, mete.

apposite *a.* relevant, apt, fitting, appropriate, apropos, befitting, proper, suited.

appraisal *n.* evaluation, valuation, assessment, rating, estimate.

appraise *v.* evaluate, valuate, assess, rate, estimate, measure, judge, put a value on.

appreciable *a.* perceptible, significant, substantial, measurable, discernible. ANT. *negligible, insignificant.*

appreciate *v.* **1.** ENJOY esteem, value, prize, regard, respect, like, cherish. **2.** BE THANKFUL FOR be obliged, be grateful, give thanks, acknowledge, credit. **3.** GROW IN VALUE increase, gain, compound, enhance, inflate. ANT. *1. overlook, disregard, ignore. 2. depreciate, decrease, deflate, lose.*

appreciation *n.* **1.** ENJOYMENT esteem, regard, respect, liking, prizing, cherishing, affection. **2.** THANKS gratefulness, gratitude, acknowledgement, thankfulness, credit. **3.** GROWTH IN VALUE increase, compounding, inflation, escalation. ANT. *1. disrespect, disregard. 2. ungratefulness. 3. depreciation, loss, deflation.*

apprehend *v.* **1.** ARREST catch, capture, *nab, *collar, take into custody, seize, incarcerate, jail. **2.** UNDERSTAND perceive, comprehend, see, *get the picture, recognize, know, grasp.

apprehensible *a.* understandable, comprehensible.

apprehension *n.* **1.** ARREST capture, seizure, incarceration, jailing, *collaring, *nabbing. **2.** UNDERSTANDING perception, comprehension, recognition, grasping. **3.** ANXIETY foreboding, dread, angst, fear, uneasiness, misgiving. ANT. *3. confidence, tranquility, reassurance.*

APPREHENSIVE *a.* [AP ri HEN siv] anxious

about the future. *He was apprehensive about his final exams.* SYN. anxious, uneasy, nervous, *edgy, dreading, fearful, full of misgiving, filled with foreboding, distressed, *uptight. ANT. *confident, cocksure, assured, worryfree.*

apprentice *n.* trainee, learner, beginner, novice, *rookie, *greenhorn, student, amateur, neophyte, pupil. ANT. *teacher, mentor, master, guru.*

apprise *v.* notify, inform, fill in, brief, tell, advise.

approach *n.* **1.** METHOD procedure, modus operandi, way, course. **2.** COMING NEAR advance, drawing near. **3.** ACCESS way, entry, passage, course, drive, route, road, pathway.

approach *v.* **1.** NEAR come, draw near, close in, advance, loom, gain on, converge. **2.** APPROXIMATE compare, come close, near, resemble, match up to, be like, equal. **3.** PROPOSE recommend, make overtures to, offer, bring up, suggest, present. **4.** SET ABOUT start, begin, get the ball rolling, tackle. ANT. *1. withdraw, depart. 4. finish up, conclude, close.*

approachable *a.* open, accessible, friendly, warm.

approbation *n.* approval, sanction, commendation. SEE APPROVAL

appropriate *v.* take, confiscate, seize, steal, expropriate, impound, claim, assume, commandeer, *pirate, pilfer, pocket.

appropriate *a.* proper, fitting, suitable, correct, apt, befitting, becoming, seemly, right, apropos, *politically correct. ANT. *inappropriate, improper, incorrect.*

appropriation *n.* **1.** ALLOTMENT allocation, funds, stipend, allowance. **2.** SEIZURE capture, confiscation, impounding, stealing, *pirating, commandeering.

approval *n.* **1.** ESTEEM regard, esteem, favor, liking, respect, acceptance, good opinion, blessing, honor. **2.** SANCTION consent, support, endorsement, imprimatur, approbation, *the okay, *the nod, *the green light, permission, authorization. ANT. *1. disapproval, rejection, disrespect. 2. denial, refusal, rejection.*

approve *v.* **1.** ESTEEM regard, favor, like, respect, accept, bless, honor. **2.** SANCTION consent, support, endorse, authorize, permit, allow, ratify. ANT. *1. disapprove, disrespect. 2. deny, refuse, reject.*

approximate *v.* approach, come close, near, equal, match, parallel, resemble.

approximate *a.* about, near, close, around, rough, estimated, in the neighborhood, in round numbers, well-nigh.

approximately *a.* about, close to, nearly, approaching, roughly, estimated, *guestimated, virtually, in round numbers, wellnigh, more or less, around. ANT. *exactly, precisely.*

appurtenance *n.* adjunct, accessory.

April *n.* "Love's spring." — Shakespeare. "The month when the green returns to the lawn, the lilac and the IRS." — Anon.

apron *n.* pinafore, garment, bib, smock, coverall.

APROPOS *a.* [AP ruh PO] timely; also, fitting or appropriate. *His speech was particularly apropos for the occasion.* SYN. timely, opportune, fitting, befitting, appropriate, relevant, apt, suitable, germane, pertinent. ANT. *untimely, inopportune, irrelevant.*

apt *a.* **1.** SUITED appropriate, fitting, relevant, germane, apropos. **2.** LIKELY inclined, prone, quick, liable, disposed. **3.** CLEVER quick, bright, adept. SEE INTELLIGENT ANT. *1. inappropriate, irrelevant. 2. unlikely. 3. slow, dull.*

aptitude *n.* ability, talent, flair, knack, gift, skill, capability, faculty, intelligence, proficiency.

aqua *n.* water, liquid, solution.

aquamarine *n.* bluishgreen.

aquarium *n.* tank, fishbowl.

aquatic *a.* marine, lacustrine, fluvial.

aqueduct *n.* conduit, pipe, channel, trough, watercourse, race.

aqueous *a.* watery.

arable *a.* plowable, tillable, fertile.

ARBITER *n.* [AR bi tur] one who judges or mediates. *An arbiter of justice.* SYN. judge, mediator, arbitrator, umpire, referee, intermediary, go-between, negotiator, authority, expert, specialist.

ARBITRARY *a.* [ARB uh trary] random, discretionary, capricious. *He didn't go by any set rules; his decision was arbitrary.* SYN. random, discretionary, capricious, dictatorial, whimsical, fanciful, unscientific, autocratic, personal. ANT. *objective, by set rules, scientific.*

ARBITRATE *v.* [AR bi TRATE] to decide or settle. *An authority will be brought in to arbitrate the dispute.* SYN. decide, settle, mediate, reconcile, negotiate, judge, moderate, adjudicate, referee, umpire.

arbitrator *n.* judge, middleman. SEE ARBITER

arbor *n.* bower, pergola, trellis.

arboreal *a.* treelike, arborescent.

arboretum *n.* conservatory, greenhouse, hothouse, nursery, vinery.

arc *n.* semicircle, curve, arch.

arcade *n.* gallery, cloister, walkway, passageway, piazza, archway.

ARCANE *a.* [ar KANE] mysterious, secret. *Much of the universe remains arcane.* SYN. mysterious, secret, hidden, esoteric, enigmatic, incomprehensible, occult, recondite, abstruse. ANT. *known, knowable, comprehensible.*

arch *n.* **1.** VAULT ogive, dome. **2.** CURVATURE arc, bow, parabola, bend, crescent.

arch *v.* bend, curve, bow, flex, round.

arch *a.* main, chief, principal, top, primary, highest, greatest, foremost. ANT. *least, smallest, minor.*

ARCHAIC *a.* [ar KAY ik] ancient, antiquated. *The crossbow is an archaic weapon.* SYN. ancient, antiquated, obsolete, from an earlier time, outmoded, old-fashioned, passé, old-world, antediluvian. ANT. *modern, fresh, *cutting edge, new.*

archbishop *n.* chief bishop.

archenemy *n.* **1.** Satan, the Devil. **2.** CHIEF ENEMY adversary, nemesis, bete noire.

archeologist *n.* historian, anthropologist. "One whose career lies in ruins." — Anon.

archeology *n.* history, anthropology. "Frozen history." — Gregory Mason.

archer *n.* bowman.

archetype *n.* model, prototype, original, template, example, exemplar, precursor, mold, classic.

archipelago *n.* chain of islands.

architect *n.* draftsman, designer, builder, creator, engineer, planner.

architecture *n.* drafting, designing, building design. "The flowering of geometry." — Ralph Waldo Emerson. "Frozen music." — Johann Goethe.

WORD FIND

borrowed style of motherland: colonial

classical orders of Hellenic Greece and Imperial Rome: Corinthian, Doric, Ionic, Tuscan, Composite

domes, round arches and columns of early Greece: Byzantine

eighteenth-century style derived from classical, Renaissance and Baroque: Georgian

elaborately decorative European style from 1550-1700s: baroque

florid ornamentation, eighteenth-century France: rococo

French Gothic form with flaming tracery, fifteenth century: flamboyant style

futuristic chevron and zigzag style of the 1930s: art deco

Italian, classically derived, fourteenth through sixteenth centuries: Renaissance

Mediterranean style characterized by horseshoe arches, domes, tunnel vaults, geometrical ornaments: Islamic style

pointed arches, rib vaulting, flying buttresses, twelfth through fifteenth centuries: Gothic style

retro style: revival

SEE BRIDGE, BUILDING, CASTLE, CATHEDRAL, CHURCH, HOUSE

archives *n.* records, chronicles, annals, historical documents, memorabilia.

arctic *a.* frigid, cold, freezing, polar, boreal. ANT. *warm, temperate, tropical.*

ARDENT *a.* [AR dent] passionate, highly enthusiastic. *An ardent fan of the Celtics.* SYN. passionate, enthusiastic, devoted, intense, zealous, fervent, feverish, torrid, vehement. ANT. *apathetic, cool, dispassionate.*

ardor *n.* **1.** PASSION warmth, love, sensuality, desire. **2.** EAGERNESS zeal, enthusiasm, devotion, fervor, intensity. ANT. *coldness, indifference, apathy.*

ARDUOUS *a.* [AR joo us] extremely difficult. *Mowing a golf course is an arduous task.* SYN. difficult, hard, taxing, demanding, laborious, burdensome, grueling, back-breaking, trying, strenuous, Herculean, exhausting. ANT. *easy, simple, *a snap.*

area *n.* **1.** EXPANSE stretch, range, breadth, space. **2.** REGION territory, district, section, locality, tract, stretch, ward, division, lot, sector, belt, quarter, zone. **3.** REALM sphere, dominion, province, field.

arena *n.* **1.** stadium, coliseum, amphitheater, stage, ring, hippodrome. **2.** DOMINION field, area, realm, province.

argot *n.* jargon, lingo, cant, idiom, vernacular, parlance, slang.

argue *v.* **1.** PLEAD contend, maintain, hold, assert, expostulate, evince, insist. **2.** QUARREL fight, bicker, debate, haggle, quibble, *hash out, *lock horns, altercate, squabble, *have a row, *mix it up, wrangle. ANT. *agree, concur, assent.* SEE ANGRY, WORD FIND

argument *n.* **1.** CONTENTION plea, assertion, proof, pros and cons, evidence, support, reasoning, defense, line of reasoning, grounds, case. **2.** QUARRELING disagreement, fight, dispute, debate, altercation, *row, *tiff, *spat, uproar, squabble, imbroglio. "The longest distance between two points of view." — Dan

Bennett. ANT. *agreement, accord, concord.* SEE FIGHT

argumentative *a.* quarrelsome, combative, cranky, contentious, polemical, scrappy, agonistic, eristic, belligerent, pugnacious, touchy, irritable, opinionated. ANT. *agreeable, passive, conciliatory.*

aria *n.* song, air, melody, solo. SEE OPERA

arid *a.* **1.** DRY dried-up, parched, barren, dusty, sterile, bone-dry, desertlike, desiccated. **2.** DULL boring, lifeless, tedious, drab, lackluster, uninteresting. ANT. *1. wet, fertile, humid. 2. lively, colorful, interesting.*

arise *v.* **1.** STAND UP get up, rise. **2.** ASCEND move upward, climb, rise. **3.** EMANATE originate, spring, issue, well up, occur, stem from, crop up. ANT. *1. recline, lie down. 2. descend, drop.*

aristocracy *n.* nobility, noblesse, peerage, gentility, privileged class, gentry, elite, *upper crust. "The rich, the beautiful and well born." —John Quincy Adams.* ANT. *peasantry, bourgeoisie, commoners.*

aristocrat *n.* nobleman, high-born, noblewoman, peer, patrician, blue blood, lord, duke, snob. *"Fellows that wear downy hats and clean shirts—guilty of education and suspected of bank accounts." —Ambrose Bierce.* ANT. *peasant, commoner, bourgeois.*

ARISTOCRATIC *a.* [uh RIS tuh KRAT ik] high-born. *He was aristocratic, but he was not a snob.* SYN. of noble birth, blue-blooded, well-born, genteel, pedigreed, mannerly, civil, worldly, sophisticated, gracious, gentlemanly, courtly, chivalrous, gallant, cultivated, refined, classy, snobbish, haughty, *snotty, hoity-toity, affected, pretentious. ANT. *bourgeois, lower-class, common.*

ark *n.* boat, refuge.

arm *n.* **1.** LIMB extremity, forearm. **2.** BRANCH extension, offshoot, appendage, projection.

arm *v.* equip, furnish, issue, outfit, accoutre, provide, fit out, load. ANT. *disarm.*

armada *n.* fleet, squadron, argosy, flotilla, navy, convoy, flight.

armaments SEE ARMS

armchair *n.* easy chair, rocking chair, recliner. SEE CHAIR.

armed *a.* outfitted, equipped, accoutred, fitted out, *armed to the teeth, *bristling with arms, loaded, fortified, supplied, *packing a rod. ANT. *disarmed.*

armistice *n.* truce, cease-fire, peace.

armor *n.* protective covering, shield, sheathing, mail.

WORD FIND

SUIT OF ARMOR

arm, from elbow to shoulder: brassard

armpit plate: pallette

back and breast plate: cuirass

bearer: armiger, squire

chain: mail

foot: solleret

hand: gauntlet

head: basinet, beaver, visor, armet, sconce, helmet

jacket or tunic: jupon

joint: gusset

leg, knee to ankle: greave

neck: gorget

shoulder: ailette, pauldron

thigh: cuisse, tasset

trunk: tasset

SEE AMMUNITION, BOMB, BULLET, GUN, MISSILE, NUCLEAR BOMB, WAR, WEAPON

armory *n.* arsenal, depot, drill hall.

arms *n.* weapons, armaments, ordnance, munitions, armor, ammunition. SEE AMMUNITION, BOMB, BULLET, GUN, MISSILE, NUCLEAR BOMB, WAR, WEAPON

arm's length, at *a.* at a distance, aloof, unfriendly.

arms, up in *a.* in an uproar, hostile, prepared for war.

army *n.* **1.** HORDE legion, mass, multitude, throng, swarm. **2.** ARMED FORCES troops, infantry, soldiers, division, battalion, ground forces. *"A body of men assembled to rectify the mistakes of the diplomats." —Josephus Daniels.*

WORD FIND

absent without leave: AWOL

bursts from antiaircraft guns: flak

clandestine movement: ratline

collective term for ammo, guns, explosives: ordnance

combat fatigue: shell shock

discharge for physical or mental problem: section eight

drab camp uniform: fatigues

eating facility: mess

emergency call-up troops: reserves

enemy ground to be won: bridgehead

enemy role during NATO exercise: orange forces

finishing off defeated enemy: mopping up

form up and come to attention: fall in

fortification, small, of concrete or sandbags: pillbox

friendly role during NATO exercise: blue forces

hiding material: camouflage

i.d. piece on chain: dogtag

infantryman, slang: grunt

items: materiel

jeep: hum-vee

kilometer, slang: click

largest unit: army group

liberty that ends at midnight: Cinderella liberty

lowest grade soldier: buck private

medal for wounds received: Purple Heart

mess hall duty: K.P. (kitchen police)

military store: PX, post exchange

missing in action: MIA

movement of troops: deployment

multilanguage message to return captured soldier, with reward: blood chit

negotiator sent behind enemy lines: parlimentaire

passing safely through minefield: breaching

phonetic alphabet: Alpha, Bravo, Charlie, Delta, Echo, Foxtrot, Golf, Hotel, India, Juliet, Kilo, Lima, Mike, November, Oscar, Papa, Quebec, Romeo, Sierra, Tango, Uniform, Victor, Whiskey, X-ray, Yankee, Zulu.

ranks, in ascending order: (enlisted men) Private E-1, Private E-2, Private First-Class E-3; (noncommissioned officers) Corporal E-4, Sergeant E-5, Staff Sergeant E-6, Platoon Sergeant E-7, Master Sergeant E-8, First Sergeant E-8, Sergeant Major E-9, Command Major Sergeant E-9, Sergeant Major of the Army E-9; (warrant officers) Warrant Officer, grade one; Chief Warrant Officer, grade two; Chief Warrant Officer, grade three; Chief Warrant Officer, grade four; (commissioned officers) Second Lieutenant, First Lieutenant, Captain, Major, Lieutenant Colonel, Colonel, Brigadier General, Major General, Lieutenant General, Four Star General, Five Star General of the Army

recruit training facility: boot camp

request for fire: call for fire, all available

shelter, lodging: billet, barracks

shield from enemy: defilade

shore foothold: beachhead

simultaneous fire at target from multiple guns: salvo

subdivision of a unit: echelon

sweeping line of gunfire: enfilade

tank, armored group: armored division

temporary ammo storage: munitions dump

trial for crime: court-martial

unit separated from larger group: detachment

units, in ascending order of size: unit (at least two soldiers), squad (10), platoon (4 squads), company (2 platoons), battalion (2 companies), group (2 battalions), brigade (2 groups), division (3 brigades), corps (2 divisions), field army (2 corps)

vulnerable troops at high risk: cannon fodder

SEE AIR FORCE, AMMUNITION, BOMB, BULLET, GUN, MARINES, NAVY, NUCLEAR BOMB, WAR, WEAPON

aroma n. scent, odor, smell, fragrance, bouquet, savor. SEE ODOR

aromatic a. fragrant, odoriferous, redolent, pungent, savory, scented, spicy. ANT. unscented, stinky.

arouse v. rouse, enliven, stimulate, awaken, stir, inflame, excite, fire up, shake up, disturb, incite, provoke. ANT. put to sleep, lull, pacify.

ARRAIGN v. [uh RANE] to bring before a court and accuse one of a crime. The suspected murderer was arraigned in court today. SYN. accuse, call to account, charge, indict, incriminate, serve a summons, blame, *point the finger at. ANT. exonerate, absolve, acquit.

arrange v. 1. PUT IN ORDER organize, straighten, position, rearrange, sort, classify, alphabetize, systematize. 2. PLAN devise, scheme, design, make preparations, map out, draw up. 3. SETTLE resolve, straighten out, determine, come to terms. ANT. 1. mix up, jumble, mess up, disorder.

arrangement n. 1. ORDER organization, system, positioning, classification, lineup, configuration, design. 2. PLAN scheme, design, preparation, provision, *game plan. 3. MUSICAL COMPOSITION score, chart.

arrant a. notorious, flagrant, out-and-out, glaring, unmitigated.

array n. 1. GROUPING arrangement, alignment, lineup, order, muster, marshaling, congregation, collection. 2. FINERY clothing, attire, dress, garments, *getup, *threads. ANT. 1. disarray, disorder, mess.

arrest n. apprehension, capture, taking into custody, *collar, *bust.
WORD FIND
book in which arrests are recorded at police station: blotter

photo taken of suspect: mug shot

reading of rights, rule: Miranda rule

record of a criminal's arrests and convictions: rap sheet
SEE DETECTIVE, POLICE

arrest v. **1.** TAKE INTO CUSTODY apprehend, capture, seize, *collar, *bust. **2.** HALT stop, check, obstruct, delay, slow. **3.** FIX hold, seize, absorb, engross.

arrival n. **1.** COMING landing, entrance, appearance, homecoming, advent. **2.** NEWCOMER visitor, traveler, tourist. ANT. *1. departure, exit.*

arrive v. **1.** COME appear, show up, enter, disembark, land; take place, occur, happen. **2.** SUCCEED attain, reach the top, *make good. ANT. *1. depart, leave, exit. 2. fail, *blow it, lose.*

arrogance n. conceit, imperiousness, haughtiness, overconfidence, snobbery, hauteur, hubris, airs, cockiness, insolence, swaggering pomposity, egotism, presumption, condescension. ANT. *modesty, humility.*

arrogant a. conceited, imperious, cocky, insolent, superior, pompous, swaggering, egotistical, haughty, presumptuous, condescending, overbearing, hoity-toity, self-important, supercilious, *high and mighty. ANT. *modest, self-effacing, humble.*

arrow n. shaft, bolt, dart, projectile, missile.

WORD FIND

barb: fluke
bowstring notch: nock
case: quiver
crossbow: bolt
feather, put on: fletch
feather: vane
like an arrow: sagittal
maker: fletcher
user: archer, bowman

arsenal n. armory, stockpile, munitions dump, depot, magazine, cache.

arson n. fire-setting, *torching, pyromania.

art n. **1.** CREATIVITY craft, artistry, craftsmanship, handiwork, workmanship, finesse, knack, flair. **2.** CUNNING slyness, artfulness, artifice, craftiness. **3.** WORKS OF ART painting, sculpture, depiction, abstract, simulation, representation, illustration. "By means of appearances ... the illusion of a loftier reality."—Ralph Waldo Emerson. "An instant arrested in eternity."—James Huneker "[T]he shadow of humanity."—Henry James. "[A] sublime excrement."—George Moore.

WORD FIND

SCHOOLS AND STYLES
absurd: dada

aggressive painting method: action painting
cubed and other geometrically distorted forms: cubism
cursive, flowing lines, swirling motifs style, late nineteenth century: art nouveau
dark realism, early twentieth century: ashcan school
emotion and color, focus on: expressionism
experimental or unorthodox: avant-garde
geometrical and curvilinear style of the 1920-1930s: art deco
graphic, optical effects: op art
hallucinatory, dreamlike, subconscious imagery: surrealism
idyllic nature scenes, France, nineteenth century: Barbizon School
modern, minimalist style, graffiti, cartoons: new wave
Monet's vague outline style: impressionism
nonrepresentational: abstract
nonrepresentational style that focuses on emotion and the act of painting itself: abstract expressionism
nonschooled: folk art
points or tiny dots creating a whole: pointillism
realistic, photographic: photorealism, hyperrealism, tromp l'oeil, magic realism, representational
rich ornamentation, curved lines, sixteenth through eighteenth century: baroque
traditional forms: academic art
Warhol's (Andy) bigger-than-life depictions of everyday objects: pop art
SEE DRAWING, PAINTING, SCULPTURE

artery n. channel, vein, blood vessel, canal.

artful a. **1.** CLEVER adroit, skillful, ingenious. **2.** CUNNING sly, crafty, shrewd, wily. ANT. *1. unskilled, inept. 2. artless, naive.*

article n. **1.** STORY piece, news release, report, write-up, feature. **2.** ITEM object, thing, bit, piece, *thingamajig.

articulate v. express, enunciate, voice, pronounce, utter, make clear, elucidate.

ARTICULATE a. [ar TIK yuh lut] expressive, eloquent, well-spoken. *An articulate talk show host.* SYN. expressive, eloquent, well-spoken, intelligible, lucid, smooth-talking, fluent, facile. ANT. *inarticulate, tongue-tied, stammering, mumbled.*

ARTIFICE n. [ART uh fis] ingenuity or cleverness; also, cunning, trickery. *He succeeded in fooling us through artifice.* SYN. ingenuity, cleverness, inventiveness, skillfulness, wile, ruse, trickery, contrivance, cunning, craftiness, duplicity, machination, guile, artfulness, deceit, finesse. ANT. *honesty, artlessness, naivete.*

artificial *a.* **1.** UNNATURAL man-made, synthetic, fake, ersatz, counterfeit, imitation, manufactured, *bogus. **2.** AFFECTED mannered, forced, phony, unnatural, theatrical, feigned, *put on, pretentious, contrived. ANT. *1. natural, organic, authentic. 2. sincere, genuine, real.*

artillery *n.* gunnery, cannons, howitzer. SEE WEAPONS

artisan *n.* SEE ARTIST

artist *n.* **1.** EXPERT master, *pro, virtuoso, talent. **2.** ARTISAN craftsman, painter, portraitist, sculptor, technician, designer. "An exhibitionist by profession."—Vincent van Gogh. "One who doesn't see things as they are, but as he is."—Anon. ANT. *1. amateur, tyro.* SEE ART, DRAWING, PAINTING, SCULPTURE

artistic *a.* aesthetic, artful, tasteful, graceful, ornamental, decorative, stylish, pleasing to the eye, brilliant, masterful. ANT. *crude, gross, unattractive, tasteless.*

artistry *n.* quality, skill, talent, virtuosity, creativity, flair, style, finesse, touch, feel, genius.

ARTLESS *a.* [ART less] unskilled, uncultured, simple, naive. *As artless as a child.* SYN. **1.** UNSKILLED untalented, unschooled, inartistic. **2.** CRUDE plain, simple, primitive, natural. **3.** NAIVE simple, ingenuous, innocent, guileless, unsophisticated, childlike, genuine, direct, natural. ANT. *1. artful, skilled, talented, schooled. 2. artful, sophisticated, worldly. 3. sophisticated, self-conscious, insincere, unnatural.*

arty *a.* pretentious, *artsy-fartsy, highbrow.

ascend *v.* rise, arise, climb, surmount, scale, levitate, soar, escalate. ANT. *descend, drop, fall.*

ascendancy *n.* supremacy, control, domination, power, preeminence.

ascension *n.* scaling. SEE ASCENT

ascent *n.* **1.** CLIMB rise, ascension, progression. **2.** UPWARD SLOPE acclivity, upgrade, elevation, incline, gradient. ANT. *1. descent, fall, drop. 2. declivity, descent.*

ascertain *v.* learn, verify, find out, determine, certify, *pin down, establish, uncover, discover.

ascetic *n.* abstainer, celibate, religious fanatic, monk, anchorite.

ascetic *a.* austere, abstinent, abstemious, self-denying, strict, puritanical. ANT. *hedonistic,*

self-gratifying, indulgent.

ascribe *v.* attribute, credit, assign, charge, connect, associate, link.

ashamed *a.* embarrassed, humiliated, mortified, chagrined, humbled, *red-faced, guilty, conscious-stricken, sheepish, abashed, disgraced, flustered, shamefaced. ANT. *proud, high and mighty, arrogant.*

ashen *a.* pale, pallid, gray, wan, white, sallow, cadaverous. ANT. *rosy, ruddy.*

ashes *n.* cinders, soot, embers.

asinine *a.* stupid, moronic, idiotic, sophomoric, silly, absurd, foolish. ANT. *brilliant, wise.*

ask *v.* **1.** QUESTION query, pose a question, interrogate, quiz. **2.** REQUEST appeal, solicit, express a desire for. **3.** INVITE summon, request, call upon.

askance *a.* **1.** SIDEWAYS obliquely, sidelong, askew. **2.** SUSPICIOUSLY OR DISAPPROVINGLY disdainfully, dubiously, skeptically.

askew *a.* awry, aslant, sidelong, crooked.

asleep *a.* slumbering, *snoozing, *catching some ZZZs, *catching forty winks, napping, dozing, *comatose, hibernating, dormant.

aspect *n.* **1.** LOOK air, mien, bearing, manner. **2.** FEATURE facet, side, angle, point, element, view.

aspen *n.* poplar tree.

asperity *n.* harshness, roughness, sharpness, nastiness, ill temper, venom, irritability, crossness, hostility, acrimony, surliness, irascibility. ANT. *mildness, softness, good cheer.*

aspersion *n.* disparagement, slander, abuse, defamation, innuendo, smear, slur, vilification, blot, denigration, mud-slinging, calumny.

asphalt *n.* bitumen, tar, pavement.

asphyxiate *v.* suffocate, smother, choke, strangle, throttle.

aspirant *n.* contender, applicant. SEE CANDIDATE

aspiration *n.* ambition, goal, yearning, dream, goal, desire, objective, aim, wish, enterprise, hope, hitching one's wagon to a star. "The desire of the moth for the star."—Shelley.

aspire *v.* strive for, desire, try for, wish for, hope for, hunger for, thirst for, shoot for, aim for.

ass *n.* **1.** DONKEY burro, jackass, jenny, jack, beast of burden. **2.** BUTTOCKS rear, rump, *buns, *butt, behind, *caboose, *cheeks, derriere, *duff, *keester, *kazoo, seat, *stern, *tush, *tokus, gluteus maximus. **3.** FOOL idiot, *boob, jerk, clown, *nincompoop, *dolt.

assail *v.* attack, assault, accost, jump on, lay into, set upon, *rip into, *light into, impugn.

assailant n. attacker, assaulter, accoster, molester, mugger, aggressor, adversary, enemy, foe.

assassin n. killer, slayer, executioner, *hit man, *liquidator, sniper, gunman, *trigger man. SEE MURDERER

assassinate v. kill, slay, execute, gun down, *hit, *liquidate. SEE MURDER

assassination n. killing, slaying, execution, *hit, *liquidation. "The extreme form of censorship." — George Bernard Shaw. SEE MURDER

assault n. **1.** PHYSICAL OR VERBAL ATTACK offense, affront, insult, beating, pounding, pummeling, mugging, molestation, rape, battery, violence. **2.** RAID siege, blitz, storming, foray, offensive, invasion.

assay n. examination, test, analysis, probe, investigation, assessment.

assay v. examine, test, analyze, probe, investigate, assess.

assemblage n. group, assembly, collection, cluster, aggregation, congregation.

assemble v. **1.** PUT TOGETHER fit, piece, connect, construct, compile, puzzle out, compose, throw together. **2.** GATHER amass, congregate, muster, band, convene, meet. ANT. 1. disassemble, disconnect, dismantle. 2. scatter, disband, disperse.

assembly n. **1.** FITTING TOGETHER connection, construction, compilation, piecing together. **2.** GATHERING mass, congregation, mustering, band, meeting, convention, crowd, multitude, mob. ANT. 1. disassembly, disconnection. 2. scattering, disbanding, dispersal.

assent n. agreement, concurrence, consent, acceptance, accord, approval. ANT. disagreement, dissent.

assent v. agree, concur, accept, consent, concede, approve, grant, acquiesce, go along. ANT. dissent, disagree.

assert v. state, declare, affirm, aver, pronounce, claim, profess, attest, say. ANT. deny, controvert.

assertion n. statement, declaration, affirmation, pronouncement, profession, proclamation, averment, claim, avowal. ANT. denial, disavowal.

assertive a. outspoken, direct, forthright, unreserved, uninhibited, blunt, brash, confident, assured, aggressive. ANT. shy, reserved, inhibited.

assess v. **1.** IMPOSE levy, tax, dun, fine, charge. **2.** EVALUATE appraise, measure, estimate, judge, consider, weigh.

assessment 1. DUNNAGE charge, taxing. **2.** EVALUATION appraisal, estimate.

asset n. **1.** VALUABLE resource, possession, property, cash, inventory. **2.** QUALITY strength, gift, blessing, advantage. ANT. 1. liability. 2. liability, handicap, disadvantage.

asshole n. Sl. **1.** ANUS rectum, *butthole, *poop chute, *bunghole, *kazoo. **2.** JERK *shithead, *dickhead, *dipshit, *horse's ass, *pissant, *prick, *dink, *shit, *schmuck, bastard, idiot, son of a bitch.

ASSIDUOUS a. [uh SID yoo us] hard-working, diligent, devoted. An assiduous striving for success. SYN. hard-working, diligent, devoted, persistant, constant, persevering, tenacious, unremitting, tireless, attentive, earnest. ANT. casual, lax, lazy, laid-back.

assign v. **1.** DESIGNATE appoint, name, choose, commission, nominate, charge, entrust, cast. **2.** ALLOCATE allot, distribute, consign, give, dispense, dole out. **3.** ATTRIBUTE ascribe.

assignment n. task, duty, job, lesson, homework.

ASSIMILATE v. [uh SIM uh LATE] to absorb, digest. Also, to adjust, integrate. The new math is difficult to assimilate. It takes time to assimilate in another country. SYN. **1.** ABSORB digest, metabolize, incorporate. **2.** ADJUST integrate, adapt, acclimatize, fit in, homogenize, *do as the natives do, *go native, naturalize. ANT. 1. regurgitate, reject. 2. reject, maladapt, separate.

assist v. help, aid, support, lend a hand, accommodate, attend, serve, contribute, collaborate. ANT. hinder, hamper.

assistance n. help, aid, support, a hand, accommodation, service, contribution, collaboration. ANT. hindrance, obstruction.

assistant n. helper, aide, deputy, attendant, supporter, collaborator, contributor, adjunct, aid-de-camp, gal Friday, right-hand man, *gopher.

associate n. colleague, co-worker, peer, partner, teammate, affiliate, ally, companion, confederate, consort, accomplice, friend, fellow.

associate v. **1.** THINK OF TOGETHER link, identify, correlate, group, affiliate, relate, pair. **2.** MINGLE WITH hang out, hobnob, befriend, fraternize, consort, run with. ANT. 1. disassociate, separate. 2. shun, estrange, alienate.

association n. **1.** GROUP society, club, organization, fraternity, corporation, confederation, league, alliance, union, partnership. **2.** FRIENDSHIP fellowship, relationship, affiliation, fraternization, companionship, alliance. **3.** LINKING TOGETHER correlation, pairing, lumping together, relationship, connection, juxtaposition.

assorted *a.* diverse, varied, different, miscellaneous, sundry, mixed. ANT. *same, matching, identical, uniform.*

assortment *n.* miscellany, mixture, diversity, variety, potpourri, melange, jumble, mixed bag.

ASSUAGE *v.* [uh SWAYJ] to relieve or soothe. *To assuage his appetite, he ate some popcorn.* SYN. relieve, soothe, ease, alleviate, mitigate, allay, pacify, calm, mollify, lessen, lull, *take the edge off. ANT. *aggravate, exacerbate, intensify.*

assume *v.* **1.** TAKE ON take up, adopt, acquire, undertake. **2.** SEIZE take, appropriate, usurp, commandeer. **3.** FEIGN pretend, simulate, affect. **4.** PRESUME suppose, take for granted, believe, hypothesize, imagine, think, guess, speculate, infer, suspect. ANT. *1. throw off, abandon, renounce.*

assumed *a.* **1.** FICTITIOUS pretend, make-believe, sham, false, bogus, feigned, fake, phony. **2.** SUPPOSED presumed, tacit, inferred, hypothesized. ANT. *1. real, true. 2. known.*

assumption *n.* supposition, presumption, inference, hypothesis, guess, theory, belief, given, hunch, suspicion.

assurance *n.* **1.** CONFIDENCE security, sureness, courage, boldness, self-assurance, conviction, *guts, pluck. **2.** PROMISE OR PLEDGE guarantee, vow, oath, word, warranty. ANT. *1. insecurity, doubt, uncertainty.*

assure *v.* convince, reassure, guarantee, affirm, encourage, certify, pledge, secure, insure, ensure.

assured *a.* **1.** GUARANTEED sure, certain, secure. **2.** CONFIDENT self-assured, self-possessed, bold, assertive, poised, unflinching, unhesitating, cocksure, brassy. ANT. *1. uncertain, unsure, gamble. 2. insecure, timid, self-doubting.*

astern *a.* aft, abaft, rearward.

astonish *v.* amaze, surprise, astound, shock, flabbergast, dumbfound, startle, take aback, *bowl over, stupefy.

astonishing *a.* amazing, astounding, surprising, shocking, breathtaking, dumbfounding, awesome, *eye-popping, startling, dazzling, bewildering, extraordinary.

astonishment *n.* amazement, surprise, shock, awe, bewilderment, wonder, stupefaction, marvel.

astound *v.* astonish, amaze, bewilder, shock, surprise, flabbergast, dumbfound, startle, take aback, *bowl over, stupefy, boggle, render speechless, electrify, stagger, confound, *blow one's mind.

astounding *a.* astonishing, amazing, bewildering, shocking, surprising, startling, *eye-popping, stupefying, mind-boggling, electrifying, staggering, confounding, *mind-blowing, wondrous. ANT. *ho-hum, boring, ordinary.

astray *a.* adrift, off course, lost, afield, wrong, *off the mark, *off in left field.

astringent *a.* biting, harsh, sharp, cutting, acerbic, severe, rough, acrid. ANT. *mild, soft.*

astrology *n.* horoscopy, reading of the stars, divination. "The excellent foppery of the world." —Shakespeare.

WORD FIND

chart of positions of planets, stars, relationship to birth: horoscope

diagram: scheme

legendary astrologer: Merlin

one of twelve sectors in celestial sphere: house

table of positions of stars and planets at specific times: ephemeris

astronaut *n.* spaceman, cosmonaut, sailor of the stars. "Envoys from mankind." —Anon.

astronomer *n.* stargazer, cosmologist, astrophysicist.

astronomy *n.* stargazing, cosmology, astrophysics.

WORD FIND

eclipse, or passage of one celestial body in front of another: occultation

great circle spanning horizons: meridian

location of celestial object in sky: azimuth, declination, right ascension

path of sun on celestial sphere: ecliptic

point of sky directly overhead: zenith

star motion unrelated to earth's rotation: proper motion

table showing future positions of celestial objects: ephemeris

unit of distance, by speed of light: light year, 5,880,000,000,000 miles; parsec, 3.26 light years

unit of distance, equal to that from the earth to the sun: astronomical unit, 92,900,000 miles

SEE COMET, CONSTELLATION, METEOR, MOON, PLANET, SPACE, STAR

ASTUTE *a.* [uh STOOT] clever, sharp or cunning. *The astute mind of the successful*

businessman. SYN. clever, sharp, cunning, crafty, shrewd, wily, quick, keen, intelligent, sagacious, brilliant, bright, *on the ball. ANT. *dumb, naive, retarded, slow, obtuse.*

asunder *a.* apart, separate, in pieces.

asylum *n.* **1.** SANCTUARY refuge, shelter, haven, safe harbor, hospice. **2.** HOSPITAL psychiatric hospital, sanitarium, mental institution, insane asylum, *nut house, *booby hatch, *laughing academy, *loonybin, *madhouse.

atheist *n.* nonbeliever, agnostic, skeptic, free thinker, infidel, *doubting Thomas, heathen. "A man who has no invisible means of support."—John Buchan. "A man who believes himself an accident."—Francis Thompson. "An orphaned heart."—Jean Paul Richter. ANT. *believer, the faithful.*

athlete *n.* *jock, competitor, sportsman, champion.

athletic *a.* strong, fit, skilled, muscular, mesomorphic, sthenic, strapping, vigorous, robust, hardy, staunch, brawny, stout, wiry, supple, coordinated. ANT. *weak, feeble, sedentary, asthenic.*

WORD FIND

competition combo of five track and field events: pentathlon

competition combo of skiing and rifle shooting: biathlon

competition combo of swimming, biking and long-distance running: triathalon, *iron man contest

competition combo of ten track and field events: decathlon

atmosphere *n.* **1.** AMBIENCE aura, surroundings, air, *vibes, feeling, environment. **2.** SKY air, heavens, smog, biosphere.

WORD FIND

ion-rich layer, reflects radio waves, in thermosphere: ionosphere

layer of oxygen in stratosphere, protects earth from ultraviolet radiation: ozone layer

rising column of warm air: thermal

stratum from 0-10 miles up: troposphere

stratum from 10-30 miles up: stratosphere

stratum from 30-50 miles up: mesosphere

stratum from 50-300 miles up: thermosphere

stratum from 300 miles to space: exosphere

trapping of solar radiation and heat by carbon dioxide buildup: greenhouse effect

SEE AIR, RAIN, SNOW, WEATHER, WIND

atoll *n.* coral island.

atom *n.* particle, jot, bit, iota, scintilla, shred, bit. "A specter threatening us with annihilation."—Max Born.

atomic *a.* SEE NUCLEAR

atomic bomb *n.* SEE NUCLEAR BOMB

atomize *v.* separate, disintegrate, vaporize, spray, pulverize.

ATONE *v.* [uh TONE] to make up for a bad deed; to make amends. *Atone for your sins.* SYN. amend, make amends, redeem, do penance, repent, confess, expiate, make reparations, shrive.

atonement *n.* amends, reparations, redemption, expiation, penance, restitution, compensation, redress. "The blood of Jesus Christ . . ."—Bible, John 1:7.

atrocious *a.* evil, brutal, appalling, cruel, bad, monstrous, unspeakable, vicious, despicable, horrible, abominable, heinous, outrageous. ANT. *good, pleasant, lovely, benevolent.*

ATROCITY *n.* [uh TRAW suh tee] a cruelty, brutality or outrageous thing or act. *Drive-by shootings and other atrocities.* SYN. cruelty, brutality, outrage, monstrosity, unspeakable act, horror, savagery, barbarity, crime, abomination. ANT. *kindness, good deed.*

atrophy *n.* degeneration, wasting, deterioration, withering, emaciation, decline, weakening.

atrophy *v.* degenerate, waste, deteriorate, wither, emaciate, decline, weaken.

attach *v.* **1.** FASTEN tie, stick, secure, bind, link, hook, affix, connect, tack, pin. **2.** AFFILIATE join, associate, enlist. **3.** ASCRIBE attribute, assign, accredit, apply, place. ANT. *1. detach, loosen, free. 2. drop out, quit, dissociate.*

attaché *n.* consul, envoy, aide. SEE DIPLOMAT

attachment *n.* **1.** FASTENING tying, connection, joining. **2.** DEVOTION regard, affection, crush, affinity, bond, esteem, fondness, love. **3.** ACCESSORY appendage, appurtenance, fixture, addition, extension, supplement. ANT. *1. detachment, separation. 2. repulsion, aversion.*

attack *n.* **1.** ASSAULT offensive, raid, invasion, siege, ambush, blitz, aggression, strike, incursion, onslaught. **2.** ONSET OR RECURRENCE OF AN ILLNESS bout, relapse, throe, seizure, convulsion, spell, turn for the worse.

attack *v.* **1.** ASSAULT strike, jump on, raid, besiege, invade, ambush, assail, pounce on, molest, set upon, take the offensive, aggress, mug. **2.** VERBALLY ASSAULT *rip into, *tear apart, criticize, abuse, malign, bash, defame, scold, *rake over the coals, damn, censure, *dis, *jump down one's throat, impugn, *bad-mouth, denounce, revile. **3.** TO BEGIN WORK ON tackle, dive into, undertake, *jump into with both feet. ANT. 1. *retreat, defend, lay low.* 2. *flatter, compliment, praise.* 3. *procrastinate, avoid.*

attacker n. assailant, aggressor, offender.

attain v. achieve, accomplish, get, procure, secure, acquire, obtain, realize, fulfill, *make it, win. ANT. *fail, lose, fall short.*

attainment n. achievement, accomplishment, getting, procurement, securing, acquirement, obtaining, realization, fulfillment, winning, success, coup, skill.

attempt n. try, endeavor, shot, *crack, undertaking, *stab, *the old college try, venture, bid.

attempt v. try, endeavor, make an effort, undertake, take a shot at it, *take a crack at it, *take a stab at it, *give it the old college try, venture, make a bid for it, strive.

attend v. 1. LOOK AFTER minister to, serve, tend, take care of, nurse, assist, doctor. 2. TO BE PRESENT appear, show up, go to, turn up. 3. ACCOMPANY come with, go hand in hand, escort, be associated with.

attendance n. 1. PRESENCE appearance. 2. TURNOUT crowd, house, audience.

attendant n. servant, aide, assistant, orderly, steward, valet, consort, escort.

attention n. 1. CONCENTRATION mindfulness, consciousness, awareness, heed, notice, thoughtfulness, regard. 2. OBSERVATION notice, recognition, regard, consideration, scrutiny. ANT. 1. *absent-mindedness, abstraction, inattention.* 2. *oversight, disregard.*

attentions n. consideration, courtesy, devotion, civility, care, respect, service.

attentive a. 1. MINDFUL observant, alert, conscious, aware, sharp, thoughtful, noticing, keen, heedful, watchful. 2. CONSIDERATE thoughtful, gracious, courteous, solicitous, accommodating, gallant. ANT. 1. *neglectful, unobservant, heedless.* 2. *inconsiderate, rude, negligent.*

attenuate v. thin, dilute, weaken, rarefy, dilute, lessen, decrease, water down, diminish. ANT. *fortify, strengthen, intensify.*

attest v. bear witness, certify, verify, confirm, substantiate, support, bear out, testify, warrant, vouch for, pledge, affirm, swear, authenticate. ANT. *refute, deny, belie.*

attic n. garret, loft, dormer, clerestory, storage room.

attire n. dress, clothing, apparel, garb, costume, raiment, *duds, *togs, outfit, garments, *threads.

attire v. dress, clothe, garb, deck out, fit out,

outfit, *doll up, costume, accoutre.

attitude n. 1. OUTLOOK mind, disposition, frame of mind, temperament, feeling, view, perspective, *mindset, demeanor, bias. 2. POSTURE stance, manner, bearing, pose, mien, carriage, air.

attitude problem n. *hair across the ass, *chip on one's shoulder.

attorney n. counselor, legal representative, DA, barrister, solicitor, *ambulance chaser. SEE LAWYER

attract v. 1. DRAW pull, magnetize. 2. ALLURE lure, invite, tempt, interest, charm, captivate, fascinate, beguile, bewitch, *turn on, *spellbind. ANT. 1. *repel, repulse.* 2. *repel, repulse, turn off.*

attraction n. appeal, temptation, magnetism, affinity, pull, charm, interest, allure, bewitchment, fascination, enticement, *chemistry, charisma. ANT. *repellant, repulsion, aversion.*

attractive a. appealing, charming, enticing, *nice, beautiful, handsome, winning, fascinating, magnetic, charismatic, tempting, alluring, bewitching, fetching, cute, adorable, pretty, stunning, sexy, comely, *built, *hot, tantalizing, *hunky, *va-va-voom, *foxy. ANT. *repulsive, repellant, ugly, *butt-ugly.*

attribute n. quality, characteristic, trait, feature, distinction, quirk, facet, virtue.

attribute v. assign, ascribe, credit, charge with, blame, impute, account for.

ATTRITION n. [uh TRISH un] a wearing away or reduction, loss by natural means. *The company lost more employees by attrition than by forced layoffs.* SYN. weakening, erosion, reduction, decimation, disintegration, diminution, dwindling, decline. ANT. *buildup, reinforcement, fortification.*

attune v. adapt, adjust, harmonize, acclimate, assimilate.

atypical a. unusual, uncommon, untypical, odd, irregular, abnormal. ANT. *typical, usual.*

au courant a. informed, up-to-date, conversant.

auction n. sale, vendue.

auburn a. reddish-brown, golden-brown, nut brown, chestnut brown, henna.

AUDACIOUS a. [aw DAY shus] brave, bold. Also, not affected by shame or a sense of propriety. *An audacious foray into enemy territory.* SYN. 1. brave, bold, daring, plucky, *ballsy, courageous, dauntless, stalwart, unflinching, *gutsy, adventurous, intrepid. 2. shameless, brazen, outrageous, cheeky, brassy, impertinent, rude, forward, insolent, saucy, *ballsy. ANT. 1. *cowardly, fearful, timid*. 2. *deferential, polite*.

audacity n. **1.** COURAGE bravery, daring, nerve, pluck, backbone, *guts, *balls, *spine, grit, derring-do, mettle, boldness. **2.** SHAMELESS-NESS brashness, impudence, effrontery, *gall, *nerve, *balls, *cheek, arrogance, impertinence, brass, presumption. ANT. 1. *cowardice, fear, spinelessness*. 2. *courtesy, decorum, propriety*.

audible a. perceptible, hearable, discernible, intelligible, clear. ANT. *inaudible, silent, unintelligible*.

audience n. spectators, crowd, onlookers, viewers, house, fans, patrons, turnout, market.

audit n. examination, accounting, review, investigation.

audition n. tryout, trial, hearing, *open mike.

auditor n. accountant, inspector, analyst, bookkeeper.

auditorium n. assembly room, hall, concert hall, gallery, theater, ampitheater, playhouse, lecture hall.

augment v. enlarge, add, increase, extend, enhance, broaden, thicken, maximize, build up, amplify, strengthen, boost. ANT. *decrease, reduce, attenuate*.

augur n. prophet, seer, oracle, prognosticator, diviner, fortune-teller, psychic.

augur v. predict, prophesy, divine, forecast, bode, portend, herald, presage, forewarn.

augury n. **1.** PREDICTION prophesy, divination, forecast, forewarning, soothsaying, forecasting. **2.** OMEN portent, sign, harbinger, herald, forewarning.

AUGUST a. [aw GUST] awe-inspiring, magnificent, worthy of great respect. *The august cathedral is a national landmark*. SYN. grand, magnificent, glorious, imposing, sublime, noble, stately, dignified, regal, supreme, eminent, lofty, distinguished. ANT. *lowly, pedestrian, humble*.

aura n. ambience, atmosphere, mood, feeling, *vibes, air, spirit, nimbus, emanation.

aurora n. aurora australis (southern lights), aurora borealis (northern lights).

auspices n. sponsorship, patronage, aegis, sanction, assistance, authority, guidance, protection, supervision.

AUSPICIOUS a. [aw SPISH us] favorable, of positive conditions or character. *The economy is improving; it is an auspicious time for opening a new business*. SYN. favorable, propitious, positive, felicitous, fortunate, timely, opportune, promising, good, lucky, rosy, golden. ANT. *unfavorable, untimely, unfortunate, ominous*.

AUSTERE a. [aw STEER] severe, stern or plain in appearance, character, etc. Also, self-denying, strict. *The prison's austere facade was chillingly bleak*. SYN. **1.** severe, stern, harsh, grim, stiff, cold, forbidding, rigid, serious, sober, solemn, plain, unadorned. **2.** ascetic, self-denying, strict, abstemious, stark. ANT. 1. *bright, cheery, sunny, warm, frivolous, ornate*. 2. *indulgent, extravagant*.

authentic a. genuine, real, bona fide, true, actual, simon-pure, *kosher, certified, *the real McCoy, *honest-to-goodness, legitimate. ANT. *bogus, phony, fake, spurious*.

authenticate v. validate, certify, confirm, warrant, guarantee, attest, vouch, affirm, substantiate, corroborate, document. ANT. *invalidate, falsify, discredit*.

author n. **1.** WRITER novelist, playwright, storyteller, screenwriter, poet, bard, historian, chronicler, biographer, dramatist, journalist, *hack, wordsmith. "A person who you can silence by shutting his book." —Max Gralnik. SEE BOOK, NOVELIST **2.** ORIGINATOR creator, architect, designer, father, founder.

WORD FIND

best-selling author with staying power: brand-name author

multiple books, author of: polygraph

pen name: pseudonym, nom de plume, allonym, ananym, anonym

publicizes author and books: publicist

sells author's books, handles contracts: literary agent

writes a book for someone else who may or may not take credit: ghost writer

authoritarian n. dictator, tyrant, despot, disciplinarian, martinet.

authoritarian a. dictatorial, tyrannical, repressive, totalitarian, strict, dogmatic, rigid, despotic, imperious, autocratic, domineering. ANT. *libertarian, permissive, liberal, democratic*.

authoritative a. official, validated, authentic, true, genuine, documented, sound, certified, reliable, trustworthy, scholarly. ANT. *questionable, frivolous, unsubstantiated*.

authorities n. the powers that be, City Hall, officials, government, officialdom, *the law.

authority n. **1.** POWER jurisdiction, rule, license, charge, control, command, dominion, administration, influence. "A halter." —Adelard of Bath. "Tyranny unless tempered by freedom." — Stefan Zweig. **2.** EXPERT specialist, professional, scholar, connoisseur, *walking encyclopedia, trusted source.

authorize v. permit, give the okay, empower, entitle, license, allow, sanction, *give the green light, warrant, commission.

autocracy n. dictatorship, despotism, totalitarianism.

autocrat n. dictator, tyrant, despot, authoritarian, overlord, *iron-fisted ruler.

automated a. servo-mechanized, mechanized, computerized, programmed, motorized.

automatic a. **1.** SELF-OPERATING mechanical, self-propelling, self-programmed, servo-mechanized, automated. **2.** INVOLUNTARY unconscious, reflex, unpremeditated, spontaneous. ANT. *1. manual, labor-intensive. 2. voluntary, conscious.*

automaton SEE ROBOT

automobile n. car, vehicle, sedan, *wheels, station wagon, hatchback, subcompact, *bucket of bolts, *clunker, *shitbox, *lemon, *gas-guzzler, convertible, *lowrider, *horseless carriage, roadster, town car, *crate, coupe, *hot rod, *jalopy. "Man's most successful effort to produce the mule." — Anon. "Man's greatest invention — until he got into the driver's seat." — Anon.

WORD FIND

book listing prices of used cars: blue book

bump absorbers: shock absorbers, suspension system, leaf springs, springs, torsion bars

cables used to recharge dead battery: jumper cables

cutting tool used in a car accident: Jaws of Life

dashboard warning lights: idiot lights, hazard lights

divider between engine and passenger compartment: firewall

engages and disengages engine from transmission: clutch

engine speed gauge: tachometer

frame: chassis

gearbox: transmission

gears shifted manually: manual transmission

license plate customized with owner's name or pet word: vanity plate

mechanic's rolling board used for underbody inspection: creeper

mileage meter: odometer

radar detector: *fuzzbuster

shifting to low gear to help slow car: down-shift

speed automator: cruise control

tailpipe afterburner, burns harmful gases: catalytic converter

used car in perfect condition: cherry

wheel-locking clamp used to stop parking scofflaws: Denver boot

wheel shaft: axle

SEE ACCIDENT, DRIVE, MOTOR, ROAD, TRUCK

AUTONOMOUS a. [aw TON uh mus] acting independently. *An autonomous island government, free of the mainland's dictates.* SYN. independent, self-governing, self-ruling, self-reliant, sovereign. ANT. *dependent, subject, overruled, occupied.*

autonomy n. independence, sovereignty, self-rule, self-reliance, home rule, freedom. ANT. *dependence, subjugation.*

autumn n. fall, harvest time, Indian summer. "A second spring when every leaf's a flower." — Albert Camus.

auxiliary a. **1.** SUPPORTING assisting, aiding, adjuvant. **2.** SUBSIDIARY subordinate, supplementary, accessory, additional, secondary, reserve. ANT. *2. main, primary.*

avail n. use, usefulness, benefit, help, aid, advantage, profit.

avail v. utilize, help, assist, aid, serve.

available a. handy, ready, accessible, on hand, at hand, obtainable, on tap, free, at one's disposal. ANT. *unavailable, out.*

avalanche n. **1.** SNOWSLIDE landslide. **2.** INUNDATION cataclysm, deluge, flood, torrent, barrage.

WORD FIND

air current produced by: avalanche wind

overhang of ice and snow, known for starting avalanches: cornice

SEE MOUNTAIN, MOUNTAIN CLIMBING

avante-garde n. vanguard, *cutting edge, groundbreakers, innovators, pioneers, trailblazers.

AVARICE n. [AV ur is] unhealthy desire for wealth, greed. *Her avarice compelled her to hobnob with wealthy bachelors.* SYN. greed, cupidity, acquisitiveness, covetousness, rapacity, gluttony, miserliness, "A mere madness, to live like a wretch, and die rich." — Robert Burton. "The spur of industry." — David Hume. ANT. *generosity, benevolence, charity.*

AVARICIOUS a. [AV ur ISH us] greedy. *She was after his money; she was avaricious.* SYN. greedy, covetous, acquisitive, rapacious, piggish, hoarding, predatory, *tight, selfish, *gold-digging, gluttonous. ANT. *generous, giv-*

ing, beneficent.

avenge *v.* revenge, retaliate, take vengeance, *pay back, *get even, punish, vindicate, wreak vengeance. ANT. *forgive, excuse, overlook.*

avenue *n.* **1.** ROAD roadway, drive, lane, boulevard, highway, thoroughfare, promenade, street, parkway, artery, expressway. **2.** WAY means, route, path, course.

average *n.* norm, par, standard, mean.

average *a.* ordinary, typical, usual, common, standard, *garden variety, middling, intermediate, fair, moderate, median, run-of-the-mill, so-so, everyday. ANT. *exceptional, above par, extraordinary.*

averse *a.* loath, ill-disposed, opposed, hostile, unfavorable, disinclined, hesitant, unwilling, against. ANT. *agreeable, willing, eager.*

AVERSION *n.* [uh VUR zhun] an intense dislike or repugnance. *I have an aversion to pickled beets.* SYN. dislike, repugnance, loathing, antipathy, revulsion, disgust, hostility, hatred, detestation. ANT. *liking, attraction, fondness.*

avert *v.* **1.** TURN AWAY shift, turn aside. **2.** PREVENT ward off, avoid, thwart, deter, preclude, forestall, nip in the bud. ANT. *invite, cause, exacerbate.*

aviator *n.* pilot, flyer, airman, ace, aviatrix.

avid *a.* **1.** EAGER enthusiastic, fervent, ardent, flaming, rabid, fanatical, burning, zealous. **2.** DESIROUS greedy, avaricious, rapacious, covetous, voracious. ANT. *1. lukewarm, blasé, bored. 2. indifferent, uninterested.*

avocation *n.* hobby, pastime, interest, pursuit, sideline.

avoid *v.* evade, dodge, steer clear of, bypass, elude, sidestep, hedge, duck, shirk, avert, eschew, shun, *give the slip, refrain. ANT. *embrace, meet head on, confront, invite.*

avoidance *a.* evasion, dodging, bypassing, sidestepping, hedging, shirking, ducking out, averting, eschewing, shunning, refraining.

avow *v.* declare, admit, acknowledge, avouch, aver, confess, profess, announce, swear. ANT. *disavow, deny.*

avowal *n.* declaration, admission, acknowledgement, confession, profession, announcement, assertion, affirmation. ANT. *disavowal, denial.*

await *v.* wait for, anticipate.

awake *a.* **1.** CONSCIOUS active, alert, wakeful, astir, wide-eyed, *bright-eyed and bushy-tailed, up. **2.** ALERT watchful, attentive, sharp, circumspect, vigilant, observant. ANT.

1. asleep, unconscious, comatose. 2. inattentive, dull, off guard.

awaken *v.* wake, rouse, get up, stimulate, activate.

awakening *n.* revival, rousing, invigoration, stimulation, realization, consciousness, rebirth.

award *n.* prize, citation, medal, trophy, honor, reward, decoration, compensation.

award *v.* bestow, present, grant, confer, endow, compensate.

aware *a.* conscious, cognizant, in touch, knowing, mindful, *wise to, wary, sharp, apprised, awake, enlightened, *know the score, versed, *hip, *with it, *plugged in, grounded, au courant. ANT. *unaware, ignorant, *out to lunch, unconscious.*

away *a.* gone, removed, off, absent, out, abroad, remote.

awe *n.* wonder, fear, reverence, astonishment, amazement, stupefaction, veneration, respect, worship, admiration, shock. ANT. *disrespect, disregard, apathy, indifference.*

awesome *a.* impressive, overwhelming, intimidating, moving, formidable, astonishing, amazing, *eye-popping, breathtaking, wonderful, wondrous, stunning, *mind blowing, stupefying, excellent, *bad, *cool, *dynamite, *gnarly, *gone, immense, super, *ripping, *out of this world, *unreal. ANT. *unimpressive, *ho-hum, *lame, *lightweight, *bush league, trivial.*

awful *a.* **1.** HORRIBLE bad, ugly, dreadful, terrible, atrocious, unpleasant, horrendous, ghastly, despicable, inferior, contemptible, rotten, *crappy, appalling, frightful, terrifying. ANT. *good, nice, pleasing.*

awkward *a.* **1.** CLUMSY bumbling, oafish, ungraceful, bungling, ungainly, maladroit, inept, *klutzy, blundering. **2.** UNWIELDY cumbersome, bulky, ponderous. **3.** UNCOMFORTABLE embarrassing, inappropriate, untimely, thorny, delicate, trying, ticklish. ANT. *1. coordinated, graceful. 2. handy, convenient. 3. appropriate, relaxing, smooth.*

awning *n.* canopy, canvas, shelter, sunshade, marquee.

awry *a.* **1.** CROOKEDLY askew, obliquely, aslant. **2.** AMISS wrong, off course, astray, askew. ANT. *1. straight, evenly. 2. right, well, correctly.*

ax *n.* broadax, hatchet, pickax, maul, tomahawk.

axiom *n.* maxim, truth, truism, principle, dictum, precept.

axiomatic *a.* self-evident, unquestionable, certain, understood, acknowledged, known, absolute, fundamental. ANT. *questionable, dubious, in question.*

axis *n.* **1.** PIVOT spindle, shaft, hinge. **2.** ALIGNMENT alliance, coalition, league, union.

axle *n.* spindle, rod, bar, shaft, axis, arbor.

B

babble n. prattle, babel, gibberish, spluttering, mumbling, blabbing, jabber, burble, blubbering, drivel.

babble v. prattle, blab, gibber, *yak, jabber, burble, blather, murmur, sputter, mutter, gush, splutter, blat, prate, gurgle.

babe in the woods n. easy mark, sucker, dupe, innocent.

babel n. confusion, tumult, clamor.

baby n. **1.** INFANT newborn, babe, neonate, *bambino, papoose, tot, nursling, nipper, toddler. "An alimentary canal with a loud voice at one end and no responsibility at the other."—Elizabeth Adamson. "It is all gut and squall."—Charles Brown. "An inestimable blessing and bother."—Mark Twain. "A perfect example of minority rule."—Anon. **2.** SNIVELER whiner, crybaby, *whimp.

WORD FIND

abandoned and found: foundling
ailment: croup
bathtub: bathinette
bed: cradle, bassinet
bounce on one's knee or swing up and down in one's arms: dandle
breastfeeder, hired: wet nurse
carriage: buggy, pram, stroller, perambulator
chewy toy: teething ring, pacifier
contented, happy cry: crow
cry loudly: squall
cry weakly: whimper, mewl
dead at birth: stillborn
diaper irritation: diaper rash
embryo implant: test-tube baby
foreskin removal from male: circumcision
illegitimate: love child, bastard
multiple: twins, triplets, quadruplets, quintuplets, sextuplets
murder of: infanticide
outfit: layette
premature infant: preemie
rubber soother: pacifier
soft spot on head: fontanelle
song: lullaby
talk: babble, coo, gurgle
tooth eruption: teething
walking: toddling
whine and whimper: pule

SEE BIRTH, CHILD, CHILDREN, PREGNANCY

baby v. spoil, indulge, dote on, pamper, coddle, mollycoddle, overprotect, shelter, smother.

baby a. small, wee, miniature, tiny, young, teensy, pocket-sized.

babyish a. childish, infantile, juvenile, immature.

bacchanal n. SEE ORGY, PARTY

bachelor n. single, stag, playboy, man about town. "A man who is footloose and fiancé free."—F.G. Kernan. "One who savours the chase but does not eat the game."—Anon.

back n. backside, posterior, spine, tail end, hind, rear, stern, rump. SEE ASS

back v. **1.** SUPPORT assist, sponsor, *go to bat for, abet, boost, stand behind, promote, endorse. **2.** REVERSE go backwards, backtrack, return, turn tail, rebound, regress, recoil. ANT. 1. undermine, reject, denounce. 2. progress, advance.

back a. **1.** REAR hind, end, posterior. **2.** DISTANT remote, faraway, outermost, rural, secluded. **3.** PAST earlier, previous, dated, bygone. ANT. 1. front, anterior, head. 2. future, upcoming.

back and forth adv. to and fro, from side to side, vacillating.

backbite v. slander, malign, *backstab, defame, vilify, gossip, smear, *badmouth, *dump on, *tell tales out of school.

backbone n. **1.** SPINE spinal column, vertebrae. **2.** FOUNDATION mainstay, basis. **3.** COURAGE strength, character, mettle, *guts, grit, spunk, fortitude, pluck, resolve. ANT. 3. timidity, cowardice, spinelessness.

backbreaking a. strenuous, arduous, taxing, laborious, crippling, crushing, bankrupting. ANT. light, easy, *child's play.

back down v. give in, cave in, concede, submit, *wimp out, acquiesce, surrender. ANT. hold one's ground, stand firm.

backer n. supporter, sponsor, promoter, booster, underwriter, angel, financier, advocate, benefactor, patron, investor.

backfire v. go awry, flop, reverse, blow up in one's face, boomerang, miscarry, *bomb. ANT. *go off without a hitch, work.

background n. **1.** DISTANCE backdrop, horizon, offing. **2.** EXPERIENCE upbringing, environment, grounding, family, past, education, circumstances. ANT. 1. foreground.

backhanded a. equivocal, ambiguous, left-handed, underhanded, sarcastic.

backing n. support, sponsorship, help, aid, assistance, boost, advocacy, patronage, encouragement, endorsement. ANT. detraction, undermining.

backlash *n.* repercussion, reaction, backfire, retaliation, response, recoil, impact, effect, consequence, wake, backwash.

backlog *n.* accumulation, reserve, excess, stock, hoard.

back-pedal *v.* retract, take back, recant, retreat, renege, back down.

backslide *v.* slip, slide, sin, relapse, deviate, go astray, lapse, leave the straight and narrow, leave the path of righteousness.

back talk *n.* lip, sass, mouth, guff, insolence.

backup *n.* auxiliary, extra, substitute, alternate.

backward *a.* **1.** TOWARD THE REAR rearward, in reverse, behind. **2.** IN REVERSE upside-down, inside-out, wrong, *bassackwards. **3.** SHY hesitant, reticent, bashful, reserved, timid, demure. **4.** RETARDED slow, behind, simple, inept, stupid, rustic, impeded, laggard, dull. ANT. *3. confident, bold, forward. 4. advanced, quick, brilliant.*

backwoodsman *n.* rustic, yokel, *hillbilly, *hick, *hayseed.

bad *a.* **1.** BELOW STANDARD inadequate, poor, *lousy, *crappy, substandard, unacceptable, awful, faulty, unsatisfactory, *cheesy, slipshod, deficient, inferior, below par, worthless, shoddy. **2.** WICKED immoral, evil, corrupt, vile, sinful, demonic, satanic, diabolical, mischievous, mean. "All that proceeds from weakness." — Friedrich Nietzsche. **3.** SPOILED rotten, putrid, decayed, tainted, moldy. **4.** UNPLEASANT unfavorable, unfortunate, terrible, revolting, awful, dreadful, disagreeable, horrible, distressing, dire, tragic, negative. **5.** SEVERE powerful, destructive, serious, dangerous, grave, horrible. **6.** INCORRECT erroneous, inaccurate. **7.** SORRY low, down, distressed, troubled, gloomy, melancholy, depressed, remorseful. ANT. *1. excellent, good, superior. 2. moral, good, virtuous. 3. fresh, preserved. 4. pleasant, favorable, good. 5. harmless, trivial, light. 6. correct, accurate. 7. good, proud, glorious.*

bad breath *n.* halitosis, *dragon breath.

badge *n.* **1.** emblem, shield, medal, medallion, insignia, symbol, sign.

badger *v.* bother, nag, harass, pester, bug, needle, hassle, plague, hound, annoy, provoke, peeve, *ride.

badly *a.* inadequately, poorly, unacceptably, abominably, awfully, unsatisfactorily, deficiently, slipshod, below par, wrong, ineptly, terribly. ANT. *excellently, perfectly, superbly.*

baffle *v.* **1.** CONFUSE perplex, muddle, stump, confound, throw, befuddle, daze, delude, mix up, puzzle. **2.** THWART hinder, check, foil, obstruct, impede, bar, frustrate.

baffling *a.* inscrutable, perplexing.

bag *n.* sack, pouch, pack, satchel, tote, carryall, haversack, gunny-bag, duffel, valise, suitcase, portmanteau, briefcase.

bag *v.* snare, capture, catch, take, trap, kill, seize.

bagatelle *n.* trifle.

baggage *n.* luggage, bags, suitcases, valises, trunks, things, paraphernalia, effects, gear.

baggy *a.* sagging, droopy, puffy, limp, unpressed, loose, slack, fat, billowing. ANT. *smooth, tight, pressed, tailored.*

bagpipe *n.* SEE MUSICAL INSTRUMENT

bail *n.* bond, security, deposit, surety, warranty, release.

BAILIWICK *n.* [BAL i wik] one's area of special interest or expertise. *My personal bailiwick is paleontology.* SYN. interest, authority, field, sphere, jurisdiction, realm, domain, territory, area of expertise, department, beat.

bait *n.* lure, allurement, attraction, bribe, enticement, *come-on, inducement.

bait *v.* **1.** LURE attract, entice, bribe, induce, seduce, tantalize, tempt, draw, interest. **2.** GOAD tease, pick on, harass, rile, provoke, annoy, irk, hector, badger, *ride. ANT. *1. repel, repulse. 2. pacify, please, mollify.*

bake *v.* roast, cook, broil, heat.

balance *n.* **1.** EQUILIBRIUM parity, equity, equalization, symmetry, correspondence, equipoise, equality. **2.** MENTAL STABILITY composure, self-control, poise, *cool head, stability. ANT. *1. imbalance, inequality. 2. instability, irrationality.*

balance *v.* **1.** TO MAKE EQUAL equalize, counterpoise, stabilize, level, counteract, stabilize, equilibrate, steady, match, offset, *walk a fine line, *level the playing field. **2.** COMPARE consider, differentiate, weigh, contrast, evaluate. **3.** ACCOUNT square, debit, credit, tally, audit, compute, calculate, sum up.

balcony *n.* **1.** PORCH platform, terrace, deck, overhang, veranda, portico. **2.** GALLERY loge, upper deck, mezzanine, *peanut gallery, cheap seats.

bald *a.* **1.** HAIRLESS bare, glabrous, shaven, *head like a cueball, *skinheaded, *chrome-domed. **2.** UNADORNED plain, stark, austere, bare, barren. **3.** FRANK blunt, outright, direct, overt, out-and-out, baldfaced, flagrant, glaring. ANT. *1. hairy, furry, woolly, hirsute. 2. ornate, decorated, embellished. 3. indirect, disguised, subtle.*

balderdash *n.* bunk, rot, *bullshit, poppycock. SEE NONSENSE

bale *n.* bundle, packet, bunch, parcel.

baleful *a.* harmful, sinister, threatening, evil, ominous, deadly, injurious, pernicious, wicked, hazardous, malignant. ANT. *harmless, innocuous, benign.*

balk *v.* **1.** FRUSTRATE thwart, foil, hinder, impede, prevent, check, retard. **2.** HESITATE recoil, refuse, object, demur, draw back, shy away from, flinch, stop short. ANT. *1. facilitate, clear, help.*

balky *a.* stubborn, contrary, resisting, resistant, obstinate, mulish, intractable, ornery, unruly. ANT. *cooperative, tractable.*

ball *n.* **1.** ORB sphere, globe, spheroid, apple, round, bullet. **2.** DANCE prom, masque, shindig, hoedown, *hop.

ballad *n.* song, love song, folk song. SEE SONG

ballerina *n.* SEE BALLET

ballet *n.* dance, toe dancing, choreography, adagio.

WORD FIND
attire: tutu, tights, leotard
director: impresario
female dancer: ballerina, prima ballerina
jump and land in same position: saute
jump straight in the air with quick changes of leg position: entrechat
jump with legs clung together: soubresaut
knee-bend: plié
leap from one foot to the other: jete
male dancer: danseur
mincing steps on tiptoes: pas de bourrée
posturing on one leg: arabesque
practice: barre work
practice room bar: barre
running steps: pas couru
secondary, non-principal dancer: coryphee
shoes: toe shoes, ballet shoes
sliding on soles of feet: glissading
solo: pas seul
spin in which head is held still, then turned after body: spotting
split performed in midair: pas ciseaux, grand ecart
step: pas
steps performed on tiptoes: temps de point, en pointe
whirlaround: pirouette

balloon *n.* aerostat, lighter-than-air craft.

WORD FIND
altitude-measuring device: altimeter
anchor line: tether, dragrope, mooring line
ascent/descent speed-measuring device: variometer
basket: gondola
bottom sleeve, where hot air is blown in: appendix, mouth
broadest portion: equator
burner's lighter: sparker
gas: hot air, helium, hydrogen
ground crew: chase crew
ground director of balloon activity: balloonmeister
high-speed launch used in windy conditions: blastoff
interior of bag: envelope
pilot, passenger: aeronaut
propane gas heater: burner
rate of descent: sink
weights, sandbags, used to control altitude: ballast
SEE BLIMP

balloon *v.* inflate, swell, expand, bloat, puff out, dilate, billow. ANT. *deflate, contract, shrink.*

ballot *n.* ticket, slate, vote, poll. "The rightful and peaceful successors of bullets." — Abraham Lincoln.

balls *n.* *guts, nerve, courage, daring, effrontery, *chutzpah.

ballyhoo *n.* uproar, talk, hype, *hot air, puffery, promotion, *spiel, babble, pitch, *B.S., hoopla.

balm *n.* salve, remedy, cure, comfort, soothing agent, curative. ANT. *irritant, abrasive.*

balmy *a.* **1.** MILD fair, gentle, pleasant, temperate, tranquil, calm, soothing. **2.** CRAZY insane, foolish, *nuts, *cuckoo, daft, *crackers, eccentric, weird. ANT. *1. stormy, blustery, inclement. 2. sane, normal, stable.*

baloney *n.* *crap, rot, bunk. SEE NONSENSE

bamboo *n.* cane, grass, reed.

bamboozle *v.* trick, cheat, hoodwink, deceive, dupe, confuse, buffalo, swindle, take, defraud, pull the wool over one's eyes, con.

ban *n.* prohibition, embargo, proscription, interdiction, boycott, taboo, restriction, *blacklisting, stoppage, injunction. ANT. *approval, sanction, allowance.*

ban *v.* prohibit, restrict, stop, banish, boycott, forbid, disallow, bar, exclude, outlaw, close, *blackball. ANT. *allow, sanction, approve, legalize.*

BANAL *a.* [buh NAL; BANE ul] dull, overused, common. *The dialogue was too predictable and tired; it was banal.* SYN. dull, overused, common, tired, trite, hackneyed, insipid, stale, vapid, lackluster, hum-drum, clichéd, platitudinous, flat, inane, unoriginal. ANT. *original, rich, deep, fresh, provocative.*

banality n. cliché, platitude, triteness, commonplace, bromide.

band n. **1.** GROUP gang, association, company, assembly, mob, crush, throng, bunch, troop, posse, tribe, pack. **2.** MUSICAL GROUP ensemble, trio, quartet, orchestra, combo.
WORD FIND
advisor: manager
circuit of shows: tour
books shows: agent, booking agent
fan of: *groupie
main act, following warm-up act: headliner
publicizes, promotes: publicist, promoter
road, set-up crew-member: *roadie
session followed by break: set
speakers: amplifiers, amps, PA system
unrehearsed, impromptu performance: jam
SEE MUSIC, MUSICIAN, RECORDING
3. STRIP swath, strap, tie, ribbon, sash, cord, fillet, thong.

bandage n. gauze, swath, dressing, compress, *Bandaid.

bandanna n. handkerchief, neckerchief, kerchief.

bandit n. thief, robber, crook, desperado, outlaw, brigand, *mugger, hoodlum, thug, burglar, highwayman, hold-up man.

bandy v. exchange, give-and-take, pass back and forth, *ping pong, circulate, pass along.

BANE n. [BANE] harm, destruction. *A wolfpack is the bane of the deer yard.* SYN. death, ruin, evil, downfall, scourge, plague, destruction, curse, undoing, poison. ANT. *blessing, good.*

bang n. **1.** NOISE boom, thump, crack, report, eruption, clang, crash, burst, explosion, pop, thud, peal, salvo, slam, clap, shot. **2.** BLOW hit, whack, slam, thwack, rap, smack, belt, punch, clout. **3.** THRILL *Sl.* *kick, *jollies, *charge.

bang v. **1.** MAKE NOISE boom, peal, explode, thump, crack, clang, slam, thud, sound, pop, clap. **2.** STRIKE hit, whack, slam, pop, shoot, clap, punch, clout, smack, rap, beat, pummel.

banish v. exile, expel, eject, remove, ban, proscribe, excommunicate, deport, outlaw, dismiss, oust, relegate, drum out. ANT. *adopt, invite, embrace.*

banjo n. SEE MUSICAL INSTRUMENTS

bank n. **1.** FINANCIAL INSTITUTION savings and loan, S&L, thrift institution, trust company, treasury, credit union, Federal Reserve Bank, mortgage company. "A place where they lend you an umbrella in fair weather and ask for it back when it begins to rain." — Robert Frost.
WORD FIND
bad check-writing: kiting
clerk: teller
messenger/*gopher: runner
panicked withdrawals on fear of bank closure: bank run
storage space for customer's valuables: safe deposit box
teller's small window: wicket
SEE SECURITIES
2. EMBANKMENT slope, hill, ledge, mound, levee. **3.** ROW tier, course, string, line, array, series.

bankrupt a. insolvent, *gone belly up, ruined, wiped out, broke, *busted, penniless, in the red. ANT. *solvent, profiting, flourishing, in the black.*
WORD FIND
bankruptcy procedure/code section: Chapter Eleven

bankruptcy n. insolvency. SEE BANKRUPT

banner n. flag, pennant, ensign, streamer, standard, pennon, bunting, colors.

banner a. successful, outstanding, leading, exceptional, foremost, record, red-letter.

banquet n. feast, dinner, meal, roast, *spread, repast.

bantam n. feisty runt, little spitfire, little scrapper, *cocky little bastard, whippersnapper, swaggerer, strutting half-pint, cock of the walk.

banter n. teasing, ribbing, jesting, joking, joshing, repartee, badinage, ridicule, kidding, persiflage, raillery.

banter v. tease, rib, jest, joke, josh, ridicule, kid, *ride.

baptism n. initiation, purification, sacrament, ritual, rite, christening, sprinkling, annointing, immersion, consecration. "The vehicle to heaven, the public agent of the Kingdom, the gift of adoption." — Saint Basil.
WORD FIND
basin: baptistery, font, laver
cloth: chrisom
immersion, by: holobaptism
robe: chrisom
water: laver

baptize v. initiate, purify, annoint, cleanse, immerse, christen, indoctrinate, consecrate, sanctify, sprinkle.

bar n. **1.** RAIL OR ROD stick, strip, stake, pole, shaft, crosspiece, boom, spar, paling. **2.** IM-

PEDIMENT barrier, obstruction, obstacle, constraint, block, snag, restraint, barricade, restriction, stumbling block. **3.** PUB saloon, tavern, gin mill, cocktail lounge, *watering hole, lounge, beer garden, dramshop. **4.** LEGAL SYSTEM lawyers, attorneys, counselors, bar association, solicitors, barristers, judiciary, legal fraternity. **5.** BAND stripe, strip, striation, ribbon, score, line.

bar v. **1.** STOP impede, obstruct, prohibit, hinder, block, barricade, restrict, restrain, prevent, constrain, interdict. **2.** BOLT secure, lock, seal, close, latch. **3.** EXCLUDE prohibit, ostracize, ban, banish, blackball, blacklist, segregate, spurn, boycott, shut out, freeze out. ANT. *1. facilitate, aid, abet. 2. unlock, open, free. 3. include, welcome, embrace.*

barb n. insult, dig, cutting remark, putdown, affront, criticism.

barbarian n. savage, *animal, clod, ignoramus, Neanderthal, philistine, lout, primitive, caveman, lowbrow, redneck, *pig, brute, ruffian, hooligan, dolt, Hun.

barbaric a. savage, animalistic, ignorant, cloddish, primitive, brutish, cruel, lowbrow, rough, doltish, uncultured, vulgar, wild, ill-mannered. ANT. *civilized, cultured, refined.*

barbarity n. barbarism, savagery, ignorance, cloddishness, brutality, cruelty, roughness, vulgarity, wildness, ruthlessness, brutishness. ANT. *civility, nicety, refinement.*

barbarous a. savage, animalistic, coarse, ignorant, inhuman, primitive, uncivilized, brutish, uncouth, rude, wild, rough, doltish, uncultured, vulgar, ill-mannered, vicious, philistine. ANT. *civilized, refined, humane, cultured.*

barbecue v. flame broil, roast, rotisserie, grill, sear, cook out.

barber n. hair stylist, hairdresser, beautician, haircutter.

bare a. **1.** UNCLOTHED naked, nude, stripped, in the buff, exposed, *in the raw, *in one's birthday suit, disrobed, *wearing nothing but goosebumps. **2.** PLAIN barren, stark, spare, austere, Spartan, unfinished, unadorned, empty. **3.** UNDISGUISED bald, plain, stark, unvarnished, glaring, straightforward, flagrant ANT. *1. clothed, dressed. 2. ornate, elaborate, decorated. 3. hidden, covered up, camouflaged.*

barefaced a. shameless, brazen, bold, frank, audacious, rude, bumptious, outspoken, insolent, impudent. ANT. *reserved, polite, respectful.*

barely a. hardly, scarcely, just, slightly, merely.

bargain n. **1.** AGREEMENT understanding, pledge, contract, deal, arrangement, promise, covenant. "A transaction in which each participant thinks he has cheated the other." — Anon. **2.** GOOD DEAL steal, good value, a bon marche. "Something you can't use at a price you can't resist." — Franklin Jones.

bargain v. negotiate, dicker, haggle, come to terms, deal, higgle, promise, contract, trade, barter.

barge n. flatboat, scow, freight carrier.

bark n. **1.** WOOF yip, yelp, howl, yawp, bowwow, bay, arf, growl. **2.** COVERING skin, husk, peeling, hide, shell, pod.

bark v. **1.** WOOF yip, yelp, howl, yawp, yap, bowwow, bay, arf, growl. **2.** SHOUT bellow, holler, yell, snap, growl, bluster, roar, snarl, thunder.

barmy a. eccentric, odd, peculiar, daft, *batty.

barn n. byre, cowbarn, stables, stalls, shed.

WORD FIND

barn and other farm buildings, collectively: farmstead

erection of: barnraising

fodder storage building next to: silo

grain storage building: granary

upper portion where hay is stored: hayloft

SEE FARM

baron n. nobleman, aristocrat, lord.

baroque a. ornate, elaborate, florid, embellished, busy, overworked, rococo, ostentatious, fanciful. ANT. *plain, stark, austere.*

barrage n. **1.** SUSTAINED ATTACK bombardment, shelling, salvo, battery, volley, assault, enfilade, onslaught, hail, fusillade, wall of fire, rain of fire. **2.** PROFUSION deluge, inundation, rain, mass, plethora, torrent.

barrel n. cask, keg, hogshead, drum, firkin, vessel, butt, cylinder.

WORD FIND

maker: cooper

part: stave

stopper: bung

barren a. **1.** DESOLATE sterile, empty, bare, depleted, void, unproductive, arid, stark. **2.** CHILDLESS infertile, sterile, infecund, unbearing. **3.** DULL boring, uninteresting, stale, uninspiring. ANT. *1. fertile, lush, rich, fruitful. 2. fertile, fecund. 3. interesting, inspiring.*

barricade n. barrier, roadblock, blockade, bar, impediment, rampart, bulwark.

barricade v. bar, block, impede, shut off, fortify, obstruct, secure, defend.

barrier *n.* **1.** PHYSICAL OBSTRUCTION bar, obstacle, barricade, impediment, check, roadblock, wall, rampart, bulwark, fortification, boom, palisade. **2.** HANDICAP limitation, impediment, hindrance, difficulty, obstacle, stumbling block, hurdle, obstacle.

barrister *n.* attorney, counselor. SEE LAWYER

barrow *n.* handcart, pushcart, wheelbarrow, handbarrow.

bartender *n.* barkeep, barmaid, *mixmaster.

barter *v.* trade, exchange, swap.

base *n.* **1.** FOUNDATION support, bottom, stand, pedestal, bed, foot, ground structure. **2.** BASIS essence, core, foundation, source, backbone, root, fundamental, heart, principle. **3.** HEADQUARTERS center, station, home, post, camp.

base *v.* ground, derive, build, establish, rest, construct.

base *a.* **1.** INFERIOR lowly, cheap, impure, debased. **2.** CONTEMPTIBLE low, mean, ignoble, dishonorable, indecent, disgraceful, despicable, sordid, degenerate, unprincipled, incorrigible, disreputable; slavish, wretched, servile, menial, cringing. ANT. 1. *superior, pure.* 2. *noble, virtuous, principled.*

baseball *n.* ball, national pastime. "A game which consists of tapping a ball with a piece of wood, then running like a lunatic." — H.J. Dutiel. "An allegorical play about America, a poetic, complex, and subtle play of courage, fear, good luck, mistakes, patience...." — Saul Steinberg.

WORD FIND

ambidextrous hitter: switch hitter
batter's spot: batter's box
batting practice: fungo
bench shelter: dugout
British game evolved from: rounders
dirt track skirting outfield wall: warning track
double play from shortstop 6 to second baseman 4 to first baseman 3 6-4-3 doubleplay
fan's fanciful game of: Rotisserie League Baseball
fielding goof: error
game with few hits: pitcher's duel, shutout
half/partial swing: check swing
high-bouncing hit: chopper
hits in place of pitcher: designated hitter
home run with bases loaded: grand slam
league championship: pennant, world series
line drive: clothesline
locker room area: clubhouse
minor league: bush league, farm club, A,

AA, AAA
off-season fans: hot stove league
pitcher and catcher, collectively: battery
pitcher's illegal motion: balk
pitcher's warmup area: bullpen
pitch: fastball, curveball, spitball, forkball, sinker, slider, *beanball, split-fingered fastball, change-up, off-speed pitch, palmball, knuckleball, breaking ball, lollipop, screwball
players' nickname: boys of summer
player who blows crucial play: goat
powerful throwing arm: cannon, bazooka, rifle
practice catching fly balls: shag flies
RBI: runs batted in
short flyball: blooper, squibber, pop-up
spectacular catch: shoestring catch, circus catch
strike out oneself or someone else: fan
tiny, infield hit: bunt, nubber

baseless *a.* unsubstantiated, unfounded, groundless, unwarranted, flimsy.

bash *n.* *Sl.* celebration, *wing-ding, spree. SEE PARTY

bash *v.* smash, whack, hit, strike, slam, punch, *clobber, crush, *bop.

bashful *a.* shy, timid, shrinking, embarrassed, blushing, modest, backward, demure, self-conscious, withdrawn, sheepish, retiring, coy. ANT. *brash, confident, swaggering, loud.*

basic *n.* fundamental, rudiment, essential, nuts and bolts.

basic *a.* fundamental, rudimentary, essential, primary, vital, elementary, key, necessary. ANT. *nonessential, superfluous, extra.*

basin *n.* washbowl, sink, vessel, tub, font.

basis *n.* base, foundation, support, root, grounding, nucleus, source, center.

bask *v.* **1.** WARM ONESELF IN THE SUN *catch some rays, sunbathe. **2.** LUXURIATE revel, delight in, wallow, eat up.

basket *n.* container, receptacle, hamper, wickerwork, creel, pannier, scuttle.

basketball *n.* *hoops, *brownball, ball.

WORD FIND

blocking a shot as it descends toward basket: goaltending
blocking out opponents with body to position for a rebound: boxing out
blocking the path of a defender so teammate can get open for a pass or a shot: setting a pick
bouncing the ball while moving: dribbling
directs the offense: point guard

double-teaming the ball-carrier in an attempt to steal ball: trap

dribbling, stopping, holding the ball, then dribbling again: double-dribble

forward with strong rebounding ability: power forward

foul in which ball-carrier runs into stationary defender: charging, offensive foul

foul shot: free throw

grossly inaccurate shot: air ball, brick

hitting several shots in a row: hot, on fire, in a groove

leaping ability, measurement: hang time

missing several shots in a row, descriptive term: cold, ice cold

pass caught high in the air and slam-dunked: alley-oop

perfect shot that touches only net: swish

positions: guards, forwards, center

running downcourt quickly with ball for uncontested shot: fast break

shots: layup, jump shot (J), hook shot, three-point shot, finger-roll, slam-dunk, bank shot, Hail Mary, pullup, reverse dunk, fall-away, scoop shot

slamming ball down into the hoop: slam-dunk

taking more than two steps without dribbling: traveling, walking

turning the ball over in the palm while dribbling, a violation: palming

bastard n. **1.** ILLEGITIMATE CHILD *love child, whoreson, misbegot. **2.** SCOUNDREL asshole, jerk, son of a bitch, cad, rascal, son of a whore.

bastardize v. debase, defile, degrade, adulterate, corrupt, ruin, spoil.

BASTION n. [BAS chun] a stronghold or fortified place. *Harvard, a bastion of higher education. The marksmen took refuge behind the bastion.* SYN. stronghold, fortification, fortress, citadel, rampart, bulwark, refuge, garrison.

bat n. club, stick, staff, racket, cudgel, bludgeon, baton, shillelagh, *lumber, truncheon.

bat v. **1.** hit, smack, whack, swing at. **2.** wink, blink, flutter.

batch n. lot, bunch, cluster, assortment, group, pack, aggregate, collection, quantity.

bath n. wash, soak, cleansing, ablution, rinse, sponge bath, tub, shower, wash-up, steep, sauna.

bathe v. wash, soak, cleanse, clean, rinse, sponge off, freshen up, scrub, douche, lave, shower, steep.

bathing suit n. swimming trunks, shorts, swimsuit, bikini, *cutoffs, T-strap, maillot, *jams, one-piece, leotard, string bikini.

bathos n. sentimentality, triteness, insipidness, mush, *schmaltz, mawkishness, melodrama, bleeding heart, wishy-washyness.

bathroom n. restroom, toilet, men's room, ladies' room, *john, *head, latrine, washroom, commode, necessary, water closet, *can, outhouse, *shithouse, privy, *loo, lavatory, powder room.

baton n. stick, bat, staff, rod, club, wand, scepter, truncheon, mace.

batter v. beat, pound, strike, pummel, *sock, thrash, smash, wallop, dash, demolish, mangle, break, shatter, crush.

battery n. **1.** ELECTRICAL STORAGE UNIT dry cell, storage cell. **2.** ASSAULT beating, mugging, thrashing. **3.** SERIES array, line, string. **4.** GUNNERY artillery.

battle n. war, skirmish, conflict, clash, scuffle, engagement, combat, assault, fight, *run-in, tussle, confrontation, squabble.

battle v. fight, clash, skirmish, war, engage, confront, squabble.

battlement n. SEE CASTLE

bauble n. trinket, trifle, knickknack, gewgaw, bagatelle.

bawdy a. indecent, lewd, coarse, improper, obscene, raunchy, dirty, indelicate, lascivious, licentious, ribald. ANT. *clean, proper, chaste.*

bawl v. **1.** SHOUT yell, bellow, holler, bark, thunder, cry, howl. **2.** CRY wail, weep, blubber, sob, snivel, whimper, squall.

bawl out v. Sl. SEE SCOLD

bay n. **1.** bight, cove, inlet, gulf, estuary, strait, lagoon, harbor. **2.** alcove, niche, nook.

bay v. bark, howl, yelp, bellow.

bazaar n. marketplace, shop, fair.

beach n. shore, strand, coast, seaside, littoral.
WORD FIND

arm of land connecting two land masses: isthmus, tombolo

channel, small: rill

cross-current swimming hazard: riptide

debris, cargo washed ashore from lost ship: flotsam and jetsam

embankment or headland: bluff, promontory

harbor-protecting structure extending into water: jetty

ledge or shelf of sand deposited by sea over time: berm

marine vegetation washed ashore: wrack

mineral in beach sand: garnet, feldspar, quartz

narrow arm of land extending into water: spit

pillowlike object, egg-casing of skate: mermaid's purse

receding tide: ebb tide

ridge of coral or rock skirting shore: barrier reef

ripples in sand left by swash: swashmarks

sand bar connecting two land masses: tombolo

sea spray: spindrift

shells: abalone, baby bonnet, clam, cockle, conch, cone, cowrie, horn, limpet, mussel, nautilus, oyster, periwinkle, razor, scallop, triton, wentletrap

shelter/bathhouse: cabana

small beach between two cliffs: pocket beach

small rock island at head of promontory: stack

waves: plunger, spiller, comber, train, graybeards, eagre, tidal bore

wave's shallow sweep up beach: swash

SEE OCEAN

beacon *n.* signal light, warning light, smoke signal, guide, lighthouse, bonfire.

bead *n.* droplet, drop, pearl, spheroid, pellet, pill.

beak *n.* bill. SEE NOSE

beam *n.* **1.** SUPPORT girder, brace, rafter, boom, crosspiece, joist, stud, board, two-by-four. **2.** LIGHT ray, shaft, stream, swath, streak.

beam *v.* **1.** TRANSMIT emit, flash, broadcast. **2.** RADIATE glow, shine, glisten. **3.** SMILE BROADLY grin, take on a cheerful glow, radiate. SEE SMILE

bear *n.* bruin, ursus, grizzly, brown bear, black bear, polar bear.

bear *v.* **1.** HOLD UP support, brace, buttress, uphold, sustain, shoulder. **2.** CARRY convey, bring, lug, tote, haul, move. **3.** TOLERATE endure, suffer, stomach, stand, withstand, put up with, abide. **4.** PRODUCE YOUNG give birth to, produce, beget, yield, reproduce, bring forth.

bearable *a.* tolerable, endurable.

beard *n.* whiskers, stubble, five o'clock shadow, bristles, *rat's nest.

WORD FIND

anchorlike, short, pointy, fringe extending up to bottom lip: anchor

curly, thick, square-cut: Trojan beard

ducktail-like: ducktail beard

forked: swallowtail beard

goatlike chin tuft: goatee, Satyric tuft

long, bushy: Jewish

long tuft extending beneath lower lip, worn by Napoleon III: Imperial

medium, no mustache: Lincolnesque

pointed, short, no sideburns: Van Dyke

rounded: aureole

sideburns, bushy, shaped: muttonchops

slender, pointed: stiletto

spade shaped: spade beard, Shenandoah

Spanish style, pointed, medium length: cadiz

square-cut, long: tile

tuft of hair under bottom lip: barbiche

twisted or twined: screw beard

SEE MUSTACHE

bearing *n.* manner, carriage, air, posture, mien, attitude, demeanor, presence, comportment.

bearings *n.* orientation, location.

beast *n.* animal, creature, savage, brute, swine. SEE BARBARIAN, MONSTER

beastly *a.* savage, brutish, barbaric, heathen, wild, uncivilized, primitive, fiendish, monstrous, vile, boorish, feral, coarse, disagreeable, nasty. ANT. *humane, civilized, cultured, refined.*

beat *n.* **1.** CADENCE rhythm, pulse, pulsation, meter. **2.** CIRCUIT walk, rounds, route, precinct.

beat *v.* **1.** BATTER pound, strike, hammer, bang, pummel, thrash, *thump, hit, smack, flog, cuff, *whomp, *slug, *belt, box, *whale on, punch. **2.** MOLD fashion, forge, shape. **3.** DEFEAT win over, vanquish, rout, best, subdue, *kick butt, outstrip, outdistance, prevail over, *smoke the competition, *leave the competition in one's wake, lick, top. **4.** PULSATE throb, palpitate, vibrate, thump. **5.** WHIP stir, mix.

beat *a.* tired, exhausted.

beaten *a.* licked, vanquished, discouraged, demoralized.

beatific *a.* blissful, serene, angelic, heavenly.

beatitude *n.* blessedness, happiness, bliss, serenity, saintliness, peace.

beau *n.* boyfriend, lover, suitor, swain, sweetheart, fiancé.

beaut *n. Sl.* lulu.

beautician *n.* hairdresser, manicurist, coiffurist.

beautiful *a.* **1.** ATTRACTIVE pretty, handsome, becoming, comely, fair, lovely, good-looking, *nice, gorgeous, captivating. **2.** EXCELLENT great, fantastic, superb, splendid. ANT. *1. ugly, unattractive, homely, repulsive. 2. awful, terrible, rotten.*

beautify *v.* dress up, decorate, fix up, adorn, primp, make up, *gussie up, enhance, glamorize. ANT. *deface, spoil.*

beauty n. **1.** ATTRACTIVENESS prettiness, comeliness, fairness, loveliness, good looks, appeal, pulchritude, allure, charm. "A fading flower." — Bible. "Silent eloquence." — French proverb. "God's handwriting." — Emerson. "The power by which a woman charms a lover and terrifies a husband." — Ambrose Bierce. **2.** BELLE goddess, *babe, *fox, *looker, *knockout, sex symbol, enchantress, siren, *vision, *dreamboat, *doll, Venus. ANT. 1. ugliness, repulsiveness, plainness. 2. hag, Quasimodo, dog, eyesore.

beckon v. summon, call, signal, wave, hail, invite, motion.

becloud v. confuse, muddle, obfuscate, darken, veil, obscure, shroud, mask, bewilder, make unclear. ANT. clear up, clarify.

becoming a. **1.** SUITABLE appropriate, proper, fitting, befitting, seemly, comme il faut, right, correct. **2.** ATTRACTIVE comely, flattering, pretty, beautiful. ANT. 1. unsuitable, inappropriate, unbefitting. 2. unflattering, unattractive.

bed n. **1.** BUNK mattress, *sack, cot, berth, hammock, pallet. "The heaven upon earth to the weary head." — Thomas Hood. **2.** LAYER stratum, seam, deposit.

bedazzle v. bewilder, confuse, daze, dazzle, overwhelm, blind.

bedlam n. confusion, uproar, pandemonium, turmoil, noise, chaos, hubbub, madness, madhouse, hullabaloo.

bedraggled a. wet, dirty, limp, sopping, filthy, soggy, disheveled, drenched, unkempt, soiled, sodden, muddy. ANT. dry, clean, neat.

bedroom n. chamber, bedchamber, boudoir, bed-sitter.

bed-wetting n. enuresis, incontinence.

bee n. bumblebee, honey bee, killer bee, drone, worker, Queen bee. "Nature's confectioner." — John Cleveland.

beef n. Sl. complaint, gripe, grouse.

beefy a. brawny, fleshy, burly, strong, powerful, strapping, Herculian, robust, solid, hulklike, husky. ANT. skinny, anorexic.

beehive n. hive, beegum, skep, colony, apiary.

beer n. ale, lager, malt, bitter, *suds, *stout, *cold one, *brew, *brewski, *Clydesdale piss, *panther piss. "That which drowns all care." — Robert Herrick.

WORD FIND
cask: keg, puncheon, tun
cup/glass: mug, stein, toby, schooner
foam: head, froth, bead
ingredients: hops, malt (mash), yeast
manufacturer: brewery
mixed with ginger ale: shandygaff
spiced: flip
SEE ALCOHOL, DRINK, MOONSHINE, WINE

befall v. happen, occur, come to pass.

befitting a. appropriate, suitable, seemly, right.

beforehand a. earlier, previously, sooner, prior to.

befriend v. make friends, *get chummy with, get acquainted, get to know, help, stand up for, take under one's wing. ANT. reject, shun.

befuddle v. confuse, muddle, mix up, confound, perplex, fluster, stupefy, boggle, rattle. ANT. clear one's mind, sober.

beg v. **1.** PANHANDLE scrounge, *cadge, *bum off from, solicit, *sponge off. **2.** ASK FOR beseech, implore, plead, petition, solicit, entreat.

beget v. bear, father, create, generate, engender, propagate, reproduce, sire, bring forth, effect, give rise to.

beggar n. panhandler, *moocher, *bum, mendicant, tramp, parasite, *sponger, leech, pauper, derelict, loafer, scamp, fakir. "The only free man in the universe." — Charles Lamb.

begin v. **1.** START commence, set in motion, launch, initiate, arise, happen, go ahead, embark, open, get the ball rolling. **2.** COME INTO BEING start, commence, arise, flower, crop up, issue, sprout, originate, inaugurate, spring, get under way, found. ANT. end, conclude, stop.

beginner n. novice, tyro, virgin, neophyte, *greenhorn, *rookie, *tenderfoot, amateur, trainee, apprentice. ANT. veteran, old hand, expert.

beginning n. **1.** INITIATION onset, start, commencement, opening, launching, debut, outset, genesis, inception. "A quarter of the journey." — Henry Bohn. **2.** ORIGIN source, root, fountain, seed, germ. ANT. 1. ending, closing, conclusion, finale.

begrudge v. resent, envy, hold against, be jealous, stint.

beguile v. **1.** TRICK mislead, cheat, bamboozle, dupe, *burn, *rope in, deceive, delude. **2.** CHARM enchant, bewitch, captivate, delight, amuse, divert, distract. ANT. 2. bore.

behave v. **1.** ACT conduct, deport, comport, perform, function. **2.** MIND! shape up, *mind one's manners, *mind one's Ps and Qs, *keep one's nose clean, smarten up, be good.

behavior n. **1.** CONDUCT deportment, comportment, demeanor, manner, bearing, ways, etiquette. "The finest of the fine arts." — Emerson. "No truer index to intelligence." — Ibn Gabirol 2. ACTION performance, functioning, operation, reaction, response.

behead v. decapitate, decollate, guillotine, execute.

behest n. order, command, bidding, request, word, edict, demand, urging, decree, say-so, desire.

behind n. buttocks, backside, *ass, rump, *tush, bottom, stern.

behind a. BACK in back of, rearward, trailing, aft.

behold v. look at, regard, observe, notice, view, watch, *feast your eyes on, consider, scrutinize, examine, gaze upon. ANT. ignore, overlook, disregard.

beholden a. obligated, indebted, owing.

behoove v. benefit, befit, be worthwhile, suit, be incumbent upon.

being n. 1. ENTITY creature, organism, person, soul, spirit. 2. EXISTENCE reality, life. ANT. nonexistence.

belabor v. dwell on, go on about, *beat a dead horse, pound, hammer home, rehash, repeat, overwork.

belated a. tardy, overdue, late, delayed, past due. ANT. timely, prompt.

belch v. 1. BURP eruct. 2. EMIT spew, discharge, spout, erupt, disgorge, expel.

BELEAGUER v. [be LEE gur] to beseige or harass. The beleaguered army finally surrendered. SYN. beseige, harass, beset, plague, pester, annoy, badger, bother, hound, hector, persecute, victimize, close in on.

belie v. misrepresent, disguise, falsify, defy, negate, contradict, twist, conceal.

belief n. 1. CONVICTION certainty, faith, trust, assumption, presumption, acceptance, confidence, credence, hope, feeling, guess, understanding, notion, judgment, position, hypothesis, credo, dogma. "The most complete of all distinctions between man and the lower animals." — Charles Darwin.

believable a. convincing, plausible, credible, reliable, acceptable. ANT. unbelievable, farfetched.

believe v. accept, hold, maintain, presume, know, have faith, swear by, give credence to, trust, suspect, *take as gospel, suppose, assume, guess, surmise. ANT. disbelieve, doubt.

believer n. adherent, devotee, follower, apostle, disciple, zealot.

belittle v. disparage, depreciate, put down, diminish, degrade, deride, malign, *take down

a peg, *knock, discredit. ANT. build up, aggrandize, put on a pedestal.

bell n. campana, carillon, chimes, dinger. "The publicity of God." — R.L. Bruckberger. "The music bordering nearest heaven." — Charles Lamb.

WORD FIND
clapper: tongue
ring by striking with hammer: chime
ringer: sexton
sound: clang, dong, ting, tinkle, tintinabulation, ring, knell, peal, toll, reverberation
tower: belfry

BELLICOSE a. [BEL i KOSE] belligerent, quarrelsome, warlike. He was eager to fight; he was a notoriously bellicose man. SYN. belligerent, quarrelsome, warlike, hostile, pugnacious, aggressive, combative, volatile, contentious, peppery. ANT. peaceful, passive.

BELLIGERENT a. [buh LIJ ur unt] quarrelsome, hostile, quick to fight. Belligerent inner city gangs started the riot. SYN. bellicose, pugnacious, quarrelsome, militant, war-mongering, warlike, hostile, aggressive, combative, volatile, contentious, peppery. ANT. peaceful, passive, pacific.

bellow v. roar, shout, holler, thunder, squall, boom, bark, bawl, howl, bluster.

BELLWETHER n. [BEL WETH er] a leader, any thing or person used as an indicator. IBM has long reigned as a bellwether among computer companies. SYN. leader, pacesetter, pilot, standard-bearer, guide, *the one to watch, model, role model, indicator, *barometer.

belly n. abdomen, stomach, tummy, *gut, *spare tire, paunch, *middle-aged spread, potbelly, *breadbasket.

bellybutton n. navel, umbilicus.

belonging n. relationship, camaraderie, community, kinship, familiarity. ANT. alienation, anomie, rejection.

belongings n. things, possessions, stuff, personal effects, worldly goods, chattels.

beloved a. loved, dearest, cherished, adored, darling, precious, worshipped, revered, treasured, esteemed.

below a. beneath, down, under, low, underneath.

belt n. band, sash, girdle, strap, cord, thong, cinch, cummerbund.

belt v. hit, smack, wallop, thrash, beat, whip. SEE BEAT

bemoan v. grieve, lament, mourn, bewail, deplore, rue, cry over.

bemuse v. confuse, puzzle, bewilder, befuddle, disconcert, addle, confound, daze, mix up, muddle, stupefy.

bench n. 1. SEAT settee, pew, bleacher. 2. COURT judiciary, bar, tribunal.

benchmark n. standard, model, gauge, measure, yardstick, bellwether, touchstone, exemplar.

bend v. 1. CURVE crook, twist, arc, flex, bow, curl, coil, snake. 2. GIVE IN yield, acquiesce, *cave in, bow down, capitulate, surrender.

benediction n. blessing, invocation, prayer, grace, benison, consecration. ANT. curse, damning, malediction.

benefactor n. patron, supporter, financier, underwriter, donor, angel, philanthropist, contributor.

beneficial a. helpful, advantageous, rewarding, valuable, good, favorable, propitious, useful, gainful. ANT. harmful, useless.

beneficiary n. recipient, heir, heiress.

benefit n. gain, good, profit, help, favor, service, reward, worth, avail, *perk. ANT. loss, harm.

benefit v. gain, profit, help, favor, serve, reward, advance, do good. ANT. harm, disfavor, impair.

benevolence n. kindness, goodwill, charity, humanitarianism, goodness, altruism, generosity, compassion, sympathy. "One of the distinguishing characteristics of man. It is the path of duty." —Mencius. ANT. meanness, ill will, cold-heartedness, misanthropy.

BENEVOLENT a. [buh NEV uh lunt] kindly, doing good, charitable. The United Way and other benevolent organizations. SYN. kind, charitable, generous, humane, good, altruistic, compassionate, sympathetic, philanthropic, benign, giving, beneficent. ANT. mean, selfish, cold-hearted, malicious, misanthropic.

BENIGN a. [bi NINE] 1. kindly 2. advantageous 3. harmless. 1. Uncle Harry's bark is worse than his bite; he's really quite benign. 2. The weather turned out to be rather benign for the tournament. 3. John's tumor was found to be benign. SYN. 1. kindly, benevolent, merciful, sympathetic, genial, gracious, good-hearted, altruistic, compassionate. 2. beneficial, favorable, propitious, auspicious, healthful, helpful, fortunate. 3. harmless, slight, curable, superficial, innocuous, inconsequential. ANT. 1. mean, selfish, malicious, misanthropic. 2. harmful, inopportune, unfortunate. 3. malignant, severe.

bent n. propensity, penchant, inclination, leaning, proclivity, liking, predilection, ability, flair, fondness, aptitude.

bent a. crooked, curved, twisted, bowed, contorted, warped, hooked, doubled over. ANT. straight.

bent on a. determined, bound, intent, fixed.

bequeath v. leave, will, consign, hand over, bestow, impart, endow, give.

BEQUEST n. [bi KWEST] something given to someone in a will. She received a bequest of $1000. SYN. inheritance, gift, endowment, bequeathal, legacy, estate, dower.

berate v. scold, upbraid, rebuke, dress down, reproach, tongue-lash, *bawl out, *give one hell, *jump down one's throat, vituperate, *rake over the coals.

bereavement n. loss, deprivation, grief, sorrow, heartache, mourning.

bereft a. bereaved, left desolate, deprived, lorn, lonely, destitute, wanting, lacking.

berserk a. deranged, violent, crazed, mad, amuck, insane, maniacal, frenzied, murderous. ANT. serene, calm, rational.

beseech v. implore, plead, beg, solicit, pray, entreat, urge, press, supplicate.

beset v. plague, harass, hound, torment, badger, bother, surround, *bug, hassle, beseige, victimize, vex, beleaguer.

beside prep. next to, close to, adjacent to, alongside, abreast of, bordering, by.

besides a. in addition, as well, moreover, plus, also.

besiege v. 1. SURROUND hem in, encircle, enclose, close in on, crowd, lay siege to. 2. HARASS beleaguer, badger, plague, torment, beset, overwhelm, hound, pressure.

besmirch v. soil, sully, dishonor, taint, tarnish, smear, muddy, disgrace. ANT. glorify, honor.

best v. beat, outdo, defeat, outdistance, outclass, conquer, win over, dominate, *wipe the floor with, prevail, *thrash. ANT. lose, *choke.

best a. finest, utmost, *topflight, *top drawer, unsurpassed, superior, first-rate, choice, preeminent, peerless, unequaled, nonpareil, supreme, tops. ANT. worst, lowest.

bestial a. animalistic, wild, untamed, savage, fierce, primitive, unrefined, feral, base, barbaric, brutish, inhumane, monstrous. ANT. humane, civilized, civil.

bestow v. present, give, endow, bequeath, confer, award, consign, donate.

best-seller n. hit. "A book which somehow sold well simply because it was selling well." —

Daniel Boorstin. SEE BOOK, NOVEL

bet *n.* wager, stake, gamble, parlay, *long shot, risk, proposition, chance.

WORD FIND

bet one's winnings from a previous race on another: parlay

horseracing bet choosing first and second place finishers, not necessarily in correct order: quiniela

horseracing bet choosing first and second place finishers: perfecta

horseracing bet choosing first, second and third-place finishers: trifecta

horseracing bet choosing winners in two races: daily double

horseracing bet in which winnings are shared: pari-mutuel

betray *v.* **1.** BREAK FAITH turn traitor, deceive, *pull a Judas, sell out, stab in the back, *sell down the river, *two-time, *double-cross, *fink, *rat on. **2.** REVEAL give away, show, disclose, tell on, unmask, divulge, expose. ANT. *1. be loyal, be faithful. 2. hide, cover up.*

betrayal *n.* treachery, disloyalty, breech of faith, double-crossing, duplicity, treason, *Judas kiss, perfidy. ANT. *faithfulness, loyalty.*

betrayer *n.* traitor, Judas, conspirator.

betrothal *n.* engagement, vow, pledge to marry.

better *v.* improve, enrich, advance, promote, upgrade.

better *a.* finer, superior, surpassing, topping, first-rate, preeminent, peerless, supreme, excelling. ANT. *worse, inferior, lower.*

betterment *n.* improvement, enrichment, advancement, promotion, upgrading.

between *prep.* amidst, among, within, in the thick, intermediate.

beverage *n.* drink, refreshment, pop, liquid, ale, cooler, liquor, draft.

bevy *n.* group, flock, bunch, band, knot, gaggle, covey, pack, crowd, clique, party, throng.

bewail *v.* bemoan, lament, mourn, wail, cry, deplore, grieve, weep, rue, pine for. ANT. *shriek with joy, celebrate, rejoice.*

beware *v.* be wary, be careful, watch, stay on guard, heed, be on the lookout, stay on one's toes.

bewilder *v.* confuse, puzzle, befuddle, confound, perplex, mystify, baffle, befog, strike dumb, set adrift, disorient, disconcert. ANT. *inform, clarify.*

bewilderment *n.* confusion, puzzlement, befuddlement, perplexity, mystification, bafflement, *discombobulation. ANT. *understanding, clear-headedness, lucidity.*

bewitching *a.* enchanting, charming, beguiling, spellbinding, mesmerizing, captivating, fascinating, seductive, enticing, hypnotizing, alluring. ANT. *repulsive, dull.*

beyond *a.* past, yonder, inaccessible, unattainable.

bias *n.* partiality, inclination, preference, prejudice, bent, predilection, leaning, proclivity, one-sidedness, *mind-set, favoritism, bigotry. ANT. *impartiality, fairness, objectivity.*

bias *v.* influence, sway, prejudice, indoctrinate, brainwash, twist, slant.

BIBLE *n.* **1.** HOLY SCRIPTURES the Good Book, Word of God, Gospel, Old Testament, New Testament. "That great medicine chest of humanity."—Heinrich Heine. "The book of books, the storehouse and magazine of life and comfort."—George Herbert. "A window in this prison world, through which we may look into eternity."—Timothy Dwight. "God's chart for you to steer by."—Henry Ward Beecher. "Obscene stories . . . voluptuous debaucheries . . . cruel and torturous executions . . . unrelenting vindictiveness with which more than half of [it] is filled . . . it would be more consistent that we call it the word of a demon than the word of God. It is a history of wickedness that has served to corrupt and brutalize mankind."—Thomas Paine. **2.** GUIDEBOOK manual, text, handbook, vade mecum, authority.

bicker *v.* squabble, fight, quarrel, wrangle, spar, debate, haggle, argue. ANT. *agree, concur.*

bicycle *n.* bike, two-wheeler, *wheels, velocipede.

WORD FIND

forerunner with giant front wheel, small rear wheel: ordinary

four-wheeler: quadricycle

one-wheeler: unicycle

safety bar: *sissy bar

seat: saddle

three-wheel passenger vehicle: pedicab, trishaw

two-seater: tandem, bicycle built for two

bid *n.* **1.** OFFER proffer, tender, proposition, submission, proposal. **2.** ATTEMPT try, effort, endeavor, crack.

bid *v.* **1.** OFFER proffer, tender, proposition, propose, submit. **2.** COMMAND call, order, request, instruct, ask, charge.

bidding *n.* command, request, order, charge, direction, behest, mandate, dictate, demand, injunction, invitation.

bide *v.* wait, stay, continue, remain, linger,

dwell, *sit tight.

big *a.* **1.** LARGE huge, sizable, immense, gigantic, prodigious, ample, substantial, vast, *heavy-duty, colossal, *Brobdingnagian, massive, voluminous, hulking, gargantuan. **2.** IMPORTANT weighty, consequential, powerful, prominent, eminent, significant, *major league, momentous, *big-time, paramount, major. ANT. *1. small, tiny, pint-sized.* **2.** *insignificant, trivial, *small potatoes.*

big-hearted *a.* kind, generous, giving, benevolent, noble, compassionate, gracious, forgiving, altruistic, magnanimous, sweet. ANT. *cold-hearted, mean, malevolent, selfish.*

bigot *n.* zealot, fanatic, racist, sexist, *male chauvinist pig, chauvinist, *Archie Bunker. "He who will not reason." — William Drummond.

BIGOTRY n. [BIG uh tree] intolerance for those who are different or have different ideas, narrow-mindedness. *Archie Bunker was famous for his numerous racist and sexist remarks; he represented the epitome of bigotry.* SYN. intolerance, narrow-mindedness, prejudice, closed-mindedness, unfairness, bias, racism, sexism, chauvinism, provincialism, discrimination. "The disease of ignorance, of morbid minds." — Thomas Jefferson. ANT. *tolerance, open-mindedness, fairness.*

big shot n. *big wheel, *big cheese, *VIP, *bigwig, *big gun, high muck-a-muck, somebody, *heavy-hitter, *biggest toad in the puddle. ANT. *nobody, *bush-leaguer, *second banana, *lightweight.*

bigwig n. SEE BIG SHOT

bilateral *a.* reciprocal, mutual, two-sided.

bilge n. Sl. hogwash, rubbish, rot. SEE NONSENSE

bilk v. swindle, cheat, defraud, *fleece, *rip-off, rook, *gyp, *take.

bill n. **1.** CHARGE invoice, debt, account, tab, *score, *bad news, check, statement. **2.** PROGRAM list, schedule, roster, docket, agenda. **3.** ANNOUNCEMENT handbill, circular, advertisement, bulletin. **4.** PIECE OF LEGISLATION act, draft, measure, proposal. **5.** BEAK neb.

bill v. charge, tally, invoice, debit, put on one's tab.

billet n. quarters, lodging, barracks.

billiards n. pool.

WORD FIND

ball's recoil after impact: draw

miss: scratch

shot in which ball first strikes cushion: bricole

shot in which cue ball is bounced off cushion

or strikes two balls in succession: carom

shot in which cue is held perpendicularly: massé

stick: cue

white ball: cue ball

billow v. swell, surge, undulate, wave, roll, puff up, balloon. ANT. *flatten, collapse, deflate.*

bind n. *fix, quandary, predicament, dilemma, *pickle.

bind v. **1.** TIE fasten, secure, wrap, rope, gird, lash, strap, truss, bundle, join. **2.** OBLIGATE require, restrict, confine, prescribe, compel, force. ANT. *1. untie, unbind, unravel, loose.*

binge n. spree, bender, fling, tear, orgy.

biography n. life story, bio, autobiography, memoirs.

bird n. fowl, feathered friend, Anseriformes, Charadriiformes, Columbiformes, Falconiformes, Galliformes, Passeriformes, Psittaciformes. "Dame nature's minstrels." — Gavin Douglas. "The merry minstrels of the morn." — James Thomson.

WORD FIND

bare spots on underbelly used to warm eggs: brood spots

beak that curves or hooks: aquiline

bird of prey: raptor

cage/enclosure: aviary

calls/songs: trill; cheep; chirp; pipe; warble; coo; whistle; caw; chirrup; chip; chatter; chitter; squawk; twitter; mewl; cluck; croak; peep; honk; quack; cackle; trumpet; ululate; sweet, plaintive call; mournful note; high, lisping note; rasping note; cheery, lilting melody; discordant screams of jays; forlorn hooting of an owl; liquid ululation of a loon; shrill fluting; piccolo note; caroling notes; exuberant song; wheedling voice; discordant rasp of a starling

claw: talon

collar of hair or feathers: ruff

crest on fowl: comb

domination order: pecking order

earliest known: Archaeopteryx

eggs, group of: clutch

eggs, to sit on: brood

expert on: ornithologist

eyelike spot in peacock tail: ocellus

falcons used as hunters, sport: falconry

feathers, shedding: molting

fleshy neck component on turkey: wattle

flying: flitting, darting, soaring, swooping, banking, diving, spiraling, wheeling, wheeling in intricate chandelles, rising

on a thermal
grooming: preening
group of: flock; bevy (quail), charm (finches), chattering (starlings), colony (gulls), convocation (eagles), covey (grouse), exaltation (larks), fall (woodcock), flight (doves or swallows), gaggle (geese), herd (swans), host (sparrows), murder (crows), murmuration (starlings), muster (peacocks), nye (pheasants), parliament (owls), rookery (sea birds), siege (herons), skein (flying geese), team (ducks).
migratory route: flyway
mythical: phoenix, roc
nest: aerie
plumage that is soft and fluffy: down
referring to: avian
reservation: sanctuary
second stomach: gizzard, craw, crop
throat patch: gorget
wingless: apterous
young bird: chick, fledgling, nestling

birth *n.* **1.** CHILDBIRTH delivery, bearing, parturition, labor. "The sudden opening of a window through which you look out upon a stupendous prospect . . . "—William Dixon. **2.** INCEPTION genesis, beginning, start, debut, emergence, onset, origin.

WORD FIND

anesthesia used locally to ease mother's pain: epidural
breathing/relaxation technique: Lamaze method
contractions: labor
dead, infant delivered: stillbirth
delivery assistant: midwife
delivery through mother's abdominal wall: Caesarian section, C-section
feet or buttocks-first presentation: breech presentation
membranes covering head during delivery: caul
peaceful, low-key delivery method: Leboyer delivery
profession: obstetrics
spontaneous abortion: miscarriage
uterine muscular action: contractions
vaginal incision, creates more room for passage of baby's head: episiotomy
SEE BABY, PREGNANCY

birth control *n.* contraception, planned parenthood, abortion. "Copulation without population."—Anon.

biscuit *n.* bread, roll, muffin, scone, cracker, popover.

bisexual *a.* *swinging both ways, *AC-DC, androgynous, hermaphroditic.

bit *n.* **1.** PIECE fragment, fraction, portion, particle, section, snippet, segment. **2.** MOMENT second, minute, jiffy, flash, *quick as a wink, time, spell, instant.

bitch *n.* *Sl.* complainer, *rag, *witch, nag, *rotten egg, *stinker, *ball-buster, grumbler, nitpicker, whiner, critic.

bitch *v.* *Sl.* complain, nag, *rag, *beef, *bellyache, *crab, gripe, grouch, *kick up a fuss, *piss and moan, *raise a big stink.

bitchy *a.* *Sl.* complaining, fault-finding, nagging, catty, back-stabbing, malicious, vindictive, *ball-busting, *full of piss and vinegar, critical, crabby, negative, *whiny, fussy, picky, grouchy. ANT. *sweet, kind, warm.*

bite *n.* mouthful, morsel, spoonful, chunk, snack, nosh.

bite *v.* nip, chew, champ, chomp, gnaw, munch, nibble, snap, sink one's teeth into, hold, clamp.

biting *a.* **1.** CAUSTIC bitter, cutting, penetrating, piercing, stinging. **2.** SARCASTIC cutting, caustic, nasty, bitter, stinging, acerbic, scathing, sharp. ANT. *1. gentle, balmy, soothing.*

bitter *a.* **1.** ACRID tart, sour, harsh, acidic, vinegary, acerbic. **2.** GRIEVOUS distressing, heartbreaking, wretched, sorrowful, painful, sad, disturbing, cruel. **3.** SEVERE piercing, harsh, cutting, penetrating, stinging, sharp. **4.** RESENTFUL hostile, sarcastic, nasty, begrudging, spiteful, contemptuous, cynical, peevish, malevolent. ANT. *1. sweet, honeyed. 2. happy, joyous. 3. mild, gentle. 4. friendly, warm, charitable, forgiving.*

bizarre *a.* weird, strange, odd, outlandish, unusual, peculiar, freaky, wild, extraordinary, *way out, *off the wall, fantastic, grotesque, nightmarish, surreal. ANT. *ordinary, normal, everyday.*

blab *v.* **1.** TELL A SECRET *spill the beans, *let the cat out the bag, divulge, let slip, blurt out, *squeal. **2.** CHATTER prattle, *yak, gab.

blabbermouth *n.* *bigmouth, tattletale, busybody.

black *a.* **1.** COLOR ink, jet, raven, carbon, gunmetal, pitch, sable, ebony, tar, soot, coal, coffee, pepper. **2.** DARK inky, unlit, shadowy, murky, dusky, gloomy. **3.** NEGRO colored, African, Afro-American, Negroid. **4.** BLEAK gloomy, dismal, grim, dreary, somber, forlorn, mournful, funereal. **5.** THREATENING ominous, foreboding, forbidding, menacing. **6.** EVIL wicked, diabolical, satanic, nefarious. ANT. *1. white, snowy. 2. sunny, bright, illuminated. 4. cheerful, bright, hopeful. 5. auspicious, favorable. 6. good, angelic, saintly.*

blackball *v.* ostracize, ban, exclude, blacklist, bar, snub, reject, proscribe. ANT. *enlist, welcome, embrace.*

blacken *v.* **1.** DARKEN smudge, black, begrime. **2.** DEFAME slander, smear, tarnish, drag through the mud, *knock, libel, *badmouth. ANT. *1. lighten, brighten. 2. glorify, honor, respect.*

blackguard *n.* villain, scoundrel, rogue.

black magic *n.* necromancy, sorcery, witchcraft.

blackmail *n.* extortion, hush money, *the squeeze, milking, bleeding.

black out *v.* lose consciousness, swoon, pass out. SEE FAINT

bladder *n.* sac, bag, pouch, pocket.

blade *n.* cutting edge, knife, cutter, razor, scalpel. SEE KNIFE

blah *a.* Sl. bland, *humdrum, dull, *dull as dishwater, stale, insipid, tedious, flat, monotonous. ANT. *electrifying, original, colorful, spirited.*

blame *n.* **1.** CONDEMNATION accusation, attribution, incrimination, imputation, impeachment, complaint, recrimination. **2.** RESPONSIBILITY onus, liability, fault, guilt, culpability, accountability.

blame *v.* accuse, condemn, *point the finger at, fault, charge, hold responsible, *pin on, attribute, indict, impute, censure, rap.

blameless *a.* innocent, *clean, inculpable, above suspicion, above reproach, virtuous, unimpeachable, faultless, spotless. ANT. *guilty, at fault, culpable.*

blanch *v.* whiten, bleach, fade, wash out, pale.

bland *a.* dull, lackluster, uninteresting, insipid, flat, *blah, mediocre, vapid, unstimulating, plain. ANT. *stimulating, exciting, rich.*

blank *n.* nothing, zero, void, nill, emptiness, space.

blank *a.* **1.** CLEAR empty, vacant, white, unmarked, untouched, clean, barren, unused. **2.** EXPRESSIONLESS lifeless, dull, vacuous, vacant, dead, glassy, indifferent, deadpan, apathetic. ANT. *1. filled, marked, used. 2. lively, thoughtful.*

blanket *n.* cover, quilt, comforter, afghan.

blanket *v.* cover, bury, carpet, envelope, enclose, overlay.

blare *v.* blast, roar, blow, trumpet, peal, clamor, bellow, resound.

blarney *n.* **1.** FLATTERY apple-polishing, *asskissing, wheedling, fawning, cajolery, *sweet talk, *snow job. **2.** *BUNK *balderdash. SEE NONSENSE

blasé *a.* nonchalant, unmoved, apathetic, jaded, bored, sophisticated, lukewarm, unfazed, cloyed, weary, sated, casual. ANT. *enthusiastic, eager.*

blasphemous *a.* irreverent, irreligious, sacrilegious, impious, profane, disrespectful, ungodly. ANT. *reverent, religious, pious.*

BLASPHEMY *n.* [BLAS fuh mee] any show of disrespect toward the divine, irreverence. *Cursing God for your misfortune is blasphemy.* SYN. irreverence, sacrilege, profanity, disrespect, impiety, desecration, cursing, denouncing. "Denying the being or providence of God . . . " — William Blackstone. ANT. *reverence, piety, respect.*

blast *n.* boom, surge, roar, explosion, burst, crack, blowup, bang, detonation, eruption, gust, shock wave. SEE WIND

blast *v.* explode, blowup, raze, detonate, level, annihilate, demolish, boom, burst, roar, blare.

blast-off *n.* launch, liftoff.

BLATANT *a.* [BLAYT unt] loud, glaring or conspicuous. *Wearing Bermuda shorts to the board meeting shows a blatant disregard for dress codes.* SYN. loud, glaring, conspicuous, obvious, obnoxious, brazen, flagrant, showy, flashy, prominent, plain, boisterous, overt, naked, baldfaced. ANT. *subtle, quiet, unobtrusive.*

blather *n.* drivel, foolishness, claptrap, twaddle, *bull. SEE NONSENSE

blaze *n.* fire, flames, conflagration. SEE FIRE

blaze *v.* flame, flash, flare, flicker, radiate. SEE BURN

bleach *v.* whiten, blanch, lighten, fade, wash out, insolate.

bleak *a.* **1.** DESOLATE bare, barren, unsheltered, treeless, desert, stark, raw. **2.** DEPRESSING grim, dreary, gloomy, dismal, mournful, disheartening, cheerless, black, somber. ANT. *1. lush, overgrown. 2. cheery, sunny, bright, hopeful.*

bleed *v.* hemorrhage, ooze, gush, trickle, run, spurt, flow.

bleeding heart *n.* sentimental fool, liberal, *softy, sympathizer, *sucker for a sob story.

blemish *n.* flaw, fault, mark, defect, stain, spot, blotch, mole, disfigurement, imperfection, deformity, freckle, speckle, birthmark.

blend *n.* mixture, combination, compound, composite, amalgam, concoction, fusion.

blend *v.* mix, combine, compound, amalgamate, mingle, stir in, merge, meld, alloy, scramble. ANT. *separate, divide.*

bless *v.* hallow, consecrate, sanctify, ordain, anoint, exalt, glorify, canonize, declare holy. ANT. *curse, damn.*

blessed *a.* **1.** SACRED holy, consecrated, redeemed, sacrosanct, hallowed, sainted, saved, beatified. **2.** FAVORED gifted, fortunate, lucky. ANT. *unholy, cursed, condemned.*

blessing *n.* **1.** SANCTIFICATION invocation, benediction, prayer, grace, dedication. **2.** FAVOR good fortune, luck, godsend, benefit, gift, boon, good. ANT. *1. curse, condemnation. 2. misfortune, adversity, bad luck.*

blight *n.* affliction, plague, curse, scourge, infliction, pestilence, calamity, bane, curse.

blight *v.* ruin, damage, destroy, afflict, devastate, cripple, kill, wither, frustrate, inflict.

blimp *n.* airship, dirigible, zeppelin.

WORD FIND

balloon portion: gas bag

gas: helium

ground crew: riggers

inner airbags inflated or deflated as a ballast control: ballonets

mooring post on ground: mast

passenger/crew compartment: car, gondola

rigid, cigar-shaped dirigible: zeppelin

weights hung from car: ballast bags

SEE BALLOON

blind *a.* **1.** SIGHTLESS unsighted, *blind as a mole, *blind as a bat, *blind as a post, stone-blind, groping. **2.** IGNORANT dense, stupid, unaware, heedless, unseeing, *thick, obtuse, myopic, shortsighted, unperceptive. ANT. *1. seeing, sighted. 2. sharp, understanding, perceptive.*

blindness *n.* sightlessness, impaired vision, glaucoma, color blindness, astigmatism, cataracts, myopia, tunnel vision, typhlosis. SEE EYE

blink *v.* **1.** WINK bat, flutter. **2.** TWINKLE glimmer, sparkle, scintillate, shimmer.

bliss *n.* rapture, joy, contentment, happiness, elation, euphoria, ecstasy, delight, heaven, nirvana. SEE HAPPINESS

blister *n.* swelling, patch, bubble, bleb, pimple, boil, canker, ulcer.

BLITHE *a.* [BLĪTHE] cheerful and carefree. *She was frequently in blithe spirits on Sunday.* SYN. cheerful, carefree, sunny, lighthearted, buoyant, airy, jovial, merry, cheery, gleeful,

playful. ANT. *miserable, depressed, black, downhearted.* SEE HAPPY

blitz *n.* attack, onslaught, blitzkrieg, charge, raid, strike, offensive.

blizzard *n.* snowstorm, northeaster, blow, gale, snow squall, blast, whiteout.

bloat *v.* balloon, swell, dilate, billow, inflate, expand, puff. ANT. *contract, deflate, shrivel.*

bloc *n.* alliance, group, affiliation, faction, cabal, ring, coalition.

block *n.* **1.** MASS chunk, hunk, brick, lump, bar, cube, square, cake. **2.** OBSTRUCTION obstacle, impediment, bar, snag, stop, barrier, hindrance.

block *v.* obstruct, impede, bar, stop, hinder, close off, occlude, interfere with, intercept, stymie, thwart, barricade, arrest, dam. ANT. *open, free, clear, facilitate.*

blockade *n.* barricade, barrier, obstruction, stop, bar, closure, hindrance, roadblock.

blockhead *n.* idiot, ignoramus, *Charlie Brown, *chowderhead. SEE MORON

blond *n.* "A brunette with a top secret." — Dan Bennett

blond *a.* golden-haired, flaxen-haired, sandy-haired, platinum, peroxide-blond, *tow-headed, strawberry-blond. SEE HAIR

blood *n.* **1.** LIFE-FLUID hemoglobin, gore, plasma. "A very special kind of sap." — Johann Goethe. **2.** KINSHIP kindred, ancestry, pedigree, extraction, lineage, relatives.

bloodbath *n.* massacre, holocaust, murder, slaughter, carnage.

blood, in cold *a.* cruelly, intentionally, indifferently, unfeelingly.

bloodcurdling *a.* terrifying, horrifying, frightening, spine-chilling, hair-raising.

bloodless *a.* pallid, wan, pale, colorless, dead, anemic.

bloodshed *n.* bloodletting, slaughter, massacre, carnage, gore, bloodbath, murder, butchery.

bloodthirsty *a.* homicidal, murderous, savage, barbaric, brutal, ruthless, sadistic, cruel, inhuman, *psycho. SEE INSANE, VIOLENT

bloom *n.* blossom, flower, floret, efflorescence.

bloom *v.* blossom, flower, flourish, flare, develop, thrive, come of age, germinate, bear fruit. ANT. *wither, die.*

blooper *n.* Sl. mistake, *goof, blunder, *boo-boo, gaffe, *muff, slip, *boner, *screwup.

blossom *n.* bloom, flower, floret, posy, bud.

blossom *v.* bloom, flower, effloresce, flourish, flare, develop, come of age, germinate, bear fruit.

blot *n.* spot, smudge, stain, smear, streak, blemish.

blot v. splotch, spot, smudge, stain, soil, smear, streak, blemish.

blotch n. spot, splotch, blot.

blouse n. pullover, slipover. SEE SHIRT

blow n. **1.** WIND gale, tempest, blast, gust, squall, whirlwind. **2.** HIT punch, smack, slug, shot, bash, knock, rap, swat, slap, jolt, clout. **3.** MISFORTUNE reversal, shock, tragedy, upset, calamity, catastrophe. ANT. 3. *blessing.*

blow v. **1.** MOVE AIR bluster, puff, gust, squall, huff, whiffle, rush, swirl, flow, waft, exhale, breathe. **2.** SOUND toot, trumpet, pipe, honk, whistle. **3.** FAIL *choke, lose, miss, *goof, *screw up, muff, bungle.

blow away v. **1.** kill, gun down. SEE MURDER **2.** STUN *throw for a loop, impress, fill with awe.

blow up v. **1.** INFLATE fill, expand, pump up, swell. **2.** EXPLODE burst, detonate, rupture, erupt, pop, demolish. ANT. 2. *deflate.*

blue a. COLOR sky-blue, cobalt, azure, ultramarine, indigo, slate, navy, aquamarine, turquoise, lapis lazuli, royal, powder, electric, robin's egg. **2.** MOOD down, melancholy, depressed, sad, despondent, downhearted, down in the dumps.

bluff n. bank, cliff, promontory, headland, ridge, hill, precipice, palisade, scarp. **2.** SHAM *four-flushing, *bull, deception, *humbug.

bluff v. **1.** MISLEAD deceive, delude, *bamboozle, dupe, fake, *bullshit, shuck and jive.

bluff a. frank, blunt, rough, coarse, gruff, straightforward, abrupt.

blunder n. mistake, *goof, fumble, *boo-boo, *muff, gaffe, *flubup.

blunder v. *goof, fumble, botch, *muff, *flub, *drop the ball, err, *screw up, bungle, misstep, miscalculate.

blunt v. make dull, deaden, flatten, soften.

blunt a. **1.** DULL rounded, unpointed. **2.** FRANK candid, upfront, plainspoken, point-blank, straightforward, abrupt, brusque, gruff, curt, terse, direct, bluff. ANT. 1. *sharp, pointed.* 2. *soft-pedaling, mealy-mouthed, subtle, gentle, euphemistic.*

blur n. stain, blot, haze, blotch, smear.

blur v. **1.** SMUDGE smear, stain, splotch. **2.** DIM cloud, obfuscate, obscure, shadow, veil, shroud. ANT. 2. *clarify, sharpen, define.*

blurt v. blab, tattle, blabber, gush, spout, let slip.

blush v. flush, redden, color, glow, turn scarlet, bloom. "Virtue's color." —English proverb. "Notice to be careful." —Edgar Howe. ANT.

blanch, pale.

bluster n. boasting, bluff, bragging, braggadocio, swaggering, bullying, bravado, crowing, strutting, ranting, gasconade.

bluster v. boast, bluff, brag, swagger, strut, bully, crow, rant, show off, intimidate, storm.

blustery a. windy, gusty.

board n. **1.** PLANK two-by-four, beam, slat, stick, lumber, timber, clapboard, slat, panel. **2.** COMMITTEE directors, council, trustees, advisers, cabinet. **3.** ROOM AND BOARD keep, provisions, meals.

board v. **1.** GO ABOARD get on, enter, embark. **2.** ACCOMMODATE feed, lodge, house, quarter. **3.** COVER WITH WOOD sheathe, panel, enclose. ANT. 1. *disembark, deplane, detrain, leave.*

boast n. bragging, bluster, vainglory, bravado, gasconade, braggadocio, *hot air, vaunt.

boast v. brag, *toot one's own horn, crow, bluster, show off, puff, *pat oneself on the back, swagger, strut, gasconade, gloat, flaunt, *blow. ANT. *eat humble pie, downplay.*

boastful a. bragging, blustering, vaunting, pompous, vain, arrogant, conceited, *full of hot air, vainglorious, strutting, swaggering. ANT. *humble, modest, self-effacing.*

boat n. vessel, watercraft, tub, ship; motorboat, sailboat.

WORD FIND

air-propelled: airboat

double-hulled sailboat: catamaran

emergency vessel: lifeboat

fishing: trawler, dragger, longliner, dogger, smack, whaler, sportfisherman

flat-bottomed carrier: barge, scow

flat-bottomed, pole-propelled: punt, ark

flat-bottomed vessel used in construction on water: pontoon

gondolier's song: barcarole

house on water: houseboat

Italian: gondola, vaporetto

log, hollowed out: dugout, pirogue

motorboat, small: runabout

narrow-hulled racing boat rowed by as many as eight: shell

narrow, racing boat rowed by one, two or four rowers: scull

old: hulk

Oriental, flat-bottomed river and coast boat: sampan, junk

pleasure cruiser: cabin cruiser, yacht

race/event: regatta

racing boat: cigarette boat, hydrofoil

rowboat: canoe, kayak, dinghy, shell, dory,

gig, skiff, umiak (eskimo)
service craft: tender
shuttle of passengers, freight: ferry
steam-propelled: paddle steamer, steamboat
triple-hulled sailboat: trimaran
SEE NAVY, SAIL, SHIP, SUBMARINE

bob v. wobble, bounce, waver, quiver.

body n. **1.** PHYSIQUE figure, frame, build, form, flesh and bones, *bag of bones, anatomy, torso, trunk. "A pair of pincers set over a bellows and a stewpan, the whole fixed upon stilts." —Samuel Butler. "A machine which winds its own springs." —Julien Mettrie. "A cell state in which every cell is a citizen." —Rudolf Virchow. **2.** CORPSE cadaver, carcass, corpus delecti, mummy, skeleton, *dead meat, *stiff, remains, carrion. **3.** MASS group, collection, union, bulk, bunch, majority, crowd, throng. **4.** MAIN PIECE chassis, fuselage, frame, assembly.

bog n. marsh, quag, mire, fen, swamp, quagmire, slough, morass.

bog down v. mire, get stuck, sink, impede, slow, stall.

bogus a. fake, counterfeit, phony, *sham, artificial, imitation, fraudulent, ersatz, spurious, pseudo. ANT. genuine, real, authentic.

Bohemian n. gypsy, artist, dilettante, poet, nonconformist, *free spirit, vagabond. "A person who works to live but does not live to work." —Heathcote Williams.

boil n. blister, swelling, furuncle, pustule, bleb, abscess, carbuncle, pimple, fester, sore.

boil v. **1.** COOK steam, parboil, seethe, churn, bubble, simmer, stew, steep, heat, brew. **2.** RAGE fume, seethe, rave, burn, storm.

boisterous a. rough, rambunctious, rowdy, loud, raucous, wild, obstreperous, vociferous, turbulent, uproarious, unrestrained, unruly. ANT. quiet, laid-back, calm, restrained.

bold a. **1.** DARING brave, fearless, courageous, undaunted, adventurous, audacious, confidant, plucky, intrepid, lionhearted, *ballsy. **2.** BRAZEN insolent, *saucy, *brassy, *cheeky, fresh, forward, impudent, brash, rude, *gutsy, *ballsy. **3.** PRONOUNCED striking, loud, bright, flashy, conspicuous, prominent, vivid, colorful, eye-catching. ANT. **1.** cowardly, meek, timid. **2.** courteous, polite, shy, deferential. **3.** understated, subtle, weak, pale.

bolster v. prop up, reinforce, support, strengthen, fortify, buttress, shoulder, brace, shore up. ANT. undermine, weaken.

bolt n. **1.** FASTENER bar, lock, latch, rod, catch, pin, peg, screw, spike, coupling. SEE NAIL, SCREW **2.** LIGHTNING flash, stroke, thunderbolt, shaft, chain. SEE LIGHTNING, STORM, THUNDER

bolt v. dart, spring, dash out, rush, flee, make a break for it, jump, leap, scoot, *hotfoot, *skedaddle.

bomb n. **1.** EXPLOSIVE charge, shell, missile, mine, grenade, depth charge, atom bomb, hydrogen bomb, *physics package, torpedo, incendiary, blockbuster, warhead, dud, *egg.

WORD FIND

antipersonnel mine with fanning fragmentation: claymore mine

boom: report

explosive chemical used in bombs: TNT, trinitrotoluene, nitroglycerin

explosive portion of bomb, missile, etc.: warhead

fire-starting bomb: incendiary bomb

fragmenting, shrapnel-producing bomb: fragmentation bomb, antipersonnel bomb

fuel detonated in midair: fuel-air bomb

gasoline-filled bottle stuffed with rag: Molotov cocktail

guided bomb: smart bomb

jelled gas incendiary: napalm

lead pipe containing home-made charge: pipe bomb

multiple bombs released from canister: cluster bomb

puttylike substance holding charge: plastic explosive

smoke-producing: smoke bomb

stink-producing: stink bomb

timed charge: time bomb

SEE AIR FORCE, ARMY, MISSILE, NUCLEAR BOMB, WAR, WEAPON **2.** FLOP failure, fiasco, disaster, *turkey, *dog, loser, *washout. ANT. **2.** success, triumph, hit.

bomb v. **1.** FAIL flop, fizzle, wash out, *die. **2.** BOMBARD shell, assault, blitz, pepper, barrage, strafe, *drop the big one.

WORD FIND

intense bombing: saturation bombing, carpet bombing

BOMBASTIC a. [bom BAS tik] pompous, high-sounding speech or writing. He tried too hard to make an impression; his speech was wordy and bombastic. SYN. pompous, high-sounding, grandiloquent, grandiose, flaunting, pretentious, turgid, euphuistic, inflated, fustian, windy, flamboyant, flowery. ANT. understated, restrained, subtle.

bona fide a. genuine, authentic, legitimate,

real. ANT. *counterfeit.*

bonanza n. windfall, gold mine, *cash cow.

bond n. **1.** ALLEGIANCE tie, relationship, loyalty, connection, attachment, affinity. **2.** GUAR-ANTEE warranty, contract, security, pledge, covenant, agreement.

bond v. attach, tie, bind, connect, fasten, stick, join, fuse, weld.

bondage n. servitude, slavery, serfdom, subjection, subjugation, enslavement, captivity, bonds, shackles. ANT. *freedom, liberty, emancipation.*

bonds n. ties, shackles, fetters, manacles, chains, reins, yoke, handcuffs, bindings.

bone n. ossicle, marrow, cartilage; skull, mandible, vertebrae, rib, humerus, femur, tibia, sternum, clavicle. SEE SKELETON

boner n. *Sl.* mistake, goof, blunder.

bones, feel in one's v. *Sl.* sense, perceive, expect.

bones, make no v. *Sl.* admit, confess, own up, level.

bone up n. *Sl.* study, brush up, read up, cram.

bonus n. extra, premium, reward, gift, fringe benefit, *perk, tip, recompense, dividend.

bony a. skinny, scrawny, anorexic, malnourished, rawboned, lean, gaunt, emaciated, angular. ANT. *fat, brawny, blubbery.*

book n. volume, hardcover, softcover, paperback, novel, work, opus, tome, publication, best-seller, booklet, pamphlet, treatise, manual, text. "A garden carried in the pocket." —Arabian proverb. "The world carried in the hand." —Anon. "For company the best friends." —Richard Whitlock. "Portable pieces of thought." —Susan Sontag. "The true university." —Thomas Carlyle. "The compasses and telescopes and sextants and charts which other men have prepared to help us navigate the dangerous seas of human life." —Jesse L. Bennet.

WORD FIND

alphabetical/page-number guide to words and terms: index

avoider of: bibliophobe

back list of sources, related works: bibliography

back: spine

blank page: flyleaf

book published at author's expense: vanity book

burner or destroyer of: biblioclast

burning or destruction of: biblioclasm

category: genre

collecting passion: bibliomania

compilation of various works: anthology

condensed or shortened: abridged

end comment: epilogue

hardcover republished in paperback: reprint

inscription, front: dedication

introduction: foreword

ISBN: International Standard Book Number

jacket description: flap copy, blurbs

large, illustrated book: coffee table book

large paperback: trade paperback

literary works: belles lettres

logo of publisher: colophon

lover of: bibliophile

overstocked book: remainder

printed before 1500 A.D.: incunabula

stealer of books: biblioklept

strange (subject matter): curiosa

title page: frontispiece

vocabulary list: glossary

voracious reader of: bookworm, bibliobibuli

SEE AUTHOR, NOVEL, NOVELIST, WRITER

boom n. **1.** THUD thunder, report, crack, roar, rumble, crash, bang, shot, explosion, detonation. **2.** INCREASE growth, expansion, upturn, prosperity, growth spurt, bull market. ANT. *2. recession, depression, decline.*

boom v. **1.** THUD thunder, report, crack, roar, rumble, crash, bang, shoot, explode, detonate. **2.** INCREASE grow, expand, upturn, prosper, thrive, flourish. ANT. *2. recede, decline.*

boondocks n. *boonies, *sticks, *North Overshoe, *East Jesus, backwater, backwoods, hinterland, wilderness, nowhere.

boor n. clod, lout, oaf, churl, clodhopper, *yahoo, yokel, bumpkin, rustic.

boorish a. ill-mannered, rude, awkward, uncouth, unrefined, churlish, cloddish, vulgar, rustic, coarse. ANT. *refined, sophisticated, cultured.*

boost n. **1.** PUSH UP lift, elevation, hand up. **2.** INCREASE raise, hike, expansion, upgrade, gain. **3.** PROMOTION support, encouragement, assistance, backing, fostering, advancement, plug. ANT. *2. decrease, cutback. 3. disparagement, undermining, knock.*

boost v. **1.** RAISE push up, hoist, lift, elevate. **2.** INCREASE heighten, raise, hike, jack up, enlarge, inflate. **3.** PROMOTE support, advance, further, plug, foster, advocate. ANT. *1. lower, drop. 2. decrease, lower. 3. undermine, disparage, knock.*

boot n. shoe, overshoe, footwear, clodhopper.

WORD FIND

ankle-high boot worn horseback-riding:

jodhpur

Eskimo boot made from hide: mukluk

hiking boot with ridged sole: wafflestomper

leather, above the knee in front, below the knee in back: Wellington

military: combat boot, jackboot

old fashioned woman's boot laced up the front: granny

rubber/waterproof: galosh

tooled leather, square or pointed toes: cowboy boot

wading boot: hip boot, wader

white, calf-high, worn with mini skirt in the 1960s: go-go boot

SEE SHOE

booth *n.* stall, stand, kiosk, shed, enclosure.

booty *n.* loot, spoils, plunder, prize, winnings, *haul.

booze *n.* liquor, alcohol, spirits, drink, *hard stuff. SEE ALCOHOL, BEER, DRINK, MOONSHINE, WINE

bordello *n.* brothel, *whorehouse, *cathouse, *house of ill repute, bagnio.

border *n.* margin, edge, side, line, verge, fringe, rim, brink, boundary, outer limit, perimeter, periphery, borderland.

borderline *a.* indefinite, doubtful, marginal, unclear, vague, halfway, ambiguous, equivocal, unclassifiable, one way or the other. ANT. *absolute, decisive.*

bore *n.* *drag, *yawn, tiresome person, *pill, *wet blanket, *stick in the mud, soporific. "A fellow talking who can change the subject back to his topic . . . faster than you can change it back to yours." — Lawrence Peter. "One who lights up a room when he leaves." — Anon.

bore *v.* **1.** DRILL tunnel, burrow, gouge out, auger, mine, ream. **2.** TIRE weary, put to sleep, fatigue, tax, cloy, annoy. ANT. *2. excite, stimulate.*

boredom *n.* tedium, ennui, monotony, apathy, dullness, doldrums, jadedness, indifference, weariness, humdrum, flatness. "What happens when we lose contact with the universe." — John Ciardi. ANT. *excitement, stimulation.*

boring *a.* tedious, tiresome, wearisome, dull, monotonous, humdrum, unstimulating, uninteresting, prosaic, mundane, *ho-hum, stale, routine. ANT. *exciting, stimulating.*

born *v.* delivered, brought into this world.

born *a.* inherent, natural, innate.

borrow *v.* **1.** TAKE TEMPORARILY use, take a loan, obtain, scrounge, *mooch, *hit up, *bum,

*sponge. **2.** ADOPT FOR ONE'S OWN USE appropriate, imitate, steal, plagiarize, copy, pirate, use. ANT. *1. lend, give, return. 2. originate, invent.*

bosom *n.* **1.** BREAST chest, bust. **2.** HEART emotions, soul, spirit, core, depths, inside.

boss *n.* chief, head, master, supervisor, foreman, superintendent, overseer, taskmaster, *head honcho, *big cheese, *whip, employer, director, executive, manager, administrator, *biggest toad in the puddle. "[One who] exists to make sensible exceptions to general rules." — Elting Morrison. ANT. *employee, subordinate, underling.*

boss *v.* command, control, direct, manage, administrate, supervise, lead, run, press, lord over, domineer, dictate, throw one's weight around, tyrannize. ANT. *submit, follow, jump on command.*

botch *v.* bungle, *screw up, spoil, *goof, muff, foul up, fumble, flub, louse up.

bother *n.* annoyance, irritation, burden, trouble, aggravation, inconvenience, pother, *pain, *headache, *pain in the ass, difficulty, nuisance.

bother *v.* **1.** ANNOY harass, trouble, pester, irritate, agitate, burden, vex, aggravate, distress, put out, irk, harry. **2.** TAKE THE TROUBLE inconvenience oneself, take pains, *go out of one's way, worry about.

bothersome *a.* annoying, troublesome, irksome, aggravation, burdensome, inconvenient, difficult, vexatious, irritating.

bottle *n.* container, decanter, jug, vial, carafe, flask, flagon, jar, phial.

bottleneck *n.* obstacle, blockage, jam, hindrance, snag, congestion, obstruction, *tight squeeze.

bottom *n.* **1.** BASE foundation, bed, seat, footing, floor, ground, nadir. **2.** ROOT basis, core, essence, gist, source, origin. **3.** REAR buttocks, *fanny, butt, rump, seat, derriere, *tush, *buns, *stern.

bough *n.* limb, branch.

boulevard *n.* avenue, parkway, concourse. SEE STREET

bounce *v.* **1.** SPRING BACK rebound, bob, bound, recoil, jump, hop, carom, ricochet. **2.** JOUNCE jolt, shake.

bound *v.* **1.** JUMP leap, bounce, spring, vault, gambol, bounce, hop. **2.** RESTRICT restrain, limit, confine, enclose, circumscribe, demarcate.

bound *a.* **1.** TIED fastened, wrapped, secured, trussed. **2.** DESTINED certain, doomed, fated,

headed, sure, ordained, assured, determined.
3. OBLIGATED pledged, required, liable, compelled.

boundary *n.* border, borderline, line, frontier, verge, periphery, edge, rim, margin, brink, hem, limit, confines, outer limit, bounds, perimeter, demarcation.

boundless *a.* limitless, endless, infinite, immeasurable, vast, inexaustable, unbounded, perpetual, innumerable, everlasting. ANT. *limited, finite.*

bounteous SEE BOUNTIFUL

bountiful *a.* generous, plentiful, abundant, ample, copious, prolific, lavish, bounteous, fat, teeming, *jam-packed, *dime a dozen, luxuriant. ANT. *spare, scant, sparse, lean.*

bounty *n.* gift, reward, present, bonus, benefit, largess, premium, allowance.

bouquet *n.* **1.** BUNCH posy, spray, garland, nosegay. **2.** SCENT aroma, fragrance, essence, perfume, trace, breath, smell.

BOURGEOIS *a.* [boor ZHWAW] of the middle-class, boring, conventional and materialistic. *He described himself as a Bohemian; he abhorred our bourgeois ways.* SYN. middle-class, working-class, proletarian, conventional, common, rigid, boring, *square, *politically correct, materialistic, conservative, traditional, respectable, uncultured, philistine. ANT. *Bohemian, unconventional, nonconforming.*

bout *n.* **1.** MATCH contest, battle, struggle, round, go, competition. **2.** PERIOD spell, course, round, turn, shift, term, stint.

bow *n.* **1.** BEND curtsy, genuflection, nod. **2.** PROW

bow *v.* **1.** BEND stoop, curtsy, genuflect, nod, salaam, kneel. **2.** SUBMIT yield, give in, *cave in, *knuckle under, concede, defer, *kowtow, acquiesce, surrender, lay down. ANT. **2.** *fight, dominate, resist.*

bowels *n.* **1.** INTESTINES guts, entrails, viscera, innards, insides. **2.** INTERIOR depth, core, insides, heart, innermost part.

bowl *n.* dish, receptacle, saucer, basin, vessel, tureen, boat, urn.

bowling *n.* tenpins, candlepins, duckpins, kegling, skittles, bocci.

WORD FIND

area most likely to yield strike: pocket
body movement of bowler after shot: body English
bowler: kegler
central pin: kingpin, headpin
curving shot: hook

gutter, in the: gutter ball
knock down ten with one shot: strike, mark
knock down ten with two shots: spare, mark
one game: string
pin-setting machine: pinsetter
shot that leaves a gap between pins: split
spin imparted on the ball: English
unit of game, 1/10th: frame
wide split: goalposts, mule ears, bed posts

box *n.* carton, container, crate, receptacle, case, package, bin, chest, trunk, canister, coffer.

box *v.* fight, spar, fisticuff, tussle, punch, cuff, jab, sock, hit, strike, slug, deliver blows, pound, clout, pummel, *whale, beat.

boxer *n.* fighter, prizefighter, pugilist.

boxing *n.* pugilism, fighting, sparring.

WORD FIND

black eye: mouse
crossover punch: cross
dazed: punch drunk
ear deformation: cauliflower ear
exchange punches: mix it up
hold, embrace: clinch
illegal blow: rabbit punch, below the belt, low blow, kidney punch, head butt
inning: round
jab and cross: one-two punch
movement: bob and weave, dance, footwork, on one's bicycle
powerful punch: haymaker, Sunday punch
practice partner: sparring partner
practice with partner: spar
practice with self: shadow box
punching bag: speedbag, heavy bag, crazy bag
punch with less than full strength: pull a punch
quick, straight punch: jab
ring floor: canvas, apron
stamina program: roadwork
sweeping hook: roundhouse
tic: draw
trainer, assistant: cornerman, cut man, handler
upswinging punch: uppercut, bolo punch
varied punches delivered quickly: combination, flurry
wait of eight seconds after knockdown: mandatory eight-count, standing eight-count
weight and measurements of opponents: tale of the tape
weight division lightest to heaviest: flyweight, bantamweight, featherweight, lightweight, welterweight, middleweight, light heavyweight, heavyweight, cruiser-

weight

win by injuring, disabling opponent: knockout, technical knockout, TKO

win by points: decision

win not agreed on by all officials: split decision

boy *n.* lad, youth, youngster, sprig, junior, *little shaver, *nipper. "One who has a wolf in his stomach." — German proverb. "Of all the wild beasts, the most unmanageable." — Plato.

boycott *v.* *blackball, blacklist, shun, reject, refuse, ban, ostracize, shut out, spurn, proscribe, strike.

boyfriend *n.* sweetheart, *honey, beau, *steady, suitor, lover, date, swain, flame, *main squeeze.

brace *n.* support, prop, reinforcement, strut, stay, buttress, truss, stanchion.

brace *v.* reinforce, strengthen, support, prop, bolster, tighten, shore up, fortify.

bracing *a.* invigorating, stimulating, exhilarating, refreshing, energizing, restorative. ANT. *tiring, soporific, draining.*

brackish *a.* salty, saline, briny.

brag *v.* boast, gloat, *blow one's own horn, crow, vaunt, swagger, strut, flaunt, puff, *talk big, *shovel it, *blow hard. ANT. *downplay, *hide one's light under a bushel basket, be modest.*

braggart *n.* bragger, boaster, *blowhard, *windbag, *gasbag, *bag of wind, show-off, egotist, blusterer, braggadocio, peacock, trumpeter.

braid *v.* plait, weave, twine, interlace, knot.

brain *n.* **1.** SMART PERSON genius, intellectual, scholar, savant, wizard, prodigy, thinker, mastermind, Einstein, *egghead, sage, wit, mental giant. **2.** MIND *gray matter, *thinking cap, *bean, encephalon, *noodle, *upper story. "An apparatus with which we think that we think." — Ambrose Bierce. "An invention of the universe in order to study itself." — Anon.

WORD FIND

abnormally small brain: microencephalon

ancient portion, regulates hunger, thirst, fighting, sex: limbic system, reptilian brain

base, regulates breathing and circulation: medulla oblongata

body temperature and blood pressure regulator: hypothalamus

connector of right and left hemispheres: corpus callosum

egg-shaped patch controlling speech muscles: Broca's area

exam of brain waves: electroenchephalogram (EEG).

heat, cold, pain, pressure sensor: thalamus

inflammation: encephalitis, meningitis

left or right side: hemisphere

muscular coordinator in back of skull: cerebellum

nerve cell: neuron

outer brain area controlling perception, reasoning, memory: cerebrum

outer layer: cortex, dura mater

seizure disease caused by electrical disturbances: epilepsy

superhuman right-brain functioning: idiot savant syndrome

ANT. *1. idiot, moron, imbecile.* SEE INTELLIGENCE, THOUGHT

brainwash *v.* indoctrinate, convert, influence, persuade.

brainy *a.* brilliant. SEE CLEVER, INTELLIGENT, SMART

brake *n.* restraint, curb, constraint, check, control.

brake *v.* stop, slow, decelerate, halt, curb.

branch *n.* **1.** LIMB bough, arm, twig, offshoot. **2.** UNIT division, subdivision, department, bureau, wing, affiliate, arm, chapter, office. **3.** TRIBUTARY channel, feeder, stream.

branch *v.* fork, spread, divide, bifurcate, diverge, grow.

brand *n.* make, trade name, line, variety.

brand *v.* **1.** MARK sear, burn in, label. **2.** STIGMATIZE mark, disgrace, taint, *give a black eye.

brandish *v.* wave, exhibit, shake, show, flourish, hold menacingly, flaunt, wield, swing.

brash *a.* **1.** RECKLESS rash, impetuous, hasty, mindless, incautious, headlong, foolhardy, unwary, impulsive. **2.** PUSHY bold, cocky, impudent, nervy, rude, cheeky, forward, flip, brazen. ANT. *1. thoughtful, cautious, wary. 2. courteous, reserved, respectful.*

brassy *a.* bold, brazen, loud, impudent, insolent, arrogant, cheeky, nervy, cocky, brash, forward, shameless, loudmouthed. ANT. *shy, retiring, respectful, timid.*

brat *n.* imp, *holy terror, *little bastard, spoiled child, *enfant terrible, *punk.

bravado *a.* bluff, bluster, swaggering, strutting, cockiness, *show, *crowing, bombast, muscle-flexing, macho posturing. ANT. *timidity, mousiness, cowering.*

brave *v.* face, defy, dare, confront, challenge, *stand up to.

brave *a.* courageous, bold, fearless, valiant, lionhearted, dauntless, heroic, plucky, *gutsy, *ballsy, intrepid, daring, spunky, manly, foolhardy, macho. ANT. *timid, mousy, cowardly, fainthearted, *chicken.

bravery n. courage, fearlessness, boldness, *guts, *balls, daring, spunk, valor, pluck, heroism, intrepidness, manliness, mettle. "Falling but not yielding." — Latin proverb. "Fear sneering at itself." — Maxwell Bodenheim. ANT. *timidity, cowardice, mousiness, fearfulness.*

brawl n. fight, tussle, *scrap, donnybrook, *rumble, *slugfest, imbroglio, uproar, row, fracas, quarrel, altercation, melee, riot, *free-for-all.

brawn n. muscles, strength, huskiness, *beefiness, robustness, power, might.

brawny a. muscular, herculean, beefy, burly, sinewy, powerful, strapping, rugged, husky, solid, stout.

brazen a. bold, brassy, impudent, shameless, audacious, cheeky, brash, cocky, loudmouthed, frank, forward, *ballsy. ANT. *quiet, shy, reserved.*

breach n. **1.** OPENING hole, break, crack, fissure, gap, cleft. **2.** VIOLATION nonobservance, transgression, infringement, noncompliance, infraction, contravention. **3.** ALIENATION split, separation, falling-out, schism, friction, estrangement, parting of the ways.

breadth n. **1.** WIDTH broadness, span. **2.** RANGE extent, scope, span, area.

break n. **1.** FRACTURE crack, rupture, tear, split, fissure, collapse, rift, breach, rent. **2.** PAUSE recess, breather, intermission, lull, letup, rest, hiatus, respite. GOOD FORTUNE opportunity, shot, opening, stroke of luck, chance.

break v. **1.** FRACTURE crack, rupture, tear, split, shatter, collapse, breach, fall apart, bust, burst, snap, pop, smash, pulverize, splinter, demolish, total, disintegrate, mangle. **2.** WEAKEN impair, undermine, diminish, degrade, incapacitate, cripple. **3.** PAUSE rest, recess, take a breather, suspend, stop. ANT. *1. repair, mend, fix. 2. strengthen, fortify. 3. resume, begin.*

breakdown n. **1.** FAILURE malfunction, collapse, short circuit, disruption, mishap. **2.** ITEMIZATION analysis, list, categorization.

breakthrough n. PROGRESS advance, discovery, innovation, invention, leap forward, finding.

breakup n. separation, disintegration, rift, split, disbanding, dissolution.

breast n. **1.** CHEST bosom, bust, mammary gland, tit, *boob, teat, udder, *bazooms,

*hooters, *headlights, *knockers, *jugs, *maracas. **2.** HEART soul, core, inner self, spirit, psyche.

breath n. whiff, puff, air, respiration, sigh, wheeze, whisper, gasp, inhalation, exhalation, aspiration.

breathe v. inhale, exhale, respire, draw a breath, gasp, pant, wheeze, huff, blow, heave, suck, snore, snort, sniff, hyperventilate.

breather n. break, recess, pause, rest, respite, time out.

breathless a. short of breath, out of breath, shortwinded, winded, asthmatic, gasping, wheezing, choking, panting, puffing, suffering from apnea, suffering from dyspnea.

breathtaking a. electrifying, awe-inspiring, shocking, exciting, stunning, astounding, heart-stopping, thrilling, hair-raising, moving.

breed n. strain, variety, type, class, genus, race, kind, line, species.

breed v. **1.** REPRODUCE procreate, propagate, bear young, beget, generate, hatch, produce, engender. **2.** TO CAUSE bring about, lead to, produce, foster, create, effect, spawn.

breeding n. cultivation, training, upbringing, development, schooling, rearing, conditioning, manners, refinement. "Concealing how much we think of ourselves and how little we think of the other person." — Mark Twain.

breeze n. **1.** GENTLE WIND zephyr, breath, whiff, sough, draft, waft. SEE WIND **2.** *CINCH *snap, *nothing, *duck soup.

breezy a. **1.** WINDY blustery, drafty, gusty, airy, windswept, fresh. **2.** LIGHTHEARTED easygoing, casual, sprightly, lively, playful, spirited, brisk, animated, vivacious, effervescent. ANT. *1. still, dead calm, becalmed. 2. depressed, morose, spiritless.*

BREVITY n. [BREV i tee] briefness, conciseness. *The speech was too long; the audience begged for brevity.* SYN. briefness, shortness, conciseness, succinctness, terseness, compactness, pithiness, economy, pointedness. ANT. *long-windedness, wordiness, lengthiness.*

brew v. **1.** STEEP boil, ferment, cook, stew, seethe. **2.** DEVISE concoct, invent, cook up, contrive, hatch, formulate, engineer.

brewery n. distillery.

bribe n. payoff, *hush money, graft, *kickback, *boodle, sop, baksheesh, *grease, inducement, incentive.

bribe v. pay off, buy off, *grease the palm, suborn, corrupt, entice.

bric-a-brac n. knickknacks, trinkets, baubles, gewgaws, bibelots, virtu.

bridge n. span, overpass, arch, viaduct, footbridge, catwalk, connector, link, connection, tie, bond.

WORD FIND

arched roadway over a valley: viaduct

cable and girder-supported: bridle-chord bridge, suspension bridge

dual beams or trusses that project beyond their supports, are connected: cantilever bridge

enclosure used in water for repair of: cofferdam

fear of: gephyrophobia

float-supported: pontoon bridge

opens and closes for boat traffic: drawbridge, bascule, swing bridge, lift bridge

protective railing or wall: balustrade, parapet

railroad bridge framework: trestle

support: pier, pile, abutment

bridge v. span, cross, traverse, connect, link, join, unite.

bridle n. restraint, rein, halter, bit, leash, muzzle, check, curb.

bridle v. restrain, check, hold back, curb, arrest, inhibit, muzzle.

brief n. summary, synopsis, condensation, outline, sketch, precis, abridgement.

brief v. inform, fill in, summarize, outline.

brief a. **1.** SHORT-LIVED short, fleeting, quick, fast, short-term, instantaneous, momentary, swift, transitory. **2.** SHORT, CONCISE *short and sweet, succinct, abbreviated, to the point, condensed, summarized, compressed, pithy. ANT. 1. long, prolonged, time-consuming. 2. long-winded, wordy, time-consuming.

briefing n. rundown, outlining, summary, *lowdown, instruction, orientation.

brigade n. troop, unit, group, outfit, company, battalion, contingent, legion.

brigand n. bandit, outlaw, robber, desperado, pirate.

bright a. **1.** LIGHT shining, brilliant, blinding, glowing, luminous, radiant, dazzling, blazing, glaring, intense, incandescent, vivid, sparkling, resplendent, effulgent. **2.** SMART intelligent, clever, sharp, quick, witty, brainy, brilliant, astute. **3.** HOPEFUL promising, cheering, golden, rosy, encouraging, auspicious, sunny. **4.** CHEERFUL lively, vivacious, happy, sprightly, merry, lighthearted, joyous, blithe. ANT. 1. dark, dim, gloomy, black. 2. stupid, moronic, retarded, bovine, dull. 3. dark,

black, grim, hopeless. 4. grim, morose, depressed.

brighten v. **1.** LIGHTEN illuminate, intensify, furbish, shine, polish, perk up. **2.** CHEER UP lift spirits, perk up, enliven, hearten, buoy, uplift, gladden. ANT. 1. darken, blacken, tone down. 2. depress, sadden, make glum.

brilliant a. **1.** BRIGHT shining, incandescent, blinding, radiant, glowing, dazzling, blazing, intense, resplendent, scintillating, sparkling, vivid. **2.** SMART intelligent, clever, sharp, quick, witty, brainy, astute, ingenious, wise, scholarly. ANT. 1. dull, dark, tarnished, grimy. 2. dull, slow, *bovine, stupid, dim-witted.

brim n. rim, edge, verge, lip, margin, brink.

brine n. salt water, sea water, saline solution; souse.

bring v. **1.** CONVEY carry, bear, transport, take, retrieve, fetch, deliver. **2.** EFFECT cause, make, produce, prompt, start, institute, induce, force, compel.

brink n. verge, edge, borderline, threshold, limit, brim, line.

brisk a. **1.** QUICK swift, energetic, lively, sprightly, vigorous, bustling, hustling, *peppy. **2.** BRACING invigorating, cool, chilly, nippy, biting, exhilarating, stimulating. ANT. 1. slow, torpid, lethargic, dull. 2. somnolent, sleepy, tiring.

bristle v. get angry, seethe, *see red, *raise one's hackles, *get one's dander up, flare, *boil, get indignant, *snap.

brittle a. fragile, crisp, delicate, breakable, frail, crumbly. ANT. solid, rock-hard, unbreakable.

BROACH v. [BROACH] to introduce a topic or start a discussion. Ken broached a new subject. SYN. introduce, start, begin, open, bring up, launch, put forth.

broad a. **1.** WIDE vast, voluminous, capacious, deep, fat, expansive, ample, commodious, sweeping, large, immense. **2.** EXTENSIVE comprehensive, blanket, sweeping, universal, general, far-reaching, compendious, catholic, widespread. **3.** OBVIOUS apparent, clear, plain, explicit, straightforward. ANT. 1. narrow, tight. 2. limited, specific, confined. 3. unapparent, veiled.

broadcast v. transmit, *beam, put on the air, *air, televise, telecast, relay, radio, cable, spread, disseminate, scatter, announce, report.

broaden v. widen, enlarge, expand, deepen, extend, increase, augment, supplement. ANT. narrow, reduce.

broad-minded a. liberal-minded, open-minded, tolerant, fair, impartial, unprejudiced, unbiased, undogmatic, catholic, free-thinking, accepting, open. ANT. *close-minded, narrow-minded, bigoted, dogmatic.*

brochure n. pamphlet, booklet, folder, circular, leaflet, flier, throwaway.

broil v. flame-broil, sear, grill, barbecue, heat, cook, roast, burn, singe.

broke a. penniless, poor, impoverished, bankrupt, insolvent, destitute, ruined.

broken a. 1. BUSTED fractured, ruptured, shattered, splintered, torn apart, pulverized, damaged, smashed, mangled. 2. NOT WORKING nonfunctioning, broken down, in disrepair, out of order, *on the blink, *on the fritz, *busted, *kaput, *dead. 3. DEFEATED beaten, crushed, vanquished, disheartened, humbled, fallen. ANT. 1. *whole, intact.* 2. *functioning, running, *humming.* 3. *invincible, indomitable, triumphant.*

broken-hearted a. heartbroken, grief-stricken, mournful, forlorn, despairing, dejected, inconsolable, desolate, crushed. ANT. *euphoric, elated, joyous.*

broker n. agent, dealer, intermediary, negotiator, go-between, middle-man.

bromide n. platitude, trite saying, cliche.

brooch n. pin, clip, ornament, breastpin, clasp.

brood n. offspring, young, hatchlings, clutch, litter, spawn, children.

brood v. worry, agonize, fret, ruminate, deliberate, *stew over, mope, muse, meditate, think over.

brook n. stream, creek, *crick, rill, runnel, tributary, branch.

brook v. take, stand for, tolerate, abide, bear, put up with, condone.

brothel n. bordello, *whorehouse, *cathouse, house of ill repute, house of prostitution, bagnio, bawdyhouse, *sporting house.

brotherhood n. fellowship, fraternity, comradeship, kinship. "All for one and one for all." —Alexandre Dumas.

brouhaha n. uproar, hubbub, commotion, wrangle, stir, clamor, *to-do, ruckus.

browbeat v. intimidate, bully, cow, badger, terrorize, harass, threaten, domineer, *bulldoze, tyrannize, hector.

brown n. auburn, chestnut, chocolate, sorrel, coffee, brunette, fawn, ochre, umber, mahogany, cocoa, dun, tan, beige, cinnamon, ginger, rust, nutbrown, bister, sepia, henna, earth, fox.

browse v. glance, skim, scan, flip through, peruse, skip over.

bruise n. contusion, black and blue mark, ecchymosis, discoloration, blemish, wound, *hickey.

bruise v. contuse, jam, wound, bump, discolor, injure, mark, mar.

bruiser n. bully, fighter, boxer, hulk.

brunt n. blow, impact, shock, force, full force.

brush n. 1. BROOM whisk, besom, duster. 2. TOUCH sweep, stroke, scrape. 3. CONFRONTATION clash, encounter, run-in, skirmish, tussle. 4. BUSH scrub, thicket, undergrowth, shrubs, coppice, brake, bramble, brier, bracken.

brush v. 1. SWEEP scrub, whisk, wash, wipe, buff, paint, scuff, dust off. 2. TOUCH sweep, stroke, scrape, glance, graze, caress, tickle.

brush-off n. *cold shoulder, *kiss-off, snub, rejection, slight, rebuff.

brush up v. study, bone up, *cram.

BRUSQUE a. [BRUSK] blunt or rough in manner. *The clerk was always discourteous and brusque.* SYN. blunt, rough, abrupt, curt, gruff, short, bluff, terse, discourteous, snippy, sharp, rude. ANT. *courteous, considerate, gracious.*

brutal a. 1. VICIOUS savage, cruel, cold, barbaric, inhuman, ferocious, heartless, bloodthirsty, brutish, ruthless, harsh, hellish, pitiless. 2. HARSH rigorous, tortuous, trying, merciless, hard, painful. ANT. *kind, caring, humane, gentle.*

brutality n. viciousness, savagery, cruelty, coldness, barbarism, ferocity, inhumanity, heartlessness, brutishness, harshness. ANT. *kindness, caring, humaneness, gentility.*

brute n. beast, savage, barbarian, monster, animal, fiend, *Neanderthal, caveman, ogre, swine, devil.

bubble n. globule, droplet, sphere, burble, spheroid, orb, bead, bleb.

bubble v. boil, percolate, simmer, seethe, effervesce, burble, froth, foam, fizz, popple.

buccaneer n. pirate, corsair, privateer.

buck n. stag, deer.

bucket n. pail, vessel, cask, can, scuttle, pot, pitcher, container, holder.

buckle n. clasp, clip, fastener, snap, hitch, hasp.

buckle v. 1. CLASP clip, fasten, snap on, hitch. 2. BEND contort, warp, crimp, bulge, break, collapse, cave in, crumple, give way. ANT. 1. *unbuckle, unfasten, release.* 2. *straighten.*

buckle down v. apply oneself, get serious, *put one's nose to the grindstone.

BUCOLIC a. [byoo KOL ik] of rural or pastoral life; rustic. *A bucolic panorama of rolling* *hills, grazing cows and old stone walls.* SYN. rustic, rural, countrified, pastoral, agrarian, Arcadian. ANT. *urban, citified, metropolitan.*

bud *v.* sprout, open, bloom, flower, blossom, shoot.

buddy *n.* pal, chum, friend, comrade, companion, sidekick, crony, alter ego, *bro.

budge *v.* **1.** MOVE inch, shift, stir, roll, dislodge, push, propel, nudge. **2.** BEND give in, acquiesce, yield.

budget *n.* financial plan, appropriation, estimate, overhead, expenses. "A mathematical confirmation of your suspicions." — A.A. Latimer. "A system of going into debt systematically." — Anon.

budget *v.* apportion, allocate, estimate, ration, allow.

buff *n.* devotee, enthusiast, fanatic, expert, connoisseur, *bug, *freak, nut.

buff *v.* clean, shine, polish, rub, burnish, smooth.

buffer *n.* cushion, pad, shock absorber, guard.

buffet *n.* sideboard, counter, credenza, shelf, salad bar, cold table, smorgasbord.

buffet *v.* pummel, beat, cuff, strike, slug, slap, drub, knock, punch, smack, wallop, pound, *hit up-side the head.

buffoon *n.* clown, fool, jester, joker, prankster, comedian, harlequin, *boob, bozo, zany, merry-andrew.

bug *n.* **1.** INSECT vermin, pest. **2.** FLAW defect, fault, imperfection.

bug *v.* **1.** BOTHER annoy, irritate, irk, pester, vex, nettle, badger, plague, disturb. **2.** WIRETAP eavesdrop, spy.

build *n.* physique, shape, figure, body.

build *v.* **1.** CONSTRUCT erect, put together, assemble, raise, fabricate, *knock together, engineer, contrive, *throw up. **2.** ESTABLISH start, set up, initiate, institute, found, create. **3.** FORM shape, mold, model, fashion, create. **4.** INTENSIFY compound, escalate, mount, amplify, magnify, grow, swell. ANT. *1. disassemble, demolish, raze.*

building *n.* structure, edifice, construction, erection, high rise, *skyscraper, superstructure, framework.

WORD FIND

arches, series of: arcade

brickwork laid in checkered pattern: checkerwork, basketweave

brickwork with alternating courses of bricks laid sideways (stretchers) and head-ways (headers): English bond

brickwork with every other brick laid head-

ways (header): Flemish bond

concrete embedded with steel mesh, bars: reinforced concrete

face: facade

gallery between two main stories: mezzanine

inscribed stone: cornerstone

inscription on: epigraph

material: brick, mortar, concrete, reinforced concrete, stone, wood, adobe

monstrous ornament: gargoyle, grotesque

nonopening window: deadlight

outside corner: quoin

rooftop safety wall: parapet

round, domed: rotunda

shelflike projection: cornice

support: joist, beam, girder, pier, buttress, flying buttress

window design, arrangement: fenestration

wing: annex, ell, bay

SEE ARCHITECTURE, CASTLE, CATHEDRAL, HOUSE

bulge *n.* bump, swelling, protuberance, lump, hump, prominence, outgrowth. ANT. *hollow, hole.*

bulge *v.* swell, protrude, distend, puff, balloon, stick out. ANT. *contract, shrivel.*

bulk *n.* **1.** SIZE mass, volume, amount, magnitude, body, extent. **2.** BIGGEST PART main, majority, most, lion's share, preponderance, better part.

bulky *a.* massive, unwieldy, cumbersome, huge, ponderous, prodigious, mammoth, sizable, unmanageable, hulking, voluminous. ANT. *small, wieldy, manageable, pocket-sized.*

bull *n.* **1.** ANIMAL taurus, bullock, male, steer, ox. **2.** *Sl.* BULLSHIT *bilge, *blarney, *baloney, bushwa, *BS, *hogwash, lies, bunk, *crock of shit, *hokum, *horsefeathers, *malarkey, *rot, *rubbish, nonsense.

bull *v.* charge, drive, thrust, press, bulldoze, *muscle.

bullet *n.* shot, ball, shell, cartridge, trajectile, slug, *lead, pellet, missile.

WORD FIND

bulletproof garment: bulletproof vest

bulletproof shield: mantelet

cartridge with no projectile: blank

container: cartridge

covering: jacket

diameter: caliber

glowing, military: tracer

pointed: spitzer

receptacle: clip, magazine

shotgun pellets: birdshot, buckshot

shotgun projectiles used in riots to stun, not kill: baton rounds soft, expands when it hits, causing severe damage: dumdum

trajectory deviation: drift

SEE AMMUNITION, GUN

bulletin n. report, flash, statement, announcement, notification, communication, dispatch, publication.

bullfight n. corrida, spectacle.

WORD FIND

assistant on horseback, lances bull's neck: picador

assisting team: cuadrilla

barbed dart: banderilla

cheer: ole

fighter: matador, torero

matador's emergency shelter: burladero

picador's lance: pic

red cape waved: capa

wave of red cloth: capeador

bullheaded n. headstrong, stubborn, mulish, obstinate.

bullish a. optimistic, confident, rising.

bully n. tyrant, thug, tormentor, terrorizer, bruiser, ruffian, rowdy, *browbeater, *dink, swaggerer, oppressor, dictator, *biggest toad in the puddle. SEE BOSS

bully v. domineer, tyrannize, torment, *lord over, threaten, oppress, dictate, *call the shots, intimidate, hector, browbeat.

bulwark n. fortification, rampart, earthwork, bank, wall, reinforcement, barrier, defense, stronghold, bastion, protection.

bum n. loafer, idler, derelict, panhandler, drunk, hobo, vagrant, ne'er-do-well, beggar, tramp, transient.

bumbling a. blundering, stumbling, bungling, clumsy, uncoordinated.

bump n. 1. COLLISION crash, thud, thump, scrape, tap, jolt, blow, jostle, knock, sideswiping, *fenderbender, impact, crack, nudge. 2. SWELLING lump, bulge, welt, knob, gnarl, nodule, protuberance, dent, *ding.

bump v. 1. HIT thump, collide with, run into, butt, scrape, tap, jar, bang, graze, sideswipe, jostle, smash into, bang. 2. DISPLACE depose, replace, remove, dislodge.

bumpkin n. hick, *hayseed, yokel, rustic, *goat-roper, clodhopper, yahoo, *cider squeezer, farmer.

bumptious a. arrogant, conceited, pushy, forward, overbearing, cocky, haughty, presumptuous. ANT. bashful, diffident, retiring.

bumpy a. rough, jolting, lumpy, jerky, jarring, rugged, *washboard, *spine-shattering, *kidney-crushing, choppy, *chuckholed,

*potholed. ANT. smooth, silky, graded.

bunch n. group, cluster, collection, lot, mass, clump, quantity, assortment, bundle, host, multitude, heap, batch, throng, swarm, number, galaxy, *mess, *oodles.

bundle n. 1. MASS bunch, lot, cluster, heap, group, pile, batch, collection. 2. PACKAGE parcel, packet, box, carton, sheaf, bale, stack, roll.

bungalow n. cottage. SEE HOUSE

bungle v. botch, *screw up, *muff, *blow it, *goof, mess up, blunder, fumble, misstep, miscalculate, *drop the ball. ANT. succeed, *pull it off, *score.

bungling a. inept, incompetent, clumsy, blundering, maladroit.

bunk n. 1. BED cot, berth. 2. Sl. NONSENSE *malarky, *baloney, *hokum, *rubbish, twaddle. SEE BULL, NONSENSE

buoy n. dan, float, marker, beacon, bell.

WORD FIND

mooring: dolphin

type: can, nun, bell, whistle

buoy v. uplift, boost, raise, lift, hearten.

buoyant a. cheerful, lighthearted, resilient, blithe, optimistic, sprightly, mirthful, sanguine, carefree, jaunty. ANT. depressed, somber, down.

burden n. load, weight, cross to bear, obligation, stress, millstone, albatross, onus, strain, hardship, responsibility, encumbrance, affliction, workload, incubus.

burden v. load, weigh down, saddle with, encumber, strain, obligate, bog down, hamper, oppress, tax, yoke. ANT. unburden, lighten, free.

bureau n. 1. DRESSER chest of drawers, chest, chiffonier, highboy. 2. DEPARTMENT division, branch, agency, office, commission.

BUREAUCRACY n. [byoo ROK ruh see] any form of government administration, especially that which is inefficient and bound by its own red tape. A bureaucracy requires a contract submitted in quadruplicate when a handshake would do. SYN. government administration, civil service, officaldom, *the Establishment, *powers that be, city hall, the system, the authorities, *Big Brother. "That great clog in the wheel." —Marc McCutcheon. "A giant mechanism operated by pygmies." —Honore de Balzac. "The anonymous 'they,' the enigmatic 'they' who are in charge." —Joseph Heller.

bureaucrat n. government official, civil servant, administrator, politician, clerk, public servant, pencil-pusher, *desk-jockey, *red tape dispenser.

BURGEON v. [BUR jun] grow, proliferate. *The deficit is burgeoning out of control.* SYN. grow, proliferate, flourish, develop, sprout, thrive, mushroom, bud, spread, multiply, expand. ANT. *dwindle, diminish.*

burglar n. thief, cat burglar, crook, mugger, prowler, *picklock, robber, housebreaker.

burial n. interment, inhumation, funeral, entombment, last rites, *deep six. SEE CEMETERY

burlesque n. parody, satire, caricature, farce, lampoon, travesty, *send-up, spoof, vaudeville, comedy, *schtick, skits, striptease.

burly a. big, heavy, muscular, strong, beefy, brawny, stout, hefty, hulking, rugged, thickset. ANT. *skinny, anorexic, slight.*

burn v. **1.** BE ON FIRE OR SET FIRE incinerate, ignite, torch, blaze, flame, light, smolder, kindle, reduce to ashes, rage, go up in smoke, consume, cremate, deflagrate, combust, singe, sear, broil, char, scorch, brand, cauterize. **2.** CONSUME use up, expend, squander. **3.** CHEAT swindle, bilk, take, *rip off. ANT. *1. extinguish, quench. 2. conserve, save.*

burning a. **1.** FLAMING blazing, on fire, raging, aflame, fiery, ignited, smouldering, smoking. **2.** SERIOUS dire, crucial, compelling, important, critical, crucial, vital, urgent, pressing. **3.** FERVENT feverish, passionate, frenzied, ardent, enthusiastic. ANT. *1. extinguished, out, quenched. 2. insignificant, trivial. 3. apathetic, cool, unconcerned.*

burnish v. polish, smooth, brighten, furbish, buff, shine, gloss, rub.

burp v. belch.

burrow n. hole, tunnel, warren, dugout, diggings, den, lair.

burrow v. dig, excavate, tunnel, hollow out, furrow.

burst n. explosion, outburst, blowout, eruption, discharge, outpouring, spurt.

burst v. pop, explode, crack open, rupture, fly apart, blow up, shatter, rip, bust, split, erupt, disintegrate.

bury v. **1.** INTER entomb, inhume, sepulcher, lay to rest. **2.** EMBED sink, submerge, implant, engulf. **3.** COVER conceal, hide, cache, stash, secrete. ANT. *1. exhume, dig up. 3. expose, air.*

bush n. **1.** SHRUB hedge, plant, thicket, brier, bramble, undergrowth, scrub. **2.** BACKCOUNTRY woods, jungle, the wild, outback.

bushed a. exhausted, spent, *pooped. ANT. *energetic, peppy.* SEE TIRED

bush-league a. second-rate, *minor league, *small potatoes. SEE INFERIOR

business n. **1.** OCCUPATION profession, trade, job, career, vocation, calling, work, livelihood, *racket, pursuit. **2.** COMMERCE industry, trade, enterprise, manufacturing, merchandising, buying and selling, mercantilism, marketing. "The art of extracting money from another man's pocket without resorting to violence."—Max Amsterdam. "Riding a bicycle. Either you keep moving or you fall down."—John Wright. **3.** RESPONSIBILITY concern, department, province, affair, duty, interest, subject, matter. **4.** FIRM company, corporation, concern, enterprise, market, store, factory, office, organization, conglomerate, mill.

businesslike a. methodical, efficient, organized, orderly, systematic, professional, industrious. ANT. *disorganized, slipshod, unprofessional.*

businessman/woman n. merchant, trader, industrialist, entrepreneur, tycoon, capitalist, investor, employer.

bust n. chest, bosom, breast.

bustle n. activity, commotion, hubbub, hurly-burly, uproar, tumult, flurry, stir, *comings and goings, to-do, pother. ANT. *stillness, calm, peace.*

busy a. **1.** ACTIVE bustling, full, *buzzing, *humming, *popping, *hopping, jumping, *on the go, lively. **2.** ENGAGED preoccupied, employed, unavailable, working, active, involved, tied down, tied up. ANT. *1. idle, still, quiet. 2. free, at leisure, lazing around.*

busybody n. meddler, pry, gossip, snoop, blabbermouth, *buttinski.

butcher v. **1.** SLAUGHTER dress, clean, cure, pack, smoke. **2.** KILL slaughter, kill, murder, massacre, slay. **3.** BUNGLE botch, make a mess of, *screw up, ruin.

butt/buttocks n. bottom, seat, rump, *tush, *ass, derriere, *fanny, *stern, backside, gluteus maximus.

butt n. subject, target, victim, scapegoat.

butt v. ram, horn, thrust, strike, drive, batter, collide, jab, jam.

buttress n. support, prop, brace, reinforcement, abutment, stanchion, shore, beam, pier, arch.

buttress v. reinforce, strengthen, fortify, bolster, shore up, prop up.

buxom n. full-figured, *busty, shapely, plump, voluptuous, *built, *stacked, zaftig, *topheavy. ANT. *skinny, bony, *flat.*

buy v. **1.** PURCHASE acquire, bargain for, pay for,

procure. **2.** BRIBE corrupt, *pay off.

buzz *n.* hum, drone, whir, hiss, whizz.

bygone *a.* former, past, previous, gone by, olden, erstwhile, defunct, forgotten, lost. ANT. *present, current, in the here and now.*

bypass *v.* go around, avoid, detour around, sidestep, circumvent.

byproduct *n.* outgrowth, offshoot, spin-off, side effect.

bystander *n.* observer, onlooker, witness, eyewitness, spectator, passerby.

byword *n.* proverb, adage, motto, maxim, slogan, saying, catchword, watchword, dictum, truth, principle.

C

cab n. taxi, cabriolet, hack, hansom.

cabal n. **1.** FACTION junta, camarilla, clique, ring, band. **2.** CONSPIRACY plot, intrigue, scheme.

cabaret n. nightclub, boite, dinner theater, cafe, supper club, honky-tonk, disco.

cabin n. **1.** COTTAGE shack, loghouse, camp, hovel, hut, lodge, chalet, chalet, shanty, bungalow. **2.** COMPARTMENT quarters, stateroom, room, chamber.

cabinet n. **1.** CUPBOARD commode, bureau, chest, chiffonier, chifforobe, box, case, file, etagere, console. **2.** ADMINISTRATION advisers, council, ministry, board, *brain trust.

cable n. **1.** WIRE cord, line, rope, chain. **2.** OVERSEAS TELEGRAM wire, cablegram.

cache n. stockpile, hoard, stash, supply, store, *nest egg, respository, reserve.

cackle v. chuckle, chortle. SEE LAUGH

CACOPHONOUS a. [kuh KOF uh nus] harsh-sounding, jarring, especially designating incongruent sounds heard over one another. *No one could tell whether the cacophonous heavy-metal band was in tune or not.* SYN. harsh-sounding, jarring, dissonant, discordant, strident, inharmonious, unmelodious, grating, raucous, noisy. ANT. *euphonic, euphonious, harmonious, melodious.*

cactus n. desert plant, saguaro, cholla, prickly pear, cereus, mescal. SEE DESERT

cad n. scoundrel, bounder, heel, rogue, rat, rascal, lout, scamp, knave.

cadaver n. corpse, body, *stiff, carcass, remains, mummy.

cadaverous a. pale, ghastly, gaunt, haggard, pallid, ashen, deathly, chalky, ghostly, bloodless. ANT. *rosy, ruddy, glowing.*

cadence n. modulation, meter, rhythm, beat, measure, pulse, tempo, swing.

cadre n. nucleus, core, infrastructure, framework.

cafe n. coffeehouse, bistro. SEE RESTAURANT

cafeteria n. lunchroom, commissary. SEE RESTAURANT

cage n. **1.** enclosure, jail, pound, lockup, pen, prison, trap.

cage v. confine, trap, enclose, pen, imprison, impound, coop up, lock up. ANT. *free, release.*

CAGEY a. [KAY jee] tricky, not easily caught or fooled. *A fox is a cagey animal.* SYN. tricky, sly, cunning, wary, leery, shrewd, wily, cautious, crafty, careful. ANT. *unwary, trusting,*

naive.

cahoots n. Sl. partnership, league, collusion, alliance, conspiracy.

CAJOLE v. [kuh JOHL] to persuade with flattery, coax. *She cajoled him for hours; he finally gave in.* SYN. persuade, coax, wheedle, *sweet talk, blandish, pander to, *butter up, flatter, stroke, *kiss up, beguile, inveigle.

cajolery n. palaver, persuasion, coaxing. SEE FLATTERY

cake n. **1.** BAR block, lump, brick, slab, cube. **2.** LOAF batter cake, layer cake, torte, pastry.

calamitous a. disastrous, catastrophic, ruinous, devastating, cataclysmic, grievous, fatal, tragic, dire. ANT. *blessed, beneficial, favorable.*

calamity n. disaster, catastrophe, devastation, cataclysm, fatality, misery, blow, adversity, ruination, misfortune. "A mighty leveller." — Edmund Burke. "The test of integrity." — Samuel Richardson. ANT. *blessing, good fortune, boon.*

calculate v. compute, figure, reckon, add up, sum up, count, evaluate, surmise, judge, forecast.

calculating a. shrewd, scheming, crafty, designing, manipulative, plotting, artful, wily, sharp. ANT. *artless, naive.*

calculation n. computation, figuring, counting, reckoning, summation, evaluation, estimation.

caldron n. boiler. SEE KETTLE

caliber n. **1.** QUALITY value, worth, character, ability, virtue, distinction. **2.** DIAMETER bore, gauge.

calibrate v. rectify, graduate, correct, fix, measure, tweak.

calisthenics n. exercises, workout, aerobics.

call n. **1.** SHOUT exclamation, yell, whoop, announcement, outcry. **2.** SUMMONS request, convocation, appeal, draft. **3.** INVITATION solicitation, bidding. **3.** ANIMAL CRY hoot, shriek, bleat, low, bellow, trumpet, ululation. SEE BIRD, SHOUT

call v. **1.** SHOUT exclaim, announce, yell, cry, holler, hail, whoop. **2.** SUMMON request, convoke, muster, convene, direct. **3.** NAME designate, label, title, term, christen, dub. **4.** VISIT drop in, ring.

call girl n. *hooker, *streetwalker. SEE PROSTITUTE

calling n. vocation, metier, occupation, profession, trade, business, pursuit, line, forte, passion, *thing, *bag, *racket.

call off v. cancel, postpone, *scrub, abort, *kill.

CALLOUS a. [KAL us] unfeeling, having no pity. *The callous rioters looted neighborhood stores.* SYN. unfeeling, pitiless, merciless, cold, uncaring, heartless, insensitive, hardboiled, indifferent, cruel, cold-blooded. ANT. *sympathetic, caring, thoughtful.*

CALLOW a. [KAL oh] inexperienced, immature. *Some sixteen-year-olds are too callow to be trusted behind the wheel.* SYN. inexperienced, immature, unseasoned, naive, unsophisticated, childish, juvenile, sophomoric, uninitiated, green, unfledged. ANT. *mature, experienced, worldly.*

calm a. **1.** STILL motionless, tranquil, quiet, undisturbed, halcyon, windless, smooth, placid, serene. **2.** RELAXED unperturbed, cool, collected, unruffled, unexcited, sedate, tranquil, dispassionate, composed, staid, unflappable, placid. ANT. *1. turbulent, rough, disturbed. 2. nervous, anxious, frenzied, panicky.*

calumny a. slander, defamation, malicious statement, libel, smear, mud-slinging, smirch, false accusation, aspersion, slur. ANT. *praise, compliment, acclaim.*

camaraderie n. fellowship, companionship, bonhomie, brotherhood, friendship, comradeship, conviviality, esprit de corps, fraternization, loyalty, *buddy-buddy atmosphere.

camel n. dromedary, beast of burden, ruminant.

camera n. 35mm, *Polaroid, video camera, camcorder, *Brownie, *Kodak, *Nikon.

WORD FIND
flash receptacle: hot shoe
focusing system: range finder, viewfinder
lens for shooting tiny objects: macro lens
lens producing haze or color effect: filter
lightmeasuring device: light meter, exposure meter, photometer
light producer: flash
long-distance lens: telephoto lens, zoom lens
opening, amount of: aperture
opens and closes when shot is taken: shutter
stand: tripod, highhat
wide field of view lens: wide angle lens, fisheye, bugeye
SEE PHOTOGRAPHY

camouflage n. disguise, concealment, facade, cover-up, cryptic coloration, blind, dissimulation, front, masquerade, veil, shroud, mimicry.

camouflage v. disguise, conceal, cover up, masquerade, obscure, obfuscate, shroud, veil,

hide, simulate, mimic. ANT. *expose, reveal, display.*

camp n. **1.** ENCAMPMENT bivouac, cantonment, shelter. **2.** GROUP faction, clique, sect, party, circle.

camp v. bivouac, encamp, pitch a tent, rough it, lodge, sleep out.

campaign n. **1.** OPERATIONS offensive, strategy, battle plan. **2.** DRIVE crusade, movement, project, push.

campaign v. electioneer, run, solicit votes, canvass, crusade, lobby, barnstorm.

campus n. grounds, yard, quad, dorm, alma mater. SEE SCHOOL

campy a. affected, effeminate, artificial, ostentatious, garish, posturing, flaunting, outlandish, theatrical, *faggy.

can n. container, receptacle, vessel, tin.

canal n. waterway, conduit, channel, race, aqueduct, passage, trench, culvert, duct, tube.

cancel v. **1.** CALL OFF stop, revoke, *kill, break off, void, annul, discontinue, rescind, countermand, abort. **2.** OFFSET counter, neutralize, counterbalance, make up for, nullify.

cancer n. carcinoma, tumor, malignancy, sarcoma.

WORD FIND
blood/marrow: leukemia
breast removal: mastectomy
cause, substance: carcinogen
deadly form: malignant
harmless form: benign
mass: tumor, neoplasm, growth
medical branch: oncology
removable: resectable
skin: melanoma, basal cell tumor
spread of: metastasis
treatment: chemotherapy, radiation
tumor removal: lumpectomy
SEE OPERATION

candid a. open, honest, frank, up-front, straightforward, blunt, direct, four-square, heart-to-heart. ANT. *mealy-mouthed, insincere, indirect.*

candidate n. nominee, aspirant, contender, office-seeker, party favorite, hopeful, entrant, *dark horse.

candle n. taper, rush, torch, glim.

WORD FIND
burning center: wick
holder: sconce, candelabra, chandelier, girandole, menorah
lighter: taper
maker: chandler
material: wax, carnauba, tallow

wick's end: snuff

CANDOR n. [KAN dur] truthfulness, frankness. *In all candor, Mary, you have dragon breath.* SYN. truthfulness, frankness, honesty, straightforwardness, bluntness, outspokenness, openness, directness, forthrightness, plain-speaking. ANT. *deception, indirectness, duplicity, *doublespeak.*

candy n. sweet, confection, bonbon, kiss, lozenge, taffy, caramel, toffee, jellybean, jawbreaker, fudge, drop, wafer, lollipop, nougat, praline, sweetmeat, brittle, cotton candy, peanut brittle, mint, sucker, gumball, chocolate bar, penny candy.

cane n. stick, walking stick, staff, crook, rod.

canker n. lesion, sore, ulcer, blister, cold sore.

cannibal n. man-eater, headhunter, savage, barbarian, carnivore. "A man who loves his neighbor with sauce."—Jean Riguax.

cannon n. gun, howitzer, mortar, heavy artillery, ordnance, *Big Bertha, *Long Tom.

WORD FIND

case of projectiles: canister

cast iron balls: grapeshot

continuous firing: cannonade, barrage, salvo

gunner: cannoneer

kick: recoil

shipboard antiaircraft guns: pompom

SEE ARMY, GUN, WEAPON

canny a. shrewd, clever, cautious, careful, cagey, wiley, sly, smart, streetwise, worldly, wary, crafty, sagacious. ANT. *naive, careless, unsophisticated, dim-witted.*

canoe n. boat, dugout, pirogue, bongo, kayak.

WORD FIND

air chambers: sponsons

angled stroke used to avoid fatigue on long excursions: Canadian stroke

apparel and equipment of canoeist: duffle

braking stroke: jam stroke

carrying canoe over land between water bodies: portaging

deviate from course or float sideways: yaw

distance above water line to gunwales: freeboard, draw, draft

left side facing forward: port

line used to tie or tow: painter

right side facing forward: starboard

side edges, upper: gunwales (pronounced "gunnels")

underside strip: keel

SEE BOAT, RIVER, SHIP

canon n. law, decree, doctrine, principle, dogma, edict, statute.

canopy n. awning, cover, sunshade, baldachin, tilt, tarp.

cant n. **1.** INSINCERITY piety, *lip service, hypocrisy, pretense, sanctimony. **2.** JARGON argot, lingo, dialect, slang, vernacular, patter.

cant v. tilt, angle, overturn, slant, lean, tip, incline.

cantankerous a. bad-tempered, ornery, crabby, touchy, surly, grouchy, irritable, contentious, grumpy, crotchety, testy, cranky, bearish. ANT. *cheerful, easygoing, good-humored.*

canteen n. flask, bottle, jug.

canter v. lope, saunter, amble, trot, gallop.

canvas n. duck, tent cloth, sailcloth, coarse cloth.

canvass v. analyze, poll, examine, solicit, survey, study, investigate, discuss, electioneer.

canyon n. valley, gorge, gulch, ravine, gully, chasm, pass.

cap n. hat, headgear, beret, beanie, tam-o'-shanter. SEE HAT

cap v. top, crown, surpass, beat, transcend, eclipse, defeat.

capability a. ability, know-how, capacity, proficiency, wherewithal, aptitude, *the right stuff, means, power, skill, mind, talent.

capable a. able, competent, skilled, trained, apt, adept, learned, proficient, deft, adept, equal to, expert, masterly, adroit, talented, *having the right stuff. ANT. *incapable, incompetent, inept.*

capacious a. spacious, roomy, commodious, voluminous, big, ample. ANT. *tiny, cramped.*

capacity n. **1.** VOLUME proportions, size, dimensions, magnitude, range, contents, space, limit, room. **2.** ABILITY capability, means, power, competence, faculty, aptitude, *the right stuff, mind, talent, skill, proficiency. **3.** POSITION role, responsibility, function.

cape n. **1.** MANTLE cloak, wrap, poncho, shawl, capote, pelisse. **2.** PENINSULA headland, point, promontory.

caper n. prank, escapade, *high jinx, *shenanigans.

caper v. jump, skip, gambol, prance, romp, frisk, leap about.

capital n. **1.** SEAT OF GOVERNMENT principal city. **2.** WEALTH funds, moneys, stock, savings, assets, resources, venture capital, investment capital. "That part of wealth which is devoted to obtaining further wealth."—Alfred Marshall.

CAPITALISM n. [KAP i tuh LIZ um] free enterprise, business and the pursuit of wealth by private citizens for private gain. *Capitalism is the economic engine that drives*

America. SYN. free enterprise, free market, commercialism, mercantilism, *dog eat dog, laissez-faire, private ownership, market economy, private investment. "The unequal sharing of blessings. . . . " — Winston Churchill. ANT. *socialism, communism.*

capitalist n. investor, entrepreneur, financier, tycoon, businessman.

capitalize on v. take advantage of, cash in on, exploit, profit by, utilize.

CAPITULATE v. [kuh PICH yoo LATE] to give up, give in, yield. *The opposing side agreed to capitulate on several points.* SYN. give up, give in, yield, surrender, acquiesce, accede, come to terms, submit, bow, cave in, knuckle under. ANT. *stand firm, stand one's ground, fight.*

caprice n. whim, impulse, notion, vagary, whimsy, eccentricity, fancy, fickleness.

CAPRICIOUS a. [kuh PRISH us] subject to change on a whim, unpredictable. *Fred is always changing his mind; he is as capricious as the wind.* SYN. fickle, whimsical, unpredictable, unstable, frivolous, impulsive, inconsistent, indecisive, wayward, flighty, crotchety, quirky, *any way the wind blows. ANT. *constant, stable, predictable.*

capsize v. overturn, tip, upset, *turn turtle, roll over, keel over.

capsule n. pill, tablet, pellet, ampule, wafer.

captain n. cap'n, master, skipper, boss, chief, manager, head, commanding officer, leader, *old man.

caption n. heading, title, subtitle, legend, inscription.

captivate v. attract, charm, fascinate, spellbind, enamor, enchant, enthrall, bewitch, mesmerize, hypnotize, *knock/sweep off one's feet. ANT. *repel, repulse, turn off.*

captive n. prisoner, internee, convict, hostage.

captive a. imprisoned, confined, held, bound, obliged.

captivity n. imprisonment, incarceration, restraint, bondage, custody, detention.

capture n. apprehension, seizure, landing, *bagging, catch, taking, acquisition, netting, recovery, taking into custody, trapping, cornering. ANT. *release, liberation.*

capture v. catch, apprehend, seize, *bag, *nab, *collar, land, snare, net, corner, trap, *round up. ANT. *release, liberate.*

car n. sedan, coupe, roadster, *clunker. SEE AUTOMOBILE, TRUCK

caravan n. train, cavalcade, procession, company, motorcade, column.

carcass n. corpse, cadaver, body, remains, carrion.

cardinal a. principal, main, chief, utmost, central, prime, foremost, fundamental. ANT. *insignificant, unimportant.*

cards n. playing cards, tarot cards. "The Devil's books." — English proverb.

WORD FIND

authority: Hoyle

card pile remaining after deal: talon, stock

card with value determined before game: wild card

cheat: sharper, card shark, blackleg

game: bridge, baccarat, monte, whist, blackjack, crazy eights, concentration, war, three card monte, old maid, poker, pinochle, canasta, solitaire, gin, rummy, gin rummy, hearts, cribbage, slapjack, casino

jack, queen or king: face card

outranking suit, card: trump card

same suit group: flush

tie-breaking game: rubber match

care n. **1.** CAREFULNESS caution, regard, consideration, thought, diligence, pains, prudence, conscientiousness, mindfulness, exactitude, vigilance. **2.** CONCERN worry, anxiety, bother, trouble, burden, problem, tribulation, distress. **3.** CUSTODY charge, protection, supervision, safekeeping, administration, guidance, tutelage, keep. ANT. *1. carelessness, negligence.*

care v. **1.** BE CONCERNED mind, worry, fret, take pains. **2.** REGARD love, hold dear, prize, cherish.

careen v. tip, tilt, lurch, totter, pitch, sway, lean.

career n. profession, occupation, vocation, lifework, job, livelihood, metier, business, field, *thing.

carefree a. happy-go-lucky, insouciant, footloose, lighthearted, untroubled, breezy, *laid-back, blasé, blithe, devil-may-care, cheerful. ANT. *troubled, careworn, burdened.*

careful a. **1.** CAUTIOUS wary, circumspect, heedful, vigilant, leery, guarded, prudent, alert, attentive. **2.** METICULOUS painstaking, thorough, fussy, scrupulous, demanding, conscientious, rigorous, fastidious, punctilious, attentive. ANT. *1. careless, reckless, negligent. 2. careless, slipshod, sloppy.*

careless a. unattentive, heedless, reckless, lax, unwary, slipshod, sloppy, slapdash, indiscreet, remiss, neglectful, absentminded, hasty, thoughtless, imprudent, casual, offhand, rash, unconcerned, lackadaisical. ANT.

careful, attentive, cautious, meticulous, rigorous.

caress *v.* stroke, touch, fondle, pet, pat, brush, graze, rub, snuggle, cuddle.

caretaker *n.* custodian, superintendent, supervisor, janitor, curator, warden, conservator, maintenance man.

careworn *a.* haggard, tired, exhausted, worried, anxious, troubled, heavy-hearted.

cargo *n.* freight, load, shipment, payload, consignment, lading.

CARICATURE *n.* [KAR uh kuh chur] an exaggerated portrait or depiction of someone or something, usually for satirical effect. *Gross caricatures of politicians frequently appear in editorial cartoons.* SYN. cartoon, portrait, sketch, depiction, exaggeration, parody, satire, spoof, farce, takeoff, send-up, lampoon, travesty, mockery, imitation, *aping, humorous distortion. "The most penetrating of criticisms." — Aldous Huxley. "Exaggeration of a fact." — Robert Zwickey.

CARNAGE *n.* [KAR nij] bloody slaughter. *The carnage of war.* SYN. slaughter, bloodshed, massacre, bloodbath, butchery, holocaust, decimation, gore, mass murder, annihilation.

CARNAL *a.* [KAR nul] of bodily, not spiritual, pleasure, sensual. *Carnal fantasies.* SYN. sensual, sexual, of the flesh, bodily, animal, voluptuous, lustful, corporal, lascivious, prurient, erotic, wanton. ANT. *spiritual, moral, godly.*

carnival *n.* festival, fair, gala, celebration, jamboree, fiesta, jubilee, Mardis Gras, *carny.

carnivorous *a.* flesh-eating, meat-eating, predatory. ANT. *herbivorous.*

carol *n.* melody, tune. SEE SONG

carom *v.* rebound, glance, ricochet.

carouse *v.* drink, party, frolic, *get high, *catch a buzz, wassail, make merry, cut loose, revel, *tie one on, *get hammered, *chug-a-lug, guzzle, *knock down a few, quaff. ANT. *sober up, *swear off.*

carp *v.* complain, find-fault, nag, *bitch, scold, nitpick, *moan and groan, knock, belittle, cavil, criticize. ANT. *praise, compliment.*

carpenter *n.* woodwright, woodworker, builder, joiner, contractor, subcontractor.

carpentry *n.* woodworking, building.

> **WORD FIND**
> aligned, fitted perfectly: true, plumb
> cutting and sizing of lumber before use: millwork
> drive nails at an angle: toenail
> frame supporter for worker: scaffold
> grooves, cut: dado, rabbet
> joint: miter, mortise
> nail length, designation: penny
> out of vertical alignment: out-of-plumb
> sawing stand: sawhorse
> tools: saw, plane, miter box, chisel, bevel, level, adze, sander
> SEE HOUSE, TOOL

carpet *n.* rug, mat, Oriental, Persian, area rug, bearskin, moquette, runner, shag, Wilton.

carriage *n.* **1.** VEHICLE coach, rig, buggy, wagon, cabriolet, brougham, surrey, hansom, landau, phaeton, stagecoach, calash, buckboard. **2.** POSTURE bearing, demeanor, pose, posture, comportment, mien, cast, attitude.

carry *v.* **1.** CONVEY transport, lug, haul, tote, bear, bring, transfer, *schlep. **2.** SUPPORT hold up, shoulder, bear, sustain, buttress.

cart *n.* wagon, truck, handcart, dray, wheelbarrow.

cart *v.* haul, carry, lug, transport, convey, truck.

CARTE BLANCHE *n.* [KART BLANSH] a granting of power, freedom or authority to do as one wishes. *His bosses gave him carte blanche to run the department as he saw fit.* SYN. free rein, license, freedom, authority, power, blank check, sanction, free hand, permission, discretion.

cartel *n.* association, trust, monopoly, syndicate.

carton *n.* box, package, crate, container, case.

cartoon *n.* caricature, drawing, sketch, line drawing, funny, comic strip, parody, joke. SEE CARICATURE

carve *v.* cut, slice, hew, incise, chisel, sculpt, form, fashion, whittle, chip.

Casanova *n.* *womanizer, Don Juan, *ladykiller, *heartbreaker, *Romeo, *skirtchaser, *stud, Lothario, wolf, sex addict.

cascade *n.* waterfall, shower, cataract, falls, deluge, watercourse, torrent, *stairstep. SEE RIVER

cascade *v.* fall, tumble, plummet, plunge, spill, flood, rush, gush, descend, spew, *stairstep.

case *n.* **1.** EXAMPLE instance, sample, occurrence, affair, matter, event, illustration, situation, circumstance. **2.** SUBJECT client, patient, illness. **3.** LAWSUIT suit, action, claim, litigation. **4.** BOX holder, receptacle, container, package, carton, casing, covering, sheathing, jacket.

cash *n.* money, currency, coins, change, legal tender, *dough, *scratch, *bread, liquid assets. SEE MONEY, WEALTH

cashier n. teller, counter person, bursar, clerk.

casing n. covering, wrapper, sheath, jacket, skin, hull.

cask n. barrel, keg, hogshead, firkin, vat, kilderkin, vessel, tun, butt.

casket n. coffin, sarcophagus, box, pall. SEE CEMETERY

CASSANDRA n. [kuh SAN druh] one who foretells doom or spreads alarm but is disregarded, after the mythological character of the same name. *The economist warned of a stock market crash but was regarded as just another Cassandra.* SYN. alarmist, *Chicken Little, voice of doom, prophet of doom, scaremonger, seer, prognosticator, fortune teller.

cast n. **1.** THROW pitch, toss, shot, fling, heave, sling, hurl. **2.** MOLD form, model, impression, shape. **3.** PERSONAE company, troupe, dramatis personae, actors, actresses, players, performers, repertory, characters. **4.** APPEARANCE complexion, aspect, look, shade, air, semblance.

cast v. **1.** THROW fling, hurl, pitch, heave, *chuck, toss, sling, launch, let fly. **2.** SPREAD scatter, shed, broadcast, disperse, strew, sprinkle. **3.** EMIT radiate, project, send out. **4.** CHOOSE pick, assign, select, *typecast. **5.** MOLD form, shape, set.

castaway n. outcast, pariah, *reject, waif, stray, derelict, exile, vagabond, leper.

caste n. class, group, position, station, rank, status, place, clan, grade, social order.

CASTIGATE v. [KAS tuh GATE] to criticize harshly or punish. *The dictator liked to castigate his underlings in public.* SYN. punish, criticize, chastise, scold, rebuke, discipline, reproach, admonish, *take to task, reprimand, berate, bawl out, blister, *rake over the coals, lambaste, tongue-lash. ANT. *praise, compliment, laud.*

castle n. fortress, citadel, stronghold, keep, manor, chateau, mansion, alcazar.

WORD FIND

attack on: siege

bottlery: buttery

bridge spanning moat: drawbridge

candle storeroom: chandlery

castle used as a prison: bastille

circular turret with a conical roof: pepperbox turret

crossbow storage room: ballistraria

domestic official in charge of supplies: chamberlain, seneschal, steward

door, huge, grated: portcullis

doorman: usher

fort surrounded by fortified village: castellum

gateway, minor: postern

governor of: castellan

holes or slits through which archers shoot: archeria, arrow loops, loopholes, balistraria, murder holes

knight's practice yard: tiltyard

lady of: chatelaine

lights: rushlights

main inner tower, keep: donjon

mass of earth: bastion, rampart

mobile tower used by attackers to reach castle defenders: belfry

notched parapet: battlement

notches, solid area between: merlon

notch in parapet: crenel

outer wall ringing castle: curtain wall

owner: lord

privy: garderobe

roof wall: parapet

seating platform of lord: dais

siege engine used against: catapult, mangon, trebuchet

small tower above main structure: turret

sunny family room: solar

timber tower: brattice

tower/structure protecting a drawbridge: barbican, gatehouse

trench around: moat

turret that overhangs: bartizan

underground prison: dungeon

waste receptacle: cess pit

yard area within outer walls: ward, bailey, courtyard

castrate v. emasculate, geld, neuter, *fix, sterilize, effeminize, eunuchize; debilitate, weaken.

casual a. **1.** CHANCE accidental, random, serendipitous, fortuitous, *flukey, unexpected. **2.** RELAXED nonchalant, cool, blasé, unconcerned, carefree, apathetic, devil-may-care, *laid-back, indifferent. **3.** NONDRESSY informal, sporty, for-play. ANT. *1. planned, predetermined, arranged. 2. intense, serious, *meaning business. 3. formal, dressy.*

casualty n. victim, fatality, dead, loss.

cat n. feline, kitty, kitten, tomcat, pussy, grimalkin, tabby, mouser, Angora, Burmese, Manx, Persian, Siamese. "A pygmy lion."—Oliver Herford. "A hedonist of the sloth family."—Unknown.

WORD FIND

black and white: piebald

blue gray to slate gray coloring: blue
bred from long line of its own kind: purebred
breeding female: queen
castrated male: gib
domesticated cat living in the wild: feral
father: sire
frill around head in longhaired breed: ruff
hairball: furball
intoxicant: catnip
"kneading" of paws on human's stomach: milk treading
long-bodied, long-limbed: rangy
lover of: ailurophile
mating cry: caterwaul
mixed breed: mongrel, moggie
mother: dam
neutering of female: spaying
newborn kitten group: litter
patches of white on feet: mittens, gloves
paw soles: pads
phobic: ailurophobe
pinkish gray coloring: lilac, lavender
sexually receptive period of female: heat
short-legged: cobby
sneer of male as it smells urine of sexually receptive female: flehmen response
striped: tabby, tiger
thin, long tail: whip
tortoiseshell and white coloring: calico
trace colorings: ghost markings
whiskers: vibrissae
white marking from forehead to nose: blaze
white or colored patch under neck: locket
white undercoat with dark tips: chinchilla

cataclysm n. upheaval, disaster, eruption, catastrophe, calamity, devastation, debacle.

catalog n. list, file, inventory, directory, index.

catalog v. list, classify, index, inventory, file.

CATALYST n. [KAT uh list] one that makes something happen, gets something started or hastens a process. *Martin Luther King was a catalyst for change.* SYN. stimulus, motivator, *spark, *sparkplug, spur, *mover and shaker, activist, agitator, *whip.

catapult n. launcher, siege engine, slingshot, sling, trebuchet.

catastrophe n. disaster, misfortune, calamity, cataclysm, ruin, debacle, devastation, tragedy, mishap, blow, hardship, misadventure.

catcall n. shout, whistle, hiss, boo, *Bronx cheer, *raspberry, jeer, heckle, hoot.

catch n. 1. CAPTURE snatch, seizure, trap, grab, snare, grasp. 2. CLASP latch, clip, fastener, lock, hook and eye. 3. TAKE haul, prize, plunder, booty, spoils. 4. DRAWBACK hitch, trick, gimmick, snag.

catch v. 1. APPREHEND capture, seize, snatch, grasp, grip, nab, net, snare, clutch, trap, bag. 2. DISCOVER surprise, *nail, expose, detect, come upon. 3. COME DOWN WITH AN ILLNESS contract, get, develop, break out with, be infected by, fall ill with. 4. UNDERSTAND comprehend, see, grasp, get, follow, perceive.

catching a. contagious, infectious, communicable, spreading, epidemic, pandemic. ANT. *noncommunicable.*

CATCH-22 n. [KACH twen tee TOO] a no-win situation. *The government's contradictory regulations frequently put people in Catch-22 situations.* SYN. no-win situation, lose-lose situation, paradox, contradiction, quagmire, quandary, dilemma, Gordion knot, horns of a dilemma.

catchword n. byword, watchword, buzz word, motto, slogan, shiboleth.

categorical a. absolute, direct, unequivocal, positive, unqualified, explicit, express, total, unconditional, without exceptions. ANT. *conditional, qualified.*

categorize v. classify, designate, sort, group, label, assign, name, catalog.

category n. class, classification, division, variety, type, kind, sort, order, grade, denomination, genre.

cater v. 1. PROVIDE furnish, serve, provision, feed. 2. INDULGE humor, gratify, serve, wait on, pamper, spoil, baby, pander.

caterwaul v. howl, yowl, mewl, screech, wail, meow, squall, cry, whine.

CATHARSIS n. [kuh THAR sis] a purification or cleansing of the soul; release from mental turmoil. *Venting tensions in a self-help group provided Ellen with the catharsis she longed for.* SYN. purification, cleansing, release, relief, renewal, expurgation, replenishment of spirit, rebirth, fresh start, wiping clean.

cathedral n. basilica, chapel. SEE CHURCH

CATHOLIC a. [KATH uh lik] universal, general. *His tastes were catholic; in other words, his tastes were broad.* SYN. universal, general, broad, all-inclusive, comprehensive, liberal, all-encompassing, ecumenical, global. ANT. *limited, narrow, sectarian.*

cattle n. livestock, cows, bulls, steers.

catty a. malicious, spiteful, mean, vicious, nasty, malevolent, back-biting, back-stabbing, *bitchy, malignant, venomous. ANT. *kind, warm, friendly.*

caucus n. meeting, assembly, convention, conference, gathering, session, conclave.

cauldron n. kettle, pot, boiler.

cause n. **1.** DETERMINANT agent, reason, root, antecedent, motive, source, origin, mover, occasion, stimulus, mainspring. **2.** IDEAL principle, end, objective, enterprise, goal, purpose.

cause v. **1.** EFFECT induce, bring about, produce, incite, provoke, generate, breed, motivate, give rise to, precipitate.

CAUSTIC a. [KAW stik] biting, burning or corrosive, as acid. *Wear gloves when handling caustic substances. She was a caustic-tongued witch.* SYN. corrosive, burning, biting, acid, astringent, erosive, sharp, stinging, sarcastic, sardonic, bitter, scathing, cutting, vitriolic, excoriating, acid-tongued, saber-tongued. ANT. *soothing, sweet, honey-tongued, smooth.*

cauterize v. burn, sear, char, singe.

caution n. **1.** WARINESS care, prudence, heed, vigilance, discretion, guardedness, circumspection, alertness. "The eldest child of wisdom." —Victor Hugo. "What we call cowardice in others." —Oscar Wilde. **2.** WARNING admonition, caveat, advisement, *red flag, *word to the wise, advisory. ANT. *1. rashness, recklessness.*

caution v. warn, admonish, advise, alert, forewarn, *raise a red flag, counsel; *better safe than sorry, *stay on one's toes, *watch one's step, *look before one leaps, *sleep with one eye open.

cautious a. wary, careful, heedful, circumspect, prudent, discreet, guarded, on guard, alert, on one's toes, vigilant, chary. ANT. *rash, reckless, imprudent.*

cavalcade n. procession, parade, column, train, line, caravan.

CAVALIER a. [kav uh LEER] arrogant; indifferent to important matters. *The coach took a cavalier attitude toward the rules of good sportsmanship.* SYN. arrogant, haughty, indifferent, casual, supercilious, devil-may-care, lofty, curt, cocky, disdainful. ANT. *obliging, caring, conscientious.*

cave n. cavern, grotto, tunnel, hole, *yawning chasm, hollow, underground chamber, subterranean passage, catacomb.

WORD FIND

carved out from this rock: limestone

crawl space: crawl, crouchway

dripping water and mineral formation: dripstone

entrance area exposed to daylight: twilight zone

explorer: spelunker

exploring: spelunking

geological area with many caves, sinkholes: karst

high, narrow passage: canyon

iciclelike formation hanging from roof: stalactite

iciclelike formation on floor: stalagmite

inhabitant: troglodyte, troglobite, troglophile

joined stalactite and stalagmite: column

large chamber: gallery

pool of water edged with calcite: gour

study of: speleology

tiny, thin stalactite: soda straw

underwater passage: sump, syphon

vertical shaft: chimney, pitch

CAVEAT n. [KAV ee at] warning. *The accountant gave us a strong caveat about filing our taxes accurately.* SYN. warning, caution, notice, forewarning, admonition, advisory, advisement, *word to the wise.

cavernous a. hollow, yawning, deep-set, sunken, abysmal, enormous, huge, gaping, roomy, commodious, chambered.

cavil v. quibble, object, find-fault, *nitpick, carp, criticize, pick.

cavity n. hole, hollow, pit, cleft, chamber, crevice, fissure, pocket, niche.

cavort v. frolic, prance, romp, *carry on, *cut up, act up, horseplay, gambol, frisk, caper.

cease v. end, stop, discontinue, desist, halt, refrain, finish, conclude, quit.

ceaseless a. unending, relentless, incessant, neverending, perpetual, constant, nonstop, continuous, unremitting. ANT. *ending, fleeting, finite, limited.*

cede v. surrender, give up, yield, abdicate, *hand over, grant, relinquish, transfer, resign.

ceiling n. **1.** TOPSIDE roof, plafond, rafters. **2.** MAXIMUM limit, restriction, highest point.

celebrate v. **1.** COMMEMORATE observe, honor, memorialize, remember, ceremonialize, solemnize. **2.** *PARTY *paint the town red, *whoop it up, *raise the roof, *go out on the town, *go out with a bang, *have a blowout, splurge, revel, carouse, *live it up. **3.** PRAISE honor, extol, laud, pay homage to, acclaim, worship, hail, pay tribute to, exalt.

celebrated a. famous, renowned, eminent, prominent, noted, illustrious, acclaimed, popular, lionized, great. ANT. *obscure, little-known, unknown.*

celebration n. **1.** COMMEMORATION observance,

ceremony, honoring, memorial, remembrance, anniversary. **2.** PARTY *blowout, fiesta, gala, jubilee, *bash, *wingding, festival, spree, frolic, *blast, *rumpus, revelry.

celebrity *n.* **1.** FAMOUS PERSON star, superstar, *somebody, *bigwig, notable, idol, *celeb, *big name, personage, personality, VIP, sex symbol. "Someone who is known for being known." — Studs Terkel. "A person who works hard all his life to become well known, then wears dark glasses to avoid being recognized." — Fred Allen. **2.** FAME renown, notoriety, stardom, eminence, prominence, distinction, note. ANT. *1.* nobody, *bush leaguer, unknown. *2.* oblivion, obscurity.

celerity *n.* speed, quickness, alacrity, haste, dispatch, expedition, swiftness. ANT. *slowness, *snail's pace, leisureliness.*

celestial *a.* **1.** HEAVENLY divine, sublime, supernal, angelic, ethereal, blessed, eternal, supernatural. **2.** ASTRAL astronomical, universal, heavenly, extraterrestrial, stellar, sky, planetary, galactic.

CELIBATE *a.* [SELL uh but] abstaining from sex. *With sexually transmitted diseases running rampant, many singles choose to remain celibate.* SYN. abstinent, continent, upright, virtuous, pure, untouched, virginal, maiden, single, unwed, chaste. ANT. *promiscuous, wanton, sexual.*

cell *n.* **1.** UNIT germ, microorganism, bacterium. **2.** SMALL ROOM compartment, chamber, vault, keep, cloister, coop, booth, lockup.

cellar *n.* basement, downstairs, vault.

cement *v.* join, unite, bond, glue, mortar, bind, seal, fix.

cemetery *n.* graveyard, necropolis, memorial grounds, burial ground, churchyard, golgotha, *bone yard, *city of the dead. "The last resort." — Anon. "The country home I need." — Mark Twain.

WORD FIND

ashes of cremated body: cremains
burial place, vault: tomb
burial site, unit: plot
empty tomb, marker for one whose remains are elsewhere: cenotaph
grave robber: ghoul
gunfighter's, American West: Boot Hill
incinerator: crematory
inscription on gravestone: epitaph
large cemetery: necropolis
memorial building, place: shrine
mound of earth over grave: barrow
mourning statues: weepers

pauper's: Potter's field
preparation facility for the dead: mortuary
RIP: rest in peace
sarcophagus, elaborately carved: solium
sculpted representation of the dead on a monument: effigy
sculptural depiction of the crucifixion: Calvary
stone: headstone, tombstone, gravestone, monument, memorial
tomb housing: mausoleum
underground vaults: catacombs, crypt, cubiculum
urn or vault for bones: ossuary
urn vault: cinerarium
vault: sepulcher
SEE COFFIN, FUNERAL, MONUMENT

censor *n.* bowdlerizer, arbiter of good taste, expurgator, inspector, Mrs. Grundy, guardian of morals, prude. "A man who knows more than he thinks you ought to." — Laurence J. Peter.

censor *v.* prohibit, squelch, cut, edit out, abridge, clean up, delete, sanitize, bowdlerize, restrict, inspect, expurgate, review, purge.

censure *n.* disapproval, condemnation, reprehension, rebuke, admonition, criticism, objection, remonstrance, reproof. ANT. *approval, blessing, praise.*

censure *v.* disapprove, condemn, rebuke, admonish, criticize, object, remonstrate, denounce, reproach, reprimand. ANT. *approve, bless, praise.*

center *n.* **1.** MIDDLE POINT middle, median, focal point, dead center, bull's-eye, midst, hub, pivot, core, heart, nucleus, inside, pith.

center *v.* concentrate, focus, converge, direct, join, unify, fix.

central *a.* **1.** INNERMOST middle, interior, median, inner, nuclear. **2.** VITAL key, indispensable, main, prime, dominant, chief, ruling, fundamental. ANT. *1.* outermost, peripheral. *2.* peripheral, incidental, marginal.

centralize *v.* concentrate, converge, focus, consolidate, unify, amalgamate, join. ANT. *decentralize, disperse.*

CEREBRAL *a.* [suh REE brul] of or appealing to the intellect. *His philosophy reveals some advanced thinking; it's very cerebral.* SYN. intellectual, intelligent, brainy, erudite, scholarly, smart, analytical, thoughtful, deep, recondite, abstruse.

ceremonial *a.* ritual, formal, ceremonious.

ceremonious *a.* ceremonial, polite, proper, formal, solemn, stately, punctilious, rigid, prim, courtly, starchy, dignified, decorous. ANT. *informal, casual, *laid-back.*

ceremony n. **1.** RITUAL observation, rite, service, function, formality, solemnity, custom, observance. "The wine of human experience." —Morris Cohen. **2.** ETIQUETTE protocol, punctilio, formality, decorum, propriety, prescription. ANT. *2. informality.*

certain a. **1.** SURE positive, cocksure, convinced, undoubting, assured, satisfied. **2.** UNQUESTIONABLE doubtless, *beyond a shadow of a doubt, indubitable, definite, indisputable, incontestable, unequivocal, incontrovertible, firm, unambiguous. ANT. *1. uncertain, unsure, doubting. 2. questionable, doubtful, *up in the air.*

certainty n. **1.** CONVICTION authority, certitude, confidence, assurance, infallibility. **2.** FACT truth, reality, *sure thing, *sure bet, actuality, *luck. ANT. *1. doubt, skepticism. 2. uncertainty, fantasy, unknown.*

certificate n. document, documentation, instrument, voucher, warrant, license, permit, certification, testimonial, credential, diploma.

certify v. vouch, verify, notarize, attest, assure, guarantee, validate, accredit, authenticate, confirm, depose.

cessation n. stop, termination, ending, stoppage, letup, ceasing, halt, pause, suspension, discontinuance, close. ANT. *continuation, persistence.*

cesspool n. sewer, cesspit, sump, cloaca, septic tank.

C'EST LA VIE [say lah VEE] that's life, such is life. *Our team lost again; oh well, c'est la vie!* SYN. that's life, such is life, oh well, that's how the cookie crumbles, what can you do?, that's reality.

chafe v. **1.** RUB wear, erode, scrape, abrade, rasp, scour, shred. **2.** IRRITATE *rub the wrong way, annoy, irk, rankle, vex, gall, harass, nag, aggravate.

chaff n. waste, garbage, refuse, rubbish, trash, discards, remains, wastrel, dross.

CHAGRIN n. [shuh GRIN] annoyed embarrassment. *To my chagrin, I discovered that I had left my wallet at home.* SYN. embarrassment, mortification, humiliation, shame, distress, disgruntlement, dismay, annoyance, discomfiture, discomposure, frustration. ANT. *pride, satisfaction.*

chain n. **1.** LINKS cable, fetter, shackle, irons, manacle, mail. **2.** SERIES course, string, train,

line, succession, sequence.

chain v. tie, shackle, fetter, secure, tether, hitch.

chair n. **1.** SEAT stool, bench, rocker, easy chair, straight-backed chair.

WORD FIND

armless, leather-made, with steel frame: Barcelona chair

bench: settee, settle

folding canvas chair: director's chair

high-backed with side wings: wing chair

king's: throne

reclining: recliner

sling, canvas: butterfly chair, sling chair

spindle-backed, wooden: Windsor chair

suspended on poles and carried: sedan

tabletopped arm for writing, chair with: tablet chair

wicker, with rounded back: basket chair

SEE COUCH

2. SEAT OF AUTHORITY office, appointment, fellowship.

chairman n. chairperson, director, principal, leader, president, moderator, chief, master of ceremonies.

chalice n. goblet, vessel. SEE CUP

challenge n. **1.** DIFFICULTY obstacle, trial, test, *hurdle, problem. **2.** PROVOCATION dare, ultimatum, *throwing down the gauntlet, threat, summons, bid.

challenge v. **1.** PRODUCE DIFFICULTY test, try, make demands, tax. **2.** PROVOKE dare, give an ultimatum, *throw down the gauntlet, threaten, gage, defy, summon, beard, make a stand, face off, cross, stare down. **3.** QUESTION contest, dispute, object, take exception, disagree.

chamber n. room, bedroom, boudoir, parlor, sitting room.

champagne n. *bubbly. SEE WINE

champion n. **1.** VICTOR winner, titleholder, *champ, *top dog, conqueror, vanquisher, *number one, medalist. **2.** SUPPORTER backer, advocate, upholder, friend, abettor, defender. ANT. *1. loser, *also-ran, *poor sport. 2. opponent, detractor.*

champion v. support, defend, fight for, stand up for, advocate, back, uphold, espouse, take up the cause. ANT. *oppose, counter, reject.*

chance n. **1.** LUCK fortuity, fortune, serendipity, fate, destiny, *wheel of fortune, providence, *toss of the dice. "A nickname for Providence." —Nicolas Chamfort. "The instrument of Providence." —Horace Walpole. **2.** POSSIBILITY odds, likelihood, probability, prospect, *long shot. **3.** RISK gamble, *toss of the dice, *crap shoot, jeopardy, hazard. **4.** OPPORTUNITY shot, try, opening, occasion, turn.

chance v. **1.** RISK gamble, *roll the dice, take a shot, wager, *go out on a limb, *tempt fate, hazard, speculate, try one's luck. **2.** HAPPEN occur, transpire, come to pass, befall.

chance a. fortuitous, accidental, casual, random, lucky, inadvertent, unplanned. ANT. *planned, designed, arranged.*

chancy a. risky, uncertain, *iffy, dicey, speculative, *a roll of the dice, dangerous. ANT. *certain, guaranteed, assured.*

change n. **1.** ALTERATION modification, transformation, variation, conversion, metamorphosis, shift, remodeling, reformation, adaption, mutation, *about-face, *chameleon, transmutation, refinement, flux, vicissitude. "What people fear most." — Fyodor Dostoyevski. "The unknown." — Eleanor Roosevelt. "Truths being in and out of favor." — Robert Frost. **2.** SOMETHING DIFFERENT novelty, variation, switch, change of pace.

change v. **1.** ALTER modify, transform, vary, convert, metamorphose, shift, remodel, reinvent, reform, adapt, mutate, transmogrify, *do an about-face. **2.** SUBSTITUTE transfer, exchange, switch, alternate, swap, trade, replace, interchange.

changeable a. variable, alternating, erratic, irregular, chameleon, protean, capricious, fickle, labile, mercurial, inconsistent, mutable, transformable, shifting, volatile, *blows hot and cold. ANT. *steady, invariable, regular, stable.*

channel n. conduit, course, strait, waterway, groove, runnel, culvert, trough, run, canal, chase, furrow, rut, trench, sluiceway, flume.

channel v. route, direct, guide, send, funnel, lead, siphon.

chant n. song, plainsong, recitation, psalm, canticle, hymn, Gregorian chant. SEE SONG

chant v. singsong, intone, vocalize, speak in a monotone, utter, recite.

chaos n. disorder, confusion, upheaval, turmoil, disarray, anarchy, jumble, unrest, mess, commotion, pandemonium, disorganization, bedlam, turbulence, *Chinese fire drill. ANT. *order, organization, regularity, tranquility.*

chaotic a. disordered, confused, in disarray, jumbled, messy, turbulent, out of control, topsy-turvy, tumultuous, anarchic, disorganized, random, stormy. ANT. *ordered, organized, systematic.*

chaperone n. escort, overseer, guardian, protector, babysitter.

chaperone v. escort, accompany, attend, protect, babysit, supervise, safeguard, keep an eye on.

chaplain n. clergyman, minister, priest, rabbi, reverend, parson, padre.

chapter n. division, section, episode, part, portion, phase, period.

char v. scorch, sear. SEE BURN

character n. **1.** PERSONALITY nature, makeup, individuality, temperament, constitution, appearance, type, sort, kind, qualities. "[W]hat (a man) would do if he knew he would never be found out." — Thomas Macaulay. **2.** INTEGRITY reputation, standing, position, repute, distinction, honor, status. "Moral order seen through the medium of an individual nature." — Ralph Waldo Emerson. "Mastery over your thoughts and actions." — Mohandas Gandhi. "What God and the angels know of us." — Horace Mann. **3.** ODD PERSON eccentric, oddball, nut, *odd duck, personality, *weirdo, *fruitcake, *original. **4.** ROLE impersonation, portrayal, part. **5.** WRITTEN SYMBOL cipher, mark, figure, letter.

characteristic n. attribute, trait, feature, quality, peculiarity, aspect, mark, distinction, individuality, earmark, idiosyncrasy.

characteristic a. typical, representative, indicative, distinguishing, illustrative, idiosyncratic, marked, peculiar, individual. ANT. *atypical, anomalous.*

characterize v. **1.** PORTRAY describe, represent, depict, sketch. **2.** DISTINGUISH specify, define, style, brand, stamp.

charade n. pretense, fiction, lie, travesty, act.

charge n. **1.** FEE debit, *damage, bill, cost, amount, price. **2.** CARE custody, burden, duty, trust, onus, obligation, ward. **3.** ACCUSATION allegation, indictment, citation. **4.** ATTACK offensive, *blitz, assault, raid. **5.** ORDER command, directive, demand, instruction, mandate, behest, bidding.

charge v. **1.** BILL levy, debit, *ring up, demand payment. **2.** DEBIT ONE'S CREDIT ACCOUNT take on account, put on one's tab, incur a debt, buy on credit. **3.** BURDEN load, weigh, tax, saddle, entrust. **4.** ACCUSE allege, indict, impute, blame, incriminate, *point the finger at, impeach. **5.** ATTACK raid, blitz, assault, storm, rush, assail. **6.** ORDER command, direct, demand, instruct, mandate, bid.

CHARISMA n. [kuh RIZ muh] personal magnetism or charm that inspires others to follow one's lead. *John F. Kennedy had great charisma.* SYN. charm, magnetism, appeal, confidence, *star power, presence, dominance, *it, *pizzazz, sex appeal, power, voice of authority, poise, *je na sais quoi AN INDESCRIBABLE SOMETHING, allure, *the lure of a Svengali.

charitable *a.* **1.** GENEROUS giving, benevolent, philanthropic, freehanded, humanitarian, magnanimous, bighearted. **2.** KIND forgiving, lenient, humane, benevolent, sympathetic, bighearted, soft, merciful, easy. ANT. *1. cheap, stingy, tightfisted, selfish. 2. mean, cruel, thoughtless, intolerant.*

charity *n.* **1.** GENEROSITY benevolence, philanthropy, freehandedness, humanitarianism, magnanimity, altruism, softheartedness. **2.** ALMS contribution, welfare, donation, assistance, aid, benefaction, dole, endowment. "The spice of riches." — Hebrew Proverb. "A debt of honor." — Immanuel Kant. "Doing good for good-for-nothing people." — Elizabeth Barret Browning. **3.** KINDNESS forgiveness, tolerance, lenience, benevolence, sympathy, mercy, softheartedness, compassion. ANT. *1. cheapness, stinginess, miserliness. 3. meanness, cruelty, intolerance.*

charlatan *n.* quack, fake, mountebank, *rip-off artist, imposter, fraud, swindler.

charm *n.* **1.** APPEAL attractiveness, allure, grace, magnetism, charisma, enchantment, fascination, *it, *je ne sais quoi, *pizzazz. "A glow within . . . that casts a most becoming light on others." — John Mason Brown. "A way of getting the answer yes without asking any clear question." — Albert Camus **2.** SPELL OR LUCKY PIECE incantation, magic, sorcery, amulet, talisman, good-luck piece, fetish.

charm *v.* enchant, enamor, fascinate, attract, allure, please, bewitch, captivate, mesmerize, hypnotize, win over, beguile, *sweep off one's feet, spellbind. ANT. *repel, repulse, turn off, disgust.*

charming *a.* attractive, appealing, alluring, magnetic, charismatic, enchanting, beguiling, bewitching, fascinating, winsome, captivating, smooth, irresistible. ANT. *1. repellant, repulsive, disgusting, gross.*

charred *a.* scorched, seared, burned, blackened, singed, carbonized.

chart *n.* map, graph, diagram, outline, blueprint, layout, plot, table, scheme.

chart *v.* map, outline, plot, diagram, draft, plan, draw up, design, graph, scheme.

charter *n.* agreement, contract, franchise, treaty, covenant, sanction, authority, license, permit.

charter *v.* hire, lease, rent, reserve, commission, employ.

chary *a.* **1.** CAREFUL cautious, wary, guarded, mindful, circumspect, suspicious, leery. **2.** SPARING cheap, tight, miserly, niggardly, frugal, stingy. ANT. *1. imprudent, rash, reckless. 2. generous, freehanded.*

chase *v.* **1.** PURSUE follow, track, trail, go after, shadow, *bird-dog. **2.** CHASE OFF oust, drive away, shoo, evict, throw out.

chasm *n.* abyss, gorge, canyon, void, crevasse, gap, gulch, fissure, ravine, rift, bottomless pit, crater. SEE CANYON, CAVE, HOLE

CHASTE *a.* [CHAYST] virtuous, pure or moral. *She was a somewhat puritanical woman and chose to remain chaste.* SYN. virtuous, pure, moral, untouched, clean, *squeaky-clean, decent, abstinent, celibate, modest, righteous, immaculate, uncorrupted, virginal. ANT. *immoral, dirty, lewd, wanton, sleazy, promiscuous.*

chasten *v.* **1.** PUNISH chastise, castigate, correct, admonish, discipline, scold, penalize. **2.** REFINE purify, cleanse, purge.

CHASTISE *v.* [chas TIZE] to punish or discipline. *He was chastised for being foulmouthed.* SYN. punish, discipline, scold, condemn, castigate, admonish, beat, chasten *rake over the coals, *jump down one's throat, *lay into, thrash, ream, spank, whip, *call on the carpet. ANT. *reward, bless.*

chastity *n.* virtue, morality, purity, decency, abstinence, celibacy, righteousness, modesty, virginity, innocence. "A woman's lack of temptation and a man's lack of opportunity." — Anon. "A monkish and evangelical superstition." — Percy Bysshe Shelley. ANT. *promiscuity, nymphomania, adultery, lewdness.* SEE VIRGINITY

chat *v.* talk, converse, gab, jaw, *chew the fat, gossip, *shoot the breeze, *rap, palaver, chitchat, prattle, *schmooze.

chateau *n.* manor, palace, stronghold. SEE CASTLE

chattels *n.* belongings, personal possessions, *things, *stuff, personal effects.

chatter *v.* prattle, *gibber-jabber, jabber, prattle, babble, blab, chitchat, cackle, palaver, prate.

chatterbox *n.* talker, *windbag, gossip, blabbermouth.

CHAUVINISM *a.* [SHO vin izm] blind loyalty to one's own kind, race, sex, etc., with disdain for those who are different. *The sexes earn unequal pay partly due to male chauvinism.* SYN. jingoism, supremacy, male dominance, female dominance, blind patriotism, provincialism, racism, sexism, narrow-mindedness, ethnocentrism, prejudice, bias, bigotry, intolerance, homophobia, nationalism. ANT. *liberality, broad-mindedness.*

chauvinist n. jingo, supremacist, blind patriot, provincialist, racist, sexist, nationalist, bigot, *male chauvinist pig, ethnocentrist.

cheap a. **1.** LOW-PRICED inexpensive, bargain-priced, reasonable, marked-down, cut-rate, economical, *rock-bottom, *dirt-cheap, dime-a-dozen. **2.** POOR QUALITY worthless, inferior, shoddy, *chintzy, *cheesy, tacky, *two-bit, *crappy, *schlock, shabby, common. **3.** STINGY tight, penny-pinching, miserly, niggardly, stinting, grudging. **4.** CONTEMPTIBLE despicable, low, sordid, vulgar, base. ANT. *1. expensive, priceless, steep, exorbitant 2. superior, select, sterling quality. 3. generous, giving. 4. admirable, noble.*

cheapen v. depreciate, degrade, lower, downgrade, diminish.

cheapskate n. Sl. penny-pincher, tightwad, miser, niggard, *nickel-squeezer.

cheat n. **1.** SWINDLE *rip-off, con, fleecing, sham, deception, *fast shuffle, fraud, flimflam, *dirty pool, trick. **2.** SWINDLER *rip-off artist, con, sham artist, chiseler, sharper, flimflam man, crook, rogue, imposter, fraud.

cheat v. defraud, swindle, *rip off, con, burn, bilk, sucker, *rook, screw, fleece, *bamboozle, gouge, *soak, snooker, finagle, double-cross.

check n. **1.** RESTRAINT stop, block, obstacle, limitation, control, damper, curb. **2.** EXAMINATION inspection, review, inquiry, investigation, *look-see.

check v. **1.** RESTRAIN stop, block, obstruct, limit, control, dampen, curb, constrain, foil, harness. **2.** EXAMINE inspect, review, inquire, investigate, look into, *eyeball, scrutinize. **3.** AGREE correspond, conform.

checkered a. **1.** PLAID tattersall, tartan. **2.** VARIED diversified, irregular, patchwork, motley. ANT. *consistent.*

check out v. investigate, look into, probe, scrutinize, inspect, *eyeball.

cheek n. jowl, chop, jaw.

WORD FIND

descriptive: high cheek bones, rawboned, apple cheeks, sunken, pouchy.

cheek by jowl a. close, crowded, intimate, side-by-side, familiar.

cheeky a. impudent, insolent, saucy, impertinent, brazen, bold, brash, audacious, *nervy, *ballsy, forward. ANT. *timid, shy, mousy.*

cheer n. **1.** HURRAH acclamation, shout of approval, *yay, rah, applause, bravo. **2.** CHEERFULNESS high spirits, gladness, gayness, happiness, joyfulness, optimism, joviality, jubilance, buoyancy. "A kind of daylight in the mind." — Joseph Addison. ANT. *1. boo, raspberry, hiss. 2. depression, downheartedness.*

cheerful a. lighthearted, happy, joyful, blithe, buoyant, sunny, optimistic, sanguine, jocund, roseate, gay, carefree, debonair. ANT. *depressed, gloomy, downhearted, glum.*

cheerless a. gloomy, glum, depressed, dark, black, grim, melancholy, funereal, bleak, dismal, dreary, somber, forlorn, despairing. ANT. *cheerful, sunny, lighthearted.*

cheese n. pressed curds, American, Swiss, Brie, Edam, Gouda, Limburger, Jack, Parmesan, Gruyere, cream, mysost, cottage, cheddar. "Milk's leap toward immortality." — Clifton Fadiman.

cherish v. love, adore, hold dear, care for, revere, fancy, hold in high esteem, admire, like, worship, prize, idolize, foster, protect, treasure. ANT. *despise, reject, hate.*

chest n. **1.** THORAX breast, bosom, pectorals. **2.** BOX trunk, crate, casket, cabinet.

chew v. masticate, chomp, champ, grind, crunch, munch, nibble, gnaw.

chew out v. Sl. reprimand, berate. SEE SCOLD

chic a. stylish, elegant, fashionable, smart, *snazzy, current, swank, dapper, chichi.

CHICANERY n. [shi KAY nuh ree] deception, trickery. *A con artist uses all manner of chicanery to separate you from your money.* SYN. deception, trickery, deceit, fraud, subterfuge, double-dealing, underhandedness, dishonesty, cheating, duping, sophistry.

chichi a. SEE CHIC

chicken n. **1.** FOWL hen, biddy, rooster. **2.** *SCAREDY CAT *wimp, *wuss, sissy.

chide v. reprove, scold, *dress down, upbraid, rebuke, reproach, admonish, tell off, give a good talking to, criticize, take to task.

chief n. head, boss, leader, *top dog, *big cheese, president, director, supervisor, master, ringleader, captain, commander, *biggest toad in the puddle, honcho, *cock of the walk. ANT. *subordinate, underling.*

chief a. main, principal, leading, prime, greatest, biggest, supreme, paramount, ruling, cardinal. ANT. *least, smallest.*

chiefly *a.* mainly, principally, primarily, first and foremost, above all, largely, mostly. ANT. *lastly.*

child *n.* **1.** youngster, juvenile, kid, youth, toddler, tyke, nipper, *little shaver, lad, lass, tadpole, adolescent, *teenybopper, moppet, brat, *rug rat, *munchkin. "An ever-bubbling fountain in the world of humanity." — Friedrich Froebel. **2.** INNOCENT naif, babe in the woods.

childbirth SEE BABY, BIRTH, PREGNANCY

childhood *n.* youth, boyhood, girlhood, school days, puberty, adolescence. "A garden of god . . . each day a festival radiant with laughter and play." — Micah Lebensohn. "That wonderful time when all you need to lose weight is to bathe." — Anon.

childish *a.* immature, sophomoric, babyish, adolescent, infantile, juvenile, naive, callow, unsophisticated. ANT. *mature, adult, grown-up.*

chill *n.* cold, frigidity, iciness, rawness, briskness, frostiness, nip, shivers.

chilly *a.* **1.** COLD freezing, frigid, raw, biting, icy, brisk, frosty, shivery, anesthetizing, wintry, nippy, arctic. **2.** UNFRIENDLY cold, icy, aloof, cool, hostile, frigid, unsociable. ANT. *1. hot, *roasting, muggy. 2. friendly, warm, congenial.*

chime *v.* ring, peal, toll, knell, sound, tinkle, jingle, tintinnabulate. SEE BELL

CHIMERA *n.* [kye MEER uh] something impossible or fanciful, after the monster of Greek mythology. *Hank's desire to be president was just a chimera.* SYN. fancy, dream, impossibility, daydream, whim, *castle in the air, *pie in the sky, *fool's paradise, *pipe dream, fantasy, illusion, delusion.

chimney *n.* smokestack.

china *n.* dishes, tableware, porcelain, crockery.

chink *n.* opening, slit, fissure, crack, crevice, cleft, hole, gap, rift.

chintzy *a.* **1.** SHABBY tacky, cheap, sleazy, frowzy, *schlock. **2.** STINGY cheap, miserly, tight, stinting. ANT. *1. elegant, classy, stylish. 2. generous.*

chip *n.* fragment, piece, bit, shard, scrap, sliver, shred, flake, dent, mark, nick, scratch, break, crack, flaw, fault.

chip *v.* fragment, nick, crack, crumble, break off, sliver, fracture, splinter, scratch, flake.

chipper *a.* cheerful, buoyant, high-spirited, cheery, sunny, bright, vivacious, zippy, lively, sprightly, gay, jaunty. ANT. *grim, glum,*

slothful, melancholy.

chirp *v.* tweet, chip, peep, trill, warble, twitter. SEE BIRD

chisel *v.* cut, gouge, carve, engrave, sculpt, tool, incise.

chivalrous *a.* honorable, courageous, noble, gallant, valiant, brave, courteous, courtly, heroic, lionhearted, quixotic, gentlemanly. ANT. *dishonorable, cowardly, brutish, barbaric.*

chivalry *n.* honor, courage, nobility, gallantry, valor, knight-errantry, bravery, courtesy, courtliness, heroism, lionheartedness. ANT. *cowardice, dishonor, rudeness, discourtesy.*

chock-full *a.* packed, chock-a-block, overflowing, brimming, stuffed, crammed, bursting, filled to capacity, *jam-packed. ANT. *empty, barren, devoid.*

choice *n.* selection, preference, choosing, election, determination, vote, decision, druthers, volition, option, desire, pick, wish.

choice *a.* best, superior, excellent, select, first-rate, cream-of-the-crop, vintage, prime. ANT. *poor, fair, ordinary, inferior.*

choke *v.* **1.** STRANGLE throttle, garrote, asphyxiate, suffocate, smother, stifle, wring. **2.** CLOG obstruct, block, close off, occlude, dam, seal, shut, constrict, restrict. ANT. *2. unclog, free, open.*

choleric *a.* quick-tempered, irritable, angry, hotheaded, irascible, touchy, grouchy, *short-fused, testy. ANT. *easy-going, mild-mannered, imperturbable.*

choose *v.* select, pick, elect, wish for, desire, opt for, decide on, determine, prefer, want, single out, call for, fancy, appoint.

choosy *a.* picky, fussy, finicky, particular, selective, persnickety, fastidious, exacting, over-particular, discriminating. ANT. *undiscriminating, *easy.*

chop *n.* blow, whack, swipe, knock, *wallop, *plug, smack, hit.

chop *v.* cut, hew, lop, hack, fell, split, cleave, slash, slice, dice, mince, rend, sever.

choppy *a.* rough, stormy, wavy, violent, bumpy, turbulent, frothy, wild. ANT. *calm, serene, glassy.*

chore *n.* task, job, duty, burden, work, responsibility, charge, bother, *drag, *pain. ANT. *pleasure, recreation, entertainment.*

chortle *v.* chuckle, snort, snicker, snigger, crow, laugh with glee, guffaw, crackle, giggle. SEE LAUGH

chorus *n.* **1.** CHOIR chorale group, glee club, ensemble, choristers. SEE MUSIC **2.** AGREEMENT unison, harmony, concert.

christen v. baptize, name, designate, dub, title.

chronic a. long-term, recurrent, perpetual, constant, habitual, prolonged, protracted, lingering, persistent, stubborn, unabating, continual. ANT. *short-term, temporary.*

chronicle n. history, narrative, accounting, record, annals, archive, chronology, register, log, calendar, journal, diary.

chronological a. in order, ordered, sequential, consecutive, successive, serial, dated.

chubby a. plump, rotund, portly, pudgy, stout, fleshy, *roly-poly, round, *zaftig, tubby, flabby, full-figured, *porky. ANT. *skinny, anorexic, bony.*

chuck v. throw, toss, hurl, heave, pitch, fling, discard, *eighty-six, *shitcan, dump, junk, abandon, get rid of.

chuckle v. chortle, laugh, snicker, snigger, giggle, smile, cluck. SEE LAUGH

chum n. friend, buddy, pal, *bro, companion, comrade, crony, *sidekick, alter ego, *homeboy, *main man, *pardner.

chummy a. friendly, companionable, *palsy-walsy, affectionate, *buddy-buddy, intimate, inseparable, thick, *kissy-huggy, familiar. ANT. *hostile, distant, alienated, estranged.*

chump n. fool, dupe, idiot, *sucker, dope, patsy.

chunk n. hunk, piece, lump, clump, mass, portion, wad, slab, wedge.

chunky a. thick, stocky, thickset, *built like a fireplug, *built like a brick shithouse, stubby, squat, stout, chubby, pudgy. ANT. *skinny, anorexic, *built like linguine, *like a beanpole, willowy.* SEE FAT

church n. chapel, cathedral, house of worship, temple, synagogue, basilica, meeting house, mosque, tabernacle, the Lord's house, bethel, abbey, sanctuary, denomination, sect, faith, affiliation. "God between four walls."—Victor Hugo. "A hospital for sinners."—L.L. Nash. "Wherever one hand meets another helpfully."—John Ruskin.

WORD FIND

altar area reserved for clergy: chancel, sanctuary, presbytery

balcony for choir: choir loft

baptism basin: font

baptism room/section: baptistery

bell ringer: sexton

bell tower: belfry

bench: pew

bishop's church: cathedral

Buddhist: pagoda

central portion/ main area for congregation: nave

collection/revenue: tithe, benefice

confession booth in the Catholic church: confessional

council of bishops: synod

crucifixion sculptures: Calvary

cup: chalice

district: parish

division, difference of opinion: schism

faith/denomination: (Christian) Roman Catholic, Protestant, Methodist, Presbyterian, Lutheran, Mormon, Episcopalian, Unitarian, Baptist, Eastern Orthodox, Pentecostal, Church of the Nazarene, Seventh Day Adventists, Unification Church; Orthodox Judaism; Islam; Hindu; Buddhist

gallery above side aisle: triforium

governing body: classis

grave digger: sexton

high-ranking clergy: prelate

house of clergyman: parsonage, rectory

Italian cathedral: duomo

Jewish house of worship: synagogue

jurisdiction of archbishop: archdiocese

jurisdiction of bishop: diocese

land/property: glebe

laws of: canon

lay authority: elder

light-admitting upper wall: clerestory

members: congregation, fold, flock, Ecclesia

Moslem: mosque

mosque tower: minaret

nunnery: convent

office, endowed: benefice

outreach church supported by larger church: mission

preaching platform: pulpit

reading stand: lectern, ambo

repository for sacraments: ambry

rite: baptism, benediction, communion, mass

semicircular projection and vaulted roof area at east end behind altar: apse

storage room for altar vessels: sacristy

storage room for clergy and choir's robes: vestry

study of architecture, decoration: ecclesiology

table or raised platform: altar

tower: steeple, spire, belfry

underground vault/burial place: crypt

vestibule: narthex, galilee porch

west-side chapel: galilee

window, arched: lancet window

window, large, round, stained glass: catherine wheel, rose window, marigold window

yard, enclosed: parvis

SEE CLERGY, MONASTERY, RELIGION

churchman n. SEE CLERGY

churlish a. surly, mean, grouchy, boorish, loutish, crude, cantankerous, thorny, cranky, cross, huffy, grumpy, dour, sullen, ill-tempered. ANT. *nice, pleasant, civil.*

churn v. stir, agitate, shake, seethe, whip, heave, swirl, whisk, beat.

chute n. waterfall, rapids, trough, passage, slide, channel, gutter, runway, flume.

CHUTZPAH n. [HOOTS puh] nerve, brass, fearlessness. *It takes a lot of chutzpah to cut in line.* SYN. nerve, brass, gall, *balls, audacity, boldness, backbone, spine, cheek, brazenness, arrogance. ANT. *cowardice, mousiness, spinelessness.*

cigar n. stogie, toby, Havana, *smoke, corona, cheroot, panatella, *weed, perfecto.

cigarette n. *smoke, *coffin nail, *butt, *cancer stick, *gasper, *fag, *Kent, *Pall Mall, *Salem, *Kool, *Winston, *Camel, *Marlboro, *Chesterfield. "Killers that travel in packs." —Mary S. Ott.

cinch n. Sl. breeze, snap, *walk on the beach, *child's play, *piece of cake, *duck soup, no sweat. ANT. *killer, *ballbuster, Herculean task.

cinders n. embers, coals, clinkers, slag, ashes.

cinema n. film theater, the movies. SEE MOVIE

cipher n. 1. ZERO nothing, naught, nil, *zip, *goose egg. 2. CODE cryptography. ANT. 1. *infinity*

circa a. about, approximately, roughly.

circle n. 1. RING loop, oval, disc, orb, round, compass, hoop, halo, wheel, orbit, sphere, globe, circuit, coil, circlet, crown. 2. CYCLE revolution, series, period, progression, round. 3. ASSOCIATES group, coterie, crowd, clique, fraternity, sorority, gang, assembly. 4. SPHERE OF INTEREST domain, realm, range, field, province, dominion, bailiwick.

circle v. go around, circumnavigate, encircle, surround, ring, encompass, circumscribe, wheel, roll, loop, pivot, reel.

circuit n. 1. COURSE path, route, cycle, lap, pass, round, tour, run. 2. CIRCLING revolution, orbit. 3. BOUNDARY periphery, border, perimeter, margin, fringe, confines, brink.

CIRCUITOUS a. [sur KYOO i tus] roundabout or indirect. *Much to my irritation, the cabbie took a circuitous route to the airport.*

SYN. roundabout, indirect, circular, meandering, rambling, *long way, *far afield, labyrinthine, devious, *off the beaten path. ANT. *direct, straight.*

circular n. advertisement, flier, handbill, insert, brochure, leaflet, announcement, letter.

circular a. 1. ROUND spherical, spheroid, disklike, globular, oval. 2. CIRCUITOUS roundabout.

circulate v. 1. CIRCLE revolve, mill, move around, wander, tour, course, make the rounds. 2. DISTRIBUTE spread, pass out, disperse, disseminate, publicize, announce.

circulation n. 1. FLOW movement, coursing, circling, rotation, round, tour, revolution. 2. DISTRIBUTION dissemination, transmission, spread.

circumference n. girth, perimeter, periphery, ambit, outline, compass, circuit.

CIRCUMLOCUTION n. [SUR kum loh KYOO shun] an overly wordy or indirect way of saying something. *Circumlocution is the tendency to use ten words when one would do.* SYN. periphrasis, long-windedness, prolixity, rambling, verbosity, redundancy, wordiness, repetition, roundaboutness, *beating around the bush, digression. ANT. *directness, brevity, conciseness.*

CIRCUMSCRIBE v. [SUR kum SKRIBE] to draw a line around, to set limits. *Points of interest on the map were circumscribed. The rule book clearly circumscribes unsportsmanlike conduct.* SYN. 1. enclose, circle, encircle, surround, outline, encompass. 2. bound, confine, limit, restrict, restrain, prohibit, check, hem in, curb, impede, demarcate.

CIRCUMSPECT a. [SUR kum SPEKT] cautious, careful. *John is always circumspect around skunks.* SYN. cautious, careful, wary, mindful, chary, leery, apprehensive, guarded, prudent, vigilant, heedful, scrupulous, judicious. ANT. *careless, reckless, rash.*

circumstance n. situation, case, instance, occasion, incidence, occurrence, matter, episode, condition, contingency, concern, place, time.

circumstances n. course of events, turn of events, situation, predicament, attending factors, condition, state of affairs.

circumstantial a. incidental, indirect, extrinsic, secondary, extraneous, conditional, external, collateral, ancillary, inferred, presumed, deduced, implied, inconclusive. ANT. *central, principal, crucial, firm, concrete.*

circumvent v. get around, dodge, bypass,

avoid, elude, shun, skirt, sidestep, thwart, stymie, outflank, foil, contravene, outwit.

circus *n.* *big top, hippodrome, spectacle, tent show, exhibition, performance, extravaganza. "A show that smells." — Anon.
WORD FIND
arena: ring
procession: caravan, cavalcade
subordinate show: sideshow
swing: trapeze
worker/laborer: rouster, roustabout

cistern *n.* tank, reservoir, vat.

citadel *n.* fortress, fort, stronghold, safehold, bastion, tower, refuge. SEE CASTLE

citation *n.* **1.** SUMMONS subpoena, warrant, charge, call. **2.** CITING quoting, quotation, quote, reference, passage, excerpt, source, extract, text. **3.** HONORABLE MENTION accolade, recognition, commendation, award, reward, kudos.

cite *v.* **1.** SUMMON subpoena, put out a warrant, charge, call. **2.** QUOTE reference, note, excerpt, extract, refer to, provide a source.

citizen *n.* inhabitant, native, resident, subject, national, denizen, freeman, taxpayer, burgher, cosmopolite, *just another brick in the wall, *John/Jane Q. Public. "The most important office." — Louis Brandeis.

city *n.* metropolis, municipality, megalopolis, town, *burg, downtown, suburb, urban complex, boomtown, community, asphalt jungle, urban sprawl, capital, borough. "A herding region." — Elbert Hubbard. "A human zoo." — Desmond Morris. "A stone forest." — John Priestly. "The centre of a thousand trades." — William Cowper. "Millions of people being lonesome together." — Henry Thoreau.
WORD FIND
districts: ward, business district, residential district, ghetto, slums, tenement district, inner city, *skid row, *red light district, tenderloin, hell's kitchen, Chinatown, Little Italy, barrio, greenbelt
official: alderman, councilor, mayor
SEE NEW YORK

civic *a.* municipal, civil, metropolitan, urban, community, communal, public.

civil *a.* **1.** CIVIC municipal, community, communal, public, urban, metropolitan, civilian. **2.** POLITE courteous, well-mannered, proper, civilized, obliging, gracious, urbane, genteel, refined, diplomatic. ANT. *rude, unrefined, barbaric, beastly.*

civilization *n.* **1.** SOCIAL ORGANIZATION culture, refinement, sophistication, education, civility, acculturation, polish, breeding, taming, socialization. "Restrictions, standards, courtesy, indirect methods, justice, reason." — Jose Ortega y Gasset "To convert a man, a beast of prey, into a tame and civilized animal, a domestic animal." — Friedrich Nietzsche. "A concerted effort to remedy the blunders and check the practical joking of God." — Henry Louis Mencken. "A series of victories over nature." — William Harvey. "The lamb's skin in which barbarism masquerades." — Thomas Bailey Aldrich. **2.** HUMANITY society. ANT. **1.** *wildness, wilderness, savagery, barbarism, laws of the jungle.*

civilized *a.* cultured, refined, sophisticated, educated, civil, acculturated, polished, bred, tamed, humane, socialized, socially organized. "To have some quality of consideration for all who cross our path." — Agnes Repplier. ANT. *wild, raw, crude, savage, barbaric.*

clad *a.* dressed, clothed, attired.

claim *v.* **1.** DEMAND take, seek, petition, *have dibs on, exact, expropriate, attach. **2.** ASSERT maintain, insist, allege, proclaim, declare, hold, profess, defend, contend.

clairvoyant *a.* psychic, perceptive, telepathic, extrasensory, prescient, prophetic, second-sighted.

clam *n.* mollusk, quahog, cherrystone, littleneck, steamer.

clamber *v.* climb, scale, *crab, climb with all fours, scrabble, ascend, crawl, shinny. SEE MOUNTAIN CLIMBING

clammy *a.* damp, moist, dank, cold, slimy, mucous, sticky, pasty, sweaty.

clamor *n.* **1.** uproar, outcry, racket, hullabaloo, ballyhoo, hue and cry, babel, shouting, din, noise, hubbub, tumult, chaos, bedlam, commotion, pandemonium, upheaval, brouhaha, disruption. ANT. *silence, tranquility, serenity, peace.*

clamor *v.* cry out, demand, *put up a fuss, call out, shout, *raise the roof, bellow, howl, yell, insist.

clamorous *a.* noisy, loud, confused, uproarious, tumultuous, chaotic, disruptive, deafening, ear-piercing, vociferous. ANT. *quiet, silent, peaceful.*

clamp *n.* vise, hold, grip, clasp, bracket, clip.

clan *n.* tribe, family, dynasty, group, clique, circle, coterie, band, fraternity, society, gang, ring.

CLANDESTINE *a.* [klan DES tin] secret or

undercover, an activity associated with illicit activities. *A clandestine meeting of drug lords.* SYN. secret, undercover, hidden, concealed, surreptitious, *cloak and dagger, *hush-hush, covert, underground, furtive, underhanded, sneaky, conspiratory, back room. ANT. *public, aboveboard, open.*

clang v. ring, clank, reverberate, resound, peal, bong, toll, gong, chime.

clannish a. cliquish, insular, provincial, snobbish, selective, sectarian, parochial, narrow, tribal, exclusive, class conscious, caste conscious. ANT. *friendly, open, broad-minded, accepting, worldly.*

clap n. explosion, crack, thunder, peal, bang, shot, burst, report.

clap v. applaud, give a hand, cheer, slap, strike, rap, whack, slam.

CLAPTRAP n. [KLAP TRAP] pretentious writing or talk designed to win attention. *That all men are unfeeling Neanderthals is feminist claptrap.* SYN. bombast, hogwash, grandstanding, fustian, pretentiousness, insincerity, speciousness, sensationalism, platitude, inflation, sophistry, *bunk, *bilge, twaddle.

clarify v. elucidate, clear up, make plain, explain, show, define, illuminate, simplify, *shed light on, interpret. ANT. *confuse, muddle, obfuscate, *make clear as mud.*

clarity n. clearness, lucidity, plainness, intelligibility, comprehensibility, explicitness, legibility, simplicity, transparency, purity. ANT. *obscurity, haze, fog, fuzziness, distortion.*

clash v. 1. CONFLICT disagree, argue, fight, quarrel, *butt heads, wrangle, feud, scuffle, *lock horns, tussle. 2. CRASH clatter, clang, rattle, jangle, bang. 3. MISMATCH contrast, don't go with, are ill-suited together. ANT. 1. *agree, harmonize, correspond.*

clasp n. catch, hook, snap, fastener, clip, buckle, hasp, pin.

clasp v. grasp, grip, embrace, hold, clutch, clench, squeeze.

class n. 1. SORT kind, category, type, group, caste, genus, grade, species, stripe, variety, breed, division, ilk, order. 2. SOCIAL RANK position, stratum, status, sect, birth, lineage, extraction, place, echelon, hierarchy, pedigree, caste, station, rank, standing. 3. BODY OF STUDENTS study group. 4. COURSE subject, period, lesson, curriculum. 5. Sl. HIGH STYLE elegance, excellence, quality, flair, polish, distinction, fineness, refinement.

class v. SEE CLASSIFY

classic n. model, standard, example, masterpiece, paragon, exemplar, chef-d'oeuvre, ideal, paradigm, archetype, magnum opus.

classic a. 1. EXCELLENT first-class, model, exemplary, superior, extraordinary, quintessential, finest, best, vintage, standard, ideal. 2. TRADITIONAL established, conventional, tried-and-true, regular, standard, prototypical. ANT. 1. *inferior, second-rate, poor.* 2. *radical, *new wave, avant-garde.*

classical a. SEE CLASSIC

classification n. 1. ARRANGEMENT division, grouping, categorization, cataloging, ordering, grading, sorting, *pigeonholing, typing, labeling, assignment. 2. CATEGORY division, group, class, variety, order, grade, type.

classified a. confidential, secret, top secret, private, restricted.

classify v. categorize, arrange, group, catalog, order, grade, sort, *pigeonhole, type, label, assign, organize, rank, systemize.

classy a. first-class, fine, elegant, superior, excellent, high-class, polished, smart, stylish, chic, swanky, fashionable. ANT. *low-class, cheap, chintzy, *slummy.*

clatter v. rattle, crack, smash, clank, clang, jangle.

clause n. article, provision, term, specification, condition, part, section, paragraph, sentence, passage, *catch.

claw n. talon, nail, pincer, hook, spur, nipper.

claw v. scratch, rip, tear, pierce, lacerate, hook, slash, dig, puncture, gouge, gash.

clay n. earth, dirt, loam, mud, soil, sod.

clean v. wash, cleanse, launder, scrub, bathe, freshen up, scour, purify, disinfect, sterilize, deterge, swab, spruce up, shampoo, dust, sanitize, decontaminate. ANT. *soil, dirty, begrime, pollute, mess.*

clean a. 1. NOT DIRTY spotless, washed, fresh, *spic and span, unsoiled, immaculate, *clean as a whistle, laundered, *squeaky clean, scrubbed, antiseptic, scoured, sanitary, bright, sparkling, pure, disinfected, sterile, clear, unpolluted. 2. VIRTUOUS upright, moral, pure, chaste, sinless, innocent, decent, wholesome, respectable, lily-white. 3. FAIR sportsmanlike, honest, aboveboard, respectable, by the rules. 4. TRIM plain, uncluttered, simple, sharp. 5. COMPLETE thorough, entire, whole, clear-cut. ANT. 1. *dirty, filthy, grubby, unsanitary, grimy.* 2. *immoral, filthy, indecent.* 3. *unfair, unsportsmanlike, *below-the-belt.* 4. *busy, ornate, cluttered.* 5. *incomplete, uncertain.*

cleanse v. SEE CLEAN

clear *v.* **1.** CLEAN wipe, tidy, sweep, free, empty, open, rid, remove, liberate, disentangle. **2.** EXONERATE liberate, free, *let off the hook, release, find innocent, absolve, exculpate, acquit, vindicate, *restore one's good name. **3.** PASS OVER miss, *make, steer clear of, hurdle, vault. **4.** CLEAR UP clarify, illuminate, explain, elucidate. ANT. *1. mess up, soil, tangle. 2. find guilty, incriminate. 4. obfuscate, confuse, muddle.*

clear *a.* **1.** APPARENT understandable, clear-cut, obvious, perspicuous, crystal-clear, plain, lucid, transparent, incontrovertible, evident, comprehensible, explicit, unmistakable. **2.** UNOBSTRUCTED open, free, unblocked, unclogged, unhindered, unobstructed, empty. **3.** TRANSPARENT crystal, glassy, see-through, diaphanous, pellucid, translucent, limpid. ANT. *1. unclear, hazy, foggy, fuzzy, incomprehensible. 2. obstructed, blocked, hindered, jammed. 3. opaque, cloudy, fuzzy.*

clearance *n.* *okay, *go, *green light, goahead, authorization, sanction.

clear-cut *a.* clear, definite, distinct, unquestionable, unmistakable, explicit, obvious, express.

clearheaded *a.* rational, of sound mind, lucid, alert, sharp, keen, wide-awake, sane, levelheaded, sensible, composed. ANT. *muddled, confused, hazy, irrational.*

clearly *a.* obviously, plainly, apparently, unquestionably, unmistakably, incontrovertibly, conspicuously, undoubtedly, transparently, positively, overtly, indubitably. ANT. *questionably, doubtfully, unclearly, debatably.*

cleavage *n.* cleft, fissure, gap, chasm, rift, valley.

cleave *v.* **1.** STICK adhere, cling, cohere, hold fast, be faithful, be true. **2.** SPLIT divide, chop, carve, sever, slice, part, rend, rip, cut.

cleft *n.* opening, crack, crevice, break, gap, chink, fissure, slit, schism, split, rift.

CLEMENCY *n.* [KLEM un see] forgiveness, lenience, mercy. *The crook was granted clemency in exchange for information.* SYN. forgiveness, lenience, mercy, mildness, compassion, charity, amnesty, sympathy, softening, quarter, mitigation, easing, softheartedness. ANT. *vindictiveness, cruel and unusual punishment, strictness, harshness, heavy-handedness.*

clench *v.* grip, grasp, hold firm, clutch, clasp, hold, constrict, close. ANT. *loosen, release.*

clergy *n.* ecclesiastics, men of the cloth, ministry, priesthood, churchmen, holy order, prelacy, patorate, presbytery, rabbinate. SEE CLER-GYMAN

clergyman *n.* ecclesiastic, minister, priest, rabbi, preacher, canon, cleric, *dominie, reverend, curate, father, pastor, parson, prelate, chaplain, bishop, cardinal, rector, vicar, man of the cloth, deacon, evangelist, theologian, shepherd, pontiff, man/woman of God. "Ambassadors for Christ." — Bible "A human Sunday." — Samuel Butler.

WORD FIND

abbey's superior female: abbess

abbey's superior male: abbot

assists priest or minister with candles, offerings: acolyte, altar boy

bishop-assisting priest who oversees a territory: archdeacon

bishop, highest ranking: archbishop

cape, short, worn by pope, cardinal and bishop: mozzetta

cathedral superior: dean

collar worn by priest: clerical collar

council of: synod

deacon's wide-sleeved tunic worn over alb: dalmatic

England, parish priest in: vicar

garment, general term: vestment

hat, squarish, with three or four projections, Roman Catholic: biretta

hat worn by bishop: miter

high-ranking minister who oversees a diocese: bishop

Hindu's spiritual teacher: guru

house of: rectory, parsonage, manse

Jewish minister: rabbi

long open cloak worn by bishop: cope

Lutheran, Baptist or Pentecostal minister: pastor

monk/friar's robe: frock

mosque official who calls faithful to prayer from minaret: muezzin

mosque's prayer leader: imam

Muslim authority: ayatollah

pope: pontiff

pope's assistant, second-highest in Catholic hierarchy: cardinal

pope's office: papacy

pope's palace home: Vatican

robe, long and white, worn by priest for Mass: alb

Roman Catholic's highest-ranking: pope

salary: prebend

school for: seminary

sleeveless mantle worn by priest at communion: chasuble

square cloth worn by priest over shoulders:

amice
strip one of power due to unethical behavior:
defrock
synagogue's prayer leader/singer: cantor
vestment, full-length, usually black, worn by
priest: cassock
waist cord of alb: cincture
white, wide-sleeved, knee or hip-length garment: surplice
SEE CHURCH, RELIGION

clerical a. ecclesiastical, churchly, ministerial,
priestly, pastoral, religious. ANT. secular, lay.

clerk n. salesman/woman, cashier, teller, office
worker, bookkeeper, *desk jockey. SEE OFFICE
WORKER

clever a. intelligent, adroit, bright, ingenious,
smart, dexterous, shrewd, quick, witty, facile, *brainy, versatile, sharp, savvy, inventive, capable, handy, resourceful, imaginative. ANT. stupid, bovine, dull, moronic.

cliché n. banality, trite remark, bromide, *chestnut, old saw, *old line, *tired line, hackneyed expression, platitude, *old story, stereotype. "Only something well said in the
first place." — William Granger.

clichéd a. trite, hackneyed, tired, worn out, stereotyped.

click v. 1. TICK clack, snap, clink, chink, rattle.
2. WORK TOGETHER SUCCESSFULLY come to-
gether, fit, fall into place.

client n. customer, patron, consumer, buyer,
*regular.

clientele n. clients, customers, patrons, following, trade, business, regulars, market.

cliff n. precipice, bluff, scarp, escarpment, overlook, overhang, ledge, headland, promon-
tory, peak, summit, palisade, crag. SEE MOUN-
TAIN

climate n. 1. WEATHER clime, temperature, me-
teorological conditions. 2. ATMOSPHERE air,
ambience, feel, tone, undertone, sense, aura,
spirit, character, mood, disposition.

climax n. culmination, highest point, peak,
acme, pinnacle, crest, zenith, maximum,
summit, critical mass, apex, turning point,
climacteric. ANT. anticlimax, low, nadir. SEE
ORGASM

climb v. ascend, scale, mount, clamber, shinny,
*climb hand over hand, rise, swarm, esca-
lade, scramble up, descend. SEE MOUNTAIN
CLIMBING

clime n. SEE CLIMATE

clinch v. 1. FASTEN secure, fix, make fast, set,
attach, bolt. 2. WIN CONCLUSIVELY OR SETTLE
finish off, close, culminate, confirm, decide,

put all doubts to rest, sew up, cap, *put on
ice.

clincher n. crowning blow, finisher, closer,
deathblow, culmination, capper, *coup de
grace, settler, finishing touch.

cling v. stick, adhere, hold, clasp, cleave to, cohere, embrace, be attached to, cherish. ANT.
release, let go, repel.

clinic n. dispensary, infirmary, sick bay, hospital, outpatient ward.

clinical a. scientific, analytic, objective, detached, impersonal, dispassionate, unemotional. ANT. personal, subjective, involved.

clink v. jingle, jangle, tinkle, ring, tink.

clip n. fastener, clasp, holder, pin, hasp.

clip v. 1. ATTACH fasten, pin, couple, hook, grip.
2. CUT snip, crop, trim, bob, shorten, shave,
shear, scissor, *buzz, prune, mow. 3. REDUCE
shorten, curtail, abridge. ANT. 3. lengthen, increase.

CLIQUE n. [KLIK] an exclusive group or circle
of people, sometimes of a snobbish nature.
High school is notorious for its cliques. SYN. coterie, group, crowd, in crowd, circle, band,
clan, set, gang, faction, bunch, crew, pack.

cloak n. 1. CAPE mantle, wrap, dolman, overcoat, robe, pelisse, capote. 2. DISGUISE cover,
mask, masquerade, guise, concealment,
front, pretext.

cloak v. cover, conceal, hide, mask, disguise,
veil. ANT. uncover, reveal, unmask.

clobber v. punch, pound, beat, wallop, pummel, hit, strike, belt, drub, thrash, *slug,
*sock.

clock n. timepiece, chronometer, timer, watch,
hourglass.

clod n. dolt, moron, idiot, simpleton, dunce,
halfwit, ignoramus, oaf, nitwit, blockhead,
*chowderhead.

clodhopper n. hick, yokel, bumpkin, hayseed,
rustic, farmer, hillbilly, *cider squeezer.

clog n. blockage, obstacle, jam, congestion,
stoppage, barrier, occlusion, encumbrance,
clot, bottleneck.

clog v. block, obstruct, jam, congest, stop, bar,
occlude, encumber, clot, close, choke, fill,
impede, stuff, cram, gum up. ANT. open, free,
clear.

cloister n. 1. SECLUDED REFUGE asylum, retreat,
sanctuary, haven, monastery, abbey, convent. 2. COVERED WALKWAY colonnade, arcade, courtyard, ambulatory, promenade,
archway, gallery.

CLOISTERED a. [KLOIS terd] secluded,
sheltered. Monks enjoy a cloistered lifestyle.

SYN. secluded, sheltered, reclusive, solitary, sequestered, hidden, shielded, remote, aloof, segregated, hermitic, insular. ANT. *public, conspicuous.*

close n. ending, finale, finish, completion, windup, culmination.

close v. 1. SHUT seal, lock, secure, bolt, bar, shutter. 2. COMPLETE finish, *wind down, *call it a day, end, cease, finalize, *put to bed, fold up, terminate, stop, discontinue, shut down. 3. JOIN unite, merge, fuse, couple, connect. ANT. *1. open, broach. 2. begin, start, open. 3. separate, divide.*

close a. 1. NEAR proximate, at hand, handy, next to, immediate, *under one's nose, *within shouting distance, bordering, nigh, in close proximity, approaching, contiguous, neighboring. 2. DENSE cramped, thick, compact, packed, congested, crowded, solid, confined, narrow, stuffed. 3. INTIMATE friendly, familiar, chummy, inseparable, *buddy-buddy, attached, *thick with, *cosy with. 4. SIMILAR comparable, alike, like, much the same, analogous, near, akin. 5. OP-PRESSIVE humid, stuffy, airless, muggy, unventilated, heavy, stifling, suffocating, thick. 6. STINGY tight, miserly, tight-fisted, niggardly, *penny-pinching, penurious. ANT. *1. far, distant, remote. 2. loose, roomy, commodious. 3. unfamiliar, distant, cool. 4. dissimilar, opposite, contrasting. 5. airy, breezy, fresh. 6. generous, free-spending, extravagant.*

closefisted a. tightfisted, tight, cheap, stingy, miserly, niggardly, penny-pinching, parsimonious, penurious. ANT. *generous, giving, openhanded.*

closemouthed a. uncommunicative, taciturn, quiet, reserved, laconic, tight-lipped, reticent, retiring, mute. ANT. *talkative, loquacious.*

closet n. storeroom, cupboard, locker, compartment, wardrobe, cubbyhole.

clot n. grume, embolism, lump, mass, coagulation, occlusion.

clot v. coagulate, congeal, set, thicken, clog, coalesce, solidify. ANT. *thin, liquefy, flow.*

cloth n. fabric, textile, material, weave, dry goods.

clothe v. dress, attire, fit out, garb, don, vest, put on, outfit, deck out, doll up, tog, costume, caparison, adorn. ANT. *strip, undress.*

clothes n. pl. SEE CLOTHING

clothing n. apparel, dress, attire, garb, wear, garments, habiliments, wardrobe, getup, duds, *threads, *rags, costume, finery, outfit,

vestment, tog, *civvies. "The reflection of one's self-respect." "Two-thirds of beauty." — Welsh proverb. SEE BOOT, COAT, DRESS, HAT, JACKET, PANTS, SHIRT, SHOE, SKIRT, SWEATER

cloud n. vapor, mist, fog, haze, steam, puff, veil, billow, overcast, gloom, nebula. "The only birds that never sleep." — Victor Hugo.

WORD FIND

aircraft trail: contrail

boiling, billowing or breastlike, severe thunderstorm: mammatocumulus

bulging: billowing

cauliflowerlike, fair-weather cloud: cumulus, stratocumulus

circle around sun or moon: halo

continuous, layered, low: stratus

descriptive: buttermilk sky

feathery tuft: cirrus, mare's tail

fleecy cumulus cloud: woolpack, sheep, altocumulus

gray, thick and shapeless rain cloud: nimbostratus

horsetail-like cirrus cloud: mare's tail

mass broken off by wind: rack

rain-producing: nimbus

referring to: nubilous

ripples or bands: cirrocumulus, mackeral sky

study of: nephology

swift-moving, dark storm patch: scud

thunder and lightning: thunderhead

thunderhead's anvil-shaped top: incus

veils, thin and white, covering most of sky: cirrostratus

wisp trailing from rain cloud: virga

SEE FOG, RAIN

cloud v. befog, darken, obscure, veil, dim, cloak, blind, muddle. ANT. *clear, illuminate.*

cloudy a. 1. OVERCAST gray, dreary, dismal, hazy, murky, partly sunny, nubilous, lowery, lowering, turbid, leaden, misty, foggy, murky. 2. OBSCURE vague, indistinct, blurry, nebulous, fuzzy, unclear, hazy, confused, muddled, mysterious. ANT. *1. clear, sunny, bright, radiant. 2. clear, distinct, certain.*

clout n. 1. BLOW rap, hit, whack, clip, *sock. 2. INFLUENCE power, weight, *pull.

cloverleaf n. interchange, overpass, on-off ramp. "Our national flower . . . the concrete cloverleaf." — Lewis Mumford. SEE STREET

clown n. buffoon, jester, joker, merry-andrew, comic, *cutup, prankster, zany, mime, harlequin, card, wit.

CLOY v. [KLOY] to make sick of something from having too much. *Try to eat a pound of* chocolate and it will soon cloy. SYN. sicken, satiate, surfeit, displease, nauseate, glut, sate, overdo, gag, weary, pall. ANT. entice, tantalize.

club n. **1.** STICK bat, cudgel, billy, mace, truncheon, blackjack, bludgeon, shillelagh. **2.** ASSOCIATION organization, society, fraternity, sorority, clique, affiliation, coterie, alliance, lodge, order. "A wealthy man's saloon."— Anon.

club v. hit, strike, bat, batter, cudgel, baste, beat, clout, blackjack, slug.

clue n. hint, tip, tipoff, *lead, sign, telltale, inkling, inference, pointer, implication, *dead giveaway, evidence, suggestion, trace, mark.

clump n. **1.** CLUSTER aggregation, bunch, group, lump, mass, clod, thicket, bushes. **2.** THUMP clomp, stomp, bump, bang, thud, *thunk.

clumsy a. **1.** KLUTZY oafish, inept, ungainly, bumbling, maladroit, awkward, gauche, graceless, fumbling, *all thumbs, *having two left feet, clodish, butterfingered, blundering, lumbering, uncoordinated. **2.** UNWIELDY awkward, cumbersome, bulky, unmanageable, ponderous. ANT. 1. coordinated, graceful, nimble, adroit. 2. handy.

cluster n. bunch, clump, mass, group, body, crowd, assembly, knot, collection, congregation.

clutch v. grasp, snatch, seize, grip, grab, catch, nab, snare, clench, hold, squeeze. ANT. release, drop.

clutches n. power, control, grip, hands, rule, possession, custody.

clutter n. mess, disorder, jumble, litter, trash, disarray, hodgepodge, chaos. ANT. order, neatness, tidiness.

clutter v. mess, disorder, jumble, litter, *trash, strew about, scatter. ANT. neaten, order, arrange, clean.

coach n. **1.** TRAINER teacher, tutor, instructor, mentor, *whip, taskmaster, drillmaster, athletic director. **2.** CARRIAGE stage, brougham, landau, phaeton, coupe, buggy.

coach v. train, teach, tutor, instruct, *whip into shape, drill, direct, guide, school, cram.

coachman n. driver, jehu, hack, whip.

coagulate v. clot, curdle, mass, lump, congeal, gel, thicken, set, condense, cake. ANT. thin, liquefy.

COALESCE v. [KOH uh LES] to come together or merge as one, fuse. The two factions coalesced in order to fight a common enemy. SYN. come together, merge, unite, fuse, weld, consolidate, blend, cohere, integrate, incorporate, combine, mingle. ANT. divide, fragment, split, separate.

COALITION n. [KOH uh LISH un] an alliance or union. The coalition of environmentalists will be lobbying for cleaner air. SYN. alliance, union, association, confederacy, faction, league, bloc, partnership, cartel, consolidation, cooperative, merger.

coarse a. **1.** ROUGH gritty, scratchy, grainy, harsh, unpolished, bumpy, bristly, unrefined. **2.** INFERIOR poor, second-rate, shoddy, common, mediocre. **3.** VULGAR unrefined, crude, rough-hewn, crass, uncouth, offensive, uncultured, earthy, foulmouthed, ill-mannered, churlish, impolite. ANT. 1. smooth, polished, refined. 2. superior, first-rate, high quality. 3. refined, cultured, polite, gentlemanly, well-mannered.

coast n. shore, beach, strand, seaboard, seaside, littoral. SEE BEACH

coast v. glide, slide, skim, glissade, drift, roll.

coat n. **1.** FUR pelt, fleece, wool, hide, pelage, fell. **2.** COATING covering, finish, layer, lamination. **3.** OVERCOAT jacket, wrap, tog, topcoat, windbreaker.

WORD FIND

classic with black velvet collar: chesterfield
formal: tails, tuxedo
full-length: maxi
large overcoat: greatcoat
long, loose with wide sleeves cut in one piece with shoulders: raglan
long raincoat or overcoat with several pockets, belt: trenchcoat
midlength: midi
raincoat: slicker, trenchcoat
sportcoat: blazer
toggle-buttoning: toggle coat, duffel coat
waterproof coat with drawstring hood: stadium coat
woman's long coat with large pockets: duster
woolen, plaid and short: mackinaw
SEE JACKET

coax v. cajole, wheedle, persuade, talk into, lure, press, *rope in, beg, *butter up, beguile, blandish, play up to, con, sweet talk, inveigle.

cocaine n. narcotic, *coke, *snow, *crack, *happy dust, *joy powder, *snort, *toot.

cock n. rooster, cockerel.

cock v. prick, raise, stick up.

cockeyed a. **1.** CROOKED askance, askew, lopsided, cross-eyed, awry, off-center. **2.** RIDICULOUS silly, foolish, preposterous, stupid, absurd, whacky, *cockamamie, insane, *nuts.

ANT. *1. straight, centered. 2. sane, rational.*

cocksure *a.* confident, self-assured, unblinking, unflinching, sure, positive, certain, cocky, arrogant, overconfident, full of oneself, egotistical, bloated, swaggering, strutting, overbearing, smug, brash. ANT. *unsure, uncertain, timid, mousy, shy, tentative.*

cocktail *n.* mixed drink, aperitif. "Drinks that passion the night." — Anon. SEE ALCOHOL, DRINK, GLASS, LIQUEUR, WINE

WORD FIND

bourbon, bitters, soda, sugar: old-fashioned

bourbon, boiling water, sugar, cloves, cinnamon: hot toddy

bourbon, mint leaves, syrup: mint julep

gin, cream, creme de cacao, nutmeg garnish: Alexander

gin, grenadine, cream: pink lady

gin, vermouth, olive: martini

glass: cocktail glass, cooler, delmonico, highball, snifter, wine glass

Kahlua, cream: sombrero

red wine, fruit juice and brandy: sangria

rum, sweet and sour: Daiquiri

Scotch, drambuie: rusty nail

Scotch, vermouth, cherry garnish: Rob Roy

sloe gin, Southern Comfort, orange juice: slow comfortable screw

sloe gin, sweet and sour, soda, cherry garnish: sloe gin fizz

tequila, sweet and sour, rim of glass frosted with salt: Margarita

vodka, beef bouillon: bull shot

vodka, Kahlua: black Russian

vodka, orange juice, Galliano: Harvey Wallbanger

vodka, orange juice: screwdriver

vodka, worcestershire sauce, tomato juice: Bloody Mary

whiskey, ginger ale: highball

whiskey IRISH, hot coffee, whipped cream: Irish coffee

whiskey, sweet and sour, cherry: whiskey sour

whiskey, vermouth with cherry: Manhattan

cocky *a.* SEE COCKSURE

coddle *v.* pamper, mollycoddle, baby, indulge, spoil, cater to, cosset, dote on.

code *n.* **1.** SECRET WRITING cipher, cryptograph, cryptogram. **2.** LAWS regulations, standards, rules, canon, ethics, system, charter.

codicil *n.* appendix, addendum, rider.

codify *v.* classify, order, group, catalog, file, organize, arrange.

COERCE *v.* [koh URS] to force one to do something by intimidation or threats. *Tom didn't want to forge the check; he was coerced into it by his peer group.* SYN. force, compel, persuade, bully, impel, strong-arm, pressure, railroad, constrain, impel, scare, make, cow, intimidate, *twist one's arm.

coercion *n.* force, pressure, duress, bullying, persuasion, strong-arm tactics, railroading, constraint, scare tactics, intimidation, threats, menacing, *heat, *arm-twisting.

coffee *n.* espresso, cafe au lait, cafe noir, cappuccino, *mud, *machine oil, brew, *battery acid, *joe, *java, *pick-me-up, *decaf, mocha, *crude, *blackstrap, *paint remover. "Break fluid." — R.R. Anderson.

coffer *n.* chest, strongbox, safe, vault.

coffers *n.* treasury, funds, finances, capital, means, assets, reserves.

coffin *n.* casket, pine box, catafalque, sarcophagus, pall, *wooden overcoat. "An ornamental . . . box which no one cares to open." — Elbert Hubbard. SEE CEMETERY, FUNERAL

COGENT *a.* [KOH junt] strongly convincing. *His argument was cogent.* SYN. convincing, compelling, persuasive, effective, forceful, powerful, meaningful, conclusive, sound, potent, weighty. ANT. *unconvincing, ineffective, weak.*

cogitate *v.* ponder, consider, meditate, weigh, think over, contemplate, deliberate.

cognate *a.* alike, akin, associated, related, kindred, common, generic, affiliated, connected. ANT. *unlike, unrelated, different.*

COGNIZANT *a.* [KOG ni zunt] aware; conscious. *Are you cognizant of the deteriorating environment?* SYN. aware, conscious, informed, familiar, knowing, acquainted with, enlightened, mindful, apprised, in the know, understanding. ANT. *ignorant, unaware, oblivious.*

cohere *v.* **1.** STICK adhere, cling, attach, bind, hold, unite, join. **2.** AGREE harmonize, correspond, concur, coincide.

coherence *a.* agreement, consistency, harmony, correspondence, concurrence, congruity, unity, cohesion, accord. ANT. *incoherence, inconsistency.*

COHERENT *a.* [ko HEER unt] intelligible; making sense. *He'd had a few drinks but he was still coherent.* SYN. intelligible, rational, logical, lucid, articulate, understandable, comprehensible. ANT. *incoherent, unintelligible, confusing, nonsensical.*

cohort *n.* associate, colleague, companion, sidekick, supporter, buddy, pal, chum, accomplice, ally, comrade.

coiffure n. hairdo, *do, cut, permanent, trim. SEE HAIR

coil n. ring, helix, circle, spiral, vortex, loop, convolution, corkscrew, curlicue, braid.

coil v. wind, spiral, twist, turn, loop, twirl, corkscrew, snake, twine, convolute, sinuate.

coin n. piece, specie, copper, change, money, legal tender, coinage, *pin money.

coin v. devise, invent, make up, create, conceive, originate, think up, dream up, fabricate, compose; mint, neologize.

coincide v. agree, equal, synchronize, square, accord, dovetail, fit, correspond, harmonize, jibe, match, be synonymous, be concurrent. ANT. disagree, differ.

coincidence n. happenstance, chance, fluke, fortuity, accident, serendipity, synchronicity, *fickle finger of fate.

coincidental a. chance, accidental, fortuitous, fluky, serendipitous, lucky, casual, circumstantial.

coitus n. sexual intercourse, copulation, fornication, *roll in the hay, *screwing. SEE SEX

cold n. virus, *bug, cough, runny nose, *sniffles, fever, coryza, nasal congestion. "An ailment cured in two weeks with a doctor's care, and in fourteen days without it." — C.C. Furnas.

cold a. CHILLY frigid, wintry, icy, freezing, arctic, nippy, cool, raw, biting, brisk, bitter, numbing, *anesthetizing, below zero, frosty, piercing, stinging, algid, hyperboreal, gelid, drafty, Siberian, bone-chilling, *teeth-chattering cold. 2. UNFRIENDLY OR ALOOF icy, distant, frosty, stony, apathetic, unsociable, remote, unapproachable, closed. 3. COLD-BLOODED uncaring, unfeeling, cruel, mean, icy, cool, stony, insensitive, heartless, distant, soulless, brutal, callous, ruthless, merciless. ANT. 1. hot, sweltering. 2. warm, friendly, open. 3. sympathetic, humane, merciful.

cold-blooded a. SEE COLD

coldhearted a. SEE COLD

coliseum n. arena, stadium, ampitheater, bowl, theater.

collaborate v. work together, cooperate, team up, conspire, collude, join forces, coauthor.

collaborator n. contributor, partner, coworker, colleague, *partner in crime, coauthor, confederate, quisling.

collapse n. 1. CAVE-IN fall, cataclysm, toppling, breakdown, failure, foundering, buckling, crash, undoing, downfall, disintegration. 2. FALLING ILL breakdown, fainting, succumbing, seizure, prostration, loss of consciousness.

collapse v. 1. CAVE IN fall, crumple, crumble, topple, break, give way, give out, fail, founder, buckle, slump, fold up, *collapse like a house of cards. 2. FALL ILL keel over, break down, succumb, wilt, be stricken, lose consciousness, slump over, swoon.

collar v. nab, seize, catch, capture, nail, apprehend, bring into custody. SEE ARREST

collate v. sort, order, group, arrange, juxtapose.

collateral n. security, insurance, warranty, surety, pledge, guarantee, bond.

collateral a. secondary, ancillary, subordinate, indirect, supporting, corroborating, parallel, incidental, supplementary. ANT. primary, fundamental.

colleague n. associate, coworker, confederate, cohort, collaborator, partner, confrere, *partner in crime, compatriot, peer, teammate.

collect v. 1. ACCUMULATE OR ASSEMBLE gather, harvest, reap, amass, hoard, save, round up, pile up, squirrel away, compile; congregate, flock, group, muster, convene, meet, cluster. 3. OBTAIN acquire, solicit, raise, *pass the hat, get. 4. PICK UP get, fetch, gather, take away 5. PULL ONESELF TOGETHER gather one's wits, calm down, *get it together, regain one's composure, relax.

collected a. composed, calm, cool, level-headed, unruffled, unperturbed, self-possessed, poised, unflappable, placid, at ease, nonchalant. ANT. agitated, nervous, flustered, perturbed, ill-at-ease.

collection n. 1. ACCUMULATION cumulation, mass, group, assortment, assembly, pile, gathering, stockpile, store, hoard, cluster, congregation, aggregation, compilation, anthology, hodgepodge. 2. OFFERING tithe, offertory, contribution, alms.

collective n. cooperative, co-op, company.

collective a. combined, composite, aggregate, mutual, corporate, common, cumulative, compound, joint, unified.

college n. university, school, academy, institution, seminary, alma mater, *halls of ivy, vocational school, polytechnic, graduate school, campus. "[Where one] may learn the 'principles' of salesmanship from a Ph.D. who has never sold anything, or the 'principles' of marketing from a Ph.D. who has never marketed anything." — Abraham Flexner. "A place where pebbles are polished and diamonds are dimmed." — Robert Ingersoll. **WORD FIND**

advanced degree: postgraduate degree, master's, doctorate

advanced studies after graduation: postgraduate work

agricultural college: cow college

brotherhood: fraternity

charge for instruction: tuition

course: major, minor, elective

dining hall: refectory

exams: midterms, finals

general knowledge studies: liberal arts

girl: coed

graduate: alumnus

graduates: alumni

graduate "with great praise" or honors: magna cum laude

graduate "with highest praise" or highest honors: summa cum laude

graduation ceremony: commencement

grounds: campus, quad, quadrangle

half year: semester

housing: dorm, dormitory

leave of absence, professor's: sabbatical

official: dean, regent, provost, registrar

permanence of position granted to professor: tenure

president: chancellor, prexy

relating to: collegiate

sisterhood: sorority

student: freshman, *(Frosh); sophomore; junior; senior

teacher: professor

treasurer: bursar

SEE DEGREE, SCHOOL, UNIVERSITY

collide *v.* **1.** CRASH INTO bump, meet head-on, smash, plow into, bang, hit, sideswipe, *t-bone. **2.** DISAGREE clash, conflict, oppose.

collision *n.* crash, *smashup, *fenderbender, impact, bump, accident, *crack-up, blow, jolt, pileup, wreck.

COLLOQUIAL *a.* [kuh LOH kwee ul] designating informal or conversational speech, writing, etc. *A relaxed, colloquial form of writing is often best.* SYN. conversational, informal, everyday, *street, chatty, casual, familiar, vernacular, folksy, homey, simple, unaffected, unstudied. ANT. *formal, literary, pedantic.*

colloquy *n.* talk, conversation, dialogue, discussion, chat, discourse, council, conference.

COLLUSION *n.* [kuh LOO zhun] a conspiracy. *Fred worked in collusion with the drug cartel to smuggle narcotics.* SYN. conspiracy, secret agreement, intrigue, *dirty dealings,

complicity, *cahoots, deceit, racket, scheme, fraud.

colony *n.* **1.** SETTLEMENT community, outpost, dependency, province, possession, territory. **2.** GROUP community, band, flock.

color *n.* **1.** HUE tint, shade, tinge, cast, tone, coloring, pigment, dye, paint, stain. **2.** COMPLEXION color, tone, bloom, blush, flush, ruddiness, rosiness, glow.

color *v.* **1.** PAINT dye, tint, tinge, stain, suffuse, cast, daub, wash, blazon, imbue. **2.** BLUSH redden, glow, flush, bloom, brighten, burn, flame, turn crimson.

colored *a.* distorted, influenced, biased, partial, exaggerated, jaundiced, prejudiced, misrepresented, affected. ANT. *unbiased, objective.*

colorful *a.* **1.** BRIGHTLY OR VARIOUSLY COLORED vivid, vibrant, multihued, chromatic, striking, showy, gaudy, pavonine, iridescent, rainbowlike, florid, loud, kaleidoscopic, screaming, variegated, graphic, eye-catching, picturesque, psychedelic. **2.** INTERESTING unusual, dynamic, eccentric, distinctive, unique, offbeat, glamorous, extravagant. ANT. **1.** *achromatic, pallid, lackluster.* **2.** *dull, drab, nondescript, *ho-hum, *as distinctive as a plain brown wrapper, *as distinctive as a brick in the wall.*

colorless *a.* **1.** ACHROMATIC blanched, pale, pallid, lackluster, bleached, washed-out, neutral, faded, dull, gray, transparent. **2.** UNINTERESTING dull, drab, nondescript, *ho-hum, *as distinctive as a plain brown wrapper, lifeless, vapid, *as eye-catching as a brick in the wall. ANT. **1.** *chromatic, vivid, vibrant, pavonine.* **2.** *colorful, distinctive, glamorous.*

colors *n.* flag, banner, standard, insignia, badge.

colossal *a.* huge, gigantic, gargantuan, massive, titanic, monstrous, towering, immense, monumental, Brobdingnagian, enormous, *humongus, awe-inspiring, mammoth, herculian, prodigious, staggering, mighty, commanding. ANT. *microscopic, tiny, pocket-sized, pint-sized, insignificant, Lilliputian.*

colossus *n.* giant, titan, monster, leviathan, behemoth, mammoth, mountain, Gargantua, Goliath, Cyclops, Hercules, Samson, Godzilla. ANT. *midget, dwarf, *shrimp, *pipsqueak.* SEE MONSTER, STATUE, WHALE

colt *n.* foal, yearling. SEE HORSE, ROOKIE

coltish *a.* frisky, frolicsome, playful, gamboling, spirited, romping, perky. ANT. *lethargic, slothful.*

column *n.* **1.** PILLAR support, pilaster, post, pier, upright, shaft pylon.

WORD FIND
base: plinth, pedestal
classical orders: Ionic, Doric, Corinthian, Composite, Tuscan
eight columns, having: octastyle
five columns, having: pentastyle
four columns, having: tetrastyle
man-figure column: atlas
porch, columned: portico
series of: colonnade
six columns, having: hexastyle
ten columns, having: decastyle
top: capital
two columns, having: distyle
woman-figure column: caryatid
2. LINE row, file, formation, string, procession, train.

coma n. unconsciousness, stupor, catalepsy, oblivion, deep sleep. SEE SLEEP

comatose a. unconscious, cataleptic, stuporous, insensate, *out of it, lifeless, unresponsive, inert, sluggish.

comb v. **1.** SEARCH seek, look over thoroughly, rake, scour, *beat the bushes. **2.** DRESS HAIR fix, arrange, brush, style, smooth, unsnarl.

combat v. fight, struggle, contend, battle, oppose, contest, war, clash, skirmish. ANT. make peace, pacify, surrender, cooperate.

combatant n. fighter, warrior, soldier, contender, battler, assailant, enemy, foe, antagonist. ANT. peacemaker, dove.

combative a. contentious, antagonistic, pugnacious, belligerent, aggressive, quarrelsome, militant, hawkish, hostile. ANT. peaceful, passive, deferential.

combination n. **1.** COMBINING mixture, mix, amalgam, amalgamation, blending, aggregation, conglomeration, assemblage, joining, union, compound, composite, consolidation. **2.** ASSOCIATION alliance, union, affiliation, coalition, league, faction, federation, partnership, bloc.

combine v. **1.** MIX join, unite, amalgamate, blend, aggregate, conglomerate, assemble, compound, consolidate, merge, wed, mingle. ANT. separate, divide.

combustible a. flammable, inflammable, ignitable, burnable, explosive, incendiary.

combustion n. burning, ignition, flame, kindling, incineration, blazing, oxidation.

come v. **1.** APPROACH near, draw near, close in, move toward, advance. **2.** SHOW UP show, appear, make an appearance, arrive, pop in, roll in, turn up, *blow in, drop in, materialize, check in. **3.** TAKE PLACE occur, arrive, happen, fall, arise, ensue, transpire, come to pass. ANT. **1.** go, leave, depart.

comeback n. **1.** REVIVAL resurgence, rebirth, return, recovery, rally. **2.** SNAPPY REPLY retort, rejoinder, riposte, repartee, witticism, esprit de l'escalier, answer.

comedian n. comic, comedienne, joker, clown, humorist, funnyman, wit, entertainer, buffoon, jester, *zany, cutup, *card, *top banana. ANT. straight man.

comedy n. **1.** FARCE burlesque, vaudeville, slapstick, parody, satire, lampoon, travesty, comedy of errors, comedy of manners, send-up, takeoff, sitcom, *schtick, *bit, skit, *stand-up. **2.** HUMOR joking, jesting, silliness, hilarity, gags, buffoonery, cutting up, parody, satire, drollery, *poking fun, slapstick, physical comedy, black comedy, *one-liners. "A funny way of being serious."— Peter Ustinov. "The very last alternative to despair."— Franklin Marcus. ANT. **1.** tragedy. **2.** solemnity, seriousness, gloom.

comely a. attractive, beautiful, fair, lovely, pretty, handsome, pleasing, *nice, good-looking, cute, bonny, winsome, fine. ANT. ugly, *butt-ugly, repulsive, plain, homely.

come-on n. Sl. inducement, enticement. SEE LURE

comet n. celestial body, *iceball, orbital debris, *cosmic wanderer, *stellar nomad, *ethereal snowball.

WORD FIND
icy center: nucleus
mistaken for a: meteor, fireball
nucleus and coma: head
orbital point farthest from sun: aphelion
orbital point nearest to sun: perihelion
surrounding gas and particles, envelope: coma
trailing particles: tail
vast repository of: Oort Cloud

come upon vi. meet, encounter, chance, come across, bump into.

comeuppance n. punishment, retribution, just deserts, discipline.

come up with vi. invent, create, think up, originate, produce, propose, suggest, put forth.

comfort n. **1.** WELL-BEING ease, peace, tranquility, happiness, coziness, creature comforts, satisfaction, luxury, contentment. "That stealthy thing that enters the house as a guest, and then becomes a host, and then a master."— Kahlil Gibran. **2.** SOLACE consolation, relief, reassurance, sympathy, commiseration, cheer, support, succor, lift, alleviation, help. ANT. *1. discomfort, agony, pain. 2. aggravation.*

comfort *v.* console, soothe, reassure, unburden, support, uphold, alleviate, hearten, bolster, cheer, mitigate, solace, relieve, salve, gladden, assuage. ANT. *aggravate, trouble, burden.*

comfortable *a.* **1.** FEELING GOOD at ease, at peace, tranquil, cozy, satisfied, content, carefree, untroubled, serene, *in a bed of roses, *in clover, satisfactory, agreeable, relaxed, pleasant. **2.** WELL-OFF FINANCIALLY prosperous, well-to-do, wealthy, sufficient, ample. ANT. *1. uncomfortable, miserable, troubled. 2. broke, poor, destitute, squalid.*

comic *n.* SEE COMEDIAN

comical *a.* funny, hilarious, laughable, humorous, whimsical, jocular, zany, amusing, slapstick, farcical, loony, droll, rich, side-splitting, wacky, witty, ludicrous. ANT. *tragic, solemn, serious, grave.*

coming *n.* advent, arrival, emergence, nearing, approach, forthcoming.

coming *a.* approaching, advancing, forthcoming, nearing, impending, imminient, next, at hand, anticipated, on the horizon, in the offing.

command *n.* **1.** ORDER imperative, charge, dictate, directive, prescription, ultimatum, fiat, injunction, behest, word. **2.** CONTROL rule, power, authority, leadership, government, dominion, influence, supremacy, say-so, direction, upper hand.

command *v.* **1.** ORDER demand, charge, dictate, direct, make, prescribe, decree, require, bid, enjoin, summon, *give the word, exact, compel, warrant, give an ultimatum. **2.** CONTROL rule, govern, oversee, direct, supervise, lead, direct, dominate, dictate, run, head, master, reign.

commandeer *v.* appropriate, expropriate, confiscate, usurp, hijack, seize, take.

commander *n.* leader, captain, chief, boss, head, *head honcho, commanding officer, *CO, *brass, skipper, superior, *biggest toad in the puddle, *Sir, *Ma'am. ANT. *subordinate, underling, follower, toady, *kiss-up.*

commanding *a.* **1.** AUTHORITATIVE powerful, in charge, dictatorial, dominating, ruling, controlling, supervisory, governing, imposing, impressive, imperious. **2.** OVERLOOKING wide, expansive, dominating, prominent, far-reaching, towering.

commandment *n.* edict, law. SEE COMMAND

commemorate *v.* honor, memorialize, remember, observe, salute, pay tribute, immortalize,

solemnize, celebrate. ANT. *dishonor, neglect, ignore.*

commence *v.* begin, start, initiate, launch, open. ANT. *end, terminate.*

commencement *n.* **1.** BEGINNING, start, outset, onset, opening, genesis, dawn, inauguration. **2.** GRADUATION CEREMONIES graduation. ANT. *1. ending, termination.*

WORD FIND
address: valedictory
square, flat hat: mortarboard
SEE GRADUATION

commend *v.* **1.** RECOMMEND extol, laud, praise, acclaim, endorse, acclaim, applaud, compliment. **2.** ENTRUST turn over, assign, relegate, consign, confer, confide, transfer. ANT. *1. disparage, smear, criticize.*

commendable *a.* praiseworthy, laudable, meritorious, admirable, exemplary, noble, estimable, excellent. ANT. *contemptible, despicable, rotten.*

commendation *n.* recommendation, praise, acclaim, approval, kudos, rave, *pat on the back, *good word, plaudit, *points, tribute, award, *thumbs up. ANT. *criticism, disparagement, demotion.*

COMMENSURATE *a.* [kuh MEN sur it] equal; proportionate. *The pay scale is commensurate with experience.* SYN. equal, proportionate, coextensive, corresponding, parallel, coinciding, to scale, appropriate, relative, in accord, fitting, compatible. ANT. *disproportionate, divergent, inconsistent.*

comment *n.* remark, commentary, observation, statement, utterance, mention, *crack, criticism, word, opinion.

comment *v.* remark, observe, state, utter, mention, *make a crack, criticize, critique, say a word or two, opine, touch on, make note, expound, mention, point out.

commentary *n.* comment, analysis, remark, observation, exposition, criticism, critique, interpretation, review, opinion.

commentator *n.* reporter, analyst, reviewer, critic, pundit, interpreter, observer, editorialist.

commerce *n.* business, trade, marketing, exchange, buying and selling, merchandising, *wheeling and dealing, industry, mercantilism, traffic. "The great civilizer." — Robert Ingersoll. SEE BUSINESS

commercial *n.* advertisement, ad. SEE ADVERTISEMENT, ADVERTISING

commercial *a.* **1.** MERCANTILE business, trade, marketing, exchanging, profit-making, merchandising, industrial, entrepreneurial, retail, wholesale. **2.** MARKETABLE salable, in demand, *hot.

commingle v. mingle, blend. SEE MIX

COMMISERATE v. [kuh MIZ uh RATE] to pity or feel sorry for. *Twins turning forty commiserate together.* SYN. pity, feel sorry for, sympathize, condole, share one's sorrow, grieve with, console, ache for, bleed for, comfort.

commission n. **1.** AUTHORIZATION relegation, entrusting, power, authority, charge, trust, vesting. **2.** BOARD committee, delegation, council, agency. **3.** COMPENSATION fee, share, cut, remuneration, royalty, payment, allowance, stipend.

commission v. appoint, assign, delegate, authorize, order, enlist, consign, charge, engage, invest, hire, contract for.

commit v. **1.** PERPETRATE do, effect, execute, perform, *pull off, enact, transact, carry out. **2.** ENTRUST charge, vest, appoint, delegate, relegate, engage, consign. **3.** INCARCERATE imprison, place in custody, confine, institutionalize, hospitalize. **4.** PLEDGE devote, obligate, bind, swear, give one's word, dedicate, engage.

commitment n. pledge, promise, dedication, vow, promise, undertaking, charge, obligation, responsibility, liability.

committee n. board, council, panel, commission, task force, cabinet, steering committee, ad hoc committee. "A thing which takes a week to do what one good man can do in an hour." — Elbert Hubbard. "An arrangement enabling one to share the blame with others." — Franklin P. Jones.

commode n. potty, *john. SEE TOILET

commodious a. spacious, roomy, capacious, large, ample, vast, extensive. ANT. *cramped, tight, small.*

commodity n. product, article, goods, item, thing, merchandise, property, object, ware.

common a. **1.** ORDINARY commonplace, average, everyday, usual, typical, standard, routine, regular, general, stock, *run-of-the-mill, universal, familiar, prevailing, widespread. **2.** COMMUNITY communal, collective, shared, public, mutual. **3.** BASIC simple, rudimentary. **4.** LOW sleazy, base, vile, mean, cheap, inferior, course, second-rate, vulgar. ANT. *1. extraordinary, uncommon, rare. 2. private, individual. 3. advanced, complex. 4. superior, refined, high-class.*

commonly a. usually, as a rule, generally, regularly, routinely, normally, ordinarily, on average, habitually. ANT. *rarely, seldom, *once in a blue moon.*

commonplace a. SEE COMMON

common sense n. good sense, savvy, sound judgment, native intelligence, *horse sense, prudence, acumen, levelheadedness, instinct, wisdom, experience. "The shortest line between two points." — Ralph Waldo Emerson "Genius dressed in its working clothes." — Ralph Waldo Emerson. ANT. *stupidity, ignorance, rashness.*

commotion n. turmoil, hubbub, stir, uproar, agitation, to-do, bustle, flurry, excitement, hurly-burly, turbulence, ruckus, disquiet, rumpus, chaos. ANT. *peace, tranquility, serenity, stillness.*

communal a. common, shared, mutual, community, collective, joint, public, shared, cooperative. ANT. *private, individual.*

commune n. cooperative, collective, *kibbutz, community.

commune v. **1.** TALK converse, confide, confer with, discuss, communicate, speak intimately with. **2.** PONDER think, meditate, reflect, contemplate, muse.

communicable a. contagious, infectious, catching, transmittable, spreadable.

communicate v. convey, transmit, disclose, impart, pass on, interface, reveal, touch base, tell, report, announce, proclaim, converse, express, correspond, inform, broadcast, enlighten, inform, relate.

communication n. **1.** CONVEYANCE correspondence, contact, interchange, disclosure, exchange, transmission, intercourse, expression, interface, interplay, interaction. **2.** CORRESPONDENCE communique, report, dispatch, news, message, bulletin.

communicative a. talkative, open, forthright, expressive, loquacious, expansive, unreserved, candid, *gabby, voluble. ANT. *closed, taciturn, reserved.*

communion n. **1.** INTIMACY sharing, rapport, exchange, give and take, disclosure, closeness, communication, harmony, fellowship, union, oneness. **2.** SACRAMENT Holy Communion, Mass, Eucharist, breaking of bread. ANT. *1. alienation, distance.*

communique n. report, bulletin, announcement, communication, message, dispatch.

communism n. collectivism, Bolshevism, Marxism, Leninism, socialism. "What is thine is mine, and all of mine is thine." — Plautus. "Abolition of private property." —

Communist Manifesto. ANT. *capitalism.*

community n. neighborhood, borough, suburb, bedroom community, hamlet, district, public, people, residents, citizenry, population, group.

commute v. **1.** CHARGE substitute, alter, modify, reverse, adjust, mitigate, soften. **2.** TRAVEL shuttle, drive, carpool, bus.

compact n. agreement, contract, treaty, bond, bargain, deal, understanding, arrangement, pact, covenant.

compact v. pack, condense, compress, concentrate, consolidate, squeeze together, contract, cram. ANT. *loosen, expand, blow up.*

compact a. **1.** DENSE solid, compressed, pressed, thick, close, firm, tight-knit, impermeable. **2.** SMALL portable, tiny, handy. **3.** SHORT concise, brief, succinct, pithy, condensed, abridged. ANT. *1. loose. 2. large, ponderous. 3. elongated, prolonged, expanded.*

companion n. friend, partner, sidekick, comrade, confederate, colleague, fellow, alter ego, chum, buddy, associate, escort, mate, counterpart, double. SEE FRIEND

companionable a. friendly, warm, easy-going, congenial, sociable, good-natured, *buddy-buddy, outgoing, gregarious, agreeable, clubby, jolly. ANT. *nasty, aloof, cold, antagonistic, unfriendly.*

company n. **1.** COMPANIONSHIP friendship, fellowship, *chumminess, society, presence. **2.** VISTOR guest, caller, friends over. **3.** GROUP band, party, troupe, throng, gathering, assembly, entourage. **4.** FIRM corporation, business, concern, establishment, partnership, enterprise, outfit.

comparable a. similar, alike, akin, near, corresponding, approaching, analogous, cognate, parallel, close, equal, on a par with. ANT. *dissimilar, different, *like apples and oranges.*

compare v. **1.** EXAMINE FOR DIFFERENCES OR SIMILARITIES contrast, weigh, inspect, size up, correlate, match, relate, stack up against, scrutinize, differentiate. **2.** RESEMBLE correspond, take after, approximate, equal, *hold a candle to. **3.** LIKEN equate, identify with, match, tie.

comparison n. **1.** EXAMINATION OF DIFFERENCES OR SIMILARITIES contrasting, inspection, sizing up, correlation, differentiation, matching, weighing, measurement, scrutiny, study. **2.** RESEMBLANCE correspondence, approximation, relation, similarity, likeness, connection, affinity. **3.** LIKENING equating, identification with, matching, parallel, analogy.

compartment n. cell, unit, cubicle, room, capsule, bay, stall, booth, nook, cubbyhole, pigeonhole, niche, receptacle, slot, section, division, category.

compassion n. sympathy, empathy, feeling, heart, pity, mercy, love, charity, ruth, grace, commiseration, concern, kindness. ANT. *indifference, cold-bloodedness, disregard.*

compassionate a. sympathetic, feeling, kindhearted, merciful, loving, charitable, concerned, magnanimous, humane, tender, soft, clement. ANT. *indifferent, cold-blooded, unfeeling.*

compatible a. congruous, harmonious, sympathetic, agreeable, simpatico, congenial, accordant, *in sync with, *on the same wavelength, in rapport, consistent. ANT. *incompatible, incongruous.*

COMPEL v. [kum PEL] to force. *Conscience compels one to file a tax return honestly.* SYN. force, make, drive, oblige, insist, coerce, constrain, press, require, command, necessitate, bully.

COMPENDIUM n. [kum PEN dee um] a summary. *We were provided with a compendium of the most salient points.* SYN. summary, abstract, abridgement, synopsis, brief, digest, precis, syllabus, condensation.

compensate v. **1.** REMUNERATE reimburse, recompense, pay, repay, make restitution, refund, *make good. **2.** OFFSET neutralize, counterbalance, counteract, countervail, balance, equalize, cancel out.

compensation n. **1.** REMUNERATION reimbursement, recompense, pay, repayment, restitution, refund, allowance, recoupment, stipend, *take, consideration, benefit, settlement, reward, wages, salary.

compete v. vie, contend, contest, go up against, rival, take on, combat, tussle, spar, *lock horns, face off, *match wits, grapple, battle, *go head to head.

competence n. adequacy, ability, capability, proficiency, skill, *know-how, *the right stuff, *what it takes, expertise, mastery, adroitness, finesse, fitness. ANT. *incompetence, inadequacy, inability.*

competent a. adequate, able, capable, proficient, skillful, expert, masterly, adroit, fit, qualified, sufficient, equal, *on the ball, sharp, *up to snuff. ANT. *incompetent, inadequate, unable, lacking.*

competition n. **1.** CONTEST match, bout, rivalry, contention, championship, clash, encounter, engagement, meet, tournament, trial, one-on-one, emulation, struggle, *dog-eat-dog, battle, conflict, dogfight, tug-of-war, battle royal, free-for-all, fight to the death, *one-upmanship, fight for supremacy, *jockeying for position. **2.** OPPOSITION rival, competitor, challenger, opponent, contender, adversary.

competitive *a.* rivaling, aggressive, striving, *high-octane, ambitious, combative, feisty, *cutthroat, *dog-eat-dog, *go-getting, *tough as nails, grueling, Olympian, adversarial.

competitor *n.* contender, rival, opposition, adversary, challenger, competition, opponent, contestant.

compilation *n.* **1.** COLLECTION assembly, assemblage, accumulation, assortment, anthology. **2.** COMPILING gathering, collecting, assembling, accumulating, consolidating.

compile *v.* gather, accumulate, assemble, amass, consolidate, congregate, group, organize, anthologize, order.

COMPLACENT *a.* [kum PLAY sunt] to be satisfied with oneself to the point of smugness. *The former Olympian had grown so complacent that he neglected to practice.* SYN. satisfied, self-satisfied, smug, contented, at ease, pleased with oneself, self-assured, unconcerned, untroubled, *full of oneself, secure. ANT. *insecure, troubled, uneasy, unsatisfied.*

complain *v.* gripe, grumble, *bitch, protest, crab, *kick, *piss and moan, *raise a fuss, gripe, *beef, *bellyache, nag, carp, find fault, pick, grouse, whine, *squawk. ANT. *praise, compliment, laud.*

complaint *n.* **1.** GRIEVANCE *beef, criticism, gripe, protest, stink, cavil, grumble, problem, grouse, charge, objection. **2.** MALADY illness, disorder, ailment, affliction, disease, pain.

complaisant *a.* agreeable, obliging, pleasing, solicitous, gracious, accommodating, deferential, conciliatory, compliant. ANT. *disagreeable, contrary, difficult.*

complement *n.* **1.** *ROUNDING-OFF crown, finishing touch, consummation, completion, clincher, balance, supplement, rest, remainder. **2.** TOTAL aggregate, the entirety, sum, *the works, *the whole shooting match.

complement *v.* round out, complete, crown, consummate, supplement, clinch, perfect.

complementary *a.* completing, crowning, finishing, filling, consummating, perfecting, fulfilling, corresponding, reciprocal, parallel.

complete *v.* finish, conclude, fulfill, end, realize, *wrap up, accomplish, actualize, close,

*wind up, *call it a day, finalize, crown, *put to bed. ANT. *start, begin, break ground.*

complete *a.* **1.** WHOLE entire, full, total, all, intact, plenary, uncut, unabridged, undivided, integral. **2.** THOROUGH absolute, total, perfect, dyed-in-the-wool, utter, outright, unqualified, full-fledged, unmitigated. **3.** FINISHED done, concluded, fulfilled, ended, realized, *wrapped up, *polished off, accomplished.

completion *n.* finish, conclusion, fulfillment, end, realization, *wrapping up, accomplishment, closing, *winding up, finalization, crowning, consummation. ANT. *start, beginning.*

complex *a.* complicated, intricate, difficult, knotty, convoluted, tangled, unfathomable, inscrutable, manifold, perplexing, Gordian, labyrinthine, undecipherable, cryptic, abstruse, involved. ANT. *simple, easy, clear.*

complexion *n.* **1.** SKIN COLORING tone, cast, hue, tinge, tint, pigmentation.

WORD FIND

aged: leathery, lined like an old boot, parchmentlike, like scalded milk, liver-spotted, age-spotted, cadaverous, gaunt, craggy, furrowed, mottled, withered, pendulous, rosaceous, moled, weatherbeaten, rawboned

brown/black: ebony, pitch, brown as the Congo/Mississippi/Rio Grande, honey, golden brown, leathery, lentil, mahogany, dark as a mill pond, molasses, russet, mottled, nutbrown, obsidian, olive, raven, raisin, tawny, tarnished penny, weathered acorn

healthy: peaches and cream, apple-cheeked, scrubbed, rosy, glowing, ruddy, pink, blushing

pink/red: scarlet, crimson, burned, rosy, lobster

sickly: cadaverous, leaden, ashen, ghastly, pale, pallid, wan, blanched, pasty, chalky, jaundiced, sallow, flushed, clammy

white: alabaster, lily-white, ivory, milky, creamy, beige, fair

2. character, aspect, appearance, quality, look, bearing, cast.

complexity *n.* complication, intricacy, involvement, entanglement, knot, Gordian knot, perplexity, maze, labyrinth, convolution. ANT. *simplicity, clarity.*

compliance *a.* yielding, ascent, conforming, obedience, observation, acquiescence, deference, complaisance. ANT. *noncompliance, dis-*

obedience.

complicate *v.* entangle, *mess up, convolute, confuse, make complex, snarl, bedevil, *add fuel to the fire, confound, involve, embrangle. ANT. *simplify, clarify.*

complicated *a.* complex, intricate, involved, entangled, knotty, difficult, convoluted, perplexing, elaborate, manifold, labyrinthine, abstruse, problematic, recondite, deep, incomprehensible. ANT. *simple, easy, straightforward.*

complication *n.* problem, difficulty, complexity, knot, hitch, snag, entanglement, obstacle, stumbling block, *fly in the ointment.

COMPLICITY *n.* [kum PLIS i tee] participation as an accomplice in a wrongdoing. *There was apparent complicity between the unhampered drug runners and town officials.* SYN. conspiracy, collusion, collaboration, partnership, confederacy, abetment, machination, intrigue, *backdoor arrangement.

compliment *n.* praise, tribute, *good word, *pat on the back, commendation, flattery, acclaim, kudos, *posy, homage, blandishment. ANT. *insult, disparagement.*

compliment *v.* praise, pay tribute to, *pat on the back, commend, flatter, puff up, *give a posy, *take one's hat off to, cheer, laud, salute, *stroke, *slather, *kiss up. SEE FLATTER

complimentary *a.* **1.** FLATTERING laudatory, commendatory, congratulatory, favorable, approving, cajoling, *ass-kissing, *apple polishing. **2.** FREE gratis, on the house, gratuitous. ANT. *insulting, critical, disparaging.*

comply *v.* yield, ascent, conform, obey, observe, acquiesce, defer, respect, abide by, adhere, follow. ANT. *disobey, disregard.*

component *n.* part, element, ingredient, constituent, fundamental, unit, factor.

component *a.* constituent, fundamental, basic, essential, composing, integral.

comport *v.* behave, conduct, act, carry, bear, acquit, deport.

compose *v.* **1.** CONSTITUTE make up, comprise, form, be part of. **2.** CREATE write, invent, author, formulate, devise, fashion, make, produce. **3.** CALM tranquilize, collect, simmer down, cool down, *chill, *get it together, contain, allay. ANT. 3. *lose it, break down.*

composed *a.* tranquil, calm, collected, cool, *together, levelheaded, nonchalant, self-possessed, unruffled, unperturbed, serene. ANT. *nervous, distraught, catatonic, tense.*

composite *n.* combination, mixture, consolidation, blend, amalgam, compound, synthesis, fusion.

composite *a.* combined, consolidated, mingled, blended, melded.

composition *n.* **1.** CREATION synthesis, invention, fabrication, formulation, devising, making. **2.** WRITING opus, essay, paper, work, creation, piece, draft, exposition, dissertation, thesis, arrangement. **3.** STRUCTURE arrangement, organization, formulation, constitution, form, makeup, content, fabric.

composure *n.* tranquility, calm, cool, self-possession, serenity, equanimity, poise, *head, aplomb, presence of mind, equilibrium. ANT. *nervousness, anxiety, panic.*

compound *n.* composite, blend, mixture, combination, amalgam, consolidation, concoction, synthesis.

compound *v.* combine, consolidate, blend, mix, amalgamate, concoct, synthesize, fuse.

compound *a.* combined, composite, complex, manifold, synthesized, conglomerate, multiform. ANT. *simple, pure, elemental.*

comprehend *v.* understand, get, grasp, realize, see, fathom, apprehend, catch, recognize, appreciate, *get the picture, discern.

comprehension *n.* understanding, grasp, realization, apprehension, recognition, perception, cognizance, discernment.

comprehensive *a.* all-inclusive, extensive, exhaustive, thorough, complete, encyclopedic, sweeping, *across the board, in depth, umbrella. ANT. *limited, narrow, exclusive.*

compress *v.* compact, pack, condense, press, contract, constrict, squeeze, shrink, wring, squash, shorten, reduce. ANT. *expand, stretch, enlarge.*

comprise *v.* include, contain, consist of, make up, form, compose, constitute, incorporate, embody.

compromise *n.* concession, *give-and-take, agreement, conciliation, deal, *happy medium, trade-off, *middle ground, balance, accommodation, golden mean. "Simply changing the question to fit the answer." —Merrit Malloy. "A deal in which two people get what neither of them wanted." —Anon.

compromise *v.* **1.** GIVE AND TAKE strike a deal, trade off, bargain, find the middle ground, strike a balance, accommodate, find a happy medium, make concessions, agree, *give your shirt but keep your pants, *split the difference. **2.** ENDANGER jeopardize, imperil, expose, implicate, discredit.

COMPULSION *n.* [kum PUL shun] a strong drive or force, a compelling impulse. *He had* *a strange compulsion to giggle at the funeral.* SYN. drive, force, pressure, constraint, coercion, need, urge, urgency, obsession, desire, impulse.

compulsive *a.* compelling, obsessive, uncontrollable, irresistible, urgent, crazed.

COMPULSORY *a.* [kum PUL suh ree] mandatory, required. *The tests are compulsory; no one can skip them.* SYN. mandatory, required, obligatory, requisite, imperative, forced, nonelective. ANT. *voluntary, elective, optional.*

COMPUNCTION *n.* [kum PUNK shun] the uncomfortable feeling caused by guilt, conscience. *He felt no compunction over his crimes; he had no conscience.* SYN. guilt, conscience, qualm, uneasiness, misgiving, regret, self-reproach, shame, pangs of guilt, contrition, remorse, penitence, twinge.

computation *n.* calculation, reckoning, estimation, figuring, tallying, account.

compute *v.* calculate, reckon, figure, tally, account, count, add, subtract, sum, determine, work out, measure, total.

computer *n.* calculator, adding machine, data processor, microprocessor, *number cruncher, *PC, *laptop, *micro, supercomputer.

WORD FIND
auxiliary device: peripheral
aversion: cyberphobia
byte: 8 bits of memory space
calculating, rows and columns program: spreadsheet
California manufacturing mecca: Silicon Valley
chip: microprocessor, integrated circuit
data storage area: memory
data storage medium: disk, diskette, floppy disk, cartridge
device enabling computer to communicate over phone: modem
device enabling computer to read, write info on disks: disk drive
disrupting prank program: virus, worm
easy to use: user-friendly
enthusiast: hacker, *chiphead
EPROM: erasable memory chip
giant computer serving multiple users: mainframe
GIGO: garbage in, garbage out
inoperable: down
instructions: program
keyboard and monitor portion: terminal
language/program: AGOL, BASIC, COBOL, FORTRAN, PASCAL, PROLOG
linkage of several computers: network
linked to a main computer: on-line
list of options on screen: menu
long printout, slang for: *wallpaper
messages sent between two computers: e-mail
MS-DOS: Microsoft Disk Operating System
nonphysical components, info, programs: software
on-screen symbol showing where next character will appear: cursor
palm-sized external device for moving on-screen cursor: mouse
paper printout: hard copy
paper-propelling device: tractor feed
physical components of: hardware
program that protects against virus: vaccine, antidote, *DDT
read-only memory chip: ROM
secret opening designed into program to allow access at later date: trap door
superimposed screen within screen: window
transfer data from main to small or remote computer: download
transfer data from remote source to central computer: upload
transfer data to memory: store
TV-like screen: monitor

comrade *n.* friend, companion, partner, pal, buddy, associate, sidekick, confederate, chum, colleague, coworker, confrere. ANT. *stranger, enemy.*

con *v. Sl.* *rip off, cheat, swindle, defraud, trick, deceive, bamboozle.

conceal *v.* hide, cover, secrete, cloak, obscure, disguise, stash, lie low, camouflage, shield. ANT. *display, show, spotlight.*

concealment *n.* covering, hiding, cover-up, disguising, shielding, camouflaging, front, secretion, hiding place, hideaway, blind, shield, cover, refuge.

concede *v.* admit, grant, yield, acknowledge, acquiesce, avow, confess, yield, *cave in, fold, come around, give up. ANT. *fight, deny, reject, refute.*

CONCEIT *a.* [kun SEET] an overblown sense of one's positive attributes, egotism. *His swaggering conceit was sickening.* SYN. egotism, pride, vanity, bigheadedness, arrogance, vainglory, self-love, immodesty, narcissism, swagger, self-worship, self-importance. ANT. *modesty, self-effacement, humility.* "God's gift to little men." —Bruce Barton. "The quicksand of success." —Arnold Glasow.

conceited *a.* egotistical, proud, vain,

bigheaded, arrogant, vainglorious, *full of oneself, *in love with oneself, puffed up, immodest, narcissistic, swaggering, strutting, self-worshipping, self-important. ANT. *modest, self-effacing, humble.

conceivable a. imaginable, possible, thinkable, comprehensible, credible, believable. ANT. inconceivable, impossible.

conceive v. **1.** FORM develop, create, think up, invent, concoct, dream up, devise, originate, fabricate, hatch, *cook up, imagine. **2.** UNDERSTAND comprehend, apprehend, see, imagine, grasp, realize, follow.

concentrate v. **1.** THINK center, focus, *rack one's brains, study, fix one's attention toward, consider, absorb oneself in, engross oneself in, ponder, scrutinze, *zero in on. **2.** COLLECT, GATHER assemble, amass, intensify, focus, converge, consolidate, congregate, center, cluster. ANT. 2. spread out, scatter.

concentration n. **1.** THINKING centering, focus, study, fixation, consideration, absorption, engrossment, pondering, scrutiny, attention, single-mindedness. **2.** COLLECTION, GATHERING assemblage, mass, intensification, focus, converging, consolidation, congregation, centralization, cluster, agglomerate. ANT. 1. diversion, absentmindedness, mind-wandering. 2. spread, scattering, dispersal.

concept n. idea, thought, notion, conceptualization, *brainchild, conviction, view, image, impression, theory, hypothesis.

conception n. **1.** BEGINNING origination, birth, genesis, inception, start, formation, germination, dawn. **2.** IDEA thought, notion, conceptualization, conviction, view, image, impression, theory, hypothesis.

concern n. **1.** AFFAIR care, business, matter, interest, department, job, worry, responsibility. **2.** WORRY trouble, anxiety, unease, disquiet, apprehension, distress. **3.** BUSINESS ESTABLISHMENT company, firm, outfit, house.

concern v. **1.** BEAR ON deal with, regard, involve, pertain to, touch, relate to, affect, interest. **2.** WORRY trouble, make anxious, put ill-at-ease, disquiet, distress, disturb, bother, pain.

concerned a. **1.** INVOLVED WITH interested, active, caring, attentive, solicitous, connected, mixed up in. **2.** WORRIED anxious, troubled, ill-at-ease, disquieted, distressed, disturbed, bothered, pained, uneasy. ANT. 1. disinterested, detached, removed. 2. indifferent, nonchalant, untroubled.

concerning prep. regarding, about, with reference to.

concert n. **1.** AGREEMENT harmony, concord, accord, union, unison, league, cooperation, collaboration. **2.** SHOW recital, *jam, gig, performance, symphony, philharmonic. ANT. 1. disunity, disagreement, discord.

concerted a. united, joined, joint, cooperative, collaborative, interactive, combined, mutual. ANT. individual.

concession n. yielding, granting, giving-in, conceding, capitulation, compromise, assent, acknowledgement, trade-off, allowance, permit, right.

CONCILIATORY a. [kun SIL ee uh tor ee] willing to make peace, placatory. The warring gangs were largely conciliatory after the riots. SYN. placatory, placative, appeasing, pacific, peacemaking, reconciling, mollifying, yielding, amicable, accommodating, deferential. ANT. bellicose, aggressive, belligerent.

CONCISE a. [kun SISE] brief and to the point. A concise letter to the editor is always best. SYN. brief, to the point, succinct, short, pithy, pointed, terse, compact, summary, *boiled down, *in a nutshell, crisp, laconic. ANT. long-winded, wordy, verbose, rambling.

conclave n. secret meeting, council, synod, meeting, session, congress, assembly, *powwow.

conclude v. **1.** END close, finish, terminate, complete, wind up, *wrap up, stop, consummate, *knock off, *call it a day, break off. **2.** INFER deduce, reason, decide, assume, surmise, presume, suppose, reckon, figure. **3.** SETTLE resolve, come to terms, work out, decide. ANT. 1. start, open, commence.

conclusion n. **1.** ENDING closing, finish, termination, completion, winding up, *wrap up, stopping, consummation, finale, denouement. **2.** INFERENCE deduction, reckoning, supposition, figuring, presumption, assumption, judgment. **3.** SETTLEMENT resolution, coming to terms, agreement, understanding. ANT. 1. start, opening, commencement.

conclusive a. decisive, final, settled, determining, convincing, definitive, incontestable, clinching, unmistakable, undeniable, absolute, resolving, irrefutable, *litmus test. ANT. inconclusive, *iffy, questionable, uncertain.

concoct v. compound, invent, devise, create, *whip up, formulate, hatch, fabricate, *slap together, prepare, think up, dream up.

concoction n. compound, mixture, invention, creation, formulation, fabrication, brew, preparation, contrivance, medley, synthesis.

concomitant *a.* attendant, accompanying, associative, accessory, supplementary, auxiliary.

CONCORD *n.* [KON kawrd] harmony, peaceful relations. *The former enemies have now lived in concord for thirty years.* SYN. harmony, peace, agreement, accord, friendship, unity, goodwill, understanding, rapport. ANT. *discord, disagreement, conflict.*

concourse *n.* **1.** CONGREGATION throng, confluence, convergence, mob, gathering, flock, assemblage, multitude, crush. **2.** PASSAGE mall, walkway, promenade, boulevard, esplanade, path.

concrete *a.* **1.** REAL actual, material, definite, solid, substantial, factual, physical, tangible. **2.** SPECIFIC distinct, explicit, particular, precise, express. ANT. *1. abstract, theoretical. 2. general, vague.*

concubine *n.* mistress, *live-in lover, kept woman, odalisque.

concur *v.* **1.** HAPPEN TOGETHER coincide, parallel, synchronize. **2.** BE IN ACCORD agree, assent, consent, harmonize, approve, accede, correspond. ANT. *2. disagree, differ.*

concurrent *a.* **1.** HAPPENING TOGETHER coinciding, parallel, synchronized, coincident, simultaneous. **2.** IN AGREEMENT in accordance, harmonizing, consistent, corresponding, in rapport, compatible. ANT. *in disagreement, differing, contradictory.*

concussion *n.* shaking, agitation, jolt, blow, shock, jarring, impact, bang, bump, pounding, buffeting.

condemn *v.* **1.** CRITICIZE censure, denounce, decry, reprove, deprecate, vilify, rebuke, disapprove, disparage, pass judgment on. **2.** DOOM sentence, damn, convict, adjudge, punish, *send up the river. ANT. *1. praise, commend, laud. 2. liberate, absolve.*

condemnation *n.* criticism, censure, disapproval, remonstration, deprecation, rebuke, reproach, denunciation, judgment, sentencing, damning, punishment. ANT. *praise, approval, absolution.*

condensation *n.* **1.** ABRIDGEMENT reduction, compression, consolidation, summary, brief, synopsis, outline, digest. **2.** LIQUEFACTION dew, moisture, precipitation, *sweating.

condense *v.* **1.** ABRIDGE reduce, compress, shorten, consolidate, summarize, synopsize, outline, contract, boil down, concentrate, curtail, encapsulate. ANT. *expand, lengthen, enlarge.*

CONDESCEND *v.* [KON di send] to lower oneself to the level of another with lesser status. Also, to talk down to someone. *Our teacher was willing to condescend and take the advice of students. He fancied himself a big shot and spoke condescendingly to everyone.* SYN. **1.** descend, humble oneself, bend, *come down off one's high horse, vouchsafe, deign, stoop, lower oneself, yield. **2.** talk down to, patronize, talk down one's nose, regard with hauteur.

condescending *a.* superior, arrogant, *high and mighty, patronizing, lofty, snobbish, disdainful, lordly, pretentious, *snooty, haughty, imperious. ANT. *down-to-earth, unpretentious, unassuming.*

condition *n.* **1.** PROVISION stipulation, qualification, proviso, consideration, requirement. **2.** STATE situation, order, circumstance, stage, predicament, position, *lay of the land. **3.** HEALTH fitness, shape, constitution, state. **4.** AILMENT malady, illness.

condition *v.* get fit, train, prepare, get in shape, build up, work out.

conditional *a.* subject to, dependent, contingent, limited, relative, provisional, qualified, *with strings attached, tentative. ANT. *unconditional, unrestricted.*

condolence *n.* sympathy, commiseration, consolation, compassion, pity, comfort, support, solace.

condom *n.* contraceptive, prophylactic, *rubber, *safe, *skin, *protection, *raincoat, *Coney Island whitefish, *Trojan.

CONDONE *v.* [kun DOHN] to overlook or forgive a negative action. *The church does not condone infidelity.* SYN. overlook, forgive, pardon, *look the other way, ignore, excuse, let go, make allowances for, wink at. ANT. *condemn, damn, denounce.*

CONDUCIVE *a.* [kun DOO siv] leading to or promoting. *Rain pattering on the roof is conducive to good sleep.* SYN. leading to, promoting, contributing, instrumental, helpful, ancillary, tending, favorable. ANT. *adverse, counter, deleterious.*

conduct *n.* **1.** BEHAVIOR manner, comportment, bearing, demeanor, ways. **2.** MANAGEMENT administration, direction, supervision, rule, organization, regulation, leadership.

conduct *v.* **1.** BEHAVE deport, demean, act, bear, acquit. **2.** MANAGE administer, direct, supervise, rule, organize, regulate, execute, handle. **3.** LEAD guide, escort, show the way, usher, marshal.

conductor *n.* leader, director, guide, manager,

marshal, supervisor, usher, maestro.

conduit *n.* pipe, tube, channel, duct, drain, sewer, canal, course, passage, trough, race.

confection *n.* sweet, candy, comfit, dainty.

confederacy *n.* alliance, league, union, federation, coalition, bloc.

confederate *n.* ally, associate, accomplice, colleague, abettor, collaborator, partner, co-conspirator, cohort. ANT. *adversary, foe.*

confederation *n.* SEE CONFEDERACY

confer *v.* **1.** GIVE bestow, grant, present, award. **2.** HAVE A CONFERENCE talk, discuss, speak, parley, consult, deliberate, *powwow.

conference *n.* talk, discussion, meeting, consultation, seminar, dialogue, *powwow, convention, *bull session, symposium. "A gathering of important people who singly can do nothing, but together can decide that nothing can be done." — Fred Allen.

confess *v.* admit, acknowledge, reveal, disclose, allow, *own up, *come clean, *fess up, level, divulge, *open up, *spill it. ANT. *deny, cover up, keep secret.*

confession *n.* admission, acknowledgement, revelation, disclosure, allowance, leveling, declaration, profession, avowal. "A medicine to the erring." — Cicero.

confidant *n.* friend, intimate, bosom buddy, companion, lover, alter ego. SEE FRIEND

confide *v.* **1.** SHARE INTIMATE INFORMATION confess, disclose, divulge, share feelings, reveal, *unload, intimate, *get off one's chest. **2.** ENTRUST charge, consign, relegate, trust, commit, assign.

confidence *n.* **1.** BELIEF trust, reliance, sureness, faith, dependence, assurance. **2.** SELF-CONFIDENCE self-esteem, self-assurance, courage, self-reliance, heart, faith in oneself, mental toughness, pluck, backbone, spine, nerve. "The feeling you have before you know better." — Anon. ANT. *1. uncertainty, doubt. 2. insecurity, diffidence, self-doubt.*

confident *a.* self-confident, self-assured, cocky, plucky, bold, dauntless, faithful, sure, secure, certain, positive, convinced, presumptuous. ANT. *insecure, unsure, diffident.*

confidential *a.* secret, private, privy, classified, *off the record, *between you, me and the bedpost, personal, restricted. ANT. *public, open.*

configuration *n.* arrangement, outline, contour, form, conformation, structure, figure, build, shape.

confine *v.* enclose, restrict, shut in, imprison, restrain, limit, keep, jail, coop up, incarcer-

ate, intern, hold, detain, bound, quarantine. ANT. *free, liberate, release.*

confinement *n.* restriction, shutting in, imprisonment, enclosure, keeping, incarceration, holding, detainment, bounding, quarantine, detention, captivity. ANT. *freedom, liberation, release.*

confirm *v.* **1.** STRENGTHEN firm up, establish, buttress, reinforce. **2.** VALIDATE ratify, prove, establish, attest, substantiate, vouch, sanction, authenticate, affirm. ANT. *1. weaken, contradict. 2. disprove, question, contradict.*

confirmation *n.* validation, ratification, proof, verification, authentication, substantiation, affirmation, corroboration, support, sanction, nod, okay. ANT. *question, contradiction, repudiation.*

confirmed *a.* **1.** SUBSTANTIATED validated, proven, verified, authenticated, corroborated. **2.** ESTABLISHED deep-rooted, *dyed-in-the-wool, deep-seated, habitual, chronic, inveterate, ingrained. ANT. *1. unconfirmed, unsupported, questionable. 2. new, sometimes.*

confiscate *v.* seize, appropriate, take, impound, expropriate, preempt, sequester, commandeer, usurp.

conflagration *n.* fire, blaze, inferno, firestorm, holocaust, wildfire, hellfire.

conflict *n.* **1.** FIGHT battle, war, clash, combat, struggle, contest, tussle. **2.** DISAGREEMENT clash, contention, discord, dissension, hostility, argument, opposition, dispute, confrontation. ANT. *1. peace, amity. 2. agreement, accord.*

conflict *v.* **1.** FIGHT battle, wage war, clash, combat, struggle, contest, tussle. **2.** DISAGREE clash, contend, oppose, differ, *lock horns, square off, be at odds with, spar. ANT. *1. settle, conciliate. 2. agree, harmonize.*

conflicting *a.* contradictory, contrary, inconsistent, incompatible, discrepant. ANT. *corresponding, congruous.*

confluence *n.* **1.** CONVERGENCE juncture, meeting, union. **2.** CROWD throng, gathering, assembly.

conform *v.* **1.** MAKE THE SAME correspond, match, be like, harmonize, fit, jibe, assimilate. **2.** ADAPT adjust, accommodate, integrate, suit, follow, fall into line, *go with the flow, comply, *do as the Romans do, *swim with the stream. ANT. *deviate, *march to the beat of a different drum, differ.*

conformation *n.* shape, build, form, structure, figure, configuration.

conformist *n.* follower, *yes man, *sheep, *one

of the herd, *brick in a wall, emulator. ANT.
nonconformist, rebel, free spirit.

conformity n. **1.** AGREEMENT correspondence,
harmony, affinity, congruity, accord, likeness, similarity. "The herd-fear."—E. Stanley Jones. **2.** COMPLIANCE obedience, observance, assent, yielding, acquiescence,
submission. ANT. *1. disagreement, incongruity,
difference. 2. noncompliance, disobedience, rebellion.*

confound v. confuse, puzzle, mix up, bewilder,
perplex, mystify, flabbergast, nonplus, daze,
muddle, dumbfound. ANT. *clarify.*

confront v. face, oppose, stand up to, challenge, cross, encounter, *go up against,
meet, dare, defy, beard, brave. ANT. *avoid,
back away from, retreat from, dodge.*

confrontation n. meeting, challenge, encounter, crossing of paths, showdown, face-off,
set-to, contest, dare, defiance, fight. ANT.
avoidance.

confuse v. **1.** BEWILDER mix up, perplex, throw
off, baffle, mystify, muddle, bemuse, puzzle,
confound. **2.** DISORDER jumble, mix up, mess
up, disarrange, discombobulate, disarray,
*foul up, mingle, blend. ANT. *2. straighten,
order.*

confusion n. **1.** BEWILDERMENT perplexity, bafflement, mystification, puzzlement, disorientation, fog, daze, befuddlement. **2.** DISORDER
jumble, mess, disarray, disorganization, tangle, upheaval, labyrinth, muddle, *snafu, anarchy, chaos, bedlam, pandemonium. ANT. *1.
lucidity, clarity. 2. order, organization, tidiness.*

congeal v. solidify, thicken, jell, set, stiffen, coagulate, clot, curdle.

CONGENIAL a. [kun JEEN yul] friendly,
compatible, having similar tastes. *The party
atmosphere was low-key but congenial.* SYN.
friendly, compatible, agreeable, suitable,
pleasant, cordial, kindred, companionable,
convivial, sociable, like-minded, sympathetic, affable, harmonious, *en rapport.
ANT. *hostile, incompatible, disagreeable.*

CONGENITAL a. [kun JEN i tul] existing at
birth. *A congenital heart defect.* SYN. inborn,
natal, natural, connate, inherent, innate, intrinsic, hereditary, in the blood, genetic.
ANT. *acquired.*

congested a. overcrowded, clogged, blocked,
overfilled, stuffed up, plugged, occluded,
jammed, glutted, packed, choked. ANT. *clear.*

congestion n. overcrowding, clogging, blockage, stuffiness, plug, cramming, jam, occlusion, repletion, fullness, bottleneck.

conglomerate n. composite, aggregate, hodgepodge; chain, multinational, partnership,
company, trust, firm.

conglomerate a. clustered, massed, amassed,
combined, aggregate, mixed, composite.

congratulate v. felicitate, hail, commend, salute, applaud, toast.

congregate v. gather, mass, cluster, collect,
flock, group, crowd together, muster, convene, throng, concentrate. ANT. *scatter, disperse.*

congregation n. assembly, group, mass, cluster,
collection, flock, crowd, throng, gathering,
parishioners.

congress n. assembly, council, association, conference, delegation, legislature, legislative
body, government, committee, caucus, session, Parliament, Senate, House of Representatives, Capitol Hill. "The great commanding theatre . . ."—Thomas Jefferson.

WORD FIND

assistant party leader in House or Senate:
whip

break: recess

committee that sets rules for debate on bills:
Rules Committee

debate's time-limiting process: cloture

influencing of member by special interest
group: lobbying

House of Commons: lower legislative house
of British Parliament

House of Lords: upper legislative house of
British Parliament

House: U.S. House of Representatives

kill or remove a bill from consideration: table
a bill

legislative house: chamber

meeting of House and Senate: joint session

member: congressman, senator, representative, legislator, statesman

messenger/*gofer of: page

minimum member attendance necessary to
transact business: quorum

newly elected member: freshman

official controlling access, maintaining order: sergeant at arms

presides in House of Representatives:
Speaker of the House

presides in Senate after Vice President: president pro tempore

proposed legislation: bill

Senate: upper legislative body of U.S. Congress

speaking and work area of: floor

speech, long-winded: filibuster

transcript of daily debates, votes, House and Senate: *Congressional Record*
SEE ELECTION, GOVERNMENT, POLITICS

congressman *n.* senator, representative, legislator, statesman, politician. "[One] who votes for all appropriations and against all taxes." — Henry Ashurst.

congruent *a.* corresponding, in agreement, harmonious, parallel, consonant. ANT. *incongruent, disagreeing.*

CONJECTURE *n.* [kun JEK chur] a guess or inference made from incomplete information. *The evidence was comprised of little more than conjecture.* SYN. guess, guesswork, inference, deduction, supposition, surmise, assumption, speculation, theory, hypothesis, inkling, *shot in the dark. ANT. *fact, certainty.*

conjecture *v.* guess, infer, deduce, assume, suppose, surmise, speculate, theorize, hypothesize, gather.

conjugal *a.* matrimonial, connubial, nuptial, marital, wedded.

conjunction *n.* combination, union, alliance, juxtaposition, connection, meeting, merger, joining.

conjure *v.* summon, call upon, beckon, raise, invoke, make magic, cast a spell, bewitch.

connect *v.* join, link, unite, tie, bind, couple, attach, wed, merge, hitch, cohere, yoke. ANT. *disconnect, detach, separate.*

connection *n.* **1.** LINK tie, coupling, bond, juncture, union, association, relationship, marriage, network, attachment. **2.** ASSOCIATE friend, relative, kin, sibling, acquaintance, contact, go-between, agent.

CONNIVE *v.* [kuh NIVE] to conspire in a wrongdoing or at least look the other way. *They connived their way to wealth.* SYN. conspire, scheme, collude, plot, *be in cahoots with, look the other way, intrigue, finagle, have a hand in, cabal, cooperate.

CONNOISSEUR *n.* [KON uh SUR] an expert, especially on the fine arts or in matters of taste. *A wine connoisseur.* SYN. expert, authority, cognoscente, aesthete, afficianado, buff, dilettante, virtuoso, judge, specialist, devotee, epicure, gourmet, critic, maven, *nut, freak.

connotation *n.* inference, allusion, implication, suggestion, sense, undercurrent, meaning, reference, nuance, hint.

connote *v.* suggest, convey, denote, imply, infer, hint at, mean, indicate, designate, signify, allude to.

connubial *a.* conjugal, marital, matrimonial, nuptial, wedded, married, spousal.

conquer *v.* vanquish, defeat, overcome, overpower, overthrow, subdue, master, beat, dominate, win, triumph. ANT. *surrender, lose, fall, bow.*

conqueror *n.* victor, winner, champion, master, vanquisher, subduer, conquistador. ANT. *loser, victim, the defeated.*

conquest *n.* victory, triumph, win, defeat, domination, overthrow, coup, subjugation, subjection, occupation, spoils, plunder, booty, winnings.

conscience *n.* moral judgment, principles, *little voice, scruples, ethics, standards, integrity, sense of right and wrong, superego. "That inner tribunal." — Anton Boisen. "One's soul companion." — Evelyn Brenzel. "The muzzle of the will." — Elbert Hubbard. "A thousand witnesses." — Richard Taverner. ANT. *indifference, cold-bloodedness.*

conscientious *a.* **1.** MORAL principled, ethical, virtuous, upright, honest, scrupulous, good, upstanding, honorable. **2.** CAREFUL thorough, painstaking, particular, responsible, attentive, exacting, thoughtful, diligent, meticulous. ANT. *1. immoral, unprincipled, unscrupulous. 2. slack, slipshod, careless.*

conscious *a.* **1.** AWAKE AND AWARE alert, perceiving, sentient, cognizant, responsive, recognizing, apprehending, mindful, knowing, apprised, *on the ball. **2.** DELIBERATE intended, intentional, calculated, willful, premeditated, designed, on purpose. ANT. *1. unconscious, dead, oblivious. 2. accidental, unplanned, inadvertent.*

consciousness *n.* awareness, alertness, thoughts, cognizance, familiarity, recognition, knowledge, perception, mind, mindfulness, concern, heed. ANT. *unconsciousness, oblivion, ignorance.*

CONSECRATE *v.* [KON suh KRATE] to make or declare sacred or holy. *Fans gathered to consecrate the shrine of Elvis Presley.* SYN. sanctify, exalt, honor, hallow, bless, devote, dedicate, annoint. ANT. *desecrate, defile, revile.*

consecutive *a.* successive, sequential, serial, progressive, orderly, in order, in turn, serial, following, succeeding. ANT. *random, irregular.*

CONSENSUS *n.* [kun SEN sus] an opinion held in common, agreement. *The committee finally reached a consensus.* SYN. agreement, unanimity, concord, accord, unison, harmony, concordance, single-mindedness. ANT. *disagreement, dissension, discord.*

consent n. permission, approval, assent, okay, nod, *go-ahead, acceptance, agreement, *say-so, sanction, allowance. ANT. *dissent, refusal, veto.*

consent v. agree, permit, approve, allow, grant, accept, sanction, *give the green light, *give the nod, okay, assent, acquiesce. ANT. *refuse, veto, object.*

consequence n. **1.** RESULT outcome, effect, upshot, aftermath, fallout, repercussion, reaction, reverberation, wake. **2.** DISTINCTION status, influence, stature, standing, eminence, rank, prestige, notability, power. ANT. *1. cause, source. 2. insignificance, unimportance.*

consequential a. important, significant, weighty, notable, substantial, momentous, serious, far-reaching, considerable, *heavy. ANT. *inconsequential, insignificant, trivial.*

consequently a. therefore, hence, thus, so, accordingly, ergo.

conservation n. preservation, protection, safeguarding, management, saving, supervision, maintenance, husbandry, environmentalism. ANT. *neglect, squandering, denuding.*

conservative n. traditionalist, right-winger, diehard, champion of the status quo, moderate, obstructionist, *stick-in-the-mud. "A man who believes nothing should be done for the first time."— Alfred Wiggam.

CONSERVATIVE a. [kun SURV uh tiv] favoring traditional, nonprogressive ways, moderate. *He doesn't like change; his politics are conservative.* SYN. **1.** traditional, rightwing, rightist, conventional, die-hard, unchanging, stable, old line, hidebound, opposed to change, unprogressive. **2.** CAUTIOUS moderate, safe, middle-of-the-road, careful. ANT. *1. radical, liberal, progressive.*

conserve v. preserve, save, protect, keep, guard, safeguard, maintain, husband, sustain. ANT. *squander, exhaust, denude.*

consider v. ponder, heed, regard, study, think about, deliberate, contemplate, mull over, inspect, ruminate, note. ANT. *ignore, forget, nevermind.*

considerable a. **1.** LARGE sizable, big, substantial, appreciable, respectable, tidy, extensive, great. **2.** IMPORTANT significant, noteworthy, momentous, weighty, distinguished, consequential, substantial, respectable. ANT. *small, insignificant, trivial.*

considerate a. thoughtful, kind, benevolent,

conscientious, respectful, accommodating, polite, solicitous, magnanimous, gracious, tactful. ANT. *inconsiderate, rude, thoughtless.*

consideration n. **1.** THOUGHT study, regard, attention, reflection, contemplation, analysis, review, examination. **2.** THOUGHTFULNESS kindness, benevolence, respect, accommodation, courtesy, solicitude, tact. **3.** FACTOR concern, issue, extent, problem, point. **4.** COMPENSATION recompense, fee, payment, remuneration, reward. ANT. *2. thoughtlessness, rudeness, carelessness.*

consign v. hand over, deliver, entrust, commit, convey, transfer, remit, deposit, assign.

consignment n. assignment, entrusting, delivery, transferal, trust, conveyance, remittance, deposit.

consistency n. agreement, harmony, correspondence, coherence, compatibility, consonance, similarity, uniformity, congruity. ANT. *inconsistence, incongruity, disagreement.*

consistent a. **1.** IN AGREEMENT harmonious, corresponding, coherent, compatible, similar, uniform, homogenous, accordant. **2.** UNCHANGING steady, constant, regular, undeviating. ANT. *1. inconsistent, incompatible. 2. changing, inconsistent.*

consist of vi. comprise, include.

consolation n. solace, comfort, sympathy, compassion, condolence, succor, relief, support, pity, alleviation. ANT. *grief, discouragement.*

console v. comfort, solace, sympathize, condole, soothe, relieve, support, pity, alleviate, cheer, commiserate. ANT. *grieve, distress, dishearten, depress.*

consolidate v. combine, merge, unite, amalgamate, strengthen, band, concentrate, unify, league, mass, firm up. ANT. *separate, disband, weaken.*

consonant a. in agreement, harmonious, accordant, corresponding, consistent, congruent, parallel, coherent. ANT. *disagreeing, discordant, incongruent.*

consort n. partner, companion, husband, wife, spouse, mate, associate, friend.

consort v. associate, fraternize, keep company with, *hang out with, mingle, mix with, *run with, *chum with.

consortium n. partnership, association, alliance, league.

CONSPICUOUS a. [kun SPIK yoo us] attention-grabbing, striking. *A stretch limousine is conspicuous in rural America.* SYN. attention-grabbing, striking, noticeable, obvious, outstanding, prominent, unusual, overt, arresting, distinguished, glaring, flagrant, loud, *sticking out like a sore thumb. ANT. *inconspicuous, hidden, indistinct.*

CONSPIRACY *n.* [kun SPEER uh see] a working together in secret to commit a wrongdoing, a plotting. *A conspiracy to remove the president from power.* SYN. plotting, plot, scheme, intrigue, connivance, collusion, cabal, treachery, machination, foul play, web, *wire-pulling.

conspirator *n.* schemer, plotter, accomplice, engineer, collaborator, colluder, *wire-puller, subversive, traitor, *backstabber, betrayer.

conspire *v.* plot, scheme, intrigue, connive, collude, machinate, engineer, collaborate.

constant *a.* **1.** UNCHANGING steady, regular, invariable, firm, permanent, solid, fixed, stable. **2.** PERPETUAL endless, never ending, relentless, continual, nonstop, unremitting, sustained, incessant, persistent. **3.** FAITHFUL loyal, steadfast, devoted, tried-and-true. ANT. *1. variable, unstable. 2. intermittent, occasional, sporadic. 3. disloyal, unfaithful, fickle.*

constellation *n.* **1.** GATHERING cluster, collection, array, assemblage, group, body. **2.** A FORMATION OF STARS configuration, asterism. "Celestial hieroglyphics." — Marc McCutcheon).

WORD FIND

NORTHERN HEMISPHERE
Andromeda: Andromeda
arrow: Sagitta
bear, great: Ursa Major BIG DIPPER
bear, little: Ursa Minor LITTLE DIPPER
Berenice's Hair: Coma Berenices
Cassiopeia: Cassiopeia
Cepheus: Cepheus
charioteer: Auriga
dolphin: Delphinius
dragon: Draco
filly: Equuleus
fox: Vulpecula
giraffe: Camelopardallis
Hercules: Hercules
herdsmen: Bootes
hunting dogs: Canes Venacti
lion, little: Leo Minor
lizard: Lacerta
lynx: Lynx
lyre: Lyra
northern crown: Corona Borealis
Pegasus: Pegasus
Perseus: Perseus
sea serpent: Hydra

serpent bearer: Ophiuchus
serpent: Serpens
shield: Scutum
swan: Cygnus
triangle: Triangulum
SOUTHERN HEMISPHERE
air pump: Antlia
altar: Ara
bird of paradise: Apus
centaur: Centaurus
chameleon: Chameleon
clock: Horologium
compasses: Circinus
crane: Grus
crow: Corvus
cup: Crater
dog, greater: Canis Major
dog, lesser: Canis Minor
dove: Columba
flying fish: Volans
furnace: Fornax
hare: Lepus
hunter: Orion
Indian: Indus
keel: Carina
mariner's compass: Pyxis
microscope: Microscopium
net: Reticulum
octant: Octans
painter: Pictor
peacock: Pavo
Phoenix: Phoenix
poop deck: Puppis
river: Eridanus
sail: Vela
sculptor: Sculptor
sculptor's tool: Caelum
sextant: Sextans
southern cross: Crux
southern crown: Corona Australis
southern fish: Piscis Austrinus
southern fly: Musca
southern triangle: Triangulum Australe
square: Norma
swordfish: Dorado
table: Mensa
telescope: Telescopium
toucan: Tucana
unicorn: Monoceros
water snake: Hydrus
whale: Cetus
wolf: Lupus
ZODIAC
archer: Sagittarius
bull: Taurus

crab: Cancer
fishes: Pisces
goat: Capricornus
lion: Leo
ram: Aries
scales: Libra
scorpion: Scorpius
twins: Gemini
virgin: Virgo
water bearer: Aquarius

CONSTERNATION *n.* [kon stur NA shun] dismay or shock that leaves one feeling helpless or confused. *The sudden collision filled him with consternation.* SYN. dismay, shock, fear, anxiety, panic, bewilderment, confusion, alarm, stupefaction, horror, terror. ANT. *composure, calm, presence of mind.*

constituency *n.* electorate, voters, district.

constituent *n.* **1.** COMPONENT part, element, unit, ingredient, rudiment. **2.** VOTER elector, balloter, citizen.

constitute *v.* **1.** COMPRISE form, make up, consist of, incorporate, integrate, compose. **2.** APPOINT name, empower, authorize, install, nominate, deputize. **3.** ESTABLISH create, institute, develop, set up, originate, found.

constitution *n.* charter, code, law, rules, canon, Bill of Rights. "A means of assuring that depositories of power cannot misemploy it." — John Stuart Mill.

constitutional *a.* lawful, legal, statutory, chartered, prescribed.

constrain *v.* **1.** FORCE compel, drive, press, coerce, oblige, make, impel, pressure, prevail upon. **2.** RESTRAIN confine, curb, restrict, check, limit, shut in, bar, hold down, incarcerate, imprison.

constraint *n.* **1.** FORCE pressure, obligation, compulsion, coercion, duress, necessity. **2.** RESTRICTION limitation, restraint, check, curb, control, repression, inhibition, confinement. **3.** UNEASE inhibition, reticence, reserve, shyness, diffidence, bashfulness, self-consciousness, restraint.

constrict *v.* **1.** NARROW squeeze, bind, tighten, shrink, contract, clamp, cramp, compress, pinch, strangle, choke. **2.** LIMIT restrict, hold in, impede, arrest, block, curb. ANT. *1. expand, widen, loosen. 2. free, liberate.*

constriction *n.* narrowing, contraction, squeezing, strangulation, compression, stricture, clamping, cramping, pinching, clenching, choking, stenosis, bottleneck. ANT. *opening, loosening.*

construct *v.* build, assemble, put together, erect, *throw up, *slap together, fabricate, engineer, raise, frame, fashion, form. ANT. *raze, demolish, tear down.*

construction *n.* **1.** CONSTRUCTION building, erection, assembling, fabrication, raising, framing, putting up, fashioning, manufacturing, formation. **2.** BUILDING structure, framework, assembly. **3.** EXPLANATION interpretation, rendition, translation, reading.

constructive *a.* helpful, useful, beneficial, practical, valuable, positive, effective.

construe *v.* explain, interpret, translate, spell out, infer, read, understand.

consulate *n.* embassy.

consult *v.* refer to, check with, confer, inquire, seek advice, discuss, talk, deliberate, ask, *pick one's brains, compare notes.

consultation *n.* conference, meeting, discussion, talk, conversation, deliberation, council, *powwow, parley, hearing, session.

consume *v.* **1.** INGEST eat, drink, swallow, devour, guzzle, absorb, down, *gobble, *wolf, *scarf, *polish off. **2.** EXPEND use up, deplete, exhaust, spend, waste, squander, drain, fritter away, finish. **3.** DESTROY level, raze, demolish, annihilate, wreck, ruin, devastate, lay to waste. **4.** ENGROSS absorb, engage, arrest, preoccupy, fix, fascinate, rivet. ANT. *2. save, collect, hoard.*

consummate *v.* complete, perfect, fulfill, achieve, finish, crown, effectuate, *put the finishing touch on, cap, clinch, realize.

CONSUMMATE *a.* [kun SUM it] supremely accomplished, complete. *A consummate violinist.* SYN. accomplished, skilled, supreme, superior, best, ultimate, unsurpassed, superlative, masterful, excellent, complete, thorough, inimitable, peerless. ANT. *run-of-the-mill, mediocre, amateurish.*

consummation *n.* completion, perfecting, fulfillment, finishing, crowning, *finishing touch, cap, realization, attainment.

consumption *n.* use, expenditure, utilization, depletion, loss, devouring, exhaustion, reduction, exploitation. ANT. *conservation, preservation.*

contact *n.* **1.** TOUCHING meeting, connection, union, contingence, proximity, junction, collision. **2.** CONNECTION acquaintance.

contact *v.* **1.** TOUCH meet, graze, impinge, strike, brush. **2.** COMMUNICATE WITH get in touch with, call, seek, reach, look up, find, approach.

contagious *a.* communicable, catching, transmittable, transmissible, spreading, infectious, epidemic, endemic.

contain v. **1.** HOLD accommodate, carry, receive, have a capacity for. **2.** COMPRISE include, consist of, involve, embody, incorporate. **3.** KEEP IN CHECK hold in, restrain, control, suppress, repress, stifle.

contaminate v. pollute, adulterate, spoil, taint, sully, corrupt, defile, poison, degrade, befoul. ANT. *purify, cleanse, sterilize.*

contamination n. pollution, adulteration, spoilage, corruption, defilement, degradation, poisoning, fouling, taint, impurity.

contemplate v. **1.** LOOK AT watch, gaze at, behold, survey, eye, consider, regard, scrutinize. **2.** THINK ABOUT ponder, mull over, brood over, meditate, reflect, ruminate, dwell on, *chew on, consider, *turn over in one's mind.

contemplative a. thoughtful, intent, introspective, absorbed, pensive, meditative, reflective, ruminative, musing, rapt. ANT. *thoughtless, blank, vacuous.*

contemporary a. **1.** MODERN present-day, up-to-date, here and now, current, late, *hot, new, *cutting edge, recent, now, *fresh as today, extant. **2.** COEXISTING coincident, attending, simultaneous, synchronous, concurrent, of the same time. ANT. *1. old, yesterday, historical, past, ancient.*

contempt n. **1.** DISDAIN scorn, repugnance, disgust, disrespect, disregard, derision, revulsion, abhorrence. **2.** DISGRACE shame, dishonor, humiliation, disrepute. ANT. *respect, esteem, honor.*

contemptible a. despicable, shameful, low, detestable, wretched, abhorrent, wicked, mean, loathsome, disgusting, ignominious, shabby, cheap, repugnant. ANT. *honorable, respectable, admirable.*

contemptuous a. disdainful, scornful, disrespectful, arrogant, sneering, insolent, insulting, derisive, *high and mighty, supercilious, condescending, haughty. ANT. *complimentary, deferential, respectful.*

contend v. **1.** MAINTAIN assert, claim, hold, state, declare, argue, insist, prescribe. **2.** VIE struggle, strive, contest, battle, wrestle, tussle, fight, scuffle, clash.

contender n. contestant, competitor, rival.

content n. **1.** MEANING intent, essence, significance, idea. **2.** SATISFACTION happiness, pleasure, comfort, fulfillment, gratification, delight, contentment.

content v. satisfy, please, comfort, delight, gratify, gladden, cheer. ANT. *discontent, trouble,*

upset.

content a. satisfied, happy, pleased, comfortable, at ease, carefree, fulfilled, complacent, serene. ANT. *discontented, miserable, troubled.*

contention n. **1.** DISPUTE argument, disagreement, debate, controversy, squabble, altercation, fight, wrangling, *beef, *bone to pick, quarrel. **2.** STRIVING struggle, contest, battle, fight. **3.** ASSERTION point, stand, claim, opinion, belief, view, plea. ANT. *1. agreement, accord, harmony.*

CONTENTIOUS a. [kun TEN shus] quarrelsome. *He couldn't get along with anyone; he was contentious.* SYN. quarrelsome, belligerent, testy, disputatious, argumentative, combative, nasty, disagreeable, *short-fused, petulant, antagonistic. ANT. *easygoing, accommodating, placatory, peaceable.*

contentment n. satisfaction, happiness, pleasure, comfort, ease, fulfillment, complacency, serenity, tranquility. "The only riches, the only quietness . . . " — George Pettie. "Natural wealth." — Plato. ANT. *discontent, dissatisfaction, misery.*

contest n. competition, match, struggle, rivalry, battle, challenge, meet, round, duel, trial, war, marathon, tourney.

contest v. argue, debate, dispute, challenge, oppose, call into question, object to, conflict, contend, vie, fight, scrap, square off, battle. ANT. *acquiesce, cave in, give in, surrender.*

contestant n. contender, competitor, combatant, opponent, rival, adversary, challenger.

context n. frame of reference, framework, relationship, connection, substance, circumstances, meaning.

contiguous a. touching, meeting, contacting, connecting, next to, abutting, adjoining, nearby, proximate, adjacent, close. ANT. *distant, removed, remote.*

continence n. self-restraint, moderation, self-control, forbearance, refraining, abstinence; virtue, chastity. ANT. *incontinence, indulgence, excess.*

contingency n. possibility, emergency, eventuality, chance occurrence, accident, fortuity, uncertainty, happening, probability.

CONTINGENT a. [kun TIN junt] dependent, subject to. *When we schedule the outing is contingent upon the weather.* SYN. dependent, subject to, conditional, hinging on, controlled by, incidental to, provisory.

continual a. never ending, perpetual, unending, incessant, relentless, unceasing, constant, nonstop, eternal, unremitting, around-the-clock. ANT. *finite, ending, sporadic, intermittent.*

continuance n. persistence, prolongation, protraction, perpetuation, duration.

continue v. **1.** KEEP ON persist, carry on, persevere, extend, maintain, sustain, press on, prolong, progress, remain, abide. **2.** RESUME carry on, restart, begin again, pick up where one left off, proceed, renew. ANT. *stop, end, cease.*

continuity n. continuance, continuation, persistence, prolongation, protraction, perpetuation, endurance, constancy, extension. ANT. *interruption, stoppage, intermittence.*

continuous a. constant, never ending, perpetual, unbroken, connected, uninterrupted, unremitting, incessant, nonstop, infinite, protracted. ANT. *intermittent, broken.*

contort v. twist, turn, wrench, distort, screw up, warp, knot, convolute, gnarl, torture, misshape. ANT. *straighten, smooth.*

contour n. outline, profile, shape, form, figure, lines, curves, silhouette.

contraband a. illegal, black-market, bootleg, unlawful, illicit, *hot, forbidden, prohibited, smuggled, taboo, trafficked.

contraceptive n. birth control device, condom, diaphragm, IUD, *the pill, prophylactic, sponge, shield, spermicide, *rubber.

contract n. agreement, arrangement, understanding, deal, covenant, pact, transaction, compact, bond, gentleman's agreement, obligation, pledge, legal document.

contract v. **1.** COMPRESS reduce, narrow, squeeze, shorten, tighten, condense, recede, constrict, cramp, wither. **2.** MAKE AN AGREEMENT agree, bargain, come to terms, bound, *hammer out a deal, put in writing, pledge, promise, guarantee, covenant. ANT. *1. expand, swell. 2. renege, back out.*

contraction n. compression, reduction, narrowing, squeezing, shortening, tightening, condensing, recession, cramping, withering, shrinkage. ANT. *expansion, swelling, enlargement.*

contradict v. differ, deny, controvert, refute, counter, *fly in the face of, negate, gainsay, repudiate, belie, cancel out. ANT. *agree, corroborate, correspond.*

contradiction n. differing, denial, refutation, disagreement, negation, confliction, discrepancy, gainsay, inconsistency. ANT. *agreement, corroboration, correspondence.*

contradictory a. differing, conflicting, inconsistent, contrary, discrepant, disagreeing, incongruous, antithetical, at variance. ANT. *consistent, agreeing, corresponding.*

contraption n. device, machine, contrivance, gadget, rig, mechanism, appliance, widget, *doohickey, *thingamajig, *Rube Goldberg device.

contrary a. **1.** OPPOSITE contradictory, antithetical, reverse, different, counter, incompatible, incongruous, inimical, conflicting. **2.** DISAGREEABLE cantankerous, antagonistic, hostile, inimical, averse, antipathetic, at odds. ANT. *1. identical, consistent. 2. agreeable, accommodating.*

contrast n. difference, dissimilarity, opposition, variation, differentiation, disparity, antithesis, polarity, distinction, divergence. ANT. *likeness, similarity, mirror image.*

contrast v. **1.** COMPARE differentiate, discriminate, set off, distinguish, weigh. **2.** DIFFER vary, oppose, diverge, contradict, mismatch, conflict.

contravene v. **1.** OPPOSE go against, contradict, reject, repudiate, disagree, gainsay. **2.** VIOLATE cross, disobey, infract, transgress.

contribute v. give, provide, donate, bestow, furnish, supply, grant, dispense, help, hand out, *chip in, *pitch in.

contribution n. donation, gift, handout, helping hand, offering, present, charity, input, benefaction, bestowal.

CONTRITE a. [kun TRITE] feeling or showing remorse, guilt. *He was obviously contrite; he apologized ten times.* SYN. remorseful, guilty, repentant, regretful, penitent, sorry, apologetic, compunctious, rueful, troubled, ashamed, conscience-stricken. ANT. *indifferent, unrepentant, proud.*

contrition n. remorse, repentance, regret, guilt, sorrow, compunction, shame, penitence, self-reproach, ruth, qualms. ANT. *indifference, apathy, pride.*

contrivance n. **1.** DEVICE gadget, creation, appliance, mechanism, machine, contraption, implement, invention, *Rube Goldberg device. **2.** DESIGN scheme, invention, artifice, fabrication, machination, ingenuity, trick.

contrive v. **1.** DEVISE invent, create, improvise, *rig, design, construct, fabricate, *throw together. **2.** DESIGN plan, plot, scheme, connive, engineer, swing, conspire, machinate, finagle, formulate.

CONTRIVED a. [kun TRIVED] overly planned or designed, with a forced or unnatural effect. *The plot was ruined by unlikely coincidences; it was too obviously contrived.* SYN.

forced, unnatural, unspontaneous, labored, phony, manipulated, fake, affected, artificial, strained. ANT. *natural, spontaneous, artless.*

control *n.* command, power, rule, order, direction, mastery, management, supervision, regulation, government, *upper hand, *the whip, influence, jurisdiction, dominion.

control *v.* command, rule, order, direct, master, manage, supervise, run, regulate, govern, influence, dominate, guide, *hold sway over, lead, quarterback, reign, call the shots, dictate, preside over, *be in the driver's seat, *rule with an iron hand, manipulate.

controversial *a.* debatable, moot, arguable, polemical, contestable, questionable, suspect, controvertible, disputable, at issue, unsettled.

controversy *n.* debate, argument, dispute, issue, disagreement, moot point, war of words, brouhaha, fuss, flak, quarrel, wrangling, polemics, embattlement. "A battle in which spittle or ink replace the . . . cannon ball." — Ambrose Bierce.

controvert *v.* oppose, argue, dispute, deny, gainsay, refute, rebut, challenge, contest, debate. ANT. *agree, affirm, go along.*

contusion *n.* bruise, black-and-blue mark, discoloration, injury, bump, *mulberry patch.

CONUNDRUM *n.* [kuh NUN drum] a problem without an apparent solution; a puzzle; a mystery. *Solving the world's population problem is a political conundrum.* SYN. problem, puzzle, mystery, enigma, riddle, brainteaser, *mind-boggler, *hard nut to crack, *stumper, question mark, mystery.

convalesce *v.* recuperate, recover, rehabilitate, restore, revive, get better.

convalescence *n.* recuperation, recovery, rehabilitation, restoration, revival, rejuvenation, cure, return to health, strengthening. "That part that makes the illness worth while." — George Bernard Shaw.

convene *v.* convoke, summon, round up, call up, assemble, gather, congregate, meet, muster, rally, get together.

convenience *n.* **1.** SERVICE usefulness, utility, suitability, benefit, expedience, handiness. **2.** APPLIANCE OR SERVICE time-saver, accessory, comfort, luxury, amenity, facility, help, *life-saver. **3.** SPARE TIME free moment, leisure, chance, opportunity. ANT. **2.** *inconvenience, trouble, bother, *a pain.*

convenient *a.* **1.** SERVICEABLE handy, accommodating, useful, advantageous, beneficial, conducive, helpful, timesaving. **2.** NEARBY at

hand, accessible, central, adjacent, handy, next-door, close, proximate. ANT. *1. inconvenient, troublesome, unsuitable. 2. remote, distant, inaccessible.*

convent *n.* nunnery, abbey, cloister.

convention *n.* **1.** MEETING assembly, gathering, caucus, council, *powwow, congress, convocation. **2.** CUSTOM practice, code, habit, tradition, orthodoxy, etiquette, law.

conventional *a.* **1.** CUSTOMARY usual, traditional, normal, accepted, regular, standard, orthodox, routine, prevailing. **2.** COMMON unoriginal, everyday, run-of-the-mill, conforming, pedestrian, trite, prosaic, undistinguished, humdrum. ANT. *unconventional, unorthodox, radical, avant-garde, original.*

converge *v.* meet, come together, join, intersect, merge, unite, mingle, connect. ANT. *separate, divide.*

conversant *a.* familiar, knowledgeable, acquainted with, au courant, informed, up-to-date, versed, learned, experienced, au fait, abreast. *hip. ANT. *unfamiliar, unacquainted with, ignorant, oblivious.*

conversation *n.* talk, dialogue, discourse, discussion, exchange, communication, chat, colloquy, interlocution, conference, intercourse, gab, *rap, palaver, tete-a-tete, give-and-take, *small talk. "The image of the mind. As the man is, so is his talk." — Publius Syrus. "Our account of ourselves." — Ralph Waldo Emerson.

conversationalist *n.* talker, *blabbermouth, *bag of wind, *bigmouth, *blowhard, *motormouth, *windbag, *yakker.

converse *n.* opposite, reverse, antithesis, obverse.

converse *v.* talk, discuss, communicate, chat, hold a dialogue, confer, discourse, gab, *chew the fat, *rap, *shoot the breeze, confabulate, commune, *schmooze, *flap one's chops, *jibber-jabber, *yack.

conversion *n.* change, changeover, transformation, transmutation, switch, metamorphosis, reversal, remodeling, modification, *about-face, *turnaround, adaptation.

convert *n.* proselyte, novitiate, neophyte, catechumen.

convert *v.* change, transform, transmutate, switch, metamorphose, reverse, remodel, modify, *do an about-face, *do a turnaround, adapt.

convey *v.* **1.** TRANSPORT carry, conduct, transfer, bring, send, move, transmit, forward, deliver, bear, haul. **2.** COMMUNICATE tell, relate, pass along, disclose, reveal, send.

conveyance n. transport, transfer, carrying, transmission, movement, carriage, communication, vehicle.

convict n. criminal, outlaw, prisoner, malefactor, felon, *jailbird, lawbreaker, *con, inmate.

convict v. find guilty, imprison, *send up the river, sentence, condemn.

conviction n. 1. BELIEF faith, opinion, sentiment, tenet, dogma, view, principle, persuasion, doctrine. 2. ASSURANCE certainty, confidence, surety, fervor, earnestness. ANT. 2. uncertainty, doubt.

convince v. prove, sway, persuade, satisfy, *talk into, prevail upon, *sell, *make one see the light, *bring around.

convincing a. persuasive, incontrovertible, solid, satisfying, plausible, powerful, credible, conclusive, sound. ANT. unconvincing, questionable, dubious.

CONVIVIAL a. [kun VIV ee ul] fond of the party life, festive. A convivial mob poured into the bar. SYN. festive, jovial, sociable, fun-loving, merry-making, gregarious, jolly, cheerful, *back-slapping, lively, genial. ANT. grim, sober, solemn, reserved, antisocial.

convocation n. assembly, gathering, convention, congregation, get-together, conference, meeting, council.

convoke v. summon, call together, muster, assemble, gather.

convolution n. coil, loop, twisting, whorl, roll, spiral, helix, curlicue.

convoy n. escort, guard, attendant, accompaniment, protection, defense, contingent, security.

convoy v. escort, guard, accompany, attend, protect, defend, shield, secure, guide, shepherd, chaperon.

convulsion n. spasm, seizure, fit, throe, paroxysm, tremor, twitch, tic, *spaz, *the shakes, *floorgasm.

cook n. chef, baker, chef de cuisine, short-order cook, sous-chef.

cook v. bake, broil, roast, fry, stir fry, deep fry, braise, boil, steam, simmer, fricasee, frizzle, heat, barbecue, grill, sear, blacken, stew, brown, microwave, *nuke, poach, coddle, parboil, saute. "[Cooking] An art; a noble science." — Robert Burton.

cookie n. snap, macaroon, fig bar, chocolate chip cookie, *Oreo, sugar cookie.

cool v. 1. CHILL refrigerate, freeze, frost. 2. COOL IT Sl. simmer down, calm down, moderate, dampen, soften, temper, *chill, *take it easy, *don't sweat it. ANT. 1. heat, warm. 2. go crazy, *have a nutty, *throw a fit, rage.

cool a. 1. CHILLY cold, nippy, wintry, brisk, frosty. 2. CALM collected, composed, relaxed, self-possessed, sedate, tranquil, nonchalant, unflappable, laid-back. 3. UNFRIENDLY aloof, distant, icy, frigid, remote, standoffish, unapproachable, frosty, superior. 4. Sl. EXCELLENT great, *neat, *nifty, *groovy, *rad, *funky, awesome, *bad, *bitchen, *boss, *def, *fresh, *hot. ANT. 1. hot, *roasting. 2. agitated, ruffled, *bent out of shape, *unglued. 3. warm, friendly. 4. *uncool, no good, bad.

coop n. pen, cage, enclosure, hutch.

cooperate v. comply with, go along, work with, accommodate, aid, collaborate, pull together, *play ball, pool resources, help, contribute, further. ANT. oppose, undermine.

cooperation n. collaboration, assistance, help, give-and-take, concert, complicity, compliance, participation, *playing ball, pooling of resources, accommodation. ANT. opposition, undermining, autonomy.

coordinate v. organize, arrange, order, group, systematize, integrate, mesh, synchronize, classify, sort, regulate.

cope v. manage, weather, endure, contend, suffer, get by, face, *cut it, *hack it, deal with, handle.

COPIOUS a. [KOH pee us] abundant, abounding, plentiful. We prepared a copious spread of food for Thanksgiving. SYN. abundant, plentiful, plenty, ample, bounteous, overflowing, lavish, replete, generous, liberal, fat. ANT. scant, sparse, meager.

copout v. Sl. quit, back down, withdraw, *blow off, *worm out, renege, skip, *chicken out, *tap dance.

copse n. thicket, grove, wood, scrub, coppice, boscage.

copulate v. have sexual intercourse, make love, *make out, fornicate, *fool around, sleep together, breed, *screw, *go all the way, *ball, *bang, *bop, *diddle, *dip one's wick, *frig, *get off, *hump, *jump someone's bones, *nail, *pork.

copy n. duplicate, reproduction, replica, imitation, facsimile, *carbon copy, likeness, representation, counterfeit. ANT. original, model.

copy v. 1. DUPLICATE reproduce, replicate, imitate, clone, simulate, represent. 2. IMITATE ape, emulate, pattern, model, mimic, simulate, act like, mirror, impersonate, embody, mock.

coquet v. flirt, tease, toy with, wink at, strut, vamp, titillate, dally, philander.

coquette n. flirt, tease, vamp, hussy, heartbreaker. "A woman without any heart, who makes a fool out of a man that hasn't got any head."—Madame Deluzy.

cord n. line, rope, twine, string, cable, wire, binding.

cordial a. warm, friendly, hearty, sociable, genial, affable, amiable, gracious, hearty, heartfelt. ANT. cold, distant, unsociable.

core n. center, nucleus, heart, kernel, root, *meat, crux, essence, bottom line, *nitty-gritty, gist.

cork n. plug, stopper.

corner n. 1. BEND crook, angle, convergence, intersection, junction, juncture. 2. PREDICA-MENT *pickle, *jam, *squeeze, tight spot, impasse.

corner v. trap, back into, catch, bring to bay.

corny a. trite, banal, stupid, stereotyped, hackneyed, sentimental, sappy, insipid, mushy, unsophisticated, *hokey. ANT. sophisticated, original, powerful.

corollary n. deduction, inference, result, outcome, consequence, end, aftereffect, upshot, precipitate.

corporal a. bodily, physical, material, carnal.

corporate a. united, combined, joint, allied, collective, common.

corps n. unit, crew, team, force, band, division, troupe, regiment, battalion, company, squadron, outfit.

corpse n. body, cadaver, *stiff, carcass, remains, bones, the deceased. "A human been."—Kay Goodman. "[L]ike the cover of an old book, its contents torn out, and stript of its lettering and gilding ... yet the work itself shall not be lost, for it will appear once more in a new and more beautiful edition."—Ben Franklin.

corpulent a. fat, obese, plump, chubby, fleshy, beefy, rotund, tubby, stout, portly, roly-poly, blubbery. ANT. skinny, anorexic, bony.

correct v. 1. RECTIFY set right, redress, amend, fix, adjust, better, mend, revise, reform, doctor. 2. CHASTISE reprimand, scold, reprove, admonish, dress down, censure, rebuke, discipline. ANT. 2. praise, compliment, approve.

correct a. 1. ACCURATE exact, *right, true, precise, *on the button, *on the nose, *on the money, unmistaken, flawless. 2. PROPER suitable, fitting, appropriate, befitting, seemly, *politically correct, *kosher, acceptable. ANT. 1. incorrect, wrong, inaccurate. 2. im-

proper, inappropriate.

correction n. rectification, modification, adjustment, amendment, improvement, righting, reparation, change.

corrective a. remedial, rectifying, counter, reparative, curative, healing, therapeutic.

correlate v. equate, relate, compare, contrast, parallel, correspond, connect.

correspond v. 1. AGREE harmonize, conform, be consistent, be compatible, match, go together, coincide, concur, jibe, fit. 2. COMMUNICATE BY LETTER write, *drop a line, keep in touch. ANT. 1. clash, disagree, differ.

correspondence n. 1. AGREEMENT harmony, conformity, consistency, compatibility, match, coinciding, accordance, congruity. 2. COMMUNICATION letters, *faxes, messages, mail, dispatches. ANT. 1. disagreement, incongruity.

corresponding a. equivalent, parallel, analogous, correlative, reciprocal, alike, synonymous, complementary, conforming, consistent.

corridor n. hall, passageway, walkway, gallery, aisle.

CORROBORATE v. [kuh ROB uh RATE] to confirm or support the information given by another. Several witnesses came forward to corroborate the defendant's alibi. SYN. confirm, support, attest to, verify, certify, authenticate, prove, substantiate, validate, strengthen. ANT. contradict, refute.

corrode v. dissolve, wear, deteriorate, waste, rust, erode, oxidize.

corrosive a. erosive, caustic, acidic, biting, mordant, scathing, cutting, acerbic, wasting, consuming.

corrugated a. ridged, crinkled, wrinkled, creased, ribbed, furrowed, pleated, fluted, rough. ANT. smooth, flat.

corrupt v. demoralize, pervert, debase, spoil, pollute, taint, abase, adulterate, infect, ruin, defile, degrade, debauch, taint.

corrupt a. 1. DISHONEST deceitful, unethical, unprincipled, unscrupulous, crooked, untrustworthy, shady, underhanded, venal, deceptive. 2. IMMORAL depraved, perverted, degenerate, low, evil, rotten, debased, warped, unprincipled. 3. IMPURE contaminated, adulterated, unclean, tainted, defiled, polluted, infected. ANT. 1. honest, honorable, scrupulous. 2. moral, virtuous, upright. 3. pure, clean, unaltered.

corruption n. 1. DISHONESTY deceit, deception, underhandedness, deception, crookedness, *shadiness, fraud, unscrupulousness. **2.** IMMORALITY depravity, perversion, evil, degeneration, baseness, decadence, wickedness, impurity, turpitude, iniquity. **3.** CONTAMINATION adulteration, tainting, defilement, pollution, infection. ANT. *1. honesty, scruples. 2. morality, virtue. 3. purity.*

cortege n. train, retinue, entourage, escort, attendants, procession, court.

cosmetic a. beautifying, enhancing, corrective, superficial.

cosmetics n. makeup, beautifiers, preparations, *warpaint. "Crease paint." — Raymond Cvikota.

cosmic a. **1.** OF SPACE interstellar, universal, interplanetary, galactic. **2.** LIMITLESS infinite, vast, neverending, immense, grandiose, measureless. ANT. *2. microscopic, finite, limited, infinitesimal.* SEE SPACE, UNIVERSE

cosmopolitan a. worldly, international, global, universal, metropolitan, sophisticated, cultured, cultivated, urbane, unprovincial. ANT. *provincial, small-town, insular.*

cosmos n. *great beyond, macrocosm, creation. SEE CONSTELLATION, MOON, PLANET, SPACE, STAR, UNIVERSE

cosset v. pamper, fondle, coddle, pet.

cost n. **1.** EXPENSE charge, price, value, worth, amount, expenditure, payment, outlay, bill. **2.** LOSS injury, harm, forfeit, expense, detriment, damage, sacrifice, price.

costly a. **1.** EXPENSIVE high-priced, steep, exorbitant, dear, pricey, excessive, *stiff. **2.** SACRIFICING painful, injurious, harmful, ruinous. **3.** VALUABLE precious, priceless, luxurious, sumptuous, opulent, exquisite, grand, lavish. ANT. *1. cheap, bargain-priced, economical. 2. painless, harmless. 3. worthless, cheap.*

costume n. outfit, clothing, apparel, garb, attire, dress, ensemble, *getup, raiment, vestments, guise.

coterie n. group, circle, clique, set, club, association, crew, band.

cottage n. house, cabin, shanty, bungalow, shack, chalet, camp.

couch n. sofa, divan, davenport, lounge.

couch v. express, voice, phrase, frame.

cougar n. mountain lion, puma, panther.

cough v. hack, *bark, gasp, rasp, wheeze, hem, hawk, whoop, clear throat.

council n. meeting, assembly, conference, *powwow, convention, gathering, convocation, session, caucus, congress.

counsel n. **1.** ADVICE guidance, instruction, direction, recommendation, *word to the wise, suggestion, opinion, warning. **2.** ATTORNEY lawyer, legal representative, counselor, advocate, barrister, solicitor.

counsel v. advise, guide, instruct, direct, recommend, *give a word to the wise, suggest, warn, steer, prompt, advocate.

counselor n. advisor, attorney, lawyer, advocate, guide, instructor, teacher, mentor, confidant.

count n. total, sum, tally, number, outcome, calculation, score, *bottom line.

count v. **1.** ENUMERATE tally, number, total, add up, tick off, sum, calculate, compute. **2.** CONSIDER regard, deem, esteem, rate. **3.** INCLUDE take into account, number among. **4.** MATTER carry weight, rate, *cut ice.

countenance n. **1.** APPEARANCE aspect, face, expression, features, look, mien, visage, cast, air, semblance. **2.** APPROVAL support, acceptance, sanction, encouragement, blessing, backing.

countenance v. approve, condone, allow, permit, put up with, stand for, tolerate, support, back, sanction. ANT. *disapprove, reject, prohibit.*

counter n. stand, table, shelf, display case, *checkout counter.

counter v. counteract, answer, respond, retaliate, return, come back, oppose, check, neutralize, offset.

counter a. contrary, opposite, contrasting, antithetical, inverse.

counteract v. neutralize, offset, negate, annul, oppose, check, cancel.

counterfeit n. imitation, copy, reproduction, forgery, fake, sham, fraud, phony, replica. ANT. *original, model, *real McCoy, genuine article.*

counterfeit a. *bogus, fake, phony, imitation, sham, fraudulent, *fishy, not genuine, *not kosher, forged, spurious, pseudo. ANT. *real, actual, authentic, genuine.*

countermand n. cancel, override, revoke, repeal, recall, rescind, retract, reverse, overrule.

counterpart n. equivalent, match, correspondent, twin, correlate, duplicate, copy, parallel, mate, analogue, peer.

countless a. innumerable, infinite, multitudinous, untold, *slew, *umpteen, *oodles, limitless, legion, incalculable, many. ANT. *few, finite.*

countrified a. rural, rustic, agrarian, pastoral, *down-home, simple. ANT. *citified, urban, metropolitan.*

country *n.* **1.** NATION motherland, fatherland, land, commonwealth, state, union, realm, republic. **2.** RURAL AREA backwoods, *boonies, *the sticks, woodlands, wilds, farmland, *cow country, outback, bush.

COUP *n.* [KOO] a brilliant maneuver or victory, a masterstroke. Also, a coup d'etat. *The chess match ended with an unexpected coup by the challenger.* SYN. masterstroke, maneuver, achievement, accomplishment, stroke, exploit, coup d'etat, action, move, stunt, feat.

COUP DE GRACE *n.* [KOO de GRAHSS] a deathblow, a finishing blow. *A resounding slam dunk was the coup de grace.* SYN. deathblow, finishing blow, finishing stroke, mortal blow, the clincher, knockout punch.

COUP D'ETAT *n.* [koo day TAH] a violent overthrow of a government or ruler. *The unrest was followed by a coup d'etat and the assassination of the dictator.* SYN. overthrow, change of government, coup, power grab, revolution, uprising, takeover, power play.

couple *n.* pair, duo, twosome, brace.

couple *v.* joint, link, unite, pair, attach, connect, yoke, hitch. ANT. *uncouple, detach, disconnect.*

courage *n.* bravery, fearlessness, valor, lionheartedness, *guts, nerve, *balls, boldness, dauntlessness, derring-do, self-assurance, daring, pluck, backbone, *spine. "[L]ies halfway between rashness and cowardice."—Cervantes. "Being scared to death—and saddling up anyway."—John Wayne. "Grace under pressure."—Ernest Hemingway. ANT. *cowardice, mousiness, *wimpiness, faintheartedness.*

courageous *a.* brave, fearless, valorous, valiant, lionhearted, *gutsy, nervy, *ballsy, dauntless, bold, daring, plucky, stout, manly, *macho, gallant, intrepid, *gritty. ANT. *cowardly, spineless, fearful, *wimpy.*

courier *n.* messenger, carrier, emissary, runner, envoy, *gofer.

course *n.* **1.** PROGRESSION way, advance, proceeding, passage, flow. **2.** ROUTE path, trail, way, channel, run, track. **3.** PROCEDURE mode, plan, scheme, policy. **4.** CLASS curriculum, subject, program, lessons.

course *v.* run, flow, traverse, race, rush, surge, speed, tumble.

court *n.* **1.** COURTYARD enclosure, quadrangle, plaza, square, patio, atrium. **2.** ATTENDANTS entourage, staff, retinue, cortege. **3.** COURT OF LAW court of justice, judiciary, bench, bar, forum, tribunal, municipal building, hall of justice.

WORD FIND

action: suit

appearance before judge without formal trial: hearing

arrest order for failure to appear: bench warrant

blatant show of disrespect for court rules: contempt of court

bond forfeited if accused fails to show up for court: bail

calendar of cases: docket

court order: injunction

court system: judiciary

DA: district attorney, prosecutor

damages awarded beyond plaintiff's loss to punish defendant: punitive damages, exemplary damages, double damages

decision: judgment

decision won without proceedings, for failure of one party to show: default judgment

defendant's suit against plaintiff: countersuit, counterclaim

defending party in a court action: defendant

disposition of case by negotiating guilty plea for lesser charge: plea bargaining

fail to appear after posting bail: jump bail

faulty trial that is voided: mistrial

filer of court action: plaintiff, petitioner

general jurisdiction court: superior court

hearing of charges, entering of plea by accused: arraignment

hears appeals from lower court decisions: court of appeals

higher court that reviews lower court decisions: appellate court

highest: Supreme Court

inquiry, judicial: inquest

intermediary who settles cases out of court: mediator

judge's private room: chambers

jury, citizen's obligation to serve on: jury duty

jury member: juror

jury member's verdict, surveying each: polling the jury

jury's decision: verdict

jury selection process: impaneling

jury spokesman: foreman

jury, trial without: bench trial

jury, twelve-member: petit jury, jury

jury, 12-23 members, evaluates accusations, returns indictments: grand jury

jury unable to reach consensus: hung jury

jury, unethical contact with by lawyer: jury
tampering

lawyer: counsel, attorney, barrister BRIT., solicitor BRIT., advocate

lawyer provided by government for the poor:
public defender

lawyer's assistant: paralegal

local criminal and civil court: municipal
court

location/jurisdiction: venue

loss claimed by plaintiff: damages

lowest court, holds sessions at different
places: circuit court

lying while under oath: perjury

military court proceedings: court-marshal

minor claims court: small claims court

officer/guard who maintains order in court-
room: bailiff

order to appear in court: subpoena, summons

order to arrest someone: warrant

order to restrict comments about case outside court: gag order

order to search a location for evidence:
search warrant

party to a lawsuit: litigant

pledge to tell nothing but the truth: oath

present or argue a case in court: plead

private suit: civil action

punishment handed down by judge: sentence

questioning of opposing party witness by
lawyer: cross examination

retrial from lower court to higher: appeal

ruling, plea for: motion

seat of judge: bench

seat of witness while testifying: witness
stand, witness box

similar earlier case used as model in later
case: precedent

simulated trial by law students: moot court

suit filed on behalf of a group: class action
suit

suspend proceedings: adjourn, recess

suspension of sentencing: stay

sworn statement: affidavit

transcribes court proceedings word-for-
word: court reporter, stenographer

unsanctioned court that ignores appropriate
legal procedures: kangaroo court

will and estate processing court: probate
court, surrogate court

witness who is absolutely vital: material witness

witness who is biased against opponent: hostile witness

witness's pretrial statement given while under oath: deposition

written statement charging one with crime:
indictment

SEE LAW

court v. woo, pursue, keep company with, date,
take out, curry favor with, pander to, flatter,
blandish, cajole, fawn over, *brown-nose,
*kiss up to. ANT. *reject, shun, avoid.*

courteous a. polite, well-mannered, civil, mannerly, respectful, considerate, gracious, refined, gentlemanly, cultivated, formal, ladylike. ANT. *rude, impolite, ill-mannered.*

courtesan n. prostitute, mistress, harlot, kept
woman, concubine. "The aristocracy of
whoredom." —Anon.

courtesy n. politeness, good manners, civility,
respect, consideration, graciousness, refinement, gentleness, formality, tact. "The art of
concealing natural impulses." —Anon. "The
art of choosing among one's real
thoughts." —Abel Stevens. ANT. *rudeness,
discourtesy, informality.*

courtly a. dignified, refined, polite, mannerly,
stately, cultivated, gentlemanly, polished,
well-bred, proper, elegant, respectful, suave.
ANT. *rude, unrefined, rough, ill mannered.*

cove n. bay, inlet, harbor, anchorage, bight, estuary, lagoon.

COVENANT n. [KUV uh nunt] a contract or
binding agreement. *They made a covenant to
perform their duties on time.* SYN. agreement,
contract, compact, pact, pledge, promise,
trust, commitment, arrangement, concordat.

cover n. 1. COVERING coverup, wrapping, sheet,
blanket, tarpaulin, canopy, sheath, folder,
spread, canvas, binding. 2. SHELTER refuge,
retreat, haven, sanctuary, hiding place, protection.

cover v. 1. WRAP encase, enshroud, overspread,
overlay, envelop, cloak, dress, coat. 2. HIDE
conceal, shield, veil, screen, cloak, bury,
camouflage, secrete, disguise. 3. INCLUDE encompass, incorporate, contain, deal with,
comprise, embrace, embody. 4. TRAVERSE
cross, pass through, range over. 5. REPORT
detail, recount, chronicle, tell. ANT. *1. uncover, unwrap, expose. 2. expose, reveal, show.*

COVERT a. [KOH vurt] secret, covered up.
A covert military action. SYN. covered, covered up, secret, hidden, undercover, clandestine, underground, concealed, cloaked, camouflaged, *under wraps, *hush-hush,
surreptitious. ANT. *open, overt, up-front.*

COVET v. [KUH vit] to wish for or desire, especially that of another's. *Do not covet thy neighbor's wife.* SYN. desire, wish for, want, long for, hunger for, crave, yearn for, lust after, itch for, fancy. ANT. *reject, ignore, spurn.*

covetous a. desirous, avaricious, greedy, acquisitive, lustful, rapacious, yearning, longing, grasping, grabby, envious.

covey n. flock, party, band, bevy, group, cluster, clique.

cow n. bovine, ruminant, bull, heifer, calf, *bossy.

WORD FIND

barn: byre, stable

beef breeds: Angus, Beefalo, Belted Galloway, Brahman, Charbray, Hereford, Texas Longhorn

chew cud: ruminate

cornstalks, hay, straw food: fodder

dairy breeds: Brown Swiss, Guernsey, Holstein, Jersey

dehorned animal: pollard

diseases: foot-and-mouth disease, mastitis, scours

hairy portion of tail: switch

milk gland: udder

moo: low

neck fold on some breeds: dewlap

regurgitated food that is rechewed: cud

stomachs: abomasum, omasum, reticulum, rumen

cow v. intimidate, bully, unnerve, frighten, daunt, threaten, buffalo, bully, terrorize, browbeat. ANT. *fortify, embolden, puff up.*

coward n. *gutless wonder, *scaredy-cat, *baby, *chicken, *wimp, *wuss, milquetoast, poltroon, dastard, *invertebrate, *sissy, *mouse, *candy ass. "One who in a perilous emergency thinks with his legs."—Ambrose Bierce. "A man in whom the instinct of self-preservation acts normally."—Sultana Zoraya. ANT. *daredevil, hero, *macho man.*

cowardice n. timidity, fearfulness, faintheartedness, *wimpiness, *mousiness, pusillanimity, timorousness, *chicken-heartedness, *cold feet. "To know what is right and not do it."—Confucius ANT. *bravery, fearlessness, *guts, *balls, daring.*

cowardly a. fearful, timid, frightened, fainthearted, *babyish, *chicken, *wimpy, *mousy, dastardly, craven, *gutless, spineless, timorous, shrinking, *yellow. ANT. *brave, courageous, *gutsy, daring.*

cowboy n. cowpuncher, bronco, cowpoke, rancher, *buckaroo, drover, *vaquero, cattle herder, *gaucho.

WORD FIND

breaker of wild horses: bronc buster

calf: dogie

capture of wandering cattle: roundup

cattle identification mark: brand

competition: rodeo

food wagon on the range: chuck wagon

foreman: trail boss

hat: Stetson

herd horses: wrangle

horse herder: wrangler

leather breeches: chaps, chaparejos, leggins

pistol: Colt 45

ranch company: outfit

rides alongside herd: flank rider, swing rider

rides at front of herd: point rider

rides behind herd: drag rider

rides wide of herd and rounds up wandering cattle: outrider

rifle: Winchester

rope: lariat, lasso

sack for personal belongings: war bag

staple: frijoles, beans, jerky

steal cattle: rustle

string of horses assigned to rider: mount

unbranded cow: maverick

unbroken horse: bronco

SEE COW, HORSE

cower v. cringe, shrink, flinch, quail, blench, wince, tremble, kowtow, grovel, skulk. ANT. *strut, swagger, tower over.*

COY a. [KOY] shy or affectedly shy, demure. *With men, she was always coy.* SYN. shy, demure, modest, retiring, bashful, shrinking, diffident, blushing, sheepish, self-conscious, *playing hard-to-get, coquettish. ANT. *bold, aggressive, forward, cheeky.*

cozy a. snug, comfy, cushy, warm, snuggled, secure, safe, intimate.

crabby a. *bitchy, surly, irritable, *cranky, snappish, cross, petulant, grouchy, testy, moody, *touchy, *on the rag. ANT. *sweet, pleasant, good-humored.*

crack n. 1. SNAP clap, crackle, pop, slap, bang, thunder, boom, report. 2. FRACTURE break, split, cut, fragment, splinter, tear, rent, cleft, fissure, rupture. 3. HIT blow, clout, clip, whack, pound, bang.

crack v. 1. SNAP clap, crackle, pop, slap, bang, thunder, boom. 2. FRACTURE break, split, cut, fragment, splinter, shatter, smash, tear, cleave. 3. HIT strike, clip, whack, clout. 4.

LOSE COMPOSURE *lose it, go crazy, *bug out, have a nervous breakdown, *go to pieces. **5.** SOLVE OR BREAK, AS A CODE decipher, decode, work out, figure out.

crack *a.* *crackerjack, first-rate, superior, ace, expert, proficient, master.

crackerjack *a.* SEE CRACK

crackpot *n.* eccentric, *nut, *birdbrain, crackbrain, crank, *screwball.

crack-up *n.* collision, accident, wreck. SEE ACCIDENT

cradle *n.* birthplace, origin, source, fountain, beginning, wellspring.

craft *n.* **1.** SKILL expertise, artistry, facility, mastery, dexterity, ability, knack, know-how. **2.** CUNNING artfulness, deceit, craftiness, shrewdness, slyness, artifice, guile, trickery, ruse. **3.** TRADE handiwork, job, line, business, vocation. ANT. *1. incompetency, clumsiness, inability. 2. honesty, naiveté.*

craftsman *n.* artisan, artist, artificer, technician, smith, talent, *wiz.

craftsmanship *n.* artistry, handiwork, detail work.

crafty *a.* cunning, shrewd, sly, *foxy, wily, artful, deceitful, underhanded, sharp, designing, scheming, *slippery. ANT. *honest, naive, artless.*

craggy *a.* steep, rugged, rocky, jagged, stony, precipitous, scraggy.

cram *v.* **1.** STUFF fill, crowd, press, compress, ram, squeeze, pack, load, choke, condense. **2.** STUDY *burn the midnight oil, read up, *bone up, *hit the books.

cramp *n.* contraction, spasm, *charlie horse, kink, crick, twinge, stitch, knot.

cramp *v.* restrict, restrain, confine, hinder, hamper, constrict, check, limit, impede, clamp, stymie, inhibit.

crank *n.* eccentric, *crackpot, character, *nut.

cranky *a.* irritable, ill-tempered, grouchy, surly, moody, ugly, *ornery, grumpy, grouchy, *like a bear, testy, ill-humored, choleric. ANT. *sweet, pleasant, good-humored.*

cranny *n.* opening, crevice, fissure, cavity, gap, chink, cleft, furrow.

crap *n.* **1.** EXCREMENT *shit, dung, poop. **2.** JUNK trash, garbage, refuse.

crash *n.* **1.** BANG clatter, clangor, racket, din, blast, crack, thunder, boom. **2.** COLLISION smashup, wreck, impact, crack-up, pileup, accident, *wipeout, crunch, bump, *fenderbender, *rear-ending, *T-bone, *sideswipe. **3.** BANKRUPTCY financial collapse, failure, ruination.

crash *v.* **1.** BANG clatter, clang, explode, blast, crack, thunder, boom. **2.** SMASH impact, wreck, shatter, total, crack up, disintegrate, collide, bump, jolt, blindside, tumble, *go end over end, *go ass over teakettle, *plow into, ditch, *go down in flames. **3.** GO BANKRUPT fail, collapse, *go belly up.

CRASS *a.* [KRASS] ignorant and insensitive, indelicate. *We were mortified by his crass jokes.* SYN. ignorant, stupid, insensitive, unfeeling, coarse, vulgar, boorish, uncouth, rough, lowbrow, gross, unrefined, philistine, crude. ANT. *sensitive, refined, delicate.*

crate *n.* box, case, carton, container, receptacle.

crater *n.* pit, craterlet, hole, caldera, cavity.

crave *v.* **1.** DESIRE long for, yearn for, hunger for, want, covet, thirst for, lust after, ache for, need, require. **2.** BEG implore, beseech, plead for, entreat, solicit, supplicate, pray for. ANT. *detest, loathe, spurn, reject.*

craven *a.* cowardly, fearful, dastardly, timid, timorous, yellow, fainthearted, *chicken, *wimpy, gutless, spineless, pusillanimous. ANT. *brave, courageous, fearless, daring.*

craving *n.* desire, longing, yearning, want, need, hunger, thirst, hankering, *yen, lust.

crawl *v.* creep, go on all fours, *belly, worm, inch, wriggle, drag, *go at a snail's pace, writhe, grovel.

craze *n.* fad, mania, rage, *latest thing, fashion, trend, passion.

crazed *a.* SEE CRAZY

crazy *a.* **1.** MENTALLY UNSTABLE insane, deranged, demented, psychotic, *nuts, cracked, *out of one's mind, daft, *touched, *out to lunch, *moonstruck, maniacal, mad, *flipped out, flaky, wacky, loco, *potty, *psycho, *loony, buggy, *mad as a March hare, *crazier than a shithouse rat, *off the wall, *mental, berserk, hysterical, *gone around the bend, *apeshit, *off one's trolley. SEE NEUROSIS, NEUROTIC, PSYCHOSIS. **2.** NOT SENSIBLE impractical, unrealistic, ludicrous, *cockamamie, *harebrained, fantastical, absurd, ridiculous, foolish, silly, unsound, irrational. **3.** ARDENT fond, mad, devoted, wild, zealous, enthusiastic, passionate. ANT. *1. sane, stable, levelheaded, lucid, rational. 2. sensible, realistic, practical. 3. cool, indifferent, apathetic.*

creak *v.* squeak, grate, rasp, groan, squeal, screech, squawk.

crease *n.* fold, ridge, pleat, wrinkle, crimp, crinkle, rumple.

crease v. fold, pleat, wrinkle, crimp, crinkle, rumple, pucker.

create v. originate, make, think up, develop, invent, design, author, compose, produce, spawn, give rise to, found, formulate, dream up, establish, innovate, fabricate, coin, *hatch, launch, start, conceive.

creation n. **1.** CONCEPTION birth, genesis, inception, origination, nativity, generation, establishment, formation. **2.** INVENTION work, handiwork, brainchild, production, piece, innovation. **3.** HEAVEN AND EARTH universe, life, cosmos, world, nature. "The shaping of an indifferent matter into a world of value." — J.E. Boodin.

creative a. inventive, artistic, imaginative, resourceful, clever, ingenious, original, innovative, gifted, visionary, inspired, Promethean. ANT. *unoriginal, mindless, sterile, stale, unimaginative.*

creativity n. inventiveness, originality, resourcefulness, cleverness, inspiration, vision, ingenuity, genius, fertility, fecundity, talent. "Discontent translated into art." — Eric Hoffer. ANT. *sterility, barrenness, mindlessness, infertility.*

creator n. inventor, maker, architect, God, father, originator, mastermind, founder, designer.

creature n. beast, animal, *critter, *varmint, living being, mammal, vertebrate, man. SEE ANIMAL, MONSTER

credence n. acceptance, belief, trust, credibility, reliance, faith, confidence, assurance, credit, stock. ANT. *disbelief, doubt, distrust.*

credentials n. references, qualifications, documents, authorization, testimonial, certificate, license, letter of reference, diploma, title, papers.

credibility n. believability, reliability, trustworthiness, soundness, integrity, plausibility, dependability. ANT. *implausibility, questionability.*

credible a. believable, reliable, trustworthy, sound, plausible, dependable, honest, solid, conceivable, likely. ANT. *incredible, unbelievable, doubtful.*

credit n. **1.** BELIEF trust, faith, honesty, credibility. **2.** RECOGNITION acclaim, praise, tribute, notice, commendation, pat on the back, *Brownie points, acknowledgement. **3.** DEBT on account, deferred payment, charge, time, installment plan. "Imaginary riches" — Thomas Peacock. ANT. 1. *disbelief, mistrust.* 2. *blame, disapproval.* 3. *cash.*

credit v. **1.** BELIEVE trust, accept, *buy, have faith in, trust, *take stock in. **2.** ASSIGN TO recognize, accredit, attribute, ascribe, acknowledge. ANT. 1. *disbelieve, distrust.*

creditable a. commendable, laudatory, meritorious, praiseworthy, worthy, respectable, exemplary, honorable. ANT. *unworthy, disgraceful, despicable.*

credo n. belief, creed, tenet, principles, code.

credulous a. gullible, naive, trusting, believing, *born yesterday, unsuspecting, unsophisticated, *thick, green. ANT. *incredulous, suspicious, disbelieving, wary, cynical.*

creed n. faith, religion, belief, ideology, principles, persuasion, tenet, doctrine, conviction, dogma.

creek n. stream, brook, crik, rill, run, rivulet, runnel, spring.

creep n. Sl. jerk, *dink, *geek, *goon, *sleazebag, *scumbag, weirdo.

creep v. crawl, worm, snake, writhe, move stealthily, *belly, wriggle, *crab, grovel, slink, skulk, steal, sneak.

creeps, the n. Sl. *heebie-jeebies, fear, repugnance, *the willies, *the horrors, *the jumps.

creepy a. scary, gruesome, spine-tingling, hair-raising, horrible, disturbing, nightmarish, eerie, revolting, sinister, weird, macabre, chilling, *skin-crawling.

crescent n. half-moon, demilune, meniscus, sickle. SEE MOON

crest n. **1.** COMB tuft, cockscomb, topknot, plume, mane. **2.** TOP summit, crown, ridge, peak, pinnacle, head, apex.

crestfallen a. disappointed, dejected, down, depressed, discouraged, downhearted, dispirited, sad, melancholy, low. ANT. *joyful, euphoric, *up.*

crevice n. fissure, crack, gap, cleft, cranny, rent, split, groove, fracture, slit, gash, crevasse, chasm, opening.

crew n. group, band, team, company, squad, troupe, mob, gang, party, set, bunch, posse, clique.

crib v. Sl. cheat, copy, plagiarize, lift.

crime n. lawlessness, wrongdoing, offense, malfeasance, malefaction, antisocial behavior, transgression, corruption, felony, misdemeanor.

criminal n. lawbreaker, outlaw, felon, convict, crook, *hood, larcenist, culprit, desperado, mafioso, scofflaw, recidivist. "A person with predatory instincts who has not sufficient capital to form a corporation." — Howard

Scott.

criminal *a.* **1.** ILLEGAL unlawful, illicit, felonious, illegitimate, *shady, crooked, larcenous, homicidal. **2.** VILLAINOUS wicked, evil, nefarious, degenerate, corrupt, errant.

crimp *n.* fold, crease, pleat, wrinkle.

cringe *v.* shrink, flinch, cower, wince, quail, blench, recoil, grovel, quiver, crouch, bow and scrape. ANT. *stand tall, strut, swagger.*

crinkle *v.* wrinkle, crumple, crimple, pucker, crease, crimp, fold, twist, crackle, rustle. ANT. *smooth, straighten, press.*

cripple *v.* disable, handicap, incapacitate, paralyze, maim, debilitate, immobilize, hamstring, *sideline, *bench, impair, weaken. ANT. *invigorate, strengthen, fortify.*

crisis *n.* turning point, emergency, trouble, *moment of truth, *point of no return, crossroad, catastrophe, disaster, *zero hour, predicament, exigency, *crunch, *pickle, strait, *critical mass. "God's call to us to reach a new level of humanity." —Samuel Miller.

crisp *a.* **1.** BRITTLE crunchy, crumbly, friable, firm, fresh. **2.** CHILLY invigorating, bracing, brisk, refreshing, nippy. **3.** SHORT pithy, succinct, brief, terse, sharp, blunt, pointed. **4.** NEAT tidy, trim, clean, smart, *snappy, spruce. ANT. *1. soft, withered. 2. hot. 3. dull, wordy, verbose. 4. sloppy, slovenly.*

CRITERION *n.* [kri TEER ee un] something on which a judgment can be based, a test or standard. *When hiring an employee, our most important criterion is sales ability.* SYN. standard, test, rule, measure, guideline, barometer, gauge, scale, yardstick, guidepost, touchstone.

critic *n.* **1.** REVIEWER analyst, judge, expositor, connoisseur, authority, expert, arbiter, commentator. "A legless man who teaches running." —Channing Pollack. "Brushers of noblemen's clothes." —George Herbert **2.** FAULTFINDER complainer, *nitpicker, *nagger, carper, censor, detractor, quibbler, belittler, attacker.

critical *a.* **1.** FAULTFINDING cutting, censorious, carping, 'nitpicking, derogatory, disparaging, captious, unflattering, severe, quibbling, disapproving. **2.** EXACTING particular, judicial, discerning, discriminating, fussy, precise, finicky, demanding, hairsplitting. **3.** CRUCIAL decisive, serious, grave, important, momentous, significant, pivotal, dire, climacteric, vital, urgent. ANT. *1. approving, accepting, complimentary. 2. undiscerning, un-*particular, *easy. **3.** *trivial, insignificant.*

criticism *n.* **1.** ANALYSIS critique, assessment, review, judgment, evaluation, examination, appraisal, commentary. "The avocation of assessing the failures of better men." —Nelson Algren. "A disinterested endeavor to learn and propagate the best that is known and thought in the world." —Mathew Arnold. "Growing important and formidable at very small expense." —Samuel Johnson. **2.** DISAPPROVAL faultfinding, disparagement, belittling, censure, carping, diatribe, *nitpicking, quibbling, *knock, *slam, pan, *swipe, *Bronx cheer, brickbats. ANT. *2. approval, compliment, praise, raves.*

criticize *v.* **1.** ANALYZE critique, assess, review, judge, evaluate, examine, appraise, dissect, comment on. **2.** FINDFAULT disapprove, censure, disparage, belittle, *nitpick, quibble, *knock, *slam, *pan, *swipe, bash, blast, *trash, scathe, *roast, attack, *let have it with both barrels, ridicule, scarify. ANT. *2. approve, laud, praise, applaud, cheer.*

critique *n.* analysis, review, assessment, commentary, write-up, report, *pan, *slam, *trashing, rave.

crony *n.* friend, companion, comrade, ally, pal, *chum, *buddy, *sidekick, colleague, accomplice.

crook *n.* **1.** BEND curve, hook, bow, angle, turn. **2.** CRIMINAL felon, thief, swindler, robber, embezzler, burglar, *con.

crooked *a.* **1.** BENT curved, hooked, bowed, angled, twisted, awry, tortuous, warped, misshapen, skewed, serpentine, lopsided, deviating, zigzag. **2.** DISHONEST corrupt, deceitful, shady, fraudulent, shifty, underhanded, tricky, designing, crafty. ANT. *1. straight, level, aligned. 2. honest, honorable, aboveboard, trustworthy.*

crop *n.* harvest, yield, production, produce.

crop *v.* cut, trim, clip, chop, snip, shear, shorten, pare, lop, prune, mow.

cross *n.* **1.** CRUCIFIX crux, rood. "Ladders that lead to heaven." —Samuel Smiles.

WORD FIND

cross-bearer: crucifer

cross-shaped: cruciate, cruciform

cross with circle behind crossbeam: Celtic cross

cross with v-shaped ends: Maltese cross

Egyptian cross with loop on top: ankh, ansate cross

horizontal beam: transom

2. CROSS TO BEAR, BURDEN weight, suffering,

adversity, load, albatross, affliction, misfortune, pain.

cross v. **1.** TRAVERSE span, pass over, extend, go across, bridge, ply, ford. **2.** INTERSECT converge, meet, join, bisect, crisscross, entwine. **3.** MIX mingle, blend, crossbreed, hybridize, fuse. **4.** HINDER oppose, thwart, frustrate, foil, check, deny, impede, stymie, interfere with. ANT. **4.** *help, aid, assist.*

cross a. angry, irritable, crabby, testy, touchy, annoyed, surly, snappy, *pissed, *put out, peeved, ill-tempered, *full of piss and vinegar, waspish, choleric. ANT. *happy, cheerful, good-humored.*

cross-examine v. question, interrogate, *pump, *give the third degree, *put on the hotseat, *grill, *go over with a fine-tooth comb, scrutinize.

cross-eye n. strabismus, walleye, exotropia.

crossing n. crossway, passage, bridge, crossroad, junction.

crotchety a. grouchy, irritable, cross, touchy, cantankerous, surly, *ornery, testy, peevish, cranky, eccentric. ANT. *pleasant, good-humored, sweet.*

crouch v. bend, stoop, bow, hunker down, *scooch down, hunch, cower, cringe.

crow n. raven, rook, jackdaw.

crow v. brag, boast, bluster, strut, *toot one's own horn, exult, gloat, vaunt. ANT. *minimize, be humble, *eat crow.*

crowd n. **1.** THRONG crush, flood, multitude, horde, mass, confluence, pack, press, *everybody and his brother, mob, gathering. "The collective wisdom of individual ignorance."—Thomas Carlyle. "A fatal condition to thought."—Anon. **2.** GROUP circle, set, clique, clan, coterie, bunch, gang, faction, crew.

crowd v. throng, press, congest, cluster, mass, surge, swarm, pile, squeeze, jam, crush, huddle, squash, *squish, *stand cheek by jowl, jostle, elbow, mob. ANT. *disperse, scatter, thin out.*

crowded a. thronged, congested, massed, swarming, squeezed together, jammed, crushed, huddled, squashed, *squished, mobbed, standing room only, *wall to wall, *sardined, teeming, *standing cheek by jowl, *breathing down each other's necks. ANT. *empty, deserted.*

crown n. **1.** TOP crest, head, pinnacle, zenith, summit, apex, culmination, tip, vertex. **2.** TIARA coronet, diadem, circlet. **3.** ROYALTY sovereignty, monarchy, the throne. ANT. *bottom, base.*

crown v. cap, complete, perfect, finish, complete, fulfill, climax, top off.

crucial a. critical, vital, essential, decisive, pivotal, central, dire, pressing, climactic, momentous, life-threatening, important. ANT. *unimportant, insignificant, trivial, incidental.*

crucify v. torture, torment, hang, nail to a cross, rack, excruciate, persecute, brutalize, harrow.

crude a. **1.** ROUGH OR UNREFINED IN MANNER coarse, earthy, *gross, tactless, unpolished, uncouth, crass, vulgar, ignorant, churlish. **2.** RAW OR UNFINISHED rough, natural, green, unrefined, ungraded, unpolished, rough-hewn, primitive, unprocessed. ANT. **1.** *refined, cultured, polished, civilized.* **2.** *refined, finished, polished.*

cruel a. vicious, ferocious, inhuman, inhumane, mean, savage, brutal, merciless, barbarous, sadistic, cold-blooded, heartless, bestial, bloodthirsty, ruthless. ANT. *kind, benevolent, compassionate.*

cruelty n. viciousness, ferocity, inhumanity, meanness, savagery, brutality, barbarity, sadism, cold-bloodedness, heartlessness, bestiality, ruthlessness. ANT. *kindness, compassion, benevolence.*

cruise v. sail, navigate, travel, voyage, rove, wander, journey, drift.

crumb n. fragment, bit, tidbit, morsel, sliver, scrap, shred, speck, splinter.

crumble v. break apart, fall to pieces, disintegrate, fragment, crack, fritter, powder, shred, decay.

crumple v. **1.** RUMPLE wrinkle, pucker, crinkle, crease. **2.** FALL APART collapse, give way, buckle, topple, fall to pieces, cave in.

crunch v. grind, munch, chew, chomp, masticate, gnaw, champ.

crusade n. campaign, movement, cause, drive, mission, expedition, march, push, battle.

crusader n. champion, campaigner, reformer, visionary, *mover and shaker, fighter, *voice for change.

crush n. infatuation, *puppy love, fancy, passion, fondness, liking, *the hots.

crush v. **1.** MASH squash, press, compress, squeeze, pulverize, crunch, powder, *squish, grind, granulate, trample. **2.** DEFEAT overpower, overwhelm, vanquish, obliterate, humiliate, *blow away, subdue, conquer, squelch, beat down. ANT. **2.** *surrender, lose, bow down.*

crust n. coating, shell, skin, hull, rind, layer,

border, caking, encrustation.

crusty a. surly, sour, testy, cranky, crabby, gruff, peevish, irascible, ill-tempered, bearish, grouchy. ANT. *easygoing, good-natured, pleasant.*

crutch n. prop, support.

crux n. core, essence, heart, meat, *meat and potatoes, nitty-gritty, gist, root, nub, basis.

cry n. **1.** WEEPING bawling, wailing, whimpering, sobbing, sniveling, blubbering, howling, bewailing, lament. **2.** SHOUT yell, exclamation, call, holler, outcry, utterance, scream, squawk, shriek, yelp, bellow. **3.** PLEADING appeal, entreaty, supplication, imploration, plea, *cri de coeur, request, prayer.

cry v. WEEP bawl, wail, whimper, sob, snivel, squall, blubber, howl, burst into tears, break down, mewl, pule, *boohoo, moan, dissolve into tears, convulse with tears, choke up, shed tears, blink back tears.

WORD FIND

body language: curls into a fetal position; clenching/lurching/knotting stomach; throat closing spastically; throat raw; swallows lump in throat; nostrils dilate; chest grows heavy; gulps air spastically; chokes; splutters; screws knuckles into eye sockets

face: snarl of agony, grimace, scarlet, swollen/puffy, contorts grotesquely, twists in anguish, pouts, tremulous, bottom lip curls, eyes take on wounded look, features stricken, eyes transfixed with shock and grief, eyes brim with tears

voice: quavers, cracks, shrill, constricts, rises hysterically, rises an octave, strangled; takes on a hitch, raw with agony, speaks in ragged bursts SEE GRIEVE, MOURN, SCREAM, TEARS

2. SHOUT yell, exclaim, holler, call, utter, sing out, bellow, hail, crow, scream, yelp, vociferate, squawk

crypt n. tomb, vault, chamber, mausoleum, grave, catacomb, sepulcher. SEE CEMETERY

CRYPTIC a. [KRIP tic] mysterious, hidden. *A cryptic message from the psychic.* SYN. mysterious, hidden, enigmatic, secret, mystic, occult, vague, obscure, ambiguous, arcane, esoteric, veiled. ANT. *clear, open, straightforward.*

crystal a. clear, transparent, limpid, pellucid.

cuddle v. snuggle, hug, embrace, nestle, nuzzle, curl up, clasp, pet, caress, fondle, squeeze.

cudgel n. club, bat, bludgeon, stick, shillelagh.

cue n. signal, sign, intimation, tip, tip-off, hint, prompt, indication, nod, wink.

cuff v. slap, buffet, hit, strike, box, clout.

cul-de-sac n. deadend, alley, impasse, blind alley, trap.

cull v. choose, select, pick, single out, glean, opt for, winnow, garner, collect, sift, sort out.

culminate v. [KULL muh NATE] to come to the conclusion or peak, to climax. *The derby will culminate with the awarding of prizes.* SYN. peak, climax, conclude, finish, end, complete, perfect, crown, cap, top off, *come to a head. ANT. *open, begin, commence, *get the ball rolling.*

culmination n. conclusion, peak, climax, finish, end, completion, crowning, cap, consummation, apex, height, zenith, pinnacle. ANT. *beginning, opening, commencement.*

CULPABLE a. [KUL puh bul] responsible for a wrongdoing, to blame. *She was culpable in the car accident.* SYN. responsible, blameworthy, to blame, accountable, guilty, at fault, liable, amiss, in the wrong, sinful. ANT. *innocent, blameless.*

culprit n. offender, guilty party, wrongdoer, malefactor, miscreant, evildoer, criminal, felon, rascal, sinner, *bad guy.

cult n. followers, following, believers, school, affiliation, clique, band, sect, faction, faith, idolization, devotees, disciples, *underground.

cultivate v. **1.** PREPARE GROUND FOR GROWING plow, till, fertilize, dress, hoe, rake, manure, tend, sow, nurture, foster, plant, farm. **2.** DEVELOP enrich, educate, train, improve, school, enlighten, discipline, refine, civilize. **3.** SEEK THE FRIENDSHIP OF befriend, court, ingratiate, *get on one's good side, *suck up to, *kiss up to, *brownnose, *get cozy with, *play up to, promote, foster. ANT. 1 *sterilize*, pollute. 2. *retard, stunt.* 3. *alienate, distance, slight.*

cultivation n. **1.** FARMING agriculture, crop-raising, agronomy, gardening, husbandry, tillage. **2.** DEVELOPMENT education, training, schooling, enlightenment, discipline, refinement, scholarship, erudition, culture.

culture n. **1.** EDUCATION AND SOCIAL GROWTH advancement, development, refinement, elevation, improvement, training, accomplishment, erudition, enlightenment, gentility, urbanity, manners, polish, civility. "The best that has been said and thought in the world."—Mathew Arnold. "The developing of an avid hunger for knowledge and beauty."—Jesse Bennet. "Anything that people do and monkeys don't."—Anon. **2.**

INSTITUTIONS AND BELIEFS civilization, the arts, customs, folkways, mores, convention, lifestyle. ANT. *1. regression, degeneration, decline.*

cultured *a.* cultivated, refined, polished, learned, educated, civilized, enlightened, accomplished, well-bred, erudite, genteel, high-class. ANT. *regressive, primitive, uncultured, illiterate.*

cumbersome *a.* heavy, clumsy, awkward, bulky, unmanageable, unwieldy, hefty, ponderous, massive, incommodious. ANT. *light, compact.*

cunning *n.* "A sinister or crooked wisdom." — Frances Bacon.

cunning *a.* **1.** CRAFTY shrewd, wily, artful, cagey, sharp, guileful, foxy, sly, slick, *streetwise. **2.** INGENIOUS imaginative, clever, skillful, inventive, dexterous, intelligent, masterly, resourceful. ANT. *1. artless, naive, honest. 2. stupid, unimaginative, moronic.*

cup *n.* glass, goblet, mug, tumbler, chalice, demitasse, stein, vessel.

cupboard *n.* cabinet, shelf, closet.

cupidity *a.* greed, avarice, acquisitiveness, rapaciousness, graspingness, covetousness, want, hunger. ANT. *unselfishness, generosity.*

cupola *n.* dome, belfry.

cur *n.* scoundrel, knave, cad, villain, blackguard, *dog, *scumbag, wretch, rogue, *snake, *weasel.

curator *n.* custodian, keeper, conservator, caretaker, steward, guardian.

curb *n.* restriction, check, restraint, control, bar, hindrance, stop, brake, bridle, damper.

curb *v.* restrict, check, restrain, control, bar, hinder, stop, brake, bridle, dampen, slow, limit, inhibit. ANT. *push, facilitate, help.*

curdle *v.* congeal, coagulate, clot, clabber, thicken, solidify, ferment, sour. ANT. *thin, liquefy.*

cure *n.* remedy, antidote, corrective, medicine, cure-all, panacea, treatment, regimen, *quick fix, elixir, prescription, nostrum.

cure *v.* remedy, correct, treat, medicate, fix, heal, restore, alleviate, relieve, repair, doctor, rehabilitate.

cure-all *n.* panacea, elixir, catholicon, nostrum, patent medicine.

curfew *n.* *lights out, prohibition, ban, restriction.

curiosity *n.* **1.** INQUISITIVENESS interest, concern, *nosiness, questioning, prying, *thirst for knowledge. "To eat of the forbidden fruit." — Robert Burton. "The lust of the mind." — Thomas Hobbes. "The mother of science." — Charles Singer. "A peep-hole in the brain." — Elbert Hubbard. **2.** CURIO novelty, oddity, rarity, conversation piece, objet d'art, bibelot, wonder, marvel. ANT. *indifference, apathy.*

curious *a.* **1.** INQUISITIVE interested, concerned, *nosy, questioning, prying, *thirsty for knowledge, inquiring, snooping, wondering, inquisitorial. **2.** ODD strange, rare, novel, peculiar, exotic, quaint, weird, unique, marvelous, queer, unusual. ANT. *1. indifferent, apathetic, unconcerned. 2. common, ordinary, usual, everyday.*

curl *n.* curve, loop, coil, wave, turn, roll, twist, swirl, whorl, convolution, spiral, corkscrew, ringlet, curlicue.

curl *v.* curve, coil, twist, bend, loop, wind, turn, snake, meander.

curmudgeon *n.* grouch, bear, *crank, crab, *grump.

currency *n.* money, cash, legal tender, coins, bills. SEE MONEY

current *n.* flow, course, stream, rush, run, tide, river, flux, draft.

current *a.* contemporary, present, now, present-day, modern, up-to-date, in vogue, prevalent, in progress, fashionable, *cutting edge, *leading edge. ANT. *past, bygone, historical, old, dated.*

curse *n.* **1.** JINX spell, *evil eye, evil, *whammy, voodoo, charm, incantation, execration, anathema, damnation, malediction. **2.** SWEARING oath, profanity, expletive, *gutter word, *cuss word, *dirty word, *four-letter word, obscenity. ANT. *1. blessing, benediction.*

cursed *a.* **1.** JINXED doomed, star-crossed, bedeviled, ill-fated, plagued, damned, stricken, blighted. **2.** HATEFUL detestable, loathsome, damnable, execrable, wicked, evil, abominable, fiendish. ANT. *1. blessed, favored. 2. commendable, honorable.*

CURSORY *a.* [KUR suh ree] quick and superficial; unthorough. *She made a cursory inspection and moved on.* SYN. quick, hasty, superficial, casual, perfunctory, hurried, slight, desultory, unmethodical, fleeting, shallow. ANT. *thorough, comprehensive, in-depth.*

CURT *a.* [KURT] brief to the point of rudeness; brusque. *He gave a curt introduction and left.* SYN. abrupt, terse, rude, snappy, short, short and sweet, gruff, unceremonious, sharp, laconic, impolite. ANT. *couteous, polite, loquacious, long-winded, fawning.*

curtail *v.* shorten, cut, abbreviate, abridge,

downsize, boil down, trim, reduce, diminish. ANT. *lengthen, draw out, expand.*

curtain *n.* drape, shade, blind, valance, portiere, veil, cover, backdrop.

curvaceous *a.* shapely, voluptuous, *built, *stacked, statuesque, *wasp-waisted, full-figured, zaftig, buxom. ANT. *anorexic, *built like linguine, bony.*

curve *v.* bend, arc, bow, turn, veer, twist, hook, loop, spiral, coil, swerve, curl, crook.

cushion *n.* pillow, pad, bolster, mat, buffer, fender.

cushion *v.* absorb, dampen, soften, check, protect, muffle, deaden, pillow, stifle.

cushy *a. Sl.* easy, *comfy, pleasant, agreeable.

custodian *n.* caretaker, guardian, conservator, janitor, keeper, maintenance man, steward, *super, watchman, curator.

custody *n.* **1.** GUARDIANSHIP keeping, safekeeping, care, protection, wardship, holding, watch, supervision. **2.** CONFINEMENT incarceration, imprisonment, detention, jail, arrest, restraint.

custom *n.* **1.** PRACTICE habit, convention, rule, fashion, mode, routine, way, law, *right thing to do. *The plague of wise men and the idol of fools." — Thomas Fuller. "The great guide to human life." — David Hume. **2.** TAX levy, toll, tariff.

customary *a.* usual, conventional, accustomed, established, set, routine, regular, accepted, habitual, fashionable, normal, traditional, orthodox. ANT. *unusual, offbeat, unfamiliar, untried.*

customer *n.* patron, shopper, buyer, consumer, browser, prospect, client.

cut *n.* **1.** INCISION gash, laceration, slash, slit, nick, tear, slice, wound, opening; kerf. **2.** REDUCTION decrease, diminution, cutback, decrement, excision, lowering. **3.** SHARE percentage, *piece of the pie, slice, allowance, allotment, quota, kickback. **3.** INSULT *putdown, offense, *dig.

cut *v.* **1.** INCISE gash, lacerate, slash, slit, nick, tear, slice, wound, open, sever, carve, split, shear, rip, hack, dice, section, lay open, lance, pierce, scotch. **2.** CUT DOWN OR TRIM fell, crop, mow, lop off truncate, harvest, prune, clip, chop. **3.** REDUCE decrease, diminish, cut back, downsize, excise, lower, lessen, crop, pare, trim, shave. **4.** INSULT slight, snub, affront, spurn, *give the cold shoulder, shun.

cut and dried *a.* **1.** SETTLED fixed, set, prepared. **2.** ROUTINE unoriginal, ordinary.

cute *a.* adorable, attractive, cunning, pretty, darling, cherubic, charming, sweet, *cute as a bug's ear, *dollfaced.

cutthroat *a.* ruthless, *dog-eat-dog, merciless, *every man for himself, pitiless, *hard as nails. ANT. *compassionate, merciful, benevolent.*

cutting *a.* insulting, biting, sarcastic, scathing, sharp, sardonic, nasty, mean, caustic, venomous, acerbic, vicious, malevolent. ANT. *complimentary, flattering, kind.*

cycle *n.* progression, sequence, succession, rotation, round, series.

cyclone *n.* tornado, twister, hurricane, windstorm, whirlwind, monsoon.

cynic *n.* skeptic, nonbeliever; *doubting Thomas, scoffer, realist, pessimist, naysayer, killjoy, misanthrope. "A man who tells you the truth about your own motives." — Russel Green. "A man who, when he smells flowers, looks around for a coffin." — H.L. Mencken. ANT. *optimist, *Pollyanna, believer.*

CYNICAL *a.* [SIN ik ul] mistrusting and looking for hidden motives in others. *Frank said he wanted to raise money for charity, but Mary was cynical.* SYN. skeptical, unbelieving, doubting, questioning, scoffing, pesimistic, negative, naysaying, misanthropic, sneering, sardonic, mocking, distrustful, suspicious. ANT. *trusting, optimistic, positive.*

cynicism *n.* "A euphemism for realism. Seeing things as they really are, instead of the way we'd like them to be." — Harry Ruby. "Idealism gone sour." — Will Herberg. SEE CYNICAL

cyst *n.* vesicle, sac, blister, bleb.

czar *n.* autocrat, tsar, ruler, emperor, overlord, king.

D

dab n. bit, touch, drop, pat, smidgen, speck, dollop, pinch, soupcon.

dab v. daub, touch, smear, smudge, pat, tap.

dabble v. *play around, *mess around, toy with, *fiddle with, putter, tinker, dillydally, trifle.

dabbler n. amateur, hobbyist, tinkerer, dillettante, novice, putterer, layman, nonprofessional. ANT. master, expert, professional.

daft a. *nutty, *loony, idiotic. SEE CRAZY

dagger n. knife, dirk, bodkin, stiletto, poniard, Bowie knife, switchblade, bayonet.

WORD FIND

Arabian, double-edged, curved blade: jambiya

handle: hilt, haft, grip, dudgeon

Irish/Scottish, double-edged: skean

knob at butt end: pommel

Medieval: anlace, bodkin, misericord, rondel, swordbreaker

slide projections at the hilt: quillons

daily a. everyday, day in and day out, quotidian, circadian, per diem.

dainty a. **1.** DELICATE exquisite, charming, fine, fragile, precious, lovely, elegant, refined, graceful. **2.** DISCRIMINATING fussy, finicky, particular, fastidious, *persnickety, choosy, refined, overrefined. ANT. *1. rough, ugly, ponderous, *built like a brick shithouse, junky. 2. unparticular, easy to please.*

dais n. podium, platform, rostrum, stage.

dale n. dell, glen. SEE VALLEY

dalliance n. flirtation, coquetry, *cow eyes, *making eyes at, love affair, affair, *fling, *fooling around, relationship, *hanky-panky.

dally v. dawdle, waste time, *drag feet, lag, put off, idle, delay, procrastinate, *fiddle and diddle, dillydally, shilly-shally. ANT. *hurry, rush, *get a move on.*

dam n. bank, dike, levee, wall, barrage, obstruction, check, barrier.

dam v. block, obstruct, check, close, bar, impede, stop, slow, restrict. ANT. *release, free.*

damage n. destruction, injury, loss, harm, breakage, hurt, depreciation, deterioration, wreckage, spoilage, impairment, disfigurement.

damage v. injure, harm, destroy, break, hurt, depreciate, wreck, ruin, impair, cripple, deface, weaken, incapacitate, mar, mutilate, ravage, vandalize.

damages n. cost, expenses, compensation, penalty, reimbursement, amends.

damn v. condemn, criticize, doom, slam, denounce, attack, curse, disparage, censure, excoriate, pan, swear at, objurgate, blast. ANT. *praise, commend, give one's blessings.*

damnation n. "Everlasting fire." — Bible. "Everlasting torments." — John Sergieff.

damned a. detestable, cursed, infernal, *darned, loathsome, *dang, confounded, *blasted, rotten, revolting.

damp a. wet, moist, dank, humid, clammy, misty, drizzly, soggy.

dampen v. **1.** MOISTEN wet, sprinkle, spray, rinse, humidify. **2.** DEPRESS deaden, muffle, lower, lessen, check, cool, diminish, moderate, chill, mute. ANT. *1. dry, dehydrate. 2. enliven, intensify, increase.*

damsel n. maiden, girl, woman, lass.

dance n. ballroom dance, capering, ballet, waltz, polka, square dance, *shindig, hop, prom. "Poetry of the foot." — John Dryden.

WORD FIND

bend backwards under pole: limbo

Bohemian, lively: polka

Brazilian, dips, leaps: samba

Brazilian, like samba: bossa nova

Brazilian, sensual coupling: lambada

Caribbean, like rhumba: beguine

classical ballroom: waltz

country and western swinging two-step: Texas two-step

Cuban: rhumba, conga, mambo

death dance: danse macabre

French, high-kicking, skirt-lifting: cancan

glissade backwards: moonwalk

group single file procession, three steps and kick: conga

Hawaiian: hula

Italian, whirling folk dance: tarantella

Latin American quickstep and shuffle: cha-cha

Latin American, with stylized posturing: tango

legs scissoring in opposite directions: split

lively folk dance; jig

lively French dance, eighteenth century: cotillion

Middle Eastern female solo, stomach undulations: belly dance

modern jazz: jazz dance

Negro, nineteenth century: Juba

1920s: Charleston

1930s-1940s, hopping: shag
1930s, jitterbuglike: Lindy hop
1940s, acrobatic somersaults, splits: jitterbug
1960s, Chubby Checker: twist
1970s, hip-touching: bump
1980s, prostrate movements: breakdance
1990s, running in position: running man
Oriental head motions: sundari
Polish: polonaise
Russian dance, squatting, arms folded: cossack
sailor's: hornpipe
Scottish, lively folk dance: reel
secret, all-night dance party: *rave
shaking of body part: shimmy
solo male dance around Sombrero: Mexican hat dance
Spanish: flamenco, fandango, bolero, tango
spin: pirourette
square dance: quadrille, hoedown
square dance steps: California twirl, cloverleaf, Dixie chain, do si do, promenade, sashay.
stately eighteenth-century dance: minuet
steps: choreography
tap steps: soft shoe, falling off the log, dig, brush, chug, coffee grinder
two-step, ballroom: fox-trot
wooden shoes dance: clog
SEE BALLET

dance v. caper, step, *trip the light fantastic, *boogie, *cut a rug, swing, step, prance, *disco, *beat feet, twist, shimmy, strut, prance, sway, hop, *get down, *shake your booties, rock, wiggle one's hips, jig, skip, leap, gambol, romp, *slink, contort, flex, undulate, careen, shuffle, *hoof, clomp, *jockey, *pose, *posture, thrust, quiver, dip, gyrate, convulse, glissade, *have a floorgasm.

dancer n. danseuse, ballerina, danseur, *hoofer, terpsichorean.

dandle v. bounce on knee, toss up and down.

dandy a. great, excellent, wonderful, swell, terrific.

danger n. peril, threat, hazard, menace, endangerment, *thin ice, jeopardy, vulnerability, *storm clouds on the horizon, pitfall, *between Scylla and Charybdis, *sword of Damocles. "The spur of all great minds."—George Chapman. ANT. safety, security.

dangerous a. perilous, threatening, hazardous, unsafe, menacing, jeopardous, risky, precarious, chancy, *touch and go, *ticklish, unhealthy, dire, *hanging over one's head like the sword of Damocles, *between Scylla and

Charybdis. ANT. safe, secure, protected.

dangle v. hang, drag, droop, flap, depend, swing, wave, flutter.

dank a. damp, wet, chilly, clammy, moist, slimy, dewy, muggy, humid.

dapper a. neat, trim, smart, dashing, swank, stylish, well-groomed, spruce, natty, *spiffy. ANT. sloppy, unkempt, disheveled.

dappled a. mottled, spotted, speckled, stippled, flecked, piebald, variegated, particolored. ANT. uniform, solid.

dare v. 1. VENTURE gamble, risk, brave, hazard, face, brook, adventure, *run the gauntlet, have the nerve. 2. DEFY challenge, beard, face, oppose, square off, mock, throw down the gauntlet, look in the eye, provoke, confront, taunt. ANT. 1. pass, beg off, retreat. 2. run away, retreat, knuckle under, *blink.

daredevil n. thrill-seeker, adventurer, showoff, *hotdog, swashbuckler, stuntman, ace, fool.

daring a. adventurous, brave, bold, venturesome, plucky, *gutsy, *ballsy, nervy, courageous, fearless, intrepid, reckless, rash, *having icewater in one's veins. ANT. fearful, afraid, *chicken, *mousy, timid, cautious, *wimpy.

dark n. nightfall, evening, dusk, twilight, midnight.

dark a. 1. BLACK aphotic, dim, dusky, gloomy, unlit, nebulous, inky, shadowy, somber, gauzy, murky. 2. COMPLEXION swarthy, ebony, black. 3. DREARY dismal, bleak, gloomy, stygian, depressing, somber, grim, morbid. 4. WICKED evil, satanic, sinister, hellish, infernal. ANT. light, bright, sunny. SEE BLACK, COMPLEXION

darling n. sweetheart, *honey, *honeybunch, love, beloved, *pet, *sweetie, precious, dear, *apple of one's eye.

dart v. flit, dash, rush, bolt, scurry, shoot, spurt, scoot, bound, run, race, fly, tear, speed.

dash n. 1. RACE run, sprint. 2. A LITTLE trace, bit, smidgen, sprinkle, hint, pinch, taste, drop.

dash v. 1. RUN sprint, race, bolt, speed, zip, rush, dart, bound, charge, shoot, scoot, scamper, tear. 2. SMASH break, hit, strike, shatter, throw, hurl, slam, fling, sling, splash. 3. FRUSTRATE confound, discourage, dampen, thwart, circumvent, foil, ruin, spoil, dishearten. ANT. 3. encourage, aid.

dashing a. elegant, debonair, splendid, jaunty, stylish, dapper, swank, chic, fashionable, sharp, flamboyant, rakish.

dastardly a. cowardly, fainthearted, timid, craven, mean, base, low, rotten. ANT. *courageous, brave, noble.*

data *n.* information, report, facts, figures, evidence, measurements, statistics, numbers, document, *readout.

date *n.* **1.** APPOINTMENT engagement, tryst, meeting. **2.** ESCORT companion, partner, lover, *pickup.

dated *a.* out-of-date, obsolete, antiquated, passé, old-fashioned, outmoded, old hat, antediluvian, prehistoric. ANT. *current, *cutting edge, *leading edge, modern contemporary.*

daub *v.* coat, cover, smear, smudge, plaster, dab, paint, splatter, spot, stain.

daunt *v.* intimidate, scare, frighten, unnerve, threaten, faze, discourage, dismay, cow, dispirit, overawe. ANT. *encourage, embolden.*

DAUNTLESS *a.* [DAWNT less] fearless; bold. *A dauntless raid on the enemy camp.* SYN. fearless, bold, brave, unafraid, courageous, intrepid, valorous, stouthearted, unflinching, resolute. ANT. *fearful, afraid, timid, irresolute.*

dawdle *v.* *fiddle and diddle, delay, procrastinate, waste time, dally, *drag one's feet, loiter, *poke, piddle, shilly-shally, fritter. ANT. *hurry, rush, *beat feet, *get a move on.*

dawn *n.* **1.** DAYBREAK sunrise, sunup, morning, aurora, cockcrow, first light, wee hours, *holy light of dawn. "The time when men of reason go to bed." — Ambrose Bierce. "That single hour of the twenty-four, when crime ceases, debauchery is exhausted, and even desolation finds a shelter." — Benjamin Disraeli. **2.** BEGINNING start, rise, advent, opening, coming, emergence, birth, onset. ANT. *1. sunset, dusk, twilight. 2. close, end, dusk.*

day *n.* light of day, sunup to sundown, twenty-four hours. "Each day is a little life." — Arthur Schopenhauer. "A miniature Eternity." — Ralph Waldo Emerson. **2.** PERIOD time, heyday, age, time, epoch.

daydream *n.* fantasy, reverie, *castle in the air, figment of the imagination, musing, visualization, fancy, imagining, pipe dream, *woolgathering.

daze *n.* stupor, bewilderment, shock, trance, confusion, *lala land, befuddlement.

daze *v.* confuse, bewilder, shock, befuddle, stupefy, stun, perplex, addle, numb, confound, muddle, dumfound.

dazzle *v.* amaze, blind, overwhelm, astonish, bewilder, confuse, awe, *bowl over, daze, *blow away, dumfound.

dazzling *a.* brilliant, blinding, sparkling, glittering, flashy, shining, radiant, resplendent, ablaze, prismatic, meteoric.

dead *a.* **1.** LIFELESS deceased, expired, passed away, departed, perished, extinct, still, defunct, resting in peace, *pushing up daisies, late, stiff, *gone to meet one's maker, *out of one's misery, *kaput, *gone belly up, *down for the count, *crowbait, *buzzard bait, *stone cold, *worm food, *dead as a coffin nail, *carrion, lost, *on ice. **2.** UNRESPONSIVE flat, apathetic, wooden, paralyzed, numb, emotionless, frigid, unfeeling, insensible, insensate, cool, lukewarm. **3.** INOPERATIVE not working, out of order, *on the blink. **4.** ENDED extinguished, snuffed out, terminated, squelched, quenched, smothered, finished. **5.** UNPRODUCTIVE exhausted, unprofitable, sterile, stagnant, useless, barren, spent, worn out. **6.** TOTAL complete, utter, entire, out-and-out, absolute, sure, downright. **7.** BORING dull, tiresome, tedious, stale, bland, *blah, vapid. ANT. *1. alive, lively, animate. 2. lively, spirited, responsive. 3. operating, working. 4. growing. 5. productive, fruitful, fertile. 6. partial, uncertain. 7. lively, interesting, engrossing, riveting.* SEE DEATH, DIE

deaden *a. v.* dampen, dull, numb, muffle, mute, blunt, check, moderate, diminish, suppress, dim, tone down, stifle. ANT. *amplify, enliven, turn up.*

deadlock *n.* stalemate, impasse, *Catch 22, standstill, gridlock, standoff, *Gordian knot, *logjam, *hung jury.

deadly *a.* fatal, lethal, deathly, mortal, malignant, toxic, killing, dangerous, virulent, death-dealing, pernicious, baneful. ANT. *harmless, benign, innocuous.*

deadpan *a.* expressionless, blank, *poker-faced, stony, wooden, unreadable.

deafening *a.* ear-splitting, noisy. SEE LOUD

deal *n.* arrangement, understanding, contract, transaction, compact, bargain.

deal *v.* **1.** DISTRIBUTE dole out, allocate, allot, mete out, hand out, dispense, apportion. **2.** DEAL WITH attend to, reckon with, concern, take care of, cope, face, treat, manage, handle. **3.** BARGAIN dicker, negotiate, trade, buy and sell, do business, barter, give and take.

dealings *n.* relations, transactions, business, arrangements, trade, commerce, exchange.

dean *n.* senior, elder statesman, ranking member, elder, veteran; headmaster, preceptor, administrator.

dear *n.* darling, sweetheart, angel, saint.

dear *a.* **1.** BELOVED precious, loved, treasured,

cherished, favored, darling, prized, admired, *near to one's heart. **2.** EXPENSIVE costly, *pricey, *steep, exorbitant, extravagant. ANT. 1. *loathed, despised.* 2. *cheap, reasonable.*

DEARTH n. [DURTH] scarcity, lack. *A dearth of funds has kept me from vacationing in Hawaii.* SYN. scarcity, lack, deficiency, insufficiency, want, shortage, paucity, inadequacy, scantiness, stint, need. ANT. *sufficiency, abundance, plenty.*

death n. demise, end, dying, decease, passing, expiration, parting, termination, release, rest, extinction, mortality, in extremis, *curtains, *lights out, *last roundup, *finis, *grim reaper, *show stopper, afterlife, fatality, oblivion, repose. "When the soul shall emerge from its sheath." — Marcus Aurelius. "A black camel, which kneels at the gates of all." — Abd-El-Kader. "An eternal night." — Algernon Swinburne. "The undiscovered country." — Shakespeare. "The grand perhaps." — Robert Browning. "A pale horse." — Bible. "The port where all may refuge find." — William Alexander.

WORD FIND
after death, occurring: posthumous
DOA: dead on arrival
fear of: necrophobia, thanatophobia
gurgle at last breath: death rattle
herald of: banshee
investigation of: inquest, autopsy, postmortem
march: dirge
mercy killing: euthanasia
notice: obituary, necrology
omen: knell
reminder or symbol of: memento mori, death's head
study of: thanatology
watch: vigil
SEE AFTERLIFE, CEMETERY, CORPSE, DEAD, DIE, FUNERAL, HEAVEN, IMMORTALITY

deathless a. eternal. SEE IMMORTAL

deathly a. horrible, dreadful, terrible, appalling, macabre, ghastly.

DEBACLE n. [di BAH kul] a disaster or sudden collapse. *Thousands lost money in the stock market debacle.* SYN. disaster, collapse, overthrow, catastrophe, ruin, breakdown, rout, washout, downfall, bankruptcy, devastation. ANT. *success.*

debase v. degrade, lower, devalue, adulterate, pollute, corrupt, cheapen, depreciate, defile, demean, disgrace. ANT. *elevate, raise.*

debatable a. undecided, questionable, moot,

controversial, dubious, disputable, doubtful, unsettled, contestable, *the jury's out. ANT. *settled, certain, decided.*

debate n. argument, dispute, war of words, contention, wrangle, controversy, contest, deliberation, disagreement, forensic. "Feud for thought." — Cynthia Scott. "The shortest cut between two minds." — Kahlil Gibran.

debate v. argue, dispute, *wage a war of words, contend, wrangle, controvert, contest, disagree, deliberate, bicker, *hash out, *lock horns, rebut.

DEBAUCHERY n. [di BAW chuh ree] excess, wild living, indulgence. *The rowdiness and debauchery of a frat party.* SYN. indulgence, excess, profligacy, over-indulgence, whoring, immoderation, womanizing, carousal, dissipation, intemperance, *fast living, revelry. ANT. *chastity, clean-living, moderation, abstinence, celibacy.*

DEBILITATE v. [di BIL i TATE] to weaken or handicap. *His illness would soon debilitate him.* SYN. weaken, handicap, enervate, enfeeble, cripple, fatigue, exhaust, disable, prostrate, devitalize. ANT. *strengthen, invigorate.*

debility n. weakness, infirmity, enfeeblement, handicap, enervation, prostration, languor, frailty, asthenia. ANT. *strength, power, vigor.*

DEBONAIR a. [deb uh NARE] friendly, gracious and suave. *The prince was charming and debonair.* SYN. friendly, gracious, suave, charming, jaunty, genial, pleasant, urbane, nonchalant, refined, genteel, gentlemanly. ANT. *coarse, crude, rude, unrefined, unfriendly.*

debris n. rubble, trash, ruins, rubbish, scraps, fragments, remains, junk, litter, waste, *crap.

debt n. obligation, liability, bill, debit, arrears, deficit, pledge, due, burden, *red ink. "The slavery of the free." — Publilius Syrus. "A trap which a man sets and baits himself, and then deliberately gets into." — Josh Billings.

debunk v. disprove, expose, refute, unmask, ridicule, deflate.

debut n. premiere, *coming out, first time out, introduction, launch, entrance, opener, inauguration. ANT. *farewell, swan song.*

decadence n. deterioration, decay, debasement, corruption, decline, regression, degeneration, downfall, degradation, fall. ANT. *growth, progression, revitalization.*

DECADENT a. [DEK uh dunt] decaying or deteriorating, in morals, art or other institution. *A decadent lifestyle led to their downfall.* SYN. decaying, deteriorating, declining, corrupt, degraded, *gone to hell, *gone to the dogs, degenerating, on the wane, *on the way out, *circling the drain, debauched. ANT. *growing, progressing, vital, vigorous.*

decamp v. bolt, flee, escape, *head for the hills.

decapitate v. behead, decollate, guillotine, ax.

decay n. rot, spoilage, decomposition, decline, disintegration, putrefaction, deterioration, degeneration, decrepitude. ANT. *growth, vigor.*

decay v. decline, deteriorate, degenerate, atrophy, waste away, wane, rot, decompose, putrefy, wither, disintegrate. ANT. *grow, thrive.*

deceased a. passed on. SEE DEAD

deceit n. dishonesty, deception, fraud, trickery, cheating, double-dealing, *BS, craft, *funny business, underhandedness, chicanery. "The smiler with the knife under the cloak."— Geoffrey Chaucer. "That glib and oily art."—Shakespeare. ANT. *honesty, truthfulness, fairness.*

deceitful a. dishonest, deceptive, fraudulent, double-dealing, *full of it, crafty, underhanded, treacherous, duplicitous, insincere, artful, shifty. ANT. *honest, truthful, straightforward.*

deceive v. mislead, delude, trick, hoodwink, *pull the wool over one's eyes, dupe, defraud, *buffalo, *con, burn, *screw, beguile, *BS.

decency n. propriety, respectability, righteousness, seemliness, modesty, appropriateness, goodness, good manners, decorum. ANT. *indecency, impropriety.*

decent a. **1.** RESPECTABLE righteous, seemly, proper, moral, correct, modest, appropriate, good, fitting, virtuous, prudent. **2.** ADEQUATE sufficient, passable, tolerable, enough, satisfactory, ample, standard, reasonable. **3.** KIND generous, obliging, thoughtful, gracious, accommodating. ANT. *1. improper, inappropriate. 2. inadequate, insufficient, poor. 3. selfish, coldhearted, inconsiderate.*

deception n. lie, fraud, trick, chicane, deceit, hoax, sham, subterfuge, artifice, treachery, *bullshit, ruse, imposture, sleight of hand, con.

deceptive a. dishonest, misleading, fraudulent, tricky, deceitful, treacherous, bogus, spurious, fallacious, shifty. ANT. *honest, truthful, straightforward.*

decide v. settle, determine, choose, opt, judge, commit oneself, elect, guess, rule, make up one's mind, *fish or cut bait, *shit or get off the pot, resolve. ANT. *vacillate, waver, *ride the fence, hem and haw, waffle.*

decided a. definite, certain, absolute, unequivocal, clear, express, sure, unmistakable, settled, undeniable, positive, emphatic. ANT. *dubious, doubtful, uncertain.*

decimate v. slaughter, massacre, destroy, obliterate, wipe out, annihilate.

decipher v. figure out, read, decode, make out, solve, interpret, work out, understand, crack, unravel, puzzle out.

decision n. **1.** SETTLING determination) choice, judgment, election, guess, conclusion, resolution, preference, *roll of the dice. **2.** VERDICT judgment, ruling, finding, decree, sentence. ANT. *vacillation, wavering, waffling, indecision.*

decisive a. conclusive, certain, firm, absolute, unqualified, unmistakable, convincing, undeniable, final, clinching, crucial, critical. ANT. *inconclusive, questionable, inconsequential.*

deck v. outfit, adorn, decorate, clothe, trim, ornament, festoon, array, embellish, beautify.

declaration n. statement, assertion, announcement, communication, utterance, affirmation, proclamation, attestation, testimony.

declare v. state, assert, announce, communicate, utter, affirm, proclaim, attest, testify, profess, avow.

decline v. **1.** REFUSE turn down, reject, forgo, spurn, pass on, demur, *turn thumbs down. **2.** WANE degenerate, deteriorate, lessen, weaken, diminish, ebb, peter out, die out, slump, decay, sink, backslide. **3.** SLOPE slant, incline, pitch. ANT. *1. accept, take. 2. grow, wax, rise.*

decompose v. rot, putrefy, biodegrade. SEE DECAY

decontaminate v. clean, purify, sterilize.

decorate v. adorn, ornament, beautify, embellish, festoon, dress, trim, deck, garnish, *do up, *jazz up.

decoration n. n. **1.** ADORNMENT ornament, embellishment, festoon, dressing, trim, garnish, frill, embroidery. **2.** MEDAL award, honor, citation, emblem, badge, purple heart, ribbon.

decorous a. proper, appropriate, fitting, mannerly, conventional, correct, refined, dignified, comme il faut, suitable, civilized. ANT. *misbehaving, rowdy, improper.*

DECORUM n. [di KOR um] proper manners, propriety. *The children were told to behave with decorum.* SYN. propriety, respectability, conformity, civility, etiquette, good manners, good taste, dignity, grace, protocol.

ANT. *bad manners, impropriety, incivility.*

decoy n. lure, bait, enticement, *plant, *shill, magnet, seduction, pitfall, phony, trap, fake, facade.

decrease n. lessening, lowering, shrinkage, reduction, decline, weakening, lightening, contraction, depreciation, drop. ANT. *increase, growth, expansion.*

decrease v. lessen, diminish, lower, shrink, reduce, decline, weaken, lighten, contract, depreciate, dwindle, plummet, drop, sink. ANT. *increase, grow, expand, burgeon.*

decree n. order, act, mandate, command, ruling, edict, ordinance, injunction, fiat, statute, command, dictum.

decree v. order, mandate, command, rule, ordain, enact, proclaim, dictate, prescribe, require.

decrepit a. broken down, weakened, deteriorated, old, worn, dilapidated, antiquated, rickety, withered, enfeebled. ANT. *strong, robust, powerful.*

decry v. disparage, belittle, deflate, detract, deprecate, criticize, *slam, rap, condemn, censure, denounce. ANT. *praise, compliment.*

dedicated a. committed, devoted, determined, wholehearted.

deduce v. infer, gather, figure, conclude, reason, assume, judge, presume, *have a hunch, reckon, surmise.

deduct v. subtract, take off, decrease, remove, withdraw, reduce, cut, write off. ANT. *add, increase.*

deduction n. inference, conclusion, line of reasoning, assumption, judgment, presumption, hunch, reckoning, finding, understanding.

deed n. act, feat, exploit, enterprise, work, achievement, accomplishment, turn, stunt. "Something attempted, something done." — Longfellow. "A freeway to self-esteem." — Anon.

deem v. judge, consider, believe, think, hold, suppose, daresay, regard, understand, imagine, fancy.

deep a. **1.** OF GREAT DEPTH far-reaching, bottomless, cavernous, low, abysmal, unfathomable, immeasurable, subterranean. **2.** PROFOUND abstruse, mysterious, unfathomable, philosophical, complicated, abstract, arcane, intense. **3.** ENGROSSED absorbed, preoccupied, wrapped up, concentrated, immersed, lost. **4.** STRONG intense, dark, rich, heavy, full, powerful. **5.** BASS low, guttural, booming, rumbling, resonant. ANT. *1. shallow, superficial. 2. trivial, simple, shallow. 3. distracted.*

4. *light, weak, diluted.* **5.** *high, shrill.*

deep-seated a. deep-rooted, ingrained, *dyed in the wool, inherent.

deer n. ruminant, whitetail, elk, caribou, buck, doe, roe, quadriped.

WORD FIND

bellowing cry: bell
branch of antler: point
feeding area; yard
female: doe, hind
like a: cervine
male adult: stag, buck, hart
meat: venison
odiferous secretion: musk
pair of antlers: rack
sexual period: rut
soft covering of antler: velvet
tail: flag
track or trail of: slot
young: fawn

deface v. mar, deform, sully, blemish, disfigure, spoil, damage, soil, mutilate, vandalize, scratch.

de facto a. actual, real, in fact, in reality.

defamation n. slander, denigration, smear, slur, mud-slinging, blot, innuendo, libel, disparagement, character assassination.

defamatory a. slanderous, libelous, denigrating, derogatory, disparaging, scandalous, insulting, calumnious, smearing, injurious. ANT. *flattering, complimentary, honoring.*

DEFAME v. [di FAME] to put down, especially in a libelous or slanderous way. *He proceeded to defame every politician in office.* SYN. slander, libel, smear, put down, mud-sling, blacken, scandalize, malign, disgrace, disparage, insult, smirch, denigrate. ANT. *flatter, compliment, honor.*

default v. shirk, *welsh, fail, *stiff, *skip out, *run out on, dodge. ANT. *pay in full, satisfy.*

defeat n. loss, beating, rout, slaughter, debacle, blow, whipping, thrashing, knockout, licking, *Waterloo, reversal, *drubbing, fall, upset, downfall. ANT. *win, victory, triumph.*

defeat v. vanquish, beat, conquer, subdue, win over, overthrow, best, lick, whip, rout, slaughter, unseat, trounce, *smoke, prevail over. ANT. *lose, knuckle under, concede.*

defect n. imperfection, flaw, failing, mistake, deficiency, drawback, *bug, irregularity, error, shortcoming, weakness, chink. ANT. *strength.*

defect v. leave, desert, change allegiance, born, turn traitor, abandon, renounce, reject, forsake. ANT. *embrace, uphold, remain.*

defective *a.* imperfect, flawed, irregular, deficient, faulty, lacking, marred, unsound, inoperative, *out of commission. ANT. *perfect, sound, intact.*

defend *v.* **1.** PROTECT fight for, guard, fend off, withstand, hold at bay, shield, secure, ward off, preserve. **2.** SUPPORT advocate, back, uphold, stick up for, stand behind, *go to bat for, plead, justify. ANT. *offend, attack, let down one's guard.*

defense *n.* **1.** PROTECTION guard, shield, fortification, shelter, screen, bulwark, stronghold, armament. **2.** JUSTIFICATION explanation, excuse, stand, argument, plea, story, apologia, support. ANT. *1. offense, aggression.*

defenseless *a.* powerless, vulnerable, unprotected, unguarded, unarmed, helpless, weak, impotent, exposed, open to attack. ANT. *guarded, fortified, defended.*

defer *v.* **1.** DELAY postpone, put off, hold off, suspend, *put on the back burner, procrastinate, stall, table. **2.** COMPLY submit, yield, acquiesce, accede, capitulate, give in, assent, agree. ANT. *1. expedite, rush.*

DEFERENCE *n.* [DEF ur uns] yielding to another's will, usually out of respect or courtesy. *In deference to her mother, the toddler finally quit screaming.* SYN. submission, regard, consideration, respect, thoughtfulness, yielding, compliance, courtesy, obeisance. ANT. *opposition, rebellion, disrespect.*

deferential *a.* respectful, submissive, compliant, courteous, considerate, obedient, obeisant, acquiescent, regardful, reverential. ANT. *disrespectful, disobedient, rude.*

defiance *n.* rebellion, disobedience, resistance, opposition, challenge, insolence, revolt, *throwing down the gauntlet, disregard, contempt. ANT. *conformance, acquiescence, deference.*

defiant *a.* rebellious, disobedient, resistant, opposing, challenging, insolent, revolting, *throwing down the gauntlet, fractious, unruly. ANT. *conforming, obedient, acquiescent.*

deficiency *n.* imperfection, lack, shortcoming, insufficiency, inadequacy, failing, flaw, defect, weakness, drawback. ANT. *sufficiency, adequacy, perfection.*

deficient *a.* imperfect, lacking, insufficient, inadequate, failing, flawed, defective, weak, substandard, wanting, *below par, incomplete, faulty. ANT. *sufficient, flawless, perfect.*

deficit *n.* shortage, shortfall, lack, loss, red ink.

defile *v.* dirty, befoul, tarnish, pollute, taint, sully, corrupt, smear, besmirch, soil, contaminate, degrade. ANT. *purify, cleanse.*

define *v.* explain, spell out, describe, outline, delineate, map out, detail, characterize, label, illustrate, construe.

definite *a.* **1.** CERTAIN positive, sure, absolute, fixed, assured, guaranteed, settled, decided. **2.** EXACT clear, unambiguous, explicit, specific, precise, unmistakable, express, concrete. ANT. *1. uncertain, iffy, indefinite. 2. unclear, ambiguous, vague.*

definitely *a.* absolutely, positively, surely, certainly, doubtless, without question, indubitably, categorically, *no ifs ands or buts. ANT. *maybe, possibly, uncertain.*

definition *n.* meaning, elucidation, explanation, characterization, description. "The enclosing a wilderness of ideas within a wall of words." —Samuel Butler.

DEFINITIVE *a.* [di FIN uh tiv] defining absolutely, conclusive. *The definitive Hall of Famer is Babe Ruth.* SYN. absolute, precise, actual, decisive, thorough, consummate, conclusive, complete, exact, clear-cut, perfect. ANT. *questionable, debatable, inexact.*

deflate *v.* **1.** COLLAPSE contract, deplete, shrink, empty, exhaust, flatten, puncture. **2.** HUMBLE *take the wind out of one's sails, put down, *take down a peg, humiliate, *puncture one's aura of invincibility, mortify. ANT. *1. inflate, fill, swell. 2. puff up, hearten, flatter.*

deflect *v.* turn aside, swerve, bounce off, diverge, divert, veer, twist, hook, ricochet, deviate.

deformed *a.* misshapen, malformed, disfigured, grotesque, distorted, misproportioned, bent out of shape, twisted, warped, contorted, unnatural, hunchbacked, gnarled.

deformity *n.* malformation, disfigurement, distortion, contortion, abnormality, birth defect, hunchback, club foot, hump, harelip.

defraud *v.* cheat, swindle, dupe, *rip off, fleece, bamboozle, bilk, rook, *con, take for a ride, *sucker.

defray *v.* cover cost, pay.

DEFT *a.* [DEFT] skillful. *A deft carpenter.* SYN. dexterous, handy, adroit, adept, clever, proficient, *crackerjack, ingenious, facile. ANT. *unskilled, inept, bumbling.*

DEFUNCT *a.* [di FUNGKT] no longer in existence. *The company that made horse-drawn carriages is defunct.* SYN. nonexistent, dead, extinct, deceased, obsolete, no more, gone, bygone, *kaput, out of business. ANT. *existing, thriving, living, operating.*

defy *v.* rebel, resist, challenge, flout, disregard,

oppose, brave, frustrate, ignore, fly in the face of, dare, *thumb one's nose at. ANT. *obey, comply, acquiesce.*

degenerate n. deviant, pervert, wretch, *pig, deviate, *lowlife, fiend, psychopath, *psycho, *sleazebag.

degenerate v. deteriorate, degrade, rot, decay, fail, sink, regress, decline, fall, backslide, slip, *go to the dogs.

degenerate a. deteriorated, degraded, debauched, dissolute, corrupt, debased, decadent, failing, sinking, regressive.

degrade v. lower, debase, corrupt, diminish, demean, abase, humiliate, disgrace, shame, dishonor, downgrade, discredit. ANT. *honor, put on a pedestal, worship.*

degrading a. debasing, lowering, corrupting, diminishing, downgrading, humiliating, disgraceful, shameful, cheapening, demeaning. ANT. *uplifting, honorable, dignifying.*

degree n. **1.** STEP notch, grade, point, rung, tier, stage, rank, peg. **2.** LEVEL intensity, extent, magnitude, capacity. **3.** ACADEMIC TITLE diploma, certificate, sheepskin, credentials, shingle, testimonial.

WORD FIND

B.A.: Bachelor of Arts

baccalaureate: bachelor's degree

between bachelor's and doctorate: master's degree

B.S.: Bachelor of Science

C.E.: Civil Engineer

D.D.S.: Doctor of Dental Science

D. Th.: Doctor of Theology

graduating with great honor or praise: magna cum laude

graduating with highest praise: summa cum laude

graduating with honors: cum laude

highest degree: doctorate, Ph. D.

LL.D.: Doctor of Laws

M.A.: Master of Arts

M.B.A.: Master of Business Administration

M.D.: Doctor of Medicine

Ph.D: Doctor of Philosophy

recognition of achievement, not schooling: honorary degree

Sc.D.: Doctor of Science

S.J.D.: Doctor of Judicial Science

SEE COLLEGE

dehydrate v. dry, desiccate.

deign v. deem worthy, see fit, stoop, condescend.

deity n. god, goddess, supreme being, idol.

dejected a. depressed, disheartened, saddened, low, dispirited, *bummed, melancholy, downhearted, heavyhearted, blue, disconsolate, *down in the mouth. ANT. *cheerful, happy, euphoric.*

delay n. postponement, deferment, detention, stall, hindrance, impediment, procrastination, suspension, prolongation, hold, stop. ANT. *rush.*

delay v. postpone, put off, defer, detain, stall, hinder, impede, procrastinate, suspend, prolong, hold, stop, wait. ANT. *expedite, rush, hurry.*

delectable a. delightful, pleasing, pleasurable, enjoyable, satisfying, delicious, tasty, *scrumptious, heavenly, luscious, savory, ambrosial, toothsome. ANT. *disgusting, nauseating.*

delegate n. representative, deputy, spokesperson, agent, appointee, proxy, envoy, intermediary.

delegate v. appoint, commission, deputize, authorize, charge, commission, empower, nominate, assign, give.

delete v. strike out, omit, cancel, erase, scratch, remove, eliminate, exclude, expunge, drop. ANT. *include, insert, add.*

DELETERIOUS a. [DEL i TEER ee us] harmful, destructive. *Rock salt is deleterious to a car's paint.* SYN. harmful, injurious, hurtful, pernicious, bad, noxious, detrimental, destructive, damaging, malignant. ANT. *beneficial, helpful, advantageous.*

deliberate v. think about, reflect, ponder, consider, weigh, muse, cogitate, turn over, ruminate, mull, contemplate.

deliberate a. intentional, willful, designed, on purpose, premeditated, meant, calculated, planned, conscious, knowing. ANT. *accidental, unintentional, rash, impulsive.*

deliberation n. thought, contemplation, consideration, circumspection, study, debate, reflection, forethought, pondering, weighing. ANT. *thoughtlessness, carelessness, impulsiveness.*

delicacy n. **1.** FRAILTY OR FINENESS fragility, tenderness, lightness, daintiness, airiness, exquisiteness. **2.** GOURMET FOOD tidbit, dainty, appetizer, morsel, goody, rarity, treat, bonne bouche, caviar. **3.** SENSITIVITY consideration, tact, grace, subtlety, finesse, diplomacy. ANT. *1. toughness, durability, sturdiness. 3. insensitivity, thoughtlessness, roughness.*

delicate a. **1.** FRAIL fragile, fine, tender, light, dainty, airy, exquisite, diaphanous, slight. **2.** SENSITIVE considerate, tactful, graceful, subtle, diplomatic, discreet, careful. **3.** DIFFICULT *sticky, *ticklish, precarious, critical, sensitive, tenuous. ANT. *1. tough, durable, sturdy. 2. insensitive, inconsiderate, rude.*

delicious *a.* tasty, delightful, *lip-smacking good, appetizing, delectable, luscious, scrumptious, ambrosial, mouth-watering, heavenly, *fit for a king, *yummy, toothsome.

delight *n.* pleasure, joy, happiness, gratification, enjoyment, thrill, glee, felicity. ANT. *misery, disgust.*

delight *v.* please, make happy, gratify, thrill, gladden, charm, *tickle, enchant, fill with joy, cheer. ANT. *depress, *piss off, anger.*

delightful *a.* pleasing, gratifying, thrilling, gladdening, charming, joyful, enjoyable, happy, agreeable, delectable, thrilling, enchanting. ANT. *miserable, depressing, unpleasant.*

delineate *v.* **1.** OUTLINE sketch, draft, draw, diagram, rough out. **2.** PORTRAY depict, describe, define, characterize, limn, detail.

delinquency *n.* offense, misdeed, wrongdoing, infrcation, transgression, violation, misconduct, dereliction, negligence.

delinquent *n.* criminal, lawbreaker, outlaw, malefactor, offender, miscreant, culprit, scamp, rascal, *hood.

delinquent *a.* lawbreaking, criminal, irresponsible, derelict, remiss, neglectful, faulty, slack, negligent.

delirious *a.* confused, incoherent, disordered, muddled, hallucinating, irrational, raving, *out of it, bewildered, deranged, babbling. ANT. *rational, lucid, clearheaded.*

deliver *v.* **1.** TRANSFER carry, convey, transport, bring, send, transmit, forward, surrender. **2.** FREE liberate, save, rescue, emancipate, release. **3.** THROW send, discharge, pitch, shoot, toss, launch, fire. ANT. *2. enslave, shackle.*

deliverance *n.* rescue, emancipation, liberation, freeing, saving, salvation, release.

delivery *n.* transfer, transport, transmittal, transmission, forwarding, consignment, distribution, shipment.

dell *n.* vale. SEE VALLEY

delude *v.* deceive, mislead, fool, *lead up the garden path, *hoodwink, dupe, misrepresent, beguile, *sucker, brainwash, kid.

deluge *n.* flood, inundation, torrent, downpour, cloudburst, spate, cataract, ocean, sea, *rain of biblical proportion, avalanche.

deluge *v.* **1.** FLOOD inundate, drench, drown, swamp, flush, overflow, submerge, immerse, overwhelm, overrun, engulf, *snow under.

DELUSION *n.* [di LOO zshun] a belief that is unsupported by the facts. *Mary thought she was a queen; she was suffering from delusions.* SYN. fancy, illusion, mirage, vision, self-deception, misconception, fantasy, *pipe dream, *fool's paradise, figment of the imagination, paranoia, megalomania, delusions of grandeur, folie a deux.

deluxe *a.* superior, luxurious, first-rate, first-class, select, sumptuous, choice, elegant, grand, rich, elite, *posh. ANT. *cheap, *cut-rate, run of the mill.*

DEMAGOGUE *n.* [DEM uh GAWG] a leader who panders to the emotions of the masses in order to win them over. *He knew how to push the voters' buttons; he was a rabble-rouser and a demagogue.* SYN. rabble-rouser, *grandstander, agitator, inciter, opportunist, troublemaker, instigator, *firebrand, mountebank. "[One who] appeals to passions and prejudices rather than to reason . . . " — James Fenimore Cooper. "One who tells you what you want to hear. A statesman tells you what you need to hear." — Max Rafferty.

demand *n.* requirement, bid, call, order, charge, request, command, petition, ultimatum, injunction, appeal.

demand *v.* order, insist on, press, ask, bid, compel, requisition, exact, command, necessitate, require, urge, summon, implore.

demean *v.* lower, debase, humble, degrade, depreciate, *take down a peg, disgrace, humiliate, demote, shame. ANT. *elevate, *put on a pedestal, idolize, honor.*

demeanor *n.* behavior, manner, deportment, conduct, comportment, bearing, disposition, attitude, air, actions.

demented *a.* insane, crazy, psychotic, deranged, maniacal, unstable, *flipped out, hysterical, mad, schizophrenic, irrational, *nuts. ANT. *sane, rational, stable.* SEE CRAZY, NEUROTIC

demise *n.* death, passing, end, expiration, downfall, termination, *lights out, fall. ANT. *birth, beginning.* SEE DEATH

democracy *n.* government by and for the people, republic, representative government, constitutional government, commonwealth. "Government by amateurs." — Maxwell Anderson. "Gives every man the right to be his own oppressor." — James Lowell. "Mob rule." — Polybius.

DEMOCRATIC *a.* [dem uh KRAT ik] representing the common people, especially with issues of equality. *A democratic government is a fair and just government.* SYN. equal, common, populist, popular, self-governing, constitutional, egalitarian, libertarian, representative, of and for the people, tolerant, fair-minded. ANT. *dictatorial, authoritarian, despotic, autocratic, intolerant.*

demolish *v.* destroy, wreck, raze, level, annihilate, ruin, *trash, obliterate, tear down, fell, wipe out, smash. ANT. *build, create.*

demolition *n.* destruction, wreckage, razing, leveling, *trashing, annihilation, obliteration, smashing, tearing down.

demon *n.* devil, fiend, satan, imp, monster, ogre, savage, evil spirit, ghoul, *fallen angel. SEE MONSTER

demonic *a.* demoniac, fiendish, possessed, hellish, frenzied, bedeviled, bewitched, devilish, diabolical, satanic, monstrous. ANT. *angelic, saintly.*

demonstrate *v.* **1.** SHOW illustrate, exhibit, explain, describe, *walk one through, set forth. **2.** MAKE EVIDENT prove, establish, substantiate, corroborate, evince, authenticate, validate, verify, document. **3.** PROTEST picket, rally, strike, march, parade.

demonstration *n.* **1.** SHOW illustration, exhibition, explanation, description, *walk through, presentation. **2.** EVIDENCE proof, substantiation, corroboration, authentication, validation, verification, documentation. **3.** PROTEST picketing, rally, strike, march, parade, *sit-in.

demonstrative *a.* affectionate, *touchy-feely, expressive, outpouring, emotional, gushing, expansive, warm, unrestrained, open. ANT. *reserved, restrained, distant, cold, uptight.*

DEMORALIZE *v.* [di MOR uh lize] to sap one's morale or confidence. *The hometown team suffered a demoralizing defeat.* SYN. deflate, dishearten, discourage, sap, *take the wind out of one's sails, *take the fight out of, *take the starch out of, crush, undermine, shake one's confidence, dispirit. ANT. *encourage, hearten, puff up.*

demote *v.* lower, degrade, downgrade, *bust, *bench.

demur *v.* object, take exception, disagree, dissent, protest, remonstrate, refute. ANT. *agree, concur, acquiesce.*

DEMURE *a.* [di MYOOR] quiet, reserved or shy. Also, affecting shyness. *She was demure in church but boisterous among friends.* SYN. quiet, reserved, sedate, shy, low-keyed, modest, coy, bashful, blushing, unassuming, self-

effacing, timid, retiring. ANT. *loudmouthed, bold, brash, aggressive.*

den *n.* **1.** LAIR hole, cave, burrow, diggings, tunnel, retreat, nest. **2.** STUDY library, sanctuary, cloister, retreat.

denial *n.* rejection, refusal, dismissal, negation, veto, no, turndown, refutation, repudiation, prohibition, declination, contradiction, disallowance. ANT. *acceptance, affirmation, approval.*

denigrate *v.* belittle, defame, calumniate, *badmouth, vilify, malign, put down, slander, assail, criticize, *give a black eye. ANT. *honor, flatter, compliment.*

DENIZEN *n.* [DEN i zun] an inhabitant. *The denizens of Alaska know how to stay warm.* SYN. inhabitant, resident, native, dweller, citizen, occupant.

denomination *n.* **1.** NAME designation, title, appellation, label, moniker, *handle, class, group, classification, category, type, heading. **2.** SECT faith, church, school, persuasion, affiliation.

denote *v.* mean, designate, signify, indicate, symbolize, tag, represent, connote, stand for, suggest.

denounce *v.* condemn, censure, criticize, attack, proscribe, disparage, impugn, castigate, decry, vilify, damn, stigmatize. ANT. *honor, praise, laud.*

dense *a.* **1.** THICK compressed, compact, solid, firm, tight, concentrated, packed, impenetrable. **2.** STUPID dumb, bovine, dull, *lamebrained, *brain-drained, *slow on the uptake, thick, *dense as a post. ANT. *1. porous, sparse, thin. 2. smart, sharp, quick.* SEE MORONIC, STUPID

dent *n.* indentation, hollow, concavity, dint, *ding, dimple, depression, furrow, notch, scratch.

denude *v.* expose, lay bare. SEE STRIP

denunciation *n.* condemnation, censure, criticism, fulmination, disapproval, castigation, indictment, vilification, reprobation, harangue. ANT. *praise, compliment, advocation.*

deny *v.* **1.** REFUSE turn down, reject, veto, say no, turn thumbs down, prohibit, disallow. **2.** CONTROVERT dispute, gainsay, contradict, disclaim, forswear, refute, repudiate. ANT. *1. allow, *give the green light, okay, pass. 2. concede, affirm.*

depart *v.* **1.** LEAVE go, set out, be off, run along, *hit the road, *split, exit, embark, *shove off, *scram, *beat it, pull out, evacuate. **2.** DIVERGE digress, deviate, veer, stray, wander, swerve. ANT. *1. come, arrive. 2. *stay on the straight and narrow, abide.*

department n. division, section, office, branch, unit, subdivision, bureau, sector, district, precinct.

departure n. **1.** LEAVING going, setting out, running along, exit, leavetaking, withdrawal, exodus, embarkation, parting, adieu, withdrawal. **2.** DIVERGENCE digression, deviation, veering, straying, wandering. ANT. *1. coming, arrival.*

depend v. **1.** RELY ON bank on, trust, count, bet on, *pin one's faith on, turn to. **2.** BE DETERMINED BY hinge on, be subject to, hang on, be contingent on.

dependable a. reliable, bankable, trustworthy, steady, unfailing, responsible, tried-and-true, *good as one's word, loyal, staunch, steadfast. ANT. *unreliable, irresponsible.*

dependence n. reliance, faith, confidence, belief, stock, trust, expectation; need, addiction, dependency.

dependent a. **1.** RELIANT helpless, defenseless, vulnerable, clinging, *tied to mother's apron strings, needful, addicted. **2.** DETERMINED BY hinging on, subject to, hanging on, contingent on. ANT. *1. autonomous, self-reliant, independent.*

depict v. describe, portray, detail, outline, sketch, characterize, limn, represent, paint, show, delineate, narrate, tell.

deplete v. use up, exhaust, run out, consume, empty, drain, spend, bleed, bankrupt, finish, expend. ANT. *restock, replenish, fill.*

DEPLORABLE a. [di PLOR uh bul] bad, wretched or grievous. *The boy's bedroom was in a deplorable state.* SYN. bad, wretched, grievous, disgraceful, shameful, abominable, lamentable, despicable, pitiable, reprehensible, depressing, scandalous. ANT. *agreeable, pleasing, acceptable.*

deplore v. **1.** EXPRESS OR FEEL SORROW lament, grieve, weep, mourn, sorrow, bemoan, rue, bewail. **2.** DISAPPROVE OF censure, condemn, criticize, abhor, hate, object to, reject, decry.

deploy v. spread, distribute, station, position, spread out, arrange, use, utilize.

deport v. expel, banish, exile, extradite, cast out, expatriate, *kick out, *give the boot, ostracize.

deportment n. behavior, conduct, carriage, demeanor, actions, manner, mien, bearing, air, posture.

DEPOSE v. [di POZ] to remove from a position of power. *They are planning to have the presi-*dent deposed. SYN. remove, oust, *kick out, dismiss, impeach, unseat, *unhorse, eject, *can, drum out, dethrone, overthrow, *send packing, *ride out on a rail. ANT. *install, seat, empower.*

deposit n. installment, down payment, security, pledge, warranty, collateral.

deposition n. testimony, written statement, sworn statement, affidavit.

depot n. **1.** STATION terminal. **2.** WAREHOUSE storehouse, repository, station, armory, magazine.

depraved a. corrupt, debased, immoral, wicked, bad, perverted, vile, shameless, *dirty, warped, evil, low, lecherous, sinful, nasty, iniquitous, debauched. ANT. *virtuous, chaste, moral, clean-living.*

depravity n. corruption, wickedness, perversion, immorality, vileness, shamelessness, evil, lechery, sin, nastiness, debauchery, debasement, vice, degeneracy. ANT. *virtue, morality, clean-living, holiness.*

DEPRECATE v. [DEP ruh KATE] to express one's disapproval toward; to speak out against. *The radio host liked to deprecate environmental extremists.* SYN. put down, belittle, condemn, *slam, disparage, mudsling, disapprove, frown on, reproach, censure, rail against. ANT. *approve of, praise, extol, laud.*

depreciate v. **1.** LOSE VALUE cheapen, downgrade, drop, deflate, diminish, shrink, soften, depress, devalue, decay, wane, fall, ebb. **2.** BELITTLE diminish, put down, disparage, denigrate, deprecate, ridicule, underestimate, minimize, find fault, slight. ANT. *1. appreciate, increase, grow, boom. 2. value, esteem, appreciate.*

depreciation n. devaluation, downgrade, drop, fall, deflation, shrinkage, depression, *bear market, decay, waning, slump.

depress v. **1.** SADDEN dishearten, distress, *bum out, burden, dispirit, weigh down, demoralize, weary, enervate. **2.** DEVALUE cheapen, degrade, diminish, weaken, depreciate, lower, lessen. **3.** PUSH DOWN press down, level, lower, step on. ANT. *1. cheer, hearten, buoy. 2. appreciate, heighten. 3. pull.*

depressed a. downhearted, melancholy, *blue, *bummed out, *down in the dumps, disconsolate, dejected, unhappy, low, woebegone, dispirited, down, sad, glum, suicidal, sullen, *down in the mouth, in the doldrums. ANT. *happy, euphoric, joyful.*

depression n. **1.** DOWNHEARTEDNESS melancholia, *blues, dejection, unhappiness, sadness, doldrums, *blahs, *blue funk, sorrow, heavy-heartedness, despair, gloom. **2.** HOLLOW dent, impression, indentation, recess, concavity. ANT. *1. euphoria, happiness, joy.*

deprivation *n.* loss, privation, need, want, hardship, withholding, dispossession.

deprive *v.* keep from, take away, divest, strip, withhold, deny, shut out, remove, dispossess, cut off, confiscate.

depth *n.* **1.** LOWNESS deepness, bottom, draft, drop, pitch. **2.** PROFOUNDNESS wisdom, insight, perception, astuteness. ANT. *1. height, shallowness. 2. shallowness, superficiality.*

deputy *n.* assistant, representative, agent, delegate, appointee, aide, surrogate, proxy, substitute, *second-in-command, emissary, envoy.

deranged *a.* irrational, insane, crazy, unstable, *off the wall, *nuts, demented, psychotic, berserk, mad, lunatic, *out of one's mind, *flipped, *schizo. ANT. *rational, sane, lucid, stable.* SEE CRAZY, NEUROTIC

derelict *n.* vagrant, outcast, *bum, hobo, tramp, beggar, *ne'er-do-well, *good-for-nothing, pariah.

derelict *a.* neglectful, delinquent, remiss, irresponsible, lazy, slack, careless, lax, shiftless, laggard. ANT. *responsible, conscientious, dutiful.*

DERIDE *v.* [di RIDE] to laugh at; ridicule. *Citizens of the nineteenth century often derided the automobile.* SYN. laugh at, ridicule, scoff, jeer, mock, taunt, make fun of, heckle, kid, *rib, *razz, *roast. ANT. *take seriously, respect, esteem.*

DE RIGUEUR *a.* [de ree GUHR] necessary or proper; required by the rules of etiquette. *Hats were de rigueur for the first half of the century.* SYN. necessary, called for, fashionable, compulsory, a must, proper, right, correct, required, fitting, comme il faut. ANT. *unnecessary, demode.*

derision *n.* ridicule, scoffing, disrespect, *dig, insult, mockery, sneering, scorn, satire, contempt, jeer, lampoon, laughingstock, *Bronx cheer. ANT. *respect, esteem.*

derisive *a.* ridiculing, sarcastic, disdainful, mocking, taunting, *smart-alecky, jeering, insulting, *razzing, disrespectful. ANT. *respectful.*

derivation *n.* origin, source, root, beginning, inception, wellspring, ancestry.

derivative *a.* borrowed, copied, unoriginal, imitative, derived, rehashed, uninventive, secondary, warmed-over, *lifted. ANT. *original,*

new, inventive.

derive *v.* draw, gain, obtain, extract, get, gather, reap, receive.

derive from *vi.* come from, descend, originate, stem from, arise, emanate, spring from.

DERNIER CRI *n.* [DAIR nee ay CREE] the latest thing, the last word. *A ponytail worn by a man is dernier cri.* SYN. the latest cry, the latest thing, the latest fashion, the last word, the in thing, all the rage, mode, fad, look, in vogue.

DEROGATORY *a.* [di ROG uh TOHR ee] disparaging or disapproving. *One more derogatory comment from the class clown would infuriate the teacher.* SYN. disparaging, disapproving, belittling, deprecatory, censorious, critical, perjorative, unflattering, detracting, disdainful, contemptuous. ANT. *flattering, complimentary, approving.*

derriere *n.* seat, backside, rear, *tush. SEE BUTTOCKS

derring-do *n.* valor, daring, courage. SEE BRAVERY

descend *v.* go down, drop, fall, decline, lower, plunge, plummet, submerge, dip, sink, slope, rappel. ANT. *ascend, go up, rise.*

descendant *n.* offspring, progeny, child, seed, offshoot, scion, son, daughter, grandchild, heir. ANT. *ancestor, forebear, parent.*

descent *n.* **1.** MOVING DOWN fall, drop, lowering, sinking, tumble, plunge, plummet, dive, decline. **2.** SLOPE grade, incline, declivity, gradient, slant. **3.** LINEAGE ancestry, forefathers, pedigree, family tree, roots, parentage, genealogy. ANT. *1. ascent, rise.*

describe *v.* illustrate, portray, paint a mental picture, show, detail, explain, depict, chronicle, illuminate, relate, sketch, specify, limn.

description *n.* portrayal, depiction, detailing, chronicle, sketch, explanation, illumination, specification, characterization, elaboration, report, *blow by blow, rundown.

DESECRATE *v.* [DES uh krate] to abuse or disrespect that which is sacred. *The hoodlums descrated the shrine by covering it with grafitti.* SYN. profane, defile, abuse, violate, commit sacrilege, pervert, dishonor, debase, degrade, blaspheme, contaminate. ANT. *worship, honor, consecrate.*

desert *n.* wasteland, barrens, *parched Eden, *Devil's backyard, badlands, flats, dunes, *desiccated landscape, *neglected plot in God's garden, no man's land, dustbowl, *Euclidian plane, *scorched plain, *thirsty terrain, wilderness, Sahara, Gobi, Kalahari, Mojave. "The sea-like, pathless, limitless waste." — Longfellow "An old man in a dry season." — T.S. Eliot. "A wild of sand." — Addison.

WORD FIND

ancient desert mountain reduced to eroded nubbin: inselberg
characterized by mesas, gulleys, channels, erosion: badlands
dried-up river bed: arroyo
dune, crescent-shaped: barchan
dune, huge, whalelike: whaleback
dune, long or elongated: seif dune, sword dune
dune, pyramidlike: pyramid
dune, ridged or wavy: transverse dune
dune, starlike: star
fertile area, fed by spring: oasis
mosaiclike ground of colorful, polished pebbles: desert pavement, gibber plain, reg
mountain that is eroded and flattened on top: mesa, butte
nomadic Arab: Bedouin
optical illusion: mirage
pertaining to: eremic
plain that becomes temporary lake after rain: playa
plants: barrel cactus, century plant, cereus, cholla, creosote bush, ironwood, Joshua tree, mesquite, ocotillo, prickly pear cactus, sagebrush, saguaro
rain that evaporates before hitting ground: phantom rain
salty plain left by evaporation of lake: salt flat
sandy area of the Sahara: erg
semidesert plain: steppe
valley that is flat and arid: bolson

desert *v.* abandon, leave behind, forsake, leave, give up, *walk, *leave high and dry, strand, quit, maroon, renounce, *bail out, *leave in the lurch. ANT. *remain, stay, stick with.*

deserted *a.* empty, abandoned, desolate, solitary, barren, derelict, lonely, uninhabited, *godforsaken, vacant, forlorn. ANT. *crowded, mobbed, inhabited.*

deserter *n.* traitor, defector, fugitive, truant, renegade, runaway, refugee, escapee, derelict, turncoat, *AWOL.

deserts *n.* retribution, payback, punishment, reward, comeuppance, revenge, penalty, recompense, due.

deserve *v.* earn, merit, be entitled to, due, *get what is coming, warrant, expect to get, should be given.

deserving *a.* meritorious, worthy, due, commendable, laudable, praiseworthy.

DESHABILLE n. ALSO, **DISHABILLE** [DAYS ab ee yay] in a state of undress or partial undress; also, in one's night clothes. *She lounged around the breakfast table in deshabille.* SYN. undress, partial dress, in a state of sloppiness, informal dress, partially covered.

desiccate *v.* dry, dehydrate, drain, deplete, shrivel.

design *n.* **1.** COMPOSITION draft, arrangement, motif, plan, pattern, scheme, depiction, idea, sketch, outline, conception, blueprint, diagram, model. **2.** INTENTION purpose, objective, aim, goal, plan, *game plan, target, project. **3.** SCHEME plot, intrigue, machination, plan.

design *v.* **1.** COMPOSE draft, arrange, plan, pattern, invent, contrive, create, sketch, outline, conceive, blueprint, diagram, model, *cook up, fashion. **2.** INTEND purpose, aim, plan, aspire to, mean.

designate *v.* **1.** INDICATE specify, signify, point out, denote, assign, connote, mark, name. **2.** NAME entitle, christen, dub, label, denominate, nickname, baptize. **3.** APPOINT elect, name, nominate, choose, select, assign.

designation *n.* **1.** NAME title, label, appellation, moniker, tag, nickname, honorific. **2.** APPOINTMENT delegation, nomination, selection, assignment.

designing *a.* conniving, plotting, crafty, conspiring, tricky, scheming, double-dealing, artful, calculating, foxy, Machiavellian. ANT. *innocent, artless, open.*

desirable *a.* **1.** AROUSING DESIRE attractive, seductive, fetching, enticing, alluring, tantalizing, sexy, tempting, *hot. **2.** WORTHWHILE beneficial, good, pleasing, agreeable, preferable, profitable, advantageous. ANT. *1. repulsive, repellant. 2. undesirable, worthless, useless.*

desire *n.* want, longing, hunger, thirst, need, *hankering, ache, wish, appetite, passion, lust, libido, fervor, urge, yearning, mania, itch. "The warm beast . . . that lies curled up in our loins and stretches itself with a fierce gentleness." — Albert Camus. "A perpetual rack." — Robert Burton. ANT. *aversion, revulsion.*

desire *v.* want, long for, hunger for, thirst after, crave, need, *hanker for, ache for, covet, wish for, lust after, yearn for.

desist *v.* stop, cease, discontinue, refrain, halt, end, conclude, quit, suspend, hold, arrest.

ANT. *go, continue, persist.*

desolate *a.* **1.** BARREN abandoned, forsaken, deserted, lonely, uninhabited, isolated, solitary, empty, bleak, remote, *godforsaken, stark. **2.** FORLORN wretched, bereft, abandoned, friendless, forsaken, lonesome, alone, isolated, estranged, despondent, miserable, downhearted. ANT. *1. crowded, inhabited, mobbed. 2. happy, cheerful, befriended.*

despair *n.* hopelessness, depression, dejection, despondency, desperation, discouragement, melancholy, gloom, resignation, anguish, misery. ANT. *hope, euphoria, happiness.*

despair *v.* lose hope, to feel defeat, resign, lose faith, lose heart, despond. "An epitome of hell." — Robert Burton. "The worst poison." — Heinrich Heine. ANT. *hope, look up, think positive.*

desperado *n.* outlaw, criminal, thug, bandit, gunman, lawbreaker, highwayman.

desperate *a.* **1.** RECKLESS careless, dangerous, frantic, headlong, foolhardy, rash, out of control, *on a crash course, frenzied, death-defying. **2.** DESPAIRING hopeless, beyond help, *at the end of one's rope, *back to the wall, incurable, irretrievable, futile, *sunk, lost, critical, grave. **3.** EXTREME critical, grave, serious, crucial, urgent, acute, drastic, compelling. ANT. *1. careful, cautious, prudent, rational. 2. hopeful, optimistic. 3. trivial, minor, casual.*

desperation *n.* **1.** DESPAIR hopelessness, futility, despondency, depression, melancholy, dejection, discouragement, gloom. **2.** RECKLESSNESS carelessness, frenzy, foolhardiness, rashness, impetuosity, daring, imprudence. ANT. *1. hope, optimism. 2. caution, wariness, prudence.*

despicable *a.* contemptible, vile, loathsome, shameful, disgraceful, awful, beastly, sickening, base, abhorrent, cheap, rotten, unforgivable, detestable. ANT. *honorable, praiseworthy, laudable.*

despise *v.* disdain, hate, loathe, abhor, scorn, spurn, look down on, revile, execrate, detest, *can't stand. ANT. *admire, respect, like.*

despite *prep.* in spite of, regardless of, notwithstanding.

DESPONDENT *a.* [di SPON dunt] deeply depressed, filled with despair. *Alice was despondent after her mother died.* SYN. depressed, despairing, miserable, downhearted, inconsolable, melancholy, forlorn, sorrowful, disheartened, glum, *bummed out, heartbroken, *down in the dumps, suicidal. ANT.

euphoric, joyful, optimistic, buoyant, cheerful.

DESPOT *n.* [DES put] an absolute ruler, an autocrat. *The despot completely oppressed the citizenry.* SYN. autocrat, tyrant, dictator, *strong man, *Hitler, oppressor, lord, master, authoritarian.

destination *n.* goal, stop, journey's end, objective, station, terminal, end of the line, port of call.

destiny *n.* fate, lot, destination, future, design, doom, predestination, serendipity, fortune, karma, *wheel of fortune. "A tyrant's authority for crime and a fool's excuse for failure." — Ambrose Bierce. "Not a thing to be waited for, it is a thing to be achieved." — William Jennings Bryan. "An invention of the cowardly and the resigned." — Ignazio Silone.

DESTITUTE *a.* [DES ti TOOT] profoundly poor, impoverished. *The destitute who live on the streets.* SYN. poor, penniless, indigent, impoverished, broke, *down and out, *dirt poor, lacking, bankrupt, homeless, ruined, *wiped out. ANT. *rich, wealthy, *rolling in dough.*

destroy *v.* demolish, annihilate, wreck, devastate, wipe out, *total, raze, extirpate, ruin, ravage, obliterate, eradicate, *cream, level, waste, quash, *gut, *nuke, crush. ANT. *create, build, preserve.*

destruction *n.* wreckage, demolition, annihilation, ruins, devastation, ravaging, liquidation, havoc, extinction, eradication, slaughter, decimation. "A primitive instinct which occasionally comes out despite our veneer of civilization." — Anon. ANT. *building, creation, preservation.*

destructive *a.* injurious, pernicious, harmful, ravaging, ruinous, catastrophic, fatal, damaging, deleterious, disastrous, malevolent, noxious. ANT. *creative, constructive, preserving.*

DESULTORY *a.* [DES ul TOHR ee] moving from one thing to another randomly or haphazardly. *She examined the shoes in desultory fashion.* SYN. random, haphazard, unmethodical, disconnected, rambling, aimless, irregular, chaotic, unsystematic, erratic. ANT. *methodical, planned.*

detach *v.* disconnect, separate, sever, loose, unhitch, uncouple, divide, free, remove. ANT. *attach, fasten.*

detached *a.* **1.** DISCONNECTED separated, removed, severed, unfastened, unconnected, unhitched, loose, apart. **2.** DISINTERESTED removed, remote, objective, impartial, aloof, dispassionate, neutral, unbiased. ANT. *1. attached, fastened, connected. 2. interested, biased, partial.*

detachment a. objectivity, aloofness, unconcern, impartiality, indifference, remoteness, neutrality, isolation. ANT. *interest, partiality, bias.*

detail n. particular, item, point, fact, feature, specific, component, part, *nuts and bolts, aspect, element, minutiae.

detain v. hold, stop, slow, arrest, restrain, delay, impede, confine, keep, retard. ANT. *free, liberate, speed.*

detect v. notice, spot, find, discover, uncover, sense, catch, espy, sleuth, *sniff out, ferret out, discern, unmask, *stumble on. ANT. *miss, overlook, ignore.*

detection n. discovery, spotting, notice, finding, uncovering, sensing, revelation, exposure, espial, ferreting out, *sniffing out.

detective n. sleuth, private investigator (P.I.), *private eye, *dick, operative, *gumshoe, hawkshaw, undercover agent, secret agent, shadow, *tail, *G-man, *snoop. SEE POLICE

DETENTE n. [day TONT] an easing of hostilities between nations. *Following the treaty was an extended period of detente.* SYN. relaxation, cooling off, easing, peace, quietude, relief, tranquility, harmony, softening, suspension of hostilities, quiescence, accord, truce, amity. ANT. *hostility, cold war, war, animosity.*

detention n. holding, retention, restraint, arrest, confinement, duress, delaying, incarceration, custody, internment. ANT. *freedom, liberation.*

deter v. prevent, stop, scare off, inhibit, check, dissuade, curb, hinder, bar, stall, cool, daunt, dampen, preclude, discourage. ANT. *encourage, speed, facilitate.*

deteriorate v. decay, degenerate, fall apart, crumble, degrade, decline, *go downhill, *go to the dogs, corrode, rot, decompose, depreciate. ANT. *improve, grow, strengthen.*

determination n. **1.** RESOLUTENESS perseverance, steadfastness, fortitude, resolve, tenacity, *backbone, drive, willpower, grit, *stiff upper lip, persistence, single-mindedness, mettle, stick-to-itiveness, indomitability. **2.** DECISION conclusion, ascertainment, finding, judgment, settlement, resolution, verdict, opinion.

determine v. **1.** DECIDE conclude, ascertain, find, judge, settle, resolve, confirm, verify,

*nail down, *sew up, establish. **2.** AFFECT THE COURSE OF decide, influence, control, direct, govern, regulate, shape.

determined a. resolute, steadfast, purposeful, firm, *hell-bent, fixed, intent, tenacious, driven, single-minded, settled, stalwart, dogged. ANT. *waffling, wavering, lukewarm.*

deterrent n. check, curb, obstacle, stumbling block, bar, defense, impediment, hindrance, discouragement, restraint.

detest v. hate, loathe, despise, abhor, dislike, execrate, *feel sick at the sight of, reject. ANT. *like, admire, love.*

detestable a. hateful, despicable, loathsome, abhorrent, abominable, sickening, execrable, revolting, obnoxious, beastly, disgusting, contemptible. ANT. *admirable, likable.*

detonate v. explode, set off, discharge, blow up, fire, touch off.

detour n. bypass, *go-around, alternate route, deviation.

detract v. lessen, diminish, take away from, undermine, minimize, devaluate, depreciate. ANT. *enhance, increase, add to.*

DETRIMENTAL a. [det ruh MEN tul] causing harm. *Neglecting to wax your car is detrimental to its finish.* SYN. harmful, injurious, damaging, deleterious, bad, disadvantageous, inimical, destructive, pernicious. ANT. *beneficial, advantageous.*

devastate v. lay waste, ruin, destroy, demolish, wipe out, *total, level, desolate, ravage, raze, gut, *trash, *blow away, ransack, pillage.

devastation n. waste, ruin, destruction, havoc, desolation, ravaging, demolition, wreckage, annihilation, *trashing.

develop v. **1.** EXPAND grow, enlarge, elaborate, evolve, advance, mature, flourish, progress, fill out, blossom, bear fruit, enrich, broaden, flesh out, amplify. **2.** GENERATE begin, start, commence, originate, establish, arise, break, transpire, unfold. **3.** CONTRACT acquire. ANT. *1. die, shrivel, regress, shrink, degrade.*

development n. **1.** GROWTH expansion, enlargement, elaboration, evolution, advancement, maturation, progress, filling out, flowering, blossoming, enrichment, broadening, fleshing out, amplification. **2.** HAPPENING event, occurrence, circumstance, change, issue, result, advance. ANT. *1. decline, regression, shriveling, withering, death.*

deviate v. diverge, turn aside, veer, depart, stray, drift, wander, swerve, part, meander, err, detour, digress. ANT. *follow the straight and narrow, stay on course.*

device n. 1. INSTRUMENT apparatus, contrivance, tool, appliance, mechanism, rig, machine, gadget, *contraption, outfit, gear, *thingamajig. 2. SCHEME plan, contrivance, design, ploy, ruse, trick, artifice, gimmick, deus ex machina, stunt, machination.

devil n. 1. SATAN Lucifer, Prince of Darkness, Beelzebub, Mephistopheles, archfiend, el diablo, Lord of the Flies, the Serpent, *Old Harry, *Old Scratch, *the Deuce, *the Dickens, the Adversary, fallen angel. "A liar, and the father of it." — Bible. "The most diligent preacher of all others; he is never out of his diocese." — Hugh Latimer. 2. BAD PERSON, SPIRIT OR CREATURE demon, fiend, imp, ogre, savage, brute, rogue, hellion, evildoer, beast, villain, scoundrel, brat.

devilish a. fiendish, villainous, beastly, hellish, evil, diabolical, brutish, mischievous, demonic, impish, troublemaking, naughty, wicked, infernal, cruel, sinister. ANT. angelic, saintly, good, virtuous.

devil-may-care a. careless, reckless, happy-go-lucky, foolhardy, rash, nonchalant, cavalier, heedless, casual. ANT. cautious, careful.

DEVIL'S ADVOCATE n. one who argues for but doesn't necessarily agree with the unpopular side of an issue in order to illustrate all perspectives. Talk show hosts often play the devil's advocate for argument's sake. SYN. pleader, apologist, mediator, medium, devil's counsel, defender, devil's champion, devil's surrogate, polemicist.

devious a. deceptive, roundabout, crafty, tricky, wily, guileful, sly, treacherous, crooked, dishonest, evasive, underhanded, scheming, shifty. ANT. honest, aboveboard, straightforward.

devise v. invent, conceive, form, contrive, formulate, *cook up, create, *whip up, plot, scheme, concoct, construct, shape.

devoid a. empty, lacking, destitute, vacuous, depleted, denuded, stripped, vacant, bare, wanting, barren. ANT. full, replete.

devote v. dedicate, give, pledge, commit, vow, consign, apply, direct.

devoted a. dedicated, faithful, true, committed, loyal, staunch, zealous, dutiful, devout, constant, earnest, steadfast. ANT. indifferent, disloyal.

devotee n. fan, fanatic, enthusiast, afficianado, buff, lover, supporter, addict, *nut, adherent, *hound, *fiend.

devotion n. DEDICATION commitment, adherence, allegiance, devoutness, faithfulness, loyalty, fidelity, steadfastness, piety, zeal, reverence. ANT. indifference, apathy, disloyalty.

devour v. swallow up, eat, consume, gobble up, wolf, gulp, stuff, gorge, bolt, *polish off, guzzle, gormandize, dispatch.

devout a. pious, religious, believing, faithful, reverent, worshipping, earnest, holy, orthodox, zealous, ardent, heartfelt, sincere. ANT. atheistic, agnostic, unbelieving.

dewy-eyed a. innocent, childlike, naive.

dexterity n. skill, adroitness, deftness, cleverness, expertise, know-how, knack, touch, aptitude, facility, nimbleness, finesse. ANT. ineptitude, clumsiness.

dexterous a. skillful, adroit, deft, clever, expert, handy, adept, nimble, proficient, savvy, clever, facile. ANT. clumsy, inept, uncoordinated.

diabolic a. satanic, hellish, devilish, infernal, fiendish, evil, demonic, wicked, villainous, Mephistophelean, malevolent, vicious, cruel, beastly. ANT. heavenly, saintly, benevolent, angelic.

diagnosis n. identification, conclusion, determination, hunch, opinion, analysis, educated guess. "One of the commonest diseases." — Karl Kraus.

dialect n. speech, local tongue, provincialism, vernacular, patois, idiom, lingo, argot, slang, cant, colloquialism, accent, pidgin.

dialogue n. talk, discussion, conversation, verbal exchange, interlocution, confabulation, communication, conference, tete-a-tete, *rap session, discourse, *powwow, *heart-to-heart.

diametrical a. opposite, contrary, conflicting, converse, reverse, antithetical, different. ANT. alike, similar, matching.

diaphanous a. transparent, sheer, *see-through, translucent, thin, flimsy, gauzy, delicate, chiffon. ANT. opaque, thick.

diary n. journal, chronicle, account, log, record, daybook. "The lavatory of literature." — Elbert Hubbard.

DIATRIBE n. [DI uh tribe] a bitter denunciation or criticism. The talk show host launched into a scathing diatribe. SYN. invective, criticism, denunciation, harangue, castigation, tirade, abuse, vituperation, *tongue-lashing, rebuke.

dice n. *bones, *rollers, die, cube.

dicey a. risky, chancy, hazardous, a gamble, ticklish, *iffy.

dicker v. haggle, bargain, negotiate, *hash out

a deal, higgle, quibble, *talk down, barter.

dictate *n.* directive, rule, order, direction, command, mandate, law, ordinance, decree, bidding, dictum, requirement.

dictate *v.* **1.** PRESCRIBE order, command, direct, rule, charge, lay down the law, demand, enjoin, *call the shots, impose, ordain. **2.** READ ALOUD compose, utter, draft, record.

dictator *n.* tyrant, despot, autocrat, authoritarian, *Hitler, totalitarian, oppressor, overlord, *lord and master, strongman, czar, taskmaster. "Jealous gods monopolizing power, destroying all rivals, compelling exclusive loyalty." — Walter Lippmann. "Rulers who always look good until the last ten minutes." — Jan Masaryk.

dictatorial *a.* tyrannical, despotic, autocratic, authoritarian, *Hitleresque, totalitarian, oppressive, overbearing, ironhanded, lordly, high-handed, absolute, *whip-cracking, imperious, domineering. ANT. *democratic, liberal, tolerant.*

diction *n.* vocabulary, wording, articulation, enunciation, expression, eloquence, usage, pronunciation, phraseology, language, inflection, elocution.

dictionary *n.* lexicon, glossary, word book, reference book, vocabulary. "The most interesting book in our language." — Albert Nock.

dictum *n.* **1.** PRONOUNCEMENT dictate, declaration, assertion, decree, command, edict, order. **2.** SAYING maxim, adage, proverb, truism, axiom, aphorism.

DIDACTIC *a.* [dye DAK tik] instructional or educational, especially involving morals. Also, overly preachy or instructional; pedantic. *A didactic speech. Didactic lessons of Sunday school.* SYN. instructional, educational, informative, enlightening, expository, edifying, moralizing, pedantic, preachy, homiletic, pedagogic, sermonizing.

die *v.* **1.** PERISH expire, pass away, decease, succumb, depart, drop dead, *croak, *kick the bucket, *buy the farm, *cash in one's chips, *bite the dust, *kick off, *give up the ghost, *go belly up, *slip one's cable, *permanently change one's address, *meet one's Maker. "Go the way of all earth." — Bible. SEE DEAD, DEATH **2.** DWINDLE wane, ebb, fade, weaken, abate, decline, subside, slacken, *fizzle out, *peter out, recede, diminish.

diehard *n.* *bitter-ender, zealot, fanatic, ultraconservative, reactionary, stick-in-the-mud.

diet *n.* **1.** DAILY FOOD INTAKE food and drink, sustenance, nourishment, nutrition, victuals, foodstuffs, provisions, fare. **2.** FOOD ABSTINENCE abstinence, fasting, regimen, regime, *weight-watching, calorie counting. "A system of starving yourself to death so you can live a little longer." — Jan Murray. "The only discipline that shows a gain by showing a loss." — Anon.

differ *v.* **1.** CONTRAST vary, stand apart, clash, diverge, be distinguished from, deviate from. **2.** DISAGREE clash, oppose, dispute, conflict, be at variance, take issue, contend, contradict, *lock horns. ANT. *1. resemble, correspond, match. 2. agree, concur, accede, *see eye to eye.*

difference *n.* **1.** DISSIMILARITY contrast, antithesis, variance, opposition, distinction, asymmetry, differentiation, inconformity, unlikeness, deviation. **2.** DISAGREEMENT argument, dispute, contention, clash, controversy, dissension, conflict, debate, quarrel, opposition, contradiction. ANT. *1. similarity, likeness, correspondence, mirrorimage. 2. agreement, concurrence, accord.*

different *a.* **1.** DISSIMILAR distinct, contrasting, antithetical, opposite, asymmetrical, unlike, variant, *like night and day, divergent, clashing, disparate, incompatible. **2.** SEPARATE distinct, delineated, differentiated, singular, individual, another, exclusive. **3.** VARIOUS several, sundry, assorted, diverse, numerous, miscellaneous, mixed. ANT. *1. the same, alike, resembling, matching. 2. together, whole.*

differentiate *v.* distinguish, set apart, make a distinction, contrast, separate, characterize.

difficult *a.* **1.** HARD laborious, arduous, demanding, strenuous, tough, *Herculean, back-breaking, wearisome, burdensome, *Sisyphean, formidable. **2.** COMPLICATED abstruse, intricate, perplexing, recondite, hard, *brain-draining, complex, knotty, enigmatic, unfathomable, problematic. **3.** UNMANAGEABLE intractable, obstinate, unaccommodating, hard to please, unruly, refractory, trying, stubborn, *a pain, fussy. ANT. *1. easy, simple, *a snap, *child's play. 2. simple, uncomplicated, obvious. 3. easy to please, easygoing, accommodating.*

difficulty *n.* problem, complication, pain, struggle, trouble, bother, trial, *hard row to hoe, dilemma, hardship, obstacle, *fix, *deep shit, snag, impasse, quagmire, hassle, *tough sledding, plight, mess, *hot water, *deep water, straits, *hornet's nest, *Gordian knot, *can of worms, deadlock, gridlock, *pickle. "God's errands and trainers, and only through them can one come to the fullness of manhood."—Henry Ward Beecher. "A harsh nurse who roughly rocks her foster-children into strength and athletic proportion."—William Jennings Bryan.

DIFFIDENT *a.* [DIF i dunt] lacking confidence, timid. *She became diffident with people in authority.* SYN. timid, shy, bashful, hesitant, unassertive, unsure of oneself, shrinking, timorous, modest, unassuming, insecure, reluctant, fainthearted. ANT. *self-confident, bold, assertive.*

diffuse *a.* **1.** SPREAD OUT dispersed, scattered, strewn, disseminated, extensive, prevalent, distributed, circulated. **2.** WORDY long-winded, verbose, profuse, rambling, prolix, loquacious, discursive. ANT. *1. concentrated, focused. 2. brief, terse, pithy.*

diffusion *n.* spreading, dispersal, scattering, dissemination, distribution, circulation, propagation.

dig *n.* insult, crack, knock, cutting remark, wisecrack, *slap in the face, taunt, jeer, *low blow, barb. ANT. *compliment, praise.*

dig *v.* excavate, hollow out, shovel, spade, delve, hoe, scoop out, till, unearth, dredge, quarry, sift, root out, mine, exhume, *backhoe.

digest *n.* summary, synopsis, abridgement, abstract, condensation, precis.

digest *v.* **1.** ABSORB FOOD assimilate, break down, consume, eat, dissolve. **2.** UNDERSTAND comprehend, absorb, take in, get, grasp, mull over, reflect, ponder, assimilate.

dignified *a.* self-respecting, poised, distinguished, stately, noble, regal, lofty, classy, refined, solemn, formal, imperious, *distingue, decorous. ANT. *undignified, goofy, foolish, sophomoric.*

dignify *v.* elevate, exalt, honor, uplift, aggrandize, ennoble, raise, solemnize, add a bit of class. ANT. *demean, degrade, lower.*

dignitary *n.* *VIP, official, *bigwig, *bigshot, personage, *name, somebody, celebrity, *high muck-a-muck, star, lion. ANT. *nobody, *lightweight, *Joe Blow.*

dignity *n.* self-respect, poise, nobility, stateliness, courtliness, honor, stature, loftiness, solemnity, class, formality, pride, presence. "The quality that enables a man who says nothing, does nothing and knows nothing to command . . . respect."—John W. Raper. ANT. *sheepishness, goofiness, cringing servitude.*

DIGRESS *v.* [di GRESS] to depart or stray from the main subject at hand. *The speech was long-winded; the speaker liked to digress.* SYN. stray, depart, ramble, drift, wander, divagate, deviate, *go off on a tangent, get sidetracked, rove, *beat around the bush.

digression *n.* straying, departure, rambling, drifting, wandering, divagation, deviation, roving, aside, detour.

dilapidated *a.* broken down, in disrepair, crumbling, tumbledown, decaying, falling down, *on its last legs, in ruins, worn out, run-down, rickety, deteriorated, *shot. ANT. *sound, solid, intact, *good as new.*

dilate *v.* widen, expand, enlarge, broaden, extend, swell, distend. ANT. *contract, shrink, constrict.*

dilatory *a.* procrastinating, delaying, putting off, dallying, tardy, postponing, lagging, behind, shilly-shallying. ANT. *on time, prompt, timely.*

dilemma *n.* difficulty, predicament, bind, quandary, plight, impasse, *pickle, *box, *fix, *Catch-22, puzzle, hard choice, problem, Hobson's choice.

DILETTANTE *n.* [DIL i TAHNT] one who dabbles in or has an amateur's knowledge of the arts. *She painted only as a hobby; she was a dilettante.* SYN. dabbler, amateur, hobbyist, layman, nonprofessional, trifler, putterer, tyro, *lightweight. ANT. *professional, master, expert.*

DILIGENT *a.* [DIL uh junt] hard working or industrious, careful and meticulous. *A diligent work force will make our company thrive.* SYN. hard-working, industrious, careful, meticulous, painstaking, sedulous, assiduous, dogged, persistent, busy, unrelenting, steadfast, plugging, tireless, active, toiling. ANT. *lazy, laggard, sluggish, slack.*

dilute *v.* thin, water down, reduce, weaken, diminish, rarefy, attenuate, *cut, adulterate, moderate. ANT. *concentrate, enrich, strengthen.*

dim *a.* **1.** POORLY LIT faint, dusky, gauzy, gloomy, shadowy, gray, blurry, indistinct, vague, murky, fuzzy, subdued. **2.** DIM WITTED stupid, bovine, slow, dense, *thick, *dumb as a post. ANT. *1. bright, blinding, brilliant. 2. smart, intelligent, bright.*

dimension *n.* size, extent, range, scope, magnitude, proportion, scale, measure, measurement, span.

diminish *v.* lessen, reduce, decrease, lower, shrink, dwindle, wane, ebb, weaken, fade, depreciate, slacken, abate. ANT. *grow, enlarge, expand.*

diminution n. lessening, reduction, decrease, lowering, shrinkage, decline, weakening, depreciation, slackening, abatement. ANT. *growth, expansion, enlargement.*

diminutive a. tiny, small, little, miniature, pintsized, minute, petite, *teeny, Lilliputian, *baby, microscopic, puny. ANT. *huge, gigantic, enormous.*

dimwit n. idiot, simpleton, dunce. SEE MORON

din n. noise, uproar, cacophony, racket, clamor, commotion, tumult, *hubbub, *hurly-burly, babel, bedlam, clangor. ANT. *silence, peace, stillness.*

dine v. eat, sup, lunch, feast, break bread, banquet, feed, *pig out. ANT. *fast.*

diner n. cafe, eatery, lunch counter. SEE RESTAURANT

dinghy n. rowboat. SEE BOAT

dingy a. grimy, dirty, sooty, smoky, soiled, drab, smudgy, shabby, tarnished, dim, faded, smeared. ANT. *sparkling, brilliant, clean, bright.*

dinner n. meal, supper, repast, feast, banquet.

dinosaur n. saurian, sauropod, *terrible lizard, prehistoric creature.

WORD FIND

aquatic: mosasaur

armored, spiked: ankylosaurus

duck-billed: hadrosaur

era: Mesozoic

large herbivore: brontosaurus

longest herbivore: supersaurus

meat-eating, ferocious: tyrannosaurus rex, allosaurus, iguanodon

period: Triassic, Jurassic, Cretaceous

plate-backed: stegosaurus

tallest herbivore: ultrasaurus

three-horned, beaklike mouth: triceratops

winged: pterodactyl

dip v. 1. DUNK immerse, duck, lower, submerge, wet, plunge, sink. 2. DECLINE decrease, slip, drop off, descend, droop, plummet, plunge.

diploma n. certificate, sheepskin, degree, parchment.

diplomacy n. "The art of saying 'Nice doggie' till you can find a rock." —Wynn Catlin. SEE DIPLOMATIC

diplomat n. ambassador, statesman, envoy, consul, representative, politician, negotiator, mediator, go-between, minister, emissary, attache. "A man who says 'perhaps' when he means no." —Elbert Hubbard. "A person who can tell you to go to hell in such a way that you actually look forward to the trip." —Caskie Stinnett. "An honest man sent abroad to lie for his country." —Henry Wooton. "One who can put his oar in the water without rocking the boat." —Anon.

diplomatic a. tactful, discreet, gracious, smooth, conciliatory, sensitive, prudent, politic, suave, subtle, artful. "The art of letting someone have your way." —Daniele Vare. ANT. *rude, tactless, uncivil, indelicate, blunt.*

dire a. 1. TERRIBLE disastrous, horrible, calamitous, dreadful, fearful, appalling, grievous, distressing, shocking, catastrophic. 2. URGENT critical, pressing, crucial, exigent.

direct v. 1. CONDUCT manage, orchestrate, guide, control, *head up, oversee, supervise, *quarterback, *call the shots, *be in the driver's seat, boss. 2. AIM point, guide, train, indicate, target, steer, orient, show, usher. 3. ADDRESS focus, devote, fix, funnel, aim. ANT. 1. *follow, obey.*

direct a. 1. STRAIGHTFORWARD frank, honest, explicit, forthright, point-blank, blunt, open, unequivocal, candid. 2. UNDEVIATING straight, unswerving, true, *as the crow flies, *in a beeline. 3. IMMEDIATE unimpeded, firsthand, face-to-face. ANT. 1. *indirect, mealymouthed, roundabout.* 2. *roundabout, deviating, circuitous.*

direction n. 1. MANAGEMENT orchestration, guidance, control, supervision, leadership, administration, care, command. 2. POINT OF THE COMPASS course, way, orientation, bearing, heading, route, tack, trajectory. 3. INSTRUCTION guidance, advice, specifications, prescription, guidelines, recipe. 4. ORDER command, charge, instruction.

directive n. order, command, mandate, instruction, direction, charge, ruling, injunction, ordinance.

directly a. 1. STRAIGHT *as the crow flies, * in a beeline, undeviatingly, *spang. 2. IMMEDIATELY without delay, promptly, at once, *first thing, pronto, speedily, straightaway. ANT. 1. *indirectly, roundabout, circuitously.* 2. *eventually, later.*

director n. leader, orchestrator, manager, overseer, administrator, supervisor, head, *whip, *kingpin, executive, foreman, overlord, *biggest toad in the puddle, general, quarterback, captain.

direful a. SEE DIRE

dirge n. funeral hymn, epicedium, threnody, lament, elegy, death march, mass.

dirigible n. balloon, zeppelin. SEE BLIMP

dirt n. 1. SOIL filth, grime, mud, muck, dust,

dung, mire, ooze, loam, earth, residue, *crap, *crud, *gunk, *gook, clay. **2.** OBSCENITY pornography, filth, smut, indecency. **3.** GOSSIP rumor, scandal, scoop, talk, exposé, muck, *keyhole journalism.

dirty v. soil, stain, muddy, besmirch, mess, spot, begrime, foul, pollute, smudge, smatter, defile.

dirty a. **1.** SOILED filthy, unclean, grimy, *grungy, stained, spotted, begrimed, unsightly, squalid, messy, foul, greasy, grubby, polluted, muddy, smudged, *scuzzy, *gross, unsanitary. **2.** OBSCENE pornographic, X-rated, filthy, smutty, indecent, prurient, blue, risque, off-color, ribald, *raunchy, *raw, explicit, scatological. **3.** UNFAIR unsportsmanlike, dishonorable, dishonest, low, *cheap, rotten, mean, below-the-belt. ANT. 1. clean, sanitary, spotless, sparkling. 2. wholesome, clean, G-rated. 3. fair, sportsmanlike, clean.

disability n. handicap, incapacity, infirmity, defect, weakness, restriction, malady, injury, impairment, paralysis, affliction.

disable v. cripple, impair, incapacitate, lame, hamstring, damage, weaken, debilitate, *put out of action, handicap, prostrate, paralyze, disarm. ANT. enable, strengthen.

disabled a. crippled, impaired, incapacitated, lame, injured, weakened, *out of action, handicapped, prostrate, paralyzed, bedridden, confined to a wheelchair, paraplegic, quadraplegic. ANT. sound, strong, fit, conditioned, powerful.

disadvantage n. drawback, liability, handicap, weakness, impediment, detriment, hurdle, stumbling block, limitation, failing, minus, burden. ANT. advantage, plus, benefit.

disadvantaged a. underprivileged, handicapped, deprived, unequal, impoverished, poor.

disadvantageous a. unfavorable, detrimental, injurious, deleterious, inopportune, adverse, harmful, detracting, unlucky. ANT. favorable, opportune.

DISAFFECTED a. [dis uh FEK tid] no longer feeling loyalty or affection for someone or something; alienated. *Government betrayed him and he became disaffected.* SYN. alienated, estranged, discontented, disloyal, unfriendly, separated, hostile, dissatisfied, disgruntled. ANT. affectionate, loyal, contented.

disagree v. differ, be at odds, dissent, conflict, contradict, contest, contend, argue, clash, oppose, take issue, dispute, see things differ-

ently. ANT. agree, concur, correspond.

disagreeable a. **1.** UNPLEASANT offensive, repugnant, objectionable, repellant, distasteful, disgusting, repulsive, obnoxious, odious, negative, unwanted. **2.** QUARRELSOME grouchy, bad-tempered, contentious, contrary, petulant, standoffish, cross, peevish, surly, irritable, nasty, churlish. ANT. 1. pleasant, welcome, nice. 2. easygoing, pleasant, good-humored.

disagreement n. dispute, difference of opinion, dissent, contention, argument, quarrel, controversy, division, squabble, discord, opposition, spat, falling-out. ANT. agreement, accord, harmony.

disallow v. reject, veto, prohibit, deny, proscribe.

disappear v. **1.** VANISH fade, go away, dissolve, recede, evaporate, *vamoose, *go south, evanesce, leave no trace, *fade into the woodwork, dematerialize, vaporize, wane, cease, pass, escape, depart, hide. ANT. appear, materialize, show.

disappoint v. let down, sadden, deflate, *dash one's hopes, *burst one's bubble, fall short, fail, disillusion, displease, disenchant, frustrate, dishearten. ANT. live up to expectations, hearten, encourage, fulfill, satisfy.

disappointed a. let down, saddened, deflated, disillusioned, disenchanted, displeased, unfulfilled, unsatisfied, frustrated, disheartened. ANT. satisfied, fulfilled, happy.

disappointment n. letdown, disillusionment, disenchantment, displeasure, unfulfillment, frustration, dissatisfaction, dud, *bitter pill to swallow, *bust, *drag, *bummer, setback, failure, rude awakening, washout, blow. "The bankruptcy of a soul that expends too much in hope and expectation." — Eric Hoffer. "The nurse of wisdom." — Boyle Roche. ANT. satisfaction, fulfillment, happiness.

disapproval a. rejection, disfavor, censure, dislike, disparagement, detraction, displeasure, deprecation, dissatisfaction, *thumbs down, animadversion, *boo, *hiss, *Bronx cheer, *raspberry. ANT. approval, favor, acceptance.

disapprove v. reject, frown on, disfavor, censure, dislike, disparage, condemn, criticize, take a dim view of, object to, *nix, *give thumbs down, dismiss, deprecate, denounce. ANT. approve, accept, embrace, praise.

disarm v. disable, weaken, take the teeth out of, *defang, neutralize, mollify, charm, conciliate, pacify, win over.

DISARMING a. [dis ARM ing] winning one

over by charm or removing hostility. *A disarming smile mollified his ire.* SYN. winning, charming, winsome, appealing, irresistible, appeasing, ingratiating, likable, pleasing, agreeable, conciliatory. ANT. *offensive, obnoxious, irritating.*

disarrange *v.* mix up, disorder, scramble, muss, mess, jumble, ruffle.

disarray *n.* disorder, disarrangement, mess, jumble, confusion, tangle, *shambles, chaos, dishevelment, hodgepodge, clutter.

disaster *n.* catastrophe, misfortune, calamity, accident, tragedy, debacle, adversity, *act of God, cataclysm, ruin, blow, hardship, reverse, holocaust.

disastrous *a.* catastrophic, calamitous, unfortunate, tragic, cataclysmic, ruinous, dire, devastating, desolating, adverse.

disavow *v.* abjure, disown, repudiate, deny, disclaim, reject, gainsay, contradict, *weasel out of, *wash one's hands of, recant, retract. ANT. *admit, own up.*

disband *v.* break up, dissolve, fold, separate.

disbelief *n.* doubt, incredulity, questioning, skepticism, rejection, distrust, dissent. ANT. *belief, faith, credulity.*

disburse *v.* pay out, expend, outlay, spend, *shell out, dole out, allocate, mete out.

discard *v.* throw out, reject, toss, dismiss, *can, scrap, dump, eject, junk, jettison, *eighty-six, *scratch, shed. ANT. *keep, retain.*

discern *v.* perceive, detect, apprehend, sense, see, notice, ascertain, observe, make out, spot, distinguish. ANT. *miss, overlook.*

DISCERNING *a.* [di SUR ning] perceptive and sharp. *She was discerning with her fashion choices.* SYN. perceptive, sharp, sagacious, discriminating, astute, hawk-eyed, critical, shrewd, judicious, intelligent, wise, mindful. ANT. *unperceptive, unobservant, mindless.*

discharge *n.* **1.** RELEASE liberation, pardon, acquittal, setting free. **2.** DISMISSAL *the axe, *the boot, *sack, *walking papers, *pink slip, ejection, ouster, *the gate, firing, layoff. **3.** DETONATION firing, shot, explosion. **4.** EMMISION expulsion, ejection, exudation, excretion, flow, seepage, oozing. ANT. *1. capture, holding, incarceration.*

discharge *v.* **1.** RELEASE set free, liberate, let go, emancipate, dismiss, acquit, pardon. **2.** DISMISS fire, lay off, *sack, *give the boot, *give walking papers, *give the axe, *give pink slip, *show the gate/door, eject, oust, *can, relieve of duties, excuse. **3.** DETONATE fire, shoot, explode, set off. **4.** EMIT eject,

exude, excrete, flow, gush, seep, OOZE, spew. ANT. *capture, hold, incarcerate.*

disciple *n.* follower, believer, devotee, believer, supporter, apostle, adherent, proselyte, pupil.

disciplinarian *n.* authoritarian, tyrant, martinet, taskmaster, *whipcracker, drill sergeant, bully.

discipline *n.* **1.** FORTITUDE, TRAINING drilling, willpower, self-control, mental toughness, regimen, practice, self-regulation, firmness, diligence, mettle, earnestness, iron will, *grit, *moxie, commitment. **2.** PUNISHMENT penalty, consequence, correction, castigation, reprimand. **3.** BRANCH OF STUDY specialty, field, subject, curriculum, course. ANT. *1. laziness, sloth. 2. reward.*

discipline *v.* **1.** TRAIN drill, harden, self-regulate, test one's mettle, commit, *bite the bullet, toughen, control, exercise, *whip into shape, practice. **2.** PUNISH penalize, correct, castigate, reprimand, *call on the carpet. ANT. *1. let oneself go, slip, neglect. 2. reward.*

disclaim *v.* deny, repudiate, denounce, disown, disavow, abjure, forswear, reject, renounce. ANT. *admit, acknowledge, own up.*

disclaimer *n.* denial, disavowal, retraction, repudiation.

disclose *v.* reveal, tell, divulge, let slip, make known, *spill the beans, confess, impart, expose, *bare one's soul. ANT. *hide, cover up, withhold.*

disclosure *n.* revelation, confession, exposé, admission, divulgence, declaration, publication.

discolor *v.* stain, bleach, fade, spot, wash, tinge, weather.

discomfit *v.* thwart, foil, frustrate, defeat, disconcert, fluster, distress, perplex, faze, unsettle, discompose, ruffle.

discomfort *n.* uneasiness, distress, pain, anxiety, irritation, soreness, ache, suffering, malaise, annoyance. ANT. *ease, pleasure.*

DISCONCERTED *a.* [DIS kun SERT ed] perturbed, disturbed, ruffled. *He saw the policeman and was disconcerted.* SYN. perturbed, disturbed, ruffled, uncomfortable, uneasy, flabbergasted, anxious, upset, taken aback, confused, rattled, shaken up, flustered. ANT. *calm, composed, at ease.*

disconnect *v.* detach, unhook, uncouple, separate, disengage, undo, unlink, loose, sever, break off. ANT. *connect, attach, engage.*

disconsolate *a.* inconsolable, depressed, dejected, suicidal, cheerless, downhearted, heartbroken, forlorn, desolate, melancholy, gloomy, hopeless, crushed. ANT. *euphoric, joyous, happy.*

discontent n. dissatisfaction, unhappiness, uneasiness, displeasure, disquiet, unfulfillment, vexation, wanting, dysphoria, restlessness. "The first step of progress." — Thomas Edison. "A perverse and fretful disposition." — Cicero. ANT. *contentment, satisfaction, ease.*

discontinue v. stop, end, cease, terminate, *knock off, finish, quit, *call it quits, desist, suspend, hold off. ANT. *resume, start.*

DISCORD n. [DIS kord] disagreement; conflict. *The new proposal was met with discord.* SYN. disagreement, dissension, conflict, variance, disunity, disharmony, contention, clashing, difference of opinion, dissonance. "A sleepless hag who never dies." — John Wolcott. ANT. *accord, harmony, agreement.*

discordant a. conflicting, dissonant, unharmonious, incongruous, contrary, inimical, harsh, jarring, sour, strident, incompatible. ANT. *harmonious, euphonious, compatible.*

discourage v. **1.** DISHEARTEN dispirit, demoralize, dampen one's spirits, unnerve, *throw cold water on, daunt, intimidate, cow, *dash one's hopes, *take the wind out of one's sails. **2.** DETER dissuade, hinder, impede, restrain, curb. ANT. *encourage, hearten, embolden.*

discouraging a. demoralizing, disheartening, hopeless, daunting, dismaying, dissuasive, dispiriting, deflating, intimidating. ANT. *encouraging, heartening, uplifting.*

discourse n. dialogue, speech, conversation, talk, discussion, communication, chat, lecture, colloquy, *confab, address.

discourteous a. rude, inconsiderate, impolite, ill-mannered, uncivil, brusque, ungracious, indelicate, cavalier, fresh, boorish. ANT. *polite, courteous, civil.*

discover v. find, uncover, discern, detect, learn, espy, unearth, notice, come across, realize, bring to light, spot, descry. ANT. *miss, overlook, pass over.*

discovery n. finding, uncovering, detection, unearthing, strike, espial, breakthrough.

discredit v. **1.** DAMAGE ONE'S REPUTATION disgrace, dishonor, detract, defame, disparage, censure, degrade, tear down, depreciate, demean. **2.** CAST DOUBT ON refute, disprove, discount, disbelieve, question, challenge, reject, scoff. ANT. **1.** *praise, honor, laud.* **2.** *credit, verify, support.*

DISCREET a. [dis KREET] unobtrusive and tactful, properly reserved. *If you must burp, please be discreet.* SYN. tactful, unobtrusive, reserved, proper, judicious, diplomatic, restrained, prudent, modest, quiet, low-profiled, circumspect, careful, sensitive. ANT. *indiscreet, insensitive, tactless, obtrusive, conspicuous.*

discrepancy n. inconsistency, variance, difference, incongruity, conflict, error, divergence, disparity. ANT. *consistency, agreement.*

discrete a. distinct, individual, separate, different, independent, detached.

discretion n. **1.** PRUDENCE judgment, diplomacy, sagacity, tact, common sense, circumspection, caution, consideration, maturity, wisdom. "That honorable stop." — Shakespeare. "Leaving a few things unsaid." — Elbert Hubbard. **2.** FREEDOM OF CHOICE volition, will, liberty, choice, inclination, preference.

discriminate v. **1.** SHOW PREJUDICE favor, show bias, treat unfairly. **2.** DISTINGUISH differentiate, separate, contrast, compare, tell the difference, judge, draw a distinction, discern, segregate.

discriminating a. selective, choosy, picky, fussy, judicious, critical, particular, finicky, astute, discerning.

discrimination n. prejudice, bias, favoritism, bigotry, inequity, racism, sexism, chauvinism.

discursive a. rambling, digressive, excursive, wandering, roving, circumlocutory, rhapsodic, prolix. ANT. *succinct, direct, to the point.*

discuss v. talk over, deliberate, converse, confabulate, *hash over, *kick around, argue, dissert, debate, confer, review.

discussion n. talk, deliberation, conversation, confabulation, conference, debate, argument, consultation, *powwow, parley, *rap session, *bull session, seminar, symposium.

DISDAIN n. [dis DANE] scorn or contempt. *I felt nothing but disdain for the man.* SYN. scorn, contempt, hatred, disgust, dislike, detestation, loathing, abhorrence, haughtiness, *snottiness, snobbishness. ANT. *admiration, respect.*

disdain v. despise, loathe, hate, hold in contempt, abhor, sicken at the sight of, spurn, reject, look down one's nose at. ANT. *admire, respect.*

disease n. sickness, illness, affliction, ailment, malady, disorder, ill health, condition, syndrome, *bug, debility, infection, virus, infirmity, pathology, plague. "The taxes laid upon this wretched life." — Lord Chesterfield. "Death's servant." — Francis Rous. "Fear made manifest on the body." — Mary Baker Eddy.

WORD FIND

blood: anemia, hemophilia, leukemia, pernicious anemia, sickle-cell anemia

bone: osteoporosis, osteoarthritis, rickets

brain and nervous system: Alzheimer's, aphasia, apoplexy (stroke), encephalitis, epilepsy, Huntington's chorea, hydrocephalus, meningitis, multiple sclerosis (MS), Parkinson's disease, wet brain

bubonic plague: Black Death

cat: FAIDS. Feline Acquired Immune Deficiency Syndrome

cause of: virus, germ, contagion, microbe, bacillus, pathogen

circulatory: aneuryssm, arteriosclerosis, atherosclerosis, hypertension, ischemia, peripheral vascular disease, phlebitis, thrombosis

contagious: chicken pox, diptheria, measles, tuberculosis, plague, whooping cough

deficiency: scurvy, beriberi, pellagra, rickets

digestive: appendicitis, cirrhosis of the liver, colitis, Crohn's disease, diabetes, diverticulitis, dysentery, gastroenteritis, gallstones, hepatitis, hiatal hernia, jaundice, pancreatitis, peptic ulcer, typhoid fever

dog: distemper, heartworm, mange, rabies

ear: tinnitus, vertigo

eye: cataract, conjunctivitis, detached retina, glaucoma, lazy eye, pinkeye, retinitis pigmentosa, strabismus, stye, trachoma

flu: influenza, grippe

food poisoning: botulism, salmonella, trichinosis

German measles: rubella

germ destroyer: antibiotic, antibody

gums: gingivitis, periodontal disease, pyorrhea

heart: angina pectoris, arrhythmia, athletic heart syndrome, cardiac arrest, congestive heart failure, coronary artery disease, heart attack, heart murmur, ischemic heart disease, mitral valve prolapse, myocardial infarction, pericarditis, rheumatic heart disease, tachycardia

identification: diagnosis

imagined: hypochondriasis

immune dysfunction: AIDS, Acquired Immune Deficiency Syndrome

joints: arthritis, gout, rheumatism

kissing disease: mononucleosis

livestock: anthrax, foot-and-mouth disease, listeriosis, mange, mastitis

lockjaw: tetanus

lungs, breathing: apnea, asthma, black lung disease, bronchitis, cystic fibrosis, dyspnea, emphysema, pleurisy, pneumonia, tuberculosis

mononucleosis, form of: Epstein-Barr syndrome

muscles: muscular dystrophy, myasthenia gravis, tendinitis, myopathy

nose: rhinitis, sinusitis

origin: etiology

peculiar to or found in only one region: endemic

predicted outcome: prognosis

recurring: chronic

sexually transmitted: venereal disease, herpes, gonorrhea (*clap), genital warts, chlamydia, syphilis.

skin: carbuncle, dermatitis, eczema, hives, impetigo, lupus, psoriasis, rosacea, scabies, vitiligo

spine, curvature of: scoliosis

spreading: contagious

spreading rapidly: epidemic

strep throat, related to: rheumatic fever, scarlet fever

swollen salivary glands: mumps

tick, transmitted by: Lyme disease, Rocky Mountain spotted fever

tropical: malaria, sprue, dengue fever, leprosy, yellow fever

warning symptom: prodrome

widespread: pandemic

SEE BRAIN, CANCER, HEART, NEUROSIS

disembowel v. eviscerate, gut, draw.

disenchanted a. disillusioned, undeceived, seeing the real world, disabused, cynical, worldly-wise. ANT. spellbound, naive, enchanted.

disengage v. detach, release, free, unfasten, extricate, remove, loose.

disfigure v. deface, mar, scar, deform, mutilate, blemish, maim, distort.

disgorge v. vomit, discharge, spew, empty. SEE VOMIT

disgrace n. dishonor, shame, blot, degradation, odium, humiliation, *black eye, discredit, obloquy, defamation, scandal, opprobrium, ignominy, disrepute. "To stumble twice against the same stone." — Cicero. ANT. honor, credit, grace.

disgrace v. dishonor, shame, blot, degrade, humiliate, *give a black eye, discredit, defame, scandalize, smear, taint, embarrass. ANT.

honor, credit, glorify.

disgraceful *a.* dishonorable, shameful, degrading, humiliating, discrediting, defaming, scandalizing, embarrassing, ignominious, odious. ANT. *honorable, reputable, admirable.*

disgruntled *a.* angry, cross, unhappy, peeved, annoyed, put out, discontented, grouchy, irritable, dissatisfied, disappointed, sulky. ANT. *contented, satisfied, happy.*

disguise *n.* cover-up, costume, mask, charade, camouflage, facade, guise, getup, pretense, masquerade, cloak, veil, incognito.

disguise *v.* cover up, mask, camouflage, put up a facade, masquerade, cloak, veil, counterfeit, dissemble, put on a false front, feign. ANT. *expose, reveal, unmask.*

disgust *n.* revulsion, repulsion, distaste, loathing, abhorrence, aversion, dislike, nausea, repugnance, detestation. ANT. *liking, delight.*

disgust *v.* revolt, repel, sicken, nauseate, *make one sick, offend, repulse, *turn one's stomach, *turn off, *gross out, appall. ANT. *delight, attract, charm.*

disgusting *a.* repugnant, loathsome, revolting, repellant, sickening, nauseating, *stomach-turning, repulsive, *gross, offensive, distasteful, noisome, nasty, vulgar, vile, foul. ANT *delightful, attractive, charming, appetizing.*

dish *n.* plate, platter, bowl, vessel, saucer, utensil.

dishearten *v.* discourage, dispirit, dampen, *take the wind out of one's sails, *shake up, daunt, unnerve, *take the starch out of, crush, *put a wet blanket on, *pour cold water on, dash, deject. ANT. *encourage, hearten, embolden.*

disheveled *a.* in disarray, unkempt, sloppy, messy, slovenly, rumpled, wrinkled, bedraggled, *grubby, mussed, blowzy, uncombed. ANT. *neat, *put together, sharp, groomed.*

dishonest *a.* untruthful, deceitful, insincere, fraudulent, shady, corrupt, untrustworthy, false, misleading, shifty, treacherous, disingenuous, crooked, two-faced. ANT. *honest, trustworthy, straightforward.*

dishonor *n.* disgrace, shame, embarrassment, humiliation, discredit, degradation, ignominy, opprobrium, obloquy, scandal, odium, *fall from grace, smear, blot, *black eye. ANT. *honor, esteem, admiration.*

dishonor *v.* disgrace, shame, discredit, degrade, scandalize, smear, blot, *give a black eye, besmirch, tarnish, *drag through the mud.

DISILLUSION *v.* [dis i LOO szhun] to remove faulty perceptions and see things as they really are. *Children eventually become disillusioned with Santa Claus.* SYN. disenchant, disabuse, disappoint, enlighten, *bring down to earth, *burst one's bubble, open one's eyes, *clue in, shatter illusions. ANT. *enchant, spellbind, deceive.*

disinclined *a.* unwilling, reluctant, loath, averse, indisposed, opposed, resistant, hesitant. ANT. *willing, eager.*

disinfect *v.* sterilize, sanitize, purify, cleanse, decontaminate, antisepticize, *zap.

disingenuous *a.* insincere, deceitful, lying, artful, false, uncandid, dishonest, crooked, underhanded, two-faced. ANT. *sincere, honest, *real.*

disintegrate *v.* fall apart, crumble, shatter, break up, atomize, pulverize, turn to dust, decompose, decay, erode.

disinterested *a.* indifferent, apathetic, unconcerned, dispassionate, uninvolved, impartial, unprejudiced, unbiased, neutral. ANT. *concerned, biased, prejudiced, involved, riveted.*

disjointed *a.* disconnected, loose, displaced, incoherent, disordered, disorganized, discontinuous, broken, separated, rambling, choppy. ANT. *connected, coherent.*

dislike *n.* hatred, abhorrence, loathing, scorn, detestation, distaste, disapproval, aversion, antipathy, repugnance, repulsion. ANT. *approval, acceptance, love.*

dislike *v.* hate, abhor, loathe, *get turned off by, despise, deplore, scorn, *turn up one's nose at, disapprove, *look down on, frown upon, detest. ANT. *like, fancy, love.*

disloyal *a.* unfaithful, traitorous, treacherous, back-stabbing, two-faced, treasonous, perfidious, double-crossing, *like a snake in the grass. ANT. *faithful, true, loyal.*

dismal *a.* dreary, gloomy, bleak, depressing, cheerless, grim, black, desolate, melancholy, forlorn, miserable, somber. ANT. *cheerful, sunny, uplifting, bright.*

dismay *n.* consternation, horror, discomposure, fright, apprehension, terror, discouragement, trepidation, *cold feet, alarm, dread.

dismay *v.* daunt, dishearten, trouble, frighten, disconcert, appall, intimidate, horrify, cow, discompose, unnerve, shake, fluster, rattle, consternate.

dismiss *v.* **1.** LET GO send away, discharge, release, turn out, expel, rid, excuse, dispense with, free, banish, clear, oust, evict. **2.** FIRE lay off, *give the axe, *give the boot, *give walking papers, *send packing, *show the door, *give pink slip, terminate, *can, *sack, set adrift, *bounce. **3.** PUT OUT OF ONE'S MIND dispel, disregard, banish, *pooh-pooh.

dismissal n. discharge, release, expulsion, ousting, eviction, *walking papers, layoff, *sack, *pink slip, removal.

disobedience n. rebellion, noncompliance, defiance, insubordination, transgression, revolt, recalcitrance, contumacy, insubmission. "The rarest and the most courageous of the virtues, is seldom distinguished from neglect, the laziest and most common of the vices." — George Bernard Shaw.

disobedient v. rebellious, noncompliant, defiant, insubordinate, unruly, recalcitrant, insubmissive, fractious, contrary, stubborn, mischievous. ANT. *obedient, compliant, dutiful.*

disobey v. defy, rebel, revolt, reject, transgress, oppose, flout, contradict, *thumb one's nose at, disregard, overstep, resist. ANT. *obey, comply, *knuckle under, abide by.*

disorder n. **1.** DISARRAY jumble, confusion, mess, disarrangement, clutter, disorganization, untidiness, chaos, muddle. **2.** DISTURBANCE commotion, upset, agitation, unrest, chaos, turbulence, imbroglio, clamor, rumpus, *hullabaloo, fracas, anarchy, ferment, discord. **3.** AFFLICTION ailment, malady, infirmity, sickness, illness, disease, syndrome. ANT. *1. order, organization, arrangement. 2. peace, calm, tranquility.*

disorder v. mix up, mess, disarrange, jumble, confuse, shuffle, clutter, disorganize, muddle, disturb, scatter, muss up. ANT. *order, arrange, neaten.*

disorderly a. **1.** IRREGULAR messy, disarranged, jumbled, confused, shuffled, cluttered, mixed up, disorganized, muddled, scrambled, scattered. **2.** UNRULY disruptive, unmanageable, riotous, *out-of-line, unlawful, rowdy, uncontrollable, wayward, obstreperous. ANT. *1. orderly, arranged, organized. 2. orderly, well-behaved, peaceful.*

disoriented a. lost, confused, mixed-up, dazed, muddled, bewildered.

disown v. repudiate, reject, renounce, disclaim, forsake, disavow, cast off, divorce oneself from, disinherit. ANT. *claim, accept, admit, adopt.*

DISPARAGE v. [di SPAIR ij] to belittle, put down. *The coach disparaged the team after yet another loss.* SYN. belittle, put down, criticize, deprecate, denigrate, depreciate, deflate, defame, malign, *dump on, ridicule, discredit.

ANT. *praise, commend, laud.*

DISPARITY n. [dis PAIR uh tee] a gap or state of inequality, difference. *There is often a disparity between thoughts and deeds.* SYN. gap, inequality, difference, incongruity, discrepancy, imbalance, disproportion, inconsistency. ANT. *equality, correspondence, consistency.*

dispassionate a. unfeeling, unemotional, calm, detached, indifferent, neutral, disinterested, unprejudiced, unbiased, objective, judicial, impartial. ANT. *passionate, involved, interested, biased.*

dispatch n. **1.** MESSAGE communication, communique, news, report, bulletin, flash, note. **2.** SPEED promptness, swiftness, alacrity, celerity, quickness, haste, expedition. ANT. *2. sloth, sluggishness.*

dispatch v. **1.** SEND OFF consign, forward, issue, transmit, speed, express, post. **2.** EXPEDITE hurry, dash off, quicken, push, dispose of, *zip off. **3.** KILL slay, execute, murder, assassinate, put to death, *waste. SEE KILL, MURDER

dispel v. dispense with, rid, scatter, drive away, dismiss, banish, oust, eject, rout, disperse, remove, dispose of.

dispensable a. unnecessary, disposable, nonessential, inessential, expendable, superfluous. ANT. *indispensable.*

dispensation n. **1.** DISTRIBUTION apportionment, allocation, disbursement, allotment, assignment, consignment. **2.** SHARE allotment, quota, portion, consignment, allocation. **3.** ADMINISTRATION management, regulation, direction, operation, supervision.

dispense v. give out, distribute, allocate, apportion, dole out, assign, mete out, supply, disperse, parcel out.

dispense with a. dispose of, get rid of, do without, relinquish. forgo, waive, forswear.

disperse v. scatter, distribute, strew, disseminate, spread, broadcast, sow, circulate; diffuse, disband, dissipate.

dispirited a. dejected, depressed, downhearted, melancholy, blue, glum, discouraged, *down in the dumps, disheartened, despondent, disconsolate. ANT. *cheerful, euphoric, happy.*

displace v. **1.** MOVE dislocate, shift, dislodge, unsettle, transfer, dispossess, relocate, disturb, force out, uproot. **2.** SUPPLANT replace, supersede, succeed, crowd out, take over, usurp.

display n. exhibit, exhibition, presentation, advertisement, exposition, layout, spread, staging, panorama.

display v. exhibit, show, present, showcase, advertise, lay out, stage, flaunt, demonstrate, parade, spotlight. ANT. *hide, conceal, camouflage.*

displease v. annoy, offend, anger, irritate, disturb, irk, disappoint, bother, upset, dissatisfy, disgruntle, *piss off, repulse, pall, insult. ANT. *delight, satisfy, *tickle.*

displeasure n. annoyance, dissatisfaction, anger, irritation, disappointment, disgruntlement, dislike, distaste, unhappiness. ANT. *delight, satisfaction, happiness.*

disposal n. **1.** THROWING OUT discarding, dumping, junking, dispatching, scrapping, removal. **2.** ORDER placement, distribution, array, arrangement, disposition, grouping. **3.** SETTLEMENT conclusion, dispensation, determination, transfer, end. **4.** POWER liberty, authority, control, direction.

disposed a. inclined, apt, willing, prone, liable, predisposed, likely.

dispose of 1. THROW OUT discard, dump, toss, scrap, junk, *shitcan, *chuck, *eighty-six. **2.** SETTLE determine, decide, end, finish up.

disposition n. **1.** TEMPERAMENT temper, nature, mood, humor, frame of mind, outlook, character, *mind-set, tendency, proclivity, bent. **2.** ORDER placement, distribution, arrangement, grouping, array.

dispossess v. divest, deprive, expropriate, strip, confiscate, oust, expel, eject.

disproportionate a. unequal, unbalanced, lopsided, inordinate, uneven.

disprove v. debunk, invalidate, refute, confute, negate, expose, controvert, belie, *shoot holes in, discredit. ANT. *prove, validate.*

disputable a. debatable, arguable, dubious, moot, questionable, controversial.

dispute n. argument, debate, controversy, disagreement, conflict, altercation, difference of opinion, contest, *beef, wrangle, dissension, *fuss, *bone of contention, row, imbroglio. ANT. *agreement.*

dispute v. argue, debate, disagree, conflict, contest, contend, controvert, *lock horns, wrangle, quarrel, doubt, controvert, bicker, quibble. ANT. *agree, concur, *find common ground.*

disquiet n. restlessness, anxiety, worry, trouble, distress, unrest, unease, angst, fretfulness. ANT. *serenity, tranquility, calm.*

disquiet v. trouble, disturb, bother, disrupt, distress, worry, fret, shake up, fluster, discompose, rattle. ANT. *calm, compose, relax.*

disregard v. ignore, nevermind, skip, overlook, forget, omit, *pay no mind, *turn a deaf ear, slight. ANT. *heed, notice, consider.*

disrepair n. deterioration, decay, dilapidation, ruin, wreckage.

disreputable a. dishonorable, disgraceful, low, shady, cheap, unprincipled, shameful, scandalous, sordid, ignominious, ignoble, unsavory. ANT. *respectable, honorable, classy, noble.*

disrespect a. irreverence, incivility, disregard, discourtesy, impoliteness, rudeness, impertinence, insolence, impudence, flippancy, lèse-majesté. ANT. *respect, reverence, civility, deference.*

disrespectful a. irreverent, uncivil, discourteous, impolite, rude, impertinent, insolent, impudent, flippant, contemptuous, insulting, *smart-alecky, *out of line, ill-mannered. ANT. *respectful, civil, reverent, deferential.*

disrobe v. undress, strip, bare, *peel, slip out of, *shuck, uncover, shed, *drop one's drawers.

disrupt v. interrupt, upset, disturb, disorder, unsettle, agitate, *discombobulate, interfere with, break up, disorganize, disconcert.

disruptive a. interrupting, upsetting, disturbing, unsettling, agitating, disconcerting, distracting, *discombobulating, trouble making. ANT. *calming, quieting.*

dissatisfied a. displeased, unfulfilled, unhappy, discontented, disappointed, critical, disgruntled, malcontented, frustrated, disaffected. ANT. *satisfied, pleased, content.*

dissect v. cut up, separate, examine, analyze, inspect, scrutinize, explore, study, *go over with fine-tooth comb.

dissemble v. disguise, hide, cover up, mask, dissimulate, conceal, feign, *put on a front, cloak, camouflage. ANT. *reveal, show, expose.*

DISSEMINATE v. [di SEM uh NATE] to distribute, spread or scatter. *The head office will disseminate the new information.* SYN. distribute, spread, scatter, disperse, broadcast, propagate, promulgate, circulate, sow, diffuse.

DISSENSION n. [di SEN shun] disagreement, difference of opinion. *There was dissension over the issue.* SYN. discord, disagreement, difference of opinion, contention, conflict, strife, dissent, argument, variance, friction, *flak. ANT. *accord, agreement, harmony.*

dissent n. disagreement, difference of opinion, contention, conflict, dissension, argument, dispute, discord, schism, nonconformity, opposition. ANT. *agreement, accord, concurrence.*

dissent v. disagree, contradict, differ, argue, dispute, oppose, vary, reject, contend, protest. ANT. *agree, concur, assent.*

dissertation n. thesis, treatise, paper, discourse, study, composition, disquisition, essay, exposition.

disservice n. wrong, harm, injustice, injury, disfavor, damage.

dissident n. dissenter, protestor, nonconformist, objector, separatist.

dissident a. disagreeing, differing, dissenting.

dissimilar a. unlike, different, distinct, divergent, opposite, contrasting, antithetical, disparate, *like night and day. ANT. *like, similar, matched.*

dissimulate v. hide, conceal. SEE DISSEMBLE

DISSIPATE v. [DIS uh PATE] to scatter, thin out, dispel, disappear, exhaust. *The snow finally began to dissipate.* SYN. scatter, thin out, disperse, dispel, disappear, dissolve, exhaust, ebb, deplete, disintegrate, vanish. ANT. *conserve, save, concentrate.*

dissociate v. separate, part, disconnect, detach, segregate, break off, divorce, estrange, distance.

dissolute a. abandoned, immoral, debauched, unrestrained, intemperate, depraved, unbridled, perverted, lecherous, licentious, wanton. ANT. *virtuous, moral, restrained, abstinent.*

dissolution n. dissolving, disintegration, decay, decomposition, death, end, passing, termination, demise, extinction, collapse, disappearance.

dissolve v. **1.** MELT diffuse, liquefy, deliquesce, thaw. **2.** END terminate, close, finish, break up, discontinue, disband, disperse, evaporate. **3.** ANNUL void, cancel, invalidate, nullify, rescind, repeal. **4.** VANISH fade, disappear, blur, dematerialize. ANT. *1. thicken, congeal, harden. 2. begin, start, open. 3. validate. 4. materialize, appear.*

dissonant a. **1.** INHARMONIOUS harsh, discordant, cacophonous, jarring, grating, raucous, sour, strident. **2.** DISAGREEING incompatible, discordant, incongruous, clashing, divergent, opposing, at variance. ANT. *1. harmonious, euphonious, melodious. 2. agreeing, compatible, consonant.*

DISSUADE v. [dis WADE] to discourage or talk out of. *I would dissuade any family member from bungee-jumping.* SYN. discourage, talk out of, deter, advise against, disincline, *throw cold water on, persuade not to, stop. ANT. *talk into, persuade to, encourage.*

distance n. **1.** SPACE span, length, remoteness, range, area, expanse, interval, stretch, sweep, spread, width, remove, horizon, far reaches, extent. **2.** COLDNESS reserve, aloofness, unfriendliness, stiffness. ANT. *2. warmth, closeness, intimacy.*

distant a. **1.** FAR far off, remote, removed, afar, away, yonder, far-flung, outlying, out of range, outback, isolated. **2.** COLD reserved, aloof, unfriendly, *at arm's length, stiff, cool, frigid, formal, withdrawn. ANT. *1. close, near, at hand. 2. warm, close, intimate, friendly.*

distaste n. dislike, aversion, repulsion, revulsion, abhorrence, disgust, repugnance, disinclination, displeasure. ANT. *liking, attraction.*

distasteful a. disgusting, repulsive, revolting, abhorrent, repellent, offensive, unsavory, unappetizing, obnoxious, unpalatable, disagreeable, tasteless, *gross, nauseating. ANT. *appealing, savory, attractive, pleasing.*

distended a. bloated, swollen, inflated, enlarged, turgid, expanded, bulging, puffed out, ballooned, blown up. ANT. *shriveled, sunken, deflated.*

distill v. extract, purify, boil down, decoct, refine, ferment, concentrate, separate, condense, press out, brew, vaporize.

distillation n. essence, distillate, concentrate.

distinct a. **1.** CLEAR obvious, plain, clear-cut, unambiguous, defined, unmistakable, specific, explicit, manifest. **2.** SEPARATE individual, unlike, different, unassociated, detached, sole, disparate, discrete. ANT. *1. unclear, vague, fuzzy. 2. associated, joined, linked.*

distinction n. **1.** DIFFERENTIATION discrimination, distinguishment, difference, peculiarity, feature, mark, characteristic, earmark. **2.** RECOGNITION honor, eminence, achievement, credit, prominence, repute, merit, prestige, renown, consequence.

distinctive a. unique, distinguishing, characteristic, singular, different, peculiar, individual, special, idiosyncratic, unusual. ANT. *common, ordinary, nondescript.*

distinguish v. **1.** SEE THE DIFFERENCE differentiate, discriminate, separate, judge, tell apart, ascertain, characterize, classify. **2.** DISCERN make out, perceive, see, notice, detect, observe, apprehend, catch, spot, recognize.

distinguished a. **1.** EMINENT renowned, famous, prominent, acclaimed, notable, illustrious, celebrated, excellent. **2.** DIGNIFIED stately, elegant, grand, magnificent, august, princely, lordly, imposing, *distingue. ANT. *1. un-*

known, ordinary, pedestrian. 2. undignified, undistinguished, lowly.

distort v. 1. MISSHAPE contort, deform, twist, warp, gnarl, wrench, screw, knot, disfigure. 2. MISREPRESENT misconstrue, falsify, lie, misinterpret, alter, twist, slant, pervert, stretch, varnish, embellish.

distortion n. misrepresentation, lie, misinterpretation, alteration, stretch, embellishment, falsification, exaggeration, perversion, *BS, fabrication, embroidery. ANT. truth, accuracy.

distract v. 1. DIVERT sidetrack, draw away, catch one's attention, entertain. 2. BEWILDER confuse, perplex, befuddle, fluster, discompose, confound, trouble, unsettle.

distraction n. diversion, amusement, entertainment, beguilement, interruption, divertissement, interference, annoyance.

distraught a. anxious, upset, worried, agitated, disturbed, troubled, perturbed, overwrought, crazed, frantic, *out of one's mind, harassed. ANT. calm, composed, relaxed, tranquil.

distress n. pain, suffering, anxiety, anguish, difficulty, strain, unhappiness, sorrow, discomfort, agony, angst, torture.

distress v. upset, worry, trouble, strain, disturb, bother, burden, aggrieve, pain, plague, hurt, tax, torment, harass. ANT. comfort, console, soothe, relieve.

distribute v. 1. APPORTION allot, parcel out, allocate, prorate, issue, ration, deliver, mete, divide, *dole out, disseminate, *divvy, dispense, spread. 2. CLASSIFY arrange, group, order. ANT. 1. collect, gather, concentrate.

distribution n. 1. APPORTIONMENT allotment, allocation, parcel, division, rationing, spreading, delivery, propagation, scattering. 2. CLASSIFICATION arrangement, grouping, order.

district n. area, region, precinct, section, quarter, zone, locale, community, parish, ward.

distrust n. mistrust, disbelief, doubt, suspicion, wariness, leeriness, incredulity, misgiving, skepticism. ANT. trust, belief, faith.

distrust v. mistrust, disbelieve, question, doubt, suspect, be wary of, be leery of, have reservations about. ANT. trust, believe, have faith in.

disturb v. 1. BOTHER trouble, disquiet, disrupt, distress, ruffle, interrupt, annoy, plague, irritate, discommode, perturb, *hassle, *bug, intrude upon. 2. DISARRANGE disorder, disorganize, jumble, mix up, upset, unsettle.

disturbance n. disruption, commotion, interruption, interference, upset, tumult, annoyance, agitation, perturbation, bother, uproar, rumpus.

ditch n. trench, channel, gully, excavation, trough, gutter, cut, waterway, dike, moat.

ditch v. Sl. dump, junk, discard, abandon, unload, get rid of, desert.

ditto n. the same, likewise, the above, the aforementioned.

dive n. 1. PLUNGE drop, vault, *header, nosedive, descent, swoop, leap, submergence, immersion, bellyflop, cannonball, half twist, full twist, jackknife, gainer, half gainer, swan dive, backflip. 2. Sl. *DUMP hole, bar, honkytonk, tavern.

dive v. plunge, drop, plummet, vault, *do a header, nosedive, pitch, descend, submerge.

diverge v. 1. SEPARATE come apart, spread, depart, deviate, divide, split, branch off. 2. DIFFER disagree, vary, conflict, oppose, be at odds. ANT. 1. converge. 2. agree.

divergence n. 1. SEPARATION split, fork, branching, parting, deviation, division, digression. 2. DIFFERENCE disagreement, conflict, variance, odds, incongruity. ANT. 1. convergence. 2. agreement.

diverse a. 1. DIFFERENT unlike, disparate, distinct, dissimilar, varied, discrete. 2. MULTIFORM diversified, sundry, varied, manifold, multifarious, assorted. ANT. 1. similar, like, identical.

diversify v. vary, branch out, expand, variegate, assort, modify.

diversion n. entertainment, amusement, distraction, pastime, divertissement, fun, pleasure, frolic, sport.

diversity n. variety, difference, assortment, multiplicity, heterogeneity, miscellany, medley. ANT. sameness, homogeneity.

divert v. 1. TURN ASIDE change course, deflect, sidetrack, avert, swerve. 2. DISTRACT OR AMUSE entertain, draw, absorb, regale, beguile.

diverting a. distracting, amusing, entertaining, absorbing, beguiling, engrossing, magnetic.

divest v. strip, dispossess, deprive, confiscate, relieve of, seize, remove, bare, denude.

divide v. 1. SEPARATE sever, cleave, part, split, cut, rend, halve, quarter, bisect, sunder, disjoin, disconnect, segregate, section. 2. APPORTION distribute, share, allocate, mete out, dole, dispense, *divvy up, portion, ration, deal. 3. CLASSIFY group, categorize, label, sort, arrange. ANT. 1. join, unite, fuse.

divination n. prophecy, soothsaying, augury, prognostication, fortune-telling, foretelling, premonition, forecast.

WORD FIND

by bird actions: auspice

by celestial positions: astrology

by choosing random passage in book, especially the Bible: bibliomancy

by communication with the dead: necromancy

by dirt figures: geomancy

by divining rod: rhabdomancy

by entrails of animals: haruspicy

by lots: sortilege

by numbers: numerology

by water: hydromancy

divine v. foretell, predict, prophesy, forecast, foresee, prognosticate, surmise, guess, infer, portend.

divine a. godlike, holy, sacred, omnipotent, omnipresent, omniscient, heavenly, deified, supreme, sanctified, perfect, celestial, angelic, superhuman. ANT. *earthly, mortal*

division n. **1.** PART section, segment, unit, department, branch, sector, subdivision, component, piece, cut, chunk. **2.** DISAGREEMENT difference of opinion, variance, discord, dissension, dissent, rift, feud, argument. ANT. *agreement, unity, accord.*

divorce n. disunion, separation, *split, breakup, dissolution, annulment, parting. "A hash made of domestic scraps." — Ed Wynn. "Holy deadlock." — A.P. Herbert.

divorce v. **1.** SEPARATE dissociate, split, sever, part, detach. **2.** END MARRIAGE dissolve, annul, split up, break up.

divulge v. reveal, disclose, make known, confess, confide, tell, let slip, impart, expose, *spill the beans, *spill one's guts, blab, leak. ANT. *keep secret, conceal, hide.*

divvy up vt. apportion. SEE DIVIDE

dizzy a. **1.** UNSTEADY light-headed, vertiginous, off balance, reeling, wobbly, *punch-drunk, whirling, giddy, groggy, bewildered, confused. **2.** SCATTERBRAINED silly, flighty, frivolous, harebrained, foolish, giddy.

do v. **1.** PERFORM execute, carry out, complete, undertake, see to it, make, cause, bring about, produce, fulfill, engineer, *swing, effect. **2.** COMPLETE fulfill, accomplish, dispatch, clinch, consummate, dispose of. **3.** SUFFICE serve, pass muster, be adequate, measure up, suit, meet one's needs. **4.** ACT behave, conduct, comport, deport, operate. **5.** TRAVEL THROUGH visit, cover, tour, pass through, explore, experience.

DOCILE a. [DOS ul] easy to train and handle,

tractable. *The poodle is considerably more docile than the coyote.* SYN. tractable, malleable, trainable, pliant, manageable, obedient, gentle, accommodating, submissive, compliant, obliging, meek. ANT. *defiant, stubborn, vicious, untrainable, *unbreakable.*

dock n. pier, wharf, landing, quay, marina, slip, berth.

docket n. agenda, calendar, program, schedule, ticket.

doctor n. physician, medical practitioner, M.D., general practitioner, osteopath, medic, intern, specialist, resident, medicine man, healer, *doc, *pill pusher, *bones, *sawbones, *quack, witch doctor. "An angel when he comes to cure, a devil when he asks for pay." — English proverb. "Death's pilotfish." — G.D. Prentice "The flower of our civilization." — Robert Louis Stevenson.

WORD FIND

ambulance attendant: paramedic, emergency medical technician (EMT)

anesthesia administrator: anesthetist, anesthesiologist

animals: veterinarian

association: American Medical Association, AMA

bone, joint and muscle specialist: orthopedist

children's: pediatrician

digestive system: gastroenterologist

disease authority: pathologist

drug authority: pharmacologist

ear, nose and throat specialist: otolaryngologist

epidemic authority: epidemiologist

eye: ophthalmologist

feeling patient's body with hands to aid diagnosis: palpation

foot: podiatrist

heart: cardiologist

hormone specialist: endocrinologist

knee hammer: percussor

listening for body sounds through stethoscope: auscultation

manipulator of bones and spine: chiropractor

medical examiner: coroner

mental disorders: psychiatrist

national health chief: Surgeon General

nervous system: neurologist

newborns: neonatologist

oath of: Hippocratic oath

prayer, cures by: faith healer

pregnancy and birth: obstetrician

radiology: radiologist
rectum, anus: proctologist
skin: dermatologist
tapping chest, back, abdomen, aid in diagnosis: percussion
trainee: intern
tumor specialist: oncologist
urinary tract, kidneys, prostate: urologist
women's reproductive system: gynecologist
SEE DISEASE, HOSPITAL, MEDICINE, NURSE, OPERATION, SURGERY

doctor *v.* **1.** MEND fix, treat, repair, attend, nurse, medicate, *patch up. **2.** ALTER tamper with, falsify, change, distort, adulterate.

doctrinaire *a.* obstinate, dogmatic, impractical, unrealistic, rigid, speculative, authoritarian, inflexible. ANT. *practical, flexible, open-minded.*

doctrine *n.* principle, belief, conviction, precept, opinion, convention, tenet, dictum, dogma, creed, gospel.

document *n.* paper, record, certificate, form, report, instrument, testimony, contract, writ.

document *v.* support, verify, authenticate, substantiate, prove.

dodder *v.* shake, tremble, totter, falter, shuffle, quiver, potter.

doddering *a.* feebleminded, senile, faltering, weak, infirm, decrepit, shaky, tottering, shuffling, quivering, *dotty.

dodge *n.* stratagem, subterfuge, sidestep, evasion, escape, ruse, feint, trick, maneuver, ploy.

dodge *v.* avoid, evade, sidestep, elude, escape, *give the slip, duck, get around, *weasel out of, swerve, parry, skirt, bob and weave. ANT. *encounter, meet, confront.*

doer *n.* *go-getter, *mover and shaker, activist.

doff *v.* remove, take off, shed, strip, shuck, disrobe, undress.

dog *n.* canine, hound, *mutt, mongrel, cur, *pooch, puppy, bitch, *flea bag, tyke, *man's best friend. "The one absolutely unselfish friend." — George Vest. "A liberal. He wants to please everyone." — William Kunstler. "The god of frolic." — Henry Ward Beecher.
WORD FIND
Australian wild dog: dingo
back portion between shoulder blades: withers
bark: bay, howl, yelp
breeds: Afghan, Airedale, Alaskan malamute, Alsatian, basset hound, beagle, Belgian sheep dog, bloodhound, border terrier, borzoi, Boston terrier, boxer, bulldog, bull mastiff, bull terrier, Chesapeake Bay retriever, Chihuahua, chow, cocker spaniel, collie, dachshund, Dalmatian, deerhound, Doberman pinscher, elkhound, English setter, English springer spaniel, English toy spaniel, foxhound, fox terrier, German shepherd, golden retriever, Great Dane, Great Pyrenees, greyhound, griffon, harrier, hound dog, husky, Irish setter, Irish wolfhound, Labrador retriever, Lhasa apso, Maltese, mastiff, Mexican hairless, miniature poodle, Newfoundland, Norwegian elkhound, Old English sheepdog, Pekingese, pointer, Pomeranian, poodle, pug, rat terrier, retriever, Rottweiler, Russian wolfhound, Saint Bernard, Saluki, Samoyed, schnauzer, Scottish terrier, setter, Shih tzu, Skye terrier, spaniel, spitz, springer spaniel, staghound, Sussex spaniel, terrier, toy poodle, toy spaniel, water spaniel, Welsh collie, Welsh corgi, whippet, wirehaired terrier, wolfhound, Yorkshire terrier
bristling neck and back hairs: hackles
cheeks, lower: chops
chest hairs or coloration: apron
chest, lower: brisket
chin hairs: beard
claw, vestigial: dewclaw
coat, black or dark brown: sable
coat, gray or black on white: badger-marked
coat, gray or streaked with gray: grizzle
coat, multicolored: parti-colored
coat, patchy or spotted with two or more colors: pied
coat, reddish brown or purplish brown: liver
coat, streaked or spotted: brindle
coat, white with black spots: harlequin
coat, yellowish blond
coat, yellowish-brown: fawn
disease: distemper, rabies, mange
domed or rounded skull: apple head
ears that are loose and dangling: lop ears
father: sire
fear of: cynophobia
female: bitch
foot cushions: pads
fringe around neck: frill, ruff
fringe on tail, back of legs: feather
hell's guardian: Cerberus
history: cynology
house: kennel
light-colored streak on head: blaze

lineage, especially from same breed: pedigree

long-legged, slight: racy

lover of: philocynic

low to the ground, thickset: cloddy

mixed breed: mongrel

mother: dam

mouth, nose and jaws: muzzle

muzzle that is dark on some breeds: mask

muzzle that is sharply pointed: snipy

nose of more than one color: butterfly nose

ovaries, remove: spay

range over field looking for game: quarter

sagging back: swayback

sculpted tufts left on sheared dog, esp. poodle: pompon

short-bodied: cobby

tail, bushy: brush

tail, curled: ringtail

tail, cut short: bobtail, docked tail

tail, feathery: plume

tail, straight, stiff: whip

tail, twisted: screwtail

worm parasite: heartworm

dogged *a.* stubborn, willful, persistent, obstinate, mulish, determined, intent, steadfast, tenacious, resolute, plodding, unflagging, persevering.

DOGMA *n.* [DAWG muh] beliefs and principles. *My own religious dogma is not unlike others.* SYN. beliefs, principles, doctrine, conviction, creed, gospel, teachings, credo, tenet, article of faith, view, opinion. "A hard substance which forms in a soft brain." — Elbert Hubbard.

DOGMATIC *a.* [dawg MAT ik] stubbornly clinging to one's own beliefs and refusing to consider those of others; overpositive. *Our minister is too dogmatic to consider other views.* SYN. overpositive, closed-minded, opinionated, doctrinaire, biased, authoritarian, narrow-minded, emphatic, prejudiced, fanatical, imperious, dictatorial. ANT. *liberal-minded, open-minded, tolerant, receptive.*

doings *n.* actions, deeds, acts, exploits, affairs, events, *goings-on. happenings, transactions.

doldrums *n.* listlessness, depression, *blahs, malaise, boredom, *blues, *dumps, *blue funk, slump, torpor, tedium.

dole *n.* welfare, charity, handouts, gift, alms, subsidy, food stamps, relief.

doleful *a.* mournful, melancholy, grief-stricken, downhearted, depressed, melancholy, sorrowful, dejected, disconsolate, sad, *down in the dumps, forlorn, woebegone. ANT. *cheer-*

ful, euphoric, happy.

dole out *v.* distribute, hand out, allocate, dispense, mete, allot, parcel, divide, share.

dolorous *a.* sad, sorrowful, painful, grievous, heartrending, miserable, woebegone, wretched, anguished, lamentable, pitiable. ANT. *cheerful, happy, upbeat.*

dolt *n.* dullard, simpleton, blockhead, dunce, *airhead, idiot, *dimwit, *chowderhead, ignoramus, *nitwit, *lunkhead, numskull, moron. ANT. *genius, *Rhodes scholar, *rocket scientist.*

domain *n.* territory, realm, sphere, area, terrain, bailiwick, province, dominion, estate, empire, concern, kingdom, turf.

dome *n.* roof, cupola, hemisphere, vault, rotunda, onion dome, stupa, geodesic dome.

domestic *n.* servant, maid, butler, cook, *live-in.

domestic *a.* **1.** HOUSEHOLD home, residential, family, private. **2.** NATIVE indigenous, homegrown, homemade.

domesticate *v.* tame, break, train, housebreak, gentle, *bust, master, subdue, civilize.

domicile *n.* home, residence, house, abode, dwelling, habitation, castle, *roof over one's head, *pad, living quarters, apartment, condo.

dominant *a.* ruling, controlling, supreme, *having the upper hand, reigning, prevailing, preeminent, *in the driver's seat, authoritative, domineering, presiding, lordly, overruling, superior, ascendant, uppermost, proponderant, predominant, paramount, foremost. ANT. *subordinate, inferior, submissive, deferential.*

dominate *v.* rule, control, *have the upper hand, reign, prevail, preside, lord over, govern, master, tyrannize, overshadow, command, overrule, predominate, eclipse, *rule the roost, *run the show, *call the shots, dictate, subdue, overpower, bully, cow, loom over, dwarf, rule with an iron hand, *stand head and shoulders above. ANT. *submit, cringe, defer.*

domineer *v.* SEE DOMINATE

domineering *a.* overbearing, oppressive, high-handed, *ironhanded, bossy, controlling, lordly, high and mighty, tyrannical, imperious, pushy, authoritarian, bullying, *whip-cracking. ANT. *submissive, deferential, cringing.*

dominion *n.* rule, realm, domain, sovereignty, authority, jurisdiction, command, reign, control, supremacy.

donate *v.* give, contribute, pledge, *chip in, grant, confer, bestow, bequeath, make a gift of.

donation *n.* contribution, gift, pledge, present, alms, aid, relief, handout, grant, offering, benefaction.

done *a.* finished, completed, accomplished, fulfilled, concluded, realized, terminated, executed, consummated, ended. ANT. *unfinished, unfulfilled,* *up in the air.*

done for *a.* doomed, *had it, beaten, defeated, ruined, finished, *sunk, *washed up, exhausted, tired, dead.

donkey *n.* ass, mule, burro, jackass, jenny, beast of burden.

Don Juan *n.* *ladies' man, Lothario, Casanova, *lady-killer, Romeo, *make-out artist, *wolf, stud, *skirt-chaser, *smooth operator, playboy.

donnybrook *n.* brawl, free-for-all, fight, fray, fracas, melee, fisticuffs, riot, *rumble.

donor *n.* contributor, benefactor, supporter, giver, backer, patron, grantor, subscriber, *angel.

do-nothing *n.* *bum, idler, loafer, sloth, malingerer, moocher, lazybones, *goof-off, laggard, shirker, *couch potato, *lard-ass, goldbricker, slacker. ANT. *go-getter.*

doodad *n.* thingamajig, doohickey, whatzit, thingamabob, *goofus, whatchamacallit, gizmo, widget, doomajigger, gadget, *whangdoodle, widget.

doohickey *n.* SEE DOODAD

doom *n.* disaster, ruin, condemnation, death, extinction, Last Judgment, downfall, destruction, tragedy, damnation, annihilation, bane.

doom *v.* condemn, damn, consign to death, destine to ruin, sentence.

doomed *a.* condemned, damned, sentenced to death, consigned to ruin, destined for destruction, done for, kaput, *had it, *washed up.

door *n.* entrance, passage, exit, opening, hatch, gate, portal, access.

dope *n.* *Sl.* **1.** DRUG narcotic, *fairy powder, opiate, *weed, *pot, *reefer, heroin, cocaine, *happy dust, hash, *smoke. **2.** IDIOT dolt, *dummy, *nitwit, *birdbrain, moron, *retard, dunce. **3.** FACTUAL INFORMATION scoop, skinny, news, *score, *poop, *lowdown, inside information.

dope *v.* drug, dose, sedate, knock out, *spike, anesthetize, *slip a Mickey Finn.

dopey *a.* stupid, idiotic, moronic, retarded, silly, mindless.

DORMANT *a.* [DOOR munt] inactive, asleep. *A dormant volcano.* SYN. inactive, asleep, quiet, resting, still, becalmed, latent, inert, passive, hibernating, quiescent, torpid. ANT. *active, alive, awake.*

dose *n.* measure, portion, amount, quantity, allotment, *shot.

dossier *n.* file, record, profile, report, history.

dot *n.* point, spot, speck, period, mark, mote, iota.

dotage *n.* second childhood, senility, decrepitude, old age, feeblemindedness.

dote on *v.* lavish attention on, indulge, spoil, wait on, coddle, make of, fuss over, treasure, prize, hold dear. ANT. *neglect, ignore, abuse.*

doting *a.* lavish, indulgent, spoiling, coddling, demonstrative, devoted, adoring, lovesick, pampering. ANT. *neglectful, abusive.*

double *n.* duplicate, twin, replica, look-alike, *dead ringer, *spitting image, clone, counterpart, match, mate, stand-in.

double *a.* paired, twin, two-sided, dual, twofold, binary, duplex, duple.

double back *v.* backtrack, retrace steps, return, backpedal.

double-dealing *n.* treachery, duplicity, betrayal, disloyalty, two-timing, double-crossing.

DOUBLE ENTENDRE *n.* [DUB ul on TON druh] a word or statement having two meanings, a risque ambiguity. *The comedian couldn't be as frank as he wanted, so he used a lot of double entendres.* SYN. ambiguity, double meaning, play on words, innuendo, equivocation, equivoque, tergiversation, pun.

doubt *n.* uncertainty, question, hesitation, mistrust, indecision, misgiving, skepticism, suspicion, lack of faith, lack of conviction, qualm, apprehension, irresolution, dubiety, question mark. ANT. *certainty, faith, confidence, trust.*

doubt *v.* question, be uncertain, hesitate, mistrust, suspect, lack faith, lack conviction, misgive, waver, *smell a rat, be dubious, harbor suspicion, be skeptical, disbelieve. "The beacon of the wise." —Shakespeare. ANT. *believe, trust, accept.*

doubter *n.* skeptic, disbeliever, doubting Thomas, questioner, cynic, scoffer, freethinker, iconoclast.

doubtful *a.* **1.** QUESTIONABLE dubious, unclear, hazy, uncertain, unsure, debatable, inconclusive, ambiguous, clouded, undetermined, problematic. **2.** UNLIKELY improbable, far-fetched. **3.** DISBELIEVING suspicious, distrustful, hesitant, unsure, uncertain, questioning, skeptical, wavering, irresolute. ANT. *1. certain, sure, clear. 2. likely, probable. 3. believing, convinced.*

DOUR *a.* [DOUR] sullen, gloomy. *An unsmiling, dour clerk.* SYN. sullen, gloomy, morose, surly, glum, sour, stern, hard, grim, severe, forbidding, harsh, ill-humored. ANT. *cheerful, good-humored, beaming.*

douse *v.* **1.** IMMERSE wet, drench, submerge, sink, plunge, splash, soak, duck, dunk, sprinkle, saturate, slosh, rinse. **2.** EXTINGUISH put out.

dovetail *v.* fit, join, mortise, intersect, interlock, correspond, jibe.

dowdy *a.* shabby, sloppy, frumpy, bedraggled, slovenly, wrinkled, frowzy, unkempt, messy, unstylish, unfashionable, disheveled, *dressed in a potato sack. ANT. chic, smart, put together, *dressed to the nines, sharp.*

down *a.* **1.** DEPRESSED unhappy, melancholy, miserable, downhearted, blue, dejected, disconsolate, low, disheartened, dispirited. **2.** BELOW earthward, groundward, floor level, to the bottom, under, underneath, nether, at the foot of, sub. ANT. *1. up, cheerful, euphoric, high. 2. up, skyward, above.*

down-and-out *a.* broke, penniless, bankrupt, *shit-out-of-luck, destitute, impoverished, *in the poorhouse, *on the streets, *on the skids, derelict. ANT. *on the rise, rich, successful, *on top.*

downcast *a.* dejected, sad, unhappy, miserable, depressed, melancholy, blue, *down in the mouth, *down in the dumps, disheartened, discouraged. ANT. *up, cheerful, happy.*

downfall *n.* **1.** RUIN collapse, crash, debacle, breakdown, undoing, overthrow, destruction, comeuppance, defeat. **2.** DOWNPOUR cloudburst, rain shower, torrent, deluge, thunderstorm. ANT. *1. *rise to the top, ascension.*

downhearted *a.* sad, unhappy, dejected, miserable, depressed, melancholy, blue, *down in the mouth, *down in the dumps, hopeless, disheartened, discouraged. ANT. *up, cheerful, euphoric, hopeful, optimistic.*

downright *a.* total, complete, absolute, out and out, thorough, categorical, outright, unqualified, utter, unmitigated, sheer. ANT. *partial, qualified, semi.*

down to earth *a.* realistic, sensible, no-nonsense, reasonable, practical, sober, plainspo-

ken, pragmatic, earthy, levelheaded, matter-of-fact, *real, natural, true. ANT. *unrealistic, fantastic, impractical, pretentious.*

downtrodden *a.* oppressed, subjugated, dominated, tyrannized, abused, cowed, trampled upon, mistreated, afflicted, *jackbooted, helpless, persecuted.

downturn *n.* decline, drop, dip, slide, slump, depression, reversal, *bear market.

downy *a.* fluffy, soft, feathery, velvety, fleecy, silky, fuzzy. ANT. *rough, coarse, hard.*

doze *v.* nap, sleep, snooze, *nod off, slumber, drowse, *catch forty winks, catnap.

drab *a.* dull, lackluster, *blah, colorless, boring, dreary, faded, somber, dingy. ANT. *colorful, bright, vivid.*

DRACONIAN *a.* [dray KO nee un] harsh or severe, especially concerning a law or code; named after the code of Draco, from 621 B.C. *Some favor taking Draconian measures to fight crime.* SYN. harsh, severe, strict, cruel, extreme, rough, brutal, serious, dire, ironhanded, drastic, punitive. ANT. *slight, light, inconsequential, petty.*

draft *n.* **1.** WIND breeze, current, puff, whiff, breath, waft, sigh, sough. **2.** MILITARY CONSCRIPTION induction, selection, lottery, recruitment, registration, call of duty. **3.** OUTLINE OR PICTURE rough, blueprint, sketch, overview, formulation, skeleton, drawing.

draft *v.* **1.** CONSCRIPT induct, recruit, register, select, call up, enlist. **2.** ROUGH IN sketch, outline, delineate, formulate, compose, fashion, shape.

drag *v.* **1.** HAUL pull, lug, tow, hale, trail. **2.** PROGRESS SLOWLY *go at a snail's pace, crawl, lag, plod, poke along, inch along. **3.** PROTRACT extend, prolong, draw out. ANT. *1. push, shove. 2. rush, fly, speed. 3. shorten.*

dragon *n.* monster, firedrake, serpent. SEE MONSTER

drain *n.* outlet, conduit, channel, pipe, sewer, watercourse, plumbing.

drain *v.* **1.** DRAW empty, bleed, pump out, withdraw, remove, siphon, tap, broach, milk, release, discharge, filter, flush. **2.** USE UP exhaust, expend, suck dry, consume, deplete, tax, sap, bleed dry. ANT. *fill, replenish.*

drama *n.* play, show, screenplay, production, melodrama, dramatic arts, tragedy, *tearjerker, dramatization, stagecraft, theatrics. "A slice of life artistically put on the boards." —Jean Jullien.

dramatic *a.* intense, exciting, emotional, striking, vivid, melodramatic, climactic, moving, tense, histrionic, suspenseful, electrifying, gripping, riveting. ANT. *blah*, **ho-hum, prosaic*.

dramatize *v.* play up, emphasize, exaggerate, sensationalize, embellish, *lay it on thick, amplify, intensify, *ham it up. ANT. *play down, understate*.

drastic *a.* extreme, severe, dire, strong, harsh, exorbitant, radical, intensive, extensive, extravagant, draconian. ANT. *slight, petty, modest*.

draw *n.* 1. TIE stalemate, *photo finish. 2. ATTRACTION pull, magnetism.

draw *v.* 1. PULL TOWARD attract, haul, tow, drag, lug, hale, trail, attract. 2. SKETCH depict, portray, outline, trace, delineate, compose, paint, caricature, draft, compose, fashion, rough out. 3. DISPLACE 4. ATTRACT allure, entice, lure, tempt, seduce, captivate, mesmerize, pull in, bring forth. 5. ELICIT induce. 6. DEDUCE extract, formulate, derive, infer, conclude, gather. ANT. *1. push, shove. 4. repel, repulse*.

drawback *n.* disadvantage, weakness, snag, hitch, hindrance, liability, flaw, handicap, impediment, failing, shortcoming. ANT. *advantage, bonus*.

drawing *n.* 1. PICTURE illustration, sketch, diagram, design, outline, pen and ink, depiction, portrayal, study, work of art, figure, caricature, draft. 2. LOTTERY selection.

drawn *a.* haggard, gaunt, worn, exhausted, fatigued, unhealthy, pale, taut, tense. ANT. *rested, refreshed, glowing*.

dread *n.* fear, trepidation, horror, apprehension, qualm, misgiving, dismay, angst, anxiety, *the creeps, awe, *the willies, *heebie-jeebies.

dread *v.* fear, shudder at the thought of, anticipate with horror, shrink, worry, apprehend, *have cold feet, blanch at the thought of. ANT. *look forward to*.

dreadful *a.* terrible, unpleasant, horrible, frightful, appalling, distressing, grievous, awful, ghastly, hideous, shocking.

dream *n.* 1. SLEEP VISIONS OR REVERIE daydream, hallucination, *REM sleep, hypnogogic imagery, nightmare, night terrors, incubus, fantasy, figment of the imagination, vision. "The ghost of a shadow." — Joseph Devlin. "Children of an idle brain." — Shakespeare. "The imaginary gratification of unconscious wishes." — Sigmund Freud. "You eat, in dreams, the custard of the day." — Alexander Pope. SEE SLEEP. 2. ASPIRATION goal, ambi-

tion, *pipe dream, flight of fancy, aim, wish, desire, *castle in the air, *castle in Spain, fantasy. 3. PLEASURE delight.

dream *v.* fantasize, daydream, imagine, muse, fancy, envisage, visualize, conjure up, hallucinate, conceive, lose oneself in reverie.

dreamer *v.* visionary, fantast, daydreamer, castle-builder. "One who can only find his way by moonlight, and his punishment is that he sees the dawn before the rest of the world." — Oscar Wilde.

dream up *vt.* think up, concoct, *cook up, devise, invent, hatch, imagine.

dreary *a.* gloomy, dismal, bleak, gray, cheerless, depressing, drab, colorless, somber, mournful, funereal. ANT. *sunny, bright, cheerful*.

dredge *v.* clean, deepen, widen, dig up, unearth.

dregs *n.* 1. SEDIMENT residue, grounds, dross, deposits, settlings, lees. 2. RIFFRAFF scum, refuse, losers, *bums.

drench *v.* wet, soak, saturate, sop, drown, immerse, submerge, wash, slosh, flood.

dress *n.* 1. CLOTHING outfit, garb, attire, apparel, costume, habit, habiliment, ensemble, raiment, vestments, *togs, *duds. "The soul of a man." — Shakespeare. 2. WOMAN'S GARMENT frock, gown, evening dress, skirt, shift, ensemble, formal, wraparound.

WORD FIND

African chemise with bell-shaped sleeves: dashiki

African, long, flowing: seloso

African shift: Ethiopian shirtdress

ankle-length dress popular in late 1960s: maxi

bell-shaped dress with tight bodice: dirndl

black ankle-length dress with high neckline, ruffled sleeves: granny dress

bloused-top dress: blouson

bubble-shaped dress of the 1950s: bubble dress

calf-length dress introduced in the 1960s: midi

chemise: shift

child's sleeveless dress with bib-top apron: pinafore

full, puffed: bouffant

full, triangular: tent dress

glittery, beaded, sequined: diamante

Hawaiian: muumuu

Hindu, wrapped and draped: sari

Indian fringed and beaded: buckskin

Japanese wraparound with sash: yukata, kimono

kiltlike dress with wrap skirt: kiltie

knitted: sweater dress

loose-fitting gown: peignoir

1920s dress with short skirt and long torso: flapper

poor European dress with puffed sleeves, drawstring neckline: peasant dress

pregnant, for women who are: maternity dress

robelike, full-length, embroidered around neck: caftan

Roman-inspired, one shoulder bare: toga

rump protrusion of the nineteenth century: bustle

sack: chemise

shapeless, long: Mother Hubbard

shirtlike, buttoned top, with full or straight skirt: shirtwaist dress

short evening dress: cocktail dress

short-skirted dress of 1960s, 1980s: mini-dress

snug and narrow with slashed back: sheath

straight-cut, no waistline: chemise, sack

strapless or halter-style: sundress

wraparound: wrap

SEE SKIRT

dress v. 1. CLOTHE garb, attire, vest, deck out, outfit, slip into, wear, clad, don, costume. 2. DECORATE trim, embellish, adorn, garnish, beautify, festoon, deck. ANT. *strip, undress, disrobe.*

dresser n. 1. CHEST OF DRAWERS bureau, chiffonier. 2. PERSON fashion plate, *clotheshorse, dandy.

dressing-down n. scolding, reprimand, upbraiding, *tongue-lashing, castigation, censure, *bawling-out, reproach, talking to.

dressy a. fashionable, chic, stylish, formal, *dressed to the nines, smart, sharp, classy, elegant, flashy, *dressed to kill, *hot.

dribble v. trickle, weep, run, drip, leak, ooze, drizzle, seep, drivel, slobber, drool.

drift n. 1. HEAP pile, mound, hill, mass, deposit, bank, dune, accumulation. 2. FLOW current, course, movement, bearing, direction, trend. 3. MEANING gist, intention, purport, tenor, essence, sense.

drift v. 1. HEAP pile up, mound, mass, deposit, bank, accumulate. 2. WANDER float, waft, meander, stray, rove, ramble, be borne along by the current/tide/wind.

drifter n. wanderer, vagabond, transient, vagrant, nomad, hobo, tramp, derelict.

drill n. practice, exercise, training, discipline, regimen, repetition, dry run, warm up.

drill v. practice, exercise, train, discipline, test, warm up, ground.

drink n. liquid, beverage, refreshment, thirst quencher, soda, soft drink, *pop, punch, nectar of the gods, swallow, sip, swig, taste, *hit, *booze, liquor, shot, nip, *slug, potation, *hard stuff, *rot gut, firewater, draft, quaff, jigger, *snort, *pull. "The social lubricant." —Edward Strecker. SEE COCKTAIL, LIQUEUR, LIQUOR, MOONSHINE

drink v. swallow, sip, down, guzzle, *chug-a-lug, swig, quaff, *take a hit, *take a shot, have a taste, quench one's thirst, gulp, imbibe, drain, swill, *wet one's whistle, wash down, tipple, *bend the elbow, *gargle, *have a nip.

drinkable a. potable, palatable.

drip v. dribble, trickle, leak, drop, weep, seep, sprinkle, splash, run.

drive n. 1. RIDE spin, *cruise, tour, whirl, joyride, outing, jaunt, *Sunday drive, road trip, journey, excursion. 2. CRUSADE campaign, cause, push, appeal. 3. DETERMINATION get-up-and-go, aggressiveness, ambition, momentum, vigor, energy, hustle, enterprise, *head of steam, self-motivation.

drive v. 1. OPERATE A VEHICLE steer, control, pilot, ride, *cruise, tour, *take a spin, take a road trip, tool down the highway, motor, wheel, speed, travel, *burn up the highway. 2. PUSH propel, urge, force, press, goad, spur, move, shove, induce, pressure, compel, prod. 3. HIT throw, strike, ram, shoot, hurl, thrust.

drivel n. nonsense, *hogwash, twaddle, foolishness, falderal, gibberish, babble, *rot, *humbug, balderdash, bull, blather.

drivel v. slobber, drool, dribble, slaver, salivate.

driver n. motorist, commuter, jehu, whip, coachman, chauffeur, operator.

DROLL a. [DROLE] amusing in an odd way. *His droll sense of humor tickled us.* SYN. amusing, comical, entertaining, whimsical, quaint, humorous, eccentric, queer, peculiar, jocular.

drone v. buzz, hum, purr, whirr, murmur, hiss, bombilate, thrum, intone.

drool v. dribble, slobber, drivel, slaver, salivate, foam at the mouth.

droop v. sag, hang down, slouch, loll, slump, bend, dangle, wither, wilt, languish, bow, settle, stoop, flag.

drop n. 1. DROPLET globule, bead, teardrop, pearl, speck, pinch, splash, dewdrop, drip, blob, driblet, smidgen, trace, dab. 2. FALL pitch, descent, slope, precipice, plunge, chasm, hole. **3.** DECLINE decrease, fall, downswing, lowering, tumble, slump, reduction, fall-off, depreciation. ANT. *2. ascent, rise. 3. increase, rise, elevation.*

drop *v.* **1.** FALL dive, plunge, descend, plummet, pitch, tumble, *nose-dive, go down, topple, slump, *keel over, collapse. **2.** ABANDON give up, let go, dismiss, discontinue, cease, end, quit, desert, *write off, forsake, *scrub, leave. **3.** DECREASE decline, fall, lower, reduce, depreciate, tumble, slump, diminish, slacken. ANT. *1. rise, ascend, elevate. 2. take up, adopt. 3. increase, appreciate, rise.*

drop off *vi.* deliver, deposit, unload, leave.

drop out *vi.* quit, abandon, *turn one's back on, abandon, withdraw, forsake, leave.

droppings *n.* dung, excrement, manure, guano, *crap, *doo-doo, *squat, *turd, scat.

drought *n.* dry spell, dehydration, aridity, dearth, shortage, scarcity, want, insufficiency.

drown *v.* **1.** GO UNDER AND PERISH submerge, asphyxiate, suffocate, sink, submerge, flood, inundate, engulf, swamp. **2.** OVERWHELM overpower, overcome, stifle, smother, suppress.

drowsy *a.* sleepy, tired, dozy, half asleep, *out of it, lethargic, drifting off, groggy, somnolent, listless, sluggish. ANT. *alert, awake, energetic, wide-eyed.*

drub *v.* thrash, hit, beat, whip, wallop, pound, club, cane, lash, switch.

drudge *v.* work hard, toil, labor, *break one's back, *do the dirty work, slave away, *keep nose to the grindstone, plod, grind, sweat.

drudgery *n.* menial labor, chore, slave labor, toil, backbreaking work, manual labor, *daily grind, taskwork.

drug *n.* medicine, narcotic, remedy, cure, opiate, dope, pharmaceutical, prescription, pill.
WORD FIND
addict: *junkie, *hophead, *dope fiend, *druggie, *space cadet, *burnout
addict's alternative to heroin: methadone
*angel dust: PCP
cocaine that is smoked: crack
*cranki methamphetamine
depressant, muscle-relaxer: barbituate, *downer
ether-purified cocaine: *freebase
hallucinogen: LSD, DMT (Dimethyltryptamine), *ecstasy, mescaline, peyote, *psychedelic, *STP
*ice: methamphetamine in smokable form
laughing gas: nitrous oxide

LSD: lysergic acid diethylamide, *California sunshine, *acid
mix of cocaine, amphetamine and heroin: *speedball
mood-altering: psychotropic drug
muscle-building hormone: anabolic steroid
narcotic: heroin
opium-derived: opiate
painkiller: analgesic, codeine, Demerol, morphine, Percodan
poppy-plant, derived from: opium
sex drive arouser: aphrodisiac
sleep-inducing: hypnotic, soporific, tranquilizer, sedative, Quaalude, Seconal
*smack: heroin
stimulant: amphetamine, Dexedrine, *speed, *upper
tranquilizer: sedative, Valium
vomiting, causes: emetic
SEE COCAINE, CURE, HEROIN, OPIUM, MARIJUANA, MEDICINE, NARCOTIC

druggist *n.* pharmacist, apothecary, chemist. BRIT.

drum *n.* SEE MUSICAL INSTRUMENT

drunk *a.* intoxicated, inebriated, under the influence, *three sheets to the wind, *hammered, *high, *buzzed, besotted, soused, *pickled, *lit, *tanked, *stewed to the gills, *bombed, *blitzed, *smashed, *blotto, *drunker than a brewer's fart, *drunk as a lord. ANT. *sober, clearheaded.*

drunk(ard) *n.* alcoholic, *lush, problem drinker, *boozer, inebriate, *wino, *rummy, barfly, *sot, dipsomaniac, *alchy, *boozehound. "Like a whiskey bottle, all neck and belly and no head." — Austin O'Malley. "One who beats everyone to the punch." — Anon. "A person who tries to pull himself out of trouble with a corkscrew." — Edward Baldwin.

dry *a.* **1.** DEHYDRATED dessicated, waterless, arid, parched, thirsty, droughty, evaporated, anhydrous, withered. **2.** DULL boring, uninteresting, prosaic, tedious, flat, blah, *ho hum, wearisome, *dull as dishwater, insipid, monotonous, sterile. **3.** DROLL humorous, sarcastic, satirical, deadpan. ANT. *1. wet, moist, saturated. 2. interesting, fascinating.*

dual *a.* double, twofold, twin, duplex, binary, matched.

dub *v.* name, christen, label, title, designate, term, nickname, tag, style, confer, denominate, baptize, knight.

DUBIOUS *a.* [DOO bee us] doubtful or causing doubt, questionable, uncertain. *I was du-*

bious about her chances of winning the lottery. SYN. doubtful, questionable, uncertain equivocal, indefinite, unclear, unsure, disputable, suspect, debatable, moot. ANT. *certain, sure, indisputable.*

duck *v.* **1.** LOWER bow, crouch, stoop, dip, double over, drop, bob, bend, hunker down. **2.** EVADE dodge, sidestep, elude, avoid, parry, swerve, shun, steer clear. **3.** IMMERSE submerge, dunk, dip, plunge, sink. ANT. *1. rise, straighten. 2. meet, confront.*

duct *n.* conduit, pipe, channel, passage, tube, airway, chimney, smokestack, funnel.

dud *n.* failure, bomb, lemon, bust, loser, *dog, washout, fizzle, *flop, disappointment. ANT. *success, *cocker, winner.*

dude *n. Sl.* **1.** GUY man, *buddy, friend, *bro'. **2.** AN OVERDRESSED MAN dandy, fop, Beau Brummel, coxcomb, fashion plate, *peacock, clotheshorse.

duds *n.* SEE CLOTHING

due *n.* compensation, payment, recompense, *what is coming, rightful claim, reward, *comeuppance, *just deserts.

due *a.* **1.** OWED in arrears, payable, unpaid, outstanding, unsatisfied, not met, mature. **2.** APPOINTED TO ARRIVE expected, scheduled, anticipated, slated, booked. **3.** FITTING appropriate, deserved, merited, justified, entitled, warranted. ANT. *3. undue, inappropriate.*

due to *prep.* attributable, because of, accountable.

duel *n.* combat, contest, fight to the death, clash, engagement, shootout, challenge, joust.

dues *n.* membership fee, charge, obligation, levy, toll, assessment, payment, tax.

dull *a.* **1.** STUPID slow, unintelligent, *thick, dense, bovine, retarded, obtuse, doltish, *dumb as a post, dim-witted, half-witted, ignorant. **2.** BORING tedious, *ho-hum, blah, uninteresting, prosaic, dry, tiresome, bland, vapid, *dull as dishwater, humdrum, stale, lackluster, soporific. **3.** SUBDUED quiet, muted, deadened, faded, softened, muffled. **4.** UNSHARPENED blunt, unhoned, edgeless. ANT. *1. sharp, intelligent, quick-witted, bright. 2. exciting, stimulating, colorful, dramatic. 3. overstated, overdone, flashy, loud. 4. sharp, honed.*

dullard *n.* dolt, dunce, *retard, idiot, *dope, *blockhead, *chowderhead, *meathead, *nitwit, imbecile, *half-wit. ANT. *genius, *brain, *Rhodes scholar.*

dumb *a.* **1.** STUPID unintelligent, slow, *thick, dense, bovine, moronic, retarded, obtuse, doltish, dim-witted, *dumb as a post, ignorant. **2.** UNABLE TO SPEAK mute, speechless, still, mum, silent, voiceless, tongue-tied. ANT. *1. smart, intelligent, bright. 2. loquacious, verbose, *motor-mouthed.*

dumbfound *v.* stun, nonplus, strike dumb, flabbergast, astound, take aback, stagger, paralyze, nonplus, render speechless, stupefy.

dummy *n.* **1.** FIGURE mannequin, straw man, scarecrow, model, puppet, muppet, doll, figure. **2.** MOCK-UP model, imitation, substitute, copy, representation. **3.** IDIOT *lamebrain, *airhead, simpleton, dolt, *nitwit, *dimwit, ignoramus, dunce, moron, *chowderhead, numskull. ANT. *3. genius, *brain, *Rhodes scholar, *rocket scientist.*

dump *n.* **1.** REFUSE YARD junkyard, rubbish heap. **2.** RUNDOWN, MESSY PLACE hole, *pigpen, *pigsty, slum, *rathole, *toilet, *sewer hole.

dump *v.* throw out, drop, get rid of, cast off, empty, *deep six, *shitcan, chuck, scrap, unload, junk, ditch, discard. ANT. *load, fill.*

dunce *n.* idiot, moron, dolt, *nitwit, *half-wit, *lamebrain, *airhead, simpleton, ignoramus, *retard, *chowderhead, numskull.

dung *n.* excrement, droppings, feces, scat, manure, muck, guano, *cow chips, *cow pies, *crap, *butt muffin, *poop.

WORD FIND

dunghill: midden

study of: scatology

dungeon *n.* prison, keep, hold, donjon, stronghold. SEE CASTLE

dunk *v.* dip, sink, immerse, submerge, duck, soak, souse, sop.

dupe *n.* victim, *easy mark, *chump, gull, *sucker, *patsy, *pushover, dummy, fall guy, *sap, pawn, *babe in the woods. ANT. *nobody's fool, quick study.*

dupe *v.* *put one over on, trick, fool, take in, delude, *pull the wool over one's eyes, *rope in, deceive, cheat, *snooker, *buffalo, *snow, *bullshit.

duplicate *n.* copy, reproduction, carbon copy, match, counterpart, mate, mirror image, facsimile, clone, twin, dead ringer. ANT. *original.*

duplicate *v.* copy, reproduce, replicate, clone, *Xerox, *run off, match, double, counterfeit, parallel, ditto.

DUPLICITY *n.* [doo PLIS i tee] deceptiveness, the act of double-dealing or being two-faced. *Shady politicians are skilled in the art of duplicity.* SYN. deceptiveness, deception, double-dealing, being two-faced, guile, treachery, backstabbing, *two-timing, deceit, disloyalty, artifice, hypocrisy, dishonesty, *Judas kiss. ANT. *honesty, loyalty, artlessness, straightforwardness.*

durable *a.* lasting, tough, rugged, sturdy, enduring, strong, permanent, sound, stout, *built like a brick shithouse, stable, solid. ANT. *fragile, flimsy, cheap, shoddy.*

duration *n.* period, time, age, span, term, run, stretch, era, lifetime extent, continuation, course.

duress *n.* coercion, constraint, threat, pressure, force, arm-twisting, compulsion. ANT. *free will.*

dusk *n.* twilight, sundown, sunset, gloom, nightfall, gloaming, evening, moonrise.

dusky *a.* dark, dim, gauzy, murky, gloomy, veiled, twilight, swarthy, gray, shadowy, unlit, somber. ANT. *sunny, bright, radiant.*

dust *n.* particles, lint, grit, ashes, powder, soot.

dusty *a.* dirty, sandy, granular, *linty, sooty, powdery, undusted. ANT. *dusted, clean, polished.*

dutiful *a.* conscientious, diligent, obedient, devoted, regardful, accommodating, obliging, faithful. ANT. *lazy, slack, negligent*

duty *n.* **1.** RESPONSIBILITY charge, task, commission, obligation, trust, requirement, function, assignment, job, burden. **2.** TAX customs, excise, levy, tariff, toll, impost, assessment.

dwarf *n.* midget, runt, pygmy, gnome, *shrimp, Lilliputian, *squirt, bantam, elf, *peewee, *half-pint, *micro. ANT. *giant, colossus.*

dwarf *v.* eclipse, overshadow, outshine, stand head and shoulders above, tower above, excel, dominate, stunt.

dwell *v.* **1.** LIVE reside, inhabit, stay, abide, *crash, keep house, quarter, lodge, *roost, *bunk, take shelter, domicile. **2.** LINGER OVER think about, pause, harp on, ponder.

dwelling *n.* home, house, residence, domicile, habitation, lodging, abode, homestead, quarters, diggings, castle, *pad, den.

dwindle *v.* diminish, decline, decrease, lessen, fade, wane, shrink, ebb, waste away, slacken, die down, drop, decay. ANT. *increase, grow, expand.*

dye *n.* color, tint, pigment, tinge, stain.

DYED-IN-THE-WOOL *a.* through and through, to the very core, deep-down. A *dyed-in-the-wool conservative.* SYN. through and through, to the core, deep-down, out and out, complete, utter, absolute, true, genuine, full-fledged. ANT. *partial, superficial.*

dying *a.* **1.** EXPIRING perishing, fading, declining, *going downhill, *circling the drain, *at death's door, moribund, doomed, slipping away, *one foot in the grave. "The last gasp." — Bible. "A great leap in the dark." — Thomas Hobbes "That dreadful season." — Joseph Addison. "A natural appointment from which there is no hope of escape." — Jonathan Miller. **2.** DISAPPEARING passing, declining, becoming extinct, receding, going out. ANT. *thriving, flourishing, rejuvenating.*

dynamic *a.* active, energetic, vital, vigorous, forceful, aggressive, alive, powerful, spirited, effective, potent, driving, compelling. ANT. *lifeless, dead, ineffectual, weak.*

dynamite *n.* explosive, TNT, nitroglycerin.

dynamo *n.* generator, *go-getter, *bundle of energy, *live wire, *spark plug, work horse, *ball of fire, hard worker, mover and shaker.

dynasty *n.* lineage, ascendancy, regency, rule, house, command, crown, regime, empire.

E

each *a.* every, all, respective, any, individual.

each *adv.* apiece, per, individually, a person, *a head, *a shot.

eager *a.* enthusiastic, anxious, *champing at the bit, desirous, itching, *gung ho, agog, impatient, *rarin' to go, fervent, ardent, hungry, intent, zealous. ANT. *apathetic, indifferent, lukewarm.*

eagle *n.* raptor, bird of prey, Falconiforme.

WORD FIND

group of: convocation
hooked beak, describing: aquiline
nest: aerie
SEE BIRD

ear *n.* hearing organ, auditory organ. "The road to the heart." — Voltaire "The gates to the mind." — Moses Ibn Ezra.

WORD FIND

balance, inner organ of: labyrinth
bones of: anvil (incus), hammer (malleus), stirrup (stapes): ossicles
deformity: cauliflower ear
doctor: otologist
earache: otalgia
eardrum: tympanic membrane
external portion: auricle, pinna
hereditary disorder causing progressive deafness: otosclerosis
instrument: otoscope
nerve: auditory nerve
nerve deafness: sensorineural deafness
ringing in: tinnitus
spiral inner cavity: cochlea
study of: otology
swimmer's ear: otitis externa
vestigial point: Darwin's tubercle
wax: cerumen
whirling, dizzy sensation due to inner ear impairment: vertigo

early *a.* **1.** NEAR THE BEGINNING preceding, prior, initial, young, aboriginal, primal, primeval, primitive, antediluvian, maiden, original, starting, ancient. **2.** TOO SOON premature, ahead of time, beforehand, preceding, advanced, immature, precocious.

earmark *n.* characteristic, feature, mark, hallmark, trait, quality, signature, peculiarity, trademark, stamp.

earmark *v.* set aside, reserve, designate, slot, allocate, assign, hold, tag, label.

earn *v.* **1.** MAKE MONEY net, *clear, gross, profit, take in, take home, pull in, gain, realize, collect, get, draw. **2.** DESERVE merit, be entitled to, warrant, achieve, be worthy of.

EARNEST *a.* [UR nist] serious, sincere, nononsense, determined. *An earnest attempt. An earnest student.* SYN. serious, sincere, nononsense, determined, heartfelt, wholehearted, devoted, resolute, intent, *meaning business, ardent, fervent, diligent. ANT. *halfhearted, frivolous, insincere, apathetic.*

earnings *n.* pay, wages, salary, net, gross, *take-home, income, profit, compensation, proceeds, gain, return, receipts.

earth *n.* **1.** GROUND soil, land, dirt, clay, loam, humus, turf, mud, terra firma. **2.** PLANET world, globe, sphere, biosphere, Gaea, terrene, orb, terra, terra firma, *spaceship Earth, vale. "One voice in the cosmic fugue." — Carl Sagan. "The frozen echo of the silent voice of God." — S.M. Hageman. "Footstool of our God" — Isaac Watts. "A spot, a grain, an atom." — John Milton. "The lonely menagerie." — Marc McCutcheon.

WORD FIND

center of, pertaining to: geocentric
green earth color: terre verte
inhabitant: earthling, tellurian
outermost shell: crust, lithosphere
personification of: Gaea
pertaining to: terrene
shape: oblate spheroid
study of its shape, size: geodesy
study of its structure: tectonics, geology
subsurface: asthenosphere, mantle, core

earthly *a.* terrestrial, terrene, worldly, *down to earth, physical, mundane, global, physical, corporeal, mortal, temporal. ANT. *spiritual, ethereal, otherworldly, divine, heavenly.*

earthquake *n.* tremor, temblor, quake, seism, *earthshake, shock, convulsion, upheaval, cataclysm, *wake-up call. "A moving experience." — Marc McCutcheon

WORD FIND

center of: epicenter
continental dynamics causing: plate tectonics
following tremor: aftershock
fracture in rock strata, origination of quake: fault
ground waves causing initial roar: primary waves, compressional waves
ground waves causing side-to-side shaking: Love waves

magnitude scale: Richter scale, Mercalli intensity scale
pertaining to: seismic
preceding tremor: foreshock
recorder of earth's vibrations: seismograph
sea wave caused by: tsunami
study of: seismology
SEE VOLCANO

earthy a. *down to earth, folksy, uninhibited, down-home, unsophisticated, coarse, *real, crude, *hard-boiled, unrefined, lusty, ribald, rough, gross. ANT. *sophisticated, refined, dainty, prissy.*

ease n. **1.** COMFORT well-being, peace, rest, contentment, *peace of mind, relaxation, tranquility, relief, serenity, leisure. **2.** EASINESS facility, readiness, effortlessness, freedom, *a snap, *child's play, *duck soup, *a walk on the beach, a breeze, *a cinch. ANT. *1. discomfort, pain, difficulty. 2. difficulty, hardship.*

ease v. alleviate, loosen, relieve, moderate, comfort, mitigate, diminish, assuage, lighten, simplify, mollify, quiet, smooth. ANT. *aggravate, worsen.*

easily adv. **1.** EFFORTLESSLY with ease, readily, handily, without difficulty, swimmingly, facilely, dexterously. **2.** BY FAR *hands down, far and away, decidedly, unquestionably, clearly. ANT. *1. arduously, laboriously, with difficulty. 2. barely, hardly.*

easy a. **1.** NOT HARD effortless, simple, slight, light, uncomplicated, painless, *cinchy, *child's play, *a snap, *piece of cake, *nothing to it, *duck soup. **2.** FREE FROM TROUBLE OR PAIN relaxed, carefree, untroubled, tranquil, peaceful, serene, comfortable, luxurious, undemanding, secure, pleasant. **3.** EASYGOING relaxed, lenient, gentle, tolerant, soft, mild, permissive, moderate, lax, informal, benign. ANT. *1. difficult, arduous, laborious. 2. burdensome, hard, troubled. 3. strict, harsh, stern.*

easygoing a. placid, careless, undemanding, relaxed, lenient, gentle, tolerant, permissive, lax, informal, *happy-go-lucky, *devil-may-care, laid-back. ANT. *uptight, intense, stern, severe, harsh.*

eat v. **1.** INGEST FOOD consume, dine, feast, devour, lunch, break bread, sup, *chow down, gorge, scoff, *put on a feedbag, gobble, wolf, nibble, nosh, bolt. **2.** CORRODE erode, dissolve, wear away, rot, decay, disintegrate, waste.

eavesdrop v. listen in, pry, spy, wiretap, *bug, *snoop, bend an ear.

ebb v. recede, decline, fall back, diminish, subside, decrease, wane, retreat, fade, flag, abate, withdraw. ANT. *grow, increase, build, wax.*

EBULLIENT a. [i BUL yunt] boiling or bubbling over with excitement. *The crowd was absolutely ebullient with the hometown's victory.* SYN. exuberant, bubbling over with excitement, exhilarated, high-spirited, electrified, effervescent, elated, enthusiastic, irrepressible, *going nuts, zestful, wild. ANT. *subdued, sedate, apathetic, somber.*

eccentric n. *nut, character, queer duck, original, oddball, *weirdo, nonconformist, *ding-a-ling, crank, loner, individual, free spirit.

eccentric a. odd, peculiar, weird, *nutty, queer, off-center, flaky, unconventional, idiosyncratic, *off the wall, deviant, *kinky, different, *daft, *potty, irregular, nonconforming. ANT. *normal, conventional, ordinary.* SEE CRAZY

eccentricity n. quirk, peculiarity, oddity, idiosyncracy, abnormality, foible, idiocrasy, curiousity, irregularity, singularity, *kink.

ecclesiastical a. churchly, religious, ministerial, parochial, pastoral, clerical. ANT. *lay, secular, mundane.*

echelon n. level, hierarchy, rank, class, position, place, tier, order.

echo n. answer, reverberation, rebound, reflection, reply, replication, repercussion, repetition, parroting. "Something that always has the last word." — German proverb. "The shadow of a sound." — Horace Smith.

ECLECTIC a. [i KLEK tik] selecting the best from various sources, that which has been selected from diverse sources. *Fran's taste in music is eclectic.* SYN. selective, comprehensive, wide-ranging, assorted, broad, diverse, liberal, multifaceted, catholic, heterogenous. ANT. *limited, narrow, specialized.*

eclipse n. occultation, shadowing, obliteration, obscuring, darkening, penumbra.

eclipse v. **1.** BLOCK obscure, cover, darken, hide, conceal, dim, veil, overshadow. **2.** OUTSHINE exceed, surpass, overpower, overshadow, outdo, transcend, stand head and shoulders above, dwarf.

economical a. **1.** FRUGAL conservative, thrifty, economizing, efficient, *penny-wise, tight, prudent, saving, scrimping. **2.** INEXPENSIVE cheap, *dirt cheap, cost-effective, reasonable, budget, low-priced. ANT. *wasteful, extravagant. 2. expensive, costly, dear.*

economize v. save, be frugal, *tighten one's belt, pinch pennies, conserve, scrimp, cut corners, stint, cut back. ANT. *waste, squander, *piss away.*

economy n. thrift, saving, frugality, conserving, austerity, prudence, skimping, penny-pinching. "To pitch your scale of living one degree below your means." — Henry Taylor. "The art of making the most of life." — George Bernard Shaw. ANT. *extravagance, wastefulness, spending.*

ecstasy n. rapture, euphoria, bliss, elation, transport, exaltation, ebullience, heaven, joy, exhilaration, seventh heaven. ANT. *misery, depression, gloom.*

ecstatic a. rapturous, euphoric, elated, blissful, transported, exalted, ebullient, in heaven, in seventh heaven, overjoyed, thrilled. ANT. *miserable, depressed, down.*

eddy n. current, vortex, countercurrent, whirlpool, swirl.

edge n. **1.** MARGIN border, boundary, verge, outline, perimeter, skirt, rim, fringe, periphery, limit, brink. **2.** ADVANTAGE leg up, handicap, head start, upper hand.

edgy a. nervous, on edge, tense, uptight, anxious, *wired, jumpy, jittery, *keyed up, restless, ill at ease, *a bundle of nerves. ANT. *calm, tranquil, relaxed.*

edible a. palatable, consumable, fit to eat, comestible, digestible, esculent.

edict n. decree, command, proclamation, law, fiat, manifesto, enactment, ruling, act, regulation, ordinance.

edification n. enlightenment, education, improvement, betterment, learning, uplifting, instruction, guidance, teaching.

edifice n. building, structure, skyscraper, tower, construction, highrise.

edit v. revise, correct, *blue pencil, refine, check, rewrite, polish, proofread, redact, doctor, cut, delete, condense, *clean up.

editor n. reviser, redactor, rewriter, copy editor. "A bit of sandpaper applied to all forms of originality." — Elbert Hubbard.

edition n. issue, copy, number, printing, volume.

editorial n. essay, opinion piece, think piece, article, commentary.

educate v. teach, instruct, train, enlighten, school, edify, tutor, coach, cultivate, *show the ropes, inform, drum into.

educated a. trained, enlightened, schooled, learned, literate, cultivated, erudite, scholarly, refined, well-read, well-grounded, knowledgeable. ANT. *ignorant, naive, illiterate.*

education n. training, enlightenment, schooling, learning, edification, erudition, scholarship, literacy, book-learning, instruction, study, grounding, cultivation. "A companion which no misfortune can depress." — Joseph Addison. "A better safeguard of liberty than a standing army." — Edward Everett. "Character development." — William O'Shea. "A chest of tools." — Herbert Kaufman. "All the minds of past ages." — Bernard de Fontenelle.

educational a. informative, instructional, enlightening, academic, edifying, illuminating, scholastic, didactic.

educator n. teacher, instructor, tutor, mentor, trainer, coach, professor.

educe v. evoke, bring out, draw forth, elicit.

eerie a. weird, unsettling, creepy, macabre, unnatural, spooky, bizarre, strange, unearthly, uncanny, frightening.

efface v. erase, obliterate, rub out, cancel, wipe out, fade, expunge, eradicate.

effect n. **1.** RESULT consequence, upshot, reaction, response, aftermath, end, fallout, wake, repercussion. **2.** INFLUENCE impact, force, weight, power, clout, efficacy.

effect v. bring about, cause, actualize, produce, achieve, make, create, generate, accomplish.

effective a. **1.** PRODUCTIVE successful, compelling, sufficient, forceful, efficacious, useful, powerful, persuasive. **2.** OPERATIVE functional, serviceable, in effect, active. ANT. *ineffectual, ineffective, impotent, inadequate.*

effects n. belongings, possessions, goods, things, property, stuff, chattels.

effeminate a. feminine, unmanly, soft, ladylike, womanish, emasculate, *limp-wristed, *faggy, delicate, *queer, sissyish. ANT. *masculine, virile, macho, manly.*

effervescence n. **1.** FIZZ bubbles, foam, froth, carbonation. **2.** VIVACITY high spirits, exuberance, vitality, liveliness, *zip, spirit, buoyancy, animation, ebullience. ANT. *1. flatness. 2. lifelessness, listlessness, torpor.*

effervescent a. **1.** FIZZY bubbly, foaming, frothy, carbonated. **2.** VIVACIOUS spirited, exuberant, vital, lively, *zippy, buoyant, animated, ebullient. ANT. *1. flat. 2. dead, lifeless, listless.*

effete a. **1.** BARREN unproductive, fruitless, sterile. **2.** SPENT worn out, exhausted, used up, *burned out, enervated, weak. ANT. *fertile, vital, vigorous.*

EFFICACY a. [EF uh kuh see] the capacity to bring about the desired end, effectiveness. *The efficacy of the space agency will be tested with the new mission.* SYN. effectiveness, power, productiveness, capacity, competency, potency, vigor, proficiency, capability, efficiency.

efficient *a.* effective, effectual, potent, productive, capable, causative, proficient, dynamic, economical, workmanlike, able. ANT. *inefficient, ineffectual, wasteful.*

effort *n.* **1.** EXERTION strain, output, work, trouble, application, muscle, toil, pain, *elbow grease, stress, sweat. **2.** ATTEMPT try, endeavor, venture, *go. **3.** ACHIEVEMENT feat, creation, accomplishment.

effortless *a.* easy, simple, *no sweat, *piece of cake, *child's play, facile, *a snap, cinchy, no problem, *duck soup. ANT. *arduous, laborious, backbreaking.*

EFFRONTERY *n.* [i FRUN tuh ree] audacity, insulting gall. *I can't believe he had the effrontery to cut in line.* SYN. audacity, impudence, boldness, nerve, gall, cheek, insolence, presumption, arrogance, brass, impertinence, *balls, rudeness, *chutzpah. ANT. *deference, timidity, respect.*

effulgent *a.* radiant, glowing, luminous, brilliant, resplendent, shining, dazzling, bright. ANT. *dim, dull, dark.*

EFFUSIVE *a.* [i FYOO siv] gushing or highly demonstrative of one's emotions. *It made me uncomfortable to see him so effusive.* SYN. gushing, demonstrative, unrestrained, profuse, expansive, lavish, extravagant, overflowing, unreserved. ANT. *reserved, restrained, taciturn.*

EGALITARIAN *a.* [i GAL uh TARE ee un] believing in equality for everyone. *An egalitarian policy was the ideal.* SYN. equal, liberal, fair-minded, democratic, just, unbiased, unprejudiced, equitable. ANT. *unfair, inequitable, prejudiced, biased.*

egg *n.* ovum, embryo, roe, spawn, *cacklejelly.
WORD FIND
crumbed and buttered: shirred eggs
laid at same time: clutch
shape: ovoid, ovate, oval
tester: candler
white: albumen
yolk: vitellus

egghead *n. Sl.* intellectual, *brain, genius, *walking encyclopedia, *know-it-all. ANT. *ignoramus, moron.*

egg on *v.* urge, incite, prod, encourage, spur, push, prompt, goad, rally. ANT. *discourage.*

ego *n.* self, psyche, self-esteem, self-image, self-respect. "The personality as the center of the universe." —Anon.

egocentric *a.* self-centered, selfish, egotistic, self-absorbed, wrapped up in oneself, narcissistic, vainglorious, conceited.

egotism *n.* self-centeredness, selfishness, egoism, self-absorption, conceit, narcissism, vainglory, arrogance, self-worship, vanity, overconfidence. "The anesthetic given by a kindly nature to relieve the pain of being a damned fool." —Bellamy Brooks. "A case of mistaken nonentity." —Barbara Stanwyck.

egotist *n.* egoist, boaster, selfish pig, narcissist, braggart, peacock, *swellhead, *King shit, egomaniac. "A self-made man who worships his creator." —John Bright.

egotistic *a.* self-centered, selfish, self-absorbed, conceited, narcissistic, arrogant, vainglorious, self-worshipping, vain, smug, overconfident, *puffed up, *swellheaded.

EGREGIOUS *a.* [i GREE jus] extremely bad or outrageous. *Murder is an egregious sin.* SYN. bad, outrageous, flagrant, blatant, extreme, atrocious, monstrous, shocking, grievous, glaring, striking, baldfaced, appalling. ANT. *minor, trivial, petty.*

egress *n.* doorway, outlet. SEE EXIT

ejaculate *v.* discharge, climax, have an orgasm, spurt, spout, *come, *shoot one's goo, *get off, *get one's rocks off, *empty one's barrel, *pop one's cookies.

eject *v.* throw out, expel, oust, *kick out, *give the boot, evict, ditch, banish, *send packing, *show the door, *bounce, *give walking papers.

ejection *n.* expulsion, ouster, removal, dismissal, exile, *the boot, discharge, banishment, eviction, ostracism.

elaborate *v.* develop, work out, detail, flesh out, fashion, add to, enlarge, amplify, refine, explain.

elaborate *a.* complicated, complex, intricate, detailed, comprehensive, painstaking, thorough, involved, sophisticated, multifaceted, ornate, busy, showy, extravagant. ANT. *simple, plain, unadorned, stark.*

élan *n.* enthusiasm, spirit, vigor, dash, ardor, verve, vivacity, panache, flair, zest.

elapse *v.* go by, pass, transpire, expire, intervene, slip by, lapse.

elastic *a.* flexible, resilient, supple, adaptable, springy, pliant, accommodating, yielding, buoyant. ANT. *inflexible, rigid, stiff.*

elated *a.* happy, ecstatic, euphoric, delighted, excited, in high spirits, *in seventh heaven, exultant, *flying, exhilarated, gleeful, joyful, *tickled. ANT. *miserable, down, depressed,* *bummed.

elation n. happiness, joy, euphoria, delight, excitement, high spirits, glee, exhilaration, exaltation, rapture, *cloud nine, ecstasy. ANT. *misery, depression, blues.*

elbow v. push, shove, jostle, shoulder, bump, bulldoze, nudge, crowd.

elder n. senior, old-timer, veteran, superior, forefather, ancestor, matriarch, patriarch, *old fogey, *geezer, retiree, graybeard, dowager.

WORD FIND

sixty, or between sixty and seventy: sexagenarian

seventy, or between seventy and eighty: septuagenarian

eighty, or between eighty and ninety: octogenarian

ninety, or between ninety and one hundred: nonagenarian

one hundred-year-old: centenarian

elder a. older, senior, superior, higher ranking.

elderly a. aged, venerable, seasoned, ancient, *long in the tooth, mature, *over the hill, experienced, senescent, advanced in years, weathered, vintage. SEE OLD, OLD AGE, OLD-FACED

elect v. select, choose, pick, opt for, appoint, vote for, settle on, nominate, single out, cast one's ballot.

election n. selection, choosing, choice, voting, vote-casting, determination, preference, appointment, designation, nomination, referendum.

WORD FIND

ELECTIONS AND CAMPAIGNING

aid to candidate, solicits votes: electioneer

assembly every four years to elect presidential candidate: national convention

attack on opposing candidate: mudslinging, smear campaign

candidate list: ballot, ticket

convention representatives from one state: delegation

cross-party vote: crossover vote

desires and dictates of voters expressed through vote: mandate

district of voters: constituency

district, smallest voting unit: precinct

fund-raising, fund-distributing committee: political action committee (pac)

mail-in vote: absentee ballot

majority (large) of votes, victory: landslide

meeting of party to choose candidate: caucus

meeting to generate enthusiasm for candidate: rally

person not on ballot, but written in by voter: write-in

poll public opinion or solicit votes: canvass

popular candidate's trickle-down benefit to weaker party member: coattail effect

preliminary, nominating election: primary

principles of candidate or party: platform

proposal of action, to be voted on: proposition, referendum

random vote poll: straw poll

report of voting trends: poll, returns, exit poll

shake hands and smile: glad-hand

speak from town to town: barnstorm, stump

state representatives chosen to elect president and vice president: electoral college

voting enrollment: registration

SEE CONGRESS, ELECTIONEERING, POLITICS

electioneering n. campaigning, canvassing, soliciting votes, *stumping, *barnstorming, promoting. "A war in which everybody shoots from the lip." — Raymond Moley. "When the air is filled with speech and vice versa." — Anon.

elective a. chosen, optional, electoral, discretionary, voluntary. ANT. *required.*

electricity n. current, power, AC, DC, voltage, spark, charge, *juice.

WORD FIND

atom: electron

cell that converts light to electricity: photovoltaic cell

current regulator: rheostat

drop in voltage through power line: brownout

earth or other large body to which circuit is connected to prevent noise interference: ground

generator: dynamo

material capable of carrying current with little resistance: conductor

particle, electrified: ion

poor conductor and a poor insulator: semiconductor

restrictor of current's flow: insulator

stores electrical charge: capacitor

unit of: amp, ampere, ohm, volt, watt, joule

zero resistance of current: superconductivity

SEE ELECTRONICS, EXCITEMENT

electrify v. thrill, shock, startle, stun, excite, dazzle, stir, daze, jolt, *give one a charge, stagger, *take one's breath away. ANT. *bore.*

electronics n. integrated circuitry, transistors,

chips, solid state components. SEE COMPUTER, ELECTRICITY

elegance *n.* fineness, refinement, grace, opulence, luxuriousness, high style, beauty, grandeur, class, tastefulness, sophistication, poshness, polish.

elegant *a.* fine, refined, graceful, opulent, luxurious, high-styled, stylish, beautiful, grand, classy, tasteful, sophisticated, posh, cultured, fashionable, polished. ANT. *coarse, crude, unrefined, tacky.*

elegiac *a.* sad, sorrowful, mournful, plaintive.

elegy *n.* dirge, lamentation, lament, funeral song, requiem.

element *n.* component, ingredient, constituent, unit, facet, bit, feature, piece, portion, section, item, factor.

elementary *a.* basic, simple, fundamental, rudimentary, easy, *child's play, uncomplicated, primary, introductory, plain, abecedarian.

elephant *n.* pachyderm, mammal. "A mouse built to government specifications." — Robert Heinlein.

WORD FIND
call: trumpet, bellow
driver/keeper: mahout
extinct: mammoth, mastadon
female: cow
male: bull
male's violent and sexual frenzy: musth, rut
nose: trunk, snout
rider's seat: howdah
run towards: charge
solitary, vicious outcast: rogue
tooth: tusk
tusk: ivory
young: calf

elephantine *a.* mammoth, gargantuan, jumbo. SEE HUGE

elevate *v.* **1.** RAISE lift, uplift, hoist, escalate, hike up, jack up, heighten. **2.** PROMOTE advance, raise, enhance, improve, upgrade, boost, heighten, aggrandize, exalt. ANT. *lower, drop, degrade.*

elevated *a.* lofty, exalted, noble, grand, eminent, high, upstanding, distinguished, admirable, *put on a pedestal.

elevation *n.* height, altitude, eminence, high ground, prominence, rise, hill, mountain, lift.

elf *n.* gnome, fairy, hob, pixy, imp, brownie, sprite, dwarf, leprechaun.

elfin *a.* mischievous, prankish, impish, playful, sprightly, small, fleeting.

ELICIT *v.* [i LIS it] to bring out or draw forth.

He tried to elicit a response from the speaker. SYN. draw, bring out, evoke, extract, wrest, cause, exact, call forth, wring, *arm-twist, *pump, extort.

eligible *a.* qualified, worthy, suitable, appropriate, desirable, fitting, acceptable. ANT. *ineligible, disqualified.*

eliminate *v.* get rid of, remove, discard, cut, reject, omit, drop, kill, eject, oust, shut out, expel, exclude. ANT. *include, get.*

elimination *n.* removal, discard, cut, rejection, omission, dropping, killing, ejection, ouster, expulsion, exclusion. ANT. *inclusion.*

elite *n.* the best, the greatest, *upper crust, aristocracy, *creme de la creme, high society, gentry, blue bloods, nobility, clique, *haut monde, pick. ANT. *the dregs, working class, lower class.*

elitist *n.* snob, highbrow, oligarch, social climber, *snoot, *stuffed shirt, egotist.

elixir *n.* potion, curative, mixture, compound, panacea, cure-all, miracle drug, nostrum, catholicon.

elliptical *a.* oval, egg-shaped, ovoid.

elocution *n.* public speaking, speech, oratory, articulation, recitation, declamation, rhetoric, delivery, eloquence, enunciation, diction. SEE ELOQUENCE, SPEECH

elongate *v.* lengthen, extend, stretch, protract, let out, prolong. ANT. *shorten, shrink, curtail.*

elongated *a.* lengthened, extended, stretched, protracted, let out, prolonged, prolate, oblong. ANT. *shortened, contracted, curtailed.*

elope *v.* run off, abscond, run away with, slip off.

eloquence *n.* persuasiveness, fluency, forcefulness, expressiveness, rhetoric, command of language, way with words, elocution, oratory, articulation. "A gift of the mind, which makes us master of the heart and spirit of others." — Jean de La Bruyere. "What one thinks he has after a cocktail." — Warren Goldberg. "The gift of making any color appear white." — Ambrose Bierce

ELOQUENT *a.* [EL uh KWUNT] persuasive by means of one's speech, having a way with words, articulate. *There are many eloquent speakers in Washington.* SYN. persuasive, articulate, fluent, forceful, having a way with words, expressive, having a command of the language, silver-tongued, smooth, stirring, cogent, vivid, pointed. ANT. *inarticulate, tongue-tied, stumbling.*

elucidate *v.* clarify, make clear, explain, illustrate, illuminate, *shed light on, simplify, spell out, interpret. ANT. *obfuscate, confuse, muddy.*

elude *v.* avoid, evade, escape, *give the slip, dodge, *lose, *throw off the scent, get away, circumvent, baffle, thwart, foil. ANT. *confront, meet, face.*

elusive *a.* evasive, slippery, shifty, hard to catch, fleeting, eely, baffling, cagey, puzzling, wily.

EMACIATED *a.* [i MAY shee ay ted] lean and scrawny, as from starvation. *Many deer become emaciated through the winter.* SYN. lean, thin, scrawny, wasted, malnourished, anorexic, bony, skinny, skeletal, gaunt, raw-boned, drawn, wizened, hollow-eyed. ANT. *beefy, plump, fat, obese.*

emanate *v.* issue, proceed, spring, arise, appear, exude, come forth, originate, flow, discharge.

EMANCIPATE *v.* [i MAN suh pate] to free. *Lincoln wished to emancipate the slaves.* SYN. free, liberate, release, deliver, loose, unchain, unburden, enfranchise, manumit, save, rescue. ANT. *enslave, fetter, subjugate.*

emancipation *n.* freedom, liberation, release, delivery, manumission, enfranchisement. ANT. *enslavement, subjugation.*

EMASCULATE *v.* [i MASS kyuh late] to castrate or weaken; to take away a man's strength. *Kryptonite had the power to emasculate Superman.* SYN. castrate, weaken, effeminate, debilitate, enervate, render ineffectual, soften, *take the teeth out of. ANT. *strengthen, invigorate.*

EMBARGO *n.* [em BAR go] a government-imposed prohibition on the shipment or receipt of foreign commercial freight. *The president imposed an embargo on French wine.* SYN. prohibition, restriction, ban, blockage, proscription, stoppage, restaint, check, interdiction.

embark *v.* **1.** BOARD get on. **2.** COMMENCE set out, start, venture, undertake, take up, broach, launch, enter, initiate.

embarrass *v.* disconcert, make ill-at-ease, make self-conscious, abash, shame, mortify, chagrin, fluster, discompose, fluster, faze.

embarrassing *a.* disconcerting, humiliating, awkward, mortifying, uncomfortable, discomfiting, shaming, discomposing, ticklish, touchy, undignifying.

embarrassment *n.* humiliation, sname, chagrin, discomposure, mortification, discomfort, self-consciousness, *egg on one's face, uneasiness, pudency.

WORD FIND

descriptive: cheeks burn; color deeply; toes curl in one's shoes; feel hot and foolish; feel the blood rush to one's face; squirm/wriggle with embarrassment; eyes range the floor, searching desperately for a hole to crawl into; eyelids bat self-consciously; cringe inwardly; smile sheepishly; splutter with embarrassment; stammer self-consciously; ears flush scarlet

embarrassed smiling: dry grins

embarrassing occurrence: contretemps

embellish *v.* enhance, adorn, ornament, decorate, garnish, elaborate, beautify, touch up, fix up, embroider, play up, exaggerate, overstate.

embellishment *n.* enhancement, ornamentation, adornment, decoration, beautification, embroidery, exaggeration, enrichment.

embers *n.* ashes, coals, cinders, clinkers, sparks.

EMBEZZLE *v.* [em BEZ ul] to steal, especially when in a position of trust, to commit fraud. *The accountant was jailed for embezzling church funds.* SYN. steal, defraud, misappropriate, cheat, defalcate, purloin, *have one's hand in the till, filch, swindle, peculate, *cook the books.

embittered *a.* bitter, resentful, hostile, disaffected, sour, disillusioned, spiteful, cynical, irritated, sore, rankled.

emblazon *v.* ornament, color, paint, decorate, embellish.

emblem *n.* symbol, badge, design, representation, crest, trademark, coat of arms, colors, insignia, mark, attribute, image.

emblematic *a.* symbolic, representative.

embodiment *n.* representation, personification, incarnation, materialization, manifestation, realization, incorporation, exemplification.

embody *v.* represent, personify, incarnate, manifest, realize, stand for, incorporate, materialize, substantiate, symbolize.

embolden *v.* encourage, hearten, buoy, reassure, puff up, invigorate, boost, psyche up, *give pep talk. ANT. *frighten, cow, unnerve.*

embrace *v.* **1.** HUG squeeze, hold, clasp, enfold, clinch, grab, envelop, cuddle, snuggle, *bear hug. **2.** ENCOMPASS take in, include, cover, embody, comprehend, incorporate. **3.** ADOPT take up, espouse, welcome, accept, seize. ANT. *2. exclude, omit. 3. reject, spurn, shun.*

EMBROIDER *v.* [em BROY dur] to exaggerate or embellish by stretching the truth, to add untruthful details. *Some tabloids embroi-*

der the truth. SYN. exaggerate, embellish, stretch the truth, fib, varnish, aggrandize, puff up, overstate, *hype, *blow out of proportion, *make a mountain out of a molehill, fabricate, invent.

embroil v. disturb, entangle, trouble, mix up, involve, snarl, muddle, set at odds, rouse, *fan the flames.

embryonic a. rudimentary, elementary, beginning, immature, undeveloped, initial, fetal.

emend v. improve, correct, right, fix, edit, redact, revise.

emerge v. appear, arise, issue, come forth, surface, materialize, crop up, come out, spring, originate, emanate.

emergency n. crisis, exigency, trouble, urgency, plight, contingency, pinch, *pickle, bind, difficulty, clutch.

eminence n. **1.** POSITION rank, fame, standing, importance, prominency, distinction, greatness, repute, celebrity, station, loftiness. **2.** HILL rise, elevation, height, prominence, peak, summit, ridge, high ground.

EMINENT a. [EM uh nunt] high-ranking and distinguished, noteworthy. An eminent authority on economics predicted a downturn. SYN. high-ranking, distinguished, noteworthy, famous, renowned, exalted, excellent, esteemed, celebrated, prominent, illustrious, outstanding, great, dominant. ANT. little-known, obscure, undistinguished.

emissary n. representative, messenger, agent, ambassador, envoy, go-between, courier, deputy, attache.

emission n. discharge, emanation, expulsion, ejection, issuance, diffusion, transmission, outpouring, leaking.

emit v. discharge, emanate, expel, eject, issue, diffuse, outpour, leak, exhale, secrete, exude, excrete, leak.

emollient n. balm, salve, lotion, ointment, lenitive.

emollient a. soothing, softening, relieving, assuasive, healing, palliative.

emotion n. feeling, state of mind, sentiment, passion, gut reaction, sensation, heart, drive.

emotional a. **1.** FEELING sensitive, passionate, reactive, sentimental, sympathetic, ardent, susceptible, excitable, fervent, fiery, histrionic, temperamental. **2.** MOVING soul-stirring, touching, poignant, heartrending, heartfelt, disturbing. ANT. apathetic, unfeeling, impassive.

emotionless a. apathetic, cold, numb, unfeeling, indifferent, stony, stoical, insensate, dis-

passionate, heartless, matter-of-fact.

empathize a. identify with, relate to, understand, comprehend, sympathize, stand in one's shoes, *be on the same wavelength.

EMPATHY n. [EM puh thee] understanding or sharing of another's feelings, thoughts, etc. As a basketball official, I have a certain amount of empathy for baseball umpires. SYN. understanding, sympathy, accord, comprehension, rapport, communion, affinity, fellow feeling.

emperor n. ruler, sovereign, monarch, czar, dictator, empress.

emphasis n. stress, accent, underscoring, importance, force, weight, significance, prominence, highlight, attention.

emphasize v. stress, accent, underscore, highlight, accentuate, play up, spotlight, punctuate, italicize, bring to the fore. ANT. downplay, play down, soften.

EMPHATIC a. [em FAT ik] done with emphasis. He protested emphatically. SYN. insistent, forceful, impassioned, passionate, vigorous, pointed, stressed, strong, earnest, compelling, striking, vehement. ANT. vague, halfhearted.

empire n. dominion, realm, rule, kingdom, domain, sovereignty.

EMPIRICAL a. [em PIR i kul] based on observation or experience, not theory. The empirical evidence backed the scientists' claims. SYN. experiential, experimental, observed, practical, pragmatic, firsthand, factual.

employ v. **1.** MAKE USE OF use, practice, utilize, apply, put to use. **2.** ENGAGE THE SERVICES OF contract for, retain, hire.

employee n. worker, personnel, staffer, hired hand, jobholder, wage earner, *company man/woman, *working stiff, *slave.

employer n. boss, manager, owner, proprietor, chief executive officer (CEO), director, contractor, *big cheese, overseer, *front office, corporation, company, firm.

employment n. **1.** USE utilization, application, operation, usage, exercise. **2.** WORK job, position, occupation, employ, business, trade, field, profession, vocation, situation.

WORD FIND

employing more workers than is necessary: featherbedding

favoritism in which family members and friends are hired first: nepotism

emporium n. marketplace, store, trade center, mart, bazaar, mall.

EMPOWER v. [em POW ur] to give or invest

with power, legal or otherwise, to enable. *Empower the homeless to do for themselves.* SYN. enable, authorize, vest, permit, warrant, allow, entrust, validate, commission, accredit.

emptiness *n.* void, vacuity, vacuum, nothingness, space, vacancy, desolation, blankness, hole.

empty *a.* **1.** VACANT void, hollow, bare, vacuous, barren, desolate, blank, deserted, abandoned, devoid, stark, evacuated. **2.** MEANINGLESS purposeless, hollow, futile, ineffective, idle, worthless, cheap, insubstantial, vapid, vain. ANT. *1. full, crowded, replete. 2. meaningful, fruitful, effective.*

empty-headed *a.* brainless, witless, *brain-drained, ignorant. SEE STUPID

emulate *v.* copy, imitate, rival, model after, match, vie, compete, ape, contend, challenge, *take after, mimic.

enable *v.* empower, capacitate, allow, endow, authorize, invest, qualify, warrant, sanction, permit, license. ANT. *hinder, block, prevent.*

enact *v.* legislate, pass, ratify, sanction, decree, effectuate, institute, establish, order, ordain. ANT. *veto, repeal, reject, table.*

ENAMORED *a.* [i NAM urd] in love, charmed. *She is enamored with Hawaii.* SYN. in love, charmed, captivated, infatuated, enthralled, bewitched, entranced, taken, smittened, fascinated, *stuck on.

enchant *v.* mesmerize, bewitch, spellbind, charm, captivate, cast a spell on, *sweep off feet, allure, entrance, hypnotize, beguile.

enchanting *a.* mesmerizing, bewitching, spellbinding, charming, captivating, alluring, entrancing, hypnotic, beguiling, enthralling.

enchantress *n.* seductress, sorceress, witch, charmer, siren, *femme fatale, *Circe.

encircle *v.* encompass, surround, circle, circumscribe, band, ring, girdle, envelop, hoop, wreath.

enclose *v.* **1.** SHUT IN surround, *hem in, pen, confine, imprison, encompass, fence off, circumscribe, corral. **2.** INSERT enter, put in, include, add.

encompass *v.* **1.** SURROUND circle, encircle, circumscribe, ring, envelop. **2.** INCLUDE contain, comprehend, embody, comprise, take in, cover, embrace. ANT. *exclude, omit.*

encounter *n.* meeting, confrontation, conjunction, brush.

encounter *v.* meet, confront, come face to face, happen upon, chance upon, cross paths, see, accost, face, bump into.

encourage *v.* hearten, embolden, spur, inspire, rally, reassure, root for, *buck up, *psyche up, foster, steel, fortify, support, cheer, buoy, *give a shot in the arm. ANT. *discourage, dishearten, *take the wind out of one's sails, deflate.*

encouragement *n.* support, assuring, help, buoying, heartening, *bucking up, boost, reassurance, *shot in the arm, *pep talk, stimulus, lift, inspiration, cheer, fortitude, *psyching up, backing. ANT. *discouragement, disheartening, deflation.*

ENCROACH *v.* [en KROCH] to intrude or trespass, to move into another's domain. *Humans continue to encroach upon wildlife habitat.* SYN. intrude, trespass, invade, infringe, *horn in, usurp, *make inroads, interlope, impose upon, overstep the bounds, infiltrate.

encumber *v.* burden, weigh down, hinder, impede, obstruct, hold up, cramp, saddle, oppress, handicap, hamper, handicap. ANT. *free, facilitate, lighten.*

encumbrance *n.* burden, weight, hindrance, impediment, obstruction, saddle, handicap, millstone, cross.

encyclopedic *a.* broad, extensive, comprehensive, complete, diverse, wide-ranging, catholic, general, exhaustive, thorough. ANT. *limited, specific, narrow.*

end *n.* **1.** LIMIT terminus, borderline, extremity, boundary, edge, extent, tip, point, pale. **2.** FINISH completion, conclusion, close, stop, cessation, finale, finis, termination, expiration, windup, consummation. **3.** PURPOSE aim, intention, object, reason, point, objective, motivation. **4.** RESULT outcome, consequence, effect, upshot. ANT. *2. start, beginning, opening.* SEE DEATH

end *v.* stop, finish, cease, wrap up, conclude, close, terminate, wind down, consummate, expire, discontinue, desist, drop. ANT. *start, begin, open.*

endanger *v.* imperil, jeopardize, expose, tempt fate, put at risk, compromise, hazard, venture, threaten. ANT. *safeguard, protect, defend.*

endearing *a.* lovable, charming, captivating, winning, adorable, sweet, dear, cuddly.

endeavor *n.* attempt, effort, try, striving, venture, enterprise, undertaking, trial, *shot, crack, *whack, exertion.

endeavor *v.* attempt, try, strive, venture, make an effort, struggle, tackle, undertake, essay, labor, *have a go, *take a crack at.

endless *a.* interminable, neverending, eternal,

infinite, forever, unending, ceaseless, perpetual, continuous, incessant, relentless, *sisyphean, everlasting. ANT. *finite, limited, temporary.*

endorse *v.* sanction, approve, recommend, support, back, back up, vouch for, certify, advocate, stand behind, warrant, *give one's stamp of approval. ANT. *reject, repudiate.*

endorsement *n.* sanction, approval, recommendation, support, backing, certification, advocacy, warranty, *stamp of approval, authorization, okay.

endow *v.* provide, grant, fund, contribute, equip, bestow, bequeath, enrich, favor, furnish, supply, appoint, vest. ANT. *divest, deprive.*

endowment *n.* **1.** GIFT grant, contribution, bestowal, bequest, funding, donation, provision, subsidy, benefaction. **2.** ATTRIBUTE natural gift, genius, quality, talent, asset, aptitude.

endurance *n.* stamina, fortitude, perseverance, grit, *guts, *stick-to-it-iveness, backbone, staying power, tenacity, *starch, *moxie, *heart, strength, hardiness.

endure *v.* **1.** BEAR hold out, live through, withstand, tolerate, *stick it out, brave, suffer, weather, stand, *ride out, take it, *go through the mill, *hang in, brook. **2.** CONTINUE persist, last, abide, perdure, sustain, go on, outlast, survive, prevail. ANT. *1. give out, cave in, collapse, quit. 2. peter out, die, end.*

enemy *n.* foe, adversary, antagonist, opponent, rival, villain, contestant, hostile party, contender, nemesis, archenemy, *bad guy. "[One who] strengthens our nerves and sharpens our skill." — Edmund Burke. "An injured friend." — Thomas Jefferson.

energetic *a.* vigorous, peppy, active, lively, industrious, *zippy, tireless, spirited, full of vim and vigor, *bright-eyed and bushy-tailed, vibrant, sprightly, *high octane. ANT. *tired, slothful, lethargic.*

energize *v.* activate, invigorate, stimulate, spark, enliven, electrify, pep up, refresh, turn on, *pump up. ANT. *exhaust, sap, tire.*

energy *n.* power, force, steam, strength, juice, vigor, zip, *get-up-and- go, vitality, pep, zest, verve, life, punch.

ENERVATE *v.* [EN ur vate] to weaken or debilitate. *Smoking tends to enervate.* SYN. weaken, debilitate, sap, enfeeble, tire, exhaust, wear out, prostrate, fatigue, devitalize. ANT. *fortify, strengthen, invigorate.*

enfeeble *v.* weaken, deplete, enervate, debilitate, deplete, sap, emasculate, fatigue, exhaust, diminish, *take the starch out of.

enfilade *n.* barrage, gunfire, rake, sweeping fire.

enfold *v.* embrace, wrap.

enforce *v.* compel, impose, press, make, crack down, coerce, implement, oblige, *clamp down, prosecute, *strong-arm, bully.

enforcement *n.* compulsion, imposition, press, crackdown, coercion, implementation, obligation, prosecution, *strong-arm tactics, bullying, control, duress.

engage *v.* **1.** CONTRACT FOR employ, hire, enlist, commission, sign on, retain, enroll, secure, appoint, charter. **2.** ENGROSS occupy, captivate, absorb, hold, grip, rivet, arrest, interest, preoccupy, fascinate. **3.** PLEDGE promise, bind, commit, obligate, contract, betroth, affiance.

engaged *a.* **1.** BETROTHED pledged, spoken for, affianced, committed, plighted, bound. **2.** BUSY occupied, working, involved, employed, preoccupied, *tied up, operating, diverted. ANT. *2. idle, free.*

engagement *n.* **1.** BETROTHAL pledge, promise, commitment, plight, troth. "In war, a battle. In love, the salubrious calm that precedes the hostilities." — Gideon Wurdz. **2.** APPOINTMENT date, meeting, commitment, tryst. **3.** BATTLE encounter, combat, conflict, confrontation, skirmish, action.

engaging *a.* charming, pleasing, attractive, magnetic, agreeable, sweet, appealing, winning, likable, fetching, captivating, pleasant. ANT. *unattractive, repellant, unappealing.*

ENGENDER *v.* [en JEN dur] to bring about; cause. *Understanding will engender peace.* SYN. produce, bring about, cause, give rise to, effect, arouse, stimulate, generate, create, spawn, breed.

engine *n.* motor, turbine, dynamo, power plant, powerhouse, *workhorse, generator, mechanism. SEE MOTOR

engineer *n.* builder, manager, architect, designer, planner, inventor, operator.

engineer *v.* plan, devise, scheme, arrange, swing, set up, direct, *rig, mastermind, *call the shots, finagle, concoct.

engorged *a.* congested, full, filled, swollen, distended, bloated.

engrave *v.* etch, cut, incise, carve, inscribe, scratch, chisel, imprint, ingrain.

engrossed *a.* absorbed, rapt, lost in, riveted, involved, engaged, captivated, enthralled, deep in, *wrapped up in, gripped, fascinated.

engrossing *a.* absorbing, riveting, involving,

engaging, captivating, enthralling, gripping, fascinating, occupying. ANT. *boring, dull, tiresome.*

engulf *v.* surround, swallow up, overwhelm, overflow, envelop, enclose, deluge, submerge, inundate, bury.

enhance *v.* augment, better, improve, strengthen, embellish, complement, raise, increase, beautify, aggrandize, magnify. ANT. *diminish, strip, weaken.*

ENIGMA *n.* [ih NIG muh] a riddle, mystery or puzzle. *The origin of the universe remains an enigma.* SYN. riddle, mystery, puzzle, conundrum, question, secret, perplexity, *tough nut to crack, *mind-boggler, unknown.

enigmatic *a.* mysterious, puzzling, perplexing, questionable, unknown, mind-boggling, baffling, incomprehensible, unfathomable, inscrutable, bewildering, unexplainable. ANT. *known, obvious, clear, plain.*

enjoin *v.* **1.** COMMAND impose, order, dictate, prescribe, demand, ordain, decree, charge. **2.** PROHIBIT forbid, ban, proscribe, outlaw, interdict. ANT. *2. allow, permit.*

enjoy *v.* take pleasure in, delight in, relish, appreciate, revel in, savor, luxuriate in, *eat up, *get a kick out of.

enjoyable *a.* delightful, satisfying, fun, pleasing, pleasant, amusing, entertaining, delicious, gratifying, *a lot of laughs, wonderful. ANT. *miserable, rotten, unpleasant.*

enjoyment *n.* pleasure, delight, fun, amusement, relish, happiness, entertainment, gratification, satisfaction, *laughs, diversion, gusto, recreation, delectation.

enlarge *v.* increase, expand, extend, spread, augment, magnify, broaden, lengthen, stretch, inflate, grow, swell, blow up, branch out, snowball. ANT. *shrink, diminish, lessen, decrease.*

enlargement *n.* increase, expansion, extension, spreading, augmentation, magnification, broadening, lengthening, stretch, inflation, growth, swelling, snowballing. ANT. *shrinkage, decrease, lessening.*

ENLIGHTEN *v.* [en LITE un] to inform or instruct. *Obedience school will enlighten you and your dog.* SYN. inform, instruct, fill in, teach, edify, make one aware, apprise, school, illuminate, indoctrinate, ground, *open one's eyes. ANT. *put one in the dark, cloud, obfuscate, mystify.*

enlightened *a.* informed, aware, learned, educated, knowledgeable, apprised, grounded, knowing, open-minded, cultivated, *hip.

enlist *v.* sign up, enroll, draft, recruit, induct, conscript, join, volunteer, muster, register, engage.

enliven *v.* stimulate, spark, animate, *jumpstart, excite, invigorate, charge up, electrify, energize, vitalize, inflame, kindle. ANT. *dampen, extinguish, quiet.*

en masse *n.* together, as a body, in a group, jointly, as one, ensemble. ANT. *individually, separately.*

enmesh *v.* entangle, catch, snarl, trap, knot, engage.

ENMITY *n.* [EN muh tee] hatred, deep hostility. *There was obvious enmity between the divorcing couple.* SYN. hatred, hostility, antagonism, animosity, malevolence, acrimony, spite, bitterness, loathing, venom, malice, *bad blood. ANT. *love, adoration, affection.*

ENNUI *n.* [AN WEE] boredom and the listlessness that accompanies it. *The students suffered from a severe case of ennui.* SYN. boredom, listlessness, restlessness, languor, weariness, lassitude, malaise, blahs, tedium, doldrums. ANT. *excitement.*

enormity *n.* **1.** WICKEDNESS outrageousness, evil, monstrousness, atrocity, viciousness, ferocity, savagery, ruthlessness. **2.** HUGENESS largeness, vastness, size, bulk, greatness, magnitude, prodigiousness. ANT. *1. morality, goodness, virtue. 2. smallness, triviality.*

enormous *a.* huge, gigantic, stupendous, immense, vast, gargantuan, mammoth, Brobdingnagian, prodigious, massive, astronomical, colossal, titanic, monstrous, towering. ANT. *tiny, pint-sized, pocket-sized, diminutive.*

enough *a.* sufficient, ample, plenty, adequate, acceptable, satisfactory, abundant. ANT. *short, wanting, scant, deficient.*

enquire *v.* look into, explore, query. SEE INQUIRE

enquiry *n.* inquest, probe. SEE INQUIRY

enrage *v.* incense, anger, infuriate, inflame, *piss off, madden, *make blood boil, *burn up, *tee off *get Irish up, rile. SEE ANGER, ANGRY

enraged *a.* furious, incensed, irate, angry, infuriated, inflamed, mad, *gone ballistic, *pissed, *boiling.

enrich *v.* enhance, add, upgrade, improve, endow, cultivate, embellish, aggrandize, *sweeten, refine, *beef up. ANT. *degenerate, cheapen, impoverish.*

enroll *v.* register, record, enter, enlist, sign up, join, matriculate, admit.

ensconce *v.* settle, fix, curl up, nestle, seat,

place, conceal, shelter, hide, cover.

ensemble *n.* **1.** UNIT collection, group, whole, aggregate. **2.** OUTFIT *getup, suit, coordinates. **3.** ENTERTAINMENT GROUP trio, quartet, group, orchestra, band, troupe, company, repertory.

enshrine *v.* cherish, sanctify, exalt, consecrate, hallow, deify, revere, immortalize, glorify.

enshroud *v.* shroud, cover, veil, conceal, cloak, mask.

ensign *n.* flag, standard, banner, pennant, streamer, insignia.

enslave *v.* subjugate, dominate, control, enthrall, indenture, subject, yoke, fetter, master, *jackboot into submission, coerce, subdue.

ensnare *v.* snare, catch, trap, bag, snag, net, entrap, entangle, take in.

ensue *v.* follow, succeed, result, come to pass, come out of, derive, spring from.

ensuing *a.* following, succeeding, resulting, subsequent, consequent, next, after.

ensure *v.* assure, make sure, guarantee, warranty, insure, certify, secure, safeguard, confirm.

entail *v.* involve, necessitate, require, call for, occasion, include, contain, incorporate.

entangle *v.* enmesh, tangle, snarl, entrap, involve, embroil, mix up, rope in, intertwine, trap, catch up, *suck in.

entanglement *n.* knot, snare, difficulty, problem, quandary, predicament, embroilment, web, mess, involvement, mix-up.

entente *n.* understanding, agreement, accord, rapprochement, settlement, arrangement, conciliation.

enter *v.* **1.** COME OR GO IN gain entree, make an entrance, infiltrate, intrude, set foot in, penetrate, *burst in, *breeze in, trespass. **2.** BEGIN start, commence, set out, launch. **3.** JOIN enlist in, enroll, embark on, sign up. **4.** RECORD register, log in, sign up, post, inscribe. ANT. *1. exit, leave.*

enterprise *n.* **1.** UNDERTAKING venture, project, job, campaign, adventure, concern, scheme, operation, task, endeavor, cause, business, crusade. **2.** EFFORT initiative, drive, determination, ambition, gumption, intensity, aggressiveness, industry, boldness, hustle. ANT. *2. sloth, laziness.*

enterprising *a.* ambitious, industious, aggressive, bold, venturesome, audacious, earnest, resourceful, driving, hustling, inventive, energetic. ANT. *lazy, indolent, slothful, passive.*

entertain *v.* **1.** AMUSE interest, divert, engross, engage, absorb, rivet, beguile, *wow, pique, stimulate, enthrall. **2.** TO SHOW HOSPITALITY TO receive, host, accommodate, *wine and dine, feed, treat, regale, fete, have guests, give a party. **3.** CONSIDER think about, ponder, contemplate, muse over, deliberate, mind, weigh, heed.

entertainment *n.* amusement, diversion, recreation, fun, distraction, *ball, *laughs, enjoyment, merrymaking, pastime, divertissement, good time, *high time.

enthrall *v.* captivate, hold spellbound, charm, fascinate, rivet, beguile, bewitch, mesmerize, entrance, thrill, hypnotize, transfix.

enthusiasm *n.* eagerness, keenness, feeling, fervor, interest, zeal, passion, vivacity, ardor, relish, exuberance, verve, spirit, elan. "Energy that boils over and runs down the side of the pot." — Arnold Glasow. "A distemper of youth." — Ambrose Bierce. "Fire under control." — Norman Vincent Peale. "The great hill-climber." — Elbert Hubbard. ANT. *apathy, indifference, passivity.*

enthusiast *n.* zealot, fan, devotee, aficionado, fanatic, disciple, addict, buff, *freak, *nut, *bug.

enthusiastic *a.* eager, keen, fervent, interested, zealous, passionate, ardent, exuberant, spirited, wholehearted, avid, hot, rabid. ANT. *apathetic, indifferent, halfhearted.*

entice *v.* tempt, lure, tantalize, allure, inveigle, seduce, bait, draw, attract, persuade, cajole, coax.

entire *a.* total, whole, complete, full, aggregate, all, thorough, undivided, uncut, intact, unmitigated, uncompromised. ANT. *partial, incomplete.*

entitle *v.* authorize, allow, qualify, license, warrant, empower, enable, sanction.

entity *n.* being, thing, it, individual, soul, unit, existence, life, object, creature, essence.

entomb *v.* bury, inter, sepulcher, inhume, *lay to rest.

entourage *n.* attendants, train, followers, retinue, staff, court, cortege, escort, bodyguards, *toadies.

entrails *n.* intestine, viscera, internal organs, guts, bowels, innards, vitals.

entrance *n.* **1.** DOORWAY ingress, portal, access, gate, inlet, porch, vestibule, foyer, portico, threshold. **2.** ADMISSION admittance, ingress, passage, entry, approach, access.

entrance *v.* captivate, bewitch, charm, hypnotize, mesmerize, spellbind, enchant, enthrall, allure.

entrant n. competitor, contestant, entry, player, opponent.

entrap v. lure, allure, tempt, entice, *suck in, *set up, *lead on, trap, bait, inveigle, implicate, incriminate, nail.

entreat v. implore, beseech, beg, plead, petition, appeal, supplicate, pray.

entreaty n. plea, appeal, supplication, solicitation, prayer, bid, cry, request, petition, imploration.

entreé n. 1. ADMITTANCE access. SEE ENTRY 2. DISH main course, meal, supper, dinner, *piece de resistance.

entrenched a. fixed, secured, established, deep-rooted, deep-seated, embedded, ingrained, ensconced, dug in, grounded, settled.

ENTREPRENEUR n. [on truh pruh NUR] one who starts and runs her own business. *Several entrepreneurs moved in to revitalize the downtown district.* SYN. businessman/woman, industrialist, go-getter, producer, promoter, impresario, undertaker, enterpriser, capitalist, tycoon, venture capitalist, magnate, employer.

entrust v. commit, confide, turn over, consign, charge, vest, assign, delegate, invest, hand over, authorize.

entry n. 1. ENTRANCE access, door, ingress, inlet, passageway, portal, opening, gate, foyer, approach. 2. ADMITTANCE admission, access, entree; intrusion, trespass.

entwine v. braid, intertwine, wind. SEE TWIST

enumerate v. count off, list, number, tally, itemize, calculate, sum, compute, inventory, name, run down, tick off.

enunciate v. pronounce, articulate, express, utter, intone, voice, mouth, accentuate, modulate, carefully frame each word, inflect.

envelop v. enclose, encase, surround, engulf, enfold, contain, sheathe, wrap, shroud, overlay.

envelope n. wrapper, cover, case, jacket, sheathe, casing, skin, shell, hull, mailer, *jiffy bag.

envious a. covetous, jealous, resentful, begrudging, yearning, *drooling over, green with envy, emulous, discontent.

environment n. surroundings, habitat, setting, environs, milieu, domain, terrain, turf, neighborhood, territory, *stomping grounds, world, atmosphere, climate, element, medium.

environmentalist n. conservationist, ecologist, naturalist, *tree hugger.

environs n. surroundings, environment, vicinity, neighborhood, territory, outskirts, suburbs.

envisage v. visualize, conceive of, see, imagine, envision, conceptualize, picture, fancy, think of.

ENVOY n. [ON voy] a representative or messenger. *The United States sent a special envoy to its embassy in Iran.* SYN. representative, messenger, agent, emissary, courier, delegate, diplomat, ambassador, attache, minister.

envy n. covetousness, jealousy, grudgingness, rivalry, *green-eyed monster, resentment, spite, lusting, wanting, longing, greed. "The sincerest form of flattery."—John C. Collins. "The green sickness."—Shakespeare. "Self-made hurts."—ShaikhSaadi. "The tax which all distinction must pay."—Emerson.

envy v. covet, begrudge, grudge, resent, be green with envy, be jealous of, lust after, want, desire, *eat one's heart out, *drool over.

eon n. age, eternity, ages, years.

EPHEMERAL a. [i FEM ur al] lasting only a short time. *Fads are usually ephemeral.* SYN. short-lived, transient, brief, fleeting, temporary, transitory, of short duration, evanescent, momentary, *gone in a heartbeat. ANT. *long-lived, permanent, everlasting.*

epic a. huge, grand, legendary, mythical, exaggerated, fabulous, Homeric, heroic, majestic, sublime.

epicure n. gourmet, epicurian, gourmand, gastronome, connoisseur, glutton, bon vivant, hedonist.

epidemic n. spread, contagion, infection, disease, plague, pestilence, endemic, pandemic.

epidemic a. spreading, contagious, infectious, catching, widespread, endemic, pandemic, rampant, rife, prevalent. ANT. *local, limited, confined.*

epigram n. observation, witticism, aphorism, quip, adage, slogan, bon mot, pun, motto, saying. "A light vessel carrying a heavy load."—Jacob Klatzkin. "A dash of wit and a jigger of wisdom, flavored with surprise."—Elbert Hubbard.

epilepsy n. seizure disorder, catalepsy, convulsions, fits.

WORD FIND

major seizure and loss of consciousness: grand mal

medication: Dilantin

momentary unconsciousness without con-

vulsions: petite mal
symptom of impending seizure: aura

epilogue *n.* afterword, conclusion, last word, follow-up, postscript, addendum, swan song, coda.

epiphany *n.* appearance, manifestation, incarnation, realization, insight.

episode *n.* incident, event, occurrence, happening, occasion, experience, action, installment, chapter, part.

episodic *a.* intermittent, sporadic, segmented, irregular, sequential.

epistle *n.* communication, message, missive. SEE LETTER

epitaph *n.* inscription, memorial, legend, commemoration, hic jacet, *last word. "An inscription showing that virtues acquired by death have a retroactive effect." — Ambrose Bierce.

epithet *n.* nickname, name, label, pet name, appellation, designation, tag, sobriquet.

EPITOME *n.* [I PIT uh mee] the perfect representation of something. *Michael Jordan is the epitome of a great athlete.* SYN. representation, archetype, example, embodiment, typification, ultimate, quintessence, *last word, model.

epitomize *v.* typify, represent, exemplify, embody.

epoch *n.* era, period, time, age, span, interval.

equable *a.* even, steady, uniform, unvarying, consistent, regular, unchanging, constant, stable, serene, tranquil.

equal *n.* peer, counterpart, equivalent, compeer, coequal, double, fellow, match, alter ego.

equal *v.* match, accord with, line up with, align, correspond, parallel, *stack up against, mirror.

equal *a.* **1.** EVEN same, identical, balanced, uniform, alike, commensurate, parallel, *even Stephen, level, matching, comparable, *on common footing, *on a level playing field. ANT. *unequal, uneven, dissimilar, disparate.*

equality *n.* parity, par, sameness, equivalence, likeness, evenness, balance, uniformity, fairness. "The centre and circumference of all democracy." — Herman Melville. ANT. *inequality, disparity, unfairness, injustice.*

EQUANIMITY *n.* [EE kwuh NIM i tee] composure, calm. *He handled the crisis with equanimity.* SYN. composure, calmness, sangfroid, serenity, nonchalance, coolness, placidity, aplomb, tranquility, poise, presence of mind. ANT. *hysteria, panic.*

equate *v.* liken, associate, compare, relate, parallel.

EQUILIBRIUM *n.* [EE kwuh LIB ree um] balance, stability, composure. *The disaster challenged her equilibrium.* SYN. balance, stability, equanimity, calmness, levelheadedness, poise, sangfroid, composure, aplomb. ANT. *instability.*

equip *v.* outfit, furnish, rig, supply, gird, fit out, accoutre, arm, gear, appoint, *heel, provision.

equipment *n.* gear, apparatus, accessories, furnishings, supplies, contrivances, tools, rigging, trappings, appliances, fittings, tackle, machinery, paraphernalia.

EQUITABLE *a.* [EK wi tuh bul] fair, just. *An equitable arrangement was not possible.* SYN. fair, just, equal, impartial, square, evenhanded, proportionate, honest, *even Stephen, unbiased, rightful, proper. ANT. *inequitable, unfair, unjust, partial.*

equity *n.* fairness, justice, impartiality, evenhandedness, honesty, fair play, objectivity, neutrality, rightness.

equivalent *n.* equal, counterpart, same, twin, match, mirror image, double, fellow, peer, *carbon copy.

equivalent *a.* equal, same, alike, synonymous, tantamount, analogous, identical, even, commensurate, *six of one, half dozen of another, correlative, comparable.

equivocal *a.* ambiguous, vague, duplicitous, uncertain, indefinite, unclear, misleading, evasive, undecided, hazy, indeterminate. ANT. *definite, clear, plain.*

EQUIVOCATE *v.* [i KWIV uh kate] to use vague or ambiguous language, usually to evade. *The politician handled the tough question by equivocating.* SYN. hedge, evade, waffle, hem and haw, dodge, *weasel out, *beat around the bush, *cloud the issue, doubletalk, mince words, sidestep, *dance around the issue, *perform a verbal hatdance around.

era *n.* period, time, age, epoch, days, interval, span.

eradicate *v.* annihilate, uproot, erase, remove, eliminate, extirpate, exterminate, destroy, expunge, abolish, do away with, obliterate.

erase *v.* rub off, expunge, remove, wipe out, delete, efface, strike, obliterate, nullify, scratch, blue-pencil, wash out.

erect *v.* construct, build, assemble, *slap together, fabricate, raise, frame, pitch, put up, devise, form.

erect *a.* upright, straight up, standing, perpendicular, vertical.

erection *n.* **1.** CONSTRUCTION building, assembly, fabrication, framework, formation, structure, edifice. **2.** TUMESCENCE *hard-on, *blue-steeler, *woody, *boner. SEE PENIS

ergo *adv.* consequently, therefore, thus, accordingly.

erode *v.* wear away, corrode, waste, gnaw, consume, eat away, abrade, disintegrate, deteriorate.

EROGENOUS *a.* [i ROJ uh nus] pertaining to parts of the body that can be aroused by sexual stimulation. *Erogenous zones are rich in nerve endings.* SYN. erotogenic, erotic, sexual, amatory, sensuous, sensual, *hot, rousing, X-rated, libidinal, carnal.

erosion *n.* wear, deterioration, corrosion, disintegration, destruction, attrition, abrasion, wasting.

erotic *a.* amatory, sexual, carnal, lusty, sensual, erogenous, romantic, libidinous, amorous, *hot, fleshly, *blue, titillating, spicey, *kinky, lascivious, passionate.

err *v.* make a mistake, miscalculate, misjudge, misstep, *slip up, blunder, *goof, *blow it, *muff, go astray, misconstrue, misunderstand.

errand *n.* task, mission, chore, trip, jaunt, *run.

errant *a.* wrong, deviant, erring, astray, *off the straight and narrow, wayward, wandering.

erratic *a.* straying, inconsistent, deviating, eccentric, irregular, unpredictable, unreliable, shifting, peculiar, wayward. ANT. *consistent, predictable, unchanging.*

ERRONEOUS *a.* [i RO nee us] mistaken, wrong. *The theory of green cheese on the moon is erroneous.* SYN. mistaken, wrong, incorrect, false, amiss, in error, inaccurate, *all wet, fallacious, unfounded, misguided, faulty. ANT. *correct, right, accurate.*

error *n.* mistake, inaccuracy, miscalculation, wrong, erratum, blunder, flub, *slip-up, boner, blooper, lapse, gaffe, wrongdoing, *howler, *boo-boo, misconception. "The best teachers."—James A. Froude.

ersatz *a.* substitute, artificial, synthetic, fake, simulated, man-made, imitation, *bogus, counterfeit.

erstwhile *a.* former, bygone, past, late.

ERUDITE *a.* [ER yoo DITE, ER oo DITE] highly educated, learned. *Erudite professors.* SYN. educated, scholarly, learned, intellectual, well-read, well-schooled, pedantic, highbrow, brainy, literate, well-versed, book-

ish. ANT. *uneducated, ignorant, illiterate, unschooled.*

erudition *n.* learning, scholarship, schooling, knowledge, book learning, refinement, wisdom, brains, education, higher education, pedantry, literacy.

erupt *v.* burst forth, explode, blow up, discharge, spout, rupture, gush, eject, emit, vent, spew, belch. SEE VOLCANO

eruption *n.* ejection, explosion, blowup, outburst, upheaval, expulsion, cataclysm, blast, detonation, gushing, outpouring, surge, paroxysm. SEE VOLCANO

escalate *v.* increase, rise, mount, climb, intensify, heighten, grow, enlarge, deepen, worsen. ANT. *decrease, shrink, lessen.*

escapade *n.* prank, adventure, antic, caper, practical joke, stunt, tomfoolery, high jinks, *shenanigans.

escape *n.* getaway, fast break, flight, evasion, *the slip, breakout, extrication, dodging, departure, desertion, *disappearing act.

escape *v.* get away, break out, extricate, loose, liberate, break, bolt, *fly the coop, cut loose, elude, dodge, abscond, elope, *take on the lam, skip, flee, decamp, disappear.

ESCHEW *v.* [es CHOO] stay away from, avoid, shun. *He has chosen to eschew smoking for health reasons.* SYN. avoid, shun, forego, abstain, swear off, forswear, renounce, give up, shy away from, refrain from, *turn up one's nose at. ANT. *take up, indulge in, embrace.*

escort *n.* attendant, chaperon, guardian, accompaniment, companion, body guard, guide, protector, retinue, cortege, entourage, convoy.

escort *v.* accompany, attend, protect, guide, usher, chaperone, guard, conduct, look after, convoy, defend.

Eskimo *n.* Innuit, Alaskan, Aleut, Yuit.

WORD FIND
boat: umiak, oomiac, kayak
boot: mukluk
dog: husky, malamute
hooded jacket: anorak, parka
house: igloo, topek
sledge: komatik

ESOTERIC *a.* [ES uh TER ik] understood by only a few, hard to understand. *Einstein's theories are esoteric.* SYN. abstruse, arcane, recondite, profound, deep, obscure, inscrutable, mysterious, incomprehensible, occult. ANT. *understandable, simple, obvious.*

especially *adv.* specifically, particularly, exclusively, expressly, principally, specially, chiefly.

espionage *n.* spying, intelligence, undercover work, surveillance, shadowing, tailing, wiretapping, *cloak and dagger, secret service.

esplanade *n.* walk, walkway, promenade, avenue, road, sidewalk, lane, mall.

ESPOUSE *v.* [e SPOUZ] to support or take up. *The group espouses environmetalism.* SYN. take up, support, advocate, adopt, abet, champion, embrace, back, stand up for, uphold, advance. ANT. *reject, detract, spurn.*

ESPRIT DE CORPS *n.* [es SPREE de COHR] group spirit or group loyalty, common bond between members of a group. *Good companies foster a certain esprit de corps.* SYN. group spirit, common bond, group loyalty, solidarity, team morale, camaraderie, fellowship, fraternity.

essay *n.* **1.** COMPOSITION article, paper, discourse, treatise, theme, think piece, editorial, exposition, study, thesis. "A loose sally of the mind." — Samuel Johnson. **2.** TRY attempt, endeavor, bid, trial, *shot, *whack, venture.

essay *v.* try, attempt, endeavor, bid, venture, *take a shot, *take a whack, *take a stab at.

essence *n.* **1.** HEART soul, core, kernel, distillate, marrow, root, spirit, *meat, *nittygritty, gist, nature, quintessence, crux. **2.** CONCENTRATE distillate, distillation, extract, elixir.

essential *n.* necessity, must, fundamental, basic, prerequisite, requirement, rudiment, cornerstone, indispensable element. ANT. *nonessential, extra.*

essential *a.* fundamental, important, vital, crucial, basic, prime, cardinal, necessary, elementary, indispensable, requisite. ANT. *incidental, unessential, peripheral, superfluous.*

establish *v.* **1.** SET UP found, institute, create, make, organize, build, construct, erect, enact, install, place, originate. **2.** PROVE demonstrate, substantiate, verify, authenticate, show, validate, corroborate.

establishment *n.* **1.** FOUNDING formation, instituting, creation, organization, construction, origin. **2.** INSTITUTION business, enterprise, concern, foundation, firm, company, corporation, association.

estate *n.* **1.** ASSETS property, holdings, resources, wealth, fortune, belongings, possessions. **2.** MANOR acreage, holdings, dominion, domain, residence, plantation.

esteem *n.* regard, respect, admiration, approval, repute, liking, affection, veneration, reverence. ANT. *disrespect, contempt, disdain.*

esteem *v.* regard highly, respect, look up to, admire, idolize, value, prize, appreciate, revere, venerate. ANT. *disrespect, disdain, scorn.*

estimable *a.* worthy, respectable, admirable, deserving, esteemed, honorable, reputable, valued, exemplary, revered. ANT. *disrespected, disregarded, scorned, disliked.*

estimate *n.* guess, *guesstimate, calculation, rough figure, educated guess, *ballpark figure, projection, evaluation, judgment.

estimate *v.* guess, *guesstimate, calculate, give a rough figure, give an educated guess, *give a ballpark figure, project, evaluate, judge, reckon, appraise, gauge, suppose.

ESTRANGED *a.* [e STRANJD] alienated, removed from the friendship of others. *The worker quit and soon became estranged from his colleagues.* SYN. alienated, removed, dissociated, separated, at odds, distant, disaffected, *turned off, hostile, *at arm's length.

etch *v.* engrave, carve, burn into, eat into, impress, inscribe, ingrain, corrode.

eternal *a.* endless, neverending, everlasting, unending, ageless, infinite, timeless, perpetual, enduring, interminable, undying, immortal. ANT. *finite, fleeting, ephemeral, temporary.*

eternity *n.* forever, infinity, immortality, world without end, timelessness, afterlife. "Where there is no where and no when." — Arthur Schopenhauer. "The sum of all sums." — Lucretius.

ETHEREAL *a.* [i THIR ee ul] otherworldly, celestial or heavenly. Also, light, airy and delicate. *His musical compositions were haunting and ethereal.* SYN. otherworldly, celestial, heavenly, divine, unearthly, sublime, supernal, light, airy, delicate, gossamer, exquisite, tenuous. ANT. *earthly, mundane, heavy, ponderous.*

ethical *a.* right, moral, righteous, fair, just, honest, good, honorable, upright, pure, conscientious, square, decent, noble, correct. ANT. *unethical, immoral, dishonest, dishonorable, corrupt.*

ethics *n.* principles, values, standards, morality, moral code, integrity, honesty, honor, *Ten Commandments, *Golden Rule, mores, conscience, decency. "The obligations of morality." — Lajos Kossuh. "The doctrine of manners." — Maunder.

ethnic *a.* cultural, racial, tribal, folk.

etiquette *n.* manners, courtesy, civility, politeness, decorum, proper conduct, propriety, formalities, protocol, social graces. "Behaving yourself a little better than is absolutely essential." — Will Cuppy.

eulogize v. praise, extol, laud, pay tribute, honor, celebrate, extol, pay homage to, glorify. ANT. *damn, condemn, defame.*

eulogy n. praise, encomium, tribute, homage, panegyric, laudation, extolment, honor, acclamation. "Praise that is too much and too late." — Anon. ANT. *damning, condemnation, defamation.*

EUPHEMISM n. [YOO fuh miz um] a polite word or phrase used in place of an offensive word or phrase. *Heck is a euphemism for hell.* SYN. polite word, delicacy, pretense, *prudism, *nice-nellyism, substitution, mild word, *weasel word. ANT. *crude term, crass term, *gutter word.*

euphonious a. harmonious, melodious, mellifluous, pleasing. ANT. *discordant.*

EUPHORIA n. [yoo FOR ee uh] high spirits, elation. *Spring always brings on a curious euphoria.* SYN. high spirits, happiness, joy, glee, elation, ecstasy, bliss, jubilation, rapture, *seventh heaven. ANT. *misery, depression, unhappiness.*

evacuate v. 1. LEAVE withdraw, vacate, abandon, *run for the hills, hightail, clear out, *skedaddle, *bail out, decamp. 2. EMPTY discharge, remove, void, excrete, eliminate.

evade v. elude, dodge, sidestep, avoid, escape, *give the slip, bypass, duck, *steer clear of, *shake off, shirk, circumvent. ANT. *confront, face, meet.*

evaluate v. appraise, assess, size up, judge, grade, estimate, measure, assay, gauge, determine, rate, weigh.

evaluation n. appraisal, assessment, judgment, grading, estimate, measurement, assay, gauging, determination, rating, ranking.

evanescent a. transient, fleeting, ephemeral, vanishing.

evangelist n. preacher, revivalist, minister, missionary, crusader for God.

evaporate v. vaporize, dehydrate, dry up, dissipate, desiccate, vanish, disappear, disperse, evanesce.

evasion n. avoidance, dodge, elusion, escape, subterfuge, circumvention, shirking, equivocation, *song and dance. ANT. *confrontation, meeting.*

evasive a. deceitful, elusive, slippery, equivocal, shifty, hedging, tricky, shuffling, dissembling, misleading, dodging, prevaricative.

ANT. *direct, forthright, straightforward.*

even v. equalize, balance, level, align, square, make flush, smooth, straighten.

even a. 1. LEVEL, UNIFORM flat, straight, smooth, plumb, balanced, plane, flush, proportional. 2. EQUAL same, balanced, fifty-fifty, on a par, parallel, fair, identical, uniform, *even Stephen. 3. CALM tranquil, serene, peaceful, even-tempered, placid, steady, stable. ANT. *1. uneven, crooked, unbalanced. 2. unequal, disparate. 3. unstable, excitable.*

evening n. nightfall, twilight, dusk, sundown, sunset, eve, eventide, gloaming.

event n. happening, occurrence, incident, episode, affair, circumstance, situation, matter, experience, phenomenon.

eventful a. busy, active, lively, exciting, momentous, outstanding. ANT. *uneventful, slow.*

eventual a. ultimate, future, final, destined, coming, ensuing, inevitable, concluding, succeeding, resultant, consequent.

eventually a. ultimately, in the future, finally, inevitably, sooner or later, in the long run, consequently, in the end.

everlasting a. eternal, agelong, unending, enduring, infinite, immortal, timeless, undying, never ending, unremitting, interminable. ANT. *temporary, ephemeral, fleeting, finite.*

everyday a. 1. DAILY diurnal, circadian. 2. ROUTINE regular, ordinary, commonplace, customary, usual, run-of-the-mill, household, stock, workaday, *garden variety, normal. ANT. *special, rare, occasional.*

evict v. eject, remove, throw out, *show the door, expel, oust, kick out, dispossess.

evidence n. proof, substantiation, confirmation, documentation, corroboration, testimony, support, verification, indication, grounds, *smoking gun, clue.

WORD FIND

hiding of: suppression of evidence

inconclusive, indirect or inferred: circumstantial evidence

physical evidence displayed in court: exhibit

what someone other than the witness has said: hearsay

SEE COURT, LAW

evident a. obvious, clear, plain, manifest, express, visible, *plain as the nose on one's face, apparent, incontestable, palpable, conspicuous, *open and shut. ANT. *hidden, uncertain, obscure, unknown.*

evidently a. apparently, ostensibly, seemingly, as far as one can tell, doubtless, to all appearances.

evil *n.* badness, immorality, sinfulness, indecency, criminality, wickedness, villainy, diabolism, iniquity, viciousness, vileness, lawlessness, cruelty, misfortune, ruin, affliction, harm, woe, catastrophe, disaster. "Whatever springs from weakness." —Nietzsche. "Good tortured by its own hunger and thirst." —Kahil Gibran. ANT. *morality, goodness, righteousness.*

evil *a.* immoral, bad, wicked, depraved, demonic, sinful, villainous, heinous, malicious, iniquitous, atrocious, foul, black, damnable, nefarious, malevolent. ANT. *good, moral, righteous, virtuous.*

evince *v.* show, indicate, disclose, prove, display.

evoke *v.* summon, call forth, conjure up, extract, elicit, invite, cause, stimulate, rouse, awaken.

evolution *n.* *survival of the fittest, phylogeny, development, progression, succession, transformation, change, growth, mutation, metamorphosis. "The preservation of favored races in the struggle for life." —Herbert Spencer. "Men risen out of the mire." —Don Marquis. "Natural selection." —Charles Darwin.

evolve *v.* develop, progress, transform, grow, mutate, metamorphose, *reinvent oneself, advance, emerge.

EXACERBATE *v.* [ek ZAS ur bate] to make worse, aggravate. *Lashing out will only exacerbate the situation.* SYN. make worse, aggravate, intensify, worsen, inflame, *fan the flames, provoke, deepen, *rub salt into the wound, *add insult to injury, heighten. ANT. *mitigate, mollify, soften, ease.*

exact *v.* insist on, demand, require, compel, force, extort, extract, wring, *put the squeeze on.

exact *a.* **1.** PRECISE accurate, *on the button, *on the money, correct, true, *on the mark, faithful, *right on, *dead on, *bullseye, perfect, literal. **2.** CAREFUL rigorous, meticulous, exacting, painstaking, punctilious, methodical. ANT. **1.** *inexact, inaccurate, approximate, rough.* **2.** *careless*

EXACTING *a.* [ig ZAK ting] extremely demanding. *Defusing a bomb is an exacting task.* SYN. demanding, strict, difficult, meticulous, rigorous, painstaking, hard, particular, fastidious, strenuous, burdensome, trying.

exaggerate *v.* amplify, overstate, hyperbolize, *make a mountain out of a mole hill, *play up, embellish, *lay it on thick, color, embroider, *stretch the truth, puff, magnify, *blow out of proportion. ANT. *understate, play down, minimize.*

exaggeration *n.* amplification, overstatement, hype, hyperbole, embellishment, coloring, embroidery, *a stretch, magnification, tall tale, *fish story, *tempest in a teapot. "A branch of lying." —Baltasar Gracian.

EXALT *v.* [eg ZAWLT] to raise up, honor or glorify. *Exalt your champions.* SYN. raise up, honor, glorify, *put on a pedestal, elevate, extol, praise, acclaim, revere, idolize, pay tribute to, worship. ANT. *condemn, put down, ridicule.*

exalted *a.* raised up, glorified, *put on a pedestal, elevated, extolled, praised, esteemed, acclaimed, venerated, idolized, revered. ANT. *condemned, put down, ridiculed, belittled.*

examination *n.* exam, test, inspection, analysis, scrutiny, study, investigation, checkup, probe, review, survey, *once over, assessment, quiz, questionnaire.

examine *v.* **1.** LOOK OVER, TEST check out, inspect, analyze, scrutinize, study, investigate, probe, review, survey, *perform a once-over, *eyeball, assess, scan, peruse, appraise, *size up. **2.** QUIZ grill, question, interrogate, cross-examine, *pump, *give the third degree, catechize.

example *n.* sample, specimen, sampling, instance, exemplar, model, paradigm, stereotype. "The best sermon." —Ben Franklin.

EXASPERATE *v.* [eg ZAS puh RATE] to irritate profoundly. *Husband and wife tend to exasperate each other in divorce court.* SYN. irritate, annoy, ruffle, upset, madden, provoke, *get under one's skin, infuriate, rile, irk, *push one's buttons, peeve, needle, vex, rankle, *rattle one's cage, *pull one's chain. ANT. *mollify, pacify.*

excavate *v.* dig out, hollow out, unearth, burrow, dredge, scoop, tunnel, backhoe, channel, hoe, shovel out.

excavation *n.* pit, hollow, mine, ditch. SEE HOLE

exceed *v.* surpass, best, pass, transcend, eclipse, top, outdo, excel, outshine, overshadow, outrank, outdistance, overwhelm, *go above and beyond.

exceedingly *a.* extremely, very, exceptionally, especially, greatly, highly, vastly, enormously.

excel *v.* surpass, transcend, best, eclipse, top, outdo, excel, outshine, overshadow, outrank, outdistance, trump, *smoke the competition.

excellence *n.* superiority, greatness, supremacy, distinction, fineness, quality, eminence, merit, virtue, perfection. ANT. *inferiority, imperfection, mediocrity.*

excellent *a.* superior, great, supreme, superlative, fine, exceptional, first-rate, peerless, world-class, capital, *premium, champion, superb, *top-drawer, transcendent, *tops, outstanding, *bang-up, *bad, *A-1, awesome, super, *bitchen, *def. ANT. *inferior, poor, mediocre, *crappy.*

except *v.* leave out, omit, exclude, pass over, eliminate, overlook, reject, remove, bar.

exception *n.* **1.** OMISSION exclusion, barring, expulsion, rejection. **2.** IRREGULARITY anomaly, special case, exemption, departure, oddity, deviation, rarity, quirk. **3.** OBJECTION complaint, challenge, reservation.

exceptional *a.* irregular, anomalous, extraordinary, atypical, outstanding, unusual, special, abnormal, singular, rare, remarkable, freakish, unique. ANT. *normal, typical, common, everyday.*

excerpt *n.* passage, section, cut, selection, part, extract, citation, clip, scene, bit.

excess *n.* **1.** SURPLUS glut, overabundance, superabundance, overkill, fat, redundancy, surfeit, superfluity, overrun, *too much of a good thing, plethora. **2.** OVERINDULGENCE extravagance, indulgence, immoderation, intemperance, lack of restraint, exorbitance ANT. **1.** *dearth, shortage, lack.* **2.** *moderation, abstinence.*

excessive *a.* overdone, extreme, too much, inordinate, immoderate, extravagant, exorbitant, overmuch, undue, superfluous, redundant. ANT. *moderate, reasonable, called-for.*

exchange *n.* trade, barter, swap, transaction, reciprocation, interchange, truck, commutation, quid pro quo, substitution, alternate.

exchange *v.* trade, barter, swap, transact, reciprocate, interchange, *give and take, commute, substitute, alternate, bandy.

excise *n.* toll, duty, tax.

excise *v.* remove, cut out, exscind, extirpate.

excitable *a.* emotional, high-strung, temperamental, fiery, volatile, hotheaded, *high octane, explosive, passionate, skittish, tempestuous, hot-blooded. ANT. *unflappable, imperturbable, tranquil.*

excite *v.* arouse, stir, stimulate, *spark, *turn on, thrill, provoke, inspire, electrify, inflame, whet, titillate, incite, agitate, fluster, *charge up, impassion. ANT. *bore, tranquilize, calm.*

excited *a.* aroused, stirred, stimulated, *turned on, thrilled, provoked, electrified, *fired up, agitated, enthusiastic, energized, keyed up, impassioned, *hyper, *wired, electrified, *adrenalized, titillated, *charged up, flustered, frenzied, agog, *sparked, *hot, frenetic. ANT. *sedate, tranquil, bored, comatose.*

excitement *n.* agitation, stimulation, furor, arousal, electricity, passion, enthusiasm, energy, titillation, sensation, frenzy, tizzy, fever, commotion, ferment, *fireworks, flurry, *kicks, perturbation, tumult, *hubbub, *hullabaloo, *white heat, *to-do, *hoopla. ANT. *somnolence, dormancy, boredom, stagnation.*

exciting *a.* arousing, agitating, stirring, stimulating, thrilling, electrifying, energizing, inflaming, titillating, *adrenalizing, *hair-raising, invigorating, exhilarating, breathtaking, *spine-tingling, sensational. ANT. *somnolent, boring, dull.*

exclaim *v.* cry out, ejaculate, shout, burst out, cry, blurt, holler, clamor, interject.

exclamation *n.* cry, outburst, ejaculation, shout, clamor, yell, interjection.

exclude *v.* shut out, keep out, bar, reject, debar, *blackball, forbid, prohibit, ostracize, expel, oust, eject, evict, throw out, omit, rule out, refuse. ANT. *include, welcome, invite.*

exclusive *a.* **1.** RESTRICTED selective, closed, *snobbish, discriminating, preferential, privileged, clannish, segregated, cliquish, undemocratic. **2.** HIGH-PRICED posh, luxurious, *ritzy, expensive, swank, fashionable, chic. **3.** SOLE single, individual, only, complete, entire, total. ANT. **1.** *open, public, unrestricted, democratic.* **2.** *modest, cheap, *cut-rate, pedestrian.* **3.** *shared, limited.*

excoriate *v.* **1.** STRIP OFF scratch off, rub off, abrade, chafe, flay. **2.** DENOUNCE attack, censure, vilify, criticize, condemn, reproach, upbraid, chastise.

excrement *n.* feces, dung, waste, manure, stools, *squat, droppings, guano, scat, *doodoo, turd, *number two, *crap, *poop, *butt muffin, *night soil.

excrete *v.* discharge, eliminate, defecate, evacuate, void, expel, exude, eject, pass.

excruciating *a.* unbearable, agonizing, tortuous, painful, insufferable, consuming, unendurable, *teeth-gritting, *wincing, paralyzing, debilitating, racking, stabbing. SEE PAIN, PAINFUL

exculpate *v.* absolve, forgive, clear, exonerate, acquit, vindicate, pardon, liberate. ANT. *in-*

dict, condemn, convict.

excursion *n.* trip, journey, jaunt, outing, tour, expedition, junket, cruise, trek, side trip, ride, drive, hike, run.

excusable *a.* forgivable, condonable, pardonable, allowable, venial, understandable, extenuating, justifiable, reasonable, justified. ANT. *inexcusable, unforgivable, indefensible.*

excuse *n.* defense, justification, explanation, reason, rationalization, grounds, alibi, *song and dance, extenuation, *cover story, *whitewash, plea.

excuse *v.* pardon, forgive, absolve, condone, overlook, make allowances for, exonerate, acquit, reprieve, exempt, spare, liberate, *let go, extenuate.

execrable *a.* detestable, abominable, contemptible, horrible, deplorable, revolting, loathsome, sickening, odious, atrocious, despicable.

execute *v.* **1.** PERFORM do, carry out, follow out, discharge, accomplish, fulfill, achieve, effect, effectuate, complete. **2.** PUT TO DEATH kill, murder, assassinate, hang, behead, electrocute, lynch.

execution *n.* **1.** PERFORMANCE OF A DUTY implementation, discharge, accomplishment, fulfillment, achievement, completion, consummation. **2.** PUTTING TO DEATH death penalty, capital punishment, killing, hanging, beheading, lethal injection, electrocution, slaying, lynching, gassing, guillotining. **3.** STYLE manner, technique, touch, performance.

executive *n.* manager, administrator, chief executive officer (CEO), supervisor, director, head, *top brass, officer, *big wheel, *higher-up, boss, *white-collar worker, *big cheese, *big toad in the puddle. "[One] who isn't worried about his own career but rather the careers of those who work for him." — Henry Burns. "One who can delegate all the responsibility, shift all the blame, and appropriate all the credit." — Bobby Vinton.

WORD FIND

recruiter: headhunter

executive *a.* administrative, managerial, decision-making, directorial, authoritative, supervisory.

exemplar *n.* model, archetype, pattern, ideal, example, paradigm, standard, prototype, paragon, exemplification.

EXEMPLARY *a.* [eg ZEM pluh ree] serving as a model worth copying. *An exemplary student.* SYN. model, worthy, admirable, ideal, praiseworthy, illustrative, laudable, superior,

outstanding, classic, prototypical. ANT. *awful, poor, lousy, substandard.*

EXEMPLIFY *v.* [eg ZEM pluh FYE] to serve as a good example. *Babe Ruth exemplified the model homerun hitter.* SYN. epitomize, typify, represent, illustrate, demonstrate, symbolize, stand for, personify, embody.

exempt *a.* free from, excused, immune, unrestricted, discharged, privileged, unrestrained, excluded, spared from, absolved, *off the hook. ANT. *bound, liable, subject to.*

exercise *n.* **1.** WORKOUT aerobics, calisthenics, training, warm-up, gymnastics, drill, isometrics, regimen, bodybuilding, dancercise, push-up, sit-up, pull-up, jumping jacks, skipjacks, crunch, *pumping iron, weightlifting. "A modern superstition, invented by people who ate too much, and had nothing to think about." — George Santayana. **2.** USE execution, application, employment, utilization, practice.

exercise *v.* **1.** WORK OUT perform aerobics, perform calisthenics, train, drill, warm up, *pump iron. **2.** USE apply, employ, utilize, practice, execute, perform, exert.

exert *v.* **1.** USE exercise, employ, utilize, apply, employ. **2.** APPLY GREAT EFFORT push, drive, strain, struggle, *go all out, *dig deep, *bust a gut, strive, *pour it on, *pop a vein.

exertion *n.* effort, exercise, work, strain, labor, application, *muscle, pains, *elbow grease, toil, energy, struggle. ANT. *inertia, sloth, rest, relaxation.*

exhale *v.* breathe, respire. SEE BREATHE

exhaust *n.* discharge, fumes, gas, smoke, carbon monoxide, steam, outflow, outpouring, effluvium.

exhaust *v.* **1.** TIRE drain, fatigue, wear out, sap, *tucker out, *poop, enervate, *bush, tax, fag, *wear one's battery down, overtire. **2.** DEPLETE use up, empty, drain, consume, spend, clean out, expend, *blow, bankrupt. ANT. 1. *energize, refresh, invigorate, revive.* 2. *restore, stock up, conserve.*

exhausted *a.* **1.** TIRED drained, fatigued, worn out, sapped, *tuckered out, *pooped, enervated, *bushed, fagged out, overtired, *trashed out, *wiped out, *beat, *dead, rundown, *out of juice, *dog-tired. **2.** DEPLETED used up, emptied, drained, consumed, spent, cleaned out, *blown, bankrupt, expended. ANT. 1. *refreshed, invigorated, *charged up, energized.* 2. *restored, replenished, restocked, conserved.*

exhaustion *n.* weariness, fatigue, collapse,

tiredness, enervation, *burnout, prostration, *physical bankruptcy, weakness, sleepiness, faintness, dissipation. ANT. *energy, *get-up-and-go, pep.

EXHAUSTIVE a. [ex ZAWS tiv] thorough, painstaking. *She made an exhaustive search through her family tree.* SYN. thorough, painstaking, comprehensive, in-depth, complete, extensive, intensive, all-inclusive, sweeping, encyclopedic. ANT. *perfunctory, superficial, cursory.*

exhibit n. exhibition, showing, display, presentation, exposition.

exhibit v. show, display, present, expose, demonstrate, air, showcase, feature, illustrate, parade.

exhibition n. exhibit, showing, display, presentation, exposition, demonstration, spectacle, showcasing.

exhilarate v. cheer, excite, gladden, enliven, stimulate, elate, animate, delight, *perk up, thrill, invigorate, uplift. ANT. *depress, sadden, *bum out.*

exhort v. urge, admonish, prod, persuade, egg, prompt, caution, warn, goad, prevail upon, recommend, advise.

exhume v. dig up, disinter, unearth, resurrect.

exigency n. urgency, demand, pressing need, crisis, requirement, imperative, necessity, emergency, dire circumstance, *pickle, *hot water.

exile n. **1.** BANISHMENT deportation, expatriation, expulsion, uprooting, separation, ostracism, relegation. **2.** BANISHED PERSON outcast, expatriate, refugee, deportee, pariah, displaced person. "One who serves his country by residing abroad, yet is not an ambassador." —Ambrose Bierce.

exile v. banish, deport, expatriate, expel, ostracize, uproot, separate, relegate, oust, displace.

exist v. be, live, endure, breathe, survive, subsist, abide, remain.

existence n. being, life, subsistence, presence, reality, actuality. "A party. You join after its started and you leave before its finished." —Elsa Maxwell. "A series of footnotes to a vast, obscure, unfinished masterpiece." —Vladimir Nabokov.

exit n. **1.** DOORWAY egress, outlet, passage, escape-way. **2.** DEPARTURE leaving, withdrawal, egress, leave-taking, exodus, parting, farewell, goodbye, adieu.

exodus n. departure, going forth, flight, emigration, hegira, migration, fleeing, retreat, withdrawal.

EXONERATE v. [egg ZAWN ur rate] to free from charges or show that one is blameless. *The prisoner was exonerated and released.* SYN. acquit, clear, free, vindicate, absolve, excuse, exculpate, dismiss, let go. ANT. *convict, condemn, find guilty.*

EXORBITANT a. [eg ZORB uh tunt] excessive or unreasonable. *The prices for homes in Beverly Hills are exorbitant.* SYN. excessive, unreasonable, extravagant, outrageous, inordinate, out-of-line, unwarranted, disproportionate, extreme, *stiff, preposterous, ludicrous. ANT. *reasonable, modest, moderate.*

exotic a. foreign, alien, outlandish, unfamiliar, strange, peculiar, weird, unusual, different, extraordinary, imported, colorful. ANT. *native, ordinary, familiar.*

expand v. **1.** ENLARGE grow, magnify, inflate, widen, swell, distend, bloat, increase, fatten, broaden, puff up. **2.** ELABORATE detail, draw out, develop, expound upon, *flesh out. ANT. *1. shrink, contract, condense. 2. condense, shorten.*

expanse n. area, space, immensity, extent, plain, stretch, sweep, range, radius, territory, reach.

expansion n. enlargement, extension, increase, growth, development, magnification, spread, heightening, widening, broadening, lengthening. ANT. *contraction, downsizing, decrease.*

expansive a. **1.** EXTENDED extensive, sweeping, broad, comprehensive, spacious, inclusive, voluminous, large. **2.** FRIENDLY open, demonstrative, sympathetic, generous, free, outgoing, unrestrained, effusive, talkative, unrestrained. ANT. *1. confined, restricted, cramped. 2. inhibited, reserved, restrained.*

expatriate n. outcast, displaced person. SEE EXILE

expect v. **1.** ANTICIPATE look for, count on, foresee, bargain for, envisage, look forward to, assume, presume, predict, imagine. **2.** WANT require, call for, demand, count on.

expectant a. anticipating, awaiting, anxious, watching, *on tenterhooks, *with bated breath, apprehensive, *on pins and needles.

expectation n. anticipation, outlook, prospect, belief, hope, fear, supposition, presumption, likelihood, assumption, forecast.

expecting a. *with child, *in a family way. SEE PREGNANT

expectorate v. *hawk a loogie. SEE SPIT

expediency n. suitability, appropriateness, properness, usefulness, convenience, utility, advantage, effectiveness, opportunism.

EXPEDIENT *n.* [ek SPEE dee unt] resource, makeshift, contrivance, means, measure, instrument, resort, device, scheme, stopgap.

expedient *a.* serving one's immediate needs, useful. *It would be expedient to study if you want to pass the test.* SYN. useful, advantageous, practical, self-serving, prudent, profitable, fitting, sensible, proper, worthwhile, desirable. ANT. *impractical, useless, futile.*

EXPEDITE *v.* [EK spi DITE] to speed up or facilitate a process or action. *I'm going to expedite delivery by mailing the package first class.* SYN. speed up, facilitate, accelerate, hurry, quicken, hasten, precipitate, rush, *grease the wheels, advance, dispatch. ANT. *slow, bog down, hinder.*

expedition *n.* journey, voyage, trip, mission, march, tour, excursion, trek, campaign, exploration, crusade, safari, junket, enterprise.

expeditious *a.* quick, fast, speedy, prompt, efficient, swift, rapid, brisk, fleet, punctual, instant. ANT. *slow, leisurely, slothful.*

expel *v.* throw out, remove, banish, exile, dispel, eject, evict, get rid of, *bounce, oust, deport, *give the boot, *show the door, *give walking papers, expatriate. ANT. *invite, admit, welcome.*

expend *v.* use, consume, spend, exhaust, empty, drain, *blow, squander, dissipate, disburse, *shell out, deplete, *fritter away. ANT. *conserve, save.*

expendable *a.* dispensable, unimportant, replaceable, nonessential, spendable, extraneous, superfluous.

expenditure *n.* expense, outlay, spending, payment, disbursement, outgo, cost, charge, overhead, investment, consumption, use. ANT. *income, receivable.*

expense *n.* cost, outlay, price, charge, amount, payment, price tag, *out of pocket cost, expenditure, fee, burden, *bottom line, overhead.

expensive *a.* costly, high-priced, *pricey, exorbitant, dear, steep, *sky-high, stiff, unreasonable, outrageous. ANT. *cheap, low-priced, cut-rate, economical.*

experience *n.* **1.** FIRSTHAND KNOWLEDGE exposure, familiarity, practice, understanding, participation, empiricism, involvement, seasoning, encountering, worldliness, wisdom. "A good school, but the fees are high."—Heinrich Heine. "The stern lights of a ship, which illumine only the track it has passed."—Samuel Taylor Coleridge "The

fruit of the tree of errors."—Portuguese proverb. "The name everyone gives to their mistakes."—Oscar Wilde. **2.** AFFAIR event, ordeal, happening, adventure, encounter, incident, episode. ANT. *1. inexperience, naiveté.*

experience *v.* feel, undergo, encounter, taste, meet, sample, perceive, know, suffer, see, smell, hear, absorb.

experienced *a.* practiced, accomplished, seasoned, weathered, *battle-scarred, initiated, knowing, knowledgeable, worldly-wise, hardened, veteran, *been through the wringer, *been there, tested, mature. ANT. *inexperienced, green, unseasoned, naive, uninitiated.*

experiment *n.* test, trial, investigation, analysis, examination, assay, probe, inquiry, research, trial and error, try, study, *double-blind study. "A hard teacher because she gives the test first, the lesson afterwards."—Vernon Law.

experiment *v.* test, try, investigate, analyze, examine, assess, assay, prove, probe, inquire, research, study, weigh, explore, scrutinize.

experimental *a.* trial, speculative, unproven, hypthothetical, conjectural, tentative, pilot, theoretical, exploratory, test, developmental. ANT. *proven, tested.*

expert *n.* authority, specialist, professional, master, virtuoso, connoisseur, scholar, *whiz, veteran, *crackerjack, journeyman, *guru, *shark, *old hand, *know-it-all, *maven. "A man who has made all the mistakes which can be made in a very narrow field."—Niels Bohr. "The one who predicts the job will take the longest and cost the most."—Arthur Bloch. ANT. *amateur, beginner, layman, apprentice.*

expert *a.* experienced, knowledgeable, *crack, proficient, masterful, schooled, practiced, virtuoso, dexterous, skilled, *whiz-bang, *ace. ANT. *inexperienced, unschooled, lay.*

expertise *n.* knowledge, know-how, skill, prowess, authority, proficiency, finesse, *knack, mastery, specialization.

expiration *n.* ending, closing, termination, death, cessation, passing, demise, finish, departure, conclusion, *last gasp.

expire *v.* **1.** RUN OUT OR DIE lapse, end, close, cease, discontinue, *kick the bucket, pass away, terminate. SEE DIE **2.** EXHALE respire. SEE BREATHE

explain *v.* clarify, clear up, illustrate, explicate, elucidate, expound, interpret, define, *make plain, spell out, describe, account for, justify.

explanation n. clarification, illustration, explication, elucidation, exposition, interpretation, definition, description, account, justification, answer, rationalization.

EXPLICIT a. [eks PLIS it] clearly expressed, directly stated or shown. *The movie has explicit sex scenes.* SYN. clear, direct, unambiguous, definite, candid, exact, specific, frank, distinct, unequivocal, plain, straightforward. ANT. *indirect, vague, ambiguous.*

explode v. **1.** BLOW UP pop, burst, detonate, *blow, discharge, erupt, fulminate, blast, bang, thunder, burst into flames. **2.** DISCREDIT debunk, expose, refute, invalidate, *shoot down, belie, puncture.

exploit n. FEAT deed, act, achievement, accomplishment, coup, stunt, adventure, maneuver.

exploit v. use, take advantage of, utilize, capitalize on, *milk, *cash in on, abuse, *walk on, impose upon, employ.

exploration n. investigation, probe, *look-see, search, inspection, survey, canvass, examination, inquiry, scrutiny, reconnaissance, *trailblazing.

explore v. investigate, probe, look into, search out, inspect, scrutinize, survey, canvass, range over, examine, research, *blaze a trail.

explosion n. blowup, detonation, blast, boom, outburst, eruption, pop, crack, fulmination, roar, report, concussion, percussion, shot, upheaval.

explosive n. bomb, dynamite, TNT, charge, gunpowder, nitroglycerine, warhead, blasting cap, cordite, dunnite, fuel-air explosive, Molotov cocktail, napalm, petard, plastic explosive. SEE AMMUNITION, BOMB, MISSILE, NUCLEAR BOMB, WAR, WEAPON

explosive a. volatile, charged, *at the boiling point, inflammable, fulminant, volcanic, eruptive, dangerous, perilous. ANT. *stable, relaxed.*

exponent n. spokesman, representative, proponent, interpreter, explainer, advocate, champion, expounder.

exposé n. disclosure, uncovering, revelation, exposure, *kiss-and-tell, muckraking, explanation.

exposé v. **1.** UNCOVER bare, reveal, show, disclose, unmask, *let cat out of the bag, exhibit, unveil, air, divulge. **2.** LEAVE UNPROTECTED lay open, endanger, jeopardize, imperil, tempt fate, leave vulnerable, make defenseless. ANT. **1.** *cover up, hide, conceal.* **2.** *block, camouflage, protect.*

exposition n. explanation, commentary, explication, description, account, treatise, study, discourse, essay, exegesis, overview, elucidation.

exposure n. uncovering, airing, disclosure, revelation, unmasking, exposé, unveiling, showing, exhibition, baring, divulging.

EXPOUND v. [eks POUND] to set forth detail by detail, explain. *She will expound her conservative views on the news.* SYN. detail, explain, describe, set forth, state, express, elucidate, spell out, illustrate, define, delineate, comment on.

express v. communicate, articulate, say, verbalize, enunciate, convey, put across, put into words, declare, voice, tell, pronounce, state.

express a. **1.** EXPLICIT clear, certain, plain, direct, precise, distinct, obvious, specific, exact. **2.** FAST quick, swift, fleet, prompt. ANT. *1. vague, ambiguous, indirect. 2. slow, sluggish.*

expression n. **1.** COMMUNICATION articulation, verbalization, enunciation, conveyance, declaration, voicing, pronouncement, statement, utterance, elucidation, formulation, phrasing, wording. **2.** TERM phrase, word, idiom, saying, metaphor, simile. **3.** LOOK face, countenance, aspect, visage, cast, mien, *mug.

expressionless a. deadpan, poker-faced, blank, wooden, stony, vacuous, inscrutable, vacant, apathetic, *shark-eyed, unreadable.

expressive a. indicative, telling, eloquent, meaningful, evocative, revealing, vivid, pregnant, descriptive, pointed, graphic. ANT. *nondescript, empty, meaningless.*

expressly adv. **1.** PARTICULARLY purposely, precisely, strictly, exactly, especially, specifically. **2.** EXPLICITLY clearly, plainly, unambiguously, definitely, pointedly, unequivocally, categorically. ANT. **2.** *implicitly, indirectly, vaguely.*

expulsion n. discharge, exile, banishment, ejection, eviction, ouster, *the boot, expatriation, deportment, removal, exclusion. ANT. *inclusion, welcoming, receiving.*

expunge v. erase, blot out, delete, obliterate, efface, wipe out, cut, cancel, omit, extirpate, remove, eradicate.

expurgate v. censor, remove, expunge, cut, bowdlerize, clean up, sanitize, purge, soften.

exquisite a. delicate, lovely, fine, elegant, beautiful, dainty, precious, rare, consummate, superlative, splendid, ethereal, fragile. ANT. *clunky, rough, coarse, bulky, ponderous.*

extant a. existing, living, alive, surviving,

around, present, current, remaining. ANT. *extinct, defunct, dead, gone.*

extemporaneous *a.* unrehearsed, offhand, unprepared, unpremeditated, impromptu, spontaneous, ad lib, *off the cuff, *spur of the moment, *on the spot. ANT. *rehearsed, prepared, premeditated.*

extemporize *v.* improvise, ad-lib, *perform offhand, *wing it, *play it by ear, *make up as one goes along, *do off the cuff.

extend *v.* **1.** STRETCH elongate, enlarge, expand, spread, lengthen, draw out, prolong, protract, unfurl, increase, continue. **2.** OFFER accord, grant, proffer, tender, present, submit, put forth. ANT. *1. contract, shorten, shrink.*

extension *n.* enlargement, lengthening, protraction, elongation, expansion, spread, prolongation, unfurling, increase, addition, augmentation, annex, attachment. ANT. *contraction, shortening, shrinkage.*

extensive *a.* broad, far-reaching, comprehensive, expansive, considerable, vast, sweeping, large-scale, widespread, out-and-out, wholesale, thorough, lengthy, protracted. ANT. *limited, restricted, small-scale.*

extent *n.* size, area, degree, magnitude, measure, proportions, range, expanse, amount, sweep, dimensions, scope.

EXTENUATE *v.* [ek STEN yoo ate] to lessen, mitigate or provide an excuse for a wrongdoing. *Extenuating circumstances absolved him of guilt.* SYN. lessen, mitigate, justify, soften, attenuate, moderate, diminish, palliate, qualify, make allowances for.

exterior *n.* surface, face, facade, outside, shell, skin, appearance. ANT. *interior, inside.*

exterior *a.* external, outside, outer, extrinsic, extraneous, superficial, foreign, surface, outward. ANT. *internal, inner, intrinsic.*

exterminate *v.* destroy, kill, wipe out, eradicate, annihilate, eliminate, abolish, slaughter, decimate, extirpate, massacre, extinguish.

external *a.* outer, extrinsic, outside, outward, surface, superficial, exterior, foreign, extraneous. ANT. *internal, intrinsic.*

extinct *a.* died out, dead, defunct, obsolete, nonexistent, vanished, vanquished, gone, wiped out, nonextant, *fossilized, *dead and forgotten, outmoded. ANT. *living, existing, thriving.*

extinction *n.* dying out, death, downfall, destruction, annihilation, termination, *fossilization, obsolescence, disappearance, passing.

extinguish *v.* **1.** QUENCH douse, snuff out, put out, smother, *douse. **2.** DESTROY abolish, end, stifle, annihilate, quash, eliminate, exterminate, extirpate, eradicate, wipe out.

extirpate *v.* exterminate, destroy, eradicate, obliterate, annihilate, abolish, uproot, eliminate, root out, remove.

EXTOL *v.* [eks TOLE] to praise highly, laud. *Society extols its athletes.* SYN. praise, laud, acclaim, glorify, cheer, commend, exalt, celebrate, applaud, honor, *sing the praises of. ANT. *put down, disparage, discredit, condemn.*

extort *v.* extract, blackmail, coerce, *strongarm, wrest, wring, *bleed, *milk, fleece, cheat, *put the screws to, squeeze, *armtwist, bully.

extortion *n.* blackmail, *strong-arming, *armtwisting, extraction, *bleeding, *milking, *the squeeze, bullying, wringing, shakedown, graft, hush money.

extra *n.* accessory, spare, bonus, supplement.

extra *a.* additional, surplus, excess, more, accessory, extraneous, spare, superfluous, over.

extract *n.* **1.** EXCERPT clipping, quotation, citation, abstract, passage. **2.** DISTILLATION concentrate, distillate, essence, juice.

extract *v.* remove, withdraw, pull, pluck, yank, extirpate, glean, pry, wrench, cull, reap, derive, wrest.

EXTRANEOUS *a.* [ek STRAY nee us] inessential, unnecessary. *We ditched our extraneous gear to lighten the load.* SYN. inessential, unnecessary, irrelevant, extra, superfluous, incidental, peripheral, needless, immaterial. ANT. *essential, relevant, needed.*

extraordinary *a.* unusual, exceptional, remarkable, uncommon, rare, striking, singular, strange, odd, phenomenal, outstanding, marvelous, unprecedented, wondrous. ANT. *ordinary, usual, common.*

EXTRAPOLATE *v.* [ek STRAP uh late] to infer or draw conclusions from what is known, to hypothesize. *Although it is not known for sure, many scientists extrapolate that life exists on other worlds.* SYN. infer, conclude, deduce, *put two and two together, figure, guess, hypothesize, postulate, theorize, assume, presume, *make an educated guess.

extrasensory perception *n.* ESP, psychic powers, *third eye, telepathy, clairvoyance, telesthesia.

extraterrestrial *n.* alien, space being, *E.T., unearthly visitor, *little green man, *visitor from another planet.

extravagance *n.* indulgence, excessiveness,

lavishness, wastefulness, excess, immoderation, prodigality, frill, *overkill, superfluity, profligacy, exorbitance, *conspicuous consumption. "The way the other fellow spends his money."—Harry Thompson. ANT. *thrift, moderation, restraint, frugality.*

extravagant *a.* indulgent, excessive, lavish, wasteful, immoderate, prodigal, superfluous, profligate, exorbitant, conspicuous, ultra, unrestrained, spendthrift, ostentatious, extreme. ANT. *moderate, restrained, thrifty, reasonable.*

extreme *n.* outer limit, height, extremity, end, ultimate, maximum, ceiling, utmost, top, peak.

extreme *a.* drastic, beyond reason, excessive, utmost, severe, extraordinary, great, immoderate, extravagant, outrageous, imprudent, radical, overkill, undue. ANT. *conventional, normal, conservative, moderate.*

extremely *adv.* very, exceedingly, quite, exceptionally, excessively, greatly, immensely, highly, markedly, severely, intensely, inordinately.

extremist *n.* radical, fanatic, zealot, ultra, revolutionist, immoderate, *hard-liner.

extremity *n.* **1.** LIMIT edge, tip, boundary, outer limit, periphery, border, verge, terminus, margin, brink. **2.** APPENDAGE limb, leg, arm, hand, foot.

extricate *v.* free, get out of, extract, liberate, release, *get out from under, *wriggle out of, disentangle, relieve, save. ANT. *entangle, involve, embroil.*

extrovert *n.* outgoing person, socializer, ˙life of the party, gregarious person, *party animal, exhibitionist, *mixer. ANT. *introvert, loner, introspective person.*

extrude *v.* expel, push out, eject, force out.

exuberance *n.* **1.** HIGH SPIRITS liveliness, vitality, enthusiasm, ebullience, buoyancy, effervescence, zest, energy, vigor, bounce. **2.** ABUNDANCE luxuriance, lushness, profusion, lavishness, affluence, plenitude, richness. ANT. *1. depression, dullness, apathy, listlessness, low spirits. 2. scarcity, shortage.*

exuberant *a.* **1.** HIGH-SPIRITED lively, vital, enthusiastic, ebullient, buoyant, effervescent, effusive, zestful, energetic, vigorous, *full of bounce. **2.** ABUNDANT luxurious, lush, profuse, lavish, affluent, rich, flush, plentiful. ANT. *1. down, dispirited, *blue, listless. 2. short, scarce.*

exude *v.* emit, discharge, secrete, emanate, ooze, sweat, issue, well forth, excrete, trickle.

exult *v.* rejoice, jubilate, glory, celebrate, revel, *jump for joy, be joyful, make merry, crow.

EXULTANT *a.* [eg ZULT unt] jubilant, joyful, or jumping for joy. *The exultant partygoers sang for hours.* SYN. jubilant, joyful, triumphant, ecstatic, elated, gleeful, rejoicing, euphoric, overjoyed, transported, happy. ANT. *miserable, depressed, downhearted.*

exultation *n.* jubilation, rejoicing, joy, triumph, ecstasy, elation, glee, euphoria, happiness, exhilaration. ANT. *misery, depression, dejection.*

eye *n.* optical organ, eyeball, *peeper, orb, oculus, *winker, *baby blue. "The pulse of the soul; as physicians judge the heart by the pulse, so we by the eye."—Thomas Adams. "The traitor of the heart."—Thomas Wyatt. "Windows of the soul."—Guillaume Du Bartas. "Sentinels."—Cicero.

WORD FIND

blackened, bruised: shiner, mouse

blindness caused by loss of retina's rods: retinitis pigmentosa

blue eye, brown eye, having one of each: helerochroma iridis

bulging, protruding: exophthalmic

cavity: orbit, socket

close-up vision: nearsightedness, myopia

clouding of lens: cataract

color confusion: color blindness

color detectors, nerve cells: cones

colored portioned surrounding pupil: iris

corneal incisions that correct nearsightedness: radial keratotomy

crossed inwardly, one eye: esotropia, stabismus

crossed outward, one eye: exotropia

crossed outward, one eye or both: walleyed

cross-eyed, family of disorders: strabismus

dark spot that responds to light, dark: pupil

descriptive, shapes: almond, banjo, beady, bug, button, close-set, crescent, cue ball, deep-set, birdlike, fishy, goggle, hooded, lenticular, owlish, pop, rheumy, saucer, slanty, sloe, squinty, sunken, wide-set

discharge: rheum

distance vision: farsightedness, hyperopia

doctor: ophthalmologist, oculist

eyelid liner, inner: conjunctiva

feeling, showing deep: soulful

flashes of light, seeing: photopsia, scintillation

floating specks before: floaters (dead blood cells)

fluid between cornea and lens: aqueous hu-

mor
focusing body: lens
inflammation causing reddening of eyeball:
    pinkeye
inflammation of conjunctiva: conjunctivitis
inflammation on lid: sty
innermost layer where light rays are focused:
    retina
instrument: orthoscope
iris that is light-colored: walleye
jelly behind lens: vitreous humor
light sensitivity: photophobia
nerve to brain: optic nerve
Oriental skin fold: epicanthus
peripheral distortion: astigmatism
pertaining to: ocular
pressure build-up causing visual defects,
    blindness: glaucoma
pupil conctraction: myosis
seeing double: diplopia
sunken: deep-set, cavernous
transparent outer membrane: cornea
velvety and dark: sloe-eyed
white of: sclera

eye v. look at, study, scrutinize, gaze at, *eyeball, scan, ogle, *give the once-over, regard,
view.

eyeball v. SEE EYE

eyebrow n. brow, bree, *ceja.
WORD FIND
bushy, prominent: beetle-browed, caterpillar
    eyebrows

eyeglasses n. glasses, spectacles, *specs, lenses,
*eyes.
WORD FIND
circular, frameless glasses that pinch in place
    over nose: pince-nez
fake, nonprescription fashion glasses: planos
fancy, upscale: designer glasses
granny glasses worn on middle of nose: Ben
    Franklins
handle, held with a: lorgnette
heavy, dark brown frames: horn-rimmed
lenses divided for near and far sight: bifocals
mottled brown frames: tortoiseshell glasses
reading glasses with half-lenses for peering
    over: half-glasses
single lens hung from ribbon worn around
    neck: monocle

eyesight n. SEE VISION

eyesore n. ugliness, sight, fright, mess, pollution, monstrosity, pigsty, dump.

eyewash n. hogwash, *bullshit, flattery, bunk.
SEE NONSENSE

eyewitness n. bystander, observer, spectator,
onlooker, passerby, watcher.

F

fable n. myth, tale, parable, legend, allegory, story, yarn, fiction, old wives' tale, moral, fantasy. "A horror story to prepare children for the daily newspaper." —Anon.

fabled a. mythical, legendary, famous, storied, fanciful, fictitious, make-believe, fantastic.

fabric n. **1.** CLOTH material, textile, fiber, weave, dry goods, stuff.
WORD FIND
canvas: duckcloth, sailcloth
crinkled: crepe, seersucker
decorated with many small, colorful print designs: calico
drape, upholstery fabric of glazed cotton: chintz
dress fabric used in evening wear: faille
edging preventing raveling: selvage
filling: weft
fuzzy surface: nap
gingham, light: chambray
glossy: satin, etoile
goathair, angora: mohair
heavy, floral-patterned with metallic threads: brocade
heavy, used in tablecloths: damask
holes, full of: fishnet
hunting jacket fabric: mackinaw
jeans: denim, dungaree
leather, soft and napped: suede
leather, soft, goat: chamois
lustrous, tightly woven: broadcloth
man-made fiber known as artifical silk: rayon
metallic yarn fabric used in evening dresses: lame
pile, thick and soft: velveteen
plush, velvet, corduroy: pile
puckered: plisse
quantity of, fifteen to twenty yards: bolt
rib, as of corduroy: wale
rabbit, goat: angora
raised design or bumpy surface on: blister
sample of: swatch
Scottish, handwoven: Harris tweed
silk, woven: tricot
sheer: gauze, organza, batiste, voile, chiffon, gossamer
sheets, bed: muslin, percale
shiny, imitation silk: poplin
shiny, rustling: taffeta
stretchy, synthetic: spandex
suit: tweed, serge
towel, robes: terry cloth
uniform, olive green: khaki
uniforms, twilled fabric for: cavalry twill, chino
wool, combed and smoothed: worsted
wool: fleece
wool, goat: cashmere
wool, nubby type used in suits: tweed
wool, soft and brushed: flannel
wool, unprocessed: virgin wool
wrinkle-resistant, man-made: polyester
2. MAKEUP substance, structure, framework, constitution, texture.

fabricate v. **1.** MAKE manufacture, construct, assemble, piece together, create, fashion, produce, fashion, devise. **2.** LIE prevaricate, *fudge, invent, make up, concoct, hatch, fib, contrive.

fabrication n. lie, concoction, invention, fib, prevarication, falsehood, *fish story, *cock and bull story, *tall tale, web. ANT. *truth, fact.*

fabulous a. **1.** INCREDIBLE OR GREAT astounding, wonderful, excellent, *out-of-this-world, super, *primo, marvelous, amazing, exceptional, superb, *aces, fantastic. **2.** MYTHICAL legendary, fictitious, fabled, imaginary, fantastic, make-believe, fanciful. SEE MONSTER ANT. **1.** *ordinary, run-of-the-mill, routine, everyday.* **2.** *actual, real, factual.*

FACADE n. [fuh SAHD] the front or face of a person, place or thing, often with the implication of hiding something negative behind it. *His smiling face was just a facade; we knew he was really quite angry inside.* SYN. front, false front, face, mask, guise, veneer, show, *window dressing, *put-on, pretense, disguise, appearance.

face n. **1.** VISAGE countenance, features, physiognomy, *mug, *puss, front, profile, *kisser, head. "The portrait of the mind." —Samuel Coleridge. "The shorthand of the mind. " —Jeremy Collier. "A book where men may read strange matters." —Shakespeare. "The title page which heralds the contents of the human volume." —William Matthews. "Oftentimes the true index of the heart." —James Howell. SEE EXPRESSION, EYE, FROWN, MOUTH, NOSE, OLD-FACED, SMILE **2.** FRONT exterior, surface, appearance, mask, semblance, disguise, facade.

face v. confront, meet, brave, encounter, beard, withstand, bear, *fly in the face of, acknowledge, *meet head-on, brook, *bite the bullet.

facet n. aspect, side, point, angle, surface, feature, plane, side, detail, part, cut.

FACETIOUS a. [fuh SEE shus] jocular, flippant, tongue-in-cheek. *She was being facetious when she said I should run for president.* SYN. jocular, flippant, funny, humorous, playful, joking, kidding, tongue-in-cheek, not serious, *joshing, jesting, *wise, *pulling one's leg. ANT. *serious, grave, sober.*

facile a. 1. EASY simple, *cinchy, *a snap, *child's play, *a breeze, effortless. 2. FLUENT quick, ready, adroit, dexterous, smooth, superficial, glib. ANT. 1. *difficult, hard, laborious.*

FACILITATE v. [fuh SIL uh tate] to simplify, make easier. *To facilitate mailing, please include a self-addressed stamped envelope.* SYN. simplify, ease, expedite, help, quicken, further, aid, smooth, speed up, *grease the wheels, advance. ANT. *hinder, complicate, hamper, burden.*

facility n. 1. ABILITY skill, ease, dexterity, adroitness, efficiency, fluency, proficiency, effortlessness, aptitude, knack. 2. ACCOMMODATION convenience, resource, means, appliance, building, room, office.

facsimile n. copy, reproduction, replica, duplicate, likeness, carbon copy, *Xerox, double, clone, twin, *ditto, FAX.

fact n. truth, reality, datum, certainty, actuality, verity, gospel, law, scripture, particular, detail, specific, element, item.

FACTION n. [FAK shun] a group sharing a common cause, especially one within a larger group or body. *The liberal faction is working for stronger environmental controls.* SYN. group, bloc, clique, circle, part, sect, subdivision, side, camp, sector, pressure group, splinter group, coalition.

factious a. conflicting, quarrelsome, discordant, contentious, partisan, dissentious, divisive, warring, at odds, hostile, at loggerheads. ANT. *agreeing, consonant, harmonious.*

factor n. determinant, element, influence, cause, component, agent, means, instrument, circumstance, point, consideration, aspect.

factory n. manufactory, manufacturing facility, plant, mill, shop, firm, machine shop, works, foundry, assembly line.

factual a. true, actual, realistic, literal, authentic, faithful, correct, exact, sound, valid, credible, legitimate, certain, unquestionable. ANT. *untrue, false, fictitious, fanciful, made up.*

faculty n. 1. ABILITY capability, skill, aptitude, talent, facility, capacity, gift, knack, flair, instinct. 2. TEACHERS staff, instructors, academics, professors, body.

fad n. craze, vogue, mania, rage, *in thing, trend, fashion, *dernier cri, whim, furor, mode.

fade v. 1. LOSE COLOR pale, dim, wane, wash out, blanch. 2. DWINDLE disappear, vanish, slacken, wither, waste away, diminish, decline, recede, ebb, wane, languish, die out. ANT. *1. brighten, make vivid. 2. grow, increase, brighten.*

fag n. Sl. homosexual, *gay boy, *faggot, *fairy, *fem, *twinkletoes.

fail v. 1. NOT SUCCEED *blow it, *fall short, slip up, lose, go wrong, flop, miss, *bomb, *fall flat on one's face, flunk, *lay an egg, run aground, *strike out, *come a cropper. 2. WEAKEN deteriorate, dwindle, die away, wane, sink, fade, *be on one's last legs, *circle the drain, decline, sicken. 3. DEFAULT back out, neglect, forsake, renege, let down, desert, slight, disregard, ignore. 4. GO BANKRUPT crash, close, *lose one's shirt, *go belly up, *file for chapter eleven, *go broke, fold, go out of business, *drown in a sea of red ink. ANT. *1. succeed, win, achieve, triumph. 2. grow stronger, flourish, thrive. 3. carry out, follow through. 4. flourish, thrive, profit.*

failing n. fault, defect, weakness, imperfection, flaw, shortcoming, peccadillo, deficiency. ANT. *strength, strong point.*

failure n. 1. NONSUCCESS *washout, *bomb, fiasco, disappointment, defeat, mishap, *strikeout, abortion, misadventure, dud, loss, bust, *dog, *turkey, debacle. "A school in which the truth always grows strong." — Henry Ward Beecher. "Not the falling down, but the staying down." — Mary Pickford. "The highway to success." — John Keats. 2. LOSER down-and-outer, also-ran, flop, incompetent, *has-been, washout. 3. WEAKENING deterioration, dwindling, fading, decline, loss. ANT. *1. success, achievement, triumph. 2. winner, success, champion. 3. strengthening, flourishing, thriving, growth.*

faint v. pass out, black out, collapse, lose consciousness, keel over, crumple, drop, swoon.

faint a. 1. INDISTINCT vague, dim, pale, obscure, faded, soft, unclear, low, weak, ill-defined, distant. 2. WEAK *woozy, lightheaded, dizzy, drooping, limp, feeble, enervated. ANT. *1. distinct, sharp, defined. 2. strong, invigorated, energetic.*

fainthearted a. timid, cowardly, *wimpy, *yellow, *candy-assed, afraid, meek, spineless, *afraid of one's own shadow, mousy. ANT. *brave, courageous, bold.*

fair a. **1.** JUST evenhanded, equitable, unprejudiced, impartial, unbiased, *square, honest, clean, scrupulous. **2.** SUNNY bright, cloudless, clear, clement, pleasant, mild. **3.** MEDIOCRE adequate, intermediate, okay, satisfactory, good enough, *so-so, *not bad, tolerable, *comme ci, comme ca. **4.** ATTRACTIVE beautiful, good-looking, comely, handsome, pulchritudinous, lovely, pretty. **5.** LIGHT-COMPLEXIONED blonde, pale, peaches and cream, towheaded, alabaster, white. ANT. *1. unfair, one-sided, prejudiced, unjust, crooked. 2. stormy, cloudy, overcast, rainy. 3. excellent, superior, poor, inferior. 4. ugly, homely. 5. dark, swarthy, black.*

fairly adv. **1.** SOMEWHAT passably, moderately, sort of, tolerably, more or less. **2.** EQUITABLY justly, impartially, evenly, honestly, legitimately. ANT. *2. unfairly, unjustly, dishonestly.*

fairness n. justice, equity, evenhandedness, impartiality, honor, integrity, honesty, righteousness, *fair shake, *level playing field, equitableness. ANT. *unfairness, injustice, impartiality.*

fairy n. elf, pixie, nymph, leprechaun, brownie, gnome, sprite, dwarf, imp, puck, gremlin, sandman, Tinkerbell.

faith n. **1.** BELIEF conviction, trust, confidence, certainty, sureness, credence, reliance, hope, dependence. "It is an instinct, for it precedes all outward instruction." — Henry Amiel. "The response of our spirits to beckonings of the eternal." — George Buttrick. "The soul riding at anchor." — Josh Billings. "A bridge across the gulf of death." — Edward Young. "God felt by the heart, not by reason." — Blaise Pascal. **2.** RELIGIOUS BELIEF religion, persuasion, church, denomination, sect, doctrine, creed, dogma, teaching.

faithful a. **1.** LOYAL true, true-blue, trustworthy, devoted, allegiant, steadfast, staunch, patriotic, *tried and true, honorable, semper fidelis. **2.** ACCURATE exact, reliable, correct, literal, true, actual, perfect, authentic, precise. ANT. *1. disloyal, treacherous, backstabbing. 2. inaccurate, inexact, rough.*

fake n. phony, sham, counterfeit, fraud, imitation, imposture, hoax, *humbug, *three-dollar bill, forgery, fabrication, imposter, poseur, mountebank, charlatan. ANT. *genuine article, *real McCoy.

fake v. feign, counterfeit, falsify, sham, *put on, fabricate, pose, imitate, pretend, dissemble, affect.

fake a. counterfeit, phony, false, sham, fraudulent, *fakey, imitation, spurious, bogus, make-believe, pseudo. ANT. *real, genuine, authentic.*

falderal n. nonsense, gibberish, blather, *gobbledegook, *crap.

fall n. **1.** DROP plunge, tumble, descent, dive, spill, *header, *nose dive, plummet. **2.** DECLINE decrease, drop, slump, reduction, dip, depreciation, lowering, recession, lessening. **3.** DEFEAT ruin, failure, downfall, collapse, destruction, submission. **4.** AUTUMN harvest time, October. SEE AUTUMN, OCTOBER, NOVEMBER ANT. *1. ascent, elevation. 2. increase, growth, appreciation. 3. victory, ascent, win.*

fall v. **1.** DROP plunge, tumble, descend, dive, spill, topple, plummet, *do a header, *nosedive, cascade, trip, pitch, stumble, sprawl, flop. **2.** DECLINE decrease, drop, slump, reduce, dip, depreciate, lower, recede, lessen. **3.** BE RUINED OR DEFEATED succumb, be destroyed, fail, collapse, submit, capitulate, surrender, be overthrown. ANT. *1. ascend, rise, elevate. 2. increase, grow, appreciate. 3. win, ascend, be victorious.*

FALLACIOUS a. [fuh LAY shus] based on fallacy, erroneous, false. *His statements about green cheese on the moon were fallacious.* SYN. erroneous, incorrect, false, untrue, faulty, wrong, deceiving, unfounded, mistaken, spurious, invalid. ANT. *true, valid, substantiated.*

FALLACY n. [FAL uh see] a mistaken belief, false notion. *The belief that the moon is made of green cheese is a fallacy.* SYN. mistake, misconception, error, false notion, illusion, delusion, untruth, falsehood, sophistry, misapprehension, misinterpretation. ANT. *truth, fact, certainty.*

fall guy n. patsy, dupe, scapegoat, victim.

fallible a. imperfect, human, liable to make mistakes, faulty, unreliable, errant, mortal, defective, deficient. ANT. *perfect, *goof-proof, unerring, infallible.*

falling-out n. disagreement, fight, quarrel. SEE ARGUMENT

fallout n. **1.** CONSEQUENCE backlash, reaction, repercussion, aftermath, wake, effect. **2.** RAIN OF RADIOACTIVE PARTICLES settling, *rainout, contamination. SEE NUCLEAR BOMB

fallow a. inactive, idle, dormant, resting, inert, uncultivated, barren, neglected, unused, undeveloped. ANT. *productive, active, cultivated.*

false *a.* **1.** UNTRUE wrong, erroneous, inaccurate, mistaken, fabricated, *full of hot air, *all wet, in error, bogus, fallacious, dishonest, fictitious, unfounded, spurious, invalid, misleading. **2.** IMITATION fake, artificial, counterfeit, phony, ersatz, bogus, simulated, mock, sham, forged, pseudo. ANT. *1. true, factual, accurate. 2. real, genuine, authentic.*

falsehood *n.* lie, untruth, fib, fiction, fabrication, distortion, *whopper, prevarication, canard, *tall tale, perjury, fraud, *hogwash, *bullshit. ANT. *truth, fact, reality.*

falsify *v.* forge, fake, distort, misrepresent, adulterate, doctor, alter, misstate, dissemble, stretch, embroider.

falter *v.* **1.** HESITATE waver, vacillate, flinch, oscillate, hang back. **2.** STAMMER stumble, stutter, speak haltingly. **3.** STUMBLE totter, stagger, shamble, reel, teeter, dodder.

fame *n.* renown, celebrity, prominence, notoriety, recognition, distinction, stardom, eminence, standing, repute, greatness, acclaim. "Vanity." — Marcus Aurelius. "Wind." — Thomas Coryate. "The perfume of heroic deeds." — Plato. "Footprints on the sands of time." — Longfellow. "Climbing a greasy pole for $10 and ruining trousers worth $15." — Josh Billings. "A host of expendable sycophants, a lack of privacy and the alienation of old friends." — Morton Da Costa. ANT. *obscurity, anonymity, oblivion.*

familiar *a.* **1.** WELL-KNOWN acquainted, accustomed, recognizable, intimate, *old hat, common, everyday, habitual, routine, ordinary, stock. **2.** KNOWLEDGEABLE conversant with, informed, versed, aware of, apprised of, *up on, savvy, cognizant, au courant. **3.** FRIENDLY intimate, informal, close, relaxed, neighborly, *free and easy, *buddy-buddy, cozy, genial, natural, at home. **4.** BOLD over-familiar, presumptuous, forward, disrespectful, taking liberties, impudent. ANT. *1. unfamiliar, foreign, alien, extraordinary. 2. ignorant, unaware, oblivious. 3. formal, shy, aloof, stiff. 4. respectful, reserved, reticent.*

familiarity *n.* KNOWLEDGE acquaintance, association, intimacy, closeness, firsthand knowledge, conversance, understanding, cognizance, awareness, feel. "A magician that is cruel to beauty, but kind to ugliness." — Ouida **2.** FRIENDLINESS informality, neighborliness, intimacy, closeness, naturalness.

familiarize *v.* acquaint, get to know, enlighten, accustom, make conversant, inform, school,

*get a feel for, *get a handle on, acclimatize, habituate.

family *n.* **1.** CLAN household, kin, tribe, kinfolk, relatives, relations, *blood, brethren, siblings, generation, dynasty, offspring, children, brood, kids, ancestry, bloodline, forebears, lineage, pedigree. "One of nature's masterpieces." — George Santayana "The miniature commonwealth upon whose integrity the safety of the larger commonwealth depends." — Felix Adler. "The we of me." — Carson McCullers. "The first and essential cell of human society." — Pope John XXIII. "The nucleus of civilization." — Will Durant. **2.** CLASS genus, classification, division, group, order, kind, species, type.

famine *n.* starvation, hunger, shortage, scarcity, privation, want.

famous *a.* well-known, prominent, renowned, celebrated, famed, eminent, notable, illustrious, glamourized, distinguished, exalted, glorified, acclaimed, recognized, notorious. ANT. *obscure, anonymous, unknown.*

fan *n.* enthusiast, devotee, *hound, *nut, *bug, *fiend, aficiondo, addict, *freak, buff, fanatic, rooter.

fanatic *n.* zealot, extremist, radical, enthusiast, devotee, follower, militant, bigot, nut. "The gadflies that keep society from being too complacent." Abraham Flexner. "The Devil's plaything." — Armenian proverb. "A lunatic with a hobby." Leonard Levinson.

fanatical *a.* zealous, extreme, radical, devoted, militant, rabid, single-minded, monomaniacal, obsessive, fervent, dogmatic. ANT. *moderate, reasonable, open-minded.*

FANATICISM *a.* [fuh NAT uh siz um] excessive enthusiasm or zeal. *Her fanaticism led her into performing terrorist acts.* SYN. zeal, overenthusiasm, fervor, obsession, monomania, single-mindedness, devotion, passion, dogmatism, bigotry, militantism. "False fire of an overheated mind." — William Cowper. ANT. *moderation, apathy, indifference.*

fanciful *a.* imaginary, whimsical, unreal, made-up, romantic, capricious, fantastic, dreamy, fairy-tale, chimerical, illusory, flighty, quaint. ANT. *reality-based, real, down-to-earth, prosaic.*

fancy *n.* **1.** IMAGINATION fantasy, creation, illusion, visualization, whimsy, whim, conception, notion, vision, idea, picture, dream, daydream, figment, chimera, hallucination. **2.** LIKING fondness, *yen, desire, partiality, hankering, penchant, taste.

fancy *a.* fine, *done up, elegant, prime, extravagant, deluxe, ornate, embellished, frilly, special, showy, lavish, rich, elaborate, decorated. ANT. *plain, ordinary, simple.*

fanfare *n.* *hoopla, *ballyhoo, buildup, trumpeting, show, to-do, fuss, display, pomp, commotion, ruckus.

fantasize *v.* envision, dream up, daydream, imagine, visualize, picture, invent, *take a flight of fancy, muse, *build castles in the air, moon, *trip.

fantastic *a.* **1.** EXCELLENT wonderful, great, super, awesome, sensational, marvelous, first-class, *primo, *out of this world. **2.** STRANGE weird, grotesque, odd, quaint, imaginary, outlandish, *out of this world, exotic, peculiar, freakish, queer, Kafkaesque, nightmarish, hallucinatory, incredible. ANT. *1. terrible, bad, lousy, awful. 2. normal, down to earth, ordinary, prosaic.*

fantasy *n.* imagination, imagining, visualization, envisioning, dream, daydream, invention, *flight of fancy, *castle in the air, reverie, whimsy, conception, hallucination, chimera, *fool's paradise. ANT. *reality, real world.*

far *a.* distant, remote, removed, far-off, far-flung, out-of-the-way, outlying. ANT. *near, close, at hand.*

farce *n.* **1.** COMEDY slapstick, burlesque, lampoon, satire, parody, *knee-slapper, absurdity, low comedy, travesty, silliness. **2.** ABSURDITY mockery, pretense, travesty.

farcical *a.* [FARS i kul] absurd, laughable, ridiculous. *The solemn affair turned farcical when the speaker's pants fell down.* SYN. absurd, laughable, ludicrous, ridiculous, comical, funny, foolish, preposterous, droll, goofy. ANT. *serious, solemn, grave.*

fare *n.* **1.** FOOD diet, menu, victuals, rations, table, edibles, spread, *munchies. **2.** CHARGE FOR TRANSPORTATION fee, price, passage, toll, token.

farewell *n.* goodbye, *see you later, *take care, *so long, adios, cheerio, adieu, auf Wiedersehen, bon voyage, *toodle-oo, *toodles, sayonara, ciao, ta-ta, hasta la vista, arrivederci, au revoir, Godspeed.

farfetched *a.* unlikely, doubtful, improbable, remote, strained, implausible, unbelievable, *hard to swallow, *stretching things, forced. ANT. *plausible, believable, likely.*

far-flung *a.* widespread, far-reaching, wide-ranging, remote, distant.

farm *n.* farmstead, plantation, ranch, grange, barnyard, homestead, pasture, vineyard, orchard, acreage, tillage, croft, hacienda, patch, garden. "An irregular patch of nettles, bound by short term notes, containing a fool and his wife who didn't know enough to stay in the city."—S.J. Perelman.

WORD FIND

animal-raising: pastoral farming

animal used for pulling: draft animal

barren, as a field left unplanted: fallow

changing crop type grown in field periodically: crop rotation

channel cut into soil: furrow

chicken house: coop

corn storage structure: corncrib

cover crop and fodder: alfalfa

cow barn: byre

crops sold for money, not used as feed: cash crops

crop such as grass planted to prevent soil erosion: cover crop

cutting edge of moldboard plow: plowshare

cylindrical storage building for fodder: silo

descriptive: rolling patchwork; regiment of corn; pastoral quilting; stubble fields of Autumn; Irish green fields; weathered, swayback barn; plodding draft animals; rooting pigs; hens scratching in the dirt

farming: husbandry

farming to feed family only with crops: subsistence farming

feed for livestock: fodder

fertilizer: manure, compost, fish meal, bone meal

fodder that has been stored: silage

grain storage building: granary

grazing land for animals: pasture

harvesting machine that cuts, threshes, cleans, bags grain: combine

hay cutter: mower, sickle, scythe

hayfork: pitchfork

hay grass, most common in United States: timothy

hay pile (long) left to dry in field: windrow

hay pile shaped like cone: haycock

horse enclosure: corral

implement having spikes or disks for breaking clods, refining soil: harrow

implement having teeth, pulled by tractor to gather loose hay: rake

implement that breaks up soil, uproots weeds: cultivator

irrigation, farming without: dry farming

laborer: farm hand, migrant worker, bracero

natural farming without man-made pesticides, fertilizers: organic farming

pesticide spraying, especially by air: crop dusting

plant, scatter seeds: sow

rig that compresses and ties hay into blocks: baler

rig that separates seeds, grains from straw: thresher

rig that spreads manure, lime, other material: spreader

rotary blades for breaking up soil: tiller

separated husks of grain: chaff

separate seeds, grains from straw: thresh

shelf plowed into hill to prevent water runoff: terrace

silo that is horizontal: bunker silo

sowing grass to be used as pasture: ley farming

spread seeds: broadcast

stumps of crops left after harvest: stubble

subsistence farm, small: croft

tenant farmer who works for a share of the crop: sharecropper

unplowed strip of land at end of furrows: headland

wedge-shaped plow of yesterday: moldboard plow

SEE BARN, RANCH

farm v. cultivate, grow, sow, plow, till, raise crops, plant, practice husbandry, work the soil, *scratch out a meager existence, garden, homestead, ranch.

farmer n. agriculturist, cultivator, planter, grower, agrarian, agronomist, granger, sodbuster, rustic, *hayseed, *clodhopper, gardener, sharecropper, rancher, husbandman. "The staunchest soldiers." — Cato. "A handy man with a sense of humus." — Edward B. White.

farming n. husbandry, agriculture, agronomy, cultivation, crop-raising, sharecropping, harvesting, agribusiness, growing, tillage, working the land, homesteading, ranching. "Laying down roots." — Anon. "Massaging the land." — Anon. "The first and most precious of all the arts." — Thomas Jefferson. "A school of patience: you can't hurry the crops or make an ox in two days." — Emile C. Alain.

far-out a. Sl. wild, *cool, *groovy, weird, *rad.

far-reaching a. extensive, wide-ranging, widespread, broad, sweeping, pervasive.

farsighted a. foresighted, prescient, wise, shrewd, judicious, perceptive, provident, thoughtful. ANT. shortsighted, nearsighted, my-opic, tunnel-visioned.

fart n. gas, flatulence, *barking spider, *ill wind.

fart v. pass gas, *cut one, *rip one, *let her rip, *cut the cheese, *break wind.

fascinate v. spellbind, bewitch, charm, fix, attract, transfix, entrance, captivate, beguile, enthrall, engross, hypnotize.

fascinating a. spellbinding, bewitching, charming, attractive, transfixing, entrancing, captivating, beguiling, eye-popping, enthralling, engrossing, hypnotizing, riveting. ANT. boring, dull, prosaic.

fascination n. attraction, spellbinding, charm, bewitchment, captivation, trance, magnetism, enchantment, enthrallment.

fascism n. totalitarianism. SEE DICTATORSHIP

fashion n. style, mode, vogue, rage, dernier cri, trend, look, taste, fad, *latest thing, furor, way, craze, manner, design, cut. "What one wears himself; what is unfashionable is what other people wear." — Oscar Wilde. "Something that goes out of style as soon as most people have one." — Sylvia Bremer. "Beautiful things which always become ugly with time." — Jean Cocteau. "A despot whom the wise ridicule and obey." — Ambrose Bierce.

WORD FIND

calico dresses with long sleeves: prairie look

cowboy shirts, jeans, string ties, tooled-leather belts, Stetson: cowboy look

dashikis, selosos, bubas, Afros: African-American

1890-1910: leg-o-mutton sleeves, choker collars, pompadour hair: Gibson Girl

full skirts, hoop earrings, shawls: gypsy

historical fashion brought back: retro, vintage

Ivy League, upper-crust sweaters, chinos, cords, oxfords, loafers: preppy look

long torso dresses, ropes of pearls, 1920s: flapper look

male and female combined: androgynous

mod 1960s, miniskirts, polka dot shirts with white collars, bell-bottoms: Carnaby

mod 1960s, platform shoes, newsboy hats, faded dresses: funky

mohawks, spiked hair, black leather jackets, slitted skirts, safety pins, torn clothes: punk

nation, of a: ethnic

ruffled necks, wrists for both sexes, 1960s and 1970s: dandy

Scottish kilt like skirts, knee-socks, tam-o-shanter: kiltie look

tailored business or professional's clothes:

Brooks Brothers

uncoordinated 1970s look, baggy pants, challis skirts: Annie Hall look

unkempt, long hair, tank tops, tie-dyed shirts, jeans, miniskirts, love beads: hippie, Grateful Dead look

fashion v. make, form, shape, create, devise, contrive, construct, forge, sculpt, *throw together, *slap together, fabricate, mold.

fashionable a. stylish, modish, in vogue, smart, chic, *on the cutting edge, *hot, trendsetting, *hip, mod, *all the rage, *happening, swank, a la mode, chi-chi, *in, *with it. ANT. unfashionable, old-fashioned, outmoded, dated, *out.

fast v. abstain, go hungry, refrain, starve, diet.

fast a. **1.** QUICK rapid, swift, fleet, speedy, hasty, *snappy, *flying, *quicker than greased lightning, *breakneck, *in a heartbeat, *lickety-split, expeditious, instantaneous, brisk, supersonic, hypersonic, meteoric. **2.** FIXED firm, stuck, unmovable, fastened, tight, secure, permanent, staunch, inextricable, steady, fortified. **3.** WILD reckless, dissipated, loose, promiscuous, immoral, devil-may-care, lascivious, licentious, intemperate, unrestrained. ANT. 1. slow, leisurely, sluggish, slothlike. 2. movable, temporary, insecure. 3. moral, chaste, virtuous, celibate.

fast adv. **1.** QUICKLY rapidly, swiftly, speedily, hastily, expeditiously, instantly, briskly, *in a flash, *in a heartbeat, *in short order, supersonically, hypersonically. **2.** FIRMLY fixedly, securely, tight, solidly, steadfastly. ANT. 1. slowly, slothfully, leisurely. 2. loosely, insecurely.

fasten v. attach, secure, affix, hook, tie, join, couple, bind, lock, close, hitch, buckle, link, nail, weld, solder, rivet, cement. ANT.unfasten, detach, disconnect.

FASTIDIOUS a. [fa STID ee us] discriminating, meticulous, picky. Also, overly dainty and easily disgusted. He was neat and fastidious; he was always picking lint from his clothing. SYN. discriminating, meticulous, picky, critical, fussy, finicky, hypercritical, dainty, overparticular, easily disgusted, squeamish, *persnickety. ANT. undiscriminating, uncritical, slack, sloppy.

fat n. adipose tissue, bulk, chubbiness, blubber, obesity, excess, *winter storage, flesh, *spare tire, *middle-aged spread, excess, beef, lard, grease.

fat a. **1.** OVERWEIGHT obese, corpulent, chubby, plump, rotund, stout, portly, beefy, heavyset,

elephantine, blubbery, lumpy, tubby, potbellied, paunchy, walrus-like, roly-poly, *blimpy, thickset, full-figured, big-boned, *wide load, *lard-assed. **2.** RICH affluent, prosperous, well-to-do, moneyed, *well-heeled, comfortable, profitable, wealthy. ANT. 1. skinny, anorexic, bony, lean. 2. poor, poverty-stricken.

fatal a. deadly, lethal, mortal, destructive, killing, disastrous, terminal, calamitous, ruinous, death-dealing, catastrophic, pernicious.

fatality n. death, casualty, victim, dead.

fate n. destiny, providence, fortune, kismet, lot, future, *wheel of fortune, end, *the stars, luck, *lady luck, doom, God's will, karma, *handwriting on the wall. "What must be shall be."—Seneca. "The gunman that all gunmen dread."—Don Marquis.

fateful a. momentous, crucial, critical, important, decisive, portentous, apocalyptic, prophetic, deadly, lethal, fatal.

father n. **1.** MALE PARENT dad, daddy, papa, pappy, pop, pa, *old man, parent, sire, head of the household, protector, forefather, progenitor, forebear. "A man who expects his son to be as good a man as he meant to be."—Franklin Clark. "He who brings up, not he who begets, is the father."—Bible. "One ... is more than a hundred schoolmasters."—George Herbert. **2.** FOUNDER inventor, originator, author, architect, creator, sire, intitiator, maker, producer.

father v. sire, produce, beget, generate, procreate, engender, conceive, originate, create, invent, found.

fatherhood n. paternity, parenthood.

fatherland n. motherland, old country, homeland, native land.

fathom v. **1.** UNDERSTAND comprehend, *get to the bottom of, grasp, get, sense, probe, interpret, figure out, penetrate. **2.** SOUND plumb, measure.

fatigue n. tiredness, exhaustion, weariness, lassitude, listlessness, enervation, *burn-out, lethargy, malaise, weakness, languor. ANT. energy, vigor, strength.

fatigue v. tire, exhaust, wear out, enervate, *burn out, weaken, *poop, drain, wipe out, tucker out, deplete, debilitate, *bush.

fatty a. adipose, blubbery, lardy, tallowy, marbled, greasy, oily. ANT. lean.

fatuous a. stupid, silly, foolish, asinine, inane, moronic, *lamebrained, vacuous, idiotic, imbecilic. ANT. brilliant, smart, wise.

fault n. **1.** DEFECT imperfect, flaw, shortcoming,

weakness, failing, *bug, blemish, stain. "The greatest . . . is to be conscious of none." — Thomas Carlyle. **2.** MISTAKE error, slipup, lapse, blunder, *goof, blame, wrongdoing, liability, guilt, responsibility. ANT. *1. virtue, strength. 2. credit.*

fault v. blame, criticize, reproach, reprove, impugn, accuse, *wag one's finger at, shame.

faultfinder n. critic, nagger, nag, carper, caviler, *nitpicker, quibbler, Momus, *hairsplitter, *bitch, *rag, *bellyacher, censor, grumbler, *backseat driver.

faultfinding a. critical, picky, nit-picking, captious, quibbling, *hairsplitting, caviling, hypercritical, overcritical. ANT. *easygoing, forgiving, tolerant.*

faultless a. flawless, perfect, impeccable, immaculate, clean, spotless, pure, ideal, unblemished, blameless, above reproach, innocent. ANT. *faulty, flawed, imperfect.*

faulty a. imperfect, flawed, defective, deficient, impaired, lacking, incorrect, wrong, unsound, malfunctioning. ANT. *perfect, flawless, sound.*

FAUX PAS n. [foh PAH] a social blunder, a mistake in etiquette. *Forgetting the host's name at a party is a faux pas.* SYN. social blunder, misstep, mistake, error, goof, impropriety, gaffe, indiscretion, transgression, lapse, offense.

favor n. **1.** GOOD TURN service, courtesy, help, aid, accommodation, assistance, consideration, kindness, good deed, dispensation. **2.** APPROVAL esteem, goodwill, liking, regard, approbation, backing, grace, patronage. ANT. *2. disfavor, ill will, disapproval.*

favor v. like, support, back, endorse, advocate, prefer, regard highly, fancy, *go for, sanction, pick, commend, indulge, pamper. ANT. *dislike, disfavor, frown upon, reject.*

favorable a. **1.** APPROVING commending, friendly, good, kind, sympathetic, complimentary, affirmative, enthusiastic. **2.** HELPFUL advantageous, beneficial, profitable, useful, auspicious, propitious, fortunate, convenient, timely, opportune, lucky. ANT. *1. disapproving, negative, unfriendly. 2. unfavorable, adverse, untimely.*

favorite n. preference, choice, selection, *number one, *apple of one's eye, pet, darling, ideal, dearest, idol, *pick of the litter.

favorite a. best-liked, preferred, pet, dear, choice, beloved, popular, selected, ideal, *fair-haired, dearest. ANT. *disliked, unwanted.*

favoritism n. partiality, bias, prejudice, discrimination, one-sidedness, preferential treatment, unfairness, partisanship, nepotism.

FAWN v. [FAWN] to flatter, cater to and generally fall all over someone in order to please. *Mary always fawns over the boss.* SYN. cringe, flatter, *kiss up to, *bootlick, *brownnose, toady, grovel, kowtow, bow and scrape, *apple polish, truckle to.

fawning a. servile, sycophantic, deferential, slavish, groveling, subservient, cringing, flattering, *brownnosing, kowtowing, submissive, obsequious.

faze v. disturb, disconcert, bother, perturb, upset, rattle, embarrass, discompose, daunt, discomfit, *shake up, unnerve.

fear n. fright, terror, apprehension, foreboding, dread, alarm, anxiety, angst, panic, trepidation, nervousness, *butterflies, *the shakes, *cold feet, creeps, *chills, awe, uneasiness, dismay, jitters, horror, cowardice, phobia, nightmare, *feeling of impending doom. "Nature's warning signal to get busy." — Henry Link. "The soul's signal for rallying." — Henry Ward Beecher. "A slinking cat I find beneath the lilacs of my mind." — Sophie Tunnel. "The darkness where negatives are developed." — Anon. SEE FEARFUL, PHOBIA

fear v. be afraid of, dread, apprehend, shudder at the thought of, be scared, *sweat bullets over, *get the shakes over, *get cold feet, feel alarm, *break out in a cold sweat, have qualms, cower.

fearful a. **1.** AFRAID frightened, scared, terrified, apprehensive, dreading, alarmed, anxious, frantic, panicky, discomposed, nervous, shaking, awed, uneasy, dismayed, intimidated, timorous, skittish, jittery, horrified, phobic, *sweating bullets, *shitting bricks. **2.** FRIGHTENING terrifying, scary, frightful, dreadful, alarming, horrifying, chilling, nightmarish, distressing, creepy, shocking, horrible, *hair-raising, bloodcurdling, formidable, *adrenalizing, *heart-pounding, paralyzing.

WORD FIND

Body reactions/language: hackles rise, small hairs at the back of the neck stir; prickling sensation up spine; skin crawling; icy chill down spine; skin blossoming with goosebumps; quaking knees; throat closes spastically; gulp; swallow dryly; swallow a lump in throat; knot constricting throat; breath raw in one's throat; shudder; heart fluttering/pounding/palpitating/hammering/performing flip-flops; breath quickens; blood pounds in one's throat; trap door (sensation) opening in pit of belly; nauseating spurts of adrenalin coursing through veins; gasp; gulp air furiously; feel paralyzed; feel strangely semipresent or disembodied, as if in a dream; events appearing in slow motion; wring hands; sweat bullets; break out in cold sweat; skin turns clammy; stomach knots/clenches/shrivels/lurches; recoil in shock; reel; jumpy; feel weak and shaky from adrenalin

Facial expressions: gape pop-eyed, stare saucer-eyed with terror, stare catatonically, face ashen, face stricken, eyes take on a hunted look, nostrils dilate, face pales, blood drains from face, eyes dart maniacally, eyes widen in alarm, eyes transfixed, eyes watch with numbed horror, eyes watch with fascinated horror, peer wild-eyed, eyes blink with incredulity, lips form a silent O.

Voice: becomes high and hysterical, strangled cry, desperate, shrill with horror, hoarse shriek, mute, gargling scream, guttural scream, raw, constricted, strained, cracking; quavering, rises an octave. SEE ANXIETY

fearless *a.* courageous, bold, unafraid, brave, undaunted, unflinching, daring, valorous, stouthearted, bodacious, gutsy, confident, heroic, intrepid, spunky, *ballsy. ANT. *afraid, frightened, spineless, mousy, cowardly.*

feasible *a.* doable, possible, workable, attainable, achievable, practicable, viable, reachable, realistic. ANT. *impossible, unworkable, impractical.*

feast *n.* banquet, meal, spread, celebration, repast, dinner, supper, festival, eating and drinking, *feed.

feast *v.* banquet, eat, dine, wine and dine, indulge, partake, gorge, gormandize, regale, *stuff oneself, *pig out.

feat *n.* accomplishment, deed, act, exploit, achievement, stunt, adventure, venture, triumph, coup.

feather *n.* plume, plumage, penna, quill, down, eider.

feathery *a.* downy, fluffy, soft, ticklish, gossamer, ethereal.

feature *n.* **1.** CHARACTERISTIC aspect, component, element, point, item, quality, attribute, highlight, mark, trait, hallmark, property. **2.** MAIN SHOW headliner, highlight, drawing card, special attraction.

feature *v.* showcase, highlight, emphasize, spotlight, star, stress, play up, headline, give prominence to, underscore.

February *n.* "The most serious charge which can be brought against New England." — Joseph Krutch.

feces *n.* excrement, dung, stools, *crap, *shit, *squat, *poop, *doo-doo, *load, manure, guano, muck, waste.

FECUND *a.* [FEE kund] fertile and productive. *A photograph of a fecund farmscape accompanied the article.* SYN. fertile, productive, fruitful, prolific, bounteous, rich, generating, teeming, potent. ANT. *sterile, barren, impotent.*

federation *n.* confederacy, union, league, alliance, partnership, amalgamation, syndicate, fraternity, association.

fee *n.* charge, price, commission, payment, toll, due, bill, cost, expense, percentage, consideration, remuneration, compensation.

feeble *a.* weak, ineffective, frail, enervated, impotent, *wimpy, lame, powerless, fragile, inadequate, ineffectual, debilitated, sickly, slight, faint, meager. ANT. *powerful, potent, strong, effective.*

feebleminded *a.* mentally retarded, slow, dull-witted, imbecilic, stupid, dumb, moronic, *weak in the head, subnormal, *airheaded, bovine. ANT. *brilliant, *brainy, intelligent.*

feed *n.* food, fodder, ensilage, silage, forage, pasturage, vittles, *grub, provisions.

feed *v.* nourish, fuel, fill, sustain, provide, *wine and dine, serve, provision, foster, cater, maintain, give, *stuff, cram. SEE EAT

feel *n.* flair, knack, aptitude, ability, faculty, gift, talent, hang.

feel *v.* **1.** TOUCH handle, finger, caress, palpate, stroke, fondle, grasp, squeeze, probe, grope, run hands over. **2.** SENSE experience, perceive, comprehend, know, understand, discern, notice, apprehend, detect, enjoy, suffer.

feeling *n.* **1.** SENSATION experience, perception, comprehension, understanding, consciousness, awareness, impression, response, reaction, emotion, sentiment. **2.** EMOTION passion, sensitivity, sympathy, depth, ardor, fervor, enthusiasm, zest, soul, heart, spirit, tenderness. "The emotion which drives the intelligence forward in spite of obstacles." — Henry Bergson. "The unconscious conversion of instinctual impulses." — Carl Jung. **3.** OPINION point of view, idea, sentiment, impression, sense, inclination, conviction, belief, evaluation, outlook, conception.

feelings n. emotions, sensibilities, passions, ego, impulses, susceptibilities, sentiments, sympathies, soul, spirit, drives, *plucking of heartstrings, instincts.

FEIGN v. [FANE] to make up, invent or fake. *At the funeral, Joe feigned sympathy; he never cared about the deceased.* SYN. make up, invent, fake, simulate, affect, pretend, assume, pose, bluff, *put on an act, sham, dissemble.

feint n. fake, diversion, sham, bluff, ruse, subterfuge, pretense, bait, snare, ploy, dodge.

felicitous a. appropriate, apt, fitting, suitable, apropos, pertinent, relevant, timely. ANT. *inappropriate.*

fell v. knock down, cut down, level, raze, hew, mow, prostrate. ANT. *raise.*

fellow n. **1.** MAN guy, person, boy, human, *chap, *dude, gentleman, individual, *hombre. **2.** PEER equal, companion, associate, compatriot, counterpart, friend, colleague, confrere, mate, twin, match.

fellowship n. companionship, friendship, association, comradeship, fraternity, camaraderie, togetherness, brotherhood, communion. "The ability to unite." — Berl Katznelson.

felon n. criminal, larcenist, lawbreaker, convict, outlaw, malefactor, miscreant, *hood, gangster, mafioso, crook, recidivist.

FELONIOUS a. [fuh LOW nee us] evil, wicked, designating serious criminal behavior. *Armed robbery is a felonious act.* SYN. evil, wicked, base, criminal, larcenous, villainous, vicious, corrupt, lawbreaking, illegal, immoral. ANT. *virtuous, law-abiding, moral, upstanding.*

female n. girl, woman, lady, *she, femme, gal, matron, sister.

feminine a. female, womanly, girlish, ladylike, soft, gentle, genteel, effeminate. ANT. *masculine, manly, macho.*

fence n. enclosure, barrier, barricade, boundary, wall, rail, paling, palisade, hedge.

WORD FIND
cattle-enclosing: barbed wire fence
fish-catching fence made of stakes: weir
post and rail: post and rail fence
screen of wood strips: lattice
stake fence: picket fence, paling
stake fence used for defense: palisade
sunken, in ditch: ha-ha
wire mesh: chain-link fence, *Cyclone fence
woven work of twigs, branches: wattle fence
zigzagging rail fence: Virginia fence, worm

fence, snake fence

fence v. **1.** ENCLOSE surround, pen, confine, encircle, separate, bound, corral, wall, hem. **2.** FIGHT WITH SABERS OR FOILS duel, parry, engage in swordplay.

WORD FIND
deflect opponent's weapon: parry
faked movement to throw off opponent: feint
forward thrust and jump: lunge
grazing blow down opponent's blade: coulé
jump and lunge: balestra
leap: volt
offensive move made after parry: riposte
protective cup on weapon: guard
protective glove: gauntlet
protective jacket: fencing jacket, underplastron
readiness stance: on guard
run toward opponent with arm extended: fleché
score: hit
taking of opponent's blade, method of: croisé
term: touché
weapon: epee, foil, saber, rapier
SEE FEND OFF

fend off v. defend, parry, resist, ward off, dodge, repel, deflect, divert, shield from, keep at bay, protect, evade, repulse.

ferment n. agitation, excitement, commotion, uproar, turmoil, turbulence, stir, tumult, hubbub, disruption, to-do. ANT. *peace, calm, serenity.*

ferment v. agitate, excite, disturb, shake, stir, churn, provoke, foment, incite, inflame, *bring to a head, seethe, rouse. ANT. *soothe, quiet, calm.*

ferocious a. savage, fierce, violent, cruel, wild, beastly, brutish, predatory, bloodthirsty, brutal, rapacious, vicious, barbarous, merciless. ANT. *humane, gentle, mild, tame.*

ferret out v. search out, sniff out, root out, dig up, unearth, track down, chase down, hunt down, discover, probe, smoke out.

fertile a. productive, fecund, fruitful, reproductive, generative, potent, yielding, rich, teeming, prolific, bountiful. ANT. *sterile, barren, impotent, unproductive.*

fertilize v. enrich, dress, compost, manure, germinate, inseminate, impregnate.

FERVENT a. [FUR vunt] passionate, intense, heated. *A fervent desire to succeed.* SYN. passionate, intense, heated, ardent, fervid, burning, hot, earnest, raging, eager, flaming, zealous, feverish, fierce, spirited. ANT. cool, lukewarm, apathetic, dispassionate.

fervor n. passion, intensity, heat, ardor, warmth, fire, fever, eagerness, zeal, enthusiasm, gusto, spirit, zest, vigor. ANT. apathy, indifference, coolness.

fester v. 1. SUPPURATE ulcerate, drain, run, putrefy, become inflamed. 2. RANKLE rile, irk, annoy, irritate, gall, inflame, embitter.

festival n. celebration, feast, rite, observation, carnival, commemoration, fair, gala, jubilee, fiesta.

festive a. celebratory, merry, gay, mirthful, sportive, jolly, cheery, jubilant, jolly, light-hearted. ANT. gloomy, dreary, somber.

festivity n. merrymaking, celebration, gaity, play, fun, revelry, party, mirth, jollity, carousal, sport, entertainment.

festoon v. adorn, decorate, deck, garland, trim, wreathe, ornament.

fetch v. 1. GET bring, retrieve, deliver, tote, convey, obtain, transport, lug, grab. 2. SELL FOR bring in, realize.

fetching a. attractive, charming, captivating, alluring, beautiful, winsome, fascinating, tantalizing, entrancing, enticing, lovely. ANT. repulsive, unattractive, ugly.

fetid a. stinking, putrid, *stinky, malodorous, foul, rank, rancid, smelly, rotten, tainted, gamy, reeking. ANT. fresh, floral, sweet. SEE ODOR, SCENT, SMELL

fetish n. erotic fixation, obsession, idee fixe, *turn-on, mania, preoccupation.

fetter n. restraint, check, shackle, chain, binding, bond, irons, trammel, handcuffs, hobble, manacle.

fetter v. restrain, check, shackle, chain, bind, put in irons, trammel, manacle, handcuff, restrict, hold. ANT. free, loose, liberate.

fettle n. condition, shape, form, state, order, fitness.

feud n. fight, quarrel, conflict, combat, altercation, squabble, argument, contention, row, hostility, *falling-out. ANT. peace, accord, harmony.

feud v. fight, quarrel, combat, squabble, contend, clash, war, *lock horns, wrangle, dispute.

fever n. temperature, pyrexia, heat, glow, flush.

feverish a. 1. RUNNING A TEMPERATURE warm, hot, fiery, *burning up, flushed, clammy, sweaty, delirious. 2. EXCITED agitated, heated, passionate, frenetic, restless, fervid, worked up, frantic, ardent, frenzied. ANT. 1. cool, chilled, normal. 2. calm, cool, luke-warm.

few n. some, a number, a handful, several, a bunch.

few a. not many, scant, scarce, rare, negligible, skimpy, sparse, thin, meager, limited, infrequent.

fiasco n. failure, *turkey, disaster, *flop, *bomb, *dud, debacle, catastrophe, abortion, miscarriage, *washout, farce, *joke. ANT. success, hit, triumph.

fiat n. decree, command, act. SEE ORDER

fib n. lie, white lie, half-truth, untruth, falsehood, fabrication, *cock-and-bull story, prevarication, *whopper, *crock. ANT. truth, fact.

fib v. lie, tell a white lie, falsify, fabricate, prevaricate, *tell a whopper, *stretch the truth, fudge.

FICKLE a. [FIK ul] liable to change one's loyalties or affections, capricious. Mary went through four boyfriends last month; she is very fickle. SYN. capricious, changeable, unstable, inconstant, whimsical, variable, unpredictable, impulsive, *blowing hot and cold, vacillating, flighty, volatile. ANT. stable, constant, faithful, steady.

fiction n. story, fabrication, lie, yarn, tale, invention, fantasy. "The world of our dreams come true."—Courtney Cooper. "Imagining based on facts."—Margaret Banning. "Fact distorted into truth."—Edward Albee. ANT. nonfiction, truth, fact. SEE NOVEL, STORY

fictitious a. made up, imaginary, fabricated, concocted, untrue, unreal, *bogus, created, fanciful, fantastic, feigned, phony. ANT. real, factual, true.

fiddle v. fuss with, toy, diddle, tinker, adjust, finger, mess with, play.

fidelity n. faithfulness, loyalty, devotion, allegiance, constancy, dedication, fealty, reliability, integrity. ANT. infidelity, faithlessness, disloyalty.

fidget v. squirm, wiggle, twitch, twiddle, fret, jiggle, jitter, *get antsy, jump, *worm about.

field n. 1. MEADOW pasture, grassland, plain, green, clearing, glebe, range.

WORD FIND

descriptive: Audubonesque tableau of birds and flowers, tawny tussocks of fall, softly-flowered like a Monet canvas, profusion of flowers, melange of colors, soft heather meadow, sea of crested wheat, bluegrass meadow, golden alpine meadow, thatchy undergrowth, verdant, Irish green field, broad sweep, wildflower meadow, sprays of daisies and buttercups, the lush grasses of a miller's dreams

grasses: bluegrass, bunch grass, salt grass, foxtail, buffalo grass, crab grass, deer grass, fescue, orchard grass, June grass, red top, river grass, ribbon grass, cattail

grasslands of Eurasia: steppes

heather or other small shrubs: heath

marshy area covered with heather, bracken: moor

midwest plain: prairie

plain of South America: pampas

Siberian: tundra

South African grassland: veld, veldt

tropical/subtropical grassland: savanna

2. SPECIALTY line, profession, province, realm, domain, area, sphere, territory, bailiwick.

fiend *n.* devil, demon, evil spirit, Satan, Lucifer, beast, monster, ogre, villain, savage, barbarian, scoundrel, sadist, *bad actor, *bastard, *creep. ANT. *angel, saint.*

fiendish *a.* evil, satanic, diabolical, demonic, monstrous, beastly, villainous, savage, barbarous, sadistic, *creepy, brutish. ANT. *angelic, saintly.*

fierce *a.* savage, wild, cruel, violent, ferocious, intense, furious, untamed, horrible, tempestuous, unbridled, vehement. ANT. *mild, tame, gentle.*

fiery *a.* passionate, burning, ardent, *hot, fervid, peppery, hot-blooded, blazing, feverish, angry, impassioned, excitable, high-strung, volatile. ANT. *cool, calm, lukewarm, dispassionate.*

fight *n.* battle, combat, clash, brawl, wrangle, bout, war, *scrap, fray, skirmish, encounter, scuffle, tussle, row, *fisticuffs, rumble, *free-for-all, donnybrook, altercation, set-to, dispute.

fight *v.* **1.** PHYSICALLY COMBAT battle, clash, brawl, wrangle, war, skirmish, rumble, contest, wrestle, altercate, assault, spar, box, *mix it up, *lock horns, tussle, *exchange blows, *slug it out, *go at it tooth and nail. **2.** OPPOSE BY ARGUMENT argue, contradict, dispute, contest, defy, *make a stand against, squabble, resist, protest, repulse, bicker.

fighter *n.* battler, scrapper, warrior, combatant, boxer, pugilist, wrestler, brawler, soldier, aggressor, bruiser, bully, antagonist, contender.

figment *n.* fantasy, imagining, fancy, fiction, creation, invention, daydream, product of the imagination, fabrication, delusion. ANT. *reality, truth, fact.*

FIGURATIVE *a.* [FIG yur uh tiv] based on figures of speech, symbols, etc.; not literal; metaphorical. *"The show blew my mind" is a figurative statement; my brain is actually still intact.* SYN. metaphorical, symbolic, not literal, illustrative, allegorical, representative, emblematic, pictorial. ANT. *literal, exact.*

figure *n.* **1.** FORM outline, shape, configuration, cast, structure, conformation. **2.** PHYSIQUE build, body, frame, shape. **3.** ILLUSTRATION picture, diagram, drawing, depiction, sketch, pattern, design. **4.** PROMINENT PERSON celebrity, notable, personage, man, woman, character. **5.** NUMBER numeral, digit.

figure *v.* **1.** CALCULATE compute, reckon, add up, sum, tally, count. **2.** THINK reckon, believe, suppose, guess, reason, judge.

FIGUREHEAD *n.* [FIG yur hed] one with the appearance or rank of someone in charge, but who in reality has no power. *The president is just a figurehead; the real leadership comes from his cabinet members.* SYN. straw man, *front, *puppet, nominal head, *dummy, dupe, token.

filch *v.* steal, pilfer, lift, shoplift, swipe, *pinch, thieve, purloin, *power, *rip off, rob, misappropriate.

file *n.* record, documents, data, folder, dossier, information, cabinet, repository, directory, index.

file *v.* **1.** ORDER catalog, categorize, classify, alphabetize, organize, sort, index. **2.** APPLY petition, register, make an application. **3.** SMOOTH grind, rasp, abrade, grate.

fill *v.* load, pack, cram, crowd, *top off, stuff, stock, replenish, squeeze in, glut, pad, heap, inflate, feed, gorge, saturate, pervade, suffuse. ANT. *empty, drain, deplete.*

film *n.* **1.** COATING layer, sheet, membrane, covering, scum, veil, cloud, haze, mistiness, blur, fog. **2.** MOVIE *flick, picture, cinema. SEE MOTION PICTURE, MOVIE

filmy *a.* veiled, hazy, cloudy, misty, foggy, blurred, milky, murky, gauzy. ANT. *clear, transparent, sharp.*

filter *n.* strainer, sieve, purifier, clarifier, screen, sifter.

filter *v.* strain, filtrate, screen, sift, clarify, purify, refine, stream, trickle, leak, drain, effuse.

filth *n.* **1.** DIRT muck, grubbiness, mud, scum, pollution, sewage, sludge, mire, *crap, *crud, grime, nastiness, slime, foulness, dung, excrement. **2.** OBSCENITY indecency, nastiness, pornography, smut, *raunch. ANT.

2. *decency, wholesomeness, purity.*

filthy *a.* **1.** DIRTY mucky, grubby, muddy, scummy, polluted, gross, *sludgy, *crappy, *cruddy, grimy, nasty, slimy, foul, stinking, soiled, begrimed. **2.** OBSCENE indecent, nasty, pornographic, *smutty, *raunchy, lewd. ANT. 1. *clean, spotless, fresh, sanitary.* 2. *decent, *squeaky-clean, pure, wholesome.*

FINAGLE *v.* [fuh NA gul] arrange, maneuver or manipulate to get something. *Joe tried to finagle his way into the game without tickets.* SYN. arrange, maneuver, manipulate, wangle, trick, deceive, engineer, machinate, negotiate, contrive.

final *a.* last, end, concluding, closing, finishing, ultimate, terminal, completing, extreme, decisive, definitive. ANT. *first, opening, beginning.*

finale *n.* end, close, finish, cap, conclusion, termination, completion, culmination, consummation, swan song, windup, finis. ANT. *opening, beginning, start.*

finalize *v.* conclude, complete, close, cap, wind up, terminate, consummate, culminate, *sew up loose ends, *put on ice, *clinch.

finance *n.* money management, banking, investment, economics, fiscal matters.

finance *v.* pay for, back, underwrite, bankroll, subsidize, capitalize, support.

financier *n.* banker, investor, venture capitalist, underwriter, tycoon, *fat cat, *angel, treasurer, merchant, *sugar daddy.

find *v.* discover, stumble upon, come upon, chance upon, uncover, spot, ferret out, see, locate, ascertain, espy, discern, sight, detect. ANT. *lose, misplace, lose sight of, overlook.*

finding *n.* judgment, conclusion, discovery, decision, verdict.

fine *n.* penalty, assessment, amercement, forfeit, punishment, damages, *slap on the wrist.

fine *a.* **1.** SUPERIOR excellent, very good, A-1, the best, first-class, first-rate, choice, prime, select, exceptional, great, supreme, refined. **2.** IN GOOD HEALTH well, okay, satisfactory. **3.** DELICATE light, gossamer, diaphanous, airy, fragile, dainty, flimsy, refined, exquisite. **4.** THIN slender, slight, narrow. **5.** GROUND powdered, pulverized, refined. **6.** SUBTLE slight, minute. ANT. 1. *poor, inferior, mediocre.* 2. *sick, ill, *under the weather.* 3. *heavy, coarse, ponderous.* 4. *fat, broad, wide.* 5. *coarse, unrefined.* 6. *huge.*

fine *v.* levy, penalize, punish, charge, assess, amerce.

FINESSE *n.* [fi NES] delicate skill or maneuvering. *He pitched the ball with great finesse. She moved through Washington society with great finesse.* SYN. skill, adroitness, delicacy, know-how, acumen, subtlety, sophistication, savvy, knack, shrewdness, savoir faire. ANT. *clumsiness, incompetence, bumbling, awkwardness.*

finger *n.* digit, pointer, thumb, forefinger, ring finger.

finger *v.* touch, handle, squeeze, feel, palpate, poke.

finicky *a.* fussy, picky, overparticular, exacting, dainty, meticulous, choosy, fastidious, anal retentive, *persnickety, *hard to please. ANT. *easy, careless, sloppy.*

finish *n.* **1.** ENDING close, closing, completion, finale, termination, windup, fulfillment, consummation, culmination, finis, death, *curtains, cap, climax. **2.** COATING surface, shine, polish, refinement, patina, veneer, varnish, luster. **3.** REFINEMENT elegance, grace, polish, cultivation, sauvity, genteelness. ANT. 1. *beginning, start, opening.* 3. *coarseness, roughness, crudity.*

finish *v.* **1.** COMPLETE end, close, finalize, stop, terminate, wind up, fulfill, consummate, culminate, die, cap off, *sew up loose ends. **2.** DEPLETE use up, exhaust, *knock off, consume, expend, dispose of, drain, dispatch. ANT. 1. *start, begin, open.* 2. *refill, conserve, restock, replenish.*

FINITE *a.* [FI nite] limited, as distinguished from infinite. *Natural resources on earth are finite; they won't last forever.* SYN. limited, measureable, confined, bounded, countable, terminable, delimited, fixed, ephemeral, ending, exhaustable. ANT. *infinite, boundless, interminable, endless.*

fink *n.* Sl. informer, *rat, *tattletale, *snake, *weasel, bastard, *shit, *brownnose.

fire *n.* **1.** FLAME blaze, conflagration, inferno, flare, sparks, embers, combustion, wildfire, bonfire, holocaust. "The symbol of civilization." —Joseph Hertz. "God's unfailing charity." —John Oxenham. "The most tolerable third party." —Thoreau.

WORD FIND

building that is a fire hazard: firetrap
causing fire: incendiary
fear of fire: pyrophobia
firesetter with criminal intentions: arsonist, incendiary
firesetter with mental problems: pyromaniac, firebug

firesetting compulsion: pyromania

forecasting the future by peering into flames: pyromancy

god: vulcan

intense, widespread fire caused by nuclear detonation: firestorm

strip of land cleared to stop fire spread: fire-break

worshipper: pyrolater

2. ENTHUSIASM energy, drive, vigor, zeal, fervor, intensity, ardor, passion, verve, gusto, vehemence. **3.** GUNFIRE round, barrage, shelling, salvo, fusillade, volley, strafing. ANT. *2. apathy, indifference, dispassion.*

fire *v.* **1.** SHOOT discharge, shell, pull the trigger, let off, detonate. **2.** ROUSE arouse, excite, inflame, spark, stir, incite, electrify, inspire, quicken, galvanize. **3.** DISCHARGE FROM DUTIES *pink slip, lay off, dismiss, *give walking papers, *can, *show the door, *axe, *let go, give notice, *sack. ANT. *1. cease fire. 2. dampen, discourage. 3. hire.*

firearm *n.* pistol, revolver, rifle, *shooting iron. SEE GUN

fireball *n.* meteor, bolide. SEE METEOR

firebrand *n.* agitator, rabble-rouser, instigator, agent provocateur, troublemaker, rebel, revolutionist, anarchist, *sparkplug.

firecracker *n.* squib, *cherry bomb, petard, *noisemaker. SEE FIREWORKS

fireplace *n.* hearth, chimney, stove, grate, fireside, blaze, inglenook.

fireproof *a.* fire resistant, flameproof, incombustible, unburnable, nonflammable. ANT. *combustible, flammable, incendiary, explosive.*

fireworks *n.* pyrotechnics, incendiary devices, rockets, feux d'artifice.

WORD FIND

arsenic sulfide used in: realgar

child's spark-maker: sparkler

hisses and sputters: fizgig, squib

pinwheellike: catherine wheel

rotating display: girandole

small rockets: bottle rockets

spiral, rises in a: tourbillion

star: star shell

tube ejecting balls of fire: Roman candle

firm *n.* company, corporation, business, enterprise, concern, outfit, institution, house, organization, conglomeration.

firm *a.* **1.** HARD solid, stiff, rigid, compressed, compact, unyielding, stony, inflexible, set. **2.** FIXED stationary, unmovable, stable, immovable, secure, immobile, anchored, sturdy, tight, unshakable, solid, rooted. **3.** CON-STANT, RESOLUTE consistent, enduring, steady, staunch, unshakable, fixed, persevering, unwavering, true, steadfast. ANT. *1. soft, loose. 2. unstable, mobile, movable. 3. wavering, unsteady, irresolute.*

firmament *n.* sky, heavens, vault, arch, *wild blue yonder, ether, infinity.

first *a.* **1.** EARLIEST original, beginning, front, opening, maiden, initial, premiere, preceding, prior, antecedent, primal, primeval, rudimentary, elementary. **2.** HIGHEST principal, chief, head, main, foremost, supreme, greatest, top, preeminent, dominant, capital, outstanding, ranking. **3.** BASIC fundamental, rudimentary, primary, elementary, beginning. ANT. *1. last, latest, end, subsequent. 2. lowest, least, smallest. 3. advanced.*

first-class *a.* best, superior, greatest, fine, excellent, superb, supreme, A-1, tops, *top-drawer, topnotch, *primo, peerless. ANT. *inferior, second-class, *bottom of the barrel.*

first-rate *a.* SEE FIRST-CLASS

fish *v.* **1.** ANGLE troll, cast, flycast, trawl, seine, chum. **2.** SEARCH rummage, hunt, pick through.

fisherman *n.* angler, fisher, piscator, *gill-netter, lobsterman.

fishing *n.* angling, casting, trolling, trawling. "That solitary vice." —Lord Byron. "A stick and a string with a fly on one end and a fool at the other." —Anon.

WORD FIND

artificial bait: lure, jig, spinner, fly, nymph

bait: earthworm, night crawler, mayfly, nymph, baitfish, chum, herring, squid

basket used by fisherman: creel

chair in sport-fishing boat: fighting chair

dragging a line near surface behind boat: trolling

drag net along bottom: trawl

fence that corrals fish: weir

floating signal ball: bobber

gear box: tackle box

gear: tackle

illegal fishing: poaching

line with several hooks at intervals across stream: trotline

net drawn shut by two boats: purse seine

net that hangs from floats on surface: seine, gill net

rippled water showing where fish is rising to bait: rise

snarled line on reel caused by overrun: backlash, *bird's nest

spear: harpoon, gaff

taking of bait by fish: strike
up and down motion imparted on bait to lure
fish: jigging
weight: sinker

fishy *a.* suspicious, doubtful, shady, unbelievable, incredible, shady, questionable, dubious, slippery, not kosher. ANT. *plausible, believable, credible.*

fissure *n.* cleft, crack, groove, crevice, crevasse, crack, chasm, fracture, fault, rift, slit.

fit *n.* seizure, convulsion, paroxysm, spasm, attack, *spaz, throe, bout, conniption, outburst, spell, frenzy, *floorgasm.

fit *v.* correspond, accord, jibe, harmonize, match, conform, agree, *dovetail, interlock, mesh.

fit *a.* **1.** SUITABLE fitting, apt, proper, seemly, right, correct, appropriate, befitting, decorous, germane. **2.** IN SHAPE healthy, well, robust, strong, hardy, hale, vigorous, hearty, strapping. ANT. *1. unsuitable, inappropriate. 2. sickly, weak, out of shape.*

fitful *a.* intermittent, irregular, spasmodic, restless, sporadic, erratic, unstable, spotty, fluctuating, random. ANT. *regular, constant, steady.*

fitting *n.* fixture, part, accessory, component, attachment, *doohickey.

fitting *a.* proper, suitable, befitting, correct, appropriate, decorous, becoming, fit, comme il faut, right, seemly, *politically correct. ANT. *improper, unsuitable, incorrect.*

fix *n.* predicament, mess, jam, *stew, difficulty, plight, *hot water, *pickle, *between a rock and a hard place.

fix *v.* **1.** REPAIR mend, patch up, doctor, remedy, restore, recondition, tune up, overhaul, adjust, correct. **2.** ATTACH affix, secure, connect, fasten, plant, tie, couple, link, lock, implant, cement, nail. **3.** DETERMINE set, decide, establish, settle. ANT. *1. break, bust. 2. detach, loosen, remove.*

FIXATION *n.* [fiks A shun] a neurotic preoccupation with someone or something; an obsession. *He has a fixation with blue-eyed blondes.* SYN. obsession, preoccupation, monomania, mania, fetish, fascination, *thing, complex, crush, infatuation, compulsion, idee fixe.

fixed *a.* **1.** FIRMLY ATTACHED unmovable, secured, anchored, firm, stable, solid, rooted, tight, made fast. **2.** ESTABLISHED set, settled, unchangeable, decided, constant, steady, unvarying, firm, inflexible. ANT. *1. detached, loosened. 2. changeable, varying.*

fixture *n.* fitting, part, accessory, component, attachment, appurtenance, *doohickey.

fizzle *v.* fail, *flop, *bomb, die, miscarry, fall short, *lay an egg, *sputter and die, come to nothing. ANT. *succeed, triumph, *score.*

flabbergasted *a.* surprised, amazed, astonished, taken aback, dumbfounded, astounded, struck dumb, rendered speechless, shocked, staggered, *bowled over, *blown away, confounded. ANT. *nonchalant, calm, cool, unperturbed.*

flabby *a.* flaccid, soft, limp, blubbery, *doughy, slack, droopy, fat, baggy, untoned, sagging, pendulous. ANT. *firm, toned, rigid, *rock-hard.*

flaccid *a.* SEE FLABBY

flag *n.* banner, standard, ensign, colors, pennant, *Old Glory, *Stars and Stripes, *Union Jack, streamer, banderole, bunting. "The emblem of our unity, our power, our thought and purpose as a nation." — Woodrow Wilson. "The trademark of a nation." — Leonard Levinson.

WORD FIND

decorative cloth in the colors of a flag: bunting
military unit's: guidon
pirate's skull and crossbones: Jolly Roger
pole: staff, shaft
signaling pennant used on boats: burgee

flag *v.* weaken, wilt, tire, become limp, languish, wilt, droop, fade, wane, ebb, sink, diminish, die. ANT. *strengthen, invigorate, energize.*

flagellate *v.* flog, lash. SEE WHIP

FLAGRANT *a.* [FLA grunt] outrageous or glaring. *He was ejected from the game after committing his second flagrant foul.* SYN. outrageous, glaring, blatant, audacious, shameless, brazen, undisguised, gross, conspicuous, barefaced, flaunted, disgraceful, egregious, extreme. ANT. *inconspicuous, subtle, slight, sneaky.*

flail *v.* strike, thrash, flog. SEE BEAT

flair *n.* **1.** KNACK talent, aptitude, ability, genius, propensity, bent, feel, gift, faculty. **2.** TASTE style, panache, dash.

flak *n.* criticism, disapproval, opposition, censure. SEE CRITICISM

flake *n.* scale, bit, fleck, chip, sliver, peel, shaving, sheet.

flake *v.* scale, peel, shave, exfoliate, chip, shed.

FLAMBOYANT *a.* [flam BOY unt] showy or ornate, loud. *She wore flamboyant costumes to draw attention to herself.* SYN. showy, ornate, loud, colorful, flashy, florid, gaudy, dazzling, ostentatious, garish, wild, theatrical, splashy, extravagant, glamorous. ANT. *quiet, understated, modest, plain, inconspicuous, dull.*

flame *n.* **1.** FIRE flame, blaze, light, *tongue, flash. SEE FIRE **2.** LOVER sweetheart, girlfriend, boyfriend.

flame *v.* burn, blaze, flare up, kindle, flash, spark, flicker, glow, sparkle.

flammable *a.* combustible, inflammable, incendiary, igneous, explosive. ANT. *fireproof, nonflammable.*

flap *n.* **1.** FOLD cover, tab, wing, tail, fly, skirt. **2.** CONTROVERSY agitation, commotion, brouhaha, to-do, fuss, hullabaloo, *tempest.

flap *v.* slap, whack, flutter, smack, swat, lash, whip.

flare *v.* **1.** FLAME blaze, flash, flicker, glow, scintillate, sparkle, ignite, spark, glare. **2.** BURST OUT erupt, explode, blow up, pop. **3.** WIDEN broaden, spread, expand, dilate, splay. ANT. *2. die down, dampen, cool. 3. contract, narrow.*

flash *n.* **1.** FLARE streak, burst, blaze, glint, flame, radiance, strobe, coruscation, illumination, spark, scintillation, glow, discharge, explosion. **2.** INSTANT second, *heartbeat, *blink of an eye, jiffy.

flash *v.* strobe, blink, fulgurate, flicker, flare, shine, scintillate, glow, glint, shimmer.

flashy *a.* showy, loud, flamboyant, gaudy, ostentatious, garish, glaring, blinding, glitzy, glittery, pretentious. ANT. *quiet, plain, understated, modest, sober.*

flask *n.* bottle, container, flagon, phial, vial, canteen.

flat *a.* **1.** LEVEL even, flush, horizontal, plane, smooth, lying down, recumbent, supine, prostrate, prone. **2.** ABSOLUTE unequivocal, unqualified, positive, definite, direct, plain, clear. **3.** TASTELESS, DULL insipid, stale, bland, dull, boring, flavorless, lackluster, blah, spiritless, drab, uninteresting. ANT. *1. uneven, rough, bumpy, round. 2. equivocal, qualified. 3. interesting, tasty, effervescent.*

flatten *v.* **1.** LEVEL plane, smooth, spread out, lie flat. **2.** KNOCK DOWN squash, crush, *steamroll, prostrate.

flatter *v.* compliment, praise, puff up, adulate, laud, extoll, inflate, *brownnose, *kiss up to, *apple polish, toady, cajole, fawn, *suck up to, *lay it on thick, *lay it on with a trowel, *butter up, *massage one's ego, *stroke, blandish, gush, *sweet talk.

flatterer *n.* complimenter, booster, trumpeter, sycophant, *yes-man, *kiss-ass, *brown-nose, *sweet talker, *apple polisher, toady, *lickspittle, bootlicker. "Like cats, [they] lick and then scratch." — German proverb. "One who says things to your face that he would not say behind your back." — G. Millington. "A friend who is your inferior, or pretends to be so." — Aristotle.

flattery *n.* praise, compliment, adulation, tribute, eulogy, blarney, inflation, applause, sycophancy, blandishment, *ass-kissing, *brownnosing, *apple polishing, toadyism, *honeyed words, *snow job, gush, smarm, bootlicking, fawning, cajolery. "Something nice someone tells you about yourself that you wish were true." — Frank Malester. "A commodity that makes everyone sick except those that swallow it." — Anon.

flatulent *a.* **1.** GASSY windy. **2.** PRETENTIOUS pompous, windy, long-winded, bombastic, verbose.

flaunt *v.* show off, strut, display, parade, wave, flash, exhibit, spotlight, swagger, peacock, broadcast, advertise, vaunt. ANT. *hide, cover up, conceal.*

flavor *n.* **1.** TASTE savor, sapor, tincture, piquancy, tang, zing, seasoning, spiciness, saltiness, sweetness, sourness, tartness. **2.** ESSENCE character, quality, nature, spirit, feel.

flavor *v.* season, spice, *liven up, salt, lace, infuse.

flaw *n.* defect, imperfection, fault, deformity, blemish, failing, weakness, pitfall, shortcoming, chink.

flawless *a.* faultless, defect-free. SEE PERFECT

fledgling *n.* beginner, *rookie, *greenhorn, *tenderfoot, freshman, *tyro, novice, neophyte.

flee *v.* run away, escape, bolt, *cut and run, *make a quick exit, take off, decamp, *split, *beat feet, *fly the coop, *make a getaway, *make tracks, *blow, *skedaddle, *vamoose, *scram.

fleece *v.* cheat, *rip off, swindle, rook, *flimflam, *take to the cleaners, *soak, *chisel, con, hustle.

fleet *n.* flotilla, armada, squadron, convoy, navy. SEE NAVY

fleet *a.* fast, swift, quick, rapid, speedy, mercurial, hasty, expeditious, meteoric, nimble. ANT. *slow, plodding, slothful, dragging.*

fleeting *a.* transient, brief, ephemeral, temporary, quick, short-lived, momentary, *flash in the pan, *here today gone tomorrow, meteoric. ANT. *enduring, lasting, permanent.*

flesh *n.* **1.** MEAT body tissue, muscle, fat, beef,

brawn. **2.** BODY material person, human, man, woman, physical nature. ANT. *2. soul, spirit.*

fleshy *a.* fat, plump, beefy, obese, blubbery, corpulent, chubby, chunky, *tubby, meaty, porcine, portly, stout, paunchy, *jelly-bellied, pulpy. ANT. *skinny, anorexic, bony, rawboned.*

flex *v.* bend, crook, stretch, tense.

flexible *a.* **1.** PLIABLE bendable, pliant, elastic, supple, springy, ductile, malleable, rubbery, willowy, lithe, limber. **2.** ADAPTABLE yielding, adjustable, manageable, compliant, docile, tractable, amenable. ANT. *1. rigid, stiff, inflexible. 2. rigid, obstinate.*

flick *v.* snap, flip, tap, brush.

flicker *v.* waver, flutter, dance, quiver, glimmer, glint, scintillate, flash, shimmer, flare, flame.

flight *n.* soaring, air travel, hovering, gliding, planing, flying, aeronautics, volitation.

flighty *a.* frivolous, capricious, irresponsible, fickle, impulsive, scatterbrained, whimsical, harebrained, giddy, *airheaded, *ditzy, unstable. ANT. *stable, rational, thoughtful.*

flimsy *a.* **1.** FRAGILE frail, easily broken, thin, delicate, slight, shoddy, unsubstantial, ethereal, diaphanous, gossamer, rickety, cheap. **2.** INADEQUATE ineffectual, feeble, weak, lame, shallow, unconvincing, trivial, poor, incredible, implausible. ANT. *1. solid, strong, *like the Rock of Gibraltar, *built like a brick shithouse. 2. credible, solid, convincing, plausible.*

flinch *v.* recoil, wince, cringe, shrink, jump, cower, quail, start, blench, jerk, blink.

fling *v.* throw, pitch, cast, hurl, toss, sling, heave, flip, *chuck.

flinty *a.* hard, firm, stony, inflexible, rigid, unmerciful, coldhearted, hardened, heartless, unsympathetic. ANT. *soft, warmhearted, sympathetic.*

flip *n.* somersault.

flip *v.* toss, flick, throw, pitch, spin, snap.

flip out *v. Sl.* *go mental, *go berserk, *go ballistic, *have a piss hemorrhage, *go nuts, *lose it, *freak out, *flip one's lid, *go apeshit.

FLIPPANT *a.* [FLIP unt] disrespectful, irreverent. *Tom was sent to the principal's office for being flippant.* SYN. disrespectful, irreverent, impudent, impertinent, insolent, brash, fresh, cheeky, *flip, *wise, *smart-assed, cocky, rude, sassy. ANT. *respectful, reverent, polite.*

flirt *n.* tease, coquette, hussy, wolf, vamp, heartbreaker, *game-player.

flirt *v.* tease, lead on, entice, coquet, tantalize, toy, trifle, dally, vamp, *make eyes at, *wink at, *make a pass at, *hit on, *make cow eyes at, *undress with eyes, *gaze at candidly, *scorch one with eyes, *shoot a predatory look, wink salaciously, leer conspiratorially, look at hungrily, eye provocatively, smile roguishly, laugh lasciviously, lick lips provocatively.

flirtatious *a.* teasing, enticing, tantalizing, provocative, coquettish, *on the make, *come-hither, alluring, *on the prowl, *making eyes at, inviting.

flit *v.* dart, hop, flutter, hover, whisk, skim, fly, flitter, race, hurry, flap, wing.

float *v.* bob, buoy, levitate, hover, be borne along by current, ride, raft, drift, swim, waft, sail. ANT. *sink, go under, submerge.*

flock *n.* congregation, drove, pack, herd, group, gang, assemblage, band, swarm, colony, mass, throng, multitude. SEE ANIMAL

flog *v.* whip, thrash, lash, flagellate, horsewhip, beat, strap, flail, cane, flay, hide, tan.

flood *n.* deluge, inundation, torrent, overflow, outpouring, gush, rush, surge, wave, tsunami, downpour, cloudburst, gullywasher, *rain of biblical proportion, cataclysm.

flood *v.* deluge, inundate, overflow, gush, rush, surge, overwhelm, drown, engulf, submerge, swamp, flush, drench, saturate.

floor *n.* **1.** BOTTOM footing, base, flooring, planking, parquet, linoleum, rug, carpeting, walkway. **2.** STORY level, flight, tier, deck.

floor *v.* flabbergast, astound, stun, stagger, shock, throw, nonplus, dumbfound, astonish, confound.

flop *n.* failure, *bomb, *dud, *dog, loser, *turkey, disaster, *bust, fiasco, *clunker, *lemon, *lead balloon, *laugher. ANT. *success, hit, triumph, winner.*

flop *v.* **1.** FALL plop, collapse, flounder, *bellyflop, tumble, topple, *plunk down, *fall flat on one's face. **2.** FAIL *bomb, *go over like a lead balloon, *wash out, fizzle, *lay an egg, fold, *sputter and die. ANT. *2. succeed, triumph, win.*

florid *a.* ornate, showy, gaudy, ostentatious, flamboyant, flowery, elaborate, embellished, overdecorated, high-flown, garish, arabesque, rococo, baroque, ruddy, rosy, pink. ANT. *plain, simple, austere, stark, unadorned.*

flotsam *n.* wreckage, debris, cargo, odds and ends, castoffs, junk, jetsam.

flounder *v.* struggle, stumble, blunder, wallow, fumble, flop, thrash, stammer, stutter, falter, *flub one's lines.

flourish n. **1.** DECORATION embellishment, ornamentation, garnish, adornment, frill, curlicue. **2.** BRANDISHING wave, show, flaunting, exhibition, display.

flourish v. grow, thrive, prosper, blossom, flower, fatten, boom, burgeon, increase, wax, succeed, *go great guns, expand, mushroom. ANT. wither, die, shrivel, fail.

flout v. jeer, scoff, mock, scorn, ridicule, jeer at, spurn, insult, deride, taunt, *make fun of. ANT. respect, honor, revere.

flow n. current, course, gush, stream, drift, river, outpouring, spill, issuance, discharge, emanation, flux, trickle, progression, ebb, tide.

flow v. course, gush, stream, drift, issue, discharge, emanate, spout, trickle, progress, surge, run, roll, spew, ooze, ebb, proceed, cascade, well, spill.

flower n. bloom, blossom, ornamental, floweret, floret, bud, annual, perennial, spray, posy, nosegay, bouquet. "Heaven's masterpiece." — Dorothy Parker. "The sweetest thing God ever made, and forgot to put a soul into." — Henry Ward Beecher.

WORD FIND

bloom, blossom: effloresce

bouquet worn on shoulder: corsage

descriptive: teardrop petals, ruffles and lace, spikes like kitten tails, irridescent, radiant, creamy, flaming, blazing, dotting fields like fallen confetti, elegant profusion, heady perfumes of Spring

female organ that becomes fruit: pistil

grains of male germ cells: pollen

male organ: stamen

names: African violet, amaryllis, aster, azalea, baby's breath, begonia, black-eyed Susan, bleeding heart, bluebell, buttercup, camellia, candytuft, carnation, cat's paw, Chinese lantern, chrysanthemum, cockscomb, columbine, cornflower, cowslip, daffodil, dahlia, daisy, dandelion, dogwood, forget-me-not, forsythia, foxglove, foxtail, fuchsia, gardenia, gentian, geranium, gladiolus, goldenrod, heather, hibiscus, hollyhock, honeysuckle, hyacinth, impatience, Indian paintbrush, iris, jack-in-the-pulpit, jonquil, lady's slipper, larkspur, lilac, lily, lily of the valley, lotus, lupine, magnolia, mallow, marigold, mayflower, mimosa, morning glory, narcissus, oleander, orchid, pansy, peony, petunia, phlox, poinsetta, poppy, prim-rose, Queen Anne's lace, rhododendron, rose, snapdragon, sunflower, sweet alyssum, sweet William, tulip, Venus flytrap, viola, violet, water lily, wolfbane, yucca, zinnia

native flowers of a region: flora

petals, collective term: corolla

science of growing: horticulture

sepals, or protective leaves of a flower: calyx

spike, dense: spadix, spike

spot of different color in center of some types: eye

sun, follows the: heliotropic, phototropic

SEE FIELD

fluctuate v. vary, waver, oscillate, vacillate, *run hot and cold, change, *seesaw, *yo-yo, alternate, shift, rise and fall.

fluent a. flowing, smooth, easy, loose, fluid, articulate, eloquent, smooth-talking, practiced, effortless, glib, natural, *silver-tongued. ANT. halting, floundering, tongue-tied.

fluffy a. downy, feathery, soft, fleecy, flossy, woolly, silky.

fluid n. liquid, water, juice, agua.

fluid a. **1.** LIQUID liquefied, watery, flowing, streaming, pouring, running, juicy, wet. **2.** FLEXIBLE adaptable, unfixed, changeable, indefinite, adjustable. ANT. 1. solid. 2. fixed.

fluke n. stroke of luck, good fortune, windfall, *one in a million, *lucky strike, break, fortuity, godsend, serendipity, accident, fate.

flurry n. **1.** SUDDEN GUST OF WIND, SNOW OR RAIN shower, ducting, squall. SEE RAIN, SNOW **2.** COMMOTION stir, bustle, fluster, *to-do, *ado, squall, turmoil, hubbub, ferment.

flush v. **1.** BLUSH redden, color, glow, turn crimson, *burn, bloom, *turn rosy, *turn ruddy. **2.** WASH OUT flood, rinse, drench, irrigate, spray, douche, douse. ANT. 1. blanch, whiten.

flush a. **1.** FLAT level, square, plane, plumb, straight. **2.** ABUNDANT plentiful, affluent, rich, wealthy, well-supplied, well-to-do. ANT. 1. uneven, out of plumb. 2. poor, destitute, lacking.

flushed a. red, pink, ruddy, florid, glowing, aglow, blushing, red-faced, burning, scarlet-faced, blooming, feverish ANT. pale, blanched, white.

fluster n. confusion, befuddlement, agitation, nervousness, turmoil, *discombobulation, bewilderment, disturbance, excitement, commotion. ANT. calm, composure, peace.

fluster v. confuse, bewilder, perturb, befuddle, agitate, *discombobulate, disturb, *rattle, excite, stir, ruffle, disquiet. ANT. calm, quiet, compose.

flute n. SEE MUSICAL INSTRUMENT

fluting n. channels. SEE GROOVE

flutter v. flap, wave, beat, quiver, shake, sway, swing, shudder, tremble, bat, oscillate, wag, dance, flit, fly.

flux n. flow, current, course, stream, run, movement, tide, passage, surge, change, unrest, fluctuation. ANT. *stagnation, inertia, stasis.*

fly v. **1.** SOAR take wing, take flight, glide, flit, hover, jet, float, *ride the thermals, *wing, climb, dive, swoop, *hedgehop, waft, be borne along by the wind, scud, barnstorm. SEE AIRCRAFT, BIRD **2.** SPEED AWAY rush, hurry, *hightail, hustle, scoot, *make a mad dash, *go like the wind, scurry, *go off like a shot, *put the pedal to the metal, *beat feet. **3.** FLEE escape, *make a getaway, skedaddle, *cut and run, *split, *vamoose, *scram, *head for the hills, *blow.

foam n. froth, lather, suds, scum, fizz, bubbles, spume, effervescence, spindrift, head.

foam v. froth, lather, fizz, bubble, spume, effervesce, ferment, cream.

foamy a. frothy, lathery, fizzy, bubbly, effervescent, spumy, soapy, sudsy, creamy.

focus n. focal point, center, target, hub, heart, spotlight, bull's eye, nucleus.

focus v. center on, center, zero in on, pinpoint, direct, fix, concentrate, *home in on, spotlight, clear up, sharpen.

foe n. enemy, adversary, rival, opponent, antagonist, *bad guy, combatant, competitor. ANT. *friend, ally, *soul mate.*

fog n. **1.** MIST haze, cloud, brume, sea smoke, vapor, *pea soup, murk, smog, gloom.

WORD FIND

cooling point below which fog forms: dew point

dense mass of: fog bank

descriptive: diaphanous, gossamer, nubilous, ethereal, veils, gauzy, sea's breath, thick enough to curdle, as thick as New England clam chowder, thick enough to eat/shovel, creeping, dank, cloaking, shrouds, sheets of fog like the sails of Spanish galleons, ghosting over the water, wisps, fingers of fog clutching at ship riggings, soul-dampening

freezing fog that deposits frost: rime

ice crystals, containing: pogonip

surrounded by and prevented from sailing: fogbound

2. MUDDLE confusion, daze, bewilderment, haze, stupor, disorientation, perplexity, mystification.

foggy a. SEE FOG

FOIBLE n. [FOY bul] a minor weakness or fault. *Reporters regularly expose the foibles of those in the public eye.* SYN. weakness, fault, shortcoming, deficiency, flaw, failing, frailty, imperfection, quirk, vice, chink. ANT. *asset, strength, strong point.*

foil n. contrast, complement, antithesis, background.

foil v. thwart, frustrate, balk, check, baffle, impede, outsmart, circumvent, stymie, prevent, checkmate, stop, outwit, counter, hamstring, spoil, *throw up a roadblock. ANT. *aid, assist, abet, advance.*

foist v. palm off, sneak in, fob, pass off, *pull a fast one.

fold n. crease, pleat, tuck, crimp, gather, dog-ear, overlap, layer, drape.

fold v. **1.** CREASE pleat, plait, tuck, crimp, gather, double over, dog-ear, overlap, drape, hem, enclose, envelop, wrap. **2.** GO OUT OF BUSINESS fail, close, go bankrupt, *go belly up, become insolvent.

folder n. file, binder, wrapper, envelope, sheath, covering.

foliage n. leaves, leafage, greenery, umbrage. SEE TREE, FOREST, JUNGLE

folklore n. myths, legends, fables, custom, tradition, superstition.

folks n. kin, relatives, parents, flesh and blood, family.

folksy a. *down-to-earth, friendly, informal, unassuming, rustic, natural, down-home, casual, unpretentious, simple, easygoing, corny. ANT. *sophisticated, pretentious, *la-di-da.*

follow v. **1.** COME AFTER ensue, succeed, supplant, supersede, proceed, replace, take the place of, result, issue, emanate. **2.** TRAIL stay behind, *bring up the rear, shadow, tail, track, *dog, hunt down, chase, pursue, go after. **3.** ABIDE BY obey, conform to, heed, regard, mind, comply with, do what is told, emulate, copy, imitate. ANT. *1. precede, antedate. 2. trailblaze, head up, lead. 3. disregard, ignore.*

follower n. disciple, fan, adherent, apostle, partisan, pupil, devotee, member, proponent, patron, votary, proselyte, henchman. ANT. *leader, mentor, detractor.*

following n. fans, supporters, patrons, devotees, adherents, coterie, entourage, retinue, train.

following a. afterward, successive, subsequent,

next, ensuing, coming, *in the wake of, *on the horizon. ANT. *preceding.*

folly *n.* foolishness, silliness, nonsense, craziness, lunacy, absurdity, wackiness, senselessness, idiocy, fatuity. "A vigorous plant, which sheds abundant seed." — Isaac D'Israeli. ANT. *good sense, intelligence, wisdom,* *wise move.

foment *v.* instigate, incite, stir up, agitate, spark, fire, excite, arouse, provoke, spur, egg on, galvanize, *fan the flames. ANT. *extinguish, suppress, dampen, check.*

fond *a.* affectionate, loving, attached, tender, doting, close, warm, adoring, caring, devoted, *sweet on, enamored. ANT. *hostile, hating, uncaring, cool.*

fondle *v.* stroke, caress, pat, pet, embrace, rub, hug, hold, massage, squeeze, *feel up, *paw.

font *n.* source, origin, wellspring, genesis, root, seed.

food *n.* nourishment, sustenance, foodstuffs, *eats, victuals, *chow, *grub, edibles, comestibles, cuisine, fare, *vittles, ration, provisions, subsistence, meal, meat and potatoes, fodder, feed. "The first enjoyment of life." — Lin Yutang.

fool *n.* idiot, blockhead, ignoramus, moron, imbecile, ninny, nincompoop, simpleton, nitwit, harebrain, clown, ass, buffoon, *dingaling, *lunkhead, dupe, dunce, sap, oaf. "One who does not suspect himself." — José Ortega y Gasset. "The whetstone of the wits." — Shakespeare.

fool *v.* deceive, kid, trick, cheat, hoodwink, *pull the wool over one's eyes, mislead, dupe, *sucker, *scam, *take in, *bamboozle.

fool around *v.* **1.** WASTE TIME *horse around, fritter, *hang out, putter, diddle. **2.** MAKE LOVE *make out, *screw, *get horizontal, *hump, *parallel park, *bop, *go for a roll in the hay, *ball, *jump bones.

foolhardy *a.* reckless, rash, foolish, risk-taking, bold, Icarian, daring, stupid, impetuous, daredevil, imprudent, irrational, insane, adventuresome. ANT. *cautious, careful, wary.*

foolish *a.* stupid, idiotic, asinine, ignorant, imprudent, moronic, imbecilic, harebrained, clownish, oafish, *cockamamy, daft, unwise, silly, *nuts, ill-advised, *half-baked, fatuous, ludicrous, *screwy, childish. ANT. *wise, thoughtful, smart, rational, sensible.*

foot *n.* **1.** EXTREMITY hoof, pad, paw, *dog. **2.** BASE bottom, foundation, floor, pedestal. ANT. **2.** *crown, head.*

football *n.* sport.

WORD FIND

ball, slang for: pigskin

ball snapper: center

center of defensive line: nose guard, nose tackle

defends against passes and runs into the backfield: defensive back, safety, cornerback

defensive backfield: secondary

defensive players just behind linemen: linebackers

downing of ball in offense's end zone, two points to defense: safety

encroaching into opposing team's side before ball is snapped: offside, encroachment

extra point kick after touchdown: conversion

faking a handoff and running with ball hidden behind hip: bootleg

faking a handoff to running back, who pretends to run with ball hidden in arms, then passing: play-action pass

field: gridiron

five back defense: nickel defense

foul in which player without ball is hit from behind: clipping

imaginary line where ball is down: line of scrimmage

kickoff in which ball lands in receiving team's end zone: touchback

kickoff to opposing side: punt

kick that is low and tumbling, employed to force fumble: onside kick

know-it-all fan who criticizes players: armchair quarterback, Monday morning quarterback

lateral pass or handoff followed by surprise pass: flea-flicker

line-drive pass: bullet

line-of-scrimmage player: lineman

long pass requiring small miracle to be caught: Hail Mary, prayer

offensive alignment in which quarterback takes snap standing several yards back from center: shotgun

offensive back behind or near quarterback: fullback, halfback running back

passes, hands off, runs, calls plays: quarterback

pass that imparts spin on ball and keeps it from tumbling: spiral, bullet

play change called out at line of scrimmage: audible

quarterback's eluding of tacklers: scrambling

run and handoff to player running in opposite direction: reverse

score: touchdown

sideways or backwards pass: lateral

six back defense: dime defense

slamming ball down in end zone after scoring touchdown: spike

surprise run by quarterback: quarterback sneak

surprise rush: blitz

tackle with arm swung into opponent's neck or head: clothesline

tailback, halfback and fullback form a line behind quarterback: I formation

footing n. foot, foothold, foundation, establishment, position, toehold, basis, beachhead, bridgehead, vantage.

footloose a. free, unrestricted, fancy-free, unencumbered, unattached, roving, untethered, liberated, uninhibited. ANT. *restricted, bound, shackled.*

footprint n. track, footmark, impression, tread.

fop n. dandy, clotheshorse, dude, coxcomb, peacock, popinjay, fashion plate, Beau Brummel, poseur, *pretty boy.

forage v. search, look for, hunt, sniff out, scavenge, rummage, explore, root out, seek, raid, plunder.

foray v. raid, plunder, pillage, ransack, loot, ravage, attack, invade, maraud, asault.

forbear v. refrain, avoid, resist temptation, abstain, lay off, desist, shun, eschew, go without, hold back, forgo, endure, tolerate, bear.

forbearance n. restraint, self-control, abstinence, refraining, avoidance, desistance, tolerance, patience, mercy. "To forgive an enemy who has been shorn of power." —Elbert Hubbard. ANT. *impatience, intolerance.*

forbid v. prohibit, proscribe, disallow, ban, outlaw, enjoin, restrict, veto, make off limits, taboo, interdict, stop. ANT. *allow, permit, approve.*

forbidden a. prohibited, proscribed, banned, outlawed, verboten, restricted, off limits, vetoed, taboo, disallowed. ANT. *allowed, permitted, approved of.*

forbidding a. threatening, ominous, dangerous, frightening, scary, uninviting, foreboding, sinister, disagreeable, unfriendly. ANT. *inviting, friendly, alluring.*

force n. **1.** POWER strength, vigor, might, energy, velocity, momentum, pressure, horsepower, *muscle, drive, pull, weight, stress, potency, impetus. "The blind wild beast." —Alfred Lord Tennyson. **2.** COERCION compul-

sion, constraint, duress, bullying, arm-twisting, violence. **3.** MILITARY POWER army, navy, air power, troops, infantry, division, squadron, regiment. ANT. *1. impotence, weakness.*

force v. coerce, compel, oblige, arm-twist, strong-arm, constrain, pressure, press, make, *railroad, exact, push, drive, necessitate, wrest, *put the screws to.

forced a. **1.** COERCED involuntary, obligatory, compulsory, enforced, unwilling, constrained, pressured. **2.** NOT SPONTANEOUS strained, constrained, stiff, labored, contrived, unnatural, artificial, insincere, affected, self-conscious, studied. ANT. *1. voluntary, willing, unforced. 2. spontaneous, natural, genuine.*

forceful a. powerful, effective, vigorous, dynamic, potent, mighty, strong, robust, energetic, commanding, persuasive. ANT. *ineffectual, impotent, weak.*

fore a. front, first, forward, head, leading. ANT. *rear, last.*

forebear n. forefather, progenitor. SEE ANCESTOR

foreboding n. portent, bad feeling, omen, premonition, uneasiness, warning, prophecy, foreshadowing, *gut feeling, apprehension, *handwriting on the wall, *bad vibes, forewarning.

forecast n. prediction, prophecy, divination, prognostication, augury, projection, *reading of the cards, prognosis, conjecture, guess.

forecast v. predict, foresee, prophesy, foretell, divine, *read in the cards, augur, prognosticate, project, presage, envision, conjecture, guess, estimate.

forefather n. forbear, progenitor, forerunner, predecessor. SEE ANCESTOR

forefront n. front, head, *cutting edge, vanguard, fore. ANT. *rear, background.*

foregoing a. previous, former, aforesaid, preceding, prior, late, earlier. ANT. *following, ensuing.*

foreign a. **1.** NONDOMESTIC alien, exotic, unfamiliar, imported, faraway, distant, outlandish, unknown, nonnative, strange, overseas. **2.** UNCHARACTERISTIC aberrant, unnatural, abnormal, inconsistent, incompatible, unrelated, extraneous. ANT. *1. domestic, native, indigenous. 2. characteristic, compatible, natural.*

foreigner n. alien, nonnative, immigrant, outsider, stranger. ANT. *native.*

foreman n. boss, crew chief, overseer, supervisor, superintendent, spokesman.

foremost a. chief, first, leading, head, principal,

primary, preeminent, main, paramount, supreme, first, uppermost. ANT. *bottom, least, lowest.*

forensic *a.* arguable, controversial, debatable, moot, judicial.

forerunner *n.* **1.** PREDECESSOR precursor, ancestor, forebear, forefather, prototype, pioneer. **2.** HERALD announcer, harbinger, usher, messenger, portent, omen.

foresee *v.* anticipate, predict, prophesy, prognosticate, foretell, divine, envision, forecast, presage, augur.

foresight *n.* farsightedness, vision, anticipation, foreknowledge, precognition, forethought, preconception, prudence, preparedness, precaution, prophecy. ANT. *hindsight, unpreparedness.*

forest *n.* woods, woodland, timberland, weald, stand, grove, bush, copse, coppice, wilderness, wild, trees, habitat, *regiment of trees.

WORD FIND

ancient, uncut: old-growth forest, virgin forest

cleared area littered with logging debris: slash

evergreen oak thicket: chaparral

grassy clearing in: glade

ground or floor material: litter, duff, mor

leaf-shedding trees: deciduous

logging, denuding method: clear-cutting

non-leaf-shedding trees: coniferous

pertaining to trees: arboreal

thickly treed: bosky

top of trees: canopy, crowns

trees of a forest region: sylva

tropical woods receiving heavy rainfall: rain forest

wind-toppled trees and branches: windthrow, windfall, deadfall

SEE JUNGLE, TREE

foretell *v.* predict, forecast, prophesy, foresee, divine, augur, presage, prognosticate, anticipate, forebode, portend, warn.

forethought *n.* planning, foresight, prudence, anticipation, farsightedness, preparedness, precaution, provision. ANT. *afterthought.*

forever *adv.* always, everlastingly, endlessly, eternally, incessantly, continually, unceasingly, for all time, interminably, *till hell freezes over. ANT. *never.*

foreword *n.* preface, introduction, prologue. ANT. *epilogue.*

forfeit *n.* penalty, fine, forfeiture, damages, fee, loss.

forfeit *v.* lose, surrender, give up, relinquish, sacrifice, yield.

forge *v.* **1.** FORM make, manufacture, shape, fabricate, mold, contrive, fashion, hammer out, cast, devise, invent. **2.** COUNTERFEIT copy, falsify, trace, reproduce, imitate, simulate.

forgery *n.* fake, counterfeit, fraud, copy, imitation, simulation, falsification, sham.

forget *v.* **1.** *DRAW A BLANK slip one's mind, overlook. **2.** LET PASS nevermind, disregard, ignore, write off, skip, drop. ANT. *1. remember, recall. 2. regard, consider.*

forgetful *a.* absentminded, amnesic, abstracted, distracted, *out to lunch, oblivious, inattentive, daydreaming, heedless, mindless, absent.

forgive *v.* pardon, excuse, absolve, overlook, condone, *wipe the slate clean, *let off the hook, *let bygones be bygones, exculpate, acquit. ANT. *condemn, convict, damn.*

forgiveness *n.* pardon, excusing, forbearance, absolution, amnesty, reprieve, dispensation, mercy, exoneration, clemency, acquittal. "The fragrance the violet sheds on the heel that has crushed it." — Mark Twain. "Man's deepest need and highest achievement." — Horace Bushnell. "The sweetest revenge." — Isaac Friedmann. ANT. *condemnation, conviction, revenge.*

forgo *v.* do without, give up, relinquish, abstain from, renounce, eschew, refrain from, forswear, pass up, quit. ANT. *take up, keep, indulge in.*

fork *n.* branching, division, split, divergence, bifurcation, parting.

FORLORN *a.* [for LORN] miserable and without hope. *After the funeral she was grim and forlorn.* SYN. miserable, hopeless, wretched, woebegone, pitiful, pathetic, abandoned, bereft, desolate, dismal, inconsolable, despairing, lonesome, deserted. ANT. *cheerful, happy, euphoric.*

form *n.* **1.** SHAPE configuration, contour, silhouette, outline, profile, cast, structure, figure, conformation, design, frame. **2.** BODY anatomy, figure, build, frame, physique, shape. **3.** MOLD cast, frame, model. **4.** TYPE kind, sort, variety, class, genus, species, order. **5.** PROCEDURE way, ceremony, formality, ritual, custom, decorum, motions, formula, protocol, method, mode, format. **6.** DOCUMENT application, sheet, questionnaire.

form *v.* **1.** SHAPE mold, cast, frame, design, make, produce, construct, build, fabricate, *hammer out, fashion, manufacture, invent, create, concoct. **2.** ORGANIZE found, establish, start, incept. **3.** MATERIALIZE arise, appear, *take shape, crystallize, come into being. **4.** COMPRISE compose, constitute, make up.

formal *a.* **1.** CEREMONIAL decorous, orderly, customary, proper, conventional, methodical, ritualistic, systematic, official, prescribed, correct, *by-the-book. **2.** STIFF stuffy, *starched, prim, ceremonious, stilted, strait-laced, punctilious, rigid, proper, self-conscious. ANT. *informal, relaxed, casual, spontaneous.*

formality *n.* **1.** CONVENTION form, tradition, observance, protocol, practice, decorum, officiality, *red tape. **2.** PROPRIETY etiquette, ceremony, decorum. ANT. *2. informality.*

format *n.* arrangement, layout, system, shape, size, form, setup, configuration, organization, scheme, method, formula, plan.

formation *n.* creation, establishment, development, genesis, generation, production, construction, manufacture, crystallization, evolution, structure, composition.

former *a.* previous, prior, earlier, aforementioned, first, past, antecedent, preceding, bygone. ANT. *later, following, ensuing.*

FORMIDABLE *a.* [FOR muh duh bul] an intimidating thing or person that is difficult to face, surmount or overcome. *The rookie boxer and his formidable opponent. A formidable task.* SYN. intimidating, dreadful, frightening, scary, feared, awesome, difficult, hard, overwhelming, insurmountable, powerful, indomitable, staggering, tough, huge. ANT. *weak, manageable, tiny, insignificant.*

formless *a.* shapeless, amorphous, asymmetrical.

formula *n.* recipe, prescription, specifications, method, blueprint, code, system, principle, creed.

fornication *n.* intercourse, copulation, sex, adultery. SEE SEX

forsake *v.* abandon, leave behind, renounce, give up, quit, discard, forswear, reject, desert, disown, disavow, repudiate, *spurn, *wash one's hands of, *kiss off. ANT. *embrace, take up.*

fort *n.* fortress, fortification, stronghold, citadel, garrison, defense, army post, battlement. SEE CASTLE

FORTE *n.* [FOR tay] something one does particularly well or excels at. *I'm not much of a tennis player; basketball is more my forte.* SYN. specialty, strong point, strength, *bag, *cup of tea, *thing, proficiency, skill, area of expertise, bent, talent, aptitude, *long suit, metier. ANT. *weakness, foible.*

forthcoming *a.* upcoming, *on the horizon, approaching, imminent, impending, prospective, expected, pending, awaited.

forthright *a.* direct, straightforward, frank, blunt, candid, honest, plain, unambiguous, undisguised, heart-to-heart, *up front, bald. ANT. *indirect, dishonest, ambiguous, disguised, *sugar-coated.*

forthwith *adv.* immediately, at once, now, directly, without delay, tout de suite, *pronto, this instant, speedily. ANT. *eventually, gradually, slowly, later.*

fortification *n.* fort, fortress, stronghold, citadel, garrison, defense, army post, battlement, earthwork, outwork, palisade, bastion, bulwark, rampart. SEE CASTLE

fortify *v.* **1.** STRENGTHEN reinforce, brace, bulwark, secure, harden, shore up, steel, temper, buttress, build up, arm, shield, gird. **2.** REASSURE encourage, hearten, embolden, empower, strengthen, invigorate, *buck up. **3.** Enrich. ANT. *1. weaken, strip down, expose, soften. 2. demoralize, undermine, discourage.*

FORTITUDE *n.* [FORT uh tood] courage and strength in the face of adversity. *Intestinal fortitude allowed him to press on, despite the death of his wife.* SYN. strength, courage, heart, grit, endurance, mettle, backbone, *guts, resoluteness, bravery, tenacity, pluck, hardiness, *stick-to-itiveness. ANT. *weakness, cowardice, spinelessness, mousiness.*

FORTUITOUS *a.* [for TOO uh tus] occurring by chance, accidental. *A fortuitous discovery led to the invention.* SYN. chance, accidental, serendipitous, casual, random, *fluky, unforeseen, unintentional, haphazard, lucky, providential. ANT. *planned, *mapped out, arranged.*

fortunate *a.* lucky, blessed, happy, fortuitous, felicitous, propitious, favored, providential, advantageous, opportune, timely. ANT. *unfortunate, unlucky, untimely.*

fortune *n.* **1.** RICHES wealth, affluence, money, assets, treasure, estate, *miser's hoard. **2.** CHANCE luck, fate, destiny, providence, serendipity, fortuity, *wheel of fortune, happenstance, *toss of the dice. "A tide in the affairs of men." — Shakespeare. "That arrant whore." — Shakespeare. "Like glass, the brighter the glitter, the more easily broken." — Pubilius Syrus.

fortuneteller *n.* seer, soothsayer, augur, crystal ball gazer, diviner, palm reader, tarot reader, prophet, prognosticator, astrologer, psychic, sibyl.

forward *a.* bold, presumptuous, brazen, pushy, insolent, brash, impudent, cheeky, audacious, *nervy, *ballsy, fresh, pert. ANT. *backwards, shy, reserved, deferential.*

fossil *n.* remains, specimen, relic, impression, mineralized bone.

foster *v.* **1.** ADVANCE further, promote, feed, nurture, cultivate, boost, support, help, stimulate. **2.** REAR bring up, raise, care for, parent, mother, father, nurture, nurse, sustain, shelter. ANT. *1. hinder, hamper, undermine.*

foul *n.* infraction, violation.

foul *v.* **1.** MAKE DIRTY soil, defile, taint, pollute, dirty, stain, smear, contaminate. **2.** ENTANGLE catch, snarl, tangle, ensnare. ANT. *1. clean, wash. 2. untangle.*

foul *a.* **1.** DISGUSTING loathsome, stinking, dirty, *gross, disgraceful, repulsive, revolting, nasty, malodorous, rank, filthy, putrid, spoiled, polluted. **2.** INDECENT obscene, vulgar, indelicate, nasty, course, smutty, *raunchy, lewd, scatological, dirty, offensive. **3.** WICKED abominable, evil, villainous, monstrous, hellish, abhorrent, heinous, atrocious. ANT. *1. attractive, appealing, clean, pure. 2. wholesome, clean, *G-rated. 3. moral, good, virtuous.*

foul play *n.* SEE MURDER

found *v.* establish, organize, originate, develop, start, create, launch, institute.

foundation *n.* **1.** BASE, BASIS groundwork, bedrock, footing, underpinning, substructure, support, rudiment, fundamental, root, grounds. **2.** FINANCING ORGANIZATION institution, establishment, charity, endowment.

founder *n.* originator, creator, organizer, father, designer, architect, establisher.

founder *v.* **1.** TAKE ON WATER AND SINK go down, capsize, swamp, wallow, lurch, submerge, run aground, shipwreck. **2.** COLLAPSE fall, break down, fail, stumble, trip, go under, falter, bog down.

fountain *n.* **1.** SPOUT jet, fount, spray, gush, geyser, font, spring. **2.** SOURCE origin, wellspring, birthplace, root, beginning.

foxy *a.* sly, wily, crafty, cunning, shrewd, tricky, artful, sharp, devious, deceitful, scheming, crazy, vulpine. ANT. *artless, stupid, naive.*

foyer *n.* hall, lobby, entrance, reception area, receiving area, waiting room, vestibule, anteroom.

fracas *n.* fight, brawl, quarrel, wrangle, argument, *scrap, row, melee, ruckus, uproar, scuffle, free-for-all, fistfight, donnybrook, altercation, *rumble.

fraction *n.* part, fragment, division, segment, piece, slice, portion.

FRACTIOUS *a.* [FRAK shus] unruly, troublemaking, irritable. *The fractious mob demanded a recount.* SYN. unruly, troublemaking, rebellious, irritable, cross, peevish, insubordinate, touchy, unmanageable, *ornery, petulant, huffy. ANT. *agreeable, peaceful, docile, easygoing.*

fracture *n.* crack, cleft, rent, split, fissure, rupture, breach, cleavage, slit, gash, chasm, cut.

fracture *v.* crack, split, break, shatter, rupture, cut, breach, rend, cleave.

fragile *a.* delicate, frail, breakable, brittle, flimsy, fine, frangible, flimsy, dainty, tender, unsubstantial. ANT. *unbreakable, sturdy, strong.*

fragment *n.* part, fraction, segment, piece, portion, slice, splinter, chip, shard, sliver, snippet, bit, shaving.

fragmentary *a.* incomplete, partial, piecemeal, broken, disconnected, choppy, separate, fractional, imperfect, sketch. ANT. *complete, whole.*

fragrance *n.* scent, sweet smell, perfume, aroma, odor, incense, bouquet, essence, redolence. ANT. *stink, stench, reek.* SEE ODOR

fragrant *a.* sweet-smelling, aromatic, savory, redolent, spicy, balmy, heady, floral, intoxicating, ambrosial, tangy. ANT. *stinky, malodorous, foul, fetid, noxious.*

frail *a.* fragile, delicate, weak, dainty, flimsy, slight, breakable, feeble, decrepit, infirm, sickly, wispy. ANT. *strong, robust, sturdy.*

frailty *n.* weakness, failing, shortcoming, *chink in one's armour, *Achilles heel, deficiency, fallibility, foible, susceptibility. ANT. *strength, virtue.*

frame *n.* **1.** FRAMEWORK support, substructure, skeleton, underpinning, scaffolding, construction, mounting, staging, armature, rack. **2.** PICTURE FRAME mounting, casing, edging. **3.** PHYSIQUE build, body, figure, shape, anatomy.

frame *v.* **1.** BUILD construct, assemble, set up, stage, shape, fashion, form, erect, fabricate. **2.** COMPOSE conceive, create, concoct, devise, contrive, put into words, articulate.

frame of mind *n.* state of mind, disposition. SEE MOOD

frank *a.* honest, straightforward, candid, open, *straight from the heart, direct, blunt, plain, explicit, outspoken, unequivocal, unambiguous, sincere, forthright. ANT. *indirect, mealy-*

mouthed, insincere, euphemistic, disguised.

frantic *a.* frenzied, wild, excited, distraught, *unglued, agitated, *at wit's end, overexcited, beside oneself, crazy, berserk, *gone ballistic, raving, maniacal, *out of one's mind, furious, *freaked out, *wigged out. ANT. *calm, composed, serene, self-possessed, cool.*

fraternity *n.* brotherhood, brotherliness, fellowship, kinship, camaraderie, comradeship, society, club, *frat, order, house, clan.

WORD FIND
rite: rush, initiation, hazing

fraud *n.* **1.** DECEIT deception, trickery, cheating, swindle, *flimflam, ruse, *rip-off, con, extortion, scam, racket, hoax, double-dealing. **2.** CHEAT imposter, deceiver, *con artist, *rip-off artist, swindler, crook, charlatan, *shark, mountebank. ANT. 1. *honesty, trustworthiness, integrity.* 2. *honest John, *Dudley Do-right.*

fraudulent *a.* deceptive, deceitful, tricky, cheating, dishonest, crooked, criminal, illegal, bogus, shifty, treacherous, shady, *sham. ANT. *honest, moral, trustworthy.*

fraught *a.* loaded, filled, charged, full of, teeming with, laden, pregnant, replete.

fray *n.* fight, quarrel, brawl, *rumble, wrangle, melee, skirmish, battle, war, squabble, row, scuffle, clash.

fray *v.* shred, ravel, unravel, come apart, tear, tatter, rip.

freak *n.* abnormality, anomaly, weirdo, aberration, mutant, *geek, monster, monstrosity, deformity, curiosity, oddity, *oddball. SEE MONSTER

freak *v. Sl.* *freak out, *flip out, *wig out, *go apeshit, *go ballistic, *lose it.

freak *a.* anomalous, aberrant, weird, abnormal, unusual, irregular, atypical, extraordinary. ANT. *normal, typical, usual.*

freakish *a.* abnormal, anomalous, weird, aberrant, unusual, irregular, quirky, atypical, extraordinary, strange, outlandish, bizarre. ANT. *normal, regular, usual.*

free *a.* **1.** UNRESTRICTED liberated, at liberty, emancipated, footloose, independent, autonomous, self-governing, unrestrained, loose, unconfined, sovereign. **2.** COSTING NOTHING gratis, *on the house, complimentary, no charge. **3.** UNOCCUPIED clear, open, available, vacant, unused, empty, unengaged. **4.** GENEROUS lavish, liberal, openhanded, giving, munificent. ANT. *1. restricted, enslaved, dependent, imprisoned. 2. costing, *dear, expensive. 3. occupied, busy. 4.*

*cheap, stingy, *tight.*

free *v.* liberate, release, loose, let go, emancipate, unshackle, discharge, deliver, *spring, clear, extricate, unburden, disencumber, absolve. ANT. *imprison, enslave, shackle, confine, restrict.*

freedom *n.* liberty, independence, autonomy, sovereignty, self-government, emancipation, free will, license, carte blanche, privilege, *free reign, immunity, exemption, latitude, range, unrestraint. "Room to enlarge." — C.A. Bartol. "The right to be wrong, not the right to do wrong." — John Diefenbaker. ANT. *slavery, bondage, restriction, confinement.*

free-for-all *n.* fight, brawl, melee, *rumble, fray, donnybrook.

free spirit *n.* maverick, nonconformist, bohemian, eccentric.

freezing *a.* frigid, icy, cold, arctic, chilling, numbing, anesthetizing, *bone-chilling, biting, frosty, wintry, raw. ANT. *hot, sweltering.*

freight *n.* cargo, shipment, load, lading, tonnage.

frenetic *a.* frenzied, wild, overexcited. SEE FRANTIC

frenzy *n.* mania, madness, delerium, hysteria, fit, furor, outburst, rage, tantrum, spell, agitation, paroxysm, derangement. ANT. *stability, composure, calmness, equanimity.*

frequent *a.* numerous, regular, habitual, recurrent, common, continual, daily, everyday, incessant, periodic, usual, often. ANT. *seldom, rare, infrequent.*

frequent *v.* attend regularly, visit often, haunt, *hang out at, patronize.

fresh *a.* **1.** NEW up-to-date, *hot, current, modern, newborn, recent, bright, sparkling, unused, *hot off the presses, untouched, vernal, *spring-fresh. **2.** ADDITIONAL new, more, further. **3.** VIGOROUS energetic, lively, vital, bright-eyed, rested, revived, full of vim and vigor, vibrant, alert, bouncing. **4.** ORIGINAL imaginative, creative, new, unconventional, novel, untried, *cutting edge. **5.** REFRESHING cool, clean, bracing, pure, invigorating. **6.** INEXPERIENCED raw, green, untried, new, untrained, *wet behind the ears. **7.** SASSY rude, smart-alecky, cheeky, flippant, disrespectful, *smartass, *wiseass, impudent, bold, *nervy, ballsy. ANT. *1. old, worn, dated, stale. 3. tired, exhausted, weary. 4. trite, hackneyed, cliched. 5. stale, musty, polluted. 6. experienced, tried, veteran. 7. polite, shy, quiet, deferential.*

fret *v.* worry, brood, agonize, stew, mope, anguish, fuss, lose sleep over, chafe, *work oneself up, *give oneself an ulcer, *eat one's heart out, fume. ANT. *relax, ignore.

fretful *a.* discontented, irritable, annoyed, peevish, cross, grouchy, cranky, *bitchy, touchy, testy, *ornery, grumbling, anxious, whiny. ANT. *relaxed, cheerful, good-humored, unperturbed.*

friable *a.* crumbly, fragile, powdery, brittle.

friction *n.* **1.** ABRASION rubbing, erosion, attrition, grinding, scraping, chafing, rasping, wearing. **2.** DISAGREEMENT discord, conflict, opposition, animosity, antagonism, dispute, clash, hostility, strife. ANT. *2. agreement, accord, harmony.*

friend *n.* confidant, pal, *buddy, companion, sidekick, alter ego, chum, playmate, *soul mate, *bro, crony, amigo. "A person with whom you dare to be yourself." — Frank Crane. "The medicine of life." — Bible. "The best mirror." — George Herbert. "Someone you can be silent with." — Anon. "One who walks in when the rest of the world walks out." — Walter Winchell. ANT. *enemy, adversary, stranger.*

friendly *a.* sociable, amiable, warm, approachable, amicable, *buddy-buddy, companionable, neighborly, affectionate, hospitable, *chummy, outgoing, intimate, close, familiar. ANT. *hostile, distant, cool, aloof, standoffish.*

friendship *n.* companionship, comradeship, fellowship, camaraderie, neighborliness, relationship, intimacy, amity, affection, rapport, affinity, pact, tie. "To feel as one while remaining two." — Anne Swetchine. "The wine of life." — Edward Young. "A holy tie." — John Dryden. ANT. *hostility, distance, coolness.*

fright *n.* fear, terror, alarm, apprehension, scare, panic, trepidation, horror, shock, awe, *the creeps, *the willies, dread. ANT. *courage, calm, composure.* SEE ANXIETY, FEAR, FEARFUL

frighten *v.* scare, terrify, panic, shock, fill with dread, petrify, awe, *adrenalize, horrify, unnerve, *send chills down spine, spook, alarm, startle, intimidate, *curdle one's blood, *paralyze, *scare shitless. ANT. *encourage, embolden, reassure.*

frightening *a.* scary, terrifying, shocking, dreadful, petrifying, awesome, *adrenalizing, unnerving, chilling, *spooky, alarming, startling, intimidating, *bloodcurdling, *paralyzing, traumatic, horrifying. ANT. *encouraging, reassuring, heartening.*

frigid *a.* **1.** FREEZING icy, cold, arctic, frosty, wintry, hyperborean, *anesthetizing, biting, bit-

ter, brisk, Siberian, polar, glacial, gelid. **2.** STIFF formal, cold, icy, cool, distant, remote, aloof, austere, unsociable. **3.** UNRESPONSIVE lifeless, unfeeling, passionless, inhibited, passive, cold, chilly, frosty. ANT. *1. hot, sweltering, warm. 2. warm, friendly, sociable. 3. passionate, *hot-blooded, orgasmic.*

frill *n.* ornament, trimming, decoration, extra, luxury, ruffle, extravagance, superfluity, embellishment, frippery.

fringe *n.* **1.** DECORATIVE EDGING border, margin, trimming, ruff, hem, skirting, flounce. **2.** BORDER margin, outskirts, edge, periphery, verge, perimeter.

frisk *v.* **1.** FROLIC gambol, romp, cavort, prance, dance, play, wiggle. **2.** *Sl.* SEARCH shake down, inspect.

frisky *a.* lively, playful, spirited, frolicsome, zippy, active, kittenish, *peppy, coltish, spry. ANT. *lifeless, dead, comatose.*

fritter *v.* waste, squander, *blow, spend, dissipate, throw away, lavish, *piss away. ANT. *save, conserve.*

frivolous *a.* trivial, trifling, silly, impractical, petty, unimportant, foolish, extravagant, shallow, *piddling, pointless, worthless, unnecessary. ANT. *important, vital, necessary.*

frock *n.* tunic, robe, gown, garment.

frolic *n.* fun, play, sport, romping, merriment, antics, mirth, joking, game-playing, gaiety, amusement, tomfoolery.

frolic *v.* play, romp, make merry, have fun, joke, *cut up, *cut loose, *whoop it up, play games, frisk, gambol, cavort, *raise hell, *fool around.

front *n.* **1.** FORE, face, facade, head, exterior, anterior, foreground, top, obverse, beginning. **2.** PRETENSE facade, mask, false front, look, air, demeanor, expression, countenance, guise, exterior. ANT. *1. rear, back.*

front *a.* fore, lead, first, forward, topmost, anterior.

frontier *n.* **1.** BORDERLAND boundary, far reaches, perimeter, limit, verge. **2.** UNCIVILIZED TERRITORY outskirts, remote region, far reaches, outland, hinterland, outpost, no-man's-land.

frosty *a.* **1.** FREEZING hoary, rimy, icy, frigid, frozen, cold, raw, nippy, bone-chilling, anesthetizing. **2.** UNFRIENDLY cool, icy, aloof, distant, remote. ANT. *1. hot, sweltering. 2. friendly, warm.*

froth *n.* bubbles, foam, fizz, spume, suds, spray, head, lather, effervescence, spindrift, scum.

frothy *a.* **1.** BUBBLY foamy, fizzy, spumous, effervescent, *scummy, lathery, soapy. **2.** TRI-FLING light, worthless, trivial, frivolous, shallow, foolish. ANT. *important, deep, serious.*

frown *v.* **1.** SCOWL glower, *give a dirty look, glare, *shoot daggers, *scorch with one's eyes, *narrow eyes with contempt, lower, gloom. SEE ANGRY **2.** FROWN UPON *look down on, dislike, object to, disapprove of, *take a dim view of, discourage. ANT. *1. smile, grin. 2. approve of, accept, like.*

frozen *a.* icy, frigid, cold, chilled, iced, cooled, solidified, wintry, glacial, numb, arctic. ANT. *thawed, melted.* SEE COLD, SNOW

FRUGAL *a.* [FROO gul] careful not to be wasteful, thrifty. *He's so frugal he manages to pay for everything in cash.* SYN. thrifty, economical, unwasteful, conserving, sparing, saving, penny-pinching, stingy, scrimping, *nickel-squeezing, parsimonious, tight. ANT. *extravagant, wasteful, lavish, spending.*

fruit *n.* **1.** PRODUCE drupe, harvest, crop. **2.** RE-WARD return, yield, profit, benefit, result, consequence, outcome.

fruitful *a.* fertile, productive, rich, prolific, profitable, bounteous, advantageous, gainful, worthwhile, successful. ANT. *fruitless, worthless, unproductive.*

FRUITION *n.* [froo ISH un] a fulfillment, a bearing of fruit. *A number of her investments have come to fruition.* SYN. fulfillment, realization, consummation, maturity, achievement, ripeness, attainment. ANT. *incompletion, nonfulfillment.*

fruitless *a.* futile, vain, useless, unproductive, worthless, unsuccessful, unrewarding, pointless, barren, infertile. ANT. *fruitful, productive, worthwhile.*

frumpy *a.* dowdy, frumpish, dull, plain, unfashionable, colorless, slovenly, shabby, wrinkled, *as fashionable as a potato sack/burlap bag. ANT. *fashionable, stylish, chic.*

frustrate *v.* thwart, foil, check, balk, circumvent, hamstring, cripple, short-circuit, arrest, stymie, defeat, discourage, baffle, obstruct, impede, inhibit, exasperate. ANT. *advance, promote, encourage, abet.*

frustration *n.* defeat, circumvention, discouragement, obstruction, check, nonfulfillment, failure, disappointment, miscarriage, bafflement, dissatisfaction, thwarting. ANT. *success, advancement, encouragement, fulfillment.*

fry *v.* brown, singe, pan fry, sizzle, deep fry, sear, saute, French fry.

fuel *n.* combustible, gas, oil, propellant, wood, kindling, coal.

fuel *v.* charge, stoke, fire, fan, *tank up, feed, nourish. ANT. *extinguish, quench, dampen.*

fugitive *n.* runaway, exile, absconder, escapee, refugee, truant, renegade, deserter, outlaw.

fugitive *a.* fleeing, runaway, escaped, wanted, evading.

fulfill *v.* complete, satisfy, realize, achieve, consummate, carry out, accomplish, bring to fruition, perfect, meet, make good, perform, effect. ANT. *fall short, *miss the mark, fail.*

fulfillment *n.* completion, satisfaction, realization, achievement, consummation, accomplishment, fruition, perfection, culmination, attainment. ANT. *failure, miscarriage, incompletion.*

full *a.* **1.** FILLED glutted, gorged, sated, brimming, crammed, stuffed, *chock-full, bursting, stocked, crowded, teeming, replete, chockablock, saturated, overflowing, bulging. **2.** COMPLETE whole, entire, thorough, comprehensive, exhaustive, maximum, total, integral. ANT. *1. empty, barren, vacant, hungry, starving. 2. incomplete, partial.*

full-blooded *a.* purebred, thoroughbred, unmixed.

full-bodied *a.* rich, concentrated, strong, undiluted.

full-fledged *a.* developed, trained, schooled, skilled, qualified, experienced.

full-grown *a.* adult, fully developed, ripe. SEE MATURE

fully *adv.* **1.** COMPLETELY totally, entirely, comprehensively, wholly. **2.** ADEQUATELY sufficiently, amply.

fulminate *v.* denounce, denunciate, censure, criticize, damn, curse, shout down, *knock, condemn, remonstrate, thunder, swear at, revile.

fumble *v.* grope, mishandle, bungle, *drop the ball, *flub, botch, blunder, muff, flounder, bobble, mess up.

fume *n.* smoke, exhaust, gas, steam, vapor, effluvium, exhalation, pollution, reek, smog, stench, miasma.

fume *v.* rage, rant, rave, seethe, boil, blow up, explode, bluster, *get steamed, *blow one's stack, *fly off the handle, *go ballistic.

fun *n.* amusement, entertainment, enjoyment, pleasure, diversion, play, sport, good time, romping, *blast, frolic, recreation, merriment, pastime, jollity, *jollies. ANT. *misery, torture, agony, monotony.*

function *n.* **1.** ROLE job, use, purpose, duty, task, business, occupation, employment, responsibility, activity, concern. **2.** AFFAIR ceremony, gala, social, formal, *get-together, reception, party.

function v. act, work, serve, operate, perform, run.

functional a. working, operative, serviceable, performing, practical, useful.

fund n. reserve, savings, treasury, capital, nest egg, account, endowment, stock, mutual fund, *stash, hoard, pool, *kitty.

fund v. pay for, finance, bankroll, endow, back, capitalize, grant, subsidize, contribute, underwrite, *pick up the check.

fundamental n. basic, essential, element, rudiment, principle, foundation, ABCs, cornerstone, *nitty-gritty, heart, nucleus. ANT. extra, peripheral, supplement.

fundamental a. basic, essential, primary, elementary, rudimentary, principal, underlying, cardinal, chief, indispensable, integral, foundational. ANT. secondary, peripheral, auxiliary.

funds n. money, cash, capital, currency, finances, means, *dough, *bread, reserve, assets, resources, nest egg, *loot, *piggy bank, *stash.

funeral n. obsequies, exequies, burial, inhumation, interment, entombment, last rites, services, cremation. "The last bedtime story."—Leonard Levinson. "A consolation to the living than of any service to the dead."—Saint Augustine.

WORD FIND

announcement: obituary

automobile/coach that carries coffin to cemetery: hearse

bell toll signaling death: knell

bugle call at military funeral: taps

burial at sea: deep six

burial cloth or sheet: shroud, winding sheet

Catholic Mass for: Requiem Mass

churchyard gateway sheltering coffin at service: lich gate

coffin carriers: pallbearers

euphemism, burying: lay to rest

friends, relatives of deceased: bereaved, mourners

mourn aloud by weeping, wailing, etc.: lament

pile of wood on which corpse is burned: pyre

praise for deceased: eulogy

prayer for deceased: requiescat

procession: cortege, death march

RIP: rest in peace

song of lament: dirge, elegy, requiem, threnody

undertaker: mortician

watch or viewing of the deceased, often with festivities: wake, vigil

SEE CEMETERY, COFFIN, DEATH, MOURNING

funereal a. somber, depressing, black, gray, grim, mournful, sepulchral, dreary, doleful, dismal, grave, lugubrious, gloomy, melancholy. ANT. cheerful, euphoric, bright, upbeat.

funnel v. channel, direct, conduct, siphon, pour, filter, focus, conduct.

funny a. **1.** HUMOROUS comical, hilarious, laughable, *side-splitting, amusing, *a scream, droll, absurd, riotous, hysterical, ludicrous, ridiculous, farcical, silly, jocular, *tickling. **2.** PECULIAR strange, odd, weird, bizarre, unusual, outlandish, abnormal, *offbeat, different, queer. ANT. 1. serious, grave, grim, morbid. 2. ordinary, normal, usual.

furious a. **1.** ANGRY enraged, infuriated, outraged, irate, *beside oneself, *boiling, *pissed, *on the warpath, fuming, mad, inflamed, incensed, livid, *up in arms, *spitting tacks, *bent out of shape, rabid, *ripped. **2.** VIOLENT overpowering, intense, fierce, wild, ferocious, stormy, turbulent, raging, vicious, savage. ANT. 1. calm, unperturbed, pleased. 2. mild, meek, weak.

furnish v. supply, equip, provide, stock, outfit, provision, fit, turn out, rig, appoint, accouter, give.

furnishings n. gear, trappings, appointments, decor, fittings, equipment, accessories.

furor n. uproar, craze, excitement, frenzy, commotion, rage, outburst, mania, disturbance, *ado, *to-do, ruckus, *big stink. ANT. apathy, indifference, dispassion.

furrow n. channel, groove, rut, trench, ditch, cut, trough, track, line, seam, crease, wrinkle.

furry a. hairy, woolly, shaggy, bushy, downy.

further v. advance, forward, assist, foster, facilitate, promote, aid, contribute to, abet. ANT. hamper, hinder, thwart.

further a. additional, more, added, supplementary, other, new.

furthermore adv. in addition, additionally, also, moreover, what's more, too.

FURTIVE a. [FUR tiv] secret, sneaky. He shot a furtive glance at his desk partner's notes. SYN. secret, sneaky, stealthy, surreptitious, covert, clandestine, sly, wary, hidden, underhand, conspiratorial, skulking, concealed, shifty. ANT. open, overt, aboveboard.

fury n. anger, rage, wrath, furor, frenzy, indignation, madness, fire, ire, tantrum, fit, dudgeon, storm, squall, tempest, hot blood, huff, rampage, fierceness. ANT. *calm, serenity, tranquility, indifference.*

fuse *v.* merge, meld, smelt, combine, blend, compound, unite, integrate, commingle, weld, alloy, consolidate. ANT. *divide, separate, split.*

fusion *n.* union, amalgamation, coalescence, melding, blend, mixture, consolidation, compound, merger, combination, coalition. ANT. *separation, division, splitting.*

fuss *n.* bother, ado, fluster, pother, trouble, turmoil, disturbance, agitation, stir, fretting, flutter.

fussy *a.* particular, picky, choosy, meticulous, persnickety, discriminating, finicky, fastidious, dainty, hard-to-please, nit-picking. ANT. **easy, careless.*

futile *a.* vain, useless, hopeless, fruitless, ineffective, unproductive, for naught, pointless, unavailing, idle, **on a wild goose chase.* ANT.

fruitful, productive, worthwhile.

future *n.* tomorrow, offing, time to come, hereafter, *down the road, *over the horizon, prospect, fate, destiny. "The shape of things to come." — H.G. Wells. "That period of time in which our affairs prosper, our friends are true and our happiness is assured." — Ambrose Bierce. "The past returning through another gate." — Arnold Glasgow. "Not what it used to be." — Anon.

future *a.* coming, expected, prospective, anticipated, imminent, impending, next, *on the horizon, forthcoming, approaching, scheduled, eventual, projected, succeeding, subsequent. ANT. *past, former, bygone.*

fuzz *n.* hair, fur, fluff, down, wool, nap, lint.

fuzzy *a.* **1.** HAIRY furry, fluffy, downy, woolly, napped, linty, frizzy. **2.** UNCLEAR blurry, vague, cloudy, dim, hazy, obscure, misty, out of focus. ANT. **2.** *clear, focused, sharp.*

G

gab n. chatter, talk, jabber, conversation, babble, *chitchat, *tongue-wagging, *rap, prattle, palaver, gossip.

gab v. chatter, talk, jabber, converse, babble, *yak, *chitchat, *rap, prattle, *jaw, *shoot the breeze, gossip.

gabby a. talkative, loquacious, windy, garrulous, long-winded, voluble, wordy, verbose, *motor-mouthed, blabbermouthed, chatty, babbling. ANT. reserved, taciturn, quiet, mute.

gadabout n. wanderer, fun-seeker, rambler, roamer, playboy.

gadfly n. *pain in the neck, irritant. SEE PEST

gadget n. contraption, *widget, apparatus, appliance, device, mechanism, instrument, tool, *gizmo, contrivance, *doohickey, *thingamajig, machine, *Rube Goldberg device.

gaffe n. blunder, goof, mistake, *boner, faux pas, *boo-boo, slip, misstep, indiscretion, lapse, transgression, pecadillo, error.

gag n. joke, practical joke, prank, trick, wisecrack, caper, jest, *leg-pulling.

gag v. **1.** CHOKE retch, heave, gasp, upchuck, vomit, puke, *blow lunch, *blow chunks, *ralph, *hurl, *spew. **2.** SILENCE muzzle, shut up, censor, squelch, hush, muffle, suppress, *put a lid on.

gaiety n. happiness, cheer, mirth, joy, high spirits, elation, revelry, merriment, lightheartedness, glee, joie de vivre, festivity, jollity, gladness, hilarity, jubilation, buoyancy. ANT. somberness, depression, downheartedness, melancholy.

gain n. profit, increase, proceeds, growth, earnings, yield, winnings, advancement, improvement, enrichment, progress, headway. ANT. loss, decline.

gain v. profit, increase, grow, earn, yield, acquire, attain, get, advance, improve, enrich, progress, win, make headway. ANT. lose, decline, fall.

gainful a. profitable, productive, worthwhile, rewarding, remunerative, paying, lucrative, fruitful, beneficial. ANT. unprofitable, unrewarding.

gainsay v. deny, contradict, controvert, dispute, refute, oppose, negate, disagree, repudiate. ANT. affirm, uphold, *own up.

gait n. stride, walk, step, carriage, motion, run, tread, pace, gallop, canter.

WORD FIND

descriptive: limp; hobble; lumber; plod; stagger; shuffle; totter; traipse; trudge; shamble; pert wiggle; military gait; goosestepping; portly waddle; long, fluid stride; bowlegged stride; grace of a porteuse; loose-boned gait; willowy gait; strut; swagger; feline grace; voluptuous sway; mincing steps; authoritative gait

SEE WALK

gala n. celebration, festival, bash, fiesta, party, jubilee, *blowout, *blast, *wingding, *shindig.

galaxy n. *island universe, star cluster, Milky Way, Andromeda. SEE SPACE

gale n. wind, gust, squall, blow, blast, breeze, tempest, northeaster, hurricane, cyclone, tornado. SEE WIND

gall n. *nerve, brass, *chutzpah, *balls, impudence, insolence, brashness, sauciness, *cheek, audacity, *guts, effrontery. ANT. timidity, deference, mousiness, shyness.

gall v. irritate, annoy, *rub the wrong way, rankle, vex, irk, agitate, peeve, *piss off, provoke, inflame, chafe, nettle. ANT. please, delight.

gallant a. **1.** BRAVE daring, courageous, valorous, heroic, chivalrous, noble, valiant, lionhearted, intrepid, dauntless, high spirited, knightly. **2.** POLITE gracious, courteous, noble, mannerly, courtly, gentlemanly, kindly, well-bred, attentive, considerate. ANT. 1. cowardly, timid, mousy. 2. rude, impolite, discourteous, coarse, crude.

gallantry n. **1.** BRAVERY daring, courage, valor, heroism, chivalry, nobility, dauntlessness, fearlessness, *derring-do, intrepidity. **2.** POLITENESS graciousness, courtesy, suavity, tact, nobility, manners, gentleness, kindness, courtliness, attentiveness, duty. "To remember one is a gentleman in spite of one's birth and training." —Elbert Hubbard. ANT. 1. cowardice, mousiness, timidity. 2. rudeness, crudeness, discourtesy.

gallery n. **1.** WALKWAY passage, hall, corridor, veranda, porch, arcade, loggia, colonnade. **2.** BALCONY bleachers, grandstand. **3.** EXHIBIT art museum, exhibition hall, showplace, showroom, salon.

galling a. annoying, irritating, nettlesome, vexing, aggravating, chafing, rankling, irksome, peeving, exasperating. ANT. pleasing, delightful.

gallop v. run, race, sprint, hurdle, dash, bolt, *hightail, canter, lope, rack, trot, *clippety-clop. SEE HORSE

GALVANIZE v. [GAL vuh nize] to stimulate or rouse into action, to jolt. *The plight of the spotted owl galvanized the environmental movement.* SYN. stimulate, rouse, stir, spur, goad, excite, *fire, *spark, energize, electrify, jolt, wake up, vitalize, invigorate. ANT. *dampen, inhibit, deaden, *pull the plug.*

gambit n. maneuver, action, move, play, tactic, strategy, plan, ploy, stratagem, ruse, trick.

gamble n. bet, wager, stake, speculation, chance, risk, *shot in the dark, *outside chance, *long shot, *toss of the dice, *a ride on the wheel of fortune, *flier.

gamble v. bet, wager, chance, speculate, risk, *take a shot in the dark, *toss the dice, *take a flier, *spin the wheel of fortune, try one's luck, *shoot the works, *go for broke, hazard, prospect, *play the ponies, *play the numbers.

gambler n. "One who plays the fool." — Anon.

gambling n. "The sure way of getting nothing for something." — Wilson Mizner. "This tyrant vice." — David Garrick.

gambol v. frolic, frisk, caper, romp, cavort, bounce, prance, spring, rollick, sport, dance about, leap about.

game n. **1.** CONTEST match, competition, tournament, tourney, meet, showdown, round, bout, test of skill. **2.** AMUSEMENT entertainment, pastime, diversion, play, sport, recreation, fun, merriment, romp, clowning, test of skill.

game a. brave, courageous, bold, dauntless, fearless, plucky, *gutsy, daring, spirited, eager, enthusiastic, willing. ANT. *unwilling, *chicken, afraid.*

gamely adv. bravely, courageously, boldly, dauntlessly, fearlessly, pluckily, eagerly, enthusiastically, willingly. ANT. *unwillingly, timidly, cowardly.*

gamut n. range, extent, sweep, scope, area, reach, compass, spectrum.

gang n. group, band, pack, mob, tribe, party, squad, herd, company, clique, crowd, crew, troop, coterie, club, ring, league, fraternity, *boys in the hood, juvenile delinquents.

gangling a. lanky, tall, thin, awkward, skinny, spindly, rangy, loosely built. ANT. *husky, stout, brawny, obese.*

gangster n. mobster, Mafioso, criminal, *soldier, thug, hoodlum, *hood, racketeer, *goon, crook, godfather, *consigliere, hit man, gunman, tough.

gap n. opening, break, hole, aperture, breach, cleft, separation, rent, crevice, chasm, space, crack, fissure, hiatus, lacuna, void, interruption.

gape v. gawk, look saucer-eyed, stare, ogle, stare at goggle-eyed, *rubberneck, peer, stare openmouthed, stare in astonishment.

garb n. clothes, clothing, apparel, outfit, dress, wear, vestments, costume, attire, gear, *duds, *threads.

garb v. dress, clothe, outfit, attire, fit out, apparel, clad, deck, vest, array.

garbage n. waste, refuse, scraps, leavings, remains, rubbish, trash, offal, *slop, dregs, *crap.

garble v. confuse, mix up, distort, jumble, slur, mumble, misrepresent, twist, misstate, misunderstand.

garden n. vegetable garden, flower garden, plot, bed, patch, nursery. "The richer realm." — Alice Brown. "The purest of human pleasures." — Francis Bacon. "The best place to seek God . . . you can dig for Him there." — George Bernard Shaw. "Man's effort to improve his lot." — Anon.

WORD FIND

cultivation science: horticulture

enclosed garden: garth

fertilizer: bone meal, manure, compost

first: Eden

glass container, small garden in: terrarium

greenhouse display: conservatory

greenhouse-like box, small: cold frame

Japanese teahouse, bonsai, water: tea garden, Japanese garden

pest: aphid, cutworm, borer

pleasure ground or garden on an estate: pleasance

protective organic cover of straw, leaves, peat moss: mulch

rock: rock garden, rockery

section: bed, plot

sheltered from elements: greenhouse, hothouse

shrubs sculpted into shapes of animals, objects: topiary

skill for growing: green thumb

soil: humus, loam

soilless growing method using nutrient-rich solution: hydroponics

tool: hoe, trowel, rake, *Garden Weasel, sprinkler

tree and shrub: arbor, arboretum

wartime garden grown to boost food production: victory garden

watering: irrigation

gargantuan *a.* gigantic, huge, colossal, enormous, immense, monstrous, Brobdingnagian, Herculean, mammoth, stupendous, towering, massive, elephantine, prodigious, *humongous. ANT. *tiny*, *pint-sized, miniature, Lilliputian.*

garish *a.* flashy, showy, gaudy, glaring, loud, ostentatious, cheap, blatant, ornate, tawdry, glittering, bright. ANT. *subtle, understated, plain, modest, conservative.*

garland *n.* wreath, festoon, laurel, crown, coronet.

garment(s) *n.* clothing, attire, outfit, dress, costume, vestment, apparel, wear, *duds, *threads, *getup, uniform, *rags.

garner *v.* collect, reap, harvest, store, gather, assemble, *squirrel away, amass, accumulate.

garnish *n.* embellishment, adornment, ornament, decoration, dressing, enhancement, trimming.

garnish *v.* embellish, adorn, ornament, decorate, dress, enhance, bedeck, trim.

GARRULOUS *a.* [GAR uh lus] talkative. *They're a garrulous family; they'll talk your ear off.* SYN. talkative, loquacious, long-winded, windy, verbose, *motor-mouthed, *loose-lipped, babbling, windy, effusive, wordy, glib. ANT. *quiet, reserved, taciturn.*

gas *n.* vapor, fume, air, exhalation, steam, smoke, effluvium, miasma, oxygen, carbon dioxide, carbon monoxide, methane, propane.

gash *n.* cut, slice, slash, slit, tear, rent, split, laceration, incision, wound.

gash *v.* cut, slice, slash, slit, tear, rent, split, lacerate, incise, wound, rend, hack, hew.

gasp *n.* heave, pant, sharp intake of air, huff, gulp.

gasp *v.* heave, pant, huff, inhale sharply, gulp.

gate *n.* entry, entrance, door, opening, gateway, portal, access, egress, ingress, turnstile.

gather *v.* **1.** MASS amass, collect, accumulate, assemble, reap, harvest, muster, garner, glean, stockpile, hoard. **2.** INFER assume, guess, surmise, reckon, deduce, presume, conclude, judge. ANT. *disperse, scatter.*

gathering *n.* congregation, assembly, collection, crowd, mass, throng, bunch, concentration, gang, band, meeting, convention, muster, conference, convocation, council, caucus.

GAUCHE *a.* [GŌSH] tactless, lacking social

grace. *Telling the queen a dirty joke is considered gauche.* SYN. tactless, clumsy, boorish, uncultured, uncouth, ill-mannered, crude, unrefined, cloddish, crass, unsophisticated, ignorant, graceless. ANT. *gracious, refined, cultured, suave.*

gaudy *a.* showy, flashy, cheap, garish, ostentatious, loud, tacky, tasteless, eye-catching, tawdry, glaring, pretentious. ANT. *tasteful, understated, modest, conservative.*

gauge *n.* measure, standard, yardstick, criterion, test, touchstone, barometer, indicator, benchmark, guideline.

gauge *v.* measure, evaluate, appraise, assess, estimate, guess, calculate, judge, weigh, quantify, figure, compute, calibrate.

GAUNT *a.* [GAWNT] emaciated and hollow-eyed, as if from starvation, old age, sickness, etc. *The old man looked gaunt on his death bed.* SYN. emaciated, thin, haggard, hollow-eyed, bony, sickly, cadaverous, spindly, rawboned, wasted, scrawny, skeletal, drawn, *like death warmed over, anorexic. ANT. *strapping, robust, well-fed, fat.*

gauzy *a.* sheer, diaphanous, *see-through, transparent, gossamer, filmy, hazy, unsubstantial, translucent. ANT. *opaque, heavy, thick.*

gawk *v.* gape, stare in astonishment, stare saucer-eyed, ogle, look goggle-eyed, *rubberneck.

gawky *a.* clumsy, ungainly, awkward, oafish, graceless, bumbling, bungling, cloddish, maladroit, uncoordinated. ANT. *coordinated, graceful.*

gay *a.* **1.** HAPPY joyous, joyful, cheerful, sunny, festive, merry, mirthful, jolly, in high spirits, gleeful, vivacious, lighthearted, buoyant, animated, effervescent. **2.** BRIGHT brilliant, vivid, intense, showy, flashy, colorful. **3.** HOMOSEXUAL *queer, *bent, lesbian, *faggy, *flaming, *light on one's feet, *swish, *limp-wristed, *dykey.

gaze *v.* stare, peer, ogle, eye, *eyeball, look, scrutinize, inspect, watch, survey, scan, regard, study, admire, glare, *scorch with one's eyes.

gear *n.* **1.** EQUIPMENT apparatus, rigging, accessories, tools, implements, paraphernalia, outfit, kit, trappings, accoutrement, *stuff, effects. **2.** MACHINE PART cog, toothed wheel, sprocket, flywheel, cam. **3.** CLOTHING apparel, outfit, attire, costume, *togs, *duds.

geld *v.* castrate, neuter, sterilize, emasculate, alter, *fix.

gem *n.* jewel, precious stone, semiprecious stone, *rock, *ice, bauble.

WORD FIND

blue: sapphire, aquamarine, turquoise, hyacinth

carved in relief: cameo

cutting device: lap

diamond look-alike: zircon

engraving: glyptics

expert, cutter, polisher, dealer: lapidary

fake: paste, rhinestone

flaw: feather

imperfectly transparent gem: loupe

iridescent: pearl, moonstone, opal, cat's eye

green: emerald, beryl, aquamarine, jade, peridot

magnifying glass used by jeweler: loupe

oblong shape, cut in: baguette

plane or individual cut: facet, culet, bezel, bezil

purple: amethyst

red: ruby, garnet, carnelian, sard, avena

setting, groove and flange: bezel

study of: gemology

transparent: diamond

weight: carat, karat

yellow: topaz

SEE JEWELRY

genealogy *n.* descent, pedigree, lineage, family tree, ancestry, blood line, extraction, parentage.

general *a.* **1.** COMMON popular, regular, conventional, routine, normal, everyday, familiar, usual, prevalent, accepted, widespread. **2.** COMPREHENSIVE universal, all-inclusive, catholic, blanket, sweeping, extensive, broad, worldwide. **3.** INEXACT approximate, vague, unspecific, ill-defined, indefinite. ANT. *1. uncommon, irregular, unconventional. 2. exclusive, restricted. 3. exact, specific, defined.*

generality *n.* generalization, loose statement, broad statement, sweeping statement, abstraction.

generalize *v.* speculate, hypothesize, make sweeping statement, make broad statement, *paint with a broad brush.

generally *adv.* **1.** COMMONLY regularly, conventionally, usually, routinely, normally, typically, ordinarily. **2.** MAINLY mostly, for the most part, chiefly, ordinarily, on the whole, as a rule. ANT. *1. rarely, seldom, irregularly.*

generate *v.* produce, create, start, give rise to, invent, fashion, make, cause, initiate, originate, spawn, father, mother, found, give birth to, beget.

generation *n.* **1.** CREATION production, formation, invention, inception, fashioning, making, initiation, origination, spawning, founding, genesis. **2.** AGE period, era, epoch, eon, day, span.

generic *a.* general, universal, common, comprehensive.

generous *a.* **1.** GIVING charitable, unselfish, bighearted, openhanded, lavish, munificent, beneficent, benevolent, philanthropic, liberal, unstinting. **2.** PLENTIFUL bounteous, abundant, copious, ample, rich, lavish, liberal, overflowing. ANT. *1. cheap, stingy, *tight. 2. scanty, spare, meager.*

genesis *n.* origin, beginning, birth, creation, inception, start, generation, formation, dawn, commencement. ANT. *death, finish.*

genial *a.* cheerful, friendly, amiable, warm, sympathetic, cordial, sunny, pleasant, agreeable, good-natured, nice, convivial, sociable. ANT. *unfriendly, moody, standoffish, grouchy.*

genius *n.* **1.** MENTAL GIANT *brain, *whiz, intellectual, *wunderkind, prodigy, *Einstein, expert, virtuoso, *egghead, *rocket scientist. **2.** GREAT ABILITY OR INTELLECT talent, gift, facility, knack, endowment, flair, wisdom, ingenuity, propensity, grasp, inventiveness. "Nothing more than our common faculties refined to a greater intensity." — Benjamin Haydon. "Nothing but labor and diligence." — William Hogarth. "Perseverance in disguise." — Henry Austin. "Originality, the opening of new frontiers." — Arthur Koestler. ANT. *1. moron, imbecile, ignoramus, idiot.*

GENRE *n.* [ZHAHN ruh] a type, kind or category. *Stephen King writes primarily within the horror genre.* SYN. type, kind, category, class, sort, classification, school, variety, style, genus.

GENTEEL *a.* [jen TEEL] refined and polite. Also, affectedly refined. *He never burped out loud; he was too genteel for that.* SYN. refined, polite, cultured, respectable, mannerly, civil, courtly, behaved, gentlemanly, ladylike, formal, prudish, pretentious, *la-di-da, *highfalutin, affected, pompous, *stuffy, hoity-toity. ANT. *1. unrefined, coarse, crude, uncultured, rude, earthy, *down-home.*

gentility *n.* refinement, politeness, manners, civility, courtliness, courtesy, polish, sophistication, culture, respectability, nobility. ANT. *coarseness, vulgarity.*

gentle *a.* **1.** SOFT light, delicate, calm, quiet,

easy, tender, slight, mellow, faint, temperate. **2.** KINDLY agreeable, mild, docile, tender, soft, quiet, placid, peaceful, meek, serene, tame. ANT. *1. rough, hard, violent. 2. violent, vicious, rough.*

gentleman n. **1.** MAN fellow, *guy, chap, *dude. **2.** REFINED MAN OR RICH MAN patrician, lord, aristocrat, nobleman, *gent, *blue-blood, courtier. "To speak as the common people do, to think as wise men do." — Roger Ascham. "A man who can disagree without being disagreeable." — Anon.

gentlemanly a. genteel, mannerly, courtly, refined, polite, courteous, gallant, civil, honorable, cultivated, noble.

gentry n. aristocracy, upper class, *upper crust, nobility, gentlefolk, elite.

genuine a. **1.** REAL authentic, legitimate, *the real McCoy, bona fide, certified, actual, honest, true, unadulterated. **2.** SINCERE honest, frank, ingenuous, forthright, heartfelt, unaffected, earnest, natural. ANT. *1. counterfeit, fake, bogus. 2. insincere, affected, disingenuous.*

genus n. class, classification, sort, kind, type, category, order.

germ n. **1.** MICROBE microorganism, *bug, virus, bacterium, bacillus, pathogen. **2.** SOURCE root, beginning, origin, seed, embryo, fountainhead, spark.

GERMANE a. [jur MANE] relevant, pertinent. *Your comment is not germane to the subject at hand.* SYN. relevant, pertinent, related, appropriate, applicable, to the point, apropos, related, material, apt. ANT. *irrelevant, immaterial, unrelated.*

germinate v. sprout, bud, flower, grow, develop, spring up, shoot, generate.

gestation n. pregnancy, incubation, maturation, development.

gesticulate v. SEE GESTURE

gesture v. gesticulate, motion, signal, wave, pantomime, mime, express with hands, *use body language, *use body English, sign.

get v. **1.** OBTAIN acquire, attain, come by, secure, net, take, *bag, gain, receive, seize, earn, win, procure, reap, harvest, gather, achieve. **2.** UNDERSTAND comprehend, grasp, see, follow, fathom, take in, apprehend. **3.** BE AFFLICTED WITH catch, *come down with, contract.

ghastly a. **1.** FRIGHTFUL horrible, hideous, gruesome, shocking, dreadful, horrendous, appalling, revolting, macabre, grisly. **2.** CADAVEROUS ghostly, pale, haggard, blanched,

corpselike, deathly, ashen.

ghost n. spirit, specter, apparition, phantom, *spook, phantasm, poltergeist, wraith, doppelgänger, shade, shadow. "A shadow of its former self." — Anon. "The outward and visible sign of an inward fear." — Ambrose Bierce.

ghostly a. spectral, phantom, spiritual, phantasmic, spooky, spiritual, haunted, unearthly, wraithlike, supernatural, ghastly, eerie, illusory.

ghoulish a. monstrous, hideous, fiendish, vampiric, gruesome, diabolical, necrophilic, cold-blooded, horrible.

giant n. titan, gargantua, colossus, behemoth, *whopper, *bruiser, hulk, Goliath, Brobdingnagian, Amazon, Cyclops, ogre, giantess. ANT. *midget, dwarf, *shrimp, *Lilliputian.*

giant a. huge, gigantic, gargantuan, mammoth, colossal, enormous, prodigious, Brobdingnagian, titanic, Herculean, elephantine, towering. ANT. *tiny, microscopic, *Lilliputian.*

gibberish n. babble, gibber, *gobbledegook, mumbojumbo, jabber, chatter, nonsense, twaddle, drivel, blather, prattle, jargon.

gibe v. taunt, jeer, mock, scoff, ridicule, tease, *ride, deride, make fun of, sneer at, heckle, *razz, rib.

giddy a. **1.** DIZZY light-headed, *woozy, reeling, unsteady, faint, vertiginous. **2.** FLIGHTY frivolous, fickle, *bubbleheaded, capricious, silly, *airheaded, scatterbrained, *ditzy. ANT. *levelheaded, sober, stable, serious.*

gift n. **1.** PRESENT gratuity, donation, giveaway, contribution, offering, token, gesture, favor, benefaction, bonus, grant, tip. **2.** TALENT natural ability, knack, faculty, aptitude, endowment, flair, bent, genius.

gifted a. talented, endowed, skilled, expert, accomplished, masterly, proficient, adept, ingenious, intelligent.

gigantic a. huge, big, titanic, gargantuan, colossal, *whopping, Brobdingnagian, Herculean, enormous, stupendous, towering, prodigious. ANT. *tiny, microscopic, Lilliputian.*

giggle v. laugh, titter, snigger, chuckle, snicker, *teehee, chortle, cackle.

gild v. embellish, decorate, gloss over, embroider, dress up, enhance, touch up, garnish, whitewash, sugarcoat.

gimcrack n. knickknack, bauble, gewgaw, trinket, doodad, novelty, whatnot, bagatelle.

gimmick n. device, scheme, catch, subterfuge, artifice, wrinkle, ruse, ploy, trick, contrivance, *dodge.

gingerly a. delicately, lightly, carefully, cautiously, gently, warily, guardedly, discreetly, charily, timidly. ANT. *recklessly, boldly, rashly.*

gird v. encircle, surround, enclose, circumscribe, band, encompass, secure, reinforce, fortify.

girl n. female, lass, lassie, maiden, miss, *filly, damsel, wench, *chick, *babe, *dame, mademoiselle, debutante, belle, tomboy, *muchacha. "Innocence playing in the mud, beauty standing on its head, and motherhood dragging a doll by the foot." — Allan Beck.

gist n. essence, substance, main point, pith, crux, heart, core, point, drift, thrust, *bottom line.

give v. 1. CONTRIBUTE, BESTOW donate, present, hand over, confer, award, dispense, deliver, transmit, provide, *fork over, convey, *shell out, entrust. 2. IMPART express, communicate, send, deliver, offer, announce, state. 3. CONCEDE yield, bend, surrender, relinquish. 4. COLLAPSE buckle, cave in, fall.

give-and-take n. compromise, cooperation, reciprocity, *mutual back-scratching, interchange, trade-off, collaboration.

glacial a. icy, snowy, frozen, gelid, frigid, frosty, arctic, polar, wintry.

WORD FIND

altering of land mass by glacier: glaciation

boulder pushed far from its native land by: glacial erratic

bowllike gouge carved out of mountain side by glacier: cirque

breaking away of large chunks from head of glacier: calving

cave in a glacier: glaciere

chunks of glacier floating in ocean: iceberg

epoch: pleistocene

expert: glaciologist

gravel and rocks deposited by: drift, till, drumlin, esker, kame, moraine

mountain peak surrounded by: nunatak

period of cold in which glaciers grow and expand: ice age

pinnacle of ice on: serac

scratches, grooves left on bedrock by passing glacier: striations

snow that gradually becomes glacial ice: neve, firn

glad a. 1. HAPPY delighted, *tickled, *tickled to death, *tickled pink, pleased, thrilled, gratified, cheerful, joyous, upbeat. 2. DELIGHTFUL happy, pleasing, gratifying, cheering. 3. WILLING eager. ANT. *1. sad, depressed, unhappy. 2.* miserable, awful, terrible. *3. unwilling, reluctant.*

gladden a. cheer, make happy, hearten, please, brighten, delight, *tickle pink, *raise one's spirits, elate. ANT. *bring down, *bum out, depress.

glamorous a. fascinating, charismatic, alluring, captivating, charming, magnetic, bewitching, enchanting, dazzling, provocative.

glamour n. allure, charm, appeal, fascination, *razzle-dazzle, charisma, magnetism, attraction, bewitchment, *star power.

glance n. look, glimpse, peek, peep, gander, *once-over.

glance v. 1. LOOK glimpse, peer, peek, peep, view, observe, *get a load of, *take a gander, *give a once-over, eye, *eyeball. 2. GRAZE sideswipe, brush, carom, kiss, ricochet, skim, bounce off, touch.

glare v. 1. SHINE flash, gleam, blaze, dazzle, light, radiate, blind, flame, glow. 2. SCOWL frown, *stare down, glower, lower, *scorch with one's eyes, *look at piercingly, *stare icily. SEE ANGRY

glaring a. 1. BRIGHT blinding, dazzling, brilliant, intense, overpowering, shining, harsh, flashy, blazing. 2. FLAGRANT obvious, conspicuous, blatant, extreme, open, overt, prominent, undisguised. ANT. *1. dim, subdued. 2. subtle, covert, negligible, inconspicuous.*

glass n. cup, tumbler, goblet, mug, chalice, beaker, pony.

glasses n. *specs, lenses. SEE EYE GLASSES

glassy a. 1. TRANSPARENT clear, crystal, glossy, vitreous, lucid, smooth, slick. 2. EXPRESSIONLESS glazed, lifeless, vacuous, empty, dazed, deadpan, fixed. ANT. *2. expressive.*

glaze n. varnish, lacquer, gloss, coat, finish, patina, luster.

glaze v. varnish, lacquer, gloss, coat, finish, polish, paint.

gleam n. flash, beam, light, brilliance, sparkle, glimmer, glow, twinkle, scintillation, shimmer.

gleam v. shine, beam, flash, light, radiate, sparkle, glimmer, glow, twinkle, scintillate, shimmer.

glean v. collect, gather, harvest, reap, cull, take in, extract.

glee a. joy, gaiety, happiness, merriment, exultation, elation, verve, mirth, gladness, jubilation, felicity. ANT. *depression, misery, melancholy.*

gleeful a. joyous, gay, happy, merry, exultant,

elated, mirthful, glad, jubilant, exhilarated, blithe. ANT. *depressed, miserable, melancholy.*

GLIB *a.* [GLIB] spoken or given too easily, too offhandedly or too superficially to be taken seriously, as a piece of advice. *He had all the answers; he was glib; he was full of hot air.* SYN. facile, superficial, smooth-tongued, quick, ready, slick, smooth-talking, fluent, fast-talking, voluble. ANT. *thoughtful, sincere, deep, profound.*

glide *v.* slide, glissade, float, skim, plane, waft, coast, drift, skate, slip, flow, wing.

glimmer *v.* gleam, glow, flicker, sparkle, glare, coruscate, beam, glitter, twinkle, scintillate, flash.

glimpse *n.* look, peek, peep, glance, fleeting look, flash.

glimpse *v.* catch a peek, peep, look, glance, see, eye, *eyeball, spot, *get a load of, take in, spy.

glisten *v.* shine, sparkle, flash, glimmer, shimmer, gleam, glint, scintillate, glitter.

glitch *n. Sl.* error, malfunction, *bug, snag, *SNAFU.

glitter *n.* sparkle, glint, glimmer, gleam, sheen, shine, brilliance, radiance, scintillation, luster, twinkle.

glitter *v.* sparkle, glint, glimmer, gleam, shine, radiate, scintillate, twinkle, coruscate.

gloaming *n.* dusk, twilight, nightfall, sundown.

gloat *v.* crow, exult, strut, brag, vaunt, triumph, *rub it in, boast, *lord over, *take malicious pleasure in. ANT. *downplay, deprecate.*

global *a.* worldwide, international, intercontinental, universal, planetary, pandemic, widespread, extensive, far-reaching. ANT. *local, regional, confined.*

globe *n.* sphere, orb, spheroid, earth, planet, world, ball, *spaceship Earth, biosphere.

gloom *n.* **1.** DARKNESS dimness, murk, shadow, obscurity, shade, dusk, blackness, cloudiness. **2.** SADNESS depression, hopelessness, melancholy, despair, woe, grief, sorrow, dejection, unhappiness, desolation, heavyheartedness. ANT. *1. brightness, sunniness, light, radiance. 2. happiness, cheerfulness, joy.*

gloomy *a.* **1.** DARK dim, murky, shadowy, dismal, obscure, dusky, gauzy, black, cloudy, dreary, somber. **2.** SAD depressed, depressing, hopeless, dismal, melancholy, woeful, glum, sorrowful, dejected, unhappy, desolated, joyless, heavyhearted, despondent, saturnine, black, bleak, funereal. ANT. *1. bright, light, radiant, sunny. 2. happy, elated, euphoric, bright.*

glorify *v.* **1.** EXALT honor, idolize, revere, worship, deify, elevate, venerate, immortalize, beatify, sanctify. **2.** PRAISE extol, celebrate, honor, *put on a pedestal, *talk up, *sing the praises of, hail, acclaim, celebrate, flatter, lionize. ANT. *degrade, condemn, dishonor, disgrace.*

glorious *a.* divine, splendid, magnificent, wonderful, grand, marvelous, superb, excellent, heavenly, sublime, spectacular, resplendent.

glory *n.* **1.** HONOR admiration, fame, renown, celebrity, praise, acclaim, esteem, adoration, veneration, prestige, notoriety. "Goads and spurs to virtue." — Francis Bacon. "A torch to kindle the noble mind." — Silius Italicus. **2.** BEAUTY splendor, magnificence, radiance, grandeur, resplendence, majesty, brilliance. ANT. *1. dishonor, degradation, disgrace. 2. ugliness.*

gloss *n.* shine, luster, sheen, shimmer, glow, gleam, polish, brilliance.

gloss *v.* **1.** SHINE make lustrous, polish, buff, rub, burnish, varnish. **2.** SMOOTH OVER cover up, mask, disguise, *sugarcoat, soft-pedal, *whitewash, doctor.

glossary *n.* lexicon, word list, nomenclature.

glossy *a.* shiny, lustrous, shimmering, gleaming, glowing, polished, burnished, sleek, silky, glassy. ANT. *dull, tarnished.*

glow *n.* radiance, light, gleam, brightness, glimmer, shine, luminosity, illumination, incandescence, effulgence, phosphorescence. SEE BLUSH

glow *v.* radiate, light, gleam, glimmer, shine, illuminate, incandesce, shimmer, glare. SEE BLUSH

glower *v.* frown, scowl, glare, lower, stare blackly, *shoot a dirty look, *scorch with one's eyes. SEE ANGRY

glowing *a.* **1.** RADIANT aglow, luminous. **2.** COLORED red, ruddy, rosy, flushed, florid, radiant, aglow, blooming. **3.** ENTHUSIASTIC complimentary, laudatory, favorable. ANT. *1. dull, dim. 2. pale, blanched, pallid. 3. negative, unenthusiastic, critical.*

glue *n.* cement, paste, fixative, adhesive, *stickum, mucilage.

glum *a.* sullen, gloomy, morose, down, low, dispirited, long-faced, sulky, dismal, cheerless, lugubrious, sad. ANT. *cheerful, happy, joyous, elated.*

glut *n.* excess, surplus, overabundance, superfluity, surfeit, surplus, flood, inundation, overflow, plethora, repletion. ANT. *dearth, scarcity, lack, shortage.*

glut *v.* fill, flood, surfeit, sate, satiate, inundate, clog, choke, oversupply, stuff, congest, overload.

glutton *n.* *pig, *hog, gourmand, *garbage disposal, eater, epicure, *garbage gut, *chow hound, overeater. "One who takes the piece of pastry you wanted."—Anon. "One who digs his grave with his teeth."—French proverb.

gluttonous *a.* voracious, gourmandizing, insatiable, ravenous, *piggish, *hoggish.

gnarled *a.* knotted, knotty, twisted, contorted, tortured, crooked, distorted, arthritic, wrinkled. ANT. *smooth.*

gnash *v.* grind, grit, grate, rasp, clamp.

gnaw *v.* **1.** MUNCH nibble, chew, bite, champ, eat away. **2.** BOTHER nag, *eat at, trouble, worry, plague, torment.

gnome *n.* fairy, elf, dwarf, troll, pixie, leprechaun, imp.

go *n.* **1.** ENERGY animation, drive, vigor, zest, pep, life, force. **2.** TRY attempt, whirl, stab, shot, crack.

go *v.* **1.** PROCEED advance, begin, move, start, set out, get the ball rolling, travel, make headway, progress. **2.** LEAVE depart, retire, run, *split, *scram, decamp, withdraw, slip away, *hit the road, vamoose, quit, *shove off, *beat it, *blow. **3.** FUNCTION perform, run, work, operate, act. **4.** PASS elapse, slip away, transpire, expire. **5.** EXTEND lead, stretch, span, reach. ANT. *1. stop, stay, freeze. 2. remain, stay.*

goad *n.* stimulus, spur, prod, inducement, impetus, catalyst, urge, motive, incentive, *kick in the pants, *swift kick.

goad *v.* stimulate, spur, prod, induce, urge, motivate, impel, incite, spark, egg on, coerce, prompt, *kickstart, provoke.

goal *n.* aim, ambition, end, purpose, objective, target, design, intention, destination.

goat *n.* scapegoat, *fall guy, whipping boy, butt, *patsy.

gobble *v.* bolt, wolf, gulp, stuff, cram, choke down, devour, *shovel, gorge, *suck up, swallow whole.

gobbledygook *n.* gibberish, jargon, cant, *officialese, claptrap, legalese, nonsense, *bunk, *rot, *bafflegab.

go-between *n.* intermediary, middleman, medium, second, arbitrator, mediator, agent, broker, referee.

goblin *n.* spirit, bogeyman, *spook, hobgoblin, imp, elf, puck, gnome, kobold.

God/god *n.* **1.** GOD Supreme Being, Father in Heaven, Heavenly Father, the Almighty, the All-Powerful, the All-Wise, the All-Merciful, the All-Seeing, Lord of Lords, King of Kings, the Creator, Brahma, Allah, Adonai, Lord, Jehovah, Holy Spirit, the Man Upstairs. "Love."—The Bible. "A superior reasoning power . . . revealed in the incomprehensible universe."—Albert Einstein. "Conscience."—Mohandas Gandhi. "A light that is never darkened."—Francis Quarles. "A mighty fortress."—Martin Luther. "Personified incomprehensibility."—George Lichtenberg. "That which has no definition."—Joseph Albo. "A vengeful, pitiless, and almighty fiend."—Percy Bysshe Shelley. "An infantile fantasy . . . necessary when men did not know what lightning was."—Edward Anhalt. "A gaseous vertebrate."—Ernst Haeckel. **2.** GOD goddess, deity, divinity, spirit, idol. ANT. *1. the Devil, Satan, Lucifer, Prince of Darkness. 2. mortal, physical being.*

WORD FIND

appearance of: theophany

belief in god other than that of Jewish, Christian or Muslim faith: paganism

cry of praise to God: hosanna

disbelief in: atheism

disbeliever: atheist

half god, half human: demigod

Hindu deity on earth: avatar

humans created by God not evolved, belief that: creationism

human traits imagined in: anthropomorphism

Latin: Dominus

one, belief in more than: polytheism

one, belief in only: monotheism

questioner of God's existence: agnostic

questioning of God's existence: agnosticism

Son of God: Jesus Christ

study of: theology

universe and its natural laws are God, belief that: pantheism

SEE CHURCH, MYTHICAL DEITIES, RELIGION

God-fearing *a.* pious, devout, faithful, devoted, reverent, holy, religious. ANT. *atheistic, godless, heathen.*

godforsaken *a.* desolate, forlorn, lonely, abandoned, wretched, cheerless, forgotten, condemned.

godless *a.* atheistic, heathen, impious, pagan, sacrilegious, blasphemous, freethinking, agnostic, wicked, unholy. ANT. *pious, devout, God-fearing.*

godly *a.* religious, God-fearing, devout, pious, righteous, holy, spiritual, reverent, born-again, saintly, good, moral. ANT. *godless, sinful, atheistic, blasphemous, sacrilegious.*

godsend *n.* blessing, gift, windfall, miracle, manna, benediction, boon.

gold *n.* **1.** COLOR yellow, gilt, straw, tawny, flaxen, blond, honey, auric. **2.** METAL precious metal, nugget. "The touchstone whereby to try men."—Thomas Fuller.

goldbrick *v. Sl.* shirk, loaf, *goof off, malinger.

golden *a.* **1.** SEE GOLD **2.** ADVANTAGEOUS best, opportune, favorable, auspicious, timely, propitious, providential, rosy. ANT. *2. black, unfavorable.*

golf *n.* "A plague invented by the Calvinistic Scots as a punishment for man's sins."—James Reston. "A good walk spoiled."—Mark Twain. "A sport in which many impressive scores are attained by a lead pencil."—Anon.

WORD FIND

aid: caddy

average number of shots deemed necessary for each hole: par

ball position after coming to rest: lie

closely cropped green around hole: putting green

club: baffy, blade, brassie, chipping iron, cleek, iron, mashie, niblick, putter, driver, wood, wedge, spoon

curving drive: hook, slice

curving fairway: dogleg

extra shot allowed in casual game: Mulligan

fee to play: greens fee

flagstick: pin

grounder fairway, green, links, course

hole made in one stroke: ace, hole in one

lockers, club building: clubhouse

long grass area: rough

par, scoring one stroke over: bogey

par, scoring one stroke under: birdie

par, scoring three strokes under: albatross, double eagle

par, scoring two strokes over: double bogey

par, scoring two strokes under: eagle

plug that ball sits on: tee

poor golfer: duffer, hacker

sand hazard: sand trap, bunker; *beach

shots: drive, putt, chip shot, loft, pitch, hook, slice

shouted warning: fore!

turf hacked out by club: divot

gone *a.* departed, left, removed, away, absent, vanished, missing, extinct, *AWOL, out, off, lost, used up, consumed, finished.

good *n.* **1.** ADVANTAGE benefit, welfare, profit, gain, interest, well-being. **2.** VIRTUE goodness, morality, value, worth, uprightness.

good *a.* **1.** SATISFACTORY adequate, acceptable, worthy, OK, all right, fine, excellent, first-rate, choice, super, great, commendable, prime, marvelous, select, sufficient, beneficial, reputable, recommended, effective. **2.** MORAL virtuous, righteous, wholesome, honorable, upright, conscientious, exemplary, respectable, noble, chaste. **3.** KIND humane, benevolent, sympathetic, compassionate, giving, charitable, merciful, altruistic. **4.** WELL-BEHAVED mannerly, respectful, polite, considerate. **5.** UNSPOILED fresh, uncontaminated, untainted, fit, sound. **6.** SKILLED able, proficient, competent, accomplished, adept, capable, talented. **7.** GENUINE authentic, real, bona fide, valid, true, sound, *kosher. **8.** CONSIDERABLE big, large, sizable, respectable, substantial, extensive. ANT. *1. unsatisfactory, bad, poor, second-rate. 2. immoral, sinful, wicked. 3. cruel, mean, vicious. 4. rude, impolite, unruly. 5. spoiled, tainted. 6. unskilled, bad, inadequate. 7. fake, counterfeit, phony. 8. scant, trivial, piddling.*

goodbye *interj.* farewell, bye-bye, *so long, Godspeed, *toodle-oo, *toodles, *ta-ta, adieu, adios, ciao, sayonara, hasta la vista, arrivederci, au revoir, auf Wiedersehen, see you later, *later, *see you later alligator.

good-humored *a.* SEE GOOD-NATURED

good-looking *a.* attractive, beautiful, handsome, pretty, cute, comely, lovely, becoming, fair, *nice, *foxy, *bonny. ANT. *ugly, repulsive.*

good-natured *a.* easygoing, cheerful, amiable, genial, pleasant, good-humored, agreeable, nice, even-tempered, complaisant, kindly. ANT. *grouchy, touchy, standoffish.*

goodness *n.* virtue, excellence, righteousness, uprightness, morality, integrity, kindness, wholesomeness, benevolence. ANT. *badness, wickedness, evil.*

goods *n.* **1.** PERSONAL PROPERTY belongings, possessions, things, stuff, effects. **2.** MERCHANDISE wares, stock, inventory, commodities.

goodwill *n.* benevolence, kindliness, altruism, favor, friendliness, humanitarianism, graciousness, goodness. ANT. *ill will, hostility.*

goof *v. Sl.* bungle, mess up, blunder, fail, *screw up, miscalculate.

goofy *a. Sl.* silly, foolish, stupid, sophomoric, childish, *nerdy, *ditzy, *daffy, dopey.

goon n. *geek, *bozo, clown, *boob, *dork, *goober, lummox, freak, moron, *throwback, *Neanderthal.

gore n. bloodshed, slaughter, carnage. SEE MURDER

gore v. pierce, puncture, stab, impale, gouge, horn, hook.

gorge n. canyon, chasm, pass, valley, gap, ravine, gully, defile.

gorge v. bolt, stuff, cram, wolf, swallow whole, gulp, gobble, devour, *shovel in, overeat, satiate, glut.

gorgeous a. beautiful, magnificent, splendid, sumptuous, attractive, stunning, lovely, ravishing, exquisite, luxurious, resplendent. SEE GOOD-LOOKING

gormandize v. devour, gorge, *pig out, overeat, stuff, gobble, wolf.

gory a. bloody, bloodstained, sanguinary, murderous, savage, horrible.

gossamer a. delicate, diaphanous, airy, fine, feathery, cobwebby.

gossip n. **1.** RUMORS hearsay, chatter, talk, scandal, *dirt, *lowdown, *scuttlebutt, report, mudslinging, *grapevine, *small talk, *buzz. "Foul whisperings." — Shakespeare. "Murder by language." — Roland Barthes. **2.** RUMORMONGER tattler, tattletale, *big mouth, *blabbermouth, busybody, snoop, prattler. "One with a sense of rumor." — Anon.

gourmet n. epicure, epicurean, gastronome, connoisseur, bon vivant, gourmand. "Just a glutton with brains." — Philip Haberman.

govern v. **1.** RULE administer, direct, supervise, manage, oversee, dictate, run, reign, order, occupy the throne, regulate, *lay down the law, hold sway, *pull the strings, exercise authority. **2.** HOLD IN CHECK curb, inhibit, bridle, restrain, control, arrest, regulate.

government n. regulation, administration, governing body, control, *Big Brother, Washington, *Uncle Sam, the state, *powers that be, management, supervision, guidance, bureaucracy, rule, command, reign, authority, leadership, dictatorship, regime, senate, congress, ministry. "The biggest organized social effort for dealing with social problems." — Felix Frankfurter. "The people." — John Quincy Adams. "The Santa Claus of something-for-nothing and something-for-everyone." — Barry Goldwater. "A kind of gangsterism." — Frank Lloyd Wright. "A baby. An alimentary canal with a big appetite at one end and no sense of responsibility at the other." — Ronald Reagan.

WORD FIND
absence of: anarchy
authoritarian: totalitarianism
autonomy: sovereignty
betrayal of: treason
citizens in authority: commonwealth, democracy, republic
clergy, headed by: hierocracy, theocracy, hagiarchy
dictated by one ruler or small group: dictatorship, despotism, tyranny
experts, by: technocracy
female: matriarchy, gynarchy, gynecocracy
king's: monarchy
male lineage, handed down through: patriarchy
Medieval system of lords and vassals: feudalism
military, by: stratocracy, martial law
oppressive, one-party system: fascism
preserving cultural diversity: pluralism
privileged class, by: aristocracy, oligarchy, plutocracy
secret police, controlled by: police state
seizure of: coup d'etat
self-governing: autonomous
without: acracy
SEE CONGRESS, ELECTION, POLITICS

governor n. ruler, regulator, director, administrator, supervisor, head, bureaucrat, magistrate.

gown n. dress, frock, robe, negligee.

grab v. snatch, seize, clutch, grasp, pluck, catch, capture, bag, nab, take, latch on to, get one's hands on.

grace n. **1.** BEAUTY AND CHARM loveliness, attractiveness, elegance, appeal, pulchritude. **2.** GOOD FORM fluidity, symmetry, finesse, ease, *poetry in motion, form, agility, dexterity, poise, refinement, coordination. **3.** MANNERS thoughtfulness, savoir faire, decorum, tact, charm, cultivation, etiquette. **4.** MERCY forgiveness, clemency, leniency, compassion, reprieve, quarter, good will. **5.** PRAYER benediction, thanksgiving, request for blessings. **6.** GOD'S FAVOR love, virtue, divine influence, holiness. "The outward expression of the inward harmony of the soul." — William Hazlitt. ANT. *1. ugliness, repulsiveness. 2. clumsiness, awkwardness. 3. boorishness, rudeness, bad manners. 4. condemnation, damnation, ill will.*

grace v. decorate, adorn, beautify, bedeck, ornament, enhance, garnish, dignify, honor, distinguish.

graceful *a.* **1.** HAVING GOOD FORM fluid, coordinated, poised, dexterous, agile, refined, adroit, nimble, lissome, lithesome, supple, *graceful as a porteuse, smooth, balanced, elegant. **2.** CHARMING appealing, attractive, elegant, mannerly, cultivated, winsome, tactful, urbane. ANT. *1. clumsy, awkward. 2. rude, obnoxious, boorish, unrefined.*

gracious *a.* kind, courteous, hospitable, cordial, polite, benevolent, accommodating, considerate, well-mannered, friendly, affable, charitable. ANT. *ungracious, rude, inconsiderate.*

grade *n.* **1.** SLOPE incline, gradient, slant, rise, pitch, ascent, descent. **2.** RANK status, standing, position, class, station, stage, increment, rating, mark.

grade *v.* **1.** RANK rate, evaluate, classify, sort, brand, order, label. **2.** LEVEL flatten, smooth.

gradient *n.* grade, slope, incline, slant, rise, pitch, ascent, descent.

gradual *a.* progressive, successive, slow, incremental, piecemeal, step-by-step, bit-by-bit, leisurely, measured, steady, by degrees. ANT. *abrupt, sudden, instantaneous.*

graduate *n.* alumnus, alumna, grad, bachelor.

graduate *v.* **1.** COMPLETE SCHOOL receive a diploma, receive a degree, complete one's education. **2.** GRADE measure, calibrate, mark off.

graduation *n.* commencement, advancement. SEE COLLEGE, SCHOOL

graft *n.* **1.** transplant, implant, scion, splice, slip. **2.** corruption, spoils, *take, *payola, bribe, *hush money, *skimming, kickback, boodle.

graft *v.* implant, transplant, splice, insert, affix.

grain *n.* **1.** SEED kernel, grist, cereal, wheat, oats, barley, rice, rye, millet. **2.** PARTICLE granule, bit, speck, fleck, mote, dot. **3.** TEXTURE surface, weave.

grand *a.* **1.** MAGNIFICENT impressive, great, majestic, imposing, striking, glorious, splendid, excellent, superb, ambitious, marvelous, sumptuous, monumental, stately, august, awesome, huge, palatial, lofty. **2.** MAIN principle, head, chief, leading, supreme, preeminent. **3.** EXCELLENT great, good, superb, fabulous, first-rate. ANT. *1. lowly, pedestrian, paltry, modest. 2. secondary, lesser, minor. 3. poor, lousy, second-rate.*

grandeur *n.* magnificence, greatness, splendor, majesty, glory, resplendence, vastness, augustness, beauty, distinction, eminence. ANT. *insignificance, modesty.*

GRANDILOQUENT *a.* [gran DIL uh kwent]

using big words to try to impress, bombastic. *Many politicians are grandiloquent but have little to say.* SYN. bombastic, pompous, pretentious, high-flown, fustian, *windy, inflated, verbose, magnific, turgid, rhetorical. ANT. *plainspoken, *folksy, simple, unpretentious.*

grandiose *a.* grand, magnificent, impressive, imposing, extravagant, ambitious, cosmic, epic, homeric, pompous, theatrical, *highfalutin. ANT. *down to earth, modest, humble.*

grant *n.* gift, contribution, donation, present, endowment, award, bestowal, charity, scholarship.

grant *v.* **1.** GIVE confer, transfer, bestow, award, impart, present, contribute, donate. **2.** CONCEDE acknowledge, admit, accede, yield, go along with. ANT. *refuse, deny.*

graphic *a.* vivid, clear, lifelike, striking, pictorial, picturesque, realistic, explicit, descriptive, effective, expressive. ANT. *vague, obscure.*

grapple *v.* **1.** STRUGGLE wrestle, scuffle, battle, tussle, combat, *lock horns, confront, fight. **2.** GRIP hold, seize, clutch, snatch, squeeze, catch.

grasp *n.* **1.** GRIP hold, clutch, clasp. **2.** COMPREHENSION understanding, perception, mastery, knowledge, cognition.

grasp *v.* **1.** GRIP grab, hold, clutch, clasp, catch, snatch, clinch, grapple, nab. **2.** COMPREHEND understand, get, see, sense, follow, apprehend, appreciate. ANT. *1. loose, release, let go.*

grasping *a.* avaricious, greedy, acquisitive, hungry, covetous, rapacious, miserly, *grabby, venal, desirous. ANT. *generous, giving.*

grass *n.* lawn, turf, sward, pasture, meadow, alfalfa, barley, Bermuda grass, bluegrass, broomcorn, buckwheat, bulrush, bunch grass, cane, crab grass, darnel, eelgrass, fescue, foxtail, hay, horsetail, lemon grass, millet, oat, orchard grass, redtop, ribbon grass, rice, rush, rye, sedge, sorghum, timothy, wheat, witch grass. "The hair of the earth."—Thomas Dekker.

WORD FIND

clump: hassock, tussock, tuft
decaying matter beneath: thatch
dried: hay
hay: timothy
individual: blade, spear, shoot, leaf
new growth: fog
SEE FIELD

GRASS ROOTS *n.* the common people, ordinary taxpayers. *A grass roots movement to clean up the environment.* SYN. common people, taxpayers, the masses, middle class, rank and file, *little guys, hoi polloi, electorate, Middle America.

grate v. **1.** SHRED grind, rasp, fray, mince, abrade, grit, file. **2.** IRRITATE *rub the wrong way, annoy, *get on one's nerves, irk, nettle, peeve, fret.

grateful a. thankful, appreciative, indebted, beholden, obliged, much obliged. ANT. *ungrateful, unappreciative.*

gratification n. satisfaction, enjoyment, pleasure, fulfillment, contentment, delight, happiness, reward, gratuity.

gratify v. please, satisfy, fulfill, content, make happy, delight, gladden, favor, oblige, indulge. ANT. *displease, dissatisfy, disappoint.*

gratifying a. pleasing, satisfying, fulfilling, contenting, delightful, gladdening, rewarding, enjoyable. ANT. *displeasing, disappointing.*

grating n. framework, grille, grid, latticework, grate.

grating a. **1.** HARSH rasping, jarring, grinding, strident, scraping, screeching, piercing. **2.** IRRITATING annoying, irksome, nettlesome, vexatious, exasperating, abrasive. ANT. *1. fluid, melodious, pleasing. 2. pleasing, agreeable.*

gratis a. free, complimentary, *on the house, no charge, gratuitous.

gratitude n. appreciation, thankfulness, gratefulness, thanks, acknowledgement, recognition, sense of obligation. "The exchequer of the poor." — Shakespeare.

GRATUITOUS a. [gruh TOO i tus] uncalled for or unjustified, also, given freely or without charge. *Movies today are filled with gratuitous violence.* SYN. **1.** uncalled for, unjustified, unnecessary, unwarranted, needless, superfluous, inessential, unprovoked, baseless. **2.** free, gratis, complimentary, *on the house. ANT. *1. necessary, relevant, justified, warranted.*

gratuity n. gift, tip, present, fee, extra, *perk, lagniappe, recompense, bonus, offering, vail, cumshaw.

grave n. tomb, resting place, crypt, vault, sepulcher, burial pit, mausoleum, catacomb, barrow. "The last inn of all travelers." — William Davenant. "The footprints of angels." — Longfellow. "The threshold of eternity." — Robert Southey. "The last resort." — Anon. SEE CEMETERY, COFFIN, FUNERAL, MONUMENT

grave a. **1.** SERIOUS important, momentous, weighty, critical, crucial, *life and death, vi-

tal, pivotal, urgent, ominous, grievous, dangerous, threatening. **2.** SOLEMN grim, somber, dignified, serious, sedate, gloomy, sober, subdued, staid, dour, quiet, saturnine. ANT. *1. trivial, unimportant, insignificant, inconsequential. 2. cheerful, beaming, silly, merry.*

graveyard n. necropolis, *boneyard. SEE CEMETERY

gravitate v. be drawn to, be attracted, head toward, converge, incline, fall, settle, sink.

gravity n. **1.** GRAVITATION pull, attraction, pressure, force, weight. **2.** SERIOUSNESS importance, weightiness, consequence, magnitude, significance, urgency, import, enormity. ANT. *1. repulsion. 2. insignificance, triviality, frivolity.*

gray a. **1.** SILVERY ash, leaden, pearly, smoky, gunmetal, battleship gray, stone, slate, dove-colored, salt and pepper, grizzled. **2.** OVERCAST gloomy, dismal, dim, dreary, somber.

graze v. **1.** TOUCH scrape, brush, glance, kiss, skim, skin, scratch. **2.** FEED forage, browse, crop, munch, pasture.

grease n. fat, oil, lard, tallow, drippings, lubricant.

grease v. lubricate, oil.

greasy a. oily, fatty, buttery, lardy, oleaginous, slick, slippery, waxy, unctuous, smeared.

great a. **1.** LARGE big, huge, grand, immense, prodigious, gigantic, massive, tremendous, stupendous, enormous, gargantuan, extensive, boundless, voluminous, countless, extreme, prolonged, numerous. **2.** INTENSE strong, pronounced, extraordinary, considerable, powerful. **3.** IMPORTANT significant, momentous, consequential, influential, critical. **4.** CELEBRATED eminent, illustrious, famed, distinguished, esteemed, prominent, exalted, noted, renowned, heroic. **5.** EXCELLENT superb, super, fantastic, exceptional, awesome, first-rate, outstanding, terrific, wonderful, *crack, *aces, proficient, skilled. ANT. *1. small, lesser, tiny, miniscule. 2. mild, minor, light, weak. 3. insignificant, unimportant, inconsequential. 4. obscure, unknown, ordinary. 5. mediocre, terrible, lousy, awful.*

greed n. avarice, *grabbiness, acquisitiveness, covetousness, gluttony, rapaciousness, insatiability, graspingness, cupidity, want, hunger. ANT. *generosity, charity.*

greedy a. avaricious, covetous, *grabby, *piggish, *hoggish, acquisitive, gluttonous, rapacious, insatiable, grasping, hungry, selfish, stingy. ANT. *generous, giving, charitable.*

green a. **1.** COLOR aquamarine, emerald, grass,

kelly, pea, lime, beryl, sap, apple, moss, sea green. **2.** YOUNG AND GROWING youthful, blooming, budding, developing, vigorous, robust, fresh, spreading, flourishing, burgeoning, verdant. **3.** INEXPERIENCED unseasoned, untried, *wet behind the ears, naive, new, untrained, ignorant, raw. ANT. *2. withered, wilted, dying. 3. experienced, veteran, seasoned, mature.*

greenhorn n. newcomer, tenderfoot, novice, amateur, *babe in the woods, neophyte, beginner, tyro, rookie, pup. ANT. *veteran, *old hand.*

greet v. welcome, hail, receive, salute, meet, wave to, usher in, address, recognize.

greeting n. salutation, acknowledgement, respects, hello, hail, nod, welcome, *how do, salute, bow, reception.

GREGARIOUS a. [gri GAIR ee us] outgoing and sociable, liking the company of others. *Gregarious partygoers.* SYN. sociable, outgoing, friendly, social, extroverted, companionable, affable, genial, *chummy, folksy. ANT. *introverted, reclusive, aloof.*

grief n. sorrow, sadness, heartache, anguish, woe, misery, bereavement, desolation, mourning, melancholy, agony, despair, despondency. "An iron chain."— Stephen Vincent Benet. ANT. *joy, euphoria, happiness.*

grief-stricken a. sad, heartsick, anguished, heavyhearted, devastated, despairing, heartbroken, desolate, melancholy, miserable, despondent. ANT. *happy, joyful, cheerful.*

grievance n. complaint, gripe, wrong, injustice, injury, hardship, *axe to grind, *stink, objection, *beef, *bone to pick.

grieve v. **1.** MOURN lament, ache, sorrow, rue, bewail, bemoan, *eat one's heart out, weep, cry, shed tears, be heartsick. **2.** AFFLICT WITH GRIEF aggrieve, hurt, sadden, pain, break one's heart, wound, crush. ANT. *1. rejoice, revel, *party. 2. cheer, hearten.*

grievous a. serious, severe, harmful, appalling, atrocious, deplorable, egregious, flagrant, heinous, intolerable, outrageous, monstrous, grave, distressing, sad, sorrowful. ANT. *harmless, trivial, insignificant.*

grill v. **1.** BROIL sear, flame-broil, barbecue, fry, cook. **2.** QUESTION cross-examine, quiz, interrogate, pump, *give the third degree.

grim a. gloomy, harsh, severe, stern, sullen, somber, hard, morose, surly, miserable, dour, menacing, bleak, hopeless, forbidding, sinister, horrible, ghastly, gruesome, resolute, determined. ANT. *bright, cheerful, pleasant.*

grimace n. pained expression, wry face, face, twisted face, scowl, frown, glare, look of distaste.

grime n. dirt, soot, grit, smudge, filth, soil, mud, dust, *crud, *gook.

grimy a. dirty, filthy, *grungy, sooty, smudged, soiled, muddy, *cruddy, befouled, begrimed, dingy. ANT. *clean, spotless, bright, unsoiled.*

grin v. smile, beam, smirk, simper, *grin like a Cheshire cat. SEE SMILE, TEETH

grind n. drudgery, tedium, treadmill, routine, rut, chore.

grind v. **1.** PULVERIZE crush, mash, grit, grate, rasp, powder, mill, granulate, triturate, crush, disintegrate. **2.** SHARPEN hone, smooth, whet, polish, burnish. **3.** GNASH grit, grate, rasp, crunch.

grip n. **1.** HOLD clasp, clutch, clench, grasp. **2.** COMPREHENSION understanding, perception, mastery, grasp. **3.** CONTROL mastery, command.

grip v. grasp, hold, clasp, clutch, clench, squeeze.

gripe n. complaint, *beef, grumble, protest, grouch, *bitch, grievance, pain, grouse.

gripe v. complain, *beef, grumble, protest, grouch, *bitch, grouse, *piss and moan, nag, whine, cry, bellyache.

grisly a. terrifying, horrible, ghastly, frightful, hideous, dreadful, gruesome, sickening, shocking, macabre, gory. ANT. *pleasant, heartwarming, lovely.*

grit n. **1.** DIRT sand, dust, soot, particles, powder. **2.** COURAGE perseverance, toughness, pluck, determination, tenacity, mettle, backbone, heart, fortitude, *guts, *moxie. ANT. *2. cowardice, weakness, mousiness.*

gritty a. **1.** DIRTY sandy, dusty, sooty, granular, powdery. **2.** COURAGEOUS persevering, tough, plucky, determined, tenacious, *gutsy, steadfast, resolute, game, mettlesome. ANT. *2. cowardly, weak, mousy.*

grizzled a. gray, salt and pepper, silvery.

groan n. moan, grumble, whine, complaint, mutter, gripe, howl, murmur, lament, whimper.

groan v. moan, grumble, whine, complain, mutter, gripe, howl, murmur, lament, whimper.

groggy a. dazed, *dopey, dizzy, *punch-drunk, *punchy, shaky, sluggish, stupefied, numbed, sleepy, *out of it, woozy, reeling, confused. ANT. *lucid, alert, steady.*

groom n. bridegroom, husband, spouse, partner.

groom v. **1.** CLEAN UP tidy, neaten, prepare,

dress, freshen up, brush, comb, curry, primp, *fix up, preen, tend to one's toilette. **2.** TRAIN prepare, educate.

groove n. **1.** CHANNEL score, rut, furrow, canal, cut, striation, scratch, flute, trench, indentation, line. **2.** RUT habit, routine, custom, *same old thing.

groovy a. Sl. *cool, excellent, great, *neat, *far-out, wonderful.

grope v. feel about, finger, seek blindly, paw, probe, fumble, fish for, poke around, grabble.

gross a. **1.** DISGUSTING, INDELICATE vulgar, foul, crude, indecent, obscene, *out of the gutter, *barnyard, unseemly, tasteless, offensive. **2.** TOTAL whole, aggregate, comprehensive, all, before taxes. **3.** FLAGRANT blatant, obvious, glaring, apparent, outrageous, egregious, shocking, heinous, plain, shameful. **4.** OBESE fat, overweight, big, corpulent, stout, burly, *blubbery. ANT. *1. seemly, tasteful, decent. 2. net, after taxes, take-home. 3. subtle, minor. 4. skinny, anorexic.*

grotesque a. strange, ridiculous, fantastic, bizarre, freakish, odd, incongruous, distorted, weird, peculiar, fanciful, surrealistic, misshapen, ugly, *gross, deformed, monstrous. ANT. *normal, ordinary, realistic.*

grouch n. complainer, faultfinder, grumbler, *bitch, nag, whiner, crab, curmudgeon, *sourpuss, *bear, *grump.

grouch v. complain, find fault, grumble, *bitch, nag, whine, crab, *grump, sulk, gripe, grouse, bellyache, growl, *piss and moan.

grouchy a. *grumpy, *bitchy, grumbling, complaining, whining, crabby, sulky, *full of piss and vinegar, surly, testy, cross, cantankerous, *like a bear. ANT. *good-humored, easygoing, agreeable.*

ground n. earth, soil, land, terra firma, turf, sand, terrain, real estate.

ground v. teach, educate, train, base, familiarize, prime, instruct, indoctrinate.

groundless a. baseless, unjustified, unwarranted, idle, unsupported, conjectural, gratuitous, unfounded.

grounds n. **1.** AREA land, estate, holding, lot, acreage, terrain, property, tract, surroundings. **2.** BASIS base, foundation, rationale, premise, reason, argument, cause, motive.

groundwork n. preparation, foundation, footing, underpinning, infrastructure, fundamentals, preliminaries, base, planning.

group n. **1.** ASSEMBLAGE body, mass, collection, party, bunch, band, crowd, gang, pack, crew, congregation, herd, flock, throng, aggrega-

tion. **2.** CLASS classification, variety, category, division, branch, set, circle.

group v. classify, categorize, divide, sort, assign, grade, systematize, arrange, bunch.

grouse v. grumble, complain. SEE GROUCH

grove n. stand, orchard, wood, copse, coppice, thicket, boscage.

grovel v. *bow and scrape, kowtow, cringe, beg, *kiss up, *brownnose, toady, *fall all over, demean oneself, fawn, *bootlick, *kiss feet, cower, *suck up to, wheedle, cower, *applepolish, kneel before, worm. ANT. *defy, challenge, dominate.*

grow v. **1.** DEVELOP spread, increase, enlarge, expand, lengthen, double, flourish, thrive, mature, burgeon, progress, sprout, spring up, germinate, blossom, mushroom. **2.** PRODUCE cultivate, raise, generate, nurture, propagate. ANT. *1. die, wither, shrink.*

growl v. snarl, grumble, rumble, gnarl, howl, *give a throaty warning, roar, bark, make a guttural noise.

grown-up a. mature, adult, full-grown, of age. ANT. *immature, childish.*

growth n. **1.** DEVELOPMENT spread, increase, expansion, lengthening, branching out, maturing, burgeoning, progress, germination, blossoming, blooming, evolution. **2.** TUMOR mass, lump, cancer.

grub v. dig, root, poke, probe, forage, unearth, search, hunt, ferret about, dig, delve, uproot.

grubby a. messy, dirty, grimy, soiled, unclean, filthy, *grungy, foul, begrimed, slovenly, *scuzzy, squalid. ANT. *clean, tidy, fresh.*

grudge n. resentment, grievance, malice, spite, hard feelings, bitterness, *bone to pick, ill will, *axe to grind, rancor. ANT. *good will, benevolence.*

grudge v. begrudge, resent, mind, envy, hold against.

grueling a. exhausting, trying, arduous, backbreaking, hard, taxing, draining, strenuous, laborious, fatiguing, demanding, punishing. ANT. *easy, effortless, *no sweat.*

gruesome a. grisly, horrifying, repulsive, disgusting, hideous, frightful, ghastly, revolting, repellant, appalling, monstrous, horrific, repugnant. ANT. *lovely, charming, delightful.*

gruff a. **1.** RUDE brusque, surly, blunt, grouchy, grumpy, abrupt, rough, curt, sour, bearish, nasty, short. **2.** HOARSE throaty, harsh, croaking, husky, rough, gutteral. ANT. *genial, polite, sweet. 2. resonant, smooth.*

grumble v. complain, groan, gripe, bellyache, *bitch, *piss and moan, fuss, grouch, growl, squawk, snarl.

grumpy v. grouchy, *bitchy, surly, crabby, bearish, cross, cranky, peevish, *pissy, cantankerous, testy, moody, irritable, touchy. ANT. *cheerful, happy, good-humored.*

guarantee n. warranty, pledge, assurance, bond, promise, contract, word of honor, covenant, surety, security, oath.

guarantee v. warrant, promise, pledge, assure, *give one's word of honor, back, certify, *stand behind, vouch for, ensure, insure, protect, contract, underwrite.

guarantor n. warrantor, sponsor, backer, insurer, bondsman, underwriter.

guard n. security officer, protector, guardian, watchman, sentinel, sentry, lookout, escort, custodian, warder, cordon.

guard v. watch, protect, defend, attend, cover, shield, lookout, secure, safeguard, place under surveillance, screen, escort, *ride shotgun, patrol.

guarded a. wary, cautious, circumspect, careful, mindful, leery, watchful, apprehensive, suspicious, reserved, discreet. ANT. *careless, reckless, rash.*

guess n. estimate, *guestimate, conjecture, hypothesis, calculation, presumption, speculation, assumption, supposition, *shot in the dark, *ballpark figure, reckoning, hunch.

guess v. estimate, *guestimate, calculate, hypothesize, conjecture, presume, speculate, assume, suppose, *take a shot in the dark, *give a ballpark figure, reckon, figure, deduce, infer, theorize, gather, imagine.

guest n. visitor, company, caller, roomer, renter, boarder, lodger, client, customer. "[Those who] are often welcomest when they are gone." — Shakespeare. "A nuisance after three days." — Plautus.

guffaw n. roar, howl, burst of laughter. SEE LAUGH

guidance n. counseling, counsel, advice, direction, instruction, word to the wise, suggestion, recommendation, leadership, navigation.

guide n. leader, director, captain, pilot, navigator, escort, chaperon, mentor, guru, teacher, example, exemplar, model, beacon, landmark, lodestar.

guild n. society, association, union, fraternity, sorority, federation, league, club, group, company, alliance, coalition.

GUILE n. [GILE] slyness, craftiness, artfulness. *He managed a passing grade through pure guile; he used crib notes.* SYN. slyness, craftiness,

artfulness, cunning, trickery, artifice, deceit, duplicity, fraud, dishonesty, treachery. ANT. *honesty, naivete, candor.*

guileless a. open, honest, frank, candid, naive, innocent, artless, ingenuous, sincere, truthful, unsophisticated. ANT. *sly, crafty, artful.*

guilt n. **1.** BLAME culpability, culpa, reprehensibility, criminality, guiltiness, crime, sin, wrongdoing, liability, **2.** REMORSE regret, shame, conscience, contrition, disgrace, self-reproach, penitence, compunction. "The avenging fiend that follows us behind with whips and stings." — Nicholas Rowe. ANT. *1. innocence, *clean hands, clear conscience.*

guilty a. **1.** TO BLAME culpable, responsible, blameworthy, at fault, wrong, reprehensible, *caught red-handed, in flagrante delicto, sinful, liable. **2.** REMORSEFUL regretful, ashamed, conscience-stricken, contrite, disgraced, compunctious, sorry, sheepish, hangdog. ANT. *innocent, faultless, blameless.*

guise n. appearance, semblance, aspect, cover, facade, disguise, form, mode, pretense, garb, dress, costume.

guitar SEE MUSICAL INSTRUMENT

gulf n. **1.** INLET bay, estuary, harbor, cove, sound. **2.** CHASM abyss, gap, rift, cleft, void, canyon, breach, hollow.

GULLIBLE a. [GULL uh bul] easily fooled, credulous. *Gullible people believe anything told them by the media.* SYN. credulous, naive, easily fooled, trusting, innocent, unsophisticated, unsuspicious, *born yesterday, green, *wet behind the ears. ANT. *wary, skeptical, wise, suspicious.*

gully n. ditch, ravine, culvert, channel, trench, gutter, watercourse, gorge, valley, gulch.

gulp v. swallow, bolt, wolf, gobble, choke down, guzzle, swill, *chugalug, swig, quaff.

gumption n. courage, boldness, initiative, *starch, resourcefulness, enterprise, *get up and go, hustle, drive.

gun n. firearm, revolver, pistol, *six-shooter, *shooting iron, rifle, carbine, shotgun, *peashooter, *Saturday night special, *thirty-eight, *forty-five, *equalizer, *rod, *piece, *enforcer, *heater, *roscoe. "[That which] makes men equal, a citizen's musket fires as well as a nobleman's." — Heinriche Heine. "Temper's relief valve." — Marc McCutcheon.

WORD FIND

ammunition receptacle, clip, magazine, cylinder

antique: blunderbuss, breechloader, Colt

six-shooter, flintlock, gatling gun, musket, muzzle loader
attack rifle: assault rifle
back explosion: backfire
barrel end: muzzle
barrel portion receiving bullet: chamber
bead: sight
bore: caliber, gauge
brush: swab
butt: stock
case: holster
cock: hammer
colored finish on metal parts: blueing
gunfire: fusillade, enfilade, volley, salvo
handle: grip
knife mounting: bayonet
locking mechanism: safety
manufacturer: Colt, Magnum, Luger, Winchester, Smith and Wesson, Beretta, Remington, Uzi
plug placed in muzzle for safety: tampion
quieting attachment: silencer, suppressor
rear portion: breech
recoil after firing: kick
revolver's ability to shoot without first cocking hammer: double-action
revolving cartridge holder: cylinder
trigger needing only slight pull: hair trigger
single-shot pistol: derringer
sliding rod that pushes cartridge into firing chamber: bolt
SEE AMMUNITION, ARMY, BULLET, CANNON, WAR, WEAPON

gung ho *a. Sl.* enthusiastic, eager, *fired up, ardent, fanatical.

gunman *n.* killer, triggerman, assassin. SEE MURDERER

gurgle *v.* burble, babble, murmur, tinkle, ripple, bubble.

guru *n.* advisor, mentor, teacher, guide, leader, master, maharishi, swami.

gush *n.* outpouring, flow, spurt, cascade, flood, rush, flush, surge, stream, spill, jet, discharge.

gush *v.* **1.** POUR OUT flow, spurt, cascade, flood, rush, flush, surge, stream, spill, spew. **2.** EXAGGERATE *lay it on thick, *get carried away, be effusive, blather, bubble over, overstate, *carry on. ANT. **2.** *understate, restrain oneself.*

gust *n.* wind, rush, blow, burst, breeze, surge, squall, gale, blast, puff, draft. SEE WIND

gusto *n.* enjoyment, appreciation, zest, relish, exhilaration, enthusiasm, delight, pleasure, passion, ardor. ANT. *apathy, indifference.*

gut *n.* stomach, belly, abdomen, *tummy, innards, intestines, bowels, *spare tire, *beer gut, *middle-aged spread, paunch.

gut *v.* eviscerate, clean out, disembowel, dress, decimate.

gut *a.* instinctual, intuitive, inner, internal, visceral, deep, heartfelt, emotional.

gutless *a.* cowardly, timid, fearful, mousy, *wimpy, fainthearted, spineless, *chicken, *yellow, *lily-livered, weak, *candy-assed. ANT. *brave, courageous, *gutsy, *ballsy.*

guts *n. Sl.* courage, bravery, backbone, pluck, nerve, *balls, heart, spunk, daring, boldness, *spine, *grit, *moxie, fortitude. ANT. *cowardice, timidity, faintheartedness.*

gutsy *a. Sl.* courageous, brave, plucky, *nervy, *ballsy, spunky, daring, bold, *gritty, intrepid, game. ANT. *cowardly, fainthearted, spineless.*

gutter *n.* channel, trough, trench, ditch, conduit, drain, culvert, sewer, canal, watercourse, runnel, gully.

guttural *a.* throaty, harsh, rasping, hoarse, gruff, *whiskey-voiced, croaking, deep, glottal, gravelly, thick.

guy *n.* man, fellow, gentleman, chap, *dude, person, teen, boy, lad, *bro, *buddy.

guzzle *v.* swill, swig, *chug-a-lug, *down, quaff, tipple, *knock back, gulp, drain, *polish off, *choke down.

gymnastics *n.* athletics, acrobatics, vaulting, calisthenics, exercises, somersaults.

gyp *v.* *rip-off, cheat, swindle, defraud, bilk, trick, bamboozle, hoodwink, rook, *gull.

gypsy *n.* wanderer, nomad, roamer, vagrant, vagabond, migrant, drifter, rover, gadabout, Bohemian.

gyrate *v.* revolve, spin, twirl, whirl, rotate, circle, wheel, gyre, pirouette, spiral.

H

habit n. routine, custom, practice, tendency, convention, way, rut, pattern, mode, proclivity, manner, mannerism, inclination. "A cable. We weave a thread of it everyday, and at last we cannot break it." — Horace Mann.

habitat n. natural environment, home, terrain, haunt, natural element, *stomping grounds, biosphere, range, domain, realm, natural surroundings.

habitation n. home, dwelling, lodging, residence, domicile, abode, quarters, house, chambers, roost, place, *pad, shelter.

habitual a. routine, usual, customary, established, fixed, set, hardened, inveterate, regular, everyday, accustomed, chronic, repetitious, persistent, ingrained, rooted. ANT. *irregular, unusual, infrequent.*

habituated a. inurred, used to, accustomed, familiar, acclimated, seasoned, adapted, hardened, conditioned.

hack v. chop, slice, axe, cleave, slash, cut, sever, hew, gash, lop off, shear, fell.

HACKNEYED a. [HAK need] commonplace; dull from overuse, trite. *Clichés are hackneyed expressions.* SYN. commonplace, trite, banal, pedestrian, unimaginative, unoriginal, stock, overworked, tired, shopworn, inane, threadbare, clichéd, stale. ANT. *fresh, original, imaginative.*

hag n. witch, crone, harridan, ogress, virago, demon, enchantress, beldam, battle-ax, shrew.

HAGGARD a. [HAG urd] having a wild-eyed, drawn or gaunt appearance from exhaustion, sickness, etc. SYN. wild-eyed, wild, drawn, gaunt, wasted, drained, unruly, exhausted, careworn, run-down, hollow-cheeked, emaciated, ghastly, mad, insane. ANT. *fresh, rested, vigorous.*

haggle v. argue, bargain, wrangle, dicker, higgle, deal, *drive a hard bargain, chaffer, barter, *hash out a deal, quibble.

hail v. greet, wave to, call to, hello, accost, salute, welcome, *tip one's hat to, nod to, flag down, signal.

hair n. locks, mane, tress, down, *mop, fur, strand, tuft, curls, fuzz, fringe, bristle, whiskers. "The only thing that will really prevent baldness." — Drew Berkowitz.

WORD FIND

arrange: coif, set, style, perm

auburn dye: henna

back comb: tease

bald crown surrounded by ring of fringe: tonsure

bald: glabrous

baldness, common: male pattern baldness

band: filet, snood

beehive-like style of 1950s, 1960s: beehive

bowl-like: Beatle cut, *Moe

braided rows close to head: cornrows

braid: plait, cue, cueue, pigtail, tress, fishbone braid, French braid

colors: ash, ash blond, auburn, black, bleach blond, blond, blue-gray, brown, brunet, carrot, chestnut, cinnamon, coal black, cocoa, copper, dusky, fair-haired, fiery, flaxen, frosted, ginger, golden, gray, grizzled, hoary, honey, jet-black, nutbrown, nutmeg, peroxide blond, platinum blond, polished wood, premature gray, raven, russet, rust, sable, salt and pepper, silver, snowy, strawberry blond, tawny, technicolor (dyed, punk), titian, towheaded, violent red, washed out, white.

curl: ringlet, corkscrew

curled-ends style with bangs: flip

curl pressed against face with saliva: spit curl

curly like a poodle: poodle cut

cut short: crop

Dorothy Hamill style of 1970s: wedge

ducktail-like style of 1950s: ducktail

fake: toupee, *rug, wig, implant

forehead fringe: bangs

graying, premature: poliosis

hairy, abnormally: hirsute, hirsutism

high sweep of hair combed back from forehead: pompadour

Jamaican braids: dreadlocks, Rastafarian dreadlocks

knot: chignon, bob, bun

mass, tangled or bushy: shock

matted, tangled hairs: elflocks

neck hairs: hackles

Negro, kinky, puffy, 1960s, 1970s: Afro

point of hair tapering to forehead: widow's peak

puffed-out mass, style: bouffant

punk: mohawk, porcupine, spiked, shaved, dyed

remove: epilate, depilate, bob

remover: depilatory, electrolysis

roll: bun, chignon

shaved trails in a slanted or sculpted buzz

cut: *fade, *gumby

short haircut for men: buzz, flattop, crew cut, butch, *fade

short haircut for women: bob

standing cone ending in ponytail: empire cone

stick-up tuft: cowlick

straight-cut style with bangs: page boy

textures: billowing, bouncy, bristly, bushy, coarse, cornsilk, crimped, crinkly, dollish, downy, eiderdown, fine (baby fine), fleecy, flowing, flyaway, frazzled, frizzy, fuzzy, greasy, kinky, knotted, lacquered, listless, lustrous, luxurious, matted, nappy, oily, rat's nest, rigid, ropey, satiny, shaggy, shocked, silky, snarled, stringy (like twine), thatched, wispy, withered, wizened, woolly.

waves style: marcel

hairdresser n. hair stylist, barber, coiffeur, beautician.

hairless a. SEE BALD, HAIR

hair-raising a. bloodcurdling, breathtaking, frightening, terrifying, hackle-raising, spine-tingling, electrifying, shocking, chilling, horrifying.

hairy a. hirsute, shaggy. SEE HAIR

hale a. vigorous, sound, healthy, robust, fit, hearty, spry, hardy, well, *in the pink, *full of vim and vigor, *in fine fettle. ANT. *sickly, weak, frail, failing.*

half-baked a. stupid, sophomoric, harebrained, premature, crude, impractical, *birdbrained, idiotic, imbecilic, moronic, *half-assed, dumb. ANT. *practical, brilliant, well-formulated.*

halfhearted a. unenthusiastic, lukewarm, blasé, indifferent, apathetic, dispassionate, cool, perfunctory, tepid, spiritless. ANT. *enthusiastic, eager, ardent, wholehearted.*

half-wit n. dimwit, nitwit, *pea brain. SEE MORON

hall n. hallway, corridor, passageway, entrance, foyer, vestibule, gallery.

HALLMARK n. [HALL mark] an identifying characteristic or telltale sign. *The hallmark of a sluggish economy is a drop in interest rates.* SYN. characteristic, telltale sign, identifying mark, sign, symbol, indicator, badge, earmark, index.

hallowed a. holy, sacred, venerated, revered, sanctified, worshipped, honored, consecrated, blessed, beatified, divine.

hallucination n. vision, illusion, hypnogogic image, delusion, fantasy, figment of the imagination, apparition, delirium, mirage, phantasmagoria.

halt n. stop, end, close, termination, pause, freeze, stay, recess, standstill, break, discontinuance.

halt v. stop, end, close, terminate, pause, freeze, stay, recess, stand still, take a break, discontinue, cease and desist, suspend.

halting a. hesitant, *jerky, unsteady, disconnected, stuttering, stammering, faltering, stumbling, tentative, clumsy.

halve v. divide, split, cut in two, bisect.

hamlet n. small town, crossroads. SEE VILLAGE

hammer n. beetle, clawhammer, sledge, maul, mallet, gavel.

hammer v. pound, beat, batter, bang, hit, pummel, drive, tap, strike, nail, *clobber, fashion, form, forge.

hamper v. impede, hinder, handicap, hamstring, slow, inhibit, encumber, obstruct, frustrate, retard, restrict, hobble, curb. ANT. *help, assist, facilitate.*

hamstring v. cripple, handicap. SEE DISABLE

hamstrung a. crippled, handicapped. SEE DISABLED

hand n. 1. FIST palm, *mitt, *paw, *duke. 2. HELPER worker, employee, laborer, aide, assistant, help. 3. HELP assistance, aid, lift, support, boost.

handicap n. disability, impediment, encumbrance, disadvantage, impairment, limitation, millstone, difficulty, burden, restriction, stumbling block.

handicap v. disable, impede, hamstring, cripple, encumber, impair, limit, burden, restrict, inhibit, weigh down, hamper.

handkerchief n. kerchief, bandanna, neckerchief, hanky, *snot rag.

handle n. grip, haft, hilt, butt, knob, holder, crank, stock, pull.

handle v. 1. TOUCH feel, examine, finger, poke, hold, fondle, stroke, caress, rub, palpate. 2. MANAGE take care of, direct, supervise, oversee, govern, control, administer, deal with, steer.

hand out vt. distribute, dispense, disburse, deal out, parcel, mete, give out, deliver.

handsome a. 1. ATTRACTIVE good-looking, *hunky, comely, fine, fair, manly, dignified, gorgeous, majestic, statuesque, *foxy, luscious, macho, beautiful. 2. GENEROUS liberal, considerable, abundant, princely, magnanimous, ample. ANT. 1. *ugly, repulsive, *gross.* 2. *meager, small, niggardly.*

handy a. 1. CONVENIENT accessible, close at

hand, nearby, at one's fingertips, within reach. **2.** DEXTEROUS deft, clever, adroit, skilled, adept, proficient, masterful, *crackerjack. ANT. *1. inconvenient, inaccessible. 2. unskilled, inept, clumsy.*

hang *v.* **1.** SUSPEND dangle, drape, depend, stick, pin, affix, sling, fall, swing, be pendent. **2.** EXECUTE lynch, *string up, *send to the gallows, *invite to a necktie party, gibbet, noose.

hangdog *a.* shamefaced, cringing, crestfallen, cowering, browbeaten, abject, miserable, wretched, conscience-stricken. ANT. *saintly, triumphant, innocent.*

hang-up *n. Sl.* problem, inhibition, difficulty, quirk, disturbance, preoccupation, phobia, fear.

hankering *n.* desire, craving, yearning, want, thirst, itch, yen, ache, longing, *fire in one's belly, drive.

hanky-panky *n. Sl.* trickery, *funny business. SEE MISCHIEF

haphazard *a.* unmethodical, unorganized, slapdash, uncoordinated, aimless, casual, *willynilly, indiscriminate, *hit or miss, careless, random, arbitrary. ANT. *planned, organized, designed.*

hapless *a.* unfortunate, cursed, unlucky, starcrossed, jinxed, hopeless, luckless, wretched, woeful. ANT. *fortunate, lucky.*

happen *v.* occur, take place, befall, transpire, materialize, come about, come to pass, develop, ensue, spring, pass, result, arise.

happening *n.* event, occurrence, incident, experience, occasion, episode, incidence, affair, circumstance.

happiness *n.* joy, gladness, contentment, bliss, delight, jubilation, pleasure, cheer, high spirits, peace of mind, elation, rapture, euphoria, *seventh heaven, exuberance, felicity, ecstasy. "It is all within yourself, in your way of thinking." — Marcus Aurelius "[Something that] makes up for height what it lacks in length." — Robert Frost. "Tranquility and occupation." — Thomas Jefferson. "Freedom from suffering." — Arthur Schopenhauer. "The mastery of passions." — Alfred Lord Tennyson. "Good friends, good books and a sleepy conscience." — Mark Twain. "A mental state aided by wine, women, and tobacco." — Anon. ANT. *misery, depression, melancholia.*

happy *a.* **1.** GLAD joyful, content, blissful, delighted, jubilant, pleased, cheerful, in high spirits, at peace, elated, euphoric, in *seventh heaven, exuberant, ecstatic, gleeful, *tickled pink, *walking on air, chipper, overjoyed, *happier than a pig in shit, *high. **2.** FORTUNATE lucky, felicitous, auspicious, opportune, favorable, propitious, timely. ANT. *1. depressed, miserable, downhearted, suicidal, sad, glum. 2. inauspicious, inopportune, unlucky.*

happy-go-lucky *a.* carefree, untroubled, *devil-may-care, lighthearted, casual, easy, easygoing, nonchalant, insouciant, *living the life of Riley, unconcerned. ANT. *stressed, worried, anxious, careful, concerned.*

harangue *n.* tirade, diatribe, exhortation, lecture, *chewing-out, speech, sermon.

harangue *v.* exhort, *chew out, lecture, spout off, rant, sermonize, preach, declaim, rant and rave, go on about, *get on one's soapbox.

harass *v.* disturb, trouble, torment, pester, plague, bother, *bug, badger, distress, worry, *pull one's chain, *rattle one's cage, irritate, attack, intimidate, persecute, hound, harry, vex, ride, beset.

HARBINGER *n.* [HAR binj ur] a sign of things to come, a forerunner, herald. *April rain is a harbinger of May flowers.* SYN. sign of things to come, forerunner, herald, precursor, omen, usher, messenger, premonition, portent, signal.

harbor *n.* **1.** ANCHORAGE port, dock, pier, mooring, wharves, landing, bay, inlet, cove. **2.** HAVEN refuge, retreat, shelter, sanctuary, port, port in a storm.

harbor *v.* **1.** SHELTER house, lodge, quarter, berth, hide, protect, secrete, conceal, cover, shield, guard. **2.** TO ENTERTAIN IN THE MIND hold, maintain, believe, cling to, foster, imagine, indulge, nurse.

hard *a.* **1.** FIRM rigid, stiff, rock-solid, stony, inflexible, concrete, set, compacted, like iron, like steel, unyielding, impregnable. **2.** DIFFICULT arduous, demanding, tough, laborious, burdensome, exhausting, strenuous, backbreaking, rigorous, painstaking, Herculian, *murder, draining. **3.** COMPLICATED complex, knotty, involved, incomprehensible, perplexing, bewildering, thorny. **4.** STRONG powerful, severe, heavy. **5.** UNFEELING callous, unfriendly, hostile, cold, merciless, harsh, cruel, hard-boiled, hard-hearted, unsympathetic, pitiless, ruthless, unrelenting. **6.** HARSH rough, severe, trying, intolerable, unbearable, torturous, insufferable, difficult, bad. ANT. *1. soft, pliable, flexible. 2, 3. easy,* *simple, effortless.* **4.** *weak, light.* **5.** *warm, sympathetic, compassionate.* **6.** *soft, easy, mild.*

hard-and-fast *a.* set, invariable, strict, binding, unalterable, exacting, unbending, inflexible, incontrovertible. ANT. *flexible, variable, changeable.*

hard-boiled *a.* SEE HARD, TOUGH

hard-core *a.* **1.** ABSOLUTE express, unqualified. **2.** FIRM unyielding, resistant, rigid, staunch, steadfast, stubborn, inveterate, die-hard, unwavering.

harden *v.* **1.** STIFFEN solidify, thicken, set, toughen, indurate, compact, cement, temper, steel, freeze, petrify. **2.** ACCUSTOM strengthen, steel, inure, season, case harden, toughen, acclimatize, gird, callous. ANT. *1. soften, weaken, thin.*

hard-hearted *a.* cold, callous, cruel, merciless, pitiless, unsympathetic, unfeeling, *coldhearted, inhuman, uncaring, *icewater in one's veins. ANT. *compassionate, sympathetic, warmhearted.*

hardly *a.* scarcely, barely, just, rarely, only.

hard-nosed *a.* hardheaded, stubborn, bullheaded, mulish, pigheaded, obstinate, tough, uncompromising, indomitable. ANT. *flexible, open-minded.*

hardship *n.* adversity, misfortune, suffering, privation, burden, affliction, *hard knock, trial, tribulation, bad luck, grief, infelicity, trouble, hard times, disaster, catastrophe, rigor, travail. ANT. *good fortune, blessing, boon.*

hardy *a.* robust, vigorous, strong, tough, rugged, powerful, strapping, fit, healthy, *tough as nails, hearty, hale, sound, in good shape. ANT. *weak, sickly, frail.*

harebrained *a.* stupid, reckless, rash, foolish, idiotic, imbecilic, silly, half-witted, brainless, scatterbrained. ANT. *smart, *brainy, sensible.*

harlot *n.* whore, prostitute, strumpet, hussy, slut, tramp, loose woman, wench, trollop, streetwalker, *hooker, lady of the evening.

harm *n.* injury, hurt, damage, destruction, adversity, waste, wrong, detriment, abuse, loss, ruin. ANT. *help, good, benefit.*

harm *v.* hurt, injure, damage, wound, cripple, maim, molest, impair, destroy, wrong, abuse, ruin, misuse, wreck, spoil. ANT. *help, benefit, do good.*

harmful *a.* injurious, hurtful, damaging, destructive, detrimental, wounding, crippling, abusive, adverse, noxious, deleterious, inimical, pernicious, ruinous, disastrous. ANT. *beneficial, helpful, harmless.*

harmless *a.* benign, innocuous, safe, innocent, unoffensive, powerless, impotent, *a pussycat, gentle, *defanged. ANT. *harmful, deleterious, noxious, injurious.*

harmonious *a.* compatible, agreeable, in rapport, peaceable, amicable, friendly, in accord, congenial, in tune, simpatico, likeminded, unified, blending. ANT. *discordant, clashing, incompatible.*

harmonize *v.* correspond, agree, unify, get in tune, attune, blend, coincide, *be of one mind, jibe with, accommodate, accord, integrate. ANT. *disagree, clash.*

harmony *n.* agreement, correspondence, unification, blending, accord, integration, concurrence, rapport, consonance, rapprochement, coordination, compatibility. ANT. *discord, dissonance, disagreement.*

harried *a.* pressured, stressed, troubled, *at wit's end, beset, agitated, put-upon, overtaxed, plagued, harassed.

HARROWING *a.* [HAIR o wing] frightening, distressing. *A harrowing roller coaster ride.* SYN. frightening, distressing, upsetting, traumatic, disturbing, terrifying, bloodcurdling, hair-raising, tormenting. ANT. *soothing, pacifying, tranquilizing, relaxing.*

harry *v.* torment, harass, worry, agitate, beset, trouble, plague, pester, pressure, annoy, bother, *stress out, nag, bug, weary.

harsh *a.* **1.** ROUGH coarse, jagged, craggy, rugged, sharp, unpleasant, grinding, jarring, discordant, grating, clashing. **2.** SEVERE cruel, unfeeling, hard, tough, merciless, stern, brutal, hard-boiled, unbending, cold-blooded. ANT. *1. smooth, pleasant, melodious, musical. 2. soft, mild, easy, gentle.*

harvest *n.* gathering, reaping, return, yield, crop, fruit, profit, product.

harvest *v.* reap, gather, pick, collect, amass, glean.

hash *n.* mixture, hodgepodge, mess, jumble, potpourri, mishmash, medley, miscellany, muddle.

hassle *n.* *Sl.* problem, difficulty, bother, *pain, dispute, squabble, argument, disagreement, tussle.

hassle *v.* bother, harass, *give a hard time, annoy, plague, pester, *bug, hound, harry.

haste *n.* speed, swiftness, quickness, fleetness, dispatch, celerity, hurry, hustle, rapidity, rush, velocity, promptness. ANT. *slowness, sluggishness, delay.*

hasten *v.* hurry, rush, speed, race, *step on it, *get a move on, go quickly, scurry, *ride like the wind, hustle, fly, accelerate, expedite, sprint, *get the lead out, *beat feet. ANT. slow, delay, *drag one's feet, procrastinate.

hasty a. quick, fast, swift, rushed, fleet, rapid, expeditious, abrupt, prompt, *on the double, *pronto, brisk, instantaneous, *quick as a wink, *in a heartbeat, brief, rash, impetuous, reckless. ANT. slow, leisurely, careful.

hat n. cap, chapeau, headgear, headdress, *lid.

WORD FIND

Australian cowboy hat with brim turned up on one side: bush hat

bejeweled, decorated skullcap for evening wear, weddings: Juliet

beret with pompom in the middle: tam, tam-o-shanter

bowler: derby

box: bandbox

brimless, round, small hat of 1920s: pillbox

collapsible opera hat: gibus

cowboy: Stetson, ten-gallon hat

Crockett's, Davy: coonskin cap

derby: bowler

French Foreign Legion cap with havelock: kepi, Legionnaire's

graduate's square with tassel: mortarboard

high-domed hat worn by English police: bobby

high-domed hat worn by polo players: chukka

Jewish embroidered skullcap: yarmulka

knitted winter hat: watch cap

knitted winter hat with a long tail sometimes fitted with pompom: stocking cap

marching band's tall hat with feather cockade: shako

Mexican broad hat made of straw or felt: sombrero

pancakelike cap: beret, tam

pith helmet: topee

scarf wound around head: turban

Scottish Highland Military's creased cloth cap with badge and black ribbons: glengarry

seventeenth-century tall black hat, silver buckle: Puritan

Sherlock Holmes's tweed hat: deerstalker

snap-brim hat with low, flat crown: porkpie

snap-brim hat with puffed crown: newsboy

soft, domelike hat pulled down over forehead, for women: cloche

soft, felt hat creased down middle of crown: fedora, homburg

soft hat that can be crushed, carried in pocket: crusher

stovepipelike hat with tall crown, silky finish: top hat

straw hat, man's: Panama

straw hat with oval crown: boater, picture hat

straw, parasollike hat worn by Chinese: coolie

straw, yellow and broad: leghorn

tall, fur hat worn by British army: busby

three-cornered: tricorne

Turkish hat shaped like truncated cone, decorated with tassel: fez

World War II folding dress cap, olive or khaki-colored: garrison cap

SEE CAP

hatch v. create, concoct, bring forth, devise, design, produce, *cook up, conceive, invent, originate, formulate, *dream up.

hate n. loathing, dislike, abhorrence, detestation, odium, aversion, scorn, disgust, contempt, venom, repugnance, enmity, hostility, animosity, malice. ANT. love, liking, affection.

hate v. loathe, dislike, abhor, detest, scorn, regard with disgust, regard with contempt, feel hostile toward, despise, be sickened by, abominate, shrink from, disdain, have an aversion to. ANT. love, like, admire.

hateful a. loathsome, detestable, despicable, abhorrent, abominable, odious, nasty, mean, damnable, repugnant, foul, heinous, malicious. ANT. loving, nice, wonderful.

hatred n. loathing, dislike, abhorrence, detestation, odium, aversion, scorn, disgust, contempt, venom, repugnance, enmity, hostility, animosity, malice. "Self-punishment." —Hosea Ballou. "Burning down your own house to get rid of a rat." —Harry Emerson Fosdick. "The coward's revenge." —George Bernard Shaw. ANT. love, affection, friendliness.

HAUGHTY a. [HAWT ee] arrogant and disdainful of others, high and mighty. She had a haughty way of peering down her nose at us. SYN. arrogant, disdainful, high and mighty, snobbish, lordly, condescending, patronizing, stuck-up, self-important, vain, conceited, imperious, superior, *hoity toity, supercilious, *sniffy, *above it all. ANT. modest, humble, down to earth, folksy.

haul v. pull, drag, tow, draw, lug, move, carry, truck, transport, convey, cart, take.

haunt n. purlieu, hangout, stomping gound, gathering place.

haunt v. 1. FREQUENT hang out at. 2. TROUBLE worry, torment, plague, disquiet, disturb. 3.

*SPOOK inhabit, appear, possess, manifest, terrorize, materialize, scare.

HAUTEUR n. [ho TUR] haughtiness, arrogance. *He regarded us with his usual hauteur.* SYN. haughtiness, arrogance, disdain, snobbishness, condescension, pride, self-importance, imperiousness, superiority, presumptuousness, conceit, airs. ANT. *modesty, folksiness.*

have v. **1.** BE IN POSSESSION possess, hold, own, retain, keep, enjoy. **2.** EXPERIENCE endure, suffer, entertain, bear, undergo, know.

haven n. refuge, asylum, safe harbor, sanctuary, shelter, sanctum, port in a storm, retreat, hideaway.

havoc n. destruction, devastation, ruin, disaster, catastrophe, demolition, waste, chaos, desolation, shambles, calamity.

hawker n. peddler, huckster, street vendor, salesman, pitchman.

hayseed n. Sl. yokel, bumpkin, hick, clodhopper, rustic, farmer, hillbilly, hobnail, *rube, *goat-roper, *Bubba, *Arky, *Clem, *Okie, *brush ape. ANT. *city slicker, sophisticate, cosmopolitan.*

haywire a. Sl. crazy, confused, *bonkers, berserk, amok, disordered, *out of kilter, *out of whack, *psycho, out of order.

hazard n. danger, threat, peril, risk, jeopardy, pitfall, *thin ice, *house of cards, insecurity, endangerment, cause for alarm, quicksand.

hazard v. risk, chance, venture, wager, gamble, stake, dare, attempt, try, *go out on a limb, *go for broke.

hazardous a. dangerous, threatening, perilous, imperiling, endangering, life-threatening, risky, unsafe, chancy, menacing, *hairy, *dicey, precarious. ANT. *safe, secure, harmless.*

hazy a. **1.** CLOUDY foggy, misty, murky, nebulous, dim, gauzy, steamy, smoky, veiled, blurred, filmy, fuzzy. **2.** VAGUE obscure, indefinite, confused, indistinct, dim, muddled, unintelligible, nebulous. ANT. *1. clear, sunny. 2. clear, distinct, lucid.*

head n. **1.** SKULL cranium, brain, noggin, *belfry, *noodle, *bean, dome. "The palace of the soul." —Lord Byron. "The dupe of the heart." —La Rochefoucauld. **2.** CROWN top, summit, peak, tip, apex, acme, pinnacle, cap, crest, vertex, height. **3.** LEADER boss, chief, president, director, CEO, commander, ringleader, principal, chairman, *big cheese, *biggest toad in the puddle, *top dog, captain, ruler. ANT. *2. foot, base. 3. follower, un-*

derling.

head v. lead, direct, command, boss, preside, chair, captain, run, rule, control, govern, supervise, oversee.

headache n. *pain, *pain in the neck, trouble, bother, annoyance, nuisance, problem.

heading n. **1.** TITLE caption, headline, line. **2.** COURSE bearing, direction.

headline n. caption, heading, title, banner, screamer. SEE NEWSPAPER

headlong a. reckless, dangerous, incautious, rash, foolhardy, breakneck, impetuous, uncontrolled, at full tilt, ungoverned. ANT. *cautious, careful, prudent.*

headstrong a. stubborn, self-willed, pigheaded, bullheaded, willful, obstinate, mulish, unyielding, wayward, defiant, intractable. ANT. *docile, obedient, yielding.*

headway n. advance, improvement, procession. SEE PROGRESS

heady a. intoxicating, stimulating, powerful, inebriating, exhilarating, exciting, arousing.

heal v. cure, make well, mend, restore, remedy, repair, treat, recover, alleviate, patch up, fix, doctor, nurse, revive, renew, medicate, rejuvenate.

healer n. physician, shaman, medicine man. SEE DOCTOR

health n. fitness, soundness, well-being, vitality, strength, vigor, hardiness, shape, condition. "To eat what you don't want, drink what you don't like and do what you'd rather not." —Mark Twain.

healthy a. **1.** GOOD FOR YOU salubrious, healthful, wholesome, salutary, beneficial, nutritious, nourishing, invigorating, restorative, sustaining, energizing. **2.** IN GOOD SHAPE fit, strong, sound, well, vital, vigorous, hardy, hearty, *bright-eyed, robust, hale, trim, *in the pink, *in fine fettle, lusty, lively, energetic. ANT. *1. unhealthy, noxious, pernicious, deleterious. 2. failing, sickly, diseased, weak.*

heap n. pile, mound, stack, mass, bank, accumulation, clump, load, agglomeration, stockpile, jumble, bunch, abundance, *lots, plenty.

heap v. pile, mound, stack, amass, bank, accumulate, clump, load, gather, group, cluster.

hear v. listen, heed, pay attention to, receive, hearken.

hearing n. interview, audience, inquiry, day in court, inquisition, inquest, review, trial, presentation.

hearsay n. rumor, gossip, *grapevine report, scuttlebutt, word of mouth, talk, secondhand information, *talk of the town.

heart n. **1.** BLOOD-PUMPING ORGAN muscle, *pump, *ticker.

WORD FIND

angina drug used to widen blood vessels: nitroglycerin

artery, large: aorta

artery-repairing procedure: angioplasty, bypass

chest pain from lack of blood flow: angina pectoris

damage to heart muscle due to insufficient blood supply: heart attack, myocardial infarction

decreased blood flow to: ischemia

defect sign: murmur

device used to regulate heartbeat: pacemaker

drug used to strengthen heartbeat: digitalis

enlarged heart caused by strenuous exercise: athletic heart syndrome

fluttering or pounding beat: palpitation

inflammation: pericarditis

occluded arteries: atherosclerosis

out-of-control heart contractions: fibrillation

pertaining to: cardiac

pumping failure or weakening: congestive heart failure

rapid heartbeat: tachycardia

readout of electrical impulses: electrocardiogram (EKG)

rhythm disturbance: arrhythmia

stoppage: cardiac arrest

study of: cardiology

2. CENTRAL CORE nucleus, pith, center, kernel, essence, crux, seat, hub. **3.** EMOTIONS compassion, love, sympathy, feeling, passion, soul, humanity, sensitivity, affection, pity. "The tabernacle of the human intellect." — Moses Maimonides. "The organ that sees better than the eye." — Yiddish proverb. "A free and fetterless thing—a wave of the ocean, a bird on the wing." — Longfellow. **4.** COURAGE *guts, bravery, spirit, *spunk, valor, grit, nerve, backbone, mettle, fortitude. ANT. *3. coldness, hatred, indifference. 4. cowardice, timidity.*

heartache n. heartbreak, anguish, grief, sorrow, misery, sadness, despair, broken heart, agony, heartsickness, desolation, woe, suffering, melancholy.

heartbreak n. grief, anguish. SEE HEARTACHE

heartbreaking a. sad, pitiful, heart-wrenching, heartrending, painful, agonizing, disappointing, tragic, grievous, poignant, bitter, unendurable, crushing, devastating. ANT. *cheering, heartening.*

heartbroken a. sad, disappointed, crushed, devastated, heartsick, desolate, dejected, miserable, disheartened, despondent, depressed, crestfallen. ANT. *cheered, heartened, buoyed.*

heartburn n. reflux, pyrosis.

hearten v. encourage, cheer up, embolden, buoy, raise one's spirits, fortify, *give a shot in the arm, boost up, buck up, comfort. ANT. *discourage, dishearten, *take the wind out of one's sails.*

heartfelt a. sincere, feeling, real, deep, genuine, serious, ardent, fervent, honest, impassioned, profound. ANT. *insincere, phony, feigned.*

heartless a. cold, cruel, brutal, inhuman, callous, merciless, pitiless, unfeeling, *thick-skinned, uncaring, mean, insensitive, hard. ANT. *compassionate, sympathetic, feeling.*

hearty a. **1.** WARM friendly, genial, cordial, affectionate, jovial, enthusiastic, whole-hearted, passionate, unrestrained, effusive. **2.** STRONG healthy, robust, hardy, vigorous, sturdy, energetic, stout, *in fine fettle. ANT. *1. cool, reserved, restrained, half-hearted. 2. frail, feeble, weak, sickly.*

heat n. **1.** HIGH TEMPERATURE warmth, hotness, fever, fire, torridity, sultriness. **2.** ANGER passion, rage, ardor, zeal, fervor, intensity, excitement, vehemence. ANT. *1. coldness, frigidity. 2. indifference, apathy, coolness.*

heated a. passionate, hot, raging, angry, ardent, fervent, intense, excited, vehement, violent, fiery, volcanic. ANT. *cool, calm, mild.*

heathen n. pagan, non-Christian, non-Jew, non-Muslim, infidel, nonbeliever, atheist, idolater, agnostic, skeptic. ANT. *believer, Christian, Jew, Muslim.*

heave v. **1.** RAISE, THROW hurl, cast, toss, hoist, lift, fling, shoot, fire, pitch, chuck. **2.** VOMIT throw up, puke, *ralph, disgorge, discharge, *upchuck, spew, spit up, *blow chunks.

heaven n. paradise, hereafter, afterworld, bliss, kingdom of God, glory, providence, ecstasy, utopia, *Shangri-la, *happy hunting ground, nirvana, city of light, Elysium, transport, happiness. "To be one with God." — Confucius. "Fulfilled desire." — Edward Fitzgerald. ANT. *hell, Hades, purgatory, torment.*

heavenly a. blissful, glorious, divine, beautiful, holy, sublime, wonderful, extramundane, spiritual, beatific, ethereal. ANT. *hellish, horri-*

ble, demonic.

heavy *a.* **1.** HEFTY weighty, burdensome, overweight, unmanageable, ponderous, substantial, massive, huge, titanic, obese. SEE FAT **2.** INTENSE great, large, strong, abundant, extreme, powerful, overwhelming, violent, rough, deep, extensive, prolonged, profound. **3.** SERIOUS profound, grave, weighty, important, critical, vital, crucial. **4.** BURDENSOME oppressive, distressing, hard, harsh, onerous, intolerable, harsh. ANT. *1. light, weightless, featherlike. 2. light, mild, weak, brief. 3. trivial, unimportant, petty. 4. easy, light, tolerable.*

heckle *v.* harass, annoy, hassle, pester, *wise off, jeer, bait, taunt, tease, *ride, bother, *give a hard time, *bug.

hectic *a.* feverish, confused, rushed, chaotic, frenzied, frenetic, excited, wild, riotous, furious, tumultuous. ANT. *relaxed, calm, tranquil.*

hector *v.* bully, browbeat, pester, bait, badger, bother, torment, threaten, intimidate, harry, plague, menace, dominate.

hedge *n.* bush, hedgerow, boundary, shrubbery, windbreak, fence, barrier.

hedge *v.* avoid, lessen, evade, dodge, sidestep, equivocate, *stonewall, *hem and haw, temporize, *pass the buck, *waffle, duck.

HEDONIST *n.* [HEE dun ist] a pleasure-seeker, one who indulges. *He partied every Saturday night; he was a dyed-in-the-wool hedonist.* SYN. pleasure-seeker, bon vivant, indulger, *party animal, profligate, glutton, voluptuary, epicure, gourmand, debauchee. ANT. *prude, Puritan, bluenose.*

heed *n.* attention, mind, notice, consideration, regard, thought.

heed *v.* mind, regard, pay attention to, consider, take notice, note, follow, hear, look at.

heedless *a.* inattentive, unmindful, careless, unobservant, thoughtless, reckless, rash, negligent, disregardful. ANT. *attentive, mindful, observant.*

hefty *a.* heavy, weighty, large, massive, powerful, bulky, gigantic, ample, husky, brawny, rugged, muscular. ANT. *puny, weak, wispy.*

height *n.* **1.** ALTITUDE elevation, tallness, highness, loftiness. **2.** TOP, CLIMAX crest, crowning point, acme, zenith, high point, limit, peak, summit, pinnacle, apex, culmination.

heighten *v.* increase, intensify, enlarge, magnify, amplify, raise, lift, elevate, augment, strengthen, extend. ANT. *lower, lessen, shorten.*

HEINOUS *a.* [HA nus] evil or wicked to the extreme, abominable. *The heinous war crimes*

will never be forgotten. SYN. evil, wicked, abominable, atrocious, hellish, monstrous, loathsome, ghastly, horrid, shocking, unspeakable, revolting, outrageous, damnable, sickening, despicable, grisly. ANT. *saintly, angelic, good, moral.*

heir *n.* heiress, inheritor, beneficiary, recipient, successor.

heist *n. Sl.* holdup, *stickup. SEE ROBBERY

hell *n.* Hades, Gehenna, nether world, abyss, fire and brimstone, inferno, underworld, Pandemonium, Abaddon, abode of the damned, limbo, infernal regions, purgatory, pit, perdition, torment, depths. "Where their worms die not, and the fire is not quenched." — Bible. "A vast, unbottom'd, boundless pit." — Robert Burns. "A brimstone sea of boiling fire." — Francis Quarles. "Every man is his own." — Henry Louis Mencken. "God's penitentiary." — Charles Jaynes. ANT. *heaven, paradise, bliss.*

hellion *n.* troublemaker, rascal, *rowdy, devil, rogue.

hellish *a.* infernal, satanic, demonic, diabolical, fiendish, horrible, black, evil, wicked, stygian, terrible, cruel, pitiless. ANT. *heavenly, blissful.*

helmet *n.* headgear, head protector, hard hat.

help *n.* assistance, aid, hand, succor, support, boost, contribution, lift, service, guidance.

help *v.* **1.** ASSIST aid, lend a hand, support, boost, contribute, lift, serve, guide, accommodate, do a favor, succor, abet, *pitch in, oblige, *go to bat for, *stick up for, back, promote, rescue, save, extricate, *throw a lifeline. **2.** IMPROVE alleviate, ameliorate, mitigate, relieve, remedy, cure, allay, better, benefit. ANT. *1. hinder, hamper, *throw up a roadblock. 2. make worse, aggravate.*

helper *n.* assistant, aide, hand, helpmate, *right-hand man, *gofer, laborer, handmaid, henchman, subordinate, girl/man Friday, colleague, partner.

helpful *a.* useful, beneficial, constructive, accommodating, of service, valuable, conducive, invaluable, profitable, practical. ANT. *harmful, useless, worthless.*

helpless *a.* powerless, impotent, useless, inadequate, incompetent, incapable, weak, vulnerable, defenseless, infirm, dependent, spineless, lost. ANT. *capable, independent, powerful.*

helter-skelter *a.* disorderly, arbitrary, confused, random, haphazard, hurried, pell-mell, hit-or-miss, jumbled, chaotic. ANT. *orderly,* *arranged.*

hem n. edge, border, edging, skirt, trim, fringe, verge, ruff.

henchman n. follower, helper, underling, aide, flunky, bodyguard, subordinate, *yes-man, hatchet man, advisor, attendant.

herald n. messenger, usher, forerunner, harbinger, precursor, omen, sign, indication, portent, symptom.

herald v. usher in, announce, foretell, harbinger, portend, trumpet, precede, presage, broadcast.

Herculean a. powerful, courageous, strong, mighty, formidable, tough, brawny, muscular, *built, gigantic, colossal, heroic, laborious, arduous, hard, rough, backbreaking, strenuous, *ball-busting. ANT. *puny, weak, easy.*

herd n. drove, flock, bunch, drift, mass, swarm, mob, bevy, crush, crowd, throng, horde.

hereditary a. inborn, inherited, congenital, genetic, inbred, ancestral, innate, inherent.

heresy n. apostasy, unorthodoxy, nonconformity, freethinking, blasphemy, heterodoxy, infidelity, dissension, atheism, agnosticism. "Only another word for freedom of thought."—Graham Greene. "Experiments in man's unsatisfied search for truth."—H.G. Wells.

heretical a. unorthodox, infidelic, nonconforming, unbelieving, freethinking, heterodox, impious, schismatic, heathen. ANT. *orthodox, faithful.*

heritage n. legacy, inheritance, ancestry, tradition, birthright, lot. "Scriptures ... which have been absorbed into our blood."—Sholom Asch.

hermit n. recluse, solitary, loner, *lone wolf, anchorite, misanthrope.

hero n. heroine, champion, idol, conqueror, victor, star, role model, principal, public figure, lion, protagonist, leading man. "One who is afraid to run away."—English proverb. "The shortest lived profession on earth."—Will Rogers. "One who thinks slower than a coward."—William Rotsler.

heroic a. brave, courageous, fearless, bold, noble, gallant, valiant, lionhearted, manly, *gutsy, *ballsy, *bigger than life, virile, gritty, altruistic, exalted. epic. ANT. *cowardly, fainthearted, dastardly.*

heroin n. narcotic, drug, *horse, *snow, *smack. SEE DRUG

heroism n. bravery, courageousness, fearlessness, boldness, nobility, gallantry, valiance,

valor, manliness, *gutsiness, *ballsiness, virility, grit, altruism. "Unbounded courage and compassion joined."—Joseph Addison. "Endurance for one moment more."—George Kennan. "It is always either doing or dying."—Roswell Hitchcock.

hesitant a. reluctant, irresolute, faltering, undecided, balking, tentative, wavering, halting, unsure, stalling, dallying. ANT. *decided, firm, confident.*

hesitate v. pause, hem and haw, falter, balk, waver, stall, wait, *dillydally, *waffle, dither, hang back, pussyfoot, *drag one's feet.

HETEROGENEOUS a. [HET ur o GEE nee us] made up of dissimilar elements, different, incongruous. *America is known for its heterogeneous society.* SYN. dissimilar, different, incongruous, diverse, motley, varied, mixed, miscellaneous, disparate, unrelated. ANT. *homogeneous, like, same, uniform.*

HIATUS n. [hi AYE tus] a break, gap or rest, often in one's work. SYN. break, interruption, lapse, discontinuity, interim, gap, pause, blank, rest, suspension, time out.

hibernate v. winter, sleep, hole up, lie low, lie dormant.

hick n. yokel, *hayseed, farmer, rustic, bumpkin, *hillbilly, *rube, clodhopper, *Okie, *Arky, *Clem.

hidden a. concealed, covered, covert, secret, under wraps, cloaked, clandestine, veiled, undercover, secreted, indiscernible, obscure, latent, occult, cryptic, invisible. ANT. *open, exposed, *in the spotlight, overt.*

hide v. conceal, secrete, cover, *put under wraps, cloak, veil, obscure, lie low, cache, shield, mask, camouflage, disguise, *drop out of sight, *hole up. ANT. *expose, reveal, show.*

hideous a. horrible, dreadful, appalling, terrible, ugly, awful, monstrous, grotesque, sickening, repulsive, gruesome, frightful, ghastly, grisly, repugnant, macabre. ANT. *lovely, beautiful, attractive.*

HIERARCHY n. [HYE uh RAHR kee] an order of rank, pecking order. *He was second in command in the company hierarchy.* SYN. order, pecking order, ranking, grouping, strata, *chain of command, *ladder, caste system.

high a. 1. LOFTY tall, towering, soaring, steep, sky-high, *cloud-kissing, *cloud-piercing, elevated, skyward, alpine, vertiginous. 2. IMPORTANT powerful, superior, prominent, excellent, exalted, ranking, eminent, chief, leading, uppermost. 3. EXTREME excessive, great, intensified, dear, expensive, exorbitant, extravagant, costly, *steep. **4.** HIGH-PITCHED soprano, shrill, treble, piercing. **5.** HAPPY euphoric, elated, ecstatic, joyful, cheerful, exuberant, rhapsodic. **6.** UNDER THE INFLUENCE OF DRUGS OR DRINK *buzzed, under the influence, intoxicated, *stoned, *flying, *hammered, *baked, *blitzed, *coked out, delirious, *fried, *hopped up, *out of it, *tripping, *wired, *spaced out. ANT. *1.* low, short. *2.* low, insignificant, piddling. *3.* modest, low, cheap. *4.* low, bass. *5.* low, depressed, *down in the dumps. *6.* sober, lucid, clearheaded.

high and mighty a. lordly, arrogant, presumptuous. SEE HAUGHTY

highbrow n. longhair, thinker, *egghead, scholar. "The kind of person who looks at a sausage and thinks of Picasso."—Alan Herbert. "A person educated beyond his intelligence."—Brander Mathews. SEE INTELLECTUAL

highbrow a. erudite, scholarly, intellectual, learned, cultivated, bookish, cultured.

high-class a. superior, first-rate, best, supreme, *tops, upper-class, *upper-crust, top-flight, select, deluxe, quality, plush. ANT. low-class, ordinary, mediocre.

highfalutin a. pretentious, high-flown. SEE POMPOUS

high-flown a. high-sounding, bombastic, grandiloquent, lofty, grandiose, pretentious, stilted, inflated, extravagant, turgid, showy, flowery. ANT. folksy, down to earth, plain.

high-handed a. overbearing, domineering, imperious, tyrannical, dictatorial, arbitrary, oppressive, ironhanded, authoritarian.

highlight n. high point, memorable part, feature, focus, focal point, peak, climax, best part.

highlight v. spotlight, underline, underscore, feature, play up, headline, punctuate, accentuate, emphasize, stress. ANT. downplay, obscure.

high-minded a. ethical, moral, principled, honorable, noble, upright, conscientious, virtuous, honest, righteous. ANT. unethical, immoral, unprincipled.

high-strung a. nervous, tense, uptight, wound up, *hyper, *wired, edgy, skittish, jumpy, excitable, taut, temperamental, snappy. ANT calm, relaxed, placid.

highway n. road, street, freeway, drive, parkway, turnpike, expressway, thoroughfare, boulevard, *main drag, causeway, autobahn, toll road, beltway.

hijack v. seize control, commandeer, steal, *hold up, skyjack, *carjack.

hijacker n. robber, skyjacker, *carjacker, kidnapper, abductor.

hike n. walk, journey, walkabout, ramble, trek, march, tramp, odyssey.

hike v. walk, journey, ramble, backpack, trek, march, tramp, rove, *hoof it, range.

hilarious a. funny, side-splitting, *hysterical, humorous, *a riot, *a scream, uproarious, amusing, merry, boisterous, gay, jolly, mirthful, gleeful, noisy. ANT. grim, grave, sad, depressing.

hill n. elevation, rise, knoll, hillock, hummock, knob, hump, bluff, gradient, slope, highland, prominence, mound, tor, dune. ANT. crater, canyon, hollow, valley.

WORD FIND

hilly: rolling, tumulose
land between hills: intervale
SEE MOUNTAIN

hillbilly n. *hayseed, *Clem, clodhopper. SEE HICK

hillock n. SEE HILL

hinder v. obstruct, block, impede, slow, stop, prevent, check, deter, thwart, frustrate, hamper, interfere, foil, forestall, stand in the way, *hamstring. ANT. help, enable, facilitate, free.

hindrance n. impediment, obstruction, encumbrance, stumbling block, obstacle, restriction, restraint, constraint, snag, handicap.

hinge v. depend, be contingent, rest, hang, revolve.

hint n. **1.** CLUE indication, tip, *tip-off, suggestion, telltale, implication, allusion, sign, lead, innuendo, intimation. **2.** TRACE tinge, touch, suggestion, taste, sprinkling.

hint v. give a clue, suggest, indicate, intimate, imply, indicate, allude to, insinuate, *put a bug in one's ear, infer, tip, cue.

hip a. Sl. *with it, sophisticated, *in the know, aware, stylish, savvy, worldly-wise, experienced, astute, *cool. ANT. ignorant, *out of it, unaware.

hire v. employ, engage, enlist, take on, commission, secure, appoint, delegate, put to work, retain, contract for, rent, charter, lease. ANT. fire, let go, *pink slip.

historic a. momentous, consequential, important, notable, significant, unforgettable, famous, celebrated, renowned, outstanding, extraordinary. ANT. unimportant, insignificant, inconsequential, obscure.

historical a. documented, factual, real, actual,

authentic, true, recorded, verifiable, chronicled, past, bygone, former. ANT. *mythical, fictitious, made-up, contemporary, modern.*

history n. **1.** CHRONICLE record, documentation, account, annals, saga, chronology, memories, diary, memoirs. "The witness of the times . . . the messenger of antiquity." — Cicero. "A voice forever sounding across the centuries the laws of right and wrong." — James Froude. "A sort of mask, richly colored." — John Quincy Adams. "The great dust heap." — Augustine Birrell. "A fraud agreed upon." — Napoleon I. "The propaganda of the victorious." — Anon. "That terrible mill in which sawdust rejoins sawdust." — Edith Sitwell. **2.** THE PAST yesteryear, bygone era, *good old days, *water under the bridge, antiquity.

HISTRIONIC a. [HISS tree AWN ik] theatrical, overly dramatic. *His histrionic show of temper made him the center of attention.* SYN. theatrical, dramatic, melodramatic, overplayed, overacted, affected, stagy, thespian, forced, unnatural, *put-on. ANT. *natural, unaffected, understated.*

histrionics n. theatrics, melodramatics, dramatics, show, acting, affectation, display, playacting, performing.

hit n. **1.** BLOW strike, knock, bump, impact, smack, whack, tap, rap, thump, *conk, cuff, punch, slap, swat. **2.** SUCCESS triumph, winner, *smash, sensation, best-seller, sellout.

hit v. strike, knock, bump, smack, whack, tap, rap, thump, *conk, cuff, punch, slap, swat, belt, bang, wallop, sock, pound, bash, beat, bop, slug.

hitch n. problem, snag, impediment, hindrance, stumbling block, *snafu, catch, difficulty, *glitch, bug, complication.

hitch v. join, connect, fasten, link, bind, attach, harness, couple, yoke, unite.

hit man n. Sl. *triggerman, assassin. SEE KILLER, MURDERER

hoard n. stockpile, store, cache, supply, reserve, stash, *nest egg, collection, accumulation.

hoard v. stockpile, store, cache, put away, *squirrel away, amass, stash, hide, save, collect, accumulate. ANT. *squander, waste, spend.*

hoarse a. husky, throaty, rough, harsh, rasping, gravelly, croaking, *whiskey-voiced, scratchy, roupy, guttural, ragged.

hoary a. **1.** WHITE OR GRAY salt and pepper, grizzled, snowy-haired. **2.** OLD elderly, ancient, aged, venerable.

hoax n. prank, trick, *put-on, *fake-out, joke, *spoof, ruse, fraud, deception, *crock, *humbug.

hoax v. trick, *put on, *fake out, deceive, *con, *hoodwink, fool, delude, *pull the wool over one's eyes, *sucker, dupe.

hobble v. **1.** LIMP hitch, shamble, falter, dodder, walk lamely, stumble, stagger, *shortleg. **2.** RESTRICT fetter, hinder, hamper, *hamstring, cripple, impede, handicap, inhibit.

hobby n. pastime, avocation, diversion, sideline, *thing, leisure time activity, pursuit, play, *bag, fun, *cup of tea.

hobgoblin n. bogey, bugbear, apparition, evil spirit, *spook, puck, elf, imp, fairy.

hobo n. tramp, *bum, transient, drifter, vagrant, derelict, *stiff, migrant worker, rover.

hockey n. ice hockey, field hockey, sport.

WORD FIND ICE HOCKEY

avoid being scored against while short-handed: kill a penalty

bumping opponent away from play: check, body check

cup: Stanley

disk: puck

drop of puck by referee between two players: face-off

fake a move to shake off opponent: deke

free shot on goal: penalty shot

goaltender: goalie

hard, driving shot: slapshot

holding crook of opponent's stick to stop movement: hooking

illegally striking opponent with stick: slashing, spearing, high sticking

illegal shot from behind center red line: icing

penalty situation in which team has a one-man advantage: power play

positions: center, forwards, wings, backline, defensemen

rectangle in front of goal: crease

roughness penalty, excessive: roughing

three goals scored by one player in a single game: hat trick

vehicle that restores ice surface: Zamboni

hocus-pocus n. magic, trickery, legerdemain, sleight-of-hand, prestidigitation, hoax, conjuring, deception, incantation, *abracadabra, mumbo jumbo, gibberish.

hodgepodge n. mixture, miscellany, jumble, melange, potpourri, medley, patchwork, *goulash, mess, *mishmash, hash, *mixed bag.

hog n. **1.** PIG swine, *oinker, shoat, piglet, sow, boar. **2.** GLUTTON gourmand.

hog v. *Sl.* be greedy, take all, monopolize.

hogwash n. *BS, *baloney, balderdash, *bilge.
SEE NONSENSE

hoi polloi n. the common people, the masses, commoners, rank and file, the working class, the crowd, citizenry, plebians, proletariat, *Middle America. ANT. *aristocracy, high society, upper class.*

hoist v. raise, lift, pull up, elevate, raise aloft, jack up, erect.

hold n. influence, grip, control, sway, pull, effect, *clout.

hold v. 1. GRIP clutch, grasp, clasp, clench, carry, embrace, squeeze, palm, cradle, handle, wield. 2. POSSESS have, retain, keep, own, secure, maintain, contain. 3. BELIEVE maintain, think, feel, reckon, view, deem, assume, surmise, espouse, swear by. 4. CHECK restrain, restrict, suspend, postpone. 5. PERSIST continue, last, endure, stay, remain. 6. SUPPORT uphold, bear, shoulder.

hole n. 1. OPENING space, aperture, gap, orifice, vent, cavity, rift, slot, break, puncture, perforation, excavation, hollow, crater, pit, dugout, well, burrow. 2. PREDICAMENT *box, *pickle, jam, dilemma, fix, spot, bind, plight, *hot water, *tight squeeze.

holiday n. celebration, festival, commemoration, fiesta, jubilee, holy day, observance, anniversary, vacation, day off, day of rest, long weekend. "Overrated disturbances of routine." — Edward Lucas.

HOLIER-THAN-THOU a. acting as if one is more virtuous than another, self-righteous. *We were sickened by his hypocritical, holier-than-thou judgments.* SYN. sanctimonious, self-righteous, pious, self-satisfied, smug, snobbish, *squeaky clean, judgmental.

holiness a. sanctity, sacredness, godliness, divinity, blessedness, grace, saintliness, piety, virtue. "A sweet, pleasant, charming, serene, calm nature." — Jonathan Edwards. "A fire whose outgoing warmth pervades the Universe." — Plotinus.

holler v. yell, bellow, thunder. SEE SHOUT

hollow n. depression, concavity, indentation, cavity, dent, dimple, sink, bowl. SEE HOLE

hollow a. 1. EMPTY vacant, void, unfilled. 2. CONCAVE deep-set, indented, sunken, cavernous. 3. MEANINGLESS empty, vain, futile, worthless, useless, insincere.

holocaust n. destruction, annihilation, genocide, mass killing, massacre, carnage, extermination, catastrophe, disaster, devastation, conflagration, firestorm, inferno.

holy a. godly, divine, sacred, hallowed, sacrosanct, consecrated, blessed, saintly, virtuous, religious, righteous, pious, faithful, spiritual. ANT. *ungodly, unholy, profane, diabolical, demonic.*

HOMAGE n. ['(H) ĂM - ij] something done, said or given to honor or show respect for another. *We paid the president homage by saluting him.* SYN. honor, respect, tribute, exaltation, esteem, admiration, reverence, allegiance, obeisance, deference, recognition.

home n. 1. RESIDENCE house, domicile, abode, habitation, dwelling, quarters, place, castle, lodging, roost, *diggings, *pad. "Where we love." — Oliver Wendell Homes. "A place where you can scratch any place you itch." — Henry Ainsley. "The abode of the heart." — Elbert Hubbard. 2. HOME BASE OR ORIGIN birthplace, native land, fatherland, habitat. SEE HOUSE

homeless a. destitute, *down-and-out, vagrant, displaced, derelict, evicted, dispossessed, exiled, forsaken, impoverished.

homely a. 1. UGLY plain, unattractive, *short on looks. 2. SIMPLE plain, unpretentious, unsophisticated, homey, modest, folksy, informal, comfortable. ANT. *1. beautiful, pretty, handsome. 2. pretentious, sophisticated, showy.*

homespun a. plain, unpretentious, homemade, homely, simple, unsophisticated, folksy, simple, down-home, modest, informal. ANT. *sophisticated, pretentious, refined.*

homey a. comfortable, cozy, relaxed, familiar, informal, folksy, domestic, intimate, friendly, unpretentious. ANT. *sophisticated, formal.*

homicidal a. murderous, bloodthirsty, violent, maniacal.

homicide n. murder, killing, manslaughter, slaughter, slaying, assassination, *hit, shooting. SEE MURDER

HOMOGENEOUS a. [HO mo JEE nee us] made of like or similar elements. *A nation with only one ethnic group is a homogeneous society.* SYN. similar, like, identical, kindred, uniform, consistent, unmixed, the same. ANT. *heterogeneous, dissimilar.*

homosexual n. gay man, gay woman, lesbian, invert, bisexual, transsexual, *faggot, *queer, *fruit, *dyke, *fairy, *fay, *Nancy boy, *pansy.

homosexual a. gay, lesbian, *queer, *faggy, *flaming, *bent, *fruity, *kinky, *light on one's feet, *limp-wristed, *pink, *swish, bisexual, transsexual, inverted.

hone v. sharpen, file, whet, grind.

honest *a.* **1.** TRUTHFUL trustworthy, upstanding, scrupulous, moral, ethical, veracious, reputable, straight, *on the level, honorable, aboveboard, conscientious, principled, credible, believable. **2.** CANDID frank, direct, straightforward, forthright, sincere, genuine, real, outspoken, outright, blunt. ANT. *1. dishonest, deceitful, disreputable. 2. indirect, insincere.*

honesty *n.* **1.** TRUTHFULNESS veracity, integrity, trustworthiness, scrupulousness, probity, principle, morality, virtue, conscientiousness; credibility. "The ability to resist small temptations." — John Ciardi. **2.** CANDOR frankness, directness, straightforwardness, forthrightness, sincerity, outspokenness, bluntness. ANT. *1. dishonesty, deceit, deception. 2. indirectness, insincerity.*

honeyed *a.* sweetened, sugarcoated, candied, syrupy, flattering, smooth-tongued, ingratiating, cajoling.

honor *n.* **1.** REGARD respect, esteem, admiration, veneration, reverence, dignity, glory, deference, homage, exaltation, recognition, approval. **2.** INTEGRITY character, honesty, morality, virtue, principles, decency, righteousness, rectitude, nobility, dignity. "The moral conscience of the great." — William D'Avenant. "The morality of superior men." — Henry Louis Mencken. "A mistress all mankind pursue." — Paul Whitehead. ANT. *1. dishonor, shame, disgrace, 2. dishonor, dishonesty, immorality, perfidy, treachery.*

honorable *a.* virtuous, scrupulous, honest, moral, ethical, principled, decent, righteous, noble, trustworthy, upright, good. ANT. *dishonorable, disreputable, dishonest.*

honorary *a.* honorific, titular, in name only.

hoodlum *n.* *hood, criminal, thug, ruffian, gangster, mobster, *tough, *goon, *hooligan, *punk, rowdy, troublemaker.

hoodwink *v.* dupe, mislead, deceive, confuse, trick, *pull the wool over one's eyes, delude, cheat, fool, bamboozle.

hook *n.* **1.** GRAPPLE grapnel, crook, catch, hasp. **2.** BEND crook, dogleg, curve, angle, loop, arc, hairpin turn.

hook *v.* hitch, catch, gaff, grab, seize, snag, secure, fasten, couple.

hooked *a. Sl.* *having a monkey on one's back. SEE ADDICTED

hooker *n. Sl.* whore, lady of the evening, streetwalker. SEE PROSTITUTE

hooligan *n.* rowdy, *punk, *tough. SEE HOODLUM

hoopla *n. Sl.* excitement, to-do, fuss, fireworks, brouhaha, bustle, furor, ballyhoo.

hoot *v.* jeer, shout in disapproval, scorn, catcall, deride, boo, *razz, howl, mock, scoff at.

hop *v.* jump, leap, bound, hurdle, vault, spring, bounce, skip, dance, romp, caper, prance, gambol.

hope *n.* optimism, faith, confidence, trust, expectation, wish, desire, want, aspiration, dream, anticipation, expectancy, prospect, belief, fancy. "The poor man's bread." — George Herbert. "Eating the air on promise of supply." — Shakespeare. ANT. *hopelessness, despair, pessimism.*

hope *v.* have faith, trust, be optimistic, expect, wish, desire, want, aspire, dream, anticipate, believe, fancy, look forward to, count on. ANT. *despair, doubt.*

hopeful *a.* **1.** OPTIMISITC *keeping the faith, looking forward to, anticipating, expectant, confident, sanguine. **2.** PROMISING encouraging, bright, favorable, heartening, reassuring, auspicious, propitious. ANT. *1. pessimistic, hopeless. 2. black, bleak, hopeless, foreboding.*

hopeless *a.* **1.** FUTILE lost, desperate, irrevocable, bleak, discouraging, vain, foreboding, incurable, threatening, grave, unobtainable, impossible. **2.** DESPAIRING desperate, demoralized, lost, disconsolate, miserable, heartbroken, depressed, suicidal, *broken, dispirited. ANT. *1. hopeful, bright, promising. 2. hopeful, optimistic, confident, encouraged.*

horde *n.* crowd, mass, throng, multitude, mob, pack, swarm, bunch, gang, group, band, press.

horizon *n.* skyline, vista, purview, field of vision, limit, range, offing, azimuth.

horizontal *a.* flat, level, flush, plane, straight, supine, prone, recumbent. ANT. *vertical, upright.*

horn **1.** OUTGROWTH tusk, antler, spike, cornu. **2.** SEE MUSICAL INSTRUMENTS

horny *a. Sl.* *hot, lustful, *turned on, amorous, passionate, lascivious, erotic, goatish, feverish, salacious, libidinous, sex-crazed, randy, *hot as a three-dollar pistol.

horrendous *a.* SEE HORRIBLE

horrible *a.* horrendous, terrible, awful, frightful, horrid, appalling, dreadful, horrifying, abominable, hideous, ghastly, shocking, gruesome, disgusting, terrifying, repulsive, atrocious. ANT. *wonderful, lovely, charming, delightful.*

horrid *a.* SEE HORRIBLE

horrify *v.* dismay, shock, frighten, terrify, appall, scare, *curdle one's blood, *curl one's hair, *scare the daylights out of, *make one's skin crawl, *send chills up one's spine, sicken, nauseate, disgust, revolt, fill with morbid fascination, paralyze, petrify. ANT. *calm, soothe, reassure.*

horror *n.* fear, terror, fright, dread, trepidation, dismay, revulsion, repulsion, disgust, loathing, abhorrence, aversion.

hors d'oeuvre *n.* tidbit, finger sandwich, canape. SEE APPETIZER

horse *n.* equine, steed, mount, nag, pony, *bronc, stallion, mare, *plug, *crowbait.

WORD FIND

COLORS AND MARKINGS

beige with black mane: buckskin
beige with brown or light mane: dun
black and white: piebald
black speckles: medicine hat
bluish gray: grulla, smokey
bronze or coppery: chestnut, sorrel
brownish sprinkled with gray and white: roan
palomino color: buttermilk, golden
patches of white over any coat color except black: skewbald
piebald or spotted: calico, pinto, dappled, paint
reddish brown with black mane: bay
stripe extending down back: eel stripe, dorsal stripe
white above fetlock: stocking
white below fetlock: sock
white marking around nostril: snip
white marking between eyes: star
white streak on face: blaze, race
white with white mane: palomilla
yellowish cross of sorrel and dun: claybank

BREEDS

appaloosa, Arabian, Cleveland bay, Clydesdale, Dartmoor, Exmoor, French Trotter, Hackney, Holstein, hunter, Lipizzaner, Morgan, palomino, Percheron, quarter horse, saddlebred, Shetland, Shire, standardbred, Suffolk, Tennessee Walking Horse, thoroughbred

GENERAL

back, highest portion of: withers
bangs: forelock
barnyard play area: paddock
bent-backed: swaybacked, hogbacked
breeding mare: brood mare
breeding period of mare: heat
bushy tail: broomtail
care and feeding of, for a fee: livery

castrated male: gelding
cattle horse: cutting horse
comb: currycomb
command to turn left: haw
command to turn right: gee
cry of: neigh, whinny, snort
disease: staggers, distemper, loco, spavin, heaves
equipment: appointments, breastplate, bridle, bit, cheek straps, crownpiece, throatlatch, headband, blinder, cavesson, reins, saddle, halter, hackamore
feeding trough: manger
female under age four: filly
gait: walk, trot, lope, canter, gallop, rack, volt, fox trot
gentle farm horse: dobbin
half-turn: caracole
Indian: pinto, cayuse, mustang
joint above hoof: fetlock
leap, playful four-legged: gambado
leap straight up: capriole
male under age four: colt
measurement of four inches: hand
mythological: Pegasus, centaur
nervous movement sideways or backwards: jib
newborn: foal
nose and mouth area: muzzle
pen: corral
pertaining to: equestrian, equine
race: steeplechase, derby
riding competition: gymkhana
riding pants, boots: jodhpurs
rising and falling in English riding style: posting
shelter: stall, stable
short-legged horse: cob
sideways gait: volt
smooth, refined gait for show: dressage
stand up on rear legs: rear
strong horse used for pulling: draft horse
stud's herd: harras
sweat: lather
trained: broken, bridlewise
trot in place for show: piaffe
upjerk of head: bridle
wild or half-wild: mustang, bronco
winker: blinder

horseman *n.* equestrian, rider, jockey, roughrider, cowboy, broncobuster.

horseplay *n.* clowning, foolishness, antics, fun, hijinks, tomfoolery.

hose *n.* hosiery, stockings.

hospitable *a.* gracious, accommodating, sociable, friendly, welcoming, neighborly, convivial, genial, cordial, helpful. ANT. *unwelcoming, inhospitable, unfriendly.*

hospital n. medical center, infirmary, clinic, sanatorium, sick bay, dispensary, ward, institution, treatment facility, hospice. "That blend of penitentiary and third-class hotel."—Henry Sigerist. SEE DOCTOR, MEDICINE, NURSE, OPERATION, SURGERY

hospitality n. accommodation, welcome, friendliness, graciousness, sociability, neighborliness, geniality, cordiality, warmth. "A genial hearth, a hospitable board, and a refined rusticity."—William Wordsworth

host n. multitude, group, throng, legion, horde, flock, myriad.

hostage n. pawn, captive, security. SEE PRISONER.

hostile a. unfriendly, antagonistic, malevolent, bellicose, belligerent, enemy, contrary, aggressive, nasty, contentious, warring, pugnacious, cold. ANT. *friendly, warm, amiable, peaceful.*

hostility n. unfriendliness, antagonism, malevolence, hatred, ill will, enmity, animus, opposition, aggression, venom, bellicosity, virulence, bad blood, anger, nastiness. HOSTILITIES war, conflict, dispute, clash. ANT. *friendliness, good will, unity, peace.*

hot a. **1.** TORRID blazing, fiery, burning, scorching, steaming, boiling, blistering, roasting, sweltering, feverish, sizzling, sultry, tropical. **2.** SPICY peppery, sharp, biting, burning, piquant, zesty, pungent. **3.** PASSIONATE ardent, fiery, intense, fervent, vehement, impassioned, angry, raging, furious, violent. **4.** AROUSED SEXUALLY *horny, lustful, lascivious, salacious, libidinous, randy. **5.** NEW AND POPULAR trendy, fresh, in vogue. ANT. *1. cold, wintry, frigid. 2. bland, mild. 3. indifferent, apathetic, lukewarm. 4. turned off, repulsed, cold.*

hotel n. motel, inn, motor inn, resort, lodging, tavern, hostel, *flophouse.

hotheaded a. hot-tempered, quick-tempered, touchy, explosive, volatile, testy, *short-fused, combustible, rash, impetuous. ANT. *even-tempered, levelheaded, easygoing.*

hound v. chase, nag, badger, harass, pester, pursue, dog, *bug, ride, *hassle, persecute, go after.

house n. home, residence, shelter, abode, habitation, domicile, homestead, castle, mansion, duplex.

WORD FIND

attic access hole: scuttle
beam supporting floor or ceiling: joist

board siding: clapboard
flooring of wood forming geometric pattern: parquet
foundation without basement: slab
frame made of heavy timbers: post-and-beam construction
framing member, vertical: stud
glass-enclosed lookout on top of roof: belvedere
glass: glazing
ornamentation, elaborate: gingerbread
passage between garage and house: breezeway
projection, with window, on sloping roof: dormer
roof dome or domelike structure: cupola
roof framing member: rafter, purlin, ridgeboard
roof overhang: eaves
roof walkway: widow's walk
roof with double slope on each side: gambrel
roof with four sides, no gables: hip roof
roof with two slopes on all four sides: mansard roof
stair railing spindles: balusters
styles: adobe, bothy, brownstone, bungalow, cabin, cajun cottage, Cape Cod, chateau, colonial, cottage, Creole townhouse, Dutch Colonial, Elizabethan, English magpie, Federal, gambrel, Georgian, gingerbread, Gothic Revival, Greek Revival, Italianate, octagon, pueblo, Queen Anne, Romanesque, row house, saltbox, Second Empire, split level, Tudor, Victorian
tile mortar: grout
upper wall portion between slopes of roof: gable
wall not requiring plaster: drywall, sheetrock, gypsum wallboard
window framework: sash
window strips or bars: mullions
window that projects: bay window
SEE ARCHITECTURE, CASTLE, HOME

hovel n. shed, hut, shack, cabin, shanty, lean-to, *dump, *rattrap, *hole.

hover v. float, hang, linger, flutter, stay suspended.

howl v. wail, waul, bay, bellow, yowl, cry out, bawl, moan, whine, ululate, caterwaul.

hub n. center, axis, core, pivot, focal point, *nerve center, heart, middle.

hubbub n. noise, uproar, tumult, commotion, clamor, racket, confusion, pandemonium, hullaballoo, stir, fuss, *ruckus, unrest. ANT.

quiet, silence, stillness.

hubris n. arrogance, insolence. SEE PRIDE

huckster n. salesman, peddler, tradesman, hawker, vendor, concessionaire, merchant.

huddle v. mass, gather, pack, crowd, cluster, bunch, converge, herd, confer, *powwow.

hue n. color, tint, shade, tone, tinge, cast.

huff n. snit, bad mood, *stew, tiff, rage, resentment, fit of anger, tantrum.

huffy a. touchy, irritable, easily offended, testy, sensitive, hypersensitive, petulant, peevish, cross, crabby, waspish, nettled, irate. ANT. *cheerful, good-humored.*

hug n. embrace, squeeze, clasp, clinch, *bear hug. "A roundabout way of expressing emotion." — Gideon Wurdz.

hug v. embrace, squeeze, clasp, clinch, hold, clutch, *bear hug, take in one's arms, cuddle.

huge a. gigantic, colossal, immense, enormous, gargantuan, prodigious, humongous, great, whopping, tremendous, king-size, titanic, monstrous, massive, jumbo, stupendous, Brobdingnagian, mountainous, monumental, towering, elephantine, staggering, *eclipsing. ANT. *tiny, small, miniature, Lilliputian, microscopic.*

hulking a. heavy, large, clumsy, bulky, unwieldy, ponderous, massive, awkward, cumbersome, weighty, unmanageable. ANT. *compact, petite.*

hullabaloo n. uproar, noise, confusion. SEE HUBBUB

hum v. drone, buzz, whir, croon, intone, purr, murmur, sound, throb, bombinate.

human n. man, woman, person, Homo sapiens, being, *naked ape, creature. "A pair of pincers set over a bellows and a stewpan, the whole fixed upon stilts." — Samuel Butler. "A proper engine for the soul to work with." — Joseph Addison. "A little cave-dwelling virus mutated." — John D. MacDonald.

human a. **1.** ANTHROPOID anthropomorphic, manlike, hominine, bipedal, civilized, mortal. **2.** SEE HUMANE

humane a. compassionate, kind, sympathetic, merciful, good, understanding, humanitarian, forgiving, pitying, tolerant, magnanimous. ANT. *inhumane, cruel, unfeeling, vicious, merciless.*

humanitarian n. good Samaritan, philanthropist, do-gooder, *Robin Hood, altruist, benefactor.

humanity n. **1.** HUMAN RACE mankind, humankind, men and women, people, the masses, society, man. **2.** COMPASSION kindness, goodness, sympathy, benevolence, mercy, magnanimity, goodwill, brotherly love.

humble a. **1.** MODEST self-effacing, unassuming, unpretentious, reserved, deferential, meek, demure, self-conscious, subservient, diffident, obsequious, lowly. **2.** LOWLY shabby, simple, plain, ordinary, poor, undistinguished, rough, plebian, humdrum, unrefined, inconsequential. ANT. *1. arrogant, pretentious, haughty, proud, conceited. 2. rich, superior, ostentatious, illustrious, distinguished.*

humble v. degrade, deflate, *take the wind out of one's sails, *bring down a peg, shame, humiliate, demean, disgrace, *make one feel small, *make one eat crow, *make one eat humble pie. ANT. *exalt, *put on a pedestal, inflate, puff up.*

humbug n. *bullshit, *BS, baloney, nonsense, balderdash, *eyewash, *bunk, claptrap, poppycock, *hogwash, rubbish, *rot.

humdrum a. monotonous, boring, tedious, *ho-hum, dull, tiresome, routine, prosaic, uninteresting, *blah, flat, insipid, somnolent. ANT. *interesting, stimulating, fascinating, riveting, exciting.*

humid a. moist, damp, wet, vaporous, muggy, steamy, clammy, sticky, *close, dank, sultry, foggy, misty. ANT. *dry, arid.*

humiliate v. embarrass, mortify, shame, disgrace, chagrin, *make a fool out of, abash, put to shame, degrade, deflate, demean, humble, abase. ANT. *honor, exalt, *put on pedestal.*

humiliation n. embarrassment, mortification, shame, disgrace, chagrin, degradation, deflation, humbling, humble pie, losing face, *put-down, belittling. ANT. *honor, exaltation.*

HUMILITY n. [hyoo MIL uh tee] humbleness, modesty, the absence of arrogance or pride. *She accepted the award with great humility.* SYN. humbleness, modesty, unpretentiousness, lowliness, meekness, reserve, diffidence, sheepishness, obsequiousness, self-abasement. "Nothing else but a right judgment of ourselves." — William Law. "A noble mind in a low estate." — Jane Porter. "The pride of the humble." — Anon. ANT. *arrogance, pride, haughtiness.*

humor n. **1.** COMEDY funniness, jest, wit, facetiousness, jocularity, buffoonery, slapstick, drollery, whimsy, parody, satire. **2.** MOOD temperament, disposition, spirits, frame of mind, bent. "Truth in an intoxicated condition." — George Jean Nathan. "Pleasantry in pain." — Moritz Saphir. "Playful aggression." — Emil Draitser.

humorist n. comedian, comedienne, *stand-up, joker, comic, jester, wit, clown, caricaturist, mimic.

humorous a. funny, comical, laughable, ludicrous, hilarious, *side-splitting, facetious, tickling, farcical, amusing, droll, jocular, whimsical. ANT. serious, grave, somber.

hump n. bulge, protuberance, hunch, swelling, lump, mound, bump, knob, swell, hummock, hill.

hunch n. feeling, suspicion, guess, idea, premonition, inkling, intuition, notion, foreboding, impression.

hunch v. hump, bend, bow, huddle, crouch.

hunger n. appetite, starvation, famine, ravenousness, voraciousness, famishment, *sweet tooth, *munchies, stomach pangs, desire, craving, longing, yen, want, need, lust, drive, thirst. "The best sauce in the world." — Miguel de Cervantes. ANT. satiety.

hungry a. starving, famished, ravenous, malnourished, peckish, voracious, hankering, *got the munchies, *could eat a horse, craving, salivating. ANT. full, sated, gorged.

hunk n. chunk, lump, piece, clod, slab, block, portion, square, loaf, glob, slice.

hunt n. search, chase, pursuit, trailing, quest, coursing.

hunt v. 1. LOOK FOR search high and low, ferret out, scour, seek, quest for, leave no stone unturned, turn everything upside down, rummage, probe, fish for, investigate. 2. PURSUE AND KILL hound, trail, chase, track, *beat the bushes, stalk, course, poach.

hurdle n. obstacle, obstruction, stumbling block, barrier, impediment, difficulty, complication, block, snag.

hurdle v. jump over, clear, vault, leap, spring, hop, bound, negotiate.

hurl v. throw, chuck, fling, sling, heave, toss, pitch, lob, launch, catapult, propel.

hurried a. hasty, quick, rushed, speedy, swift, breakneck, superficial, cursory, perfunctory, slapdash. ANT. slow, leisurely, careful.

hurry n. haste, speed, swiftness, rush, celerity, hustle, dispatch, expeditiousness, bustle.

hurry v. hasten, quicken, pick up the pace, *step on it, rush, run, lose no time, hustle, *get a move on, zip, fly, race, speed, scurry, *make tracks, expedite, *get the lead out, *beat feet. ANT. slow, decelerate, delay.

hurt n. injury, harm, pain, wound, trauma, soreness, ache, pang, *boo-boo, sting, stitch, pinch, twinge, throb.

hurt v. 1. PHYSICALLY injure, harm, pain, torture, wound, damage, punish, abuse, sting, pinch, ache, throb, bite, sear, gnaw, stab, chafe, smart, pierce. 2. EMOTIONALLY insult, wound, cut to the quick, grieve, anguish, sadden, depress, affront, offend, abuse, distress, upset, torment, crush, *rake over the coals.

hurt a. injured, harmed, pained, wounded, traumatized, sore, aching, stinging, throbbing, bleeding, bruised, stricken, damaged, offended, crushed, devastated, distressed.

hurtful a. injurious, harmful, painful, wounding, traumatizing, deleterious, pernicious, damaging, destructive; cutting, nasty, cruel, spiteful, mean. ANT. helpful, benign, beneficial.

hurtle v. fly, rush, plunge, charge, hurl, scramble, *zip, *go hell-bent for leather, tear.

husband n. spouse, groom, *hubby, *old man, mate, alter ego, sidekick, companion. "A hero in his own home until the company leaves." — Warren Goldberg.

husband v. preserve, manage, economize. SEE CONSERVE

hush n. silence, stillness, peace, quiet, lull, quietude, vacuum.

hush v. silence, quiet, mute, shut up, stifle, muffle, mute, suppress, gag, shush.

husk n. shell, hull, pod, shuck, peel, covering, case, bark.

husky a. 1. HOARSE harsh, rough, throaty, rasping, croaking, whiskey-voiced, gruff, raucous, guttural. 2. BRAWNY muscular, stout, beefy, burly, *Herculean, powerful, strapping, strong, athletic, hefty. ANT. 1. clear, fluid, fluting, shrill. 2. anorexic, scrawny, puny.

hussy n. loose woman, wench, *tart, Jezebel, strumpet, slut, whore, trollop, minx.

hustle v. 1. HURRY *get a move on, bustle, scramble, rush, *hotfoot, make haste, fly, run, *step on it, *work like hell, *move. 2. PUSH shove, jostle, force, knock about, elbow, nudge, shoulder.

hut n. shelter, shack, camp, cabin, cottage, lean-to, shed, hovel, shanty, hutch.

hutch n. 1. PEN coop, cote, shed, cage, confine. 2. CHEST box, cabinet, locker, trunk.

hybrid n. cross, crossbreed, half-breed, mixed breed, mongrel, *mutt, composite, mixture, conglomerate, combination, mulatto. ANT. thoroughbred.

hygiene n. cleanliness, hygienics, sanitation, washing, regimen.

hygienic a. clean, sanitary, healthful, pure, disinfected, aseptic, sterile, germfree, prophylactic, wholesome. ANT. *dirty, infected, germ-infested.*

hymn n. spiritual, psalm, paean, choral, anthem, song of praise, canticle. SEE SONG

hype n. *Sl.* exaggeration, promotion. SEE HYPERBOLE

HYPERBOLE n. [hi PUR bul ee] an exaggeration, often used in figures of speech. *"I'm so hungry I could eat an elephant" is a statement illustrating the use of hyperbole.* SYN. exaggeration, overstatement, aggrandizement, *hype, embellishment, *PR, enlargement, inflation, magnification. ANT. *understatement.*

hypercritical a. overcritical, hard to please, severe, fussy, exacting, rigid, strict, overparticular, captious, persnickety, hairsplitting, finicky. ANT. *easy to please, unparticular.*

hypnotic a. soporific, somnolent, sleep-inducing, sedative, numbing, spellbinding, mesmerizing, mesmeric, entrancing, stupefying.

hypnotize v. spellbind, entrance, mesmerize, stupefy, bewilder, enchant, enthrall, charm, bewitch, sedate, put to sleep.

hypocrisy n. lip service, pretense, insincerity, phoniness, imposture, falsity, pietism, sanctimoniousness, Pharisaism, duplicity, two-facedness, crocodile tears. "A mouth that prays, a hand that kills." — Arabian proverb. ANT. *sincerity, genuineness, honesty.*

hypocrite n. pretender, *con, Pharisee, fake, dissembler, phony, tartuffe, deceiver, Janus, *bullshit artist, whited sepulchre, Holy Willie, poser.

hypocritical a. insincere, phony, hollow, dishonest, Janus-faced, deceptive, fake, Pecksniffian, pretending, sanctimonious, unnatural, pious, self-righteous, dissembling, artificial, duplicitous, pretentious. ANT. *sincere, genuine, real, honest.*

hypothesis n. theory, supposition, proposition, assumption, conjecture, speculation, guess, thesis, inference, deduction, idea, *shot in the dark.

HYPOTHETICAL a. [hye puh THET i kul] assumed, unproven, uncertain. *There are numerous hypothetical explanations for UFOs.* SYN. assumed, unproven, uncertain, conjectural, speculative, supposed, presumed, inferred, guessed, academic, theoretical, presumptive. ANT. *factual, established, actual, confirmed.*

hysteria n. hysterics, frenzy, madness, delirium, craze, panic, mania, anxiety, agitation, fit, outburst.

hysterical a. **1.** OUT OF CONTROL wild, crazed, frenzied, mad, delirious, panicked, manic, agitated, raving, carried away, rabid, *nuts, berserk. **2.** COMICAL funny, *side-splitting, uproarious, ludicrous, *a riot. ANT. *1. calm, rational, composed.*

I

icky *a. Sl.* *yucky, *gross, disgusting, distasteful, sickening, repulsive, sticky, gluey.

ICONOCLAST *n.* [iye KON uh KLAST] one who attacks popular institutions, beliefs, public figures, etc., or who views such modern icons with skepticism and cynicism. *The true iconoclast believes that nothing is sacred.* SYN. cynic, skeptic, critic, detractor, nonconformist, image-shatterer, denouncer, dissenter, nonbeliever.

icy *a.* **1.** FREEZING frozen, frigid, frosty, gelid, glacial, chilly, wintry, biting, cold. **2.** UN-FRIENDLY cold, aloof, distant, chilly, frigid, hostile, stony. ANT. *2. friendly, warm, genial.*

idea *n.* thought, notion, concept, view, plan, design, inkling, scheme, theory, insight, belief, understanding, *brainstorm, inspiration.

ideal *n.* model, archetype, epitome, paragon, standard, example, acme, ne plus ultra, exemplar, ultimate, inspiration.

ideal *a.* **1.** PERFECT model, supreme, consummate, exemplary, optimal, classic, faultless, best, excellent, utopian. **2.** CONCEPTUAL imaginary, visionary, fanciful, abstract. ANT. *1. imperfect, flawed. 2. real, actual.*

idealist *n.* dreamer, visionary, optimist, Pollyanna, romantic, utopian. "Those who gaze at the moon and fall in the gutter." — Anon. "One who, on noticing that a rose smells better than a cabbage, concludes that it will also make a better soup." — Henry Louis Mencken. ANT. *realist, cynic, skeptic, pragmatist.*

idealistic *a.* unrealistic, visionary, optimistic, utopian, Pollyannish, dreaming, romantic, naive. ANT. *realistic, skeptical, cynical.*

identical *a.* matching, alike, same, indistinguishable, twin, duplicate, corresponding, exact, synonymous, uniform, *carbon copy. ANT. *different, distinct, dissimilar.*

identify *v.* recognize, determine, distinguish, know, pick out, place, *tag, *spot, *peg, name, label, earmark.

identity *n.* individuality, self, oneself, ego, personality, character, identification, uniqueness.

idiocy *n.* foolishness, stupidity, imbecility, lunacy, craziness, madness, wackiness, absurdity, silliness.

idiom *n.* language, tongue, dialect, vernacular, lingo, parlance, jargon, colloquialism, expression, phrasing.

idiosyncrasy *n.* peculiarity, mannerism, quirk, singularity, characteristic, bent, trait, distinction, habit, quality, eccentricity.

idiot *n.* moron, imbecile, *retard, fool, nincompoop, simpleton, half-wit, lamebrain, *numskull, *chowderhead, *airhead, *dufus, ignoramus, dolt, *boob, blockhead, *pinhead. ANT. *genius, *Rhodes scholar, *brain, rocket scientist.*

idiotic *a.* moronic, stupid, retarded, foolish, imbecilic, simple, half-witted, *lamebrained, *numb, ignorant, dumb, asinine. ANT. *brilliant, intelligent, clever.*

idle *a.* **1.** WORTHLESS useless, vain, futile, frivolous, unproductive, pointless, irrelevant. **2.** UNUSED inactive, out of action, down, still, unemployed, quiet, dead, mothballed, empty, vacant. **3.** LAZY unemployed, slothful, shiftless, indolent, lethargic, loafing, sluggish, resting. ANT. *1. useful, valuable, productive. 2. in use, active, working. 3. active, busy, employed.*

idol *n.* hero, god, role model, star, superstar, celebrity, luminary, favorite, darling, icon.

idolize *v.* look up to, admire, revere, worship, venerate, deify, hero-worship, honor, *put on a pedestal, *worship the ground one walks on.

IDYLLIC *a.* [iye DIL ik] pastoral and peaceful; rustic and simple. *They chose an idyllic spot to build their house.* SYN. rustic, charming, peaceful, pastoral, unspoiled, romantic, simple, picturesque, heavenly, blissful.

iffy *a.* uncertain, unsettled, doubtful, questionable, *up in the air, dubious, unresolved, tentative, chancy. ANT. *certain, settled, sure.*

ignite *v.* **1.** LIGHT set fire, burst into flames, touch off, kindle, blow up, put a match to, flare up, burn. **2.** EXCITE arouse, agitate, spark. ANT. *douse, extinguish, smother.*

ignoble *a.* dishonorable, base, low, contemptible, despicable, shameful, corrupt, rotten, mean, disgraceful, vile, deplorable. ANT. *noble, honorable, admirable, good.*

IGNOMINY *n.* [IG num MIN ee] shame and dishonor. *He suffered the ignominy of a jail sentence.* SYN. shame, dishonor, disgrace, infamy, disrepute, discredit, odium, degradation, loss of face, humiliation. ANT. *honor, glory.*

ignoramus *n.* idiot, moron, *retard, simpleton, dunce, fool, half-wit, *airhead, bonehead, dolt, *dummy, *pea-brain. "Someone who doesn't know about what you learned yesterday." — Anon. ANT. *intellectual,* *Rhodes scholar,* *brain.*

ignorance *n.* stupidity, inexperience, unenlightenment, illiteracy, denseness, naivete, unfamiliarity, unconsciousness, empty-headedness, innocence, nescience, greenness. "The only thing more costly than an education." — Anon. "The only slavery." — Ralph Ingersoll. ANT. *knowledge, experience, intelligence.*

ignorant *a.* uneducated, inexperienced, unschooled, stupid, retarded, unenlightened, illiterate, dense, *thick, naive, unfamiliar, unaware, unconscious, empty-headed, innocent, unlettered, obtuse, oblivious, mindless, moronic, sophomoric, nescient, green, *dense as a post, *numb as a hake. "To walk in the night." — Anon. "Confident in everything." — Charles Spurgeon. "What everybody is, only on different subjects." — Will Rogers. ANT. *educated, aware, experienced, schooled, conscious.*

ignore *v.* disregard, overlook, skip, *pass over, slight, nevermind, discount, *turn deaf ear on, neglect, pay no attention to, *bury one's head in the sand, *give the cold shoulder. ANT. *regard, mind, heed.*

ilk *n.* sort, kind, class, type.

ill *n.* harm, injury, hurt, pain, trouble, misfortune, damage, evil, misery, calamity, bad luck, tribulation. ANT. *good fortune.*

ill *a.* **1.** SICK ailing, sickly, unwell, afflicted, *laid low, *green around the gills, *under the weather, *out of sorts, *off one's feed, *out of commission, bedridden, feverish, nauseated, diseased. **2.** EVIL bad, wicked, harmful, malicious, sinful, wrong, nefarious, immoral, foul, nasty. ANT. *1. healthy, well, sound. 2. good, moral, kind.*

ill-advised *a.* unwise, imprudent, misguided, stupid, foolish, short-sighted, harebrained, *half-baked, rash, injudicious. ANT. *wise, prudent.*

ill-at-ease *a.* uncomfortable, self-conscious, anxious, nervous, uneasy, apprehensive, awkward, insecure, shy, bashful. ANT. *relaxed, calm, confident.*

illegal *a.* against the law, unlawful, prohibited, forbidden, criminal, banned, illicit, outlawed, wrongful, felonious, shady, *black market. ANT. *legal, lawful, licit.*

illegible *a.* unreadable, indecipherable, unintelligible, *hard to make out, scrawled, scribbled, *clear as mud, *hen scratching. ANT. *legible, readable.*

WORD FIND

illegible handwriting: griffonage
poor handwriting: cacography

illegitimate *a.* *born out of wedlock, misbegotten, bastard, baseborn, *love child, illegal, unlawful.

ill-fated *a.* doomed, unlucky, star-crossed. SEE UNFORTUNATE

illicit *a.* unlawful, prohibited, improper. SEE ILLEGAL

illiterate *a.* uneducated, unschooled, unlettered. SEE IGNORANT

ill-mannered *a.* rude, beastly, discourteous, impolite, crude, coarse, uncivil, boorish, tacky, rough, vulgar. ANT. *courteous, mannerly, civil.*

ill-natured *a.* moody, ill-tempered, contentious, ill-humored, grouchy, irritable, crabby, touchy, sour, surly, waspish, cantankerous. ANT. *good-natured, easygoing, amiable.*

illness *n.* sickness, affliction, disorder, malady, ailment, disease, infirmity, syndrome, indisposition, poor health, complaint, *bug, virus. "A great leveler. At its touch, the artificial distinctions of society vanish away." — Max Thorek.

illogical *a.* unscientific, unsound, fallacious, senseless, wacky, *screwy, inconsistent, invalid, incongruous, unreasonable, wrong, irrational, *cockeyed. ANT. *sound, correct, logical.*

ill-suited *a.* unsuitable, incompatible. SEE INAPPROPRIATE

ill-tempered *a.* nasty, moody, explosive, ill-natured, contentious, grouchy, irritable, crabby, touchy, sour, surly, waspish, cantankerous. ANT. *even-tempered, easygoing, good-natured.*

illuminate *v.* **1.** LIGHT UP brighten, spotlight, radiate, beam, shine. **2.** EXPLAIN elucidate, clarify, throw light on, shed light on, clear up, define, enlighten, expound. ANT. *1. darken, dim. 2. obfuscate, muddy, obscure.*

illumination *n.* **1.** LIGHT luminescence, radiation, radiance, glow, shine. **2.** EXPLANATION elucidation, clarification, enlightenment, knowledge, instruction, wisdom, insight, understanding.

illusion *n.* apparition, mirage, hallucination, misconception, pipe dream, vision, phantasm, figment of the imagination, delusion, fallacy, deception.

illusory *a.* unreal, deceptive, imaginary, false,

delusory, visionary, hallucinatory, fanciful, spurious, chimerical. ANT. *real, concrete, true.*

illustrate *v.* **1.** MAKE CLEAR explain, demonstrate, illuminate, cite, elucidate, expound, clear up, make plain, describe, clarify, give an example, exemplify. **2.** DRAW depict, paint, portray, sketch, diagram, delineate, decorate, adorn.

illustration *n.* **1.** DEMONSTRATION exemplification, example, anecdote, story, analogy, sampling, case in point, instance. **2.** DRAWING depiction, painting, portrayal, sketch, diagram, cartoon, reproduction, design, figure, artwork, picture.

illustrious *a.* famous, renowned, distinguished, celebrated, prominent, eminent, notable, well-known, outstanding, acclaimed, esteemed. ANT. *obscure, unknown, undistinguished.*

ill will *n.* hostility, animosity, hate, malice, dislike, enmity, antipathy, hard feelings, spite, venom, grudge. ANT. *goodwill, friendliness, love.*

image *n.* **1.** REPRESENTATION picture, form, likeness, resemblance, imitation, copy, *carbon copy, mirror image, reproduction, facsimile, replica. **2.** IMPRESSION concept, idea, conception, mental picture, perception, thought.

imaginary *a.* fantasized, fancied, unreal, fantastic, visionary, invented, fictitious, *dreamed-up, made-up, conceived, mythical, hypothetical. ANT. *real, actual, true.*

imagination *n.* mind's eye, mental imagery, fabrication, visualization, *mental gymnastics, fantasy, illusion, reverie, dream world, figment, fancy, *castle in Spain, delusion, creativity, enterprise, inventiveness. "The true magic carpet." — Norman Vincent Peale. "A ladder to the fourth dimension." — Elbert Hubbard. "A warehouse of facts, with poet and liar in joint ownership." — Ambrose Bierce.

imaginative *a.* creative, inventive, original, innovative, *far-out, artistic, visionary, clever, ingenious, inspired, fanciful, fantastic, surreal. ANT. *unimaginative, unoriginal, prosaic, shallow.*

imagine *v.* **1.** PICTURE think of, fantasize, conceive, visualize, envision, conceptualize, dream, invent, fancy, create, conjure up. **2.** ASSUME believe, think, deduce, expect, conjecture, suspect, infer, surmise, suppose, guess.

imbecile *n.* idiot, moron, *retard, cretin, *pinhead, simpleton, dimwit, fool, dolt, *mental midget, *dummy, *chowderhead, dope, blockhead, ignoramus. ANT. *genius, *Rhodes scholar, rocket scientist, *brain.* SEE MORON

imbibe *v.* drink, partake, consume, quaff, swallow, guzzle, sip, *swig, *swill, *tipple, *chug-a-lug, *hit the sauce.

IMBROGLIO *n.* [im BROL yo] a confusing or complicated situation causing misunderstanding and, sometimes, a fight. *The police are experts at disentangling neighborhood imbroglios.* SYN. predicament, entanglement, confusion, disagreement, mess, complication, confusion, problem, difficulty, dilemma, quandary, trouble, *Catch-22, stalemate, squabble.

imbue *v.* infuse, saturate, suffuse, permeate, steep, fill, impregnate, instill, pervade, inspire.

imitate *v.* copy, mimic, match, emulate, follow suit, ape, impersonate, clone, simulate, replicate, mirror, parrot, caricature, model after.

imitation *n.* simulation, copy, fake, replica, likeness, facsimile, *phony, counterfeit, *sham, fraud, clone, parody, caricature, impersonation, impression. "The sincerest form of flattery." — Charles Colton. ANT. *genuine article, *the real McCoy, original.*

imitation *a.* simulated, fake, artificial, synthetic, ersatz, phony, bogus, mock. ANT. *authentic, genuine, real.*

immaculate *a.* clean, pure, flawless, *squeaky clean, uncorrupted, spotless, unsoiled, faultless, sinless, untainted, perfect, above reproach, pristine, virginal. ANT. *dirty, unclean, tainted, sinful, defiled.*

immaterial *a.* irrelevant, impertinent, unimportant, insignificant, trivial, inconsequential, meaningless, extraneous. ANT. *important, vital, central, relevant.*

immature *a.* young, undeveloped, incomplete, unfinished, imperfect, unseasoned, *green, infantile, babyish, childish, juvenile, sophomoric, inexperienced, *wet behind the ears, raw, unfledged, callow, puerile. ANT. *mature, adult, experienced, seasoned.*

immeasurable *a.* infinite, boundless, vast, inestimable, incalculable, limitless, unfathomable, inexhaustible, countless, neverending. ANT. *finite, measurable, limited.*

immediate *a.* **1.** INSTANTANEOUS instant, now, present, current, sudden, prompt, swift, hasty, without delay. **2.** NEAR next, close, direct, neighboring, adjacent, adjoining, contiguous. ANT. *1. slow, leisurely, eventual. 2. distant, remote.*

immediately *a.* instantly, at once, without delay, now, presently, *in a wink, *in a heartbeat, *licketysplit, forthwith, *pronto, directly, *PDQ, *in a New York minute, *tout de suite, *before you can say "Jack Robinson" *before you can say "Bob's your uncle," *in a jiffy. ANT. *eventually, later.*

immense *a.* huge, gigantic, colossal, gargantuan, prodigious, vast, enormous, massive, towering, Brobdingnagian, tremendous, stupendous, staggering, *humongous, monstrous. ANT. *tiny, miniature, microscopic.*

immerse *v.* **1.** DIP submerge, sink, dunk, douse, duck, plunge, soak, baptize. **2.** ABSORB engross, involve, engage, occupy.

imminent *a.* impending, approaching, threatening, at hand, on the verge, close, immediate, looming, nearing, on the horizon. ANT. *far, distant.*

immobile *a.* stationary, unmovable, fixed, stable, motionless, rooted, riveted, still, frozen, paralyzed. ANT. *mobile, movable.*

immoderate *a.* excessive, unreasonable, extreme, extravagant, unrestrained, too much, inordinate, overblown, unwarranted. ANT. *moderate, reasonable, just enough.*

immodest *a.* bold, shameless, unseemly, indecent, unblushing, risque, unrestrained, brazen, *cheeky. ANT. *modest, restrained, shy.*

immoral *a.* wrong, evil, sinful, bad, wicked, nasty, depraved, unethical, unprincipled, corrupt, unscrupulous, degenerate, *loose, debauched, perverted, disreputable. ANT. *moral, upright, virtuous, good.*

immortal *n.* SEE GOD/GOD

immortal *a.* deathless, everlasting, eternal, undying, indestructible, enduring, lasting, timeless, never ending, ageless, perpetual. ANT. *mortal, temporary, ephemeral.*

immortality *a.* **1.** DEATHLESSNESS everlastingness, indestructiblility, endurance, eternity, infinity. "To rise upon some fairer shore."—J.L. McCreery. **2.** FAME renown, celebrity, glorification, commemoration. "When a man dies but his words live."—Carl Crow. "The genius to move others long after you yourself have stopped moving."—Franklin Rooney. ANT. *mortality, death, obscurity, oblivion.*

immune *a.* invulnerable, resistant, safe, protected, exempt, unsusceptible, defended, inoculated, spared. ANT. *vulnerable, susceptible, liable.*

immunity *n.* protection, resistance, defense, inoculation, safety, exemption, privilege, exception, impunity. ANT. *vulnerability, liability, susceptibility.*

IMMUTABLE *a.* [i MYOO tuh bul] unchangeable. *The rules of the club are strict and immutable.* SYN. unchangeable, unalterable, inflexible, permanent, fixed, irreversible, unbreakable, stable, *carved in stone. ANT. *changeable, variable, flexible.*

imp *n.* devil, demon, brat, troublemaker, puck, sprite, hellion, hobgoblin, rascal, hellcat, scamp, tyke, mischievous child. ANT. *angel, little saint.*

impact *n.* **1.** COLLISION crash, bang, striking, slam, bump, smash, blow, whack, crunch, jolt, concussion, thump, rock, meeting, percussion. **2.** EFFECT repercussion, force, influence, power, consequences, results, brunt.

impair *v.* injure, damage, weaken, hinder, debilitate, harm, hurt, lessen, worsen, diminish, undermine, deteriorate, disable, enfeeble. ANT. *strengthen, improve, fortify.*

impale *v.* pierce, transfix, stab, run through, lance, spear, stick, prick, spike, puncture, skewer.

impart *v.* communicate, make known, inform, tell, announce, pass on, relate, transmit, proclaim, convey, divulge.

IMPARTIAL [im PAR shul] completely fair and unbiased. *We need an impartial judge to make the right decision.* SYN. fair, unbiased, neutral, disinterested, just, unprejudiced, objective, detached, equitable, dispassionate, nonpartisan. ANT. *partial, biased, partisan.*

impasse *n.* dead end, cul-de-sac, deadlock, stalemate, gridlock, *Catch-22, morass, standstill, standoff, dead stop.

impassioned *a.* passionate, ardent, fervent, intense, fiery, vehement, enthusiastic, excited, burning, torrid, powerful, rousing, emotional. ANT. *indifferent, apathetic, cool, dispassionate.*

impassive *a.* emotionless, calm, placid, stoic, stony, cool, indifferent, apathetic, stolid, dispassionate, unfeeling, matter-of-fact, reserved, phlegmatic. ANT. *impassioned, ardent, fervent.*

impatience *n.* restlessness, eagerness, agitation, expectancy, *ants in one's pants, restiveness, itchiness, excitement. ANT. *patience, calm.*

impatient *a.* restless, eager, agitated, expectant, restive, itching, *antsy, *chomping at the bit, hurried, nervous, anxious, edgy, annoyed. ANT. *patient, nonchalant, calm.*

IMPECCABLE *a.* [im PEK uh bul] flawless, without fault or sin. *The general's record was impeccable.* SYN. flawless, faultless, perfect, immaculate, spotless, unblemished, irreproachable, virtuous, sinless, pure. ANT. *flawed, imperfect, defective.*

impede *v.* block, hinder, obstruct, delay, hamper, check, thwart, bar, foil, inhibit, slow, stymie, stop, hold up, retard. ANT. *help, facilitate, advance.*

impediment *n.* barrier, obstacle, hindrance, block, stumbling block, obstruction, restriction, bar, check, holdup, delay, deterrent. ANT. *help, advancement, aid.*

impending *a.* imminent, coming, approaching, close, at hand, nearing, on the horizon, in the offing, forthcoming, looming, threatening.

impenetrable *a.* 1. IMPERVIOUS dense, hard, solid, thick, bulletproof, impassable, unaccessible. 2. INCOMPREHENSIBLE unfathomable, inscrutable, unknowable, arcane, baffling, inexplicable, esoteric, mysterious. ANT. 1. *penetrable, accessible, passable.* 2. *knowable, understandable, clear, simple.*

imperative *a.* necessary, urgent, compelling, pressing, important, mandatory, obligatory, requisite, essential. ANT. *unnecessary, voluntary, unimportant.*

imperfect *a.* flawed, faulty, defective, deficient, unfinished, insufficient, below par, substandard, immature. ANT. *perfect, flawless.*

imperfection *n.* flaw, fault, defect, deficiency, failing, blemish, shortcoming, malformation, weakness, inadequacy, disfigurement. ANT. *perfection, faultlessness.*

imperil *v.* endanger, jeopardize, hazard, *play with fire, risk, chance it, expose, *put one's life on the line. ANT. *safeguard, protect.*

IMPERIOUS *a.* [im PEER ee us] domineering and overbearing. *He peered down his nose at us with his usual imperious expression.* SYN. domineering, overbearing, lordly, arrogant, haughty, high-handed, tyrannical, bossy, authoritarian, commanding. ANT. *deferential, mousy, bashful.*

impersonal *a.* unfriendly, detached, remote, distant, cold, businesslike, formal, cool, disinterested, objective, neutral. ANT. *friendly, warm, personal.*

impersonate *v.* imitate, ape, caricature, do an impression, mimic, double as, represent, mock, parody, pretend to be.

impertinent *a.* 1. IRRELEVANT not germane, immaterial, unrelated, extraneous, beside the point. 2. INSOLENT rude, impudent, disrespectful, saucy, brash, inappropriate, fresh, *smart-alecky, *flip, *mouthy. ANT. 1. *relevant, germane.* 2. *polite, respectful.*

impervious *a.* inaccessible, dense. SEE IMPENETRABLE

IMPETUOUS *a.* [im PECH oo us] acting thoughtlessly or without careful consideration. *The impetuous youth drove without brakes and crashed into a wall.* SYN. rash, impulsive, headlong, hasty, careless, spontaneous, reckless, foolhardy, precipitate, spur-of-the-moment. ANT. *thoughtful, careful, prudent, cautious.*

impetus *n.* incentive, stimulus, spur, motive, spark, instigation, motivation, goad, catalyst, drive, force.

impinge *v.* trespass, encroach, infringe, invade, intrude.

impious *a.* irreverent, sacrilegious, blasphemous, ungodly, atheistic, irreligious, agnostic, sinful, iconoclastic, profane, immoral. ANT. *pious, religious, devout.*

impish *a.* mischievous, troublesome, naughty, prankish, devilish, *bratty, rascally, roguish, puckish, pert. ANT. *angelic, saintly.*

implacable *a.* inflexible, inexorable, unappeasable, unforgiving, relentless, merciless, vengeful, vindictive, unbending. ANT. *placable, merciful, forgiving.*

implausible *a.* unbelievable, improbable, unlikely, incredible, questionable, doubtful, dubious, inconceivable, farfetched. ANT. *plausible, believable, likely, credible.*

implement *n.* tool, utensil, instrument, device, contrivance, mechanism, apparatus, appliance, gadget, contraption.

implement *v.* start, fulfill, carry into effect, perform, accomplish, bring about, execute, enable.

implicate *v.* involve, point the finger at, accuse, embroil, name, incriminate, entangle, insinuate, connect, associate. ANT. *exclude, acquit, exonerate.*

implication *n.* association, involvement, connection, link, inference, incrimination, suggestion, assumption, ramification.

IMPLICIT [im PLIS it] not expressed explicitly but implied or suggested. *There was an implicit understanding that Joe was guilty.* SYN. implied, suggested, unspoken, tacit, inferred, understood, unexpressed, deduced, hinted. ANT. *explicit, spoken.*

implied *a.* suggested, implicit, unspoken, inferred, hinted at, tacit, deduced, alluded to, indicated, insinuated.

implore v. beg, beseech, ask, plead, entreat, appeal to, request, pray, supplicate.

imply a. suggest, hint, infer, allude to, indicate, point to, refer, insinuate, signify, mean.

impolite a. rude, discourteous, ill-mannered, unrefined, disrespectful, boorish, crude, indelicate, ungracious, uncivil. ANT. *polite, courteous, respectful.*

importance a. consequence, significance, weight, moment, substance, value, magnitude, gravity, greatness, seriousness.

important a. consequential, significant, weighty, *heavy, momentous, substantial, valuable, great, serious, critical, vital, crucial, paramount, far-reaching, big, huge, influential, *major league, decisive. ANT. *unimportant, trivial, insignificant, inconsequential.*

impose v. place, set, dictate, charge, enjoin, assign exact, demand, lay, force, prescribe, fix, order, require, obtrude, *shove down one's throat, intrude.

IMPOSING a. [im PO zing] grand, awesome, having a powerful presence. *New York has many imposing skyscrapers.* SYN. grand, awesome, impressive, powerful, majestic, monumental, towering, massive, commanding, striking, magnificent, mighty, stupendous. ANT. *unimpressive, insignificant.*

impossible a. inconceivable, unachievable, unfeasible, unobtainable, insurmountable, unreachable, beyond reason, unthinkable, preposterous, absurd, hopeless. ANT. *possible, conceivable, feasible.*

impostor n. pretender, masquerader, fake, phony, fraud, con man, mountebank, impersonator, charlatan, humbug.

IMPOTENT a. [IM puh tunt] powerless, weak, ineffective. Also, unable to engage in sexual intercourse. *The marshall was impotent without his six-shooter.* SYN. powerless, weak, ineffective, helpless, debilitated, incapacitated, emasculate, prostrate, inadequate, worthless. ANT. *potent, strong, powerful.*

impoverished a. poor, destitute, poverty-stricken, indigent, penniless, impecunious, ruined, needy, broke, insolvent, bankrupt, *strapped, *hard up. ANT. *rich, wealthy, affluent.*

impractical a. unworkable, impracticable, unrealistic, useless, wild, starry-eyed, chimerical, impossible, unfeasible, speculative, ideal. ANT. *practical, workable, viable, realistic, down-to-earth.*

impregnable a. unyielding, firm, secure, invincible, invulnerable, indestructible, impenetrable, strong, indomitable. ANT. *pregnable, yielding, vulnerable.*

impregnate v. inseminate, fertilize, fecundate, procreate, make pregnant, *knock up.

impress v. **1.** AFFECT influence, move, sway, stir, touch, grab, faze, strike, overwhelm, inspire, excite. **2.** IMPRINT dent, indent, stamp, mold, engrave, emboss, mark.

impression n. **1.** EFFECT influence, mark, impact, feeling. **2.** FEELING notion, sense, inkling, hunch, idea, suspicion, belief, perception. **3.** IMPRINT dent, indentation, stamp, mold, engraving, mark.

impressionable a. susceptible, moldable, gullible, receptive, vulnerable, suggestible, inexperienced, naive, pliable, sensitive. ANT. *worldly-wise, impervious, sophisticated, hardened.*

impressive a. effective, powerful, striking, awesome, extraordinary, profound, dramatic, imposing, moving, wondrous, admirable, momentous, breathtaking. ANT. *unimpressive, *blah, *ho-hum, ordinary.*

imprint n. impression, stamp, signature, trademark, seal.

imprison v. jail, incarcerate, immure, lock up, confine, cage, impound, put behind bars, *throw in the slammer, hold in custody, detain. ANT. *release, free, liberate.*

improbable a. unlikely, doubtful, questionable, implausible, dubious, unrealistic, unbelievable, impossible, farfetched, unheard of. ANT. *probable, likely, reasonable.*

impromptu a. unrehearsed, extemporaneous, improvised, ad-lib, off the cuff, unprepared, spontaneous, offhand, *off the top of one's head, spur-of-the-moment. ANT. *rehearsed, prepared, planned.*

improper a. unsuitable, inappropriate, unfitting, wrong, out of place, inapt, imprudent, uncalled for, incorrect, indecent, unseemly, indecorous, impolite, indelicate, offensive. ANT. *proper, correct, appropriate, fitting.*

impropriety n. slip, faux paus, gaffe, mistake, blunder, indecency, misstep, fault, bad taste, bad form.

improve v. make better, better, upgrade, reform, rework, correct, *touch up, *doctor, revise, enhance, mend, fix, refine, polish, enrich, ameliorate, promote, heal. ANT. *worsen, damage, impair.*

improvement n. enhancement, enrichment, amelioration, betterment, change for the better, betterment, progression, advance, upgrade, rectification, furtherance, revision. ANT. *worsening, impairment, decline.*

improvise *v.* invent, *wing it, *play by ear, make do, fake it, extemporize, make up, contrive, ad-lib, jury-rig.

imprudent *a.* unwise, rash, careless, indiscreet, thoughtless, foolhardy, reckless, injudicious, unthinking, irresponsible, impulsive, impetuous, unwary. ANT. *prudent, wise, cautious.*

IMPUDENT *a.* [IM pyoo dunt] boldly disrespectful, impertinent. *The impudent student was removed from the classroom.* SYN. bold, disrespectful, impertinent, shameless, insolent, saucy, rude, cheeky, brazen, audacious, fresh, *mouthy, *smart-alecky. ANT. *respectful, reverent, deferential.*

IMPUGN *v.* [im PYOON] to attack or criticize, especially for dishonesty or lack of integrity, to refute. *The attorney impugned the witness for stretching the truth.* SYN. attack, criticize, refute, call into question, vilify, challenge, assail, negate, cast aspersions, rebuke, impeach.

impulse *n.* urge, drive, instinct, itch, spur, goad, desire, feeling, whim, notion, impetus, incitement.

impulsive *a.* spontaneous, impetuous, spur-of-the-moment, extemporaneous, precipitate, unpremeditated, offhand, sudden, thoughtless, rash, hasty, whimsical. ANT. *premeditated, cautious, planned.*

IMPUNITY *n.* [im PYOO ni tee] freedom from penalty or punishment. *The looters thought they could steal with impunity.* SYN. exemption, freedom, immunity, license, privilege, without liability, *free hand, amnesty. ANT. *punishment, liability, comeuppance.*

impure *a.* **1.** CONTAMINATED polluted, dirty, adulterated, tainted, infected, sullied, foul, defiled, unclean. **2.** IMMORAL unchaste, defiled, indecent, corrupted, degenerate, sinful, depraved, unvirginal. ANT. *1. pure, clean, untainted. 2. moral, upright, wholesome.*

impurity *n.* contaminant, pollutant, foreign matter, defilement.

impute *v.* attribute, ascribe, blame, charge, assign, credit, cite, implicate, accuse, associate.

inaccuracy *n.* error, mistake, fault, blunder, defect, miscalculation, bungle, slip, flub, *screwup, *boo-boo, *boner.

inaccurate *a.* inexact, imprecise, wrong, incorrect, false, faulty, erroneous, mistaken, slipshod, *way off, flawed, fallacious, *wide of the mark, unreliable, *all wet. ANT. *accurate,*

precise, correct.

inactive *a.* idle, inert, immobile, down, inoperative, dormant, disengaged, still, unemployed, lazy, lethargic, sedentary, slothful. ANT. *active, busy, bustling.*

inadequate *a.* deficient, unsatisfactory, lacking, unfit, wanting, insufficient, too little, short, scanty, scarce, incompetent, impotent, incapable, unqualified. ANT. *adequate, satisfactory, sufficient, capable.*

inadvertent *a.* accidental, unplanned, unintentional, undeliberate, unwitting, undesigned, not on purpose, involuntary. ANT. *on purpose, designed, intentional, deliberate.*

INANE *a.* [i NANE] empty, silly or foolish, pointless. *The TV show was poorly written and inane.* SYN. empty, silly, foolish, senseless, pointless, fatuous, insipid, thoughtless, ludicrous, stupid, idiotic, mindless. ANT. *deep, profound, intelligent, meaningful.*

inapplicable *a.* unsuited, unfit, inapt, irrelevant, immaterial, impertinent, incompatible, inappropriate. ANT. *applicable, suitable, relevant.*

inappropriate *a.* unsuitable, unfitting, improper, incompatible, inapt, incorrect, out of line, wrong, unseemly, indecorous. ANT. *appropriate, fitting, suitable.*

inapt *a.* SEE INAPPROPRIATE

inarticulate *a.* mute, incoherent, indistinct, garbled, unintelligible, tongue-tied, speechless, taciturn, reticent, shy. ANT. *articulate, expressive, intelligible.*

inattentive *a.* absentminded, daydreaming, *out to lunch, negligent, distracted, unobservant, faraway, preoccupied, unconscious, heedless. ANT. *sharp, observant, *on the ball, aware.*

inaugurate *v.* **1.** INDUCT install, invest, instate. **2.** BEGIN commence, start, initiate, launch, set in motion, get under way.

inauguration *n.* **1.** INDUCTION installation, investiture, instatement, *swearing in. **2.** BEGINNING commencement, start, initiation, launch, outset, institution.

inborn *a.* innate, inbred, congenital, natural, indigenous, inherent, inherited, native, in the genes, in the blood. ANT. *acquired, learned.*

incalculable *a.* inestimable, immeasurable, countless, infinite, innumerable, unnfathomable, endless, limitless, unknowable. ANT. *measurable, finite, limited.*

incapable *a.* unable, inept, incompetent, unskilled, inadequate, insufficient, helpless, impotent, ineffective, unfit, powerless. ANT. *capable, able, competent.*

incapacitated *a.* disabled, crippled, handicapped, debilitated, unfit, disarmed, put out of action, *hamstrung, paralyzed, immobilized.

incarcerate *v.* jail, imprison, lock up, *throw in the slammer, confine, hold in custody, impound. ANT. *free, release, liberate.*

incautious *a.* unwary, careless, rash, reckless, imprudent, impetuous, injudicious, *devil-may-care, bold, unthinking, impulsive. ANT. *careful, wary, prudent, judicious.*

incendiary *a.* rebellious, troublemaking, rabble-rousing, inflammatory, agitating, provocative, stirring, ardent.

incensed *a.* enraged, angry, outraged, furious, wrathful, infuriated, *up in arms, mad, *pissed, irate, indignant, *ticked off, fired up. SEE ANGRY

incentive *n.* motivation, motive, inducement, stimulus, goad, provocation, impetus, spur, consideration, enticement, lure.

inception *n.* start, beginning, origin, outset, birth, commencement, debut, conception, initiation. ANT. *end, close, finish, death.*

INCESSANT *a.* [in SES unt] never ceasing, nonstop. *I'm sick of your incessant complaining.* SYN. unceasing, neverending, relentless, constant, perpetual, continual, unremitting, unending, persistent. ANT. *infrequent, sporadic, intermittent, occasional.*

incident *n.* event, occurrence, happening, experience, affair, episode, occasion, circumstance, matter, scene, encounter.

incidental *a.* casual, accidental, chance, random, odd, *fluky, concidental, secondary, minor, subordinate, unimportant, insignificant, negligible. ANT. *main, central, basic.*

incidentally *adv.* by the way, parenthetically, speaking of that, by the by.

incipient *a.* beginning, commencing, developing, newborn, nascent, initial, embryonic, developing, early.

incision *n.* slit, slash, scratch, gash. SEE CUT

INCISIVE *a.* [in SYE siv] sharp, penetrating to the heart of a matter. *An incisive newspaper story on the homeless changed his attitude.* SYN. sharp, penetrating, trenchant, acute, cutting, biting, piercing, to the point, keen, crisp, probing. ANT. *shallow, superficial, dull.*

incite *v.* instigate, spark, prompt, rouse, stir, spur, provoke, goad, inflame, whip up, agitate, encourage, *egg on. ANT. *dissuade, dampen, stop.*

incivility *n.* rudeness, discourtesy, disrespect, impoliteness, bad manners, tactlessness, roughness, coarseness. ANT. *civility, courtesy, politeness.*

inclement *a.* rough, stormy, harsh, severe, raw, nasty, foul, violent. ANT. *clement, mild, nice.*

inclination *n.* disposition, tendency, proclivity, bent, penchant, propensity, leaning, drift, bias, predilection, preference.

incline *n.* slant, slope, grade, cant, tilt, leaning, rise, pitch, ramp.

incline *v.* slant, slope, cant, tilt, lean, pitch, grade, rise, recline, list.

inclined *a.* disposed, prone, tending, liable, likely, predisposed.

include *v.* involve, incorporate, comprise, hold, embody, contain, comprehend, take into account, number, accommodate, embrace. ANT. *exclude, preclude, omit.*

incognito *a.* in disguise, masked, concealed, clandestine, anonymous.

incoherent *a.* unintelligible, illogical, disjointed, disconnected, incohesive, indistinguishable, rambling, muddled, inarticulate, mumbling. ANT. *coherent, intelligible, understandable, clear.*

income *n.* revenue, profit, gross, net, earnings, pay, *take-home, wages, salary, yield, receipts, gain, proceeds.

incomparable *a.* peerless, unequaled, matchless, unrivaled, superior, supreme, beyond compare, superlative, second to none. ANT. *run-of-the-mill, average, *just another brick in the wall.*

incompatible *a.* unsuited, incongruous, clashing, contrary, contradictory, mismatched, inharmonious, conflicting, opposite, *different as night and day. ANT. *compatible, harmonious, suited, *like hand in glove.*

incompetent *a.* inadequate, incapable, unskilled, inept, unfit, bumbling, useless, *all thumbs, unqualified, bungling, inexpert. ANT. *competent, skilled, capable, expert.*

incomplete *a.* unfinished, lacking, deficient, wanting, imperfect, immature, short, insufficient, rough, fragmentary. ANT. *complete, finished, done.*

incomprehensible *a.* beyond comprehension, unintelligible, baffling, *beyond me, bewildering, *over one's head, unfathomable, unexplainable, deep, profound, mysterious, *clear as mud. ANT. *clear, plain, understandable.*

inconceivable *a.* unimaginable, unthinkable, unbelievable, incredible, incomprehensible, *mind-boggling, hard to grasp, unheard of, fantastic. ANT. *believable, reasonable, plausible.*

inconclusive *a.* undetermined, indefinite, unresolved, *up in the air, ambiguous, vague, open, uncertain, doubtful. ANT. *conclusive, definite, certain.*

INCONGRUOUS *a.* [in KON groo us] not fitting together, incompatible, inharmonious. *The new sports dome looked incongruous among the Victorian mansions.* SYN. incompatible, inharmonious, incongruent, discordant, conflicting, odd, inconsistent, discrepant, clashing, out of place, jarring, unsuited, inappropriate. ANT. *congruous, suitable, compatible, consistent.*

inconsequential *a.* insignificant, unimportant, immaterial, neglible, *small time, *no great shakes, trivial, trifling, piddling. ANT. *consequential, significant, important.*

inconsiderate *a.* thoughtless, insensitive, unthinking, rude, inattentive, boorish, ungracious, discourteous, self-centered. ANT. *considerate, sensitive, thoughtful.*

inconsistent *a.* **1.** IRREGULAR erratic, variable, unstable, changing, fickle, inconstant. **2.** INCOMPATIBLE contradictory, contrary, incongruous, divergent, out of step, conflicting, at odds, incoherent. ANT. **1.** *regular, steady, consistent.* **2.** *compatible, harmonious, congruent.*

INCONSPICUOUS *a.* [in kon SPIK yoo us] not standing out, attracting little attention. *The shoplifter tried to remain as inconspicuous as possible.* SYN. undistinguished, unapparent, indistinct, unnoticeable, low-profile, invisible, hidden, unostentatious, plain, unobtrusive, *fading into the woodwork, *like another brick in the wall. ANT. *conspicuous, distinguished, obvious, *standing out like a sore thumb.*

inconstant *a.* irregular, erratic, variable, unstable, changing, intermittent, unsteady, fickle. ANT. *constant, steady, stable.*

incontrovertible *a.* indisputable, beyond doubt, established, certain, incontestable, solid, undeniable, irrefutable. ANT. *debatable, questionable, doubtful.*

inconvenient *a.* bothersome, troublesome, inopportune, untimely, burdensome, disadvantageous, cumbersome, discommoding. ANT. *convenient, advantageous, timely.*

incorporate *v.* include, involve, embody, comprise, unite, join, integrate, consolidate, merge, combine, associate.

incorrect *a.* wrong, in error, inaccurate, erroneous, faulty, false, inexact, fallacious, *way off. ANT. *correct, right, accurate.*

INCORRIGIBLE *a.* [in KAWR i juh bul] incapable of improving or becoming reformed. *The incorrigible youth was destined for the county jail.* SYN. hardened, hopeless, beyond help, irreformable, irredeemable, lost, intractable, incurable, recidivous, *unbreakable, *dyed in the wool. ANT. *correctable, reformable, curable.*

incorruptible *a.* honest, moral, honorable, virtuous, noble, principled, ethical, righteous, irreproachable, innocent, *squeaky clean. ANT. *corrupt, dishonest, immoral, dishonorable.*

increase *n.* GROWTH rise, enlargement, addition, expansion, enhancement, escalation, upsurge, intensification, broadening, burgeoning. ANT. *decrease, reduction, shrinkage.*

increase *v.* grow, rise, enlarge, add, expand, enhance, escalate, surge, intensify, broaden, burgeon, amplify, swell, advance, heighten, augment, *snowball, mushroom, multiply, build, inflate, double, triple. ANT. *decrease, reduce, shrink, deflate.*

incredible *a.* unbelievable, improbable, inconceivable, farfetched, unimaginable, extraordinary, fantastic, awesome, miraculous, wonderful, astonishing, fabulous, *unreal. ANT. *credible, believable, ordinary.*

INCREDULOUS *a.* [in KREJ oo lus] unbelieving, skeptical. *The cop looked incredulous; clearly he didn't believe the driver's story.* SYN. unbelieving, doubting, skeptical, suspicious, dubious, distrusting, mistrusting, unconvinced, cynical. ANT. *credulous, trusting, believing, gullible.*

increment *n.* addition, accession, step, increase, rise, gain, augmentation, accretion.

incriminate *v.* accuse, charge, *point the finger at, blame, involve, implicate, *blow the whistle on, *squeal.

incurable *a.* fatal, deadly, terminal, uncorrectable, hopeless, inoperable. ANT. *curable, remedial.*

incur *v.* acquire, bring upon oneself, bargain for, contract, provoke.

incursion *n.* inroad, infiltration, encroachment, advance, penetration, invasion, raid, foray.

indebted *a.* obligated, beholden, bound, owing, appreciative, thankful, grateful.

indecency *n.* obscenity, foulness, offensiveness, vulgarity, filthiness, *raunchiness, vileness, incivility, crudity, impropriety.

indecent a. obscene, foul, offensive, vulgar, filthy, *raunchy, vile, crude, *dirty, *X-rated, pornographic, lewd, unseemly, indecorous, indelicate, improper. ANT. *decent, modest, *clean, wholesome.*

indecisive a. **1.** UNCERTAIN wavering, faltering, vacillating, waffling, irresolute, wishy-washy, hesitant, undecided, *of two minds. **2.** IN-CONCLUSIVE unclear, indeterminate, unsettled, *up in the air. ANT. *1. certain, positive, resolute. 2. conclusive, settled.*

indeed adv. truly, certainly, surely, verily, by all means, positively, really.

indefatigable a. tireless, untiring, inexhaustible, unflagging, energetic, unfaltering, dogged, unremitting, persevering, diligent, tenacious. ANT. *slothful, sluggish, anemic.*

indefensible a. inexcusable, unjustifiable, unforgivable, untenable, weak, insupportable. ANT. *defensible, excusable, justifiable.*

indefinite a. uncertain, imprecise, ambiguous, undetermined, inexact, vague, indeterminate, unspecific, unknown, indistinct, ill-defined. ANT. *definite, specific, precise, unambiguous.*

INDELIBLE a. [in DEL uh bul] leaving a lasting impression. *The Kennedy assassination left an indelible impression in my mind.* SYN. fixed, permanent, enduring, indestructible, unforgettable, ingrained, nonerasable, unfading, fast. ANT. *erasable, temporary, fading.*

indelicate a. coarse, rough, crude, gross, offensive, indecorous, tactless, unrefined, indecent, immodest, rude, lewd. ANT. *delicate, refined, decent.*

indent v. dent, depress, dimple, push in, mark, impress, hollow.

independence n. self-determination, self-government, self-reliance, self-sufficiency, autonomy, freedom, liberty. "Resistance to the herd spirit." —Daniel Mason. "The privilege of the strong." —Friedrich Nietzsche. "To live after your own nature." —Thoreau. ANT. *dependence, subordination, subjugation.*

independent a. self-determining, self-governing, self-reliant, self-sufficient, autonomous, sovereign, free, nonpartisan, separate. ANT. *dependent, subordinate, controlled.*

indescribable a. beyond words, inexpressible, nondescript, extraordinary, incredible, strange, wondrous.

indestructible a. unbreakable, lasting, durable, permanent, enduring, immortal, deathless.

indeterminate a. indefinite, inexact, vague, uncertain, inconclusive, unclear, unspeci-

fied.

indicate v. signify, denote, mark, show, point out, express, tell, suggest, demonstrate, imply, designate, specify, symbolize.

indication n. sign, signal, symptom, hint, testimony, evidence, manifestation, intimation, clue, telltale, suggestion, attestation, warning, portent.

indicator n. pointer, dial, gauge, register, sign, guide, index, barometer.

INDICT v. [in DITE] to charge with a crime, accuse. *He was indicted by the grand jury.* SYN. charge, accuse, arraign, cite, incriminate, impute, prosecute, impeach.

INDICTMENT n. [in DITE munt] a formal charge of a crime, a written accusation. *The grand jury handed down an indictment against three gang members.* SYN. charge, accusation, imputation, arraignment, incrimination, implication, complaint, blame, allegation, summons, prosecution, impeachment.

indifference a. apathy, disinterest, unconcern, nonchalance, impassiveness, lack of interest, detachment, stoniness, disregard, insensitivity. "The worst sin toward our fellow creatures." —George Bernard Shaw. ANT. *interest, concern, passion.*

INDIFFERENT a. [in DIF ur unt] unconcerned, not interested, apathetic. *She didn't care who won the election; she was indifferent.* SYN. unconcerned, disinterested, apathetic, impassive, detached, nonchalant, cool, lukewarm, removed, blasé, uninvolved. ANT. *interested, concerned, passionate, involved.*

INDIGENOUS a. [in DIJ uh nus] originating in a specific region, native. *Cactus is indigenous to the American southwest.* SYN. native, aboriginal, natural, endemic, original, homegrown, domestic; innate, inherent, intrinsic. ANT. *foreign, imported, naturalized.*

INDIGENT a. [IN di junt] poor. *The indigent family had no money for luxuries.* SYN. poor, poverty-stricken, needy, impoverished, penniless, destitute, *bad off, *hard up, *broke, *down and out, *struggling to keep the wolf from the door. ANT. *wealthy, rich, well off.*

indignant a. angry, incensed, irate, peeved, *sore, furious, wrathful, miffed, *bent out of shape, fuming, resentful, exasperated. ANT. *pleased, happy, joyful.*

indignation n. anger, fury, wrath, rage, resentment, offense, displeasure, ire, exasperation, irritation, gall. ANT. *delight, pleasure.* SEE ANGER

indignity n. insult, affront, humiliation, embarrassment, outrage, *slap in the face, abuse, slur, disrespect, *snub.

indirect *a.* **1.** ROUNDABOUT circuitous, wandering, divergent, tortuous, digressive, deviating, oblique, sidelong. **2.** INCIDENTAL secondary, unintentional, ancillary, circumstantial. **3.** DISHONEST backhanded, deceitful, sneaky. ANT. *1. direct, straight. 2. primary, direct. 3. direct, honest, straightforward.*

indiscreet *a.* imprudent, unwise, injudicious, careless, thoughtless, inconsiderate, insensitive, hasty, rash. ANT. *discreet, sensitive, considerate.*

indiscretion *n.* imprudence, injudiciousness; blunder, impropriety, mistake, gaffe, misstep, faux pas, lapse, *slip, gaucherie, transgression, offense.

indiscriminate *a.* random, careless, unparticular, casual, uncritical, undiscriminating, haphazard, promiscuous, unmethodical, hit-or-miss, unselective. ANT. *discriminating, selective.*

indispensable *a.* necessary, essential, vital, needed, requisite, required, crucial, fundamental, basic, critical. ANT. *extraneous, dispensable, superfluous.*

indisposed *a.* ill, sick, *under the weather, ailing, *laid up, *out of sorts, *out of action, *feeling crappy.

indisputable *a.* irrefutable, incontestable, undeniable, clear, beyond doubt, incontrovertible, unquestionable, *open and shut, solid. ANT. *questionable, debatable, dubious.*

indistinct *a.* vague, fuzzy, ambiguous, obscure, faint, dim, hazy, unclear, unintelligible, blurry, undefined, out of focus, nebulous, undecipherable. ANT. *distinct, clear, sharp, defined.*

individual *n.* person, human being, body, soul, character, man, woman, guy, girl, boy, personality.

individual *a.* single, separate, distinctive, sole, lone, exclusive, peculiar, particular, unique, singular, characteristic, specific, special, personal. ANT. *group, general, common, universal.*

individuality *n.* personality, character, distinction, difference, uniqueness, singularity, idiosyncrasy, peculiarity, originality, self, temperament.

INDOCTRINATE *v.* [in DAWK truh nate] to teach or instruct, to transfer one's beliefs to another. *The cult thoroughly indoctrinates new members with its beliefs.* SYN. teach, instruct, school, imbue, enlighten, train, implant, instill, *beat into one's head, brain-

wash, program. ANT. *deprogram.

INDOLENT *a.* [IN duh lunt] lazy. *He was homeless because he was indolent, not unlucky.* SYN. lazy, idle, slothful, *allergic to work, listless, inactive, shiftless, do-nothing. ANT. *industrious, bustling, *go-getting.*

indomitable *a.* invincible, unyielding, unconquerable, undefeatable, unbeatable, insurmountable, dogged, steadfast, staunch, resolute, tough. ANT. *yielding, weak, *wimpy.*

indubitably *adv.* certainly, unquestionably, undoubtedly, surely, undeniably, definitely.

induce *v.* bring on, persuade, encourage, produce, influence, talk into, instigate, incite, prompt, cause, abet, prevail upon, sway, effect.

inducement *n.* incentive, motive, *carrot, stimulus, spur, enticement, instigation, reason, cause, *come-on.

induct *v.* bring in, install, instate, swear in, inaugurate.

indulge *v.* gratify, humor, satisfy, spoil, pamper, coddle, accommodate, splurge, treat oneself, *baby oneself.

indulgence *n.* luxury, self-gratification, immoderation, extravagance, treat, excess, satisfaction, *wishfulfillment, intemperance, spoiling, pampering, *babying, catering, splurging.

indulgent *a.* immoderate, extravagant, excessive, *weak, intemperate, pampering, *babying, splurging, lenient, overpermissive.

industrious *a.* hardworking, bustling, on the go, busy, *busy as a bee, hustling, *high octane, aggressive, productive, assiduous, diligent, dynamic, vigorous, constructive. ANT. *indolent, lazy, slothful.*

industry *n.* **1.** BUSINESS manufacturing, enterprise, trade, commerce. **2.** HARD WORK effort, industriousness, labor, toil, diligence, enterprise, activity.

inebriated *a.* drunk, intoxicated, tipsy, *bombed, *smashed, *loaded, *hammered, *sloshed, *drunk as a lord, *drunker than a brewer's fart, *lit to the gills, *under the table. ANT. *sober.*

ineffective *a.* ineffectual, impotent, useless, inadequate, incompetent, vain, futile, unproductive, powerless, fruitless. ANT. *effective, powerful, potent.*

ineffectual *a.* SEE INEFFECTIVE

inefficient *a.* deficient, unfit, inapt, inept, incompetent, *below par, ineffective, wasteful, time-wasting, slow, disorganized, sloppy. ANT. *efficient, effective.*

INEPT *a.* [in EPT] awkward, clumsy, incompetent; unsuitable. *Every beginning carpenter is inept.* SYN. awkward, clumsy, incompetent, unfit, unskilled, bungling, *all thumbs, ungraceful, oafish, maladroit, wrong, unsuitable, inappropriate. ANT. *competent, skilled, graceful, appropriate.*

inequitable *a.* unequal, unfair, uneven, unjust, unbalanced, biased, partial, one-sided. ANT. *equal, fair.*

INERT *a.* [in URT] inactive, motionless. *The substance had completed its chemical reaction and was now inert.* SYN. inactive, still, motionless, lifeless, dead, unresponsive, quiescent, dormant, passive, static, sleepy, sluggish. ANT. *active, moving, reactive.*

inertia *n.* inactivity, stillness, lifelessness, quiescence, passivity, stasis, stagnation, paralysis, sluggishness, laziness. ANT. *activity, motion, business.*

inevitable *a.* unavoidable, inescapable, inexorable, assured, certain, irrevocable, unpreventable, ordained, fated, destined, predetermined. ANT. *avoidable, escapable, preventable.*

inexcusable *a.* unforgivable, unpardonable, unacceptable, outrageous, indefensible, unjustifiable, reprehensible, intolerable. ANT. *forgivable, understandable, acceptable.*

inexhaustible *a.* **1.** UNLIMITED limitless, boundless, infinite, bountiful, measureless, endless. **2.** TIRELESS unflagging. ANT. *1. limited, finite. 2. tiring.*

INEXORABLE *a.* [in EK sur uh bul] unchangeable and unrelenting, inevitable. *Americans have two inexorable fates: death and taxes.* SYN. unchangeable, unalterable, inescapable, inevitable, *carved in stone, unmovable, inflexible, unremitting, unyielding. ANT. *changeable, alterable, flexible.*

inexpensive *a.* cheap, reasonable, bargain, low-priced, *dime-a-dozen, nominal, economical, sale-priced, *budget. ANT. *expensive, costly, exorbitant.*

inexperienced *a.* green, unseasoned, unfamiliar, unschooled, virgin, unfledged, immature, innocent, young, untrained, raw, callow, ignorant, *wet behind the ears, rookie, naive, unsophisticated. ANT. *practiced, veteran, seasoned, sophisticated.*

inexplicable *a.* unexplainable, mysterious, baffling, puzzling, bewildering, incomprehensible, undecipherable, inscrutable. ANT. *explainable, understandable, explicable.*

infallible *a.* unerring, accurate, unfailing, flawless, perfect, reliable, dependable, trustworthy, foolproof, impeccable. ANT. *fallible, inaccurate, imperfect, erring.*

INFAMOUS *a.* [IN fuh mus] having a bad or scandalous reputation, notorious. *The infamous gangster went on trial today.* SYN. notorious, disreputable, disgraceful, scandalous, villainous, dishonorable, shameful, wicked, evil, low, wretched, reprehensible, despicable. ANT. *virtuous, illustrious, noble, revered.*

infamy *n.* bad reputation, scandalous reputation, disgrace, dishonor, disrepute, shame, villainy, evil, wickedness, notoriety, ignominy, opprobrium. ANT. *honor, nobility, repute.*

infant *n.* newborn, tot, toddler. SEE BABY

infantile *a.* babyish, childish, juvenile, immature, spoiled.

infatuated *a.* enamored, smitten, charmed, bewitched, beguiled, taken with, spellbound, in love, *stuck on, *hung up on, *gaga over, *hot for, *having a crush on, *carried away with. ANT. *repulsed, disgusted, repelled.*

infect *v.* contaminate, poison, taint, pollute, affect, disease, defile, corrupt, befoul.

infectious *a.* catching, contagious, spreading, communicable, transmittable, transferable, epidemic, pestilent, poisonous, toxic, virulent.

INFER *v.* [in FUR] to deduce or come to a conclusion, to suppose something from a set of facts. *The police infer that a lack of eye contact may point to a guilty conscience.* SYN. deduce, conclude, gather, suppose, assume, presume, *put two and two together, figure, arrive at, guess, surmise, reckon, judge.

inference *n.* deduction, conclusion, assumption, presumption, corollary, supposition, figuring, guess, reckoning, judgment, interpretation, reasoning.

inferior *a.* poor, bad, awful, second-rate, *bush-league, lousy, mediocre, substandard, low, *junky, *two-bit, subordinate, minor, junior. ANT. *superior, first-rate, *top-drawer, senior.*

infernal *a.* hellish, diabolic, Stygian, fiendish, demonic, satanic, devilish, hateful, outrageous, evil, damned, damnable. ANT. *heavenly, angelic, saintly, godly.*

inferno *n.* hellfire, conflagration. SEE HELL

infertile *a.* barren, sterile, unproductive, unfruitful, infecund, impotent, depleted, exhausted, fallow. ANT. *fertile, productive, fecund.*

infest *v.* overrun, swarm, populate, spread, pervade, flood, fill, overwhelm, teem.

infidel n. nonbeliever, atheist, non-Christian, non-Muslim, pagan, heathen, heretic, dissenter, idolater, agnostic. ANT. *believer, follower.*

infidelity n. unfaithfulness, disloyalty, betrayal, treachery, perfidy, adultery, cheating, *two-timing. ANT. *fidelity, loyalty, faithfulness.*

infiltrate v. pass through, creep in, penetrate, intrude, invade, impregnate, permeate.

infinite a. endless, boundless, limitless, unlimited, countless, immeasurable, innumerable, inexhaustible, astronomical, vast, immense, never ending, eternal, ceaseless, perpetual. ANT. *finite, limited, ending.*

INFINITESIMAL a. [IN fin i TES uh mul] infinitely small, microscopic. *The odds of winning the contest were infinitesimal.* SYN. infinitely small, microscopic, tiny, minute, imperceptible, negligible, inappreciable, atomic, miniscule, slight. ANT. *gigantic, huge, enormous, great.*

infinity n. endlessness, limitlessness, continuum, eternity, inexhaustibility, infinitude, immeasurability, forever, perpetuity, vastness. "A fathomless gulf, into which all things vanish."—Marcus Aurelius. "A dark illimitable ocean, without bound."—John Milton.

infirm a. weak, feeble, sick, faint, shaky, fragile, ailing, frail, debilitated, unsound, powerless, faltering, decrepit. ANT. *strong, robust, sound, powerful.*

inflame v. fire, spark, ignite, agitate, excite, incite, impassion, fan the fire, aggravate, enrage, rile, intensify. ANT. *dampen, extinguish.*

inflammable a. combustible. SEE FLAMMABLE

inflammatory a. fiery, explosive, incendiary, provocative, inciting, rabble-rousing, riotous, instigative.

inflate v. blow up, swell, increase, dilate, distend, expand, puff up, bloat, stretch, grow, balloon. ANT. *deflate, contract, shrink.*

inflexible a. **1.** HARD unyielding, rigid, firm, stiff, unmalleable. **2.** STUBBORN unyielding, adamant, firm, uncompromising, obstinate, rigid, unbending, intractable, fixed, pigheaded. ANT. *1. flexible, soft, malleable. 2. compromising, yielding.*

inflict v. impose, deal out, administer, visit upon, wreak, bring to bear.

influence n. power, pull, control, clout, weight, authority, leadership, pressure, force, effect, dominance, sway.

influence v. sway, control, persuade, move, incline, affect, act on, impact upon, impress, direct, turn, shape, *pull strings, manipulate.

influential a. powerful, persuasive, weighty, compelling, authoritative, effective, consequential, potent, inspiring, charismatic, forceful, important.

inform v. tell, let know, advise, apprise, fill in, enlighten, notify, communicate to, *squeal, *rat on, tattle, snitch, fink.

informal a. casual, relaxed, unofficial, unceremonious, simple, workaday, down-home, breezy, *laid-back, loose, natural. ANT. *formal, ceremonious, stiff, official.*

information n. data, facts, intelligence, knowledge, *dope, *lowdown, news, communication.

informative a. educational, enlightening, instructive, edifying, informational, illuminating, explanatory.

informer n. informant, tattletale, *rat, *fink, snitch, *stool pigeon, *squealer, *weasel, whistle-blower, betrayer.

infraction n. violation, infringement, breach, lawbreaking, transgression, offense, malfeasance, trespass.

infrequent a. rare, seldom, occasional, odd, unusual, exceptional, irregular, limited, *few and far between. ANT. *frequent, often.*

infringe v. trespass, violate, transgress, intrude, encroach, contravene.

infuriate v. enrage, anger, *make one's blood boil, outrage, madden, *burn up, incense, rile, inflame, *get one's dander up. ANT. *pacify, mollify.*

infuse v. instill, impart, imbue, inspire, inculcate, fill, ingrain, infect, implant, suffuse, permeate, introduce.

ingenious a. clever, brilliant, intelligent, resourceful, creative, inventive, shrewd, imaginative, skillful, proficient, *crack. ANT. *uncreative, stupid, unimaginative, *lame.*

ingenuity n. cleverness, brilliance, intelligence, resourcefulness, creativity, inventiveness, shrewdness, imagination, skill, proficiency, genius.

INGENUOUS a. [in JEN yoo us] unsophisticated, unworldly, naive, artless and honest. *Most young children are naturally ingenuous.* SYN. unsophisticated, unworldly, naive, artless, honest, simple, up-front, innocent, childlike, open, sincere, genuine, candid, frank, direct. ANT. *disingenuous, artful, sophisticated, deceitful, insincere.*

ingest v. swallow, consume, eat.

inglorious a. shameful, dishonorable, disgraceful, ignominious, odious, scandalous, disreputable, infamous, reprehensible. ANT. *honorable, commendable.*

ingrained *a.* deep-rooted, fixed, planted, inherent, intrinsic, innate, *built-in, indelible, dyed-in-the-wool, permanent. ANT. *surface, superficial.*

INGRATIATE *v.* [in GRA she ate] to court favor with someone or purposely try to get on his or her good side. *She employed an ingratiating manner to appease her boyfriend.* SYN. court, blandish, *kiss up, *brownnose, charm, flatter, *get on one's good side, *butter up, curry favor, cajole, kowtow.

ingratitude *n.* ungratefulness, unthankfulness.

ingredient *n.* element, component, part, constituent, item.

inhabit *v.* live, abide, reside, lodge, dwell, occupy, stay at, populate.

inhabitant *n.* resident, occupant, lodger, tenant, renter, boarder, citizen, native, denizen.

inhale *v.* breathe, draw a breath, gasp, inspire, sniff.

INHERENT *a.* [in HEER unt, in HER unt] existing naturally, as an inborn trait, innate, native. *The drive to survive is inherent in every living thing.* SYN. natural, inborn, innate, native, existing, instinctive, hereditary, built-in, ingrained, fundamental, essential. ANT. *extrinsic, alien, foreign, unnatural.*

inheritance *n.* legacy, bequest, estate, birthright, endowment, gift.

inhibit *v.* hinder, restrain, check, repress, arrest, cramp, hold back, obstruct, constrict, impede, forbid, prohibit. ANT. *free, encourage, let.*

inhibited *a.* shy, withdrawn, self-conscious, reticent, reserved, guarded, uptight, bashful, self-censoring, stiff. ANT. *spontaneous, outgoing, uninhibited.*

inhibition *n.* **1.** SHYNESS self-consciousness, withdrawal, reticence, reserve, guardedness, uptightness, bashfulness, self-censorship, stiffness. **2.** RESTRAINT restriction, hindrance, check, constriction, blockage, prohibition. ANT. *1. spontaneity, outgoingness, unrestraint. 2. freedom, liberty.*

inhospitable *a.* unfriendly, forbidding, unkind, ungracious, hostile, cold, unwelcoming, aloof, unsociable. ANT. *hospitable, friendly, warm.*

inhuman *a.* beastly, cruel, inhumane, brutal, cold-blooded, merciless, pitiless, heartless, savage, animal, vicious, barbaric, unfeeling, ferocious, malicious. ANT. *human, humane, compassionate, kind.*

inhumane *a.* SEE INHUMAN

inhumanity *n.* beastliness, cruelty, brutality, cold-bloodedness, savagery, viciousness, barbarity, maliciousness. ANT. *humanity, compassion, kindness.*

inimitable *a.* unequaled, unmatched, preeminent, incomparable, unparalleled, unrivaled, unsurpassed, peerless, supreme.

iniquity *n.* wickedness, evil, injustice, sinfulness, wrong, immorality, wrongdoing, godlessness, abomination, infamy, crime. ANT. *virtue, righteousness, morality, justice.*

initial *a.* first, original, primary, beginning, earliest, inaugural, opening, commencing, maiden, embryonic. ANT. *last, final, closing.*

initiate *v.* **1.** START originate, begin, commence, introduce, usher in, institute, launch, establish, kick off, pioneer. **2.** TEACH instruct, train, acquaint with, familiarize with, tutor, train, indoctrinate, inculcate. **3.** INDUCT instate, enroll.

initiation *n.* start, beginning, commencement, entrance, introduction, institution, launch, kickoff, inception, debut, induction.

initiative *n.* **1.** FIRST STEP first move, start, lead, beginning, kickoff. **2.** ENTERPRISE ambition, resourcefulness, hustle, drive, *get up and go, dynamism, push, aggressiveness.

inject *v.* insert, introduce, put in, implant, infuse, imbue, inoculate, *shoot up, *mainline.

injure *v.* harm, damage, hurt, wound, maim, bruise, impair, cripple, weaken, disfigure, mangle, afflict, mutilate, abuse.

injurious *a.* harmful, damaging, hurtful, wounding, maiming, bruising, impairing, crippling, pernicious, weakening, deleterious, disfiguring, destructive. ANT. *healing, helpful, reconstructive.*

injury *n.* harm, damage, hurt, wound, impairment, *boo-boo, indignity, disfigurement, mutilation, trauma, bruise, cut, gash, contusion, laceration, sprain, break, fracture, hemorrhage, scar, abrasion, concussion, dislocation, whiplash.

injustice *n.* unfairness, inequity, mistreatment, inequality, wrong, injury, crime, miscarriage, outrage, offense, inequity, discrimination, bias, grievance. ANT. *justice, fairness, equity.*

inkling *n.* hint, suggestion, indication, glimmer, idea, clue, notion, suspicion, trace.

inn *n.* lodging, hotel, motel, motor inn, motor court, bed and breakfast, hostel, resort, roadhouse.

INNATE *a.* [i NATE] naturally present, as

from birth. *Infants have an innate ability to grasp.* SYN. inborn, natural, native, hereditary, in the blood, inherent, inherited, intrinsic, indigenous, inbred. ANT. *acquired, foreign, alien, learned, unnatural.*

inner *a.* **1.** INTERIOR inside, internal, inward, central, middle. **2.** PRIVATE personal, intimate, mental, psychic, interior, *gut, spiritual, emotional, psychological, secret. ANT. *1. outer, external, exterior. 2. outer, public, surface.*

innocence *n.* **1.** FREEDOM FROM GUILT blamelessness, clean hands, virtue, inculpability, clear conscience, purity, righteousness. **2.** SIMPLICITY naivete, harmlessness, unsophistication, unworldliness, ingenuousness, artlessness, gullibility, unfamiliarity. "The unbounded hope, the heavenly ignorance."—Lord Byron. ANT. *1. guilt, unclean hands, corruption. 2. artfulness, worldliness, sophistication, disengenuousness.*

innocent *a.* **1.** FREE FROM GUILT blameless, pure, *clean, inculpable, above suspicion, sinless, unimpeachable, guilt-free, guiltless, uncorrupt, immaculate, irreproachable. **2.** SIMPLE, AS A CHILD naive, childlike, harmless, unsophisticated, unworldly, ingenuous, artless, gullible, guileless, pure of heart. "Those who not only are guiltless themselves but who think others are."—Josh Billings. ANT. *1. guilty, to blame, culpable, corrupt. 2. sophisticated, worldly, artful, disengenuous.*

INNOCUOUS *a.* [i NOK yoo us] harmless, dull, or causing no controversy or offense. *Her comments were largely innocuous.* SYN. harmless, benign, inoffensive, innocent, painless, insipid, banal, dull, bland, mild, safe, *blah. ANT. *harmful, malignant, noxious, offensive.*

innovation *n.* change, invention, novelty, *new wrinkle, modernization, *new thing, *latest thing, *cutting edge, *last word.

INNUENDO *n.* [IN yoo EN do] a remark or reference made indirectly that implies something negative. *He never insulted the company directly, but by innuendos and subtle hints.* SYN. insinuation, oblique remark, intimation, suggestion, hint, allusion, implication, reference, overtone, *winking compliment, veiled sarcasm.

innumerable *a.* countless, numberless, myriad, *umpteen, incalculable, infinite, untold. ANT. *finite, limited, measurable.*

inoculation *n.* immunization, injection, shot, vaccination.

inoffensive *a.* unobjectionable, innocuous, harmless, clean, innocent, quiet, unobtrusive, wholesome. ANT. *offensive, objectionable.*

inopportune *a.* untimely, inconvenient, ill-timed, unseasonable, disadvantageous, inauspicious, unfavorable. ANT. *opportune, timely.*

inordinate *a.* excessive, immoderate, extravagant, unreasonable, disproportionate, uncalled for, exorbitant, unwarranted. ANT. *reasonable, proportionate, moderate.*

inquire *v.* **1.** ASK question, query, quiz, interrogate, pry, feel out, grill, pump, seek information, cross-examine. **2.** LOOK INTO investigate, probe, examine, scrutinize, inspect, *sniff out, study, track down, *leave no stone unturned.

inquiry *n.* **1.** QUESTIONING query, quiz, interrogation, inquisition, *Q and A, grilling, *third degree, cross-examination. **2.** INVESTIGATION probe, examination, scrutiny, inspection, study, analysis, exploration.

inquisitive *a.* curious, prying, nosy, inquiring, questioning, interested, *dying to know, probing, intrusive, *snooping, *hungry for knowledge. ANT. *uninterested, indifferent.*

inroad *n.* advance, encroachment, incursion, intrusion, trespassing, infiltration, foray, onslaught, infringement.

insane *a.* mentally ill, psychotic, *psycho, *nuts, deranged, crazy, demented, schizophrenic, *cracked, *loony, maniacal, paranoid, mad, *mental, *out of one's mind, *off one's rocker, lunatic, *loco, scatterbrained, not of sound mind, *cuckoo, *flipped out, sick, touched, *wigged out. ANT. *sane, rational, normal.*

insanity *n.* mental illness, psychosis, derangement, dementia, schizophrenia, paranoia, madness, lunacy, craziness, unbalance, psychopathy, diseased mind, loss of reason. "A perfectly rational adjustment to the insane world."—R.D. Laing.

WORD FIND

alcoholic's: delirium tremens, hallucinosis, Korsakoff's psychosis

amnesic flight from reality: fugue state

brain lobe removal treatment: prefrontal lobotomy

conscience, without: antisocial personality; sociopathic

corpse, sexual attraction to: necrophilism

delusion that one is great or powerful: delusions of grandeur

deteriorating behavior due to long-term

stress: decompensation
emotional agitation, extreme: hysteria
excessive, irrational talking: logorrhea
hands, delusion one has lost one or both: achiria
memory loss, profound: amnesia
mood swings disorder: manic-depressive psychosis
multiple personality: multiple personality, split personality
nonstop talking: logomania
odor hallucination: phantosmia
overeating, pathologic: hyperphagia
perception of sights, sounds, smells that aren't there: hallucination
persecution, delusions of: paranoia
pregnant, delusion that one is: pseudocyesis
primitive behavior, reverting to: atavism
psychosis involving thought processes, moods, emotion: schizophrenia
schizophrenia marked by constant silly grin: hebephrenia
shock therapy: electroconvulsive therapy
stupor marked by muteness, motionlessness: catatonia
unstable or rapidly changing moods: lability
SEE MANIA, NEUROSIS, PHOBIA

insatiable a. unquenchable, ravenous, voracious, unappeasable, gluttonous, greedy, unsatisfiable, wanting, desiring, *hungry for more. ANT. satiable, satisfiable.

inscrutable a. unfathomable, mysterious, enigmatic, impenetrable, unknowable, indecipherable, hidden, incomprehensible, unreadable, secret. ANT. knowable, readable, obvious.

insecure a. 1. UNSURE uncertain, anxious, lacking confidence, doubtful, diffident, timid, shy, apprehensive. 2. UNSAFE defenseless, vulnerable, unprotected, unguarded, exposed, dangerous, hazardous, perilous, precarious. ANT. 1. confident, sure. 2. safe, guarded, defended, invulnerable.

insensitive a. unfeeling, thoughtless, inconsiderate, indifferent, obtuse, callous, unconcerned, hardened, thick-skinned, unrefined. ANT. sensitive, considerate, thoughtful.

insert v. put in, inject, implant, introduce, pop in, tuck in, enter, imbed, place, stick, root, inlay, *shoehorn. ANT. remove, extract.

inside n. interior, middle, innards, soul, guts, heart.

INSIDIOUS a. [in SID ee us] working in a treacherous or sneaky way and quietly producing severe results. Cancer is frequently insidious; by the time victims learn they have it, it may be too late. SYN. treacherous, sneaky, sly, tricky, quietly damaging, guileful, underhanded, subtle, stealthy, slippery, covert, shady, Machiavellian. ANT. overt, blatant, innocuous.

insight n. awareness, observation, wisdom, sensitivity, intuitiveness, intuition, understanding, grasp, perception, discernment, sagacity, ken.

insignia n. emblem, badge, mark, patch, decoration, regalia.

insignificant a. inconsequential, unimportant, trivial, trifling, meaningless, petty, negligible, *no great shakes, inappreciable, not worth mentioning, piddling, picayune, minor. ANT. important, weighty, meaningful.

insincere a. ungenuine, *fake, dishonest, phony, disingenuous, *put-on, deceitful, hypocritical, two-faced, pretended, slick, pretentious, fulsome. ANT. sincere, genuine, honest, *real.

insinuate v. imply, suggest, indicate, hint, intimate, allude, cast innuendos.

INSIPID a. [in SIP id] dull, lifeless, bland. Television programming is growing ever more insipid. SYN. dull, lifeless, bland, vapid, tasteless, prosaic, flavorless, *blah, uninteresting, boring, tiring, colorless, weak, *lame. ANT. interesting, stimulating, exciting, colorful.

insist v. demand, require, command, *lay down the law, stand firm, urge, contend, maintain, aver.

insolence n. disrespect, boldness, impertinence, impudence, arrogance, nerve, gall, *balls, cheek, effrontery, back talk, *lip, *guff, haughtiness. ANT. respect, deference, courtesy.

INSOLENT a. [IN suh lunt] boldly disrespectful, arrogant. Insolent youths disrupted the class. SYN. disrespectful, bold, impertinent, impudent, arrogant, *nervy, *ballsy, *smartalecky, *wise, *flip, cheeky, insulting. ANT. respectful, deferential, courteous.

INSOLVENT a. [in SAWL vunt] unable to pay one's bills or debts. The company became insolvent and declared bankruptcy. SYN. indebted, ruined, *behind, *broke, wiped out, bankrupt, penniless, in arrears, *in the red, *in the hole, *strapped, *hard up. ANT. solvent, in the black, profitable.

insouciant a. carefree, lighthearted, buoyant, happy-go-lucky, untroubled, devil-may-care, airy, free and easy, sunny. ANT. anxious, troubled, worried.

inspect v. examine, scrutinize, look over, check, eye, scan, study, survey, peruse, probe, *give the once-over.

inspection n. examination, scrutiny, check, scan, study, survey, perusal, probe, *once-over, audit, inventory.

inspiration n. motivation, stimulus, provocation, prompting, spur, sparking, igniting, idea, *flash, spark, flight of fancy, vision, insight.

inspire v. influence, stimulate, impel, arouse, prompt, motivate, spur, encourage, spark, stir, excite, ignite, inflame, trigger, give rise to. ANT. discourage, stifle, dampen.

instability a. unstableness, unsteadiness, shakiness, imbalance, precariousness, insecurity, variability, inconstancy, impermanence, vacillation, fickleness, capriciousness, volatility. ANT. stability, equilibrium, steadiness.

install v. put in, place, fix, set, situate, position, locate, establish, induct, instate, inaugurate, invest.

installment a. 1. INSTALLATION emplacement, fixing, positioning, locating, establishment. 2. SEGMENT portion, section, part, fragment, division, chapter, serial.

instance n. example, case, situation, sampling, exemplification, time, particular, occasion.

instant n. moment, split second, *heartbeat, *wink/blink of an eye, *flash, *jiffy, *twinkling, *nothing flat.

instant a. immediate, quick, sudden, direct, fast, prompt, swift, instantaneous, split second, quick, direct, abrupt. ANT. slow, delayed.

instantly adv. immediately, at once, instantaneously, now, directly, tour de suite, *PDQ, without delay, forthwith.

instigate v. incite, foment, initiate, urge on, egg on, spur, prompt, goad, start, begin, encourage, *whip up, kindle, spark, rally. ANT. discourage, stop, check, quell.

instigator n. troublemaker, *spark, *sparkplug, spur, rabble-rouser, initiator, fomenter, incendiary, *provocateur, *agent provocateur.

instill v. infuse, imbue, implant, impart, inculcate, indoctrinate, introduce, engender, brainwash, program, inject, impress.

instinct n. 1. DRIVE intuition, impulse, *gut feeling, urge, sense, prompting. 2. APTITUDE tendency, bent, knack, talent, proclivity.

instinctive a. innate, inborn, inbred, inherent, natural, reflexive, automatic, impulsive, intuitive, unthinking, involuntary, *gut. ANT. acquired, learned, unnatural.

institute n. institution, organization, company, establishment, society, association, union, school, academy, college.

institute v. begin, establish, set up, found, originate, develop, *usher in, create, organize, launch, fix, introduce.

institution n. 1. SEE INSTITUTE 2. CUSTOM law, practice, convention, principle, system, code, tradition, bylaw.

instruct v. 1. TEACH school, train, show how, educate, tutor, enlighten, edify, indoctrinate, inform, drill, acquaint. 2. ORDER command, direct, charge, enjoin.

instruction n. 1. EDUCATION teaching, direction, training, grounding, tutelage, drilling, enlightenment, edification, indoctrination. 2. COMMAND demand, direction, order, directive, mandate, charge.

instructor n. teacher, educator, trainer, tutor, coach, mentor, master, professor, counselor, guide, pedagogue.

instrument n. 1. TOOL implement, appliance, apparatus, contrivance, device, mechanism, utensil, machine, contraption, *gizmo. 2. SEE MUSICAL INSTRUMENT 3. MEANS agent, vehicle, medium, tool, way, mechanism.

instrumental a. helpful, useful, effectual, valuable, serviceable, of assistance, contributory, influential, vital, determining.

insubordinate a. disobedient, defiant, rebellious, uncompliant, contrary, refractory, uncooperative, dissentious, *too big for one's britches. ANT. subordinate, deferential, obedient, compliant.

insubordination n. disobedience, defiance, rebellion, noncompliance, noncooperation, dissension, revolt, insurrection, resistance. ANT. subordination, obedience, deference.

insubstantial a. 1. SLIGHT flimsy, airy, tenuous, light, gossamer, ethereal, delicate, weak. 2. IMAGINARY unreal, immaterial, intangible, phantom, illusive, impalpable. ANT. substantial, hefty, real.

insufferable a. intolerable, unbearable, unendurable, agonizing, impossible, too much, excruciating, torturous. ANT. tolerable, bearable.

insufficient a. deficient, lacking, inadequate, wanting, short, not enough, incomplete, shy, scant, missing, unsatisfactory, incommensurate. ANT. enough, sufficient, plenty.

INSULAR a. [IN suh lur] isolated like an island, detached. *The hermit lived an insular lifestyle in the woods.* SYN. isolated, detached, separated, sequestered, insulated, lonely, cloistered, secluded, cut off, provincial, narrow-minded. ANT. *connected, urban, *in touch, broad-minded.*

insult n. affront, *put-down, slight, *slap in the face, dig, offense, snub, denigration, abuse, attack, *cheap shot, slam, impudence. ANT. *compliment, praise, *pat on the back.*

insult v. affront, *put down, slight, cut, *slap in the face, dig, offend, snub, denigrate, abuse, attack, slam, *cut to the quick, ridicule, *dump on, belittle. ANT. *compliment, praise, flatter.*

insulting a. offensive, abusive, hurtful, disparaging, cutting, disrespectful, derogatory, ridiculing, denigrating, insolent. ANT. *complimentary, flattering, respectful.*

insurance n. security, protection, guarantee, pledge, assurance, warranty, backing, indemnity, safeguard.

insurgent n. rebel, revolutionist, mutineer, insurrectionist.

insurmountable a. insuperable, unconquerable, invincible, unassailable, unbeatable, formidable, impossible, hopeless, impassable. ANT. *surmountable, superable.*

INSURRECTION n. [in suh REK shun] a rebellion or revolt against established authority. *The insurrection of the masses stunned the king.* SYN. rebellion, revolt, uprising, revolution, mutiny, sedition, insubordination, coup, overthrow.

intact a. whole, undamaged, all together, unbroken, sound, unimpaired, complete, unharmed, unscathed, all in one piece. ANT. *broken, damaged, shattered.*

INTANGIBLE a. [in TAN juh bul] that which cannot be physically perceived, impalpable. *The soul is intangible.* SYN. impalpable, imperceptible, invisible, untouchable, incorporeal, unapparent, immaterial, indefinite, elusive. ANT. *tangible, palpable, physical.*

integral a. essential, central, basic, indispensable, fundamental, elemental, necessary, component. ANT. *inessential, unnecessary.*

integrate v. unify, unite, combine, mix, merge, consolidate, combine, amalgamate, fuse, desegregate. ANT. *divide, separate, segregate.*

integrity n. 1. UPRIGHTNESS goodness, honesty, honor, morality, virtue, character, incorruptibility, rectitude, probity, decency. 2. COMPLETENESS wholeness, unity, soundness. ANT. 1. *improbity, immorality, dishonor, corruption.* 2. *fragmentation, unsoundness.*

intellect n. brain power, reason, sense, intelligence, *brains, comprehension, understanding, wits, judgment, cognition, intuition, aptitude, genius, *smarts, mental agility.

intellectual n. *brain, *egghead, thinker, scholar, genius, *Einstein, pundit, academic, savant, mental giant, philosopher, highbrow, *walking encyclopedia, *know-it-all. "A person educated beyond his intellect." — Horace Porter. "Those who are all head but can't sew on a button." — Anon. "A man who takes more words than necessary to tell us more than he knows." — Dwight D. Eisenhower. ANT. *moron, imbecile, ignoramus, idiot.*

intellectual a. smart, intelligent, *brainy, cerebral, learned, scholarly, educated, well-schooled, literate, bookish, erudite.

intelligence n. 1. SMARTNESS intellect, mind, brain power, brains, *smarts, *gray matter, *IQ, reasoning, sense, comprehension, understanding, wits, judgment, aptitude, genius, brilliance, cleverness, acumen, wisdom, astuteness, sagacity, creativity. "The thing that enables a man to get along without an education." — Albert Wiggam. 2. INFORMATION news, report, data, facts, *lowdown, surveillance.

intelligent a. smart, intellectual, *brainy, brilliant, bright, wise, astute, clever, sharp, knowledgeable, ingenious, perceptive, witty, resourceful, creative, quick, sagacious, *having a good head on one's shoulders, sensible. ANT. *stupid, moronic, dense, ignorant.*

intelligible a. clear, comprehensible, understandable, plain, distinct, umistakable, unambiguous. ANT. *unintelligible, unclear, incomprehensible.*

intend v. plan, have in mind, mean, aim at, aspire to, propose, expect, design, figure on, plot, scheme, devise.

intended a. planned, designed, meant, devised, intentional, expected, set, prearranged, deliberate, premeditated. ANT. *unintentional, accidental, unplanned.*

intense a. concentrated, acute, strong, severe, powerful, deep, extreme, violent, sharp, fierce, potent, high, vivid, passionate, earnest, ardent, fervent, vigorous. ANT. *mild, light, weak, gentle.*

intensify v. concentrate, strengthen, deepen, sharpen, heighten, magnify, amplify, escalate, raise, *beef up, step up, redouble. ANT. *weaken, lighten, diminish.*

intensity n. force, concentration, strength, power, magnitude, severity, potency, vigor, depth, volume, ferocity, violence, sharpness, passion, earnestness, ardor, fervor. ANT. *weakness, lightness, emptiness.*

intensive *a.* concentrated, thorough, profound, exhaustive, strengthened, stepped-up, increased, heightened, comprehensive, in-depth. ANT. *weakened, diluted, diminished.*

intent *n.* intention, purpose, goal, aim, design.

intent *a.* determined, resolved, resolute, intense, concentrated, set, steadfast, committed, *hell-bent.

intention *n.* purpose, intent, goal, aim, design, plan, object, end, target.

intentional *a.* deliberate, planned, intended, designed, calculated, meant, willful, on purpose, premeditated, voluntary. ANT. *unintentional, accidental, unplanned.*

inter *v.* bury, entomb, lay to rest, inhume, consign to the grave. ANT. *exhume, dig up.*

intercede *v.* mediate, arbitrate, advocate, plead for, petition for, step in, intervene, interpose.

intercept *v.* stop, head off, cut off, catch, seize, arrest, check, confiscate, impound.

intercourse *n.* **1.** COPULATION sexual relations, coitus, lovemaking, *screwing, *humping, mating, carnal knowledge, *balling, *going all the way, *jumping one's bones, *making out, *scoring, *roll in the hay, *parallel parking. **2.** COMMUNICATION exchange, interchange, interplay, correspondence, connection, liaison.

interest *n.* **1.** CURIOSITY engagement, attention, engrossment, attraction, notice, regard, concern. **2.** SHARE claim, stake, investment, right, involvement, percentage. **3.** ADVANTAGE benefit, welfare, profit, gain. ANT. *indifference, boredom, apathy.*

interesting *a.* engaging, engrossing, fascinating, riveting, entertaining, diverting, absorbing, stimulating, intriguing, enthralling, provocative, gripping. ANT. *boring, dull, insipid.*

interfere *v.* *butt in, intervene, meddle, intercede, obtrude, intrude, interpose, horn in, hinder, impede, obstruct.

interim *n.* meantime, interval, interlude, break, pause, interruption, hiatus, intermission.

interim *a.* temporary, stopgap, intervening, provisional, makeshift.

interior *n.* inside, center, innards. ANT. *exterior.*

interior *a.* inner, internal, inside, inward, innermost, central. ANT. *exterior, outer.*

interject *v.* throw in, insert, interrupt, interpose, introduce.

interloper *n.* intruder, meddler, trespasser, busybody, outsider.

interlude *n.* pause, recess, break, intermission, rest, lull, interval, interim.

intermediary *n.* go-between, mediator, middle-man, agent, medium, negotiator, arbitrator, intermediate, referee, interceder, broker.

intermediate *a.* intervening, in-between, halfway, middle, median, midway, intervening, compromising.

interment *n.* burial, entombment, inhumation.

interminable *a.* endless, eternal, neverending, everlasting, limitless, ceaseless, continuous, incessant, nonstop, infinite, constant. ANT. *fleeting, finite, limited.*

intermingle *v.* mix, blend, combine, commingle, compound, merge, amalgamate, fuse.

intermission *n.* break, pause, recess, interim, interlude, breather, time-out, rest, lull, interruption.

intermittent *a.* sporadic, irregular, periodic, off and on, broken, now and then, occasional, alternate, infrequent. ANT. *regular, constant.*

internal *a.* inner, interior, within, inside, gut, innate, intrinsic. ANT. *external, outer.*

international *a.* worldwide, multinational, global, intercontinental, universal, cosmopolitan. ANT. *domestic, local.*

interpret *v.* **1.** CONSTRUE read, understand, view, define, explain, explicate, clarify, shed light on, spell out, illuminate. **2.** TRANSLATE transcribe, paraphrase.

interrogate *v.* question, ask, probe, cross examine, quiz, query, grill, pump, *give the third degree, inquire, *pick one's brains.

interrupt *v.* **1.** INTRUDE *butt in, break in, cut in, *chime in, interject, inject, horn in, speak out of turn, obtrude, disturb, interfere. **2.** STOP suspend, halt, discontinue, break off.

intersect *v.* cross, traverse, bisect, divide, crosscut.

intersperse *v.* sprinkle, strew, scatter, pepper, distribute, diffuse, disseminate, broadcast.

interval *n.* pause, rest, break, recess, intermission, hiatus, interim, gap, space, period, spell, lull.

intervene *v.* step in, intercede, interfere, mediate, arbitrate, interpose, come between, obtrude, meddle.

interview *n.* *Q and A, inquiry, press conference, probe, talk, conference, exchange, meeting, parley, dialogue, *tete-a-tete, examination, hearing.

intestines *n.* bowels, guts, viscera, entrails, innards, alimentary canal.

intimacy *n.* closeness, fellowship, communion, friendship, understanding, acquaintance, confidentiality, sharing, disclosing, chumminess, familiarity, affection. ANT. *alienation, isolation, aloofness, estrangement.*

intimate v. suggest, announce, state, *tip off, hint at, tell, *let the cat out of the bag, *spill the beans, leak, insinuate, imply, allude.

intimate a. **1.** PERSONAL private, confidential, privy, secret, innermost, *gut. **2.** CLOSE familiar, friendly, acquainted, dear, chummy, personal, bosom. **3.** COZY romantic, quiet, comfortable, warm, snug. **4.** SEXUAL carnal, adulterous, erotic, impure, lustful. ANT. *1. public.* *2. distant, remote, aloof, formal.* *3. crowded, loud, uncomfortable.*

intimation n. suggestion, hint, clue, inkling, allusion, insinuation, implication, tip, innuendo.

intimidate v. scare, frighten, cow, threaten, daunt, bully, unnerve, terrify, terrorize, awe, appall, silence, coerce, strong-arm, twist one's arm.

intolerable a. insufferable, unbearable, unendurable, agonizing, excruciating, unacceptable, too much, extreme, monstrous, unreasonable, outrageous. ANT. *tolerable, acceptable.*

intolerant a. bigoted, illiberal, closed-minded, narrow-minded, prejudiced, uncharitable, inconsiderate, biased, chauvinistic, sexist, racist, *homophobic, xenophobic, misanthropic, contemptuous, disdainful, arrogant. ANT. *tolerant, liberal, open-minded.*

intoxicated a. drunk, inebriated, tipsy, besotted, *high, *smashed, *hammered, *loaded, *buzzed, *drunker than a brewer's fart, *drunk as a lord, *tanked, under the influence, soused, *drunk as a lord, *three sheets to the wind. ANT. *sober, *on the wagon.*

INTRACTABLE a. [in TRAK tuh bul] unmanageable, uncontrollable or stubborn. *The two-year-old is famous for his intractable demeanor.* SYN. unmanageable, uncontrollable, stubborn, disobedient, rebellious, obstinate, ungovernable, difficult, headstrong, contrary, unruly, wild, intransigent. ANT. *obedient, docile, compliant, easy.*

INTRANSIGENT a. [in TRAN si junt] uncompromising and stubborn. *Smith was intransigent; nobody could negotiate with him and win.* SYN. uncompromising, stubborn, obstinate, mulish, pigheaded, unbending, unyielding, rigid, steadfast, die-hard, resolute, *hard-nosed, persistent. ANT. *compromising, yielding, flexible, *easy.*

INTREPID a. [in TREP id] fearless, courageous. *The intrepid explorers bushwacked their way deeper into the jungle.* SYN. fearless, courageous, brave, dauntless, bold, daring,

*gutsy, *ballsy, adventurous, valiant, lionhearted, game, plucky, heroic. ANT. *cowardly, frightened, mousy, *wimpy, craven.*

intricate a. complex, complicated, involved, convoluted, knotty, labyrinthine, elaborate, sophisticated, thorny, perplexing, tough. ANT. *simple, uninvolved, easy.*

intrigue n. plotting, scheme, machination, conspiracy, maneuver, finagling, manipulation, trickery, double-dealing, cabal.

intrigue v. **1.** PLOT scheme, machinate, conspire, maneuver, finagle, manipulate, trick, double-deal. **2.** INTEREST fascinate, pique one's interest, attract, grab, captivate, excite, appeal, draw, arouse.

INTRINSIC a. [in TRIN sik] naturally or inherently belonging. *His success was partially due to an intrinsic aggressiveness.* SYN. inherent, natural, essential, innate, internal, inbred, native, inherited, built-in, basic, fundamental, constitutional. ANT. *extrinsic, external, outer.*

introduce v. **1.** ACQUAINT present, familiarize. **2.** START begin, open, *get the ball rolling, launch, set in motion, usher in, lead off, *kick off, initiate. **3.** PUT IN insert, add, inject, interject, work in, enter, instill, infuse.

introduction n. **1.** START beginning, opening, lead, commencement, *intro, launching, initiation. **2.** PREFACE foreword, prologue, preamble, prelude. ANT. *end, afterword.*

introductory a. opening, beginning, starting, initial, preliminary, first, inaugural, preparatory, prefatory. ANT. *concluding, final.*

introspective a. [IN truh SPEC tiv] observing one's own thoughts, feelings, inner self, etc. *Joe was always analyzing his own mind; he was introspective.* SYN. introverted, self-analyzing, self-examining, soul-searching, pensive, contemplative, meditative, self-occupied, consciousness-raising, in deep thought. ANT. *outer-directed, extroverted.*

intrude v. obtrude, invade, interfere, barge in, *horn in, infringe, meddle, *butt in, interpose, *gate-crash, encroach, trespass, interlope.

intrusive a. obtrusive, invasive, unwelcome, unwanted, meddlesome, interfering, *nosy, officious, *overstepping one's bounds.

intuition n. sense, sixth sense, hunch, feeling, instinct, insight, *feeling in one's bones, *gut instinct, *vibes, inkling, perception, discernment, apprehension.

intuitive a. instinctive, *gut, innate, natural, inherent, automatic, *seat of the pants, perceptive, psychic.

inundate *v.* flood, deluge, engulf, drown, swamp, submerge, overwhelm, overpower, glut, bury.

inure *v.* habituate, accustom, harden, desensitize, season, toughen, temper, acclimate.

invade *v.* encroach, trespass, attack, assault, assail, strike, storm, swarm, blitz, occupy, overrun, intrude, interlope, *gate-crash.

invalid *n.* sick person, convalescent, cripple, shut-in, patient.

invalid *a.* **1.** NULL AND VOID unenforceable, impotent, nonviable, inoperative, useless, worthless, not binding. **2.** FALSE unfounded, wrong, untrue, fallacious, baseless, unsubstantiated, unproven. **3.** SICKLY weak, feeble, bedridden, disabled, crippled, infirm, frail. ANT. *1. valid, viable, binding. 2. true, substantiated, correct. 3. strong, able-bodied.*

invalidate *v.* void, nullify, annul, cancel, repeal, countermand, revoke, negate, disqualify, quash. ANT. *validate.*

invaluable *a.* valuable, priceless, precious, indispensable, helpful, *worth its weight in gold. ANT. worthless.*

invariable *a.* unvarying, unchanging, constant, steady, consistent, unwavering, stable, regular, uniform, unbroken, undeviating. ANT. *variable, varying, changing, inconstant.*

invasion *n.* attack, assault, strike, storm, encroachment, trespass, incursion, intrusion, onslaught, infringement, offensive, blitz.

INVECTIVE *n.* [in VEK tiv] a verbal attack, insults, criticism. *He continued his invective until she was in tears.* SYN. verbal attack, verbal abuse, censure, tongue-lashing, vilification, diatribe, tirade, disparagement, condemnation, harsh words, sarcasm.

inveigh *v.* verbally attack, rail against, assail, vituperate, censure, denounce, vilify, criticize, scold, castigate, condemn, remonstrate.

inveigle *v.* entice, lure, seduce, *suck in, tempt, tantalize, manipulate, cajole, bait, *string along, *rope in, *lead on.

invent *v.* **1.** CREATE devise, come up with, think up, originate, design, shape, conceive, forge, fabricate, improvise, concoct, develop, fashion. **2.** LIE fabricate, fib, prevaricate, *tell a white lie, distort, trump up, make up.

invention *n.* **1.** CREATION innovation, concoction, *brainchild, original, design, composition, fabrication, construction, contrivance, formulation, discovery. "Bringing out the secrets of nature and applying them for the happiness of man." — Thomas Edison. **2.** LIE

fabrication, fib, prevarication, white lie, distortion, falsehood, *tall tale.

inventive *a.* creative, ingenious, imaginative, resourceful, artistic, gifted, *brainy, visionary, clever, constructive, productive, fertile, *having a Da Vinci-like mind.

inventor *n.* creator, originator, father, discoverer, designer, deviser, innovator, craftsman, builder, tinkerer, pioneer. "A man with wheels in his head." — Anon.

inverse *a.* reversed, inverted, opposite, back to front, turned, contrary, transposed. ANT. *obverse.*

invest *v.* **1.** INVEST MONEY venture, speculate, risk, put money into, *plow profits back into, intrust, *salt away. **2.** GRANT POWER empower, authorize, confer, sanction, enable, license, entrust, ordain, charge. ANT. *1. divest. 2. divest, strip of power.*

investigate *v.* look into, inquire, probe, examine, explore, inspect, research, delve into, review, nose around, scrutinize, sift, muckrake, *check out, *case.

investigation *n.* inquiry, probe, inspection, inquest, *fact-finding mission, search, analysis, review, exploration, scrutiny, study.

investigator *n.* examiner, analyst, reviewer, inspector, inquirer, inquisitor, fact finder, research, detective, *sleuth, *private eye.

INVETERATE *a.* [in VET ur it] habitual, long-standing, chronic. *She was an inveterate liar.* SYN. habitual, long-standing, chronic, deeply rooted, long-established, ingrained, deep-seated, incurable, entrenched, hardcore, dyed-in-the-wool. ANT. *reformed, cured.*

invidious *a.* insulting, offensive, hateful, malicious, spiteful, hostile, odious, slighting, baleful, discriminatory. ANT. *complimentary, flattering, sweet.*

invigorating *a.* energizing, enlivening, refreshing, stimulating, vitalizing, restorative, bracing, strengthening, animating. ANT. *tiring, somnolent, weakening.*

invincible *a.* unconquerable, unbeatable, indestructible, indomitable, invulnerable, insuperable, impregnable, mighty, powerful, inviolable. ANT. *vulnerable, weak, conquerable.*

invisible *a.* imperceptible, imperceivable, impalpable, intangible, hidden, indiscernible, out of sight, unseen, transparent. ANT. *visible, perceivable, palpable.*

invitation *n.* bidding, summons, call, request, solicitation.

invite *v.* ask for, beckon, summon, request, solicit, bid, court, woo, petition.

inviting a. alluring, enticing, tempting, attractive, captivating, magnetic, seductive, appealing, welcoming, beguiling. ANT. *repulsive, repellent, forbidding.*

invoke v. call on, call forth, summon, petition, entreat, request, implore, supplicate, appeal to, conjure, solicit.

involuntary a. unintentional, reflexive, automatic, instinctive, spontaneous, unpremeditated, unthinking, uncalculated, forced. ANT. *voluntary, intentional, calculated.*

involve v. include, comprise, engage, contain, incorporate, concern, affect, entail, encompass, comprehend, implicate.

invulnerable a. indestructible. SEE INVINCIBLE

iota n. jot, speck, scintilla, bit, shred, whiff, mite, smidgen, atom, dot, particle, fleck.

IRASCIBLE a. [i RAS uh bul] quick-tempered or easily angered. *Mike was irascible; we walked on eggshells around him.* SYN. quick-tempered, easily angered, touchy, testy, irritable, bad-tempered, *short-fused, grouchy, cantankerous, grumpy, ornery, crabby, snappish. ANT. *easygoing, good-humored, mild-mannered, serene.*

irate a. angry, mad, furious, infuriated, incensed, *up in arms, livid, indignant, wrathful, inflamed, *foaming at the mouth, *gone ballistic. SEE ANGRY

ire n. anger, rage, fury, indignation, wrath, displeasure, choler, vexation, dudgeon, passion, irritation, *Irish. SEE ANGER

irk v. annoy, irritate, *bug, aggravate, nettle, peeve, bother, harass, fret, gall, *get on one's nerves, *try one's patience, *get under one's skin.

irksome a. annoying, irritating, aggravating, nettlesome, bothersome, vexing, troubling, troublesome, wearisome, tiring.

iron a. hard, strong, powerful, tough, firm, unyielding, unbending, rigid, steel, stony, cruel, merciless. ANT. *soft, weak, yielding.*

ironclad a. unalterable, fixed.

IRONIC a. [i RON ik] opposite of or incongruous with what is expressed or expected. *He said he loved steamed clams, but he was speaking ironically; clams actually nauseated him.* SYN. sarcastic, mocking, contradictory, paradoxical, double-edged, sardonic, satirical, unexpected, surprising.

irony n. double meaning, contradiction, sarcasm, incongruity, paradox, satire, mocking, lampoon, twist, wit. "Jesting hidden behind gravity." — John Weiss.

irrational a. senseless, unthinking, unreasonable, foolish, illogical, crazy, mindless, unwise, stupid, unsound, unscientific, halfbaked, *cockamamy, idiotic. ANT. *rational, sane, sensible, wise.*

irreconcilable a. irreparable, unresolvable, conflicting, hostile, incompatible, contrary, at odds, intransigent, inflexible. ANT. *resolvable, compatible.*

irrefutable a. undeniable, unquestionable, certain, indisputable, sure, proven, incontrovertible, beyond a shadow of a doubt. ANT. *debatable, questionable, moot.*

irregular a. **1.** VARIABLE erratic, uneven, fitful, random, sporadic, inconsistent, changeable, disordered, spasmodic. **2.** ANOMALOUS abnormal, deviant, unusual, odd, unexpected, strange, eccentric, singular, peculiar, quirky. **3.** UNEVEN asymmetrical, crooked, variable. ANT. *1. regular, consistent, even. 2. normal, typical, usual. 3. even, symmetrical.*

irrelevant a. impertinent, immaterial, unrelated, beside the point, not germane, unconnected, inapplicable, neither here nor there, extraneous. ANT. *relevant, pertinent, germane.*

irreligious a. atheistic, impious, faithless, agnostic, unholy, ungodly, profane, heathen, pagan. ANT. *religious, pious, faithful.*

irreparable a. beyond repair, irrevocable, ruined, irretrievable, *consigned to the scrap heap, *done, *shot, *kaput, hopeless. ANT. *repairable, salvageable.*

irrepressible a. unrestrainable, insuppressible, uncontrollable, uninhibited, unbridled, vivacious, lively, effervescent, buoyant.

irreproachable a. beyond reproach, blameless, faultless, inculpable, unblemished, above suspicion, *squeaky clean, virtuous, innocent, pure, upright. ANT. *reproachable, to blame.*

irresistible a. overwhelming, overpowering, powerful, potent, compelling, invincible, unconquerable; fascinating, charming, alluring, captivating, seductive. ANT. *resistible, powerless.*

irresolute a. wavering, indecisive, vacillating, undecided, dubious, wishy-washy, doubtful, hesitant, undetermined, *hot and cold, halfhearted. ANT. *resolute, resolved, firm, determined.*

irresponsible a. careless, unreliable, undependable, devil-may-care, untrustworthy, lax, immature, unaccountable, reckless, capricious. ANT. *responsible, dependable, reliable.*

IRREVERENT a. [ir REV ur unt] disrespectful. *With today's irreverent comedians, even the pope is the subject of dirty jokes.* SYN. disrespectful, contemptuous, mocking, sneering, *wise, rude, impudent, insolent, insulting, *smart-alecky, impious, blasphemous, profane. ANT. *reverent, respectful, civil.*

irrevocable *a.* irreversible, unchangeable, fixed, final, unalterable, permanent, irretrievable, *carved in stone. ANT. *reversible, changeable.*

irritable *a.* grouchy, touchy, cantankerous, irascible, crabby, testy, moody, snappy, grumbling, quick-tempered, petulant, grumpy. ANT. *good-humored, good-natured, even-tempered.*

irritate *v.* **1.** ANNOY *bug, agitate, nettle, disturb, *get under one's skin, try one's patience, exasperate, irk, *drive one up a wall, peeve, *get on one's nerves, plague. **2.** MAKE SORE inflame, aggravate, hurt, chafe, sting, rub, worsen. ANT. *1. please, delight, humor. 2. relieve, soothe.*

isolate *v.* seclude, separate, segregate, dissociate, sequester, set apart, confine, remove, quarantine.

isolation *n.* seclusion, separation, segregation, dissociation, sequestration, loneliness, solitude, confinement, removal, quarantine.

issue *n.* **1.** SUBJECT topic, matter, question at hand, bone of contention, controversy, problem. **2.** RESULT consequence, outcome, end, upshot, conclusion, effect. **3.** INSTALLMENT copy, number.

issue *v.* **1.** PUT OUT give out, distribute, circulate, dispense, disseminate, deliver. **2.** EMIT pour forth, emanate, exude, gush, effuse, stream, ooze.

itch *n.* **1.** URGE TO SCRATCH prickling sensation, tickling, irritation, crawling sensation. **2.** DESIRE craving, urge, yen, thirst, hunger, appetite, hankering, passion.

item *n.* article, thing, part, piece, bit, element, matter, paragraph, story, feature.

itemize *v.* detail, enumerate, count, inventory, tally, list, record, specify, spell out, codify.

itinerant *a.* wandering, roaming, traveling, roving, transient, rambling, journeying, wayfaring, vagabond, nomadic, migratory. ANT. *rooted, settled*

itinerary *n.* route, course, way, tour, path, plan, schedule, agenda, *game plan.

J

jab v. poke, thrust, punch, hit, strike, prod, stab.

jabber v. chatter, gibber, prattle, babble, *run off at the mouth, yak, prate, palaver.

jacket n. **1.** COVER case, wrapper, wrapping, sheath, skin, envelope. **2.** COAT blazer, windbreaker.

WORD FIND

black, waist-length, wide-lapelled: Eton jacket

Eskimo: anorak

fringed deerskin: buckskin jacket

khaki-colored with four large front pockets: safari jacket, bush jacket

knitted, sweaterlike: cardigan

leather flight jacket: bomber jacket

lightweight jacket of waist-length: golf jacket, windbreaker

parka with hood: snorkel

plaid wool: lumber jacket

seaman's: pea jacket, pea coat, reefer

sleeveless: bolero

winter, insulated: parka

woman's loose jacket: paletot

wool with blanketlike patterns: mackinaw

World War II army jacket: Eisenhower jacket, battle jacket

SEE COAT

JADED a. [JAY did] wearied or worn out, as from overindulgence. *He saw it all and grew jaded.* SYN. wearied, worn out, tired, sated, played out, exhausted, cloyed, surfeited, dulled, gorged, inured, bored. ANT. *enthusiastic, interested.*

jagged a. broken, serrated, rough, uneven, ragged, notched, saw-toothed, crenelated, ridged, denticulate. ANT. *smooth, even, level.*

jail n. prison, penitentiary, house of correction, *slammer, lockup, brig, stockade, hoosegow, *clink, *cooler, penal institution, *the big house, *pokey, *the academy.

jail v. imprison, lock up, incarcerate, put behind bars, cage, hold, confine, intern, impound. ANT. *release, free, liberate.*

jam n. trouble, scrape, bind, *hot water, *pickle, hole, predicament, mess, plight.

jam v. **1.** SQUEEZE IN cram, ram, pack, stuff, press, wedge, tamp, *squish, squash, overcrowd, *stuff to the gills. **2.** CLOG plug, obstruct, congest, stick, *gum up the works, *bottleneck.

jamboree n. celebration, party, gathering, revelry, festival, outing, carnival, jubilee, *wingding.

jangle n. clang, rattle, ring, reverberation, jingle, clatter, clangor, cacophony, racket.

jangle v. clang, rattle, ring, reverberate, jingle, clatter, chime, crash.

janitor n. custodian, caretaker, cleaning man, *super, handyman, maintenance man, superintendent.

jar n. vessel, container, bottle, receptacle, jug.

jar v. **1.** SHAKE vibrate, jog, jounce, jolt, shock, jerk, rattle, rock, jiggle. **2.** *FAZE shock, disquiet, disturb, upset, unsettle, shake up, surprise, discompose.

jargon n. **1.** LINGO vernacular, cant, argot, parlance, tongue, slang, idiom, dialect, phraseology, shop talk, *officialese, legalese. **2.** GIBBERISH gobbledygook, mumbo jumbo, nonsense, blather, babble, drivel, twaddle.

jaundiced a. prejudiced, biased, partial, narrow-minded, warped, embittered, jealous, envious, hostile, critical. ANT. *impartial, fairminded.*

jaunt n. short trip, excursion, outing, drive, tour, cruise, stroll, *spin, day trip, airing.

jaunty a. sprightly, carefree, buoyant, self-confident, bouncy, frisky, pert, lighthearted, lively, breezy, debonair.

jealous a. **1.** ENVIOUS green-eyed, green with envy, begrudging, resentful, desirous, covetous. **2.** WATCHFUL guarded, proprietary, possessive, protective, vigilant, wary. ANT. **2.** *trusting.*

jealousy n. envy, *green-eyed monster, resentment, grudge, begrudging, covetousness, spite, distrust, paranoia, suspicion. "Jealousy is all the fun you think they had." — Erica Jong. "The fear or apprehension of superiority." — William Shenstone.

jeer v. mock, taunt, hoot, heckle, scoff, ridicule, sneer, laugh at, tease, hector, deride, boo, hiss. ANT. *cheer, applaud, praise.*

jeopardize v. endanger, imperil, hazard, risk, put in jeopardy, chance, threaten, tempt fate.

jeopardy n. danger, hazard, peril, trouble, *double-trouble, threat, menace, insecurity, exposure, vulnerability, liability. ANT. *safety, security.*

jerk n. Sl. *dink, fool, asshole, *bozo, *chump, *creep, *dipshit, *dork, *dweeb, *goober, *horse's ass, *jack-off, *jerk-off, *peckerhead, *weenie.

jerrybuilt *a.* shoddy, flimsy, defective, rickety, unstable, *junky, faulty, unsound, thrown together, cheap. ANT. *solid, sturdy, sound.*

jest *n.* joke, gag, wisecrack, witticism, *funny, bon mot, *one-liner, prank, banter, riposte.

jest *v.* joke, kid, fool, quip, poke fun at, *josh, *pull one's leg, wisecrack, tease, banter, gibe.

jester *n.* joker, clown, comic, comedian, buffoon, humorist, wit, *card, zany, prankster, *cutup, *stand-up.

jet *n.* **1.** SEE AIRCRAFT **2.** SPURT gush, stream, fountain, spout, spray, squirt, spring, geyser, spritz.

jet *v.* spurt, gush, stream, spout, spew, spray, squirt, spring, shoot, discharge, issue.

jettison *v.* eject, dump, get rid of, chuck, expel, cast off, discard, unload, *deep-six, heave.

jetty *n.* breakwater, sea wall, barrier, groin, riprap.

jewel *n.* **1.** GEM stone, precious stone, semiprecious stone, *rock, birthstone, bauble, baguette, bijou, diamond, emerald, opal, ruby, sapphire, pearl. SEE GEM **2.** RARITY treasure, prize, find, pride and joy, work of art, one in a million.

jewelry *n.* jewels, gems, precious stones, semiprecious stones, bauble, ornament, chain, necklace, choker, locket, cameo, brooch, pin, ring, earring, nose ring, tiara, crown, bracelet, anklet, beads, bijou, chatelaine, rhinestone, adornment, trinket, gewgaw, gimcrack, *ice. "Orators of love." —Samuel Daniel. SEE GEM

Jezebel *n.* whore, hussy, strumpet, harlot, loose woman, wanton, trollop, witch, *bitch, harridan.

jibe *v.* harmonize, correspond, match, fit, accord, agree, dovetail, conform, square, go together.

jiffy *n.* instant, moment, second, *blink of an eye, *heartbeat, *two shakes of a lamb's tail, flash, twinkling. ANT. *eternity, lifetime.*

jiggle *v.* wiggle, shake, shimmy, twitch, joggle, jig, bib, vibrate, rock, bounce.

jilt *v.* reject, dump, cast off, drop, *give the mitten, spurn, break off, forsake, *give the brush off, ditch, *drop a bomb on.

jingle *v.* clang, tinkle, tingle, jangle, ring, clang, chime, ding, tintinnabulate.

jinx *n.* curse, spell, hex, invocation, evil eye, *whammy, *double whammy, voodoo, hoodoo, black magic, *bete noire.

jitters *n.* shakes, shivers, anxiety, nervousness, trembling, quaking, *heebie-jeebies, *willies, quivering.

jittery *a.* shaky, nervous, anxious, trembling, quaking, quivering, tense, uptight, uneasy. ANT. *relaxed, calm.*

job *n.* **1.** TASK chore, work, project, business, assignment, mission, responsibility, duty, obligation, role, charge, function, errand, venture, commission, burden. **2.** EMPLOYMENT occupation, business, livelihood, career, trade, post, position, vocation, profession, craft, *racket.

jocular *a.* joking, humorous, funny, jesting, playful, comical, fun, prankish, droll, jocose, lighthearted, jovial, sportive. ANT. *serious, grave, grim, solemn.*

jocund *a.* cheerful, gay, blithe, in high spirits, lighthearted, breezy, happy-go-lucky, optimistic, buoyant, genial, merry. ANT. *depressed, sad, miserable.*

jog *v.* **1.** RUN trot, speedwalk, dash. SEE RUN **2.** SHAKE jerk, nudge, jostle, poke, jab, prod, bump, tap.

join *v.* **1.** CONNECT fasten, unite, fuse, link, couple, merge, attach, combine, unify, hitch, splice, tie, consolidate, bind. **2.** ENROLL sign up, enlist, associate with, become a member, subscribe to. ANT. **1.** *disconnect, detach, divide, separate.*

joint *n.* connection, hinge, coupling, junction, link, union, articulation, bend.

joint *a.* combined, mutual, cooperative, shared, united, concerted, allied, collaborative, collective, hand in hand.

joke *n.* **1.** JEST *one-liner, gag, witticism, wisecrack, quip, humor, bon mot, *funny, drollery, pun, *rib-tickler, prank, *knee-slapper. "The cayenne of conversation." —Paul Chatfield. "Sport to one ... death to another." —William Hazlitt. **2.** LAUGHINGSTOCK butt, object of ridicule, target, clown, goat.

joker *n.* jester, clown, comic, comedian, *stand-up, humorist, wisecracker, *wiseass, prankster, *card, *cutup, wit, *punster.

jolly *a.* high-spirited, merry, jovial, cheerful, playful, mirthful, jocular, joyous, glad, gleeful, gay, lively, exuberant. ANT. *depressed, miserable, somber.*

jolt *n.* jerk, shake, blow, jar, start, jump, jounce, bump, jog, slam, lurch, shock, surprise, *bolt out of the blue, bombshell.

jolt *v.* jerk, shake, jar, start, jounce, bump, jog, slam, jostle, rock, shock, surprise, stun, stagger, *take one's breath away, shake up, startle.

jostle v. bump, push, elbow, shove, nudge, crash, shoulder, crowd, scuffle, *bulldoze, herd.

journal n. chronicle, record, diary, narrative, history, memoir, log, daybook, account, minutes, ledger, register.

journalism n. news-gathering, reporting, writing, news, print media, fourth estate. "The first power in the land." — Samuel Bowles.

journalist n. reporter, newspaperman/woman, correspondent, writer, newshound, columnist. "Alarmists." — George Riddell. "Puppets. They simply respond to the pull of the most powerful strings." — Lyndon Johnson. SEE NEWSPAPER

journey n. trip, wayfaring, tour, excursion, travel, expedition, odyssey, voyage, drive, journey, peregrination, trek, cruise, safari, adventure, junket, hike.

journey v. travel, take a trip, tour, voyage, drive, cruise, trek, roam, globe-trot, ramble, range, wander.

jovial a. playful, genial, cheerful, merry, mirthful, happy, gleeful, blithe, jocund, glad, high-spirited, effervescent. ANT. *miserable, depressed, somber.*

joy n. happiness, delight, euphoria, high spirits, gladness, bliss, glee, elation, cheer, jubilance, rapture, transport. ANT. *misery, depression, desolation, despair.*

joyful a. happy, delightful, euphoric, elated, high-spirited, glad, blissful, gleeful, cheerful, jubilant, rapturous, transported, ecstatic, high. ANT. *miserable, depressed, despondent.*

joyous a. SEE JOYFUL

jubilant a. joyful, elated, overjoyed, rejoicing, exultant, exhilarated, triumphant, celebrating, thrilled, euphoric, *beside oneself, *on cloud nine. ANT. *miserable, dejected, despondent, downhearted.*

judge n. 1. JUSTICE magistrate, jurist, *his Honor. "Nothing but the law speaking." — Benjamin Whichcote. "A law student who marks his own papers." — Henry Louis Mencken. SEE COURT 2. ARBITRATOR arbiter, adjudicator, mediator, referee, umpire, conciliator.

judge v. 1. ADJUDICATE try, adjudge, hear, sit, rule, give a verdict, decide, settle, determine, arbitrate, mediate, referee, umpire. 2. ESTIMATE guess, surmise, reckon, infer, deduce, gather, arrive, size up. 3. APPRAISE rate, assess, rank, evaluate, value, size up.

judgment n. 1. SENSE common sense, wisdom, intelligence, prudence, discernment, under-standing, savvy, brains, acumen, reasoning. 2. LEGAL DECISION order, decree, ruling, decision, adjudication, sentence, verdict, award, damages. 3. OPINION estimate, determination, appraisal, assessment, deduction, conclusion, conviction.

judicial a. 1. LEGAL judiciary, juristic, forensic. 2. CRITICAL careful, thoughtful, analytical, discriminating, discerning, perceptive, keen. 3. Unbiased. ANT. 2. *obtuse, undiscriminating.* SEE FAIR

JUDICIOUS a. [joo DISH us] having or using sound judgment. *A judicious decision.* SYN. wise, sound, sensible, sage, sagacious, mindful, careful, well-considered, rational, thoughtful, astute, keen, persipacious, discriminating. ANT. *injudicious, senseless, thoughtless, irrational, careless.*

jug n. vessel, receptacle, container, pitcher, jar, bottle, vase.

juice n. fluid, extract, distillation, liquid, serum, sap, nectar, essence.

juicy a. 1. MOIST succulent, dripping, watery, liquid, saturated. 2. INTERESTING provocative, racy, sexy, spicy, sensational, fascinating, colorful, risqué. ANT. 1. *dry, dehydrated.* 2. *dry, dull, bland.*

jumble n. mixture, hodgepodge, mishmash, medley, melange, tangle, miscellany, mess, confusion, assortment, goulash, hash.

jumbled a. mixed, scrambled, strewn about, disorganized, cluttered, thrown together, disarranged, tangled, confused, in disarray. ANT. *organized, ordered.*

jumbo a. huge, gigantic, king-size, industrial size, oversized, immense, prodigious, elephantine, Brobdingnagian.

jump n. 1. LEAP hop, bound, vault, hurdle, spring, pounce, rise, leapfrog, buck, frolic, bounce. 2. INCREASE upsurge, advance, upturn, boost.

jump v. 1. LEAP hop, bound, vault, hurdle, spring, dive, pounce, rise, leapfrog, bounce, lunge, buck. 2. RECOIL start, flinch, wince, bolt, jerk. 3. INCREASE surge, advance, escalate, rise, gain, boost.

jumpy a. nervous, restless, jittery, skittish, edgy, on edge, fidgety, *on pins and needles, *having hair-trigger nerves, uneasy, tense. ANT. *relaxed, calm, tranquil.*

junction n. juncture, convergence, joining, meeting, union, link, connection, crossing, intersection, crossroads, confluence.

juncture n. 1. CONNECTION joint, joining, junction, coupling, hookup, link, seam, convergence, meeting, union. **2.** POINT OF TIME moment, point, stage, period. **3.** CRITICAL MOMENT crisis, turning point, crossroad, *zero hour, exigency, emergency.

jungle n. rain forest, forest, woods, bush, *the wild, the wilderness.

WORD FIND

descriptive: lush, moss-bearded trees, festooned and encrusted with parasites, tangled gardens, steaming, rampant foliage, leafy mosaic, ferns like lacy parasols, soaring monoliths

flowering parasite growing from cracks of trees: bromeliad, orchid, epiphyte

misty jungle: cloud forest

rotting floor debris: litter

uppermost story: canopy

vine, great: liana

vine, killer: strangler

vines, slang: bush rope

junior a. lower, lesser, subordinate, inferior, minor, secondary. ANT. *senior, superior.*

junk n. trash, scrap, refuse, waste, rubbish, debris, castoffs, salvage, garbage, crap, remnants, bits and pieces.

junk v. throw out, scrap, heave, dump, discard, dispose of, *shitcan, trash.

jurisdiction n. **1.** AUTHORITY authorization, power, command, sanction, control, dominion, rule, sovereignty. **2.** REALM OF AUTHORITY domain, sphere, bounds, province, bailiwick, district, area, territory, reach.

jurist n. lawyer, attorney, attorney-at-law, counsel, counselor, legal advisor, judge, justice, magistrate.

just a. **1.** FAIR impartial, unbiased, equitable, evenhanded, dispassionate, objective, nonpartisan, right. **2.** RIGHTEOUS upright, decent, virtuous, moral, ethical, honorable, proper, scrupulous, principled, good. **3.** DESERVED justified, worthy, merited, earned, due, fitting, rightful. **4.** ACCURATE right, correct, precise, sound, valid, true. ANT. *1. unfair, partial, biased. 2. corrupt, immoral, unprincipled. 3. undeserved, unearned. 4. inaccurate, imprecise.*

just adv. **1.** ONLY merely, simply. **2.** BARELY hardly, narrowly, *by the skin of one's teeth.

justice n. **1.** RIGHTEOUSNESS virtue, rectitude, uprightness, integrity, honor, honesty, morality, goodness. **2.** FAIRNESS impartiality, equity, evenhandedness, fair play, objectivity. "To give everyone his due." — Cicero. **3.** LAWFULNESS rightness, legitimacy, validity, legality. **4.** PENALTY OR REWARD recompense, compensation, reparation, just deserts, redress, retribution. ANT. *1. immorality, dishonor, corruptness. 2. unfairness, partiality, bias.*

justify v. vindicate, absolve, warrant, legitimize, show just cause, substantiate, answer for, defend, rationalize, support, exonerate, excuse.

jut v. project, protrude, stick out, extend.

juvenile n. youngster, kid, boy, girl, youth, minor, teenager, adolescent, lad, lass.

juvenile a. childish, young, immature, childlike, babyish, teenaged, adolescent, pubescent, undeveloped, inexperienced, naive, *wet behind the ears. ANT. *adult, old, experienced.*

juvenile delinquent n. punk, hooligan, hoodlum, malefactor, rowdy. "Other people's children in trouble." — Jerry Dashkin.

JUXTAPOSE v. [JUK stuh POSE] to place side by side. *He had to juxtapose the pieces in order to see where they fit.* SYN. appose, place side by side, pair, place parallel to one another.

K

KAFKAESQUE *a.* [KAHF kuh ESK] surreal or nightmarish, as the writings of Franz Kafka. *As the drug took effect, the captive's surroundings took on an increasingly Kafkaesque quality.* SYN. surreal, nightmarish, weird, bizarre, fantastic, freakish, monstrous, unbelievable, dreamy.

keen *a.* **1.** SHARP cutting, razor-sharp, knife-edged, honed, pointed. **2.** PIERCING cutting, incisive, penetrating, trenchant. **3.** ASTUTE acute, sharp, bright, perceptive, intelligent, discerning, quick, shrewd, wise, clever, discriminating. **4.** ENTHUSIASTIC eager, interested, avid, *gung ho, ardent, zealous, *psyched. ANT. *1. dull, blunt. 2. dull. 3. dull, obtuse, dense, stupid. 4. indifferent, apathetic, lukewarm.*

keep *v.* **1.** HOLD retain, possess, have, own, save, store. **2.** TAKE CARE OF maintain, tend, look after, support, board, provide for, protect, mind, guard, watch over. **3.** CELEBRATE observe, commemorate, memorialize, regard. **4.** RESTRAIN keep back, hold in check, prevent, curb, check, obstruct, detain, arrest, stop. ANT. *1. throw out, discard, release. 2. neglect, ignore. 3. disregard, ignore. 4. free, let loose, liberate.*

keeper *n.* guardian, protector, custodian, watchman, warden, caretaker, conservator, curator.

keepsake *n.* memento, reminder, souvenir, memorial, token, remembrance.

keg *n.* barrel, cask, drum, hogshead, container, tank, butt, firkin, tun.

ken *n.* perception, understanding, knowledge, cognizance, grasp, comprehension, range of vision.

kernel *n.* seed, grain, pit, stone, germ, nut, core, essence, heart, gist, center, crux, marrow.

kettle *n.* cauldron, pot, boiler, vessel, vat, stewpot, teakettle.

key *n.* **1.** SOLUTION answer, clue. **2.** GUIDE manual, code.

keyboard *n.* organ, synthesizer. SEE MUSICAL INSTRUMENTS

keystone *n.* principle, cornerstone, linchpin, support, foundation, ground, basis.

kick *n.* **1.** THRILL *bang, *charge, *rush, enjoyment. **2.** THRUST jolt, recoil. **3.** COMPLAINT gripe, objection, *bitch. **4.** STIMULATION zing, bite, punch, snap, potency, power, sharpness.

kick *v.* **1.** BOOT punt, drop-kick. **2.** OBJECT complain, gripe, *bitch, protest, remonstrate, grumble. **3.** *Sl.* QUIT give up, *go cold turkey, stop.

kickback *n. Sl.* percentage, payment, *payola, payoff, graft, cut, bribe, *money under the table.

kid *n.* child, juvenile, adolescent, youth, teenager, boy, girl, youngster, tot, lad, lass.

kid *v.* tease, fool, *pull one's leg, *put on, make fun of, *josh, play a joke on, make sport of, *rib.

kidnap *v.* abduct, *shanghai, *snatch, seize, hold for ransom, hijack, skyjack, pirate.

kill *v.* **1.** MURDER put to death, execute, slay, do in, dispatch, get rid of, assassinate, exterminate, *waste, slaughter, *rub out, destroy. SEE MURDER **2.** END stop, abort, halt, case, terminate, turn off, cancel. **3.** VETO defeat, reject, *give thumbs down, turn down.

killer *n.* murderer, slayer, assassin, executioner, ripper, homicidal maniac, *hit man, serial killer, gunman. SEE MURDERER

killing *n.* murder, homicide, slaying, manslaughter, execution, extermination, assassination, slaughter, foul play, death, fatality.

killjoy *n.* *wet blanket, spoilsport, *gloomy Gus, *partypooper, *prophet of doom, naysayer, *stick in the mud.

kin *n.* relatives, kinsfolk, kindred, sibling, family, blood relative, relations.

kind *n.* type, sort, variety, class, order, category, breed, strain, genus, brand, genre.

kind *a.* nice, compassionate, considerate, good, benevolent, generous, charitable, bighearted, understanding, loving, sympathetic, humane, gentle, *bleedingheart, friendly, soft, merciful, forgiving, Christian, tenderhearted. ANT. *mean, cruel, cold, brutal.*

kindhearted *a.* SEE KIND

kindle *v.* **1.** SET ON FIRE ignite, burn, torch, fuel, inflame. **2.** AROUSE excite, inflame, *fire up, agitate, incite, egg on, stir up, stimulate, fan the fire.

kindly *a.* kind, nice, compassionate, considerate, good, benevolent, generous, charitable, bighearted, understanding, gracious, loving, sympathetic, humane, gentle, friendly, softhearted, merciful, forgiving, Christian. ANT. *mean, cruel, cold, brutal.*

kindly *adv.* nicely, compassionately, benevolently, generously, charitably, bigheartedly, understandingly, lovingly, sympathetically, humanely, gently, mercifully, agreeably. ANT. *meanly, cruelly, coldly, brutally.*

kindness *n.* **1.** NICENESS compassion, consideration, goodness, benevolence, generosity, charity, bigheartedness, understanding, graciousness, love, magnanimity, sympathy, humanity, gentleness, friendliness, mercy, forgiveness. "The golden chain by which society is bound together." —Johann Goethe. **2.** GOOD TURN good deed, service, accommodation, helping hand, generosity, charity, assistance, relief. ANT. *1. meanness, cruelty, coldness, brutality.*

kindred *a.* similar, like, related, matching, corresponding, parallel, close, allied. ANT. *different, opposite, unrelated.*

kinetic *a.* energetic, dynamic, active, lively, in motion.

king *n.* monarch, His Majesty, crowned head, sovereign, ruler, emperor, czar, overlord, chief, leader, boss, *top dog, *kingpin, *head honcho, *big cheese, *biggest toad in the puddle. "A name of dignity and office, not of person." —John Milton. "A highly paid model for postage stamps." —Anon.

kingdom *n.* monarchy, realm, empire, dominion, domain, sovereignty, country, nation, territory, turf, sphere.

kink *n.* **1.** CURL twist, bend, screw, coil, curlicue, crinkle, knot, crimp. **2.** MUSCLE SPASM cramp, *charley horse, knot, stitch, twinge, crick. **3.** ECCENTRICITY peculiarity, quirk, idiosyncrasy, singularity. **4.** DIFFICULTY defect, hitch, knot, snarl, *glitch, complication.

kinky *a.* **1.** CURLY snarled, knotted, frizzy, tangled, twisted, matted. **2.** PERVERTED bizarre, strange, eccentric, twisted, peculiar, depraved, warped, sick, outlandish, unconventional. ANT. *1. straight, smooth. 2. normal, conventional, ordinary.*

kinship *n.* relationship, kin, blood ties, close connection, affinity, association.

KISMET *n.* [KIZ met] fate; destiny. *His early death was attributed to kismet.* SYN. fate, destiny, fortune, Providence, *what is written in the stars, predestination, lot, portion.

kiss *n.* peck, *smack, *wet one, *French kiss, *tongue, osculation, smooch, *soul kiss. "A word invented by the poets as a rhyme for "bliss."" —Ambrose Bierce. "The sure, sweet cement, glue and lime of love." —Robert Herrick.

kiss *v.* peck, *smack, *smooch, *neck, osculate, blow, *suck face, *tongue, *French, *pucker

up, *give a hickey.

kit *n.* gear, outfit, set, equipment, implements, rigging, supplies, tools, utensils, instruments, tackle, case, bag, pack.

knack *n.* ability, skill, talent, dexterity, aptitude, gift, propensity, genius, flair, command, *head, know-how.

knave *n.* rascal, bastard, villain, rogue, cad, scoundrel, cur, louse, fiend, snake, *SOB, scamp, cheater.

knead *v.* press, work, fold over, mix, rub, massage, manipulate, squeeze.

knickknack *n.* bric-a-brac, ornament, *whatnot, bauble, gewgaw, trinket, doodad, gimcrack, bibelot, objet d'art, conversation piece.

knife *n.* dagger, switchblade, blade, dirk, stiletto, scalpel, bowie knife, butter knife, jackknife, penknife, Swiss Army knife, cutlery. SEE DAGGER, SWORD

knife *v.* stab, run through, stick, cut, slash, impale, pierce, wound, lance.

knit *v.* purl, crochet, loop, cable, knot, intertwine, bind, weave.

knob *n.* protuberance, lump, bump, projection, nub, node, bulge, tumor, prominence, swelling.

knock *v.* **1.** STRIKE bump, strike a blow, hit, bang, punch, pound, pummel, batter, thump, rap, *slug, slap, smack, floor. **2.** CRITICIZE *pan, find fault, belittle, pick apart, *slam, *badmouth, disparage, *rake over the coals. ANT. *2. praise, laud, applaud.*

knoll *n.* hillock, hill, mound, rise, hummock, hump, elevation, swell.

knot *n.* **1.** TIE twist, loop, bow, braid, plait, intertwinement, tangle, entanglement, mat, kink, snarl. **2.** LUMP bump, protuberance, knob, gnarl, nub, node. **3.** BUNCH group, aggregation, mob, swarm, gathering, mass, assemblage. **4.** COMPLEX PROBLEM complexity, Gordian knot, puzzle, difficulty, horns of a dilemma, labyrinth.

knotty *a.* complex, puzzling, baffling, perplexing, complicated, troublesome, labyrinthine, intricate, thorny, involved. ANT. *simple, easy, elementary.*

know *v.* **1.** UNDERSTAND apprehend, comprehend, grasp, realize, *get it, fathom, recognize, appreciate, see, *have the hang of, *have down pat, have memorized, *know backward and forward, *have down cold. **2.** BE ACQUAINTED WITH be familiar with, be intimate with, be close to, be on good terms with, associate with. **3.** DISTINGUISH discern, recognize, discriminate, differentiate.

know-how *n*. expertise, skill, capability, ability, experience, savvy, talent, proficiency, knack, flair, command, mastery, *the right stuff. ANT. *ignorance, inexperience, incompetence.*

knowing *a*. knowledgeable, informed, aware, conscious, perceptive, astute, schooled, educated, learned, enlightened, intelligent, sophisticated, worldly, shrewd, clever, bright, insightful, wise. ANT. *unenlightened, ignorant, obtuse, dense.*

know-it-all *n*. *walking encyclopedia, *brain, intellectual, *professor, *blowhard, *windbag.

knowledge *n*. **1.** ACQUAINTANCE familiarity, awareness, understanding, apprehension, conversance, appreciation, consciousness, cognizance, realization, perception, enlightenment, experience, recognition, memory. "The wing wherewith we fly to heaven." — Shakespeare. "An unending adventure at the edge of uncertainty." — Jacob Bronowski. "The only instrument of production that is not subject to diminishing returns." — J.M. Clark. **2.** EDUCATION schooling, erudition, learning, scholarship, instruction, enlightenment. **3.** INFORMATION facts, data, *lowdown, lore, science, wisdom. ANT. *ignorance, unfamiliarity, unconsciousness.*

knowledgeable *a*. learned, schooled, well-read, erudite, educated, scholarly, literate, conversant, au courant, experienced, informed, knowing, abreast of, wise, worldly, sophisticated. ANT. *ignorant, unaware, unschooled.*

knurled *a*. knotty, knobby, bumpy, gnarled, warty.

kook *n. Sl.* *nut case, *loony tune, *fruitcake, *wacko, weirdo, *screwball, eccentric, character, *ding-a-ling.

kosher *a. Sl.* all right, okay, proper, correct, acceptable, approved, fitting, permitted. ANT. *unacceptable.*

kowtow *v*. bow, kneel, stoop, genuflect, bow and scrape, kiss feet, *kiss up, *brownnose, toady, cringe, grovel, fawn.

kudos *n*. credit, praise, honor, glory, fame, acclaim, applause, laudation, esteem, plaudits, recognition, prestige.

L

lab *n.* SEE LABORATORY

label *n.* **1.** TAG sticker, ticket, stamp, sign, brand, name, logo, trademark, seal, identification. **2.** CHARACTERIZATION stereotype, classification, generalization, epithet.

label *v.* **1.** TAG classify, differentiate, identify, name, designate, ticket, stamp, mark, brand. **2.** CHARACTERIZE stereotype, classify, generalize, brand.

labor *n.* **1.** WORK effort, toil, *sweat of one's brow, exertion, struggle, *plugging, *blood, sweat and tears, energy, *grind, strain, *grunt work, *elbow grease. "The grand conqueror, enriching and building up nations more surely than the proudest battles."—William Channing. "The capital of our workingmen."—Grover Cleveland. **2.** BIRTH PROCESS contractions, parturition. SEE BIRTH, BABY, PREGNANCY ANT. *1.* rest, leisure, relaxation.

laboratory *n.* lab, testing room, testing ground, analysis lab, chemistry lab, workshop.

labored *a.* strained, with great effort, forced, excessive, overworked, overwrought, stiff, studied, unnatural. ANT. effortless, natural, spontaneous.

laborer *n.* worker, blue-collar worker, hand, *grunt, unskilled worker, drudge, peon, *hardhat, wage earner, employee.

laborious *a.* hard, arduous, difficult, backbreaking, strenuous, burdensome, heavy, ponderous, tough, *Herculean, demanding. ANT. easy, light, effortless, *child's play.

labyrinth *n.* maze, convolution, network, complexity, intricacy, knot, tangle, winding way, Gordian knot.

lace *n.* netting, mesh, tatting, openwork, web, embroidery, macrame, braid, filigree.

lacerate *v.* tear, rip, cut, gash, slash, rend, mutilate, stab, mangle, slice, wound.

laceration *n.* tear, jagged tear, rip, cut, gash, slash, scratch, rent, slice, mutilation, wound.

lack *n.* want, deficiency, need, dearth, insufficiency, shortage, shortfall, paucity, privation. ANT. overflow, excess, abundance.

lack *v.* miss, need, want, fall short, be found wanting, require.

lackadaisical *a.* listless, languid, spiritless, indifferent, apathetic, unmotivated, languorous, impassive, lethargic, careless, laid-back, half-hearted, lazy. ANT. eager, spirited, enthusiastic, energetic.

lackey *n.* toady, servant, footman, slave, stooge, *brownnose, *yes-man, flunky, underling, inferior.

lackluster *a.* dull, drab, colorless, bland, flat, *blah, boring, lifeless, dead, *ho-hum. ANT. vivid, radiant, colorful, interesting.

LACONIC *a.* [luh KON ik] employing few words, terse. *The laconic waiter grunted a one-word reply.* SYN. terse, brief, short, concise, to the point, succinct, short and sweet, pithy, curt, taciturn, quiet, reticent. ANT. loquacious, talkative, wordy, garrulous.

lacy *a.* filigreed, webbed, tatted, delicate, meshy, frilly.

lad *n.* boy, young man, youth, fellow, kid, chap, guy.

lady *n.* woman, female, gal, gentlewoman, matron, *dame, *chick, girl, *filly, senhorita, mademoiselle. "One who makes a man behave like a gentleman."—Russel Lynes.

ladylike *a.* refined, cultured, well-bred, genteel, proper, feminine, courtly, dignified, matronly, polite, well-mannered, prim. ANT. rough, crude, uncouth, boorish, *gross.

lag *v.* fall behind, wane, ebb, flag, slow, linger, poke, drag, stall, dawdle, delay, trail, dally, procrastinate, *take one's sweet time. ANT. rush, race, accelerate, surpass.

laggard *n.* straggler, slowpoke, dawdler, lagger, dallier, *slug.

lair *n.* den, hole, burrow, cave, nest, hideaway, hideout, retreat, lie, refuge, sanctuary.

LAISSEZ-FAIRE *n.* [LESS ay FEHR] allowance to do as one pleases without interference, regulation or control, a "hands-off" government policy. *The government's laissez-faire policy allows some businesses to set their own rules.* SYN. *hands-off policy, free enterprise, nonintervention, noninterference, permissiveness, deregulation, inaction, free hand, latitude, *enough rope to hang oneself with.

lake *n.* pond, tarn, pool, basin, reservoir, loch, Great Salt Lake, Erie, Ontario, Superior, Michigan, Huron, Tahoe, Geneva, Champlain, Mead, Loch Ness, Titicaca, Victoria, Baikal, Crater, Dead Sea. "Earth's living jewels."—Anon. "The earth's eye."—Thoreau.

WORD FIND

bend of a river, cut off: oxbow lake

crater lake: caldera

desert, temporary, shallow: playa

diminishing process from lake to pond to marsh to swamp: eutrophication, succession

epoch when most lakes formed: Pleistocene

expert on: limnologist

glacial: ice scour, kettle, moraine lake

glacial series of, resembling beads: paternoster lakes

Great Lakes forming glacier: Wisconsin ice sheet

mountain lake: tarn

mountainside basin: cirque

oscillations of: seiche

outlet: bayou

pertaining to: lacustrine

skimming insect: boatman

SEE MARSH, POND, RIVER, SWAMP

lambaste v. scold, berate, dress down, *rake over the coals, reprimand, castigate, cuss out, censure, rebuke, *chew out, *jump down one's throat.

lame a. **1.** DISABLED crippled, handicapped, gimpy, hamstrung, limping, hobbled, sidelined, impaired, stiff, sore. **2.** WEAK feeble, poor, inferior, ineffectual, inadequate, unsatisfactory, insufficient, flimsy. ANT. **1.** *fleet-footed, agile, nimble.* **2.** *sound, strong, effective.*

lament v. mourn, grieve, weep, wail, cry, sob, shed tears, sorrow, commiserate, bewail, deplore, rue, *eat one's heart out.

lamentable a. grievous, deplorable, regrettable, woeful, pitiable, heartbreaking, distressing, sad, sorrowful, wretched. ANT. *happy, fortunate, welcome.*

lamentation n. lament, grieving, mourning, wailing, weeping, crying, sobbing, moaning, commiseration, plaint, dirge.

lamp n. lantern, beacon, illuminant. SEE LIGHT

LAMPOON v. [lam POON] to satirize or parody, to ridicule. *The comedy troupe loves to lampoon the president.* SYN. satirize, parody, mock, ridicule, make fun of, caricature, burlesque, *send up, pasquinade.

lance v. pierce, cut open, incise, stick, prick, puncture, stab.

land n. **1.** GROUND earth, soil, terra firma, turf, sand, loam, dirt. **2.** TERRAIN expanse, stretch, sweep, topography, lowland, highland. **3.** PROPERTY real estate, grounds, acreage, plot, lot, parcel, holding. **4.** COUNTRY, AREA nation, region, motherland, fatherland, old country, district, territory.

land v. **1.** SET DOWN touch down, alight, dock, drop anchor, arrive. **2.** *BAG obtain, get, win, secure, catch, acquire, *collar.

landlord n. landholder, lessor, proprietor, slumlord.

landmark n. guide, marker, milestone, guidepost, beacon, benchmark, watershed.

landscape n. expanse, view, panorama, sweep, vista, scene, scenery, surroundings, prospect.

landslide n. avalanche, mudslide, rockslide, collapse.

lane n. way, path, route, passage, alley, avenue, course, access, road, trail.

language n. verbalization, vocalization, communication, linguistics, speech, parlance, tongue, expression, articulation, wording, vernacular, vocabulary, idiom, idiolect, phraseology, prose, lingo, jargon, cant, slang, slanguage, dialect, diction, colloquialism, localism, Americanism, syntax. "A man's language is an unerring index of his nature." — Laurence Binyon. "The armory of the human mind." — Samuel Taylor Coleridge. "Man's deadliest weapon." — Arthur Koestler. "A city to the building of which every human being brought a stone." "A series of squeaks." — Alfred North Whitehead.

LANGUID a. [LAN gwid] lacking vitality or energy, weak. *The day after the party, we sat around languidly.* SYN. weak, drooping, listless, faint, enervated, lethargic, languorous, sluggish, dull, slow, apathetic, indifferent. ANT. *vigorous, vital, energized.*

LANGUISH v. [LAN gwish] to grow weak, listless or dull, flag. *After the drought, the delicate flowers languished, then died.* SYN. weaken, flag, grow listless, tire, fade, wilt, wither, droop, decline, ebb, sicken, *fizzle out, *go downhill. ANT. *flourish, revive, thrive, strengthen.*

languor n. weakness, listlessness, sluggishness, languidness, faintness, lethargy, torpor, fatigue, apathy, indifference. ANT. *vigor, strength, zest, vitality.*

lanky a. tall, skinny, lean, bony, slender, spare, twiggy, gangling, skin-and-bones, spindly, *lean as linguine, *built like a broomstick, *could fall through a flute and not sound a note. ANT. *stout, hulking, fat, Herculean.*

lantern n. lamp, torch, flashlight. SEE LIGHT

lap v. lick, splash, slosh, slap, ripple.

lapse n. **1.** SLIP error, fault, flub, blunder, mistake, omission, oversight, *screwup, lapsus linguae, lapsus calami. **2.** GAP passage, break, pause, lull, interval, interim.

larceny n. stealing, theft, petty larceny, burglary, robbery, shoplifting, pilfering, embezzlement, swindling, fraud.

large *a.* big, sizable, great, huge, gigantic, immense, colossal, prodigious, hefty, towering, enormous, *jumbo, voluminous, *whopping, massive, gargantuan, vast, extensive, expansive, roomy, spacious, commodious, capacious, generous. ANT. *tiny, small, microscopic, minute, sparse, paltry.*

largely *adv.* mostly, chiefly, mainly, for the most part, principally, by and large, to a great extent, overall, generally.

largess *a.* generosity, charity, giving, gift-giving, philanthropy, benefaction.

LASCIVIOUS *a.* [luh SIV ee us] lustful, expressing lust, lewd. *She eyed him lasciviously.* SYN. lustful, lewd, wanton, licentious, *horny, lecherous, *hot, libidinous, carnal, goatish, salacious, blue, *raunchy, lurid, obscene. ANT. *celibate, pure, chaste, frigid.*

lash *v.* **1.** THRASH whip, beat, flog, switch, strike, flail, flagellate, swat, scourge. **2.** CENSURE rebuke, attack, criticize, tongue-lash, berate, scold, chastise, lambaste, *chew out.

lass *n.* girl, female, young woman, maid, maiden, lassie, miss, *filly, colleen, mademoiselle.

lassitude *n.* fatigue, weariness, languor, torpor, lethargy, listlessness, exhaustion, malaise, sluggishness, tiredness. ANT. *vigor, energy, vitality.*

lasso *n.* lariat, rope, thong, noose.

last *v.* endure, survive, persist, persevere, keep on, remain, continue, outlast, hold out. ANT. *die, wear out, give out.*

last *a.* **1.** FINAL ending, closing, concluding, terminal, ultimate, climactic, finishing, trailing, rearmost. **2.** LATEST newest, current, recent, up-to-the-minute. ANT. *1. first, beginning, opening. 2. oldest, earliest.*

lasting *a.* enduring, permanent, continuing, durable, undying, persisting, everlasting, indestructible, immortal, abiding, perdurable. ANT. *short-lived, fleeting, temporary, ephemeral.*

lastly *adv.* finally, in closing, ultimately.

latch *n.* lock, catch, hook and eye, bolt, fastening, hasp, clasp.

latch *v.* lock, bolt, fasten, secure, hook, close.

late *a.* **1.** TARDY overdue, behind, delayed, lagging, slow, held up. **2.** RECENT new, modern, current, up-to-the-minute, fresh. **3.** DECEASED dead, extinct, defunct, bygone, former, past, previous. ANT. *1. punctual, on time. 2. early, old. 3. existing, living.*

lately *adv.* of late, recently, a short time ago, now.

LATENT *a.* [LAYT unt] existing or present beneath the surface, hidden. *He possessed a latent talent that only occasionally emerged.* SYN. dormant, hidden, under the surface, inactive, quiescent, *closet, slumbering, potential, smoldering, undeveloped. ANT. *apparent, obvious, active, developed.*

lateral *a.* sideways, sidewise, sidelong, oblique, slanting, glancing, flanking.

lather *n.* foam, froth, suds, spume, cream, bubbles.

LATITUDE *n.* [LAT uh tood] freedom to act without restrictions. *The governor was given complete latitude to choose the state's fate.* SYN. freedom, liberty, free hand, carte blanche, license, leeway, *slack, room, play, run, independence. ANT. *restriction, confinement.*

lattice *n.* framework, openwork, screen, trellis, grid, grating, fretwork.

LAUD *v.* [LAWD] to praise or acclaim. *The critics lauded his latest work.* SYN. praise, acclaim, applaud, extol, hail, compliment, sing the praises of, cheer, celebrate, commend. ANT. *disparage, criticize, denigrate.*

laudable *a.* praiseworthy, commendable, admirable, excellent, exceptional, good, exemplary, superb, worthy, meritorious. ANT. *awful, contemptible, terrible, shameful.*

laudatory *a.* commendatory, praising, approving, eulogizing, complimentary, favorable, acclamatory, flattering. ANT. *condemning, critical.*

laugh *n.* chuckle, giggle, snigger, snicker, chortle, guffaw, roar, cackle, *tee-hee, horselaugh, belly laugh, *great gust/gale of laughter, howl, fit of laughter, titter, snort, hoot, *raspy chuckle, *wheezing chuckle, shriek, scream, squeal, unrestrained laughter.

laugh *v.* chuckle, giggle, snigger, snicker, chortle, guffaw, roar, cackle, *tee-hee, convulse with glee, double over with laughter, howl, titter, snort, hoot, chuckle hoarsely, shriek, scream, squeal.

laughable *a.* absurd, ridiculous, hilarious, ludicrous, comical, funny, stupid, silly, sidesplitting, amusing, *a scream, hysterical, nonsensical. ANT. *serious, sad, depressing.*

laughter *n.* giggling, chuckling, *great gales of laughter, howling, squealing, shrieking, tittering, snickering, merriment, hilarity, mirth, glee, jollity. "A smile that burst." — Patricia Nelson. "A noisy smile." — Steven Goldberg. "A universal bond that draws all men closer." — Nathan Ausubel. "A tranquilizer with no side effects." — Arnold Glasow.

launch v. **1.** START inaugurate, begin, commence, institute, *start the ball rolling, usher in, break ground, open. **2.** SET OFF send forth, propel, discharge, fire off, catapult, set afloat.

laurels n. fame, honor, credit, kudos, renown, glory, praise, laudation, tribute, commendation, recognition.

lavatory n. washroom, toilet, rest room. SEE BATHROOM

lavish v. shower, spend, squander, deluge, heap, give, waste, pour, fritter, be generous with. ANT. limit, stint.

lavish a. generous, liberal, extravagant, profuse, abundant, bountiful, immoderate, excessive, unsparing, lush, prodigal. ANT. sparing, scant, meager.

law n. regulation, code, ordinance, rule, principle, statute, restriction, control, act, commandment, enactment, mandate, legislation. "Reason free from passion."— Aristotle. "The embodiment of the moral sentiments of the people."—William Blackstone. "The expression and the perfection of common sense."—Joseph Choate. "The backbone which keeps man erect."—S.C. Yuter.

WORD FIND

evidence that incriminates oneself, refusal to give: taking the Fifth

habitual lawbreaker: scofflaw, recidivist

ignorance of the law is no excuse: ignorantia legis non excusat

jargon, law: legalese

lawlessness: anarchy

lured into a crime by police: entrapment

punishment, laws regarding: penal code

puritanical or overly strict laws: blue laws

reading of rights rule on arrest: Miranda rule

science and philosophy of law: jurisprudence

second prosecution, law against: double jeopardy

time limit for judicial action: statute of limitations

unjust imprisonment, writ preventing: habeas corpus

SEE COURT, MURDER

lawbreaker n. criminal, violator, felon, offender, outlaw, transgressor, miscreant, delinquent, culprit, malefactor, scofflaw, recidivist.

lawful a. legal, allowable, legitimate, licit, within the law, sanctioned, permissible, constitutional, rightful. ANT. illegal, unlawful, il-

licit.

lawless a. anarchic, ungoverned, unchecked, unruly, felonious, criminal, nihilistic, barbarous, uncivilized, savage, chaotic. ANT. lawful, civilized, law-abiding.

lawn n. yard, grass, grounds, turf, sward, greensward, green.

lawsuit n. suit, action, litigation, case, claim, prosecution, dispute. "A machine which you go into as a pig and come out as a sausage."—Ambrose Bierce. SEE COURT

lawyer n. attorney, counselor, counsel, legal advisor, advocate, jurist, member of the bar, public defender, solicitor BRIT., barrister BRIT. "Perilous mouths."—Shakespeare. "A learned gentleman who rescues your estate from your enemies and keeps it himself."— Henry Brougham. "Those who earn a living by the sweat of their browbeating."—James Huneker. "One skilled in the circumvention of the law."—Ambrose Bierce. SEE COURT

lax a. slack, loose, remiss, careless, negligent, inattentive, devil-may-care, sloppy, casual, inexact, *asleep at the wheel. ANT. careful, conscientious, strict.

lay n. position, layout, arrangement, configuration, form, orientation.

lay v. **1.** PUT place, set, set down, leave, deposit, rest, position. **2.** KNOCK DOWN fell, level, flatten, floor. **3.** PRODUCE bear, bring forth, generate, deposit. **4.** IMPOSE place, exact, assess, levy. **5.** Sl. COPULATE *make out, *screw, *go all the way, *hump.

lay a. amateur, nonprofessional, ordinary, secular, unschooled.

layer n. stratum, thickness, bed, course, tier, ply, fold, overlap, sheet, row, zone.

layman n. amateur, nonprofessional, laic, neophyte, novice. ANT. professional, expert.

layoff n. dismissal, discharge, firing, *downsizing, cutback, unemployment.

lazy a. indolent, slothful, unwilling to work, *allergic to work, idle, shiftless, malingering, sleepy, loafing, inert, unindustrious, unmotivated. ANT. industrious, enterprising, hardworking, hard-driving, *busy as a beaver.

lead n. **1.** FIRST PLACE edge, top spot, vanguard, jump, head, spearhead, cutting edge. **2.** CLUE tip, hint, indication, sign. ANT. 1. rear, tail.

lead v. **1.** GUIDE direct, show the way, conduct, usher, shepherd, escort. **2.** HEAD command, direct, govern, supervise, run, *take the helm, rule, dominate, take charge. **3.** INFLUENCE persuade, incline, guide, direct, affect, *sell on, prevail upon, prompt, cause. **4.** PRE-

CEDE go before. **5.** EXCEL surpass, outdo, outshine, outperform, head the pack, rank first, stand head and shoulders above.

leader n. head, chief, commander, director, boss, supervisor, manager, captain, maestro, ruler, general, governor, dean, *biggest toad in the puddle, *big cheese, bellwether, pacesetter, pioneer, trailblazer, groundbreaker, vanguard. "A man who has the ability to get other people to do what they don't want to do and like it." — Harry S. Truman. "The wave pushed ahead by the ship." — Leon Tolstoy.

leadership n. command, control, direction, guidance, influence, domination, sway, mastery, charisma, potency, authority, counsel. "Action, not position." — Donald McGannon. ANT. *subservience, subordination, obedience.*

leading a. foremost, preeminent, chief, main, dominant, supreme, outstanding, greatest, ranking, most important. ANT. *secondary, minor, lesser.*

league n. alliance, association, confederation, federation, coalition, organization, union, affiliation, partnership, fraternity.

leak n. seepage, drip, trickle, oozing, stream, dribble, discharge, opening, rupture, crack, puncture, gash, break, breach.

leak v. **1.** DISCHARGE seep, drain, drip, trickle, ooze, stream, spurt, dribble, flow. **2.** DIVULGE reveal, *spill the beans, disclose.

lean v. **1.** INCLINE slant, slope, cant, bend, tilt, pitch, list. **2.** RELY ON depend on, count on for support. **3.** TEND incline, be disposed, gravitate toward, have a preference for.

lean a. **1.** THIN spare, emaciated, anorexic, skin and bones, rawboned, gaunt, slim, slender, svelte, skinny, *lean as linguine, malnourished. **2.** UNPRODUCTIVE meager, poor, scanty, unprofitable. ANT. *1. fat, plump, rotund. 2. productive, profitable, rich.*

leaning n. tendency, inclination, disposition, preference, proclivity, propensity, bias, weakness, mindset, penchant.

leap n. jump, spring, vault, hop, bound, bounce, hurtle.

leap v. jump, spring, vault, hop, bound, bounce, hurtle, soar, rise, leapfrog.

learn v. **1.** ACQUIRE KNOWLEDGE *pick up, master, understand, comprehend, apprehend, grasp, realize, absorb, become educated. memorize, become versed in, *get the hang of, study, pore over, *cram. **2.** DISCOVER find out, hear, detect, determine, stumble upon.

learned a. educated, schooled, erudite, scholarly, literate, well-read, knowledgeable, lettered, intellectual, pedantic, bookish. ANT. *ignorant, unschooled, illiterate.*

learning n. education, schooling, enlightenment, study, edification, erudition, research, training, scholarship, cultivation, inquiry, questioning, growth, knowledge. "Dust shaken out of a book and into an empty skull." — Ambrose Bierce. "A companion on a journey to a strange country . . . a strength inexhaustible." — Hitopadesa.

lease v. let, rent, hire out, sublease, lend.

leash n. lead, line, rein, tether, rope, choker.

leash v. tie, restrain, tether, hitch, chain, collar, restrict.

least a. smallest, slightest, fewest, minimum, poorest, lowest, minutest, last. ANT. *greatest, largest, most.*

leave n. **1.** PERMISSION okay, consent, authorization, allowance, liberty, concession, indulgence, tolerance. **2.** TIME OFF furlough, leave-of-absence, sabbatical, break, *R&R. ANT. *1. refusal, denial.*

leave v. **1.** GO depart, exit, *split, take one's leave, vacate, withdraw, *shove off, decamp, flee, *cut out, bid farewell, run along, take off. **2.** ABANDON drop, desert, quit, give up, relinquish, forsake. ANT. *1. arrive, come.*

lecherous a. lustful, lewd, lascivious, libidinous, salacious, carnal, wanton, *horny, licentious, randy, *dirty-minded, *raunchy. ANT. *chaste, pure, celibate.*

lechery n. lewdness, lust, lasciviousness, salaciousness, carnality, *horniess, nymphomania, *dirty-mindedness, *raunchiness. ANT. *chastity, purity, celibacy.*

lecture n. **1.** TALK address, speech, discussion, discourse, oration, disquisition, sermon, lesson, instruction. **2.** SCOLDING *dressing down, reprimand, rebuke, criticism, reproach, *talking-to, remonstrance, admonishment, sermon.

lecture v. **1.** TALK give a speech, address, discuss, discourse, orate, give a lesson, give instruction, expound, preach, hold forth. **2.** SCOLD *dress down, reprimand, rebuke, criticize, reproach, remonstrate, admonish, sermonize, preach.

ledge n. shelf, overhang, projection, ridge, mantle, shoulder, outcrop.

leer n. salacious look, lascivious look, ogle, lustful stare, stare, once-over, lecherous look, sidelong glance, sneer.

leer v. eye lustfully, eye salaciously, eye lasciviously, eye lecherously, stare, give once-over, eye hungrily, ogle, look sidelong, smirk.

leery *a.* wary, guarded, suspicious, distrusting, cautious, chary, skeptical, uncertain. ANT. *trusting, unsuspecting.*

leeway *n.* room, margin, space, latitude, breathing space, elbow room, freedom, slack, range.

LEFT-HANDED *a.* [LEFT-HAND ED] referring to an insincere or dubious compliment, one that is actually insulting. *She told him he had the ability to sing semiprofessionally, another of her subtle left-handed compliments.* SYN. insincere, dubious, backhanded, ambiguous, questionable, ironic, veiled, sardonic, mocking. ANT. *sincere, unambiguous, genuine.*

leftover *n.* remnant, remainder, surplus, leaving, scrap, remains, oddments.

LEFT-WING *a.* [LEFT WING] liberal, leftist, radical. *Left-wing democrats wanted to preserve the entire forest, regardless of lumbering jobs lost.* SYN. liberal, leftist, radical, progressive, far left, red, communistic. ANT. *right-wing, conservative, rightist.*

LEGACY *n.* [LEG uh see] something passed down from a previous generation or ancestor. *Drug abuse is now commonplace, a legacy of the "anything goes" 1960s.* SYN. inheritance, bequest, heritage, *hand-me-down, gift, heirloom, birthright, carryover.

legal *a.* lawful, licit, allowable, sanctioned, permitted, constitutional, right, just, authorized, legitimate, judicial. ANT. *illegal, illicit, unlawful.*

legalize *a.* make lawful, legitimize, allow, sanction, authorize, decriminalize, permit, license, legislate. ANT. *outlaw, prohibit.*

legend *n.* **1.** MYTH fable, lore, tale, story, fiction, narrative, allegory. **2.** CELEBRITY giant, star, superstar, hero, prodigy.

legendary *a.* **1.** MYTHICAL fabled, fanciful, fantastic, fictional, imaginary, traditional, romantic, epic. **2.** REMARKABLE immortal, great, celebrated, extraordinary, acclaimed, renowned, heroic.

legible *a.* readable, decipherable, clear, plain, easy-to-read, intelligible. ANT. *illegible, unreadable.*

legion *n.* mass, multitude, crowd, throng, pack, army, swarm, horde, mob, scores.

legislation *n.* bill, act, law, statute, code, ordinance, rule, regulation, charter, constitution.

legislator *n.* lawmaker, lawgiver, politician, representative, congressman, senator, selectman, assemblyman, councilman.

legislature *n.* congress, senate, house of representatives, parliament, assembly, council.

legitimate *a.* **1.** LAWFUL legal, licit, *legit, statutory, constitutional. **2.** GENUINE authentic, *for-real, true, *legit, *on the level, *kosher, *OK ANT. *1. unlawful, illegal, illicit. 2. fake, dishonest, fraudulent.*

leisure *n.* repose, ease, freedom, liberty, rest, recreation, relaxation, unemployment, idle hours, respite, *downtime. "The time you don't get paid for and enjoy spending." — Hyman Berston. ANT. *labor, work, employment.*

leisurely *a.* slow, unhurried, deliberate, casual, relaxed, laid-back, easy, lazy, *poky. ANT. *hurried, breakneck, rushed.*

lemon *n.* *dud, *dog, loser, *piece of crap, *hunk of junk, reject. ANT. **piece of work, success.*

lend *v.* **1.** LOAN entrust, let use, accommodate, advance, oblige. **2.** IMPART give, provide, furnish, contribute.

length *n.* **1.** DISTANCE span, extent, reach, measure, size, dimension, expanse. **2.** DURATION span, period, term.

lengthen *v.* stretch, elongate, protract, extend, expand, increase, prolong. ANT. *shorten, cut.*

lengthy *a.* long, protracted, drawn out, extended, prolonged, extensive, elongated, interminable, long-winded. ANT. *brief, short.*

lenient *a.* soft, mild, easy, merciful, tolerant, permissive, liberal, indulgent, charitable, kind, forgiving, compassionate. ANT. *strict, harsh, tough, unforgiving.*

leprechaun *n.* fairy, elf, little old man, dwarf, gnome, brownie, sprite, pixie, goblin.

lesion *n.* injury, damage, hurt, wound, sore, trauma, cut, laceration, bruise, contusion, impairment, *boo-boo.

less *a.* fewer, smaller, slighter, shorter, lower, not as great, inferior, minor, subordinate, lower, secondary. ANT. *more, greater, superior.*

lessen *v.* decrease, diminish, reduce, lower, abate, slacken, dwindle, shrink, fall off, cut, contract, downsize, pare, fade, subtract, moderate. ANT. *increase, multiply, expand.*

lesson *n.* instruction, class, exercise, lecture, assignment, drill, study, homework, teaching.

let *v.* **1.** ALLOW permit, authorize, enable, grant, *give the go-ahead, *give the green light, give permission, license. **2.** LEASE rent, sublease, hire out, charter.

letdown *n.* disapointment, disillusionment, anticlimax, disenchantment, *comedown, frustration, *washout, blow, *bubble-burster. ANT. *fulfillment, satisfaction, dream-come-true.*

lethal a. fatal, deadly, mortal, killing, death-dealing, murderous, dangerous, poisonous, pernicious, malignant. ANT. *harmless, benign.*

lethargic a. drowsy, sluggish, tired, weary, fatigued, listless, sleepy, torpid, languid, *out of it, lazy, slothful, apathetic, somnolent, dragging, comatose. ANT. *energized, lively, hyperactive.*

lethargy n. drowsiness, sluggishness, tiredness, fatigue, listlessness, sleepiness, somnolence, torpor, languor, malaise, laziness, slothfulness, apathy. ANT. *liveliness, vigor, *get-up-and-go.*

letter n. note, dispatch, message, missive, communication, memo, reply, acknowledgement, billet-doux, *fax. "Servant of parted friends." —Charles Eliot. "An unannounced visit." —Friedrich Neitzsche.

letters n. belleslettres, learning.

letup n. stopping, pause, cessation, interlude, break, lapse, lull, recess.

levee n. bank, embankment, dam, mound, breakwater.

level n. **1.** HEIGHT elevation, altitude, story, floor, stratum, extent. **2.** RANK position, grade.

level v. **1.** GRADE smooth, plane, flatten, even out. **2.** RAZE flatten, knock down, fell, wreck, demolish, destroy.

level a. even, flat, flush, plane, uniform, straight, smooth, balanced, equable, proportionate, in line. ANT. *uneven, tilted.*

levelheaded a. sensible, reasonable, prudent, composed, even-tempered, cool, calm, self-possessed, unruffled, unflappable, poised. ANT. *unreasonable, thoughtless, irrational, wild.*

leverage n. weight, influence, *pull, *clout, power, control, upper hand, advantage.

leviathan n. giant, colossus, monster, behemoth, titan, hulk, mammoth, whale, sea monster. ANT. *shrimp, midget, gnat.*

LEVITY n. [LEV i tee] light or unserious behavior, frivolity. *His jokes added much-needed levity to the occasion.* SYN. lightness, frivolity, lightheartedness, foolishness, silliness, buoyancy, mirth, merriment, whimsy, giddiness. ANT. *seriousness, gravity, somberness.*

levy n. tax, tariff, toll, assessment, duty, revenue, dues, fee, collection, imposition.

levy v. impose, exact, assess, tax, fix, lay on, charge, collect, wrest, tithe.

lewd a. lascivious, lecherous, lustful, libidinous, salacious, licentious, obscene, vulgar, indecent, immodest, suggestive, X-rated, lurid. ANT. *chaste, pure, upright, wholesome, clean.*

lexicon n. dictionary, thesaurus, glossary, word book, vocabulary.

liability a. **1.** RESPONSIBILITY accountability, burden, blame, obligation. **2.** DEBT indebtedness, obligation, due, debit. **3.** DRAWBACK disadvantage, hindrance, handicap, impediment, encumbrance, millstone, burden. ANT. *1. immunity. 2. asset. 3. advantage, plus.*

liable a. **1.** RESPONSIBLE accountable, answerable, obligated, subject, bound. **2.** LIKELY apt, probable, prone, disposed, given, subject, open, susceptible. ANT. *1. immune, exempt. 2. unlikely.*

liaison n. **1.** ALLIANCE connection, affiliation, hookup, union, association, linkup, communication. **2.** LOVE AFFAIR romance, fling, amour, tryst, *hanky-panky.

liar n. prevaricator, fabricator, fibber, *bullshit artist, deceiver, perjurer, cheater, dissembler, *con artist.

LIBEL n. [LYE bul] published statements that are untrue, malicious, and damaging to one's reputation. *The tabloid was recently sued for libel.* SYN. slander, defamation, smear, malicious gossip, falsehood, dirty lie, yellow journalism, innuendo, aspersion.

libel v. slander, defame, smear, scandalize, malign, denigrate, *drag through the mud, slur, discredit, *give a black eye.

libelous a. slanderous, defamatory, scandalous, denigrating, untrue, false, malicious, injurious, maligning, discrediting, made up.

liberal n. progressive, reformer, leftist, left-winger, libertarian, radical. "A man too broadminded to take his own side in a quarrel." —Robert Frost.

liberal a. **1.** GENEROUS giving, free-handed, charitable, openhanded, lavish, philanthropic, bountiful, unsparing. **2.** ABUNDANT plentiful, ample, copious, rife, rich, lavish, large. **3.** NONRESTRICTIVE loose, unrestrictive, free, unstrict. **4.** TOLERANT broad-minded, open-minded, unprejudiced, accepting, unbiased, indulgent. **5.** PROGRESSIVE reformist, left-wing, leftist, radical. ANT. *1. stingy, cheap, tightfisted. 2. sparse, skimpy. 3. strict, literal. 4. intolerant, prejudiced, close-minded. 5. conservative, right-wing.*

liberate v. free, release, emancipate, loose, unshackle, deliver, manumit, unbind, extricate, rescue. ANT. *enslave, subjugate, shackle.*

liberation n. freedom, liberty, release, emancipation, unshackling, deliverance, manumission, salvation, extrication, rescue. ANT. *enslavement, subjugation, imprisonment.*

liberty n. freedom, release, emancipation, liberation, autonomy, self-determination, nonrestriction, independence, privilege, license, sovereignty, latitude, unrestraint. "A power to do as we would be done by." — John Quincy Adams. ANT. *enslavement, restriction, restraint.*

libidinous a. lustful, *hot, *horny, lascivious, lewd, randy, sensual, carnal, lecherous, turned on, *hot as a three-dollar pistol. ANT. *turned off.*

libido n. sex drive, urge, lust, desire, *horniness, *hot pants, hot blood, sexuality, Eros.

license n. **1.** PERMIT permission, authorization, entitlement, privilege, grant, right. **2.** FREEDOM liberty, latitude, free hand, indulgence, presumption, immoderation, unrestraint, looseness, excess, boldness. ANT. *1. prohibition, restriction. 2. restriction, restraint.*

license v. permit, authorize, allow, sanction, warrant, certify, accredit.

licentious a. lascivious, lewd, immoral, libidinous, wanton, abandoned, lecherous, carnal, promiscuous, lustful, debauched, smutty, unrestrained. ANT. *chaste, prudish, wholesome, restrained.*

lick n. **1.** HIT punch, *whack, smack, blow, slap, jab. **2.** MUSICAL PHRASE *riff.

lick v. **1.** LAP tongue, kiss, graze, brush. **2.** BEAT whip, defeat, trounce, overpower, *shellac, trample, *kick one's ass.

lid n. cover, top, cap.

lie n. prevarication, fabrication, fib, falsehood, story, *cock-and-bull story, little white lie, *whopper, untruth, perjury, fiction, deceit, misrepresentation, distortion, stretching of the truth, barefaced lie. "The refuse of fools and cowards." — Lord Chesterfield. "An art in a lover." — Helen Rowland. ANT. *truth, gospel truth, fact.*

lie v. **1.** PREVARICATE fabricate, fib, falsify, *tell a little white lie, perjure, deceive, misrepresent, distort, stretch the truth, fudge, con. **2.** REST recline, stretch out, be recumbent, be prone, be supine, sprawl, lounge. ANT. *stand.*

life n. **1.** EXISTENCE being, vitality, animation, viability, consciousness, flesh and blood, organism. "A vapor, that appeareth for a little time, and then vanisheth away." — Bible. "A little gleam of time between two eternities." — Thomas Carlyle. "A play. It's not in its length, but its performance that

counts." — Seneca. **2.** LIVELINESS vigor, spirit, energy, animation, zest, vivacity, heart, enthusiasm. **3.** LIFE SPAN life expectancy, duration, longevity, course, length, period. **4.** TRIALS AND TRIBULATIONS peaks and valleys, the human condition, vicissitudes, *hand one is dealt, survival of the fittest. "A bridge of groans across a stream of tears." — Philip Bailey. "One long process of getting tired." — Samuel Butler. "Like eating artichokes — you've got to go through so much to get so little." — T.A. Dorgan. "A B-picture script." — Kirk Douglas. "An onion, and one peels it crying." — French proverb. "A bitch . . . then you die." — Anon. ANT. *death, nonexistence, oblivion.*

lifeless a. **1.** DEAD deceased, extinct, *dead as a coffin nail, *stone dead, defunct, *down for the count, comatose, unconscious, inanimate, inert. **2.** COLORLESS dull, lackluster, flat, *blah, insipid, wooden, tiresome, spiritless. ANT. *1. alive, living, vital. 2. spirited, lively, colorful.*

lifelike a. natural, realistic, true-to-life, faithful, true, graphic. ANT. *unnatural.*

lift n. **1.** HOIST heave, raising, boost, pull up. **2.** RAISING OF SPIRITS boost, *shot in the arm, *pick-me-up, encouragement.

lift v. **1.** HOIST elevate, heave, raise, boost, jack up, erect, upraise, hike, heft. **2.** STEAL swipe, pinch, pocket, shoplift, pilfer. **3.** REMOVE cancel, annul, rescind. ANT. *1. drop. 3. impose.*

light n. **1.** RADIANCE luminescence, illumination, radiation, glow, shine, incandescence, effulgence, flash, glare, brilliance, glimmer. **2.** LAMP beacon, lantern, candle, torch, flare. ANT. *1. dark, gloom, blackness.*

light v. **1.** ILLUMINATE spotlight, shine, irradiate, brighten. **2.** IGNITE kindle, spark, set fire to, inflame. **3.** get down, descend, alight, land, settle, perch. ANT. *1. darken, dim. 2. extinguish, douse.*

light a. **1.** BRIGHT illuminated, radiant, brilliant, shining, luminous, glowing, aglow, well-lit, lambent, sunny, gleaming. **2.** PALE faded, fair, bleached, blanched, washed-out. **3.** OF WEIGHT weightless, slight, ethereal, *featherlight, wispy, insubstantial, airy, lighter than air, unheavy, sheer, scant. **4.** WEAK mild, slight, soft, faint, gentle. **5.** SIMPLE easy, effortless, undemanding, untaxing, *no sweat. **6.** CHEERFUL, HUMOROUS amusing, gay, merry, blithe, funny, entertaining, frivolous, trifling. ANT. *1. dark, black, gloomy. 2. dark, deep,* *vivid.* 3. *heavy, hefty, massive.* 4. *strong, powerful, hard, harsh.* 5. *hard, demanding, taxing.* 6. **heavy, deep, serious.*

lighten *v.* 1. REDUCE decrease, ease, unload, remove, lessen, empty, disencumber, alleviate, mitigate. 2. LIFT cheer, perk up, buoy, gladden. 3. BRIGHTEN illuminate, light up, irradiate. ANT. 1. *increase, burden, weigh down.* 2. *depress, discourage.* 3. *darken.*

lighthearted *a.* carefree, cheerful, happy, buoyant, sunny, jovial, playful, upbeat, blithe, glad, untroubled, joyous. ANT. *downhearted, heavyhearted, grave, depressed.*

lightly *adv.* slightly, softly, faintly, gently, daintily, delicately, sparingly, gingerly, easily, carefully. ANT. *heavily, ponderously.*

lightning *n.* electrical discharge, bolt, thunderbolt, flash, chain lightning, stroke, jag. SEE CLOUD, THUNDER

likable *a.* winning, agreeable, charming, attractive, nice, pleasing, pleasant, appealing, sweet, good-natured, warmhearted, friendly. ANT. *repellent, mean, unappealing.*

like *v.* 1. FANCY enjoy, care for, delight in, *get a kick out of, be partial to, *dig, love, adore, take pleasure in, be fond of, appreciate, relish, *have a soft spot for, esteem. 2. WANT choose, prefer, care, feel inclined. ANT. 1. *dislike, hate, abhor, detest.*

like *a.* similar, alike, uniform, approximating, much the same, comparable, corresponding, close, equivalent, homologous, akin. ANT. *different, unlike.*

likelihood *n.* probability, good chance, prospect, possibility, potentiality.

likely *a.* probable, apt, promising, liable, expected, anticipated, presumable, plausible, *in the cards, destined. ANT. *unlikely, improbable, doubtful.*

liken *v.* relate, link, equate. SEE COMPARE

likeness *n.* 1. RESEMBLANCE semblance, similarity, correspondence, sameness, uniformity, analogy. 2. FACSIMILE replica, image, representation, depiction, portrait, picture, photo, copy, model. ANT. 1. *difference, dissimilarity.*

liking *n.* fondness, fancy, affinity, taste, appetite, inclination, partiality, preference, attraction, *soft spot. ANT. *aversion, hatred.*

limb *n.* appendage, member, part, extremity, leg, arm, wing, branch, bough.

limber *a.* flexible, pliant, elastic, supple, agile, loose, pliable, malleable. ANT. *stiff, rigid, inflexible.*

limbo *n.* nowhere. SEE OBLIVION

limit *n.* boundary, end, extent, margin, maximum, ceiling, border, brink, utmost, farthest reach, termination.

limit *v.* restrict, bound, confine, put a ceiling on, inhibit, restrain, constrict, hem in, curb, ration, check, circumscribe.

limitation *n.* restriction, check, curb, impediment, stumbling block, stricture, bar, block, hindrance, handicap, qualification.

limited *a.* restricted, bound, confined, restrained, checked, circumscribed, controlled, curbed, fixed. ANT. *unlimited, unrestricted.*

limitless *a.* unlimited, boundless, unrestricted, infinite, neverending, immeasurable, incalculable, innumerable, vast. ANT. *limited, finite.*

limp *v.* hobble, falter, favor one leg, drag one foot, walk lamely, stagger, shuffle, hitch, move haltingly, hop, totter, take mincing steps.

limp *a.* flaccid, drooping, wilted, soft, slack, flabby, weak, lax. ANT. *rigid, firm, stiff, strong.*

limpid *a.* clear, transparent, pellucid, crystal, like glass, translucent. ANT. *cloudy, muddy.*

line *n.* 1. LONG MARK score, underscore, underline, stripe, stroke, dash, streak, slash, demarcation. 2. ROW course, column, series, succession, queue, procession, chain, series, train, string, file, tier. 3. CORD string, twine, rope, cable, filament, thread, strand. 4. LINE OF WORK business, calling, specialty, interest, vocation, profession, *racket. 5. LINEAGE ancestry, descent, breed, stock, pedigree.

lineage *n.* descent, ancestry, stock, family, strain, bloodline, genealogy, heredity, succession, extraction.

linger *v.* stay, remain, hang back, hang around, loiter, dawdle, dillydally, poke about, wait, procrastinate, delay, hesitate.

lingo *n.* language, dialect, jargon, vocabulary, vernacular, argot, tongue, speech, slang, idiom.

linguist *n.* polyglot, bilinguist, translator, interpreter.

liniment *n.* ointment, salve, balm, lotion, embrocation, unguent.

link *n.* 1. CONNECTION component, section, coupling. 2. ASSOCIATION attachment, tie, connection, bond, contact.

link *v.* associate, connect, attach, unite, tie, bond, couple, join, splice, bind, relate.

lionize *v.* celebrate, acclaim, glorify, exalt, elevate, idolize, immortalize, worship, revere.

lip *n.* 1. RIM brim, edge, verge. 2. *Sl.* IMPUDENCE

*mouth, back talk, insolence, rudeness, *sass, *wising off, *crap.

LIP SERVICE n. [LIP SERVICE] insincere agreement, empty talk or gesture. *Politicians pay a lot of lip service to their constituents.* SYN. insincerity, empty talk, empty gesture, token agreement, tokenism, show, hollow words, flattery, smooth talk, duplicity.

liquefy v. dissolve, thaw, melt.

liquid n. fluid, water, solution, aqua, juice, extract, broth, soup.

liquid a. fluid, running, flowing, aqueous, wet, moist, watery, juicy, molten. ANT. *solid, dry.*

liquidate v. **1.** SETTLE pay off, dispose of, make good, square, satisfy, discharge. **2.** CLOSE OUT sell out, convert to cash, sell stock. **3.** KILL murder, *knock off, slay, *rub out, *bump off, exterminate, assassinate.

liqueur n. liquor, alcohol, flavored drink, cordial, apertif, appetizer.

WORD FIND
almond-flavored: amaretto
bourbon and spice: Wild Turkey
cherry and almond: maraschino
chocolate and vanilla: creme de cacao
coconut and rum: ron coco
coffee flavor with vanilla: kahlua
cognac and orange: grand marnier
French cherry: creme de cerise
French raspberry: framboise
Greek, anise-flavored: ouzo
green, licorice flavor: absinthe
herbed brandy: benedictine, chartreuse
Irish whiskey, honey and orange: Irish mist
Israeli, chocolate and orange: sabra
Jamaican, coffee and spice: tia maria
Japanese, honeydew melon: midori
licorice-flavored: anise, pernod, sambuca
mint and menthol: creme de menthe
peach: Southern Comfort
plum gin: sloe gin
scotch, heather, honey and herbs: drambuie
SEE ALCOHOL, COCKTAIL, DRINK, LIQUOR, MOONSHINE, WINE

liquor n. alcohol, booze, spirits, whiskey, *hard stuff, firewater, *rotgut, demon rum, intoxicant, inebriant, potation, rum, gin, vodka, Scotch, rye. SEE ALCOHOL, COCKTAIL, LIQUEUR, MOONSHINE, WINE

lissom a. lithe, limber, supple, agile, flexible, pliant, loose, graceful, light on one's feet. ANT. *stiff, heavy, awkward.*

list n. checklist, rundown, inventory, roll, roster, directory, tally, lineup, schedule, index, series, menu.

list v. **1.** inventory, record, tally, schedule, tabulate, itemize, note, post, index, record, file. **2.** lean, tilt, slant, incline, pitch, slope, tip.

listen v. hear, absorb, harken, pay attention, prick up one's ears, catch, *tune in, monitor, heed, overhear, eavesdrop. "The only way to entertain some folks." — Kin Hubbard. ANT. *ignore, disregard, turn a deaf ear on.*

listless a. languid, weary, apathetic, indifferent, lethargic, sluggish, *out of it, passive, fatigued, drowsy, dead, torpid, leaden, spiritless, *blah. ANT. *energetic, lively, spirited.*

litany n. list, listing, repetition, recital, rendition, rundown, account, compilation.

literal a. exact, true, actual, word-for-word, faithful, real, accurate, verbatim, *to the letter, undeviating, precise. ANT. *figurative, metaphorical, loose, imprecise, paraphrased.*

literally adv. exactly, actually, word-for-word, real, nonfiguratively, faithfully, verbatim, *to the letter, precisely. ANT. *figuratively, metaphorically, imprecisely, loosely.*

literary a. bookish, literate, scholarly, erudite, cerebral, formal, artistic, stuffy.

literate a. schooled, educated, well-read, able to read and write, scholarly, lettered, knowledgeable, cultured. ANT. *illiterate, ignorant, uneducated.*

lithe a. flexible, limber, pliant, supple, bendable, lithesome, lissome, loose, agile, nimble. ANT. *stiff, rigid.*

lithesome a. SEE LITHE

LITIGATE v. [LIT uh GATE] to take a dispute to court, to sue. *The damaged party threatened to litigate.* SYN. try in court, contest in court, file suit, bring suit, sue, prosecute, bring legal action.

litigation n. lawsuit, suit, legal action, legal proceedings, prosecution, filing of charges, court case, trial. "A machine which you go into as a pig and come out of as a sausage." — Ambrose Bierce.

LITIGIOUS a. [li TIJ us] quick to threaten with or file lawsuits, contentious, quarrelsome. *America has become one of the most litigious societies on earth.* SYN. contentious, quarrelsome, argumentative, combative, belligerent, given to file lawsuits, *sue-happy, *lawsuit happy. ANT. *accommodating, compromising, peaceful.*

litter n. trash, rubbish, refuse, garbage, *crap, debris.

litter v. strew, clutter, mess, scatter.

little a. **1.** SMALL tiny, wee, diminutive, miniature, pint-sized, undersized, dinky, shrimpy.

Lilliputian, itsy-bitsy, minute, puny, microscopic. **2.** SCANT insufficient, few, meager, skimpy. **3.** BRIEF fleeting, passing, short, momentary, limited. **4.** WEAK insignificant, inconsequential, ineffective, faint, feeble, powerless, trivial, slight. **5.** YOUNG immature, juvenile, undeveloped. ANT. *1. big, huge, gigantic. 2. ample, sufficient. 3. protracted, prolonged. 4. strong, powerful. 5. big, adult.*

liturgy *n.* ritual, service, rite, ceremony, worship.

livable *a.* habitable, comfortable, satisfactory, adequate, tolerable, homey, *equipped with creature comforts. ANT. *uninhabitable, intolerable.*

live *v.* **1.** EXIST live and breathe, draw breath, survive, be alive, function, subsist, persist, endure, last. **2.** RESIDE dwell, inhabit, occupy, lodge, *hang one's hat. ANT. *1. die, expire, perish.*

live *a.* **1.** LIVING alive, breathing, animate, vital, conscious, *alive and kicking, viable. **2.** LIVELY energetic, dynamic, hot, operative, active, vigorous, spirited. ANT. *1. dead, inanimate, lifeless. 2. dead, cold.*

livelihood *n.* living, occupation, job, work, employment, trade, profession, vocation, business, source of income, subsistence.

lively *a.* full of life, energetic, active, *peppy, bustling, vivacious, vigorous, *hyper, frisky, spry, effervescent, perky, *bubbly, *high octane. ANT. *dead, sluggish, leaden, listless.*

livid *a.* **1.** BLACK AND BLUE bruised, discolored. **2.** FURIOUS enraged, infuriated, irate, mad, beside oneself with rage, incensed, indignant, red in the face. ANT. *2. calm, peaceful, composed.*

living *n.* livelihood, subsistence, source of income, job, support, *bread and butter, occupation.

living *a.* alive, existing, animated, breathing, vital, vigorous, lively, conscious, viable, active. ANT. *dead, extinct, inanimate.*

load *n.* **1.** FREIGHT cargo, shipment, lading, haul, payload, consignment, burden, contents, goods. **2.** BURDEN weight, encumbrance, millstone, cross, albatross, hardship, worry, care, oppression, *excess baggage.

load *v.* fill, pack, stack, stuff, lade, pile, cram, weigh down, saddle, burden, encumber. ANT. *unload, empty, unburden.*

loaf *v.* lounge about, *goof off, laze, idle, *sit on one's butt, *not lift a finger, vegetate, *lie down on the job, shirk, malinger.

loafer *n.* idler, *lazybones, *layabout, *couch potato, *sofa spud, deadbeat, slacker, *goof-off, do-nothing, ne'er-do-well, shirker, malingerer. "A person who is trying to make weekends meet." — Anon. ANT. *hustler, go-getter, doer.*

loan *n.* advance, credit, allowance, mortage, *fronting.

loathe *v.* dislike, hate, abhor, look upon with disgust, regard contemptuously, feel sick at the sight of, despise, detest, reject, scorn. ANT. *like, love, admire.*

loathing *n.* hatred, dislike, abhorrence, disgust, revulsion, repugnance, contempt, aversion, distaste. ANT. *love, admiration, adoration.*

loathsome *a.* abhorrent, disgusting, revolting, despicable, detestable, contemptible, distasteful, abominable, hateful, repugnant, deplorable. ANT. *admirable, likable, wonderful.*

lob *v.* toss, throw, loft, flip, pitch, fling.

lobby *n.* **1.** HALL entrance, corridor, foyer, vestibule, reception area, anteroom. **2.** PRESSURE GROUP special interest group, political action group, influence peddlers, lobbyists.

LOBBY *v.* [LAW bee] to try to influence others, especially politicians and their votes. *The paper companies plan to lobby in Washington for stronger lumbering rights.* SYN. influence, *influence-peddle, *pull strings, persuade, pressure, sway, solicit votes, sell, push, politick.

local *a.* regional, neighborhood, community, municipal, divisional, district, close to home, civic, parochial, provincial, native, limited, narrow, confined. ANT. *national, international, worldwide, foreign.*

locality *n.* locale, spot, place, area, neighborhood, position, site, point, region, zone, district.

localize *v.* confine, limit, narrow, restrict.

locate *v.* **1.** FIND detect, come across, uncover, discover, place, track down, pinpoint, unearth, root out, sniff out, ferret out. **2.** ESTABLISH settle, occupy, take root, house, take up residence, squat.

located *a.* situated, stationed, placed, positioned, based.

location *n.* place, spot, site, position, point, zone, locale, locality, area, neighborhood, district, neck of the woods.

lock *n.* **1.** bolt, catch, padlock, latch, hook, bar, deadbolt, clamp. **2.** tress, curl, ringlet, tuft. SEE HAIR

lock *v.* secure, latch, bolt, padlock, bar, close, shut.

locker *n.* chest, footlocker, trunk, cabinet,

compartment, closet.

locomotion n. motion, movement, progression, traveling, driving, walking. ANT. *inertia, stasis.*

locution n. phrasing, phraseology, language, ideolect, dialect, pronunciation, accent, brogue.

lodestar n. **1.** NORTH STAR pole star, Polaris. **2.** GUIDE ideal.

lodge n. summer house, cabin, camp, cottage, chalet, hostel, resort hotel, hunting lodge.

lodge v. **1.** STAY room, house, abide, *put up, reside, live, bunk, *hole up, sojourn. **2.** BECOME STUCK stick, wedge, fix, catch.

lodger n. guest, tenant, boarder, renter, roomer.

lodging n. accommodation, hotel, motel, inn, bed and breakfast, hostel, boarding house, rooming house, quarters, room and board, pied-a-terre, billet.

loft n. attic, garret, storeroom, upper level, studio, gallery, clerestory.

loft v. throw, toss, launch skyward.

lofty a. **1.** VERY HIGH sky high, elevated, soaring, towering, vertiginous, tall, aerial, cloud-kissing, heavenly, celestial. **2.** NOBLE OR SUBLIME exalted, elevated, great, grand, esteemed, renowned, celebrated, distinguished, majestic. **3.** HAUGHTY arrogant, high and mighty, lordly, supercilious, self-important, *snotty, *stuck-up, *on one's high horse, *uppity, pompous, proud. ANT. *1. low, earthbound, short. 2. ignoble, low, common. 3. modest, humble, down to earth.*

log n. **1.** TREE LIMB OR TRUNK stump, timber, branch, block, pole, beam, wood. **2.** RECORD BOOK journal, register, account, daybook, diary, chronicle.

WORD FIND

game, knock opponent off rolling log: birling

logger: lumberjack

logging slope run: flume, sluice

mass of in river: drive

pile: rollway

log v. record, report, enter, note, register, chronicle, take down, keep an account, tally.

loge n. box, balcony, compartment, stall.

logic n. reasoning, argumentation, deduction, induction, syllogization, analysis, rationale, sense, good sense, sound judgment. "The anatomy of thought."—John Locke. "The architecture of human reason."—Evelyn Waugh. "The armory of reason."—Thomas Fuller.

logical a. reasonable, sensible, commonsensical, rational, sound, analytical, intelligent, smart, deductive, scientific, plausible. ANT. *illogical, nonsensical, unscientific.*

loiter v. hang around, linger, idle, lounge, tarry, hover, mill around, poke, *hang, loaf, vegetate, dawdle.

loll v. **1.** LOUNGE lean, recline, sprawl, relax, slouch, lie on, repose, hang. **2.** DROOP hang, dangle, trail, sag.

lone a. solitary, sole, isolated, lonely, single, individual, unaccompanied, deserted, forsaken. ANT. *paired, accompanied.*

lonely a. **1.** FRIENDLESS AND FEELING EMPTY lonesome, companionless, lone, forsaken, isolated, solitary, secluded, reclusive, *like a hermit, forlorn, desolate, deserted, abandoned, forgotten, estranged, shut in. **2.** REMOTE, OUT OF THE WAY unfrequented, uninhabited, deserted, isolated, secluded, unpopulated, sequestered, cloistered. ANT. *1. befriended, popular. 2. crowded, mobbed, frequented.*

loner n. *lone wolf, solitary, hermit, recluse, introvert, outcast, misanthrope.

lonesome a. SEE LONELY

long a. **1.** EXTENSIVE extended, expanded, lengthy, elongated, protracted, prolonged, stretched out, drawn out. **2.** TAKING TOO MUCH TIME overlong, interminable, long-winded, unending, endless, dragging, tedious. ANT. *1. short, brief. 2. brief, short, concise.*

long v. yearn, hunger, desire, crave, thirst, want, hanker, wish for, pine, *lust after, *have the hots for.

longing n. yearning, desire, hunger, craving, thirst, want, hankering, yen, wish, *itch.

longing a. yearning, desirous, wanting, craving, hungry, wishful, pining.

longshot n. outside shot, outside chance.

long-standing a. long-established, deeply rooted, long-lived.

long-winded a. wordy, verbose, prolix, *windy, diffuse, rambling, circumlocutory, overlong, endless, interminable. ANT. *brief, short, to the point.*

look n. **1.** EXPRESSION, APPEARANCE face, aspect, bearing, guise, impression, air, fashion. **2.** GLANCE glimpse, eye, regard, stare, gander, inspection, *once-over, scrutiny, examination.

look v. **1.** SEE regard, behold, check out, inspect, examine, view, observe, scrutinize, notice, *take a gander, *feast one's eyes on, survey, watch, *eyeball, *get a load of, gaze, stare, glimpse, glance. **2.** APPEAR seem, strike one as, exhibit, resemble, manifest.

look-alike n. twin, double, carbon copy, clone, mirrorimage, *dead ringer, match, *spitting image, duplicate.

lookout n. **1.** WATCH guard, eye, vigilance, heed, surveillance. **2.** SENTINEL guard, sentry, watchman, patrol, spotter. **3.** LOOKOUT STATION tower, perch, crow's nest, watchtower, observatory.

loom v. appear, take shape, materialize, rise up, emerge, threaten, menace, impend, cast a long shadow. ANT. disappear, vanish, recede.

loony a. Sl. crazy, nutty, demented, lunatic, *daffy, *cuckoo, *wacky, mad, daft, foolish, stupid, *out of one's gourd, irrational. ANT. sane, rational, sober.

loop n. circle, ring, hoop, bow, noose, spiral, coil, eyelet, bend, circuit.

loop v. circle, encircle, ring, wind, coil, curl, knot.

loose v. SEE LOOSEN

loose a. **1.** NOT TIGHT slack, relaxed, lax, limp, baggy, unbinding. **2.** UNRESTRAINED unbound, unfastened, untied, undone, unrestricted, unconstrained, unsecured, unattached, free. **3.** INEXACT indefinite, imprecise, vague, broad, roundabout. **4.** SEXUALLY IMMORAL lascivious, licentious, promiscuous, lewd, lecherous, abandoned, debauched, unrestrained, libidinous, perverted, *having the morals of an alley cat. ANT. 1. tight, snug, binding. 2. restrained, bound, tied. 3. exact, precise. 4. chaste, celibate, moral.

loosen v. **1.** SLACKEN relax, unbind, ease up, moderate, relieve tension. **2.** FREE untie, unbind, let go, liberate, unfasten, untether, undo, unlock. ANT. 1. tighten, restrict, bind. 2. tie, bind, fasten.

loot n. plunder, spoils, stolen goods, booty, take, haul, pillage.

loot v. plunder, rob, steal, despoil, pillage, *rip off, swipe, lift, ransack, pilfer, burglarize.

lop v. trim, cut, remove, prune, sever, truncate, chop off, clip, shear, pare.

lope v. stride, spring, *move right along. SEE WALK.

lopsided a. uneven, asymmetrical, one-sided, unbalanced, disproportional, top-heavy, *cockeyed, awry, irregular. ANT. even, symmetrical, balanced.

LOQUACIOUS a. [loh KWAY shus] talkative, gabby. Talk show hosts are naturally loquacious. SYN. talkative, gabby, garrulous, chatty, longwinded, voluble, babbling, verbose, *bigmouthed, *motor-mouthed, *having the gift of gab. ANT. taciturn, reticent, reserved.

lord n. nobleman, master, ruler, monarch, governor, baron, viscount, king.

lordly a. **1.** NOBLE grand, stately, dignified, gracious, lofty, princely, regal, royal. **2.** HAUGHTY arrogant, overbearing, high and mighty, imperious, domineering, insolent, condescending, supercilious, *snotty, superior. ANT. 1. low, common, humble. 2. modest, humble, down to earth, subservient.

lose v. **1.** MISLAY misplace, lose track of, lose sight of. **2.** BE DEFEATED fail, fall, *blow it, *flunk, *go belly up, be outclassed, be outdistanced, fall short, surrender, *eat one's dust, *meet one's Waterloo, *take a beating, be humbled, *take a dive, *bomb, flop, *lay an egg, *take a bath. **3.** ELUDE evade, escape, avoid, *give the slip, rid, *throw off the trail, outdistance, *leave in one's wake. ANT. 1. find, stumble upon, locate. 2. win, defeat, triumph, outclass, vanquish.

loser n. failure, *Charlie Brown, *schlemiel, also-ran, *dud, *flop, *dog, *sad sack, *foul ball, *turkey, *poor slob. ANT. winner, champion, hero.

loss n. **1.** COST debit, deficit, debt, forfeiture. **2.** SEE DEFEAT **3.** DAMAGE deprivation, detriment, disadvantage, harm, injury, impairment, privation, misfortune, destruction, removal. ANT. 1. profit, gain, surplus. 2. win. 3. gain, return.

lost a. **1.** MISPLACED mislaid, missing, disappeared, vanished, gone, strayed, down the drain, irretrievable. **2.** OFF TRACK disoriented, astray, *going around in circles, off-course, adrift. **3.** DESTROYED ruined, wiped out, wrecked, obliterated. **4.** WASTED squandered, misspent, exhausted. **5.** DEEP IN THOUGHT absorbed, dreaming, rapt, preoccupied, engrossed, abstracted, far away. **6.** BEWILDERED confused. ANT. 1. found, uncovered, retrieved. 2. oriented, on course, having one's bearings. 3. preserved, saved.

lot n. **1.** PARCEL OF LAND plot, acreage, tract, real estate, subdivision. **2.** PORTION share, allotment, allowance, interest, part, percentage. **3.** FORTUNE fate, *hand one is dealt, destiny, portion, status, doom, *the way the cookie crumbles. **4.** A GREAT DEAL much, quantity, piles, slews, loads, scores, tons, abundance, plenty, oodles.

lothario n. womanizer, lady-killer, seducer, rake, lover, *wolf, philanderer, Don Juan,

Casanova, Romeo.

lotion n. cream, ointment, balm, salve, embrocation, conditioner, liniment, unguent.

loud a. **1.** BLARING earsplitting, deafening, piercing, thundering, booming, stentorian, intense, clamorous, noisy, vociferous, *enough to wake the dead, powerful, roaring, cacophonous. **2.** GAUDY flashy, garish, blinding, splashy, ostentatious, vivid, cheap. ANT. *1. quiet, low, soft, silent. 2. tasteful, understated.*

loudmouthed a. bigmouthed, obnoxious, blustering, bellowing, vociferous, boisterous, strident, clamorous. ANT. *reticent, shy, quiet, taciturn.*

lounge n. **1.** LOBBY waiting room, reception room, anteroom. **2.** COCKTAIL LOUNGE club, bar, saloon, disco.

lounge v. relax, recline, lie about, repose, stretch out, sprawl out, loll, loaf, vegetate, idle, laze.

lousy a. Sl. poor, rotten, inferior, awful, terrible, *crappy, shoddy, inadequate, shabby, bad, disgusting, contemptible, atrocious. ANT. *good, great, high class.*

lout n. boor, oaf, clodhopper, clod, bumpkin, hayseed, dolt, clown, *lug, *slob, yahoo, *lummox.

loutish a. boorish, clumsy, stupid, oafish, cloddish, dense, rough, churlish, *like a bull in a china shop. ANT. *refined, gracious, urbane, suave.*

lovable a. endearing, adorable, sweet, dear, warmhearted, winning, amiable, cute, cuddly, lovely, likable, charming, angelic. ANT. *repugnant, nauseating, loathsome.*

love n. endearment, devotion, adoration, fondness, affection, warmth, esteem, friendship, closeness, intimacy, attachment, regard, passion, infatuation, crush, enchantment, amour, ardor, rapture, desire, longing, *hots. "Our highest word, and the synonym of God." — Ralph Waldo Emerson. "An alliance of friendship and animalism." — Charles Colton. "Friendship set on fire." — Jeremy Taylor. "The heart's immortal thirst to be completely known and all forgiven." — Henry Van Dyke. "Spiritual fire." — Emanuel Swedenborg. "Two minds without a single thought." — Philip Barry. "A perpetual hyperbole." — Francis Bacon. "When another' person's needs are as important as your own." — Abe Burrows. ANT. *hate, disgust, contempt, repulsion.*

love v. **1.** ADORE be fond of, cherish, worship, hold dear, treasure, idolize, think the world of, like, be crazy about, long for, desire. **2.** *MAKE OUT hug, kiss, cuddle, neck, embrace, make love, romance, have sex, engage in foreplay, *have the hots for. ANT. *1. hate, dislike, loathe, detest.*

love affair n. affair, fling, romance, intrigue, liaison, relationship, tryst, adultery, amour.

lovely a. beautiful, pretty, attractive, exquisite, fair, gracious, winning, charming, handsome, good-looking, comely, fetching, captivating, pleasing, graceful, nice, personable. ANT. *ugly, repulsive, hideous.*

lovemaking n. *making out, foreplay. SEE SEX

lover n. **1.** SWEETHEART flame, steady, *honey, *significant other, mate, sex partner, suitor, paramour, stud, Romeo, beau, boyfriend, girlfriend, mistress, lothario, Don Juan, Casanova, heartthrob. **2.** FAN aficionado, devotee, enthusiast, buff, *freak, *bug, *nut.

lovesick a. longing, pining, *out of it, *gone, lovelorn, *having it bad.

loving a. affectionate, warm, tender, giving, fond, devoted, caring, doting, kind, friendly, demonstrative, solicitous, passionate, amorous, romantic, sexual, erotic, ardent. ANT. *hateful, mean, cold, brutal.*

low a. **1.** CLOSE TO THE GROUND ground-level, low-lying, low-hanging, low-slung, short, squat, bottommost. **2.** DECREASED diminished, drained, depleted, dried up, exhausted, shallow, expended, running out. **3.** UNHAPPY depressed, melancholy, *bummed out, miserable, blue, downhearted, dejected, glum, discouraged, sad, heavyhearted. **4.** SMALL little, paltry, slight, modest, slim, puny, deficient, humble. **5.** MEAN despicable, bad, evil, base, depraved, contemptible, disgraceful, wretched, reprehensible, ignoble, vulgar, nasty. **6.** QUIET hushed, subdued, soft, muted, muffled, whispered, murmured. **7.** POOR plebian, humble, lowborn. ANT. *1. high, tall, skyscraping, towering. 2. full, replenished, overflowing. 3. high, happy, joyous. 4. large, generous, high. 5. honorable, noble, nice. 6. loud, amplified. 7. wealthy, highborn, aristocratic.*

lower v. **1.** DROP bring down, let down, let fall, depress, descend, submerge, dip, sink. **2.** REDUCE decrease, diminish, lessen, downgrade, depreciate, modify, cut, slash, shorten, soften, abate, relieve. **3.** HUMBLE degrade, dishonor, shame, humiliate, disgrace, debase, demean. ANT. *1. raise, lift, elevate. 2. increase, boost, add, extend. 3. respect, honor.*

lower *a.* inferior, under, lesser, secondary, minor, subordinate, junior. ANT. *higher, superior.*

low-key *a.* subdued, understated, subtle, restrained, toned down, mellow, muted, quiet. ANT. *loud, intense, blatant.*

lowly *a.* inferior, humble, modest, common, ordinary, plain, simple, poor, plebian, proletarian, baseborn, obscure. ANT. *superior, highborn, lofty.*

loyal *a.* faithful, trustworthy, true, allegiant, *tried and true, *true-blue, devoted, patriotic, dedicated, staunch, reliable, dependable. ANT. *disloyal, unfaithful, treacherous.*

loyalty *n.* faithfulness, allegiance, devotion, dedication, patriotism, fidelity, duty, honor, reliability, dependability, steadfastness, staunchness, trustworthiness. ANT. *disloyalty, backstabbing, treachery, perfidy.*

lubricate *v.* grease, oil, slicken.

LUCID *a.* [LOO sid] clear, easy to understand. Also, clearheaded. *The report was straightforward and lucid.* SYN. clear, crystal-clear, transparent, understandable, comprehensible, plain, intelligible, easy to grasp, distinct, apparent, obvious, unambiguous, clearheaded, rational, of sound mind, sensible. ANT. *unclear, cloudy, unintelligible, irrational.*

Lucifer *n.* Satan. SEE DEVIL

luck *n.* **1.** FORTUNE fate, chance, lot, destiny, wheel of fortune, fortuity, happenstance, *fickle finger of fate, *toss of the dice, providence, kismet. **2.** GOOD FORTUNE *break, success, windfall, godsend, opportunity, serendipity, fluke, *shit luck. "An explanation of the other fellow's success." —Harry Thompson.."The best is created, not waited for." —Anon. ANT. **2.** *misfortune, bad break.*

LUCRATIVE *a.* [LOO kruh tiv] producing profit or riches. *His oil business turned out to be highly lucrative.* SYN. profitable, profit-producing, wealth-producing, income-producing, remunerative, money-making, high-paying, gainful, prosperous, rewarding, worthwhile. ANT. *unprofitable, money-losing, unprosperous, income-draining.*

lucre *n.* money, riches, wealth.

LUDICROUS *a.* [LOO di krus] laughable, absurd. *The medical beliefs of the early Victorians were often ludicrous.* SYN. laughable, absurd, ridiculous, stupid, preposterous, comical, hilarious, outlandish, crazy, silly, uproarious, nonsensical, *cockamamy. ANT. *serious, sensible, respectable.*

lug *v.* carry, drag, haul, tow, *schlep, hump, tug, pull, tote.

luggage *n.* baggage, trunks, carry-on, suitcases, valises, packs, bags, gear, effects.

lukewarm *a.* unenthusiastic, halfhearted, cool, apathetic, indifferent, tepid, impassive, uncaring, uninterested. ANT. *enthusiastic, passionate, hot.*

lull *n.* quiet period, calm, pause, letup, break, quiet, respite, hush, spell, breather, silence.

lull *v.* calm, soothe, reassure, sedate, pacify, quiet, put to sleep, tranquilize, allay. ANT. *agitate, arouse, excite.*

lulu *n. Sl.* *dilly, *corker, *dandy, *humdinger, *doozy, *ripsnorter, *something to write home about.

lumber *v.* clump, plod, stump, trudge, stamp, *clomp, drag, waddle, move heavily, move awkwardly.

luminary *n.* celebrity, star, *superstar, *VIP, notable, personality, dignitary, *big name, *bigshot, *bigwig, *toast of the town. ANT. *nobody.*

luminous *a.* **1.** BRIGHT glowing, aglow, shining, illuminated, lighted, brilliant, radiant, lit, resplendent, luminescent, lustrous. **2.** CLEAR understandable, lucid, comprehendable, intelligible, perspicuous, plain, obvious. ANT. **1.** *dark, dim, black.* **2.** *cloudy, confusing, vague.*

lummox *n.* oaf, clod, *klutz, *big ape, lunkhead, lout, clodhopper.

lump *n.* clump, chunk, mass, gob, ball, hunk, piece, bulk, scrap, bump, protuberance, swelling, bulge, prominence, node, knot.

lunacy *a.* craziness, insanity, psychosis, madness, dementia, folly, foolishness, idiocy, *wackiness, *nuttiness, stupidity, silliness, imbecility. ANT. *sanity, rationality, sensibleness.*

lunatic *n.* psychopath, maniac, madman, psychotic, *schizo, *psycho, *whacko, *nut, *kook, *loony, *screwball, crackbrain.

lunatic *a.* SEE CRAZY

lunch *n.* luncheon, dinner, bite to eat, brunch, meal, dejeuner.

lunge *n.* thrust, plunge, charge, pounce, jump, rush, spring, leap, pass, jab, stab.

lunge *v.* thrust, plunge, charge, pounce, jump, rush, spring, leap, pass, jab, stab.

lurch *v.* pitch, jerk, heave, slip, roll, stagger, sway, lunge, plunge, toss, reel, tilt.

lure *n.* enticement, bait, temptation, *carrot, *magnet, *come-on, attraction, tease, inducement, allurement, draw, hook, bribe. ANT. *repellent.*

lure v. entice, bait, tempt, *hold out a carrot, attract, tease, induce, draw, hook, bribe, allure, seduce. ANT. *repel.*

LURID a. [LOOR id] shocking, horrifying or sensational, as a grisly crime. *The news show provided all the lurid details of the murder.* SYN. shocking, horrifying, sensational, startling, vivid, graphic, horrid, gruesome, appalling, grisly, revolting.

luscious a. delicious, delightful, delectable, *scrumptious, tasty, flavorful, toothsome, palatable, mouth-watering, ambrosial, *yummy, rich. ANT. *disgusting, nauseating, sickening.*

lush a. rich, luxurious, luxuriant, profuse, dense, thick, flourishing, prolific, abundant, green, verdant. ANT. *sparse, scanty, thin.*

lust n. desire, *burning desire, passion, libido, want, hunger, longing, craving, urge, Eros, sex drive, hot blood, itch, licentiousness, lechery, heat. "The brutish passion." — Robert Burton. "A means for the satisfaction of animal needs." — Mohandas Gandhi. "A honeyed poison." — John Taylor.

lust v. desire, want, hunger for, long for, crave, itch for, pant after, *have the hots for, ache for, be consumed with desire.

luster n. shine, glow, gloss, sheen, radiance, shimmer, gleam, burnish, glint, brilliance, dazzle. ANT. *dullness, drabness.*

lustrous a. shining, glowing, bright, glossy, radiant, shimmering, gleaming, burnished, glinting, brilliant, dazzling. ANT. *dull, drab.*

lusty a. vigorous, hearty, strong, robust, hardy, full of life, hale, energetic, healthy, vital, virile. ANT. *weak, sickly, frail.*

luxuriant a. **1.** LUSH teeming, vigorous, abundant, profuse, rich, luxurious, dense, thick, copious, overgrown. **2.** EXTRAVAGANT excessive, florid, ornate, busy, overdone, rococo, showy, sumptuous. ANT. *1. sparse, thin, scanty. 2. understated, plain.*

luxurious a. rich, extravagant, sumptuous, splendid, plush, ostentatious, fancy, indulgent, posh, lush, immoderate, *ritzy, comfortable, sensuous. ANT. *poor, shoddy, shabby.*

luxury n. extravagance, indulgence, riches, wealth, affluence, superfluity, opulence, *bed of roses, sumptuousness, abundance, lavishness, comfort, ease, immoderation, *high living, hedonism, treat, frill, extra. "Positive hindrances to the elevation of mankind." — Thoreau. ANT. *poverty, want, deprivation, bare necessity.*

lying n. dishonesty, untruthfulness, prevarication, deceit, fibbing, dissembling, fabrication, storytelling, insincerity, mendacity. "A form of creativity; talking the truth is being only a reporter." — Eric Hoffer. ANT. *honesty, truth-telling.*

lying a. dishonest, untruthful, deceitful, fibbing, dissembling, mendacious, fabricating, insincere, prevaricating. ANT. *truthful, honest.*

lynching n. hanging, *stringing up, *necktie party, execution, *mob justice, murder, vigilante justice.

lyric a. songlike, poetic, musical, melodic, melodious, tuneful, mellifluous.

M

MACABRE a. [muh KAHB ruh] gruesome, ghastly, denoting the horrors of death. *A macabre account of torture.* SYN. gruesome, ghastly, horrifying, horrible, grim, grisly, deathly, morbid, frightful, lurid, eerie, ghostly, spooky, unearthly.

MACHIAVELLIAN a. [MAK ee uh VEL ee un] deceitful and crafty, wily. *The politician was Machiavellian in his dealings with rivals.* SYN. deceitful, crafty, wily, duplicitous, expedient, cunning, scheming, conniving, devious, sly, unscrupulous. ANT. *honorable, straightforward, honest.*

MACHINATION n. [mak uh NAY shun] a plot or scheme, especially of devious intent. *He won the nomination through behind-the-scenes machinations.* SYN. plot, plotting, scheme, scheming, engineering, string-pulling, design, contrivance, ploy, maneuver, artifice, *skulduggery, *backdoor dealing, device.

machine n. mechanism, apparatus, device, appliance, engine, motor, contraption, vehicle, *workhorse, automoton, robot, gadget.

machinery n. SEE MACHINE

mad a. **1.** INSANE crazy, psychotic, psychopathic, schizophrenic, *nuts, deranged, demented, *out of one's mind, unstable, unbalanced, *loony, *off one's rocker, *mental, *wacky, foolish, harebrained. **2.** ANGRY enraged, furious, infuriated, incensed, irate, peeved, *pissed, livid, *gone ballistic. SEE ANGRY ANT. *1. sane, rational, stable, of sound mind. 2. pleased, delighted, happy.*

madcap a. reckless, wild, impulsive, crazy, rash, imprudent, foolish, foolhardy. ANT. *prudent, sensible, cautious.*

maddening a. infuriating, aggravating, exasperating, enraging, galling, provoking, riling, troubling, irritating, annoying, outrageous.

made-up a. fictional, fictitious, invented, fabricated, contrived, thought up, dreamed up, concocted. ANT. *true, factual, real.*

madhouse n. insane asylum, *loony bin, mental hospital, *laughing academy, mental institution, psychiatric hospital, *nuthouse, *booby hatch, chaos, bedlam.

madman n. psychopath, psychotic, *psycho, lunatic, schizophrenic, maniac, sociopath, *sicko, *kook, *nut.

madness n. insanity, craziness, psychosis, lunacy, schizophrenia, dementia, derange-

ment, mental illness, *nuttiness, mania, delusion of grandeur. "That reckless fire." —Edmund Gosse. "A common calamity; we are all mad at some time or other."—Johannes Mantuanus. SEE NEUROSIS

maelstrom n. **1.** WHIRLPOOL vortex, eddy, swirl, Charybdis. **2.** AGITATION turmoil, turbulence, uproar, madness, confusion, unbalance.

Mafia n. *the mob, Cosa Nostra, organized crime, the underworld, Black Hand, the Syndicate, gangland.

WORD FIND
advisor to chief: consigliere
business enterprises: loan sharking, money laundering, drug trafficking, gambling, labor racketeering, counterfeiting, extortion, prostitution, gangland killings
chief: capo
code of silence: omerta
low-ranking member: soldier
member: Mafioso
second-in-command: caporegime

magazine n. periodical, publication, journal, digest, monthly, weekly, quarterly, *rag, review, *slick.

magic n. **1.** SUPERNATURAL POWERS wizardry, witchcraft, sorcery, black magic, necromancy, conjuring, mysticism, voodoo, hoo doo, occultism, diabolism. **2.** TRICKERY legerdemain, sleight-of-hand, prestidigitation, hocus-pocus, *smoke and mirrors, conjuring.

WORD FIND
gold from metal art: alchemy
magic words: incantation, abracadabra, presto, mumbo jumbo, sesame
symbol: pentacle
SEE OCCULT

magical a. enchanting, bewitching, charming, spellbinding, mesmerizing, entrancing, fascinating, hypnotic, seductive.

magician n. **1.** ONE WITH SUPERNATURAL POWERS wizard, sorcerer, witch, necromancer, mystic, conjurer, warlock, Merlin, shaman. **2.** TRICKSTER prestidigitator, illusionist, legerdemainist, sleight-of-hand expert, Houdini.

MAGNANIMOUS a. [mag NAN uh mus] high-minded or noble, quick to forgive and not hold grudges. *John was magnanimous in his loss, conceding that his opponent was the better man.* SYN. noble, forgiving, high-minded, big, generous, liberal, tolerant, charitable, ungrudging, benevolent, chivalrous. ANT. *grudging, petty, unforgiving.*

MAGNATE *n.* [MAG nate] a powerful or influential business person. *The oil magnate made a large donation to the library.* SYN. *big shot, *bigwig, tycoon, capitalist, industrialist, baron, leader, power, giant, VIP, *bigtime operator, *biggest toad in the puddle.

magnetic *a.* drawing, pulling, attractive, irresistible, arresting, tugging, grabbing, seductive, alluring, captivating, charismatic. ANT. *repellent, repulsive.*

magnetism *n.* attractiveness, charisma, drawing power, hold, irresistibility, charm, appeal, dynamism, animal magnetism, sex appeal, pull.

magnificent *a.* grand, beautiful, stately, glorious, exalted, spectacular, grandiose, wonderful, splendid, majestic, imposing, awe-inspiring, elegant, gorgeous, sumptuous, breathtaking. ANT. *modest, humble, *nothing to write home about.*

magnify *v.* enlarge, blow up, intensify, enhance, increase, expand, amplify, *beef up, heighten, concentrate, exaggerate, blow out of proportion, overstate. ANT. *minimize, reduce, diminish.*

magnitude *n.* **1.** SIZE extent, greatness, bigness, dimensions, vastness, measure, mass, volume, expanse, bulk. **2.** IMPORTANCE influence, consequence, weight, degree, moment, significance, import, enormity, prominence. ANT. *1. smallness. 2. insignificance.*

maiden *n.* maid, girl, miss, lass, virgin, school girl, damsel, *jailbait, *chick.

maiden *a.* new, untried, virgin, fresh, first, inaugural, initial, original.

mail *n.* letters, postcards, correspondence, post, packages, parcel post, *junk mail, circulars.

mail *v.* post, send, dispatch, address, ship, transmit, *fax, send it UPS.

maim *v.* cripple, handicap, mutilate, disable, hurt, injure, wound, incapacitate, mangle, hamstring, dismember, damage, break.

main *a.* principal, chief, primary, central, prime, major, critical, important, head, predominant, foremost, essential, crucial, outstanding. ANT. *secondary, minor, subordinate, lesser.*

mainly *adv.* principally, chiefly, primarily, predominantly, essentially, mostly.

mainstay *n.* chief support, backbone, anchor, pillar, strength, prop, staff, foundation, buttress.

maintain *v.* **1.** KEEP UP look after, service, repair, mend, care for, take care of, sustain, preserve, conserve. **2.** CONTINUE WITH carry on, prolong, keep, keep going, keep alive, sustain, perpetuate, support. **3.** ASSERT declare, hold, contend, state, claim, testify, affirm, insist, argue. ANT. *1. neglect, let go, destroy, ruin. 2. stop, quit, kill, end. 3. deny, disavow.*

maintenance *n.* **1.** UPKEEP servicing, repair, care, grooming, preservation, conservation. **2.** SUSTENANCE support, livelihood, income, allowance, alimony, child support.

majestic *a.* grand, stately, lofty, dignified, regal, princely, kingly, imperial, distinguished, palatial, imposing. ANT. *modest, humble, lowly.*

majesty *n.* grandeur, stateliness, loftiness, dignity, regalness, magnificence, nobility, splendor.

major *a.* **1.** BIGGER larger, greater, chief, superior, dominant, main, principal. **2.** IMPORTANT chief, principal, primary, foremost, top, critical, outstanding, significant. ANT. *1. smaller, lesser. 2. minor, secondary.*

majority *n.* **1.** THE MOST greater part, preponderance, bulk, more than half, mass, lion's share. **2.** ADULTHOOD voting age, age of consent, maturity, manhood, womanhood, drinking age. ANT. *1. minority, less than half, few. 2. minority, childhood.*

make *n.* brand, kind, variety, model, style.

make *v.* **1.** FORM construct, fabricate, create, originate, concoct, manufacture, build, assemble, compose, produce, devise, shape, fashion, *slap together, cook up, brew. **2.** CAUSE bring about, effect, effectuate, start, generate, produce, do, accomplish. **3.** FORCE compel, impel, coerce, prevail upon, press, pressure, oblige, railroad, arm twist, *strongarm, require. **4.** ELECT appoint, vote in, designate, name, assign, install. **5.** EARN bring in, clear, *take home, gross, net, reap, gain. ANT. *1. disassemble, dismantle, destroy, obliterate. 5. spend, pay, *blow, lose.*

make-believe *n.* fantasy, imagination, pretending, dream, fancy, fiction, invention, pretense.

makeshift *a.* temporary, expedient, *slapdash, emergency, stopgap, thrown-together, jury-rigged, improvised, on-the-spot, substitute. ANT. *permanent.*

maladjusted *a.* maladapted, unadapted, unfit, neurotic, disturbed, *messed up, *warped, abnormal, stressed. ANT. *adjusted, adapted, normal, fit.*

maladroit *a.* awkward, clumsy, bumbling, *klutzy, blundering, bungling, *having two left feet, *all thumbs, *like a bull in a china shop, uncoordinated, cloddish, oafish. ANT. *graceful, coordinated, adroit, dexterous.*

malady *n.* disease, disorder, illness, sickness, ailment, affliction, infirmity, disability, complaint, infection, *bug.

MALAISE *n.* [ma LAYZ] uneasiness or queasiness, especially that which manifests itself at the start of an illness. *He fell into a state of malaise and rarely got off the couch.* SYN. uneasiness, queasiness, weakness, sickness, tiredness, exhaustion, *the blahs, discomfort, lassitude. ANT. *vigor.*

malarky *n. Sl.* rot, poppycock, baloney, bull. SEE NONSENSE

malcontent *n.* complainer, faultfinder, grumbler, *bitch, whiner, *bellyacher, grouch, rebel.

malcontent *a.* discontented, dissatisfied, unsatisfied, unhappy, disgruntled, rebellious, complaining, faultfinding, *bitchy. ANT. *content, satisfied.*

male *n.* man, gentleman, guy, fellow, buck, *dude, boy, brother, father. ANT. *female, woman.*

male *a.* masculine, manly, *macho, virile. ANT. *female, feminine.*

malediction *n.* curse, damning, imprecation, execration, anathema, *giving the finger, vilification. ANT. *blessing, best wishes.*

MALEVOLENT *a.* [mu LEV uh lunt] malicious, wishing harm on others. *He was severely abused as a child and had a malevolent disposition.* SYN. malicious, mean, vicious, nasty, hostile, spiteful, evil, malignant, vindictive, hateful, wicked, venomous, bitter. ANT. *kind, benevolent, warm, bighearted.*

malformed *a.* deformed, misshapen, distorted, mutated, grotesque, irregular, crooked, misproportioned, freakish, stunted, hunchbacked.

malfunction *n.* breakdown, *glitch, *bug, *gremlin, *SNAFU, failure, snag, foul-up, jam, *computer virus.

MALICE *n.* [MAL iss] The desire to hurt others, ill will. *The humiliating loss filled him with malice.* SYN. ill will, spite, maliciousness, hatred, malevolence, evil intent, malignance, venom, animosity, bitterness, vengefulness, viciousness, bad blood, meanness. ANT. *love, compassion, kindness.*

malicious *a.* spiteful, hurtful, vicious, malignant, malevolent, hateful, bitter, venomous, nasty, mean, wicked, pernicious, vengeful, harmful. ANT. *loving, kind, compassionate, be-*

nevolent.

malign *v.* defame, slander, denigrate, disparage, vilify, run down, *bad-mouth, mudsling, insult, smear, revile, *drag one's name through the mud, slur.

malignant *a.* **1.** DEADLY lethal, fatal, harmful, virulent, metastatic, cancerous, pernicious. **2.** MALICIOUS malevolent, hostile, hurtful, harmful, evil, wicked, spiteful, vicious. ANT. *1. benign, harmless. 2. kind, helpful, friendly.*

malingerer *n.* shirker, slacker, loafer, clockwatcher, idler, *faker.

malleable *a.* **1.** PLIABLE flexible, movable, plastic, moldable, yielding, soft. **2.** IMPRESSIONABLE changeable, moldable, adaptable, susceptible, teachable, *like putty in one's hands, tractable, docile. ANT. *1. rigid, inflexible, hard. 2. intractable, unchangeable.*

malodorous *a.* stinking, *stinky, smelly, noxious, offensive, foul, fetid, nasty, strong, reeking, putrid, rotten, rank, vile, nauseating. ANT. *sweet-smelling, flowery.*

mammoth *a.* huge, gigantic, elephantine, colossal, gargantuan, immense, enormous, stupendous, monstrous, titanic, prodigious, massive, Brobdingnagian. ANT. *tiny, minute, microscopic, Lilliputian.*

man *n.* **1.** MALE fellow, guy, gentleman, boy, chap. **2.** HUMANKIND mankind, human being, human, Homo sapiens, hominid, person, creature, soul, mortal, earthling. "An ape with possibilities." —Roy Andrews. "A renovated ape." —Marc McCutcheon. "An intelligence served by organs." —Ralph Waldo Emerson. "An ingenious assembly of portable plumbing." —Christopher Morley. "The bad child of the universe." —James Oppenheim. "The only joker in the deck of nature." —Fulton Sheen. "The organ of the accumulated smut and sneakery of 10,000 generations of weaseling souls." —Philip Wylie. "An omniverous biped that wears breeches." —Thomas Carlyle.

manacle *n.* handcuff, shackle, iron, chain, bond.

manage *v.* **1.** OVERSEE direct, govern, supervise, control, take charge of, lead, regulate, administer, conduct, guide, pilot, command, captain, quarterback. **2.** ACCOMPLISH work, succeed, contrive, bring about, cause, effect, finagle, swing, engineer, wangle.

manageable *a.* controllable, governable, tractable, docile, obedient, compliant, tame, submissive, meek. ANT. *uncontrollable, unmanageable, noncompliant.*

management n. **1.** ADMINISTRATION overseeing, direction, government, supervision, control, leadership, regulation, guidance, operation, command. **2.** ADMINISTRATORS administration, executives, supervisors, bosses, superiors, directors, leaders.

manager n. administrator, boss, overseer, director, governor, supervisor, controller, leader, regulator, commander, foreman, officer, executive, CEO, *biggest toad in the puddle. ANT. *subordinate, employee, laborer.*

MANDATE n. [MAN dayt] the will or order of the people, as expressed through a vote or referendum, any order backed by authority. *The governor received a clear mandate from his constituents.* SYN. order, directive, command, charge, decree, edict, dictate, *word, ruling, instruction, authorization, commission.

mandatory a. required, obligatory, necessary, requisite, compulsory, demanded, needed, essential, imperative, *a must. ANT. *elective, optional, unnecessary.*

man-eater n. cannibal, anthropophagite. SEE MONSTER

maneuver n. **1.** MOVE strategy, scheme, artifice, gambit, tactic, ruse, dodge, feint, subterfuge, ploy, play, machination. **2.** MILITARY MANEUVER exercise, deployment, war game, tactics, movements, operations, flanking maneuver.

maneuver v. **1.** MANIPULATE scheme, engineer, machinate, plot, intrigue, contrive, *finagle, *pull strings. **2.** GUIDE direct, handle, steer, drive, navigate, negotiate, pilot, jockey.

mangle v. mutilate, cut, tear, hack, rip, lacerate, slice, slash, disfigure, crush, bruise, maim, damage.

mangy a. shabby, filthy, dingy, dirty, ragged, scruffy, seedy, sordid, wretched, poor.

manhandle v. strong-arm, dominate, abuse, arm-twist, rough up, bully, beat up, mistreat, *belt, *slug, batter, push around.

mania n. craze, obsession, mental disorder, compulsion, fixation, preoccupation, desire, passion, fascination, madness.

WORD FIND
alcohol: dipsomania
animals: zoomania
books: bibliomania
cats: ailuromania
children: pedomania
dancing: choreomania
death: necromania
dogs: cynomania
eating: sitomania
fire: pyromania
flowers: anthomania
food: phagomania
genius, delusion one is: sophomania
horses: hippomania
kill, desire to: dacnomania
money: chrematomania
nakedness: gymnomania
night: noctimania
pleasure: hedonomania
sex: nymphomania, aphrodisiomania
sleep: hypnomania
solitude: automania
stealing: kleptomania
sun: heliomania
talking: logomania
travel: hodomania
washing: ablutomania
wealth: plutomania
women: gynemania
woods: hylomania

maniac n. madman, lunatic, psychotic, *psycho, psychopath, sociopath, *nut, *nutcase, *mental case, *sicko, *loony.

maniacal a. crazy, insane, raving, *out of one's mind, demented, deranged, *crazed, psychotic, *psycho, *flipped out, *nuts, *wigged out. ANT. *sane, rational, stable.*

manic a. excited, agitated, *wired, *hyper, hyperactive, *worked-up, frantic, frenzied, *high, hysterical. ANT. *calm, tranquil, depressed, down.*

manifest v. show, reveal, make plain, expose, exhibit, materialize, display, illustrate, express, bring to light, demonstrate. ANT. *hide, conceal, cover up.*

MANIFEST a. [MAN uh FEST] obvious, visible, evident. *That he was sincere was manifest.* SYN. obvious, visible, evident, clear, plain, apparent, distinct, showing, glaring, in full view, unmistakable, prominent. ANT. *invisible, unapparent, uncertain, ambiguous.*

manifestation n. form, demonstration, evidence, exhibition, display, indication, example, illustration, expression, proof, testimony.

MANIFESTO n. [MAN uh FES toh] a public declaration of political doctrine and intentions. *The Communist Manifesto was required reading for the class.* SYN. proclamation, declaration, promulgation, notice, notification, announcement.

manifold a. varied, various, multifold, multifarious, multiple, multifaceted, diverse, miscellaneous, numerous. ANT. *simple, one-dimen-*

sional.

manipulate *v.* **1.** HANDLE operate, work, wield, use, finger. **2.** FINAGLE *pull strings, contrive, influence, plot, scheme, machinate, engineer, jockey, trick, *wangle, *wheel and deal.

mankind *n.* SEE MAN

manly *a.* masculine, brave, strong, courageous, macho, virile, tough, potent, red-blooded, *two-fisted, *ballsy, daring, unflinching, heroic, gritty, fearless, aggressive, chivalrous, muscular, husky. ANT. *effeminate, *wimpy, mousy, feminine, weak.*

man-made *a.* artificial, synthetic, manufactured, fabricated, handmade, unnatural, fake. ANT. *natural, real.*

manner *n.* **1.** STYLE way, mode, fashion, method, system, pattern, custom, practice. **2.** BEHAVIOR air, way, conduct, deportment, aspect, bearing, mien, posture, appearance, demeanor.

mannered *a.* affected, unnatural, pretentious, put-on, posed, phony, artificial, *fake, studied, calculated. ANT. *natural, genuine.*

mannerism *n.* habit, idiosyncrasy, quirk, peculiarity, trait, tic, characteristic gesture, affectation, put-on.

mannerly *a.* polite, courteous, well-behaved, civil, gracious, considerate, refined, nice, proper, respectful, gentlemanly, ladylike, polished. ANT. *rude, ill-mannered, discourteous.*

manners *n.* courtesy, civilities, decorum, graciousness, etiquette, politeness, formalities, social graces, good form, refinement, gentility. "The final and perfect flower of noble character." —William Winter. "The art of making those people easy with whom we converse." —Jonathan Swift. "Oil that lubricates social contacts." —Leon Harrison. ANT. *rudeness, bad manners, impoliteness, roughness.*

mansion *n.* manor, estate, chateau, villa, palazzo, castle, stately home, *showplace, *dream house, *spread.

manslaughter *n.* killing, slaying, homicide. SEE MURDER

manual *n.* handbook, guidebook, *how-to, bible, reference, primer, textbook.

manufacture *v.* **1.** MAKE produce, mass-produce, fabricate, assemble, build, construct, fashion, hammer out, turn out, cast, forge. **2.** CONCOCT make up, invent, think up, fabricate, devise, lie, embellish, *tell a tall tale.

manufacturer *n.* maker, builder, producer,

mill, assembler, assembly plant.

manure *n.* dung, excrement, *crap, droppings, much, waste matter, *do do, *cow chips, fertilizer, compost.

many *n.* a lot, abundance, scores, tons, *scads, a bunch, multitude, myriad, *galaxy, *heaps, profusion. ANT. *a few, none.*

many *a.* abundant, several, numerous, countless, multitudinous, innumerable, plentiful, copious, *umpteen. ANT. *few.*

map *n.* chart, plan, plot, graph, relief map, atlas, street guide.

mar *v.* disfigure, spoil, damage, impair, injure, blemish, deface, deform, mangle, ruin, wreck, scar, crack.

maraud *v.* raid, plunder, ransack, pillage, loot, ravage, prey upon, wreak havoc on, despoil, assault.

marauder *n.* raider, attacker, plunderer, pillager, looter, pirate, ransacker, thief, robber.

march *v.* step in time, pace, tramp, tread, parade, goose-step, walk, promenade, file, plod, strut.

WORD FIND

manner of: lockstep

marching in formations: close-order drill

margin *n.* border, edge, perimeter, verge, periphery, brink, brim, lip, hem, skirt, fringe, limit.

marginal *a.* borderline, slight, minimal, limited, negligible, insignificant, trivial.

marijuana *n.* cannabis, hemp, *pot, *weed, *grass, *dope, *ganja, *Columbian, *Indian hay, *Jamaican, *Kona gold, *Mary Jane, *Panama red, *sinsemilla, *smoke, *Maui wowie, *Thai stick.

WORD FIND

active substance: tetrahydrocannabinol, THC

block of pressed: brick

bundle weighing one kilogram: *kilo

butt end of cigarette: *roach

cigarette holding clip: *roach clip

cigarette: *reefer, *doobie, *jay, *joint, *number, *bomb

five-dollar bag: *nickel bag

ounce of: *lid

resin product: hashish, *hash

ten-dollar bag: *dime bag

water pipe: bong

SEE COCAINE, DRUG

marina *n.* harbor, dock, dockage, boat basin, moorings, berth, slip, landing, boat yard, pier, wharf.

marinate *v.* pickle, steep, soak.

marine *n.* SEE ARMY, MILITARY, NAVY

marine *a.* oceanic, sea, aquatic, pelagic, maritime, nautical.

mariner *n.* sailor, seafarer, seaman, *sea dog, *salt, bluejacket, navy man, skipper, mate, helmsman, boatswain, deckhand. SEE NAVAL OFFICER, NAVY, SHIP

marionette *n.* dummy, doll. SEE PUPPET

marital *a.* wedded, matrimonial, married, conjugal, connubial, nuptial.

maritime *a.* oceanic, sea, aquatic, pelagic, nautical, seagoing, oceangoing, naval, marine.

mark *n.* **1.** LINE, SPOT OR BLEMISH streak, tick, blot, impression, trace, blotch, dot, stain, smudge, imprint, score, scratch, cut. **2.** CHARACTERISTIC sign, hallmark, indication, symptom, symbol, brand, badge, signature, proof, evidence. **3.** STANDARD norm, rule, criterion, scale, yardstick, gauge. **4.** TARGET goal, aim, end, objective, object, bull's-eye.

mark *v.* **1.** BLEMISH streak, blot, leave an impression, blotch, dot, stain, smudge, splotch, mar, imprint, score, scratch, cut. **2.** CHARACTERIZE distinguish, brand, stamp, imprint, identify, label, indicate, symbolize, denote.

marked *a.* noticeable, obvious, distinct, conspicuous, clear, apparent, prominent, outstanding, striking, glaring, pronounced. ANT. *indistinct, undistinguished.*

market *n.* store, mart, shopping center, grocery store, outlet, mall, stall, stand, emporium, exchange.

market *v.* sell, peddle, hustle, offer for sale, hawk, wholesale, retail, exchange, trade, advertise.

marksman *n.* sharpshooter, crack shot, dead shot, good shot.

maroon *v.* strand, abandon, leave behind, cast away, desert, put ashore, forsake, isolate.

marriage *n.* union, wedding, matrimony, coupling, wedlock, tie, bond, nuptials, *wedded bliss, *tying the knot, merger. "An armed alliance against the outside world." — Gilbert Keith Chesterson. "The high sea for which no compass has yet been invented." — Heinrich Heine. "Fever in reverse: it starts with heat and ends with cold." — German proverb. "A field of battle, not a bed of roses." — Robert Louis Stevenson. "Like a bath — not so hot once you get accustomed to it." — Anon.

WORD FIND

after death of first spouse: digamy

broker, Jewish: schatchen

divorce: dissolution

estrangement: alienation of affections

failing: *on the rocks

forced, due to sexual misconduct: *shotgun wedding

hater of: misogamist

hatred of: misogamy

interracial: miscegenation, mixed marriage

invalidation of: annulment

long-term cohabitation without benefit of wedding: common-law marriage

loveless couple joined for benefits other than affection: marriage of convenience

man uninterested in: confirmed bachelor

man who has sexually unfaithful wife: cuckold

married to more than one spouse: bigamy, polygamy

married to one spouse: monogamy, monogyny, monandry

outside the bonds of marriage: extramarital

property brought into by woman: dowry

seventh-year temptation: *seven-year itch

unfaithfulness in: infidelity

vow: troth

with others: open marriage

SEE DIVORCE, WEDDING

marry *v.* wed, *tie the knot, exchange wedding vows, unite in holy wedlock, *say "I do," *hitch up, *walk down the aisle, *settle down. ANT. *divorce, *split up, separate.*

marsh *n.* bog, swamp, fen, bayou, everglade, estuary, moor, wetland, quagmire, slough.

WORD FIND

gas: methane

hollow: swale

plant: reed, sedge, cattail, bulrush

SEE LAKE

marshal *v.* order, arrange, array, manage, direct, coordinate, organize, distribute, deploy, dispose, guide.

marshy *a.* boggy, swampy, fenny, wet, soggy, spongy, mucky.

martial *a.* military, militant, warlike, hostile, combative, aggressive, bellicose, antagonistic. ANT. *peaceful, civil.*

martinet *n.* disciplinarian, drillmaster, taskmaster, *whip, tyrant, slavedriver, authoritarian, stickler.

martyr *n.* sufferer, self-sacrificer, *poor me. "A self-made hero." — Anon.

martyrdom *n.* suffering, torment, torture, anguish, self-sacrifice, persecution, crown of thorns, crucifixion, hell, vale of tears, ordeal. "Proof of the intensity, never of the correctness of a belief." — Arthur Schnitzler. "The only way in which a man can become famous without ability."—George Bernard Shaw.

marvel *n.* wonder, miracle, prodigy, sensation, spectacle, *sight to behold, *mindblower, phenomenon, rarity.

marvel *v.* wonder at, stand in awe, be awestruck, be astonished, gape at, stare at with wonder, be amazed.

marvelous *a.* **1.** WONDERFUL. sensational, phenomenal, miraculous, amazing, astonishing, surprising, extraordinary, awesome, wondrous, stunning, supernatural. **2.** GREAT excellent, fabulous, fantastic, fine, splendid, superb, *super, terrific, *out of this world, wonderful. ANT. *1.* *ho-hum, ordinary, banal, everyday. *2.* lousy, terrible, bad.

masculine *a.* manly, macho, virile, male, strong, tough, powerful, muscular, dominant, potent, butch, bold, *gutsy. ANT. effeminate, feminine, *wimpy, weak.

mash *v.* smash, crush, pulp, squash, scrunch, grind, press, pulverize.

mask *n.* disguise, cover-up, facade, masquerade, veil, concealment, false front.

mask *v.* disguise, cover up, hide, conceal, veil, camouflage, cloak, screen, masquerade.

masquerade *n.* disguise, costume, facade, put-on, guise, getup, mask, mummery, ball, costume party, *Mardis Gras, imposture, pose, pretense.

mass *n.* **1.** MATTER body, lump, solid, hunk, chunk, pile, bulk, mound, load, block, heap, deposit, gob, wad, accumulation, collection, aggregation, conglomeration, assemblage, host, number, assortment, crowd. **2.** SIZE magnitude, bulk, weight, volume, dimension, greatness.

massacre *n.* slaughter, mass killing, bloodbath, indiscriminate killing, wholesale slaughter, carnage, butchery, decimation, annihilation, genocide.

massacre *v.* slaughter, kill, butcher, slay, annihilate, decimate, kill off, liquidate, wipe out, exterminate, eliminate.

massage *n.* rubdown, back rub, kneading, manipulation, *Rolfing.

massage *v.* rub, knead, stroke, press, roll, flex.

masses *n.* common people, working class, lower class, peasantry, plebeians, proletariat, hoi polloi. "Mute, inglorious men and women who made no nuisance of themselves in the world."—Philip Howard. "The nondistinctive bulk of human kind—the average man."—Robert Zwickey. ANT. upper class, aristocracy, elite, royalty, *upper crust.

massive *a.* huge, large, tremendous, stupendous, colossal, enormous, prodigious, extensive, immense, gigantic, gargantuan, staggering, monstrous, monumental, towering. ANT. tiny, microscopic, miniscule.

master *n.* **1.** EXPERT pro, professional, *ace, authority, *whiz, veteran, *old hand, master hand, proficient, mentor, teacher. **2.** CHIEF overseer, boss, commander, director, ruler, manager, governor, leader, head, lord, *top dog, *biggest toad in the puddle. ANT. *1.* amateur, beginner, tyro, rookie. *2.* subordinate, employee, underling.

master *v.* **1.** LEARN *get the hang of, *get down, understand, *know backwards and forwards, *know inside and out, become proficient in.

master *a.* **1.** EXPERT proficient, skilled, experienced, professional, accomplished. **2.** MAIN principal, great, dominant, chief, leading, ruling, commanding. ANT. *1.* unskilled, rookie, inexperienced, amateur. *2.* secondary, subordinate, minor.

masterful *a.* expert, proficient, skilled, accomplished, experienced, crack, *crackerjack, virtuoso, dexterous, adroit. ANT. amateurish, bumbling, inept.

mastermind *n.* architect, author, engineer, leader, ringleader, wizard, genius, *brains, designer, orchestrator, instigator.

masterpiece *n.* masterwork, magnum opus, chef d'oeuvre, piece de resistance, tour de force, *jewel in the crown, showpiece.

mastery *n.* **1.** CONTROL command, rule, domination, authority, power, sway, upper hand, influence. **2.** EXPERTISE proficiency, command, skill, prowess, knowledge, ability, facility, virtuosity. ANT. *1.* submission, subservience. *2.* ineptness, ignorance.

masturbation *n.* self-gratification, onanism, autoeroticism, self-abuse, *playing with oneself, *beating the bishop, *cuffing the carrot, *jacking off, *choking the gopher, *jerking the gherkin.

match *n.* **1.** EQUAL equivalent, mate, double, twin, fellow, duplicate, peer, counterpart. **2.** COUPLE pair, pairing, partnership, duet. **3.** CONTEST competition, meet, bout, game, tournament, duel, rivalry.

match *v.* equal, go together, look alike, parallel, correspond, make a pair, mirror one another. ANT. clash, oppose.

matching *a.* twin, paired, like, coordinating, corresponding, identical, duplicate, of a set. ANT. clashing, opposing, unlike.

matchless *a.* unequaled, unparalleled, peerless,

incomparable.

mate n. PARTNER twin, counterpart, fellow, double, equal, one of a pair, peer, sidekick, alter ego, companion, *buddy, friend, lover, spouse, colleague.

mate v. pair up, couple, join up, marry, wed, breed, procreate, copulate.

material n. **1.** SUBSTANCE matter, stuff, medium, components, constituents, ingredients, elements, stock. **2.** TEXTILE fabric, cloth, dry goods. **3.** DATA facts, information, notes, text, documentation.

material a. **1.** PHYSICAL palpable, tangible, touchable, solid, concrete, corporeal, bodily, real, nonspiritual. **2.** IMPORTANT relevant, significant, consequential, weighty, fundamental, germane, momentous, vital, crucial. ANT. 1. spiritual, impalpable. 2. immaterial, irrelevant, unimportant.

materialistic a. acquisitive, greedy, *keeping up with the Joneses, *like a yuppie.

materialize v. appear, take shape, come to be, emerge, turn up, rise, issue, come about, develop, form, manifest, accomplish, realize. ANT. disappear, vanish, fade away.

maternal a. motherly, parental, nurturing, protecting, caring, devoted, doting, sheltering, loving. ANT. uncaring, cruel.

matriarch n. mother, grandmother, matron, dame, dowager, queen, empress, *ruler of the roost, *battle-ax.

matrimony n. holy wedlock. SEE MARRIAGE

matron n. **1.** MATURE WOMAN middle-aged woman, matriarch, dame, dowager, widow. **2.** WARDEN head mistress, supervisor, housemother, governess.

matronly a. dignified, sedate, mellow, mature, serious, motherly.

matted a. tangled, snarled, twisted, knotted, full of snags, *like a rat's nest, uncombed, messy, disheveled.

matter n. **1.** SUBSTANCE material, stuff, body, medium, element, object. **2.** AFFAIR issue, concern, situation, question, subject, doing, business, topic, happening, episode. **3.** CONSEQUENCE importance, weight, significance, import, gravity, magnitude. **4.** TROUBLE difficulty, problem, dilemma, upset, distress.

matter-of-fact a. unemotional, prosaic, dry, businesslike, dull, plain, unexciting, *cold-blooded, sober, phlegmatic, impassive, straightforward, direct. ANT. emotional, passionate.

mature v. grow, season, develop, ripen, bloom, flower, *come of age, grow up, evolve, settle down, mellow.

mature a. **1.** ADULT fully grown, full-grown, full-fledged, ripened, in bloom, seasoned, developed, in one's prime. **2.** WISE AND EXPERIENCED seasoned, practiced, responsible, dependable, independent, self-sufficient, settled. ANT. 1. immature, juvenile, young. 2. immature, dependent, callow.

maturity n. **1.** ADULTHOOD manhood, womanhood, majority, age of consent, full bloom, full growth, development, completion, perfection. **2.** WISDOM AND EXPERIENCE responsibility, dependability, reliability, independence, self-sufficiency, seasoning, sophistication, refinement. "The ability to live in someone else's world." — Oren Arnold. "The day you don't need to be lied to about anything." — Frank Yerby. "The ability to postpone gratification." — Sigmund Freud. "The day you have your first real laugh at yourself." — Ethel Barrymore. ANT. 1. immaturity, childhood, infancy. 2. imperfection, incompletion, dependence, irresponsibility.

MAUDLIN a. [MAWD lin] overly sentimental to the point of silliness. The drunk embraced everyone and grew increasingly maudlin. SYN. sentimental, overly sentimental, mawkish, mushy, cow-eyed, *drippy, unrestrained, teary, weepy, *schmaltzy, *cornball, overemotional, *laying it on thick, *laying it on with a trowel. ANT. cold, matter-of-fact, emotionless.

maul v. beat, injure, tear, lacerate, bruise, pound, batter, pummel, rough up, *clobber, trounce, thrash, manhandle.

mausoleum n. tomb, sepulchre. SEE GRAVE, CEMETERY

maverick n. independent, nonconformist, vanguard, trendsetter, trailblazer, pioneer, dissenter, eccentric, rebel, individual, *lone voice in the wilderness. ANT. follower, *one of the herd, conformist.

mawkish a. sickeningly sentimental, maudlin, nauseating, mushy, emotional, *schmaltzy, teary, *gushy, *sappy. ANT. emotionless, cold, matter-of-fact.

MAXIM n. [MAK sim] a saying that illustrates a basic truth. "Blood is thicker than water" is a popular maxim. SYN. saying, truth, principle, truism, adage, aphorism, proverb, axiom, tenet, saw, *bromide, cliche. "Little sermons." — Gelett Burgess. "The condensed good sense of nations." — James Mackintosh.

maximum n. top, height, zenith, peak, pinnacle, climax, culmination, high point, extreme, most, optimum, limit. ANT. *minimum, bottom.*

maximum *a.* highest, greatest, biggest, top, most, maximal, supreme, utmost, paramount. ANT. *minimum, least, smallest.*

maybe *adv.* possibly, perhaps, perchance.

mayhem *n.* destruction, violence, brutality, injury, chaos, pandemonium, havoc, disorder, riotous confusion. ANT. *calm, order.*

maze *n.* labyrinth, convolution, meander, tangle, knot, puzzle, jungle, confusion, perplexity, muddle, bewilderment.

meadow *n.* field, grassland, pasture, range, prairie, plain, lea, veldt, mead.

WORD FIND

descriptive: Audubonesque tableau of birds and flowers, grasses undulating in the breeze, windblown timothy, Irish green meadow, tawny tussocks of Autumn.

open spot in a forest: glade

SEE GRASS, FLOWER

meager *a.* scanty, sparse, scarce, thin, bare, lean, insufficient, inadequate, poor, lacking, skimpy. ANT. *plentiful, abundant.*

meal *n.* repast, *feed, feast, banquet, fare, *grub, breakfast, lunch, dinner, supper, brunch, *eats, spread, food, mess, chow, K ration, entree.

mealymouthed *a.* euphemistic, insincere, indirect, mincing, delicate, overnice, prim, oversubtle, roundabout, honeyed, vague. ANT. *direct, blunt, straightforward.*

mean *n.* average, norm, happy medium, par, middle, rule, medium.

mean *v.* **1.** HAVE IN MIND intend, plan, think of, expect, propose, aim, anticipate, want. **2.** SIGNIFY denote, indicate, designate, stand for, represent, symbolize, express, imply.

mean *a.* **1.** NASTY unpleasant, obnoxious, cruel, vicious, hurtful, rude, malicious, *dirty, rotten, rough, sour, unkind, contemptible, hostile, insulting, petty, ignoble, spiteful, brutal. **2.** STINGY miserly, cheap, penny-pinching, ungenerous, tight, parsimonious, grudging, niggardly. **3.** POOR shabby, low, second-rate, humble, modest, squalid, paltry, mediocre, menial, small. ANT. *1. noble, nice, kind. 2. generous, giving. 3. rich, first-rate, superior. 4. average, normal, medium, middle, median, mid, intermediate.*

meander *v.* wind, convolute, twist, snake, take a serpentine path, *switchback, zigzag, corkscrew, wander, go in roundabout fashion, range, ramble, *go all over the place, follow a tortuous course. ANT. *make a beeline.*

meaning *n.* intent, intention, purport, signification, denotation, sense, definition, connotation, drift, suggestion, point, thrust, interpretation, essence, content.

meaningful *a.* important, deep, profound, consequential, significant, weighty, momentous, purposeful. ANT. *meaningless, insignificant, empty.*

meaningless *a.* empty, vacuous, senseless, nonsensical, useless, worthless, pointless, inconsequential, purposeless, hollow, trivial, futile. ANT. *meaningful, deep, profound, important.*

means *n.* **1.** WAY method, resources, modus operandi, system, apparatus, mechanism, power, instrumentation, medium, expedient, agent. **2.** MONEY wealth, resources, assets, capital, cash, finances, *bucks, income.

meanwhile *adv.* meantime, at the same time, simultaneously, while, during, concurrently.

measly *a. Sl.* paltry, skimpy, meager, scanty, poor, puny, trifling. ANT. *large, substantial, generous.*

measurable *a.* quantifiable, quantitative, calculable, assessable, computable, gaugeable, determinable. ANT. *immeasurable, infinite.*

measure *n.* **1.** EXTENT, SHARE portion, part, allowance, allotment, division, quantity, quota, sum, ration, extent, dimension, scope, span, capacity, volume, magnitude. **2.** STANDARD rule, gauge, benchmark, model, yardstick, scale. **3.** ACTION act, step, course, procedure, means, expedient, move.

measure *v.* gauge, weigh, take dimensions, survey, quantify, figure, calculate, compute, appraise, size, figure, calibrate, judge.

measurement *n.* measuring, gauging, estimation, calculation, computation, assessment, dimension, volume, depth, capacity, height, width, weight, mass, density, length, density, magnitude.

meat *n.* **1.** FLESH beef, veal, fat, pork, chicken, food. **2.** GIST heart, crux, essence, core, nub.

meaty *a.* meaningful, rich, *heavy, full of substance, profound, rich, pithy, weighty, deep. ANT. *trivial, frivolous, light.*

mechanical *a.* **1.** TECHNOLOGICAL power-driven, motor-driven, machine-driven, automated, *robotic. **2.** SKILLED WITH ONE'S HANDS dexterous, deft, proficient, handy. **3.** EXPRESSIONLESS automatic, robotlike, emotionless, unfeeling, impersonal, matter-of-fact, lifeless. ANT. *1. manual, hand-powered. 2. inept, bumbling, clumsy. 3. emotional, feeling, spontaneous.*

mechanism *n.* machine, motor, generator, device, contrivance, servomechanism, apparatus, gear, component, instrument, gadget.

medal *n.* medallion, decoration, citation, ribbon, award, badge, testimonial, recognition.

meddle *v.* interfere, *stick one's nose in where it doesn't belong, *butt in, intrude, interlope, intervene, impose, horn in, *kibitz. ANT. *mind one's business, *stick to one's own knitting.*

meddlesome *a.* interfering, intrusive, meddling, officious, obtrusive, presumptuous, busybody, *snoopy, *kibitzing. ANT. *removed, restrained, indifferent.*

media *n.* press, communications industry, news industry, radio, television, publishing.

MEDIATE *v.* [MEE dee ATE] to take an intermediate position and help settle differences between two or more parties. *Better to have a third party mediate than to call in expensive lawyers.* SYN. settle, conciliate, compromise, reconcile, bring to terms, negotiate, referee, umpire, resolve differences, moderate.

mediation *n.* settlement, peaceful intervention, conciliation, compromise, reconciliation, negotiation, refereeing, moderating, making peace.

medicine *n.* medication, medicament, remedy, cure, elixir, preparation, drug, wonder drug, pharmaceutical, antibiotic, pill, inoculation, vaccine, physic, dose, treatment, therapeutics. "Consists of amusing the patient while nature cures the disease."—Voltaire "A conjectural art."—Celsus.

WORD FIND

MEDICINES AND DRUGS

acid neutralizer: antacid, bicarbonate of soda

alcohol solution of: tincture

allergy reliever that counters histamine: antihistamine

analgesic: acetaminophen, aspirin, codeine, ibuprofen, morphine, opium

angina, relieves: nitroglycerin

antibiotic: amoxicillin, ampicillin, erythromycin, penicillin, streptomycin, sulfa drug, sulfonamide, tetracycline

bacterial infection treatment derived from fungus: antibiotic

blood clotting, prevents: anticoagulant, heparin

blood serum containing antibodies: gamma globulin

blood vessel constrictor: vasoconstrictor

blood vessel widener: vasodilator

body's natural immune protein: antibody

book listings of: pharmacopoeia

breathing passages, opens: bronchodilator

cancelling out of one drug's effects by another: antagonism

circulation, steps up: epinephrine, adrenalin

cough suppressant: antitussive, codeine

cure-all: panacea, catholicon

diabetes victim's blood sugar regulator: insulin

dropper: pipette

epilepsy, seizure medication: diazepam, Dilantin

fever reducer: antipyretic, febrifuge

heart activity, decreases: beta blocker

heart stimulant: digitalis

itch reliever: antipruritic

laxative: cathartic, purgative

malaria drug: quinine

motion sickness reliever: Dramamine

muscle-building hormone: steroid

nonprescription: over-the-counter

ointment: salve, unguent, balm, emollient

organ transplant, fights rejection of: immunosuppressant

painkiller: analgesic, Demerol, methadone

Parkinson's disease, controls: L-dopa

phlegm, helps bring up: expectorant

poison counteractant: antidote, antivenin

polio vaccine: Sabin vaccine, Salk vaccine

quack: patent medicine, nostrum

reduced effectiveness of medicine over time: tolerance

relieves symptoms but does not cure disease: palliative

simulated: placebo

skin, applied to: topical

sleep, induces: hypnotic, soporific

spasm reliever: antispasmodic

study of medicines: pharmacology

tranquilizer: Librium, Miltown, Thorazine

ulcer medicine: Xantac, antacid

urine, increases excretion of: diuretic

vaccine for diptheria, pertussis and tetanus: DPT

vaccine for measles, mumps and rubella: MMR

vessel: ampule, phial, vial

vomiting, induces: emetic

PROCEDURES, SEE ALSO OPERATION

alcohol, drug, toxin removal from body: detoxification, *detox

allergy test: patch test, scratch test

blood cell count: blood count

blood filtering to aid kidney function: dialysis

brain scan by tomography: PET scan, positron emission tomography

brain's electrical activity reading: electroencephalogram, EEG

breast X-ray or imaging: mammography

broken bone alignment by force: traction

cancer treatment with X-rays, beta rays, gamma rays: radiation therapy

chemical or drug treatment for cancer, chemotherapy

choking maneuver: Heimlich maneuver

CPR: cardiopulmonary resuscitation

determination of disease: diagnosis

EEG: electroencephalogram

EKG: electrocardiogram

enhanced radiology imaging: CAT scan (computerized axial tomography)

evaluation, general: workup, physical

fat sucked out, plastic surgery method: liposuction

feeling for body abnormalities by hand: palpation

heart exam through ultrasound imaging: echocardiography

heart fitness test: stress test

heart's electrical activity reading: electrocardiogram, EKG

imaging internal body with magnetic field: magnetic resonance imaging, MRI

intravenous introduction of blood: transfusion, IV

microorganisms, lab examination of body's: culture

prediction of disease outcome: prognosis

prioritizing of most critical patients first: triage

stone destruction by sound waves: lithotripsy

tapping body part to aid in diagnosis: percussion

tissue removal for examination: biopsy

tube insertion in body part for drainage, diagnosis, etc.: intubation

uterine fluid removal during pregnancy: amniocentesis

uterine or cervical cancer test: Pap test

X-ray image live on screen: fluoroscopy

MEDICAL EQUIPMENT

bladder probe: cytoscope

bleeding, stops profuse: hemostat

blood filtering machine aiding kidney function: dialysis machine

blood pressure cuff: sphygmomanometer

breathing apparatus: respirator, resuscitator

colon discharge bag: colostomy bag

colon probe: sigmoidoscope

decompression chamber: hyperbaric chamber

ear probe: otoscope

electrocardiogram machine: electrocardiograph

gown, green surgical: *scrubs, scrub suit

grasper: forceps

hammer used to check reflexes: plessor, percussion hammer

holds body cavity open: speculum

internal probe: endoscope

joint probe: arthroscope

knife: bistoury, lancet, scalpel

knife, electrical: radio knife

larynx probe: lyngoscope

listening device, diaphragm: stethoscope

needle and syringe: hypodermic

photographs internal body by radiation: X-ray machine

pole on which medicinal fluids are hung: IV pole, *ivy pole

pump used in heart surgery: heart-lung machine

rectal probe: proctoscope, sigmoidoscope

respiratory recorder: spirograph

sterilizer, instrument: autoclave

stretcher: gurney

stomach probe: gastroscope

tissue retractor: retractor

tissue scraper: curette

tongue, moves out of the way: tongue depressor

trachea probe: bronchoscope

tube drain: catheter

X-ray screen: fluoroscope

FIELDS OF MEDICINE

aging: geriatrics, gerontology

anesthesia: anesthesiology

animal: veterinary medicine

behavioral effects of drugs: psychopharmacology

birth: obstetrics, tocology

blood: hematology

bones: osteology, osteopathy, orthopedics

children: pediatrics

cosmetic and reconstructive surgery: plastic surgery

digestive system: gastroenterology

disease identification: diagnostics

disease: pathology, etiology

ears, nose and throat: otorhinolaryngology

ears: otology

epidemics: epidemiology

eyes: ophthalmology, optometry

feet: podiatry
female reproductive system: gynecology
gums: periodontics
hearing: audiology
heart: cardiology
hormones, glands: endocrinology
immune system: immunology
internal disease, noninvasive treatment of:
    internal medicine
joints: arthrology
kidneys: nephrology
liver: hepatology
lungs and breathing: pulmonology
malformations: teratology
mental diseases, disorders: psychopathology,
    psychiatry
muscles: myology, orthopedics
needles, Chinese: acupuncture
nervous system: neurology
newborns: neonatology
obstetrics and gynecology: ob-gyn
poisons: toxicology
rectum, anus and colon: proctology
rheumatic disease: rheumatology
sexually transmitted diseases: venereology
skin: dermatology
skull: craniology
spinal alignment: chiropractic
stomach: gastrology
teeth: dentistry, orthodontics
tumors: oncology
urinary tracts: urology
veins: phlebology
viruses: virology
whole body teatment: holistic medicine
X rays, radiation: radiology
SEE ALSO BIRTH, DISEASE, DOCTOR, HOSPITAL, OP-
ERATION, PREGNANCY

medieval *a.* of the Middle Ages, of the Dark
Ages, Gothic, feudal, archaic.
WORD FIND
catapult: mangonel, trebuchet
chemistry: alchemy
duty and loyalty owed to lord by vassal: fealty
garden, villager's: croft
land grant made by lord in exchange for ser-
    vices: fief
land unit of eighteen to thirty-two acres sup-
    porting peasant: virgate
lord's tenant pledging military service: vassal
manager of lord's manor: bailiff
musical instrument: lute, lyre, rebec
peasant: serf, villein
political and social system: feudalism
singer: minstrel, troubador

sport: tilting, jousting
tax paid to a lord: tallage
town, village: bourg
tunic: gipon, jupon
yard: toft
SEE CASTLE

mediocre *a.* fair, okay, ordinary, middling, so-
so, okay, passable, tolerable, run-of-the-mill,
garden-variety, *fair to middling, second-
rate, poor, pedestrian, undistinguished. ANT.
superior, first-rate, exceptional, outstanding.

meditate *v.* think, reflect, muse, contemplate,
ruminate, ponder, brood, chew over, deliberate, focus on, cogitate, weigh, mull over.

meditation *n.* deep thought, reflection, contemplation, musing, rumination, cogitation,
concentration, reverie, chewing over, mulling over.

medium *n.* **1.** MEANS vehicle, agency, mode,
channel, way, instrument, mechanism. **2.**
ATMOSPHERE air, environment, element, climate, surroundings, setting. **3.** CLAIRVOYANT
psychic, telepathist, necromancer, seer,
mindreader.

medium *a.* mean, middle, midway, intermediate, median, average, moderate, par, standard, fair, ordinary, normal. ANT. *extraordinary, extreme, unusual.*

medley *n.* mixture, hodgepodge, miscellany,
jumble, melange, assortment, potpourri,
mishmash, variety, assortment, mixed bag.

meek *a.* mild, gentle, docile, compliant, peaceful, passive, tame, patient, timid, shy, spineless, deferential, submissive. ANT. *aggressive,
pugnacious, rebellious, domineering.*

meet *n.* competition, match, tournament, contest, game.

meet *v.* **1.** ENCOUNTER happen upon, come
upon, run across, *bump into, chance upon,
face, see. **2.** MAKE ACQUAINTANCE shake
hands with, get to know, say hello to, greet.
3. JOIN connect, touch, converge, unite,
cross, abut, intersect. **4.** ASSEMBLE gather,
congregate, convene, get together, muster,
collect. **5.** FULFILL satisfy, execute, handle,
perform, carry out, discharge. dispose of.
ANT. *1. miss, avoid. 3. separate, disconnect. 4.
disperse, break up. 5. shirk, fall short, renege.*

meeting *n.* **1.** ENCOUNTER engagement, confrontation, rendezvous, collision, convergence. **2.** ASSEMBLY gathering, conference,
*powwow, congregation, convention, get-
together, discussion, council, *confab. ANT.
avoidance, parting.

melancholy *n.* depression, unhappiness, downheartedness, blues, sadness, gloom, low spirits, funk, woe, misery, sorrow, despondency. "A hell upon earth." — Robert Burton. "The mind's disease." — John Ford. "The pleasure of being sad." — Victor Hugo. ANT. *happiness, elation, euphoria.*

melancholy a. depressed, downhearted, blue, dejected, sad, dispirited, low, glum, *down in the mouth, *down in the dumps, *bummed out, heartsick, forlorn, disconsolate, gloomy, miserable, despondent. ANT. *happy, elated, euphoric.*

melange n. mixture, hodgepodge, miscellany. SEE MEDLEY

meld v. blend, unite, merge, combine, mix, fuse, incorporate, mingle, amalgamate, compound. ANT. *separate, split.*

melee n. riot, fight, free-for-all, *rumble, brawl, fracas, donnybrook, tussle, scuffle, pandemonium, *ruckus, scrap, hubbub.

MELLIFLUOUS a. [muh LIF loo us] sweet-sounding and smooth. *The mellifluous tones echoed quietly across the stage.* SYN. smooth-sounding, sweet-sounding, honeyed, dulcet, euphonic, liquid, fluid, silver-toned, resonant. ANT. *harsh, grating, rough, discordant.*

mellow a. 1. GENTLE mild, softened, easygoing, placid, seasoned, wise, mature. 2. RIPE soft, sweet, aged, smooth, full-flavored, rich. ANT. *1. immature, aggressive, hard, troubled. 2. green, unripe, immature.*

melodious a. tuneful, musical, melodic, songlike, harmonious, euphonic, symphonic, sweet, pleasing to the ear, mellifluous. ANT. *cacophonous, discordant, unmusical.*

MELODRAMATIC a. [MEL o druh MAT ik] exaggerated or sensational, theatrical. *The teenager was being melodramatic when he said he'd die without a new pair of jeans.* SYN. exaggerated, sensational, theatrical, stagy, overemotional, histrionic, overacted, maudlin, mawkish, gushing. ANT. *understated, subtle, matter-of-fact.*

melody n. tune, song, *ditty, musical arrangement, refrain, line, run, lyric, passage, *hook.

melt v. liquefy, dissolve, soften, deliquesce, thaw, defrost.

member n. associate, enrollee, constituent, fellow, brother, sister, affiliate, part, element, component, segment.

membership n. members, associates, enrollment, constituency, rolls, roster, rank and file, fellowship, brotherhood, sisterhood, society, club, body, fraternity.

membrane n. layer, sheet, covering, lining, film, tissue, skin, sheath, mucosa.

memento n. souvenir, keepsake, remembrance, reminder, token, memorabilia, record, memorial.

memo n. SEE MEMORANDUM

memoirs n. autobiography, biography, diary, life story, reminiscences, recollections, journal, chronicle, history, *bio. "When you put down the good things you ought to have done, and leave out the bad ones you did do." — Will Rogers.

memorable a. unforgettable, important, momentous, critical, crucial, historic, powerful, leaving an indelible image, noteworthy, extraordinary, striking, remarkable, *red-letter, meaningful, *once in a lifetime. ANT. *forgettable, unimportant, ordinary, everyday.*

memorandum n. memo, note, reminder, message, notice, dispatch, minute, tickler.

memorial n. monument, statue, shrine, marker, monolith, reminder, commemoration, record, inscription.

memorial a. remembering, commemorative, retrospective.

memorize v. remember, commit to memory, store, learn by rote, learn by heart, retain, imprint on one's mind.

memory n. 1. RECALL recollection, remembrance, retention, retrospection, reminiscence, photographic memory, eidetic memory, hypermnesia, calling to mind. "The library of the mind." — Francis Fauvel-Gouraud. "What God gave us so that we might have roses in December." — James Barrie. "The warder of the brain." — Shakespeare. "A beaten path in the brain." — Anon. 2. REMINDER image, recollection, picture, thought, vision. ANT. *amnesia.*

menace n. threat, danger, hazard, peril, danger, troublemaker, sword of Damocles.

menace v. threaten, scare, frighten, intimidate, terrorize, endanger, daunt, imperil.

menacing a. threatening, scary, frightening, intimidating, terrorizing, dangerous, hazardous, looming, hanging over one's head. ANT. *reassuring, calming.*

mend v. fix, repair, restore, correct, patch up, doctor, rectify, recondition, remedy, heal, cure, right.

mendacious a. dishonest, lying, false, deceptive, misleading, deceitful, fraudulent, untruthful, dissembling. ANT. *honest, truthful.*

menial a. low, servile, mean, humble, common, subservient, unskilled, abject, ignoble, obsequious. ANT. *highborn, superior, noble, arro-*

gant.

menopause n. change of life, climacteric.

mental a. **1.** INTELLECTUAL cerebral, cognitive, thinking, phrenic, reasoning, of the mind, psychic, psychological. **2.** OF MENTAL ILLNESS mentally ill, disturbed, deranged, psychotic, insane, mad, neurotic, psychiatric.

mentality n. attitude, outlook, view, opinion, state of mind, *mind-set, way of thinking, reasoning.

mention n. reference, remark, referral, utterance, comment, note, acknowledgement, statement, indication, suggestion.

mention v. refer, remark, speak of, allude to, cite, bring up, comment on, touch on, make note of, acknowledge, indicate.

MENTOR n. [MEN tur] a teacher, guide, coach or advisor. *She couldn't have succeeded without her mentor.* SYN. teacher, guide, coach, advisor, guru, master, instructor, trainer.

mercenary n. soldier of fortune, *hired gun, professional soldier, legionnaire, hired hand.

MERCENARY a. [MUR suh ner ee] working for monetary gain and no other reason. *His motivation for fighting in the war was purely mercenary.* SYN. monetary, selfish, money-grubbing, greedy, venal, acquisitive, for financial gain. ANT. *altruistic, idealistic.*

merchandise n. goods, products, wares, stock, commodities, vendibles, line, stuff.

merchandise v. buy and sell, trade, advertise, *move, market, deal in, traffic, distribute, wholesale, do business in.

merchant n. trader, wholesaler, retailer, dealer, shopkeeper, salesman, businessman, jobber, vendor, hawker.

merciful a. compassionate, forgiving, humane, humanitarian, kind, charitable, sympathetic, sparing, lenient, pitying, mild, gentle, softhearted. ANT. *merciless, unfeeling, brutal, pitiless.*

merciless a. uncompassionate, unforgiving, inhumane, unfeeling, brutal, coldhearted, hardhearted, heartless, pitiless, stony, mean, callous, cruel, ruthless. ANT. *merciful, compassionate, kind.*

MERCURIAL a. [mur KYOOR ee ul] quick or quick to change, volatile. *She was known for her fickle, mercurial manner.* SYN. quick, changeable, volatile, unstable, quick to change, flighty, unpredictable, erratic, *blowing hot and cold, capricious, *up and down, lively. ANT. *stable, predictable, constant.*

mercy n. compassion, forgiveness, humanity, kindness, charity, sympathy, pity, lenience, clemency, softheartedness, quarter. "Nobility's true badge." —Shakespeare. ANT. *cruelty, meanness, cold-bloodedness.*

mere a. nothing more than, insignificant, trifling, little, small, minor, only, simple, bare.

merge v. unite, combine, blend, consolidate, become partners, unify, marry, join, fuse, mix, confederate, join forces. ANT. *separate, split, diverge.*

merger n. consolidation, incorporation, alliance, combination, partnership, unification, union, marriage, joining, fusion. ANT. *separation, split-up, parting.*

meridian n. zenith, apex, highest point, crowning point, acme, peak, pinnacle, summit, climax, culmination. ANT. *low point, nadir.*

merit n. worth, worthiness, value, quality, virtue, excellence, integrity, credit.

merit v. deserve, be worthy of, earn, have coming to, be entitled to, rate.

meritorious a. praiseworthy, commendable, honorable, good, worthy, admirable, laudable, deserving, exemplary, noble. ANT. *unworthy, reprehensible, despicable.*

merriment n. fun, gaiety, frolic, joy, celebration, good times, enjoyment, mirth, laughter, joviality, jollity, sport. ANT. *misery, gloom, depression.*

merry a. fun, cheerful, gay, mirthful, joyful, celebratory, jovial, jolly, laughing, happy, rollicking, festive, blithe, carefree. ANT. *miserable, gloomy, depressed.*

merry-go-round n. carousel.

mesa n. plateau, tableland, butte.

mesh n. net, netting, network, web, webbing, screen, strainer, plexus, strainer, openwork, grid, grille, lattice.

mesh v. engage, fit, interlock, come together, enmesh, dovetail, interweave, entangle.

mesmerize v. hypnotize, spellbind, entrance, enthrall, *cast a spell on, put under, enchant, bewitch, fascinate, *do a Svengali.

mess n. **1.** CLUTTER jumble, disorder, disarray, litter, eyesore, debris, unsightliness, dump, mayhem, pigpen, filth, *rat's nest. **2.** PREDICAMENT trouble, plight, difficulty, *pickle, *jam, fix, stew, *fine kettle of fish, quandary, *deep shit. ANT. **1.** *order, neatness, tidiness.*

message n. **1.** COMMUNICATION note, word, communiqué, notice, memo, wire, dispatch, bulletin, missive, intelligence. **2.** THEME meaning, idea, moral, point.

messenger n. courier, runner, carrier, bearer,

emissary, envoy, herald, delivery person.

messy *a.* cluttered, jumbled, disordered, in disarray, littered, unsightly, filthy, dirty, chaotic, untidy. ANT. *clean, neat, tidy.*

METAMORPHOSIS *n.* [MET uh MOR fuh sis] a change of form, transformation. *We studied the metamorphosis of a caterpillar to a butterfly.* SYN. change, transformation, transmutation, conversion, metastasis, alteration, evolution, transmogrification, mutation, rebirth.

metaphor *n.* figure of speech, analogy, likening, image, simile, trope, symbol. "The language of poetry." — Raphael Kraus.

METAPHYSICAL *a.* [met uh FIZ i kul] not of the physical world, supernatural. *The astronomer uses hard science along with the metaphysical to understand the universe.* SYN. incorporeal, supernatural, transcendental, philosophical, abstract, theoretical, immaterial, impalpable, speculative, spiritual. ANT. *physical, concrete, material.*

metaphysics *n.* "The attempt of the mind to rise above the mind." — Thomas Carlyle. "The art of bewildering oneself methodically." — Jules Michelet.

meteor *n.* meteorite, fireball, bolide.

meteoric *a.* dazzling, brilliant, flashing, fleeting, ephemeral, short-lived, brief, sudden, swift.

method *n.* **1.** TECHNIQUE way, system, mode, style, formula, process, manner, means, procedure, program, course. **2.** DESIGN order, arrangement, plan, scheme, regularity.

methodical *a.* systematic, orderly, ordered, constant, efficient, regular, precise, machinelike, robotic, routine, step by step, structured. ANT. *loose, unmethodical, casual.*

meticulous *a.* careful, detail-oriented, scrupulous, painstaking, precise, finicky, exact, particular, demanding, perfectionist. ANT. *lax, casual, careless, sloppy.*

metier *n.* trade, profession, line of work. SEE OCCUPATION

metropolis *n.* capital, city, municipality, downtown, urban sprawl, megalopolis. SEE CITY, NEW YORK

mettle *n.* character, courage, heart, *what one is made of, spirit, *guts, strength, spunk, *grit, makeup, nerve, backbone, resolve.

miasma *n.* effluvium, vapor, gas, fog, cloud, mist, pollution, smog, stench, reek, methane.

microbe *n.* SEE MICROORGANISM

MICROCOSM *n.* [MYE kruh KOZ um] a miniature world or reality. *Bangladesh is a microcosm of a much greater population problem.* SYN. miniature world, miniature reality, little world, miniature universe. ANT. *macrocosm.*

microorganism *n.* microbe, germ, *bug, bacillus, bacterium, virus, pathogen.

microscopic *a.* tiny, minute, infinitesimal, invisible to the naked eye, miniscule, imperceptible, *wee. ANT. *macroscopic, immense.*

middle *n.* center, midpoint, halfway point, midsection, mean, epicenter, bull's-eye, thick of things, core, focal point. ANT. *periphery, margin, extreme.*

middle *a.* central, median, center, mean, halfway, intermediate, between, inside, equidistant. ANT. *outer, peripheral.*

middle age *n.* mid-life, middle years, forties. "When everything starts to wear out, fall out or spread out." — Anon. "The old age of youth and youth of old age." — Nunally Johnson.

middle class *n.* bourgeoisie, bourgeoise, common people, hoi polloi, Middle America, citizenry, working class. "The backbone of a country." — Robert Zwickey.

middleman *n.* go-between, intermediary, broker, agent, mediator, wholesaler.

middle-of-the-road *a.* moderate, *on the fence, neutral, noncommittal, nonpartisan. ANT. *radical, leftist, rightist, liberal, conservative.*

middling *a.* okay, so-so, fair, medium, adequate, moderate, mediocre, tolerable, nothing to brag about, run-of-the-mill. ANT. *exceptional, outstanding, first-class.*

midget *n.* dwarf, homunculus, pygmy, gnome, *Lilliputian, midge, Tom Thumb, runt, shrimp, pipsqueak. ANT. *giant, titan, monster.*

midnight *n.* twelve o'clock, *witching hour, *dead of night. "Fairy time." — Shakespeare. "The outpost of advancing day." — Longfellow.

midst *n.* middle, core, thick of things, hub, nucleus, heart, center, interior. ANT. *edge, periphery, outskirt.*

mien *n.* manner, bearing, air, demeanor, carriage, deportment, act, expression, look, presence, attitude, aura.

miff *v.* insult, hurt, irritate, annoy, offend, irk, bother, *bug, aggrieve, upset, vex.

might *n.* strength, power, force, muscle, potency, command, energy, brawn, vigor, steam. ANT. *weakness, impotency.*

mighty *a.* **1.** STRONG powerful, forceful, potent, commanding, influential, muscular, omnipo-

tent, vigorous, puissant, *strong as an ox.
2. HUGE gigantic, colossal, immense, titanic, enormous, gargantuan, massive, monstrous. ANT. *1. weak, feeble, impotent. 2. tiny, small, wee.*

migrant n. drifter, vagrant, nomad, mover, wanderer, rover, itinerant, gypsy, transient, tramp, *hobo.

migrate v. emigrate, immigrate, drift, move, wander, rove, travel, range, relocate, pull up stakes, *hit the road. ANT. *remain, put down roots.*

mild a. **1.** GENTLE soft, easygoing, docile, good-natured, meek, tame, mellow, peaceful, tender, pacific, kind, passive. **2.** TEMPERATE moderate, balmy, clement, gentle, fair, sunny, halcyon. ANT. *1. harsh, severe, hard, aggressive. 2. stormy, rough, wild.*

milestone n. landmark, turning point, high point, climax, achievement, accomplishment, event.

MILIEU n. [mil YOO] environment, setting. *The classical musician was out of his milieu at the heavy metal concert.* SYN. environment, setting, surroundings, element, medium, arena, theatre, background, scene.

militant n. fighter, troublemaker, agitator, firebrand, aggressor, attacker, combatant, warrior. ANT. *dove, pacifist, peacemaker.*

militant a. combative, aggressive, contentious, belligerent, pugnacious, hostile, fierce, antagonistic, warlike, offensive. ANT. *peaceful, pacific, passive.*

military n. army, armed forces, soldiers, troops, defense, service, air force, navy, marines, militia. SEE AIR FORCE, AMMUNITION, ARMY, BOMB, GUN, MISSILE, NAVY, NUCLEAR BOMB, WAR, WEAPON

military a. fighting, armed, combative, warring, militant, martial, soldierly, militaristic, militant. ANT. *peaceful, pacific.*

milksop n. *wimp, mouse, *chicken, *wuss, coward, pansy, sissy, baby, pantywaist, milquetoast. ANT. *macho man, he-man, hero.*

Milky Way n. galaxy, *backbone of the night, *starry trail, *island universe.

mill n. factory, plant, manufactory, works, foundry, shop.

millenium n. one thousand years, one-thousandth anniversary, golden age, heaven, utopia, Second Coming.

millstone n. burden, weight, load, cross, affliction, encumbrance, albatross.

milquetoast n. SEE MILKSOP

mimic n. impersonator, imitator, mime, caricaturist, pantomimist, *copycat, ape, parrot.

mimic v. impersonate, imitate, mime, caricature, pantomime, copy, ape, parrot, burlesque, parody, mock.

mince v. **1.** CUT UP chop up, dice, cube, hash, slice, fragment. **2.** SPEAK EUPHEMISTICALLY speak delicately, euphemize, *water down, minimize, soften, gloss over, moderate.

mind n. **1.** INTELLIGENCE intellect, seat of consciousness, brains, head, thought, mentality, cognitive power, perception, wisdom, reason, wits, intuition, psyche. "That little world."—Samuel Rogers. "An empire."—Robert Southwell. "A data storage bank with feelings."—Anon. "A creation of the universe to study itself."—Anon. **2.** MEMORY recollection, remembrance. **3.** OPINION belief, view, outlook, attitude, feeling, sentiment, way of thinking, conviction, notion. **4.** SANITY reason, rationality, stability, wits, judgment, soundness of mind, *marbles.

mind v. **1.** HEED observe, pay attention to, notice, attend to, watch, abide by, follow. **2.** LOOK AFTER care for, tend, babysit, protect, nurse. **3.** CARE dislike, disapprove of, object, be opposed to, detest, care one way or another. ANT. *1. ignore, overlook. 2. neglect, ignore.*

mindful a. aware, conscious, attentive, heedful, cognizant, regardful, careful, alert, wary, on the lookout. ANT. *unaware, heedless, oblivious.*

mindless a. brainless, stupid, witless, imbecilic, oblivious, unintelligent, asinine, idiotic, moronic, sophomoric, *bubble-headed. ANT. *intelligent, brainy, brilliant.*

mine n. quarry, deposit, excavation, shaft, tunnel, pit, vein, lode, claim, diggings, bonanza.

WORD FIND

claim: stake
coal cart: corf
coal dust: culm
combustible gasses in: firedamp
discovery of ore: strike
drain: sump
entranceway: adit, portal
flume for washing out gold ore: sluice
fraudulently scatter minerals about to deceive prospective buyer: salt
glacial mineral deposit of loose particles: placer
largest vein: mother lode
lung disease caused by coal dust: black lung disease
ore deposit: vein, lode

oxygen, absence or low level in shaft: choke-damp
passageway, main: gangway
potential area containing ore: prospect
residue of: tailings
rich vein: bonanza
search for ore: prospect
stratum: seam
waterway: tailrace
SEE CAVE

mine v. dig, quarry, excavate, tunnel, prospect, extract, pan, delve.

mingle v. **1.** MIX blend, unite, merge, intermingle, combine, join, marry. **2.** SOCIALIZE associate, hobnob, *work the room, mix, fraternize, circulate, join. ANT. *1. separate, divide. 2. snub, remain aloof, stay at arm's length.*

miniature a. mini, small, tiny, baby, midget, toy, dwarf, pint-sized, pocket-sized, small-scale, bantam, minute, wee. ANT. *giant, jumbo, oversized.*

minimal a. SEE MINIMUM

minimum n. least, lowest, bottom, slightest. ANT. *maximum.*

minimum a. minimal, least, smallest, lowest, slightest, bottom. ANT. *maximum, maximal, greatest.*

minister n. **1.** CLERGYMAN cleric, pastor, preacher, parson, deacon, priest, ecclesiastic, man of the cloth, reverend, servant of God, rabbi, father. SEE CLERGYMAN **2.** ADMINISTRATOR diplomat, ambassador, envoy, consul, cabinet member, official, delegate, secretary.

minister v. administer, tend, attend, serve, care for, accommodate, wait on, help, comfort, relieve, nurse.

minor n. child, juvenile, youth, adolescent, teenager, *teenybopper, kid, schoolboy, schoolgirl. ANT. *adult.*

minor a. small, trivial, insignificant, slight, light, low grade, trifling, piddling, bush-league, secondary, inconsequential. ANT. *major, severe, extreme, significant.*

minstrel n. troubador, singer, musician, lyricist, bard, balladeer, poet.

minute n. sixty seconds, moment, instant, twinkling, jiffy, wink of an eye, *two shakes of a lamb's tail.

minute a. tiny, miniscule, microscopic, infinitesimal, teeny, atomic, molecular, puny, miniature, negligible. ANT. *huge, gigantic, massive.*

MINUTIAE n. [mi NOO shee uh] trivial details. *Don't be so concerned with minutiae.* SYN.

trivia, trivial details, unimportant details, trifles, minor details, inessentials, nonessentials, useless information.

miracle n. act of God, divine act, supernatural event, marvel, wonder, spectacle, phenomenon, sensation. "The dearest child of faith." — Johann W. Goethe. "An event which creates faith; that is the purpose ... of miracles." — George Bernard Shaw. "Life itself." — Christopher Fry. "Every cubic inch of space." — Walt Whitman.

WORD FIND
location of several: Lourdes
study of: thaumatology

miraculous a. divine, supernatural, marvelous, wonderful, wondrous, phenomenal, sensational, anomalous, supermundane, magical, superhuman, unearthly, freakish, extraordinary, mind-blowing, *unreal. ANT. *ordinary, everyday, pedestrian.*

mirage n. optical illusion, refraction of light, delusion, vision, specter, phantom, apparition, hallucination, fantasy.

mire n. bog, mud, ooze, soggy ground, slush, marsh, fen, swamp, quagmire.

mire v. bog down, sink, stick, flounder, slow, wallow, get involved.

mirror n. looking glass, reflector. "A device which tells us the truth is a terrible thing." — Abraham Pollock.

mirror v. copy, imitate, mimic, reflect, simulate, personify, emulate, ape, mock, caricature.

mirth n. merriment, gaiety, joyousness, cheer, frolic, high spirits, glee, jollity, good times, lightheartedness, laughs, hilarity, sport. ANT. *depression, gloom, misery.*

mirthful a. merry, gay, joyous, cheerful, gleeful, jolly, lighthearted, hilarious, jocular, blithe, happy, glad. ANT. *depressed, gloomy, sad.*

misadventure n. mishap, accident, disaster, miscarriage, misfortune, *screw-up, slip, catastrophe, tragedy, calamity.

misanthrope n. man-hater, cynic, hermit, loner, recluse, misogynist, grouch.

misappropriate v. steal, swindle, embezzle, pocket, defalcate, *rip off, filch, cheat.

misbegotten a. illegitimate, bastard, out of wedlock, illegal, unlawful, disreputable. ANT. *legitimate.*

misbehave v. act out, make trouble, get out of line, offend, be bad, disobey, *raise hell, *raise dickens, transgress. ANT. *behave, show good manners.*

misbehavior n. acting out, naughtiness, transgression, offensiveness, bad manners, rudeness, impropriety, misconduct, *hell-raising.

miscalculate v. err, misjudge, miscompute, make a mistake, *mess up, blunder, misconstrue, underestimate, overestimate.

miscarriage n. **1.** ABORTION spontaneous abortion, stillbirth, premature delivery. **2.** FAILURE malfunction, misfire, mistake, miss, nonfulfillment, washout, disappointment, debacle. ANT. *success, achievement, fruition.*

miscellaneous a. varied, assorted, mixed, sundry, diversified, heterogenous, multiform, motley. ANT. *uniform, homogenous.*

miscellany n. assortment, collection, combo, variety, potpourri, medley, melange, anthology, compilation, mixture, pastiche.

mischief n. **1.** PRANKS, PLAYFULNESS trick, misbehavior, trouble, devilment, deviltry, *hell, shenanigans, naughtiness, funny business, horseplay, espieglerie. **2.** HARM damage, injury, destruction, sabotage, nuisance.

mischievous a. naughty, impish, devilish, prankish, roguish, playful, troublemaking, rascally, sportive, boyish, puckish. ANT. *angelic, well-behaved, saintly.*

misconception n. erroneous notion, wrong idea, misunderstanding, distortion, misinterpretation.

misconduct n. misbehavior, bad behavior, transgression, wrongdoing, misstep, delinquency, malfeasance, impropriety.

misconstrue v. misunderstand, misinterpret, misjudge, mistake, distort. ANT. *understand.*

miscreant n. criminal, evildoer, villain, sinner, felon, hoodlum, outlaw, scoundrel, rogue, rascal.

misdeed n. crime, sin, wrongful act, misdemeanor, transgression, offense, malefaction, malfeasance, felony, violation.

misdemeanor n. misdeed, offense, misbehavior, misconduct, indiscretion, infringement, violation, naughtiness, wrong.

miser n. hoarder, penny-pincher, skinflint, cheapskate, *tightwad, *money-grubber, *Scrooge, curmudgeon, misanthrope. ANT. *spendthrift, philanthropist.*

miserable a. **1.** UNHAPPY anguished, troubled, depressed, blue, forlorn, desolate, despondent, suicidal, inconsolable, dejected, sad, melancholy, heartbroken, woebegone, glum, mournful, wretched. **2.** BAD poor, inferior, rotten, lousy, disgraceful, wretched, pathetic, pitiful, sorry, deplorable, second-rate, abysmal. ANT. *1. happy, joyous, euphoric, elated. 2. good, excellent, superb.*

miserly a. hoarding, cheap, penny-pinching, tight, money-grubbing, misanthropic, stingy, parsimonious, niggardly. ANT. *generous, charitable, philanthropic.*

misery n. **1.** SUFFERING pain, anguish, depression, melancholy, unhappiness, woe, agony, sadness, distress, torment, hardship, sorrow, heartache, desolation, despair. "A communicable disease." — Martha Graham. "Almost always the result of thinking." — Joseph Jourbert. **2.** ADVERSITY affliction, trouble, ordeal, trial, tribulation, trouble, problem, curse. ANT. *1. happiness, pleasure, euphoria.*

misfit n. nonconformist, lone wolf, *square peg in a round hole, individual, *queer duck, *fish out of water, oddball.

misfortune n. bad luck, adversity, trouble, *bad break, trial, tribulation, setback, calamity, affliction, reversal, hardship, blow, disaster, tragedy. "Knives, that either serve us or cut us, as we grasp them by the blade or the handle." — Herman Melville. ANT. *good luck, fortune, blessing, godsend.*

misgiving n. uncertainty, apprehension, qualm, doubt, hesitation, uneasiness, question, fear, distrust, suspicion. ANT. *certainty, trust, confidence.*

misguided a. misled, ill-advised, misinformed, led astray, mistaken, faulty, wrong, erroneous, *led up the garden path, *barking up the wrong tree, *off. ANT. *well-advised, correct.*

mishandle v. botch, *screw up, *flub, mismanage, mess up, bungle, fumble, *muff, blow, *foul up, *drop the ball. ANT. *succeed, master.*

mishap n. accident, miscarriage, misadventure, *screw-up, blunder, mistake, misfortune, calamity, casualty.

mishmash n. hodgepodge, jumble, conglomeration. SEE MISCELLANY

misinform v. mislead, lead astray, misstate, misguide, misrepresent, distort, lie, deceive.

misinterpret v. misconstrue, misread. SEE MISUNDERSTAND

misjudge v. miscalculate, misread, overestimate, underestimate, overrate, underrate, err, mistake, misconstrue, misunderstand.

mislead v. lead astray, misinform, misguide, deceive, *lead up the garden path, bamboozle, delude, *give the bum steer, take in, *pull the wool over one's eyes.

mismanage v. SEE MISHANDLE

mismatch n. SEE DISPARITY

misplace v. lose, lose track of, mislay, displace.

misrepresentation n. distortion, misstatement, falsification, fabrication, misquote, *stretch, perversion, adulteration, lie, exaggeration. ANT. *truth, accuracy.*

miss n. young lady, girl, lass, maiden, gal, young woman, mademoiselle.

miss v. **1.** FAIL fall short, pass over, overlook, *drop the ball, miscalculate, bobble, muff, *blow it, *choke, muff. **2.** LONG FOR pine for, yearn for, ache with nostalgia, think of fondly. ANT. *1. succeed, catch, see.*

misshapen n. deformed, malformed, grotesque, distorted, misproportioned, contorted, monstrous, ugly.

missile n. rocket, projectile, trajectile, ballistic missile, air-to-air missile, ground-to-air missile, guided missile.

WORD FIND

air-to-air: Sidewinder, Falcon, Sparrow

antiship cruise missile: Harpoon

antitank: Hellfire missile, Maverick

electronic beam, guided by: beam rider

explosive portion: warhead

guided missile: cruise missile, Tomahawk

intercepts enemy missiles: Patriot

intercontinental missile: MX, Titan

multiple warhead missile: MIRV

propulsion unit, additional: booster

radar installations, homes in on: HARM

shoulder-fired: Stinger

silo-deployed, three-stage nuclear missile: Minuteman

tank-mounted: Shillelagh

underwater, launched from: Polaris, Poseidon, Trident II

missing a. lacking, absent, elsewhere, lost, gone, away, wanting, removed, mislaid, out of sight, unaccounted for, *AWOL. ANT. *here, present.*

mission n. task, undertaking, assignment, object, objective, charge, duty, quest, errand, job, enterprise, calling.

missionary n. evangelist, proselytizer, preacher, clergyman, minister, messenger.

missive n. letter, message, note, dispatch, communication, memo, report, word, bulletin, *fax.

misspent a. wasted, squandered, misapplied, thrown away, *down the drain, *blown, prodigal, *pissed out the window. ANT. *well spent, productive.*

misstatement n. misrepresentation, innacuracy, misquote, distortion, mistake, falsification, perversion, lie, *blooper.

misstep n. error, slip, mistake, wrong move,

gaffe, lapse, faux pas, trip, transgression, blunder, oversight.

mist n. vapor, fog, drizzle, fine rain, cloud, steam, spray, brume, moisture, haze, smog. SEE CLOUD, FOG, RAIN

mistake n. error, inaccuracy, fault, blunder, gaffe, *boo-boo, *flub, slip, miscalculation, boner, misinterpretation, goof, omission, oversight, failure.

mistake v. err, blunder, *flub, miscalculate, misinterpret, goof, omit, overlook, misunderstand, underestimate, overestimate, *botch, miss, misconstrue, confuse.

mistaken a. wrong, incorrect, inaccurate, off, inexact, imprecise, erroneous, in error, fallacious, *wide of the mark, confused, *all wet, *off base, misinformed, unsound. ANT. *correct, right, accurate.*

mistreat v. abuse, maltreat, wrong, rough up, manhandle, brutalize, disrespect, *step on, *walk all over, bully. ANT. *coddle, dote on.*

mistreatment n. abuse, maltreatment, disrespect, cruelty, brutality, torment, torture, manhandling, rough treatment. ANT. *coddling, kindness.*

mistress n. **1.** MATRON madam, authority, head, matriarch, head of the household. **2.** LOVER concubine, courtesan, sweetheart, kept woman, girlfriend, *other woman.

mistrust n. distrust, suspicion, doubt, uncertainty, skepticism, apprehension, misgiving, wariness, qualm, leeriness. ANT. *trust, confidence, faith.*

mistrust v. distrust, suspect, doubt, have misgivings, question, apprehend, fear, have reservations. ANT. *trust, believe in, have faith in.*

misty a. vaporous, drizzling, foggy, moist, gauzy, cloudy, filmy, murky, steamy, hazy, fuzzy, shrouded, nebulous. ANT. *clear, transparent.*

misunderstand v. misinterpret, misconstrue, misapprehend, misconceive, get the wrong idea, misread, misjudge, miscalculate, *get signals crossed. ANT. *understand, get, see.*

misunderstanding n. **1.** MISINTERPRETATION misapprehension, the wrong idea, confusion, mix-up, misconception, mistake, misreading, false impression. **2.** ARGUMENT disagreement, difference, dispute, rift, quarrel, dissension, squabble, *falling-out.

misuse n. misapplication, abuse, misusage, corruption, misemployment, perversion.

misuse v. misapply, misemploy, abuse, corrupt, pervert, mistreat, wrong.

MITIGATE v. [MIT uh GATE] to lessen the effect or severity of something. *Mitigate the*

pain of a sprain by elevating the injured ankle.
SYN. moderate, lessen, diminish, soften, reduce, alleviate, allay, lighten, check, blunt, ease. ANT. *exacerbate, aggravate, worsen.*

mix *n.* mixture, blend, combination, combo, compound, amalgamation, composite, variety, potpourri, goulash, melange, medley.

mix *v.* **1.** BLEND combine, mingle, compound, amalgamate, jumble, suffuse, conglomerate, unite, join, merge. **2.** SOCIALIZE fraternize, hobnob, *work the room, mingle. ANT. *1. separate, divide. 2. be aloof, snub, *be a wallflower.*

mixed-up *a.* confused, muddled, lost, befuddled, perplexed, puzzled, confounded, misunderstanding. ANT. *clear, *with it.*

mixture *n.* SEE MIX

moan *n.* groan, cry, lament, wail, sigh, plaint.

moan *v.* groan, cry, lament, wail, sigh, grumble, complain, grieve.

moat *n.* trench, fosse, foss, ditch, gully, defense. SEE CASTLE

mob *n.* **1.** CROWD throng, mass, legion, flock, multitude, horde, collection, crush, host. **2.** GANG Mafia, underworld, syndicate, Cosa Nostra. "Man voluntarily descending to the nature of a beast." — Ralph Waldo Emerson. "Many heads, but no brains." — Thomas Fuller. "A many-headed beast." — Horace. "The scum that rises when the water boils." — Anon.

mob *v.* crowd, throng, swarm, surround, jostle, elbow, descend upon, attack.

mobile *a.* movable, moving, portable, locomotive, fluid, transportable, on the move, traveling. ANT. *stationary, immobile.*

mobilize *v.* ready, organize, summon, muster, assemble, call up, call to arms, round up, marshal, rally, activate. ANT. *immobilize, disperse.*

mobster *n.* goon. SEE GANGSTER

mock *v.* **1.** RIDICULE make fun of, taunt, challenge, laugh at, *poke fun at, kid, tease, scoff, jeer, burlesque, *thumb nose at. **2.** IMITATE mimic, impersonate, caricature, ape, parrot, *do, burlesque, lampoon, parody. ANT. *show respect, honor, *put on a pedestal.*

mock *a.* imitation, fake, artificial, counterfeit, simulated, mimic, *bogus, make-believe, substitute, sham. ANT. *true, genuine, real.*

mockery *n.* **1.** JOKE laughingstock, farce, travesty, *butt, fool, sham. **2.** RIDICULE taunting, kidding, disrespect, derision, scoffing, contempt, sport. ANT. *2. respect, honor, reverence.*

mode *n.* **1.** WAY manner, method, technique, style, practice, approach, procedure, methodology, form. **2.** FASHION style, look, vogue, trend, rage, craze.

model *n.* **1.** REPLICA mockup, dummy, prototype, miniature, copy, imitation, facsimile. **2.** IDEAL standard, exemplar, archetype, pattern, paragon, mold, role model, prototype. **3.** FASHION OR ARTIST'S MODEL poser, sitter, subject, dummy.

model *v.* **1.** FASHION shape, mold, design, construct, base, cast. **2.** SHOW show off, wear, display, parade.

model *a.* ideal, standard, exemplary, classic, perfect, archetypal.

moderate *n.* *middle-of-the-roader, nonliberal, nonconservative, centrist. ANT. *radical, conservative, liberal.*

moderate *v.* **1.** LESSEN soften, mitigate, restrain, check, tone down, control, regulate, reduce, slacken, ease, blunt. **2.** PRESIDE OVER control, oversee, chair, mediate, referee, lead, emcee, govern, supervise. ANT. *1. intensify, increase, aggravate.*

moderate *a.* **1.** TEMPERATE reasonable, sensible, judicious, balanced, equable, conservative, restrained, neutral, unexceptional, middling, not extreme. **2.** MILD calm, gentle, soft, low-key, quiet. **3.** AVERAGE medium, mediocre, so-so, fair, middling, ordinary, intermediate, mean, common. ANT. *1. extreme, severe, excessive. 2. harsh, severe, violent. 3. exceptional, outstanding, extraordinary.*

moderation *n.* temperance, happy medium, middle ground, discretion, restraint, judiciousness, forbearance, sobriety, golden mean. "Nothing to excess." — Anacharsis. "The silken string running through the pearl — chain of all virtues." — Thomas Fuller.

moderator *n.* master of ceremonies, emcee, chairperson, referee, speaker, presiding officer, mediator.

modern *a.* contemporary, up-to-date, new, neo, now, current, today, *cutting edge, *leading edge, *mod, fresh, late, up-to-the-minute, *hot, fashionable, modish, trendy, *in, in vogue, progressive. ANT. *out of date, outdated, old-fashioned, antiquated, ancient, antique, passé.*

modernize *v.* update, renovate, remodel, revamp, redesign, streamline, retool. ANT. *antiquate.*

modest *a.* **1.** UNASSUMING humble, self-effacing, reserved, demure, unpretentious, down to earth, shy, blushing, bashful. **2.** ORDINARY humble, limited, moderate, medium, simple, plain, small, unpretentious, homely, adequate, middling, fair, unexceptional. ANT. *1. arrogant, pretentious, *full of oneself, vain. 2. exceptional, extravagant, ostentatious.*

modesty *n.* **1.** HUMILITY humbleness, unpretentiousness, moderation, reserve, reticence, shyness, bashfulness, simplicity, plainness. "The only sure bait when you angle for praise." — Lord Chesterfield. "Meekness and wisdom combined." — Solomon Ibn Gabirol. "An index to nobility." — Solomon Ibn Gabirol. **2.** DECENCY decorum, propriety, seemliness. ANT. *1. arrogance, pretentiousness, vanity. 2. indecency, unseemliness.*

modicum *n.* bit, small amount, speck, little, iota, shred, snippet, drop, ounce, atom, whit, particle. ANT. *lot, *truckload.*

modify *v.* **1.** CHANGE alter, rework, correct, adjust, vary, innovate, reshape, reform, convert, moderate, transform, tweak, *fiddle with. **2.** LESSEN limit, moderate, reduce, soften, tone down. ANT. *2. increase, intensify.*

modish *a.* fashionable, stylish, in vogue, chic, trendy, *in, up-to-the-minute, *hot, *all the rage, smart, fresh. ANT. *old-fashioned, dated, passé.*

modulate *v.* adjust, regulate, tune, fine-tune, attune, balance, moderate, equalize, soften, tone down.

modus operandi *n.* mode of operation, method, technique, system, workings, means, way.

mogul *n.* *big shot, *bigwig, *power, magnate, tycoon, baron, *VIP, personage, *mover and shaker, *heavy hitter, *heavyweight. ANT. *nobody, *zero, peasant.*

moist *a.* damp, wet, watery, humid, muggy, dewy, dank, steamy, misty, foggy, drizzly, rainy, clammy. ANT. *dry, arid, dehydrated.*

moisten *v.* dampen, wet, moisturize.

moisture *n.* dampness, wetness, humidity, mugginess, dew, steam, mist, fog, drizzle, rain, liquid. ANT. *dryness, aridity.*

mold *n.* **1.** FORM cast, pattern, stamp, shape, impression, die, outline, cut, model. **2.** FUNGUS mildew.

mold *v.* **1.** SHAPE form, cast, make, fashion, forge, sculpt, model, construct. **2.** INFLUENCE model, shape, guide.

moldy *a.* musty, stale, decayed, rotting, moldering, crumbling, mildewed, decomposing.

mole *n.* spot, nevus, blemish, birthmark, freckle, blotch, discoloration, beauty mark.

molest *v.* **1.** PHYSICALLY OR SEXUALLY ABUSE violate, fondle, rape, *feel up, accost, make an advance, solicit, approach, *paw, assault, mistreat. **2.** BOTHER trouble, annoy, besiege, torment, plague, harass, upset, beset, irritate, pester, disturb.

MOLLIFY *v.* [MOL uh FYE] to soothe, soften or appease. *We gave the toddler a stick of gum to mollify him.* SYN. soothe, soften, appease, pacify, tranquilize, mellow, calm, tame, gentle, calm, tone down, mitigate, blunt, ease. ANT. *aggravate, intensify, exacerbate.*

mollycoddle *v.* pamper, coddle, baby, cosset, indulge, wait on, spoil.

molt *v.* shed, cast off, slough off, exuviate, exfoliate, peel.

molten *a.* melted, liquefied, red-hot, smelted, igneous, volcanic. ANT. *frozen, hardened.*

mom *n.* SEE MOTHER

moment *n.* **1.** INSTANT minute, second, hour, point in time, *twinkling, time, *jiffy, short time, *wink of an eye, flash, *two shakes of a lamb's tail, date. **2.** IMPORTANCE consequence, weight, significance, import, gravity, concern, substance, magnitude. ANT. *unimportance, insignificance.*

momentarily *adv.* shortly, in a second, immediately, briefly, any moment now.

momentary *a.* brief, fleeting, short-lived, transitory, ephemeral, transient, instantaneous, passing. ANT. *long-lived, long, prolonged.*

momentous *a.* important, consequential, weighty, of great moment, significant, decisive, critical, crucial, pivotal, earthshaking, vital. ANT. *insignificant, trivial, unimportant.*

momentum *n.* impetus, force, push, drive, thrust, energy, impulse, go, speed.

monarch *n.* ruler, king, queen, autocrat, emperor, empress, sovereign, crowned head.

monarchy *n.* kingdom, sovereign state, autocracy, absolute monarchy.

monastery *n.* abbey, friary, cloister, religious community, convent, nunnery, priory, retreat, hermitage.

monetary *a.* pecuniary, financial, capital, fiscal.

money *n.* currency, legal tender, cash, *bucks, *dough, *bread, medium of exchange, *wad, *loot, *scratch, *wampum, coin, specie, change, almighty dollar, funds, wealth, capital, riches. "A good servant but a bad master." — Henry Bohn. "Slave or master." — Horace. "A good soldier." — Shakespeare. "An eel in the hand." — Welsh proverb.

WORD FIND

Afghanistan: afghani, pul

Algeria: dinar, centime
Argentina: austral, centavo
Australia: dollar, cent
Austria: schilling, groschen
Bahamas: dollar, cent
Bangladesh: taka, paisa
Barbados: dollar, cent
Belgium: franc, centime
Bolivia: boliviano, peso boliviano
Brazil: cruzado, centavo
Bulgaria: lev, stotinka
Burma: kyat, pya
Cambodia: riel, sen
Canada: dollar, cent
Chile: peso, centesimo
China: yuan, fen
Columbia: peso, centavo
Costa Rica: colon, centimo
Cuba: peso, centavo
Czechoslovakia: koruna, haler
Denmark: krone, ore
Dominican Republic: peso, centavo
Ecuador: sucre, centavo
Egypt: pound, piaster
El Salvador: colon, centavo
Ethiopia: birr, cent
Fiji: dollar, cent
Finland: markka, penni
France: franc, centime
Germany: deutsche mark, pfennig
Greece: drachma, lepton
Guatemala: quetzal, centavo
Guinea: franc, centime
Guyana: dollar, cent
Haiti: gourde, centime
Honduras: lempira, centavo
Hungary: forint, filler
Iceland: krona, eyrir
India: rupee, paisa
Indonesia: rupiah, sen
Iran: rial, dinar
Iraq: dinar, fils
Ireland: pound, penny
Israel: shekel, agora
Italy: lira, centesimo
Jamaica: dollar, cent
Japan: yen, sen
Jordan: dinar, fils
Kenya: shilling, cent
Korea, North: won, jeon
Korea, South: won
Kuwait: dinar, fils
Lebanon: pound, piaster
Libya: dinar, dirham
Luxembourg: franc, centime

Malta: lira, cent
Mexico: peso, centavo
Monaco: franc, centime
Morocco: dirham, centime
Nepal: rupee, pice
Netherlands: guilder, cent
New Zealand: dollar, cent
Nicaragua: cordoba, centavo
Nigeria: naira, kobo
Norway: krone, ore
Oman: rial, baiza
Pakistan: rupee, paisa
Panama: balboa, cent
Peru: inti, sol
Philippines: peso, centavo
Poland: zloty, grosz
Portugal: escudo, centavo
Russia: ruble, kopeck
Saudi Arabia: riyal, halala
Singapore: dollar, cent
Somalia: shilling, cent
South Africa: rand, cent
Spain: peseta, centimo
Sri Lanka: rupee, cent
Sudan: pound, piaster
Sweden: krona, ore
Switzerland: franc, centime
Syria: pound, piaster
Taiwan: dollar, cent
Thailand: baht, satang
Trinidad/Tobago: dollar, cent
Turkey: lira, kurus
Uganda: shilling, cent
United Arab Emerates: dirham, fils
United Kingdom: pound, penny
United States: dollar, cent
Uruguay: peso, centesimo
Venezuela: bolivar, centimo
Yugoslavia: dinar, para
Zaire: zaire, likuta
Zambia: kwacha, ngwee
Zimbabwe: dollar, cent

moneyed *a.* rich, wealthy, affluent, *loaded, *well-off, *well-to-do, *flush. ANT. *poor, destitute.*

money-making *a.* profitable, lucrative, paying, gainful, successful. ANT. *unprofitable.*

mongrel *n.* mixture, crossbreed, mutt, hybrid, half-blood, half-breed, cur. ANT. *purebred, thoroughbred.*

moniker *n. Sl.* nickname. SEE NAME

monitor *n.* overseer, watchdog, supervisor, observer, advisor.

monitor *v.* oversee, watch over, observe, *keep an eye on, check, supervise, police, scan.

monk *n.* brother, monastic, friar.

monkey *n.* simian, primate, ape, chimpanzee, rhesus monkey, spider monkey, orangutan. "An organized sarcasm upon the human race." — Henry Ward Beecher.

monkey business *n. Sl.* foolishness, mischief, misbehavior, impishness, antics, high jinks, *monkeyshines, horseplay. ANT. *serious business.*

monolith *n.* slab, stone, block, monument, obelisk

MONOLITHIC *a.* [MON uh LITH ik] huge, massive, and permanent, as a monolith. *It was a monolithic government with hundreds of subbureaucracies.* SYN. massive, huge, like a rock, unyielding, gigantic, permanent, unchanging, immovable, immobile. ANT. *tiny, portable, yielding.*

monologue *n.* soliloquy, talk, discourse, lecture, speech, oration, one-man show, one-woman show. ANT. *dialogue, give and take.*

monopolize *v.* corner, appropriate, own, dominate, *hog, keep for oneself, control. ANT. *share, divide equally.*

monopoly *n.* control, corner, domination, cartel, bloc, exclusive possession. "The octopus." — Frank Norris.

monotonous *a.* boring, tiresome, wearisome, repetitious, unstimulating, unvarying, dull, ho-hum, tedious, dry, *dull as dishwater, *blah, flat, somnolent, droning. ANT. *varying, changing, stimulating.*

monotony *n.* sameness, uniformity, boredom, dullness, tedium, routine, humdrum, repetition, dreariness, flatness. ANT. *change, variation, excitement.*

monster *n.* **1.** UNNATURAL BEAST creature, mutant, miscreation, ogre, freak of nature, monstrosity, boogieman, brute, thing, *it, *lab experiment, dragon, drake, sea serpent, kraken, hydra, Loch Ness Monster (Nessie), Champ (Lake Champlain), yeti, Bigfoot, abominable snowman, Frankenstein, werewolf, vampire, ghoul, goblin, hobgoblin, zombie, incubus, succubus, troll, basilisk, harpy, centaur, griffin, gargoyle, chimera, Gorgon, Medusa, Minotaur, Phoenix, Cerberus, Argus, Cyclops, Pluto, Sphinx, Orthos, Python, Pan, roc, demon, orc, satyr, hellhound, alien, extraterrestrial, little green man, man-eater, Godzilla, the Blob, B-movie monster (Roger Corman Creation). **2.** GIANT colossus, behemoth, gargantua, goliath, titan, leviathan, mammoth, Brobdingnagian. ANT. *2. dwarf, midget, runt, baby.*

monstrosity *n.* SEE MONSTER

monstrous *a.* **1.** GROTESQUE hideous, abnormal, mutated, unnatural, repulsive, freakish, teratoid, weird, wild, outlandish, bizarre, otherworldly, beastly, frightful, shocking. **2.** HUGE gigantic, gargantuan, colossal, stupendous, hulking, enormous, titanic, immense, mammoth, towering. **3.** EVIL atrocious, satanic, revolting, heinous, hateful, gruesome, loathsome, vile, horrible. **4.** OUTRAGEOUS shocking, incredible, ridiculous, astonishing. ANT. *1. normal, natural, beautiful. 2. tiny, wee, small. 3. good, moral, angelic. 4. normal, reasonable.*

montage *n.* hodgepodge, jumble, patchwork, mosaic, mishmash, potpourri, miscellany, arrangement, scheme.

monument *n.* **1.** A MEMORIAL statue, pillar, column, monolith, obelisk, tower, stone, plinth, shrine, pyramid, tombstone, headstone, marker, cross, mausoleum, cenotaph, effigy, ossuary, sepulchre, solium, weeper. "A boast in stone." — Anon. SEE CEMETERY **2.** NOTABLE ACHIEVEMENT landmark, magnum opus, masterpiece, masterwork, chef d'oeuvre, watershed.

monumental *a.* massive, huge, prodigious, colossal, towering, grand, exalted, enduring, permanent, outstanding, exceptional. ANT. *tiny, microscopic, insignificant, forgettable.*

moo *v.* low, bellow.

mooch *v.* cadge, beg, *sponge, *bum off, *leach off, *panhandle, pilfer.

mood *n.* state of mind, frame of mind, spirit, temper, humor, vein, mind, disposition, caprice. SEE ANGER, ANXIETY, DEPRESSION, FEAR, HAPPINESS, SADNESS

moody *a.* temperamental, touchy, grouchy, labile, gloomy, glum, petulant, unpredictable, cranky, *running hot and cold. ANT. *stable, predictable, even-tempered, constant.*

moon *n.* satellite, orb, planetoid, celestial body, sphere, *dustball, Luna, Selene, Diana. "Magnificent desolation." — Edwin Aldrin. "A corpse upon the road of night." — Robert Burton. "A golden sickle reaping darkness down." "The passionless bright face." — Dinah Craik.

WORD FIND

crater: Alphonsus, Copernicus, Kepler, Plato, Tycho

descriptive: sickle, wan, albescent, sallow, sterile, stark, surrealistic

goddess: Luna, Selene, Diana, Phoebe, Astarte, Cynthis, Lucina, Hecate

halo around: nimbus
hole from meteorite impact: crater
horn of crescent: cusp
landing site, original: Sea of Tranquility
line or crack from meteorite impact: ray
line where light and dark meet: terminator
mares: (maria): Mare Imbrium, Mare Nubium, Oceanus Procellarum, Mare Tranquilititis (sea of tranquility)
mound: dome
mountains: Alps, Apennines, Caucasus, Doerfel, Leibnitz
narrow trench or valley: rill(e)
orbital point farthest from earth: apogee
orbital point nearest to earth: perigee
phases: new, crescent, quarter, gibbous, full
plain originally mistaken for sea: mare (maria)
reflected sunlight: albedo
seasonal: harvest, hunter's
shadow: umbra
study of: selenology
waxing, waning

moon v. Sl. **1.** DROP ONE'S DRAWERS *flash, *salute. **2.** DREAM daydream, fantasize, *go off into one's own world.

moonlight n. moonshine, moonbeams, albedo, effulgence, luminescence, radiance.

moonshine n. Sl. corn liquor, contraband, home brew, bootleg, *white lightning, *mountain dew, *rotgut, *stump liquor, *bathtub gin, *the stuff that looks like water and kicks like a mule.

moonstruck v. crazed, deranged, demented, possessed, loony, insane.

moor n. heath, peat bog, scrubland, swamp, tundra, wasteland, marsh, prairie.

moorings n. slip, port, harbor, anchorage, dock, marina, wharf, berth, landing, pier.
WORD FIND
deck posts around which mooring lines are secured: bitt
dock or pier post around which mooring lines are secured: bollard

moose n. deer, elk, mammal.
WORD FIND
feeding place: yard
female: cow
kin: reindeer, caribou
male: bull
sexual season: rut
young: calf

MOOT a. [MOOT] subject to discussion or debate. *Whether or not abortion is morally acceptable is a moot question.* SYN. debatable,

arguable, disputable, contestable, questionable, open to question, controversial, at issue, unsettled, theoretical, academic, conjectural. ANT. *indisputable, uncontestable, resolved.*

mop n. swab, duster, *squeegee.

mop v. swab, wipe up, sponge up, dust, *squeegee.

mope v. sulk, pout, brood, grumble, put on a long face, fret, pine, moon, languish, lose heart.

moral n. lesson, principle, truism, adage, proverb, teaching.

moral a. **1.** RIGHTEOUS virtuous, ethical, good, upright, scrupulous, honorable, honest, principled, trustworthy, fair, decent, conscientious, correct, aboveboard, just. **2.** SEXUALLY VIRTUOUS chaste, immaculate, pure, innocent, respectable, *squeaky clean. ANT. *1. immoral, unethical, unprincipled, corrupt, evil. 2. promiscuous, loose, wild.*

morale n. spirit, resolve, attitude, confidence, mood, state.

morality n. righteousness, goodness, integrity, virtue, decency, fairness, honesty, conscientiousness, honor, respectability, responsibility. "A terribly thin covering of ice over a sea of primitive barbarity." — Karl Barth. "To enjoy and give enjoyment, without injury to yourself or others." — Nicolas Chamfort "Feeling temptation but resisting it." — Sigmund Freud. ANT. *immorality, evil.*

moralize v. preach, sermonize, pontificate, lecture, pass judgment, *climb on one's moral soapbox, *look down one's holier-than-thou nose.

morals n. ideals, standards, mores, scruples, principles, ethics, ethos, manners.

morass n. **1.** MARSH bog, swamp, fen, quagmire, wetland, mire, slough, wallow. **2.** ENTANGLEMENT mess, mix-up, jam, predicament.

MORATORIUM n. [MOR uh TOR ee um] A suspension or delay of an activity. *The city has placed a moratorium on new real estate development.* SYN. suspension, delay, deferment, postponement, discontinuance, stop.

MORBID a. [MOR bid] unhealthy, unwholesome, gloomy or gruesome. *He had a morbid fascination with death.* SYN. unhealthy, sickly, pathological, morose, gloomy, black, depressed, somber, melancholy, neurotic, sick, gruesome. ANT. *healthy, wholesome, happy.*

mordant a. biting, cutting, caustic, bitter, sarcastic, acid, scathing, acerbic, venomous, pungent, acrimonious, pointed, sharp.

more *n.* additional amount, supplement, replenishment, increase, extra.

more *a.* additional, extra, further, greater, added.

more or less approximately, about, roughly, generally, thereabouts, in round numbers.

moreover *a.* in addition, furthermore, over and above, also.

mores *n.* customs, codes, manners, standards, conventions, ethos.

morgue *n.* mortuary, funeral parlor, charnel house, crematorium.

moribund *a.* dying, expiring, failing, wasting away, on one's deathbed. ANT. *robust, healthy, vital.*

morning *n.* dawn, daybreak, sunup, sunrise, A.M., forenoon, the holy light of dawn.

moron *n.* imbecile, idiot, simpleton, retardate, dope, dolt, nitwit, dullard, dunce, dummy, lamebrain, *lunkhead, *meathead, *chowderhead, *airhead, *maroon, *one with the IQ of a woodchuck, *one who cuts with a dull tool, *one two bricks shy of a load, *one slower than a glacier, *one as dense as a post, *one as numb as a flounder, *one who is dead from the neck up. "One who is content with a serene state." — Anon. ANT. *genius, savant, Rhodes scholar, Mensa member, rocket scientist.*

moronic *a.* dumb, addle-brained, bovine, asinine. SEE STUPID

morose *a.* gloomy, glum, sullen, melancholy, sour, dour, ill-humored, austere, saturnine, stern, scowling, lugubrious, surly. ANT. *cheerful, upbeat, sunny.*

morphine *n.* narcotic, pain killer, pain reliever, anesthetic, opiate, *bang, *hocus, *joy dust, *white nurse. SEE DRUG

morsel *n.* bite, tidbit, spoonful, bit, a taste, mouthful, scrap, piece, shred, speck, chunk, hunk, lump, smidgen.

mortal *a.* **1.** SUBJECT TO DEATH human, earthly, perishable, temporal, transient, fleeting, finite, ephemeral, transitory. **2.** CAUSING DEATH fatal, lethal, malignant, deadly. **3.** TO THE DEATH homicidal, murderous, deathdealing, suicidal, bloodthirsty, fatal, deadly, unrelenting. ANT. *1. immortal, permanent, everlasting. 2. benign, harmless.*

mortality *n.* **1.** IMPERMANENCE transience. **2.** DEATH ON A LARGE SCALE slaughter, carnage, bloodbath, holocaust, extermination, fatality. **3.** Death rate.

mortally *a.* gravely, seriously, fatally.

mortgage *n.* contract, pledge, title, deed, lease, loan agreement.

mortician *n.* undertaker, funeral director, embalmer.

mortification *n.* humiliation, shame, embarrassment, chagrin, humbling, humble pie, disgrace, loss of face.

mortify *v.* humiliate, embarrass, shame, humble, disgrace, dismay, deflate, bring down, *take down a notch, belittle. ANT. *honor, exalt, worship.*

mortuary *n.* funeral home, funeral parlor, morgue, charnel house, crematorium.

mosaic *n.* inlay, collage, tile-work, marquetry, parquetry, miscellany, jumble, hodgepodge.

mosey *v.* shuffle, saunter, pad, amble, stroll. SEE WALK

Moslem *n.* Muslem, Muslim, Mohammedan.

mosque *n.* temple, church, house of worship, house of God, sanctuary.

WORD FIND

prayer tower: minaret

moss *n.* lichen, liverwort, Irish moss, Spanish moss, club moss, peat moss.

mossback *n.* *old fogy, *fuddy-duddy, fossil, mid-Victorian, ultraconservative.

most *a.* greatest, largest, nearly all, majority, *lion's share, maximum, utmost, unsurpassed, unequaled, furthest. ANT. *least, smallest, lowest.*

mostly *a.* for the most part, principally, chiefly, mainly, by and large, on the whole.

mot *n.* witticism, quip, bon mot, repartee, riposte.

mote *n.* speck, particle, fragment, bit, flake, grit.

motel *n.* motor court, inn, motor inn, roadhouse, *stop and drop. SEE HOTEL

moth-eaten *a.* **1.** THREADBARE tattered, ragged, *holey, worn-out, decrepit. **2.** OLD-FASHIONED outmoded, outdated, antiquated, out of style, obsolete.

mother *n.* **1.** MOM matriarch, parent, matron, nurturer, caregiver, *hand that rocks the cradle, foster mother, adoptive mother, mother-in-law, *mama, *mum, *mumsy, *old lady. **2.** SOURCE origin, originator, womb, cradle. "What God made because He could not be everywhere." — Adapated from Jewish proverb. "God's deputy on earth." — Rahel Varnhagen.

mother *v.* nurture, raise, rear, bring up, parent, foster, nourish, protect, nurse, care for, overprotect, spoil, smother, coddle.

motherhood *n.* maternity, mothership.

motherland *n.* native land, home land, *the old country.

motherly *a.* maternal, nurturing, doting, protective, solicitous.

motif *n.* theme, pattern, subject, leitmotif, idea, strain, device, form, concept.

motion *n.* **1.** ACTION movement, change, moving, transition, drift, shift. **2.** A PROPOSAL recommendation, suggestion, proposition, submission, offering.

motion *v.* gesture, gesticulate, point, nod, beckon, shrug, pantomime.

motionless *a.* unmoving, still, inert, static, lifeless, tranquil, dead, frozen, paralyzed, inanimate, stationary, immobile, becalmed, fixed, quiet, idle.

motion picture *n.* picture show, *flick. SEE MOVIE

motivate *v.* impel, induce, move, stimulate, spur, goad, encourage, challenge, incite, prompt, inspire, start, arouse, *hold out a carrot, *light a fire under, galvanize, serve as a catalyst, *give a good, swift kick. ANT. *discourage, deflate, *take the wind out of one's sails, dishearten.*

motivation *n.* incentive, enticement, reason. SEE MOTIVE

motive *n.* motivation, purpose, reason, incentive, stimulus, rationale, driving force, grounds, enticement, aim, instigation, goal, spur, bribe.

motley *a.* heterogenous, diverse, many-colored, assorted, miscellaneous, varied, varicolored, variegated, kaleidoscopic, patchwork, jumbled, multifarious. ANT. *similar, uniform, homogeneous.*

motor *n.* engine, power plant, dynamo, turbine, generator, transformer, transducer, *workhorse; TYPES internal combustion motor, diesel, Wankel, rotary, steam, double-overhead cam, two-stroke, four-stroke, V-6, V-8, four-barrel, slant, transverse, supercharged, turbocharged, inboard-outboard.

WORD FIND
alternating current producer: alternator
carburetor replacement system: fuel injection
closes air to carburetor: choke
coolant: antifreeze, ethyl glycol
cooling system: fan, radiator, thermostat, water jackets, water pump.
cylindrical plugs that move up and down, compresses air-fuel mix: pistons
distributes electricity to spark plugs: distributor
drive train: clutch, transmission, driveshaft, differential

energy unit: horsepower, rpm REVOLUTIONS PER MINUTE
exhaust burner: catalytic converter, afterburner, turbocharger
filters dirt and dust: air filter, fuel filter, oil filter
frame: chassis
fuel vaporizer: carburetor
knocking: ping, detonation
main framework containing cylinders: engine block
main rotating shaft: crankshaft
overtaxing of: red-lining
piston housing: cylinder
sputtering after ignition turned off: dieseling
valve operator: camshaft
SEE AIRCRAFT, AUTOMOBILE, MACHINERY

motor *v.* drive, cruise, ride, tour, steer.

motorboat *n.* speedboat, power boat, outboard, cruiser. SEE BOAT, SHIP

motorcycle *n.* motor bike, dirt bike, motor scooter, minibike, moped, *hog, *wheels, *chopper, *iron horse, *rice burner, *bike, *sled. SEE MOTOR

WORD FIND
accelerator: throttle
engine shutoff: kill switch
model: Honda, Harley Davidson, Kawasaki, Suzuki, Triumph, Indian
safety bar, passenger: sissy bar
seat: saddle

motor home *n.* trailer, mobile home, RV, camper, *tin can.

motorist *n.* driver, commuter.

motorized *a.* powered, mechanized.

mottled *a.* variegated, streaked, dappled, piebald, pied, spotted, shaded, motley, splotchy, marble-patterned, flecked, particolored.

motto *n.* maxim, adage, aphorism, saying, proverb, axiom, truism, principle, slogan, epigram, saw.

mound *n.* heap, pile, mass, knoll, hump, hummock, hillock, dune. SEE HILL

mount *v.* **1.** ASCEND climb, go up, scale, surmount. **2.** INCREASE grow, pile up, burgeon, accrue, swell, mushroom, multiply, proliferate, balloon, accumulate.

mountain *n.* peak, alp, mount, summit, pinnacle, highland, elevation, ridge, pike, seamount, volcano, butte, mesa, plateau, massif, matterhorn, monadnock, nunatak, uprising, cliff. (Famous mountains) Aetna, Annapurna, Blanc, Everest, Fuji, Godwin Austen (k-2), Grand Teton, Hood, Kilamanjaro, Krakatoa, Matterhorn, McKinley,

Pelee, Pike's Peak, Rainier, Sinai, St. Helens, Vesuvius, Washington, Whitney. (Ranges) Adirondacks, Alps, Andes, Appalachian, Appenines, Canadian Rockies, Cascades, Caucasus, Himalayas, Karakoram, Pyrenees, Rockies, Sierra Madre, Sierra Nevada, Tetons, Urals, White Mountains. "The palaces of nature." — Lord Byron.

WORD FIND

air: rarefied
base: piedmont
bowllike hollow carved by glacier: cirque
chain: cordillera, range, sierra
cloud: banner
crest: arete
descriptive: bell-shaped, flinty, spired
elevation above 4800 ft.: alpine
erosion resistant: monadnock
flat-topped: butte, mesa, plateau
formation: orogeny
frozen fog: rime ice, verglas
glacial ice, surrounded by: nunatak
glow at sunrise/sunset: alpenglow
gully: couloir
humpback: shoulder
lake: tarn
leeward side: rain shadow
low between summits: saddle
needlelike peak: aiguille, matterhorn
nymph: oread
oxygen deprivation: mountain sickness
pass: col, defile
peak: horn, summit
ranges, multiple: cordillera
ridge: arete, hogback, sawback, spur
rounded: knob
rubble: scree, talus
saddle: col
sea: seamount
shadow illusion: specter of the brocken
side: flank
snow collapse: avalanche
steep, weathered rock: crag
study: orography
vestigial nubbin: inselberg
ANT. *valley, dale, dell, crater.*
SEE HILL, MOUNTAINEER, MOUNTAINEERING, MOUNTAINOUS, VOLCANO

mountaineer *n.* highlander, uplander, Sherpa, mountain climber, rock climber, adventurist.

mountaineering *n.* mountain climbing, ascending, surmounting, scaling, rock climbing.

WORD FIND

climbing without mechanical aids: free-climbing
dangerous overhang of ice and snow: cornice
descend by rope: rappel
diagonal ascent: slab
makeshift shelter: bivouac
narrow, vertical passageway: chimney
oxygen deprivation: mountain sickness
ring that connects ropes to pitons: carabiner
securing or playing out rope: belaying
short rope ladder: etrier
sideways movement across slope: traverse
sideways rope traverse: pendulum
spike, wedge or peg used to secure climber: piton
staff: alpenstock
toothed, metal traction attachment: crampon
zigzag to counter steep slopes: switchback

mountainous *a.* alpestrine, alpine.

WORD FIND

descriptive: rugged, towering, lofty, vertiginous, cloud-capped, supernal, washboard
ranges: cordillera, sierra

mountebank *n.* charlatan, swindler, quack, *rip-off artist, *con man, *grifter, cheat, imposter, *huckster, *snake oil salesman.

mounted *a.* **1.** SEATED astride, in the saddle. **2.** FITTED attached, seated, backed. SEE MOUNTING

mounting *n.* frame, backing, support, seating.

mounting *v.* growing, piling up, expanding, accruing, burgeoning, mushrooming, proliferating, accumulating, multiplying, snowballing. ANT. *diminishing, shrinking.*

mourn *v.* grieve, lament, bemoan, pine, bewail, rue, despair, miss, deplore, languish, agonize, yearn, ache, suffer, anguish.

mourner *n.* the bereaved, griever, survivor.

mournful *a.* sorrowful, bereft, desolate, woeful, heavyhearted, downhearted, forlorn, grief-stricken, anguished, heartsick, inconsolable, aching with nostalgia, disheartened, prostrate. ANT. *cheerful, sunny, joyous.*

mourning *n.* grieving, sorrowing, lamentation, lamenting, bereavement, grief, anguish.

WORD FIND

dress of: black, veil, sackcloth, mourning band, widow's weeds
ANT. *rejoicing, celebrating.*

mouse *n.* **1.** RODENT vermin, field mouse, pocket mouse, vole. **2.** SISSY coward, milquetoast, shrinking violet, weakling, *wimp, *woos.

mousy *a.* timid, quiet, shy, timorous. ANT. *bold, aggressive.*

mouth n. **1.** ORAL CAVITY lips, maw, orifice, muzzle chops, *choppers, *kisser. SEE LIPS, SMILE, TEETH **2.** END OF A RIVER outlet, estuary, delta, drain. SEE RIVER **3.** OPENING entrance, aperture.

mouthful n. bite, spoonful, morsel.

mouth off v. spout off, vociferate, vituperate, harangue, taunt, rant, rave, sass, *wise off.

mouthpiece n. spokesman, spokeswoman, PR person, attorney.

mouthwash n. mouth rinse, breath freshener, gargle.

mouth-watering a. salivary, appetizing, savory, succulent.

mouthy a. loudmouthed, vociferous, ranting, obnoxious.

movable a. portable, transportable, fluid. SEE MOBILE

move v. **1.** SET OR BE IN MOTION transport, change places, impel, propel, advance, lug, haul, budge, relocate, push, pull, go, come, travel, proceed, walk, run, fly. **2.** CHANGE RESIDENCES relocate, transfer, pull up roots, vacate, emigrate, migrate, fly the coop. **3.** AFFECT THE EMOTIONS touch, stir, arouse, play on one's sympathies, pluck TUG at the heartstrings, strike a nerve, melt the heart, stimulate, disturb. **4.** PROPOSE put forth, recommend, urge, offer, submit.

movement n. **1.** MOTION action, stirring, activity, advancement, propulsion, ascension, descension, retraction, flight. **2.** CAMPAIGN grassroots movement, crusade, undertaking, drive popular front, fundraiser, push. **3.** MUSICAL PASSAGE section, part, sequence, division, piece.

mover n. shipper, trucker, moving company.

mover and shaker n. doer, producer, *player, *heavy hitter, instigator, catalyst, generator, *whip, *wheeler and dealer, *spark plug, *lightning rod, *go-getter, enterpriser, entrepreneur, *biggest toad in the puddle, *big cheese, *chairman of the board, *kingpin, pathfinder, bellwether.

movie n. motion picture, moving picture, film, picture, show, screenplay, cinema, photoplay, silver screen, video, *talkie, *flik, documentary, docudrama, melodrama, epic, *spaghetti western, horse opera, B movie, blue movie, stag film, *skin flik. "Life with the dull parts cut out."—Alfred Hitchcock. **WORD FIND**
actor/small role: bit player, cameo appearance, extra
advertising/promotional clip: trailer

aerial shot: crane shot
award: Academy Award, Oscar
black-and-white to color process: colorization
box office smash: *boffo
captioned drawings of planned camera shots: storyboard
clapper: slate
daytime run movie: matinee
directs actors and technicians: director
double scene effect: split screen
electrician assistant: best boy
electrician in charge of lights: gaffer
end of shooting for the day: wrap
fade out effect: dissolve
gunshot wound effect: squib
head of financing and hiring: producer
joining of two pieces of film: splice
journals of the industry: trades, *Variety*, *Hollywood Reporter*
library film: stock footage
lip synchronization on short loops of film: looping
location finder: location scout
moving shot: dolly shot, trucking shot
music of: score
object: prop
past, scene from character's: flashback
photographer, motion picture: cinematographer
prints from day's shooting: dailies, rushes
proposal of movie to financiers: pitch
publicity: publicist
record dialogue and sound effects: dub, Foley
rolling credits at end of movie: crawl, closing credits
script continuity: script supervisor
set or prop assistant: grip
sets and costumes head: art director
sound effects room: Foley studio
sound recorder: sound technician, Foley artist
stop-action photography: pixillation
superimposition effect: blue screen, matte shot
studio and outside shooting area: lot, backlot
wardrobe assistant: dresser
widening shot: pull-back
wide-screen film process: Cinemascope
wide side-to-side shot: pan
writer: screenwriter, script doctor
writer's outline: treatment
zooming in effect: zoom shot

moving *a.* IN MOTION going, coming, motioning, transporting, proceeding, advancing, ascending, descending, retracting, reversing. **2.** RELOCATING transferring, vacating, pulling up roots, emigrating, migrating, flying the coop. **3.** EFFECTING THE EMOTIONS touching, stirring, rousing, stimulating, striking a nerve, plucking at the heartstrings, heart-wrenching, gut-wrenching.

mow *v.* cut, trim, shear, clip, scythe, hack, reap. SEE HARVEST

moxie *n. Sl.* courage, pluck, guts, mettle, chutzpah, *balls.

much *n.* great quantity, a lot, abundance, profusion, plethora, myriad, deluge, scores, wealth, bonanza, tons, *oodles, *all the tea in China. ANT. *nothing, zero, pittance.*

much *a.* **1.** TO A GREAT DEGREE OR EXTENT important, remarkable, considerable, significant, paramount, impressive, critical, of consequence. **2.** IN GREAT QUANTITY abundant, plentiful, ample, sufficient, profuse, lavish, generous, considerable, copious, liberal, sizable.

muck *n.* **1.** MANURE dung, compost, fertilizer, *crap, ooze. **2.** SCANDALOUS INFORMATION lowdown, *skinny, slander, gossip, *dirt, *goods. SEE MUCKRAKING

muck-a-muck *n. Sl.* big shot, *big gun, *big cheese, high muckety-muck, pooh-bah, *VIP, *bigwig, *biggest toad in the puddle.

MUCKRAKER *n.* [MUCK raker] One who investigates and reports corruption. *Newspapers train their best reporters to be muckrakers.* SYN. *whistle-blower, investigative journalist, *keyhole journalist, exposer, gossipmonger, scandalmonger, mudslinger, debunker.

MUCKRAKING *n.* [MUCK raking] investigating and reporting corruption. *Muckraking can sometimes be a journalist's most dangerous job.* SYN. whistle-blowing, investigating, exposing, *digging for dirt, gossipmongering, scandalmongering, *dragging through the mud, defaming, character assassinating.

mud *n.* mire, muck, ooze, sludge, slime, clay, slush, silt, dirt, wallow, organic matter.

muddle *v.* mix up, stir up, jumble, disorder, fumble, blunder, puzzle, scramble, ensnarl, confuse, turn upside-down, mess up, foul. ANT. *order, organize, neaten, clarify.*

muddled *a.* confused, befuddled, incoherent, addled, bewildered, disoriented.

muddy *a.* mucky, miry, sloppy, silty, slimey, slushy, gooey, dirty, oozy, soggy, swampy, boggy, soiled, filthy, grubby, organic, sedi-mentary.

mudslinging *n.* smear campaign, slander, defamation, scandalizing, libeling, name-calling, dragging one's name through the mud, *political parry and jab. ANT. *compliment, praise, tribute.*

muff *v.* bungle, botch, fumble, drop the ball, *blow it, stumble, *choke, fail, miscalculate, slip, trip up, *screw up. ANT. *succeed, accomplish.*

muffin *n.* bread, roll, biscuit, scone, bran muffin, corn muffin.

muffle *v.* stifle, deaden, dampen, mute, tone down, silence, soften.

muffler *n.* **1.** CLOTHING scarf, neckerchief, ascot. **2.** NOISE-ABSORBING DEVICE baffle, mute, silencer.

mug *n.* **1.** DRINKING VESSEL stein, tankard, flagon, cup, toby, goblet. **2.** FACE countenance, puss, grimace, mug shot. SEE FACE

mug *v.* hold up, assault, rob, purse-snatch, strong-arm, *jump, *stick up.

mugging *n.* holdup, assault, robbery, purse-snatching, *stick-up.

muggy *a.* humid, damp, moist, sticky, close, clammy, steamy, sultry, dank, sweltering, oppressive. ANT. *dry, arid.*

mulatto *n.* mixed breed, half-breed, hybrid, creole, octoroon, quadroon, *Oreo.

mule *n.* hinny, jackass, donkey, burro, jenny.

mulish *a.* obstinate, headstrong. SEE STUBBORN

mull *v.* ponder, reflect, think, consider, meditate, weigh, ruminate, deliberate, contemplate, marshal one's thoughts, chew, brood, muse, cogitate.

multicolored *a.* polychromatic, particolored, spectral, variegated, kaleidoscopic, mottled, dappled, striped, streaked. SEE COLORED

multifaceted *a.* **1.** MANY-SIDED many-faced, manifold. **2.** INTRICATE complex, complicated.

multifarious *a.* manifold, diverse, multitudinous, various, multifaceted, heterogeneous, multiplex.

multinational *a.* international, global, continental, worldwide, multicultural. ANT. *local.*

multiple *a.* many, manifold, numerous, multitudinous, several, plural, various, duplex, triplex, sundry, myriad.

multiply *v.* **1.** TO ADD increase, compound, duplicate, triple, quadruple, burgeon, proliferate, grow, spread, mushroom. **2.** PRODUCE OFFSPRING propagate, procreate, generate, breed. SEE REPRODUCE

multitude *n.* mass, throng, bunch, horde, legion, flock, mob, crowd, swarm.

mum *a.* silent, mute, tight-lipped, speechless. ANT. *effusive, talkative.*

mumble *v.* mutter, maunder, murmur, speak indistinctly, whisper, talk to oneself, *talk into one's chin/beard, drone. ANT. *project, articulate, shout, roar.*

mummify *v.* dry, shrivel, preserve, desiccate, embalm, swaddle.

mummy *n.* corpse, cadaver, the embalmed, the entombed, *stiff.

munch *v.* chew, bite, crunch, snack, nosh, chomp, nibble, gnaw. SEE CHEW, EAT

munchies *n. Sl.* **1.** SEE SNACK **2.** SEE APPETITE, HUNGER

mundane *a.* **1.** ORDINARY everyday, common, banal, trite, humdrum, routine, prosaic, stale, pedestrian. **2.** EARTHLY worldly, terrestrial, material, physical, human. ANT. *1. extraordinary, rare, exceptional. 2. spiritual, divine, out of this world.*

municipal *a.* civic, civil, metropolitan, city, urban, local, community, town; self-governing SEE CITY, TOWN

municipality *n.* city, town, village, metropolis, district, borough, suburb, bedroom community, precinct, parish, hamlet. SEE CITY

munificent *a.* generous, lavish, extravagant, bountiful, openhanded, philanthropic, liberal. ANT. *cheap, niggardly, tightfisted.*

munitions *n.* ammunition, weapons, bombs, ordnance, arsenal.

mural *n.* wall painting, panorama.

murder *n.* homicide, manslaughter, slaying, killing, assassination, shooting, execution, knifing, lynching. "One murder makes a villain, millions a hero." —Beilby Porteus.

WORD FIND

accidental or unintentional: involuntary manslaughter

automobile, from: drive-by shooting

brother: fraticide

father: patricide

gang-related: gangland killing, drive-by shooting, contract killing, *hit

hired: contract killing

infant: infanticide

(In the) heat of passion without malice aforethought: manslaughter, crime of passion

mass slaughter: massacre

mother: matricide

planned: premeditated, first-degree murder

rage, motivated by sudden: crime of passion, manslaughter

random act: *wilding

self: suicide

serial: serial killing

sister: sororicide

surprise, politically motivated: assassination

suspected: foul play

unplanned with malice aforethought: second-degree murder

murder *v.* kill, slay, slaughter, assassinate, shoot, gun down, knife, run through, lynch, strangle, suffocate, decapitate, butcher, hack to death, bludgeon to death, asphyxiate, poison, dismember, disembowel, dispatch, silence, *waste, *finish off, *rub out, *wax, *hit, *ice, *smoke, *exterminate, *grease, *eighty-six, *blow away, *pump full of lead, *take out, *put out of misery, *bump off.

murderer *n.* killer, assassin, slayer, strangler, psychopath, sociopath, sniper, lunatic, serial killer, madman, thug, executioner, *ripper, *trigger man, *gun, *hired gun, *liquidator, *hit man, terrorist.

murderous *a.* homicidal, bloodthirsty, deranged, frenzied, maniacal, savage, sociopathic, psychopathic, cannibalistic, violent, *rabid, *in a spitting rage. ANT. *tranquil, at peace.*

murk *n.* darkness, gloom, shadow, haze, fog, mist, brume. SEE FOG

murky *a.* **1.** GLOOMY dark, dismal, dusky, dreary, gauzy, funereal, somber, hazy, misty, foggy, brumous. **2.** OBSCURE unclear, vague, nebulous, esoteric, veiled, hidden, obfuscated, occult, mysterious, arcane, impenetrable. ANT. *1. sunny, bright, clear. 2. clear, distinct, in plain view.*

murmur *n.* mutter, whisper, sigh, coo, purr, mumble, sough, purl.

murmur *v.* mutter, whisper, sigh, coo, speak softly, purr, mumble.

muscle *n.* abductor, adductor, flexor, constrictor, extensor, tendon, sinew, fiber, tissue, thew, brawn.

WORD FIND

abdominal support: abdominal obliques, rectus abdominus, transversus abdominus

ankle bender: plantaris

anus: sphincter ani

arm extension, rotation, flexion: lattissimus dorsi, pectoral, supinator

back/body bender: rectus abdominus

back straightener: longissimus

breathing: diaphragm, serratus

chewing, clenching: masseter

disease of muscle wasting: muscular dystro-

phy
elbow straightener: triceps
eye focusing: ciliary
finger benders: flexor digitorum
finger straighteners: extensor digitorum
forehead/brow: corrugator, epicranial
frowning mouth: depressor, risorious
goosebumps: erector pili
head bender: longus capitus, rectus capitus
head rotator: head oblique
jaw: buccinator
kissing (puckered) lips: orbicularis oris
knee flexor: hamstring
lack of muscle coordination: ataxia
leg muscle aiding balance: soleus
leg/thigh extender: quadriceps
muscle pain: myalgia
penis erector: erector penis
rump: gluteus maximus, medius and minimus
shoulder: deltoid, trapezius
swallowing: constrictor of pharynx
testicle elevator: cremaster
tongue extender: genioglossus
upper arm: biceps, triceps
vocal cords: cricothyroid
withering muscles from lack of use: atrophy
wrist benders: flexor carpi radialis, flexor carpi ulnaris
wrist straighteners: extensor carpi radialis, extensor carpi ulnaris
2. STRENGTH power, force, weight, brawn, heft, might, leverage, *elbow grease, *oomph. ANT. **2.** *weakness, flaccidity, impotence.*

muscle *v. Sl.* jostle, *bull, ram, shoulder, shove, cow, buffalo, plow through, bulldoze, elbow one's way, strong-arm.

muscular *a.* brawny, sinewy, husky, thewy, strapping, rippling, slabbed, muscle-bound, chiseled, Herculean, sculpted, corded, *cut, *pumped, *bull-necked, Olympian, *washboardlike stomach, *hamlike biceps. ANT. *skinny, flabby, frail, undeveloped.*

muse *n.* inspiration, genius, creativity, talent.

muse *v.* ponder, meditate, reflect, ruminate, consider, mull over, brood, cogitate, chew, weigh, study, think about, turn over in one's mind, deliberate, speculate.

museum *n.* gallery, institute, archives, treasury, exhibit, collection, repository, depository, library, storehouse, *gallery of the Muses, *nation's attic, *history's attic. "Cemeteries of the arts." — Alphonse de Lamartine.

mush 1. BOILED MEAL corn meal, hasty pudding, porridge, cereal, gruel, mash. **2.** EXCESSIVE SENTIMENT treacle, pap, schmaltz, melodrama, bathos, *corn.

mushroom *n.* fungus, toadstool, meadow mushroom, truffle, champignon, chanterelle, death cup, shiitake, morel.

mushroom *v.* burgeon, spread, sprout up, grow, proliferate, thrive, pop up, boom, swell, snowball, multiply.

mushy *a.* sentimental, maudlin, gushy, *loveydovey, saccharine.

music *n.* melodies, rhythms, vocals, instrumentals, harmonies, singing, orchestrations, arrangements, tunes, sounds, tones, compositions, *canned, Muzak, longhair, rock, funk, rhythm and blues (R&B), rap, hip hop, punk, acid rock, heavy metal, top forty, boogie woogie, jazz, bebop, Dixieland, ragtime, folk, country and western, bluegrass, zydeco, swing, soul, reggae, pop, easy listening, salsa, bossa nova, classical, opera, ethnic, polka, march, baroque, primitive, new age. "The speech of angels." — Thomas Carlyle. "A fluid architecture of sound." — Roy Harris "The universal language of mankind." — Longfellow. SEE MUSICAL INSTRUMENTS, OPERA, SING, SONG

WORD FIND

GENERAL MUSIC TERMS
above correct pitch: sharp
arrangement: composition
bar: measure
beats per measure: meter
below correct pitch: flat
changing key of composition: transposing
chord with notes played individually in quick succession: arpeggio, broken chord
closing passage: coda
connection between two musical passages: bridge
dual melody: counterpoint
emphasis on a particular note: accent
highly skilled musician: virtuoso
horizontal lines on which notes are written: staff
informal rock or jazz session: jam
in-tune, pleasant-sounding: consonance
key and meter signs: signature
lowest notes or voice: bass
multiple notes played simultaneously: chord
multiple rhythms played simultaneously: polyrhythmic
out of tune, harsh-sounding: dissonance, discord
pause or silence: rest

performance of multiple song portions: medley

performing music on sight: sight reading

performing rights society: BMI

performing without notes: by ear

return to the original theme: reprise

school of music: conservatory

science of sound properties: acoustics

second or third highest voice class: alto

section or verse repeated: refrain

short composition: bagatelle

short melodic phrase on jazz or rock guitar: riff, lick

study of music: musicology

teaching of pitch and rhythm recognition: ear training

trumpeting intro: fanfare

words of song: lyrics

written music for movie or play: score

SYMPHONIC TERMS

composition of arias, duets, choruses in several movements: cantata

final movement: finale

instrumental composition preceding opera, oratorio or play: overture

instrumental composition with movements in varied keys, tempos: sonata

instrumental composition with several movements of dance music: suite

one section of a composition: movement

orchestra or musical society: philharmonic

polyphonic composition sung sequentially by two or more vocalists: fugue

work or composition of a composer: opus

MUSIC DIRECTIVES

boldly: fiero

comically: burlesco

decrease in volume: decrescendo

delicately: delicato

fast tempo: allegro, presto

loudly, very: fortissimo

moderate tempo: andante

mournfully: funerale

slow: adagio

slow, extremely: adagissimo

softly: sotto voce

softly, sweetly: dolce

softly, very: pianissimo

spoken: parlato

volume, half the singer's normal: mezza voce

volume, increase in: crescendo

wildly: furioso

musical n. revue, musical comedy, burlesque, Broadway production, show.

musical a. melodic, rhythmic, harmonious, lyrical, soulful, choral, spiritual, mellifluent, symphonic, sonorous, euphonic. ANT. *dissonant, cacophonous, discordant, noisy.*

musical instrument n. woodwind, stringed instrument, percussive instrument, keyboard instrument, brass, *noisemaker. "That which speaks all languages fluently." — Marc McCutcheon.

WORD FIND

KEYBOARD INSTRUMENTS

accordion with button keyboard: concertina

automatic piano: player piano

bell-like soundmaker in "Dance of the Sugar Plum Fairy:" celesta

electronic sound recreator: synthesizer

organ, steam whistle: calliope

piano, full-sized: grand piano

piano, largest: concert piano

piano, predecessor: clavichord, harpsichord

piano, slang: *eighty-eights, *ivories

piano, small grand: baby grand

piano, space-saving: upright

plucked instead of struck by hammers: harpsichord

squeezebox, handheld: accordion, *squeezebox

wind or electric-generated keyboard: organ

PERCUSSION INSTRUMENTS

bell: campanella

block, wooden: wood block, clog box

Caribbean tinkling drum: steel drum

clackers, wooden stick: claves

clappers clicked rhythmically: castanets

cow's bell: cowbell

crash, sizzlemaker: cymbal

Cuban drums played with fingers, hands: bongos

drum for rolls, flourishes, fills: tom-tom

hanging cymbal struck with mallet: gong

kettle drum: timpani

largest, booming drum: bass drum, *kick drum

rasping gourd: guiro

rat tat tat beatkeeper: snare drum

rattling skeleton-soundmaker: xylophone

seed-filled gourd: maraca

xylophonelike with resonant tubes: marimba

xylophonelike with steel bars: glockenspiel, bell lyre

STRINGED INSTRUMENTS

Appalachian lap instrument: dulcimer, zither

barrel organ: hurdy gurdy

bowed, quivering four-string: violin

country twanger: banjo

dulcimer struck with small hammers: hammered dulcimer
electric guitar, slang: *axe
guitar, hollow-bodied: acoustic
guitar, low-voiced four-string: bass
guitar, very small: ukelele
harplike: lyre
Hawaiian guitar with nasal tone: Hawaiian guitar
heavenly-sounding 46-string: harp
Japanese national instrument: koto
lute, East Indian long-necked: sitar
lute, small four string: mandolin
middle ages guitar: lute
rasper, husky: cello
violin, large, velvety or husky-sounding: viola
zither: dulcimer
WIND INSTRUMENTS
Alps horn: alpenhorn
alto clarinet with upcurving bell: basset horn
bass tuba: helicon, sousaphone
brass instrument with three kets, flaring bell: trumpet
clarinet nickname: *licorice stick
clarion blasters: brass
cornet with wider bore: flugelhorn
double-reeded woodwind: oboe
elephant tusk horn: oliphant
English flute: recorder
flute, small: fife, piccolo
flute, whistlelike: recorder, flageolet, fipple flute
jazz woodwind: saxophone
*licorice stick, reeded: clarinet
military horn: bugle, cornet
pan pipes: pan flute
potatolike whistle: ocarina
sad, comedic soundmaker: bassoon
Scottish skirling and droning windbag: bagpipes
slide horn: trombone
trumpet with high pitch: Bach trumpet
tuba, tenor: euphonium
wooden: woodwind

music hall n. auditorium, concert hall, amphitheater, dance hall.
musician n. performer, player, artist, singer, vocalist, instrumentalist, minstrel, session artist, studio musician, longhair, bard, drummer, guitarist, bassist, flutist, violinist, troubador. SEE SINGER
musing a. meditative, thoughtful, reflective.
musket n. breechloader, flintlock, blunderbuss. SEE GUN

muss v. mess up, tousle, tangle, disarrange, ruffle, rumple, crumple, wrinkle, dishevel, scramble, disorder, throw into disarray. ANT. neaten, order, organize, smooth.
must n. **1.** REQUIREMENT imperative, necessity, need, prerequisite, obligation, essential, exigency, fundamental. **2.** MUSTINESS mold, mildew, fungus, dry rot.
must v. have to, obligated to, required to, should, have no choice, compelled, forced, have no alternative, doomed to, bound. SEE NECESSARY
mustache n. moustache, moustachio, whiskers, *soupstrainer, *tickler, *cookie duster.
WORD FIND
chevron: chevron
descriptive: wings of a B-52, twitchy, rat's nest
dual crescents: mistletoe
long and drooping over chin: horseshoe, Fu Manchu
long and thick with turned-up ends: Hindenburg
M, resembles the letter: regent
neat, thin line: pencil line, Clark Gable
rectangular with squared ends: boxcar, toothbrush, Charlie Chaplin, Hitler
T, forms with chin tuft: Roman T
thick and overgrown over lip: walrus, soupstrainer
turned-up: handlebar, Hindenburg, Kaiser, waxed, waxed and twiddled
mustang n. range horse, wild horse, bronco, bronc, cayuse.
muster n. assembly, gathering, congregation, turnout, review, line up, group, bunch, troupe, company.
muster v. assemble, gather, summon, call the roll, mobilize, convoke, marshal, convene, rally, collect, congregate, huddle, line up. ANT. disperse, fallout, scatter, disband.
muster, pass *make the grade, *come up to snuff, pass inspection, *measure up, *come through with flying colors, *stand the test, *come up to scratch, *fall through the shithouse and come out clean.
musty a. **1.** MOULDY fusty, dusty, stale, decaying, crumbling, tainted, rancid, spoiled. **2.** WORN OUT, ANTIQUATED stale, old, aged, mossgrown, obsolete, old-fashioned, motheaten, passé. ANT. 1. fresh, unspoiled, vibrant. 2. new, modern, fresh.
mutant n. deviation, mutation, alteration, miscreation, freak of nature.
mutation n. deviation, mutant, alteration, vari-

ation, modification, miscreation, metamorphosis, transformation, accident of nature.

mute v. muffle, deaden, dampen, silence, stifle, tone down, still, quiet. ANT. *amplify.*

mute a. speechless, silent, aphonic, wordless, mum, voiceless, tongue-tied, uncommunicative, closedmouthed, still. ANT. *talkative, loquacious, communicative.*

mutilate v. tear apart, dismember, disfigure, maim, deform, rip to shreds, amputate, cut up, hack, butcher, castrate, tear limb from limb.

mutilated a. dismembered, amputated, torn limb from limb, castrated, disfigured, maimed, deformed.

mutinous a. rebellious, subversive, riotous, insurrectionary, insurgent, revolutionary, seditious, traitorous, insubordinate, malcontent. ANT. *dutiful, subservient, compliant, cooperative.*

mutiny n. rebellion, revolt, riot, uprising, insurrection, overthrow, takeover, coup, strike.

mutiny v. rebel, revolt, rise up, riot, subvert, overthrow.

mutt n. mongrel, cur, *Heinz 57 varieties. SEE DOG

mutter v. murmur, mumble, grumble, whisper, grunt, maunder, *talk into one's beard/chin, talk under one's breath, grouse, complain.

mutual a. reciprocal, give-and-take, interchangeable, common, joint, related, shared, communal. ANT. *singular, sole.*

mutual fund n. stock fund, bond fund, growth fund, investment fund.

Muzak n. *canned music, elevator music, *monotones, *snoozak.

muzzle n. **1.** SNOUT jaws, nose, mouth, chops. **2.** RESTRAINT bind, bit, bridle, strap.

muzzle v. restrain, restrict, stifle, silence, censor, shut up, mute, suppress, still, inhibit, squelch, harness.

myopic a. SEE NEARSIGHTED

myriad n. ten thousand, a thousand and one, infinity, host, profusion, multitude, abundance, *truckload, *slew, *passel, *lots, *galaxy.

mysterious a. unknowable, unexplainable, inexplicable, enigmatic, inscrutable, cryptic, unfathomable, secret, mystical, weird, arcane, esoteric, puzzling, dark. ANT. *knowable, obvious, clear, explainable.*

mystery n. **1.** AN UNKNOWN puzzle, enigma, perplexity, conundrum, secret, closed book, question mark. **2.** INSCRUTABILITY obscurity, imperceptibility, secret, inexplicability, in-

solvability. **3.** NOVEL/PLAY police procedural, detective story, *whodunit, *cat and mouse, *cloak and dagger, *cozy. ANT. *1. open book, answer, explanation, clarification.*

mystic n. seer, soothsayer, palm reader, prophet, astrologer, sorcerer, witch, astral projectionist, new age follower, *past-lifer.

mystic a. occult, esoteric, mystical, oracular, magical, arcane. ANT. *out in the open, scientific.*

mystical a. inscrutable, inexplicable, intuitive, spiritual, ethereal, metaphysical, transcendental, incorporeal, extramundane, otherworldly, supernatural. ANT. *corporeal, earthly, scientific.*

mysticism n. occultism, supernaturalism, cabalism.

mystify v. bewilder, perplex, puzzle, confuse, baffle, confound, hoodwink, *bamboozle, *buffalo. ANT. *clarify, explain, clear up.*

mystique n. aura, air, charisma, character, glamour, ambience, persona, charm, attraction, fascination, appeal, magnetism.

myth n. **1.** STORY legend, tale, fable, allegory, fiction, parable. **2.** UNTRUTH foolishness, fiction, nonsense, old wive's tale, misconception, fallacy, superstition, falsehood.

mythical a. mythological, fabled, fictitious, fabulous, imaginary, fanciful, fantastical, storybook. ANT. *actual, true, real, factual.*

WORD FIND

Argonauts leader who retrieved Golden Fleece: Jason

arts, nine goddesses of the: Muses

beautiful man: Adonis

bisexual: Hermaphroditus

dawn, goddess of: Aurora, Eos

dog with three heads guarding underworld: Cerberus

dreams, god of: Morpheus

earth, goddess of: Gaea

earth on his shoulders: Atlas

ecstasy, goddess of: Dionysus

eyed beast, hundred: Argus

fire, god of: Vulcan

fire, stole from gods: Prometheus

fish and man combined, controlled waves: Triton

flowers, goddess of: Flora

flying horse created from Medusa's blood: Pegasus

forbidden box of human misery, opened: Pandora

forever reaching for fruit and water: Tantalus

giants, race of: Titans
giant with one eye: Cyclops
god ruler: Zeus
gold, touch turned things to: Midas
gorgon, most famous: Medusa
heel, hero with vulnerable: Achilles
horse and human combined: centaur
laurel tree, turned into: Daphne
loved his own reflection and was changed to
    a flower: Narcissus
love, goddess of: Venus
love, god of: Cupid, Eros
marriage, god of: Hymen
Medusa, slew: Perseus
messenger of gods: Mercury
minotaur, slew: Theseus
moon and forest goddess: Diana
moon, goddess of: Luna, Diana, Selene
mother, married his: Oedipus
oracle of Apollo: Delphic oracle
prophet who was never believed: Cassandra
punishment, goddess of: Nemesis

Rome, founder of: Romulus
sea, god of: Poseidon
sisters of hideous form who turned onlookers
    to stone: Gorgons
sisters three who control human destiny: the
    Fates
sleep, god of: Hypnus, Somnus
stone, rolled incessantly up hill: Sisyphus
strongman: Hercules
sun, flew too near and melted wings: Icarus
sun, god of: Helios
twin protectors of seagoers: Castor and Pol-
    lux
unavenged crimes, three snake-haired fe-
    males who punish guilty in: Furies
underworld, god of: Hades, Pluto
victory, goddess of: Nike
war, god of: Mars
whirlpool, turned into: Charybdis
wisdom, goddess of: Minerva
Zeus, beautiful daughters of: Graces
SEE MONSTER

N

nab *v.* grab, snatch, seize, catch, grasp, snare, steal, snag, arrest, collar, apprehend, trap, *nail. ANT. *release.*

nag *n.* **1.** COMPLAINER *bitch, *battle-ax, whiner, needler, kvetch, faultfinder, *pain, fishwife, witch. **2.** OLD HORSE plug, swayback, *bag of bones, dobbin, *crowbait, *dogfood.

nag *v.* **1.** COMPLAIN scold, needle, badger, whine, carp, harass, grouse, henpeck, *bitch, heckle, berate, irritate, find fault. **2.** TROUBLE distress, worry, prey on, torment, bother, disturb.

nail *n.* **1.** FINGERNAIL claw, talon. **2.** FASTENER spike, brad, pin, rivet, tack, staple, hobnail, tenpenny, box nail, finishing nail, roofing nail.

nail *v.* **1.** DRIVE pound, anchor, fix, bolt. **2.** CATCH catch red-handed, nab, apprehend, seize, *pinch.

naive *a.* unsophisticated, innocent, unsuspecting, uneducated, simple, ingenuous, childlike, inexperienced, unseasoned, unworldly, unschooled, trusting, gullible, immature, *wet behind the ears. ANT. *sophisticated, experienced, wise, worldly.*

NAIVETÉ *n.* [ni eev TAY] childlike innocence or unsophisticated, lack of insight and experience. *The con man took advantage of her obvious naivete.* SYN. inexperience, childishness, innocence, simplicity, ingenuousness, artlessness, simplemindedness, credulity, gullibility. ANT. *sophistication, worldliness, experience.*

naked *a.* nude, unclothed, bare, undressed, exposed, stripped, disrobed, uncovered, *in the buff, *in the raw, *without a stitch, *in one's birthday suit, *wearing nothing but goosebumps, defenseless, vulnerable.

namby-pamby *n.* sissy, pansy, mama's boy, weakling, milquetoast, *wimp, *woos.

name *n.* **1.** APPELLATION nickname, given name, surname, Christian name, epithet, designation, title, sobriquet, *moniker, *handle, *pet name, diminutive, pseudonym, pen name, non de plume. **2.** REPUTATION character, repute.

name *v.* **1.** CHRISTEN dub, call, title, nickname, denominate, style, self-style. **2.** DESIGNATE delegate, appoint, nominate, pick.

nameless *a.* anonymous, untitled, unknown.

namely *a.* specifically, to wit, that is, i.e.

nanny *n.* nursemaid, nurse, wet nurse, mammy, babysitter, governess.

nap *n.* **1.** SNOOZE doze, siesta, catnap. SEE SLEEP **2.** FIBER fuzz, weave, fluff.

nap *v.* snooze, doze, catnap, *catch forty winks, *catch some shuteye, *drop off. SEE SLEEP

napalm *n.* incendiary, explosive, flammable gel, *Zippo.

nape *n.* scruff.

napkin *n.* linen, wipe, serviette, moist towelette.

nappy *a.* hairy, downy, shaggy, fuzzy, kinky, woolly, fleecy.

narcissist *n.* egotist, braggart, peacock. "Like all self-made men he worships his creator." — Anon.

NARCISSISTIC *a.* [nar sis SIS tic] vain, excessively interested in one's self. *An egotistical, narcissistic man won't make a good husband.* SYN. vain, self-centered, egotistical, egocentric, conceited, self-worshipping, self-infatuated, egomaniacal, self-absorbed, *wrapped up in oneself.

narcotic *n.* drug, opiate, soporific, sedative, tranquilizer, anesthetic, pain reliever, hypnotic, depressant, *downer, morphine, heroin, codeine, opium, hashish. SEE DRUG, MARIJUANA

narrate *v.* recount, tell, describe, recite, chronicle, report, portray, relate, detail.

narration *n.* recounting, telling, description, chronicling, portrayal, detailing, account, summary.

narrative *n.* account, description, tale. SEE STORY

narrator *n.* storyteller, chronicler, reporter, author, relater, recounter, raconteur; *voiceover.

narrow *v.* attenuate, hone, diminish, thin, lessen, contract, constrict, compress, squeeze.

narrow *a.* **1.** SLIM slender, thin, lean, spare, slight, attenuated. **2.** CONFINED cramped, tight, scant, sparse, meager, incapacious, close, incommodious, pinched. **3.** NARROW-MINDED prejudiced, bigoted, intolerant, small-minded. ANT. *1. fat, broad, wide. 2. capacious, roomy, spacious. 3. liberal, open-minded, tolerant.*

narrow-minded *a.* small-minded, closed-minded, bigoted, prejudiced, blind, myopic, short-sighted, tunnel-visioned, one-sided, intolerant, pigheaded, biased, deaf to reason.

ANT. *broad-minded, liberal, tolerant.*

nasty *a.* **1.** DIRTY filthy, foul, soiled, unclean, revolting, gross, offensive. **2.** INDECENT obscene, immoral, slutty, sleazy, lewd, licentious, offensive, vulgar, coarse, crude, raunchy, *morals of an alley cat. **3.** MEAN ill-tempered, disagreeable, ugly, surly, malicious, spiteful, hateful, vicious. ANT. *1. clean, unsoiled, washed. 2. decent, wholesome, pure, chaste. 3. good-humored, good-natured, kindhearted, friendly, amiable.*

nation *n.* **1.** COUNTRY state, federation, republic, commonwealth, union, empire, sovereignty. **2.** PEOPLE race, populace, natives, tribe, ethnic group.

national *a.* federal, nationwide, interstate, coast-to-coast.

nationalism *n.* provincialism, isolationism, independence. "A silly cock crowing on its own dunghill." —Richard Aldington.

nationality *n.* nativity, citizenship, tribe, clan, race, extraction, native home, lineage, bloodline, ancestry.

native *a.* aboriginal, innate, indigenous, domestic, native-born, local, *homegrown.

natty *a.* dapper, neat, trim, smart, spruce, chic, sharp, *spiffy, *snazzy, *dressed to the teeth, *dressed to the nines.

natural *a.* **1.** MADE BY NATURE organic, wild, pure, untouched, untamed, unspoiled, uncultivated, unrefined, primitive, primordial. **2.** REAL genuine, authentic, true. **3.** INHERENT instinctive, innate, genetic, inherited, natural-born. **4.** UNAFFECTED unstudied, unpretentious, spontaneous, real, sincere, earthy, down to earth, ingenuous. "A very difficult pose to maintain." —Oscar Wilde. **5.** NORMAL typical, usual, characteristic. ANT. *1. unnatural, refined, processed, man-made, synthetic. 2. phony, unreal, unnatural. 3. learned, extrinsic. 4. affected, studied, pretentious, phony. 5. abnormal, atypical.*

naturalist *n.* zoologist, botanist, field observer, environmentalist.

naturally *adv.* **1.** BY NATURE innately, instinctively. **2.** OF COURSE as one would expect, characteristically, normally.

natural selection *n.* survival of the fittest, evolution, Darwinian law.

nature *n.* **1.** CHARACTER makeup, constitution, personality, essence, identity. **2.** DISPOSITION temperament, temper, spirit, personality. **3.** PHYSICAL WORLD cosmos, universe, creation, environment, ecology, evolution, chaos, regeneration, natural forces, the wild, the great outdoors, Mother Nature. "The never idle workshop." —Mathew Arnold. "The art of God eternal." —Dante "The living, visible garment of God." —Johann W. Goethe "God under a disguise." —A.E. Taylor. **4.** KIND class, type, sort, species, stripe, category, brand.

naughty *a.* **1.** BAD mischievous, disobedient, prankish, impish, full of the devil, wayward, unruly, unmanageable, disrespectful. **2.** INDECENT nasty, lewd, obscene, improper, offensive, immoral. ANT. *1. good, well-mannered, angelic. 2. decent, moral.*

nausea *n.* queasiness, qualm, indigestion, sickness, upset stomach, bellyache, motion sickness, *witch's brew boiling up in one's belly, *belly rising up in protest, urge to vomit, throw up, regurgitate, *blow chunks, *ralph. SEE VOMIT

nauseate *v.* sicken, disgust, *gross out, turn one's stomach, revolt, disgust, *make one want to vomit.

nauseated *a.* sick, sick to one's stomach, sickened, queasy, nauseous, *green around the gills, qualmish, disgusted, repelled, repulsed.

nauseating *a.* SEE NAUSEOUS

nauseous *a.* nauseating, unsettling, sickening, revolting, repulsive, loathsome, disgusting.

nautical *a.* maritime, marine, naval, oceangoing, seagoing. SEE NAVIGATION, NAVY, OCEAN, SAIL, SHIP

navel *n.* umbilical, *belly button, *innie, *outie.

navigable *a.* passable, boatable. SEE NAVIGATE

navigate *v.* steer, direct, plot, con, pilot, skipper, guide.

navigation *n.* course plotting, course charting, guiding, piloting, steering, conning, manning the helm, taking bearings, seamanship, celestial navigation, dead reckoning.

navigator *n.* course plotter, pilot, chartsman, helmsman, seaman, aviator, explorer. SEE SAILOR

navy *n.* fleet, armada, flotilla, sea force, argosy, convoy, marine defense, squadron, task force, merchant marine.

WORD FIND
aircraft carrier runway: flight deck
aircraft carrier, slang: flattop, floating city
antimine vessel: minesweeper
antitorpedo defense: torpedo defense net
battleship nickname: floating fortress
boundary marker for mineswept area: dan buoy
disguised as merchant ship: Q ship

fuel ship: oiler, tanker

group of ships: convoy, squadron

guns/weapons of the same size or caliber: battery

heavily armed vessel: battleship

high-speed warship: destroyer

hostile shore position: beachhead

medical ship: hospital ship

mine clearing: mine sweeping

mining ship: mine

missile-armed: guided missile cruiser, guided missile destroyer

multipurpose vessel: ocean station ship

nuclear-powered submarine: Trident

officer: chief warrant officer, ensign, lieutenant, lieutenant commander, commander, captain, rear admiral, vice admiral, admiral, fleet admiral

patrol torpedo boat: PT boat

readiness condition: general quarters

simultaneous gunfire on target: salvo

sonic locator device: sonar

submarine detector: sonobuoy

two or more ship divisions: squadron

underwater vessel: submarine, U-boat

vessel that lays dan buoys: dan runner

warship capable of acting independently: frigate

SEE SHIP, SUBMARINE

naysayer n. pessimist, oppositionist, dissenter, opponent, critic, prophet of doom, defeatist.

Nazi n. fascist, nationalist.

Neanderthal n. barbarian, savage, brute, *animal, troglodyte, caveman.

near v. approach, close in, advance, move toward.

near a. close, nearby, close at hand, nigh, at close range, within shouting distance, proximate, neighboring, *cheek by jowl. ANT. distant, far.

nearing a. approaching, coming toward, closing in on, converging, impending. ANT. receding, leaving.

nearly adv. almost, not quite, just about, all but, virtually, well-nigh, roughly, about.

near miss n. near hit, close call, narrow escape.

nearsighted a. myopic, shortsighted, *blind as a mole, *blind as a post, *blind as a bat. SEE VISION

neat a. 1. ORDERLY tidy, trim, shipshape, spotless, spruce, immaculate, spic-and-span. 2. FASTIDIOUS meticulous, exacting, natty, spiffy. 3. GREAT Sl. *cool, *neato, good, excellent. ANT. 1. disorderly, untidy, sloppy, messy. 2. sloppy, unkempt. 3. bad, awful. SEE

CLEAN

neaten v. tidy, arrange, order, fix up, clean up, smooth out, spruce up.

neatly a. orderly, tidily, in good order, uniformly, smoothly, cleanly.

NEBULOUS a. [NEB u luss] cloudy, vague or unclear. *The paper was filled with nebulous guidelines.* SYN. cloudy, misty, hazy, obscure, unclear, shrouded, veiled, vague, indistinct. ANT. *clear, distinct.*

necessarily a. inevitably, of necessity, as a matter of course, perforce, like it or not, unavoidably, inescapably.

necessary a. essential, vital, needed, required, called for, requisite, prerequisite, mandatory, imperative, compulsory, fundamental, obligatory. ANT. *unnecessary, unneeded, unessential.*

necessity n. must, essential, vital component, requirement, obligation, requisite, prerequisite, need, want, basic, fundamental, dire necessity, exigency. ANT. *extra, luxury, inessential.*

necking n. Sl. kissing, *making love, *making out, cuddling, *smooching, *sucking face, *parking.

necklace n. chain, strand, choker, beads, pearls, locket, pendant, lavalier, torque, collar. SEE JEWELRY

necktie n. tie, ascot, cravat, bow tie, string tie, jabot, four-in-hand, Windsor, half-Windsor.

necromancy n. sorcery, communing with the dead, black magic, conjuring, mysticism, Satan worshipping, demonology.

necropolis n. graveyard. SEE CEMETERY

need n. 1. POVERTY destitution, indigence, penury, privation. 2. REQUIREMENT requisite, prerequisite, necessity, essential, obligation. 3. LACK want, dearth, paucity, insufficiency, shortage.

need v. require, must have, want, call for, lack, have use for, hunger for, desire, covet, got to have, can't live without.

needle v. pester, annoy, goad, heckle, provoke, nag, badger, *rag on, *bug.

needless a. unnecessary, pointless, uncalled for, unwanted, nonessential.

needlework n. needlepoint, embroidery, sewing, stitching, darning, knitting, crocheting, tatting, quilting, point lace, gros point, petit point, cross-stitch, weaving.

needy a. 1. POOR impoverished, destitute, indigent, penniless, lacking, *hard up, *broke, *down and out, *in dire straits, *without a pot to piss in nor a window to throw it out of.

2. EMOTIONALLY INSECURE *clingy, clinging, desperate.

ne'er do well n. *loser, wastrel, failure, good-for-nothing, *do-nothing, *bum, *slug, loafer.

NEFARIOUS a. [ni FAIR ee us] evil, wicked. *They committed murders and other nefarious acts.* SYN. evil, wicked, villainous, heinous, iniquitous, detestable, vicious, infamous, sinister, bad, abominable, shameful. ANT. *good, moral, decent.*

negate v. invalidate, nullify, cancel out, counteract, neutralize, void, annul, repeal.

negation n. contradiction, denial, repudiation, refutation, cancellation.

negative n. no, nay, not.

negative a. denying, nullifying, voiding, invalidating, opposing, vetoing, contradictory, contrary, conflicting, inverse.

negative attitude n. pessimism, cynicism, *chip on one's shoulder, doubt, prophecy of doom, lack of confidence.

neglect n. laxness, disregard, thoughtlessness, inattentiveness, carelessness, slackness, oversight, negligence, dereliction, indifference. ANT. *care, regard, conscientiousness.*

neglect v. disregard, ignore, overlook, slight, shirk, omit, pass over, discount, make light of, be remiss, *lie down on the job, forget, let slip, let slide, brush aside, *blow off. ANT. *regard, consider, care for.*

neglectful a. careless, remiss, derelict, negligent, inattentive, slack, lax, inconsiderate, delinquent, sloppy. ANT. *careful, conscientious, mindful.*

negligee n. nightgown, nightie, chemise, peignoir, robe, deshabille.

negligence n. disregard, carelessness, dereliction, laxness. SEE NEGLECT

negligent a. careless, derelict, inattentive, delinquent, lax, slack, remiss, disregardful, thoughtless, inconsiderate, forgetful, casual, nonchalant, devil-may-care. ANT. *caring, responsible, fostering, conscientious, attentive.*

negligible a. minute, minimal, insignificant, inconsequential, trifling, nominal, piddling, paltry, imperceptible, unimportant, minor, trivial, microscopic. ANT. *sizable, significant, considerable.*

negotiate v. **1.** BARGAIN deal, dicker, haggle, arbitrate, mediate, settle, arrange, transact, conciliate, compromise, come to terms, finagle, work out, *give one's shirt but keep one's pants, *hash out a deal. **2.** PASS THROUGH OR OVER surmount, get around, cross, clear, forge through, ford, maneuver, step nimbly around.

negotiation n. mediation, arbitration, bargaining, give and take, dickering, compromise, haggling, counteroffering.

negotiator n. mediator, arbitrator, diplomat, haggler, middleman, go-between, intermediary, *wheeler-dealer.

Negro n. black, colored person, negroid, negress, African-American, Afro American.

neigh n. whinny, nicker, whicker.

neighborhood n. community, vicinage, suburb, block, district, borough, *housing complex, *development, street, *hood, *projects, *home turf, *neck of the woods.

neighborly a. friendly, sociable, hospitable, personable, harmonious, helpful, convivial. SEE FRIENDLY

neither here nor there irrelevant, beside the point, impertinent, not germane, immaterial.

nemesis n. **1.** JUST PUNISHMENT retribution, comeuppance, just desserts, vindication, revenge, vengeance, ruin, downfall, Waterloo. **2.** AVENGER bane.

neologism n. new word, new term, new expression, *buzz word, new meaning, new interpretation.

neophyte n. beginner, novice, tyro, amateur, debutant, *rookie, *greenhorn, *tenderfoot, *new kid on the block, freshman, intern, trainee, apprentice. ANT. *veteran, *old hand, expert, master.*

NEPOTISM n. [NEP uh tizm] favoritism shown to relatives in work, politics. *Joe got work through his father's nepotism.* SYN. favoritism, partiality, bias, discrimination. "A $10 word meaning to stow your relatives in a soft berth."—Ilka Chase.

nerd n. Sl. *dork, *goofball, *geek, *jerk, *dweeb, *goober, *goon, *nebbish, *schlepper, *wimp, *trekkie.

nerve n. **1.** COURAGE bravery, strength, spirit, spunk, spine, mettle, pluck, *grit, *guts, *gumption, *balls, *chutzpah. **2.** IMPUDENCE effrontery, insolence, gall, brazenness, *balls. **3.** SENSORY PATHWAY sensor, impulse pathway, neuron. ANT. *1. cowardice, timidity, spinelessness. 2. shyness, reserve, reticence.*

nerve center n. control center, headquarters, HQ, command post, plexus.

nerveless a. **1.** WEAK impotent, powerless, helpless. **2.** MEEK spineless, cowardly, timid, reticent. **3.** COOL nonchalant, collected, unruffled, imperturbable, undisturbed, self-possessed, self-controlled.

nerve-racking *a.* distressing, stressful, disturbing, trying, grating on the nerves, aggravating, frazzling, jarring, irritating, disquieting. ANT. *soothing, calming, relaxing.*

nerves *n.* tension, stress. SEE ANXIETY

nervous *a.* anxious, tense, stressed, uneasy, *uptight, *antsy, *jittery, jumpy, excited, *keyed up, *wound up, *on edge, highstrung, flustered, ruffled, *wired, *hyper, *butterflies in the stomach, shaky. ANT. *calm, relaxed, composed, cool.* SEE ANXIOUS, FEARFUL

nervous breakdown *n.* nervous prostration, emotional collapse, *burnout, nervous exhaustion, clinical depression, hysteria.

nervous Nellie *n. Sl.* *Caspar Milquetoast, *chicken, *fraidy cat, *pantywaist, *candyass, *woos, *wimp.

nervousness *n.* anxiety, tension, stress, excitement, fluster, jitters, *butterflies, apprehension, uneasiness, angst, stage fright, *the shakes.

WORD FIND

descriptive/symptoms: throat-clearing, gulping, teeth-grinding, hand-wringing, pacing, nail-biting, stomach-knotting, hyperventilation, nervous tics and twitches, sweating.

ANT. *relaxation, calm, serenity, tranquility.*

nervy *a.* **1.** INSOLENT rude, bold, brash, forward, cocky, brassy, *cheeky, impudent, fresh, flip, flippant, *smart-assed, *wise-assed. **2.** BRAVE courageous, daring, plucky, valiant, *ballsy, *gutsy, intrepid. ANT. *1. reticent, shy, polite. 2. cowardly, spineless, *chicken.*

nest *n.* aerie, roost, *wattle and daub construction. SEE BIRD

nest egg *n.* savings, investment, *something for a rainy day, piggy bank, *the oink in one's piggy bank, *stash, *mad money, *stake.

nestle *v.* curl up against, snuggle, cuddle, huddle, nuzzle, *spoon together.

net *n.* **1.** MESH webbing, seine, screen, trawl, network, lacework, dragnet, purse net, butterfly net, snare. **2.** PROFIT earnings, gain, take-in, take-home, remainder.

net *a.* take-home, after taxes, ultimate, final, remaining.

nettle *v.* irritate, annoy, vex, needle, irk, aggravate, *get on one's nerves, *bug, *get under one's skin, hassle, *ride, rile, *drive up a wall, *rattle one's cage, *pull one's chain, pester, pick on.

nettlesome *a.* irritating, annoying, aggravating, vexatious, vexing, disturbing, perturbing, irksome, rankling, thorny.

network *n.* **1.** INTERLACING netting, mesh, webbing, lacework, latticework, reticulum. **2.** ORGANIZATION affiliations, chain, system, order, interconnection, relationship. **3.** CHANNELS labyrinth, circuitry, plexus, terminal system.

network *v.* associate, make connections, hobnob, connect, fraternize, rub elbows, drum up leads, interconnect, affiliate, consort with, enterprise.

neurosis *n.* nervous disorder, personality disorder, emotional disorder, mental illness, disordered thinking, maladjustment, dysfunction, anxiety. "The result of a conflict between the ego and the id; the person is at war with himself."—Sigmund Freud.

WORD FIND

accidental nature: accident-prone

aversion to people: misanthropy

aversion to women: misogyny

collapse, nervous: nervous breakdown

combat neurosis: shell shock, Post Traumatic Stress Syndrome

daughter's sexual attraction to father: Electra Complex

death, excessive fear of: necrophobia

depression, seasonal: SAD, seasonal affective disorder

dieting to the point of emaciation: anorexia nervosa

dieting with binging and forced vomiting: bulimia

fantasizing to escape reality: escapism

fault-finding, passively hostile character: passive-aggressive personality

fear, irrational: phobia

fire-setting, fascination with: pyromania

genitals, compulsion to expose: exhibitionism

health and symptoms, dwelling excessively on: hypochondria

heart attack, excessive fear of: cardioneurosis

infant or childlike behavior, return to: infantilism

inferiority, feelings of: inferiority complex, low self-esteem

isolation from others: withdrawal

obsession or crazed desire: mania

panic, prone to: panic disorder, panic attack

passive acceptance of another's vices and abuse: codependency

past, dwelling excessively on the: alethia

poor-me personality: martyrdom

pregnancy, imagined: pseudocyesis

psychological disturbances converted to physical symptoms: conversion disorder

rapid breathing due to anxiety: hyperventilation

reality, denial of: denial, defense mechanism

repeated thoughts, rituals: obsessive-compulsive disorder

ritual that must be carried out: compulsion

self-love, excessive: narcissism

steal, compulsion to: kleptomania

SEE FEAR, INSANITY, MANIA, NEUROTIC, PHOBIA

neurotic a. emotionally disturbed, mentally ill, irrational, unstable, paranoid, anxious, obsessive, compulsive, phobic, maladjusted, hypochondriacal, manic, accident-prone, dysfunctional, *screw loose, *splinters in the windmills of one's mind, *loopy, *twisted, *warped, *off kilter. ANT. *stable, rational, of sound mind.*

neuter n. eunuch, gelding.

neuter v. castrate, emasculate, geld, *fix, *cut, spay.

neutral a. **1.** IMPARTIAL uninvolved, nonpartisan, unbiased, nonaligned, uncommitted, indifferent, *riding the fence, dispassionate, disinterested, unaffiliated, detached. **2.** NONCOMBATIVE uninvolved, peaceful, pacifistic. **3.** COLORLESS uncolored, drab, achromatic, pale, vague, white, black, gray. ANT. *1. partial, biased, involved. 2. combative, taking sides. 3. colorful.*

neutralize v. counteract, offset, negate, cancel, dilute, counterbalance, nullify, disarm, deactivate.

never ending a. perpetual, infinite, timeless, everlasting, forever, eternal, endless, relentless, persistent, continual.

nevertheless adv. nonetheless, notwithstanding, in any event, still, yet, be that as it may.

new a. **1.** CURRENT recent, fresh, up-to-date, up-to-the-minute, contemporary, novel, modern, latest, *cutting edge, *hot. **2.** PRISTINE fresh, virginal, green, maiden, newborn. **3.** UNFAMILIAR unheard of, unknown, strange, peculiar, untried, untested, unexplored, experimental. **4.** RENEWED restored, revised, remodeled, revived. **5.** ADDITIONAL further, more, supplementary. ANT. *1. out-of-date, old, dated. 2. old, used, stale. 3. familiar, known, tried-and-true.*

newborn n. infant, neonate, infant, weanling, suckling, nursling, babe, baby, *bambino.

newfangled a. modern, new, novel, state of the art, *cutting edge.

news n. reportage, report, bulletin, information, message, account, announcement, communication, communique, dispatch, flash, press release, publication, broadcast, *scoop, lowdown, *skinny, *dope, *straight poop. "News is almost by definition bad news." — Marquis W. Childs. "When a dog bites a man that is not news, but when a man bites a dog that is news." — Charles A. Dana. "The first rough draft of history." — Philip Graham. SEE NEWSPAPER

newscast n. broadcast, telecast, dispatch, bulletin.

newscaster n. broadcaster, reporter, news anchor, announcer. SEE NEWSMAN

newsletter n. bulletin, report, journal, publication.

newsman/newswoman n. reporter, journalist, investigative reporter, anchor, stringer, correspondent, photojournalist, muckraker, *newshound.

newspaper n. journal, publication, chronicle, daily, weekly, tabloid, scandal sheet, *rag, special edition, press, Gazette, Tribune, Herald, Examiner, Express, Telegram, extra. "A circulating library with blood pressure." — Arthur Baer "A device for amusing one half of the world with the other half's troubles." — Leonard Levinson.

WORD FIND

beat the competition to a story: scoop

cancel a story: kill, spike

checks for errors: copy editor

city news supervisor: city editor

correction of an inaccuracy: retraction

early edition: bulldog, bullpup

hawking of: bootjacking

large print headline: screamer, second coming type

large story: feature

light, human interest story: bright

London press: Fleet Street

material to be printed: copy

nonstaff reporter: freelancer

number of copies sold each day: circulation

personal opinion piece: editorial

prepare for printing: put to bed

reporter's name line: byline

reference room/files: morgue

short news item: squib

short stock item: filler

story in pictures: photojournalism

story's point of origin: dateline

story's point of view: slant

syndicated pieces, press releases, prewritten

material: canned copy
trite publicity piece: puff piece
trivial news period: silly season
wire services: Associated Press, Reuters

newsworthy *a.* notable, important, remarkable, momentous, significant, consequential, weighty. ANT. *insignificant, trivial.*

New York City *n.* the Big Apple, Manhattan, Gotham, metropolis, Brooklyn, the Bronx, Queens, Harlem, Staten Island. "A city where everyone mutinies but no one deserts." —Harry Hershfield. "A beautiful catastrophe." —Charles Jeanneret. "The city of brotherly shove." —Anon.

next *adv.* following, succeeding, successively, ensuing, later, upcoming, coming up, *on the horizon.

nibble *v.* chew, munch, snack, nosh, bite, pick at, peck at, gnaw.

nice *a.* **1.** APPEALING pleasing, attractive, agreeable, pleasant, satisfactory, desirable, enjoyable. **2.** LIKABLE charming, kind, considerate, gracious, amiable, sweet, well-mannered, genial, cordial, kind, thoughtful, good-hearted. **3.** UPRIGHT virtuous, moral, chaste, genteel, seemly. **4.** REFINED delicate, proper, correct, seemly, appropriate. ANT. *1. unpleasant, unattractive, undesirable. 2. unlikable, rude, mean, nasty. 3. immoral, unseemly. 4. unrefined, indelicate.*

niche *n.* notch, corner, cranny, nook, pigeonhole, cubbyhole, recess, hollow.

nick *n.* notch, slit, gouge, indentation, scratch, cut, score, slit, gash, scrape.

nickname *n.* pet name, moniker, *handle, diminutive, cognomen, appellation.

niggardly *a.* cheap, miserly, stingy, penny-pinching, tightfisted, parsimonious, *nickel-squeezing, penurious, small, grudging. ANT. *generous, giving.*

night *n.* evening, after dusk, midnight, twilight, sundown, moonrise, bedtime, *wee hours, witching hour. "A stealthy evil raven." —Thomas Bailey Aldrich. "Vast sin-concealing chaos." —Shakespeare.

nightclub *n.* night spot, club, lounge, disco, discotheque, dance club, cabaret, supper club, comedy club, roadhouse, music hall, singles bar, honky-tonk, speakeasy, casino, *juke joint, *watering hole. "A place where the tables are reserved and the guests aren't." —Fred Casper.

nightmare *n.* **1.** BAD DREAM incubus, succubus, phantasmagoria, hallucination, hypnogogic imagery, night terrors, night sweats, *night frights. **2.** ORDEAL hell, horror, calamity, trial, tribulation, *horror show. SEE DREAM

nightmarish *a.* surreal, terrifying, ethereal, horrific, creepy, ghastly, otherworldly, unreal, weird, hallucinatory, Kafkaesque, hellish.

night stick *n.* *billy club, *billy, *hickory, *shill, cudgel.

nihilism *n.* **1.** DENIAL AND REJECTION renunciation, disbelief, atheism. **2.** ANARCHY lawlessness, subversion. **3.** NOTHINGNESS nonexistence, void.

nil *n.* nothing, zero, null, *nada, *zip, *zilch, *diddly.

nimble *a.* **1.** Agile, spry, sprightly, deft, quick, lithe, light-footed, surefooted, swift, facile. **2.** QUICK-WITTED alert, quick, sharp, quick-thinking. ANT. *1. clumsy, plodding, slow. 2. dull, slow, *dense.*

nip *n.* drink, dram, sip, jiggerful, *taste, *swallow, shot, swig, *snort.

nip *v.* bite, nibble, pinch, cut, snip, squeeze.

nirvana *n.* enlightenment, awakening, bliss, oneness, perfection, tranquility, heaven, blessedness, paradise, ecstasy. ANT. SEE HEAVEN

nit-pick *v.* split hairs, quibble, pettifog, niggle, *make a federal case out of nothing.

nitty-gritty *n. Sl.* heart of the matter, crux, core, the facts, gist, kernel, root, *brass tacks, *bottom line.

nitwit *n.* dimwit, idiot, simpleton. SEE MORON

nobility *n.* **1.** EMINENCE prominence, fame, rank, aristocracy, pedigree, peerage, upper class, noblesse, blue blood, elite, ruling class, First Family, king, queen, emperor, empress, prince, princess, marquis, earl, duke, lord, viscount, baron, baroness, knight, chevalier, squire, count, countess. **2.** INTEGRITY gentility, honor, morality, virtue, chivalry, character, moral fiber. SEE ANCESTRY, ARISTOCRACY, ROYALTY

noble *a.* **1.** EMINENT renowned, famous, illustrious, distinguished, preeminent, esteemed, acclaimed, celebrated. **2.** OF HIGH MORAL CHARACTER moral, virtuous, chivalrous, idealistic, magnanimous, lofty, heroic, honorable, principled, decent, forthright, gallant, exemplary, ethical, scrupulous, humane, benevolent, valorous. "All nobility in its beginnings was somebody's natural superiority." —Ralph Waldo Emerson. **3.** BELONGING TO NOBILITY aristocratic, highborn, princely, royal, blue-blooded, pedigreed, to the manor born, regal, titled, patrician. **4.** HAVING EXCELLENT QUALITIES superior, grand, stately, splendid, majestic, regal, august, superb. ANT. *1. unknown, obscure. 2. immoral, low, dishonorable, ignoble. 3. plebian, common, lower class, working class. 4. inferior, poor, shoddy.*

nobody *n.* nothing, zero, nonentity, flunky, *lightweight, *small fry, *bush-leaguer, *nebbish, *nobody to write home about, *bench-warmer, *second stringer, *just another brick in the wall. ANT. *somebody, *bigwig, bigshot.*

nocturnal *a.* night, nighttime, nightly, night-prowling, night-roaming, night-loving.

nod *n.* greeting, acknowledgement, gesture, signal, consenting nod. SEE GREETING

nod *v.* **1.** GREET OR ACKNOWLEDGE recognize, salute, incline the head, bow. **2.** CONSENT agree, concur. **3.** FALL ASLEEP doze off, drop off, nap.

noise *n.* clamor, din, uproar, racket, cacophony, ruckus, disturbance, blare, babel, ballyhoo, hullabaloo, outcry, tumult, crack, boom, bang, thud, crash, thump, blast, thunder, roar, bellow, rip, eruption, rumble, explosion, shot, detonation, reverberation, pop, clang, clank, clunk, twang, jingle, jangle, ring, tone, plop, kerplop, plunk, trill, peep, tinkle, whistle, ululation, warble, chirp, rattle, screech, scream, wail, shriek, squeal, shout, snap, crackle, crunch, sizzle, buzz, hiss, fizzle, honk, bleat, trumpeting, whir, clatter, scrape, grate, rasp, tick, grind, drone, hum, murmur, purr, sigh, ripple, swish, splash, whoosh, honk, echo, static, white noise, feedback, distortion. "audible grime." —Anon. ANT. *silence, peacefulness, stillness, hush.* SEE LOUD, SOUND

noiseless *a.* silent, still, soundless, hushed, noiseless as the vacuum of space, noiseless as a tomb. SEE QUIET, SILENCE

noiseproof *a.* soundproof, insulated.

noisome *a.* **1.** HARMFUL injurious, hurtful. **2.** MALODOROUS foul-smelling, stinky, smelly, fetid, reeking, rank, rancid, putrid.

noisy *a.* clamorous, cacophonous, blaring, strident, shrill, uproarious, riotous, turbulent, deafening, ear-shattering, nerve-racking. SEE LOUD

nomad *n.* Bedouin, wanderer, gypsy, itinerant, rover, roamer, rambler, vagabond, transient. SEE TRAVELER

nomadic *a.* wandering, roving, rambling, migratory, vagrant, drifting.

nomenclature *n.* terminology, classification, naming, vocabulary, taxonomy.

nominal *a.* **1.** IN NAME ONLY titular, so-called, professed, self-styled, purported, supposed. **2.** SLIGHT minor, small, trivial, minimal, inconsequential, trifling, insignificant. ANT. *1. actual, real, genuine. 2. considerable, large, exorbitant.*

nominate *v.* choose, select, appoint, propose, suggest for election, submit for approval, delegate, name, designate, denominate.

nomination *n.* selection, choice, proposal, naming, designation. SEE APPOINTMENT

nominee *n.* candidate, appointee, aspirant, office-seeker, runner, party favorite.

nonagression *n.* pacifism, nonviolence, passivity, irenicism, *dovishness.

NONCHALANT *a.* [non shuh LAUNT] having a cool or casual attitude, lacking concern. *Fred chatted nonchalantly with the audience; he wasn't nervous at all.* SYN. blasé, casual, cool, devil-may-care, lackadaisical, composed, detached, apathetic, insouciant, self-possessed, poised, carefree, disinterested, unconcerned. ANT. *earnest, anxious, concerned, wary.*

noncommittal *a.* undecided, guarded, cautious, *on the fence, equivocal, playing it safe, *playing it close to the vest, indecisive, wary. ANT. *committed, decisive, definite.*

noncompliant *a.* incompliant, disobedient, rebellious, insubordinate, unruly, rejecting, dissenting. ANT. *compliant, assenting, agreeable.*

nonconforming *a.* independent, *straying from the herd, individualistic, *marching to the beat of a different drummer, unorthodox, radical, disobedient, nonadhering, deviant. ANT. *conforming, *falling in step, obedient.*

nonconformist *n.* maverick, rebel, insubordinate, bohemian, dissenter, heretic, individual, free spirit, eccentric, deviant, renegade, hippie, yippie, beatnik, *skinhead, *square peg in a round hole. ANT. *conformist, *sheep LAMB, follower.*

nondescript *a.* **1.** INDESCRIBABLE undistinguished, unclassifiable, amorphous, undistinctive, hard to describe, plain, vague, *blending into the woodwork, *as distinctive as a plain, brown wrapper. **2.** DRAB unremarkable, colorless, common, dull, bland, *blah, prosaic. ANT. *1. distinctive, distinguished, eye-catching. 2. remarkable, colorful, eye-catching.*

nonessential *a.* unnecessary, extraneous, unimportant, unneeded, uncalled for, unrequired, superfluous, expendable, dispensable, extra. ANT. *essential, required, basic, indispensable.*

nonexistent *a.* inexistent, fictitious, null, void, made-up, make-believe, imaginary, mythical, groundless, extinct, dead, defunct, hypothetical, immaterial.

nonpartisan *a.* independent, unbiased, neutral, impartial, nonaligned, unaffiliated, objective, unprejudiced, *on the fence, open-minded, individualistic. ANT. *partisan, aligned, left wing, right wing, conservative, liberal.*

nonplus *v.* perplex, bewilder, flummox, confound, baffle, *put at a loss, dumbfound, disorient, fluster, rattle, daze, disconcert, discompose, take aback.

nonprofit *a.* not for profit, funded, underwritten, supported, sponsored, public service, subsidized, charitable, philanthropic, benevolent.

nonsense *n.* **1.** SILLINESS foolishness, absurdity, poppycock, folly, balderdash, rot, twaddle, drivel, blather, prattle, moonshine, *monkeyshines, *hooey, *baloney, *bunk, *applesauce, *crock, *crap, *marlarkey, *hogwash. **2.** TRIVIALITY garbage, trash, junk, gimcrackery, trifle. ANT. **1.** *sense, logic, wisdom, sound thinking.*

nonsensical *a.* **1.** unintelligible, meaningless, incomprehensible, senseless. **2.** ABSURD silly, foolish, scatterbrained, ridiculous, preposterous.

nonstop *a.* endless, relentless, ceaseless, never-ending, perpetual, everlasting, around the clock, continuous, ongoing, interminable, incessant.

nonviolence *n.* peace, peacefulness, pacifism, passiveness, nonaggression, dovishness, passive resistance.

nook *n.* niche, recess, cranny, corner, inglenook, retreat, alcove, cubbyhole.

noon *n.* midday, twelve o'clock, high noon, meridian.

norm *n.* standard, rule, accepted practice, criterion, the usual, benchmark, yardstick, average, mean.

normal *a.* **1.** STANDARD usual, typical, conventional, universal, traditional, regular, customary, accepted, average, *par for the course, orthodox, established. **2.** MENTALLY HEALTHY well-adjusted, sane, stable, *having all one's marbles, *all there, *together. "The only normal people are the ones you don't know very well." — Joe Ancis ANT. **1.** *abnormal, unusual, atypical.* **2.** *abnormal, sick,*

*twisted.

normally *a.* usually, typically, conventionally, traditionally, regularly, customarily, generally, as a rule, under normal circumstances.

Northern Lights *n.* aurora borealis, solar wind.

nose *n.* snout, olfactory organ, proboscis, *beak, *honk, *hooter, *snoot, *bazoo, *schnozzle, *schnozzola, *bugle. "The bone and gristle penthouse." — Stewart Robertson.

WORD FIND

blocked nasal passage disorder: deviated septum

descriptive: skewed, gumdrop, potatolike

flattened, somewhat turned-up: pug, snub

hooked like an eagle: aquiline

large: bulbous

red and grossly enlarged: rum nose, whiskey nose, toper's nose, rhinophyma

redness: rosacea

turned-up: retrousse

nose job *n.* rhinoplasty, plastic surgery, cosmetic surgery.

nosh *v.* snack, nibble, taste, pick at, munch. SEE EAT

NOSTALGIA *a.* [nuh STAL juh] a longing for the past or for one's home, homesickness. *We drove through our childhood neighborhood and ached with nostalgia.* SYN. longing, yearning, sentimentality, reminiscence, pining, remembering, mourning, aching, wistfulness. "A seductive liar." — George Ball. "Yesterdaze." — Leonard Bossard. "The longing to go back to the good old day when you were neither good nor old." — Anon.

nostalgic *a.* reminiscent, homesick, wistful, sentimental, longing, yearning, pining, romantic.

nostrum *n.* medicine, quack medicine, cure-all, panacea, *snake oil.

nosy *a.* snooping, prying, eavesdropping, curious, inquisitive, sniffing around, meddlesome, *goggle-eyed, *fence-peeping.

notable *a.* noteworthy, of note, special, important, remarkable, outstanding, of distinction, exceptional, momentous, of consequence. ANT. *inconsequential, unimportant, insignificant.*

notarize *v.* certify, attest, authenticate, endorse, witness, validate, register, sign and seal.

notary (public) *a.* registrar, certifier, signatory, witness, scrivener, recorder, clerk, public official.

notation *n.* **1.** NOTE memo, reminder, annotation, footnote, transcription, shorthand, entry, log note. **2.** MUSIC score, musical symbols.

not born yesterday *a. Sl.* wise, experienced, been around the block, savvy, seasoned, battle-scarred, been through the mill, worldly, been around, sophisticated, not born in the woods to be scared by an owl.

notch *n.* nick, gouge, groove, cleft, slice, scratch, crenel. SEE CUT

notched *a.* crenelated, serrated, saw-toothed, grooved, serriform. SEE CUT

note *n.* **1.** MEMO reminder, letter, jotting, acknowledgement, RSVP, transcription, entry, footnote, *Post-it. **2.** MUSIC tone, sharp, flat, whole note, half note. SEE MUSIC

note *v.* take note, record, regard, pay heed to, observe, notice, give thought to, consider, pay attention to.

notebook *n.* writing tablet, binder, chronicle, diary, memo book, blotter, scratch pad, journal, log, daybook, ledger.

notes *n.* shorthand, transcription, scribblings, outline, rough draft, briefs, thumbnail sketch, jottings.

noteworthy *a.* notable, of note, important, significant, of distinction, remarkable, outstanding, prominent, newsworthy. ANT. *unimportant, insignificant.*

not for profit *a.* nonprofit, charitable, philanthropic, publicly funded.

nothing *n.* **1.** ZERO naught, none, nil, *nix, *zip, *zilch, *nada, *diddly, *squat, *goose egg, *scratch. "A good thing to say, and always a clever thing to say." — Will Durant. **2.** NONEXISTENCE void, vacuum, oblivion, nothingness, inexistence, emptiness, nonentity, nullity. ANT. *1. infinity, *scads, a lot. 2. existence, being.*

nothingness *n.* nonexistence, nihility, emptiness, void, vacuum, vacancy. SEE NOTHING

nothing to it *a. Sl.* piece of cake, easy as pie, easy as ABC, *no-brainer, effortless, *cinchy, *a snap, *a breeze, *duck soup.

notice *n.* announcement, notification, bulletin, communique, warning, caution, pronouncement, mention, information, *tip, advisory.

notice *v.* observe, heed, take note of, regard, pay attention to, recognize, perceive, look at, behold, discern.

noticeable *a.* perceivable, conspicuous, observable, discernible, distinct, in plain view, palpable, obvious, *standing out like a sore thumb, *plain as the nose on one's face. ANT. *imperceivable, inconspicuous, out of sight, cam-*

ouflaged, hidden.

notification *n.* announcement, communique, warning, message, notice, statement, advisory.

notify *v.* inform, give notice, advise, warn, caution, let one know, apprise, serve notice, *tip off. SEE COMUNICATE, TELL

notion *n.* **1.** THOUGHT idea, concept, conception, opinion, view, belief, feeling. **2.** DESIRE inclination, whim, intention, fancy, caprice.

notional *a.* **1.** IMAGINARY abstract, conceptual, visionary, dreamed, fanciful. **2.** WHIMSICAL fanciful, capricious, frivolous.

notoriety *n.* infamy, ill repute, renown, stardom, eminence, prominence.

NOTORIOUS *a.* [no TOR ee us] infamous, known for something bad. *A notorious criminal.* SYN. infamous, disreputable, of ill repute, scandalous, ignominious, opprobrious, discredited, stigmatized, gossiped about, prominent, famous, celebrated, touted, eminent. ANT. *reputable, respectable, uncorrupt.* SEE FAMOUS

nourish *v.* feed, nurture, fortify, sustain, foster, promote, suckle, support.

nourishing *a.* nutritious, fulfilling, filling, fortifying, sustaining, alimentary.

nourishment *n.* nutriment, food, sustenance, subsistence, vitamins and minerals, aliment, viands, daily bread, feed.

nouveau riche *n.* new rich, parvenu, upstart, *yuppie, status seeker, arriviste.

novel *n.* narrative, story, fiction, saga, tale, yarn, chronicle, dime novel, best-seller, paperback, novelette, novella. "A short story padded." — Ambrose Bierce.

WORD FIND

characters are real persons under fictitious names: roman a clef

cheap novel of yesteryear: dime novel, penny dreadful

highbrow: literary novel

historical romance: gothic, bodice ripper, Regency romance

imaginative: sword and sorcery, fantasy, SCF, space opera

lengthy chronicle of a family or society: roman-fleuve

mystery: whodunit, police procedural

rags to riches: Horatio Alger story

real events, based on: docudrama

ridiculing life: satire

young person's maturation: Bildungsroman, come-of-age story

novel *a.* new, first of its kind, unusual, newfangled, fresh, original, unfamiliar, innovative, offbeat, unique, unprecedented, unheard of. ANT. *old hat, old-fashioned, trite.*

novelist *n.* storyteller, fiction writer, creative writer, freelance writer, wordsmith, teller of tales, *hack. SEE AUTHOR, WRITER

novelty *n.* **1.** SOMETHING NEW innovation, departure, original. **2.** FAD craze, *all the rage, *the in thing, *the latest thing. **3.** GADGET doodad, whim-wham, trifle, knickknack, trinket, gimcrack.

November *n.* autumn, fall, month, hunting season. "The gloomy month . . . when the people of England hang and drown themselves." —Joseph Addison.

novena *n.* prayers, devotions, recitations.

novice *n.* beginner, neophyte, tyro, apprentice, trainee, rookie, *greenhorn, *tenderfoot, *virgin. ANT. *veteran, expert, *old hand.* SEE AMATEUR

novitiate *n.* **1.** TRIAL PERIOD training period, probation, initiation, apprenticeship. indoctrination. **2.** NOVICE beginner, amateur, neophyte.

now *adv.* **1.** THE PRESENT at this moment, today, this instant. **2.** IMMEDIATELY at once, this minute, this instant, straightaway, without delay, *chop chop.

now and then *adv.* once in awhile, occasionally, now and again, from time to time, once every blue moon, intermittently, sometimes.

nowhere *a.* no place, *nowheresville, *boonies, *sticks, *East Jesus, *West Bumfuck, *podunk, *North Overshoe, outback, *noplaceville.

NOXIOUS *a.* [NOK shus] harmful, injurious. *The car emitted noxious exhaust fumes.* SYN. harmful, toxic, poisonous, injurious, hurtful, obnoxious, pernicious, deleterious, unhealthful. ANT. *innocuous, benign, harmless.*

nozzle *n.* spout, valve, conduit, snout, sprinkler head.

NUANCE *n.* [NOO ahns] a subtle difference, variation or gradation. *The color nuances in the painting became more apparent the closer we looked.* SYN. subtlety, gradation, shade, shading, variation, distinction, refinement.

nub *n.* knob, protuberance, lump, bump, bulge.

nubby *a.* lumpy, knotted, studded, knobbed, textured.

nubile *a.* **1.** MARRIAGEABLE of age, ripe. **2.** SEXUALLY ATTRACTIVE sexy, sexual, captivating, tempting, seductive, foxy, shapely, curvy.

nuclear *a.* atomic, subatomic, thermonuclear.

nuclear bomb *n.* atomic bomb, A-bomb, hydrogen bomb, H-bomb, thermonuclear bomb, fission bomb, nuclear warhead, neutron bomb, megaton weapon, kiloton weapon, *nuke, *the big one, *physics package, *peacekeeper.

WORD FIND

absorption of radioactive material after blast: contamination

billowing cloud after blast: mushroom cloud

blast effect that causes damaging electrical surges: electromagnetic pulse

bomb portion of missile: warhead

bomb with blast yield equivalent of millions of tons of TNT: megaton weapon

bomb with blast yield equivalent of thousands of tons of TNT: kiloton weapon

fiery side effect of blast: firestorm

illness from fallout: radiation sickness

kills people, leaves buildings intact: neutron bomb

location of detonation at, below or above ground: ground zero

minimum fissionable material necessary for chain reaction: critical mass

precipitation of radioactive material: fallout, rainout

splitting of atom: fission

unit of radiation: rem

weapon with augmented radiation properties: salted weapon

SEE EXPLOSION, MISSILE, NUCLEAR FISSION, NUCLEAR FUSION

nuclear energy *n.* atomic power, fission power.

nuclear fission *n.* atom-splitting, atom smashing, atomic reaction.

nuclear fusion *n.* atomic fusion.

nuclear physics *n.* particle physics, quantum physics, atomic science, quantum mechanics.

nuclear reactor *n.* atomic reactor, core reactor, breeder reactor.

nuclear weapons *n.* weapons of mass destruction, atomic weapons. SEE NUCLEAR BOMB

nucleus *n.* core, kernel, center, heart, pith, nut, deuteron, proton.

nude *a.* naked, unclothed, bare, stripped, *au naturel, disrobed, *in the buff, *in the raw, *without a stitch, *in one's birthday suit, *wearing nothing but goosebumps.

nudge *v.* push, poke, prod, shove, jerk, elbow, tap. SEE TOUCH

nudist *n.* naturist, Adamite, gymnosophist, *free spirit.

nudity *n.* nakedness, *the buff, *the altogether, *undress.

nugget n. lump, chunk, hunk, piece, bit, clump. SEE GOLD, ROCK

nuisance n. **1.** ANNOYANCE irritation, plague, vexation, trouble, inconvenience, bother, pain, thorn in one's side. **2.** PEST *pain in the neck, *nudnik, bane, bore. ANT. *pleasure, joy.*

nuke n. Sl. nuclear bomb, nuclear reactor, nuclear power plant. SEE NUCLEAR BOMB

nuke v. Sl. **1.** BOMB destroy, wipe out, obliterate, *blow back to the stone age, incinerate, *fry, *grease, *wax, *smoke. **2.** Sl. MICROWAVE cook, heat, warm.

null a. invalid, not binding, inconsequential, ineffectual, worthless, valueless, insignificant. ANT. *valid, effectual, valuable.* SEE VOID

nullify v. cancel, annul, negate, invalidate, repeal, revoke, veto, kill, neutralize, counteract.

numb a. **1.** BENUMBED unfeeling, deadened, dead, insensate, anesthetized, insensitive, paralyzed, stunned, narcotized, stupefied. **2.** INSENSITIVE apathetic, unfeeling, indifferent, uncaring. ANT. *1. feeling, sensitive, responsive. 2. empathetic, feeling, receptive.*

number n. **1.** DIGIT numeral, integer, ciper, round number, whole number, fraction. **2.** AMOUNT sum, total, count, aggregate, tally, quantity, score.

number v. count, tally, enumerate, add up, paginate, reckon, tick off, compute, figure up, calculate, account, audit. SEE ADD

number cruncher n. Sl. statistician, *bean counter, accountant, tabulator, calculator, computer, adding machine, *stat basher.

numberless a. innumerable, countless, infinite, incalculable, myriad, endless, many, *umpteen, measureless, copious. ANT. *numbered, finite, limited.*

numerous a. many, myriad, copious, plentiful, innumerable, a lot, profuse, numberless, plenty, *scads, several, manifold, *umpteen, considerable, rife. ANT. *few, little, sparse.*

numskull n. dolt, idiot, *blockhead. SEE MORON

nun n. sister, prioress, ecclesiast, abbess, virgin, contemplative, mother superior, reverend mother.

nunnery n. convent, abbey, cloister, sisterhood, priory.

nuptial a. matrimonial, marital, bridal, conjugal, connubial.

nuptials n. marriage ceremony, marriage, wedding, matrimony, espousal.

nurse n. medical technician, medical assistant, caregiver, attendant, registered nurse (R.N.), licensed practical nurse (L.P.N.) certified nurse's aid (C.N.A.), nurse practitioner, charge nurse, scrub nurse, orderly, therapist, *candystriper.

nurse v. **1.** CARE FOR tend, attend, treat, aid, minister to, medicate, cater to, provide therapy, medicate, *provide TLC. **2.** BREASTFEED suckle, wet-nurse.

nursemaid n. nanny, wet nurse, babysitter, governess.

nursery n. **1.** CHILD CARE CENTER day care center, nursery school, preschool. **2.** MATERNITY WARD **3.** GREENHOUSE hothouse, cold frame, hot bed.

nursing home n. convalescent home, *old folks home, rest home, retirement facility.

nurture n. raising, fostering, guidance, care, rearing, training, education.

nurture v. nourish, care for, sustain, cultivate, foster, raise, bring up, rear, mother, educate. SEE FEED

nut n. **1.** SEED kernel, fruit, peanut, *goober, acorn, chestnut, hazelnut, walnut, pinon, Brazil nut, almond, beechnut, pecan, filbert, cashew, pistachio, butternut, coconut, hickory nut. **2.** FANATIC buff, *freak, enthusiast, fan, aficianado, devotee, zealot. **3.** ECCENTRIC *kook, *flake, *butterfly case, *weirdo, *daffydill, *fuul ball, *loon, *nutter, *crackpot, mental case, *screwball, *ding-a-ling. SEE ECCENTRIC

nut house n. Sl. insane asylum, *booby hatch, *loony bin, *bughouse, *funny farm, *laughing academy, *nut college, *nut hatch, *rubber room.

nutrient n. vitamin, mineral, nutriment, food, protein, carbohydrate.

nutrition n. nourishment, sustenance, balanced diet, alimentation.

nutritionist n. dietician, diet consultant.

nutritious a. nourishing, sustaining, nutritive, body-building, alimentary, fortifying, healthy, wholesome, *good for you.

nuts a. Sl. crazy, insane, *wacko, *bonkers, *crackers, demented, deranged, *gone 'round the bend, cracked, *loony, *bananas, *cuckoo, *food for squirrels, *gaga, *googoo, *haywire, *loco, *mental, *not tightly wrapped, *off one's nut, *off one's trolley, *out of one's gourd, *potty, *psycho, *schizo, *spacey, non compos mentis, *off in the twilight zone. ANT. *sane, rational, normal.*

nuzzle v. snuggle, cuddle, nestle, lie close, hug, embrace.

nylons n. stockings, hosiery, hose.

nymph n. spirit, sprite, goddess, maiden, dryad,

oread, naiad, mermaid. SEE FAIRY

nymphomania n. lustfulness, goatishness, erotomania, carnal desire, prurience, concupiscence, libidinousness, satyriasis.

nymphomaniac n. *nympho, slut, erotomaniac, trollop, strumpet, hussy, *tart, *floozy, nymphet, loose woman, *bimbo.

O

oaf *n.* lummox, dolt, dunce, lout, simpleton, rustic, ignoramus, clod, clodhopper, ninny, *klutz, *boob. ANT. *intellectual, sophisticate, genius.*

oafish *a.* clumsy, awkward, *klutzy, stupid, ignorant, simple, rustic.

oak *n.* acorn tree, shade tree, hardwood. SEE FOREST, TREE

oar *n.* paddle, scull, pole, blade, rudder pole.

oasis *n.* **1.** SPRING watering hole, wadi, fertile area, desert arbor, *island Eden. **2.** REFUGE sanctuary, retreat, haven, sanctum, asylum.

oath *n.* **1.** PLEDGE promise, vow, declaration, swearing, word of honor, guarantee, affirmation. **2.** SWEAR WORD curse, profanity, expletive.

obdurate *a.* hardened, hard, hard-hearted, callous, heartless, unsympathetic, unmovable, stubborn, obstinate, unyielding, intractable, inflexible, dogged. ANT. *feeling, tractable, flexible.*

obedience *n.* compliance, acquiescence, submission, deference, subservience.

obedient *a.* obeying, submissive, compliant, acquiescent, tractable, obsequious, amenable, dutiful, nonresistant, servile, subservient, scraping, prostrate, docile, *at one's beck and call, *wrapped around one's little finger, *under one's thumb, *whipped, conforming. ANT. *disobedient, insubordinate, rebellious.*

obeisance *n.* **1.** GESTURE OF RESPECT bow, curtsy, genuflection, salaam, kneeling, salute. **2.** DEFERENCE homage, worship, respect, reverence, subservience, servility, obsequiousness, fawning, psychophancy. ANT. **1.** *thumbing one's nose, *giving the finger. **2.** *disrespect, irreverence, insolence.*

obeisant *a.* deferential, respecting, reverent, servile, worshipping, obsequious. ANT. *disrespectful, irreverent, insolent.*

obelisk *n.* monolith, shaft, column, monument, pillar, pylon, needle, tower.

obese *a.* fat, overweight, corpulent, plump, rotund, stout, chubby, roly-poly, blubbery, paunchy, pleasingly plump, full-figured, elephantine, *sleek as a walrus. SEE FAT

obesity *n.* corpulence, plumpness, rotundness, stoutness, paunchiness, portliness, chubbiness, overweight, fatness. "A tale of horror told by the bathroom scale."—Anon. SEE FAT

obey *v.* comply, follow orders, acquiesce, submit, yield, mind, heed, abide, relent, concur, serve, do one's bidding, carry out one's wishes, toe the line, *bend over backwards, knuckle under, *don't just jump when told—ask how high. ANT. *disobey, defy, rebel.*

OBFUSCATE *v.* [ob FUS kate] to darken, obscure or make unclear, confuse. *His irrelevant arguments only obfuscated the issue further.* SYN. obscure, confuse, muddle, darken, cloud, conceal, confound, bewilder, cover up, hide, camouflage. ANT. *clear up, clarify, elucidate.*

obituary *n.* obit, death notice, necrology. SEE DEATH, EULOGY

object *n.* **1.** THING item, subject, article, entity. **2.** PURPOSE aim, intent, goal, objective, target, end.

object *v.* disapprove, protest, oppose, demur, inveigh, except, remonstrate. ANT. *approve, assent, agree, support.*

objection *n.* disapproval, protest, remonstrance, disagreement, exception, complaint, criticism, admonition, dispute, opposition, grievance, dissatisfaction, gripe, *kick. ANT. *acceptance, agreement, approval.*

objectionable *a.* offensive, revolting, disagreeable, unbefitting, undesirable, unpleasant, inappropriate, uncalled for, unsatisfactory, out of line, unacceptable. ANT. *acceptable, agreeable.*

objective *n.* purpose, goal, intent, end, aim, target, object, quarry, point.

objective *a.* unbiased, fair, unprejudiced, unemotional, disinterested, detached, indifferent, impersonal. SEE FAIR

objectivity *a.* disinterest, neutrality, detachment, indifference, distance, fairness, evenhandedness, dispassion.

objet d' art *n.* object of art, figurine, vase, curio. SEE KNICKKNACK

objurgate *v.* scold, rebuke, berate, chastise, chide, upbraid, reproach.

obligate *v.* bind, pledge, compel, force, constrain, commit, require, necessitate, behold, indebt, contract. ANT. *free, release.*

obligated *a.* bound, beholden, indebted, required, constrained, committed, obliged, pledged, contracted. ANT. *released, freed, unbound.*

obligation *n.* duty, promise, pledge, contract, responsibility, requirement, charge, commitment, bond, liability, burden.

obligatory *a.* required, necessary, binding, requisite, mandatory, imperative, essential, compulsory, peremptory. ANT. *unrequired, optional, unnecessary.*

oblige *v.* accommodate, serve, help out, favor, aid, lend a hand, cater to, gratify. **2.** NECESSITATE compel, force, bind.

obliged *a.* **1.** REQUIRED compelled, bound, forced. **2.** indebted.

oblique *a.* **1.** SLANTING sloping, inclined, tilting, leaning, angled, deviating, askew, canted, crooked, diagonal, listing. **2.** INDIRECT evasive, devious, sly, underhanded, disingenuous, surreptitious, deceptive. ANT. *1. straight, level, horizontal. 2. straightforward, honest, open.*

obliterate *v.* **1.** ERASE expunge, wipe out, rub out, deface, scratch out, delete, blot out, remove. **2.** DESTROY annihilate, eliminate, eradicate, exterminate, do away with, incinerate, wipe out, decimate. ANT. *1. put in, enter, put in bold print, insert. 2. build up, fortify, create.*

OBLIVION *n.* [uh BLIV ee un] the state of being totally lost and forgotten. *Most people fear that their names will be lost to oblivion after death.* SYN. the forgotten, nothingness, void, *never-never land, nihility, nonexistence, space, obscurity, inexistence, extinction, unconsciousness. "The swallowing gulf." —Shakespeare." ANT. *prominence, fame, notoriety.* SEE EMPTINESS

oblivious *a.* unconscious, unaware, forgetful, absentminded, abstracted, absorbed, mindless, amnesic, preoccupied, thoughtless, *out to lunch, *off in space, *out of it. ANT. *conscious, aware, focused.*

oblong *a.* elliptical, oval, egg-shaped, elongated, rectangular.

obloquy *n.* censure, vituperation, verbal abuse, defamation, insult, discredit, dressing-down, belittlement. ANT. *compliment, praise, adulation.*

obnoxious *a.* offensive, objectionable, loathsome, odious, unpleasant, disagreeable, disgusting, revolting, hateful, insulting, repugnant, deplorable. ANT. *pleasant, agreeable, pleasing.*

obscene *a.* **1.** OFFENSIVE repulsive, foul, gross, indecent, unsavory, lewd, shameless, vulgar, revolting, distasteful, indelicate, lurid. **2.** INCITING LUST libidinous, pornographic, salacious, lewd, lascivious, nasty, smutty, *raunchy, prurient, licentious, naughty. ANT. *1. respectable, inoffensive, decent. 2. pure, chaste, prudish, puritanical.*

obscenity *n.* **1.** INDECENCY vulgarity, smut, lewdness, indelicacy, vileness, *raunch, filth, ribaldry. **2.** SWEAR WORD four-letter word, oath, cuss word, curse, expletive. ANT. *1. delicacy, decency, propriety. 2. euphemism, polite word.*

obscure *v.* **1.** MAKE INDISTINCT conceal, obstruct, hide, camouflage, muddy, obfuscate, cloud, confuse. **2.** DARKEN dim, cloud, shadow. ANT. *1. make distinct, define, make clear, spotlight, expose. 2. lighten, brighten.*

obscure *a.* **1.** INDISTINCT vague, faint, ambiguous, inconspicuous, unclear, indiscernible, imperceptible, hazy, nebulous, undistinguished, hard to make out. **2.** DARK gloomy, dusky, murky, dim, hazy, shadowy. **3.** LITTLE KNOWN unknown, unseen, elusive, inconspicuous, unheard of, remote, unsung, insignificant. ANT. *1. distinct, clear, defined. 2. bright, sunny, light. 3. famous, well-known, notorious.*

OBSEQUIOUS *a.* [ub SEE kwee us] servile, fawning or overly compliant. *The bully and his obsequious underlings started a brawl.* SYN. servile, fawning, abject, abasing, submissive, sycophantic, deferential, compliant, *brownnosing, *apple-polishing, *kissing up, *bootlicking, *ring-kissing, toadying, *falling all over oneself to please, ingratiating. ANT. *domineering, lordly, disrespectful.*

obsequy *n.* funeral rite, ceremony, service. SEE EULOGY, FUNERAL

observable *a.* perceptible, perceivable, palpable, noticeable, obvious, evident, in plain view, distinct. ANT. *hidden, obscure, camouflaged.*

observance *n.* **1.** CUSTOM rite, ritual, ceremony, celebration, commemoration, remembrance, memorial. **2.** OBSERVATION watching, notice, attention, scrutiny, lookout, inspection, examination. **3.** ABIDING BY adherence, compliance, heeding, obeying, regarding. ANT. *3. disregard, breach, noncompliance.*

observant *a.* watchful, attentive, noticing, perceptive, keen-eyed, aware, sharp-eyed, alert, mindful. ANT. *overlooking, daydreaming, ignoring.*

observation *n.* **1.** OBSERVING noticing, seeing, perception, observance, examination, attention, viewing. **2.** REMARK comment, assertion, sentiment, opinion, observance, account, declaration, thought, judgment. **3.** NOTING recording, sizing up, measuring, scrutiny, assessment.

observatory *n.* observation post, lookout,

watchtower.

observe v. **1.** WATCH see, look at, notice, view, eye, examine, study, behold, *get a load of, *take a gander at. **2.** ABIDE BY adhere, respect, recognize, follow, obey, heed, honor, maintain, regard, acknowledge, comply. ANT. *1. ignore, neglect, overlook. 2. disregard, disrespect, ignore.*

observer n. lookout, watcher, eyewitness, spectator, onlooker, bystander, examiner.

obsess v. preoccupy, haunt, beset, possess, hound, harass, torment, plague, occupy, dominate, *prey on one's mind. ANT. *ignore, forget, exorcise.*

obsessed a. preoccupied, haunted, beset, possessed, fixated, dominated, *hung up, troubled, immersed in, *gaga over, gripped, crazed.

obsession n. preoccupation, fixation, compulsion, fascination, mania, delusion, fetish, infatuation, possession, passion. SEE INSANITY, MANIA, NEUROSIS, PHOBIA

obsolete a. **1.** DISCARDED useless, abandoned, cast off, defunct, extinct, retired, forgotten. **2.** OLD-FASHIONED outmoded, antiquated, dated, passé, out of date, primitive, *old hat, ancient, worn out, Victorian. ANT. *fresh, new, modern, *cutting edge.*

obstacle n. impediment, hindrance, block, obstruction, barrier, snag, check, deterrent, impasse, bar, hurdle, restriction, stumbling block.

obstetrics n. tocology, midwifery, childbirth, labor and delivery. SEE BIRTH, PREGNANCY

obstinate a. stubborn, firm, inflexible, adamant, unyielding, resistant, tenacious, headstrong, unwavering, bullheaded, mulish, pigheaded, hardnosed, dogged, unbending, stiffnecked, cussed, *stubborn as a bobtail mule, *stubborn as crabgrass. ANT. *flexible, tractable, yielding.*

obstreperous a. noisy, boisterous, vociferous, unruly, rowdy, unmanageable, uproarious, riotous, clamorous. ANT. *peaceful, quiet.*

obstruct v. **1.** block, impede, stop up, clog, check, retard, hinder, bar, preclude. **2.** HIDE block, camouflage, screen, curtain, cover up, obscure. ANT. *1. open up, release, unstop, broach, clear. 2. reveal, expose, spotlight, unveil.*

obstruction n. impediment, obstacle, bar, barricade, block, check, stumbling block, hindrance, restriction, bottleneck, stop. ANT. *opening, gap, hole, passage.*

obtain v. get, acquire, procure, gain possession, seize, attain, net, capture, *get one's hands on, pick up, harvest. ANT. *lose, forfeit, give up.*

obtainable a. available, acquirable, attainable, winnable. ANT. *unobtainable, *out of reach.*

obtrude v. **1.** INTRUDE impose, *barge in, meddle, interrupt, *butt in, *stick one's nose in, *pry, *horn in. **2.** EXTRUDE stick out, protrude, push out, eject, thrust forward.

obtrusive a. **1.** PROJECTING protruding, prominent, protuberant, jutting out, sticking out. **2.** INTRUSIVE forward, brash, pushing, meddlesome, interfering, bold, invasive, interruptive. **3.** CONSPICUOUS glaring, overt, blatant, flagrant, striking, obvious, half-faced, outrageous. ANT. *1. flattened, smoothed, planed. 2. retiring, reticent, shy, unobtrusive. 3. inconspicuous, subtle, hidden.*

obtuse a. **1.** BLUNT dull, rounded. **2.** STUPID dull, slow, thick, dense, vapid, vacuous, peabrained, insensitive. ANT. *1. sharp, pointed. 2. sharp, intelligent, quick.* SEE MORONIC, STUPID

obverse a. **1.** FACE front, top, head. **2.** COUNTERPART opposite, reverse.

obviate v. preclude, prevent, forestall, avert, avoid, evade, circumvent.

obvious a. apparent, evident, visible, plain to see, clear, conspicuous, manifest, overt, noticeable, perceivable, glaring, palpable, patent, prominent, unambiguous, *sticking out like a sore thumb, *goes without saying. ANT. *imperceivable, mysterious, vague, inconspicuous.*

obviously adv. unmistakably, apparently, evidently, certainly, overtly, clearly.

occasion n. **1.** EVENT happening, affair, function, happening, incident. **2.** OPPORTUNITY chance, opening, golden opportunity, *shot, *crack. **3.** CELEBRATION holiday, festival, gala, carnival. **4.** TIME juncture, instance, point, case.

occasion v. cause, give occasion to, produce, bring about, prompt, induce, effect, create, bring to pass. ANT. *stop, end, quit.*

occasional a. irregular, once in awhile, sporadic, infrequent, every now and then, periodic, casual, odd, from time to time. ANT. *frequent, regular, continuous.*

occasionally a. now and then, once in awhile, from time to time, periodically, sometimes, infrequently, irregularly, once in a blue moon, sporadically. ANT. *regularly, frequently, constantly.*

occlude v. obstruct, close off, shut off, seal, plug, stop, clog, choke, block, fill. ANT. *open, clear, unstop.*

occlusion n. blockage, obstruction, seal, plug, stop, clog, block. ANT. *opening, hole, clearance.*

occult n. mystical arts, cabalism, mysticism, occultism, channeling, astrology, voodoo, alchemy, tarot, Ouija board, psychic powers, clairvoyance, exorcism, satanism, devil worshipping, sorcery, witchcraft, telekinesis, telepathy, reincarnation, possession.

occult a. supernatural, secret, hidden, magical, unexplainable, unfathomable, arcane, mystical, cryptic, esoteric, orphic. ANT. *earthly, tangible, explainable, known.* SEE MYSTERIOUS

occupancy n. residence, residency, occupation, living, tenancy, inhabitance, inhabitation, stay, tenure, lodging, possession. ANT. *leave, vacancy, absence.*

occupant n. resident, inhabitant, tenant, leaseholder, renter, lodger, dweller, homeowner, owner, lessee.

occupation n. **1.** VOCATION job, work, career, trade, profession, business, livelihood, calling, pursuit, employment. SEE JOB, WORK **2.** OCCUPANCY tenancy, possession, inhabitation. **3.** CONQUEST seizure, takeover, overthrow, subjugation, defeat, possession, rule.

occupied a. **1.** ENGAGED busy, preoccupied, engrossed, absorbed, employed, diverted. **2.** INHABITED lived in, settled, taken. **3.** CONQUERED seized, overthrown, possessed, defeated, taken, over, subjugated. ANT. *1. idle, inactive, unoccupied, at leisure. 2. uninhabited, vacant, empty. 3. sovereign, independent, self-ruled.*

occupy v. **1.** ENGAGE busy, preoccupy, engross, absorb, employ, divert, entertain. **2.** INHABIT live in, settle, take, reside in, take up residence. **3.** CONQUER seize, overthrow, possess, defeat, take over, subjugate, rule. ANT. *1. disengage, make idle, bore. 2. vacate, *fly the coop, leave, relinquish. 3. retreat, relinquish, evacuate.*

occurrence n. happening, incident, event, episode, transaction, circumstance, matter, action, experience, affair.

ocean n. sea, the deep, the abyss, deep blue sea, brine, *the drink, *Davy Jones locker, high seas, the seven seas, *bounding main, Neptune, Poseidon, expanse, *unbridgeable horizon, Arctic, Antarctic, Atlantic, North Atlantic, South Atlantic, Pacific, North Pacific, South Pacific, Indian. "The cradle of all life." — Anon "The wavy waste." — Thomas Hood. "A highway between the doorways of the nations." — Franklin Lane.

WORD FIND

bottom and its creatures: benthic realm, benthos

bottom, one region of: province

circular currents: gyres

current of Atlantic: Gulf Stream

current of Pacific that disrupts weather patterns: El Nino

depression in floor: cauldron

depth between one hundred and one thousand meters: bathyal zone

depth between one thousand and six thousand meters: abyssal zone

depth from six thousand meters down: hadal zone

depth, greatest trench: Marianas Trench

depth measurement of six feet: fathom

eddy that breaks off from main current: meander, ring

flat calm, no wind region: doldrums

foam: spume

glow of sea creatures: bioluminescence

god: Neptune

graveyards of ships: Bermuda Triangle, graveyard of the Atlantic

hills: abyssal hills

measurement of depth: bathymetry, sounding

mile, nautical: 6,082.2 feet

mountain chain in Atlantic: mid-Atlantic ridge

mountain chain in Pacific: Emperor Seamounts

mountain: seamount

seaweed region in North Atlantic: Sargasso Sea

sediment deposit, large offshore: submarine fan

shallow area, navigational hazard: shoal

spray: spindrift

study of: oceanography

tide, maximal low and high: spring tide

tide, minimal low and high: neap tide

turbulence involving bottom mud: benthic storm

waves, crash and crest of opposing: cross seas

waves: plunger, spiller, graybeard, swell, eagre (tidal bore), tsunami.

wave, tidal: tsunami

wind distance and relationship to wave height: fetch. SEE BEACH

oceanic a. marine, maritime, deep-sea, aquatic, pelagic, abyssal, nautical.

ocean liner n. cruise ship, luxury liner.

oceanographer n. marine scientist, oceanologist, hydrographer.

October n. month, harvest time, autumn, fall, Indian summer. "A carousel of swirling leaves, an arboreal danse macabre." — Marc McCutcheon.

odd a. **1.** STRANGE unusual, weird, unconventional, out of the ordinary, offbeat, unnatural, bizarre, atypical, peculiar, singular, irregular, queer, unique. **2.** UNMATCHED lone, single, unpaired, mateless. ANT. *1. usual, typical, ordinary, regular. 2. matched, paired.*

oddball n. *Sl.* *weirdo, eccentric, misfit, *crackpot, *freak, *nut, *screwball, *character, *queer duck, nonconformist. **2.** *regular Joe, *average Joe, conformist.

oddity n. curiosity, rarity, quirk, peculiarity, eccentricity, anomaly, freak.

odds n. **1.** PROBABILITY chances, likelihood, expectation, prospect. **2.** ADVANTAGE handicap, edge. **3.** AT ODDS at sixes and sevens, at loggerheads, in disagreement, misunderstanding, difference of opinion.

odds and ends n. bits and pieces, oddments, miscellany, mish mash, hodgepodge, melange, mixed bag, assortment, patchwork, remnants.

oddsmaker n. statistician, gambler, bettor, tout.

odds-on-favorite n. front-runner, best bet, chalk horse.

ode n. poem, lyric, hymn, song. SEE POEM, SONG

odious a. offensive, abhorrent, repugnant, disgusting, hateful, repulsive, detestable, revolting, loathsome. ANT. *pleasing, delightful, nice.*

odium n. **1.** HATRED ill will, loathing, disgust, repugnance. **2.** DISGRACE opprobrium. ANT. *1. love, goodwill, benevolence. 2. grace, honor.*

odor n. scent, smell, aroma, fragrance, essence, effluvium, redolence, fume, emanation, whiff, stench, stink, bouquet, perfume.

WORD FIND

types: foul, fetid, rank, goaty, musty, springfresh, herbal, floral, pungent, spicy, chemical, organic, fruity, sweet, sour, rancid, incense, civet, musk, potpourri, frankincense, sandalwood, myrrh, balsam, antiseptic, dank, stale, honeysuckle, lilac, putrid, carbolic, spindrift, ozone, fishy, diesel, ambrosial.

SEE PERFUME, SMELL

odorless a. nonfragrant, aosmic, neutral, unscented, deodorized.

odorous a. fragrant, smelly, stinky, distinct-smelling, redolent, odoriferous, aromatic, scented.

odyssey n. wandering, trek, journey, quest, sojourn, voyage, travels. SEE TRAVEL

off a. **1.** AWAY OR DETACHED removed, above, below, aside, behind, distant, not touching, separated. **2.** SHUT OFF, INOPERABLE stopped, malfunctioning, disconnected, shut down, defunct, unpowered, down. **3.** MISTAKEN incorrect, in error, wrong, inaccurate, erroneous, miscalculated. **4.** OFF DUTY on holiday, not working, on liberty, on leave. ANT. *1. on, attached, touching, astride. 2. on, functioning, running. 3. correct, accurate, right. 4. on duty, working.*

offal n. entrails, guts, refuse, rubbish, waste. SEE GARBAGE

off and on adv. intermittent, alternately, variably, fluctuating, vacillating, starting and stopping, sporadically, irregularly.

off-balance a. **1.** OFF-CENTER uncentered, unbalanced. **2.** UNSTEADY *tippy, tipping, uncoordinated, leaning, toppling, inclining. ANT. *1. centered, balanced. 2. steady, balanced, stable, counterpoised.*

offbeat a. unconventional, unorthodox, unusual, *off-center, strange, novel, *kinky, *freaky, *oddball, different, weird, atypical, *far out. ANT. *conventional, orthodox, traditional, normal.*

off-center a. misaligned, off-balanced, askew, eccentric.

off-color a. risque, improper, tasteless, indecent, inappropriate, suggestive, lewd, racy, *raunchy, dirty, offensive, indelicate, gross. ANT. *tasteful, prudish, respectable, clean.*

off course a. strayed, drifted, lost, lost one's bearings. SEE LOST

offend v. **1.** INSULT affront, annoy, slight, spite, disgust, outrage, mortify, vex, *ruffle one's feathers, *pull one's chain, *rattle one's cage, *rub one the wrong way. **2.** DO A MISDEED break the law, violate, transgress, sin. ANT. *1. please, honor, compliment, praise.*

offender n. perpetrator, culprit, lawbreaker, sinner, violator, malefactor. SEE CRIMINAL

offense n. **1.** INSULT affront, slight, injury. **2.** UMBRAGE resentment, pique, displeasure. **3.** MISDEED transgression, violation, infraction, misdemeanor, felony, wrongdoing, peccadillo, sin, charge. **4.** ATTACK, ATTACKERS assault, siege, invasion, charge, raid, offensive, blitzkrieg, blitz, run, attackers, aggressors, invaders, opposing side. ANT. *1. courtesy, compliment. 2. delight, honor. 3. good deed, benevolence. 4. defense, retreat, submission.* SEE CRIME

offensive n. attack, invasion, raid, assault, siege, charge, counteroffensive, bombing run, flanking maneuver, blitzkrieg, enfilade.

offensive a. **1.** INSULTING rude, obnoxious, revolting, disgusting, hateful, repugnant, outrageous, discourteous, distasteful, sickening, disagreeable, affronting, abominable, objectionable. SEE MEAN, OBSCENE, VULGAR **2.** AGGRESSIVE warlike, invading, pugnacious, hostile, attacking, belligerent. ANT. *1. pleasing, honoring, respectful, nice. 2. peaceful, pacific, passive, appeasing.*

offer n. proffer, proposal, proposition, overture, bid, tender, offering, submission.

offer v. proffer, present, tender, bid, propose, submit, put forward, advance, lay at one's feet, suggest, counteroffer. ANT. *withdraw, renege, take back.* SEE PROPOSE

offering n. contribution, donation, oblation, tithe, sacrifice, grant. SEE GIFT

offhand a. **1.** IMPROMPTU unprepared, casual, *at the spur of the moment, unplanned, extemporaneous, unrehearsed, unpremeditated, ad-lib. **2.** BRUSQUE curt, blunt, abrupt, informal, terse, casual. ANT. *1. rehearsed, prepared, studied. 2. tactful, mannered, polite.*

office n. **1.** PLACE OF BUSINESS OR WORK AREA department, headquarters, precinct, bureau, command center, practice, suite, *nerve center, *boiler room, base, room, work station, cubicle, compartment, niche, cubbyhole, pigeonhole, closet. **2.** POST position, service, role, function, charge, appointment.

officer n. **1.** POLICEMAN constable, magistrate, deputy, sheriff, peace officer, patrolman, *cop, *fuzz, *John Law. SEE POLICE **2.** OFFICIAL functionary, officeholder, bureaucrat, commissioner, director, minister, civil servant, secretary, commissar, corporate officer. **3.** MILITARY OFFICER MP, commissioned officer, noncommissioned officer, NCO. SEE AIR FORCE, ARMY, NAVY

office worker n. *desk jockey, *pencil driver, *bean counter, *number cruncher, *hacker, secretary, receptionist, accountant, computer programmer, controller, comptroller, clerk, payroll clerk, VP, Chief Executive Officer (CEO), *Kelly girl, file clerk, typist, word processor, billing clerk, data processor.

official n. **1.** OFFICER functionary, dignitary, administrator, public official, bureaucrat. **2.** REFEREE judge.

official a. authorized, sanctioned, certified, endorsed, approved, vested, accredited. ANT. *unofficial, unauthorized, not recognized.* SEE LE-GAL

officialese n. doublespeak, *gobblydegook, *federalese, jargon, *bloated English, *gassy prose, *verbosity, *mush, *tapioca, *departmental murk.

officiate v. oversee, preside over, chair, supervise, direct, emcee, referee, judge. SEE MEDIATE

OFFICIOUS a. [uh FISH us] offering help or advice when it is not wanted, meddlesome, especially in a domineering way. *His mother-in-law is particularly officious.* SYN. meddlesome, obtrusive, intrusive, pushy, interfering, forward, prying, domineering, bossy, overbearing, high-handed, pragmatic. ANT. *reserved, unobtrusive, knowing one's place.*

offing n. **1.** horizon, far distance. **2.** SEE FUTURE

off-key a. flat, sharp, out of tune, discordant, dissonant.

off-limits a. restricted, prohibited, forbidden, barred, out of bounds, banned, taboo, unlawful, illegal. ANT. *unrestricted, open, free.*

offset v. counter, counteract, compensate, balance, neutralize, equalize, even out, cancel out, level out.

offshoot n. branch, stem, tendril, sprout, descendant, offspring, heir, *spinoff.

offshore a. seaward, the offing, *the high seas, out to sea.

offspring n. children, progeny, descendants, brood, heirs, clutch, litter, spawn, seed, young.

offstage n. wings, backstage, green room, dressing room.

off the cuff a. impromptu, offhand, unrehearsed, extemporaneous, ad-lib, improvised.

off the record a. confidential, not for publication, on the QT, unofficial, *between you, me and the bedpost.

off-white a. antique white, ivory, blond.

often adv. frequently, repeatedly, quite a bit, oft, time and again, regularly, habitually, generally. ANT. *seldom, rarely.*

ogle v. stare, leer, goggle, gawk, gaze, *stare bug-eyed, *stare saucer-eyed, *eye salaciously, gape at.

ogre n. giant, brute, man-eater, boogieman. SEE MONSTER

oil n. crude oil, petroleum, lubricant, motor oil, machine oil, *black gold, *Texas tea, sludge, grease, ooze, lard, oleo, fat, vegetable oil, corn oil, olive oil, linseed oil, cod-liver oil, mineral oil.

oily a. **1.** VISCOUS greasy, slippery, unctious, oleaginous, fatty, lardy, tallowy, slick. **2.** EXCESSIVELY SUAVE slick, smooth, unctuous, honey-tongued, flattering. ANT. *2. sincere, artless, unpolished.*

ointment *n.* emollient, salve, unguent, medicament, balm.

okay *a.* all right, correct, sure, yes, *okey dokey, copacetic, *righto, *sure thing, *no problem.

old *a.* **1.** AGED elderly, venerable, advanced in years, matured, past one's prime, patriarchal, vintage, seasoned, *at a ripe old age, senior, retirement age. SEE OLD AGE **2.** WORN OUT decrepit, dilapidated, crumbling, decayed, deteriorated, shabby, enfeebled, senile. **3.** FORMER previous, early, past, bygone, once. **4.** LONG-STANDING age-old, of the past, from time immemorial. ANT. *1. young, newborn, immature, unseasoned. 2. new, fresh, 3. later, future. 4. recent, new.*

old age *n.* retirement age, senescence, declining years, *winter of one's life, enfeeblement, dotage, senility. "To take in sail." — Emerson. "To be left alone at a banquet — the lights dead and the flowers faded." — Gilbert Chesterson. "Whenever a man's friends begin to compliment him about looking young." — Washington Irving. "The road's last turn." — Henry Van Dyke.

old country *n.* motherland, native land, mother country, Europe.

old days *n.* olden times, *yesteryear, horse and buggy days, days gone by, *good old days, days of yore.

old-faced *a.* cadaverous, careworn, timeworn, rawboned, craggy, crow's-feet, fleshy wattle under the chin, gap-toothed, goat-skinned, haggard, hollowed cheekbones, hollowed eye sockets, jaundiced, leathery, liver-spotted, mirthful crinkles about the eyes, skin like scalded milk, mottled, prune-faced, rheumy-eyed, weathered.

old-fashioned *a.* outdated, outmoded, dated, obsolete, out of style, moss-grown, passe, fusty, antiquated, behind the times, Victorian, *horse and buggy, oldfangled, prehistoric, traditional, conservative, stodgy. ANT. *modern, fresh, fashionable, *cutting edge, new, chic.*

old maid *n.* spinster, maiden, single woman, virgin.

old man *n.* SEE OLD-TIMER

old school *a.* traditional, conservative, old-fashioned, old line, ingrained.

old-timer *n.* veteran, old hand, senior, moss-back, *antique, *fossil, Methuselah, graybeard, centenarian, nonagenarian, octogenarian, sexagenarian, golden-ager, *codger, *geezer, *old fart, *duffer, *old buzzard, *gramps, *grandma, *old girl, *old hen.

old wives' tale *n.* superstition, lore, folklore, belief, myth, fallacy.

Olympian *n.* athlete, world-class athlete, medalist, competitor.

Olympics *n.* Olympic Games, world championships, tournament, contest, challenge, international competition, Olympiad.

omen *n.* augury, portent, sign, precursor, warning, harbinger, forewarning, token, handwriting on the wall, foreboding, premonition, *storm cloud on the horizon.

OMINOUS *a.* [OM un us] pertaining to omens, portentous, foreboding. *A dark cloud on the horizon is particularly ominous to one on a sailboat.* SYN. portentous, foreboding, dreadful, prophetic, menacing, boding evil, inauspicious, threatening, sinister, cautionary. ANT. *boding well, encouraging, heartening, reassuring.*

omission *n.* exclusion, oversight, exception, deletion, neglected item. ANT. *inclusion, admission.*

omit *v.* leave out, exclude, delete, cut, overlook, erase, edit out, forget, preclude, skip, pass over, expunge, neglect, strike out, ignore. ANT. *include, put in, add to.*

omitted *a.* excluded, left out, deleted, overlooked, erased, precluded, forgotten, passed over, expunged. ANT. *included, put in, added.*

omni all, everywhere, universal.

omnibus *n.* anthology, compilation, collection, collected works, volume, edition. SEE BOOK

OMNIPOTENT *a.* [om NIP uh tent] having unlimited or infinite power. *Many dictators strive to be as omnipotent as God.* SYN. all-powerful, almighty, supreme, unlimited, godlike. ANT. *ineffectual, powerless, weak.* SEE GOD, OMNISCIENT

omnipresent *a.* all-present, pervasive, ubiquitous. SEE GOD

omniscient *a.* all-knowing, all-seeing, god-like. ANT. *ignorant, unseeing, blind, unknowing.* SEE GOD, OMNIPOTENT

on *prep.* **1.** UPON above, touching, in contact with, atop, covering, attached to. **2.** NEAR by, around, beside. **3.** ONWARD forward, ahead. **4.** OPERATING running, going, engaged, working, functioning, powered. ANT. *1. off, away from, detached from. 2. away from, distant from. 3. stop, backwards, behind. 4. off,* *stopped, unpowered.*

on and off *adv.* now and then, intermittently, start and stop.

on and on *adv.* constantly, continuously, neverending, relentless, forever, unremitting.

onanism *a.* masturbation, self-gratification.

on a roll *a.* hot, on one's game, in a groove, cooking, on fire, in a zone, hot-handed, smoking, rolling. ANT. *cold, ice cold, in a rut, in a slump.*

on call *a.* standing by, on alert, accessible, at hand, at one's beck and call, at one's disposal, at the ready.

once *n.* ONE TIME one time only, never again.

once *a.* FORMERLY previously, in the past, at one time, long ago.

once and for all *adv.* finally, decisively, conclusively, positively, at long last.

once, at *adv.* immediately, now, this instant, *pronto, straightaway, forthwith, posthaste, *before you can say Jack Robinson/Bob's your uncle, *lickety-split.

once in awhile *adv.* every now and then, every so often, occasionally, periodically, sometimes, *once every blue moon.

once-over *n.* sizing up, inspection, examination, appraising glance, scrutiny, probe, *the eye, *critical eye, *piercing look.

oncoming *a.* approaching, nearing, looming, impending, onrushing, emerging, bearing down. ANT. *leaving, receding, retreating.*

on duty *a.* on, working, *clocked in, *punched in.

one *a.* **1.** SINGLE individual, solitary. SEE NUMBER **2.** UNITED undivided, complete, whole.

one by one *adv.* in succession, one at a time, individually.

on edge *a.* jittery, anxious, wired, *hyper. ANT. *relaxed, calm.* SEE NERVOUS

one-horse *a.* insignificant, small, *tinhorn, small, *two-bit, limited, *bush, inferior, *small-townish, *piddling. ANT. *significant, of consequence, *big-time.*

one-horse town *n.* whistlestop, one stoplight town, *a U-turn and a mayor, tank town, *podunk, *filling station, *jerk town, *wide place in the road.

one-liner *n.* joke, crack, wisecrack, bon mot, witty remark.

oneness *n.* unity, singleness, togetherness, coalescence.

one-night stand *n.* **1.** ONE-NIGHT SEXUAL AFFAIR tryst, *pickup, *quickie, *wham bam thank you, Ma'am, *roll in the hay, anonymous

sex, liaison, *hump-and-dump. **2.** ENTERTAINMENT BOOKING engagement, one-nighter, *road gig.

ONEROUS *a.* [OHN ur us] burdensome, laborious or oppressive. *We were given the onerous task of mowing all thirty acres.* SYN. burdensome, laborious, oppressive, troublesome, difficult, arduous, formidable, demanding, wearisome. ANT. *easy, effortless, painless, trouble-free.*

one-sided *a.* biased, partial, prejudiced, unfair, narrow-minded, partisan. ANT. *fair-minded, democratic.*

one-track mind *n.* obsession, fixation, passion, preoccupation, fascination, single-mindedness.

one-upmanship *n.* rivaling, bettering, outsmarting, outfoxing, outwitting, outgaming, cutthroat, domination, gamesmanship, resourcefulness, artfulness, finesse, cunning, cageyness, outmaneuvering. ANT. *submission, concession, quitting.*

on guard *a.* defensive, guarded, alert, on one's toes, vigilant, watchful, cautious. ANT. *asleep, oblivious, nonchalant, carefree.*

onion *n.* shallot, scallion, leek, bulb.

on-line *a.* connected, wired, networked, linked, auxiliary, peripheral, plugged in. ANT. *off-line, disconnected, independent.*

onlooker *n.* spectator, eyewitness, bystander, observer.

only *a.* sole, single, lone, solitary.

only *adv.* singly, solely, alone, solitarily.

on paper *adv.* theoretically, hypothetically, in theory, in the abstract.

on purpose *adv.* deliberately, knowingly, intentionally, purposefully, wittingly, consciously, by intent, by design. ANT. *accidently, unwittingly, unintentionally.*

onrush *n.* rush, stampede, *blitz, storm, headlong dash, tidal wave, deluge, flood, avalanche.

onset *n.* **1.** START beginning, outset. **2.** ATTACK assault.

onslaught *n.* attack, rush, charge, assault, invasion, *blitz, offensive, strike, incursion, storming.

on tap *a. Sl.* handy, at hand, in stock, available, at one's fingertips.

on the ball *a. Sl.* *on the stick, *with it, sharp, quick, *on one's toes, ready, alert, *plugged in. ANT. *slow, unprepared, asleep.*

on the blink *a. Sl.* broken, *out of whack, *out of kilter, *on the fritz, *out of commission, in disrepair. ANT. *functioning, in good repair,* *working.*

on the brink *a. Sl.* on the verge, on the edge, at the threshold, at the limit.

on the double *a. Sl.* *double quick, *pronto, *lickety-split, *chop chop.

on the fence *a. Sl.* undecided, neutral, nonpartisan, noncommitted, half-and-half, *torn, divided, *in the middle of the road, impartial. ANT. *one-sided, biased, partial, liberal, conservative, left, right.*

on the house *a. Sl.* gratis, free, *on one, no charge, *freebie, compliments of the house.

on the level *a. Sl.* *on the up-and-up, *for real, legitimate, square, fair, straight, aboveboard, authentic. ANT. *dishonest, illegitimate, *BS, on the make, *on the prowl, out for.*

on the nose *a. Sl.* bulls-eye, precisely, exactly, *on the money.

on the wagon *a. Sl.* sworn off, sober, *dry, abstinent, abstemious.

on the whole *a. Sl.* for the most part, mostly.

on trial *adv.* under examination, in litigation, before the court, up for investigation.

onus *n.* burden, responsibility, load, weight, duty, task, obligation.

onward *a.* ahead, forward, forth, on beyond, frontward, advancing, along.

oodles *n.* slews, lots, piles, *scads, *zillions. SEE MANY

oomph *n. Sl.* **1.** ENERGY vigor, muscle, power, *elbow grease, exertion. **2.** sex appeal, *it.

ooze *n.* mud, sludge, muck, mire, slime, *goo, *crap.

ooze *v.* exude, flow, seep, percolate, squeeze out, discharge, bleed.

opalescent *a.* irridescent, rainbowlike.

OPAQUE *a.* [o PAKE] impossible to see through or impossible to understand. *The windows in the limo were opaque; nobody could see through them.* SYN. impervious, clouded, murky, misty, blurred, nebulous, filmy, hazy, foggy, nontransparent, obscure, vague, abstruse, unclear. ANT. *transparent, clear, translucent, lucid.*

open *v.* **1.** TO MAKE AN OPENING unlock, unlatch, undo, unseal, unscrew, uncork, loosen, free, untie, breach, broach, tear down, puncture, slit, pierce, rupture. **2.** SPREAD unfold, unfurl, unroll, lay out. **3.** BEGIN commence, start, inaugurate, initiate, launch, *get the ball rolling. ANT. **1.** *close, shut, cover, stop up, seal.* **2.** *fold, roll up, ball up.* **3.** *end, close, finalize.*

open *a.* **1.** UNCLOSED unsealed, accessible, agape, unlocked, unobstructed, ajar, clear, yawning. **2.** EXPOSED uncovered, unprotected, open to view, unenclosed, unconcealed. **3.** SPREAD OUT unfolded, unfurled, unrolled, laid out. **4.** OPEN TO THE PUBLIC accessible, open for business, in operation, ready to serve. **5.** FAIR-MINDED receptive, open-minded, unbiased, unprejudiced. **6.** HONEST OR CANDID frank, sincere, blunt, communicative, revealing, disclosing, intimate, *real. ANT. **1.** *closed, shut, sealed, unaccessible.* **2.** *covered, hidden, enclosed, concealed.* **3.** *closed, out of business.* **4.** *close-minded, narrow-minded, biased.* **5.** *reserved, uncommunicative, secretive.*

open-air *a.* outdoors, outside, alfresco.

open-and-shut *a.* simple, easy, obvious, incontrovertible, cut and dried, guaranteed, clear-cut, beyond argument, indisputable, *in the bag, *sew up, cinched. ANT. *arguable, moot, disputable, complex, convoluted, difficult.*

open-ended *a.* unlimited, undetermined, unrestricted.

opener *n.* **1.** MECHANICAL OPENER key, skeleton key, can opener, corkscrew, drill, punch, gouge, awl, borer, reamer, trepan, jimmy, crowbar, glasscutter, *jaws of life. **2.** OPENING ACT warmup act, supporting act.

open-eyed *a.* **1.** WATCHFUL vigilant, hawk-eyed, eagle-eyed, awake, alert, wary. **2.** WIDE-EYED saucer-eyed, pop-eyed, goggle-eyed, spellbound, enthralled, wonderstruck, thunderstruck, bug-eyed. ANT. **1.** *inattentive, lax, sleepy-eyed, unguarded.* **2.** *sleepy-eyed, droopy-eyed.*

open-handed *a.* generous, charitable, giving, unselfish, munificent, altruistic, beneficent, magnanimous. ANT. *stingy, tightfisted, penny-pinching, cheap.*

openhearted *a.* **1.** CANDID frank, sincere, open, straightforward, honest, ingenuous, genuine, *from the heart, *real. **2.** KINDHEARTED goodhearted, softhearted, benevolent, compassionate, warm, humane, *Christian. ANT. **1.** *aloof, insincere, dishonest.* **2.** *mean, cruel, cold, brutal.*

opening *n.* **1.** HOLE gap, orifice, slot, aperture, chasm, crack, rift, hollow, lacuna, gateway, doorway. **2.** BEGINNING start, commencement, initiation, introduction, inauguration, launch, *kickoff. **3.** VACANCY position, chance, availability. ANT. **1.** *closure, occlusion, blockage, seal.* **2.** *ending, closing, finale.*

opening *a.* beginning, starting, commencing, initiating, introducing, inaugurating, launching, *kicking off. ANT. *closing, ending, finalizing.*

open-minded *a.* receptive, amenable, unbiased, impartial, broad-minded, tolerant, understanding, liberal-minded, sympathetic, reasonable. ANT. *close-minded, narrow-minded, intolerant, dogmatic, bigoted.*

opera *n.* musical, melodrama, libretto, drame lyrique. "When a guy gets stabbed in the back and instead of bleeding, he sings."—Edward Gardner. "A magic scene contrived to please the eyes and the ears at the expense of the understanding."—Lord Chesterfield.
WORD FIND
bass voice, sweet and light: basso cantante
booming bass voice: basso profundo
brilliant and pure vocal tone: bel canto
comical opera: buffa
composition with several arias, duets, choruses: cantata
false high pitch of male: falsetto
highest range of male voice: tenor
highest singing voice: soprano
lead female singer: prima donna, diva
lead male singer: prima uomo
light opera: operetta
long composition of religious theme presented without scenery, costumes: oratorio
long vocal solo piece: aria
low, comical voice: basso buffo
lowest female voice: contralto
lowest male voice: bass
male castrated in seventeenth, eighteenth centuries to retain high singing voice: castrato
manager or director of opera company: impresario
midrange male voice: baritone
repetition of theme sung in succession by two or more: call and answer
short vocal solo: cavatina
SEE MUSIC, SINGING, SONG, VOICE

operable *a.* viable, serviceable, workable, feasible.

operate *v.* **1.** FUNCTION work, perform, act, conduct, manage, carry on, do, run. **2.** PERFORM SURGERY amputate, incise, excise, transplant, cauterize, cut open, explore, bypass, suture, stitch up. SEE OPERATION

operation *n.* **1.** EXERCISE project, action, campaign, maneuver, organization, venture. **2.** RUNNING performance, working, discharge, functioning. **3.** SURGICAL PROCEDURE surgery, incision, excision.
WORD FIND
anesthetic used in localized area: local anesthetic
appendix removal: appendectomy
birth delivery through abdomen: Caesarian section, C-section
blood vessel graft to improve blood flow: bypass
boring hole in skull: trepanning
brain, removal of front portion: lobotomy
brain, spinal cord or nerve surgery: neurosurgery
breast removal: mastectomy
burning away of abnormal tissue: cauterization
bypass: shunt
cornea incisions to improve vision: radial keratotomy
cutting nerve to relieve pain: denervation
cutting surgically: incising
cyst removal: cystectomy
esophagus removal: esophagectomy
exploratory: exploratory surgery
exposure of brain: craniotomy
extreme cold used to destroy abnormal tissue: cryosurgery
fallopian tube closure to prevent pregnancy: tubal ligation
gallbladder removal: cholecystectomy
general pain blocker, unconsciousness inducer: general anesthesia
gum surgery: gingivectomy
inhaled anesthetic agent: ether
joint exploration: arthroscopy
kidney removal: nephrectomy
large intestine removal: colectomy
local anesthetic agent: lidocaine, procaine
lung removal: pneumorectomy
nose enhancement: rhinoplasty
pancreas removal: pancreatectomy
passage of tube into body part: intubation
prostate gland removal: prostatectomy
removal of tissue or organ: excision
replacement of organ: transplant
restoring blood vessel flow: angioplasty
scraping of tissue: curettage
sex change: transsex surgery
sperm-blocking surgery: vasectomy
spleen removal: splenectomy
stitching of wound: suturing
tissue sampling: biopsy
tonsil removal: tonsillectomy
transplant from one body part to another: graft
tumor or mass removal: lumpectomy
uterus removal: hysterectomy
violent reaction to transplanted foreign or-

gan: rejection reaction

operational *a.* functional, fit, viable, workable, in working order, operative, usable.

operative *a.* functioning, operating, running, working.

operator *n.* **1.** TECHNICIAN worker, engineer, driver, handler, processor, keypunch operator, switchboard operator, PBX operator. **2.** SWINDLER *con artist, fraud, *ripoff artist, *flim-flam man, *shark, *hot shot, *snake.

opiate *n.* soporific, narcotic, tranquilizer, sedative, hypnotic, *downer. SEE DRUG, NARCOTIC, OPIUM

opine *v.* think, reckon, of the opinion, believe, imagine, maintain, suppose, assume, guess.

opinion *n.* conviction, belief, notion, thought, conclusion, view, idea, judgment, inference, sentiment, feeling, theory, point of view, impression, conception, finding, estimation. "Truth filtered through the moods, the blood, the disposition of the spectator."—Wendell Phillips.

opinionated *a.* biased, prejudiced, dogmatic, headstrong, obstinate, pigheaded, convinced, close-minded, narrow-minded, one-sided. ANT. *open-minded, broad-minded, tractable, neutral.*

opium *n.* narcotic, opiate, soporific, laudanum, *dope, *downer, *hop, *black snake, *leaf, *tar, *mud, *poppy hops. SEE DRUG, OPIATE

opponent *n.* adversary, enemy, rival, competitor, antagonist, foe, contender, nemesis, *sparring partner. SEE ENEMY

opportune *a.* timely, favorable, advantageous, fortuitous, felicitous, expedient, auspicious, suitable, appropriate, fitting, apropos, apt, seasonable, correct, right. ANT. *inopportune, unfavorable, untimely, unseasonable.*

opportunism *n.* exploitation, expediency, *go-getting, *making hay while the sun shines, *striking while the iron is hot.

opportunist *n.* *gold digger, operator, *go-getter, adventurer, enterpriser.

opportunity *n.* opening, chance, occasion, *window of opportunity, possibility, contingency, *shot, golden opportunity. "A knock on the door."—Anon.

oppose *v.* resist, conflict, repulse, confront, repel, counter, contest, refute, dispute, contradict, disapprove, reject, contravene, go up against. ANT. *support, embrace, advance, advocate, concur.*

opposite *n.* reverse, contrary, inverse, antithesis, counterpart, *other side of the coin, *flipside. ANT. *twin, mirrorimage, duplicate.*

opposite *a.* facing, face to face, vis a vis, inverse, obverse, contrary, contradictory, antithetical, reverse.

opposition *n.* **1.** OPPOSING INDIVIDUAL OR GROUP adversary, opponent, rival, antagonist, competitor. **2.** RESISTANCE repulsion, antagonism, conflict. **3.** OBSTRUCTION hindrance, impediment, restriction, check. ANT. *1. proponent, advocate, partnership, collaboration. 2. attraction, acceptance. 3. opening, clearance, help, aid.*

OPPRESS *v.* [uh PRESS] to force or keep down, especially by abuse of power, to tyrannize. *The dictator tries to oppress the populace through threats of violence.* SYN. subjugate, suppress, persecute, tyrannize, *step on, depress, harass, crush, stifle, burden, saddle, weigh down, dominate, subdue, squelch, *rule by yoke and whip, *rule with an iron fist, *straitjacket into conformity, *jackboot. ANT. *liberate, free, emancipate.*

oppressed *a.* downtrodden, harassed, tormented, persecuted, tyrannized, enslaved, misused, subdued, dominated, saddled, weighed down, burdened, abused. ANT. *liberated, honored, respected.*

OPPRESSION *n.* [uh PRESH un] the keeping or forcing down, especially by abuse of power; tyranny. *The inferior leader rules by oppression.* SYN. tyranny, subjugation, persecution, suppression, enslavement, domination, coercion, torment, martial law, heavy-handedness, *bullied obeisance. ANT. *freedom, liberty, justice.*

oppressive *a.* tyrannical, despotic, domineering, heavy-handed, iron fisted, severe, harsh, burdensome, ruthless, brutal, abusive. ANT. *liberating, just, fair.*

oppressor *n.* tyrant, despot, dictator, persecutor, master, slavedriver, martinet, disciplinarian, authoritarian, bully, tormentor, puppet-master. ANT. *emancipator.*

opprobrious *a.* **1.** DISGRACEFUL shameful, infamous, despicable, dishonorable, hateful. **2.** ABUSIVE offending, insulting, contemptuous, reproachful. ANT. *1. honorable, commendable. 2. complimentary, flattering.*

opprobrium *n.* disgrace, infamy, shame, dishonor, discredit, reproach, stigma. ANT. *honor, regard, esteem.*

oppugn *v.* criticize, attack, oppose, controvert, *shoot down, *blast, *light into, *rake over the coals. ANT. *concur, compliment, agree.*

opt *v.* choose, elect, decide, pick, elect.

optical *a.* visual, ocular.

optician n. optometrist, oculist.

optimal a. best, optimum, favorable, greatest, superlative.

optimism n. hopefulness, rosy outlook, positive attitude, great expectations, enthusiasm, cheerfulness, anticipation, bullishness, buoyancy, confidence, encouragement. ANT. *pessimism, negative outlook, gloomy outlook, cynicism.*

optimist n. idealist, dreamer, Pollyanna, hoper, *ray of sunshine, positive thinker. "One who makes the best of it when he gets the worst of it." — Anon "Someone who tells you to cheer up when things are going his way." — Edward R. Murrow. ANT. *pessimist, defeatist, killjoy, *gloomy Gus.*

optimistic a. hopeful, forward-looking, sanguine, cheerful, upbeat, expectant, assured, sunny, bullish, confident, anticipating, positive, *up, Pollyannish. ANT. *pessimistic, gloomy, cynical, negative.*

optimum a. optimal, greatest, foremost, most, highest, ideal, utmost, champion, consummate, prime, select, superior, tiptop. ANT. *worst, lowest, poorest.*

option n. **1.** CHOICE selection, alternative, decision, substitute, preference, election, predilection. **2.** THE RIGHT TO BUY OR SELL claim, grant, privilege, prerogative, franchise.

optional a. elective, discretionary, voluntary, free, open, volitional. ANT. *obligatory, compulsory, mandatory.*

optometrist n. optician, eye specialist, oculist.

OPULENCE n. [OP yuh lence] wealth or luxury. *The opulence of Beverly Hills was distasteful to them.* SYN. wealth, affluence, riches, prosperity, fortune, luxury, abundance, money, capital, excess, *easy street. ANT. *poverty, squalor, indigence, privation.*

opulent a. rich, wealthy, affluent, prosperous, moneyed, well-to-do, well-off, *loaded, *rolling in dough, *on easy street, *in clover, *high on the hog, abundant. ANT. *poor, penniless, indigent, destitute.*

opus n. composition, score, creation, work, piece, production, volume, title. SEE BOOK

or conj. else, otherwise, alternatively.

oracle n. prophet, seer, soothsayer, augur, diviner, fortune-teller, prognosticator, sage, priest, authority, judge.

oracular a. prophetic, prognostic, Delphic, augural, authoritative, wise, knowing.

oral a. spoken, verbal, said, voiced, verbalized, articulated, vocalized, uttered.

oral sex n. fellatio, cunnilingus, *head, *blow job, *going down on, *muff diving, *mustache ride, *69.

orange a. reddish-yellow, flaming, salmon, fox, tangerine, peach, pumpkin, tarnished sunset, ocher, tiger, apricot, burnt orange, burnt sienna, mandarin, marigold, yellow carmine, Titian, old gold, carrot.

orangutan n. ape, great ape, primate, *man of the forest.

orate v. speak, speechify, lecture, preach, sermonize, pontificate, *get up on one's soapbox, *get up on one's moral soapbox, hold forth, declaim, rhapsodize, moralize, vociferate, bluster, talk, *grandstand.

oration n. speech, address, lecture, talk, discourse, recitation, declamation, recital, disquisition, monologue.

orator n. speaker, lecturer, preacher, reciter, declaimer, sermonizer, pontificator, rhetorician, elocutionist. "One who can make men see with their ears." — Arabian proverb. "One who knows that the brain can absorb only what the seat can endure." — Anon.

oratorical a. rhetorical, eloquent, declamatory, grandiloquent, bombastic, fustian, blustering, *rabble rousing, blatherous, silver-tongued.

oratory n. rhetoric, platform rhetoric, public speaking, declamation, eloquence, grandiloquence, speechifying, preaching, sermonizing, elocution, articulation. "Platitudes plus personality." — Anon.

orb n. sphere, spheroid, globe, ball, heavenly body, celestial body, moon.

orbit n. circuit, revolution, cycle, circle, course, path, ellipse, ring, flight path, gravitational path, *gravitational tether.

orbit v. circle, round, circuit, revolve around, gravitate around, cycle around.

orc n. killer whale, grampus, cetacean, whale.

orchard n. plantation, grove, stand, vineyard, garden.

orchestra n. symphony, ensemble, band, philharmonic, quintet, quartet, combo, group. SEE MUSIC

orchestrate v. arrange, organize, conduct, lead, coordinate, direct, manage, guide, marshal, command, *hold the reins, oversee.

orchestrator n. conductor, director, manager, arranger, organizer, leader, coordinator, commander, overseer, stage manager.

orchid n. epiphyte, flower, *moccasin, *lady's slipper, *puttyroot, *Adam and Eve. SEE FLOWER

ordain v. **1.** TO INVEST WITH AUTHORITY install,

pronounce, appoint, frock, induct, instate, swear in, consecrate. **2.** ARRANGE prepare, put in order. **3.** TO DETERMINE predetermine, preordain, predestine, prearrange, fate, doom.

ordeal *n.* trial, tribulation, trying experience, difficulty, hardship, nightmare, trial by fire, torture, hell, test, strain, trouble, torment, misery, fiasco. ANT. *treat, *walk on the beach, joy, pleasure.*

order *n.* **1.** A COMMAND direction, directive, dictate, demand, mandate, prescription, assignment, bid, enjoinder, fiat, charge. **2.** ARRANGEMENT organization, system, sequence, progression, succession, alignment, grouping, classification. **3.** CONDITION state, disposition, shape, repair. **4.** RESERVATION TO PURCHASE requisition, request, booking, layaway. **5.** SOCIETY OR CLUB guild, fraternity, sorority, fellowship, lodge, council, Masons, Knights of Columbus. ANT. *2. disorder, jumble, mess.*

order *v.* **1.** GIVE A COMMAND direct, dictate, demand, mandate, prescribe, remand, enjoin, assign, bid, charge, instruct, *bark out an order. **2.** RESERVE FOR PURCHASE request, tender, bid, secure, buy, requisition, layaway. **3.** TO ARRANGE organize, systemize, put in sequence, align, group, classify, alphabetize, index, codify. ANT. *1. request, ask for nicely, beg, supplicate. 3. disorganize, disarrange, mess, jumble, mix up, scramble.*

order about *v.* dominate, badger, nag, command, *ride, lord over, henpeck, control, dictate, master, bully, *put under one's thumb. ANT. *supplicate, *cave in, defer.*

ordered *a.* orderly, arranged, well-ordered, systematic, in good form, organized, methodical, shipshape, tidy, neat. ANT. *disordered, in disarray, disorganized, messy.*

orderly *n.* hospital attendant, staff, assistant, nurse's aid.

orderly *a.* **1.** ORGANIZED systematic, arranged, well-ordered, in good form, in apple pie order, methodical, shipshape, neat, tidy, trim, uncluttered. **2.** PEACEFUL behaved, law-abiding, well-mannered, civil. ANT. *1. disorderly, in disarray, disorganized, messy. 2. rowdy, ill-mannered, riotous, uncivil.*

order, out of *a.* **1.** INOPERATIVE broken, out of commission, busted, in disrepair, *on the fritz, *shot, *out of whack. **2.** INAPPROPRIATE out of place, out of turn, indecorous, improper. ANT. *1. functioning, *running like a Swiss watch, *humming. 2. appropriate, proper.*

ordinance *n.* order, command, decree, law, rule, edict, injunction, regulation, fiat, sanction, prescription.

ordinarily *a.* usually, normally, as a rule, most of the time, customarily, generally, by and large, regularly, routinely. ANT. *rarely, seldom, infrequently.*

ordinary *a.* **1.** COMMON everyday, usual, commonplace, conventional, typical, average, normal, medial, routine, customary, general. **2.** MEDIOCRE run of the mill, so-so, nothing to write home about, banal, humdrum, pedestrian, plain, household, prosaic, bourgeois, undistinguished, garden-variety. ANT. *1. uncommon, unconventional, unusual, out of the ordinary. 2. distinguished, exceptional, extraordinary, significant.*

ordinary, out of the *a.* unusual, uncommon, strange, bizarre, odd, exceptional, off the beaten track, unheard of, incredible, wonderful, unique, one of a kind. ANT. *ordinary, normal, typical, *par for the course.*

ordination *n.* ordainment, holy orders.

ordnance *n.* artillery, weapons, armor, guns, bombs. SEE ARMS, MUNITIONS

ordure *n.* excrement, dung, feces, manure, muck, droppings, guano, cow flop, filth, *crap, *shit.

ore *n.* unrefined earth, rock, metal, iron ore, bauxite, lodestone, magnetite, pyrite, tinstone, zincite.

oread *n.* nymph, fairy, mountain nymph.

organ *n.* **1.** MUSICAL INSTRUMENT keyboard, synthesizer, pipe organ, melodeon, reed organ, calliope, harmonium, barrel organ, hurdy-gurdy, accordion. SEE MUSICAL INSTRUMENT **2.** PUBLICATION journal, newsletter, newspaper, periodical, communique, vehicle, mouthpiece, bulletin. **3.** LIVING COMPONENT part, member, element, heart, lungs, brain, liver, kidneys, bladder, gallbladder, pancreas, large intestine, small intestine, appendix, stomach, uterus.

organic *a.* **1.** LIVING alive, animate, biological. **2.** NATURAL nonchemical, untouched by man. **3.** INHERENT intrinsic, innate, native, natural. ANT. *1. inanimate, inorganic, mineral. 2. unnatural, man-made, synthetic.*

organism *n.* life-form, being, creature, animal, plant, cell.

organization *n.* **1.** A UNITED GROUP association, corporation, federation, syndication, union, alliance, company, league, institute, club, guild, corps, confederation, sorority, fraternity, cartel, brotherhood, sisterhood, coalition, affiliation, network, consortium, team. SEE ORDER **2.** ARRANGEMENT order, systemization, classification, coordination, ordering, construction, assembling, institution, disposition, standardization. SEE ORDER

organization man n. *corporate clone, *another brick in the wall, *sheep, follower, *corporate disciple.

organize v. **1.** ORDER arrange, systematize, coordinate, methodize, align, collate, *get it together, *get one's ducks in a row, *get one's act together. SEE ORDER **2.** FORM formulate, develop, create, bring together, give rise to, found, originate, establish. ANT. *1. disorder, jumble, scramble, disorganize. 2. disband, dissolve, break up, disorganize, fold.*

organized a. **1.** ORDERED arranged, systematized, coordinated, methodized, aligned, collated, classified, categorized, *ducks in a row, *got one's act together. SEE ORDERED **2.** FORMED developed, created, brought together, founded, originated, established. ANT. *1. disordered, jumbled, scrambled, disorganized. 2. disbanded, dissolved, broken up, disorganized, folded.*

organized crime n. Mafia, Cosa Nostra, mob, underworld, the syndicate, gang, Black Hand.

organized movement n. campaign, drive, crusade, popular front, grassroots movement, lobby, ground swell.

organizer n. coordinator, arranger, developer, creator, originator.

orgasm n. ejaculation, climax, spasm, convulsion, throes, paroxysm, peak, consummation, frenzy, shudder, shiver, quiver, *unfurling waves of pleasure, *melting like butter, *coming, *going over the mountain, *emptying both barrels, *getting off, *getting one's rocks off, *shooting one's wad, *shooting one's goo. SEE LOVE, ORAL SEX, ORGY, PASSION, SEX

orgasmic a. frenzied, abandoned, exhilarated, rapturous, elated, breathless, overcome, blissful, *on cloud nine, *in seventh heaven, flying, *in orbit.

orgiastic a. bacchanalian, Dionysian, debauched, wild, abandoned, wanton, saturnalian, unrestrained, out of control. ANT. *reserved, peaceful, chaste.*

orgy n. debauch, bacchanalia, carousal, saturnalia, menage a trois, threesome, foursome, love fest, *daisy chain, *group grope, *love-in, feast, bash, party, celebration, merrymaking, revelry, *tear, *binge. SEE LOVE, ORAL SEX,

ORGASM, PARTY, PASSION, SEX

Orient n. Far East, Asia, mysterious east, East Indies, Eastern Hemisphere.

orient v. **1.** TAKE ONE'S BEARINGS orientate, situate, align, locate, position, fix, face, turn, get the lay of the land. **2.** FAMILIARIZE adjust, acquaint, adapt, acclimate, accustom, reconcile, conform, get used to, habituate, condition.

Oriental a. Eastern, Asian, Far Eastern, Asiatic, Chinese, Japanese, Tai, Korean, Indian.

orientation n. **1.** BEARINGS placement, fixing, locating, position, coordination. **2.** FAMILIARIZATION adjusting, adapting, conforming, acclimating, accommodation, acculturation. **3.** INTRODUCTION initiation, breaking in, indoctrination, reception, *showing the ropes, welcoming.

orifice n. mouth, aperture, vent, opening, hole, lacuna, pore, cavity, slot, crack, gap, hollow.

origin n. **1.** INCEPTION source, root, birth, beginning, genesis, commencement, start, fountain. **2.** PARENTAGE ancestry, lineage, pedigree, extraction, descent, line. ANT. *end, death, closing.*

original n. **1.** PROTOTYPE archetype, model, exemplar, standard, mold, first draft, template. **2.** CHARACTER eccentric, oddball, nonconformist.

original a. **1.** FIRST initial, primary, earliest, fundamental, rudimentary, beginning, starting, opening, introductory. **2.** CREATIVE visionary, imaginative, resourceful, inventive, ingenious. **3.** FRESH OR UNIQUE new, groundbreaking, visionary, unusual, unconventional, novel, *cutting edge, *new wave, *new school, *new age, extraordinary, unorthodox, singular. ANT. *1. last, final, ending, ultimate. 2. banal, unoriginal, pedestrian, imitative, trite. 3. old, old hat, tired, dull, banal, hackneyed.*

originality n. ingenuity, inventiveness, vision, creativity, freshness, creative spark, imagination, novelty, newness, ingeniousness, genius, *blowing fresh wind through a stale art. "Simply a fresh pair of eyes."—Thomas W. Higginson. ANT. *imitation, plagiarism, orthodoxy, unoriginality.*

originally a. initially, first, in the beginning, at the start, *from the word go.

original sin disobedience, fall from grace, eating the apple.

originate v. start, begin, emerge, spring forth, initiate, commence, inaugurate, generate, arise.

origination n. origin, source, birthplace. SEE ORIGIN

originator n. creator, inventor, father, mother, innovator, instigator, *spark, catalyst, architect.

ornament n. decoration, embellishment, adornment, beautification, dressing, accessory, trimming, garnish, garnishment, festoon, bauble, gewgaw, torsade, tassel, trinket, spangle, knickknack, gimcrack, frill, flounce, filigree, tracery, filet, gilding, fleur-de-lis, fretwork, storiation, fluting, tooling, finial, beading, acanthus, palmette, embossing, molding, inlay, relief work, scroll work, checker-work, diamond work, floriation, astragal, swag, mosaic, wainscotting. SEE DECORATION

ornament v. decorate, adorn, dress, garnish, festoon, trim, finish, embellish, beautify.

ornamental a. decorative, garnishing, enhancing, adorning, beautifying.

ornate a. elaborate, showy, flamboyant, florid, aureate, flowery, busy, fussy, fancy, flashy, gaudy, baroque, rococo, arabesque, rich, lush. ANT. stark, plain, simple.

ornery a. mean, nasty, ugly, irritable, feisty, surly, cranky, crabby, short-tempered, *short-fused, testy, cantankerous, grouchy, obstinate, stubborn, cussed, mulish, *full of piss and vinegar, *ornery as an underfed grizzly. ANT. sweet, good-natured, nice, pleasant.

orotund a. **1.** RESOUNDING sonorous, booming, resonant, projecting, stentorian, reverberating, thundering, powerful, mighty, rich. **2.** GRANDIOSE IN SPEECH pompous, bombastic, fustian, bloated, grandiloquent. SEE ORATION, VOICE

orphan n. waif, foundling, stray, motherless child, fatherless child, castaway.

orphanage n. foster home, group home, institution, asylum, refuge.

orphaned a. left motherless, left fatherless, deprived, abandoned, forsaken.

ORTHODOX a. [ORTH uh DOKS] adhering to a particular standard, convention or doctrine, as in religion or politics; approved, recognized. Their religious practices are orthodox; they are not at all unusual. SYN. **1.** ACCEPTED traditional, approved, customary, conventional, sound, standard, established, proper, correct, official, right, recognized. **2.** ULTRACONSERVATIVE OR DOGMATIC strict, straitlaced, purist, puritanical, devout, faithful, fundamental. ANT. **1.** unorthodox, radical, unconventional. **2.** liberal, flexible, open-to-change, radical, unconventional.

orthodoxy n. **1.** BELIEF faith, creed, credo. **2.** CONFORMITY compliance, obedience. **3.** CONSERVATISM ultraconservatism, fundamentalism, puritanism, strictness, inflexibility, rigidness. ANT. **2.** nonconformity, disobedience, noncompliance. **3.** liberalism, flexibility, openmindedness, tolerance.

OSCAR n. Academy award, statuette.

oscillate v. **1.** MOVE BACK AND FORTH swing, alternate, vibrate, pulsate, librate. **2.** BE INDECISIVE vacillate, fluctuate, waver, hem and haw, change one's mind, do an about-face, equivocate, be on the fence, blow hot and cold, shilly-shally. ANT. decide, resolve, choose.

oscillation n. **1.** MOVING BACK AND FORTH swinging, alternating, vibrating, vibration, pulsating, pulsation, librating. **2.** INDECISION vacillation, wavering, hemming and hawing, changing one's mind, equivocating, blowing hot and cold, shilly-shallying, fickleness, fence-sitting. ANT. **2.** decisiveness, settling, resolving.

osmose v. diffuse, dissolve, mix, undergo osmosis.

osmosis n. diffusion, absorption, mixing, comixing, blending, comingling, dissolving.

ossified a. hardened, hard, rigid, stiffened, bony.

ossuary n. urn, receptacle, vault.

OSTENSIBLE a. [uh STEN suh bul] seeming or outwardly apparent but possibly misleading. The Peeping Tom's ostensible motivation was to make money washing windows. SYN. seeming, apparent, professed, outward, evident, manifest, pretended, external, assumed, implied, inferred.

ostentation n. showiness, pretentiousness, exhibitionism, pomp, display, gloss, affectation, flashiness, flamboyance, swank, putting on airs, immodesty, *glitz, foppery, flaunting. ANT. modesty, plainness, inconspicuous, humbleness, restraint, understatement, blending into the woodwork.

OSTENTATIOUS a. [AWS ten TAY shus] showiness, pretentiousness, overly ornate. She is as ostentatious as a peacock. SYN. showy, pretentious, pompous, affected, flashy, flamboyant, swank, immodest, grandiose, ornate, gaudy, glittery, *glitzy, foppish, garish, spotlight-seeking, *showboating. ANT. understated, subtle, modest.

ostracism n. banishment, exclusion, exile, excommunication, ejection, rejection, expulsion, shunning, blackballing, relegation; disgrace. ANT. *inclusion, acceptance, welcoming, embracing.*

OSTRACIZE *v.* [AWS truh SIZE] to banish, bar or shun. *Society tends to ostracize nonconformists.* SYN. banish, bar, shun, exclude, eject, isolate, excommunicate, blackball, relegate, shut out, oust, *give the cold shoulder, cast out, *freeze out, blacklist. ANT. *include, embrace, welcome, accept.*

other *a.* **1.** DIFFERENT dissimilar, distinct, separate, unrelated, disparate, variant. **2.** ADDITIONAL extra, further, supplementary, more, another. ANT. *1. same, alike, similar. 2. fewer, less.*

otherwise *a.* **1.** IN ANOTHER WAY differently. **2.** UNDER DIFFERENT CIRCUMSTANCES elsewise, if not, on the other hand.

otherworldly *a.* alien, extraterrestrial, unearthly, unworldly, ethereal, mystical, transcendent, spiritual, supernatural, out of this world, heavenly.

otiose *a.* **1.** LAZY idle, indolent, slothful, *do-nothing. **2.** USELESS ineffective, futile, worthless, impotent, powerless. ANT. *1. ambitious, active, busy, *go-getting. 2. effective, powerful, useful.*

ottoman *n.* footstool, hassock, divan.

ought *v.* should, is fitting, is natural, behoove.

oust *v.* eject, remove, throw out, expel, banish, depose, dismiss, overthrow, unseat, evict, discharge, *send packing, *show the door, *give the boot, *bounce. ANT. *install, induct, admit.*

ouster *n.* ejection, removal, expulsion, eviction, banishment, dismissal, discharge, overthrow. ANT. *installment, admittance, induction.*

out *a.* **1.** OUTSIDE outdoors. **2.** ABSENT away, elsewhere, gone, not here. **3.** EXTINGUISHED extinct, dead, expired, inoperable, finished, over, done. **4.** OUTMODED obsolete, old-fashioned, passe, out-of-date. **5.** UNCONSCIOUS out cold, *out like a light, *down for the count, comatose, anesthetized. ANT. *1. indoors, inside. 2. in, here, present. 3. alive, functioning, living and breathing. 4. in, *cutting edge, newfangled, modern. 5. conscious, alert, awake.*

out *n.* alibi, escape, excuse, explanation, loophole, dodge.

out *v. Sl.* unmask, reveal, *bring out of the closet, disclose, bring out into the open, tip off, publicize, announce, unburden oneself, *blow the whistle on, blab, tattle, expose. ANT. *keep secret, keep hush-hush, keep in the closet.*

outage *n.* blackout, brownout, power failure.

out-and-out *a.* outright, complete, thorough, total, utter, absolute, arrant, unmitigated, flagrant, blatant, dyed-in-the-wool, downright.

outback *n.* back country, hinterland, wilderness, wilds, *boonies, *sticks, howling wilderness, desert, barrens, wasteland. SEE DESERT

outbreak *n.* **1.** DISEASE SPREAD epidemic, pandemic, manifestation, contagion. **2.** OUTBURST eruption, flare up, upheaval, uproar. **3.** CIVIL DISCONTENT riot, insurrection, revolt, uprising, mutiny.

outbound *a.* outward bound, outgoing, out flowing, departing, leaving. ANT. *inbound, coming in, incoming, arriving.*

outbuilding *n.* auxiliary building, shed, shack, barn, outhouse.

outburst *n.* eruption, explosion, outbreak, outpouring, flare-up, outcry.

outcast *n.* pariah, exile, castaway, outsider, derelict, untouchable, vagabond, outlaw, orphan, refugee, runaway, *reject.

outcast *a.* driven out, banned, shunned, cast out, rejected, exiled, ostracized.

outclass *v.* surpass, outperform, outshine, outdo, outdistance, better, eclipse, overshadow, outmuscle, dwarf, dominate, *leave in the dust, beat, defeat, rise above, *smoke the competition, outhustle, *leave others swirling in one's wake. SEE OUTDO

out of the closet *a.* out, exposed, revealed, disclosed, out into the open, divulged, brought to light, uncovered, unveiled.

out cold *a.* unconscious, *down for the count, anesthetized. SEE OUT

outcome *n.* result, consequence, aftermath, end, upshot, *payoff, effect, aftermath, wake, repercussion.

outcrop *n.* rock shelf, mantel, protrusion, obtrusion, bedrock, *knuckle of rock.

outcry *n.* clamor, uproar, protest, outburst, exclamation, shout, scream, cry, hue and cry, howl, holler, hullabaloo.

outdated *a.* obsolete, old, antiquated. SEE OLD-FASHIONED

outdistance *v.* outrun, outmuscle, outdo, outclass, surpass, overtake, leave behind, *leave in the dust, *smoke the competition. SEE OUTDO

outdo *v.* outperform, outshine, outdistance, outmuscle, excel, eclipse, dwarf the competition, *leave others swirling in one's wake, dominate, beat, defeat, run circles around, do one better, out-Herod Herod.

outdoor *a.* out-of-doors, outside, open-air, out in the open, alfresco.

outdoorsman *n.* sportsman, woodsman, naturalist, environmentalist, camper, hunter, fisherman, trapper, adventurer.

outer *a.* outside, external, exterior, outlying, peripheral, outward, remote, fringe, extrinsic. ANT. *inner, intrinsic, proximal.*

outermost *a.* outer, outlying, peripheral, outmost, furthest out, remote, fringe. ANT. *innermost.*

outer space *n.* universe, cosmos, space, infinity, heavens, interstellar space, intergalactic space, void, vacuum, firmament, *great beyond, *wild blue yonder, all creation, macrocosm, nebulous void, galactic realm, solar system. "World without end." — Bible. "A great smelting pot." — Chuang-tzu. "The cooling fires of creation." — Anon. "The eternal horizon." — Anon. SEE COMET, GALAXY, MILKY WAY, MOON, PLANET, STAR, SUN, UNIVERSE

outfield *n.* playing field, left field, right field, center field, warning track, *deep, *shallow left, *shallow right. SEE BASEBALL

outfit *n.* rig, gear, kit, trappings, equipment, accoutrements, trousseau, getup, turnout, garb, attire, *togs, duds. SEE CLOTHING, SUIT 2. GROUP company, unit, crew, business, enterprise, battalion, troop, corps, detachment.

outfit *v.* rig, fit out, turn out, equip, provision, furnish, supply, appoint.

outflank *v.* outmaneuver, outfox, outwit, thwart.

outflow *n.* efflux, flow, effluence, effusion, outpouring, outwelling, emanation, gush, stream, spring.

out-front *a.* straight, *on the level, *on the square, honest, up front.

outfox *v.* outwit, outsmart, outguess, *run circles around, outdistance.

outgo *n.* 1. EXPENDITURE expenses, bills, outlay, disbursement, cost. ANT. *income, profit, earnings.*

outgo *v.* outdistance, outhustle, outrun. SEE OUTDO

outgoing *a.* 1. GREGARIOUS sociable, extroverted, friendly, amiable, congenial, affable, convivial, companionable, unreserved. SEE FRIENDLY 2. OUTBOUND departing, leaving. ANT. *1. introverted, reserved, solitary, aloof.*

outgrowth *n.* product, byproduct, offshoot, *spinoff, offspring, result, consequence, up-

shot, aftermath.

outhouse *n.* privy, toilet, latrine, backhouse, outbuilding, *necessary, *crapper.

outing *n.* excursion, trip, expedition, *spin, jaunt, junket, ride, drive, walk, hike, stroll.

outlandish *a.* bizarre, weird, strange, odd, queer, freakish, out of the ordinary, alien, quaint, exotic, wild, peculiar, *far-out. ANT. *ordinary, everyday, usual.*

outlast *v.* outlive, prevail, hold out, endure, stand the test of time, survive, outdistance. SEE OUTDO

outlaw *n.* criminal, felon, *bad guy, desperado, fugitive, brigand, highwayman, crook, robber, bandit, killer, gunman.

outlaw *v.* band, stop, prohibit, bar, proscribe, forbid, make illegal, disallow, restrict, limit. ANT. *legalize, allow.*

outlay *n.* expenditure, expense, disbursement, cost, outgo, charge, payment, price, fee. ANT. *income, gain, profit.*

outlet *n.* exit, opening, passage, port, vent, mouth, spout, egress, release, channel, race, conduit. ANT. *entrance, ingress, intake.*

outline *n.* 1. PROFILE form, configuration, shape, contour, silhouette, figure. 2. SYNOPSIS breakdown, *rundown, plan, draft, framework, rough draft, sketch, *thumbnail sketch.

outline *v.* rough out, sketch, delineate, summarize, draft, abstract, synopsize, frame.

outlive *v.* SEE OUTLAST

outlook *n.* 1. LOOKOUT observation post, observation tower. 2. VIEW vista, panorama, sweep, perspective. 3. ATTITUDE point of view, *mind-set, viewpoint, standpoint, perspective, frame of mind, interpretation. 4. PROSPECT expectation, hope, anticipation, forecast, future, horizon, probability.

outlying *a.* remote, distant, peripheral, frontier, rural, suburban, out-of-the-way, secluded, isolated, outer, backcountry, God-forsaken. ANT. *nearby, neighboring, next-door.*

outmoded *a.* antiquated, obsolete, outdated, old-fashioned, displaced, dated, passé, horse and buggy, old school. ANT. *new, newfangled, *cutting edge.*

output *n.* production, productivity, yield, harvest, quantity, work, efficiency, turnout, product, amount.

outrage *n.* 1. ATROCITY vicious act, violent act, crime, act of savagery, evil, abomination, monstrosity, disgrace, horror, barbarity, wrong. 2. INSULT offense, affront, blow, *slap in the face, indignity, *put down, injury, abuse. **3.** ANGER fury, indignation, wrath, rage, *spitting rage. SEE ANGER

outrage v. enrage, anger, incense, *piss off, infuriate, fill with wrath, madden, *make one's blood boil, provoke, gall, affront, insult, offend. ANT. *pacify, tickle, delight.*

outrageous a. **1.** ATROCIOUS monstrous, vicious, savage, criminal, evil, abominable, disgraceful, inhuman, barbaric, wrong, unspeakable, heinous, wicked. **2.** UNREASONABLE excessive, ridiculous, preposterous, exorbitant, unconscionable, immoderate, uncalled for, unrestrained. ANT. *2. reasonable, within reason, fair, moderate.*

outright a. out-and-out, downright, complete, total, whole, entire, wholesale, unqualified, unmitigated. ANT. *partial.*

outside n. outdoors, exterior, face, facade, front, surface, veneer, shell, covering.

outside a. **1.** EXTERIOR outer, external, surface, extrinsic, superficial. **2.** SLIGHT marginal, slim, remote, unlikely, faint, small. ANT. *1. inside, internal, intrinsic. 2. probable, certain.*

outsider n. stranger, alien, foreigner, interloper, *fifth wheel.

outspoken a. vocal, unreserved, frank, blunt, straightforward, candid, plainspoken, uninhibited, unrestrained, *not backwards about coming forward. ANT. *shy, reticent, reserved, tactful.*

outstanding a. **1.** EXCEPTIONAL extraordinary, superior, distinguished, superb, excellent, standout, great, phenomenal, remarkable, impressive, marvelous, prominent, renowned, noteworthy, sensational, *out of this world. **2.** UNRESOLVED overdue, unpaid, unsettled, due, owing, in arrears. ANT. *1. ordinary, mediocre, so-so, fair, poor. 2. paid, settled.*

outward a. outer, outside, external, exterior, surface, superficial, visible, apparent, evident. ANT. *inward, internal.*

outwardly adv. apparently, evidently, superficially, visibly, ostensibly, to the eye. ANT. *inwardly, secretly.*

outweigh v. surpass, transcend, exceed, dominate, take precedence, overshadow, eclipse, override, *tip the scales, overrule.

outwit v. outsmart, outfox, outthink, beat, *put one over on, *get the better of, outdo, outshine, fool, trick, euchre.

oval a. elliptical, ovoid, oviform, egg-shaped.

ovation n. applause, cheers, clapping, *hand, outburst, acclamation, laudation, tribute, curtain call, encore. ANT. *boos, *Bronx cheer.*

over a. finished, done, completed, closed, terminated, concluded, ended. ANT. *beginning, opening, commencing.*

over adv. above, overhead, aloft, high. ANT. *below, earthward.*

overabundance a. excess, glut, surplus, overflow, overkill, plethora, overage, spate, flood, too much, superfluity. ANT. *shortage, dearth.*

overall a. general, complete, from end to end, blanket, sweeping, comprehensive, long-range.

overbearing a. arrogant, domineering, dictatorial, high and mighty, supercilious, lordly, high-handed, tyrannical, disdainful, pompous, bossy, imperious. ANT. *shy, humble, modest, deferential.*

overblown a. excessive, exaggerated, inflated, puffed up, overdone, overworked, immoderate, disproportionate. ANT. *modest, moderate.*

overcast a. cloudy, foggy, murky, *smoggy, hazy, gray, dreary, gloomy, sunless, leaden. SEE CLOUD, CLOUDY

overcome v. defeat, beat, vanquish, conquer, subdue, *get the better of, triumph over, rise above, win, outlast, survive, weather, prevail over, surmount.

overconfident a. arrogant, cocky, cocksure, swaggering, strutting, boastful, egotistical, pompous, headed for a fall, complacent, smug, *full of oneself. ANT. *insecure, unsure, self-doubting.*

overflow v. spill over, slop over, flood, run over, deluge, drown, swamp, brim, gush, cascade, inundate, engulf.

overhaul v. restore, repair, service, fix, recondition, revamp, rebuild, check, inspect.

overhead n. expenses, costs, outlay, upkeep, disbursement.

overjoyed a. ecstatic, joyous, jubilant, thrilled, happy, elated, euphoric, delirious, *tickled, rapturous. ANT. *depressed, miserable, *bummed out.*

overlook v. **1.** DISREGARD neglect, pass over, ignore, fail to notice, miss, slight, omit, forget. **2.** EXCUSE *look the other way, disregard, *wink at, let go, let ride, make allowances for, condone, ignore. **3.** LOOK DOWN UPON front on, tower above, have a view of.

overly adv. excessively, too, exceedingly, unduly, inordinately, immoderately. ANT. *insufficiently, inadequately.*

overpower v. overcome, beat, crush, overwhelm, subdue, get the upper hand, get the better of, conquer, vanquish, master, *outmuscle, immobilize, dominate. ANT. *give in, *say uncle, surrender.

overrated a. overvalued, overesteemed, overestimated, *blown out of proportion, overpraised, exaggerated, oversold, puffed up, *hyped.

override v. surpass, prevail over, take precedence, overrule, predominate, outweigh, supersede, cancel.

overrule v. rule against, disallow, override, overturn, annul, reverse, countermand, nullify, invalidate.

overrun v. infest, swarm over, invade, spread over, permeate, cover, saturate, inundate, engulf, choke.

oversee v. supervise, manage, watch over, run, look after, direct, operate, boss, govern, rule, regulate, administer.

overshadow v. eclipse, dwarf, tower over, outshine, outclass, outdo, dominate, *stand head and shoulders above, *leave in one's wake, *steal the spotlight/limelight.

oversight n. omission, mistake, negligence, carelessness, inattention, lapse, slip, blunder, slight, slackness.

overstate v. exaggerate, inflate, *blow out of proportion, magnify, embroider, hyperbolize, *hype, embellish, play up. ANT. downplay, understate.

overt a. open, unconcealed, undisguised, obvious, patent, manifest, plain to see, bald, naked, explicit. ANT. covert, undercover, concealed.

overtake v. pass, *leave swirling in one's wake, catch up to, *outdistance, leave in the dust, reach, gain on, *blow one's doors off. ANT. fall behind, lag behind, drop back.

overthrow v. defeat, vanquish, conquer, remove from power, unseat, unhorse, dethrone, depose, overcome, topple, bring down, overpower.

overture n. proposal, offer, introduction, opening, bid, tender, presentation, suggestion, approach.

overturn v. 1. CAPSIZE turn over, knock over, flip, upset, tip, topple, upend. 2. DEFEAT conquer, vanquish, overthrow, overpower.

overview n. survey. SEE REVIEW

overweening a. arrogant, proud, cocky, cocksure, overconfident, presumptuous, haughty, disdainful, overbearing, imperious. ANT. modest, quiet, timid.

overweight a. fat, obese, roly-poly, heavy, corpulent, stout, plump, rotund, blubbery, hefty. ANT. anorexic, skeletal, emaciated.

overwhelm v. 1. BURY flood, drown, inundate, swamp, engulf, crush, smother, overpower, overflow. 2. OVERCOME crush, devastate, overpower, *blow away, stun, *bowl over, floor, paralyze, stagger, *knock off one's feet, dumbfound.

overwhelming a. overpowering, staggering, crushing, devastating, stunning, paralyzing, dumbfounding, irresistible, awe-inspiring.

overwrought a. nervous, excited, agitated, overexcited, *wired, *strung out, *hyper, worked up, in a dither, wound up, riled. ANT. relaxed, calm, tranquil.

owe v. be in debt, be bound, be under obligation, be in arrears, have a debt to pay.

own v. 1. POSSESS have, hold, keep, retain, have the rights to. 2. ADMIT acknowledge, allow, concede, confess, grant, recognize, come clean.

owner n. proprietor, possessor, landlord, holder, titleholder, keeper, holder, deed holder.

P

pace *n.* **1.** STEP gait, walk, run, stride, carriage. **2.** SPEED velocity, clip, rate, momentum, progress.

pace *v.* walk back and forth, *wear a rut in the carpet. SEE WALK

pacify *v.* appease, mollify, quiet, lull, soothe, calm, tranquilize, placate, assuage, cool, soften. ANT. *enrage, agitate, infuriate.*

pack *n.* **1.** PACKAGE parcel, load, bundle, packet, load, knapsack, bale. **2.** BUNCH group, mass, collection, crowd, throng, number, mob, flock, herd.

pack *v.* load, fill, stuff, cram, jam, stow, insert, pile, crowd, compress, ram.

package *n.* pack, parcel, box, carton, container, bundle, bale, receptacle.

packed *a.* full, stuffed, crammed, jammed, compressed, chock-full, chock-a-block, filled, overflowing, *bursting at the seams, wall-to-wall, standing room only. ANT. *empty, vacant.*

packet *n.* parcel, package, bundle, bale, envelope, sheaf.

pact *n.* agreement, compact, covenant, treaty, contract, understanding, alliance, league, arrangement, deal.

pad *n.* **1.** CUSHION pillow, mat, padding, bolster. **2.** WRITING TABLET notepad, notebook, scratch pad, memo pad.

pad *v.* **1.** STROLL saunter. SEE WALK **2.** FILL OUT stretch, expand, protract, elaborate.

paddle *n.* oar, blade, scull, pole.

paddle *v.* row, scull, oar, pole.

pagan *n.* heathen, nonbeliever, infidel, atheist, idolater.

page *n.* attendant, servant, errand-runner, messenger, *gopher.

pageant *n.* exhibition, parade, spectacle, show, extravaganza, display, procession, gala, presentation.

pageantry *n.* exhibition, parade, spectacle, show, extravaganza, display, procession, gala, grandeur, splendor, festivity, glitter, ostentation, pomp.

pain *n.* **1.** PHYSICAL HURT ache, suffering, agony, discomfort, sensation, irritation, torture, torment, soreness, tenderness, smarting, twinge, pang, spasm, throbbing, stabbing, burning, sharp pain, chafing, clamping, cramping, searing pain, stitch. "Nature's way of stopping you from accidentally cooking your own hands on the frying pan." — Anon. **2.** MENTAL ANGUISH distress, anguish, misery,

torment, anxiety, worry, grief, woe, heartache, travail. **3.** *Sl.* PAIN IN THE NECK pest, bother, headache, annoyance, trouble, nuisance.

WORD FIND

PHYSICAL PAIN

Facial expressions: wince, grimace, teeth-gritting, teeth-clamping, snarl of agony, cringe, clamp eyes shut, pout, wounded look in the eyes, face drawn and pinched, pale, blanched, twisted/contorted in pain, brows furrowed deeply

Body Language: writhing, thrashing, stiffening, convulsing, throes, doubling over, squirming, cringing, balling fists, gulping, recoiling, rocking in fetal position

ANT. *ease, comfort, relief.*

pain *v.* hurt, smart, sting, bother, irritate, harm, excruciate, distress, wound, torture, torment, afflict, annoy.

painful *a.* hurtful, agonizing, excruciating, torturous, sore, smarting, distressing, tender, aching, stinging, biting, searing, sharp, uncomfortable, unpleasant, disagreeable, difficult, grievous, trying. ANT. *comfortable, delightful, enjoyable.*

painkiller *n.* analgesic, anesthetic, palliative, anodyne, morphine, opiate. SEE MEDICINE

painstaking *a.* thorough, demanding, exacting, meticulous, careful, precise, fussy, strict, *persnickety, assiduous, conscientious, *going the extra mile. ANT. *slack, negligent, lazy.*

paint *n.* pigment, dye, coloring, tint, oil paint, latex paint, acrylic, enamel, stain, varnish, primer.

paint *v.* coat, color, tint, daub, dye, brush on, stipple, wash, stain, varnish, prime.

painter *n.* artist, portrait artist, watercolorist, old master.

painting *n.* picture, portrait, landscape, depiction, illustration, work of art, composition, masterpiece, watercolor, still life, fresco, mural, canvas, oil. "Silent poetry." — Simonedes. "A poem without words." — Confucius. "The art of protecting flat surfaces from the weather and exposing them to the critic." — Ambrose Bierce. SEE ART

pair *n.* couple, twosome, duo, couplet, matched set, twins, combo, two of a kind.

pair *v.* match, mate, couple, yoke, marry, team.

pal *n.* buddy, chum, friend, *bro, alter ego, sidekick, crony, comrade, companion, amigo, *partner in crime.

palace n. king's residence, castle, mansion, royal home, manor, alcazar, chateau. SEE CASTLE

palatial a. magnificent, luxurious, rich, ornate, majestic, grand, sumptuous, stately, huge, monumental, imposing, noble. ANT. *humble, mean, plain, poor.*

pale v. whiten, blanch, turn white. ANT. *flush, bloom, blush.*

pale a. colorless, blanched, white, bloodless, pallid, wan, cadaverous, ashen, sallow, sickly, lackluster. ANT. *ruddy, rosy, deeply-hued.*

pall n. cloud, smoke, covering, cloak, gloom, shadow, darkness, shroud, black cloth, spirit of depression, spirit of desolation.

pall v. bore, cloy, become tiresome, become dull, satiate, tire, weary, jade.

pallid a. pale, faint, wan, sallow, ashen, anemic, white, ashen, colorless, sickly, pasty. ANT. *glowing, flushed, rosy, ruddy.*

pallor n. paleness, whiteness, colorlessness, wanness, sallowness, pastiness, lack of color. ANT. *glow, ruddiness.*

PALPABLE a. [PAL puh bul] that which can be physically touched or felt, tangible, perceivable. *There is no palpable evidence of life on Mars.* SYN. perceivable, tangible, touchable, physical, solid, real, obvious, evident, visible, conspicuous, discernible, plain. ANT. *imperceptible, spiritual, abstract, invisible.*

palpitate v. flutter, throb, beat, pound, pulsate, quiver, quaver, shake, twitter, pump, hammer.

paltry a. trifling, worthless, measly, insignificant, petty, cheap, slight, piddling, meager, inconsequential, pitiful. ANT. *considerable, significant.*

pamper v. indulge, overindulge, coddle, mollycoddle, spoil, baby, cater to, *wait on hand and foot, *make things cushy for.

pamphlet n. booklet, brochure, circular, leaflet, bill, *flier, book, tract.

PANACEA n. [PAN us SEE uh] cure-all. *Scientists are still looking for a panacea to stop aging.* SYN. cure-all, catholicon, remedy, *fix-all, *magic bullet, elixir, nostrum, magic potion.

PANACHE n. [puh NASH] a dashing or flamboyant style. *The dancer had great panache.* SYN. dashing manner, flamboyance, style, self-confidence, razzle-dazzle, flair, jauntiness, spirit, elan, je ne sais quoi.

pandemonium n. *all hell, disorder, chaos, uproar, turmoil, confusion, bedlam, anarchy, *hullabaloo, tumult, ruckus. ANT. *peace, calm, order.*

pander v. cater to, satisfy, *suck up to, indulge, gratify, attend, *play up to, serve, humor.

panel n. **1.** BOARD sheet, plywood, plank, wall, partition, section, divider. **2.** COMMITTEE council, jury, review board, group, round table, conference, tribunal.

pang n. pain, spasm, twinge, ache, stab, throe, twitch, distress, discomfort, misgiving, anguish.

panhandle v. *bum, cadge, *hit up, scrounge. SEE BEG

panic n. terror, fear, alarm, fright, hysteria, loss of composure, *shakes, frenzy, consternation, *cold sweat, *sweating bullets, *rush of adrenalin. SEE FEAR, FEARFUL

panic v. be overcome with fear, *break out in a cold sweat, become hysterical, become paralyzed with fear, freeze up, become unnerved, *sweat bullets, soil one's drawers, become adrenalized, lose control, *lose it, be filled with a sense of impending doom. ANT. *relax, calm, breathe easy.* SEE FEAR

panorama n. scene, view, picture, landscape, sweep, perspective, vista, range, stretch, spectacle.

panoramic a. sweeping, far-ranging, far-reaching, extensive, bird's-eye, broad, all-encompassing.

pant v. gasp, breathe, puff, blow, wheeze, huff, huff and puff.

pants n. trousers, breeches, pantaloons, jeans, dungarees, slacks, *britches, overalls, *cords, corduroys, *Levis.

WORD FIND
army work pants: fatigues
athletic sweat pants: *sweats
bullfighter's: toreador pants
calf-length, slitted, tight-fitting: capri pants
cowboy leggings: chaps
Indian loinclothlike with broad legs tapering to ankles: dhoti
jockey: jodhpurs
khaki-colored sport pants: chinos
knee-lengths: surfers, *clamdiggers
leather: buckskins
1960s favorites: bell-bottoms, hip huggers
puffy pants gathered at waist and ankles: harem pants
shorts: Bermuda shorts, *cutoffs, *hot pants, lederhosen
skirtlike pants of various lengths: culottes
straight-cut and tight: stovepipe pants

straight-cut, cuffed, bike-riding pants of the 1940s and 1950s: pedal pushers
stretch pants: spandex pants

pantywaist n. sissy, *wimp, *wuss, *wussy, *candy-ass, pansy, *mama's boy, crybaby.

paper n. **1.** SHEET piece, stationery, letterhead, parchment, note paper, vellum, bond, onion skin, construction paper. **2.** DOCUMENT certificate, instrument, title, credentials, affidavit, deed, contract, charter, license, warrant. **3.** SEE NEWSPAPER **4.** ESSAY dissertation, thesis, composition, article, treatise, report, monograph, study.

par n. average, standard, norm, usual, equal footing, mean, parity, equality.

parable n. story, allegory, morality play, fable, tale.

parade n. procession, march, train, cavalcade, promenade, column, pageant, spectacle, autocade, motorcade, exhibition.

paradise n. heaven on earth, heaven, utopia, Shangri-la, *cloud nine, *Eden, bliss, rapture, joy, euphoria.

PARADOX n. [PAR uh DOKS] a contradictory statement that is nevertheless true. *Paradoxically, the more money he made the less happy he grew.* SYN. contradiction, self-contradiction, incongruity, inconsistency, anomaly, enigma, reverse, puzzle.

PARAGON n. [PAR uh gawn] a model of excellence. *Stephen King is a paragon of the horror fiction genre.* SYN. model, exemplar, standard, ideal, paradigm, archetype, prototype, pattern, role model, cream of the crop, creme de la creme.

parallel n. analogy, correspondence, match, twin, mirror image, counterpart, equal, equivalent, duplicate, kin.

parallel v. mirror, match, equal, equate, agree, correspond, double, imitate, approximate.

parallel a. **1.** SIDE-BY-SIDE aligned, alongside. **2.** SIMILAR correspondent, matching, alike, akin, analogous.

paralyze v. immobilize, incapacitate, disable, cripple, freeze, prostrate, debilitate, numb, anesthetize, *put out of commission.

paramount a. dominant, supreme, main, foremost, chief, leading, outstanding, principal, prime, highest, ranking. ANT. *minor, secondary, least.*

paramour n. lover, mistress, concubine, courtesan, kept woman, suitor, swain, *stud, Don Juan, Casanova, beau, boyfriend, gigolo.

parapet n. barricade, barrier, breastwork. SEE CASTLE

paraphernalia n. equipment, gear, accoutrements, tackle, stuff, things, apparatus, instruments, rigging, belongings, effects.

paraphrase v. reword, restate, transcribe, translate, rephrase, interpret, rehash, repeat roughly, summarize, abridge.

parasite n. leech, bloodsucker, *freeloader, *sponge, dependant, *moocher.

parcel n. **1.** PACKAGE packet, pack, bundle, box, carton, bale. **2.** PLOT OF LAND tract, acreage, lot, division.

parcel v. apportion, dole, divide, mete, allot, distribute, *divvy up.

parched a. arid, dry, dried up, *dry as a bone, *dry as a fossil, roasted, dehydrated, withered, wilted, scorched, evaporated, desiccated, baked. ANT. *wet, watery, waterlogged, saturated.*

pardon n. forgiveness, clemency, amnesty, reprieve, release, grace, excusal, acquittal, lenience, mercy, forbearance, exemption. ANT. *condemnation, damnation, punishment.*

pardon v. forgive, condone, excuse, indulge, *look the other way, *wink at, absolve, overlook, tolerate, acquit, let off, exonerate, exculpate. ANT. *punish, condemn, damn.*

pare v. trim, peel, skin, clip, crop, cut down, cut back, decrease, slash, curtail. ANT. *increase.*

parent n. mother, father, nurturer, sire, creator, folks, progenitor, *old man, *old lady, genitor, procreator, forerunner, predecessor, ancestor, begetter, author, inventor, architect. "The bones on which children cut their teeth."—Peter Ustinov. SEE FATHER, MOTHER

pariah n. outcast, *reject, castaway, exile, refugee, Ishmael, expatriate, undesirable, leper, untouchable.

parish n. parishioners, congregation, churchgoers, fold, assembly, flock, brethren, archdiocese, diocese, church, district.

parity n. equality, equivalence, balance, sameness, evenness, par, likeness, symmetry, uniformity, affinity. ANT. *inequality, disparity.*

park n. common, green, village green, promenade, garden, square, playground, grounds, quad, plaza.

parlance n. language, idiom, lingo, speech, tongue, vernacular, talk, wording, ideolect.

parliament n. legislature, congress, assembly, House of Lords, House of Commons.

parlor n. living room, sitting room, front room, drawing room, salon.

PAROCHIAL a. [puh ROH kee ul] limited in scope, narrow, provincial. *She had a parochial perspective and cared little about the larger* *view.* SYN. limited, narrow, provincial, restricted, local, regional, small-town, insular, myopic, prejudiced. ANT. *worldly, national, international, broad.*

PARODY *n.* [PAR uh dee] a satirical or humorous imitation of a literary or musical work. *The canine sex magazine, Playdog, was a parody of Playboy.* SYN. imitation, lampoon, takeoff, mockery, satire, spoof, *send-up, burlesque, mimicry, travesty.

parody *v.* imitate, mock, mimic, ape, lampoon, caricature, satirize, ridicule, *take off on, send up, burlesque.

paroxysm *n.* convulsion, spasm, outburst, seizure, attack, flareup, fit, eruption, throe, spell.

parrot *v.* echo, repeat, mimic, imitate, copy, ape.

parry *v.* ward off, deflect, turn aside, fend off, defend against, avert, sidestep, dodge, elude.

parsimonious *a.* [PAR suh MOH nee us] miserly, stingy. *The parsimonious old fool recycled everything.* SYN. miserly, stingy, cheap, thrifty, penny-pinching, nickel-squeezing, close, *tightfisted, sparing, close, economical, frugal. ANT. *generous, giving, charitable, free-spending.*

part *n.* **1.** PIECE component, portion, unit, ingredient, constituent, element, section, division, segment, fraction, department. **2.** ROLE function, job, duty, responsibility, involvement. **3.** ACTING ROLE character, bit part, lead, supporting role. ANT. *1. whole, total, aggregate.*

part *v.* **1.** DIVIDE separate, disunite, split, sever, cleave, dissect, break, splay, branch out. **2.** LEAVE go, depart, withdraw, break away, go separate ways, take one's leave, *split.

partake *v.* take part, participate, join in, share in, eat, *have a taste, consume.

partial *a.* **1.** INCOMPLETE limited, fragmentary, deficient, unfinished, halfway. **2.** BIASED prejudiced, one-sided, partisan, discriminatory, unbalanced, unfair, unjust. ANT. *1. complete, whole. 2. fair, impartial, neutral, objective.*

partiality *n.* bias, prejudice, favoritism, preference, one-sidedness, unfairness, leaning, partisanship, predilection, predisposition, weakness, affinity, fondness, liking. ANT. *impartiality, objectivity, fairness.*

partially *adv.* partly, incompletely, somewhat, halfway.

participant *n.* member, contributor, accessory, player, actor, partaker, a party to.

participate *v.* take part, join in, partake, be a party to, contribute, engage in, play, have a hand in. ANT. *forego, beg off.*

particle *n.* bit, speck, piece, grain, fleck, atom, molecule, whit, mote, fragment, dot, trace, iota.

particular *a.* **1.** SPECIFIC exact, precise, single, special, distinct, definite, peculiar, lone, express. **2.** FUSSY demanding, exacting, critical, finicky, picky, *persnickety, hard to please, overparticular. ANT. *1. general, unspecified. 2. unparticular, easy to please, careless.*

particularly *adv.* specifically, especially, notably, distinctly, markedly, exceptionally, explicitly, expressly.

partisan *n.* adherent, party member, supporter, devotee, follower, backer, disciple, champion, stalwart, upholder. ANT. *opponent, independent, nonconformist.*

partisan *a.* partial, biased, prejudiced, one-sided, factional, sectarian, limited, bigoted, myopic, close-minded. ANT. *nonpartisan, unbiased, open-minded, bipartisan.*

partition *n.* divider, wall, barrier, panel, screen, division, separation, demarcation, segregation.

partition *v.* separate, divide, wall off, segregate, screen, subdivide, section, apportion.

partly *adv.* partially, incompletely, somewhat, halfway.

partner *n.* ally, collaborator, colleague, associate, counterpart, accomplice, cohort, confederate, teammate, sidekick, compatriot. SEE FRIEND

party *n.* **1.** CELEBRATION *bash, revelry, gala, festivity, *blowout, get-together, *beer bash, social gathering, soiree, *do, reception, *wingding, fun and games, orgy, shindig, stag party, bachelor party. **2.** GROUP band, bunch, assemblage, assembly, company, crew, troupe. **3.** INDIVIDUAL person, participant, man, woman, human being. **4.** SECT faction, group, side, wing, denomination, alliance, set, bloc, league, confederacy, camp.

pass *n.* **1.** PASSAGE opening, defile, gap, canyon, gap, gorge, trail. **2.** TICKET admission, permit, license, furlough, *free ride. **3.** PROPOSITION advance, flirtation, overture.

pass *v.* **1.** GO BY, MOVE THROUGH go past, proceed, cross, progress, move, leave, depart, advance, flow, course, fly. **2.** OVERTAKE outdistance, leave behind, *leave in one's wake, *blow by, outrun, exceed, surpass, beat. **3.** ELAPSE flow, drag, slip by, race, proceed. **4.** DIE pass on, expire, run out, terminate, *peter out, run its course, fade, dissolve, wane, succumb. **5.** SATISFY meet requirements, pass muster, make the grade, qualify, graduate. **6.** ENACT legislate, endorse, certify, authorize, legalize, ratify, adopt, sanction. **7.** DELIVER hand over, throw, give, transfer, convey. **8.** DECLINE refuse, skip, pass up, overlook, omit. ANT. *1. stop, hold up. 2. lag, fall behind, trail. 5. fail, flunk, *blow it. 6. veto, vote down, defeat. 8. accept, take.*

passable *a.* **1.** TRAVERSABLE crossable, clear, free, unobstructed, navigable, unimpeded, accessible, penetrable. **2.** ACCEPTABLE okay, fair, mediocre, adequate, good enough, satisfactory, tolerable, so-so. ANT. *1. impassable, blocked, impenetrable. 2. unacceptable, intolerable, unsatisfactory.*

passage *n.* **1.** ACCESS path, course, corridor, hall, thoroughfare, way, door, exit, entrance, passageway, route, channel. **2.** EXCERPT section, extract, quotation, portion, selection, sentence, paragraph, verse, page, chapter. **3.** PROGRESSION passing, movement, advance, transit, trip. **4.** ENACTMENT acceptance, adoption, legislation, legalization, ratification. ANT. *3. obstruction, stoppage, blockage. 4. veto, defeat.*

passageway *n.* hall, corridor, alley, aisle, passage, gallery, path, walkway, gangway.

passé *a.* [pas SAY] old-fashioned, out-of-date. *Bell-bottom jeans have been passé since the 1970s.* SYN. old-fashioned, out-of-date, outdated, outmoded, démodé, antiquated, obsolete, stale, old, dated, discredited, unfashionable. ANT. *fashionable, stylish, *chic, *hip.*

passenger *n.* rider, commuter, *fare, traveler.

passion *n.* **1.** INTENSE EMOTION fervor, ardor, intensity, zeal, fire, heat, frenzy, vehemence, enthusiasm, devotion. "The winds necessary to put everything in motion, though they often cause storms."—Bernard de Fontenelle. **2.** ANGER rage, fury, towering rage, *lather, wrath, *dither, hot blood. **3.** LOVE adoration, fondness, affection, amour, infatuation, ardor, lust, desire, sex drive, eroticism, appetite, aching. **4.** INTENSE INTEREST obsession, mania, fixation, fancy, infatuation, liking, craze.

passionate *a.* **1.** IMPASSIONED ardent, fervid, fervent, excited, burning, hot, fiery, heartfelt, eager, emotional, enthusiastic, vehement, vigorous. **2.** LUSTFUL aroused, *turned on, desirous, *hot, *horny, erotic, amorous, libidinous, romantic, sensual. ANT. *apathetic, indifferent, turned off.*

passive *a.* inactive, unresponsive, dispassion-ate, lifeless, apathetic, impassive, unemotional, uninterested, spiritless, submissive, yielding, docile, meek, unassertive. ANT. *active, passionate, responsive.*

past *n.* yesterday, *yesteryear, history, olden days, antiquity, days of old, *good old days, yore, horse and buggy days, dark ages. "The best prophet of the future."—Lord Byron. "The misty black and bottomless pit of time."—Thomas Duffett. "A funeral gone by."—Edmund Gorse. "What's past is prologue."—Shakespeare. ANT. *future, tomorrow, days to come.*

past *a.* gone, bygone, over, forgotten, finished, old, historical, ancient, former, passed, never to return, extinct, dead and buried. ANT. *future, upcoming.*

pastime *n.* hobby, diversion, amusement, recreation, avocation, leisure time activity, sport, fun.

pastor *n.* minister, priest, clergyman, reverend, rector, chaplain, preacher, ecclesiastic.

PASTORAL *a.* [PAS tuh rul] referring to the peace and simplicity of rural life. *Many New Englanders still live a pastoral life.* SYN. rural, country, countrified, peaceful, simple, rustic, bucolic, agrarian, natural, arcadian, idyllic. ANT. *urban, metropolitan, citified, sophisticated.*

pastry *n.* baked good, sweet roll, cake, pie, tart, cream puff, Danish, turnover, croissant, eclair, doughnut.

pat *n.* tap, stroke, slap, touch, rap, caress, poke.

pat *v.* tap, stroke, fondle, slap, touch, rap, caress, poke.

pat *a.* glib, easy, facile.

patch *n.* spot, piece, plot, tract, ground, lot, strip.

patch *v.* repair, fix, mend, cover, recondition, sew up, stitch.

patchwork *n.* jumble, hodgepodge, mixture, miscellany, mishmash, conglomeration, melange, potpourri, pastiche.

patent *a.* [PATE unt] evident, obvious. *A patent lie.* SYN. evident, obvious, plain, conspicuous, apparent, clear, open, blatant, glaring, manifest, overt, flagrant, unconcealed, transparent. ANT. *covert, concealed, subtle.*

paternal *a.* fatherly, fatherlike, patriarchal, protective, solicitous. ANT. *maternal.*

path *n.* **1.** TRAIL walkway, footpath, walk, way, course, track, shortcut, rut, passage. **2.** TRAJECTORY

pathetic *a.* pitiful, piteous, sorrowful, moving, wretched, grievous, deplorable, lamentable, heartbreaking, poignant, miserable, woeful.

pathos n. pity, sadness, poignancy, suffering, heartache, sentiment, bathos.

patience n. endurance, perseverance, *staying power, stamina, stick-to-itiveness, tenacity, diligence, forbearance, tolerance, understanding, *long fuse, *type B behavior, even temper, composure. "Passion tamed." — Lyman Abbott. "The life-long martydom." — Longfellow.

patient n. sick person, case, outpatient, victim, convalescent, invalid, client.

patient a. steady, enduring, persistent, perseverant, tenacious, diligent, long-suffering, tolerant, imperturbable, easygoing, even-tempered, calm, long-fused, composed, resigned, stoical. ANT. impatient, restless, irritable, exasperated, *intolerant.

PATRIARCH n. [PAY tree AHRK] the male head of a family or group. The tribesman consulted their patriarch for guidance. SYN. head of household, chief, father, grandfather, elder, senior, ruler, sage, graybeard, wise man, master.

patrician n. aristocrat, nobleman, *blue blood, lord, *silk stocking

patrician a. aristocratic, highborn, noble, blue-blooded, upper-class, genteel, royal.

patriot n. loyalist, *flag waver, nationalist, statesman, jingoist, chauvinist. "The seed of freedom's tree." — Thomas Campbell. "The dupe of statesmen and the tool of conquerors." — Ambrose Bierce. ANT. traitor, subversive, *turncoat, *Benedict Arnold.

patriotism n. nationalism, *flag-waving, *flag-kissing, allegiance, loyalty, jingoism, chauvinsim. "A lively sense of collective responsibility." — Richard Aldington. "The passion of fools and the most foolish of passions." — George Santayana. "That pernicious sentiment, 'Our country right or wrong.'" — James Russell Lowell. ANT. treason, subversion, *flag-burning, disloyalty.

patron n. **1.** CUSTOMER shopper, client, buyer, subscriber, regular. **2.** SUPPORTER backer, sponsor, booster, benefactor, financer, champion, advocate, *angel.

patronage n. **1.** SUPPORT backing, sponsorship, benefaction, financing, aid, subsidy, advocacy, promotion. **2.** BUSINESS trade, purchasing, buying, shopping, commerce, clients, customers, clientele.

patronize v. do business with, buy at, deal with, trade at, frequent, shop at.

PATRONIZE v. [PAY truh NIZE] to talk down to as an inferior; to condescend. He always patronizes those without college degrees. SYN. *talk down to, talk to as an inferior, indulge, condescend, regard loftily, *look down one's nose at, regard superciliously, humor, suffer, endure. ANT. look up to, flatter, *kiss up to, *brownnose.

patter n. *spiel, pitch, *line, chatter, talk, monologue, recitation.

pattern n. **1.** DESIGN motif, theme, arrangement, composition, figure, scheme, device, decoration, form. **2.** MODEL guide, sample, example, exemplar, standard, prototype, mold, archetype, template.

PAUCITY n. [PAW si tee] scarcity, lack. A paucity of funds motivated him to find work. SYN. scarcity, lack, dearth, shortage, deficiency, insufficiency, absence, sparsity, rarity. ANT. wealth, surplus, excess, glut.

paunch n. potbelly, *beer belly, *beer gut, *spare tire, *middle-aged spread, *bay window, stomach, *blubbergut, bulge. ANT. washboard stomach.

pauper n. poor person, *down-and-outer, homeless person, indigent, beggar, hobo, tramp, *bum, debtor, *panhandler, *street person. ANT. millionaire.

pause n. break, stop, rest, time out, beat, delay, wait, gap, suspension, respite, halt, cessation. ANT. continuation.

pause v. break, stop, rest, take time out, delay, wait, suspend, halt, cease, take a breather. ANT. continue, carry on, proceed.

pave v. surface, blacktop, resurface, tar, overlay, lay asphalt, macadamize, level, cobble.

pavement n. blacktop, asphalt, concrete, surface, road, tar, cobble, paving stones, macadam.

pavilion n. tent, shelter, gazebo, summerhouse, belvedere.

pawn n. tool, instrument, hostage, puppet, dupe, *stooge, patsy, medium, cat's paw.

pawn v. pledge, give as security, *hock, deposit, mortgage, borrow on, venture, gamble.

pay n. wages, salary, earnings, income, *take-home, profit, remuneration, fee, compensation, commission, cut, percentage.

pay v. **1.** REMIT compensate, disburse, settle, *cough up, *foot the bill, spend, expend, *shell out, *fork over, *pick up the tab, contribute, bankroll, finance, remunerate, recompense. **2.** BE WORTHWHILE be profitable, benefit, profit, serve, be advantageous. **3.** SUFFER FOR *pay the piper, answer, atone, be punished. **4.** GIVE offer, extend.

payment *n.* remittance, installment, fee, expenditure, payout, outlay, remuneration, settlement, defrayal, recompense, sum, restitution.

peace *n.* **1.** HARMONY accord, friendship, concord, friendliness, armistice, truce, treaty, detente, brotherhood, amity, goodwill. "Liberty in tranquility." — Cicero. "War in masquerade." — John Dryden. "A short pause between wars for enemy identification." — Clemens Kirchner. "The white space between the chapters in the history books." — Leonard Levinson. **2.** QUIET stillness, silence, hush. **3.** TRANQUILITY serenity, peacefulness, quiet, placidity, relaxation, contentment. ANT. *1. war, hostilities, conflict. 2. noise, clamor. 3. discontent, agitation, disturbance.*

peaceable *a.* peaceful, friendly, gentle, nonviolent, amicable, conciliatory, peace-loving, irenic, mild, pacific, accommodating, dovish, lamblike, easygoing, agreeable. ANT. *hostile, belligerent, contentious, aggressive.*

peaceful *a.* **1.** HARMONIOUS friendly, pacific, agreeable, peaceable, nonviolent, nonaggressive, conciliatory, accommodating, dovish, easygoing, irenic. **2.** QUIET still, silent, hushed, noiseless, tranquil, serene, placid, undisturbed. ANT. *1. warring, hostile, contentious, belligerent. 2. noisy, clamorous, cacophonous.*

peacemaker *n.* diplomat, pacifist, dove, makepeace, conscientious objector, conciliator, negotiator, mediator, intermediary. ANT. *hawk, warmonger.*

peacock *n.* pea fowl, peahen.

WORD FIND
eyelike spot: ocellus
walk: strut

peak *n.* top, pinnacle, summit, mountaintop, crest, height, roof, tip, ridge, head, climax, zenith, limit, apex, maximum, acme, high point, crown. ANT. *low point, depression, foot.*

peak *v.* crest, climax, *come to a head, culminate, top, reach the zenith, crown. ANT. *bottom out.*

peaked *a.* thin, wan, pale, sickly, gaunt, haggard, emaciated, wizened. ANT. *healthy, robust, hearty.*

peal *n.* ringing, reverberation, thunder, boom, rumble, roar, crack, blast, chime, clang, tintinnabulation, clangor, toll.

peal *v.* resound, ring, reverberate, resonate, sound, clang, chime, toll, knell, bong, tintinnabulate, rumble, thunder.

peasant *n.* farmer, laborer, farmhand, serf, vassal, rustic, provincial, commoner, *hick, *hayseed. ANT. *aristocrat, nobleman.*

pebble *n.* stone, gravel. SEE ROCK

PECCADILLO *n.* [PEK uh DIL oh] a minor fault, sin or offense. *The media has a way of flushing out a politician's every peccadillo.* SYN. minor fault, petty offense, infraction, slip, lapse, misdemeanor, indiscretion, transgression, false step, shortcoming, sin, faux pas. ANT. *capital offense.*

peck *v.* pick, bite, poke, nibble, dig, prick, jab, rap, flick.

peculiar *a.* **1.** UNIQUE distinctive, singular, characteristic, individual, exclusive, special, personal, particular, limited. **2.** ODD queer, strange, weird, offbeat, different, curious, unusual, bizarre, outlandish, quaint, *off-the-wall.

peculiarity *n.* characteristc, singularity, trait, feature, oddity, mark, idiosyncrasy, distinction, quirk.

pecuniary *a.* financial, monetary, fiscal, money.

pedagogic *a.* educational, academic, professorial, teaching, scholastic, instructional, tutorial, pedantic.

PEDANTIC *a.* [puh DAN tik] overly precise or scholarly, nit-picking with facts and rules. *She was meticulously accurate with facts but had little common sense; she was pedantic.* SYN. scholarly, didactic, academic, learned, overprecise, pretentious, pompous, professorial, meticulous, bookish, nit-picking, *hairsplitting.

pedestrian *a.* [puh DES tree un] unimaginative, dull, ordinary. *The story was trite and pedestrian.* SYN. unimaginative, dull, prosaic, ordinary, trite, mediocre, run-of-the-mill, flat, banal, uninspired, uninteresting, mundane, inane. ANT. *imaginative, original, profound, interesting.*

pedigree *n.* family tree, ancestral record, genealogy, descent, lineage, line, bloodline, parentage, stock, roots, dynasty.

peek *v.* peep, spy, glimpse, eye surrepticiously, glance, peer, *have a gander.

peel *v.* pare, skin, husk, strip, scale, exfoliate, decorticate, shuck, shell.

peep *v.* **1.** SEE PEEK **2.** CHEEP chirp, tweet, pip, twit, chirrup. SEE BIRD

Peeping Tom *n.* SEE VOYEUR

peer *n.* equal, fellow, compatriot, compeer, counterpart, equivalent, *bird of a feather.

peer *v.* look closely, squint, focus in on, *eyeball, scrutinize, inspect, peep, stare, gaze, gawk.

peerless *a.* unequaled, unmatched, second to none, incomparable, superior, unparalleled, supreme, best, preeminent, greatest. ANT. *inferior, second-rate, mediocre.*

peeve *v.* irk, annoy, irritate, *bug, bother, aggravate, *rub the wrong way, nettle, vex, gall, *burn one up.

peevish *a.* irritable, touchy, cross, cranky, grouchy, snappish, moody, impatient, cantankerous, waspish, ugly, petulant. ANT. *good-humored, cheerful, easygoing.*

PEJORATIVE *a.* [pi JOR uh tiv] disparaging, negative. *His pejorative remarks upset the teacher.* SYN. disparaging, negative, derogatory, deprecatory, belittling, depreciatory, uncomplimentary, demeaning, degrading. ANT. *complimentary, flattering, favorable.*

pell-mell *adv.* helter-skelter, hastily, carelessly, recklessly, heedlessly, slapdash, hurriedly, abruptly, impetuously, wildly. ANT. *methodically, orderly, thoughtfully.*

pellucid *a.* transparent, limpid, crystal. SEE CLEAR

pelt *n.* skin, hide, coat, fur.

pelt *v.* throw things at, bombard, hurl at, shower, pepper, stone, beat, pound, wallop, belt, pummel, punch, sock, whack, thrash.

pen *n.* **1.** WRITING INSTRUMENT ballpoint, quill, style, fountain pen. "That mighty instrument of little men." — Lord Byron. "Wit's plough." — John Clarke. **2.** ENCLOSURE cage, pound, confine, corral, sty, coop, jail, prison.

penalize *v.* punish, discipline, correct, fine, impose a penalty on, *throw the book at, sentence, amerce, castigate, handicap, put at a disadvantage, disable, hamstring. ANT. *reward.*

penalty *n.* punishment, discipline, correction, fine, retribution, sentence, imprisonment, forfeit, damages, handicap, disadvantage.

penance *n.* repentance, reparation, self-punishment, confession, remorse, retribution, penalty, absolution, atonement, mea culpa.

PENCHANT *n.* [PEN chunt] a strong fondness for something. *She had a penchant for cream cheese and bagels.* SYN. fondness, liking, taste, inclination, partiality, weakness, leaning, affinity, propensity, attraction, bent, predisposition.

pendent *a.* hanging, suspended, dangling.

pending *a.* upcoming, impending, about to happen, imminent, in the offing, forthcoming, on the horizon, coming, approaching, unsettled, unresolved, *up in the air.

pendulous *a.* hanging, suspended, drooping, pendent, dangling.

penetrate *v.* **1.** GO THROUGH pierce, pass into, puncture, prick, bore through, break through, encroach, broach. **2.** SPREAD THROUGH permeate, pervade, diffuse, infiltrate, saturate, fill, infuse, suffuse.

penetrating *a.* **1.** PIERCING sharp, intrusive, cutting, biting, mordant, strong, earsplitting. **2.** DISCERNING acute, sharp, perceptive, keen, astute, sensitive, aware, intelligent, deep. ANT. **1.** *dull, blunt, muted.* **2.** *imperceptive, shallow, superficial.*

penitence *n.* repentance, sorrow, contrition, remorse, regret, penance, compunction, shame, self-reproach, regret.

penis *n.* sexual organ, male organ, genitalia, genitals, member, *peter, *rod, *dick, *pee pee, *wang, *schlong.

PENITENT *a.* [PEN i tunt] sorry, contrite, regretful. *The truly penitent shall be forgiven their misdeeds.* SYN. sorry, sorrowful, contrite, regretful, repentant, remorseful, conscience-stricken, ashamed, compunctious, atoning. ANT. *unrepentant, impenitent, conscienceless.*

penitentiary *n.* jail, federal prison, penal institution, *slammer. SEE PRISON

pen name *n.* pseudonym, non de plume, alias.

pennant *n.* banner, flag, pennon, streamer, banderole, bunting, colors.

penniless *a.* impoverished, destitute, poor, *broke, poverty-stricken, *without a pot to pee in nor a window to throw it out of, bankrupt, indigent, homeless. ANT. *rich, wealthy.*

pension *n.* annuity, retirement benefits, payment, social security, disability income.

PENSIVE *a.* [PEN siv] in deep thought, especially about sad things. *We remained pensive long after the funeral.* SYN. deep in thought, meditative, contemplative, melancholy, withdrawn, ruminative, troubled, wistful, brooding. ANT. *carefree, untroubled.*

pent-up *a.* confined, restrained, curbed, held in check, repressed, suppressed, held-in, bottled-up. ANT. *released, relieved, vented.*

penurious *a.* miserly, stingy, hoarding, frugal, thrifty, penny-pinching, cheap, parsimonious, tightfisted, mean. ANT. *extravagant, wasteful, generous.*

people *n.* **1.** HUMANS human beings, folks, humankind, human race, mankind, man, persons, populace, individuals, Homo sapiens, mortals. **2.** MASSES community, electorate, rank and file, working class, society, citizens. "A many-headed beast." — Alexander Pope. "The vulgar popular cattle." — Robert Buchanan. "A wild beast."—Niccolo Machiavelli.

pep n. energy, vim, vitality, life, zip, vigor, get-up-and-go.

pepper v. shower, rain on, pelt, bombard, sprinkle.

peppy a. lively, energetic, *zippy, snappy, vigorous, spirited, perky. ANT. *sluggish, lethargic, slothful.*

perceive v. **1.** SEE notice, discern, make out, observe, spot, detect, recognize, apprehend, sense, distinguish. **2.** UNDERSTAND comprehend, read, see, grasp, appreciate, conclude, decipher, judge. ANT. *miss, overlook.*

percentage n. portion, part, fraction, share, section, cut.

perceptible a. discernible, noticeable, apparent, visible, observable, detectable, distinguishable, obvious, conspicuous, palpable. ANT. *imperceptible, unapparent, impalpable.*

perception n. awareness, sense, feeling, discernment, apprehension, impression, insight, understanding, comprehension, recognition, cognition.

perceptive a. sensitive, sharp, alert, acute, cognizant, conscious, intelligent, insightful, wise, penetrating, intuitive, *tuned in, *on the ball. ANT. *obtuse, thick, dense, dull.*

perch n. roost, stand, seat, post.

perch v. light, alight, roost, rest, settle, sit, squat, nest.

percolate v. filtrate, filter, seep, strain, leach, drip, exude, ooze.

perdition n. damnation, hell, fire and brimstone, destruction, punishment, ruination, loss of the soul.

PEREMPTORY a. [per EMP tuh ree] final, as of the last word, with no further argument or action. *He made a peremptory order and the meeting was concluded.* SYN. final, absolute, ultimate, decisive, imperative, dictatorial, commanding, irrevocable, incontrovertible, unquestionable, authoritative, obligatory, autocratic. ANT. *wishy-washy, tentative, inconclusive, indecisive.*

PERENNIAL a. [puh REN ee ul] continuous, perpetual, returning again and again. *The Wizard of Oz is a perennial favorite with children.* SYN. continuous, continual, perpetual, everlasting, recurrent, returning, enduring, unfailing, eternal, undying, immortal. ANT. *dying, short-lived, temporary.*

perfect v. finish, polish, smooth, *get the bugs out of, *put finishing touches on, refine, accomplish, achieve, realize, complete, consummate, fulfill, effect, culminate.

perfect a. **1.** FLAWLESS faultless, immaculate, spotless, unblemished, untarnished, superlative, extraordinary, supreme, ideal, exemplary, pure, impeccable, consummate. **2.** COMPLETE whole, intact, finished, realized, utter. **3.** ACCURATE precise, exact, correct, true, right, unerring, letter-perfect, *on target, *dead on. ANT. **1.** *faulty, flawed, imperfect.* **2.** *deficient.* **3.** *inaccurate, imprecise, wrong.*

perfection n. **1.** FLAWLESSNESS excellence, ne plus ultra, precision, idealism, faultlessness, highest form, exacting standard. **2.** DEVELOPMENT achievement, accomplishment, consummation, completion, realization, fulfillment, honing, maturing.

perfectionist n. stickler, nitpicker, fussbudget, quibbler, pedant.

perfidious a. treacherous, traitoress, faithless, unfaithful, disloyal, two-faced, backstabbing, treasonous, double-dealing, dishonorable. ANT. *loyal, faithful.*

perforate v. pierce, puncture, prick, penetrate, punch, slit, bore, cut, make a hole in.

perform v. **1.** DO execute, carry out, fulfill, accomplish, act, complete, satisfy, meet, *pull off, discharge. **2.** ACT put on, take on a role, enact, present, exhibit, *ham it up, depict, portray.

performance n. **1.** EXECUTION carrying out, fulfillment, accomplishment, completion, doing, discharge, realization. **2.** SHOW entertainment, presentation, production, exhibition, spectacle, portrayal, depiction, rendition, characterization.

perfume n. fragrance, essence, scent, cologne, bouquet, emanation, aroma. "Any smell that is used to drown out a worse one."—Elbert Hubbard. "A mist used to shroud our animal heritage."—Anon.

WORD FIND

bag of: sachet

case: pomander

East Indian: patchouli

smoking: incense

sprayer: atomizer

substance used in: musk, ambergris, myrrh, attar, civet, bergamot, castor, orris

SEE ODOR

PERFUNCTORY a. [pur FUNK tuh ree] performed superficially and unenthusiastically, often as part of a routine. *The bank clerk gave me a perfunctory smile.* SYN. routine, unenthusiastic, superficial, disinterested, automatic, blasé, unthinking, apathetic, mechanical, cursory. ANT. *enthusiastic, intense, careful.*

perhaps *adv.* maybe, possibly, conceivably, perchance.

peril *n.* danger, hazard, risk, jeopardy, threat, vulnerability, insecurity, endangerment, pitfall, *sword of Damocles. ANT. *security, safety.*

perilous *a.* dangerous, hazardous, risky, *putting one in jeopardy, threatening, *playing with fire, *playing Russian roulette, *playing with a hair trigger, *treading on thin ice, ticklish, precarious, life-threatening, chancy, *dicey, menacing. ANT. *safe, secure, harmless.*

perimeter *n.* border, periphery, circumference, boundary, limit, outline, skirt, rim, edge. ANT. *center, middle.*

period *n.* time, interval, span, epoch, age, eon, era, days, season, course.

periodic *a.* recurrent, repeating, at intervals, sporadic, every so often, intermittent, regular, cyclical, daily, seasonal, weekly, monthly, annually.

peripatetic *a.* traveling, roving, itinerant, walking, moving, migrant, wandering, nomadic, roaming.

periphery *n.* perimeter, outskirts, border, circumference, boundary, limit, outline, skirt, rim, edge. ANT. *center, middle, core.*

perish *v.* die, expire, pass away, pass on, *croak, *bite the dust, *buy the farm, *kick the bucket, be destroyed, be killed, meet death, vanish, disappear. ANT. *survive, thrive.* SEE DIE

perishable *a.* liable to spoil, liable to rot, short-lived. ANT. *nonperishable, inorganic.*

PERJURY *n.* [PUR jur ee] lying while under oath in a court of law. *He committed perjury on the witness stand.* SYN. lying, dishonesty, false testimony, deception, falsification, bearing false witness, untruthfulness, prevarication.

perky *a.* lively, jaunty, spirited, energetic, vigorous, vivacious, animated, dynamic, cheerful, lighthearted.

permanent *a.* fixed, lasting, eternal, everlasting, endless, long-lived, perennial, immortal, perpetual, constant, stable, unchangeable, immutable, durable. ANT. *temporary, impermanent, short-lived.*

permeate *v.* [PUR mee ATE] to penetrate and spread throughout. *Her perfume permeated the room.* SYN. penetrate, pervade, spread throughout, saturate, imbue, diffuse, overrun, fill, osmose, suffuse, choke. ANT. dissipate.

permissible *a.* permitted, allowed, okay, legal, lawful, authorized, acceptable, approved, sanctioned, proper, *kosher.

permission *n.* authorization, okay, say-so, consent, nod, go-ahead, license, permit, allowance, approval, sanction, endorsement, liberty. ANT. *prohibition, denial, refusal, proscription.*

permissive *a.* lenient, indulgent, soft, easy, lax, liberal, accommodating, agreeable, obliging. ANT. *strict, restrictive.*

permit *n.* license, permission slip. SEE PERMISSION

permit *v.* allow, authorize, license, consent, sanction, let, endorse, tolerate, entitle, grant, give the go-ahead, *okay. ANT. *prohibit, refuse, deny, ban.*

PERNICIOUS *a.* [pur NISH us] destructive, deadly, very harmful. *He contracted a pernicious disease.* SYN. destructive, lethal, deadly, fatal, harmful, ruinous, injurious, hurtful, devastating, mortal, noxious, malignant. ANT. *harmless, benign, innocuous.*

perpetrate *v.* do, perform, carry out, commit, transact, *pull off, execute.

perpetual *a.* neverending, everlasting, unending, eternal, continuous, permanent, immortal, nonstop, incessant, ceaseless, ongoing, infinite. ANT. *temporary, short-lived, finite.*

perplex *v.* confuse, puzzle, mix up, *discombobulate, confound, muddle, befuddle, mystify, baffle, bewilder, dumbfound. ANT. *clarify, enlighten, *show the light.*

PERQUISITE *n.* [PUR kwi zit] a special privilege or fringe benefit that comes with a job. *Having unlimited use of the company car was a nice perquisite.* SYN. *perk, fringe benefit, privilege, right, extra, bonus, reward, employee benefit.

persecute *v.* harass, oppress, torment, afflict, victimize, plague, ill treat, crucify, torture, mistreat, abuse, bully, trouble. ANT. *put on a pedestal, honor, *kiss up to, serve.

perseverance *n.* *stick-to-itiveness, persistence, tenacity, steadfastness, grit, resolve, doggedness, diligence, dedication, stamina, drive, backbone. "The eternal try-angle." — Anon. "The mother of good luck." — Ben Franklin. "Patience concentrated." — Thomas Carlyle. "The greatest of all teachers." — Arabian proverb. ANT. *lack of resolve.*

persevere *v.* persist, be steadfast, continue, *keep chipping away, *never say die, *never say never, carry on, stick to it, *hang in there, be resolved, *keep plugging, *tough it out, *stay the course, be tenacious, *hammer away. ANT. *give up, quit, admit defeat.*

persist v. PERSEVERE continue, carry on, endure, *stick to it, keep up, be steadfast, *hang in there, survive. ANT. *quit, give up, die.*

persistent a. persevering, determined, dogged, tenacious, unrelenting, steadfast, resolute, diligent, untiring, stalwart, stubborn, sustained, incessant. ANT. *quitting, irresolute.*

personage n. VIP, notable, *big shot, somebody, celebrity, dignitary, public figure, star, luminary, *bigwig. ANT. *nobody, *zero, unknown.*

personal a. private, individual, own, intimate, familiar, inner, secret, confidential. ANT. *public, outer.*

personality n. **1.** CHARACTER temperament, disposition, traits, makeup, identity, individuality, self, ego, psyche. "The name we give to our collection of eccentricities." — Anon. "What you are when people are around; character is what you are when everybody goes home." — Anon. **2.** CHARISMA charm, magnetism, attractiveness, *star quality.

personify v. embody, symbolize, incarnate, represent, exemplify, anthropomorphize, humanize, illustrate.

personnel n. staff, employees, crew, workers, members, faculty, work force, labor force.

perspective n. **1.** VISTA panorama, outlook, lookout, prospect, view, aspect. **2.** POINT OF VIEW viewpoint, standpoint, position, angle, outlook, frame of reference, turn of mind, *mind-set.

perspire v. sweat, *break a sweat, glow, secrete, drip, lather, swelter, *sweat bullets.

persuade v. talk into, prevail upon, influence, motivate, induce, cajole, sell on, wear down, urge, *twist one's arm, coax, sway, prompt, brainwash. ANT. *dissuade, talk out of, discourage.*

persuasive a. influential, convincing, compelling, effective, powerful, inducing, enticing, seductive, winning, forceful, swaying. ANT. *ineffective, unconvincing.*

pert a. impudent, forward, bold, insolent, saucy, fresh, brazen, *smart-assed, *wise-ass, cheeky, nervy. ANT. *polite, shy, deferential.*

pertain v. regard, apply, relate, connect, refer, bear upon.

PERTINENT a. [PUR tuh nunt] relevant. *Stick to the subject at hand; your side comments aren't pertinent.* SYN. relevant, germane, material, applicable, fitting, pertaining, con-

nected, related, apt. ANT. *irrelevant, impertinent, immaterial.*

PERTURB v. [pur TURB] to disturb or trouble, to upset greatly. *The teacher grew perturbed with the student's rebellious attitude.* SYN. disturb, trouble, upset, agitate, distress, disconcert, discompose, unsettle, *rattle one's cage, bother. ANT. *calm, pacify, quiet.*

PERUSE v. [puh ROOZ] to read or study carefully, to scrutinize. Also, to read through casually. *She made it a habit to peruse the classifieds each morning.* SYN. scrutinize, study, read, examine, pore over, scan, inspect, review, skim, *flip through.

PERVADE v. [pur VADE] to spread throughout, permeate. *The odor of cooking fish will pervade an entire household.* SYN. spread throughout, permeate, diffuse, saturate, fill up, penetrate, imbue, osmose, disseminate. ANT. *dissipate, dispel.*

PERVASIVE a. [pur VAY siv] spreading throughout, widespread. *The weak economy gave rise to a pervasive disillusionment.* SYN. spreading, widespread, permeating, extensive, far-reaching, broad, general, rampant, epidemic, prevalent.

perverse a. **1.** DEVIANT wrong, aberrant, abnormal, odd, strange, weird, warped, backward, corrupt, wicked, depraved, perverted, immoral, degenerate, evil, bad, nasty. **2.** CONTRARY AND STUBBORN obstinate, intractable, difficult, disobedient, mulish, ornery, cantankerous, wrongheaded, unruly. ANT. **1.** *normal, proper, correct, moral.* **2.** *accommodating, yielding, tractable.*

pervert n. sexual deviant, *sex freak, sex fiend, sadist, masochist, fetishist, pedophile, sodomist, voyeur, *flasher, exhibitionist, *weirdo.

pervert v. corrupt, debase, subvert, warp, degrade, debauch, lead astray; distort, twist, butcher, slant, misconstrue, misuse, misapply.

perverted a. abnormal, deviant, depraved, warped, twisted, distorted, corrupt, immoral, debauched, sick, unnatural. ANT. *normal, healthy, proper.*

pesky a. annoying, irritating, bothersome, troublesome, aggravating, irksome, disturbing, nettlesome, tormenting, obnoxious. ANT. *agreeable, welcome, pleasing.*

pessimism n. negative thinking, negative attitude, gloom, gloom and doom, hopelessness, doubt, cynicism, skepticism, belief in Murphy's Law, *black outlook, despair. "The name that men of weak nerves give to wisdom."—Bernard De Voto. ANT. *optimism, hopefulness, positive outlook.*

pessimist n. prophet of doom, gloomy Gus, defeatist, naysayer, doubter, doubting Thomas, cynic, *killjoy, *worrywart, *wet blanket. "One who is never happy unless he is miserable."—Anon. "One who builds dungeons in the air."—Walter Winchell. "[One who] burns his bridges before he gets to them."—Sidney Ascher. ANT. *optimist, *Pollyanna.*

pest n. annoyance, *pain, *pain in the neck, nuisance, irritant, *headache, bother, gadfly, bore, *thorn in one's side.

pester v. annoy, bother, irritate, plague, *bug, hassle, harass, torment, hound, *drive nuts, *drive up the wall, bedevil, nag, get on one's nerves.

pestilence n. epidemic, pandemic, virus, plague, disease, contagion, infection, visitation, scourge.

pet v. pat, stroke, caress, fondle.

pet a. favorite, beloved, preferred, special, dear.

petite a. small, little, slight, tiny, diminutive, wee, dainty, trim, pint-sized. ANT. *huge, extra large, big.*

petition n. appeal, request, application, solicitation, entreaty, invocation, supplication, prayer.

petition v. appeal, request, ask for, apply for, solicit, entreat, pray for, supplicate.

petrified a. **1.** HARDENED solidified, calcified, mineralized, turned to stone, fossilized. **2.** PARALYZED WITH FEAR terrified, stunned, *scared stiff, transfixed, immobilized, frightened, shocked, stupefied.

petty a. **1.** UNIMPORTANT trivial, insignificant, minor, piddling, frivolous, inconsequential, *two-bit, picayune, trifling. **2.** SMALL-MINDED mean, unreasonable, ungenerous, grudging. ANT. **1.** *important, weighty, consequential.* **2.** *big, broad-minded.*

PETULANT a. [PECH uh lunt] irritable, moody. *The hot weather made her petulant.* SYN. irritable, moody, cranky, ill-tempered, grouchy, crabby, *bitchy, peevish, touchy, snappish, waspish. ANT. *good-humored, good-natured, lighthearted.*

phantom n. apparition, spirit, specter. SEE GHOST

pharmacist n. druggist, apothecary, *chemist.

phase n. **1.** PERIOD stage, time, point. **2.** ASPECT side, level, angle.

phenomenal a. extraordinary, remarkable, outstanding, unusual, exceptional, rare, wondrous, uncommon, astonishing, unbelievable, miraculous, out of this world. ANT. *ordinary, everyday, *ho-hum.*

phenomenon n. wonder, rarity, miracle, spectacle, marvel, sight, sensation, *one in a million, *one for the books, prodigy, happening.

philanderer n. adulterer, *swinger, *slut, flirt, *make-out artist, *wolf, *skirt-chaser, ladies' man, Don Juan.

philanthropic a. charitable, benevolent, giving, humane, humanitarian, altruistic, kind, generous, beneficent, magnanimous. ANT. *selfish, miserly, misanthropic.*

philanthropist n. humanitarian, giver, benefactor, Good Samaritan, donor, contributor, sponsor, booster, financier. "A rich ... old gentleman who has trained himself to grin while his conscience is picking his pocket."—Ambrose Bierce. ANT. *miser, *tightwad, misanthrope.*

PHILANTHROPY n. [fi LAN thruh pee] the giving to charity or doing of good deeds for society. *She will long be remembered for her philanthropy.* SYN. humanitarianism, charity, benefaction, altruism, munificence, generosity, public service, assistance, donation. "The wish to scatter joy and not pain around us."—Ralph Waldo Emerson. "Penance for secret guilt."—Anon. ANT. *selfishness, miserliness, misanthropy.*

philistine n. ignoramus, boor, *yahoo, *lowbrow, barbarian. ANT. *highbrow.*

philosopher n. deep thinker, logician, Aristotle, Plato, savant, sage, wise man/woman, theorist. "One who aspires to explain away all mysteries, to dissolve them into light."—Henry Amiel. "A blind man in a dark room looking for a black cat which isn't there." Lord Bowen.

philosophical a. **1.** DEEPLY THOUGHTFUL meditative, logical, cogitative, pensive, reflective, contemplative, deep, profound, learned, abstract, metaphysical. **2.** CALM AND RATIONAL composed, reasonable, tranquil, unruffled, impassive. ANT. **1.** *shallow-minded, thoughtless.* **2.** *irrational, ruffled.*

philosophy n. knowledge, logic, pursuit of truth, wisdom, deep thought, reason, metaphysics, theory. "Unintelligible answers to insoluble problems."—Franklin Adams. "The purple bullfinch in the lilac tree."—T.S. Eliot. "Common sense in a dress suit."—Oliver Braston. "A route of many roads leading from nowhere to nothing."—Ambrose Bierce.

PHLEGMATIC *a.* [fleg MAT ik] dull, hard to excite, lethargic. *Tired old Fred couldn't be moved to action; he was hopelessly phlegmatic.* SYN. unexcitable, dull, apathetic, indifferent, disinterested, dormant, unemotional, flat, unresponsive, impassive, lifeless, passive. ANT. *excitable, passionate, fervid, responsive.*

phobia *n.* irrational fear, obsessive fear, anxiety, dread, *hang-up, aversion, *thing, neurosis, maladjustment, horror.

WORD FIND

alone, being: eremiophobia
animal skin or fur: doraphobia
animals: zoophobia
blood: hemophobia
blushing: erythrophobia
bridges: gephyrophobia
burial alive: taphephobia
cancer: cancerphobia
cats: ailurophobia
children: pedophobia
cold: psychrophobia
confinement in enclosed space: claustrophobia
crowds: demophobia, agoraphobia
dark: nyctophobia
dead bodies, death: necrophobia
death: thanatophobia, necrophobia
defecation: rhypophobia
depths: bathophobia
dirt: mysophobia
disease: pathophobia
dogs: cynophobia
eating: phagophobia
fire: pyrophobia
flood: antlophobia
foreigners, strangers: xenophobia
germs: microphobia
ghosts: phasmophobia
heights: acrophobia
homosexuals: homophobia
horses: hippophobia
insects: entomophobia
knives: aichmophobia
lice: pediculophobia
marriage: gamophobia
medicine: pharmacophobia
men: androphobia
mice: musophobia
missiles: ballistophobia
money: chrematophobia
monsters: teratophobia
night: nyctophobia
noise: phonophobia, acousticophobia
number 13: triskaidekaphobia

ocean: thalassophobia
old age: gerontophobia
open spaces: agoraphobia
pain: alophobia
poison: toxicophobia
precipices: cremnophobia
responsibility: hypengyophobia
ridicule: catagelophobia
robbers: harpaxophobia
sex: coitophobia, genophobia
sharp objects: aichmophobia
sin, committing: peccatiphobia
sleep: hypnophobia
snakes: ophidiophobia
snow: chionophobia
solitude: autophobia
speaking: lalophobia
spiders: arachneophobia
stars: astrophobia
strangers: xenophobia
sunlight: heliophobia
thunderstorms: astraphobia, brontophobia
touched, being: haptephobia
water: hydrophobia
women: gynophobia
work: ergophobia
SEE NEUROSIS

phony *n.* fake, fraud, counterfeit, sham, forgery, imposter, hoax.

phony *a.* fake, counterfeit, sham, fraudulent, bogus, imitation, spurious, specious. ANT. *real, genuine, authentic.*

photograph *n.* photo, picture, print, still, snapshot, close-up, portrait, blowup, shot, *pix, negative, slide, *Polaroid, glossy, composite, photocopy.

photograph *v.* shoot, take, capture on film, snap, film, tape.

photographer *n.* *shutterbug, paparazzo, cinematographer, photojournalist.

photography *n.* picture-taking, still photography, portraiture, cinematography. "Instantaneous art."—M.F. Agha. "A form of voyeurism."—Joseph Strick.

WORD FIND

border for photo: matte
borderless or faded border photo: vignette
brushup work in lab: airbrush, retouch
chemical solution used in developing: fixer, stop bath
dawn and dusk hours: magic hour
details, bringing out: computer enhancement
dual-image photo: double exposure
enlargement for photo: blowup

enlarges photos: enlarger
exposure, long: time exposure
focus range of image: depth of field
glaring photo imperfection: overexposure
illuminate subject from behind: backlight
lab: darkroom
lens aperture setting: F-stop
lens, effects: filter, anamorphic lens, fisheye,
    long-focus lens, portrait lens, telephoto
    lens, wide angle lens, zoom lens
lens for photographing tiny objects: macro
    lens
light facing camera technique: contre jour
light-measuring device: light meter, pho-
    tometer, exposure meter
microscopic photography: photomicography
opening in camera lens: aperture
photographers, freelance celebrity: papa-
    razzo, paparazzi
photographs well, subject that: photogenic
room: studio, darkroom
sensitivity of film to light: film speed
stand, camera: tripod, high hat
three-dimensional photography: holography
three-dimensional photo: hologram, ana-
    glyph

phrase *n.* expression, figure of speech, clause,
idiom, saying, catchphrase, wording, saying,
motto, slogan.

physical *n.* medical examination, checkup,
workup.

physical *a.* material, tangible, solid, concrete,
substantial, palpable, corporeal, fleshly, mortal. ANT. *spiritual.*

physician *n.* doctor, M.D., general practitioner,
GP, *bones, medic, specialist, surgeon. SEE
DOCTOR

physique *n.* build, anatomy, body, shape, physiognomy, frame, makeup, configuration, mus-
culature.

piano *n.* *ivories, keyboard. SEE MUSICAL INSTRU-
MENT

picayune *a.* trivial, trifling. SEE PETTY

pick *n.* choice, selection, preference, favorite,
prize, elite, cream.

pick *v.* **1.** CHOOSE select, opt for, take, settle
on, single out, cull, favor, prefer. **2.** PLUCK
harvest, collect, reap. ANT. *1. reject, spurn.*

picket *n.* **1.** STAKE pale, paling, post, palisade,
upright. **2.** GUARD lookout, sentinel, sentry,
patrol, watch.

picket *v.* demonstrate, strike, boycott, protest,
sit in, march, rally, *make a stink.

pickle *n.* bind, jam, *between a rock and a hard
place, predicament, *hot water, *sticky situ-

ation, fix, scrape.

picky *a.* fussy, choosy, discriminating, finicky,
hard to please, particular, fastidious, meticulous. ANT. *easy to please, undiscriminating.*

picnic *n.* outing, cookout, barbecue, clambake.

picture *n.* **1.** REPRESENTATION illustration,
painting, drawing, likeness, sketch, draft, image, portrait, photo, photograph. **2.** SEE
MOVIE **3.** EPITOME perfect example, embodiment, model, essence.

picture *v.* imagine, envision, see, call to mind,
conceive of.

picturesque *a.* scenic, idyllic, vivid, striking,
quaint, unique, charming, breathtaking, arresting, colorful, photographic, photogenic.
ANT. *dull, ordinary, *as interesting as a brown
paper bag, nondescript.*

piece *n.* part, portion, component, bit, fragment, segment, fraction, chunk, hunk, slice,
parcel.

pier *n.* wharf, dock, landing, quay, anchorage,
slip, mooring.

pierce *v.* puncture, penetrate, perforate, stick,
cut, bore, stab, slit, incise, run through,
prick.

piercing *a.* **1.** SHRILL loud, earsplitting, deafening, high, blaring, screeching, strident, intense, penetrating. **2.** SHARP, AS A GLANCE
penetrating, intense, scorching, glaring,
acute, boring, mesmerizing, withering. ANT.
1. quiet, low.

piety *n.* religious devotion, faith, devoutness,
religion, belief, loyalty, godliness, holiness,
zeal, reverence. ANT. *irreverence, ungodliness,
unholiness.*

pig *n.* hog, swine, porker, piglet, shoat, sow,
boar.

pigheaded *a.* stubborn, obstinate, headstrong,
bullheaded, mulish, unyielding, intractable.
ANT. *tractable, yielding, flexible.*

pigment *n.* coloring, dye, tint, shade, paint,
stain.

pile *n.* **1.** HEAP mass, load, mound, stack, collection, accumulation, stockpile, quantity,
bulk, bank. **2.** SEE POST

pile *v.* heap, mass, load, stack, stockpile, amass,
bunch, mound, pyramid, hoard.

pilfer *v.* filch, steal, thieve, lift, pocket, appropriate, *walk off with, *palm, *rip off.

pilgrimage *n.* journey, expedition, sojourn,
mission, trip, excursion, *hadj, trek.

pill *n.* capsule, tablet, lozenge, drop, pellet,
dose.

pillage *n.* plundering, plunder, booty, loot,
spoils, looting, stealing, robbery, rapine.

pillage v. plunder, loot, rob, sack, despoil, steal, thieve, maraud, desecrate.

pillar n. **1.** COLUMN post, upright, support, pier, piling, shaft, colonnade, pylon. **2.** LEADER supporter, backbone, mainstay, upholder, *tower of strength.

pillow n. cushion, pad, bolster, head support.

pilot n. navigator, flyer, aviator, helmsman, coxswain, captain, wheelman.

pilot v. navigate, fly, steer, direct, guide, *man the helm, drive control.

pimp n. whoremonger, agent, procurer, panderer, *flesh peddler, madam, *hustler.

pimple n. papule, pustule, *zit, eruption, inflammation, boil, blemish, blackhead, acne.

pin n. **1.** FASTENER safety pin, straight pin, bobby pin, hat pin, catch, needle. **2.** JEWELRY brooch, clasp, breast pin, stud, badge.

pin v. **1.** FASTEN fix, affix, secure, bind, attach. **2.** HOLD DOWN OR BACK restrain, hold fast, immobilize.

pinch n. **1.** TWEAK squeeze, nip, grasp, clamp, cramp, twinge. **2.** TINY AMOUNT *smidgen, *tad, touch, bit. **3.** EMERGENCY crisis, plight, predicament, exigency, jam, pickle.

pinch v. **1.** SQUEEZE compress, clamp, crush, tweak, nip, grasp, cramp, crimp. **2.** Sl. ARREST nab, *collar, catch, apprehend, *bust.

pine v. long for, desire, yearn, want, hunger, thirst, crave, ache for, *carry a torch for.

pinnacle n. peak, summit, top, zenith, crown, apex, crest, height, high point, acme, eminence.

pinpoint v. locate, spot, *get a fix on, *home in on, *zero in on, triangulate, identify.

pioneer n. **1.** FRONTIER PERSON colonist, immigrant, settler, homesteader, squatter, trailblazer, explorer, forerunner, founder. "One who remembers when he could have bought the town for a thousand dollars." — Anon. **2.** DEVELOPER innovator, inventor, father, founder, trailblazer, groundbreaker, trendsetter. "A nail, driven wherever the country demands." — Vladimir Jabotinsky.

pioneer v. found, trailblaze, invent, father, lead, innovate, break new ground.

PIOUS a. [PYE us] devoutly religious, sometimes hypocritically so. *He was always looking down his holier-than-thou nose; he was annoyingly pious.* SYN. devout, devoted, religious, holy, zealous, faithful, reverent, spiritual, righteous, self-righteous, holier-than-thou, sanctimonious, hypocritical, unctuous. ANT. *impious, irreverent, blasphemous.*

pipe n. **1.** CONDUIT tube, pipeline, main, duct, line, conveyor, cylinder, passage, drain. **2.** SMOKING INSTRUMENT corncob pipe, meerchaum, calumet, hookah, water pipe, *bong.

PIQUANT a. [PEE kunt] sharp or stimulating, especially to the taste buds. Also, stimulating to the mind. *The sauce and the conversation were delightfully piquant.* SYN. sharp, stimulating, pungent, biting, flavorful, zesty, spicy, lively, heavily seasoned, peppery, hot, *having a kick, provocative, exciting, racy, interesting, titillating. ANT. *bland, mild, dull, uninteresting, tasteless.*

pique v. **1.** IRRITATE resent, affront, offend, wound, hurt one's feelings, gall, irk, nettle, displease. **2.** AROUSE excite, whet, stimulate, provoke, *turn on.

pirate n. buccaneer, privateer, corsair, freebooter, hijacker, sea robber, sea wolf, algerine.

WORD FIND
famous: Long John Silver, Blackbeard, Captain Kidd
flag: Jolly Roger, skull and crossbones
ship: privateer, brigantine, picaroon

pistol n. revolver, six-shooter, *Saturday night special. SEE GUN

pit n. excavation, hole, abyss, chasm, mine, burrow, cavity, hollow, tomb, grave.

pit v. **1.** GOUGE nick, dent, scratch, pock. **2.** PLAY OFF match, vie, oppose, counter.

pitch n. **1.** INCLINE slope, slant, grade, steepness, cant, tilt. **2.** TONE timbre, key. **3.** SALES PITCH spiel, patter. **4.** THROW delivery, toss, fling, sling, fastball, curve ball, knuckleball, spitball.

pitch v. **1.** THROW deliver, hurl, fling, sling, lob, cast, *smoke one by, *throw smoke, *gun. **2.** PLUNGE HEADLONG dive, dip, fall, drop, toss, topple, lurch, tumble. **3.** ERECT put up, raise.

pitcher n. **1.** JUG container, vessel, cruet, pot, ewer, bottle. **2.** BASEBALL PITCHER hurler, *fireballer, reliever, *closer, ace, *lefty, *southpaw. SEE BASEBALL

pitch in v. help, *chip in, participate, lend a hand, contribute, work.

piteous a. pitiful, pitiable, pathetic, heartbreaking, miserable, sad, wretched, deplorable, grievous, poignant.

pitfall n. trap, snare, booby trap, danger, peril, drawback, stumbling block, hazard, risk, *catch.

pithy a. concise, to the point, brief, succinct, meaningful, pointed, *meaty, tight, focused. ANT. *rambling, wordy, digressive.*

pitiful a. pathetic, piteous, pitiable, miserable,

wretched, sad, heartrending, heartbreaking, sorry, low, deplorable, grievous, lamentable. ANT. *happy, joyful, bright, humorous.*

pitiless *a.* hard, cruel, cold, unfeeling, merciless, uncompassionate, sociopathic, inhumane, inhuman, ruthless, barbarous, savage. ANT. *compassionate, merciful, caring.*

pittance *n.* *chicken feed, *drop in the bucket, *slave wages, insufficiency, modicum, small change, *peanuts. ANT. *wealth, *miser's hoard, bounty.*

pity *n.* **1.** COMPASSION mercy, feeling, sympathy, humanity, brotherly love, understanding, commiseration, tenderness, heart, ruth, softheartedness. "The scavenger of misery." — George Bernard Shaw. **2.** *CRYING SHAME shame, misfortune, crime, sorry situation, *bummer. ANT. *mercilessness, coldness, cruelty, ruthlessness.*

pity *v.* feel sorry for, sympathize, feel compassion for, *bleed for, ache for, commiserate, grieve for, condole, have mercy on.

pivot *n.* hub, turning point, axis, axle, center, fulcrum, swivel.

pivot *v.* turn, twirl, wheel, revolve, swing, rotate, spin, twist, circle.

pivotal *a.* critical, crucial, vital, focal, important, determining, decisive, paramount.

pixie *n.* imp, elf, sprite. SEE FAIRY

PLACATE *v.* [PLAY kate] to pacify or soothe one's anger, appease. *To placate the screaming baby, we gave him a bottle.* SYN. pacify, soothe, appease, quiet, mollify, assuage, propitiate, moderate, conciliate. ANT. *aggravate, exacerbate, intensify, infuriate.*

place *n.* **1.** LOCATION locale, locality, spot, site, point, whereabouts, space, position, *corner of the world, station. **2.** REGION territory, zone, district, neighborhood, area, city, town, village. **3.** RESIDENCE house, dwelling, abode, *pad, home, domicile, apartment, room, habitation. **4.** POSITION standing, rank, pecking order, station, grade, footing. **5.** ROLE function, job, responsibility, affair, duty.

place *v.* **1.** PUT locate, position, situate, lay, plant, fix, set, install, stand. **2.** IDENTIFY recognize, remember, recall, *put one's finger on.

placid *a.* peaceful, tranquil, calm, relaxed, serene, composed, imperturbable, self-possessed, quiet, gentle. ANT. *agitated, highstrung, fiery, turbulent.*

plagiarism *n.* copying, stealing, imitation, lifting, cribbing, borrowing, cheating. "Stealing

a ride on someone else's train of thought." — Russel Curran.

plague *n.* **1.** AFFLICTION scourge, epidemic, pandemic, outbreak, pestilence, contagion, bubonic plague, Black Death, calamity. **2.** ANNOYANCE nuisance, irritant, *thorn in one's side, aggravation, bother, *pain, headache.

plague *v.* annoy, irritate, trouble, bother, harass, torment, hound, vex, irk, disturb.

plain *n.* level land, expanse, grassland, field, meadow, prairie, steppe, tundra, savannah, *land as flat and featureless as a Euclidian plane.

plain *a.* **1.** CLEAR evident, obvious, apparent, visible, transparent, open, unmistakable, distinct. **2.** UNDERSTANDABLE simple, straightforward, clear. **3.** STRAIGHTFORWARD honest, frank, blunt, undisguised, unvarnished, outspoken, forthright, direct. **4.** UNEMBELLISHED unadorned, undecorated, austere, stark, colorless, severe, simple, *no frills, bare, restrained, understated. **5.** HOMELY ugly, unattractive, *not much to look at, *short on looks. ANT. 1. *unapparent, unclear, ambiguous. 2. indecipherable, incomprehensible. 3. disguised, indirect. 4. ostentatious, showy, colorful. 5. beautiful, attractive, pretty.*

PLAINTIVE *a.* [PLANE tiv] expressing sadness. *The lost fawn gave a plaintive cry.* SYN. sad, sorrowful, melancholy, mournful, pathetic, piteous, pitiful, heartrending, wistful, doleful, heartsick. ANT. *happy, cheery, perky.*

plan *n.* scheme, strategy, design, outline, idea, plot, course, agenda, schedule, program, proposal, blueprint, scenario, intention.

plan *v.* **1.** SCHEME design, outline, plot, set agenda, work out, schedule, program, propose, blueprint, organize, draft, project, map out, ready. **2.** INTEND aim, mean, count on, propose.

planet *n.* world, celestial body, heavenly body, planetoid, sphere, globe, Mercury, Venus, Mars, Earth, Saturn, Jupiter, Uranus, Neptune, Pluto. SEE MOON

plank *n.* board, stud, two-by-four, beam.

plant *n.* **1.** VEGETABLE herb, flower, weed, grass, greenery, perennial, annual, shrub, tree, seedling, shoot, cutting. **2.** FACTORY manufactory, mill, works, yard, foundry, assembly line.

plant *v.* sow, seed, set, scatter, implant, start, root, transplant, embed, install.

plastic *a.* flexible, malleable, pliable, pliant, supple, moldable, yielding, resilient. ANT. *hard, unyielding, rigid.*

plate *n.* dish, platter, china, saucer.

plateau *n.* mesa, tableland, highland, upland. SEE MOUNTAIN

platform *n.* **1.** STAGE dais, rostrum, podium, stand, scaffold, soapbox. **2.** PROGRAM policies, beliefs, plan, party line, stance, manifesto.

PLATITUDE *n.* [PLAT i TOOD] a trite or cliched remark, often given as original. *Politicians spewed platitudes to a jaded audience.* SYN. trite remark, cliche, banality, bromide, *chestnut, *saw, *familiar tune, *twice-told tale, *spent horse, *same old same-old, *corn, truism. "A dull saw that everyone borrows but no one sharpens." — Anon.

PLATONIC *a.* [pluh TAWN ik] referring to a love relationship based only on emotion, not sex. *They had a strictly platonic relationship.* SYN. nonphysical, nonsexual, emotional, spiritual, idealistic, celibate. ANT. *physical, sexual, lustful.*

platoon *n.* unit, two squads, group, detachment. SEE ARMY

plaudits *n.* applause, praise, approval, cheers, kudos, acclaim, raves, standing ovation.

plausible *a.* believable, credible, reasonable, likely, probable, tenable, sound, possible, feasible. ANT. *implausible, unlikely, impossible.*

play *n.* **1.** SHOW drama, stage play, production, performance, entertainment, melodrama, musical, comedy, farce, tragedy. **2.** FUN amusement, recreation, entertainment, sport, relaxation, game-playing, diversion, frolic, romping, pastime.

play *v.* **1.** HAVE FUN recreate, romp, amuse oneself, engage in sport, *cut loose, *let down one's hair, clown around, kid around, frolic, cavort. **2.** COMPETE vie, go up against, contend, pit oneself against. **3.** PERFORM portray, take the part of.

playboy *n.* pleasure-seeker, *swinger, stud, partyer, Lothario, Don Juan, Casanova, *skirtchaser, ladies' man, *make-out artist.

player *n.* **1.** COMPETITOR team member, athlete, *jock, contestant, opponent, participant. **2.** ACTOR actress, performer, thespian, trouper, *ham.

playful *a.* frisky, frolicsome, fun, coltish, childish, spirited, lively, jaunty, impish, prankish, mirthful. ANT. *sober, serious, grave.*

plea *n.* **1.** EXCUSE defense, explanation, justification, alibi, apology, argument. **2.** REQUEST appeal, entreaty, begging, petition, solicitation, prayer, supplication.

plead *v.* beg, appeal, implore, beseech, entreat, solicit, pray, supplicate, petition.

pleasant *a.* pleasing, pleasurable, enjoyable, gratifying, agreeable, nice, delightful, good, welcome, likable, friendly, sweet, charming, kindly, amicable, cheering, warm, gracious, good-natured. ANT. *unpleasant, painful, miserable, disagreeable.*

pleasantry *n.* quip, kidding, jest, joke, banter, repartee, crack, bon mot, witticism; polite remark, small talk.

please *v.* **1.** MAKE HAPPY gratify, satisfy, gladden, *tickle, suit, delight, cheer, warm. **2.** CHOOSE want, like, desire, be inclined.

pleasing *a.* pleasurable, gratifying, pleasant, delightful, agreeable, enjoyable, winning, charming, likable, cheering, friendly, sweet, kindly, amiable, warm, gracious, good-natured. ANT. *displeasing, disagreeable, unpleasant.*

pleasure *n.* enjoyment, delight, happiness, contentment, elation, euphoria, amusement, joy, bliss, gratification, good feeling. ANT. *displeasure, pain, misery.*

PLEBIAN, PLEBEIAN *n.* [pluh BEE un] commoner, proletarian, peasant, *plebe, man on the street, woman on the street, *John Q. Public, *Joe Blow.

plebian, plebeian *a.* common, lower-class, vulgar. *He objected to her plebeian lifestyle.* SYN. common, low, ignoble, humble, working-class, proletarian, pedestrian, mean, uncultivated, coarse, vulgar. ANT. *aristocratic, noble, highborn.*

pledge *n.* **1.** PROMISE vow, word of honor, oath, guarantee, contract, assurance, agreement. **2.** SECURITY bond, collateral, guaranty, surety, stake, earnest money.

pledge *v.* promise, vow, give one's word, guarantee, swear, contract, pawn.

plentiful *a.* abundant, bountiful, overflowing, full, *chock-full, profuse, ample, teeming, fat, great, thick, bumper, prolific, swarming, copious, replete. ANT. *scant, scarce, sparse.*

plenty *n.* abundance, *loads, wealth, profusion, lots, bunch, quantity, volume, scores, mountains, overabundance, surplus, plethora, glut, *oodles, whole slew, *miser's hoard. ANT. *shortage, scarcity, dearth.*

PLETHORA *n.* [PLETH ur uh] an overabundance. *The politician made a plethora of promises.* SYN. overabundance, excess, profusion, flood, overflow, deluge, surfeit, overkill, *too much of a good thing, glut. ANT. *shortage, scarcity.*

pliable *a.* pliant, flexible, bendable, malleable,

supple, yielding, plastic, elastic, moldable, impressionable. ANT. *rigid, unyielding, hard.*

plight n. predicament, situation, state of affairs, circumstances, trouble, tribulation, dilemma, *fix, *scrape, *pickle.

plod v. **1.** TRUDGE walk heavily, tramp, slog, drag one's feet, stamp, stomp, move laboriously, lumber. **2.** WORK STEADILY drudge, plug away, grind away, slave, sweat, toil.

plot n. **1.** AREA OF LAND lot, tract, parcel, subdivision, piece, patch, acreage. **2.** SCHEME conspiracy, plan, machination, design, intrigue. **3.** STORY theme, narrative, design, action.

plot v. **1.** SCHEME conspire, plan, design, machinate, intrigue, collude, maneuver, *make backdoor arrangements. **2.** MAP OUT chart, draft, lay out, outline.

plow v. break ground, turn over, till, harrow, furrow, cultivate, hoe, dig up, *rototill.

ploy n. maneuver, device, action, trick, move, play, tactic, gambit, stratagem, subterfuge.

pluck n. courage, fortitude, guts, mettle, spunk, backbone, spine, boldness, *balls, nerve.

pluck v. pick, pull out, yank, jerk, harvest, gather.

plug n. **1.** STOPPER cork, bung. **2.** GOOD WORD blurb, advertisement, mention.

plumb v. fathom, probe, explore, sound, *get to the bottom of, delve, penetrate, investigate.

plumb a. vertical, straight down, upright, perpendicular.

plummet v. plunge, fall, dive, drop, nose-dive, descend, crash, tumble, *rocket earthward. ANT. *ascend, rise, go up.*

plump a. fat, chubby, endomorphic, corpulent, *chunky, rotund, full-figured, stout, obese, zaftig, obese, tubby, moon-faced. ANT. *anorexic, thin, slender.* SEE FAT

plunder n. pillage, robbery, loot, booty, spoils, prize.

plunder v. rob, take, loot, pillage, ransack, appropriate, raid, despoil, sack, rape.

plunge n. drop, fall, dive, descent, nosedive, jump.

plunge v. **1.** DIVE rush, descend, fall, drop, nosedive, plummet, hustle, pitch, swoop. **2.** THROW ONESELF INTO charge, lunge, dash, leap, shoot, surge, pounce, spring, jump headlong. ANT. *1. ascend, rise, go up.*

plunk v. throw down, plop.

plural a. more than one, multiple, numerous, many.

plus n. extra, bonus, asset, advantage, benefit. ANT. *liability, negative.*

plus a. additional, added, extra, supplementary.

plush a. luxurious, rich, lush, opulent, sumptuous, posh, deluxe, elegant. ANT. *stark, austere, plain.*

ply v. work at, practice, engage in, carry on, pursue, follow, employ, use, wield.

poach v. trespass, encroach, take game illegally, steal.

pocket n. **1.** POUCH fob, sack, bag. **2.** HOLLOW opening, hole, cavity.

pocket v. take, filch, steal, nab, lift, pilfer, shoplift, appropriate, *walk off with.

pocketbook n. purse, handbag, wallet, clutch.

podium n. platform, dais, rostrum, stage.

poem n. verse, rhyme, composition, ode, sonnet, lyric, limerick.

WORD FIND

fifteen-line, three stanza with only two rhymes: rondeau

four line: quatrain

heroic narrative: epic

Japanese: haiku

love: madrigal

pastoral or rural theme: idyll

rhyme and meter, without: free verse

rhythm: meter

satirical, witty and short: epigram

study of: prosody

talentless poet: poetaster

two line: couplet

SEE POETRY

poet n. versifier, rhymer, lyricist, bard, poetaster, author. "The painter of the soul." — Isaac D'Israeli. "A nightingale who sits in darkness and sings to cheer its own solitude with sweet sounds." — Perce Bysshe Shelley.

poetic a. romantic, flowery, idyllic, symbolic, metaphoric, musical, melodic, songlike, lyrical, singsong.

poetry n. verse, rhyme, poems, song, composition, balladry. "Vocal painting." — Simonides. "The impish attempt to paint the color of the wind." — Maxwell Bodenheim. "Talking on tiptoe." — George Meredith. "Life distilled." — Gwendolyn Brooks. "The best words in their best order." — Samuel Taylor Coleridge. SEE POEM

POIGNANT a. [POIN yunt] moving or touching, especially in a painful way. *The poignant final scene moved the audience to tears.* SYN. moving, touching, painful, emotional, heartrending, heartbreaking, soulstirring, sad, pitiful, pathetic, agonizing. ANT. *insipid, vapid, flat, emotionless.*

point n. **1.** MARK dot, spot, period. **2.** LOCATION spot, place, position, site. **3.** TIME instant, moment, juncture, stage. **4.** TIP end, top, nib, head, prick, spike. **5.** FOCUS thrust, meaning, idea, core, heart, essence, theme, issue, gist, object. **6.** PURPOSE aim, object, goal, end, use, sense, value. **7.** ARGUMENT fact, idea.

point *v.* direct, aim, train, level, guide, draw a bead on.

pointed *a.* sharp, to the point, piercing, penetrating, incisive, cutting, insinuating, trenchant. ANT. *vague, meaningless, wishy-washy.*

pointless *a.* meaningless, senseless, irrelevant, inconsequential, vain, stupid, nonsensical, purposeless, worthless, inane. ANT. *meaningful, useful, purposeful.*

poise *n.* **1.** BALANCE stability, equilibrium, equipoise. **2.** DIGNITY self-assurance, aplomb, coolness, confidence, sangfroid, serenity, composure, savoir faire, equanimity, presence of mind. "The ability to be ill at ease inconspicuously." — Earl Wilson. "The ability to face the guillotine without losing your head." — Anon. "The art of raising your eyebrows instead of the roof." — Howard Newton. ANT. **1.** *imbalance, instability.* **2.** *insecurity, *loss of cool, panic.*

poison *n.* toxin, deadly chemical, venom, germ, miasma, toxic substance, carcinogen, strychnine, cyanide, arsenic, hemlock, lead, carbon monoxide, caustic soda, mustard gas, nerve gas, nightshade. ANT. *antidote.*

poison *v.* contaminate, infect, taint, envenom, make ill, kill, *slip a mickey, adulterate, pervert, defile.

poisonous *a.* toxic, venomous, virulent, carcinogenic, noxious, deadly, lethal, malignant, pernicious, vitriolic, caustic. ANT. *healthy, beneficial, benign.*

poke *v.* **1.** HIT nudge, prod, push, jab, punch, shove, butt, finger. **2.** DAWDLE loiter, putter, lag, mosey along, drag one's feet.

poker *n.* card game, draw poker, stud poker, strip poker.

WORD FIND

facial expression: deadpan, poker-faced, wooden, stony

sequence, five cards in: straight

show hands: call

stake: pot, ante, chips, kitty

suit, five cards of same: flush, royal flush

suit, four cards of same: four flush

three of a kind and a pair: full house

withdraw: fold

POLARIZE *v.* [POH luh RIZE] to take opposing sides. *Democrats and Republicans quickly polarized over the issue.* SYN. split, oppose,

counter, contradict, take side, conflict, *be on the opposite ends of the spectrum, differ, diverge. ANT. *join forces, ally, confederate, merge, unite.*

pole *n.* post, shaft, staff, rod, standard, stick, mast.

police/policeman/woman *n.* law enforcement, *arm of the law, force, law, *heat, *cops, bobby, *John Law, *fuzz, constable, officer, keeper of the peace, patrolman, highway patrol, state trooper, *badge, sheriff, marshal, deputy. "The thin line that stands between us and the barbarians." — Anon.

WORD FIND

arrest: *collar, *bust, apprehend

baton: billy club, nightstick

book of recorded arrests: blotter

bulletin or criminal alert: APB, all points bulletin

criminal running free: at large

cruiser's rotating roof light: cherry, beacon

defensive spray: pepper spray, Mace

DNA identification technique: DNA fingerprinting

drugs and prostitution squad: vice squad

fingerprinting system: Bertillon system

French: gendarme

informer: *snitch, *fink, *rat, *canary, *stool pigeon

interrogation of criminal: third degree

investigates crime-related deaths: coroner

lie detector: polygraph

London police: Scotland Yard

massive, organized crackdown of crime in one area: sweep

method of operation, criminal's: MO, modus operandi

microphone, carrying a concealed: *wired

military: MP

narcotics officer: *narc

navy ship officer: master-at-arms

networking search for criminal: dragnet, manhunt

paramilitary squad: S.W.A.T., Special Weapons and Tactics

photo of criminal: mug shot

plaster cast taken of object for evidence: moulage

reading of rights, rule: Miranda rule

record of criminal's arrests, convictions: rap sheet

register criminal at jail: book

search criminal's body: frisk

search, permission to: search warrant

section of city covered by one station: precinct

surveillance: stakeout

take law into their own hands: vigilantes

vehicle: cruiser, squad car, prowl car, *paddy wagon, Black Maria

SEE COURT, LAW

policy n. custom, code, course, procedure, *the book, rule, guideline, method, line of action, way, system.

polish n. **1.** SHINE sheen, brilliance, gloss, finish, luster, buff, glaze, varnish. **2.** REFINEMENT cultivation, finish, grace, elegance, poise, savoir faire, suavity. ANT. *1. tarnish, grime. 2. imperfection, awkwardness, coarseness.*

polite a. well-mannered, courteous, gracious, civil, considerate, thoughtful, courtly, behaved, gentlemanly, ladylike, refined, nice, diplomatic. ANT. *rude, discourteous, boorish, ill-mannered.*

politeness a. "One half good nature and the other half good lying." — Mary Little. "Consists in being easy about oneself, and in making everyone about one as easy as one can." — Alexander Pope.

politic a. diplomatic, prudent, tactful, discreet, delicate, shrewd, smooth, judicious. ANT. *tactless, rude, cloddish.*

political a. governmental, civic, civil, bureaucratic, administrative, legislative, executive.

politician n. public servant, office holder, politico, civil servant, statesman, legislator, lawmaker, democrat, republican, congressman, senator, representative, bureaucrat, *baby kisser. "Trustees of the people." — Grover Cleveland. "A dealer in promises." — Gabriel Chevallier. "One who thinks twice before saying nothing." — Anon. "A puppy attempting to follow three children at the same time." — Anon.

WORD FIND

appeals to prejudices of people to win them over: demagogue

attacks opponents, associate who: hatchetman

candidate who already holds office: incumbent

candidate who is unlikely to win: dark horse

conservative party member: Republican

conserver of the past: conservative, mossback

extremist: radical

liberal: democratic

middle-of-the-roader: moderate

older, respected politician: elder statesman

outsider who is resented: carpetbagger

party leader: whip

party, member of neither: independent

progress and reform, advocates: liberal

serves party interests over his/her own: good soldier

skilled, respected politician: statesman

sob story suckers: bleeding heart liberals

southern conservative democrats: boll weevils

veterans: old guard

weakened politician after loss of election: lame duck

SEE CONGRESS, ELECTION, GOVERNMENT, POLITICS

politics n. government, political science, legislature, civics, affairs of state, statesmanship. "War without bloodshed." — Mao Tse-tung. "The diplomatic name for the law of the jungle." — Ely Culbertson. "The moral man's compromise, the swindler's method, and the fool's hope." — John Ciardi.

WORD FIND

ambiguous language used by politicians: doublespeak, weasel words

analyst, observer, political: pundit

appointment, cushy political: political plum

backscratching, reciprocal political: logrolling

breaking the law to make a point, protest: civil disobedience

cause, one who works for a: activist

corruption, profit from: graft

demand of the people to carry out some action: mandate

dissenting group within larger body: faction, splinter group

expert investigative panel: blue-ribbon panel

group with common cause or goal: bloc

hands-off economic policy: laissez-faire

heartland of America, how issue is received in: play in Peoria

hedge or be wishy-washy on issue: waffle

hysterical investigation, finger-pointing: McCarthyism, witch hunt

influence group or attempt to influence vote: lobby

influences politician's vote on issue: lobbyist, pressure group

insults, trading of between politicians: mudslinging, smear campaign

issue used to distract public from more important issue: red herring

local projects that are sometimes wasteful, treasury for: pork barrel

member, supporter of organization, referring

to serious: card carrying, dyed-in-the-wool

minding one's own business internationally: isolationism

negotiating concession: bargaining chip

neutral: nonpartisan

nonmilitary hostility between nations: cold war

opponents, bad guys: black hats

party, dual: bipartisan

party ideology: party line

party line, following: singing from the party hymnal

passing responsibility, burden or blame to someone else: buck passing

pocketbooks, issue that affects voters': bread and butter issue

popular issue jumped on to make politician look good or to help party: bandwagon, political football

popular support for an issue: ground swell, grassroots support

powerless nation that makes threats: paper tiger

project that wastes taxpayers' money: boondoggle

research trip taken by politician: junket, fact-finding trip

speech, argument, persuasion: rhetoric

speech, crowd-rousing: stemwinder

speech, long-winded: filibuster

tactfulness, negotiation, art of: diplomacy

threat of military action: saber-rattling

uproar, controversy: brouhaha

warming of relations between two formerly hostile nations: detente

SEE ELECTION, CONGRESS, GOVERNMENT

poll *n.* survey, sampling, census, canvass, tally.

poll *v.* survey, sample, take a census, canvass, question, tally.

pollutant *n.* contaminant, toxin, toxic waste, hazardous waste, scum, filth, runoff, pollution.

pollute *v.* contaminate, poison, dirty, taint, adulterate, foul, sully, spoil, corrupt, defile.

pollution *n.* contamination, toxic waste, hazardous waste, poison, taint, adulteration, fouling, defilement, sewage, runoff, smog. "The reek that shall inherit the earth."— Anon.

pomp *n.* splendor, show, display, grandeur, spectacle, pageantry, ceremony, ostentation, pomposity. ANT. *simplicity, modesty.*

pompous *a.* pretentious, egotistic, self-important, arrogant, haughty, supercilious, overbearing, condescending, patronizing, inflated, overblown, ostentatious. ANT. *modest, humble, down to earth.*

pond *n.* marsh, bog, lagoon, pool, fish pond. SEE LAKE

ponder *v.* think about, weigh, consider, deliberate, contemplate, meditate, ruminate, reflect, cogitate, evaluate.

ponderous *a.* heavy, bulky, unwieldy, massive, prodigious, awkward, cumbersome, clumsy, laborious. ANT. *handy, lightweight, pocket-sized.*

PONTIFICATE *v.* [pawn TIF i KATE] to preach or lecture, especially in a dogmatic way; sermonize. *He liked to pontificate on the dangers of beer.* SYN. preach, lecture, sermonize, harangue, hold forth, moralize, *get up on one's moral soapbox, admonish, declaim.

pool *n.* **1.** PUDDLE pond, lagoon, spring, swimming hole, reservoir. SEE LAKE **2.** COMBINATION association, collective, trust, consortium, union, collation. **3.** FUNDS *pot, *kitty, bank, reserves.

pool *v.* combine, share, consolidate, merge, ally, join together.

poor *a.* **1.** DESTITUTE poverty-stricken, impoverished, indigent, *strapped, *broke, bankrupt, *down and out, *hard up, needy, homeless. "To always want more than you have."— Anon. **2.** INADEQUATE lacking, deficient, unsatisfactory, subpar, second-rate, inferior, insufficient, sorry, low grade, substandard, cheap, pitiable, wanting, shoddy, shabby. **3.** UNFORTUNATE pitiful, pitiable, pathetic, hapless, miserable, unlucky, wretched. ANT. *1. rich, wealthy, well-off. 2. superior, first-rate, superb. 3. lucky, fortunate, blessed.*

pop *v.* bust, explode, blow up, bang, crack, report, blow, go off.

poppycock *n.* *bull, rot, baloney, hogwash, rubbish, bunk, nonsense, balderdash, *horsefeathers, malarkey.

popular *a.* **1.** WELL-LIKED favorite, in demand, sought after, crowd-pleasing, in style, in vogue, *all the rage, beloved, *boffo, celebrated, renowned. **2.** COMMON general, public, standard, conventional, universal, prevailing. ANT. *1. unwanted, outmoded, disliked. 2. uncommon, limited.*

popularity *n.* approval, esteem, regard, acclaim, favor, adoration, acceptance, appeal, idolization, demand, fame. "A pleasant visitor who always leaves in the morning."— Anon.

population n. inhabitants, residents, populace, census, citizenry, people.

populous a. crowded, dense, overpopulated, *crawling with people, mobbed, *wall to wall, *elbow to elbow, swarming. ANT. *vacant, unpopulated.*

porch n. veranda, stoop, steps, portico, gallery, deck.

pore v. read, study, peruse, look over, examine, review, scrutinize.

pornographic a. obscene, sexually explicit, X-rated, indecent, dirty, filthy, lewd, titillating, salacious, erotic, blue, sexy, lascivious. ANT. *wholesome, G-rated, *clean.*

port n. harbor, dock, pier, wharf, berth, anchorage, landing, mooring, quay, haven.

portable a. transportable, movable, transferable, conveyable, light, compact, pocket-sized, handy. ANT. *immovable, fixed, unwieldy.*

portal n. entrance, doorway, gate, ingress, passageway, threshold.

portend v. bode, foretell, predict, presage, forewarn, foreshadow, augur, herald, harbinger, point to, bespeak.

portent n. [POR tent] a sign of things to come, a forewarning. *A storm cloud on the horizon is one portent sailors should take seriously.* SYN. sign of things to come, forewarning, omen, harbinger, herald, augury, indication, threat, presage, *handwriting on the wall.

portentious a. ominous, foreboding, threatening, menacing, doomed, prophetic, inauspicious, unpromising.

portion n. PART share, cut, section, division, ration, measure, segment, parcel, hunk, chunk, serving, allotment.

portion v. divide, apportion, segment, allocate, section, ration, dispense, dole out, mete out.

portly a. stout, large, heavy, corpulent, fat, rotund, plump, spherical, obese, pudgy. ANT. *thin, anorexic, skinny.*

portray v. depict, represent, characterize, limn, caricature, profile, mimic, delineate, simulate.

pose n. position, posture, stance, attitude, air, mien, guise, pretense, facade.

pose v. 1. STRIKE A POSE position, posture, stand, model, sit for, assume an attitude. 2. AFFECT pretend, put on, feign, posture, put on an act, show off, *put on airs, *peacock. 3. PUT FORTH ask, offer, assert, posit, propound.

posh a. luxurious, elegant, grand, *ritzy, deluxe, sumptuous, rich, opulent, *swanky, fancy. ANT. *humble, modest, low-class.*

position n. 1. LOCATION site, placement, place, locality, situation, *whereabouts, spot, point, bearings. 2. ATTITUDE stand, point of view, viewpoint, outlook, opinion. 3. POSTURE pose, stance, attitude. 4. JOB post, office, function, duty, responsibility, appointment. 5. STATUS standing, class, eminence, station, stature, prestige.

positive a. 1. CERTAIN absolute, express, explicit, definite, unqualified, categorical, sure, emphatic, precise, specific, firm. 2. BENEFICIAL useful, good, constructive, helpful, practical. ANT. *1. uncertain, qualified, equivocal. 2. negative, deleterious.*

positively adv. absolutely, certainly, surely, definitely, undeniably, categorically, doubtlessly, unquestionably, emphatically.

possess v. have, own, hold, enjoy, control, retain, occupy, be blessed with, keep, maintain.

possessed a. bedeviled, bewitched, haunted, cursed, crazed, entranced, under a spell, enthralled, demonized.

possession n. 1. OWNERSHIP custody, control, hold, proprietorship, title, occupancy. 2. PROPERTY belonging, effect, holding, *things, *stuff, worldly good.

possessive a. greedy, grasping, acquisitive, proprietary, controlling, dominating.

possibility n. chance, likelihood, odds, feasibility, prospect, probablity, plausibility, eventuality, hazard.

possible a. feasible, doable, conceivable, attainable, imaginable, obtainable, viable, potential, probable, likely. ANT. *impossible, unlikely, unthinkable.*

post n. 1. UPRIGHT shaft, pile, column, stake, support, prop, stud. 2. JOB position, office, duty, appointment, situation, role, assignment. 3. STATION lookout, beat.

post v. put up, display, affix, publicize, announce, notify, report, circulate.

posterior n. backside, rump, rear, buttock, *butt, bottom, tail, *tush.

posterior a. rear, back, hind, after, last.

posterity n. descendants, following generations, successors, heirs, offspring, progeny. ANT. *ancestors.*

postpone v. delay, defer, suspend, put off, put on hold, shelve, *issue a rain check, cancel.

POSTULATE n. [POS chuh LATE] assumption, supposition, presumption, theory, hypothesis, guess, speculation, fundamental.

postulate v. to assume without proof. *Astronomers postulate that extraterrestrial life exists in the universe.* SYN. assume, suppose, guess, theorize, hypothesize, figure, posit, surmise, take for granted, speculate.

posture n. **1.** STANCE position, pose, carriage, bearing, aspect, attitude, deportment. **2.** OPINION attitude, frame of mind, point of view, outlook. **3.** CIRCUMSTANCES condition, situation, state of affairs.

pot n. **1.** KETTLE saucepan, cauldron, boiler, vessel, pressure cooker. **2.** MARIJUANA *dope, *weed, *grass. SEE MARIJUANA

potent a. effective, powerful, strong, vigorous, compelling, forceful, *packing a punch, virile, influential, moving, weighty, efficacious. ANT. impotent, weak, powerless, helpless.

potentate n. ruler, monarch, sovereign, emperor, king, prince, crowned head, president, chieftain, dictator.

potential n. capability, untapped ability, capacity, *makings, possibility, promise, prospect, *sleeping giant.

potential a. possible, latent, unrealized, *sleeping, dormant, promising, budding, future, lurking, developing.

potion n. elixir, concoction, brew, drink, dose, medicine, *love potion, tonic, remedy, mixture.

potpourri n. mixture, hodgepodge, medley, miscellany, assortment, *mixed bag, melange, *combo, mishmash, hash.

pouch n. bag, sack, pocket, holder, receptacle, poke.

pounce v. spring, leap, swoop, jump, assault, descend upon, surprise.

pound n. enclosure, pen, holding pen, kennel.

pound v. **1.** BANG beat, strike, batter, drub, wallop, hammer, hit, pelt, thump. **2.** PULSATE palpitate, beat, throb, hammer, flutter.

pour v. **1.** LET FLOW spill, decant, slosh, drop, drip, trickle, dribble, spew, splash, funnel, stream, gush, flow, cascade. **2.** RAIN HARD *rain cats and dogs, drench, flood, *come down in buckets, *come down in sheets, soak, splatter.

pout v. sulk, mope, put on a long face, roll out one's lip, brood, *feel sorry for oneself, sniffle. ANT. smile, grin, laugh. SEE CRY

poverty n. poorness, want, need, destitution, indigence, pennilessness, privation, penury, financial distress, *wolf at the door, *Dickensian poverty, *hand-to-mouth existence, homelessness, lack, scarcity, paucity, insufficiency. "The parent of revolution and crime."—Aristotle. "The reward of honest fools."—Colley Cibber. "Life near the bone, where it is sweetest."—Henry Thoreau. ANT.

wealth, riches, affluence, plenty, abundance.

poverty-stricken a. impoverished, strapped, broke. SEE POOR

power n. **1.** PHYSICAL FORCE energy, strength, might, brawn, muscle, horsepower, potency, *punch, virility, vigor, *oomph. **2.** ABILITY capacity, capability, aptitude, *what it takes, faculty, skill, endowment. **3.** CONTROLLING FORCE mastery, authority, domination, sway, clout, weight, command, might, influence, *pull, importance, *friends in high places. "The application of intelligence to force."—Arthur Corey. "A drug, the desire for which increases with the habit."—Bertrand Russell. ANT. weakness, impotency, powerlessness, helplessness.

powerful a. **1.** PHYSICALLY STRONG mighty, potent, energetic, brawny, muscular, *built, *strapping, robust, vigorous, hulking, massive, *built like an ox. **2.** AUTHORITATIVE, EFFECTIVE commanding, dominant, in control, influential, controlling, potent, capable, forceful, preeminent, important, *carrying a lot of weight, *having a lot of clout, puissant. ANT. 1. weak, feeble, *wimpy, emasculated. 2. powerless, important, submissive, helpless.

powerless a. weak, impotent, helpless, prostrate, incapacitated, emasculated, debilitated, ineffectual, incapable, paralyzed. ANT. powerful, potent, effective.

practical a. useful, realistic, utilitarian, sensible, down-to-earth, sane, workable, practicable, functional, serviceable, pragmatic. ANT. impractical, unworkable, unrealistic.

practically adv. just about, nearly, almost, virtually.

practice n. **1.** TRAINING repetition, drilling, rehearsal, discipline, preparation, conditioning. **2.** HABIT routine, way, custom, fashion, manner, method, system, procedure, mode, wont, convention. **3.** PROFESSION occupation, firm, business, work, trade, clientele.

practice v. **1.** TRAIN drill, rehearse, prepare, condition, discipline, perfect, exercise, polish, refine. **2.** CARRY OUT do, perform, observe, follow, employ. **3.** WORK AT be employed with, pursue, ply, specialize.

PRAGMATIC a. [prag MAT ik] actual, practical, real-world, as opposed to the theoretical or speculative. He looked for pragmatic solutions, not daydreamed ideals. SYN. actual, practical, real-world, down-to-earth, utilitarian, workable, sensible, sober, hard, hardnosed. ANT. theoretical, idealistic, unrealistic.

prairie n. grassland, plain, meadow, veldt, pasture, tundra. SEE FIELD

praise n. compliments, commendation, applause, acclaim, good words, approval, tribute, recognition, laudation, extolment, cheers. "That which makes good men better and bad men worse." — Thomas Fuller. "The sweetest of all sounds." — Zenophon. ANT. *condemnation, disapproval.*

praise v. commend, compliment, flatter, applaud, acclaim, approve, pay tribute, laud, extol, hail, boost, put in a good word for. ANT. *condemn, criticize, disparage.*

praiseworthy a. commendable, admirable, laudable, meritorious, worthy, fine, honorable, sterling, excellent. ANT. *contemptible, despicable, awful.*

prank n. practical joke, trick, antic, mischief, *cheap trick, gag, caper, sport, shenanigans.

prattle n. chatter, babble, blather, twaddle, drivel, jabber, blabbing.

pray v. plead, petition, bow one's head, appeal, supplicate, implore, solicit, entreat, say grace, ask forgiveness, give thanks.

prayer n. pleading, petition, appeal, supplication, imploring, entreaty, request, thanksgiving, grace, benediction, worship, litany, communion with God. "A window to heaven." — Israel Baal Shem Tob. "A ladder on which thoughts mount to God." — Abraham Heschel. "A direct approach to the throbbing heart of the universe." — Israel Bettan.

WORD FIND

beads: rosary

enemy, prayer calling for a calamity to befall one's: imprecation

evening: vesper

Islam call to adhan: azan

Islam prayer mat: seggadeh

Jewish mourning prayer: kaddish

Jewish "standing" prayer: amidah

knee, get down on one: genuflect

meal: grace

mosque's prayer leader: imam

nine day: novena

saint's prayer made on behalf of others: intercession

shawl, Jewish: tallith

sung or spoken supplications with congregational replies: litany

synagogue's prayer leader: cantor

trust, to: amen

SEE CHURCH, CLERGY, RELIGION

preach v. deliver a sermon, sermonize, spread the gospel, moralize, teach, lecture, pontificate, evangelize, minister, exhort, get up on one's moral soapbox, counsel, admonish.

preacher n. clergyman, minister, evangelist, pastor, reverend, man of the cloth, parson, ecclesiastic, rabbi, cleric. "God's ambassador." — William Cowper. "A messenger, not an actor." — Ralph Sockman.

precarious a. insecure, risky, dangerous, chancy, unsafe, slippery, perilous, unstable, shaky, *out on a limb, *hanging by a thread, treacherous, unpredictable. ANT. *secure, safe, stable.*

precaution n. caution, case, safety measure, safeguard, insurance, provision, foresight, preparation, wariness, heedfulness, circumspection.

precede v. go before, antedate, antecede, usher in, preface, lead, predate, forerun, head up. ANT. *follow, succeed, ensue.*

PRECEDENCE n. [PRES uh duns] priority. *The baby's welfare took precedence over all other matters.* SYN. priority, preeminence, importance, preference, supremacy, rank, superiority, right, superiority, *front seat, *front burner. ANT. *back seat, *back burner, second place.*

PRECEDENT n. [PRES uh dunt] a prior instance that serves as an example, model or guideline, especially an earlier case in a law matter. *The lawyer found numerous precedents to help support his case.* SYN. example, model, guideline, standard, prior instance, classic example, pattern, paradigm, exemplar.

preceding a. previous, prior, earlier, foregoing, antecedent, former, aforementioned, preliminary, erstwhile. ANT. *following, upcoming, succeeding.*

PRECEPT n. [PREE sept] a rule to live by; maxim. *He lived by the precept, "Live and let live."* SYN. rule to live by, maxim, principle, direction, commandment, rule, axiom, canon, tenet, motto, guideline.

precinct n. division, subdivision, district, neighborhood, section, quarter, zone, ward, *neck of the woods.

precious a. 1. COSTLY valuable, priceless, inestimable, expensive, high-priced, rich. 2. BELOVED dear, loved, adored, treasured, cherished, worshipped, idolized, darling, esteemed, favorite. 3. FASTIDIOUS overrefined, particular, finicky, overnice, fussy, affected, unnatural, pretentious, flowery, dainty. ANT. 1. *cheap, worthless.* 2. *despised, hated.* 3. *sloppy, careless, cloddish.*

precipice n. drop-off, cliff, ledge, height, brink,

*vertiginous overlook, bluff, escarpment.

precipitate *v.* [pri SIP i TATE] to cause to happen sooner than desired or expected. *The embargo precipitated the rise of oil prices.* SYN. hasten, quicken, speed, expedite, accelerate, advance, trigger, instigate, drive, impel.

precipitate *a.* hasty, rash, headlong, rushed, hurried, sudden, abrupt, impetuous, reckless, impatient.

precipitous *a.* sheer, high, vertiginous. SEE STEEP

precise *a.* **1.** EXACT accurate, specific, pinpoint, correct, *on the button, *on the nose, right, *on the mark, definite, faithful, literal, flawless. **2.** FASTIDIOUS finicky, fussy, scrupulous, particular, meticulous, exacting, punctilious. ANT. *1. imprecise, inexact, approximate, rough, loose. 2. careless, casual.*

precision *n.* exactness, accuracy, perfection, correctness, fidelity, faithfulness, rectitude, *Swiss watch accuracy, attention to detail. ANT. *inaccuracy, approximation.*

PRECLUDE *v.* [pree KLOOD] to prevent something from happening. *A felony conviction precludes any chance for running for public office.* SYN. prevent, stop, make impossible, foil, avert, thwart, check, rule out, forestall, hinder, inhibit. ANT. *facilitate, allow.*

PRECOCIOUS *a.* [pre KO shus] advanced or mature for one's years. *A precocious child.* SYN. advanced, mature, premature, ahead of one's peers, progressive, bright, early-blooming, intelligent, gifted, developed. ANT. *immature, behind, slow to develop, late-blooming.*

preconception *n.* preconceived notion, prejudgment, assumption, presumption, prejudice, predisposition.

PRECURSOR *n.* [pree KUR sur] something that comes before, forerunner. *A rainy April is the precursor of May flowers.* SYN. forerunner, harbinger, herald, predecessor, usher, vanguard, antecedent, groundbreaker, trailblazer.

predatory *a.* eating, attacking, hunting, carnivorous, bloodthirsty, predacious, bestial, voracious, rapacious, omnivorous.

predecessor *n.* forerunner, precursor, antecedent, ancestor, forebear, forefather. ANT. *descendant, successor.*

predetermined *a.* preplanned, fixed, arranged, fated, destined, doomed, preordained, preset, settled.

predicament *n.* difficulty, scrape, bind, mess, plight, trouble, jam, pickle, hole, strait, *hot water, pinch, corner.

predict *v.* prophecy, forecast, foresee, foretell, divine, prognosticate, augur, envision, read the signs, guess.

prediction *n.* prophecy, forecast, prognostication, prognosis, guess, augury, divination, expectation, intuition.

PREDILECTION *n.* [PRED uh LEK shun] a natural liking or preference. *She had a predilection for ginger snaps.* SYN. liking, fondness, preference, partiality, predisposition, inclination, propensity, penchant, leaning, bias, prejudice. ANT. *aversion, dislike.*

predispose *v.* make susceptible, influence, bias, sway, prejudice, impress, prime, affect, bend.

predominant *a.* dominant, superior, leading, ruling, controlling, paramount, top, preeminent, ranking, supreme, chief. ANT. *subordinate, secondary, minor, inferior.*

preeminent *a.* dominant, superior, surpassing, unsurpassed, unrivaled, foremost, major, supreme, peerless, incomparable, unparalleled.

PREEMPT *v.* [pree EMPT] to take the place of another beforehand by rights. *The World Series will preempt normal TV programming.* SYN. appropriate, take away, usurp, claim, bump, assume, seize, commandeer.

preface *n.* foreword, prologue, introduction, prelude, preamble, overture, opening. ANT. *epilogue, postscript.*

preface *v.* introduce, begin, start, open, initiate. ANT. *close, end.*

prefer *v.* favor, choose, select, pick, opt for, be partial to, lean toward, desire, single out. ANT. *reject, pass on, dislike.*

preference *n.* **1.** FIRST CHOICE favorite, choice, selection, desire, inclination, pick, leaning, partiality. **2.** PRIORITY advantage, precedence, edge, *leg up.

pregnancy *n.* gestation, fertilization, incubation, *the family way, parturiency.

WORD FIND

abortion, spontaneous: miscarriage

before labor: antepartum

blood discharge before labor: bloody show

brown patches on pregnant woman's skin: *mask of pregnancy, chloasma

dark line on pregnant woman's belly: linea nigra

embryo, earliest form of: blastocyst

false pregnancy: pseudocyesis

fetal movement, mother's first perception of: quickening

fluid: amniotic fluid

fluid secreted from breast prior to birth: colostrum

fluid withdrawal from uterus, test: amniocentesis

genetic test sampling of placenta: chorionic
villus sampling

implantation of fertilized eggs, mechanical:
in vitro fertilization

nausea: morning sickness

optical examination of fetus through scope:
fetoscopy

organ providing nutrients and oxygen to fetus from mother: placenta

premature birth, abnormality leading to: incompetent cervix

semen, artificial deposit of: artificial insemi-
nation

sympathetic pregnancy symptoms of father:
couvade

three-month division: trimester

ultrasound picture of fetus: sonogram

uterus, development of egg outside of: ec-
topic pregnancy

SEE BABY, BIRTH

pregnant a. **1.** EXPECTING *in a family way,
gravid, *with child, parturient, gestating,
*knocked up, *having one in the oven. **2.**
MEANINGFUL important, weighty, significant,
telling.

prehistoric a. early, primitive, primeval, antediluvian, ancient, antiquated, pleistocene,
pliocene, miocene, oligocene, eocene, pa-
leocene, cretaceous, jurassic, triassic, per-
mian, paleozoic, cambrian, pre-cambrian.
ANT. *future, modern.*

prejudice n. bias, preconceived idea, preconception, predisposition, jaundiced eye, fore-
gone conclusion, bigotry, racism, sexism,
chauvinism, homophobia, intolerance, partiality, discrimination, narrow-mindedness
"An opinion without judgment."—Voltaire.
"Weighing the facts with your thumb on the
scales."—Leon Aikman. "The child of ignorance."—William Hazlitt. ANT. *open-mindedness, objectivity, fairness, tolerance.*

preliminary a. introductory, preparatory, initial, first, preceding, antecedent, opening,
precursory. ANT. *ending, final.*

prelude n. introduction, preface, preamble, beginning, opening, overture, warmup, prologue.

premature a. early, too soon, unready, green,
immature, undeveloped, unripe, precipitate,
hurried, *half-baked, *jumping the gun, untimely. ANT. *late, overdue, behind.*

premeditated a. planned, prearranged, calculated, mapped out, studied, conscious,
thought-out, intentional, deliberate, willful.
ANT. *spur-of-the-moment, in the heat of the moment, spontaneous, impulsive, unplanned.*

premier n. debut, opening night, first showing.

premise n. hypothesis, argument, postulate,
proposition, foundation, theory, supposition, basis, assertion.

premium n. reward, bonus, prize, gift, incentive, *carrot, extra, *gravy, fringe benefit,
*perk.

premonition n. foreboding, presentiment, forewarning, feeling, *gut feeling, hunch, apprehension, intuition, *bad vibes, omen, portent.

preoccupied a. busy, occupied, engaged, involved, immersed, absorbed, *wrapped up,
engrossed, removed, *lost in thought, *deep
in thought.

preparation n. **1.** MAKING READY arrangement,
development, priming, establishment,
groundwork, anticipation, *prep work, provision, framework, setting up, grooming,
training. **2.** CONCOCTION compound, mixture, composition, drug, prescription.

prepare v. ready, prime, groom, arrange, do
groundwork, *prep, set up, anticipate, plan,
develop, smooth the way, train.

preponderance n. dominance, supremacy,
bulk, weight, predominance, *lion's share,
biggest part, majority, prevalence. ANT. *lesser
part, minority.*

preposterous a. absurd, ridiculous, outrageous,
ludicrous, asinine, foolish, silly, nonsensical,
crazy, insane, impossible, unbelievable, unthinkable.

prerequisite a. [pree REK wuh zit] required,
necessary. *Math may always be a prerequisite
course* SYN. required, necessary, demanded,
essential, imperative, called for, obligatory,
mandatory, needed. ANT. *elective, unnecessary.*

PREROGATIVE n. [pree ROG uh tiv]a right
or privilege. *It was her prerogative to close the
store whenever she wished.* SYN. right, privilege, choice, authority, liberty, freedom, advantage, license, exemption.

prescribe v. direct, order, ordain, set down, recommend, dictate, assign, select, advocate,
exact, rule.

prescription n. order, direction, recommendation, directive, instruction, requirement,
preparation, concoction, medicine, drug,
dose.

presence n. **1.** ATTENDANCE existence, occupancy, being, residence, proximity. **2.** POISE

confidence, bearing, air, demeanor, charisma, personality, carriage, self-assurance, aura.

present *n.* **1.** HERE AND NOW today, now, this instant. **2.** GIFT offering, favor, benefaction, donation, premium, gratuity, give-away, bonus.

present *v.* **1.** INTRODUCE have one meet, acquaint. **2.** EXHIBIT display, show, demonstrate. **3.** PUT FORWARD advance, pose, submit, proffer, *trot out for inspection, offer, profess, declare. **4.** GIVE hand over, confer, bestow, award, entrust, donate, submit.

present *a.* **1.** CURRENT contemporary, existing, immediate, at hand, present-day, modern, at this moment. **2.** HERE at hand, in attendance, nearby, on hand, within reach. ANT. *1. past, bygone, previous. 2. absent, away.*

presentable *a.* groomed, dressed, neat and clean, fit to be seen, acceptable, respectable, suitable, *decent, passable.

presentation *n.* performance, exhibition, show, production, demonstration, display, offering, gift, bestowal, award, pitch.

presentiment *n.* foreboding, feeling, *bad vibes, premonition, apprehension, *gut feeling, intuition, hunch, presage.

presently *adv.* shortly, soon, directly, now, immediately, forthwith.

preservation *n.* conservation, maintenance, protection, conservancy, safekeeping, saving, sustenance, upkeep, perpetuation.

preserve *n.* reserve, game reserve, sanctuary, zoo, refuge, haven, park, conservation area.

preserve *v.* **1.** PROTECT save, conserve, maintain, sustain, keep up, safeguard, perpetuate. **2.** TO KEEP FRESH can, pickle, salt, cure, smoke, dry, corn, refrigerate, freeze. ANT. *1. ruin, neglect. 2. let spoil, let rot.*

preside *v.* chair, oversee, direct, control, supervise, run, officiate, *be in the driver's seat, *hold the reins, conduct, head.

president *n.* chief executive, head of state, commander-in-chief, first citizen; chief executive officer, CEO, chairman. "Chief servant."—Mohandas Gandhi. "A link in the long chain of his country's destiny, past and future."—Herbert Hoover. "A yes-man to the majority."—Anon. SEE CONGRESS, ELECTION, GOVERNMENT, POLITICS

press *n.* **1.** MEDIA reporters, newsmen, newswomen, fourth estate, TV, radio, journalists, photojournalists. SEE NEWSPAPER **2.** CROWD throng, mob, pack, swarm, horde, crush.

press *v.* **1.** PUSH squeeze, depress, crush, clamp, compress, bear down, flatten, squash, put weight on, cramp, compact, hug, embrace. **2.** IRON smooth, steam. **3.** FORCE compel, impel, constrain, move. **4.** REQUEST entreat, plead, petition, importune, solicit.

pressing *a.* urgent, importunate, high-priority, crucial, exigent, critical, vital, imperative, important, compelling, momentous. ANT. *unimportant, inconsequential, trivial.*

pressure *n.* **1.** COMPRESSION squeezing, tension, load, heaviness, weight, force, gravity. **2.** STRAIN stress, duress, demand, tension, burden, load, cross, millstone. **3.** INFLUENCE force, power, coercion, persuasion, pull, sway, compulsion, obligation, necessity, arm-twisting.

pressure *v.* compel, influence, force, push, persuade, coerce, press, drive, arm-twist, constrain, *lean on, *railroad, *put the screws to, *put the squeeze on.

prestige *n.* status, reputation, repute, stature, standing, fame, prominence, esteem, distinction, notoriety, rank, influence, power.

prestigious *a.* esteemed, distinguished, renowned, reputable, notable, eminent, great, famous, illustrious, impressive, influential. ANT. *unknown, disrespected.*

presumably *adv.* probably, ostensibly, likely, in all probability.

presume *v.* **1.** ASSUME take for granted, think, guess, surmise, suppose, believe, take it, postulate, consider. **2.** DARE venture, take liberties, have the audacity, overstep, go too far.

presumption *n.* **1.** ASSUMPTION thinking, supposition, guess, belief, suspicion, conjecture, hypothesis, premise. **2.** FORWARDNESS effrontery, audacity, gall, boldness, daring, *cheek, nerve, gall, insolence.

PRESUMPTUOUS *a.* [pree ZUMP choo us] overly bold or confident and taking too much for granted. *It was quite presumptuous of her to take the blue ribbon before the winner was even announced.* SYN. bold, nervy, confident, audacious, forward, *ballsy, rude, cocksure, brazen, lordly, arrogant, egotistical, insolent, pompous. ANT. *unassuming, modest, humble.*

pretend *v.* **1.** MAKE BELIEVE play act, imagine, put on, suppose. **2.** FEIGN fake, bluff, simulate, *put on, dissemble, fool, deceive, act, sham, counterfeit, affect.

PRETENSE *n.* [PREE tens] a falsification, put-on, show or affectation. *His claim of being rich was only a pretense to impress women.* SYN. falsification, put-on, show, affectation, imposture, fake, display, act, charade, showing off, facade, simulation, masquerade, posing, ruse, trick. ANT. *truth, reality, honest.*

PRETENTIOUS *a.* [pree TEN shus] putting on airs, especially of importance or grandness, ostentatious. *They were a bunch of pretentious snobs.* SYN. affected, self-important, bragging, showy, ostentatious, boastful, pompous, assuming, conceited, *artsy-fartsy, *la-di-da, vainglorious, snobbish, *highfalutin. ANT. *down-to-earth, unassuming, natural, modest, humble.*

pretext *n.* excuse, front, *story, alibi, cover, alleged reason, *song and dance, subterfuge, guise.

pretty *a.* attractive, comely, beautiful, lovely, nice-looking, cute, appealing, eye-catching, foxy, becoming, ravishing, fair, handsome. ANT. *ugly, plain, homely.*

pretty *adv.* fairly, moderately, reasonably, passably, adequately.

prevail *v.* **1.** WIN OVER overcome, dominate, best, succeed, triumph, conquer, master, *come out on top. **2.** PREDOMINATE be widespread, be prevalent, abound, preponderate. ANT. *1. lose, fail, give up. 2. be rare.*

prevailing *a.* superior, dominant, affective, prevalent, widespread, general, preponderant, predominant, universal, popular, current, principal, reigning, in style. ANT. *outmoded, disappearing, failing.*

prevalent *a.* prevailing, common, widespread, abundant, extensive, general, popular, pervasive, rampant. ANT. *rare, uncommon, infrequent.*

prevent *v.* stop, prohibit, preclude, avert, stave off, arrest, *nip in the bud, thwart, bar, check, restrict, block. ANT. *allow, facilitate, cause.*

prevention *n.* stoppage, prohibition, preclusion, arrest, restriction, blockage, deterrence, obstruction, forestalling, interception.

previous *a.* prior, earlier, preceding, past, antecedent, anterior, erstwhile, aforementioned. ANT. *future, succeeding, upcoming, ensuing.*

previously *adv.* earlier, in the past, before, hitherto, formerly, once, at one time, a while ago.

prey *n.* victim, the hunted, mark, quarry, kill, spoil, *sitting duck.

prey *v.* hunt, kill, victimize, eat, devour, feed on, attack, pounce, consume, exploit, use.

price *n.* cost, asking price, sticker price, charge, retail, wholesale, bill, expense, value, rate, assessment, appraisal, outlay, *damage.

priceless *a.* invaluable, precious, valuable, dear, expensive, *worth its weight in gold, *worth all the oil in Arabia, costly, prized, treasured. ANT. *cheap, *dime a dozen, worthless.*

prick *v.* pierce, stick, puncture, impale, jab, stab, cut, perforate, lance.

pride *n.* **1.** SELF-ESTEEM self-respect, self-worth, dignity, satisfaction, self-confidence, healthy ego, *amour propre. **2.** ARROGANCE conceit, hauteur, haughtiness, egotism, self-importance, vainglory, overconfidence, smugness, presumption, cockiness. "Cap and bells for a fool." — Alfred Lord Tennyson. "Pampered vanity." — Joanna Baillie.

priest *n.* father, minister, clergyman, man of the cloth, ecclesiastic, vicar, padre, chaplain, pastor, deacon. "An instrument of God." — Anon. "Crutches for the crippled life of the soul." — Franz Kafka. SEE CLERGYMAN, PREACHER

prim *a.* formal, proper, demure, correct, Victorian, straitlaced, prissy, prudish, upright, stiff, decorous. ANT. *loose, wild, unrefined, informal, casual.*

primarily *adv.* mainly, in the first place, fundamentally, first and foremost, principally, chiefly, largely.

primary *a.* **1.** FIRST original, earliest, primal, primordial, introductory, initial, beginning. **2.** MAIN principal, chief, basic, essential, fundamental, first, capital, major. ANT. *1. secondary, succeeding. 2. minor, secondary.*

prime *n.* best days, youth, springtime of life, heyday, peak, height, spring, summer.

prime *v.* prepare, *prep, ready, groom, train, break in, coach.

prime *a.* SEE PRIMARY

primeval *a.* primal, primordial, prehistoric, primitive, ancient, earliest, antediluvian, pristine. ANT. *later, recent, modern.*

primitive *a.* **1.** ANCIENT original, earliest, primal, primordial, primeval, primary, elemental, rudimentary. **2.** CRUDE rough, undeveloped, simple, uncivilized, unsophisticated, wild, natural, barbaric. ANT. *1. modern, contemporary, late. 2. refined, sophisticated, civilized.*

primordial *a.* SEE PRIMITIVE

primp *v.* groom, preen, beautify, dress up, *gussy up, *doll up, *spruce up.

principal *n.* **1.** CHIEF head, actor, performer, player, star, combatant. **2.** HEADMASTER dean.

principal *a.* main, major, chief, leading, primary, dominant, foremost, supreme, star, key, most important. ANT. *secondary, supporting, minor.*

principle n. **1.** TRUTH law, doctrine, fundamental, standard, rule, foundation, basis, criterion, precept, theory, canon. **2.** PRINCIPLES/ MORALS ethics, code, policies, guiding principle, belief, tenet, dogma, standards, credo, scruples, conscience.

print v. compose, write, imprint, run off, type, stamp, hand-letter.

printer n. typesetter, publisher, photocopier.

prior a. previous, earlier, former, antecedent, anterior, preceding, preexisting, erstwhile, aforementioned. ANT. *following, upcoming, subsequent.*

priority n. precedence, leading concern, rank, urgency, preference, weight, preeminence, seniority.

prison n. penitentiary, penal institution, jail, house of detention, house of correction, lockup, cell, *cooler, *clink, *poky, *can, *hoosegow, *slammer, *big house. "Stones of law." — William Blake. "A school to which criminals are sent to figure out what went wrong." — Anon.

WORD FIND

castle: dungeon

cell search by guards: shakedown

convicts chained together for work detail: chain gang

death penalty: capital punishment

division: ward

drunks, overnight cell for: drunk tank

early release for good behavior: parole

famous: Alcatraz, Sing Sing, Newgate

head: warden

informer: *rat, fink

inmates: convicts, *cons

isolation cell: solitary confinement

jailer: turnkey

legal expert, prisoner who becomes: jailhouse lawyer

life term, prisoner serving: *lifer

military: stockade

reforming of prisoner: rehabilitation

return to life of crime after prison: recidivism

section holding those sentenced to death: death row

ship: brig

smuggler of contraband: *mule

spousal relations visit: conjugal visit

transfer of prisoner to other jurisdiction: extradition

youth: reformatory, reform school

war camp: concentration camp

prisoner n. SEE PRISON

prissy a. *goody-goody, straitlaced, prudish, prim, *goody two shoes, overnice, fussy, fastidious, particular, puritanical.

PRISTINE a. [pris TEEN] unspoiled or pure, as something in its original state. *The pristine mountains of Alaska should be left forever wild.* SYN. unspoiled, pure, untouched, virginal, natural, primitive, primordial, unsullied, uncorrupted, clean. ANT. *spoiled, ruined, sullied.*

privacy n. solitude, separation, concealment, secrecy, isolation, sequestration, seclusion.

private a. **1.** PERSONAL secret, internal, confidential, intimate, individual, nonpublic, own. **2.** SECLUDED isolated, sequestered, reclusive, secret, concealed, cloistered, hermitic, remote, solitary. **3.** UNDISCLOSED secret, *under wraps, quiet, confidential, *hush-hush. **4.** RESTRICTED off-limits, closed to the public, exclusive. ANT. *1. public. 3. public, announced, out in the open. 4. public, unrestricted, open.*

privation n. deprivation, need, want, scarcity, lack, poverty, hardship, destitution, indigence. ANT. *wealth, affluence.*

privilege n. right, advantage, due, favor, entitlement, perquisite, liberty, prerogative, benefit, birthright.

privileged a. entitled, favored, empowered, exempt, immune, sanctioned, authorized, accommodated, given preferential treatment. ANT. *disadvantaged, underprivileged.*

privy n. latrine, toilet. SEE OUTHOUSE

prize n. award, winnings, reward, title, blue ribbon, medal, trophy, loving cup, decoration, laurel, honors, jackpot, haul, stake, spoils, booby prize.

prize v. value, regard highly, esteem, appreciate, hold dear, cherish, treasure.

prize a. award-winning, winning, choice. SEE BEST

probability n. likelihood, chance, prospect, possibility, odds, expectation, outlook.

probable a. likely, *odds-on, reasonable, expected, anticipated, possible, presumed, plausible, *in the cards, foreseeable. ANT. *unlikely, improbable, implausible.*

probation n. trial period, test period, suspension of sentence.

probe n. investigation, examination, inquiry, inquisition, exploration, study, scrutiny, feeler.

probe v. investigate, examine, inquire, look into, explore, study, scrutinize, analyze, check out, poke about, interrogate.

problem n. **1.** DIFFICULTY complication, knot, trouble, dilemma, quandary, mess, *pickle, predicament, *can of worms, *headache, *pain in the neck, *hassle, *when 2 and 2 don't make 4. **2.** PUZZLE brainteaser, question, riddle, conundrum, *stumper, *head-scratcher, *hard nut to crack.

problematic a. **1.** DIFFICULT hard, tricky. **2.** QUESTIONABLE doubtful, debatable, uncertain, unsettled, dubious, disputable, moot, suspect, hard to believe, *full of holes, undetermined. ANT. 1. easy, simple. 2. certain, settled.

procedure n. method, manner, process, course, sequence, steps, mode, practice, formula, way.

proceed v. go, go ahead, go on, continue, progress, move on, carry on, get on with. ANT. stop, halt, suspend.

proceedings n. business, matters, *doings, activities, affairs, transactions, agenda, minutes.

proceeds n. take, earnings, income, profit, receipts, gain, revenue, gross, net, gate, box office.

process n. method, workings, operation, modus operandi, procedure, course, sequence, technique, formula, way, steps, stages, mechanism.

process v. work, refine, handle, prepare, treat, convert, cook, cure, deal with.

procession n. parade, train, column, caravan, cavalcade, file, march, cortege, motorcade.

proclaim v. announce, declare, state, make known, profess, voice, broadcast, herald, advertise. ANT. hush up, cover up.

proclamation n. announcement, declaration, pronouncement, notice, statement, profession, manifesto, decree, edict.

proclivity n. inclination, tendency, propensity, disposition, predilection, penchant, weakness, leaning, bias. ANT. aversion, dislike.

procrastinate v. put off, stall, delay, *drag one's feet, *shilly-shally, postpone, dawdle, temporize, prolong, protract, play for time. ANT. *get cracking, *get a move on, expedite. "The art of keeping up with yesterday." — Don Marquis.

procreate v. produce, beget, reproduce, breed, parent, propagate, spawn, mother, father, engender, bear.

procure v. get, obtain, acquire, secure, come by, get one's hands on, get hold of, pick up, appropriate, buy, purchase, score.

prod v. POKE jab, shove, elbow, finger, punch, *goose, nudge, shove, goad, urge, rouse, motivate, spur, provoke, incite, move.

PRODIGAL a. [PROD uh gul] extremely wasteful or extravagant. Joe's prodigal grandson spent his entire inheritance within a week. SYN. wasteful, extravagant, excessive, squandering, spendthrift, lavish, immoderate, improvident, reckless. ANT. thrifty, frugal, penny-pinching.

PRODIGIOUS a. [pruh DIJ us] huge, powerful, spectacular or astounding. Climbing Mt. Everest is a prodigious undertaking. SYN. huge, massive, enormous, colossal, stupendous, Herculean, immense, monumental, tremendous, powerful, extraordinary, astounding, spectacular, phenomenal, impressive, amazing. ANT. tiny, trivial, pint-sized, common, ordinary.

PRODIGY n. [PROD i jee] a child of rare and exceptional talent or intelligence, a young genius. The young prodigy attended college at the age of twelve. SYN. wonder, genius, *whiz kid, wunderkind, sensation, marvel, *freak, phenomenon, gifted student. "A child who plays the piano when he ought to be in bed." — John Morton.

produce v. **1.** MAKE manufacture, create, bear, generate, form, fabricate, construct, invent, devise, fashion, frame, turn out. **2.** CAUSE effect, bring about, generate, result in, breed. **3.** SHOW FOR INSPECTION display, present, offer, exhibit, show, disclose.

product n. good, commodity, creation, work, handiwork, production, turnout, merchandise, result, end, yield, outcome, issue.

production n. manufacture, creation, fabrication, generation, formation, assembly, construction, invention, outpost.

productive a. fertile, rich, fecund, fruitful, prolific, profitable, gainful, creative, rewarding, worthwhile. ANT. unproductive, barren, worthless.

productivity n. output, turnout, capacity, yield, production.

PROFANE a. [pro FANE] irreverent and disrespectful, especially toward religion. Also, that which is outside of religion. His profane sense of humor got him in trouble with the church. SYN. irreverent, disrespectful, blasphemous, impious, sacrilegious, irreligious, ungodly, sinful, crude, nasty. ANT. religious, pious, devout, Christian.

profane v. desecrate, defile, debase, disrespect, violate, blaspheme, corrupt, taint, abuse. ANT. revere, respect, worship.

profanity n. swear word, swearing, cuss word, cussing, bad word, *four-letter word, dirty word, oath, expletive, obscenity, blasphemy, irreverence. "Language's natural stress vent."—Anon. ANT. *polite word, euphemism, reverence.*

profess v. **1.** AFFIRM declare, assert, admit, proclaim, tell, state, acknowledge, confess, avow, announce. **2.** TO CLAIM INSINCERELY purport, allege, pretend, feign, fake, simulate, *swear up and down, *bullshit.

profession n. **1.** OCCUPATION line of work, trade, vocation, calling, work, career, business, employment, specialty, job, field, metier. **2.** AFFIRMATION announcement, declaration, assertion, admission, proclamation, statement, confession, claim, pretense.

professional n. expert, master, pro, *old hand, veteran, specialist, virtuoso, mavin, journeyman, *crackerjack. ANT. *amateur, dabbler, hobbyist.*

professional a. expert, schooled, experienced, trained, masterly, learned, proficient, accomplished, pro, practiced, big league, au fait, accredited. ANT. *amateur, inexperienced, unschooled, incompetent.*

professor n. teacher, academic, instructor, educator, *prof, faculty member, doctor, lecturer, fellow, sage, *brain. "A talking reference library."—Anon.

professorial a. pedantic, pedagogic, scholarly. SEE ACADEMIC, COLLEGE

PROFICIENT a. [pro FISH unt] highly competent, skillful, able. *He was a proficient craftsman.* SYN. competent, skilled, able, talented, masterful, adept, expert, *crack, *crackerjack, capable, accomplished. ANT. *incompetent, incapable, inept.*

profile n. **1.** OUTLINE side view, figure, contour, form, silhouette, delineation. **2.** BIOGRAPHY review, sketch, thumbnail sketch, characterization, portrait.

profit n. gain, income, proceeds, net, revenue, return, yield, benefit, *take, earnings, *bottom line, *take-home. ANT. *loss, red ink.*

profit v. gain, benefit, yield, take, earn, make money, clear, *clean up, *make a killing, reap, *make a bundle, advance, better, learn. ANT. *lose, suffer, go bankrupt.*

profitable a. lucrative, money-making, paying, cost-effective, worthwhile, rewarding, productive, gainful, fruitful, remunerative. ANT. *unprofitable, costly, unproductive.*

PROFLIGATE a. [PROF luh git] shamelessly immoral. Also, extravagant and wasteful. A

profligate party animal. SYN. immoral, shameless, debauched, wild, wanton, degenerate, promiscuous, fast, loose, abandoned, unbridled, extravagant, wasteful, excessive, prodigal, lavish, immoderate. ANT. *moral, virtuous, principled, thrifty, economical.*

PROFOUND a. [pro FOUND] deep or intense, either physically, intellectually or emotionally. *A profound sadness. A profound silence. Her theory of galactic formation was quite profound.* SYN. **1.** INTELLECTUAL deep, intelligent, thoughtful, wise, insightful, abstruse, heavy, penetrating, esoteric, enlightened, scholarly, difficult, complex. **2.** EMOTIONAL heartfelt, deep, intense, acute, sincere, keen, heartrending, soul-stirring, moving. **3.** THOROUGH comprehensive, complete, utter, far-reaching, total, absolute. **4.** BOTTOMLESS sunken, fathomless, abysmal. ANT. *1. superficial, shallow, mindless. 2. insincere, unfeeling. 3. partial, slight. 4. shallow.*

PROFUSE a. [pro FYOOS] pouring out freely or excessively. *She thanked us profusely. He was sweating profusely.* SYN. pouring forth freely, abundant, excessive, free-flowing, overflowing, generous, copious, plentiful, extravagant, lavish, immoderate, prodigal. ANT. *sparse, thin, limited, meager, moderate.*

PROFUSION n. [pro FYOO zhun] a great pouring forth, or a great amount. *A profusion of daisies colored the meadow.* SYN. outpouring, overflow, great amount, abundance, lavish amount, extravagant supply, bounty, quantity, cornucopia, multitude, excess, flood, plethora. ANT. *dearth, lack, scarcity.*

progeny n. children, offspring, young, issue, descendants, successors, lineage, stock, posterity. ANT. *parents, ancestors, forebears.*

prognosis n. forecast, prognostication, projection. SEE PREDICTION

prognosticator n. seer, diviner, forecaster. SEE PROPHET

program n. **1.** AGENDA schedule, order of business, card, bill, slate, lineup, plan, docket, calendar, timetable. **2.** BROADCAST show, production, presentation, performance, telecast, drama, sitcom, musical. **3.** PROCEDURE plan, course, scheme, way, approach. **4.** COMPUTER PROGRAM software, instructions.

progress n. advance, development, improvement, furtherance, headway, strides forward, progression, march of progress, progression, evolution, breakthrough, gain, growth. ANT. *regression, retreat, recession.* "The law of life."—Robert Browning. "Man's ability to complicate simplicity."—Thor Heyerdahl.

progress v. move forward, develop, grow, gain, improve, make headway, evolve, advance, upgrade, improve, perfect. ANT. *regress, decline, recede, retreat.*

progression n. progress, succession, sequence, cycle, forward march, headway, continuance. ANT. *regression, recession.*

progressive a. forward-looking, modern-minded, prodevelopment, cutting edge, twenty-first century, advancing, liberal, visionary, revolutionary, evolutionary, reformist, dynamic. ANT. *conservative, unchanging, static, abiding, regressive.*

prohibit v. forbid, disallow, proscribe, interdict, ban, outlaw, restrict, prevent, stop, preclude, constrain, block, restrain, deny, put a stop to, *put a lid on. ANT. *allow, authorize, sanction, permit.*

prohibition n. ban, interdiction, proscription, nix, embargo, restriction, outlawing, disallowance, blockage, taboo. ANT. *permission, allowance, authorization.*

project n. venture, undertaking, enterprise, job, work, campaign, occupation, assignment, task, plan, scheme, proposal.

project v. **1.** PLAN propose, calculate, predict, estimate, forecast, scheme, envision, conceive, draft, outline. **2.** JUT bulge, stick out, overhang, protrude. **3.** THROW hurl, cast, shoot, propel, fling, launch.

projection n. **1.** ESTIMATE calculation, prediction, forecast, guess, approximation, figure. **2.** JUT protrusion, overhang, prominence, bump, bulge, extension, shelf.

PROLETARIAT n. [PROH li TAIR ee ut] the industrial working class or working class. *The proletariat are speaking out against higher taxes.* SYN. industrial working class, working class, laborers, blue-collar workers, commoners, lower class, rank and file, plebians, bourgeoisie, the masses, hoi polloi. ANT. *upper class, ruling class, nobility, royalty, aristocrats.*

PROLIFERATE v. [proh LIF uh RATE] to multiply, increase or spread at a fast rate. *Mushrooms proliferate on moist ground.* SYN. multiply, increase, spread, reproduce, breed, *mushroom, grow rampant, *run riot, burgeon, escalate, teem, *snowball, metastasize. ANT. *decrease, die out.*

PROLIFIC a. [proh LIF ik] richly productive, fertile. *A prolific author, he once wrote three books in one year.* SYN. productive, fertile,

fruitful, generative, creative, fecund, bountiful. ANT. *sterile, unproductive, barren.*

prolong v. extend, draw out, drag out, protract, stretch, lengthen, expand, sustain, perpetuate. ANT. *shorten, curtail, cut short.*

promenade n. walk, walkway, avenue, footpath, course, mall, stroll.

prominence n. **1.** RENOWN fame, distinction, eminence, reputation, notability, standing, importance, greatness, celebrity. **2.** JUTTING bump, projection, bulge, extrusion, eminence, peak, swelling, protrusion, protuberance, hump, lump. ANT. **1.** *obscurity, anonymity.* **2.** *depression, indentation, hole.*

prominent a. **1.** RENOWNED famous, eminent, distinguished, notable, celebrated, well-known, important, great, acclaimed. **2.** STICKING OUT jutting, projecting, conspicuous, standing out, outstanding, glaring, obvious, striking, bulging. ANT. **1.** *obscure, unknown, anonymous.* **2.** *inconspicuous, indented.*

promiscuous a. sexually active, sexually indiscriminate, oversexed, fast, loose, easy, wild, *slutty, whorish, of easy virtue, wanton, lustful. ANT. *celibate, chaste, virginal.*

promise n. **1.** WORD OF HONOR word, vow, pledge, oath, commitment, assurance, warranty, guarantee, contract, swearing. **2.** POTENTIAL hope, prospect, expectation.

promise v. **1.** GIVE ONE'S WORD pledge, vow, swear, commit, assure, *cross one's heart and hope to die, take an oath, warrant, guarantee. **2.** GIVE HOPE OF suggest, indicate, portend, bode, bespeak, show signs of.

promising a. encouraging, hopeful, full of promise, favorable, bright, up-and-coming, auspicious, rosy, *shaping up, heartening. ANT. *discouraging, disheartening, black.*

promontory n. headland, head, point, cape, projection, bluff, hill, height.

promote v. **1.** PUBLICIZE sell, advertize, *talk up, plug, tout, back, *hype, push, ballyhoo, trumpet, sing praises. **2.** FURTHER advance, foster, boost, support, cultivate, lift. **3.** UPGRADE ONE'S RANK advance, raise, *kick upstairs, move up, graduate. ANT. **1.** *criticize, condemn, censor, *bad-mouth.* **2.** *retard, inhibit, discourage.* **3.** *demote, downgrade.*

promotion n. **1.** PUBLICITY selling, advertisement, plugging, touting, backing, *hype, ballyhoo, hoopla. **2.** UPGRADE IN RANK graduation, *kick upstairs, move up, advance, raise. ANT. **1.** *condemnation, criticism, *bad-mouthing, censoring.* **2.** *demotion, downgrade.*

prompt v. urge, provoke, incite, goad, evoke, cue, stimulate, induce, spur, initiate, prod, arouse, push.

prompt a. quick, punctual, timely, swift, rapid, immediate, expeditious, meteoric. ANT. *late, slow, leisurely.*

promptly adv. at once, immediately, quickly, swiftly, in timely fashion, punctually, pronto, expeditiously, directly, *PDQ. ANT. *eventually, sooner or later, slowly.*

promulgate v. [PROM ul GATE] to proclaim or state publicly, publish. *The company will promulgate its new policies soon.* SYN. proclaim, announce, make known, publish, broadcast, declare, communicate, spread the word, present, herald.

prone a. **1.** LYING FLAT prostrate, recumbent, supine, horizontal, face-down. **2.** INCLINED disposed, given, bent, likely, of a mind to, liable, apt. ANT. *1. erect, upright, vertical. 2. disinclined.*

pronounce v. **1.** DECLARE announce, say, assert, decree, proclaim, report, state. **2.** ARTICULATE enunciate, say, vocalize, utter, sound, express, frame a word, mispronounce.

pronounced a. distinct, unmistakable, conspicuous, clear, striking, outstanding, prominent, bold, plain, obvious. ANT. *inconspicuous, subtle, concealed, hidden.*

pronouncement n. declaration, statement, announcement, assertion, proclamation, decree, notification, manifesto.

proof n. evidence, verification, confirmation, authentication, corroboration, validation, certification, substantiation, testimony, facts.

prop n. support, brace, buttress, pillar, stanchion, upright, beam, post, column, joist.

prop v. hold up, carry, support, shoulder, brace, gird, buttress, shore, stand, lean against.

propaganda n. disinformation, brainwashing, indoctrination, lies, distortion, deception, dissemination, psychological manipulation, subversive PR. "Polished lying." — Lin Yutang. "A polite euphemism for deception." — Walter Lippmann.

propagate v. **1.** BREED reproduce, multiply, generate, beget, engender, raise, mother, father, proliferate. **2.** SPREAD disseminate, promulgate, broadcast, publish, circulate, dispense.

propel v. drive, impel, push, shoot, move, launch, throw, thrust, force, send, actuate, hurl.

propellor n. prop, screw, blade, rotor, driver.

PROPENSITY n. [pruh PEN si tee] a natural inclination. *She had a propensity for Swedish meatballs.* SYN. tendency, leaning, bent, partiality, taste, liking, weakness, penchant, predilection, disposition, proclivity. ANT. *aversion, dislike.*

proper a. **1.** SUITABLE appropriate, suited, befitting, apt, right, fit, apropos, correct, sensible. **2.** SEEMLY decent, genteel, polite, correct, *politically correct, mannerly, nice, decorous, acceptable, fitting, comme il faut, refined. **3.** PECULIAR distinctive, distinguishing, own, individual, specific, personal. ANT. *1. unsuitable, ill-fitting, wrong. 2. unseemly, rude, impolite.*

property n. **1.** POSSESSIONS belongings, *things, *stuff, holdings, effects, goods, assets, wealth. **2.** REAL ESTATE land, acreage, estate, plot, lot, house. **3.** CHARACTERISTIC quality, feature, attribute, trait, distinction, mark, trademark.

prophecy n. prediction, foretelling, forecast, augury, divination, soothsaying, presage, prognostication, presentiment, second sight, revelation. "Dreaming on things to come." — Shakespeare.

prophesy v. predict, foretell, forecast, augur, divine, presage, prognosticate, soothsay, foresee, portend.

prophet n. predictor, fortuneteller, forecaster, augur, diviner, prognosticator, soothsayer, seer, astrologer, oracle, prophet of doom, Cassandra. "He who conjectures well." — Euripides.

prophetic a. predictive, oracular, foretelling, mantic, premonitory, augural, prognostic, prescient, portentous, ominous.

PROPITIOUS a. [pro PISH us] favorable, auspicious. *A propitious time to plant.* SYN. favorable, auspicious, promising, opportune, timely, good, advantageous, fortunate, conducive, providential, adverse, inopportune, unfortunate, bad.

PROPONENT n. [pro PO nunt] a supporter, backer or advocate. *A proponent of environmental protection.* SYN. supporter, backer, advocate, exponent, champion, upholder, endorser, defender, friend, booster. ANT. *opponent, detractor, critic.*

proportion n. **1.** RATIO amount, size, dimension, portion, scale, volume, fraction, measure, degree, division, percentage, quota, relationship. **2.** BALANCE symmetry.

proportions n. measurements, size, area. SEE DIMENSIONS

proposal n. suggestion, recommendation, presentation, idea, proposition, pitch, tender, plan, scheme, offer, bid.

propose v. **1.** SUGGEST recommend, present, pitch, tender, submit, proffer, advance, offer, proposition, make a bid, put forth for consideration. **2.** ASK FOR HAND IN MARRIAGE *pop the question, affiance.

proposition n. **1.** OFFER proposal, suggestion, submission, presentation, deal, proffer. **2.** FLIRTATION sexual overture, *come-on, *move.

proprietor n. owner, landlord, landlady, deed holder, master, lord of the manor.

PROPRIETY n. [pro PRYE i tee] proper behavior, decorum, good manners. *The children conducted themselves with unexpected propriety.* SYN. properness, proper behavior, decorum, good manners, conformity, seemliness, appropriateness, politeness, good form, gentility, etiquette. ANT. *impropriety, rudeness, bad manners.*

PROSAIC a. [proh ZAY ik] dull, ordinary, flat. *A prosaic story is the mark of an amateur writer.* SYN. dull, ordinary, flat, unimaginative, *ho-hum, blah, colorless, stale, humdrum, monotonous, trite, tedious. ANT. *interesting, colorful, imaginative.*

PROSCRIBE v. [proh SCRIBE] to outlaw, ban, condemn. *The church proscribes pornography.* SYN. outlaw, ban, prohibit, condemn, denounce, forbid, reject, exile, boycott, embargo, banish. ANT. *accept, allow, permit.*

prosecute v. file legal proceedings against, try, bring suit, sue, bring to trial, litigate, take to court, seek redress, arraign, indict.

prospect n. **1.** OUTLOOK expectancy, possibility, likelihood, anticipation, chance, speculation, probability, hope. **2.** VIEW panorama, scene, vista, outlook, aspect, lookout, perspective.

prospect v. search, explore, look for, seek, probe, pan.

prospective a. future, expected, likely, forthcoming, anticipated, possible, potential, coming, on the horizon, destined, probable.

prosper v. succeed, grow, thrive, make a fortune, do well, get ahead, get rich, bear fruit, arrive, *make a killing, *hit the jackpot. ANT. *fail, go bankrupt, *go belly up.*

prosperity n. success, growth, fortune, wealth, riches, affluence, boom times, *life of luxury, *easy street, plenty. "An instrument to be used, not a deity to be worshipped." — Calvin Coolidge. ANT. *poverty, failure, bankruptcy.*

prosperous a. successful, flourishing, thriving, growing, booming, fortunate, well-off, fat, wealthy, rich, affluent, *in the money, *on easy street. ANT. *failing, *going bankrupt, *going belly up, *drowning in red ink.*

prostitute n. whore, hooker, call girl, street walker, woman of ill repute, lady of the evening, working girl, harlot, slut, *hustler, fille de joie, *ho, strumpet, trollop. "Practioners of the oldest profession." — Anon. "One who relieves the tension in your wallet and other vital organs." — Anon.

WORD FIND

act, one sexual: *trick
agent: pimp
bought off, willingness to be: venality
customer: *john, *trick
district: red-light district
euphemism: adventuress, escort
group: demimonde
homosexual: *chicken
homosexual's old male customer: *chicken hawk
house: brothel, *cathouse, house of ill repute, *joy house, *sporting house, bordello, bawdy house, massage parlor
male, upper class: gigolo
mistress of rich man: courtesan
proprietor of brothel: madam
undercover: escort service, massage parlor

prostitute v. sell one's body, sell oneself out, lower oneself, demean oneself, debase, degrade, cheapen, misuse, abuse.

prostrate a. **1.** LYING FACE DOWN prone, recumbent, horizontal, flat, supine, in a position of humility, lying in submission, laid out. **2.** OVERCOME helpless, overwhelmed, overpowered, crushed, paralyzed, humbled, powerless, exhausted, weak, spent, fatigued, worn out, tired. ANT. *standing, upright, erect.*

protagonist n. principal, lead, central figure, hero, heroine, star, exponent, champion.

protect v. shield, defend, take care of, safeguard, fend, cover, stick up for, escort, screen, shelter, mother, father. ANT. *expose, leave vulnerable.*

protection n. shielding, defense, care, safeguarding, cover, escort, screen, shelter, security, preservation, safety, refuge. ANT. *exposure, vulnerability.*

protective a. protecting, shielding, defensive, safeguarding, covering, sheltering, securing, preserving, maternal, paternal.

protest n. objection, remonstrance, complaint, grievance, march, demonstration, strike, riot, boycott, rally, sit-in, *stink, fuss, picketing, challenge.

protest v. object, remonstrate, complain, file a grievance, march, picket, demonstrate, strike, riot, rally, sit in, boycott, *put up a stink, fuss, challenge, squawk.

protocol n. code of conduct, rules of conduct, formalities, conventions, custom, propriety, good form, etiquette, decorum, diplomatic code, manners.

prototype n. model, pattern, original, archetype, standard, exemplar, paradigm, first, forerunner, antecedent, *mockup.

PROTRACT v. [proh TRACT] to prolong, stretch out, lengthen. *They expect another protracted war in the Middle East.* SYN. prolong, stretch out, draw out, lengthen, extend, *drag out, elongate, sustain, keep going, pad.

protrude v. stick out, jut out, project, extrude, stand out, obtrude, bulge, swell, pop, overhang.

protuberance n. bump, projection, prominence, jut, protrusion, outgrowth, bulge, swelling, node, lump, excrescence.

proud a. **1.** PLEASED WITH ONESELF self-satisfied, self-respecting, *swollen with pride, honored, dignified, great, big, puffed up, *standing tall, winning. **2.** ARROGANT *full of oneself, *cocky, egotistical, pretentious, vainglorious, lordly, pompous, conceited, haughty, *bigheaded, strutting. ANT. *humble, modest, ashamed, low, humiliated.*

prove v. confirm, verify, evince, demonstrate, corroborate, affirm, validate, substantiate, establish, show, bear out, document, authenticate. ANT. *disprove, discredit, invalidate.*

proverb n. adage, maxim, aphorism, saying, epigram, axiom, truism, bromide, saw, cliché. "The wisdom of the streets." — William Benham. "A short sentence based on long experience." — Miguel de Cervantes.

provide v. supply, furnish, contribute, cater, provision, outfit, equip, stock, offer, bring, produce, accommodate, take care of, give, lend, render, donate.

provident a. prepared, farsighted, ready, precautious, foresighted, prudent, shrewd, economical, frugal. ANT. *unprepared, short-sighted.*

province n. **1.** TERRITORY division, district, region. **2.** RESPONSIBILITY duties, functions, bailiwick, sphere, concern, jurisdiction, department.

PROVINCIAL a. [pruh VIN shul] having a narrow outlook, as one from a small town or province, rustic. *Their provincial concerns excluded the needs of outsiders.* SYN. narrow, limited, small-town, unsophisticated, rustic, rural, countrified, insular, parochial, local. ANT. *worldly, universal, metropolitan, cosmopolitan.*

provision n. **1.** SUPPLY furnishing, accoutrement, outfitting, providing, giving, stock, stores, food. **2.** PREPARATION prearrangement, readiness, forearming. **3.** PROVISO clause, stipulation, specification, term, requirement, restriction, obligation, *fine print.

proviso n. condition, stipulation, clause, article, specification, term, requirement, restriction, obligation, rider, provision.

provocation n. provoking, incitement, cause, instigation, stimulus, motivation, inducement, grounds, offense, irritation, agitation.

PROVOCATIVE a. [pro VAWK uh tiv] provoking, stimulating, exciting. *The show was so provocative, it incited a riot.* SYN. provoking, stimulating, exciting, disturbing, aggravating, inciting, prodding, goading, offensive, instigating, angering, infuriating, arousing, erotic, sexy, seductive, titillating. ANT. *inane, insipid, dull.*

provoke v. **1.** STIMULATE excite, arouse, incite, stir up, instigate, goad, prod, generate, start, bring about, produce, evoke, kindle. **2.** ANGER infuriate, irritate, annoy, enrage, *piss off, offend, insult, *get on one's nerves, perturb, incense. ANT. **1.** *throw cold water on, inhibit, smooth over.* **2.** *mollify, appease, pacify.*

prowess n. **1.** BRAVERY courage, valor, fearlessness, daring, gallantry, spunk, *guts, mettle, heroism. **2.** ABILITY skill, expertise, talent, mastery, facility, know-how, proficiency, knack, command. ANT. **1.** *cowardice, weakness, timidity.* **2.** *incompetence, inability.*

prowl v. lurk, skulk, hunt, move with stealth, stalk, lie in wait, sneak, slink, steal, tiptoe.

proximity n. nearness, closeness, immediacy, vicinity, propinquity, adjacence.

proxy n. agent, substitute, surrogate, fill-in, deputy, alternate, second.

prude n. *goody two shoes, *goody-goody, Victorian, Mrs. Grundy, puritan, prig.

PRUDENT a. [PROOD unt] using good judgment, wise, cautious. *The prudent thing to do is buckle your seatbelts.* SYN. wise, sensible, cautious, judicious, thoughtful, discreet, sound, reasonable, careful, sage, practical. ANT. *irrational, reckless, thoughtless, mindless.*

prudish a. *goody-goody, prissy, squeamish,

Victorian, puritanical, strict, overnice, *uptight, straitlaced, prim, starchy, priggish. ANT. *wild, loose, wanton, abandoned.*

prune v. trim, clip, thin, reduce, dock, lop, snip, cut, crop, shorten.

prurient a. lustful, lewd, libidinous, salacious, lascivious, sexual, lecherous, *horny, carnal.

pry v. **1.** *STICK ONE'S NOSE IN interfere, meddle, intrude, snoop, be nosy, *butt in, interlope. **2.** OPEN wrest, force open, pull apart, lift off, raise, lever, prize, jimmy.

pseudo- a. [SOO doh] fake, counterfeit, pretended. *Faith healers and other pseudo-physicians attended the conference.* SYN. fake, counterfeit, pretended, false, bogus, sham, artificial, phony, simulated, imitation, fraudulent. ANT. *genuine, real.*

pseudonym n. assumed name, alias, pen name, nom de plume, AKA, stage name, professional name.

psyche n. soul, intellect, mind, self, ego, spirit, subconscious, anima.

psychiatrist n. doctor, psychoanalyst, psychotherapist, psychologist, *head doctor, therapist, *shrink, *headshrinker, mental health practitioner. "Someone who will listen to you as long as you don't make sense." — Maxwell Hyman. "A thought mechanic." — Anon.

psychic n. extrasensory, mind-reading, telepathic, clairvoyant, supersensory, superhuman, telekinetic, preternatural, mystic, occult.

psychological a. mental, of the mind, conscious, subconscious, unconscious, psychic, cognitive, intellectual, emotional, cerebral.

psychology n. SEE INSANITY, MANIA, NEUROSIS, PHOBIA

psychopathic a. psychotic. SEE INSANE, PSYCHOTIC

psychotic a. psychopathic, mentally ill, deranged, demented, disturbed, *nuts, delusional, unstable. SEE INSANE

pub n. tavern, bar, public house, saloon, alehouse.

puberty n. adolescence, teen years, sexual maturation, development, awkward years, pubescence.

WORD FIND

boy's change of voice: ponticello

public n. community, people, society, citizens, populace, masses, nation, *man/woman in the street, everyone.

public a. **1.** COMMON community, communal, popular, mutual, general, universal, open, unrestricted, accessible. **2.** KNOWN not private, open, plain as day, visible, overt, undisguised, disclosed, publicized. ANT. *1. private, restricted, exclusive. 2. private, confidential, secret.*

publication n. book, magazine, newspaper, newsletter, periodical, journal, bulletin, printing, pamphlet, report, dissemination.

publicity n. attention, promotion, notice, ballyhoo, advertisement, puffery, spotlight, hype, *plug, *blurb, *hoopla.

publicize v. promote, hype, get attention, announce, tout, advertise, sell, trumpet, promulgate, *plug, air, spotlight. ANT. *hush up, conceal, censor.*

publish v. issue, print, circulate, put out, distribute, promulgate, report, broadcast.

pucker v. purse, crease, wrinkle, contract, fold, crinkle.

puddle n. pool, wallow, drink, run-off, plash.

pudgy a. fat, dumpy, podgy, tubby, stout, rolypoly, chubby, squat, overweight, chunky. ANT. *thin, skinny, anorexic.*

puerile a. childish, immature, young, juvenile, infantile, babyish, callow, silly, sophomoric, foolish. ANT. *mature, adult, serious.*

puff n. breath, whiff, huff, wind, gust, draft, waft, blow, expulsion, cloud, smoke, vapor.

puff v. blow, breathe, inhale, exhale, huff, pant, wheeze, gust, draw, suck.

puffy a. swollen, baggy, inflated, bulging, puffed up, distended, bloated, billowy.

PUGNACIOUS a. [pug NA shus] given to fighting, combative. *Her brother was a pugnacious bully.* SYN. combative, quarrelsome, belligerent, given to fighting, aggressive, contentious, bellicose, antagonistic, militant. ANT. *peaceful, passive, pacifist, meek.*

pulchritude n. prettiness, attractiveness, loveliness. SEE BEAUTY

pull n. **1.** TUG yank, tow, jerk. **2.** INFLUENCE clout, power, weight, sway, authority.

pull v. tug, yank, tow, wrench, drag, haul, jerk, pluck, remove, withdraw, extract, rip out.

pulpit n. lectern, platform, podium, dais.

pulsate v. vibrate, quiver, beat, throb, pulse, palpitate, oscillate, flutter, thrum, ebb and flow.

pulse n. vibration, beat, rhythm, throb, pulsation, palpitation, oscillation, flutter, thrum, ebb and flow, contraction, cadence.

pulverize v. grind, smash, crush, crumble, powder, break up, granulate, fragment, pound, shatter, atomize.

pump v. **1.** DRAIN remove, suction, suck out,

siphon, draw. **2.** INFLATE blow up, expand, fill. **3.** QUESTION·interrogate, *grill, cross-examine, quiz, *give the third degree, probe.

pun *n.* play on words, witticism. "A low species of wit." — Noah Webster.

punch *n.* **1.** HIT belt, blow, uppercut, jab, one-two, *Sunday punch, cuff, *clip, thump, *clout, *smack, *sockdolager. **2.** FORCE wallop, impact, bite, *oomph.

punch *v.* hit, belt, jab, cuff, *clip, thump, pummel, *clout, *smack, *one-two, uppercut.

punctilio *n.* nicety, convention. SEE FORMALITY

punctilious *a.* careful, exact, fussy, finicky, strict, detail-oriented, meticulous, precise, scrupulous. ANT. *slack, careless, slipshod.*

punctual *a.* on time, prompt, on schedule, *on the dot, timely, dependable, reliable. ANT. *late, tardy.*

punctuate *v.* emphasize, accentuate, stress, underscore, underline, accent, mark.

puncture *n.* hole, opening, cut, slit, perforation, rupture, leak, *flat, *blowout.

puncture *v.* pierce, prick, cut, open, rupture, slit, perforate, put a hole in.

PUNDIT *n.* [PUN dit] one who is an authority, a learned man or woman. *A political pundit.* SYN. authority, expert, learned man/woman, sage, scholar, know-it-all, professional observer, master, savant.

PUNGENT *a.* [PUN junt] sharply flavorful or sharp-smelling. Also, sharp or biting in language or speech. *Both the meal and the conversation were pungent.* SYN. **1.** spicy, sharp, biting, acrid, harsh, bitter, acid, stinging, strong, acerbic, piquant, flavorful, peppery. **2.** biting, acid, penetrating, piercing, pointed, salty, spicy, hot, peppery, scathing, caustic, sharp-tongued. ANT. *bland, mild, dull.*

punish *v.* penalize, discipline, correct, chasten, chastise, teach a lesson, castigate, reprove, *come down hard on, *lower the boom on, fine, sentence, whip, flog, beat, thrash, torture, *slap one's wrist. ANT. *reward, praise, commend.*

punishment *n.* penalty, discipline, disciplinary action, chastening, chastisement, retribution, *one's due, comeuppance, *just deserts, castigation, penance, *the rod, reparation, fine, sentencing, whipping, beating, torture, *slap on the wrist. "A sort of medicine." — Aristotle. "Justice for the unjust." — Saint Augustine. "Sin is a suppurating wound; punishment is the surgeon's knife." — Saint John Chrysostom. ANT. reward, praise, commendation.

WORD FIND

beheader: guillotine

board with head and hand holes to lock in and humiliate offender in public: pillory

eye for an eye, tooth for a tooth: talion

frame with ankle, wrist holes to lock in offender: stocks

hanging, instrument of: gallows, gibbet

illegal: cruel and unusual

isolation from others: solitary confinement

neck, iron collar tightened around: garrote

ruler or stick to punish children: ferule

soles of feet, beating with stick: bastinado

stretching device: rack

tar and feather: tar and feather

vigilantes, execution by: lynching

yoke fastened around neck, Chinese: cangue

SEE PRISON, TORTURE

punitive *a.* penalizing, disciplinary, correctional, punishing, penal, harsh, hard, severe, strict.

punk *n.* hoodlum, *hood, hooligan, juvenile, delinquent, troublemaker, brat, *snot-nosed kid.

puny *a.* tiny, small, slight, pint-sized, little, undersized, inconsequential, trifling, runty, weak, underdeveloped, insignificant. ANT. *massive, huge, gigantic.*

pupil *n.* student, schoolboy, schoolgirl, first-grader, junior, sophomore, undergraduate, senior, scholar, disciple, apprentice.

puppet *n.* marionette, *muppet, doll, dummy, pawn, *stooge, *patsy, instrument, tool, figurehead.

purchase *n.* buy, acquisition, acquirement, procurement, bargain.

purchase *v.* buy, pay for, acquire, obtain, invest in, procure, bargain for, order, pick up.

pure *a.* **1.** UNMIXED clean, untainted, unadulterated, clear, unalloyed, undiluted, natural, genuine, real, clean, immaculate, unsullied, unpolluted, pristine. **2.** UTTER absolute, stark, out and out, sheer, downright, thorough. **3.** SINLESS, CHASTE virgin, virtuous, clean, *squeaky-clean, *pure as the driven snow, immaculate, celibate, decent, good, wholesome, moral, blameless, innocent, guiltless. ANT. *1. impure, tainted, mixed, diluted, dirty. 3. sinful, wicked, impure, unchaste.*

purge *v.* cleanse, remove, clean out, eliminate, clear, purify, excrete, expel, banish, *dump, eradicate, get rid of, exorcise.

purify *v.* clean, cleanse, sanitize, sterilize, clarify, purge, decontaminate, wash, filter, refine, distill.

puritanical *a.* straitlaced, strict, severe, austere, rigid, stiff, stuffy, prim, narrow. ANT. *wild, loose, fast, permissive.*

purloin *v.* filch, thrive, pilfer. SEE STEAL

purple *a.* violet, plum, lavender, lilac, amethyst, mauve, orchid, dahlia, fuchsia, royal, raisin, magenta, hyacinth, heliotrope.

purport *v.* mean, claim, profess, allege, hold, maintain, pretend.

purpose *n.* **1.** INTENTION aim, intent, object, objective, motivation, motive, goal, design, reason, plan, driving, force, point. **2.** DETERMINATION resolve, will, single-mindedness, drive, persistence, tenacity.

purposeful *a.* resolved, determined, deliberate, intent, committed, decided, resolute, fixed, persistent, tenacious. ANT. *unintentional, purposeless.*

purposely *adv.* on purpose, deliberately, intentionally, consciously, by design, knowingly, willingly, calculatedly. ANT. *unintentionally, unknowingly, accidentally.*

purse *n.* **1.** POCKETBOOK handbag, clutch, wallet, pouch. **2.** PRIZE award, sum, winnings, jackpot, stake.

purse *v.* close, press, pucker, contract.

pursue *v.* **1.** CHASE go after, run down, *tail, follow, give chase to, track, trail, hunt down, *bird dog, stalk, *shadow. **2.** STRIVE FOR seek, work for, go after, contend for, aspire to, aim for, try for.

push *n.* **1.** SHOVE thrust, propulsion, nudge, prod, poke, advance, drive, force. **2.** AMBITION drive, aggressiveness, determination, *oomph, vigor, energy.

push *v.* **1.** SHOVE thrust, propel, nudge, prod, poke, advance, drive, force, butt, press, ram, muscle, shoulder. **2.** URGE impel, goad, incite, prod, egg on, spur, pressure, motivate, compel, provoke. ANT. *1. pull, yank, tow.*

pushy *a.* aggressive, bumptious, obnoxious, domineering, bossy, controlling, officious, overbearing.

put *v.* **1.** SET place, position, deposit, stick, rest, lay, plunk, plop, drop, insert, park, situate, center. **2.** EXPRESS phrase, word, present, state, say, articulate, pose.

putrefy *v.* rot, decompose, spoil, decay, *go bad, deteriorate, taint, molder, *die.

putrid *a.* rotten, decomposing, spoiled, decayed, *gone bad, deteriorated, tainted, rancid, moldy, stinking, rank. ANT. *fresh, sweet, preserved.*

putter *v.* tinker, fiddle, *poke about, *mess about, trifle, *monkey with, toy, dawdle, fritter.

puzzle *n.* mystery, conundrum, problem, poser, riddle, enigma, maze, labyrinth.

puzzle *v.* perplex, confuse, bewilder, stump, baffle, mystify, confound, befog, *bamboozle.

puzzling *a.* perplexing, confusing, bewildering, stumping, baffling, mystifying, confounding, mysterious, enigmatic.

pygmy *a.* miniature, dwarf, midget, tiny, small, undersized, toy, stunted, Lilliputian.

Q

quack n. charlatan, fraud, fake, pretender, masquerader, humbug, *phony, imposter, mountebank, *con artist.

quagmire n. **1.** BOG mire, morass, slough, fen, swamp, marsh, quicksand, ooze. **2.** DIFFICULT OR INEXTRICABLE SITUATION hole, predicament, quandary, plight, corner, impasse, pinch, strait, mess, entanglement, *deep shit.

quail v. cower, draw back, flinch, cringe, recoil, wince, shrink.

quaint a. unusual, curious, strange, peculiar, charming, old-fashioned, antique, picturesque, whimsical, eccentric. ANT. modern, usual.

quake v. tremble, shudder, shiver. SEE SHAKE

qualification n. **1.** MODIFICATION restriction, limitation, stipulation, condition, requirement, proviso, caveat. **2.** ABILITY capability, skill, *the right stuff, attribute, competence, aptitude, eligibility, requisite.

qualified a. **1.** ABLE capable, skilled, *having the right stuff, competent, well-grounded, eligible, adequate, proficient, fit, certified, trained. **2.** MODIFIED limited, conditional, provisional, contingent, dependent, confined, circumscribed. ANT. 1. unqualified, incompetent, inadequate, ineligible. 2. unconditional, unqualified.

qualify v. ready, measure up, certify, make fit, entitle, make eligible, prepare, *make the cut, suit, ground, endow, enable, license.

QUALIFY v. [KWOL uh FYE] to modify or restrict. She qualified her answer. SYN. modify, restrict, limit, soften, confine, tone down, temper, mitigate.

quality n. **1.** ATTRIBUTE feature, characteristic, mark, trait, element, nature, property, peculiarity, quirk. **2.** EXCELLENCE value, superiority, distinction, worth, merit, perfection, eminence, caliber, stature, standing, class, virtue.

qualm n. uneasiness, misgiving, doubt, twinge, anxiety, sick feeling, uncertainty, pang, apprehension, compunction, scruple.

quandary n. predicament, dilemma, plight, fix, bind, strait, *pickle, corner, *Catch-22, jam.

quantity n. amount, number, measure, volume, sum, mass, bulk, portion, lot, magnitude, dose, extent, total.

quarantine v. isolate, sequester, confine, seclude, restrict.

quarrel n. dispute, disagreement, argument, fight, difference of opinion, spat, contention, row, altercation, squabble, controversy, tiff, debate, bickering, run-in, falling-out. ANT. agreement, accord.

quarrel v. dispute, disagree, argue, fight, differ, clash, *lock horns, bicker, squabble, debate, battle, wrangle, feud, contend. ANT. agree, *see eye-to-eye, accommodate.

quarrelsome a. argumentative, contentious, belligerent, combative, controversial, fiery, peppery, pugnacious, contrary, disagreeable. ANT. peaceful, agreeable, accommodating.

quarry n. **1.** PREY target, victim, prize, game, the hunted. **2.** PIT mine, excavation, rock quarry.

quarter n. **1.** DISTRICT neighborhood, barrio, precinct, section, region, zone. **2.** MERCY compassion, clemency, lenience, pity, forgiveness.

quarters n. lodging, accommodations, abode, shelter, housing, dwelling, domicile, room, place, residence, barracks.

quash v. quell, suppress, crush, put down, subdue, squelch, stamp out, squash, defeat.

queasy a. nauseated, qualmish, sickly, seasick, *green around the gills, *under the weather, out of sorts.

queer a. odd, strange, weird, bizarre, unusual, abnormal, out of the ordinary, singular, funny, *off the wall, quaint, extraordinary. ANT. normal, ordinary, usual. SEE HOMOSEXUAL

quell v. subdue, crush, put down, defeat, stamp out, conquer, suppress, quash, vanquish, end, silence.

quench v. **1.** EXTINGUISH put out, douse, smother, snuff out, subdue, suppress, quash, quell. **2.** SATISFY ONE'S THIRST slake, satiate, *hit the spot, sate, refresh, cool.

querulous a. fault-finding, complaining, critical, hard to please, caviling, grumbling, whining, *bitchy, fretful, petulant. ANT. easy to please, content, easygoing.

query n. question, inquiry, enquiry, interrogatory.

query v. ask, question, inquire, look into, interrogate, enquire, quiz, probe, pump, investigate, cross-examine.

quest n. search, seeking, hunt, pursuit, enterprise, adventure, exploration, expedition, mission, crusade.

question n. **1.** INQUIRY enquiry, query, interrog-

atory, examination, investigation, poser. **2.**
UNCERTAINTY doubt, controversy, misgiving,
hesitation, debate, confusion. **3.** ISSUE matter, subject, problem. ANT. *1. answer, reply.*
2. certainty, confidence.

question *v.* **1.** ASK inquire, enquire, query, seek
an answer, interrogate, examine, quiz, probe,
investigate, grill, cross-examine, pump. **2.**
DOUBT challenge, mistrust, suspect, disbelieve, wonder about, call into question. ANT.
1. answer, reply. 2. trust, have confidence in.

questionable *a.* **1.** DOUBTFUL debatable, in
question, controversial, unsettled, indeterminate, controvertible, ambiguous, moot,
unsure. **2.** SUSPECT fishy, shady, suspicious.
ANT. *1. certain, settled. 2. believable, legiti-*
mate, unimpeachable.

quibble *v.* *split hairs, *nit-pick, cavil, evade,
bicker, equivocate, carp, haggle, prevaricate.

quick *a.* **1.** FAST swift, rapid, speedy, fleet, expeditious, prompt, mercurial, *breakneck, *on
the double, hasty, immediate, sudden. **2.** IN-
TELLIGENT smart, quick to catch on, sharp,
astute, bright, *on the ball, acute, savvy,
alert, receptive, keen. ANT. *1. slow, slothful,*
sluggish. 2. slow, dense, stupid.

quicken *v.* **1.** SPEED UP accelerate, expedite,
hurry, speed, hasten, hustle. **2.** ENLIVEN stimulate, invigorate, stir, arouse, revive, animate, awaken, strengthen. ANT. *1. slow*
down, mire, bog down. 2. kill, deaden.

quickly *adv.* speedily, fast, expeditiously,
swiftly, hastily, rapidly, hurriedly, briskly,
full-tilt, pronto, *quicker than greased lightning. ANT. *slowly, slothfully.*

quick-tempered *a.* irritable, touchy, *short-
fused, grouchy, cantankerous, volatile, temperamental, hot-blooded, testy, waspish, fiery. ANT. *easygoing, placid, long-fused.*

quick-witted *a.* alert, *on the ball, nimble,
sharp, smart, acute, shrewd, savvy, bright,
intelligent, quick on the uptake, clever. ANT.
dull, stupid, dense.

quiet *n.* silence, peace, hush, stillness, calm,
soundlessness, noiselessness, tranquility, serenity, lull. "Noise you don't mind." — Leonard Levinson. ANT. *noise, racket, uproar, din.*

quiet *v.* hush, shush, silence, shut up, muffle,
tone down, soften squelch, muzzle, *put a
lid on, *keep down to a low roar.

quiet *a.* **1.** SOUNDLESS silent, still, peaceful,
hushed, soft, quiescent, inaudible, low,
muted, noiseless, *as silent as the vacuum of
space, *as silent as a crypt, *quiet enough to
hear a pin drop. **2.** NOT TALKATIVE close-

mouthed, silent, taciturn, reserved, mute,
tightlipped, not big on small talk, *doesn't
waste a lot of kindling to make a fire. **3.** CALM
tranquil, peaceful, motionless, undisturbed,
still, serene, placid, halcyon. ANT. *1. noisy,*
*loud, deafening. 2. loquacious, talkative, *mo-
tor-mouthed. 3. turbulent, wild, agitated.

quintessence *n.* **1.** ESSENCE heart, pith, soul,
distillation. **2.** PARAGON model, exemplar,
cream, *creme de la creme.

quip *n.* witty remark, witticism, jest, gibe, crack,
bon mot, wisecrack, joke, retort, repartee.

quirk *n.* peculiarity, oddity, characteristic, trait,
mannerism, idiosyncrasy, eccentricity, twist,
kink.

quit *v.* **1.** STOP give up, discontinue, break off,
end, *call it a day, cease, desist, *knock off,
*halt, *pack in, *hang it up, give notice. **2.**
LEAVE depart, abandon, withdraw, *cut out,
take off, relinquish, surrender, bow out, walk
out on, drop, leave flat, forsake, resign from.
ANT. *1. start, begin, commence. 2. take up, re-*
main, maintain, sustain.

quite *adv.* completely, entirely, totally, fully,
wholly, very, really, truly, surely.

quiver *n.* tremor, tremble, shake, vibration,
twitch, shudder, shiver, quaver, flutter,
throb, palpitation.

quiver *v.* shake, tremble, vibrate, shudder,
shiver, twitch, quaver, flutter, throb, palpitate.

QUIXOTIC *a.* [kwik SOT ik] idealistic or romantic in a foolish or impractical way, like
the fictional character Don Quixote. *He had*
long entertained the quixotic notion of giving
children the vote. SYN. idealistic, romantic,
foolish, impractical, unrealistic, dreamy, utopian, fanciful, chimerical, *starry-eyed, visionary, chivalrous. ANT. *practical, down-to-*
earth, realistic.

quiz *n.* test, exam, examination, pop quiz, questioning, multiple choice, Q&A, catechism.

quiz *v.* test, examine, question, grill, ask, query,
pump, inquire, interrogate, cross-examine.

quizzical *a.* **1.** QUESTIONING perplexed, inquisitive, confused, puzzled, inquiring, curious,
searching, unbelieving, bewildered, lost. **2.**
TEASING ridiculing, mocking, derisive, impudent, insolent, joking.

quota *n.* portion, share, cut, ration, allowance,
percentage, lot, part, piece, dole, measure.

quotation *n.* quote, passage, citation, excerpt,
saying, selection, extract, reference.

quote *v.* cite, parrot, recite, paraphrase, repeat,
excerpt, refer to, extract, reference.

R

rabble *n.* crowd, mob, the masses, commoners, common people, lower classes, proletariat, rank and file, hoi polloi, horde." The dregs of the people." — Cicero. "The venal herd." — Juvenal. ANT. *upper class, ruling class, aristocracy.*

rabid *a.* raging, berserk, maniacal, crazed, deranged, mad, zealous, extreme, *nuts, violent, fanatical, *foaming at the mouth. ANT. *sane, reasonable, moderate.*

race *n.* **1.** PEOPLE ethnic group, nationality, line, tribe, breed, stock, clan, folk, strain. "One of many branches in the tree of humanity." — Anon. **2.** SPRINT dash, run, marathon, footrace, heat, relay, contest, meet, steeplechase, derby.

WORD FIND

AUTO RACING

aerodynamic wing or wedge that improves car handling: spoiler

broadside crash into competitor's car or wall: T-bone

bumper-to-bumper pressure tactic: dogging

coveted front inside position at start: pole position

curve or tight turn: ess-turn, hairpin turn, chicane

custom-built, nonstock race car: formula car, Indy car

drag race, beat competitor in: shut down

drag-racing car: dragster, rail, funny car

driving directly behind lead car to create fuel-conserving vacuum: drafting, slip-streaming

flag alerting hazardous car to leave the track: black flag

flag, end of race; checkered flag

flag, final lap: white flag

flag, go: green flag

flag, hazard: yellow flag

flag, stop: red flag

flag warning of competitor on one's tail: blue flag

formula car race: Grand Prix

long-distance competition: rally

low edge of track: apron

NASCAR: National Association for Stock Car Auto Racing

noncompeting pacesetter at start of race: pace car

parachute, release at end of drag race: *hang out the laundry

passing method creating vacuum on lead car: slingshot

pass one track-length ahead of competitor: lap

pit crew's head mechanic: crew chief

production car: stock car

racing tires: *shoes, *slicks

running start: flying start

service area: pit

service mechanics: pit crew

steel support network protecting inside of car: roll cage

steel support tube protecting inside of car: roll bar

straightaway in front of grandstand: chute

straightaway race: drag race

THOROUGHBRED HORSERACING

barrier: starting gate, post

betting away from the track: offtrack betting

betting system: pari-mutuals

bugle call: Boots and Saddles

castrated male horse: gelding

close finish: photo finish, blanket finish

costumes, riders': colors, silks

crouching riding posture: monkey crouch

drug horse illegally: hop

escorts horses to post: outrider

exercise or practice run: airing

favored to win: chalk horse

first two finishers, bet on: quinella

hold back horse to keep it from winning: stiff

horse that does well on muddy track: mudder

info sheet: dope sheet

insider with "inside" information on horse: tout

length: eight to nine feet

mile, one-eighth of a: furlong

money, horse that fails to finish in the: also-ran

money-losing horse: hayburner

observation ring: walking ring

odds board: tote board

officials: clerk of the scales, stewards

pasture or saddling enclosure: paddock

peripheral visions blockers, horse's: blinkers

rider: jockey

saddle and other horse equipment, collective term: tack

short race: sprint

stable assistant: groom

straightaway, farside: backstretch

straightaway in front of grandstand: home-
stretch
surrounded position: pocket
three-year-old horse: sophomore
three-year-olds, race for: derby
track condition, broken into clods and hoof-
prints: cuppy
track condition, freshly harrowed: deep
track condition, hard and fast: pasteboard
track
two-year-old horse: juvenile
underrated horse: sleeper, dark horse
weight, adding to equalize competition:
handicap
weight assigned to horse in handicap race:
impost
weighing of jockeys with tack: weigh-in,
weigh-out
whip: gad, leather
winners of two races, correctly picking: daily
double
winning Kentucky Derby, Preakness Stakes
and the Belmont Stakes: Triple Crown
winning of three races by same jockey on
one program: hat trick
win one's first race: break maiden, graduate
win without prodding or whipping the horse:
armchair ride
withdrawal of entrant: scratch

racism n. prejudice, discrimination, bigotry,
bias, segregation, apartheid, intolerance,
white supremacy. "The snobbery of the
poor." – Raymond Aron.

rack n. frame, framework, stand, holder, scaffolding, grating, hack, flake.

racket n. 1. NOISE din, clamor, uproar, commotion, clatter, disturbance, pandemonium,
hubbub, babel, cacophony. 2. CRIMINAL AC-
TIVITY bootlegging, fraud, swindling, loan-
sharking, graft, extortion, corruption, brib-
ery, blackmail.

raconteur n. storyteller, teller of tales, spinner
of yarns. SEE AUTHOR, NOVELIST

racy a. 1. SUGGESTIVE risque, spicy, bawdy, immodest, off-color, dirty, indecent, pornographic, ribald. 2. LIVELY spirited, energetic,
vigorous, zesty, exciting, peppy, vivacious.
ANT. modest, wholesome, G-rated.

RADAR n. Radio Detecting and Ranging System, tracking device, scanning system.
WORD FIND
air surveillance, early warnings system:
AWACS, Airborne Warning and Control System
image: blip

police radar detection device: *fuzzbuster
sound: beep, racon
SEE AIR FORCE, AIRPLANE, AIRPORT

radiant a. 1. SHINING bright, glowing, beaming,
gleaming, luminous, refulgent, resplendent,
brilliant, incandescent. 2. HAPPY bright,
beaming, glowing, joyous, joyful, cheerful,
sunny. ANT. 1. dull, dim, dark. 2. gloomy,
black.

radiate v. shine, illuminate, glow, beam, pour
out, send out, shoot out, spread out, diffuse,
throw off.

radical n. extremist, fanatic, zealot, revolutionist, leftist, left-winger, iconoclast, nonconformist. "A man with both feet firmly
planted in the air." – Franklin Delano
Roosevelt. ANT. conservative, moderate.

radical a. 1. FUNDAMENTAL basic, rudimentary,
elemental, foundational. 2. EXTREME thorough, extremist, severe, progressive, fanatical, drastic, revolutionary, complete, whole,
sweeping, far left.

radio n. receiver, *boom box, *ghetto blaster,
*Walkman, Marconi, CB, crystal set, ham
radio, walkie-talkie. "Television without
eyestrain." – Max Gralnik.
WORD FIND
AM: amplitude modulation
amateur two-way radio enthusiast: ham
brief quote from someone in the news:
soundbite
broadcast sent from other station or network: feed
DJ: disc jockey
FM: frequency modulation
identification letters: call letters
morning and evening time when commuters
listen: drive time
obnoxious radio show: shock radio
overseas political radio of United States:
Voice of America
range of radio frequencies: band
station that only rebroadcasts other stations'
shows: translator
switch used by DJ to block cough or sneeze
from going over the air: cough button
type of programming: format
unlicensed station: pirate station

radius n. extent, range, scope, sphere, compass.

raffish a. careless, unconventional, casual,
wild, bohemian, rakish, vulgar, low, tawdry.

ragamuffin n. tramp, *bum, *street person,
street Arab, urchin, derelict, guttersnipe,
waif, tatterdemalion.

rage n. 1. FURY anger, wrath, tantrum, fit, ferocity, high dudgeon, hysterics, rampage, furor, *piss hemorrhage, uproar, hot blood. SEE ANGER 2. FAD craze, *in thing, fashion, *latest thing, *latest wrinkle, vogue, dernier cri. ANT. 1. *delight, calm, passivity.*

rage *v.* *blow up, *explode, *go ballistic, be furious, fume, rant and rave, *fly off the handle, *blow a fuse, boil, *blow one's top, become livid, *turn purple, *spit tacks, *see red, *blow a gasket, *flip out, *get into a lather, *get one's Irish up, *go apeshit, *have a conniption fit, storm.

ragged *a.* tattered, frayed, in shreds, worn, threadbare, shaggy, moth-eaten, torn, full of holes, seedy, shabby, jagged. ANT. *smooth, whole, new.*

raid *n.* attack, invasion, onslaught, incursion, offensive, foray, assault, charge, *bust.

raid *v.* attack, invade, storm, strike, launch an offensive, charge, sweep, maraud, assail, loot, plunder, *bust.

rail *v.* complain, criticize, *bitch out, *tongue-lash, assail, denounce, condemn, censure, castigate, chastise, *chew out. ANT. *praise, compliment, approve.*

railing *n.* baluster, balustrade, banister, handhold, fence, parapet.

railroad *n.* rail line, tracks, railway, subway, monorail, el. "Only a device for making the world smaller."—John Ruskin.

WORD FIND

barrier or stop at end of track: bumper
bed in a sleeping car: berth
brake operator: brakeman
bridge: trestle
cars owned by one company: rolling stock
crew's tail car: caboose, *doghouse, *shanty, *buggy, *van, *penthouse, *doodlebug
driver: engineman, engineer
driving compartment of locomotive: cab
elevated: el
engine employed to clear cars in yard: trimmer, *yard goat
engine: locomotive
fast train: bullet train, express train
freight car: boxcar, flatcar, gondola, hopper, livestock car, platform car, refrigerator car (*reefer), tank car, *wagon
hitching clamp: coupler
holding area for train, cars: yard
locomotive's front bumper: cowcatcher
lover of railroads: ferrophiliac
magnetically levitated train: Maglev
meal car: dining car
mountain track employing cogs to increase

traction: cog railway
passenger car: coach, dining car, Pullman sleeper, lounge car, observation car, smoking car
porter at station: redcap
rail layers: *steel gang, *spikers
rotating platform used to turn locomotives: turntable
second engine used in steep areas: booster, *rammer
shunting mechanism: switch
sidetrack dead-end: spur
signaling apparatus: semaphore
signaling framework over tracks: gantry
single rail track: monorail
sleeper, luxury: palace car
slip off tracks: derail
sorting cars in freight yard: marshaling
steam whistle's peep: crow
supervisor, fare collector: conductor
supervisor of yard: yardmaster
switching tracks: shunting
tie: sleeper, crosstie
turntable facility for switching locomotives: roundhouse
wheeled trucks that support cars: bogies
width of track: gauge
worker's hand-pumped transport: handcar
X-like railroad crossing sign: crossbuck

railroad *v.* push through, force through, rush through, expedite.

rain *n.* precipitation, rainfall, mist, drizzle, mizzle, sprinkle, spit, shower, cloudburst, downpour, squall, thundershower, *gully washer, deluge, drencher, *cats and dogs, torrent, *rain of biblical proportion, sleet, hail. "The lifeblood of mother nature." — Anon.

WORD FIND

moisture content of air: humidity
precipitation, all types of: hydrometeors
rain and evaporation cycle: hydrologic cycle
rain driven by wind: scud
study of: hyetography
sudden heavy rain: spate
temperature at which moisture condenses into rain: dewpoint
SEE CLOUD, FOG, SNOW

rain *v.* precipitate, fall, pour, drop, sprinkle, shower, spit, mist, *come down in buckets, drizzle, weep, *rain pitchforks.

raise *n.* increase, advance, pay hike, boost, promotion, jump.

raise *v.* 1. LIFT elevate, hoist, erect, run up, jack up, heighten, heave, loft. 2. INCREASE escalate, inflate, enlarge, heighten, magnify, amplify, boost, *jack up, double, triple, quadruple. **3.** AROUSE stir up, rouse, start, activate, awaken, whip up, provoke, spur, incite. **4.** REAR bring up, parent, cultivate, nurture, foster, breed. ANT. *3. dampen, inhibit.*

RAISON D'ETRE [ray ZON DET ruh] reason for being. *Protection of the company's proprietary interests was given as the security's system's raison d'etre.* SYN. reason for being, justification for being.

rake *n.* roue, playboy, lecher, swinger, *makeout artist, womanizer, Casanova, Don Juan, Lothario, wolf, philanderer.

RAKISH *a.* [RAKE ish] dashing, jaunty. Also, highly sexual or debauched. *A rakish gentleman entered the room and all the women stared at him.* SYN. dashing, jaunty, sporty, stylish, debonair, dapper, chic, sharp, debauched, oversexed, wanton, lecherous, flirtatious. ANT. *frumpy, out of style, unkempt, upright, gentlemanly, chaste, virginal.*

rally *n.* **1.** GATHERING meeting, pep rally, assembly, meet, conventional, revival, session, celebration. **2.** COMEBACK resurgence, revival, recovery, renewal, road to recovery, renaissance, rebound. ANT. *2. collapse, decline, loss, death, turn for the worse.*

rally *v.* **1.** GATHER meet, convene, assemble, reassemble, mobilize, summon together, collect, get together, unite, call to arms. **2.** RECOVER come back, surge, resurge, rise again, revive, renew, rebound, bounce back, turn around, come around, rejuvenate, *get a second wind. ANT. *1. disperse, break up. 2. decline, lose, die, take a turn for the worse.*

ram *v.* drive, hammer, slam, bang, smash, butt, crash into, hit head-on, beat, tramp.

ramble *v.* roam, wander aimlessly, drift, rove, range, stroll, traipse, meander, stray, walk, saunter, hike.

rambling *a.* digressive, discursive, circuitous, wordy, verbose, prolix, circumlocutory, roundabout, desultory. ANT. *concise, to the point.*

RAMBUNCTIOUS *a.* [ram BUNK shus] unruly, disorderly, raucous, noisy. *Most two-year-olds are rambunctious.* SYN. unruly, disorderly, raucous, noisy, unrestrained, wild, unmanageable, boisterous, *hyper, hyperactive. ANT. *docile, well-behaved, quiet.*

RAMIFICATION *n.* [RAM uh fuh KA shun] a consequence, effect or result. *One ramification of unbridled terrorism is outright war.* SYN. consequence, effect, result, outgrowth, offshoot, product, end, upshot, complication.

ramp *n.* slope, incline, rise, grade.

rampage *n.* outbreak, fury, uproar, blowup, rage, tempest, storm, running amuck, *warpath, furor. ANT. *calm, peace, contentment.*

rampant *a.* growing, spreading, uncontrolled, rife, widespread, out of hand, unchecked, out of control, unbridled, epidemic. ANT. *contained, limited, under control.*

rampart *n.* fortification, bulwark, defense, barrier, embankment, earthwork, wall, breastwork. SEE CASTLE

ramshackle *a.* rickety, falling apart, shaky, broken down, tumble-down, dilapidated, crumbling, derelict, decrepit. ANT. *sound, solid, rock-solid.*

ranch *n.* cattle farm, range land, grange, plantation, *spread.

rancid *a.* spoiled, rotten, stale, rank, reeking, bad, fetid, stinking, sour, foul, disgusting, putrid. ANT. *sweet, fresh, mouth-watering.*

RANCOR *n.* [RANG kur] long-lasting hatred and ill will. *The two parties were divided by rancor.* SYN. hatred, ill will, malice, spite, bitterness, animosity, enmity, malevolence, resentment, vindictiveness. ANT. *goodwill, friendliness, affection, love.*

random *a.* haphazard, casual, chance, accidental, unplanned, arbitrary, fortuitous, desultory, blind, hit-or-miss, aimless. ANT. *planned, designed, premeditated.*

range *n.* scope, extent, reach, limit, sphere, sweep, parameters, boundary, area, radius, expanse, territory. SEE MOUNTAIN

range *v.* roam, travel, wander, meander, rove, traverse, drift, cross, ramble.

rangy *a.* gangling, lank, lanky, slender, long-legged, *split high, leggy, thin, skinny. ANT. *squat, stout, fat.*

rank *v.* classify, align, group, station, grade, arrange, order, rate, position, sort.

rank *a.* **1.** OFFENSIVE stinking, strong, rancid, foul, bad, fetid, reeking, nauseating, revolting, rotten. **2.** LUXURIANT luxurious, lush, rich, vigorous, overgrown, flourishing, dense, proliferating, coarse. ANT. *1. sweet-smelling, sweet-tasting, mild, pleasant, fresh. 2. sparse, barren.*

rankle *v.* anger, inflame, infuriate, gall, embitter, irritate, *rub the wrong way, irk, *piss off, *fill with venom, *make blood boil, fill with resentment. ANT. *delight, pacify, mollify.*

ransack *v.* search, *tear place apart, *turn inside out, rummage, look over, rifle, *leave no stone unturned, overhaul, scour, plunder, pillage, rob.

rant v. rave, *sound off, shout, yell, roar, holler, *spout off, fume, vociferate, bluster, declaim. ANT. *whisper, murmur, talk under one's breath.*

rap n. **1.** KNOCK tap, hit, blow, stroke, slap, cuff, punch, belt. **2.** MUSIC *hip hop. **3.** Sl. CONVERSATION dialogue, talk. **4.** Sl. BLAME punishment, flak, responsibility.

rap v. **1.** KNOCK tap, hit, deliver a blow, slap, cuff, punch, belt. **2.** CONVERSE talk, chat, have a dialogue, confabulate.

RAPACIOUS a. [ruh PAY shus] plundering, predatory. *The rapacious pirates stole everything of value.* SYN. plundering, predatory, thieving, marauding, pillaging, greedy, grasping, ravenous, voracious, savage.

rape n. sexual assault, molestation, forcible intercourse, ravishment, overpowering, violation, *date rape, deflowering, plundering, pillage, sacking.

rape v. molest, sexually assault, ravish, *force oneself on, attack, overpower, violate, deflower, defile, *have one's way with, plunder, pillage, sack.

rapid a. fast, swift, quick, fleet, speedy, expeditious, mercurial, hasty, winged, *quicker than greased lightning. ANT. *slow, slothful, leisurely.*

rapport n. harmony, agreement, *seeing eye-to-eye, *common ground, closeness, understanding, affinity, compatibility, *simpatico, *good vibes. ANT. *hostility, alienation, *bad vibes, disagreement.*

rapt a. **1.** ENRAPTURED carried away, transported, rapturous, ecstatic, euphoric, emotional, joyous. **2.** ENGROSSED absorbed, captivated, preoccupied, deep, *wrapped up, spellbound, enthralled, oblivious, fascinated. ANT. *1. depressed, dejected, downhearted. 2. distracted, bored, disinterested.*

rapture n. ecstasy, euphoria, elation, joy, happiness, bliss, transport, heaven, exultation. ANT. *depression, misery, melancholy.*

rare a. **1.** UNCOMMON infrequent, scarce, unusual, unique, exceptional, *few and far between, extraordinary, singular, *once in a blue moon, at a premium, *scarce as hens' teeth, seldom found. **2.** EXCELLENT superlative, superior, fine, exquisite, select, choice, first-class, priceless, precious. **3.** UNDERCOOKED half-cooked, bloody, red, raw, underdone. ANT. *1. common, frequent, abundant, usual. 2. poor, inferior, bad. 3. well-done, burned.*

rarely adv. seldom, hardly ever, almost never, once in a blue moon, once in awhile, infrequently, scarcely. ANT. *often, frequently.*

rascal n. scoundrel, scamp, rogue, knave, imp, rapscallion, devil, cad, cur, *bastard, *SOB.

rash a. incautious, reckless, impulsive, thoughtless, careless, hasty, injudicious, devil-may-care, unwary, foolhardy. ANT. *cautious, careful, judicious.*

rasp v. scrape, grate, scratch, rub, file, grind, scour, abrade.

raspy a. scratchy, rough, whiskey-voiced, hoarse, harsh, gritty, grating, gravelly.

rate n. **1.** AMOUNT degree, proportion, ratio. **2.** PRICE fee, charge, cost, value, expense, levy, duty. **3.** SPEED tempo, pace, velocity, progress, flow.

rate v. appraise, estimate, evaluate, assess, rank, score, grade, weigh, value, deem, classify.

rather adv. moderately, pretty, somewhat, fairly, relatively, kind of, more or less.

RATIFY v. [RAT uh fi] to approve or pass officially. *They plan to ratify the amendment today.* SYN. approve, pass, sanction, support, affirm, endorse, authorize, back, warrant, *rubber stamp. ANT. *disapprove, veto, invalidate.*

rating n. rank, score, grade, mark, class, classification, evaluation, assessment.

ratio n. proportion, relationship, percentage, quota, distribution.

ration v. apportion, allot, allocate, mete out, dole out, divide, *divvy up, split up.

rational a. sane, reasonable, of sound mind, clear-thinking, sensible, levelheaded, sober, *with it, lucid, logical. ANT. *irrational, unreasonable, nonsensical, insane.*

rationale n. basis, reason, grounds, excuse, rationalization, motive, justification, logic, explanation.

rationalize v. justify, explain away, account for, make excuses for, intellectualize.

rattle v. clatter, vibrate, jangle, clink, clang, clank, knock, jiggle, bang.

raucous a. loud, noisy, rowdy, boisterous, riotous, strident, vociferous, blaring, uproarious, clamorous. ANT. *quiet, still, silent.*

raunchy a. sexual, pornographic, lustful, dirty, X-rated. SEE LEWD

ravage v. destroy, ruin, devastate, wreck, demolish, lay waste, plunder, pillage, ransack, despoil.

rave v. **1.** TALK WILDLY rant, carry on, run off at the mouth, speak deliriously, rattle on, speak incoherently. **2.** PRAISE gush, speak highly of, enthuse, carry on, rhapsodize, go on about.

3. RAGE roar, thunder, explode, storm, fume, sputter, *holler, *flip out. ANT. *criticize, disparage.*

ravenous *a.* hungry, famished, voracious, starved, starving, *could eat a horse, gluttonous, insatiable, greedy, predatory. ANT. *satiated, full, sated.*

ravine *n.* gully, gorge, gulch, arroyo, valley, ditch, wash, chasm, coulee.

ravishing *a.* attractive, enchanting, alluring, entrancing, gorgeous, bewitching, beautiful, captivating. ANT. *repulsive, ugly, disgusting.*

raw *a.* **1.** UNCOOKED rare, bloody, underdone. **2.** NATURAL unrefined, unprocessed, virgin, crude, rough, undressed, unfinished. **3.** INEXPERIENCED untrained, green, unseasoned, immature, callow, unfledged, new, ignorant, unschooled. **4.** SORE inflamed, tender, sensitive, abraded, exposed, open, bare, chafed. **5.** COLD chilly, bitter, damp, bleak, freezing, nippy, biting. ANT. *1. cooked, well done. 2. refined, processed, milled. 3. experienced, trained, seasoned. 5. warm, pleasant, balmy.*

rawboned *a.* lean, gaunt, wasted, hollow-cheeked. SEE THIN

raze *v.* tear down, level, flatten, destroy, topple, demolish, wreck, knock down, fell, *total.

reach *n.* distance, extent, range, grasp, span, stretch, sweep, compass, play.

reach *v.* **1.** ARRIVE AT come to, enter, *hit town, get in, get to, land. **2.** EXTEND THE HAND thrust out, stretch out, outstretch, strain. **3.** TOUCH grasp, get hold of, clutch, grab, seize, make contact, secure. **4.** AMOUNT TO extend, attain, arrive at.

react *v.* respond, act, counter, recoil, reciprocate, answer, return, acknowledge, reply.

reaction *n.* response, comeback, answer, feedback, counteraction, return, reflex, reciprocation, acknowledgement, recoil, backlash, fallout, repercussion.

reactionary *a.* retrogressive, right wing. SEE CONSERVATIVE

read *v.* **1.** TO INTERPRET THE PRINTED WORD comprehend, understand, construe, interpret, decipher, translate, peruse, scan, skim, pore over, flip through. **2.** UTTER recite, deliver.

readable *a.* legible, decipherable, intelligible, understandable, clear, plain.

readily *adv.* quickly, without delay, unhesitatingly, immediately, promptly, *at the drop of a hat, willingly, cheerfully, freely, *on the spur of the moment. ANT. *hesitantly, slowly, reluctantly.*

ready *v.* prepare, set up, prime, equip, prep, fit, gear up, warm up.

ready *a.* **1.** PREPARED in place, primed, set, equipped, *all systems go, *on one's toes, on call, expectant. **2.** UNHESITANT willing, eager, prompt, enthusiastic, cheerful, inclined, game. **3.** CLEVER sharp, keen, intelligent, bright, smart, astute, quick. ANT. *1. unprepared, *flat-footed, ill-equipped. 2. hesitant, unwilling, slow. 3. slow, dull.*

real *a.* actual, genuine, authentic, true, factual, valid, legitimate, bona fide, honest-to-goodness, tangible, physical, material, sincere. ANT. *unreal, fictitious, counterfeit, phony, insincere.*

realistic *a.* **1.** PRACTICAL down-to-earth, pragmatic, reasonable, having both feet on the ground, unromantic, sober, sane. **2.** REPRESENTATIONAL lifelike, true-to-life, faithful, photographic, graphic, exact. ANT. *1. impractical, idealistic, unrealistic. 2. fake, rough.*

realize *v.* **1.** UNDERSTAND apprehend, comprehend, get, recognize, be cognizant of, grasp, appreciate, perceive, conceive, discern, see. **2.** ACHIEVE fulfill, accomplish, effectuate, complete, actualize, *pull off, attain, carry out.

really *adv.* truly, honestly, in fact, certainly, surely, literally, indeed, verily.

realm *n.* area, domain, sphere, region, empire, kingdom, dominion, territory, zone, field, reach, world, arena, orbit.

reap *v.* gather, harvest, collect, bring in, pick, pluck, cut, gain, obtain.

rear *v.* raise, bring up, grow, nurture, foster, breed, parent, train, groom.

rear *a.* back, posterior, hind, tail, aft, last. ANT. *front, fore, first.*

reason *n.* **1.** EXPLANATION justification, grounds, motive, rationale, cause, why, occasion, excuse, basis. **2.** THINKING ABILITY analysis, intellect, intelligence, wisdom, sense, smarts, logic, judgment, deduction, wit, brains. "The only oracle of man." —Ethan Allen. "A harmony among irrational impulses." —George Santayana.

reason *v.* think, deduce, analyze, apply logic, judge, cogitate, draw conclusions, use one's head, deliberate, rationalize.

reasonable *a.* **1.** SENSIBLE rational, sane, logical, intelligent, sound, thoughtful, levelheaded, judicious, commonsensical, well-advised. **2.** MODERATE fair, within reason, conservative, judicious, equitable, evenhanded, right, unextreme, temperate. ANT. *1. unreasonable, irrational, nonsensical. 2. extreme, immoderate.*

reasoning n. analysis, deduction, induction, thinking, thought, logic, inference, rationale, deliberation, cogitation, ratiocination.

reassure v. assure, fill with confidence, encourage, bolster, hearten, buck up, embolden, put one's mind at ease, comfort. ANT. *unnerve, frighten, discourage, shake one's confidence.*

rebate n. reimbursement, bonus, discount. SEE REFUND

rebel n. revolutionary, insurrectionist, malcontent, nonconformist, dissenter, insurgent, mutineer, iconoclast, anarchist, independent, opponent, traitor, young Turk. ANT. *conformist, follower, *sheep.*

rebel v. revolt, defy, disobey, resist, fight, dissent, rise up, oppose, mutiny, riot, overthrow.

rebellion n. revolt, revolution, defiance, insurrection, disobedience, insurgency, resistance, dissent, opposition, uprising, mutiny. "A medicine necessary for the sound health of government."—Thomas Jefferson.

rebellious a. revolutionary, defiant, disobedient, resistant, iconoclastic, nonconforming, insurgent, insurrectionary, mutinous, recalcitrant, seditious, riotous, ungovernable. ANT. *conforming, passive, *following the herd, docile, obedient.*

rebound v. bounce back, spring back, recover, return, recoil, ricochet, boomerang.

rebuff v. refuse, snub, brush off, reject, spurn, slight, repel, check, repulse, *give the cold shoulder, *cut. ANT. *embrace, accept, welcome.*

REBUKE v. [ri BYOOK] to reprimand or criticize harshly. *He was rebuked for losing the documents.* SYN. criticize, reprimand, admonish, *chew out, berate, reprove, reproach, censure, scold, *call on the carpet, *jump down one's throat, *rake over the coals. ANT. *praise, laud, honor, *pat on the back.*

rebut v. contradict, argue, controvert, refute, disprove, invalidate, discredit, *shoot down, retort. ANT. *support, prove, validate.*

rebuttal n. counterargument, contradiction, refutation, invalidation, discrediting, retort, riposte, *comeback, disproof.

RECALCITRANT v. [ri KAL si trunt] defiant, disobedient. *The recalcitrant mule had to be gently coaxed.* SYN. defiant, disobedient, insubordinate, rebellious, resistant, refractory, intractable, fractious, contrary, stubborn. ANT. *obedient, tractable, submissive.*

recall n. recollection, memory, remembrance, reminiscence. ANT. *forgetfulness, mental block, amnesia.*

recall v. **1.** REMEMBER recollect, reminisce, call to mind, think back, evoke, look back on, review, summon. **2.** CALL BACK withdraw, repeal, rescind, revoke, retract, take back. ANT. *1. forget, suffer amnesia, *have a mental block.*

RECANT v. [ri KANT] to take back statements formerly made. *He recanted his story in view of the overwhelming evidence against him.* SYN. take back, withdraw, disavow, retract, back down, disclaim, recall, *eat one's words, reverse, revoke. ANT. *acknowledge, confirm, *own up, admit.*

recap v. SEE RECAPITULATE

recapitulate v. repeat, summarize, recount, review, restate, rehash, recap, go over again.

recede v. withdraw, back away, go down, diminish, dwindle, decline, retreat, wane, shrink, fade, ebb, regress, drain. ANT. *rise, advance, increase.*

receipt n. **1.** SALES SLIP proof of purchase, voucher, stub. **2.** RECEIVING reception, arrival, delivery, acquisition, acceptance.

receive v. **1.** GET take possession, acquire, collect, be given, obtain, pocket, gain, come by, inherit. **2.** EXPERIENCE undergo, encounter, suffer, endure, bear, sustain, meet with. **3.** TAKE IN VISITORS accommodate, greet, admit, accept, welcome, host, entertain.

recent a. late, now, current, fresh, modern, today, present-day, hot, new, up-to-date. ANT. *past, old, bygone, ancient.*

receptacle n. holder, container, vessel, repository, box, basket, bin, bag.

reception n. **1.** RECEIVING acknowledgement, welcome, greeting. **2.** PARTY function, gathering, levee, soiree.

receptive a. open, accepting, open-minded, accessible, favorable, amenable, inclined, hospitable. ANT. *closed, close-minded, unreceptive, cold.*

recess n. **1.** BREAK rest, intermission, halt, respite, breathing spell, *breather, hiatus, interlude. **2.** HOLLOW niche, indentation, nook, slot, cranny, hole, bay, alcove.

recession n. receding, withdrawal, retreat, reversal, regression, decline, downturn, slump, *hard times, economic slowdown, depression. ANT. *progression, advance, growth, *boom times.*

recipe n. formula, prescription, directions, compound, ingredients, list, blueprints, specifications.

reciprocal a. mutual, interchangeable, exchanged, alternate, interdependent, *give-and-take, corresponding, shared.

reciprocate v. give and take, interchange, exchange, return in kind, trade, repay, share, swap, retaliate, *scratch each other's back.

recite v. repeat, read, deliver, narrate, speak, tell, perform, report, relate.

recital n. **1.** CONCERT musical program, solo performance, musicale. **2.** ACCOUNT reciting, delivery, narrative, narration, retelling, story, recounting, recapitulation.

reckless a. incautious, careless, devil-may-care, heedless, headlong, breakneck, wild, daring, foolhardy, rash, negligent. ANT. *cautious, careful, responsible.*

reckon v. **1.** FIGURE UP add up, count, compute, total, tally, calculate, estimate. **2.** SUPPOSE think, surmise, imagine, gather, guess, presume, figure, fancy.

reckoning n. count, computation, figuring-up, totaling, tally, calculation, estimate, bill, account, statement, charge.

recline v. lean back, lie back, lounge, stretch out, lie down, repose, sprawl.

recluse n. hermit, loner, *lone wolf, solitary, anchorite, monk, misanthrope, troglodyte. ANT. *socializer, *social animal, *people person.*

reclusive a. solitary, secluded, isolated, lone, hermitic, cloistered, unsocial, withdrawn, misanthropic. ANT. *social, gregarious, outgoing, friendly.*

recognition n. **1.** IDENTIFICATION realization, detection, discovery, placing, recall, perception, notice, acknowledgement. **2.** APPRECIATION acknowledgement, approval, gratitude, esteem, notice, *pat on the back.

recognize v. **1.** IDENTIFY know, place, *peg, distinguish, detect, realize, recall, discover. **2.** APPRECIATE acknowledge, show gratitude, honor, salute, approve.

recoil v. draw back, shrink back, pull back, jump, withdraw, cringe, flinch, wince, start, reel.

recollect v. remember, recall, call to mind, reminisce, summon, place, evoke. ANT. *forget, draw a blank.*

recommend v. suggest, advise, back, endorse, approve, favor, prescribe, tout, put in a good word for, advocate, sanction, counsel. ANT. *disapprove, reject, advise against.*

recommendation n. suggestion, advice, endorsement, approval, prescription, *good word, counsel, testimonial, reference, plug, *word to the wise.

recompense n. payment, repayment, compensation, remuneration, restitution, reward, reparation, return.

recompense v. repay, compensate, pay back, remunerate, make restitution, reimburse, reward, return.

reconcile v. **1.** HARMONIZE settle, resolve differences, make up, make peace, conciliate, win over, appease, compromise, accord, *bury the hatchet, mediate. **2.** RESIGN ONESELF TO accept, let go, adjust to, take in stride, make the best of it, *roll with the punches. **3.** MAKE AGREE square, harmonize, equalize, rectify, straighten out. ANT. **1.** *war, aggravate, antagonize, offend.*

RECONDITE a. [REK un DITE] beyond the average person's understanding, difficult. *Her theories of creation were recondite.* SYN. difficult, abstruse, hard, deep, erudite, pedantic, complex, complicated, *over one's head, arcane, incomprehensible. ANT. *easy, simple, *child's play.*

reconnaissance n. survey, *look-see, scouting mission, observation, reconnoitering.

reconsider v. rethink, reevaluate, reexamine, *look at in a different light, change one's mind, think twice, review, amend.

record n. **1.** HISTORY register, account, chronicle, transcription, log, journal, minutes, archives, documentation, diary. **2.** PERFORMANCE HISTORY track record, book, resume, *stats. **3.** RECORDING disc, album, *45, *hot wax, single, LP, CD.

record v. register, chronicle, transcribe, take down, write down, log, take minutes, document, enter, set down, keep an account of. ANT. *erase, delete.*

recount v. tell, narrate, repeat, describe, *recap, detail, run down, relate, review.

recoup v. recover, get back, regain, make up for, compensate, reimburse, replace.

recover v. **1.** GET BACK reclaim, retrieve, win back, retake, recoup, resume. **2.** GET BETTER get well, restore one's health, regain one's strength, convalesce, heal, recuperate, come around, rally, *pull through. ANT. **1.** *lose.* **2.** *take a turn for the worse, relapse, fail.*

recreation n. amusement, leisure, activity, relaxation, *R&R, play, fun, games, exercise, sport, diversion, hobby.

recruit v. enlist, enroll, draft, induct, round up, muster, hire, sign up.

rectify v. correct, adjust, right, amend, fix, remedy, revise, straighten out, square, calibrate.

recumbent a. lying down, reclining, prone, flat, supine, prostrate, stretched out, sprawled.

ANT. *erect, standing, upright.*

recuperate *v.* get better, get well, recover, convalesce, heal, come around, mend, rally, *pull through, get back on one's feet. ANT. *take a turn for the worse, relapse, fail, *circle the drain.*

recur *v.* repeat, happen again, reappear, reoccur, return, come back, persist.

recurrent *a.* repeating, repetitive, reappearing, returning, persistent, frequent, regular, periodic, cyclical, chronic.

red *a.* crimson, blood, cherry, brick, ruby, vermillion, wine, blush, coral, ruddy, scarlet, rose, salmon, fuchsia, maroon, carmine.

redeem *v.* **1.** CASH IN recover, collect on, trade in, exchange, claim, turn in, convert. **2.** DELIVER FROM SIN atone, reform, rehabilitate, absolve, save, make up for, make amends.

REDOLENT *a.* [RED uh lunt] fragrant *The redolent sea shore.* SYN. fragrant, aromatic, scented, sweet-smelling, odoriferous, smelling, evocative, reminiscent.

REDRESS *n.* [REE dress] a setting right, compensation for a wrong. *They will seek redress for the damages done.* SYN. compensation, reparation, amends, recompense, satisfaction, righting, restitution, correction, payment.

redress *v.* rectify, set right, correct, remedy, compensate, make reparations, make restitution, satisfy, put right, square.

reduce *v.* **1.** LOWER lessen, decrease, cut, diminish, scale down, shorten, lighten, subtract, contract, trim, deflate. **2.** DEMOTE downgrade, lower in rank. **3.** SOFTEN temper, ease, moderate, dilute, mitigate, mellow, modify. **4.** SUBDUE conquer, vanquish, crush, overpower, put down, break. ANT. *1. increase, heighten. 2. promote, upgrade. 3. intensify, strengthen. 4. surrender, retreat.*

REDUNDANT *a.* [ri DUN dunt] more than what is needed, repetitive, wordy. *His speech was long-winded and redundant.* SYN. excessive, unnecessary, superfluous, repetitious, more than enough, inessential, long-winded, *de trop, wordy, verbose. ANT. *necessary, indispensable, concise.*

reef *n.* bank, bar, sand bar, ridge, shoal, atoll shelf, ledge, coral reef.

reek *n.* smell, stench, odor, stink, fetor.

reek *v.* stink, smell, *smell to high heaven, steam, vaporize, permeate.

reel *v.* stagger, sway, lurch, spin, pitch, waver, teeter, whirl, rock, fall back.

refer *v.* **1.** MAKE REFERENCE cite, allude, point to,

touch on, mention, quote, speak of, bring up. **2.** SEND direct, point, assign, recommend. **3.** REGARD relate, deal with, involve, concern, apply, pertain, cover.

referee *n.* *ref, umpire, judge, arbitrator, mediator, intermediary, go-between, moderator.

reference *n.* **1.** MENTION citation, allusion, quotation, notice, implication, intimation. **2.** RECOMMENDATION testimonial, endorsement, good word, certification.

refined *a.* **1.** CULTIVATED cultured, polished, perfected, finished, civilized, genteel, gentlemanly, courtly, ladylike, polite, well-bred, elegant. **2.** CLEANED purified, washed, filtered, strained, processed, clarified, distilled. ANT. *1. unrefined, coarse, crude. 2. unrefined, unpure, rough, raw.*

refinement *n.* cultivation, culture, polish, perfection, finish, elegance, civility, gentility, graciousness, good breeding, urbanity, delicacy. ANT. *roughness, coarseness, crudeness, vulgarity.*

reflect *v.* **1.** THROW BACK mirror, echo, reverberate, rebound, resonate, repercuss, resound, return. **2.** CONSIDER think, contemplate, ponder, ruminate, deliberate, weigh, meditate, cogitate, muse.

reflection *n.* **1.** MIRROR IMAGE image, counterpart, impression. **2.** CONSIDERATION contemplation, meditation, deliberation, rumination, thought, cogitation, pondering, musing. "Wisdom's best nurse."—John Milton.

reform *n.* correction, change for the better, improvement, advancement, betterment, renovation, progress, rectification.

refrain *v.* do without, forgo, forbear, abstain, eschew, stop, resist, pass on, *swear off, desist. ANT. *indulge, take up.*

refresh *v.* **1.** RENEW freshen, rejuvenate, invigorate, revitalize, restore, revive, breathe new life into, vivify. **2.** STIMULATE jog, activate, arouse, awaken, prompt, remind, cue. ANT. *1. wear out, drain tire, sap. 2. dull, inhibit.*

refreshing *a.* **1.** RENEWING freshening, rejuvenating, invigorating, revitalizing, restoring, reviving, bracing, energizing. **2.** NEW fresh, different, original, novel. ANT. *1. tiring, draining, sapping. 2. old, unoriginal.*

refreshment *n.* fortification, *pick-me-up, nourishment, sustenance, food, drink, bite, snack.

refuge *n.* shelter, retreat, safe haven, hiding place, hideout, asylum, sanctuary, cover, security, protection.

refugee n. emigrant, expatriate, defector, emigre, runaway, evacuee, outcast, alien, fugitive.

refund n. reimbursement, rebate, return, repayment.

refund v. pay back, reimburse, rebate, return, repay, settle, recompense, satisfy.

refurbish v. renovate, fix up, freshen up, brighten up, clean up, recondition, restore, renew, rejuvenate, revamp.

refusal n. no, rejection, *thumbs down, nix, veto, nonacceptance, denial, turndown.

refuse n. waste, trash, rubbish, litter. SEE GARBAGE

refuse v. say no, reject, *give thumbs down, nix, veto, deny, turn down, decline, demur, disapprove, spurn. ANT. okay, accept, agree.

REFUTE v. [ri FYOOT] to prove or argue to be wrong. They refuted his theories. SYN. disprove, prove false, confute, controvert, contradict, rebut, discredit, *shoot full of holes, counter. ANT. support, corroborate, prove.

regal a. royal, stately, kingly, majestic, noble, princely, august, queenly, lordly.

REGALE v. [ri GALE] to delight, amuse or entertain. He regaled us with his adventures during the war. SYN. delight, amuse, entertain, enthrall, enchant, divert, captivate, humor, charm.

regard n. 1. LOOK gaze, attention, heed, stare, mind, glance. 2. CONSIDERATION thought, concern, care, attention, heed, awareness. 3. ESTEEM respect, affection, liking, fondness, approval, admiration, appreciation. 4. MATTER aspect, point, detail. ANT. 2. thoughtlessness. 3. disregard, disrespect, dislike.

regard v. 1. LOOK AT heed, watch, see, behold, eye, observe, take in, notice, pay attention to. 2. CONSIDER take into account, think of, look upon, deem, view, judge.

regardless adv. in any event, anyway, anyhow, at any rate, nevertheless, nonetheless.

regime n. administration, government, leadership, rule, command, party, management, power.

regiment v. organize, systematize, coordinate, standardize.

region n. area, territory, zone, locality, location, district, place, ward, quarter, province, vicinity, spot, realm.

register n. record, list, book, entry, ledger, roll, daybook, registry, roster, diary.

REGRESS v. [ree GRESS] to go back, reverse, progress backwards. His behavior began to regress to that of a child. SYN. retrogress, go back, revert, retreat, degenerate, backslide, retrograde, ebb. ANT. progress, advance.

regret n. self-reproach, remorse, penitence, sorrow, self-condemnation, contrition, pangs of guilt, conscience, second thought, qualm. "The beginning of a new life." —George Eliot.

regret v. be sorry for, look back and kick oneself for, lament, bemoan, rue the day, have pangs of conscience, have second thoughts, never forgive oneself, repent, hate oneself for.

regretful a. sorry, contrite, ashamed, apologetic, conscience-stricken, guilty, penitent, self-reproachful, sadder but wiser.

regrettable a. lamentable, unfortunate, shameful, grievous, deplorable.

regular a. 1. NORMAL usual, customary, conventional, typical, routine, everyday, traditional, average, stock, ordinary, standard. 2. ORDERLY symmetrical, balanced, ordered, harmonious, even, aligned, straight, uniform. 3. CONSISTENT habitual, fixed, undeviating, recurrent, set, established, daily. ANT. 1. irregular, abnormal, unconventional. 2. disorderly, asymmetrical, uneven. 3. sporadic, irregular, infrequent.

regulate v. 1. GOVERN control, manage, direct, administer, run, maintain, oversee. 2. BALANCE equalize, adjust, time, moderate.

regulation n. 1. CONTROL government, management, adjustment, supervision, direction, moderation, tuning, timing. 2. RULE law, ordinance, statute, code, requirement, order, commandment, instruction, canon.

regurgitate v. throw up, heave, puke. SEE VOMIT

rehabilitate v. restore, reclaim, *rehab, straighten out, improve, reform, change, transform, save, redeem, change one's ways.

rehearse v. practice, go over, run through, prepare, perfect, drill, train, *have a dry run, tune up, *jam.

reign n. rule, power, dominance, dominion, sovereignty, sway, dynasty, governance, leadership, tenure, control, regime.

reign v. rule, hold power, be in power, govern, command, manage, administer, hold sway, lead, control, dominate, run the show.

reimburse v. pay back, repay, recompense, compensate, refund, make restitution, make good, settle, indemnify.

rein n. harness, bridle, control, restraint, guide.

rein v. stop, slow, restrain, control, guide, bridle, curb, check.

reinforce v. strengthen, fortify, *beef up, harden, stiffen, bolster, buttress, prop, toughen, support. ANT. *weaken, soften, undermine, cripple.*

REITERATE *v.* [ree IT uh RATE] to go over again, repeat. *Some students nodded off when the professor reiterated for the second time.* SYN. go over again, repeat, *recap, recapitulate, restate, rehash, belabor, retell.

reject *n.* castoff, outcast, discard, second, irregular, pariah, loser.

reject *v.* *nix, refuse, repulse, pass on, turn down, *give thumbs down, brush off, *give the cold shoulder, *turn one's nose up at, spurn, shun, repudiate, veto, rebuff, *spit upon, *kiss off, jilt. ANT. *accept, embrace, approve, *give thumbs up.*

rejoice *v.* be full of joy, be happy, be glad, celebrate, revel, be elated, exult, jump for joy, glory, delight. ANT. *grieve, lament.*

rejoinder *n.* answer, reply, comeback, response, retort, repartee, rebuttal, countering.

rejuvenate *v.* renew, restore, revive, invigorate, *breathe new life into, regenerate, revitalize, refresh, reanimate. ANT. *tire, sap, drain.*

relapse *n.* recurrence, reappearance, *turn for the worse, setback, decline, regression, fall, deterioration. ANT. *remission, improvement, progress.*

relate *v.* **1.** RECOUNT tell, narrate, detail, state, report, communicate, describe, give an account of, repeat. **2.** CONNECT correspond, correlate, associate, link, pertain, apply, have to do with, concern, bear upon. **3.** IDENTIFY WITH empathize, understand, *stand in another's shoes.

related *a.* associated, connected, correlated, linked, allied, affiliated, akin, kindred, cognate.

relation *n.* association, connection, affiliation, link, relationship, kinship, alliance.

relationship *n.* association, friendship, alliance, kinship, affiliation, marriage, liaison, connection, rapport.

relative *n.* relation, kin, family member, kinsman, sibling, blood relative, cognate, mother, father, brother, sister, *kissing cousin, niece, nephew, aunt, uncle, in-law. ANT. *stranger.*

relative *a.* **1.** COMPARATIVE proportional, comparable, relating to, respective. **2.** PERTAINING pertinent, relative, germane.

relax *v.* **1.** LOOSEN UP be at ease, *take it easy, rest, unwind, let oneself go, calm down, *let one's hair down, take a break, laze. **2.** SLACKEN soften, let up, lessen, ease off, loosen, diminish, relieve, lighten, moderate.

ANT. **1.** *get wound up, tense, labor, *drive oneself into the grave.* **2.** *tighten, tense up, wind up.*

relaxation *n.* **1.** REST recreation, *R&R, fun, unwinding, *cutting loose, leisure, quiet time, holiday, lounging, repose, *decompression. **2.** LOOSENING slackening, easing. ANT. **1.** *work, labor, toil, stress.* **2.** *tightening, intensification.*

release *n.* liberation, emancipation, liberty, freeing, deliverance, discharge, loosing, dismissal, acquittal, letting go. ANT. *imprisonment, incarceration, capture.*

release *v.* let go, discharge, free, liberate, emancipate, deliver, loose, dismiss, acquit, untie, unshackle.

relegate *v.* consign, assign, delegate, entrust, commission.

relent *v.* soften, let up, yield, give up, slow, ease off, mitigate, relax, slacken, drop, come around, bend, reduce.

RELENTLESS *a.* [ri LENT liss] unremitting, incessant, pitiless. *The enemy bunkers took a relentless pounding.* SYN. unremitting, incessant, persistent, sustained, pitiless, merciless, unrelenting, hard, cruel, unflagging. ANT. *relenting, brief, mercifully short, sparing.*

relevant *a.* relating, pertinent, applicable, germane, to the point, material, relative, apropos, connected, apt. ANT. *irrelevant, beside the point, unrelated.*

reliable *a.* dependable, trustworthy, responsible, conscientious, faithful, unfailing, constant, steady, trusty. ANT. *unreliable, undependable, irresponsible.*

reliance *n.* confidence, dependence, trust, belief, credit, certainty, security. ANT. *distrust, insecurity.*

relic *n.* ruin, antique, antiquity, artifact, remnant, remains, vestige, keepsake, souvenir.

relief *n.* release, alleviation, easing, relaxation, mitigation, soothing, amelioration, succor, letup, respite, palliation, balm, help. ANT. *intensification, aggravation, worsening.*

relieve *v.* **1.** EASE alleviate, release, comfort, free, relax, mitigate, soothe, palliate, assuage, diminish, quell. **2.** SET FREE unburden, take over, stand in for, substitute for, replace, release, spell.

religion *n.* belief in God, faith, spirituality, devotion, godliness, worship, piety, theology, persuasion, devoutness. "The life of God in the soul of man." —Lyman Abbott. "The opium of the people." —Karl Marx. "The elder sister of philosophy." —Walter Savage

Landor. "A universal obsessional neurosis."—Sigmund Freud. "The soul of civilization."—Will Durant.

WORD FIND

CHRISTIANITY

abandonment of one's faith: apostasy

Adam and Eve's sin of eating from tree of knowledge: Original Sin

admitting sins to priest in Roman Catholic Church: confession

amending sacrament: penance

amends for sins: atonement

amen: to trust

angel, high: archangel

angel, second order: cherubim

ascent to heaven, Christ's: Ascension

battle, location of final: Armageddon (mountain of megiddo)

biblical texts questioned by some denominations: apocrypha

birth of Christ or Second Coming: Advent

blessed with gift of tongues, healing, or prophecy: Charismatics

blessing at end of service: benediction

bread and wine, body and blood of Christ, sacrament of: Eucharist, Communion, Holy Communion, Mass

bread wafers: host

casting out of church due to transgressions: excommunication

container or chest holding Ten Commandments: Ark of the Covenant

crucifixion of Christ, commemoration: Good Friday

cursing of God: blasphemy

declaration by Pope that deceased person is blessed and worthy to pray to: beatification

declaration by Pope that deceased person is saint following beatification: canonization

dissenter: heretic

enemy of Christ: Antichrist, the beast

faith, statement of: Apostle's Creed

fellowship: communion

forgiveness of sins: absolution

forty-day period before Easter: Lent

funeral mass, Roman Catholic: requiem

God, seeing: beatific vision

gospel, one of twelve who spread: apostle

guardian or protector of specific group: patron saint

healing illness through prayer: faith healing, laying on of hands

Hebrew Bible: Old Testament

Holy Land: Israel, Palestine

kneel in worship: genuflect

laws, ecclesiastical: canon

Lamb of God icon: Agnus Dei

Last Supper, day of: Maundy Thursday

Lent, first day of: Ash Wednesday

literal interpretation of Bible, believing in: fundamentalism

nonbeliever: atheist

non-Christian: infidel

offense to God: abomination

oil, apply: anoint

oil used in Catholic confirmation: chrism

Old Testament scrolls: Dead Sea Scrolls

overlooking of transgressions in Roman Catholic Church: dispensation

prayer: Angelus

prayer beads: rosary

presiding priest at Holy Communion: celebrant

questioner or doubter: agnostic

repentance for sins: contrition

revelation of future in Bible: Apocalypse

rising of soul after death: resurrection

rites: sacraments

sacred, make: consecrate

Second Coming will arrive soon, denomination believing: Seventh Day Adventist, Second Adventists

sect: denomination

sex, priest's vow to abstain from: vow of celibacy

song from biblical text: canticle

spread of word throughout the world: evangelism

study of religion: theology

tongues, denomination known for some members who speak in: Pentecostal Church

tongues, speaking in: glossolalia

Virgin Mary: Madonna

washing before ceremonies: ablutions

water immersion ceremony: baptism

wise men's visit to Christ's birth, commemoration of: Epiphany

JUDAISM

candelabra used to mark Chanukah: menorah

discrimination against Jews: antisemitism

eight-day festival commemorating exodus of Jews from Egypt: Passover

festival of lights commemorating victory of Maccabees over the Syrians: Chanukah

food fit to be eaten: kosher

God, name of: Jehovah, Elohim, Yahweh,

YHWH, Adonai

holy day devoted to prayer, fasting: Yom Kippur

Jewish New Year: Rosh Hashanah

minister: rabbi

morning and evening prayer: Shema

non-Jew: gentile

Old Testament of Bible: Hebrew Bible, Torah

prayer leader in synagogue: cantor

rabbinical writings, interpretations and the Torah collectively: Talmud

skullcap worn by Jewish men: yarmulka

strict, orthodox Jews known for earlocks, black coats: Chasidim, Hasidim

thirteen-year-old's rite of adulthood: Bar Mitzvah

twelve-year-old girl's rite of adulthood: Bat Mitzvah

ISLAM

adherent: Moslem, Muslim

authority on Muslim law: ayatollah

call to prayer from minaret of mosque: azan

daily call to prayers: adhan

fit to eat, according to dietary laws: halal

God: Allah

holy war, fighting for Islam: Jihad

month of fasting: Ramadan

Muhammad's birthplace: Mecca

night of forgiveness: Lailat-ul-Bara'h

non-Moslem: infidel

"Peace be upon you": Salam Alaikum

pilgrimage to Mecca: hajj

prayer leader in mosque: imam

prayers required five times per day: Salat

prophet of God and founder of Islam: Muhammad

requirements of Islamic religion: five pillars of Islam

rule that women must keep covered in public: purdah

sacred stone at Mecca: Black Stone

sacred text: Koran

HINDUISM

black god, avatar of Vishnu: Krishna

communal house: ashram

elephant-headed god, symbol of luck: Ganesha

incarnation of a god: avatar

god of creation: Brahma

god of life and death: Shiva

god of love and desire: Kamadeva

god of rain and war: Indra

god who will come to destroy the world: Kalki

guidance book, "The Song of the Lord": Bhagavad Gita

meditation word or phrase repeated to clear head: mantra

mental, physical exercises to achieve well-being: yoga

merchant caste: Vaishyas

nonviolence doctrine: ahimsa

peasant, servant caste: shudras

peasants outside of caste system: untouchables

priestly caste: Brahmin

release from endless reincarnation: moksha

spiritual teacher: guru

supreme being: Vishnu

yoga adherent: yogi

warrior caste: kshyatriyas

what goes around comes around, doctrine of: karma

worship: puja

BUDDHISM

Chinese Buddhism, enlightenment through meditation: Zen

domed Buddhist shrine: stupa

enlightenment, path to: dharma

enlightenment, sudden achievement of: satori

festival: Wesak

moral rules: five precepts

nonviolence doctrine: ahimsa

one devoted to seeking enlightenment: bodhisattva

spiritual awakening, bliss: enlightenment, bodhi, nirvana

spiritual leader of Tibetan Buddhism: Dalai Lama

suffering, belief that everything leads to: dukkha

word or phrase repeated during meditation: mantra

SEE BIBLE, CHURCH, CLERGYMAN, GOD, PRAYER

religious *a.* **1.** PIOUS devout, godly, spiritual, faithful, churchgoing, theological, righteous, God-fearing, reverent, saintly. **2.** CAREFUL scrupulous, exact, conscientiousness, rigorous, meticulous. ANT. 1. atheistic, nonbelieving, impious. 2. careless, slack.

RELINQUISH *v.* [ri LING kwish] to give up, let go or renounce. *He will relinquish his office in thirty days.* SYN. give up, let go, renounce, abandon, quit, drop, surrender, forswear, leave, forsake, surrender, abdicate, resign. ANT. *hold, keep, maintain.*

relish *n.* pleasure, enjoyment, appreciation, liking, love, fondness, fancy, zest, satisfaction, gusto.

relish *v.* enjoy, take pleasure in, like, love, be fond of, appreciate, savor, adore, revel in, luxuriate in, *dig. ANT. *hate, find distasteful, detest.*

reluctant *a.* hesitant, unwilling, disinclined, slow, unenthusiastic, hanging back, leery, wary, cautious, averse, loath. ANT. *eager, willing, enthusiastic.*

rely *v.* depend, count on, bank on, have confidence in, trust, entrust, put faith in, bet on, swear by. ANT. *doubt, mistrust.*

remain *v.* stay, wait, sit tight, stay put, hold, endure, continue, abide, keep on, persist. ANT. *go, leave, change.*

remainder *n.* the rest, leftover, remnant, remains, balance, surplus, residue, overage.

remark *n.* comment, commentary, word, observation, statement, note, thought, mention, utterance, reflection.

remarkable *a.* outstanding, extraordinary, noteworthy, noticeable, unusual, exceptional, phenomenal, unique, striking, impressive, rare. ANT. *usual, ordinary, common, everyday.*

remedial *a.* healing, corrective, restorative, curing, therapeutic, curative.

remedy *n.* cure, treatment, medicine, restorative, cure-all, panacea, corrective, therapy, relief, antidote, elixir, prescription, drug.

remedy *v.* cure, treat, medicate, fix, restore, correct, relieve, revive, counteract, neutralize, alleviate, help, doctor. ANT. *aggravate, exacerbate, poison, infect.*

remember *v.* 1. RECALL recollect, call to mind, reminisce, think back, retrospect, conjure up, summon, memorize, commit to memory, retain, learn. 2. KEEP IN MIND bear in mind, don't forget. ANT. *forget, draw a blank, have amnesia.*

remind *v.* bring back, bring to mind, spur one's memory, refresh memory, make remember, *ring a bell, awaken, memories.

reminisce *v.* think back, retrospect, recollect, remember back, *ache with nostalgia, live in the past.

REMISS *a.* [ri MISS] lax or negligent in performing one's responsibilities. *He has long been remiss in his duties.* SYN. negligent, careless, lax, slack, neglectful, sloppy, lazy, inattentive, delinquent, irresponsible, derelict. ANT. *responsible, careful, dutiful.*

remit *v.* send, forward, transmit, mail, discharge.

remnant *n.* remainder, leftover, remains, excess, extra, surplus, leaving, residue, scrap, odds and ends, relic, vestige.

remodel *v.* make over, redesign, rebuild, refurbish, redo, renovate, overhaul, retrofit.

REMONSTRATE *v.* [ri MON strate] to object to or protest against. *The demonstrators continued to remonstrate outside the mayor's door.* SYN. object, protest, argue against, challenge, criticize, take issue, expostulate, take exception, oppose, denounce. ANT. *go along with, assent, agree.*

remorse *n.* guilt, penitence, self-reproach, compunction, contrition, regret, sorriness, repentance, shame, rue. "The pain of sin." – Theodore Parker. "The echo of a lost virtue." – Edward Bulwer Lytton. "The fatal egg by pleasure laid." – William Cowper. ANT. *indifference, hard-heartedness, glee, pride.*

remote *a.* 1. DISTANT far off, far-flung, isolated, secluded, God-forsaken, outlying, lonely, removed, out-of-the-way, inaccessible. 2. UNLIKELY slight, faint, slim, small, improbable, outside. 3. ALOOF distant, removed, cold, detached, faraway, withdrawn, uninterested. ANT. *1. close, at hand, nearby. 2. likely, significant, probable. 3. intimate, warm, close.*

remove *v.* 1. TAKE OFF eject, expel, extract, throw off, cut off, move, transfer, get rid of, oust, withdraw, uproot, disconnect, erase, expunge. 2. DO AWAY WITH, REMOVE FROM OFFICE kill, assassinate, take out, eliminate, do away with, execute, dismiss, depose, oust, discharge, unseat, unhorse, eject, fire, *can. ANT. *1. keep, maintain, retain. 2. hire, install.*

remunerate *v.* pay, compensate, repay, reward, recompense, reimburse, indemnify.

RENAISSANCE *n.* [REN i SAHNS] a rebirth, resurgence or revival. *The agency is hoping for a renaissance in space exploration.* SYN. rebirth, resurgence, revival, reawakening, resurgence, new day, renewal, rejuvenation, regeneration.

rend *v.* rip, split, cleave. SEE TEAR

render *v.* 1. PRESENT deliver, give, hand over, furnish, submit, tender, provide, impart. 2. CAUSE TO BE make. 3. PERFORM recite, represent, interpret, portray, play, treat, depict.

rendezvous *n.* meeting place, gathering place, appointment, engagement, date, meeting, tryst.

rendition *n.* rendering, version, interpretation, performance, presentation, arrangement, depiction, portrayal.

renegade *n.* rebel, turncoat, traitor, apostate,

betrayer, double-crosser, defector, deserter, revolutionist, Benedict Arnold.

RENEGE v. [ri NIG] to go back on one's word, to fail to follow through on an agreement. *He reneged on the deal and was sued for breach of contract.* SYN. go back on one's word, break promise, default, back out, *weasel out, *change one's tune, *cop out, backpedal. ANT. *fulfill, make good, satisfy.*

renew v. begin again, resume, make a fresh start, restore, rejuvenate, refresh, recondition, revitalize, replenish, regenerate, reinvigorate, breathe new life into.

RENOUNCE v. [ri NOUNCE] to give up, repudiate, wash one's hands of. *She renounced her belief in astrology.* SYN. give up, abandon, reject, *swear off, relinquish, quit, desert, disavow, forswear, disown, repudiate, turn one's back on, *divorce oneself from. ANT. *embrace, hold dear, claim.*

renovate v. renew, revive, clean up, fix up, recondition, restore, remodel, refurbish, redecorate, *give a face-lift, modernize, update.

renown n. celebrity, fame, reputation, prominence, notoriety, stardom, eminence, popularity, illustriousness. ANT. *obscurity, anonymity.*

renowned a. celebrated, famous, prominent, noted, eminent, popular, acclaimed, illustrious, distinguished, notorious, outstanding. ANT. *obscure, unknown.*

rent n. opening, split, rip, tear, hole, slit, fissure, rift.

rent v. lease, let, sublet, hire, charter, contract for.

renunciation n. renouncing, rejection, abandonment, relinquishment, repudiation, disavowal, spurning, forswearing. ANT. *acceptance, embracement.*

repair n. fixing, mending, restoration, service, reconditioning, patching, alignment, overhaul, correction, tune-up.

repair v. **1.** FIX mend, restore, recondition, patch, rebuild, reconstruct, align, overhaul, adjust, tinker with. **2.** GO move, head for, proceed, retire.

REPARTEE n. [REP ar TAY] witty comebacks, a series of quick and witty replies, clever conversational exchange. *He was famous for his brilliant repartee.* SYN. witty comebacks, snappy comebacks, witty replies, witty rejoinders, banter, quip, sally, lively exchange, badinage, give-and-take, jesting, riposte, mot. "A duel fought with the points of jokes." —Max Eastman. "Something we

think of 24 hours too late." —Mark Twain.

repast n. meal, food and drink, feast, banquet, eats, *feed, spread, *bite.

repay v. pay back, reimburse, return, make up for, compensate, square, requite, refund, rebate, settle, even the score, reciprocate.

repeal n. revocation, abrogation, rescission, annulment, nullification, voiding, invalidation, withdrawal, cancellation.

repeal v. withdraw, revoke, cancel, declare null and void, rescind, abrogate, invalidate, annul, abolish.

repeat n. repetition, replay, rebroadcast, rerun, rehash.

repeat v. **1.** REITERATE restate, say again, recap, recapitulate, parrot. **2.** DO AGAIN duplicate, remake, reproduce, redo, echo. **3.** TELL recount, relate.

repel v. **1.** REPULSE push back, force back, ward off, resist, drive away, fend off, check, refuse, spurn, reject, snub, *give cold shoulder. **2.** DISGUST *turn off, sicken, revolt, appall, *turn one's stomach, *gross out, *make one's flesh crawl. ANT. *1. welcome, embrace, accept. 2. attract, delight, please.*

repellent a. repulsive, disgusting, revolting, appalling, sickening, nauseating, offensive, repugnant, obnoxious.

repent v. feel sorry, be remorseful, be contrite, be conscious-stricken, rue the day, apologize, ask forgiveness, lament, deplore, be penitent.

repentance n. penitence, sorrow, remorse, contrition, guilt, compunction, sorriness, regret, pangs of conscience. "The voice of God." —Israel Baal Shem Tob. ANT. *pride, self-satisfaction.*

REPERCUSSION n. [REE pur KUSH un] an effect or consequence of some action. *Opening the borders to free trade will create serious repercussions.* SYN. effect, consequence, result, reaction, fallout, outcome, aftermath, impact, backlash, echo.

repetition n. duplication, repeat, rerun, replay, reiteration, recapitulation, recurrence, *broken record, rote, reprise.

repetitious a. repetitive, redundant, tautological, wordy, long-winded, verbose, boring, tedious, recurring. ANT. *concise, to the point, spare.*

replace v. **1.** TAKE THE PLACE OF succeed, follow, supersede, supplant, stand in, *step into one's shoes, fill in for. **2.** RETURN put back.

replenish v. fill, supply, refill, stock, restore, replace, provision, top off, reload.

REPLETE *a.* [ri PLEET] filled, full, plentiful. *The cellar was replete with wine bottles.* SYN. full, filled, plentiful, abundant, crammed, stuffed, packed, glutted, *chock-full, loaded. ANT. *empty, vacant, bare.*

replica *n.* reproduction, copy, imitation, look-alike, *knockoff, duplicate, facsimile, clone, photocopy.

reply *n.* answer, response, reaction, acknowledgement, comeback, return, rejoinder, retort.

reply *v.* answer, respond, react, acknowledge, come back, return, rejoin, *shoot back, retort.

report *n.* **1.** ACCOUNT statement, news, exposition, message, detailing, *blow by blow, communication, story, *word, rundown, summary, communique, bulletin, announcement. **2.** RUMOR gossip, talk, *word, *grapevine, *buzz, *scuttlebutt, hearsay. **3.** LOUD NOISE boom, explosion, bang, blast, detonation, crash, shot, crack, reverberation.

report *v.* **1.** COMMUNICATE give an account, state, give news, give message, detail, *give blow by blow, bring word, give rundown, summarize, announce, describe, tell, recount, relate. **2.** TURN IN tell on, *rat on.

reporter *n.* newsman, newswoman, journalist, member of the press, member of the media, correspondent, newscaster, feature writer, snoop, scribe.

repose *n.* rest, sleep, ease, relaxation, quiet, respite, peace, tranquility, leisure, break.

REPREHENSIBLE *a.* [REP ri HEN suh bul] that which deserves criticism or rebuke. *The criminals' actions were reprehensible.* SYN. blameworthy, reproachable, sinful, shameful, felonious, villainous, criminal, heinous, wicked, unforgivable, disgraceful, ignoble, despicable. ANT. *praiseworthy, honorable, virtuous, noble.*

represent *v.* **1.** STAND FOR symbolize, denote, express, exemplify, typify, embody, personify, betoken, act as, serve as. **2.** DEPICT portray, render, picture, evoke, describe, mirror, illustrate. **3.** SERVE AS AN AGENT act on behalf of, speak for, stand for, be proxy for, *go to bat for.

representative *n.* agent, proxy, stand-in, spokesperson, *mouthpiece, advocate, delegate, envoy, emissary, surrogate, congressman, councilman.

representative *a.* characteristic, typical, illustrative, model, symbolic, exemplary, indicative. ANT. *atypical, unusual, different.*

repress *v.* keep down, hold down, control, hold in, check, restrain, contrain, crush, curb, suppress, stifle, subdue, shutup.

reprieve *n.* postponement, suspension, escape, relief, stay, stay of execution, remission, delay, abeyance.

reprimand *n.* rebuke, scolding, admonishment, reproach, *bawling out, censure, chastisement, *tongue-lashing, upbraiding, castigation. ANT. *approval, praise.*

reprimand *v.* rebuke, scold, admonish, reproach, *bawl out, censure, chastise, *give a tongue-lashing, upbraid, castigate, *rake over the coals. ANT. *approve, praise, commend.*

reprisal *n.* retaliation, *eye for an eye, revenge, vengeance, retribution, redress, vindication, counterattack.

REPROACH *n.* [ri PROACH] blame, criticism. *She was above reproach.* SYN. blame, criticism, shame, discredit, rebuke, scolding, condemnation, reprimand, censure, disapproval, disgrace. ANT. *approval, credit, praise.*

reproach *v.* accuse, blame, rebuke, criticize, shame, discredit, scold, condemn, reprimand, censure, disapprove, find fault. ANT. *approve, credit, praise.*

reprobate *n.* sinner, criminal, villain, *bad guy, lost soul, profligate, miscreant, degenerate, scoundrel, evildoer, lowlife. ANT. *angel, saint.*

reprobate *a.* bad, immoral, corrupt, unprincipled, wicked, depraved, degenerate, evil, miscreant, foul. ANT. *good, virtuous, moral.*

reproduce *v.* **1.** COPY duplicate, replicate, redo, photococopy, reprint, clone, imitate, counterfeit. **2.** PROPAGATE breed, spawn, multiply, engender, procreate, proliferate.

reproduction *n.* **1.** COPY duplicate, replication, photocopy, reprint, clone, imitation, counterfeit, *mirror image, twin. **2.** PROPAGATION procreation, breeding, proliferation. ANT. *1. original, model, master.*

reproof *n.* rebuke, censure. SEE REPROACH

REPROVE *v.* [ri PROOV] to give or show one's disapproval. *She reproved the workers for making too much noise.* SYN. disapprove, rebuke, reproach, scold, admonish, censure, reprimand, condemn. ANT. *approve, praise, credit.*

REPUDIATE *v.* [ri PYOO dee ATE] to reject, have nothing to do with. *She repudiated his views.* SYN. reject, renounce, have nothing to do with, disown, cast off, disapprove, spurn, refuse, disavow, disclaim, deny. ANT. *embrace, accept, support.*

repugnant *a.* offensive, distasteful, obnoxious, repulsive, repellent, revolting, disgusting, foul, sickening, nauseating. ANT. *delightful, pleasing, appealing.*

repulse *v.* **1.** REPEL drive back, hold off, resist, check, defend, defeat. **2.** DISGUST offend, repel, revolt, sicken. **3.** REJECT rebuff, refuse, spurn, snub, *give cold shoulder. ANT. **1.** *embrace, welcome, pull in, draw.* 2. *delight, please, appeal.*

repulsive *a.* repellent, offensive, revolting, disgusting, foul, distasteful, *sickening, nauseating, *gross, repugnant. ANT. *appealing, delightful, attractive.*

reputable *a.* respectable, in good repute, esteemed, well thought of, acclaimed, honorable, honest, legitimate, principled, *on the up and up, reliable. ANT. *disreputable, questionable, shady.*

reputation *n.* repute, character, name, regard, stature, renown, *word of mouth, standing, *approval rating, estimation, *credit rating. "A bubble which a man bursts when he tries to blow it for himself." — Emma Carleton. "What people gossip behind your back." — Henry Banks.

repute *n.* SEE REPUTATION

reputed *a.* supposed, regarded, believed, assumed, presumed, alleged, thought, rumored.

request *n.* petition, solicitation, question, application, want, desire, behest, plea, demand.

request *v.* ask, petition, solicit, apply, appeal for, seek, *put in for, beg, demand.

require *v.* **1.** NEED want, lack, miss, be short of, be deficient in, desire. **2.** DEMAND order, command, obligate, call for, insist on, compel, direct, dictate.

requirement *n.* necessity, must, essential, need, imperative, requisite, prerequisite, condition, term, provision, dictate.

requisite *n.* SEE REQUIREMENT

requisite *a.* required, essential, prerequisite, needed, necessary, imperative, obligatory, called for.

RESCIND *v.* [ri SIND] to repeal or abolish. *They rescinded the order.* SYN. repeal, abolish, revoke, cancel, reverse, invalidate, declare null and void, annul, recall. ANT. *uphold, confirm, defend, shore up.*

rescue *n.* saving, recovery, delivery, extrication, relief, release, liberation, salvation, heroics.

rescue *v.* save, recover, deliver, extricate, relieve, release, liberate, free, bail out, retrieve,

*save one's bacon.

research *n.* fact-finding, investigation, inquiry, *digging, legwork, study, probing, sifting, *detective work, delving, *R&D. "The process of going up alleys to see if they are blind." — Marston Bates. "If you steal from one, it's plagiarism, if you steal from many it's research." — Wilson Mizner.

resemblance *n.* likeness, similarity, sameness, correspondence, closeness, semblance, parallel, uniformity, affinity, analogy. ANT. *difference, dissimilarity, contrast.*

resemble *v.* look alike, mirror, double, be similar to, match, bear a resemblance to, approximate, mimic, echo. ANT. *contrast.*

resent *v.* take offense, be offended, be indigent over, take exception to, dislike, bristle, harbor resentment, *get one's nose out of joint, seethe over. ANT. *appreciate, like, delight in.*

resentment *n.* offense, indignation, displeasure, annoyance, outrage, disgust, umbrage, rancor, bitterness, pique, hard feelings.

reservation *n.* **1.** RESERVE preserve, sanctuary, territory, enclave, tract, habitation, settlement. **2.** BOOKING retaining, place, *lock. **3.** QUALIFICATION condition, limitation, stipulation, reluctance, qualm, second thoughts, hesitancy.

reserve *n.* **1.** STORE cache, savings, *nest egg, stockpile, backlog, reservoir, *ace in the hole, *something for a rainy day. **2.** QUIETNESS silence, self-restraint, aloofness, reticence, shyness, inhibition, guardedness, distance, coolness.

reserve *v.* **1.** SAVE hold, hoard, store, stockpile, lay up, stash, *keep for a rainy day, conserve, *squirrel away. **2.** BOOK retain, secure, engage.

reserved *a.* self-restrained, quiet, silent, aloof, taciturn, reticent, shy, bashful, inhibited, guarded, distant, cool. ANT. *loud, demonstrative, loquacious.*

reside *v.* **1.** LIVE dwell, stay, inhabit, lodge, abide, domicile, occupy, take up residence, *hang one's hat. **2.** EXIST IN be inherent, be present, lie in, dwell.

residence *n.* home, inhabitation, house, abode, domicile, place, living quarters, address, dwelling, lodging, apartment, condo.

resident *n.* inhabitant, occupant, lodger, tenant, citizen, denizen, inmate.

residue *n.* remainder, rest, remnant, leftovers, dregs, scum, refuse, leavings.

resign *v.* **1.** QUIT step down, leave, abdicate, give notice, drop out, bail out, walk out, *hang it up, renounce. **2.** RESIGN ONESELF TO accept, live with, submit, endure, comply, endure, *grin and bear it, tolerate.

resignation n. **1.** QUITTING retirement, termination, withdrawal, leaving, notice, abdication. **2.** ACCEPTANCE submission, acquiescence, tolerance, endurance, reconciliation, passivity.

resigned a. accepting, submissive, acquiescent, tolerant, enduring, reconciled, passive, unresisting, stoical, long-suffering. ANT. *unaccepting, rebellious, resisting.*

resilient a. elastic, flexible, rebounding, springy, pliable, rubbery, bouncy, supple, recovering quickly.

resist v. fight, oppose, withstand, defy, repel, repulse, hold off, stand up against, thwart, check, weather. ANT. *surrender to, yield, give in, *cave in to.*

resistance n. fight, opposition, defiance, repulsion, withstanding, repellance, rebuff, refusal, blocking.

RESOLUTE a. [REZ uh LOOT] determined, resolved. *When it came to quitting smoking, Frank was resolute.* SYN. determined, resolved, fixed, firm, intent on, steady, tenacious, decided, purposeful, strong-willed, *dead set on, earnest, persevering. ANT. *weak-minded, irresolute, *wishy-washy.*

resolution n. **1.** DETERMINATION decidedness, purpose, resolve, tenacity, perseverance, dedication, willpower, earnestness. **2.** RESOLVING solution, sorting out, working out, outcome, end, upshot, settlement, finding. **3.** PLAN proposition, proposal, motion, objective.

resolve n. determination, resolution, purpose, decidedness, intention, earnestness, firmness, steadfastness, will, stick-to-itiveness.

resolve v. **1.** DETERMINE decide, make up one's mind, fix, intend, settle, will, *stick to one's guns. **2.** SETTLE solve, straighten out, clear up, harmonize, work out, *iron out, answer.

resonant a. resounding, reverberant, vibrant, echoing, loud, ringing, booming, full, rich, sonorous.

resort n. vacation spot, hotel, motel, *tourist trap, mineral springs, park, club, retreat.

resort v. turn to, use, utilize, take up, employ, have recourse to.

resound v. echo, reverberate, ring, repeat, clang, resonate, peal, vibrate, thunder.

resourceful a. inventive, clever, creative, ingenious, handy, quick, imaginative, capable, versatile, adaptable. ANT. *unimaginative, incapable, helpless, inefficient.*

respect n. **1.** REGARD honor, esteem, deference, admiration, reverence, consideration, fear, veneration, awe, appreciation. **2.** POINT detail, sense, aspect, way, regard. **3.** REFERENCE relation. ANT. *1. disrespect, disregard, contempt.*

respect v. **1.** REGARD HIGHLY honor, esteem, defer to, idolize, admire, revere, look up to, fear, venerate, view with awe, appreciate. **2.** OBEY comply. ANT. *disrespect, *dis.*

respectable a. **1.** WORTHY OF RESPECT admirable, estimable, worthy, reputable, honorable, dignified, good, esteemed, strong, decent, principled, correct, proper. **2.** FAIRLY LARGE appreciable, substantial, decent, sizable, tolerable, goodly. ANT. *1. disreputable, despicable, bad. 2. tiny, small, paltry.*

respectful a. deferential, regardful, courteous, reverential, submissive, obeisant, polite, well-mannered, obliging, obedient. ANT. *disrespectful, irreverent, disobedient.*

RESPITE n. [RES pit] a rest or break from something. *The rain provided respite from the heat.* SYN. rest, break, relief, lull, breather, letup, time-out, recess, reprieve, remission.

respond v. act, react, answer, come back, reply, acknowledge, feedback, retort.

response n. reaction, answer, comeback, reply, acknowledgement, feedback, retort.

responsibility n. **1.** DUTY charge, obligation, burden, onus. **2.** ACCOUNTABILITY liability, culpability, answerability. **3.** CONSCIENTIOUSNESS dependability, reliability, maturity, trustworthiness. "The price of greatness."— Winston Churchill. "A detachable burden easily shifted to the shoulders of God, Fate, Fortune, Luck, or one's neighbor."—Ambrose Bierce.

responsible a. **1.** ACCOUNTABLE liable, culpable, answerable, at fault, to blame, incumbent, duty-bound, beholden, bound. **2.** CONSCIENTIOUS dependable, reliable, mature, dutiful, trustworthy, adult, grown up, sensible, rational. ANT. *1. *off the hook, unaccountable, irresponsible. 2. immature, unreliable, undependable.*

responsive a. reactive, reacting, active, respondent, reflexive, reciprocal, receptive, answering. ANT. *unresponsive, inactive.*

rest n. **1.** RELAXATION inactivity, break, ease, respite, recess, sleep, slumber, nap, repose, breather, time-out, lull, pause, *downtime. "The end and reward of toil."—James Beattie. **2.** REMAINDER balance, remains, excess, surplus. **3.** BASE stand, holder, seat, bed, cradle.

rest *v.* **1.** RELAX take a break, recess, sleep, slumber, nap, repose, take a breather, take a time-out, lounge, stop, hold up, pause, *put feet up, retire, *crash, catch one's breath, *recharge one's batteries. **2.** LIE lay sit, stand, set, lean, prop. **3.** DEPEND rely, hinge, hang. ANT. *hustle, bustle, do double-time, work, *break a sweat.*

restful *a.* quiet, peaceful, relaxing, tranquil, recharging, restorative, serene, calming. ANT. *restless, stressful, tiring, exhausting.*

restitution *n.* reparation, compensation, recompense, redress, amends, reimbursement, remuneration, indemnity.

restaurant *n.* eatery, dining establishment, steakhouse, cafe, *greasy spoon, luncheonette, diner, cafeteria, drive-in, hamburger stand, commisary, *fast-food joint, nightclub, supper club, bistro.

restless *a.* troubled, disturbed, uneasy, stressed, *wired, unsettled, edgy, restive, fidgety, ill at ease, *uptight, anxious, agitated, uncomfortable, *ants in the pants, *hyper. ANT. *restful, quiet, content, relaxed.*

restore *v.* renew, bring back, fix, recondition, rejuvenate, rehabilitate, revive, refresh, put in good repair, regenerate, overhaul.

restrain *v.* hold, limit, check, arrest, contain, restrict, muzzle, suppress, bridle, hamper.

restrict *v.* limit, confine, check, restrain, curb, impede, inhibit, constrain, hamper, circumscribe, bind, hem in.

restriction *n.* limit, limitation, circumscription, proscription, check, curb, control, confinement, restraint, *no-no, rule, regulation, provision, condition.

result *n.* outcome, effect, consequence, upshot, product, byproduct, end, aftereffect, fruit, outgrowth, fallout, denouement.

result *v.* issue, arise, happen, develop, ensue, eventuate, stem, occur, come about.

résumé *n.* employment history, vita, curriculum vita, work history, biographical outline, *bio.

resume *v.* continue, proceed, go on, begin again, carry on, return, pick up where one left off, restart.

resurgence *n.* revival, rise, return, rebirth, renewal, resurrection, renaissance. ANT. *death, petering out, decline.*

resurrection *n.* rising from the dead, return to life, rebirth, revival, regeneration, restoration, *Lazarus effect.

resuscitate *v.* revive, bring back, revitalize, breathe life into, perform artificial respiration, perform CPR, give mouth-to-mouth resuscitation, bring around.

retain *v.* keep, hold, maintain, possess, save, own, hang on to, secure, grasp.

retaliate *v.* strike back, get even, pay back, avenge, revenge, *even the score, reciprocate, *give tit for tat, pay back in kind, give measure for measure, *take an eye for an eye. ANT. *turn the other cheek, overlook.*

retard *v.* hinder, slow, delay, obstruct, delay, block, impede, check, detain, hamper, restrict, handicap.

RETICENT *a.* [RET i sunt] reserved, quiet, restrained. SYN. *He tended to be reticent and barely spoke more than three words at a time.* SYN. reserved, quiet, restrained, taciturn, closemouthed, shy, bashful, silent, uncommunicative, *clammed up, retiring. ANT. *loquacious, *motor-mouthed, talkative.*

retinue *n.* entourage, train of attendants, cortege, court, personnel, escort, following.

retire *v.* LEAVE retreat, withdraw, depart, exit, part, run along, turn in, go to bed, *call it a day, *hit the sack, quit, resign.

retiring *a.* shy, bashful, backward, withdraw, unsociable, shrinking, quiet, reserved, reclusive, keeping to oneself, private, solitary, preferring one's own company. ANT. *outgoing, gregarious, sociable.*

retort *n.* reply, answer, comeback, snappy comeback, counter, rejoinder, repartee, rebuttal, riposte.

retort *v.* reply, answer, come back, respond, counter, rebut, rejoin, fire back, *return fire.

retract *v.* take back, recant, withdraw, backtrack, disavow, recall, *eat one's words, disclaim, back down, forswear, reverse, repeal.

retreat *n.* **1.** WITHDRAWAL flight, departure, pull-out, evacuation, escape, volte-face, *backpedaling, getaway, retirement. **2.** SAFE, QUIET PLACE sanctuary, asylum, haven, refuge, hideaway, shelter, cloister.

retreat *v.* withdraw, flee, depart, pull out, evacuate, escape, do an about-face, backpedal, get away, escape, *beat a hasty retreat. ANT. *charge, advance, progress.*

retribution *n.* requital, *payback, revenge, retaliation, punishment, vengeance, comeuppance, reprisal, just deserts, tit for tat, talion.

retrieve *v.* get, get back, fetch, recover, regain, reclaim, recoup, reacquire.

retrospect *n.* looking back, reminiscence, review, remembering, reexamination, hindsight, reflection, afterthought, *Monday morning quarterbacking.

return n. **1.** REAPPEARANCE rebound, comeback, homecoming, recurrence, rebirth, revival, renaissance, resurrection, reinstatement. **2.** PROFIT yield, interest, proceeds, net, income, gain, revenue. **3.** RESPONSE comeback, answer, rebuttal, retort, reply, rejoinder, riposte, repartee.

return v. **1.** COME BACK go back, put back, reappear, rebound, recoil, boomerang, reverse, retreat, backtrack, recur, revive, resurrect, reinstate, restore, replace, double back, retrace one's steps. **2.** PAY BACK reciprocate, requite, retaliate, replace, reimburse, recompense. **3.** GAIN show a profit, yield, earn, gain, net. **4.** RESPOND answer, come back, rebut, retort, reply, rejoin.

reunion n. reuniting, homecoming.

revamp v. renovate, revise, fix up, repair, make over, refurbish.

reveal v. disclose, expose, show, divulge, uncover, bring to light, make known, lay bare, bring out into the open, tell, confess, *let the cat out of the bag, *spill the beans, declare, announce, *blab. ANT. *conceal, cover up, keep secret.*

revel v. celebrate, delight in, *party, *party hearty, take pleasure, *cut loose, rejoice, make merry, *whoop it up, enjoy, *get a kick out of, be festive, carouse, *have a ball, bask.

revelation n. disclosure, eye-opener, exposé, exposition, news, divulgement, announcement, broadcast, bombshell, *bolt from the blue, flash, shock.

revelry n. merry-making, partying, celebration, rejoicing, festivity, gaiety, carousal, romping, carrying on, *good times.

revenge n. vengeance, retaliation, retribution, talion, *eye for an eye, reprisal, vindication, requital, *payback, *tit for tat, avenging, *getting even, countering, measure for measure. "That recoil of Nature." — Ralph Waldo Emerson. "Nothing which we don't invite." — Ralph Waldo Emerson.

revenge v. retaliate, take vengeance, avenge, *even the score, *take an eye for an eye, give measure for measure, repay, reciprocate, vindicate, settle accounts, get back at.

revenue n. return, income, gain, yield, proceeds, net, gross, earnings, receipts, profit, cash flow, wages, salary.

reverberate v. echo, reecho, resound, resonate, ring, vibrate, have repercussions, have an aftereffect, recoil, rebound, bounce back.

REVERE v. [ri VEER] to look up to, respect and honor highly. *The mayor was greatly revered in the community.* SYN. respect, honor, look up to, esteem, worship, venerate, idolize, *put on a pedestal, admire, exalt, think highly of, *kiss up to. ANT. *disrespect, despise, look down on.*

reverence n. respect, honor, esteem, worship, veneration, idolization, admiration, exaltation, awe, homage, regard. ANT. *irreverence, disrespect, contempt.*

reverent a. respectful, deferential, honoring, admiring, awed, reverential, venerating, adoring, worshipping.

REVERIE n. [REV ur ee] daydreaming, fantasizing. *I called her name twice, but she was deep in reverie.* SYN. daydreaming, fantasizing, musing, contemplation, deep thought, woolgathering, flight of fancy, trance, abstraction.

reversal n. repeal, overturning, upset, withdrawal, retraction, about-face, turnaround, switch.

reverse n. **1.** OPPOSITE inverse, converse, counterpart, antithesis, other side of the coin, mirror image, back, rear, *flip side. **2.** SETBACK defeat, check, reversal, turnabout, misfortune, misadventure, mishap, disaster, catastrophe, contretemps. ANT. *1. front, obverse.*

reverse v. **1.** GO OR TURN BACKWARDS back, *flip-flop, revert, upend, turn over, overturn, invert, transpose, *turn inside out, backtrack, backpedal, *do an about-face. **2.** CHANGE revoke, annul, repeal, withdraw, counter, overturn, rescind, recant, *change one's tune.

reverse a. backward, opposite, inverse, converse, contrasting, contrary.

revert v. go back, return, regress, backslide, degenerate, retrogress, relapse, deteriorate, hark back.

review n. **1.** EXAMINATION reexamination, reassessment, second look, another look, rundown, survey, inspection, reevaluation, retrospection. **2.** CRITIQUE evaluation, commentary, appraisal, report, *write-up, criticism, blurb, notice, rave, *pan. **3.** FORMAL INSPECTION exhibition, parade, procession, exposition, demonstration.

review v. **1.** EXAMINE reexamine, reassess, have a second look, have another look, run down, survey, inspect, reevaluate, go over again, retrospect. **2.** CRITIQUE evaluate, comment on, appraise, report on, *write up, criticize, rave, *pan, *trash, *slam.

revile v. scold, abuse, tongue-lash, curse, *jump down one's throat, *rip up one side and down the other, lambaste, upbraid, vilify, disparage. ANT. *commend, praise, compliment.*

revise v. correct, improve, change, amend, edit, *blue pencil, tighten, rewrite, polish, rectify, redraft, modify.

revision n. second draft, corrected version, amended version, editing, tightening, cutting, rewriting, polishing, modification.

revival n. rebirth, return, restoration, renaissance, rejuvenation, revitalization, resurrection, new dawn, new day, reawakening.

revive v. breathe life into, resuscitate, bring back to life, rescue from the brink of extinction, *bring around, wake up, reawaken, rejuvenate, renew, recharge, refresh, vivify, rally, recover.

revoke v. abolish, repeal, withdraw, rescind, annul, cancel, abrogate, nullify, void, declare null and void, recall. ANT. *maintain, uphold, *beef up.*

revolt n. rebellion, refusal, revolution, insurrection, uprising, mutiny, resistance, protest. SEE REVOLUTION

revolt v. **1.** REBEL refuse to cooperate, rise up against, resist, protest, mutiny, riot, oppose, defy, insurrect, boycott. **2.** DISGUST sicken, turn one's stomach, appall, nauseate, *make one's flesh crawl, repulse. ANT. *1. comply, obey, accept. 2. delight, please.*

revolting a. disgusting, repulsive, sickening, repugnant, gross, offensive, abhorrent, *stomach-turning, foul, obnoxious. ANT. *delightful, pleasing, appetizing.*

revolution n. **1.** REBELLION uprising, mutiny, revolt, insubordination, insurrection, outbreak, uproar, riot, anarchy, coup, coup d'etat, takeover, overthrow, unrest, turmoil. "A phoenix rising like a flame from the bodies of the wretched."—Luis Cernuda. "An abrupt change in the form of misgovernment."—Ambrose Bierce. "A thought in one man's mind."—Ralph Waldo Emerson. **2.** ROTATION, CIRCLE orbit, lap, circuit, cycle, spin.

revolutionary a. **1.** REBELLIOUS mutinous, insubordinate, riotous, resistant, insurrectionary, subversive. **2.** NEW progressive, radical, innovative, *cutting edge, novel, advanced.

revolve v. circle, orbit, go around, rotate, spin, wheel, gyrate, twirl, whirl.

revulsion n. disgust, repugnance, aversion, loathing, nausea, detestation, distaste, abhorrence, hatred. ANT. *liking, attraction.*

reward n. prize, payment, award, winnings, return, compensation, recompense, dividend, honor, bonus, requital, remuneration. ANT. *punishment, penalty.*

reward v. pay, award, compensate, recompense, honor, remunerate, reimburse, tip. ANT. *penalize, punish.*

rewarding a. compensating, worthwhile, enriching, fulfilling, satisfying, paying dividends, productive.

RHETORIC n. [RET ur ik] words and their artful employment in speech or writing. Also, high-blown language that says nothing. *The crowd listened to the usual political rhetoric.* SYN. expressiveness, eloquence, command of language, articulateness, fluency, elocution, *way with words, grandiloquence, magniloquence, bombast, *hot air, fustian, verbosity, *BS.

rhetorical a. **1.** EXPRESSIVE articulate, eloquent, fluent, persuasive, well-said, *silver-tongued. **2.** GRANDILOQUENT magniloquent, bombastic, fustian, verbose, pretentious, high-sounding, oratorical, inflated.

rhyme n. poem, verse, lyric, limerick, ode, alliteration.

rhythm n. beat, meter, cadence, swing, tempo, pulse, downbeat, backbeat, throb, flow.

RIBALD a. [RIB uld] vulgar, earthy or coarse, especially with sexual humor. *The men sat around the bar and told ribald jokes.* SYN. vulgar, earthy, lewd, dirty, obscene, risqué, off-color, indecent, pornographic, X-rated, gross. ANT. *wholesome, decent, G-rated, *clean.*

rich a. **1.** WEALTHY affluent, *well-off, *well-to-do, *well-heeled, *on easy street, *rolling in dough, opulent, flush, comfortable, moneyed, *filthy rich. **2.** ABUNDANT abounding, replete, well-supplied, well-stocked, overflowing, copious, plentiful, prodigal. **3.** LUXURIOUS elegant, costly, lavish, sumptuous, elaborate. **4.** FILLING heavy, sweet, *fatty, fattening. **5.** DEEP intense, full, vivid, striking, vibrant. **6.** FUNNY comical, amusing, absurd, *wacky, ludicrous, ridiculous, laughable. ANT. *1. poor, indigent, penniless. 2. scarce, scant, meager. 3. plain, poor. 4. light. 5. light, subtle, slight.*

riches n. wealth, money, affluence, opulence, possessions, fortune, *big bucks, treasure, property, abundance, resources. "A great slavery."—Seneca. "A contented mind."—Mohammed. "Not the end, but a change of worries."—Epicurus. ANT. *poverty, indigence, want.*

rickety *a.* shaky, wobbly, unstable, unsteady, teetering, tottering, fragile, *jerry-built, *tumble-down. ANT. *stable, sturdy, rock-solid, sound.*

ricochet *v.* rebound, bounce off, recoil, glance, deflect.

rid *v.* free, do away with, get rid of, purge, throw out, clear, clean, evict, disencumber, relieve, remove.

riddle *n.* puzzle, question, poser, *brainteaser, *stumper, mind-boggler, complexity, conundrum, knot, rebus, enigma, mystery.

ride *n.* drive, cruise, trip, excursion, spin, jaunt, outing.

ride *v.* **1.** TRAVEL cruise, tour, motor, commute, tool, move, float, journey, be carried along. **2.** TEASE torment, harass, *give a hard time, pester, make fun of, plague, ridicule, *kid.

rider *n.* addition, amendment, supplement, clause, attachment, appendix, codicil.

ridge *n.* **1.** CREST hill, spine, hogback, pinnacle, rise. **2.** RAISED AREA line, wale, rib, seam, cord, corrugation, seam, wrinkle, fold.

ridicule *n.* mocking, joking, taunting, teasing, making fun of, derision, poking fun at, laughter, needling, caricature, sarcasm. "The fume of little hearts." —Alfred Lord Tennyson. "These paper bullets of the brain." —Shakespeare. "The weapon of those who have no other." —Hubert Pierlot. ANT. *honor, veneration, respect, homage.*

ridicule *v.* make fun of, laugh at, poke fun at, mock, make the butt of a joke, taunt, tease, deride, needle, caricature, belittle, lampoon, roast. ANT. *honor, venerate, respect, pay homage to.*

ridiculous *a.* preposterous, absurd, ludicrous, laughable, stupid, foolish, nonsensical, senseless, idiotic, mindless, moronic, insane, crazy, *nuts, *wacky, farcical, outrageous. ANT. *sensible, rational, sober, sound.*

RIFE *a.* [RIFE] abounding, widespread, commonly occurring. *The show was rife with black humor.* SYN. widespread, abounding, abundant, plentiful, copious, profuse, numerous, bursting, overflowing, prevalent, teeming, rampant, thick. ANT. *scarce, scant, rare.*

riffraff *n.* rabble, *dregs of society, peasantry, commoners, hoi polloi, rank and file, lower class, *scum of the earth.

rifle *n.* carbine, shotgun, musket, firearm. SEE GUN

rifle *v.* search, rummage, turn inside out, ransack, steal, strip, loot, thieve.

rift *n.* **1.** OPENING fissure, cleft, crack, rent, split, crevice, fracture, breach, fault, split, tear. **2.** FALLING-OUT BETWEEN FRIENDS parting of the ways, split, separation, schism, break, disagreement, estrangement, breakup.

rig *n.* equipment, outfit, gear, tackle, apparatus, rigging.

rig *v.* **1.** equip, fit out, gear up, furnish, outfit, supply, set up, accoutre, clothe, appoint, array, slap together. **2.** manipulate, fix, tamper with, falsify, finagle, arrange, machinate, contrive.

right *n.* **1.** PRIVILEGE authority, prerogative, power, claim, license, title, birthright, say, favor, freedom, due. **2.** GOOD virtue, morality, morals, righteousness, justness, justice, integrity, uprightness, honor, correctness. "The greatest good to the greatest number." —Jeremy Bentham. **3.** CONSERVATISM rightism, orthodoxy. ANT. *2. wrong, immorality, incorrectness. 3. left, liberalism.*

right *v.* **1.** CORRECT fix, straighten out, amend, make right, mend, repair, doctor, rectify, adjust, remedy, redress, balance. **2.** PUT BACK IN UPRIGHT POSITION turn over, flip over. ANT. *1. *mess up, *screw up, ruin. 2. capsize, upend, upset.*

right *a.* **1.** VIRTUOUS upright, moral, good, righteous, honorable, scrupulous, just, honest, ethical, fair, proper, *politically correct, socially acceptable. **2.** CORRECT accurate, precise, *on the money, *on the mark, *on target, *on the nose, exact, true, perfect, valid, sound, faithful, flawless, unerring, factual. **3.** FITTING suitable, appropriate, befitting, correct, seemly, favorable, desirable, preferable, opportune. **4.** NORMAL sound, rational, sensible, sane, competent, lucid, sober. **5.** CONSERVATIVE right-wing, rightist, traditional, reactionary, orthodox, *old-line. ANT. *1. immoral, bad, unethical, wicked. 2. incorrect, inaccurate, wrong. 3. unsuitable, inappropriate. 4. irrational, insane, not of sound mind. 5. liberal, left, leftist.*

right *adv.* **1.** VIRTUOUSLY morally, righteously, honorably, justly, honestly ethically, fairly, properly. **2.** CORRECTLY accurately, precisely, *on the money, *on the mark, *on target, exactly, truly, perfectly, faithfully, flawlessly, unerringly. ANT. *1. immorally, dishonorably, unjustly. 2. incorrectly, inaccurately, imperfectly.*

righteous *a.* good, right, virtuous, moral, ethical, honest, honorable, just, fair, upright, noble, saintly, innocent, angelic. ANT. *bad, wicked, immoral, wrong.*

rightful *a.* right, just, fair, moral, ethical, proper, fitting, appropriate, legitimate, authorized, lawful. ANT. *wrong, illegitimate.*

rigid *a.* **1.** UNYIELDING inflexible, hard, stiff, unbending, firm, nonpliant, unmalleable. **2.** STRICT severe, exacting, harsh, uncompromising, inflexible, unaccommodating, stern, stringent, *bullheaded. ANT. **1.** *yielding, flexible, pliable.* **2.** *easy, compromising, accommodating, flexible.*

rigmarole *n.* babble, blather, gobbledygook, drivel, *bunk, *rot, claptrap, *bilge, hogwash, bull, twaddle. SEE NONSENSE

rigor *n.* harshness, severity, hardness, hardship, rigidity, roughness, toughness, difficulty, trial, strictness, inflexibility.

RIGOROUS *a.* [RIG ur us] harsh, severe, strict. *Life in the Arctic is rigorous.* SYN. harsh, severe, strict, hard, tough, rough, brutal, stringent, trying, austere. ANT. *easy, undemanding, soft.*

rile *v.* anger, annoy, irritate, peeve, *rub the wrong way, irk, aggravate, nettle, *get under one's skin, *get one's dander up, *get one's Irish up. ANT. *pacify, mollify, appease.*

rim *n.* edge, border, margin, perimeter, brink, fringe, verge, ring, hem, lip, brim, skirt.

rind *n.* peel, peeling, skin, husk, hull, outer layer.

ring *n.* **1.** CIRCLE band, loop, hoop, orbit. **2.** FINGER JEWELRY band, wedding band. **3.** ARENA rink, circus ring, bowl, coliseum. **4.** GROUP OR GANG mob, band, circle, party, bloc, association, bunch, syndicate, outfit, coterie, clan. **5.** CLANG ding, chime, reverberation, knell, peal, tintinnabulation, tinkle, toll, jingle.

ring *v.* **1.** CLANG ding, dong, bong, chime, reverberate, knell, peal, tintinnabulate, tinkle, toll, jingle, sound, vibrate, resonate. **2.** ANNOUNCE herald, signal, trumpet, broadcast. **3.** CIRCLE loop, orbit, encircle, circumscribe, encompass, surround, go around, gird.

ringleader *n.* leader, chief, boss, *head honcho, *big cheese, instigator, orchestrator.

rinse *v.* wash, wet, cleanse, clean, soak, flush, irrigate, drench, splash, immerse.

riot *n.* **1.** UPRISING disorder, outburst, demonstration, anarchy, uproar, protest, melee, commotion, turbulence, ruckus, rebellion, revolt, insurgence, donnybrook, free-for-all, distemper, civil unrest. **2.** SOMETHING HILARIOUS *scream, *laugh-a-minute, panic, howl. ANT. **1.** *peace, order.*

riot *v.* rise up, erupt, demonstrate, protest, raise a ruckus, *rumble, rebel, revolt, engage in a free-for-all, go on the rampage, engage in civil disobedience.

riotous *a.* disorderly, run amuck, boisterous, loud, out of control, wild, chaotic, rebellious, rambunctious, rowdy, anarchic. ANT. *peaceful, orderly, placid.*

rip *n.* tear, split, rend, slash, slit, cut, rift, rent, gash, hole.

rip *v.* tear, split, rend, slash, slit, cut, sever, hack, divide, cleave, shred.

ripe *a.* **1.** MATURE fully developed, ready, full-grown, seasoned, aged, soft, prime, mellow. **2.** READY timely, favorable, primed, set, prepared, opportune. ANT. **1.** *green.* **2.** *untimely.*

ripen *v.* mature, develop, grow, season, age, soften, mellow.

rip-off *n. Sl.* *gyp, thievery, theft, stealing, cheat, larceny, fraud, robbery, gouging, swindle, *con.

ripoff *v. Sl.* *gyp, thieve, steal, cheat, commit larceny, commit fraud, rob, gouge, swindle, *con, *stiff, *take one to the cleaners, *screw.

RIPOSTE *n.* [ri POST] a quick retort, after the quick thrust made in fencing. *His unexpected riposte took the mayor by surprise.* SYN. quick retort, snappy comeback, rejoinder, repartee, return, sally, reply, response, zinger, *returned fire, rebuttal.

ripple *n.* wave, wavelet, riffle, undulation, lap, purl, ridge, wrinkle.

ripple *v.* wave, riffle, undulate, lap, purl, swish, splash, wash.

riptide *n.* undertow.

rise *n.* **1.** ASCENT ascension, climb, lift, advancement, progression. **2.** HILL elevation, ridge, humpback, mound, knoll. **3.** INCREASE growth, jump, gain, upswing, hike, enlargement, expansion, upsurge, raise. ANT. **1.** *descent, plunge.* **2.** *depression, hole.* **3.** *drop, dip, loss.*

rise *v.* **1.** ASCEND go up, climb, lift, elevate, levitate, mount, scale, soar, go skyward, stand, get up. **2.** INCREASE grow, jump, gain, enlarge, expand, surge, raise, inflate, swell, intensify, heighten, double, triple, multiply. **3.** ADVANCE *climb the corporate ladder, *step up, progress, be promoted, get ahead, arrive. ANT. **1.** *descend, plunge.* **2.** *decrease, shrink, dip.* **3.** *recede, get demoted.*

risk *n.* danger, hazard, threat, peril, jeopardy, uncertainty, *thin ice, vulnerability, exposure, gamble, chance, insecurity. ANT. *safety, assurance, security.*

risk v. endanger, hazard, face a threat, imperil, put oneself in jeopardy, face uncertainty, expose oneself, leave oneself vulnerable, gamble, chance it, *take a shot in the dark, *roll the dice.

risky a. dangerous, hazardous, threatening, perilous, uncertain, chancy, a gamble, dicey, *treading on thin ice, *hairy, *out on a limb, ticklish, *playing with fire, insecure, venturesome. ANT. *safe, risk-free, secure, guaranteed.*

risque a. suggestive, racy, daring, dirty, improper, ribald, off-color, indecent, vulgar, bawdy, *spicy, *blue, crude, provocative, lewd. ANT. *clean, G-rated.*

rite n. ceremony, ritual, exercise, observance, solemn act, procedure, practice, custom, formality, liturgy.

ritual n. ceremony, rite, exercise, observance, solemn act, procedure, practice, custom, formality, tradition.

ritzy a. Sl. elegant, luxurious, posh, sumptuous, *classy, high-class, deluxe, *swank, *snazzy, fancy. ANT. *low-class, shabby, poor.*

rival n. competitor, opponent, combatant, adversary, contestant, contender, challenger, match, equal, enemy. ANT. *colleague, partner, confederate, friend, ally.*

rival v. compete with, equal, match, *go head to head against, *come up to, oppose, vie, contend, contest, challenge, emulate.

rival a. competing, combating, contesting, contending, opposing, vying.

rivalry n. competition, contest, vying, opposition, match, equaling, struggle, clash, contention, one-on-one, *fight for supremacy, emulation.

river n. waterway, tributary, branch, estuary, stream, brook, creek, feeder, torrent, rapids, freshet, rill. "A wet highway." — Leonard Levinson.

WORD FIND

artificial channel: sluice

brook, tiny: rill, runnel

cross a: ford

dam: weir

deposits of silt left behind by: alluvium

eddy that is foaming and violent: souse hole

embankment protecting against flooding: levee

fear of water: hydrophobia

flooding, area nearby that is susceptible to: floodplain

intertwined with several branches: braided river

island in: holm

loop of water sometimes separated from main river: oxbow

mill wheel, turns: millrace

ocean between high banks: fiord

passage of smooth water between rocks: tongue

rate of descent: gradient

referring to riverbank area: riparian

referring to rivers: fluvial

ridge of sand or silt: bar

rotating current: eddy

science of water in motion: hydraulics

sediment left in triangular mound at mouth of: delta

shallow area surrounded by deeper water: shoal

shallow stream with ripples made by cobbles or rocks: riffle

slow-moving deep water: pool

standing wave among rapids: *rooster, *haystack

steep, narrow stretch of descending water: chute

surrounding area contributing water: watershed

tidal: estuary

underground: aquifer, groundwater

upwelling or mounding water current: boil

waterfall: cataract

winding section: meander, bend

SEE LAKE, WATERFALL

rivet v. **1.** FASTEN bolt, pin, tack, secure, link, couple. **2.** FIX ONE'S ATTENTION fascinate, enthrall, grip, engross, occupy.

riveting a. gripping, fascinating, enthralling, engrossing, occupying, keeping one's attention, entrancing. ANT. *boring, dull, bland.*

road n. street, avenue, lane, thoroughfare, track, boulevard, highway, freeway, parkway, causeway, expressway, turnpike, interstate, route, *main drag, artery, alley, pavement.

WORD FIND

bump to check speed: speedbump

circle: rotary, cloverleaf, roundabout, circus

cliff edge road: corniche

concrete highway divider: jersey barrier

curve: ess, hairpin

dead-end: cul-de-sac, blind alley, impasse

descriptive: ribbon

dividing area of highway: median strip, island

edge: shoulder

elevated: skyway

French: rue

German expressway with no speed limit: autobahn
German: strasse
hole: chuckhole, pothole
overhead crossover: overpass
paving material: macadam, cobblestone, gravel, blacktop, asphalt
ringing a city: beltway
shoulder: berm
smoothing vehicle: grader, steamroller
Spanish: via
traffic jam: gridlock
zigzagging mountain road: switchback

roam v. wander, travel, wander aimlessly, ramble, rove, range, meander, stray, drift, gad about.

roar n. howl, bellow, yowl, growl, shriek, bay, cry, yell, bawl, thunder, rumble, explosion, boom, detonation, report.

roar v. howl, bellow, yowl, growl, shriek, bay, cry, yell, bawl, thunder, rumble, explode, boom, detonate, blast.

roast v. **1.** BAKE cook, brown, broil, barbecue, sear. **2.** RIDICULE make fun of, make sport of, put down, *rib, *kid, insult, slam, tease, taunt.

rob v. **1.** STEAL burglarize, burgle, hold up, stick up, *mug, *heist, thieve, filch, *swipe, loot, purloin, pilfer. **2.** DEPRIVE withhold, do out of.

robber n. crook, thief, *mugger, bandit, criminal, petty thief, *second-story man, housebreaker, hijacker.

robbery n. stealing, thievery, burglary, mugging, armed robbery, theft, *holdup, *stickup, *heist, looting, break-in, piracy.

robe n. bathrobe, gown, cassock, garment, vestment, kimono, caftan, toga, frock.

robot n. automaton, mechanical man, android, automated machine, golem.

robust a. hale, hardy, strong, vigorous, healthy, sturdy, fit, hearty, tough, potent, strapping, muscular, virile. ANT. weak, sickly, fragile.

rock n. **1.** STONE boulder, pebble, rubble, cobblestone, gravel, bedrock, crag, granite, ore.
WORD FIND
broken rock layer used as breakwater or bank: riprap
conglomeration: breccia, conglomerate
digestion aid for animal: gastrolith
drawing or carving on: petroglyph
glacier-deposited rock: till, drift, boulder train
ground layer: bedrock
layers of: strata

mass containing gems or fossils: matrix
metamorphosed by heat, pressure: metamorphic rock
mineral-lined: geode
molten: magma, lava
projecting: outcrop, ledge, knuckle, shelf
sand, silt, organic material, made from: sedimentary rock
study of: petrology
volcanic rock: igneous, pumice, obsidian, basalt
windblown sand, shaped by: ventifact
2. ROCK AND ROLL rhythm and blues (R&B), metal, heavy metal, disco, rockabilly, acid rock, punk rock, boogie, doo-wop, funk, fusion, hip-hop, rap, new wave, Motown, pop, psychedelic, reggae, surf music. SEE MUSIC

rock v. roll, pitch, swing, wobble, sway, seesaw, jiggle, lurch, teeter, totter, undulate.

rocket n. missile, projectile, spaceship, spacecraft, space capsule. SEE MISSILE, SPACECRAFT

rocket v. soar, shoot up, fly skyward, skyrocket, climb, take off like a shot, whiz, zoom.

rocky a. **1.** STONY flinty, craggy, rugged, jagged, petrous, gravelly, pebbly, bouldered, cobbled. **2.** *TIPPY shaky, teetering, wobbly, tottering, unsteady, unstable. ANT. **2.** stable, steady.

rococo a. ornate, ornamented, florid, *busy, profuse, involved, elegant, baroque, overdone, tasteless.

rod n. stick, pole, staff, shaft, cane, baton, bar, switch, mace, scepter.

rogue n. scoundrel, rascal, cad, knave, bastard, creep, scamp, villain, rapscallion, *SOB, ne'er-do-well, cur, *cheat. "A man with a perfect sense of two-timing." —Anon. ANT. *goody-two-shoes, *choirboy, *Dudley Do-Right.

roguish a. unscrupulous, cheating, dishonest, unprincipled, knavish, villainous, two-timing, crooked, mischievous, impish, devilish, prankish, fun-loving. ANT. scrupulous, upstanding, honest, principled.

roil v. cloud, muddy, agitate, stir up, disturb, churn up.

role n. function, office, character, characterization, impersonation, part.

roll n. bread, bun, brioche, scone, bagel, biscuit.

roll v. **1.** SPIN revolve, rotate, twirl, gyrate, circle, wheel, twist, spiral, reel, pivot, trundle. **2.** THUNDER reverberate, rumble, roar, resound, resonate, boom. **3.** WIND coil, ball, furl, twine.

rollicking a. lively, frisky, playful, jolly, carefree, mirthful, jovial, spirited, rip-roaring, romping, boisterous. ANT. *subdued, sad, depressed.*

roly-poly *a.* plump, pudgy, dumpy, short. SEE FAT

Roman *a.* Latin, Italian.

WORD FIND

ampitheater, large: coliseum
arena: hippodrome
assembly: forum
commander: centurion
commoner: plebeian
fighter: gladiator
garment: toga, tunic
hall or court: atrium
highway: via, Appian Way
hospital: valetudinarium
jar: amphora
merchandise house: emporium
sidewalk: crepido
stadium: circus
temple dedicated to the gods: pantheon
vehicle: chariot
wine room: apotheca

romance *n.* **1.** LOVE AFFAIR relationship, *fling, liasion, amour, *affaire d'amour, courtship. **2.** LOVE STORY novel, melodrama, *bodice-ripper, story, fantasy, fairy tale, fiction, epic. **3.** ADVENTURE love, excitement, glamour, fantasy, exoticism, mystery.

romantic *a.* **1.** LOVING amorous, passionate, sentimental, demonstrative, affectionate, tender, ardent, *hot, lustful, overemotional, *cow-eyed, *mushy, saccharine. **2.** ADVENTUROUS exotic, exciting, fabulous. **3.** NOT PRACTICAL quixotic, fanciful, unrealistic, idealistic, dreamy, farfetched, starry-eyed, visionary, fantastic. ANT. *1. antagonistic, warring, hateful. 3. practical, realistic, down-to-earth.*

romp *v.* play, frolic, cavort, frisk, rollick, gambol, prance, fool around, revel.

roof *n.* ceiling, top.

WORD FIND

lookout: belvedere
types: mansard, gambrel, shed, *catslide, dome, cupola, shingle, slate, thatch
walkway: widow's walk
window: skylight, dormer

rookie *n. Sl.* fresh recruit, *greenhorn, *tenderfoot, beginner, newcomer, freshman, raw recruit, *Johnny-come-lately, *boot, *snotnose.

room *n.* **1.** COMPARTMENT chamber, cubicle, living space, cell. **2.** SPACE clearing, clearance,

expanse, play, elbowroom, opening, range, leeway, latitude.

roomy *a.* spacious, large, capacious, commodious, voluminous, extensive, sizable, broad, wide, long, open. ANT. *cramped, tiny, confined.*

roost *n.* perch. SEE NEST

root *n.* **1.** TAPROOT rootstock, radix, tuber. **2.** SOURCE basis, seat, germ, heart, soul, nub, essence, nucleus, foundation, mainspring, origin, fountain.

root *v.* **1.** DIG UP unearth, forage, nose about, sniff out, uncover, pry out, grub. **2.** CHEER support, back, boost, applaud, hail, *egg on.

roots *n.* ancestry, lineage, background, heritage, birthplace, genealogy, family tree.

rope *n.* cord, cordage, line, strand, hemp rope, cable, painter, hawser, lanyard, shroud, ratline, guy, bungee cord, lariat, lasso, bola, tether, jump rope, hangman's noose.

roster *n.* list, roll, inventory, register, index, muster, schedule, agenda.

rostrum *n.* platform, stage, dais, podium, pulpit, lectern, *stump, soapbox.

rosy *a.* **1.** PINK ruddy, reddish, blushing, blooming, glowing, flushed, roseate, rubicund, sunburned, *apple-cheeked. **2.** OPTIMISTIC encouraging, positive, promising, hopeful, favorable, auspicious, bright, sunny. ANT. *1. pale, sallow, wan, pallid, ashen. 2. pessimistic, bleak, black, gloomy.*

rot *n.* **1.** DECAY spoilage, putrefaction, putrescence, decomposition, corrosion, deterioration, mold, blight. **2.** *Sl.* NONSENSE rubbish, *crap, *baloney, *twaddle, *hogwash. SEE NONSENSE

rot *v.* spoil, decay, putrefy, decompose, *go bad, corrode, deteriorate, mold, *stink, rust, crumble.

rotary *a.* revolving, turning, spinning, twirling, gyrating, rolling.

rotate *v.* **1.** GO ROUND revolve, spin, twirl, gyrate, wheel, turn, pivot, roll, circle, twist. **2.** ALTERNATE switch, replace, exchange places.

rote (by) *adj.* from memory, by heart, mechanically, by routine.

rotten *a.* **1.** DECAYED spoiled, putrefied, putrid, decomposed, *gone bad, rancid, sour, tainted, foul, rank, stale, stinking, corroded. **2.** IMMORAL nasty, corrupt, dishonest, evil, disgraceful, vicious, unscrupulous, bad, despicable, dirty, mean. ANT. *1. fresh, good. 2. good, honest, nice.*

rotund *a.* **1.** PLUMP stout, round, fat, obese, big, spherical, roly-poly, corpulent, *tubby, pudgy, full-figured, burly. **2.** SONOROUS full-toned, booming, stentorian, rich, resonant. ANT. *skinny, thin, anorexic.*

roue *n.* rake, debauchee, womanizer, *swinger, *wolf, *skirt-chaser, profligate, playboy, Casanova, Don Juan, Lothario, philanderer.

rough *a.* **1.** IRREGULAR bumpy, uneven, course, jagged, scaly, craggy, lumpy, wrinkled, corrugated, broken, shaggy, fuzzy, bristly. **2.** VIOLENT stormy, tempestuous, fierce, riotous, ferocious, intense, wild, furious, intense, bumpy, rocky, choppy. **3.** RUDE coarse, unrefined, crude, impolite, uncouth, vulgar, boorish, indelicate, bad-mannered, ungentlemanly, unladylike, gruff. **4.** UNFINISHED unrefined, raw, basic, crude, imperfect, unprocessed, rough-hewn, inexact, preliminary. **5.** APPROXIMATE imprecise, inexact, *ballpark, *thumbnail, sketchy, quick. ANT. *1. regular, smooth, level. 2. smooth, mild, easy, gentle. 3. polite, refined, cultured, genteel. 4. finished, refined, perfected. 5. exact, precise.*

round *n.* **1.** BOUT OR CYCLE course, series, circuit, sequence, turn, cycle, tour. **2.** GUNFIRE load, burst, salvo, barrage, enfilade, volley, fusillade.

round *v.* circle, encircle, go around, circumnavigate, make a circuit, gird, flank, encompass.

round *a.* **1.** CIRCULAR spherical, cylindrical, globular, hooplike, ringlike, ball-like, oval, ovoid, elliptical. **2.** ROTUND roly-poly, spherical, fat, plump, *chubby, stout, obese. **3.** RESONANT full, sonorous, rich. **4.** COMPLETE full, whole, unbroken, entire. ANT. *1. square, straight. 2. angular, thin, slender. 3. thin. 4. incomplete, broken.*

roundabout *a.* **1.** INDIRECT wandering, rambling, winding, circuitous, meandering, straying, deviating, circumlocutory, long. **2.** NOT STRAIGHTFORWARD indirect, evasive, oblique, digressive, devious, ambiguous, hinting. ANT. *1. direct, straight, short. 2. direct, blunt, straightforward.*

round up *v.* gather, assemble, corral, muster, herd, amass.

rouse *v.* stir, arouse, stimulate, wake, awaken, get going, *fire, rally, move, motivate, spur, prod, excite, goad, electrify. ANT. *tranquilize, put to sleep.*

rousing *a.* stirring, lively, brisk, spirited, energized, electrifying, enthusiastic, vigorous, stimulating. ANT. *sleepy, tired, dead.*

rout *n.* defeat, humiliating loss, beating, conquest, *drubbing, whipping, thrashing, *ass-kicking, shutout, debacle, retreat, flight,

*turning-tail.

rout *v.* defeat overwhelmingly, overwhelm, conquer, humiliate, beat, whip, thrash, *kick ass, shut out, vanquish, *skunk, *wipe the floor with, *shellac.

route *n.* way, course, passage, road, street, highway, path, trail, beat, round, itinerary, shortcut.

route *v.* direct, steer, dispatch, guide, channel, conduct.

routine *n.* custom, habit, pattern, treadmill, matter of course, convention, *beaten path, rut, *grind, method.

routine *a.* usual, daily, everyday, regular, habitual, customary, accustomed, normal, typical, standard, predictable. ANT. *unusual, irregular, abnormal.*

rove *v.* ramble, wander, roam, range, drift, stray, meander, gad about, travel aimlessly, hike.

row *n.* **1.** LINE chain, file, column, series, sequence, succession, course, rank, queue. **2.** QUARREL argument, fight, altercation, disagreement, dispute, *run-in, controversy, *falling-out, wrangle, conflict, *set-to, tiff.

row *v.* **1.** QUARREL argue, fight, disagree, dispute, *have a run-in, *have a falling-out, wrangle, conflict, *have a tiff. **2.** PADDLE scull, oar, stroke.

rowdy *n.* hoodlum, tough, punk, *loudmouth, ruffian, *roughneck, *bad actor, thug, hellion, troublemaker, bully, *yahoo. ANT. *gentleman, lady, choirboy.*

rowdy *a.* rough, quarrelsome, loud, noisy, boisterous, unruly, coarse, raucous, wild, roughhouse, rambunctious, trouble-making. ANT. *mild, quiet, gentle.*

royal *a.* regal, kingly, queenly, princely, noble, lordly, majestic, aristocratic, imperial, monarchical, stately, sovereign.

royalty *n.* sovereignty, kingship, queenship, regality, majesty, aristocracy, nobility, stateliness.

rub *n.* **1.** MASSAGE rubdown, stroke, kneading, caress, patting, petting, friction. **2.** OBSTACLE hindrance, check, barrier, obstruction, difficulty, catch, snag.

rub *v.* massage, rubdown, stroke, knead, caress, pat, pet, apply friction, brush, buff, wipe, burnish, abrade, scour, scrub.

rubber-stamp *v.* approve, okay, endorse.

rubbish *n.* **1.** TRASH refuse, garbage, waste, junk, litter, debris, rubble, sweepings, scraps, dregs. **2.** NONSENSE foolishness, *poppycock, *hogwash, *baloney, *hooey, *rot, *bunk, *horsefeathers, *crap, *bilge, *balderdash, humbug.

rubdown n. kneading. SEE MASSAGE

RUBE GOLDBERG DEVICE n. any overly-elaborate contraption, especially that employed for a very simple procedure, named after the cartoonist who drew such devices. *The young inventor constructed an elaborate Rube Goldberg device to make lemonade automatically.* SYN. contraption, contrivance, rig, apparatus, mechanism, appliance, gadget, *whatchamacallit, *thingamabob, *thingamajig.

rub the wrong way annoy, *bug, *ruffle one's feathers. SEE IRRITATE

ruckus n. disturbance, uproar, commotion, hubbub, rumpus, upheaval, turbulence, racket, outburst.

ruddy a. red, reddish, healthy, glowing, pinkish, *apple-cheeked, blooming, flushed, rosy, rubicund, rosy-cheeked, sunburned. ANT. *pale, pallid, wan, ashen.*

rude a. **1.** DISCOURTEOUS bad-mannered, unmannerly, impolite, ungracious, inconsiderate, coarse, insulting, ungentlemanly, unladylike, crude, vulgar, tactless, fresh, indelicate, brutal, brusque, rough. **2.** CRUDE, ROUGHLY FASHIONED rough-hewn, primitive, unfinished, unrefined, raw, simple, ill-formed, makeshift. **3.** BARBAROUS ignorant, savage, unrefined, uncivilized, uncultured, uncouth, wild, brutish. **4.** VIOLENT harsh, abrupt, rough, fierce, uproarious, savage. ANT. *1. courteous, polite, mannerly, gracious, tactful. 2. finished, refined, fully developed. 3. civilized, cultured. 4. gentle, mild, soft.*

rudeness n. discourtesy, bad manners, impoliteness, inconsideration, coarseness, lack of grace, conduct unbefitting a gentleman, conduct unbefitting a lady, crudeness, vulgarity, tactlessness, freshness, brutality, impudence, insolence. "The weak man's imitation of strength."—Eric Hoffer ANT. *courtesy, politeness, good manners, consideration.*

rudimentary a. elementary, basic, fundamental, primary, beginning, initial, original, embryonic, early, undeveloped, incomplete. ANT. *advanced, developed.*

rudiments n. fundamentals, first principles, elements, basics, essentials, ABCs, beginnings.

rue v. regret, be remorseful, lament, *be sick about, deplore, repent, bemoan, fret over, be sorry for, grieve.

rueful a. mournful, regretful, sorry, grieving, contrite, remorseful, *sick at heart over, heartsick, doleful, lugubrious, woeful. ANT. *happy, proud, joyous.*

ruffian n. hoodlum, *hood, tough, rowdy, punk, criminal, *roughneck, thug, goon, bully, *bad actor, troublemaker, *animal.

ruffle n. frill, trim, edging, flounce, pleat, border, ruff.

ruffle v. **1.** WRINKLE mess up, rumple, crinkle, crease, ripple, tousle, dishevel, disturb. **2.** IRRITATE annoy, disturb, *rattle one's cage, *rub the wrong way, *get on one's nerves, *get under one's skin, *pull one's chain, upset, aggravate, unsettle, nettle, chafe. ANT. *1. smooth, arrange.*

rug n. carpet, mat, runner, floor covering, broadloom, area rug, throw rug, braided rug, shag carpeting.

rugged a. **1.** UNEVEN, ROUGH irregular, bumpy, jagged, wrinkled, broken, craggy, unlevel, rocky, weathered. **2.** ROUGH-FACED weathered, wrinkled, lined, stony, strong, leathery, hard. **3.** STORMY tempestuous, violent, rough, harsh, severe, inclement. **4.** STRONG powerful, robust, brawny, stout, hearty, big, tough, muscular, burly. ANT. *1. smooth, flat, level. 2. baby-faced. 3. calm, balmy, mild. 4. weak, *wimpy, skinny.*

ruin n. **1.** REMAINS OF A COLLAPSED OR DECAYED BUILDING OR CITY remnants, wreckage, vestige, relics, debris, rubble. "Time's slow finger written in the dust."—Anna Barbauld. **2.** DESTRUCTION downfall, collapse, ruination, undoing, failure, decay, devastation, doom, fall, desolation, skids, extinction, Waterloo.

ruin v. destroy, wreck, devastate, wipe out, demolish, decimate, desolate, smash, crush, lay waste, bankrupt, defeat.

ruinous a. destructive, devastating, decimating, desolating, crushing, catastrophic, cataclysmic, disastrous, fatal, deadly, bankrupting.

ruins n. SEE RUIN

rule n. **1.** REGULATION law, statute, bylaw, ordinance, guideline, practice, policy, code, order, edict, tenet, principle, doctrine, precept, maxim. **2.** CUSTOM habit, routine, practice. **3.** REIGN control, authority, command, leadership, sovereignty, dominion, domination, government, power, administration.

rule v. **1.** GOVERN reign, control, assert authority, command, lead, hold power, administer, *lay down the law, *run the show, *hold the reins, *be in the driver's seat, *call the shots, supervise, dominate. **2.** DETERMINE judge, adjudicate, settle, find, deem, hand down a decision.

rule out v. exclude. SEE ELIMINATE

ruler n. leader, governor, administrator, sovereign, king, queen, prince, monarch, dictator, chief, tyrant, autocrat.

ruling n. judgment, determination, decision, settlement, verdict, adjudication, finding.

rumble n. **1.** ROLL thunder, reverberation, roar, peal, grumble. **2.** GANG FIGHT fight, donnybrook, street fight, free-for-all, riot, melee.

RUMINATE v. [ROO muh NATE] to think over or meditate on. *He went to his room to ruminate.* SYN. think over, meditate, turn over in one's mind, deliberate, *chew over, weigh, ponder, contemplate, cogitate, reflect on, muse.

rummage v. search through, fish for, go through, ransack, turn over, hunt, *turn inside out, root, comb.

rummy n. *Sl.* drunkard, drunk, lush. SEE ALCOHOLIC

rumor n. talk, *word on the street, gossip, hearsay, *grapevine talk, *scuttlebutt, report, tattle, *scoop, *lowdown. "A pipe blown by surmises, jealousies, conjectures."—Shakespeare.

rumor v. gossip, tell, tattle, *buzz, whisper, *pass on, leak.

rump n. rear, bottom, backside, hindquarters, posterior, butt, buttocks, seat, derriere, haunches, *tush, *bum, ass, *duff.

rumple v. wrinkle, mess up, muss up, crinkle, crumple, crease, ripple, fold, furrow, bedraggle, dishevel.

rumpus n. disturbance, commotion, uproar, ruckus, tumult, stir, upheaval, noise, ado, storm.

run n. **1.** SPRINT race, footrace, jog, dash, rush, clip, burst of speed, flight, bound, trot, gallop. **2.** TRIP, ESPECIALLY ONE TAKEN REGULARLY journey, route, tour, round, spin, excursion, circuit. **3.** PERIOD course, spell, span, interval, stretch, term. **4.** COURSE progression, passage, flow.

run v. **1.** SPRINT race, jog, dash, rush, bound, *beat feet, *clip, bolt, *hotfoot it, bound, scurry, scramble, hustle, trot, gallop. **2.** FLEE *skedaddle, *make tracks, escape, *beat it, *blow, take flight. **3.** ASSOCIATE WITH consort, *hang out with. **4.** GO, MOVE FREELY flow, roll, spill, discharge, gush, stream, surge, cascade. **5.** OPERATE drive, control, work, maneuver, propel, direct, pilot. **6.** CAMPAIGN FOR OFFICE *throw one's hat in the ring. **7.** SUPER-

VISE direct, manage, administer, control, head, boss, oversee, regulate, conduct, operate, *be in the driver's seat. **8.** LAST continue, elapse.

runaround n. evasion, delay, *buck-passing, excuses, *migraine merry-go-round.

runaway n. fugitive, escapee, deserter, refugee, truant.

rundown n. summary, outline, recap, synopsis, sketch, briefing, abstract, short version.

run-down a. **1.** TIRED fatigued, weary, exhausted, *dead, drained, enervated, sickly, *pooped, peaked, out of shape. **2.** IN DISREPAIR dilapidated, broken down, tumbledown, ramshackle. ANT. *energized, energetic, strong, fit.*

run-in n. fight, quarrel. SEE ARGUMENT

run-of-the-mill a. average, ordinary, common, mediocre, fair, everyday, routine, so-so, regular, *comme ci, comme ca. ANT. *extraordinary, superlative, unique.*

run out v. deplete, expire, exhaust, finish, end, close, stop, dry up.

runt n. dwarf, pygmy, midget, *shrimp, *half-pint, Lilliputian, pipsqueak, peewee.

rupture n. break, crack, burst, split, fracture, tear, rift, rip, cleavage, fissure, rent.

rupture v. break, crack, burst, split, fracture, tear, rip, cleave, rend, *bust, breach.

rural a. country, rustic, backwoods, countrified, pastoral, farm, agricultural, undeveloped, sylvan, idyllic, bucolic. ANT. *urban, metropolitan, citified.*

ruse n. trick, artifice, stratagem, deception, deceit, subterfuge, feint, *sham, maneuver, wile, contrivance.

rush n. **1.** HURRY speed, swiftness, haste, race, expedition, bustle, dispatch, flurry, hustle, quickness. **2.** RUN dash, charge, sprint, storm, stampede, scramble, race. ANT. *crawl, *snail's pace, *glacial pace.*

rush v. **1.** HURRY race, hustle, bustle, dash, make haste, *step on it, *get the lead out, *zoom, fly, sprint, scurry, scamper, hotfoot it, tear. **2.** ATTACK assault, blitz, storm. **3.** PRESSURE push, hurry. ANT. *crawl, *go at a snail's pace, *move slower than a glacier.*

rust n. oxidation. SEE CORROSION

rust v. oxidize, decay, crumble. SEE CORRODE

rustic n. country person, country cousin, farmer, *hick, yokel, bumpkin, hillbilly, *hayseed.

RUSTIC a. [RUS tik] rural, simple, plain. *They lived a rustic lifestyle.* SYN. rural, backwoods, country, agrarian, pastoral, bucolic, Arcadian, simple, plain, unrefined, unsophisticated, natural. ANT. *urban, sophisticated, citified.*

rustle *v.* shuffle, swish, crackle, crinkle, crepitate, sigh, bush, whisper, flutter.

rusty *a.* **1.** CORRODED oxidized, decayed. **2.** OUT OF PRACTICE stiff, impaired, out of shape, below par, unfit. ANT. *practiced, trained, skilled.*

rut *n.* **1.** FURROW track, groove, trench, cut, trough, score, channel, ditch. **2.** ROUTINE same-old same-old, pattern, treadmill, grind.

ruthless *a.* cruel, pitiless, merciless, heartless, brutal, vicious, mean, cold, unfeeling, savage, hard, callous, barbarous, ferocious. ANT. *compassionate, caring, merciful, soft.*

S

Sabbath *n.* Saturday, Sunday, day of rest. "The attuning of the heart to the comprehension of God." — Moses Maimonides. "A sponge to wipe out all the sins of the week." — Henry Ward Beecher.

sabbatical *n.* leave, rest, vacation, holiday, break. SEE VACATION

saber *n.* fencing weapon, cutlass, blade. SEE SWORD

sable *a.* black, dark brown, ebony, jet, raven, dark.

sabotage *n.* destruction, demolition, treachery, obstruction, wrecking, impairment, undermining.

sabotage *v.* destroy, demolish, wreck, *blow up, obstruct, impair, undermine, cripple, *gum up the works, *put out of commission, *put out of action, subvert.

SACCHARINE *a.* [SAK uh rin] excessively or sickeningly sweet. *The happy ending was too saccharine for me.* SYN. sweet, excessively sweet, sickeningly sweet, sugary, syrupy, honeyed, nauseating, cloying, maudlin, *mushy. ANT. *bitter, sour, acid.*

sack *n.* bag, pouch, satchel, knapsack.

sack *v.* **1.** FIRE discharge, *ax, *give pink slip, dismiss, *send packing, *give walking papers, lay off. **2.** *Sl.* TACKLE down, bring down. **3.** PLUNDER loot, pillage, ransack, despoil, rob.

sacrament *n.* rite, ceremony, ritual, vow, pledge, oath, baptism, confirmation, the Eucharist, penance, holy orders, matrimony.

sacred *a.* **1.** HOLY consecrated, sanctified, blessed, divine, godly, hallowed, venerated, religious. **2.** INVIOLABLE protected, guarded, defended, immune, sacrosanct. ANT. *1. profane, unsanctified. 2. violable.*

sacrifice *n.* offering, concession, loss, relinquishment, surrendering.

sacrifice *v.* give up, trade off, forfeit, let go, offer, surrender, relinquish, dispose of, cede, forgo.

SACRILEGE *n.* [SAK ruh lij] violation of something held sacred. *Taking the Lord's name in vain is a sacrilege.* SYN. violation, desecration, profanation, blasphemy, disrespect, mockery, impiety, irreverence, sin.

sacrilegious *a.* in violation, profane, impious, blasphemous, disrespectful, irreverent, godless, unholy, sinful. ANT. *holy, reverent, pious.*

SACROSANCT *a.* [SAK roh SANGKT] holy,

sacred. *The teachings of Jesus are sacrosanct.* SYN. sacred, holy, divine, godly, consecrated, hallowed, venerated, sanctified, religious, untouchable, inviolable, inviolate. ANT. *profane, impious, sacrilegious.*

sad *a.* **1.** DOWNHEARTED *blue, depressed, dejected, unhappy, sorrowful, mournful, *bummed out, despondent, *down in the dumps, woebegone, melancholy, heartsick, forlorn, *out of sorts, dispirited, brokenhearted, glum. **2.** HEARTBREAKING woeful, pitiful, tearful, poignant, moving, touching, depressing, tragic, joyless, miserable. ANT. *1. happy, joyful, euphoric, elated. 2. joyful, happy, uplifting.*

sadden *v.* depress, *bring down, grieve, dispirit, deject, dampen one's spirits, *break one's heart, make blue, distress, *bum out, make one's heart heavy. ANT. *cheer, uplift, gladden.*

saddle *n.* seat, western saddle, English saddle, mount, pad, perch.

WORD FIND

part: pommel, cinch, cantle, girth, stirrup, latigo

SEE HORSE

SADISTIC *a.* [suh DIS tik] enjoying or being sexually aroused from dominating or inflicting pain on others. *The sadistic dictator liked to torture his detractors.* SYN. cruel, domineering, bossy, strict, harsh, dictatorial, aggressive, commanding, disciplinary, severe, nasty, dirty, perverse, *raunchy, sadomasochistic. ANT. *masochistic.*

sadness *n.* downheartedness, sorrow, depression, melancholy, misery, unhappiness, cheerlessness, woefulness, gloom, despondency, broken heart, heavy heart, *the blues. ANT. *happiness, joy, euphoria, elation.*

safari *n.* hunting expedition, hunt, journey, trek, caravan, shoot, campaign.

safe *n.* strongbox, safety-deposit box, money box, vault.

safe *a.* **1.** SECURE *out of harm's way, out of danger, *out of the woods, safe and sound, sheltered, protected, guarded, invulnerable, *home free, *in the clear, impregnable. **2.** HARMLESS innocent, innocuous, tame, risk-free, okay, secure, sure. **3.** CAUTIOUS careful, conservative, wary, prudent, reliable, dependable, circumspect, guarded. ANT. *1. in danger, in peril, *on thin ice, vulnerable. 2. harmful, dangerous, risky. 3. imprudent, out of* *control.*

safeguard *n.* protection, shield, security, defense, precaution, guard, screen, safety measure.

safeguard *v.* protect, shield, secure, defend, take a precaution, guard, screen, take a safety measure, assure, insure.

safekeeping *n.* protection, security, preservation, care, custody, guardianship.

safety *n.* security, protection, shelter, invulnerability, sanctuary, refuge, safe haven, safe harbor, immunity. ANT. *danger, hazard, peril.*

sag *v.* droop, sink, hang, wilt, slump, bow, dip, settle, bend.

saga *n.* story, narrative, adventure, tale, legend, myth, epic, chronicle, history, romance, roman-fleuve.

SAGACIOUS *a.* [suh GAY shus] shrewd, sharp, having a keen power of judgment. *The sagacious police officer sized up the situation quickly.* SYN. shrewd, sharp, judicious, intelligent, acute, keen, discerning, wise, sage, smart, quick, perceptive, savvy, insightful. ANT. *stupid, undiscerning, slow.*

sagacity *n.* intelligence, good judgement, sharpness, astuteness, judiciousness, wisdom, perceptiveness, insight. ANT. *stupidity, dullness, dull-wittedness.*

sage *n.* wise man, *brain, learned man, scholar, intellectual, authority, savant, philosopher, guru, Solomon. ANT. *moron, imbecile, *retard, idiot.*

sage *a.* wise, intelligent, smart, savvy, learned, astute, sagacious, sensible, judicious, sapient, discerning. ANT. *stupid, imbecilic, dense.*

sail *v.* ply the seas, cruise, ride the bounding main, pilot, navigate, skipper, tack, float, drift, shove off, cast off.

WORD FIND

change tack: come about

close to the wind: luffing, close-hauled

come about: hard alee

crew member: hand

dead calm area of sea: doldrums

fin used in place of keel: centerboard, daggerboard

lean of vessel while sailing: heel

line fitting on deck: chock

line fixture with prongs: cleat

lines and wires: rigging

line used to hoist sail: lanyard

mast, aft-most: mizzenmast

mast, angle of: rake

mast housing on deck: tabernacle

mooring bow line: painter, bowline

overhead: aloft

pennant, yacht club: burgee

race: regatta

rigging, mast: forestay

roll up sail: furl

rope stairway to aloft: ratlines

sail, adjust angle of: trim

sail, aftermast, rigged fore-and-aft: spanker

sail, forward, triangular: foresail, for's'l (pronunciation), jib

sail, large forward: Genoa

sail, largest: mainsail

sail, large, three-cornered: spinnaker

sail, lower a: strike, take in

sail, L-shaped: blooper

sail, raise a: hoist, set

sail, reduce main: reef

sail set forward of mast, any: headsail

sail, square, set abeam: square-rigged

sail, triangular, fore-and-aft-rigged: Bermuda-rigged, Marconi-rigged

sail used in weak winds: drifter

seat used for worker aloft: bosun's chair

shallow water, sailing in: gunkholing

sideways, moving: crabbing, making leeway

spar, large vertical sail: mast

spar on bow to which headsail is attached: bowsprit

spar on which bottom of sail is attached: boom

steers, crew member who: helmsman

tack downwind: jibe

tack upwind: beat

vessel, tri-hulled: trimaran

vessel, twin-hulled: catamaran

wind indicators made of yarn tied to shrouds: telltales

wind-protected side of vessel: lee, leeward

wind, run before the: scud

wind, sail with the: run

wind, side of boat taking: windward

wires that stabilize mast: shrouds

world, sail around the: circumnavigate

zigzagging course to counter wind: tacking

SEE BOAT, NAVY, SAILBOAT, SHIP

sailboat *n.* boat, vessel, craft, pleasure craft, yacht, windjammer.

WORD FIND

TYPES

fast nineteenth century freight and transport: clipper

fifteenth-sixteenth century Spanish: caravel

fishing vessel: smack

fore-and-aft-rigged vessel with two or three masts: schooner

Oriental: sampan, junk
single-masted: sloop, cutter
small, two-masted vessel: ketch
Spanish square-rigger of fifteenth-eigh-
teenth century: galleon
square-rigged warship of eighteenth-nine-
teenth century: frigate
square-rigger with three or four masts: bark
tri-hulled: trimaran
twin-hulled: catamaran
two-masted: brigantine
warship, fast, small: corvette
SEE BOAT, NAVY, SAIL, SHIP

sailor *n.* mariner, seafarer, seaman, navy man,
sea dog, navigator, salt, shellback, skipper,
helmsman, hand, first mate, midshipman,
quartermaster, petty officer, bosun.

WORD FIND
bag: ditty bag
dance: hornpipe
hat: sou'wester, watchcap
inexperienced: lubber
kidnap: shanghai
living quarters: forecastle
one who brings bad luck: Jonah
rebellion: mutiny
song: shanty, chantey
yes: aye-aye
SEE NAVY

saint *n.* holy person, Christian, angel, martyr.
"A dead sinner, revised and edited."—Ambrose Bierce. ANT. *sinner, devil, evil-doer.*

WORD FIND
declare a: canonize
image: icon
patron saint of children: Nicholas
patron saint of sailors: Elmo
patron saint of the handicapped: Giles
qualify one for sainthood: beatify
study of: hagiography
tomb: shrine
worship: hagiolatry

saintly *a.* Christian, good, faithful, godly, pious,
holy, angelic, spiritual, religious, devout,
moral, pure, righteous, virtuous. ANT. *unholy,
immoral, sinful, wicked.*

sake *n.* **1.** BEHALF welfare, good, gain, interest,
advantage, regard. **2.** PURPOSE reason, object,
end, goal, aim.

salacious *a.* lustful, *horny, lecherous, libidinous, lewd, prurient, obscene. ANT. *chaste,
virginal, celibate, abstinent.*

salad *n.* greens, vegetarian fare, lettuce and tomato, cress salad, endive salad, coleslaw,
tossed salad, fruit salad, potato salad.

salary *n.* pay, wages, earnings, income, compensation, remuneration, *take-home, stipend.

sale *n.* **1.** SELLING trade, exchange, transfer, ven-
ding, marketing, transaction. **2.** REDUCTION
IN PRICES discount, cut, clearance sale, bargain pricing.

salesman/woman *n.* merchandiser, peddler,
pitchman, solicitor, vendor, drummer, clerk.

SALIENT *a.* [SAYL yunt] standing out, prominent, outstanding. *He wrote down the most
salient points of the lecture.* SYN. standing out,
prominent, outstanding, conspicuous, striking, important, weighty, noticeable, primary,
significant, glaring. ANT. *inconspicuous, unimportant, insignificant.*

saliva *n.* spit, spittle, drool, sputum, salivation,
slobber, slaver.

sallow *a.* pale yellow, yellowish, sickly, jaundiced, pale, pallid, wan. ANT. *rosy, glowing,
ruddy.*

sally *n.* **1.** RUSH charge, attack, assault, blitz,
foray, sortie, raid, offensive, onslaught,
thrust. **2.** QUICK REMARK witticism, quip,
*comeback, banter, repartee, mot.

sally *v.* rush out, charge, storm, raid, assault,
attack, blitz, drive.

salon *n.* **1.** SOCIAL ROOM front room, reception
area, saloon, drawing room, hall, living
room. **2.** HAIR-DRESSING ESTABLISHMENT parlor.

saloon *n.* bar, pub, drinking establishment,
*beer joint, taproom, alehouse, beer garden,
tavern, *watering hole, *speakeasy, *honky-
tonk, *ginmill, grogshop, rathskeller.

salty *a.* **1.** SALINE brackish, briny, heavily seasoned. **2.** SHARP piquant, pungent, biting. **3.**
EARTHY coarse, ribald, off-color, risque, dirty,
racy. ANT. 2. *bland, mild.* 3. *decent, G-rated,
proper.*

salubrious *a.* healthful, wholesome, salutary,
beneficial, good for. ANT. *unhealthy, harmful.*

salutary *a.* healthy, healthful, wholesome, salubrious, beneficial, good for one. ANT. *unhealthy, harmful.*

salutation *n.* greeting, hail, hello, salute,
*howdy, address.

salute *n.* recognition, respects, greeting, *snap
to attention, obeisance.

salute *v.* **1.** RECOGNIZE show one's respect, greet,
*snap to attention, show one's obeisance. **2.**
PAY TRIBUTE honor, praise, commend, applaud, recognize.

salvage *v.* save, rescue, recover, retrieve, reclaim, recondition, redeem, recycle, *dump
pick. ANT. *dump, waste, squander.*

salvation n. saving, rescue, deliverance, redemption, release, liberation, emancipation, conversion.

salve n. ointment, balm, emollient, unguent, ream, lotion, liniment.

salve v. soothe, ease, assuage, smooth over, relieve, alleviate, heal.

salvo n. discharge, firing, gunfire, broadside, fusillade, volley, cannonade, bombardment, hail, shower.

same a. **1.** IDENTICAL alike, ditto, equal, matching, twin, duplicate, comparable, equivalent, similar, corresponding. **2.** UNCHANGED changeless, constant, steady, unvarying. ANT. 1. contrasting, different, unlike. 2. changed, varied.

sample n. part, piece, bit, example, fragment, segment, cross section, portion, *swatch, *demo, bite, taste.

sample v. try, experience, partake, test, taste, take a cross section.

sanctify v. make holy, consecrate, bless, anoint, hallow, glorify, exalt, beatify, canonize, dedicate. ANT. desecrate, profane.

SANCTIMONIOUS a. [SANGK tuh MOH nee us] pretending to be holy and righteous. We were sick of his sanctimonious preaching and left. SYN. self-righteous, holier-than-thou, hypocritical, *up on one's moral soapbox, affected, overpious, unctuous, preachy, *goody-goody, false.

sanctimony n. self-righteousness, hypocrisy, sanctimoniousness, pietism, *goody-goodyness, pretense, affectation, lip service.

sanction n. authorization, approval, permission, confirmation, endorsement, *okay, accreditation, warrant, license, consent. ANT. veto, *no, disapproval.

sanction v. authorize, approve, permit, confirm, endorse, *give the okay, accredit, warrant, license, consent. ANT. veto, disapprove, prohibit.

sanctioned a. authorized, approved, permitted, confirmed, *okayed, accredited, warranted, licensed, consented. ANT. prohibited, rejected, vetoed.

sanctity n. holiness, sacredness, saintliness, godliness, inviolability, spirituality, righteousness, piety, purity. ANT. wickedness, godlessness.

sanctuary n. **1.** HOLY PLACE church, temple, chapel, sanctum, altar, shrine. **2.** REFUGE asylum, haven, retreat, safe harbor, hideaway, shelter. **3.** ANIMAL CONSERVATION AREA reserve, reservation, preserve, game preserve, wild animal park.

sane a. of sound mind, rational, lucid, clear-thinking, right-minded, compos mentis, possessing all of one's faculties, *having all one's marbles, *playing with a full deck, stable, *in one's right mind, *all there, sober, sensible, reasonable. ANT. insane, crazy, out of one's mind, deranged.

SANG-FROID n. [sahn FRWAH] composure, cool blood, coolness. Even in a crisis, she had a certain sang-froid that people respected. SYN. composure, coolness, coolheadedness, cool, cool blood, equanimity, calmness, presence of mind, equilibrium, poise, grace under pressure. ANT. anxiety, tenseness, hysteria.

sanguinary a. **1.** BLOODY bloodied, bloodstained, gory. **2.** BLOODTHIRSTY murderous, savage, predatory, homicidal, out for blood, brutal, slaughterous.

SANGUINE a. [SAN gwin] cheerful, upbeat, optimistic. Also, reddish or ruddy, as a complexion. She appeared sanguine most of the day. A sanguine complexion. SYN. **1.** cheerful, upbeat, optimistic, buoyant, happy, positive, spirited, hopeful, lighthearted, confident. **2.** reddish, ruddy, rubicund, glowing, blooming, scarlet, florid. ANT. 1. miserable, depressed, pessimistic, hopeless. 2. pale, pallid.

sanitarium n. sanitorium, resort, health spa, hospital, institution, baths, asylum.

sanitary a. clean, hygienic, healthy, uncontaminated, antiseptic, disinfected, germ-free, sterile, sterilized, wholesome. ANT. dirty, germ-ridden, unsanitary, unhealthy.

sanitize v. clean, sterilize, disinfect, make antiseptic.

sanity n. saneness, sound mind, rightmindedness, mental stability, mental health, *all one's marbles, rationality, sense, levelheadedness, good judgment, lucidity, *both oars in the water. ANT. insanity, psychosis, craziness, instability.

sap v. weaken, exhaust, undermine, drain, wear out, enervate, enfeeble, deplete, impair, bleed dry, suck dry, debilitate. ANT. invigorate, energize, strengthen

sapient a. sagacious, sage, discerning, intelligent, smart. SEE WISE

sappy a. Sl. silly, foolish, corny, fatuous, sentimental, *mushy, maudlin.

sarcasm n. mockery, jeering, snideness, ridicule, scorn, irony, satire, contempt, *cut, *dig, wisecrack, put-down. ANT. compliment, praise, approval.

sarcastic a. mocking, snide, ridiculing, scornful, ironic, satiric, contemptuous, *cutting, *digging, *wise, *smart-alecky, sardonic, nasty, caustic, sneering, jeering. ANT. complimentary, approving, positive.

SARDONIC a. [sar DON ik] mocking or sarcastic, bitter. *She has had enough of his sardonic observations.* SYN. mocking, sarcastic, bitter, nasty, disdainful, contemptuous, *cutting, cynical, jeering, *smart-mouthed, *smart-alecky, *wise, *wise-ass, acid, biting. ANT. complimentary, positive, sweet.

sash n. band, ribbon, belt, tie, scarf, cummerbund.

sashay v. strut, swagger, parade, glide, roll one's hips, wiggle pertly, slink, sway voluptuously, bounce. SEE WALK

sass n. impudence, insolence, *mouth, *lip, back talk, effrontery, disrespect, cheek, *sauce. ANT. respect, silence.

sass v. talk back, *mouth off, *give lip, be impudent, be insolent, be disrespectful, *get smart, *wise off. ANT. respect, *button one's lip, defer.

sassy a. saucy, flippant, *mouthy. SEE IMPUDENT

Satan n. the Devil, Lucifer, Prince of Darkness, Beelzebub, Mephistopheles, Lord of the Flies, Old Harry, Apollyon. SEE DEVIL

satanic a. demonic, devilish, evil, wicked, hellish, infernal, diabolical, fiendish, black-hearted, malevolent, vicious. ANT. godly, angelic, saintly.

satchel n. bag, valise, sack, suitcase.

sate v. satisfy, fill. SEE SATIATE

satellite n. moon, planetoid, orbiter, space station, weather satellite, spacecraft, *Sputnik, *Skylab.

satiate v. fill, satisfy, sate, slake, stuff, gorge, gratify, quench, glut, overload, *pig out, cloy.

satire n. caricature, ridicule, mockery, lampoon, *takeoff, parody, burlesque, *spoof, irony, sarcasm. "Moral outrage transformed into comic art." —Philip Roth.

satirical a. ridiculing, mocking, lampooning, sarcastic, ironic, *kidding, smart-alecky, tongue-in-cheek, farcical, burlesque, cynical.

satirize v. ridicule, mock, lampoon, parody, caricaturize, *kid, burlesque, *take off on, make fun of, make sport of.

satisfaction n. **1.** FULFILLMENT gratification, pleasure, contentment, enjoyment, delight, happiness, reward. **2.** SETTLEMENT compensation, restitution, reparation, recompense, reimbursement, redress, indemnity. ANT. 1. dissatisfaction, discontent.

satisfactory a. okay, acceptable, good enough, all right, sufficient, adequate, pleasing, fulfilling, suitable, up to scratch. ANT. unsatisfactory, insufficient, unacceptable.

satisfy v. **1.** FULFILL gratify, please, content, delight, make happy, reward, *fill the bill, quench, appease. **2.** MEET fulfill, answer, equal, match, comply. **3.** ASSURE convince, persuade. **4.** SETTLE discharge, make up for, compensate, make restitution, clear, pay off. ANT. 1. dissatisfy, discontent. 2. come up short, *miss the mark.

satisfying a. fulfilling, gratifying, pleasing, contenting, delightful, rewarding, quenching, satiating, *filling the bill, *hitting the spot.

saturate v. soak, imbue, fill, drench, souse, wet through, permeate, impregnate, suffuse, pervade, drown. ANT. drain, dehydrate, dry.

saturnine a. gloomy, morose, depressed, sorrowful, glum, sullen, sulky, downhearted, hopeless, dour, moody. ANT. happy, cheerful, sunny.

satyr n. lech, debaucher, playboy, *horny little devil, profligate, rake, wolf, womanizer, Don Juan, Casanova. ANT. *choir boy, celibate.

sauce n. gravy, dressing, relish, condiment, soy sauce, worcestershire sauce, Mornay sauce, white sauce, soubise.

saucy a. rude, impudent, *smart-mouthed, *mouthy, *wise, impertinent, flippant, disrespectful, insolent, *sassy, bold, fresh. ANT. respectful, shy, courteous, diplomatic.

saunter v. stroll, walk leisurely, *mosey along, amble, pad, shuffle, promenade, dawdle, stray, meander. SEE WALK

sauté v. quick fry.

savage n. primitive, aborigine, brute, barbarian, beast, monster, animal, cave man, Neanderthal, wild man, killer. "Animals in human shape." —Bernard de Fontenelle.

savage v. attack, brutalize, tear apart, maul, rip apart, beat to a pulp, kill, murder, torture.

savage a. wild, fierce, ferocious, untamed, beastly, vicious, brutal, inhuman, barbaric, bloodthirsty, predatory, animalistic, brutish, cruel. ANT. tame, gentle, civilized, broken.

savagery n. barbarity, brutality, brutishness, beastliness, monstrosity, wildness, cruelty, viciousness.

savannah n. plain, grassland, pampas, steppe. SEE FIELD

savant n. scholar, *brain, intellectual, learned person, sage, *walking encyclopedia, wise man, expert, authority. ANT. *moron, imbecile, idiot.*

save *v.* **1.** RESCUE liberate, deliver, bail out, *save one's bacon, *save one's neck, recover, free, emancipate. **2.** SQUIRREL AWAY hoard, lay aside, stash, *sock away, *put away for a rainy day, salt away. **3.** CONSERVE preserve, be thrifty, be frugal, *pinch pennies, scrimp, economize, *tighten one's belt. ANT. *1. put at risk, imperil. 2., 3. spend, expend, squander, *blow.*

savior *n.* liberator, deliverer, lifesaver, emancipator, messiah, Jesus Christ.

SAVOIR FAIRE *n.* [SAV wahr FEHR] social know-how. *He always knew what to say; he had great savoir faire.* SYN. social know-how, sophistication, cultivation, worldliness, graciousness, suavity, smoothness, social grace, poise, urbanity, tactfulness, diplomacy. ANT. *tactlessness, clumsiness, awkwardness.*

savor *n.* taste, flavor, tang, scent, odor, aroma, smell.

savor *v.* taste, smell, enjoy, relish, *smack one's lips over, luxuriate in, appreciate.

savory *a.* **1.** TASTY appetizing, delicious, mouthwatering, delectable, toothsome, ambrosial, luscious, flavorful, agreeable. **2.** RESPECTABLE reputable, decent, moral, upright, virtuous. ANT. *1. unsavory, *gross, disgusting, unappetizing. 2. unsavory, disreputable.*

savvy *n. Sl.* know-how, *smarts, understanding, shrewdness, intelligence, knowledge, experience, proficiency, grasp, awareness. ANT. *stupidity, ignorance.*

savvy *a.* in the know, knowledgeable, shrewd, astute, sharp, *on the ball, educated, experienced, intelligent, *hip, proficient. ANT. *ignorant, uneducated, stupid.*

saw *n.* **1.** CUTTING TOOL cutting instrument, blade, handsaw, circular saw, crosscut saw, hacksaw, hacksaw, coping saw. **2.** SAYING maxim, proverb, truism, adage, aphorism, epigram, cliché.

saw *v.* rend, rip. SEE CUT

saw-toothed *a.* jagged, serrated, serrate, notched.

say *v.* utter, speak, tell, assert, give voice, mouth, pronounce, vocalize, remark, phrase, state, articulate.

saying *n.* maxim, proverb, truism, adage, aphorism, epigram, cliche, slogan, saw, motto.

scab *n.* crust, incrustation, scale.

scaffold *n.* framework, platform, staging, gallows, gantry.

scald *v.* heat, injure. SEE BURN

scale *n.* **1.** SKIN layer, covering, crust, plate, scurf. **2.** GAUGE progression, order, gradation, succession, degrees, measure, calibration, ratio.

scale *v.* climb, ascend, mount, clamber up. ANT. *descend.*

scalp *v.* cheat, rob, *rip off.

scamp *n.* rascal, mischief-maker, troublemaker, imp, rogue, scoundrel, scalawag, knave, prankster, *little devil.

scamper *v.* run, hurry, scurry, scramble, dash, rush, sprint, dart, scuttle, scoot. ANT. *saunter, mosey along, creep.*

scan *v.* look at, scrutinize, study, survey, examine, inspect, search, scour, peruse, check, glance at, skim, *flip through, thumb through, browse, *give the once-over.

scandal *n.* disgrace, shocker, sin, atrocity, transgression, vice, outrage, wrongdoing, crime, infamy, *skeleton in the closet, impropriety, misconduct. "Vice enjoyed vicariously."—Elbert Hubbard.

scandalous *a.* disgraceful, shocking, sinful, atrocious, outrageous, wrong, criminal, infamous, improper, shameful, odious.

scant *a.* meager, inadequate, lacking, sparse, insufficient, deficient, tight, wanting, poor, spare, limited. ANT. *plentiful, bountiful, overflowing.*

scapegoat *n.* *fall guy, whipping boy, *goat, *patsy, victim, butt, dupe.

scar *n.* **1.** DISFIGUREMENT scab, pockmark, scar tissue, scratch, line, cut, gash, cicatrix, mark. **2.** EMOTIONAL DAMAGE psychological wound, trauma, reminder, stigma, flashbacks.

scar *v.* **1.** DISFIGURE scratch, cut, gash, blemish, mar, wound, lacerate. **2.** EMOTIONALLY DAMAGE wound psychologically, traumatize, stigmatize, brand, hurt.

scarce *a.* rare, uncommon, scanty, scant, insufficient, in short supply, *scarce as hens' teeth, not enough, meager, inadequate, at a premium, tight. ANT. *plentiful, abundant, bountiful.*

scarcely *adv.* barely, merely, only, just, hardly.

scantiness *n.* rareness, insufficiency, shortage, short supply, meagerness, inadequacy, dearth, paucity, need, poverty, sparsity.

scare *n.* fright, shock, turn, panic, terror.

scare *v.* frighten, unnerve, terrify, alarm, panic, daunt, shock, appall, *put the fear of God into, petrify, paralyze, *send chills down one's spine, *make one's hair stand on end, spook, *scare the bejeesus out of, curl one's hair, make one's blood run cold, *adrenalize, intimidate, horrify, fill with dread. ANT. *reassure, encourage, embolden.*

scarecrow n. malkin, straw man.

scarf n. muffler, neckpiece, bandanna, ascot, boa, tippet.

scary a. frightening, unnerving, terrifying, alarming, panic-inducing, daunting, shocking, appalling, petrifying, paralyzing, *bonechilling, *bloodcurdling, *spine-tingling, *hair-curling, *hair-raising, *adrenalizing, intimidating, horrifying, creepy. ANT. *reassuring, encouraging, emboldening.*

scathing a. harsh, searing, caustic, biting, acid, bitter, severe, vitriolic, cutting, sharp, nasty, pointed, brutal. ANT. *mild, bland, gentle.*

scatter v. 1. STREW sprinkle, litter, spread, broadcast, distribute. 2. SEPARATE rout, disperse, diffuse, dispel. ANT. *gather, assemble, amass.*

scatterbrained a. flighty, giddy, brainless, frivolous, *bubbleheaded, *airheaded, *dizzy, *a space case, *off in the ozone, harebrained, *ditzy, *like duh. ANT. *on the ball, *with it, *savvy, sharp.*

scenario n. outline, synopsis, script, sketch, concept, plot, story, plan.

scene n. 1. SETTING place, location, locale, backdrop, site, spot. 2. VIEW scenery, panorama, vista, landscape, prospect. 3. SEGMENT act, bit, episode, part. 4. DISPLAY OF EMOTION tantrum, fit, *spectacle, *blowup, outburst.

scenic a. picturesque, beautiful, panoramic, breathtaking, grand, spectacular, awe-inspiring, quaint.

scent n. odor, smell, fragrance, aroma, essence, bouquet, stink, whiff, trace, redolence, incense.

scented a. odorous, smelling, aromatic. SEE FRAGRANT

schedule n. agenda, program, timetable, calendar, roster, docket, plan, lineup, itinerary, slate.

scheme n. 1. PLAN plot, stratagem, ploy, machination, intrigue, conspiracy, maneuver. 2. SYSTEM arrangement, organization, order.

scheming a. crafty, underhanded, sneaky, artful, tricky, conniving, calculating, sly, foxy, slippery.

SCHISM n. [SIZ um] a separation within a group, due to disagreement over a particular issue. *A schism has formed in the church over the abortion issue.* SYN. separation, split, division, rift, splintering, break, faction, disjunction, fragmentation. ANT. *unification, union,*

harmony.

schlemiel n. *Sl.* loser, bungler, *schlimazel, *Charlie Brown, *zero, dupe, victim, *sap, *patsy, *stooge, *sucker, fool.

schlep v. *Sl.* drag oneself, drag, lug, carry.

schlock n. *Sl.* *crap, garbage, trash, *cheap stuff, junk, *dreck.

scholar n. learned person, educated person, intellectual, *brain, man of letters, *egghead, highbrow, professor, teacher, student, pupil, *walking encyclopedia, *know-it-all, authority, expert, pundit, savant, polymath. "A man, long on advice but short on action." — Elbert Hubbard. ANT. *ignoramus, idiot, *airhead, imbecile.*

scholarly a. learned, knowledgeable, educated, studious, erudite, literate, well-read, intellectual, academic, bookish, pedantic, *brainy. ANT. *ignorant, uneducated, stupid, empty-headed.*

scholarship n. 1. KNOWLEDGE education, erudition, learning, schooling, edification, enlightenment, pedantry. 2. GRANT student aid, gift, endowment, fellowship.

school n. 1. EDUCATIONAL INSTITUTE academy, high school, elementary school, university, college, institution of higher learning, alma mater, seminary. 2. SYSTEM method, style, mode, belief system, doctrine.

school v. educate, teach, instruct, train, enlighten, edify, indoctrinate, tutor.

science n. hard facts, physical laws, truths, body of knowledge, discipline. "Trained and organized common sense." — Thomas Huxley. "A knowledge of matter." — Fulton Sheen. "Pearls strung on a cord of faith." — Joshua Steinberg. "Only the tools in a box." — Frank Lloyd Wright.

WORD FIND

agriculture: geoponics, agrology

air, moving objects through: aerodynamics

air: pneumatics

animal, prebirth development: embryology

animals: zoology

aviation: aeronautics

birds: ornithology

building design: architecture

caves: speleology

cells: cytology

chemicals, applied: chemical engineering

chemistry of life processes: biochemistry

civilization, uncovering facts about early: archeology

classification, plant and animal: taxonomy

climate: climatology

color: chromatology
crime: criminology
cycles, natural: chronobiology
earth: geology
earthquakes: seismology
earth's moving plates: tectonics
energy and heat: thermodynamics
energy and matter: physics
epidemics: epidemiology
fish: ichthyology
fluids: hydraulics
fossils, animal: paleontology
heredity and genes: genetics
human beings: anthropology
human beings, extinct: paleoanthropology
gene manipulation: genetic engineering, eugenics
life processes: biology
lines, angles, planes, etc.: geometry
machinery: mechanics
mapping of terrain: topography, cartography
metals: metallurgy
monsters: teratology
motion: kinetics, dynamics
plants: botany
plants, ornamental: horticulture
population studies: demography
primitive societies: ethnography
societies and social behavior: sociology
sound: acoustics
space, study of: astronomy, astrophysics, cosmography, cosmology
time: chronometry, horology
water: hydrography
weather: meteorology

scientific a. systematic, provable, exact, empirical, physical, material, observable, mathematical, technical, technological. ANT. *unscientific, spiritual.*

scintilla n. particle, trace, iota, hint, bit, speck, atom, whit, drop, spark.

SCINTILLATING a. [SIN tuh late ing] sparkling, flashing. Also, brilliant, as of wit. *Scintillating starlight. A scintillating conversation.* SYN. **1.** SPARKLING glittering, brilliant, glinting, glimmering, twinkling, gleaming, shimmering, flashing. **2.** WITTY clever, brilliant, effervescent, lively. ANT. *dull, lackluster.*

scion n. offspring, descendant, child, heir, successor, offshoot, shoot.

scoff v. jeer, mock, ridicule, deride, snicker at, laugh at, gibe, dismiss, belittle, *pooh-pooh, discount, knock. ANT. *respect, accept, praise.*

scold v. berate, rebuke, upbraid, reprimand, reproach, *blast, *jump down one's throat,

find fault, vituperate, *chew out, *give hell, *take to task, castigate, *rake over the coals, *rip into, *let have it with both barrels, *bawl out. ANT. *commend, praise, give a pat on the back.*

scoop n. **1.** SHOVEL spade, spoon, bail, trowel, ladle. **2.** HOT NEWS *inside information, *skinny, *poop, exclusive, *lowdown.

scoot v. dart, scurry, skedaddle, hurry, *move it.

scope n. area, range, extent, span, reach, compass, radius, breadth, sphere.

scorch v. burn, blacken, char, singe, parch, sear, shrivel, brown, toast, blister.

score n. **1.** TALLY count, points, sum, total. **2.** GRADE mark. **3.** MUSICAL COMPOSITION arrangement, chart. **4.** GROOVE nick, notch, cut, gash.

score v. **1.** SUCCEED triumph, achieve, win, *rack up, *chalk up, *nail it, *hit it. **2.** CUT crosshatch, gouge, nick, notch, gash, slit.

scores n. many, multitude, lots, throng, mass, myriad, crowd, legion. ANT. *few, hardly any.*

scorn n. contempt, disdain, hatred, loathing, disgust, distaste, derision, sneering, arrogance, scoffing, mocking. ANT. *admiration, respect, esteem.*

scorn v. regard with contempt, disdain, despise, detest, hate, loathe, look down on, reject, spurn, revile, mock, ridicule. ANT. *admire, look up to, respect, like.*

scoundrel n. rascal, villain, rogue, *SOB, *bastard, cad, dog, knave, *creep, *rat, dastard, wretch, *bad egg, *bad actor.

scour v. **1.** SCRUB clean, wash, rub, abrade, brush, wipe. **2.** SEARCH OUT comb, rummage, range over, pass over, *turn upside-down, *leave no stone unturned, look high and low.

scourge n. punishment, torture, torment, affliction, plague, misery, tribulation, curse.

scourge v. punish, torture, torment, afflict, plague, chastise, curse, beat, whip, flog, thrash.

scout n. spy, patrol, outrider, advance man, reconnoiterer, picket, lookout.

scout v. spy, reconnoiter, *have a look-see, survey, investigate, explore, observe, patrol, *check out.

scow n. barge, flatboat.

scowl n. angry look, irritated look, frown, glower, *black look, *dirty look, glare, knitted brow, nasty look, lower. SEE ANGRY

scowl v. frown, glower, glare, shoot an angry look, shoot an irritated look, give a dirty look, *shoot daggers. SEE ANGRY

scraggly *a.* scrubby, ragged, uneven, irregular, straggly, rough, *like a rat's nest, ungroomed. ANT. *neat, trim.*

scraggy *a.* skinny, lean, scrawny, bony, thin, slender, gaunt.

scramble *n.* run, dash, rush, struggle, climb, race, scuffle, competition.

scramble *v.* **1.** CLAMBER climb, crawl, struggle, rush, dash, run, rush, race, scuffle, compete for, strive for. **2.** MIX jumble, stir up, disorder, mingle, tangle, confuse.

scrap *n.* **1.** BIT fragment, piece, shred, chip, speck, slice, hunk, chunk, particle, end. **2.** SALVAGE junk. **3.** FIGHT argument, quarrel, *tiff, conflict, tussle, altercation, disagreement, squabble, brawl.

scrap *v.* throw out, drop, ditch, get rid of, discard, junk, *deep six, jettison.

scrape *n.* **1.** SCRATCH scuff, abrasion, graze, scar. **2.** DIFFICULT SITUATION predicament, trouble, dilemma, quandary, fix, pickle, *mess, *hole.

scrape *v.* scratch, scuff, abrade, graze, scar, scour, rasp, shave, skin.

scrappy *a.* game, aggressive, pugnacious, plucky, gritty, contentious. ANT. *wimpy, meek.*

scratch *n.* cut, laceration, incision, scar, abrasion, scrape, gash, line, score.

scratch *v.* **1.** CUT lacerate, incise, scar, abrade, scrape, gash, score, graze. **2.** ELIMINATE cancel, drop, delete, erase, withdraw, strike.

scrawl *v.* scribble, scratch, *hen-scratch, doodle.

scrawny *a.* skinny, thin, lean, slender, *skin and bones, emaciated, anorexic, bony, gaunt, malnourished, spare, rawboned, *could slip through a flute and not sound a note. ANT. *brawny, big, beefy, fat.*

scream *n.* cry, shriek, yelp, yell, hysterical cry, strangled cry for help, gargling scream, guttural scream, wail, squeal, squall.

scream *v.* cry, shriek, yelp, cry out hysterically, wail, screech, ululate, let out a strangled cry, sing out, bawl, howl, squeal, squall.

screech *v.* SEE SCREAM

screen *n.* **1.** PARTITION divider, shield, covering, wall, fence, curtain, veil. **2.** MESH net, strainer, grating, lattice.

screen *v.* **1.** PARTITION divide, shield, cover, block, wall off, fence off, veil. **2.** SORT OUT cull, *weed out, sift, sieve, filter, strain, eliminate, winnow.

screw *v.* **1.** TWIST wind, turn, wrench, corkscrew, crank. **2.** *Sl.* CHEAT *rip off, take advantage of, defraud, *give the shaft, swindle, extort, chisel. **3.** *Sl.* HAVE SEXUAL INTERCOURSE *make out, *hump, *make love, *bop, *go all the way, *jump someone's bones, copulate.

screw up *v.* mess up, bungle, blow it, muff, botch, *flub up, goof up, mismanage, mishandle, *drop the ball, *choke.

screwy *a.* *Sl.* odd, queer, peculiar, eccentric, *nuts. SEE CRAZY

scribble *v.* scrawl, scratch, *hen-scratch, doodle, dash.

scribe *n.* scrivener, transcriber, calligrapher, writer, clerk.

scrimp *v.* be frugal, economize, save, be cheap, pinch pennies, squeeze nickels, skimp, be stingy, stint. ANT. *squander, *blow, spend.*

script *n.* **1.** HANDWRITING writing, longhand, cursive, calligraphy, penmanship. **2.** STORY dialogue, text, screenplay, manuscript.

Scrooge *n.* misanthrope, *tightwad, cheapskate, penny-pincher, skinflint, miser, hoarder, *miserable cuss, curmudgeon. ANT. *philanthropist, giver, altruist.*

scrounge *v.* dig for, hunt for, beg, scare up, forage for, bum, track down, *scrape up, panhandle.

scrub *n.* shrubs, bushes, trees, brush, thicket, bush.

scrub *v.* scour, wash, clean, rub, swab, brush, *clean with elbow grease, wipe, mop.

scruffy *a.* shabby, grubby, straggly, unkempt, ungroomed, untrimmed, unwashed, mangy, ragged, bedraggled, *like a rat's nest. ANT. *neat, tidy, trim, groomed.*

scrumptious *a.* tasty, mouth-watering, pleasing. SEE DELICIOUS

scruple *n.* hesitancy, doubt, qualm, misgiving, second thought, pang, apprehension, caution, reluctance, *little voice.

SCRUPULOUS *a.* [SKROO pyuh lus] proper and highly principled, careful to do the right thing, meticulous. *He was a scrupulous businessman.* SYN. proper, principled, moral, upright, ethical, honest, upstanding, careful, meticulous, punctilious, painstaking, exacting, particular, fussy. ANT. *unscrupulous, unprincipled, dishonest, sloppy.*

SCRUTINIZE *v.* [SKROOT uh NIZE] to look at very closely. *She scrutinized the will for her name.* SYN. look at, examine, inspect, study, pore over, eyeball, peruse, explore, probe, *scorch with one's eyes. ANT. *overlook, pass over, disregard.*

scrutiny *n.* inspection, close look, examination,

surveillance, study, probing, perusal, investigation, *eyeballing, search, exploration. ANT. *quick glance, quick glimpse.*

scuff *v.* SEE SCRAPE

scuffle *n.* struggle, fight, tussle, scrap, *set-to, commotion, *ruckus, fray, *rumble, brawl.

scuffle *v.* struggle, fight, tussle, scrap, *rumble, brawl, *mix it up.

sculpture *n.* **1.** STATUE statuary, bust, figure, figurine, bronze, carving, abstract. **2.** CARVING chiseling, molding, stonecutting. "An art that takes away superfluous material." — Michelangelo. "Mud pies which endure." — Cyril Connolly.

WORD FIND

bizarre human or animal figure: grotesque
chip off stone: stun
frame, framework: armature, butterfly
Greek statue of marble: acrolith
larger than life-size sculpture: heroic, collosal
low relief: bas-relief
medium: marble, clay, bronze
projection: relief
smaller than life-size sculpture: statuette
tool: bushhammer, calipers, mallet, rasp
trim: fettle

scum *n.* **1.** DROSS refuse, film, layer, froth, residue. **2.** LOWLIFE *sleazebag, riffraff, *dregs of society.

scurrilous *a.* vulgar, indecent, abusive, offensive, insulting, obscene, gross, foulmouthed, dirty, raunchy, *gutter-mouthed, nasty.

scurry *v.* scamper, run, race, hurry, scuttle, dash, scoot, sprint, dart, hasten, bolt, fly.

scurvy *a.* mean, contemptible, despicable, low.

scuttle *v.* **1.** RUN scurry, scamper, race, hurry, dash, scoot, sprint, dart, hasten, bolt, *beat feet. **2.** ABANDON scrap, scrub, scratch, quit, desert.

scuttlebutt *n.* *Sl.* rumor, gossip, word, grapevine news, talk.

sea *n.* ocean, the deep, *briny deep, *bounding main, *Davy Jones's locker, high seas, surf, rolling sea. SEE BEACH, OCEAN

seafarer *n.* seaman, mariner. SEE SAILOR

seal *n.* **1.** STAMP symbol, emblem, imprint, impression, logo, authentication, insignia, imprimatur. **2.** FASTENING adhesive, sealant.

seal *v.* **1.** FASTEN secure, shut tight, lock in, waterproof, make airtight, plug. **2.** SETTLE assure, determine, decide, ensure, clinch, make certain, confirm.

seam *n.* closure, connection, juncture, junction, stitches, suture.

seaman *n.* seafarer, mariner. SEE SAILOR

seamy *a.* sordid, unpleasant, squalid, disagreeable, rough, unwholesome, unsavory, objectionable, revolting, dirty. ANT. *pleasant, decent, good.*

seance *n.* communion with the dead, spiritual contact, session, sitting, conjuring.

sear *v.* scorch, burn, brown, singe, toast, char, sizzle, wither, dry up, parch, shrivel, wilt.

search *n.* hunt, exploration, quest, probe, inquisition, *shakedown, *frisking, scrutiny, investigation, study, rummaging, foraging, research.

search *v.* seek, look, hunt, explore, quest, probe, *shake down, *frisk, scrutinize, investigate, study, rummage, forage, *sniff out, *go over with a fine-tooth comb, *leave no stone unturned, *turn inside out, research, ferret, delve, ransack.

searching *a.* penetrating, piercing, probing, sharp, intent, inquisitive, curious, quizzical.

sea serpent *n.* giant squid, oarfish, kraken, Loch Ness monster. SEE MONSTER

seashore *n.* coast, strand. SEE BEACH

seasickness *n.* motion sickness, queasiness. SEE NAUSEA

season *n.* period, term, spell, interval, quarter, month, summer, spring, fall, winter, Indian summer.

season *v.* **1.** FLAVOR spice, salt, pepper, lace, marinade, smoke, cure, corn, devil. **2.** HARDEN OR SOFTEN toughen, weather, temper, acclimate, accustom, temper.

seasonable *a.* opportune, fitting, suitable, right. SEE TIMELY

seasoned *a.* hardened, softened, toughened, weathered, experienced, tempered, acclimated, accustomed, inured. ANT. *green, immature, inexperienced.*

seasoning *n.* flavoring, spice, salt, pepper, marinade, dressing, condiment, sauce, gravy, relish, Tabasco, mustard, garlic, onion powder, herbs.

seat *n.* **1.** CHAIR bench, couch, sofa, recliner, lounge, loveseat, stool, settee, throne, perch. **2.** CENTER core, location, capital, heart, hub, headquarters, place. **3.** BUTTOCKS rear, behind, rump, derriere, posterior, *tush, *duff.

seaweed *n.* kelp, sargasso, wrack, dulse.

SECEDE *v.* [si SEED] to formally withdraw or break off from a group, organization, government, etc. *The islands seceded from the mainland government.* SYN. withdraw, break off, defect, quit, renounce, separate from, split from, expatriate, pull out, disaffiliate, *wash one's hands of. ANT. *join, merge, confederate.*

secession n. withdrawal, breakup, defection, renunciation, separation, split, expatriation, pullout, disaffiliation. ANT. *union, joining, merger, confederation.*

seclude v. isolate, sequester, hide, segregate, insulate, go into retreat, withdraw, quarantine.

secluded a. isolated, sequestered, segregated, insulated, cloistered, reclusive, private, hidden, sheltered, lonesome, remote, deserted, solitary, quarantined. ANT. *public, open, frequented.*

seclusion n. isolation, sequestration, segregation, privacy, hiding, shelter, solitude, sanctuary, retreat, quarantine.

second n. instant, tick of the clock, wink, *heartbeat, moment, flash, twinkling, jiffy, *nothing flat.

second v. support, back, root for, side with, abet, advocate, further. ANT. *oppose, contradict, dispute.*

secondary a. lesser, inferior, subordinate, minor, ancillary, subsidiary. ANT. *main, first, primary.*

second-rate a. inferior, cheap, *crappy, poor, shabby, *two-bit, low-grade, middling, fair, so-so, second class. ANT. *first-rate, superior, *top drawer.*

secrecy n. concealment, covertness, confidentiality, privacy, surreptitiousness, stealth, hiding, underhandedness, sneakiness, silence. ANT. *overtness, publicity, openness.*

secret n. confidence, classified information, privileged information, *skeleton in the closet, mystery, enigma. "Something three people keep if two of them are dead." — Anon.

secret a. concealed, hidden, covert, confidential, private, surreptitious, furtive, stealthy, underhanded, sneaky, quiet, silent, hush-hush, under wraps, classified, undisclosed, clandestine, mysterious, cryptic, secluded, sequestered, out-of-the-way, undercover. ANT. *overt, public, open.*

secretary n. office worker, typist, word processor, receptionist, filer, stenographer, bookkeeper, *gal Friday, *desk jockey. SEE OFFICE WORKER

secrete v. 1. HIDE conceal, stow away, closet, seclude, shroud, veil, bury, harbor, stash. 2. RELEASE discharge, emit, excrete, ooze, exude.

secretive a. private, tight-lipped, close-mouthed, silent, evasive, surreptitious, furtive, covert, clandestine, sneaky, backdoor, stealthy, cryptic, mysterious. ANT. *open, overt, public.*

sect n. faction, party, group, denomination, body, order, cult, division, clique, splinter group.

sectarian a. partisan, party-minded, factional, denominational, cultish, cliquish, parochial, provincial, narrow-minded. ANT. *broad-minded, nonpartisan.*

section n. part, segment, piece, component, slice, hunk, chunk, parcel, quarter, division, fragment, fraction, unit, share; district, region, neighborhood, community, ward, precinct, borough.

sector n. section, segment, division, group, class, district, area, zone, region.

SECULAR a. [SEK yuh lur] unrelated to religion or the church, worldly. *The church organist sometimes played secular music.* SYN. worldly, nonreligious, laic, lay, profane, earthly, temporal, mundane. ANT. *religious, ecclesiastical, spiritual.*

secure v. 1. GET obtain, procure, acquire, pick up, attain. 2. TIE DOWN, LOCK UP bind, tighten, fasten, fix, attach, set, anchor, stabilize. 3. SAFEGUARD defend, shield, shelter, protect.

secure a. 1. SAFE sheltered, protected, defended, immune, out of harm's way, unassailable, invulnerable, in the clear, in safekeeping. 2. CONFIDENT self-assured, carefree, untroubled, certain, definite, settled. 3. FIRM stable, strong, fast, locked, set, tight, fastened, bound, anchored, tied down. ANT. *1. unsafe, insecure, unprotected, vulnerable. 2. insecure, troubled, doubting. 3. loose, unsecured, unlocked.*

security n. 1. CONFIDENCE fearlessness, assurance, peace of mind, certainty, freedom from worry. 2. PROTECTION defense, shield, shelter, safeguard, safety, immunity, refuge, invulnerability. 3. GUARANTEE pledge, assurance, collateral, bond, surety, escrow.

sedate a. calm, quiet, staid, serious, serene, impassive, sober, dignified, tranquil, placid, grave. ANT. *a nervous wreck, excited, agitated.*

sedative n. tranquilizer, hypnotic, sleeping pill, soporific, depressant, opiate, Demerol, Nembutal.

sedative a. tranquilizing, calming, relaxing, sleep-inducing, tension-relieving, sedating. ANT. *stimulating, exciting.*

SEDENTARY a. [SED un tair ee] inactive, sitting around. *She lives a sedentary lifestyle.*

SYN. inactive, *couch-potato-like, *couch-bound, *chair-bound, sitting, stationary, unmoving, vegetative. ANT. *active, busy, *on the move.

sediment n. dregs, grounds, deposit, settlings, lees, precipitate.

sedition n. rebellion, treason, incitement, rabble-rousing, mutiny, insurrection, revolt, subversion.

seditious a. rebellious, rabble-rousing, inciting, mutinous, insurrectionary, revolutionary, subversive. ANT. *loyal, subservient.*

seduce v. lure, tempt, persuade, lead astray, entice, trap, snare, beguile, *lead on, tease, debauch.

seduction n. persuasion, enticement, temptation, allurement, tantalizing, trap, beguilement, tease.

seductive a. persuasive, enticing, tempting, alluring, tantalizing, beguiling, attractive, flirtatious, sexy, bewitching. ANT. *repellent, repulsive.*

sedulous a. diligent, hard-working, busy, industrious, assiduous, tireless, constant, persistent, plodding, dogged, intense. ANT. *lazy, lagging, lax.*

see v. **1.** BEHOLD discern, eye, eyeball, perceive, regard, spot, *lay eyes on, notice, detect, look, view, peer, watch, glimpse, distinguish, *get a load of, peep, stare, make out. **2.** UNDERSTAND comprehend, get it, appreciate, catch on, *catch one's drift, fathom, recognize, perceive, grasp. **3.** IMAGINE visualize, picture, conceive, think, envisage, envision. **4.** LOOK INTO find out, discover, ascertain. **5.** MEET encounter, run into, come face to face, speak with, visit.

seed n. source, wellspring, beginning, start, nucleus, grain, kernel, nut, sperm, egg, germ.

seedy a. shabby, run-down, broken-down, dilapidated, neglected, squalid, scruffy, unkempt, mangy, bedraggled, poor. ANT. *luxurious, well-kept, groomed, sparkling.*

seek v. **1.** LOOK FOR search for, hunt, *look high and low, cast about for, quest, fish for, sniff out, ferret out, leave no stone unturned. **2.** INQUIRE request, question, ask for. **3.** PURSUE aim, set one's sights for, aspire to.

seem v. appear, have the appearance of, look like, give the impression.

seeming a. ostensible, apparent, outward, external, assumed, presumable, professed, illusory, quasi. ANT. *actual, real.*

seemly a. proper, fitting, suitable, appropriate, right, correct, becoming, decorous, prudent, in good taste. ANT. *improper, unsuitable, rude.*

seep v. leak, ooze, exude, percolate, bleed, drip, dribble, issue, sweat, weep, permeate.

seer n. prophet, prognosticator, predictor, psychic, oracle, fortuneteller, forecaster, diviner, medium, soothsayer.

seesaw n. teeter-totter.

seethe v. **1.** BOIL bubble, froth, roll, surge. **2.** RAGE *see red, *get steamed, *do a slow burn, boil over, *blow one's top, fume, be livid, *storm, *foam at the mouth.

segment n. section, piece, part, portion, fragment, fraction, division, parcel, bit, element, component, quarter.

segregate v. separate, set apart, isolate, divide, insulate, split up, dissociate, quarantine. ANT. *unite, join, integrate, desegregate.*

segregation n. separation, apartheid, isolation, division, insulation, splitting up, setting apart, exclusion, quarantine.

seize v. **1.** GRAB take, snatch, grasp, grip, clasp, pluck, catch, embrace, *jump on. **2.** CONFISCATE, CAPTURE apprehend, arrest, *nail, *collar, *nab, commandeer, impound, take by force, appropriate, usurp, kidnap, hijack.

seizure n. **1.** APPREHENSION arrest, capture, confiscation, commandeering, impounding, appropriation, kidnapping, hijacking. **2.** CONVULSION fit, attack, throe, paroxysm, epileptic episode, stroke.

seldom adv. rarely, infrequently, hardly ever, *once in a blue moon. ANT. *often, frequently.*

select v. pick, choose, elect, opt for, single out, prefer, vote for, favor, cull, weed out. ANT. *reject, turn one's nose up at.*

select a. choice, preferred, best, top-notch, A-1, prime, finest, handpicked, cream, creme de la creme. ANT. *second-rate, mediocre, run-of-the-mill.*

selection n. pick, choice, preference, election, favorite, choosing, culling, weeding out, vote. ANT. *reject.*

selective a. choosy, picky, discriminating, particular, fussy, finicky, *persnickety, discerning. ANT. *undiscriminating, *easy.*

self n. ego, individuality, entity, soul, mind, personality, being, character.

self-assured a. confident, self-confident, sure of oneself, cocky, *full of oneself, secure, self-possessed, cool. ANT. *insecure, lacking self-esteem.*

self-centered a. selfish, self-absorbed, narcissistic, *thinks the world revolves around one, conceited, self-serving, egocentric, egotistical. ANT. *other-directed, giving, generous.*

self-confidence n. self-assurance, coolness, aplomb. "The first requisite to great undertakings." —Samuel Johnson. SEE CONFIDENCE

self-conscious a. shy, bashful, ill at ease, awkward, self-aware, *redfaced, blushing, embarrassed, anxious, sheepish. ANT. self-confident, self-assured.

self-control n. self-discipline, self-restraint, willpower, self-constraint, abstemiousness, fortitude, strength. "The hardest victory." —Aristotle, ANT. impulsiveness, weakness.

self-defeating a. *shooting oneself in the foot, *cutting off one's nose to spite one's face, defeating its own purpose.

self-esteem n. pride, self-respect, healthy ego, self-regard, confidence, self-love, self-assurance, amour propre, dignity, belief in oneself. "The most voluble of the emotions." —Frank M. Colby.

self-evident a. evident, obvious, apparent, clear, manifest, self-explanatory, undeniable, plain, uncontestable, axiomatic. ANT. questionable, doubtful, uncertain.

self-image n. conception of oneself, self-esteem, self-regard, delusion of grandeur, inferiority complex.

self-important a. conceited, overbearing, arrogant, *bigheaded, egotistical, pompous, swaggering, smug, snobbish, *snotty, *high and mighty. ANT. self-effacing, modest, humble.

selfish a. self-centered, self-serving, greedy, egocentric, egotistical, *wrapped up in oneself, narcissistic, *looking out for number one, *thinks the world revolves around one, *piggish. ANT. giving, other-directed, generous.

selfishness n. self-centeredness, greediness, egocentricity, narcissism. "Consuming happiness without producing any." —Joan Tepperman.

self-reliant a. independent, *standing on one's own two feet, self-sufficient, autonomous, strong. ANT. dependent, needy.

self-respect n. self-esteem, pride, self-regard, self-worth, dignity, *the ability to hold one's head up, *the ability to stand tall. "The cornerstone of all virtue." —John Herschell. "The noblest garment." —Samuel Smiles.

self-righteous a. holier-than-thou, sanctimonious, complacent, smug, hypocritical, preachy, *goody-goody, pious, self-satisfied.

self-satisfied a. complacent, smug, pleased with oneself, proud, arrogant, *full of oneself, swelled-headed, bigheaded, content. ANT. self-effacing, humble, modest.

self-sufficient a. SEE SELF-RELIANT

sell v. deal, trade, market, wholesale, retail, peddle, vend, offer for sale, unload, auction, barter, hustle. ANT. buy, purchase.

seller n. dealer, trader, marketer, wholesaler, retailer, peddler, vendor, merchant, auctioneer, hustler, broker, agent.

sell out v. betray, double-cross, stab in the back, sell one's soul, do anything for money.

SEMANTICS n. [suh MAN tiks] dealing with language and the meanings of words, phrases, etc. They were no longer arguing over hard issues, but semantics. SYN. meanings, semiotics, lexicology, lexicography, linguistics, interpretations, connotations.

semblance n. appearance, look, aspect, air, aura, resemblance, bearing, show, face, facade, image.

semen n. seminal fluid, sperm, *cum, *goo, *jizm, *jizz.

semester n. term, period, interval, session, half-year.

SEMINAL a. [SEM uh nul] the first, originating or developmentally important, basic. Little Richard is regarded as a seminal rock and roll singer. SYN. first, originating, germinal, innovative, developmental, first of its kind, fresh, pioneering, trailblazing.

seminar n. group discussion, workshop, panel discussion, forum, conference, symposium, meeting, review.

send v. transport, transmit, deliver, transfer, convey, direct, remit, mail, post, ship, relay, wire, shoot, propel, throw, fire off, broadcast. ANT. receive, get.

send packing v. show the door, dismiss, discharge, give walking papers.

senile a. disoriented, mentally deficient, forgetful, suffering from Alzheimer's, feebleminded, *slipping, confused, in one's dotage, deteriorating. ANT. sharp, lucid, clear-thinking.

senior n. elder, senior citizen, retiree, matriarch, patriarch, grandmother, grandfather, firstborn, doyen, superior, dean. ANT. junior, inferior, subordinate.

senior a. ranking, superior, chief, preeminent, elder, older, higher, veteran. ANT. junior, inferior, lesser.

sensation n. **1.** FEELING sense, sensitivity, perception, reaction, response, sound, sight, smell, pain, tingle, itch. **2.** EXCITEMENT public interest, fuss, uproar, hit, wonder, phenomenon. ANT. 1. insentientness, anesthesia. 2. apathy, indifference, *hardly a ripple.

WORD FIND

disorder causing confused sensations, as sight for sound: synesthesia

extreme sensitivity: hyperesthesia

sensational *a.* **1.** EXCELLENT exceptional, good, superb, *out of this world, fantastic, fabulous, outstanding, extraordinary, marvelous, terrific, wonderful. **2.** STARTLING shocking, thrilling, exciting, *mind-blowing, spine-tingling, hair-raising, breathtaking, electrifying, staggering. **3.** EXAGGERATED melodramatic, lurid, *tabloid, cheap, *yellow, scandalous. ANT. *1. awful, lousy, second-rate. 2. boring, dull. 3. understated, dry.*

sensationalism *n.* exaggeration, melodrama, luridness, *tabloid journalism, *keyhole journalism, *yellow journalism, scandal, shock reporting.

sense *n.* **1.** SENSATION feeling, perception, sensitivity, responsiveness, stimulus reception, sight, hearing, smell, taste, touch. **2.** AWARENESS perception, realization, impression, feeling, consciousness, premonition. **3.** INTELLIGENCE wisdom, judgment, reason, common sense, logic, brains, *smarts, sharpness, understanding, *savvy, intuition. **4.** MEANING substance, point, content, gist, interpretation, thrust, essence, core, significance, definition.

sense *v.* feel, perceive, pick up, get the impression, have a feeling, discern, *catch some vibes, notice, *have a gut feeling, suspect.

senseless *a.* nonsensical, stupid, brainless, idiotic, foolish, insane, crazy, *nuts, mindless, *wacky, ludicrous, ridiculous, irrational. ANT. *sensible, rational, smart.*

sensibility *n.* ability to feel, sensitivity, sentience, responsiveness, receptivity, perception, perceptiveness.

sensible *a.* smart, intelligent, judicious, prudent, rational, logical, sober, sound, levelheaded, realistic, sane, reasonable, down-to-earth. ANT. *senseless, nonsensical, stupid.*

sensitive *a.* **1.** IMPRESSIONABLE responsive, acute, keen, receptive, reactive, conscious, feeling, responsive, sentient, sympathetic. **2.** EASILY HURT easily offended, touchy, hypersensitive, testy, thin-skinned, ticklish, irritable. **3.** SORE tender, painful, hurting, raw. **4.** SYMPATHETIC compassionate, understanding, empathetic, enlightened, considerate. ANT. *1. insentient, unresponsive. 2. thick-skinned. 3. calloused, numb. 4. insensitive, inconsiderate, dense.*

sensitivity *a.* **1.** RESPONSIVENESS feeling, sense, receptiveness, acuteness, keenness. **2.** SYM-

PATHY understanding, compassion, empathy, enlightenment, consideration. ANT. *1. unresponsiveness, insentience. 2. insensitivity, lack of understanding.*

sensual *a.* physical, of the body, bodily, fleshly, voluptuous, sexual, sensuous, carnal, lustful, erotic, lascivious, libidinous, *horny, licentious, lewd. ANT. *spiritual, cerebral, of the mind.*

sensuous *a.* stimulating, sensory, luxurious, pleasurable, pleasant to the touch, pleasant to the eye, rich, sumptuous, voluptuous.

sentence *n.* judgment, decision, punishment, penalty, time, prison term, *stretch up the river, doom.

sentence *v.* judge, rule, punish, penalize, give a prison term, condemn, term, doom, mete out, imprison, *send up the river, *throw the book at.

sententious *a.* **1.** CONCISE short, pithy, succinct. **2.** APHORISTIC grandiloquent, bombastic, pompous, moralizing, trite. ANT. *1. wordy, long-winded.*

sentient *a.* feeling, sensitive, conscious, perceptive, receptive, responsive. ANT. *insentient, unfeeling.*

sentiment *n.* **1.** FEELINGS attitude, opinion, thought, leaning, idea, way of thinking, view, emotion, judgment. **2.** SENTIMENTALITY romanticism, *mushiness, feeling, tenderness, emotion, *hearts and flowers. "Jam without bread." — Sydney Harris. "The poetry of the imagination." — Alphonse Lamartine.

sentimental *a.* tender, romantic, maudlin, mawkish, *mushy, emotional, softhearted, misty-eyed, weepy, nostalgic, *saccharine, *corny, *schmaltzy, *gushy, sloppy. "Having a good cry for its own sake." — Myron Schueller. ANT. *unfeeling, cold, hard, stony.*

sentimentality *n.* mawkishness, *mush, softheartedness, weepiness, nostalgia, *corniness, *schmaltz, *gush, sloppiness. "Ostentatious parading of excessive and spurious emotion." — James Baldwin.

sentinal *n.* sentry, guard, watch, lookout, picket, patrol, scout.

sentry *n.* SEE SENTINAL

separate *v.* remove, break off, divide, disconnect, detach, split, sever, divorce, take apart, single out, segregate, secede, isolate. ANT. *connect, attach, join, unite.*

separate *a.* unconnected, detached, disconnected, unattached, apart, divided, single, individual, distinct, sole, lone, independent, autonomous. ANT. *connected, attached, together, joined.*

separation *n.* division, detachment, disconnection, parting, removal, breakup, split, divorce, segregation, dissassociation, rift, secession. ANT. *union, connection, attachment.*

septic *a.* infective, putrid, putrified, rotting, contaminated. ANT. *antiseptic, sterile.*

sepulcher *n.* vault, grave, tomb, mausoleum, crypt, resting place, catacomb. SEE CEMETERY

SEPULCHRAL *a.* [suh PUL krul] gloomy, dark, dismal, as of the grave. *A sepulchral silence fell over the proceedings.* SYN. gloomy, dark, dismal, black, like the grave, funereal, deathly, morbid, mournful, dreary, heavy, Stygian. ANT. *bright, sunny, cheerful.*

sequel *n.* part two, follow-up, continuation, consequence, aftermath, outcome, epilogue, *spin-off, offshoot.

sequence *n.* series, order, succession, lineup, progression, array, cycle, train, course, string, round.

SEQUESTER *v.* [si KWEST ur] to set apart or isolate, separate. *The jury will be sequestered during the trial.* SYN. set apart, separate, isolate, seclude, hide away, secrete, remove oneself, withdraw, confine, quarantine.

SERENDIPITY *n.* [SER un DIP uh tee] accidental good fortune. *We located the treasure by pure serendipity.* SYN. good fortune, fortuity, chance, *Lady Luck, *wheel of fortune, luck, *shit luck, happy chance, happenstance, *toss of the dice, *fluke. ANT. *design, plan.*

serene *a.* **1.** PEACEFUL tranquil, placid, calm, untroubled, quiet, sedate, halcyon, undisturbed, still, composed. **2.** CLEAR unclouded, bright, fair, sunny. ANT. **1.** *wild, violent, agitated.* **2.** *stormy, cloudy.*

serenity *n.* peace, peacefulness, tranquility, placidity, calm, quiet, stillness, composure, coolness, relaxation, imperturbability. ANT. *wildness, violence, agitation.*

serf *n.* slave, villein, vassal.

serial *a.* in series, successive, continuing, consecutive, ongoing, sequential, progressive.

series *n.* chain, string, order, succession, array, procession, sequence, round, line, cycle, run.

serious *a.* **1.** SOMBER, EARNEST grave, sober, *meaning business, humorless, unsmiling, humorless, dour, stern, stony-faced, *no-nonsense, grim, staid. **2.** WEIGHTY important, crucial, *heavy, no laughing matter, consequential, life-and-death, momentous, grave, grim, critical, dangerous. **3.** SINCERE earnest,

honest. ANT. **1.** *silly, foolish, trivial.* **2.** *trivial, trifling, silly, inconsequential.* **3.** *kidding.*

sermon *n.* lecture, speech, preaching, lesson, moralizing, homily, exhortation, *fire and brimstone, discourse, exemplum.

serpent *n.* viper. SEE SNAKE

serpentine *a.* winding, twisting, coiled, snaking, tortuous, meandering, sinuous, slinky, labyrinthine.

serrated *a.* saw-toothed, jagged, serrulated, notched, crenelated.

servant *n.* domestic, butler, maid, housekeeper, cook, help, valet, chauffeur, attendant, menial, slave, *gal Friday.

serve *v.* **1.** WAIT ON provide, tend to, *be at one's beck and call, waitress, cater, deliver, minister to, help, assist, *be a gopher. **2.** BE OBEDIENT TO obey, respect, honor, be dutiful to. **3.** WORK perform, carry out, do one's duties. **4.** PASS spend, do. **5.** FUNCTION be used, perform for.

service *n.* **1.** ASSISTANCE, WORK help, labor, employment, duty, use, benefit. **2.** ARMED FORCES military, army, navy, marines, active duty. **3.** WAITING ON catering, waitressing, *gophering, serving, accommodation. **4.** CHURCH FUNCTION ceremony, worship, sermon, observance, prayer meeting. **5.** MAINTENANCE repair, upkeep, servicing.

service *v.* repair, maintain, fix, tune up, overhaul, restore.

serviceable *a.* usable, ready, operative, functional, workable, durable, utile. ANT. *inoperable, unworkable.*

SERVILE *a.* [SUR vile] submissive or subservient, like a servant or slave. *He smiled and nodded in the proper servile manner.* SYN. submissive, subservient, yielding, slavish, obsequious, fawning, groveling, deferential, cringing, sycophantic, toadying, like an Uncle Tom. ANT. *rebellious, defiant, domineering.*

servitude *n.* slavery, bondage, enslavement, indenture, serfdom, service, yoke, subjugation, serfdom. ANT. *freedom, liberty.*

session *n.* **1.** MEETING assembly, discussion, hearing, conference, council, legislative session, convention. **2.** TERM period, semester, course.

set *n.* **1.** OUTFIT collection, assemblage, array, assortment, arrangement, pair, group, series. **2.** THEATRICAL SETTING scenery, backdrop, props. **3.** GROUP clique, circle, class, pack, crowd, gang, clan, fraternity.

set *v.* **1.** PLACE position, put, stick, lay, plant, plop, situate, locate, rest, deposit, station, install, insert, mount. **2.** SETTLE UPON agree on, determine, decide, arrange, prearrange, fix, schedule, specify, establish, designate. **3.** ADJUST fix, position, ready. **4.** HARDEN stiffen, solidify, thicken, congeal. ANT. *1. pick up, remove, lift. 4. soften, loosen, liquefy.*

set *a.* **1.** SETTLED agreed on, determined, decided, arranged, prearranged, fixed, scheduled, specified, ordained, ready. **2.** USUAL routine, normal, conventional, fixed, customary, regular. **3.** HARDENED, FIXED firm, rigid, stiff, locked, positioned, secured, rooted.

setback *n.* reversal, disappointment, *stumbling block, defeat, blow, loss, trouble, relapse, upset, check, regression, *one step forward and two steps back, *square one. ANT. *advance, progress, leap forward.*

setting *n.* scene, scenery, backdrop, environment, surroundings, locale, site, milieu, mise-en-scene, time, place, period.

settle *v.* **1.** PUT IN ORDER arrange, fix, straighten out, resolve, rectify, *iron out, satisfy, clear, end. **2.** SIT sink, sag, droop, plant oneself, lay, repose. **3.** TAKE UP RESIDENCE move to, locate, colonize, populate, set up housekeeping, reside, come to roost, *put down roots, inhabit. **4.** SINK clear out, clarify, precipitate. **5.** RELAX calm, quiet, soothe, tranquilize, compose, lull, sedate. **6.** MEDIATE arbitrate, resolve, negotiate, compromise. ANT. *1. mess up, confuse. 3. pull up roots, *fly the coop, leave. 5. agitate, stress, *put on edge.*

settlement *n.* **1.** COMMUNITY colony, village, outpost, peopling. **2.** AGREEMENT arrangement, resolution, compromise, negotiation, arbitration, disposition. **3.** PAYMENT OF DEBT satisfaction, clearance, liquidation.

settler *n.* colonist, homesteader, frontiersman, pioneer, squatter, *sooner.

settlings *n.* dregs, sediment, lees.

set-to *n.* fight, fistfight, struggle. SEE FIGHT

setup *n.* arrangement, configuration, structure, system, organization, format, plan.

set up *v.* **1.** CONSTRUCT erect, raise, build, put together, assemble. **2.** CREATE start, originate, organize, establish, found, institute. ANT. *1. tear down, disassemble, dismantle, raze. 2. terminate, end.*

sever *v.* **1.** CUT cleave, split, divide, separate, cut in two, slice, rend, chop off. **2.** DISSOCIATE break off, separate, cut off, split up, discontinue, drop, divorce, disband. ANT. *1. join, attach. 2. join, unite, reunite.*

several *a.* **1.** A LOT a number, quite a few, a handful, considerable, numerous, some. **2.** SEPARATE distinct, individual, single, respective, particular, personal. ANT. *1. none, few. 2. joint.*

severe *a.* **1.** HARSH stern, strict, hard, *hardnosed, uncompromising, unsparing, rigid, unfeeling, merciless, pitiless. **2.** SERIOUS grave, forbidding, stern, unsmiling, grim, austere, cold, stony. **3.** GRIEVOUS serious, acute, violent, nasty, critical, dire, life-threatening, bad, dangerous, fierce, intense, extreme. **4.** PLAIN unornamented, spare, bare, stark, austere, undecorated. ANT. *1. softhearted, easy, compassionate. 2. light-hearted, smiling, jovial. 3. mild, minor, trivial. 4. ornate, rococo, luxurious.*

sew *v.* stitch, mend, tailor, seam, hem, embroider.

sewage *n.* waste, discharge, runoff, foul water, pollution.

sex *n.* **1.** GENDER *AC-DC. **2.** COPULATION intercourse, coitus, fornication, *making love, *making out, *birds and the bees, reproduction, procreation, *getting it on, *facts of life, *humping, *roll in the hay, *balling, *banging, *bopping, *going all the way, *jumping someone's bones, *scoring, *screwing, *sleeping with someone, *nookie. "The formula by which one and one makes three."—Leonard Levinson. "An emotion in motion."—Mae West. "An appetite placed in humans to insure breeding."—Jonathan Benter. "The poor man's polo."—Clifford Odets.

WORD FIND
abstinence: celibacy, continence
anal intercourse: sodomy
animal or human with both sets of gender organs: hermaphrodite
animals, with: bestiality
body area prone to arousal: erogenous
castrated man: eunuch
child, desire for sex with: pedophilia
corpse, attraction to or sex with a: necrophilia
demon (female) that has sex with man while he sleeps: succubus
demon (male) that has sex with woman while she sleeps: incubus
desire, drive: libido
deviance: perversion
deviant: pervert
device: vibrator, *dildo
erection, unable to achieve: impotence
exposing oneself in public for sexual arousal:

exhibitionism, flashing

gratuitous insertion of sex in movie to widen appeal: sexploitation

group sex: *gang bang, *daisy chain, orgy, menage a trois, *group grope

lack of desire: anaphrodisis

obsession with article of clothing, body part: fetishism

opposite sex, one with normal organs but characteristics of: epicene, effeminate, transexual

oral sex: cunnilingus, fellatio

oral sex, simultaneous: *sixty-nine

pleasure from being hurt, whipped, etc.: masochism

pleasure from inflicting pain on another: sadism

pleasure from receiving and inflicting pain: sadomasochism

rubbing up against another in a crowded place: frottage

self-arousal: autoeroticism, masturbation

stimulant: aphrodisiac

switching partners: swinging

tying up partner for pleasure: bondage

uncontrollable desire in man: satyriasis

unusual sex: *kinkiness

urination by one on another: *golden shower

uncontrollable desire in woman: nymphomania

unisex: androgynous

watching others have sex for pleasure: voyeurism

SEE HOMOSEXUAL, LOVE, ORAL SEX

sex appeal n. sexiness, charm, erotic charm, *oomph, magnetism, charisma, curvaceousness, virility, allure, *come-hither look.

sexism n. discrimination, prejudice, male chauvinism, sex bias.

sexless a. 1. ASEXUAL neuter. 2. HAVING NO SEX DRIVE frigid, anaphrodisic. ANT. 2. *horny, hot, nymphomaniacal, satyriasic.

sexual a. reproductive, procreative, generative, coital, carnal, erotic, *hot, *horny, lustful.

sexy a. *hot, *foxy, charming, alluring, enticing, seductive, magnetic, charismatic, erotic, sensual, attractive, curvaceous, voluptuous, titillating, flirtatious, desirable, irresistible. ANT. repellant, repulsive, *gross, disgusting.

shabby a. 1. DETERIORATED run down, ragged, dilapidated, poor, threadbare, mangy, grungy, ragged, scraggly, scruffy, ratty, seedy. 2. LOUSY disgraceful, poor, mean, shameful, terrible, bad, miserable, despicable, cheap, shoddy. ANT. 1. new, fresh, sparkling. 2. excellent, good.

shack n. shanty, hut, shed, cabin, hovel, shelter.

shackle n. restraint, handcuff, manacle, fetter, irons, chain, hobble, leg-iron.

shackle v. restrain, fetter, handcuff, *cuff, manacle, chain, hobble, tie. ANT. free, loose, release.

shade n. 1. DARKNESS shadows, cover, dimness, umbra, penumbra. 2. HUE tone, color, tint, gradation. 3. BLIND visor, shutter, drape, curtain, screen. 4. SLIGHT DIFFERENCE hint, trace, touch, suggestion, tiny degree, nuance.

shade v. darken, dim, cover, veil, shroud, mask, protect, hide, obscure, blacken.

shadow n. 1. DARKNESS dimness, shade, gloom, cover, umbra, penumbra, silhouette. 2. TRACE hint, suggestion, breath, suggestion.

shadow v. follow, trail, tail, track, watch.

shady a. 1. SHADOWY dark, cool, covered, shaded. 2. DISREPUTABLE crooked, questionable, devious, underhanded, dishonest, suspect, slippery, fishy. ANT. 1. sunny, bright. 2. reputable, honest, honorable.

shaggy a. hairy, woolly, furry, hirsute, unkempt, ungroomed, untrimmed, uncombed, snarled, tangled. ANT. neat, trimmed, bald.

shake v. 1. VIBRATE rock, tremble, quiver, quake, jog, wobble, shiver, convulse, wiggle, tremble, shudder, jounce, rattle, flutter. 2. MIX churn. 3. UNNERVE upset, discompose, disturb, disconcert, distress, rattle, unsettle, disquiet, daze. ANT. 1. stabilize. 3. calm, soothe, put one's mind at ease.

shaky a. 1. UNSTABLE unsteady, wobbly, rickety, precarious, loose, wiggly, jerry-built, teetering, unreliable. 2. NERVOUS quivering, tremulous, shivering, jittery, trembling, quaking. 3. QUESTIONABLE doubtful, uncertain, dubious, speculative, unreliable, undependable, suspect. ANT. 1. stable, secure, steady. 2. calm, relaxed. 3. certain, sure.

shallow a. superficial, surface, lacking depth, skin-deep, slight, weak, lacking character, meaningless, empty, frivolous. ANT. deep, profound, in-depth.

sham n. counterfeit, fake, imitation, fraud, phony, forgery, humbug, hoax, deception, pretense. ANT. *the genuine article, *the real McCoy.

sham a. counterfeit, false, fake, pretended, imitation, fraudulent, *bogus, phony, simulated, artificial, ersatz, spurious. ANT. genuine, real, authentic.

shaman n. priest, medicine man.

shambles n. mess, disorder, destruction, chaos, disaster area, disarray, pigsty, wreck, devastation, *bomb crater.

shame n. disgrace, dishonor, humiliation, embarrassment, loss of face, chagrin, stigma, scandal, infamy, degradation, ill-repute, ignominy, pain, mortification, guilt, remorse. ANT. *pride, self-respect.*

shame v. disgrace, dishonor, humiliate, embarrass, degrade, ridicule, mortify, fill with guilt, *take down a notch, debase, scandalize, *take the wind out of one's sails. ANT. *fill with pride, compliment, honor.*

shamefaced a. embarrassed, ashamed, disgraced, mortified, red-faced, blushing, hangdog, crestfallen, chagrined, abashed. ANT. *proud.*

shameful a. disgraceful, dishonorable, humiliating, embarrassing, mortifying, odious, scandalous, infamous, ignominious, wicked, atrocious, contemptible, despicable, dastardly. ANT. *honorable, noble, good.*

shameless a. conscienceless, unprincipled, immodest, wicked, antisocial, abandoned, unblushing, brazen, bold, outrageous, impudent, disgraceful. ANT. *ashamed, modest, principled.*

shanghai v. abduct. SEE KIDNAP

Shangri-la n. utopia, paradise, heaven on earth, Xanadu, Eden.

shanty n. shack, hovel, hut, cabin, hutch.

shantytown n. slum, ghetto, skid row.

shape n. **1.** FORM figure, outline, configuration, profile, contour, conformation, structure, lines, mold, frame, cut, pattern. **2.** STATE health, fitness, order, condition, trim, fettle.

shapeless a. formless, amorphous, irregular, nebulous, indefinite, ill-defined, asymmetrical, vague, misshapen. ANT. *well-defined, formed, symmetrical.*

shapely a. well-proportioned, fit, toned, curvaceous, well-rounded, *wasp-waisted, *hourglass, curvy, *built, *stacked, statuesque, svelt. ANT. *fat, roly-poly, obese, misshapen.*

share n. allotment, percent, apportionment, portion, allowance, cut, ration, *piece of the pie, quota, due, parcel, lot.

share v. split between one another, *divvy up, divide, allot, allocate, apportion, dole out, ration, mete out, *go Dutch, *give and take. ANT. *monopolize, *hog.*

shark n. **1.** MARINE ANIMAL fish, predator, *eating machine, man-eater, thresher, great white shark, tiger shark, hammerhead, dogfish, basking shark. **2.** SWINDLER cheat, *con man, chiseler, *rip-off artist, crook, *flimflam man. **3.** EXPERT *crackerjack, *ace, professional, *hotshot.

sharp a. **1.** HONED fine-edged, cutting, razor-sharp, knife-edge, acute, keen-edged, piercing, pointed, pronged, barbed, peaked. **2.** ABRUPT sudden, quick, rapid, precipitous, extreme. **3.** CLEAR clearly defined, distinct, crisp, in focus. **4.** SMART quick, acute, perceptive, bright, astute, *on the ball, attentive, keen, discerning, alert, canny, shrewd, clever, sensitive. **5.** CRAFTY underhanded, deceitful, cunning, designing, shrewd, wily, conniving. **6.** SEVERE intense, acute, violent, fierce, stabbing, piercing, biting. **7.** Sl. WELL-DRESSED well-groomed, chic, stylish, dapper, debonair, swank, *snappy. ANT. 1. *dull, blunted.* 2. *gradual, slow.* 3. *hazy, ill-defined.* 4. *stupid, slow, dense.* 5. *honest, artless.* 6. *mild, gentle, subtle.* 7. *disheveled, frumpy, sloppy*

sharpen v. hone, edge, whet, strop, file, grind, taper. ANT. *blunt, dull, round off.*

sharper n. swindler, cheat, *con artist, *rip-off artist, crook.

sharp-tongued a. acid-tongued, critical, vitriolic, rapier-tongued, biting, cutting, nasty, negative, mean, blunt, frank. ANT. *diplomatic, nice, mealy-mouthed.*

sharp-witted a. saber-witted, rapier-witted, quick-witted, keen, acute, intelligent, astute, *on the ball, bright, smart, alert. ANT. *dull, slow, stupid, bovine.*

shatter v. **1.** BREAK burst, explode, smash, crack, blast, break into a million pieces, fracture, split, pop, implode. **2.** DESTROY wreck, devastate, crush, demolish, ruin, *break one's heart

shave v. cut, scrape, graze, trim, shear, crop, clip, mow.

shawl n. wrap, covering, manta.

sheaf n. bundle, pile, bale, packet, package, collection.

shear v. cut, shave, clip, trim, remove, crop, trim, snip, scissor, mow.

sheath n. case, scabbard, covering, receptacle, envelope, holder, casing, wrapper, sleeve, membrane.

shed n. shack, shanty, hut, lean-to, outbuilding, shelter, hutch, outhouse, storage building, workshop, hangar.

shed v. throw off, cast off, drop, discard, slough off, molt, peel, defoliate, exude, discharge, give off, emit, pour forth, radiate, diffuse.

sheen n. shine, brightness, luster, brilliance,

gleam, glossiness, gloss, glimmer, dazzle, sparkle, burnish, shimmer.

sheep *n.* ram, ewe, lamb, ruminant, ungulate, Merino, Cheviot, Cotswold, Lincoln.

WORD FIND

caretaker: shepherd
cleaning solution: sheep-dip
cry: bleat, baa, blat
dog: shepherd, collie, shelty
flock: fold
leader: bellwether
meat: mutton
sexual period: rut, heat
wool: fleece, karakul

sheepish *a.* embarrassed, chagrined, ashamed, red-faced, blushing, shamefaced, bashful, mortified. ANT. *proud, bold, puffed up.*

sheer *a.* **1.** THIN diaphanous, see-through, gossamer, transparent, gauzy, airy, delicate, revealing. **2.** STEEP perpendicular, precipitous, vertical, abrupt. **3.** ABSOLUTE utter, complete, outright, out-and-out, pure, unadulterated, unqualified, downright. ANT. *1. opaque, thick, heavy. 2. horizontal. 3. qualified, partial, limited.*

sheet *n.* **1.** COATING, PIECE coat, layer, film, blanket, ply, leaf. **2.** LINEN bed clothing.

shelf *n.* **1.** COUNTER bracket, cupboard, mantle, bookcase. **2.** LEDGE overhang, outcropping, projection, ridge, reef.

shell *n.* **1.** MARINE ANIMAL CASING conch, mollusk, mussel shell, clamshell, periwinkle, triton, oyster, nautilus, baby bonnet, mottled Venus, scallop. **2.** CARAPACE casing, shield, defense. **3.** HULL casing, husk, pod, husk, sheath, jacket, covering. **4.** BOMB projectile, missile, shot, mortar, ball, shrapnel.

shell *v.* **1.** SHUCK husk, peel, open. **2.** BOMBARD bomb, barrage, fire upon, cannonade, strafe.

shellac *n.* varnish, resin.

shellac *v. Sl.* beat, defeat, whip, *whoop, *kick butt.

shellacking *n. Sl.* beating, whipping, flogging.

shelter *n.* protection, safe haven, refuge, asylum, *roof over one's head, sanctuary, retreat, cover, hideout, hole, *port in a storm, harbor.

shelter *v.* protect, shield, provide a roof over one's head, provide safe haven, give refuge, give asylum, give sanctuary, cover, harbor, house, hide.

shelve *v.* put aside, defer, postpone, *put on ice, *put on the back burner, drop, dismiss, scrub.

shenanigans *n.* mischief, nonsense, horseplay, pranks, trickery, *monkey-business, *hanky-panky, sport.

shepherd *v.* herd, tend, lead, care for, look after, guard, protect, watch over, escort, secure.

shield *n.* defense, protection, guard, screen, safeguard, cover, aegis, armor, buffer.

shield *v.* defend, protect, cover, guard, screen, safeguard, arm, shelter, hide.

shift *n.* **1.** MOVE change, turn, switch, variation, reversal, about-face, alteration, modification, veering, conversion. **2.** WORK PERIOD turn, stint, first shift, second shift, third shift, *graveyard shift, watch.

shift *v.* move, change, turn, switch, vary, reverse, *do an about-face, alter, modify, veer, convert.

shiftless *a.* lazy, unmotivated, inefficient, slothful, unambitious, indolent, do-nothing, unenterprising, good-for-nothing. ANT. *industrious, enterprising, go-getting.*

shifty *a.* deceitful, tricky, dishonest, evasive, devious, treacherous, conniving, artful, slick, slippery, sly, designing. ANT. *honest, trustworthy, virtuous.*

shilly-shally *v.* hesitate, wave, vacillate, hem and haw, fluctuate, *straddle the fence, hedge, be irresolute, seesaw, *blow hot and cold. ANT. *be resolved, decide, take a stand.*

shimmer *v.* **1.** FLASH glimmer, shine, gleam, glow, scintillate, glisten, glint, sparkle, glitter. **2.** WAVER ripple, shudder, sway.

shindig *n.* *wingding, entertainment, dance. SEE PARTY

shine *n.* brightness, radiance, luster, brilliance, glimmer, sheen, gloss, polish, glow. ANT. *dullness, film, patina, tarnish.*

shine *v.* **1.** LIGHT radiate, glare, blaze, gleam, luminesce, glow, glimmer, flash, illuminate, flicker, glint, sparkle, scintillate. **2.** POLISH burnish, finish, rub, buff, brighten. ANT. *2. dull, tarnish.*

shiny *a.* bright, brilliant, gleaming, glinting, glistening, glossy, polished, lustrous, sparkling, scintillating. ANT. *dull, tarnished.*

ship *n.* vessel, craft, watercraft, boat, *tub, *stormslogger, liner, cruise ship, freighter, ferry, transport. "Being in jail with a chance of being drowned." —Samuel Johnson.

WORD FIND

accommodations: first-class, cabin class, tourist class
ammunition compartment: magazine
anchor: bower, kedge, sea anchor, stream anchor

anchor chain winder, unwinder: capstan, windlass

anchoring and securing of vessel: mooring

anchor rope: hawser

bed: berth

boarding platform: gangplank

body: hull

bottom fin or backbone: keel

bottom, rounded portion of: bilges

cabin, small: cuddy

captain: skipper

cargo and debris lost from wrecked ship: flotsam and jetsam

cargo area: hold

cargo conveyance: cargo net

cargo, list of: manifest

chart and navigational instrument room: chart room

compass stand: binnacle

course change: tack

crane, hoisting apparatus: davit, derrick

crew member: hand, mate

crew quarters, structure holding: forecastle

deck: weather deck, poop deck

depth below waterline: draft, draught

drain: scupper

drive: navigate

flag: burgee, jack

floating dock that holds ship for repairs: dry dock

front: bow, prow, fore

hatch: booby hatch, scuttle, companionway

hospital: sick bay

kitchen: galley, caboose, cuddy

knot: 6,080 feet an hour

ladder: jack ladder, ratlines

lean: heel, list

left and right sides (respectively) looking from aft forward: port, starboard

living quarters: cabin

lookout perch: crow's nest

makeshift structure repairs: jury, juryrigging

meal compartment: mess room

merchant ship or fleet of same: argosy

middle: amidships

navigational house: pilot house

numbers of measurements on bow: draft marks

observation platform: bridge

officer: purser, bosun, skipper, captain

officers, upper-class passenger room: stateroom

pitch/roll indicator: clinometer

plants and animals living on ship's bottom: foul

porthole cover: deadlight

position finder: Loran

protective shielding made of ropes, tires, etc.: fender, pudding

pulley system: block

pumps, motors, winches, collective term: auxiliaries

pump that removes water: bilge pump

rear: aft, stern, astern

rising and falling fore and aft with waves: pitching

rope-belaying fixture: cleats

rope, collective term: cordage

rope: lanyard

side-to-side motion: roll

steering apparatus: helm; rudder, tiller

steer: navigate, conn

structure above deck: superstructure

supplier: chandler

tarp securer of wood: batten

toilet: head

trailing whitewater: wake

vibrations of bow over waves: panting

waiter: cabin boy

wall, compartment: bulkhead

weight of sand, rocks, concrete or iron, stabilizing: ballast

weight of water, stabilizing: ballast tanks

width: beam

window: porthole

SEE BOAT, NAVY, SAIL, SAILOR

ship *v.* send, transport, mail, convey, forward, dispatch, consign.

shipshape *a.* orderly, trim, tidy. SEE NEAT

shirk *v.* neglect, evade, avoid, get around, dodge, *goldbrick, malinger, slack off, sidestep, *funk. ANT. *be responsible.*

shirker *n.* slacker, malingerer, *goldbricker, *deadbeat, *bum, dodger, truant, evader.

shirt *n.* article of clothing, blouse, pullover, jersey, button-down shirt, dress shirt, formal shirt, shirtwaist, T-shirt.

WORD FIND

African, loose, colorful pullover: dashiki

bare midriff, knotted in front: calypso

false front: dicky

floral print: Hawaiian, aloha shirt

loose-fitting smock: camise

necked, long-sleeved, high-: turtleneck

patch pockets, having large: safari shirt, bush shirt

plaid wool: Pendleton

ruffled: dandy

short-sleeved pullover: polo shirt

sleeveless hot-weather or basketball shirt:

tanktop
striped sport pullover: rugby shirt
voluminous: blouson
western: cowboy shirt
SEE SWEATER

shiver *n.* shudder, trembling, quiver, quaver, quake, chill, goosebumps.

shiver *v.* shudder, tremble, quiver, shake, tremor, quaver, quake, have one's teeth chatter, catch a chill, *break out in goosebumps.

shoal *n.* **1.** SHALLOW sandbar, ridge, reef, ledge, bank, navigational hazard. **2.** MASS crowd, group, school, swarm, horde.

shock *n.* **1.** IMPACT blow, jolt, crash, collision, jounce, jar, concussion, bump, jerk, whiplash, brunt. **2.** SURPRISE trauma, thunderbolt, *bolt from the blue, *bombshell, *kick in the teeth, start, jolt, *eye-opener, stupefaction. **3.** TANGLED MASS bushy mass, mane, mop, tuft, thatch, *rat's nest. SEE HAIR

shock *v.* surprise, stagger, stupefy, traumatize, jolt, start, electrify, *shake up, *hit like a ton of bricks, *floor, stun, paralyze, take one's breath away, astound, daze, horrify, *flabbergast.

shocking *a.* surprising, staggering, stupefying, traumatizing, jolting, startling, electrifying, *hitting like a ton of bricks, unexpected, *flooring, paralyzing, breathtaking, astounding, horrifying, revolting, appalling, disgusting, outrageous. ANT. *expected, anticipated, met with indifference.*

shoddy *a.* inferior, poor, second-rate, second-class, bad, *crappy, cheap, *ticky-tacky, *cheesy, *junky, shabby. ANT. *superior, first-rate, *top-drawer.*

shoe *n.* footwear, footgear, loafer, pump, sneaker, running shoe.

WORD FIND

backless, woman's: mule
back of shoe: cuff
ballet slipper: toe shoe
boat shoes made of canvas and nonskid soles: deck shoes
bottom of: sole
brown and white oxford: saddle shoe
child's: Mary Jane
Chinese, flat-heeled: Chinese
flap: tongue
fringe-tongued shoe with low heel: kiltie flat
high, ankle-supporting sneakers: *hightops, basketball shoes
high-heeled strapless: pump
high-heeled, strapped: slingback

Indian, leather: moccasin
infant: bootee
instep cover: vamp
lace hole: eyelet
loaf with front slot to hold penny: penny loafer
low-heeled, woman's: flats
low shoe laced over instep: oxford
maker: cordwainer
mender: cobbler
metal tag at end of shoelace: aglet
oxford with holes or perforations for decoration: wing-tip
put on, aid to: shoehorn
raised platform sole, shoe with: platform shoe
removing device: bootjack
rope-soled canvas shoe, sometimes laced up the ankle: espadrille
sandallike with wood or cork sole: clog
sandals: clog, flip-flops, Ganymede, gladiator, thongs
sole, narrow portion of: shank
sport traction shoe: cleats
toeless: open-toed shoe
walking shoe, laced: balmoral
white oxfords: white bucks
work shoe, heavy: brogan, steel-toed shoe
SEE BOOT

shoo *interj.* scram! scat! get out! go away!

shoot *n.* sprout, new growth, bud, stem, twig.

shoot *v.* **1.** FIRE, DISCHARGE pull the trigger, *pump full of lead, *blow away, gun down, blast, open fire, barrage, strafe, kill, *smoke. SEE MURDER **2.** THROW hurl, pitch, *chuck, fling, sling, propel, send, launch. **3.** MOVE QUICKLY fly, tear, dart, spring, bound, rocket, bolt, dash, race, whiz, speed, hurtle.

shooting star *n.* meteor, fireball, bolide, comet.

shop *n.* **1.** STORE market, boutique, retail outlet, five-and-dime, emporium, mart, stall, *Mom and Pop operation. **2.** WORKSHOP studio, atelier.

shop *v.* buy, purchase, sample the merchandise, look for, market, window-shop, browse.

shopkeeper *n.* merchant, small businessman/woman, entrepreneur, retailer, trader, dealer, monger, peddler.

shopper *n.* customer, patron, browser, *shopaholic, bargain hunter.

shopping *n.* buying, purchasing, sampling the merchandise, marketing, window shopping, browsing.

shore *n.* beach, seaside, strand, coast, seaboard, waterfront, littoral, verge, brink. SEE BEACH

shore v. support, prop, stabilize, buttress, brace, reinforce, strengthen, hold up, underpin. ANT. *destabilize, weaken, loosen.*

short a. **1.** NOT TALL little, of small stature, tiny, *pint-sized, wee, diminutive, *built like a fireplug, runty, dwarfish, *sawed-off, squat, Lilliputian. **2.** BRIEF abbreviated, short-lived, momentary, to the point, fleeting, condensed, compressed, succinct. **3.** LACKING low, wanting, insufficient, tight, short-handed, scant, scarce, sparse, deficient, missing. **4.** CURT abrupt, rude, brief, terse, discourteous, brusque, gruff. ANT. *1. tall, towering, gigantic. 2. long, long-winded, eternal. 3. sufficient, full, well-supplied. 4. polite, courteous, cordial.*

shortage n. shortfall, deficit, deficiency, dearth, paucity, lack, scarcity, insufficiency, want, famine. ANT. *glut, surplus, abundance.*

shortchange v. *gyp, rook, *pull a fast one. SEE CHEAT

shortcoming n. imperfection, fault, drawback, defect, failing, weakness, flaw, peccadillo, inadequacy, liability. ANT. *strength, strong point, virtue.*

shorten v. reduce, lessen, cut, abbreviate, condense, diminish, clip, trim, slash, *boil down, edit, contract, shrink, prune. ANT. *lengthen, stretch, prolong.*

shortfall n. deficit, deficiency. SEE SHORTAGE

short-lived a. fleeting, momentary, ephemeral, transient, transitory, brief, *over in a heartbeat, *over in the wink of an eye, temporary, quick, passing. ANT. *long-lasting, immortal, permanent, neverending.*

shortly adv. soon, momentarily, any minute now, any second now, presently, quickly, directly, before you know it, *before one can say Bob's your uncle. ANT. *eventually, later.*

shortsighted a. **1.** NEARSIGHTED myopic, blind as a bat, *blind as a mole, *blind as a post, half-blind, *squinty-eyed. **2.** NOT CONSIDERING THE FUTURE unthinking, stupid, myopic, blind, imprudent, rash, reckless, incautious, *unable to see beyond the end of one's nose, having no foresight. ANT. *1. farsighted, eagle-eyed. 2. farsighted, having foresight, thoughtful.*

short-tempered a. short-fused, temperamental, touchy, irritable, grouchy, testy, crabby, cantankerous, waspish, cranky, hot-tempered, fiery. ANT. *long-fused, mild-mannered, easygoing, passive.*

shot n. **1.** DISCHARGE firing, blast, detonation, crack. **2.** BULLET buckshot, birdshot, slug, ball, pellet, BB. **3.** MARKSMAN. **4.** THROW toss, pitch. **5.** TRY attempt, turn, effort, chance, go, *crack, *stab, *the old college try. **6.** INJECTION innoculation.

shoulder v. carry, pack, bear, push, shove.

shout n. yell, holler, bellow, roar, cry, scream, exclamation, howl, whoop, shriek, outcry. ANT. *whisper, murmur, mumble.*

shout v. yell, holler, bellow, roar, cry, scream, exclaim, howl, whoop, vociferate, fulminate, thunder, shriek, raise one's voice, cry out. ANT. *whisper, murmur, mumble.*

shove n. push, drive, thrust, elbow, jostle, shoulder, press, nudge.

shove v. push, drive, thrust, elbow, jostle, *bulldoze, shoulder, strongarm, muscle, *bull, press, propel, move, nudge.

shovel n. spade, scoop, implement, *digger, posthole digger, dredge.

shovel v. dig, excavate, spade, scoop.

show n. **1.** ENTERTAINMENT exhibition, extravaganza, stage production, spectacle, exposition, program, parade, play, theatrical performance, burlesque, musical, revue, movie, drama, comedy, circus. **2.** DEMONSTRATION manifestation, exhibition, display, presentation. **3.** PRETENSE act, facade, front, affectation, pose, semblance, *Oscar performance.

show v. **1.** EXHIBIT demonstrate, display, present, reveal, expose, unveil, evince, produce, bare, trot out for inspection. **2.** APPEAR be visible, manifest. **3.** EXPLAIN instruct, demonstrate, simplify, define, *walk through, *run through, clarify. **4.** GUIDE conduct, direct, usher, point out. ANT. *1. hide, conceal, cover up. 3. mystify, confuse.*

showdown n. clash, confrontation, climax, face-off, turning point, *moment of truth, duel.

shower n. rainfall, downpour, cloudburst, drizzle, sleet, hail, sprinkle, mist, spit, deluge, *gulley washer

shower v. **1.** RAIN spray, sprinkle, drizzle, downpour, drizzle, sleet, spit. **2.** LAVISH pour forth, heap.

showoff n. *hot dog, braggart, swaggerer, exhibitionist, peacock, *showboat, *grandstander, braggadocio, blowhard.

show off v. *hotdog, brag, swagger, strut, peacock, *showboat, *grandstand, flaunt, *strut one's stuff.

showpiece n. example, *jewel in the crown, masterpiece, work of art, exceptional piece.

showy a. flashy, ostentatious, gaudy, loud, flamboyant, garish, tawdry, cheap. ANT. *understated, dull, plain.*

shred *n.* piece, fragment, strip, scrap, ribbon, sliver, snippet, band, tatter, bit.

shred *v.* rip, cut, tear, fragment, strip, cut to ribbons, snip, tatter, fray.

shrew *n.* nag, *bitch, *rag, witch, *battle-ax, henpecker, ogress, scold, virago, spitfire, harridan, vixen, *ballbuster.

shrewd *a.* **1.** SMART clever, astute, sharp, *savvy, sagacious, wise, keen, intelligent, discerning. **2.** ARTFUL cunning, wiley, cagey, sly, crafty, scheming. ANT. *1. stupid, dense, ignorant, naive. 2. artless, innocent, naive.*

shriek *n.* scream, screech, cry, piercing cry, squeal, yell, shout, wail, shrill, howl.

shriek *v.* scream, screech, cry, squeal, yell, shout, wail, howl.

shrill *a.* high-toned, high-pitched, piercing, ear-piercing, ear-shattering, thin, sharp, intense, piping, deafening, blaring. ANT. *low, quiet.* SEE LOUD

shrimp *n.* runt, pipsqueak, midget. SEE DWARF

shrine *n.* tabernacle, altar, reliquary, temple, church, chapel, mausoleum, sanctuary, holy place, monument, memorial.

shrink *v.* **1.** DIMINISH lessen, dwindle, contract, shrivel, compress, deflate, wither, shorten. **2.** DRAW BACK cower, cringe, recoil, wince, flinch, retreat. ANT. *1. grow, inflate, expand. 2. confront, face.*

shrivel *v.* shrink, wither, dry up, dehydrate, desiccate, waste away, wilt, wrinkle, contract, curl up, wizen, mummify, deflate. ANT. *bloom, expand, blow up.*

shriveled *a.* shrunken, withered, dried up, dehydrated, desiccated, wasted away, wilted, wrinkled, wizened, contracted, deflated. ANT. *swollen, plump, ballooning.*

shroud *n.* cover, winding sheet, burial sheet, cloth, wrap, cerements, pall, veil, cloak.

shroud *v.* cover, veil, wrap, cloak, conceal, keep under wraps, shield, screen, hide. ANT. *unveil, expose, reveal.*

shrub/shrubbery *n.* shrubs, bushes, brush, hedges, underbrush, thicket, scrub, copse, boscage.

WORD FIND

aromatic: mint, lavender, rosemary, bergamot

dwarfed: bonsai

ornamental or animal shapes made of: topiary

shrunken *a.* diminished, contracted, shriveled, compressed, deflated, withered, shortened, wasted away, dehydrated. ANT. *enlarged, expanded, puffed up.*

shuck *v.* shell, husk, remove, peel off, slough.

shudder *n.* tremor, trembling, shake, convulsion, quiver, shiver, quaver, quake, spasm, jerking, twitching.

shudder *v.* tremble, shake, convulse, quiver, shiver, quaver, get a chill, quake, have a spasm, jerk, twitch.

shuffle *v.* **1.** MIX jumble, disorder, shift, interchange, disarrange, displace, mess up. **2.** SCUFF THE FEET shamble, drag one's feet, scrape, limp.

shun *v.* avoid, turn away from, *give the cold shoulder to, dodge, evade, reject, snub, steer clear of, shy away from, eschew, forgo. ANT. *embrace, seek out, face.*

shunt *v.* divert, turn off, switch, shift, sidetrack

shut *v.* close, secure, lock, bolt, fasten, seal, slam, draw closed, block, bar, occlude. ANT. *open, unlock, unfasten.*

shutout *v.* *skunk, *blow out, defeat soundly.

shuttle *n.* orbiter. SEE SPACECRAFT

shuttle *v.* go back and forth, go on one's run, commute, shuttlecock, transport to and fro.

shy *a.* **1.** BASHFUL self-conscious, backward, reticent, retiring, diffident, reserved, a wallflower, ill-at-ease, nervous, self-effacing, coy, demure, shrinking, introverted, modest, humble, schizoid, quiet. **2.** LACKING short, under, deficient. ANT. *1. loud, overbearing, overconfident, bold, brash.*

shyness *n.* bashfulness, self-consciousness, reticence, diffidence, nervousness, coyness, introversion, modesty, humbleness, quietness. ANT. *loudness, overconfidence, boldness.*

shyster *n.* *Sl.* pettifogger, unethical lawyer, *ambulance chaser, *fixer.

sick *a.* **1.** UNHEALTHY ill, unwell, ailing, run down, diseased, *under the weather, *green around the gills, *off one's feed, queasy, nauseated, sickly, infected, feverish, bedridden. **2.** HEARTSICK sick at heart, heartbroken, miserable, stricken. **3.** FED UP *had it up to here with, tired, disgusted, cloyed, sated, satiated. **4.** DERANGED psychotic, *psycho, perverted, strange, sadistic. ANT. *1. healthy, well, *fit as a fiddle. 2. delighted, happy. 3. wanting more, hungry for more.*

sicken *v.* nauseate, make ill, turn one's stomach, disgust, revolt, make one want to throw up, *gross out, repel. ANT. *delight, please, attract.*

sickening *a.* nauseating, stomach-turning, disgusting, revolting, *gross, foul, vile, distasteful, repugnant, enough to make one vomit. ANT. *delightful, appetizing, attractive.*

sickle n. scythe, *bushwhacker, grass-cutter, cutting implement.

sickly a. ailing, unhealthy, in poor health, unwell, run down, diseased, *under the weather, *green around the gills, *off one's feed, weak, queasy, nauseated, infected, feverish, pale, pallid, ashen, *circling the drain. ANT. healthy, well, *fit as a fiddle.

sickness n. illness, ailment, disease, malady, affliction, infection, *bug, virus, weakness, disorder, syndrome, influenza, flu, pneumonia, queasiness, nausea, upset stomach, fever, infirmity. SEE DISEASE, ILLNESS

side n. 1. EDGE border, right, left, brink, margin, flank, front, back, top, bottom, face, aspect, quarter, surface, section. 2. VIEWPOINT aspect, standpoint, angle, facet, position. 3. ONE OF TWO OR MORE OPPOSING VIEWS OR GROUPS party, camp, team, faction, rival, competition, combatant.

side a. secondary, minor, incidental, subordinate, lesser, ancillary, flanking. ANT. main, central, chief.

sideburns n. burnsides, *mutton chops, whiskers. SEE BEARD

side by side a. juxtaposing, abreast, cheek by jowl, pari passu.

side effect n. by-product, reaction.

sidekick n. Sl. companion, friend, alter ego, buddy, pal, colleague, confederate, partner, *straight man.

sidelong a. oblique, sideways, lateral.

sidesplitting a. hilarious, hearty, a scream, convulsive. SEE FUNNY

sidestep v. dodge, avoid, evade, elude, sidetrack, bypass, go around, duck, *steer clear, *dance around. ANT. face, confront, meet head-on.

sidetrack v. divert, digress, turn off, shunt.

sidewalk n. pavement, walkway, boardwalk.

sideways adv. obliquely, laterally, edgewise, sidelong, askew.

siege n. encirclement, surrounding, investment, blockade, onslaught, offense, assault, campaign.

siege v. besiege, lay siege, encircle, surround, invest, blockade, contain, close off, beset, assault.

siesta n. rest, *catnap, snooze. SEE NAP

sieve n. sifter, strainer, filter, screen, mesh, colander.

sift v. strain, sieve, filter, screen, winnow, comb, separate, sort out, scrutinize.

sigh n. exhalation, deep breath, sough, moan, groan, murmur.

sigh v. exhale heavily, breathe out, moan, groan, lament.

sight n. 1. EYESIGHT vision, visual perception, eyes. 2. RANGE OF VISION eyeshot, view, focus. 3. SPECTACLE scene, vision, show, curiosity, picture. 4. MESS fright, horror, monstrosity, spectacle.

sign n. 1. INDICATION mark, clue, hint, intimation, suggestion, trace, *dead giveaway, evidence, earmark, signal, symptom, manifestation, beacon, spoor, trail, herald, omen, harbinger, portent, foreshadowing. 2. POSTED INFORMATION signpost, notice, pointer, marker, guidepost, warning, caution, billboard, placard.

sign v. endorse, write one's name, inscribe, autograph, authorize.

signal n. sign, indication, alert, indicator, cue, *go-ahead, *thumbs-up, gesture, nod, notice, flare, flag, siren, beacon, foghorn, semaphore.

signal v. indicate, alert, cue, *give the go-ahead, *give a thumbs-up, gesture, nod, warn, shoot off a flare, flag, semaphore.

signature n. autograph, name, inscription, *John Hancock, hand, X, endorsement, authorization, OK, identification.

significance n. 1. IMPORTANCE consequence, weight, consideration, matter, meaning, value, gravity, moment, import, interest. 2. MEANING intent, point, sense, implication, idea, drift. ANT. 1. insignificance, frivolity, unimportance.

significant a. 1. IMPORTANT consequential, weighty, considerable, meaningful, valuable, momentous, major, vital, critical, crucial. 2. MEANINGFUL indicative, suggestive, telling, expressive, symbolic. ANT. 1. insignificant, unimportant, trivial. 2. meaningless.

signify v. mean, denote, represent, indicate, stand for, suggest, imply, express, communicate, symbolize, connote.

silence n. 1. STILLNESS quiet, peace, hush, quietude, noiselessness, dead air, calm, tranquility, serenity, a *vast desert of silence, *tomblike silence, deathly silence, blackout. 2. SPEECHLESSNESS muteness, reticence, taciturnity, reservation, uncommunicativeness, secrecy. "The sharper sword."—Robert U. Johnson. "One of the hardest arguments to refute."—Josh Billings. "Unbearable repartee."—Gilbert Keith Chesterson. "The fence around wisdom."—Hebrew proverb. ANT. 1. noise, cacophony, din, uproar. 2. loquaciousness, talk, chatter.

silence v. quiet, still, shut up, hush, gag, muzzle, inhibit, censor, *squelch, strangle, put down, crush, repress.

silencer n. muffler, mute.

silent a. **1.** QUIET still, peaceful, hushed, noiseless, soundless, calm, tranquil, serene, dead, *deathly silent, *stone silent. **2.** SPEECHLESS mute, uncommunicative, taciturn, *clammed up, reticent, mum, tongue-tied. ANT. 1. noisy, cacophonous, uproarious, earsplitting. 2. talkative, loquacious, *motor-mouthed.

silhouette n. outline, profile, contour.

silky a. smooth, satiny, delicate, glossy, sleek. ANT. rough, coarse.

silly a. foolish, childish, infantile, juvenile, asinine, goofy, stupid, nonsensical, idiotic, absurd, laughable, wacky, ridiculous, zany, funny, humorous. ANT. serious, grave, mature.

silt n. sediment, settlings, alluvium, wash.

silver a. sterling, argent, shiny.

silverware n. silver, cutlery, flatware, eating utensils.

similar a. like, comparable, resembling, much the same, kindred, equivalent, akin, homologous, nearly matching, analogous. ANT. dissimilar, different, contrasting.

similarity n. likeness, resemblance, comparison, sameness, equivalence, correspondence, mirror image, semblance, homogeneity, analogy, parity, affinity. ANT. difference, contrast, opposition.

simmer v. bubble, stew, boil, seethe.

simper n. smirk. SEE SMILE

simple a. **1.** EASY *child's play, effortless, *cinchy, *a cinch, *a snap , *like falling off a log, *piece of cake, understandable, clear, straightforward, uncomplicated. **2.** MERE bare, sheer, pure, utter. **3.** PLAIN unadorned, unembellished, spare, bare, clean, austere, modest, humble, Spartan. **4.** INNOCENT artless, unsophisticated, down-to-earth, childlike, natural, naive, ingenuous, honest, real. **5.** STUPID foolish, dense, dull, dumb, moronic, slow, bovine, ignorant, witless, *clueless. ANT. 1. hard, difficult, complicated, complex. 2. qualified. 3. ornate, fancy, embellished. 4. sophisticated, artful, disingenuous. 5. smart, sharp, *on the ball.

simpleminded a. unsophisticated, stupid, dense, dull, dumb, moronic, slow, bovine, ignorant, witless, *clueless, brainless. ANT. sophisticated, smart, *savvy.

simpleton n. fool, idiot, *retard, *dumb-dumb, dunce, moron, imbecile, ignoramus, *dope, dolt, *dimwit, *lunkhead, *bonehead, *airhead. ANT. genius, savant, *Rhodes scholar.

simply adv. **1.** PLAINLY easily, naturally. **2.** MERELY only, just.

simulate v. imitate, copy, put on, act, mimic, fake, pretend, assume, pose, feign, affect, counterfeit, sham, replicate.

simulated a. imitation, artificial, synthetic, fake, counterfeit, sham, fabricated, make-believe, mock. ANT. real, authentic, genuine.

simulation n. imitation, fake, reproduction, counterfeit, sham, fabrication, copy, mockup, facsimile. ANT. the real thing, *the real McCoy.

simultaneous a. concurrent, at the same time, synchronous, coincident, concomitant, parallel, coexisting, *in sync.

sin n. offense, transgression, wrong, wrongdoing, evil, crime, felony, violation, fault, immoral act, misdeed, affront to God, wrongdoing, vice, peccadillo, wickedness. "The breaking of one's own integrity." — D.H. Lawrence. "A departure from God." — Martin Luther. ANT. good deed, virtue, kindness.

sin v. do an evil deed, do an immoral act, break a commandment, do wrong, transgress, offend God, commit a crime, fall from grace, trespass, stray from the path of righteousness. ANT. do a good deed, do a kindness.

sincere a. honest, genuine, real, heartfelt, straightforward, open, ingenuous, up front, *straight shooting, earnest, forthright, frank, candid, guileless. ANT. insincere, phony, fake.

sincerity n. honesty, genuineness, realness, heartfelt emotion, straightforwardness, openness, ingenuousness, *straight shooting, forthrightness, frankness, candidness, guilelessness. "To be consistent with your conscience." — Anon. "Just what I think, and nothing more or less." — H.W. Longfellow. "Plain dealing." — Ralph Waldo Emerson. ANT. insincerity, dishonesty, hypocrisy.

sinewy a. tough, strong, muscular, strapping, brawny, burly, athletic, toned, wiry, steely, Herculean. ANT. fat, flaccid, droopy, flabby.

sinful a. bad, evil, immoral, wicked, wrong, criminal, demonic, corrupt, vile, ungodly, shameful, disgraceful, low. ANT. virtuous, moral, upright.

sing v. *belt out a song, carry a tune, carol, croon, serenade, warble, hum, trill, pipe, cry out, yodel, bellow, sing in a booming voice, sing falsetto.

WORD FIND

singing with a falsely high voice: falsetto

singing without instrumental accompaniment: a cappella; *barbershop
SEE MUSIC, OPERA, SINGER, SONG, VOICE

singe v. burn, char, sear, brown, toast, roast, blacken.

singer n. vocalist, crooner, songster, caroler, *pop star, soloist, recording artist, minstrel, troubador, nightingale, tenor, baritone, soprano, alto, diva, prima donna. SEE OPERA, SING, SONG, VOICE

single a. **1.** ONE individual, sole, lone, singular, separate, distinct, solitary, isolated. **2.** UNMARRIED unwed, unattached, divorced, celibate, available, eligible. ANT. *1. many, several. 2. married, wed.*

single-handed a. unaided, unassisted, alone, independent.

singles bar n. bar, lounge, club, *pickup joint, *meat market.

SINGULAR a. [SING gyuh lur] unique, one of a kind. *A singular experience.* SYN. unique, one of a kind, exceptional, extraordinary, peculiar, unusual, remarkable, rare, odd, strange, different. ANT. *common, usual, ordinary.*

sinister a. threatening, ominous, inauspicious, portentious, menacing, black, malignant, malevolent, villainous, bad, evil, wicked, diabolic, satanic. ANT. *good, auspicious, divine.*

sink n. basin, washbowl, drain.

sink v. **1.** GO DOWN drop, fall, descend, sag, immerse, drown, submerge, dip, settle, slump, plunge. **2.** DECLINE decrease, diminish, fall, drop, subside, deteriorate, regress, wane, ebb. **3.** CAUSE TO SINK swamp, drown, engulf, overwhelm, scuttle. ANT. *1. rise, ascend. 2. increase, grow.*

sinuous a. **1.** WINDING curving, serpentine, wavy, bending, tortuous, meandering, undulating, coiling, twisting, snaking. **2.** DEVIOUS crooked. ANT. *1. straight, unbending.*

sip n. taste, swallow, drop, sample, lick, *swig, nip, dram, *hit.

sip v. taste, *slurp, sample, *take a swig, *take a hit, sup, siphon, suck through a straw.

sir n. seignor, monsieur, sahib, my lord.

sire n. **1.** YOUR MAJESTY **2.** FATHER genitor.

sire v. beget, father, engender, procreate, spawn, bear, generate, breed, multiply.

siren n. **1.** WARNING SIGNAL alarm, Klaxon, whistle. **2.** SEDUCTRESS enchantress, temptress, nymph, femme fatale, Lorelei, witch, charmer.

sissy n. weakling, *woos, *woosy, *wimp, *candy ass, *pansy, mama's boy, coward, *chicken, *cream puff, *fancy-pants, *pantywaist, effeminate man, *homo, homosexual, *gay boy, *faggot. ANT. *macho man, *gorilla, bull, *jock, he-man.

sit v. **1.** BE SEATED settle, plop oneself down, rest, squat, *take a load off, perch, roost, lounge, recline, straddle, sprawl, deposit oneself. **2.** MEET assemble, gather, convene, deliberate, be in session, come together.

site n. location, locale, locality, place, spot, position, plot, point, lot, area, grounds, scene, section, whereabouts.

sit-in n. protest, demonstration, strike, rally, shutdown.

sitter n. baby sitter, nanny, attendant, caretaker, wet nurse.

sitting duck n. easy target, easy pickings, *dead meat, *toast.

situate v. locate, position, place, put, install, set, set up, plant, settle, post, root. ANT. *move, withdraw, leave.*

situated a. located, positioned, placed, installed, set, set up, planted, settled, posted, rooted, established.

situation n. **1.** CONDITION predicament, plight, state, state of affairs, circumstances, position, *ball game, fix, *between a rock and a hard place, *deep do-do, *sticky wicket. **2.** PLACE locality, locale, location, spot, point, site, position. **3.** JOB employment, position, office, duty, appointment.

six-shooter n. revolver, pistol. SEE GUN

sixth sense n. intuition, *gut feelings, instinct, *feeling in one's bones, *vibes, extrasensory perception, ESP, second sight, telepathy, clairvoyance.

sizable a. big, large, considerable, great, hefty, *whopping, respectable, king-size, industrial size, huge. ANT. *small, tiny, piddling.*

size n. dimensions, measurements, proportions, scale, extent, area, magnitude, mass, square footage, volume, capacity, amount, stature, breadth, length, height, width, diameter.

size v. measure, gauge, graduate, assess, appraise, survey, size up.

sizzle v. hiss, fry, splutter, sputter, crackle, fizzle.

skate v. slide, glide, glissade, roller-skate, rollerblade, ice skate, figure skate.

WORD FIND

FIGURE SKATING

arena: rink

dance: free dance

figure of three circles: serpentine

figure of two circles: figure eight

flying spin: Arabian

flying spin ending in back camel: flying camel

glide with one skate pointing forward, the other back: spread eagle

jump and splitting apart of legs: split, stag

jump of one and a half revolutions: axel

jump of one revolution: Lutz

jump of three and a half revolutions: triple axel

jump of two and a half revolutions: double axel

jump split and touching of toes: Russian split

jump started off a back inside edge and ended on opposite foot: Salchow

machine that resurfaces ice: Zamboni

moves executed to the sound of music: freestyle, free skating

pair move in which man lifts woman overhead with her legs split: hydrant lift

pair move in which woman is revolved with head held near ice: death spiral

propelling oneself over the ice: stroking

spin in an arabesque position: camel

spin with one leg held high overhead: Bielmann spin

turn forward to back: choctaw

skedaddle *v.* run away, scoot, leave, *beat feet, vamoose, bolt, scat, *make oneself scarce, *blow, decamp, *hightail it. ANT. *loiter, hang around.*

skein *n.* coil, quantity, hank, ball, loop, twist, clump.

skeleton *n.* bones, framework, bony structure, scaffolding.

WORD FIND

breastbone, center: sternum

broken bone: Colles fracture, comminuted fracture, compound fracture, Pott's fracture

broken bone, sound of: crepitation

broken bones, realignment of: traction, countertraction

cheek: malar

collarbone: clavicle

connective tissue: cartilage

disease of bones: osteoarthritis, osteofibrosis, osteoporosis, scoliosis

ear bones: incus (anvil), malleus (hammer), stapes (stirrup)

fingers and toes: phalanges

foot bones: metatarsal

forearm: radius, ulna

funny bone between shoulder and elbow: humerus

hand bones: metacarpal

hipbone: coxae, pelvis, sacrum, coccyx

jawbone, lower: mandible

jawbone, upper: maxilla

kneecap: patella

leg, knee to ankle, outer: fibula

leg, knee to ankle: tibia

shoulder blade: scapula

skull: cranium

spinal column: vertebrae

tailbone: coccyx

thighbone: femur

upper body framework: ribs

vertebrae of neck, first: atlas

wrist bones, collectively: carpal

skeptic *n.* doubter, cynic, doubting Thomas, nonbeliever, scoffer, naysayer, questioner, freethinker, atheist, agnostic. "Not one who doubts, but one who examines."—Charles Sainte-Beauve. ANT. *believer, *sucker.*

skeptical *a.* doubting, questioning, cynical, unbelieving, scoffing, distrusting, mistrusting, dubious, incredulous, leery, unconvinced, agnostic, atheistic. ANT. *believing, gullible, trusting.*

skepticism *n.* doubt, questioning, cynicism, disbelief, scoffing, distrust, mistrust, leeriness, suspicion, agnosticism, atheism. "The mark and even the pose of the educated mind."—John Dewey.

sketch *n.* **1.** DRAWING draft, outline, rough outline, diagram, blueprint, skeleton, design, plan, brief, synopsis, apercu, survey. **2.** SKIT act, scene, vignette.

sketch *v.* draw, draft, outline, rough out, diagram, scratch out, block out, design, plot out.

sketchy *a.* rough, lacking detail, incomplete, unfinished, cursory, brief, crude, preliminary, imperfect, *half-assed, *half-baked. ANT. *detailed, thorough, complete.*

skew *v.* twist, distort, pervert, shift, misrepresent, change, falsify, misconstrue, misstate, slant, bias, embellish.

skewer *n.* pin, spit, brochette.

ski *v.* schuss, slalom, snowplow, freestyle.

WORD FIND

absorbing impact of bump by flexing knees: swallowing

acrobatic or dance-style skiing: freestyle

acrobatic side revolution like helicopter blade: helicopter

backward somersault with a twist: back moebius

bump or hump of snow: mogul

bumpy or humpy snow field: mogul field

cross-country: langlauf, Nordic skiing, rambling

form left in snow from fallen skier: sitzmark

freestyle dance: ballet

jump made in crouching position: gelendesprung

jump with skis scissored in midair: daffy

lift, covered: gondola

overhang of ice and snow known to cause avalanches: cornice

parallel turn: christie

rifle-shooting and skiing competition: biathlon

ski straight down mountain: schuss

slowing-down or stopping position: snowplow

snow, deep and soft: powder

snow, old granulated: corn

snow with hard surface: crust

turn in which one ski is lifted high in the air: kick turn, royal christie

turns, series of quick: wedelns

uphill diagonal walking method: herringbone

uphill sideways walking method: sidestepping

winding, flagged race: slalom

skid v. slide, slip, sideslip, *burn rubber, *smoke Goodyears, swerve, fishtail, glissade.

skill n. **1.** ABILITY expertise, talent, proficiency, command, competence, faculty, know-how, gift, mastery, adeptness, knack, aptitude, dexterity, adroitness, prowess, finesse. **2.** TRADE art, craft, vocation, profession, forte. ANT. *1. inability, incompetence, inexperience.*

skillful a. skilled, expert, proficient, adept, competent, experienced, schooled, adroit, dexterous, masterful, *crack, *crackerjack, practiced, accomplished, talented, gifted. ANT. *unskilled, unschooled, incompetent, inept.*

skim v. **1.** CREAM clear, remove, top. **2.** GLANCE AT HASTILY read, scan, *speed read, thumb through, flip through, peruse, spot-check, skip over. **3.** GLIDE OVER skip over, bounce over, graze.

skimp v. scrimp, stint, be stingy, be cheap, be tight, be frugal, *cut corners, *pinch pennies, scrape, conserve. ANT. *squander, waste, *blow.*

skimpy a. scanty, short, not enough, barely enough, lacking, inadequate, meager, insufficient, slight, spare, *measly. ANT. *adequate, sufficient, generous, ample.*

skin n. epidermis, dermis, derma, cuticle, hide,

pelt, membrane, *nature's shrinkwrap, coat, membrane, sheath, husk, bark, rind, covering, shell, hull.

skin v. peel, decorticate, excorticate, flay, husk, shell, shuck, shed, slough, strip, pare, scalp, trim.

skin-deep a. superficial, shallow, surface, empty, external. ANT. *deep, profound.*

skin-diving n. scuba diving, snorkeling.

WORD FIND

air flow apparatus: regulator

ascend slowly, stop, ascend: decompress

breathing tube for shallow swimming: snorkel

dangerous narcotic effect of deep water diving: nitrogen narcosis, *rapture of the deep

decompression sickness: bends

diver: frogman, aquanaut, scuba diver, pearl diver

line tied between two divers to keep them together in dark: buddy line

red signal flag with white bar: diver down flag

responsibility for fellow diver: buddy system

rubber suit: wet suit

sharing of air with another diver: buddy breathing

water pressure, lessening of: decompression

weight regulator: buoyancy compensator, weight belt

skinflick n. X-rated movie, blue movie, *porno flick, dirty movie, adult movie.

skinflint n. *cheapskate, miser, *tightwad, niggard, *Scrooge, penny-pincher, curmudgeon, hoarder, money-grubber. ANT. *spendthrift, *big spender, philanthropist.*

skinny a. thin, slender, lean, skeletal, anorexic, emaciated, bony, *thin enough to fall through a flute and not sound a note, scrawny, lank, malnourished, half-starved, raw-boned, gaunt. ANT. *fat, obese, roly-poly.*

skip v. **1.** HOP bound, spring, leap, caper, romp, jump, cavort, gambol, prance, frisk, bounce. **2.** SKIM bounce, ricochet, skate. **3.** OVERLOOK pass over, omit, exclude, leave out, forget about, disregard, nevermind, ignore.

skipper n. captain, master, mariner, pilot, seaman, officer.

skirmish n. fight, flare-up, encounter, battle, engagement, conflict, tussle, brush with the enemy, scrimmage, clash, *run-in, fray, heated exchange.

skirmish v. fight, encounter, battle, engage, conflict, tussle, scrimmage, clash, combat, have a run-in, have a heated exchange.

skirt n. **1.** BORDER margin, verge, fringe, edge, rim, periphery, perimeter. **2.** ARTICLE OF CLOTHING wrap, mini, midi, maxi.

WORD FIND

ballet dancer's: tutu

broad, nineteenth century: hoop skirt, crinoline

calico with ruffled hem: prairie skirt

grass skirt: hula skirt

Malaysian wrap: sarong

narrow, restrictive skirt of 1910: hobble skirt

narrow, slitted in back: sheath

peasant skirt: dirndl

puffy: bouffant, bubble

rear gathering, nineteenth century: bustle

rustling of silk skirt: froufrou

Scottish, man's: kilt

shorts: culottes

skit n. sketch, vignette, play, playlet, act, parody, takeoff, lampoon.

skittish a. jumpy, nervous, easily frightened, jittery, excitable, anxious, restless, edgy, restive, easily spooked. ANT. *calm, relaxed, tranquil, composed.*

skulduggery n. sneakiness, trickery, craftiness, deception, deceit, artifice, wile, treachery, machination, underhandedness, conspiracy, foul play. ANT. *honesty, innocence.*

skulk v. lurk, slink, sneak, prowl, creep, lie back in the shadows, steal, sneak, hide, pussyfoot, move stealthily.

skull n. cranium, head, sconce.

skullcap n. cap, zucchetto, yarmulke, beanie, calotte, pileus, swim cap.

skunk n. **1.** ANIMAL cognate, polecat, vermin, *stinker. **2.** BAD PERSON *SOB, bastard, *creep, stinker, scoundrel, *rat, rogue, cad.

sky n. upper atmosphere, firmament, cloudscape, vault, *the wild blue yonder, welkin, biosphere, stratosphere, mesosphere, thermosphere, exosphere, ionosphere, ether. "The roof of the world." — Willa Cather. "That beautiful old parchment in which the sun and the moon keep their diary." — Alfred Kreymborg. "Earth's ethereal armor." — Mark Clarke. "An unfolding drama in which clouds metamorphise from cotton balls to dragons and back again." — Marc McCutcheon.

WORD FIND

color: azure, cerulean, celeste

highest point: zenith

referring to: celestial

SEE ASTRONOMY, ATMOSPHERE, CLOUD, SPACE

skydiving n. parachuting, freefalling.

WORD FIND

arms at side position to increase speed of freefall: delta position

automatic deployment line attached inside aircraft: static line

auxiliary chute: reserve chute

cord that deploys parachute: ripcord

descent portion without deployment of parachute: freefall

hazard in which chute fails to unfurl completely: streamer

hazard in which chute is turned inside out after deployment: inversion

horizontal soaring: gliding

joining hands with another diver in midair: docking

landing area: drop zone

positioning the body for horizontal movement: tracking

small chute that helps deploy main chute: pilot chute

spread-eagle falling position with arms upraised: frog position

steering lines: toggle lines

supervisor of jumps: jumpmaster

skyrocket v. shoot skyward, soar, take off, shoot up, zoom, catapult, *go through the roof, *blast off to the clouds. ANT. *nosedive, plunge, plummet, spiral earthward.*

skyscraper n. high-rise, *cloudscraper, monolith, building, superstructure.

slab n. piece, hunk, chunk, plank, slice, block.

slack n. excess, play, give, leeway, looseness.

slack/slacken v. slacken, loosen, let up, relax, untighten, ease off, lessen, decrease, diminish, soften, moderate. ANT. *tighten, increase.*

slack a. **1.** SLOW idle, slow-moving, sluggish, dull, quiet, lethargic, down. **2.** NOT TIGHT loose, relaxed, not taut, sagging, drooping, limp, lax, flaccid. **3.** CARELESS, LAZY negligent, remiss, sloppy, slipshod, *asleep on the job, lax, lackadaisical, nonchalant, indifferent, indolent, uncaring. ANT. **1.** *fast, fast-moving, busy, *hopping.* **2.** *tight, taut.* **3.** *careful, meticulous, exacting.*

slacker n. shirker, idler, loafer, malingerer, *goof-off, *goldbricker, *deadbeat, clock watcher, truant.

slake v. quench, hydrate, satisfy, sate, satiate, relieve, gratify, allay, extinguish, alleviate, appease, assuage. ANT. *aggravate, increase, exacerbate.*

slam n. **1.** LOUD NOISE bang, boom, crash, wham, crack, clap, burst, impact, collision. **2.** CRITI-

CISM *dig, *pan, brickbat, disapproval, bad press, *swipe.

slam v. **1.** SHUT bang, close hard, heave, ram, push, crash, smack, dash, clobber, bat, hammer, *bodyslam. **2.** CRITICIZE *dig, *pan, *take a swipe at, shoot down, *blast, attack, *rake over the coals. ANT. *2. compliment, praise, laud.*

SLANDER n. [SLAN dur] damaging, untrue statements made publicly. *Celebrities must tolerate occasional slander against them.* SYN. lies, untruths, smear, mudslinging, defamation, denigration, misrepresentation, aspersion, false statement, libel, calumny. "The revenge of a coward." — Samuel Johnson. ANT. *praise, commendation, compliment.*

slander v. lie, misrepresent, smear, mudsling, defame, denigrate, cast aspersions, make a false statement, libel, malign, *drag one's name through the mud, slur, tarnish one's name. ANT. *praise, commend, honor.*

slang n. colloquialism, jargon, argot, lingo, vernacular, vocabulary, *slanguage, pidgin, language of the street, shoptalk, dialect, Americanisms. "Language serving its apprenticeship" — Henry T. Buckle. "Language that takes off its coat, spits on its hands, and goes to work." — Carl Sandburg. ANT. *formal language.*

slant n. **1.** INCLINE slope, pitch, lean, tilt, angle, cant, grade, camber, rake. **2.** VIEWPOINT point of view, side, position, angle, opinion, attitude. **3.** DISTORTION bias, prejudice, partiality, leaning

slant v. **1.** INCLINE slope, pitch, lean, tilt, angle, cant, grade, skew. **2.** DISTORT bias, prejudice, color, twist, weight, orient. ANT. *1. straighten, level, flatten.*

slanting a. inclined, sloping, tilting, leaning, canting, oblique, diagonal, askew, at an angle. ANT. *straight, level.*

slap n. **1.** CUFF blow, smack, hit, hand across the face, *slap upside the head, swat, buffet, clap, swipe, *belt. **2.** INSULT *crack, *shot, *dig, rebuff, offense, *put-down, snub, *cut, affront, slight.

slap v. cuff, smack, hit, *slap upside the head, swat, buffet, clap, swipe, *belt, *slap silly, spank.

slapdash a. careless, hasty, impetuous, haphazard, sloppy, slipshod, casual, harum-scarum. ANT. *careful, meticulous.*

slaphappy a. dazed, punch-drunk, dizzy, lightheaded, *woozy, reeling, giddy, silly. ANT. *sober, clearheaded.*

slash n. stroke, swipe; cut, gash, slit, wound, laceration, incision, score, tear.

slash v. **1.** CUT stroke, swipe, gash, slit, jag, wound, lacerate, incise, slice, score, tear, hack, rip open, mutilate, open. **2.** REDUCE cut, decrease, drop, lower.

slat n. strip, lath, stave, picket, paling.

slate n. ballot, ticket, list, roster.

slaughter n. massacre, bloodbath, murder, mass murder, butchering, carnage, killing, slaying, mass execution, mutilation.

slaughter v. massacre, murder, butcher, kill, slay, execute, mutilate, savage, decimate, assassinate, annihilate.

slaughterhouse n. abattoir, shambles, butchery, meat-packing house.

slave n. bondman, servant, indentured servant, chattel, drudge, serf, laborer, menial.

slave v. drudge, break one's back, work one's fingers to the bone, toil, labor, grind, sweat, plod, slog, *bust one's hump.

slavery n. bondage, servitude, forced labor, slave labor, enslavement, captivity, enthrallment, subjugation, serfdom, grind, toil. "A prison for the soul, a public dungeon." — Longinus. "Yoked with the brutes, and fettered to the soil." — Thomas Campbell.

WORD FIND

black woman servant who served as mother to white children: mammy

degrading term for slave in nineteenth-century United States: boy

elimination of: abolition

elimination, one who favored slavery's abolitionist

field supervisor on plantation: driver, overseer

free from: emancipate, manumit

fugitive slave: maroon

group of slaves tied together: coffle

master's personal slave: body servant

slave owner: master, massa

subservient, deferential slave, degrading term for: Sambo, Uncle Tom

slavish a. servile, submissive, subservient, deferential, subject, obsequious, obeisant, fawning, cowering. ANT. *domineering, intractable, arrogant.*

slay v. kill, murder, run through, slaughter, assassinate, execute, *do in, massacre, annihilate, destroy. SEE MURDER

sleazebag n. Sl. creep, *slimeball, *scumbag, *sleaze, slob, *pig, *dirtbag, *scuzzo, filthy wretch, *bum, pervert, *scum of the earth.

sleazy a. Sl. cheap, *scuzzy, dirty, foul, *creepy,

*raunchy, nasty, sick, gross, *skanky, greasy, oily, disreputable, low, contemptible. ANT. *high-class, refined, cleancut, virtuous, wholesome.*

sled n. sleigh, toboggan, bobsled, luge, cutter, sledge, pung.

sledge n. sled, sleigh, travois.

sleek a. smooth, shiny, glossy, lustrous, satiny, glistening, groomed, combed, trim. ANT. *dull, lackluster.*

sleep n. slumber, rest, somnolence, *shut-eye, *Zs, snooze, nap, catnap, dozing, *forty winks, siesta, repose, hibernation, under the spell of Morpheus, land of Nod, unconsciousness, dreaming. "A holiday from reality." — Victor Ratner. "Brother of death." — Thomas Browne. "The death of each day's life." — Shakespeare. "Our alter-life." — Anon.

WORD FIND

bedwetting: enuresis

between wakefulness and sleep: hypnagogic

breathing disorder of: sleep apnea

children's waking nightmare: night terrors

deep sleep: sopor, stupor

dream sleep: REM sleep (rapid eye movement)

drowsy: somnolent

excessive: hypersomnia

expert in: somnologist

god of dreams, Greek: Morpheus

god of sleep, Greek: Hypnos

god of sleep, Roman: Somnus

grogginess caused by sleeping too long: Rip Van Winkle syndrome

hypnotized: trance

inability to: insomnia

inducing sleep: soporific, somniferous, somnolent

internal body clock controlling: circadian rhythm

presleep visions: hypnagogic hallucinations

sex demons of: incubus, succubus

sleeping sickness: narcolepsy, encephalitis

sleepwalk: somnoambulate

sleepwalker: somnoambulist

twitch of body or leg just before sleep: myoclonic jerk, hypnagogic jerk

unconsciousness, prolonged: coma

ANT. *wakefulness, consciousness, alertness.* SEE DREAM

sleep v. slumber, snooze, drowse, *catch some Zs, rest, *hit the sack, *get some rack time, go to bed, *conk out, nod off, turn in, *saw wood, *crash, *hit the hay, take a siesta, fall under the spell of Morpheus, hibernate. ANT. *wake, regain consciousness.*

sleeper n. *up-and-comer, *late bloomer, *sleeping giant.

sleepless a. insomniac, restless, wakeful, *wired, *saucer-eyed, *tossing and turning. ANT. *sleeping, dreaming, *out like a light.*

sleepwalker n. somnambulist. SEE SLEEP

sleepy a. 1. DROWSY tired, exhausted, weary, *dead-tired, fatigued, slumberous, nodding off, *beat, *dopey, lethargic, asleep, somnolent, falling under the spell of Morpheus. 2. INACTIVE idle, still, quiet, dull. ANT. *awake, refreshed, alert, invigorated.*

sleigh n. sled, cutter, pung, *booby hut.

sleight-of-hand n. legerdemain, hand skill, deception, trickery, magic, prestidigitation, palming, feint, hocus-pocus.

slender a. thin, slim, lean, narrow, skinny, willowy, reedy, twiggy, *thin as a broomstick, svelte, lithe, spare, tenuous. ANT. *fat, obese, brawny.*

sleuth n. detective, private detective, P.I., *private eye, *private dick, *bloodhound, investigator, *sherlock, *gumshoe, shadow, *tail.

slice n. piece, cut, segment, sliver, wedge, slab, hunk, chunk, rasher, shaving, share, portion.

slice v. cut, segment, section, divide, carve, split, sever, pare, shave.

slick a. 1. SLEEK smooth, glossy, satiny, slippery, oily, greasy. 2. CLEVER tricky, crafty, smart, sophisticated, ingenious, creative, inventive, sharp. 3. SUAVE urbane, smooth, worldly. ANT. *1. rough, coarse, abrasive. 2. moronic, imbecilic, stupid. 3. clumsy, bumbling, unrefined.*

slide n. 1. CHUTE ramp, trough. 2. GLIDE slip, coast, glissade, skid.

slide v. glide, slip, coast, glissade, skid, sled, ski, skate, skim, drop, toboggan.

slight n. snub, insult, *cold shoulder, *slap in the face, *cut, insult, rebuff, *put-down, indifference, neglect. ANT. *courtesy, notice, kindness.*

slight v. snub, insult, *give the cold shoulder, *give a slap in the face, *cut, insult, rebuff, put down, neglect, overlook. ANT. *regard, notice, honor.*

slight a. 1. LIGHT frail, fragile, delicate, spare, slim, gracile, flimsy, attenuated, tenuous, weak. 2. SMALL, INSIGNIFICANT little, tiny, light, minute, fine, minor, subtle, trivial, negligible. ANT. *1. heavy, sturdy, rock-solid. 2. huge, gigantic, large, considerable.*

slim a. 1. SLENDER thin, narrow, lean, skinny,

willowy, reedy, twiggy, *thin as a broom-stick, *could fall through a flute and not sound a note, svelte, slight, tenuous. **2.** MEA-GER slight, scanty, small, *skimpy, inconsiderable, bare, deficient, scarce, remote. ANT. 1. *fat, obese, brawny.* 2. *large, considerable, great.*

slime n. mucous, mud, ooze, muck, mire, scum, sludge, *gunk, *goo.

slimy a. covered with mucous, viscid, viscous, muddy, mucky, scummy, sludgy, *gunky, *gooey, disgusting, repulsive, foul, vile, *gross.

sling n. slingshot, thong, weapon, stone-thrower.

sling v. throw, fling, hurl, cast, pitch, shoot, heave, catapult, chuck, toss, fire, launch.

slingshot n. SEE SLING

slink v. skulk, sneak, creep, steal, lurk, pussy-foot, prowl, slip quietly, tiptoe, move furtively, move stealthily.

slinky a. **1.** SKULKING sneaky, creeping, stealing, lurking, prowling, slippery, quiet, stealthy, furtive. **2.** Sl. GRACEFUL sinuous, feline, sleek.

slip n. **1.** FALL trip, stumble, misstep, slide, tumble, spill. **2.** ERROR mistake, lapse, slip of the tongue (lapsus linguae), slip of the pen (lapsus calami), *Freudian slip, faux pas, blunder, *boner, *howler, oversight. **3.** WOMAN'S UNDERGARMENT petticoat, chemise, lingerie. **4.** SLIP OF PAPER note, receipt, voucher.

slip v. **1.** FALL trip, stumble, misstep, slide, tumble, take a spill, topple, lose one's balance, take a header, go head over heels, flop. **2.** MAKE A MISTAKE make an error, err, let slip, lapse, blunder, bungle, *goof, *screw up, *blow it.

slippery a. **1.** SLICK icy, oily, greasy, slimy, waxy, smooth, sleek, satiny, glazed, wet. **2.** DECEIT-FUL deceptive, slick, *like a snake, shady, dishonest, sneaky, devious, shifty, treacherous, elusive, evasive. ANT. 2. *honest, reputable.*

slipshod a. careless, slapdash, slap-bang, sloppy, *half-assed, haphazard, shoddy, messy, slovenly, disheveled, bedraggled, unkempt. ANT. *careful, meticulous, groomed.*

slipup n. error, blunder, *goof. SEE MISTAKE

slit n. slice, tear, slash, gash, rip, rift, incision, rent, hole.

slit v. slice, tear, slash, gash, rip, incise, pierce, sever, split, rend.

slither v. slip, slide, sneak, crawl, *belly along, wriggle, slink, *snake.

sliver n. splinter, fragment, shaving, bit, snip, shard, segment.

slobber v. drool, slaver, dribble, salivate, drivel.

slob n. pig, hog, animal, *grunge, *grub, Neanderthal, *caveman.

slog v. plod, toil, laboriously make one's way, labor, grind, trudge, drag, pursue doggedly, put one foot in front of the other, persevere.

slogan n. catchphrase, motto, shibboleth, saying, jingle, battle cry, byword.

sloop n. vessel, craft. SEE SAILBOAT

slop n. slush, mush, snow, mud, swill, puddle.

slop v. spill, splash, overflow, slosh, spatter, gush.

slope n. incline, inclination, declivity, slant, pitch, grade, gradient, ramp, tilt, cant, lean, tip. ANT. *acclivity.*

slope v. incline, slant, pitch, tilt, cant, lean, tip, skew, ascend, descend.

sloppy a. messy, dirty, muddy, slushy, soiled, grubby, grimy, *grungy, wet, splattered, unkempt, bedraggled, slovenly, careless, slipshod. ANT. *neat, tidy, orderly, meticulous.*

slosh v. splash, slop, spill, overflow, spatter, gush.

slot n. **1.** HOLE slit, aperture, groove, channel. **2.** POSITION opening.

sloth n. laziness, indolence, idleness, slothfulness, shiftlessness, lack of ambition, sluggishness, lethargy, listlessness, inertia. ANT. *get-up-and-go, ambition, drive.*

slothful a. lazy, indolent, idle, shiftless, lacking ambition, unenterprising, sluggish, lethargic, listless. ANT. *energetic, ambitious, *go-getting.*

slouch n. *klutz, oaf, lout, *duffer, bumbler, clod, lazybones, idler, loafer, laggard.

slouch v. hunch, slump, droop, stoop, bend. ANT. *stand tall.*

slough n. swamp, bog, marsh, backwater, muddy hollow, mire. SEE SWAMP

slough v. shed, molt, discard, throw off, cast off, get rid of.

slovenly a. careless, slipshod, slapdash, sloppy, messy, shabby, bedraggled, unkempt, ungroomed, disheveled, untidy. ANT. *neat, trim, careful, meticulous.*

slow v. decelerate, brake, slacken, taper off, let up, restrain, check, restrict, curb, delay, hinder, moderate, take one's foot off the gas. ANT. *accelerate, speed up, *step on it.*

slow a. **1.** NOT FAST leisurely, crawling, dragging, lagging, *slower than a glacier, *slower than the Second Coming, *slower than cold molasses, snaillike, sluggish, slothful, plodding, gradual. **2.** LATE tardy, behind, delayed, overdue, detained, belated. **3.** NOT BUSY slow, inactive, sluggish, quiet, slack, off. **4.** PRO-

LONGED protracted, long, extended, interminable, drawn-out. **5.** STUPID obtuse, dull, dense, *thick, dim, dimwitted, retarded, moronic, bovine, *out to lunch, *dead from the neck up, *dumb as a box of rocks, *having the IQ of a woodchuck. ANT. *1. fast, swift, fleet, quick. 2. early, punctual. 3. busy, *hopping, *jumping. 4. brief, short, contracted. 5. intelligent, bright, smart, quick.*

slowdown n. downturn, slump, decline, fall-off, slackening, recession, depression, *bottoming out, economic cycle. ANT. *boom, upturn, expansion.*

slowpoke n. sloth, slug, laggard, snail, dawdler, foot-dragger, procrastinator.

sludge n. mud, ooze, mire, sediment, muck, oil, grease, goo, slime, *gunk, *goop, deposit, sewage, waste.

slug n. Sl. drink, swig, *hit, *shot.

slug v. hit, whack, slam, punch, *clock, pound, wallop, belt, clout, hit, whale, *coldcock, *clean one's clock, haul off on, *roundhouse.

slugfest n. fight, donnybrook, brawl, battle royal, *rumble, riot.

sluggish a. slothful, slow-moving, lethargic, listless, dull, sleepy, torpid, dragging, inactive, languid, inert, lifeless. ANT. *energetic, fast, lively.*

sluice n. channel, passage, waterway, flume, trough, floodgate.

slum n. ghetto, inner city, skid row, shanty town, warren.

slumber n. rest, *snooze, *shut-eye, land of Nod. SEE SLEEP

slumber v. rest, *snooze, *catch some shut-eye. SEE SLEEP

slump n. downturn, fall, decline, decrease, drop-off, recession, depression, crash, *falling-off, rut, *hard times. ANT. *boom, good times.*

slump v. **1.** DECREASE droop, drop, fall off, recede, crash, experience hard times, decline, slip, *go downhill. **2.** SLOUCH hunch, droop, sag, bend. ANT. *1. boom, expand. 2. stand tall, straighten.*

slur n. smear, *black eye, insult, blot, aspersion, slander, innuendo, insinuation, affront, *dig, stigma. ANT. *compliment, praise, commendation.*

slur v. **1.** SLANDER insult, smear, *give a black eye, cast aspersions, insinuate, affront, *dig, stigmatize, blot, blemish one's name, sully, disparage. **2.** MISPRONOUNCE garble, get tongue-tied. ANT. *1. compliment, praise, com-*

mend. *2. enunciate clearly.*

slurp n. Sl. sip, suck, slobber.

slut n. **1.** PROMISCUOUS WOMAN whore, prostitute, loose woman, hooker, harlot, nymphomaniac, *nympho, *floozy, *easy lay. **2.** SLATTERN *bag lady, hag, frump, sloven.

sly a. wily, foxy, cunning, crafty, tricky, clever, *cagey, artful, shrewd, sneaky, *weaselly, underhanded, furtive, secretive, stealthy. ANT. *artless, simple, naive.*

smack n. slap, blow, clout, clap, sock, hit, crack, spanking, cuff, whack.

smack v. slap, clout, clap, sock, hit, crack, spank, cuff, whack.

smack adv. directly, squarely, exactly, precisely, point-blank.

small a. **1.** LITTLE tiny, undersized, diminutive, short, wee, teeny, miniature, *pint-sized, *pocket-sized, puny, petite, Lilliputian, dwarf, pygmy, baby, minute, microscopic. **2.** SLIGHT paltry, insufficient, meager, inconsiderable, poor, picayune, modest, trivial. **3.** MINOR insignificant, trivial, light, trifling, unimportant, inconsequential, bush-league, *rinky-dink. **4.** SMALL-MINDED mean, narrow-minded, petty, selfish, cheap, ignoble, vindictive, prejudiced, grudging. ANT. *1. large, huge, gigantic, towering. 2. generous, rich, lavish, considerable. 3. important, major, big, consequential. 4. generous, liberal-minded, noble.*

small-minded a. mean, narrow-minded, petty, selfish, cheap, ignoble, vindictive, prejudice, grudging, ANT. *broad-minded, liberal-minded, noble, generous.*

small talk n. polite chatter, pleasantry, chitchat, light talk, idle chatter.

small-time a. minor, bush-league, *one-horse, petty, *low-rent, piddling, *tinhorn.

smart v. sting, burn, tingle, throb, hurt, ache, stab.

smart a. **1.** INTELLIGENT bright, brilliant, sharp, knowledgeable, educated, *savvy, astute, *brainy, learned, clever, genius, wise, keen, witty, *on the ball. **2.** NEAT spruce, trim, groomed, stylish, chic, dapper, natty, elegant, dashing. **3.** STINGING harsh, painful, rough, hard, sharp. **4.** BRISK vigorous, lively, energetic. ANT. *1. stupid, dumb, retarded, moronic, slow, dense. 2. sloppy, bedraggled, unfashionable, frumpy. 3. soft, gentle, mild.*

smart-aleck n. *wise guy, *wisenheimer, *smart ass, *comedian, *bigmouth, *know-it-all, *wise apple.

smart-alecky a. *wise, *wise-assed, *smart-assed, *smartmouthed, cheeky, flip, sassy, impudent, cocky, nervy.

smart-ass n. Sl. SEE SMART-ALECK

smash n. **1.** COLLISION crash, wreck, shattering, breakup, burst, smashup, crack, blow, collapse. **2.** SUCCESS winner, hit, sensation, sellout.

smash v. shatter, break, hit, bust, burst, wreck, crack, splinter, pulverize, disintegrate, break into a million pieces, fracture, demolish.

smashing a. great, excellent, extraordinary, outstanding, superb, wonderful, terrific, splendid, exceptional, *spot-on. ANT. lousy, awful, terrible.

smashup n. wreck, collision, accident, *fender-bender. SEE CRASH

smattering n. small amount, slight amount, sprinkling, touch, dash, trace.

smear n. **1.** STAIN spot, smudge, blot, mark, splotch, smirch, streak. **2.** SLANDER defamation, mudslinging, denigration, slur, aspersion, character assassination, blot, stain, libel. ANT. 2. honor, praise, compliment.

smear v. **1.** STAIN spot, smudge, blot, mark, splotch, smirch, streak, dirty, daub, wipe on. **2.** SLANDER defame, mudsling, denigrate, cast aspersions, character assassinate, blot, stain, libel, drag one's name through the mud. ANT. 1. clean, wash, scrub. 2. honor, praise, commend.

SMEAR CAMPAIGN n. an underhanded campaign to ruin someone's reputation. The politicians launched smear campaigns against each other. SYN. mudslinging, character assassination, slander, public denigration, defamation of character, maligning, dragging one's name through the mud.

smell n. **1.** SENSE OF SMELL olfaction, perception. **2.** ODOR scent, aroma, fragrance, stink, reek, stench, fume, perfume, bouquet, emanation, whiff, essence. SEE ODOR

smell v. sniff, inhale, sample, get a whiff of, snuff, breathe.

smidgen n. bit, tiny amount, iota, trace, speck, sprinkling, pinch, jot, whit, scintilla.

smile n. grin, smirk, simper, beam, happy look, *grin like a snarl, *alligator smile, gap-toothed smile, snaggle-toothed smile, Cheshire cat smile, idiotic grin. "An inexpensive way to improve one's looks." —Anon. ANT. frown, scowl, black look.

smile v. grin, smirk, beam, smile ear to ear, smile broadly, smile like a Cheshire cat. ANT. frown, scowl.

smirk n. smile, simper, grin, sneer, leer.

smirk v. smile, simper, grin, sneer, leer, make a

face.

smite v. strike, hit, *whack, attack, beset, defeat, punish, kill, destroy.

smitten a. taken by, *head over heels, struck, in love, enamored, *swept off one's feet, infatuated, captivated, enthralled, having a crush on, stricken.

smock n. frock, camise, coverall, shirt, garment.

smog n. air pollution, haze, smoke, fog, pall, particulate, gas cloud, soot cloud, carbon monoxide. ANT. sweet pellucid air, *ozone.

smoke n. fume, gas, soot, vapor, exhaust, smog, carbon, reek, smaze, pollution, carbon monoxide.

smoke v. fume, give off exhaust, pollute.

smoked a. dried, cured.

smokestack n. chimney, flue, funnel, *stack.

smoky a. burning, thick, smoldering, fumy, gassy, sooty, polluted, reeking, choking, hazy, smoggy, foggy.

smolder v. **1.** BURN smoke, fume, combust, char. **2.** SEETHE stew, fume, suppress one's anger, simmer, fester, steam, boil over.

smooch v. Sl. kiss, smack.

smooth a. **1.** NOT ROUGH even, level, leveled, planed, unwrinkled, unruffled, flush, glossy, glassy, slick, sleek, satiny, silky, velvety, polished, glabrous. **2.** UNTROUBLED gentle, calm, serene, uneventful, peaceful, undisturbed. **3.** SUAVE slick, urbane, graceful, silver-tongued, *having savoir faire, polished, refined, practiced, facile, flattering, oily, unctuous. ANT. 1. rough, bumpy, lumpy. 2. troubled, rough, disturbing. 3. coarse, awkward, simple, bumbling.

smorgasbord n. spread, banquet, buffet, feast, meal, appetizers.

smother v. **1.** SUFFOCATE asphyxiate, cut off one's air supply, stifle, choke, strangle, throttle. **2.** SUPPRESS stifle, hide, conceal, put down, squelch, quash, muffle. **3.** EXTINGUISH put out, cover, snuff out.

smudge n. smear, blot, stain, mark, blotch, streak, blemish, smirch, smutch, spot.

smudge v. smear, blot, stain, mark, blotch, streak, blemish, smirch, smutch, spot.

smug a. self-satisfied, complacent, proud, *full of oneself, *puffed up, superior, pompous, pleased with oneself, self-righteous, holier-than-thou. ANT. insecure, self-doubting, sheepish, humble.

smuggle v. sneak in, bring in, run, *bootleg, import illegally, traffic, deal in contraband.

smuggler n. runner, *bootlegger.

smut *n.* pornography, *porn, obscenity, dirty talk, X-rated material, *raunch, indecent material.

smutty *a.* pornographic, obscene, dirty, X-rated, *raunchy, indecent, blue, prurient, lewd, filthy. ANT. *wholesome, G-rated, clean.*

snack *n.* bite, nosh, *munchies, light meal, tidbit, nibble, morsel, refreshment.

snack *v.* have a bite to eat, nosh, nibble, eat, *munch out.

SNAFU *n. Sl.* mix-up, *screw-up, mistake, confusion, disorder, mess, disaster, chaos, difficulty.

snag *n.* catch, obstacle, difficulty, stumbling block, hindrance, road block, impediment, hitch, complication, block.

snake *n.* serpent, ophidian, viper, python, anaconda, boa constrictor, rattlesnake, coral snake, adder, cobra, garter snake.

snap *n.* 1. CRACK crackle, pop. 2. CINCH *child's play, *breeze, no problem, *walk on the beach. 3. FASTENER clip, buckle, catch.

snap *v.* 1. CRACK crackle, pop, click. 2. COLLAPSE break, crack, fracture, burst, give way. 3. BITE nip, lunge at. 4. LASH OUT yell, bark, roar, shout, scream.

snappish *a.* irritable, cross, short-tempered, touchy, testy, crabby, grouchy, quick-tempered, waspish, peevish, *short-fused, edgy. ANT. *easygoing, good-humored, mild-mannered.*

snappy *a.* 1. LIVELY vigorous, quick, swift, instant, brisk. 2. STYLISH fashionable, chic, smart, dapper, sharp, natty. ANT. *1. slow, lifeless. 2. unfashionable, frumpy, dowdy.*

snare *n.* trap, noose, net, pitfall, *booby trap, decoy, lure, *set-up, *come-on, trick.

snare *v.* trap, catch, seize, snag, capture, bag, ensnare, land.

snarl *n.* 1. GROWL rumble, grumble, throaty warning. 2. TANGLE snag, knot, kink, twist. 3. COMPLICATION disorder, confusion, SNAFU, problem, hitch, catch, difficulty, trouble.

snarl *v.* 1. GROWL rumble, grumble, threaten, warn, bare the teeth and raise one's hackles. 2. TANGLE knot, snag, kink, twist. 3. COMPLICATE confuse, make trouble, mess up, *ball up the works.

snatch *v.* grab, grasp, seize, take, clutch, grapple, *snap up, pluck, snag, *nab, get one's hands on, wrest, swipe, kidnap.

snazzy *a. Sl.* stylish, sharp, flashy, smart, showy, snappy.

sneak *n.* weasel, snake, *snake in the grass, thief in the night, dastard, *eel, scoundrel, *backstabbing SOB.

sneak *v.* creep, skulk, pussyfoot, stalk, lurk, prowl, slither, move stealthily, slink, steal, *weasel.

sneaker *n.* running shoe, *hightop, sport shoe, tennis shoe, boat shoe. SEE SHOE

sneaky *a.* underhanded, sly, secretive, undercover, backdoor, stealthy, *weaselly, feline, stealthy, furtive, surreptitious, clandestine, devious, treacherous. ANT. *open, honest, aboveboard.*

sneer *v.* smile sarcastically, smile with contempt, mock, scoff, ridicule, make fun of, curl one's lip, taunt, smile with disdain.

sneering *a.* scoffing, mocking, disdainful, scornful, derisive, ridiculing, sarcastic.

sneeze *n.* reflex, ejection, sternutation.

sneeze at disregard, take lightly.

snicker *n.* snigger, snort, sniggle, giggle, laugh, chuckle, suppressed laugh.

snicker *v.* snigger, snort, sniggle, giggle, laugh, chuckle, titter, suppress a laugh, tee-hee.

snide *a.* derisive, sarcastic, malicious, nasty, cutting, insulting, mean, hurtful, low, insinuating, sly. ANT. *nice, friendly, kind.*

sniff *n.* inhalation, sniffle, snuffle, snort, breath.

sniff *v.* inhale, snuff, snuffle, sniffle, snort, breathe.

snigger *v.* SEE SNICKER

snip *n.* cutting, snippet, piece, scrap.

snip *v.* cut, clip, shear, crop, trim, dock, bob, prune, chop, shave.

snipe *v.* ambush, take potshots, shoot, hunt, attack.

sniper *n.* ambusher, gunman, assassin, shooter.

snippet *n.* cutting, snip, piece, scrap, fragment.

snippy *a.* curt, sharp, insolent, short, snappish, abrupt, impertinent, smart-alecky, brusque. ANT. *polite, courteous.*

snit *n.* fit, pique, tizzy.

snitch *v. Sl.* 1. STEAL pilfer, lift, pickpocket, shoplift. SEE STEAL 2. INFORM ON tell on, *rat on, *squeal, tattle, turn in.

snivel *v.* cry, whine, sniffle, snuffle, fret, whimper, blubber, boo-hoo.

snob *n.* elitist, *high-hat, *stuffed shirt, upstart, highbrow, parvenu, name-dropper. "One who thinks his shit don't stink." —Anon.

snobbery *n.* snobbishness, elitism, airs, pretension, pretentiousness, haughtiness, conceit, *snootiness, hauteur, superciliousness, pride, *high horse, class conscience, condescension. "The pride of those who are not sure of their position." —Berton Braley. "Pride in status without pride in function." — Lionel Trilling.

snobbish a. snobby, *stuck-up, *uppity, putting on airs, pretentious, haughty, conceited, *snooty, supercilious, proud, *up on one's high horse, class conscious, above it all, arrogant, hoity-toity, high-falutin, high and mighty. ANT. *down-to-earth, humble, modest.*

snoop n. busybody, eavesdropper, gossip.

snoop v. spy, nose around, pry, stick one's nose in.

snooty a. haughty, snotty, la-di-da, uppity. SEE SNOBBISH

snooze v. doze, nap, drowse, *catch some Zs, take a siesta. SEE SLEEP

snore n. *sawing wood, stertor, snorting. "That tuneful serenade of that wakeful nightingale, the nose." — George Farquhar.

snort n. snuffle, sniff, sniffle, honk. SEE SNICKER

snort v. snuffle, sniff, sniffle, honk. SEE SNICKER

snotty a. impudent, offensive, insolent, cheeky, flip, sassy, smart-alecky, fresh, snooty, sniffy, arrogant. SEE SNOBBISH

snout n. nose, muzzle, nozzle, beak, trunk, proboscis, nozzle. SEE NOSE

snow n. precipitation, flurry, flurries, hydrometeors, snowflakes, sleet, hail, blizzard, drift, slush.

WORD FIND

bump or mound of snow on ski trail: mogul

collapse on mountain: avalanche

glacial snow: neve

granules, old, refrozen: corn snow

house of: igloo

old, compacted snow: firn, crust

pellets of: graupel

shelf of snow that collapses and triggers avalanche: cornice

zero visibility due to blizzard: whiteout

snow n. Sl. *coke, *blow, heroin. SEE COCAINE

snow v. 1. PRECIPITATE flurry, blizzard, storm, sleet, hail, blow. 2. Sl. DECEIVE *buffalo, *bamboozle, mislead, *bullshit, *sell a bill of goods, *fast talk, *pull the wool over one's eyes.

snowy a. niveous, wintry.

snub n. slight, affront, cold shoulder, slap in the face, rebuff, cut, oversight, neglect, ignoring, insult.

snub v. slight, give the cold shoulder, rebuff, cut, overlook, ignore, neglect, insult, shun, *give the brush-off, pass over, insult, offend.

snuff v. 1. PUT OUT smother, pinch out, douse, extinguish. 2. SNIFF smell, snort.

snuffle v. sniff, breathe, snort, snivel.

snug a. 1. PROTECTED sheltered, under cover,

secure, warm, cozy, comfortable. 2. TIGHT close, body-hugging, close-fitting, restrictive.

snuggle v. cuddle, nestle, nuzzle, hug, curl up, *spoon together, hold close.

so adv. therefore, thus, hence, ergo.

soak v. saturate, wet, drench, douse, souse, steep, sop, impregnate, drown, flood, permeate, submerge, immerse. ANT. *dry, dehydrate, desiccate.*

soaked a. saturated, wet, drenched, sopping, sodden, soggy, drowned. ANT. *dry, dehydrated.*

soap n. detergent, suds, lather, wash powder, cleaning agent, cleanser, solvent, shampoo.

soap opera n. melodrama, show, drama, program, play.

soapy a. sudsy, lathery, bubbly, foamy, frothy, saponaceous.

soar v. fly, rocket, jet, sail, glide, wing, zoom, rise, go skyward, ascend, go aloft, cruise. ANT. *nosedive, drop, plummet.*

soaring a. high, towering, lofty, vertiginous, skyscraping.

sob n. weeping, cry, sniveling, bawling, whimper, wail, blubbering, moan.

sob v. weep, cry, snivel, boo-hoo, bawl, whimper, wail, blubber, shed tears, moan, mourn, lament.

sober v. sober up, dry out, *go through a detox facility.

sober a. 1. NOT DRUNK temperate, *stone cold sober, rational, lucid, clearheaded, *on the wagon, *detoxed, *dry, in possession of one's faculties, abstemious. 2. SERIOUS solemn, grave, unsmiling, somber, dignified, sedate, staid, earnest. 3. PLAIN quiet, understated, mellow, subdued, dull, drab, simple. ANT. *1. drunk, intoxicated, inebriated, *hammered, *drunker than a brewer's fart. 2. silly, giddy, jovial. 3. flashy, loud, ostentatious.*

sobriety n. abstinence, soberness, temperance, teetotalism, moderation, self-denial, self-restraint. ANT. *drunkeness, inebriation.*

sobriquet n. nickname, pet name, agnomen, moniker, *handle, assumed name, alias.

so-called a. professed, alleged, supposed, self styled, commonly named.

soccer n. football, sport.

WORD FIND

curving pass: banana pass, banana kick, curling the ball, bending the ball

dirty player: hacker

goalie's long kick: punt

illegal position: offside

issue a card for a foul: book, card, caution

keep the ball in midair by bouncing off body parts: juggling

kick ball between defender's legs: nutmeg

kick with legs upended high overhead: bicycle kick, scissors kick

officials: linesmen, referee

out-of-bounds sidelines: touch

pass then receive quick return pass: give-and-go

penalty situation in which one team is a man short: power play

positions: back, center back, center half-back, forward, fullback, goalkeeper (goalie), halfback, sweeper, winger

run the ball downfield with one's feet: dribble

soccer field: pitch

steal the ball from opponent: tackle

stop the ball's motion with body part: trap, kill

three goals scored by same player in one game: hat trick

sociable *a.* gregarious, outgoing, extroverted, friendly, amiable, folksy, social, warm, companionable, cordial, approachable, genial. "The art of unlearning to be preoccupied with yourself." —Oscar Blumenthal. ANT. *unfriendly, aloof, cold, reclusive.*

social *a.* **1.** COMMUNAL public, community, group, common, popular, civil, civic, human. **2.** GREGARIOUS outgoing, extroverted, friendly, amiable, folksy. SEE SOCIABLE

socialism *n.* Marxism, communism.

socialize *v.* be friendly, mix, mingle, fraternize, get together, befriend, associate, entertain, hobnob, *chum with. ANT. *withdraw, be reclusive, shun.*

social security *n.* retirement income, disability insurance, unemployment insurance, old age insurance, entitlement program.

society *n.* **1.** COMMUNITY civilization, public, people, mankind, humankind, humanity, populace, culture, the world, the nation. "The vital articulation of many individuals into a new collective individual." —Thomas Carlyle. **2.** ORGANIZATION alliance, association, club, group, sorority, fraternity, brotherhood, sisterhood, affiliation, institution, league, guild. **3.** UPPER CLASS upper crust, high society, the elite, aristocracy, nobility, gentry, beau monde, haut monde. ANT. **3.** *lower class, working class, hoi polloi, commoners.*

sock *n.* stocking, hose, hosiery, footwear.

sock *v.* hit, strike, punch, belt, wallop, smack, pound, slap.

socket *n.* fitting, receiving end, chamber, holder, mortise.

sod *n.* turf, clod, sward, divot, grass chunk, clump.

soda *n.* pop, soft drink, carbonated water, soda water, beverage, cola, ginger ale, root beer.

sodden *a.* soaked, soggy, wet, sopping, saturated, waterlogged, drenched, poachy, dripping, damp, moist, steeped. ANT. *dry, dehydrated, desiccated.*

sodomize *v.* engage in anal intercourse, engage in bestiality, engage in a perverted sex act, *cornhole, *ream, *go Greek.

sodomy *n.* anal intercourse, bestiality, abnormal intercourse, deviated sex act, pederasty, perversion, *cornholing, *reaming.

sofa *n.* couch, lounge, divan, davenport, chesterfield, love seat, futon, convertible.

soft *a.* **1.** YIELDING EASILY spongy, squishy, doughy, mushy, fluffy, cushioned, pliable, supple, malleable, flexible, ductile. **2.** SMOOTH fine, silky, satiny, downy, velvety, fine, delicate. **3.** GENTLE mild, light, slight, moderate, delicate, faint, mellow, muted, subdued. **4.** TENDER compassionate, kind, softhearted, merciful, easy, easygoing, humane, lenient, forgiving. **5.** EASY *cushy, simple, plush, *piece of cake, *a snap, *no sweat, unchallenging. **6.** FAT unfit, untoned, fleshy, blubbery, doughy. ANT. **1.** *hard, rock-hard, solid, unyielding.* **2.** *rough, coarse, abrasive.* **3.** *intense, strong, loud.* **4.** *hard as nails, merciless, cold, brutal.* **5.** *hard, demanding, challenging, stressful.* **6.** *hard, toned, fit, cut.*

soften *a.* moderate, mitigate, mellow, temper, diminish, ease, lighten, lessen, assuage, mollify, tone down, slacken. ANT. *harden, intensify, toughen.*

softhearted *a.* soft, tender, compassionate, sympathetic, merciful, easy, human, lenient, forgiving, *big-hearted, *having a bleeding heart, a *soft touch. ANT. *hard, merciless, brutal.*

softly *a.* tenderly, lightly, gently, mildly, slightly, moderately, delicately, faintly, easily. ANT. *intensely, strongly, loudly.*

soft-pedal *v.* play down, tone down, understate.

soft soap *n.* praise, cajolery, blarney. SEE FLATTERY

soft touch *Sl.* *softie, *bleeding heart, dupe, *sucker.

soggy *a.* saturated, soaked, sodden, drenched,

waterlogged, sopping, poachy, dripping, moist, damp. ANT. *dry, dehydrated, desiccated.*

soil n. earth, dirt, loam, humus, topsoil, ground, clay, terra firma, turf, loess.

soil v. **1.** DIRTY muddy, begrime, stain, smudge, spot, mess, smear, foul, besmirch. **2.** DISGRACE dishonor, malign, discredit, blot, defame, taint, drag one's name through the mud. ANT. *1. clean, cleanse. 2. honor, praise.*

soiree n. party, social gathering, get-together.

sojourn n. visit, temporary stay, stopover, layover, vacation, temporary residence.

SOJOURN v. [SO jurn] to visit or stay somewhere temporarily. *She plans to sojourn with her family in California.* SYN. stay temporarily, visit, stop over, tarry, reside, vacation, lodge, linger, *hang out for awhile.

Sol n. Helios, sun god, the sun.

SOLACE n. [SAWL is] a comforting or relief from anguish. *He took solace in the fact that work would be over in one hour.* SYN. comfort, comforting, relief, easing, consolation, succor, condolence, encouragement, cheering, buoyance. ANT. *pain, anguish, exacerbation.*

solace v. comfort, console, relieve, ease, condole, cheer up, encourage, hearten, *buck up, inspirit, buoy. ANT. *pain, anguish, aggravate.*

solarium n. sunroom, sun porch.

solar system n. planetary system. SEE SPACE, SUN

soldier n. **1.** WARRIOR fighter, fighting man, GI, infantryman, *leatherneck, *grunt, *dogface, service person, airman, marine, sailor, commando, gunner, bombardier, foot soldier, Green Beret, cadet, mercenary, cannon fodder, *storm trooper, *doughboy, draftee, enlisted man, enlisted woman, guerrilla, paratrooper, POW, MIA. "Food for power."—Shakespeare. "The sinews of war."—Niccolo Machiavelli. SEE ARMY, NAVY, WAR **2.** SUPPORTER booster, party member, worker, follower, zealot.

sole a. lone, single, solitary, alone, only, exclusive.

solely adv. only, merely, entirely, singly.

SOLEMN a. [SAWL um] serious, earnest, dignified, formal. *A solemn ceremony.* SYN. serious, earnest, dignified, formal, somber, sober, funereal, *no-nonsense, staid, grave, unsmiling, ceremonious, reverential, sacred. ANT. *jovial, frivolous, lighthearted.*

solicit v. **1.** ASK FOR plead for, beg, appeal, petition, implore, beseech, supplicate. **2.** PROPOSITION tempt, entice, accost, hustle, *drum up business, tout, hawk, peddle.

SOLICITOUS a. [suh LIS uh tus] concerned, worried, showing one's concern. *The mayor appeared solicitous about our problems.* SYN. concerned, worried, caring, attentive, troubled, apprehensive, disturbed, anxious, heedful. ANT. *unconcerned, untroubled, undisturbed.*

solicitor n. attorney, counselor. SEE LAWYER

solicitude n. concern, care, worry, regard, uneasiness.

solid a. **1.** HARD dense, firm, heavy, thick, rock-solid, compact, concentrated. **2.** STRONG sound, sturdy, stable, substantial, massive, hefty. **3.** COMPLETE unbroken, continuous, undivided. **4.** GENUINE, PURE unalloyed, unmixed, 100 percent, complete. **5.** UNANIMOUS undivided, of one mind, united, unified. **6.** DEPENDABLE firm, rock-solid, reliable, constant, trustworthy. ANT. *1. fluid, porous, gaseous. 2. flimsy, airy, unstable, delicate. 3. incomplete, broken, interrupted. 4. mixed, alloyed, impure. 5. divided. 6. undependable, shaky, unreliable.*

solidarity n. unity, unanimity, union, single-mindedness, oneness, harmony, accord, concord, consensus, strength in numbers. ANT. *division, dissension.*

solidify v. harden, set, stiffen, cake, concrete, gel, jell, thicken, congeal, clot, coagulate, freeze. ANT. *liquefy, melt.*

SOLILOQUY n. [suh LIL uh kwee] the act of talking to oneself. Also, the dialogue of a stage actor revealing his thoughts to the audience. *Shakespeare liked to use the soliloquy as a dramatic tool.* SYN. monologue, aside, apostrophe.

solitary a. lone, alone, lonely, lonesome, single, companionless, friendless, separate, solo, remote, by oneself, isolated, secluded, reclusive, desolate, forlorn, sequestered, hermitical, antisocial, cloistered. ANT. *social, gregarious, popular, mixing.*

solitude n. aloneness, seclusion, isolation, loneliness, privacy, peace and quiet, withdrawal, retirement, reclusion, remoteness. "The soul's best friend."—Charles Cotton. "Divine retreat."—Edward Young. "Often the best society."—William G. Benham.

solo a. alone, lone, unaccompanied, single-handed, unassisted, unaided. ANT. *accompanied, group.*

solution n. **1.** ANSWER solving, key, explanation, resolution, clarification, uncovering, interpretation. **2.** A MIXTURE dissolving, compound, blend, combination, emulsion, suspension.

solve *v.* answer, explain, clear up, figure out, work out, clarify, uncover, crack, fathom, resolve, decode, decipher, *put the pieces together, *put two and two together, unlock, *get to the bottom of, unravel. ANT. *mystify, confuse, complicate.*

SOLVENT *a.* [SOL vent] financially stable, able to pay one's bills. *The company remained solvent, even throughout the recession.* SYN. financially fit, *out of the red, *in the black, on sound financial ground, able to pay, able to maintain cash flow. ANT. *insolvent, bankrupt,* *in the red.*

somber *a.* gloomy, dark, depressing, black, bleak, dreary, mournful, melancholy, funereal, gray, solemn, grave. ANT. *bright, sunny, cheerful, jovial.*

somersault *n.* flip, tumble, roll, revolution.

somebody *n.* celebrity, *big shot, *bigwig, *VIP, star, superstar, *name, dignitary, personage, *heavy, *high muck-a-muck, luminary. ANT. *nobody,* *zero,* *second stringer.*

someday *adv.* one day, eventually, sometime, sooner or later, one of these days, in the future.

sometimes *adv.* occasionally, at times, now and then, every now and again, once in awhile, every so often, periodically, intermittently. ANT. *never.*

somewhat *adv.* rather, to a certain extent, pretty, fairly, partly, to a certain degree, *kind of, a little.

somnambulist. *n.* sleepwalker. SEE SLEEP

somnolent *a.* sleepy, drowsy, dozy, nodding off, half-asleep, *dopey, sleep-inducing. ANT. *wide-awake, alert.*

song *n.* tune, melody, ditty, ballad, serenade, lullaby, hymn, carol, number, *oldie, *golden oldie, *moldy oldie, hit, air, aria, glee, theme song, signature song, *cut, track. "Drippings from the heart." — Anon "The licensed medium for bawling in public things too silly or sacred to be uttered in ordinary speech." — Oliver Herford.

WORD FIND

advertising: jingle

award: Grammy

busy vocals with arpeggios, trills, runs, etc.: coloratura

catchy part: hook, chorus

collection: anthology

counterpointing vocal: descant

demonstration recording for contract-seeking musicians: demo

evening: evensong, vesper

funeral: dirge, requiem

improvisation: vamp

instrumental accompaniment, sung without: a capella

jazz vocalizations imitating instruments: scat

multiple-voiced: polyphonic

multiple-voiced, singing counterpoint: madrigal

multiple-voiced with same lines begun and sung at different times: canon, round

passage: refrain

popular in more than one genre or market: crossover hit

religious or from Scriptures: anthem, canticle, chorale, psalm, hymn

repetition of theme by two or more vocalists: call and answer

sailor's: shanty, chanty

triumph, of: paean

Venetian gondolier's: barcarole

words: lyrics

SEE MUSIC, OPERA, SING, SINGER

song and dance *n.* *line, *snow job, *jive, *bull.

son of a bitch *n.* *Sl.* *SOB, bastard, scoundrel, cur, *jerk, rat, *creep, cad, rogue, rascal, *asshole, *horse's ass, louse, *son of a whore, *prick.

sonorous *a.* resonant, resounding, deep, booming, loud, reverberating, powerful, full, rich, vibrant. ANT. *mute, silent.*

soon *adv.* shortly, coming right up, directly, presently, forthwith, anon, before long, promptly.

soot *n.* carbon, ash, grit, particulate, grime.

soothe *v.* calm, comfort, quiet, ease, salve, mollify, appease, pacify, tranquilize, relax, assuage, allay, soften, settle, lull, cool, relieve, lighten. ANT. *aggravate, exacerbate, intensify.*

soothing *a.* calming, comforting, quieting, easing, mollifying, appeasing, pacifying, tranquilizing, relaxing, softening, settling, palliative, relieving. ANT. *aggravating, exacerbating, intensifying.*

soothsayer *n.* predictor, prophet, seer, fortuneteller, forecaster, augur, oracle, diviner, psychic, Cassandra.

sop *v.* soak, saturate, wet, drench, steep, immerse, dip, dunk.

sophisticated *a.* **1.** WORLDLY worldly-wise, experienced, cultured, refined, urbane, *hip, *hep, *cool, cosmopolitan, citified, mature, adult, seasoned, *with it, knowing. **2.** COMPLEX complicated, advanced, highly developed, modern, elaborate. ANT. *1. simple, naive, unseasoned. 2. simple, unsophisticated.*

sophistication *n.* worldliness, experience, culture, refinement, urbanity, *hipness, maturity, seasoning, development, advancement, experience, knowledge. ANT. *simplicity, naivete, inexperience.*

SOPHISTRY *n.* [SAWF is tree] argument or reasoning that is clever but fallacious, deceptive or misleading. *His lawyer was adept at sophistry.* SYN. fallacious argument, deceptive reasoning, subterfuge, misrepresentation, chicanery, idolism, false reasoning. "To reason correctly from a false principle."—Delos Emmons. "The lawyer's chief weapon."—Michael Axt.

SOPHOMORIC *a.* [sawf MOR ik] immature, inexperienced or foolish, like a sophomore. *His jokes were painfully sophomoric.* SYN. immature, juvenile, inexperienced, foolish, silly, unsophisticated, naive, green, callow, reckless, childish, shallow. ANT. *mature, experienced, sophisticated, seasoned.*

soporific *a.* sleep-inducing, somnolent, somniferous, sedative, hypnotic, tranquilizing, opiate, narcotic, sleepy, drowsy, tired. ANT. *stimulating, energizing, invigorating.*

sopping *a.* wet, drenched, saturated, dripping, soaked, soggy, sodden, wringing wet. ANT. *dry, dehydrated.*

sorcerer *n.* necromancer, wizard, witch, warlock, magician, shaman, sorceress, sibyl, practicer of black magic, alchemist.

sorcery *n.* black magic, black art, magic, supernatural powers, witchcraft, necromancy, wizardry, mysticism, Satanism, voodoo, spellbinding, diabolism, conjuring, alchemy.

sordid *a.* dirty, filthy, foul, rotten, wretched, bad, mean, ignoble, base, seamy, immoral, corrupt, low, wicked. ANT. *clean, wholesome.*

sore *n.* wound, injury, lesion, cut, laceration, scar, scrape, bruise, abrasion, ulceration, blister, boil, painful area, tender area.

sore *a.* **1.** PAINFUL tender, aching, burning, throbbing, stabbing, hurting, smarting, stinging, sensitive, raw, bruised, irritated. **2.** ANGRY offended, mad, *pissed, irritated, annoyed, peeved, irked, indignant, resentful. ANT. *1. numb, healed. 2. pleased, delighted.*

sorrow *n.* **1.** GRIEF lamentation, sadness, heartache, heartbreak, heavyheartedness, melancholy, despair, depths of despair, misery, woe, mournfulness, desolation, pain, depression. "That winter of one's heart."—Anon. "A rainy corner in your life."—Jean Paul

Richter "The great idealizer."—James Russell Lowell. **2.** LOSS trouble, adversity, hardship, disaster, tribulation, affliction, misfortune, bad luck. ANT. *1. joy, happiness, lightheartedness. 2. fortune, good luck, blessing.*

sorrowful *a.* grieving, grief-stricken, sad, heartbroken, heavyhearted, melancholy, plumbing the depths of despair, miserable, woeful, mournful, desolate, pained, depressed. ANT. *elated, euphoric, happy, joyous.*

sorry *a.* **1.** CONTRITE remorseful, regretful, conscience-stricken, compunctious, guilt-ridden, apologetic, repentant, penitent, ashamed. **2.** SORROWFUL pitying, commiserative, sympathetic, empathetic. **3.** POOR inferior, cheap, bad, *crappy, worthless, pitiful, pathetic, paltry, mean. ANT. *1. proud, delighted, pleased. 2. uncaring, indifferent. 3. superior, excellent.*

sort *n.* **1.** KIND type, order, style, variety, brand, class, set, make, category, genus, race. **2.** NATURE quality, ilk.

sort *v.* classify, class, arrange, order, organize, categorize, group, file, alphabetize, systemize, catalogue, grade, rank. ANT. *mix up, jumble.*

sortie *n.* raid, charge, offense, attack, assault, sally, rush, mission.

so-so *a.* okay, fair, fair to middling, not bad, tolerable, passable, mediocre, run-of-the-mill, *nothing to write home about, average. ANT. *superb, first-rate, extraordinary.*

sot *n.* drunkard, drunk, *wino, *rummy, alcoholic, *boozer, drinker, *barfly, *alky, *gin hound, *souse.

soul *n.* **1.** SPIRIT entity, mind, self, ego, psyche, conscience, anima. "A guest in our body, deserving of our kind hospitality."—Hillel. "A portion of the Deity housed in our bodies."—Josephus. "The life whereby we are joined into the body."—Saint Augustine. "A god within each human breast."—Ovid. **2.** WARMTH OF EMOTION spirit, feeling. **3.** ESSENCE heart, vital part, meat, quintessence, pith, center. **4.** PERSON human, being, man, woman, mortal, individual.

soulful *a.* emotional, with feeling, deep, moving, meaningful.

soul mate *n.* lover, friend, confidante, companion, alter ego.

soul-searching *n.* introspection, self-examination, self-analysis, reflection.

sound *n.* SEE NOISE

sound *v.* **1.** MAKE A NOISE vibrate, reverberate, echo, resound, ring, resonate, boom, thunder, detonate, thud, slam, rumble, roar, bang, crash, crack, clap, blare, burst, crunch, clang, chime, ding, ping, jangle, tinkle, buzz, hum, drone, whir, purr, creak, rustle, swish, fizz, sizzle, grate, rasp, hiss, rattle, clank, honk, trumpet, squeak, squeal, whisper. **2.** SEEM look, look like, come across, read, give the impression.

sound *a.* **1.** IN GOOD WORKING ORDER healthy, fit, whole, solid, *in good shape, intact, strong, perfect, unimpaired, *running like a Swiss watch, normal. **2.** STABLE secure, safe, firm, reliable, on solid ground, on solid footing, solvent. **3.** ACCURATE valid, sensible, logical, rational, grounded in fact, judicious, true, correct, right-minded, intelligent, commonsensical. **4.** ACCEPTED established, orthodox, recognized, *tried-and-true, traditional, standard. **5.** THOROUGH solid, complete. ANT. *1. unfit, unsound, impaired. 2. unstable, insecure, insolvent. 3. inaccurate, unsound, invalid, nonsensical. 4. new, unaccepted, radical, heterodox. 5. partial, incomplete.*

soundless *a.* still, mute, quiet. SEE SILENT

soundproof *a.* soundproofed, silent, noiseless, insulated.

soup *n.* broth, bouillon, stock, consomme, bisque, pottage, chowder, stew, gumbo, borscht, minestrone, split pea, gazpacho, bouillabaisse, lentil soup, vichyssoise.

soupcon *n.* suspicion, trace, suggestion, hint, dash, drop, pinch.

sour *v.* turn one against, *turn off, disillusion, embitter, disenchant.

sour *a.* **1.** TART acid, vinegary, sharp, *mouth-puckering, bitter, fermented, bad, rank, spoiled, curdled, rancid, repulsive, unpalatable. **2.** SURLY cross, bad-tempered, irritable, testy, touchy, nasty, crabby, ill-humored, grouchy, morose. ANT. *1. sweet, sugary, saccharine, fresh. 2. sweet, good-natured, nice.*

source *n.* **1.** SPRING wellspring, fount, fountain, origin, beginning, start, dawn, root, foundation, provenance, derivation. **2.** REFERENCE authority, author, documentation, database, *horse's mouth, informant.

sourpuss *n. Sl.* *crab, grouch, *bellyacher, *picklepuss.

souse *v.* pickle, steep, soak, saturate, brine, marinate, immerse, dunk, plunge, submerge.

soused *a. Sl.* intoxicated, inebriated. SEE DRUNK.

souvenir *n.* memento, keepsake, relic, reminder, remembrance, memorial, token, trophy.

sovereign *n.* monarch, ruler, king, queen, crowned head, prince, autocrat, emperor, empress, czar, overlord, dictator.

SOVEREIGN *a.* [SAWV run] the greatest, supreme, ruling. Also, independent from the rule of others. *We studied the evolution of a sovereign state.* SYN. greatest, supreme, ranking, leading, preeminent, chief, ruling, dominant, kingly, queenly, royal, regal, monarchal, imperial, autonomous, independent, self-governing. ANT. *dependent, powerless, following, subject.*

sovereignty *n.* supremacy, independent power, authority, domination, dominance, dominion, preeminence, rule, jurisdiction. "Some power or other from which there is no appeal." — Samuel Johnson.

sow *v.* plant, scatter, seed, broadcast, strew, disperse, spread, imbed, drill.

space *n.* **1.** UNIVERSE outer space, cosmos, infinity, heavens, ether, *eternal horizon, interstellar expanse, *the great beyond, macrocosm, galactic expanse, solar system, galaxy, cooling fires of creation, interstellar regions, void, celestial sphere, vacuum. "A handful of dust which God enchants." — Theodore Parker. "A great smelting pot." — Chuang Tzu. **2.** AREA room, expanse, range, scope, elbowroom, capacity, volume, territory.

WORD FIND

distant, bright, mysterious object: quasar

galaxy we live in: Milky Way

gas cloud, massive: nebula

measurement, unit of: light year, parsec, astronomical unit

stars, mass grouping of: galaxy

SEE ASTRONOMY, MOON, PLANET, SUN, UNIVERSE

spacecraft *n.* rocket, rocket ship, spaceship, shuttle, orbiter, capsule, space probe, satellite, Apollo, Gemini, Mariner, flying saucer, UFO.

WORD FIND

activities of astronaut outside of spacecraft: EVA, extravehicular

activity, spacewalk

agency: NASA, National Aeronautics and Space Agency

astronaut's life-support cable used outside craft: umbilical

cancel mission: scrub

cancel mission in progress: abort

cargo: payload

chamber between pressurized and unpressurized compartment: airlock

distant measuring science: telemetry

electronic monitoring systems: avionics

entry into earth's atmosphere: reentry

firing of thrusters or rockets: burn

flight path: trajectory

fuel: hydrazine, hydrogen peroxide, LOX
LIQUID OXYGEN

gravity force equal to earth: g

gravity force in earth orbit: microgravity

gravity slingshot method to boost craft further into space: gravity assist

ground station: tracking station

hazardous flying sand grains: micrometeoroids

independent system on board: module, subsystem

launchpad pit: flame pit

loss of orbital altitude due to earth's pull: decay

orbit that matches earth's rotation: geosynchronous orbit

orientation in orbit: attitude

payload, launching into space: deployment

power source: solar cells, photovoltaics SEE FUEL

propellants that ignite on contact with one another: hypergolic propellants

radio signal from earth to spacecraft: uplink

radio signal from spacecraft to earth: downlink

rocket, extra lifting: booster

rocket, slowing or reversing: retro rocket

rolling craft to diffuse external heat: barbecue mode

shuttle's nickname: *flying brick

space probe nerve center: JPL, Jet Propulsion Laboratory

space shuttle nerve center: Mission Control

speed of sound, five times the: hypersonic (above Mach 5)

speed of sound: Mach

speed of sound, twice the: Mach 2

timespan within which craft must be launched: launch window

wall: bulkhead

spacey a. Sl. *spaced out, *lost in space, *in a fog, *out to lunch, out of touch with reality, eccentric, weird, *in a zone.

spacious a. roomy, commodious, large, vast, capacious, extensive, immense, voluminous, expansive, uncrowded, generous. ANT. cramped, crowded, confined.

span n. spread, reach, width, length, height, breadth, stretch, distance, period, time.

span v. cross, traverse, extend across, stretch across, reach across, bridge, arch over.

spangle n. paillette, sequin, glitter, bead.

spank v. swat, slap, smack, hit, strike, rap, paddle one's behind, take over one's knee, cuff, lick, wallop, thrash, whip.

spar n. pole, beam, mast, sprit, boom, yard, gaff.

spare n. extra, stand-by, backup, auxiliary, substitute, fill-in, surplus, leftover.

spare v. **1.** TREAT MERCIFULLY save, free, liberate, go easy on, forgive, excuse, pardon, exempt, release, let go, reprieve. **2.** GIVE UP part with, donate, let go, do without, grant, afford.

spare a. **1.** EXTRA stand-by, backup, auxiliary, reserve, substitute, fill-in, superfluous, emergency, odd, surplus, leftover. **2.** LEAN thin, skinny, slim, slender, slight, bony, anorexic, scrawny, lanky, rawboned. **3.** SCANTY meager, sparse, modest, frugal. ANT. *2. fat, obese, flabby. 3. rich, abundant.*

sparing a. **1.** FRUGAL thrifty, economical, *tight, stingy, cheap, saving, parsimonious, miserly, stinting, grudging, niggardly. **2.** SCANTY meager, sparse, modest, spare. ANT. *1. generous, charitable, giving, lavish. 2. rich, abundant.*

spark n. **1.** FLASH flicker, scintilla, flare, sparkle, glow, discharge, glint, glimmer, trace, tinge, particle. **2.** STIMULUS spark plug, goad, spur, motivation, impetus, inspiration.

spark v. **1.** FLASH flicker, scintillate, flare, sparkle, glow, discharge, glint, glimmer. **2.** STIMULATE ignite, start, activate, goad, spur, motivate, energize, propel, inspire. ANT. *2. extinguish, douse.*

sparkle v. **1.** FLASH spark, glitter, shine, flicker, scintillate, glint, glimmer, twinkle, wink, dazzle, shimmer. **2.** BE BRILLIANT be the life of the party, shine, effervesce, dazzle, be animated, be lively, be vivacious.

sparse a. scanty, meager, slight, scarce, thin, spare, spotty, scattered, few and far between, skimpy, poor. ANT. *thick, abundant, plentiful.*

Spartan a. disciplined, strict, rigorous, demanding, severe, rigid, abstemious, austere, simple, frugal. ANT. *undisciplined, lavish, luxurious, *cushy.*

spasm n. contraction, convulsion, jerk, twitch, tic, nervous tic, seizure, fit, throe, cramp, shudder, orgasm, cramp.

spasmodic a. convulsive, fitful, spastic, twitching, intermittent, sporadic, periodic, on-and-off, irregular. ANT. *regular, steady, continuous.*

spat n. dispute, quarrel, disagreement, argument, fight, tiff, row, squabble, *run-in, falling-out, misunderstanding.

spate n. flood, deluge, outpouring, overflow, downpour, freshet, inundation, heavy rain, cloudburst. ANT. *drought.*

spatter *v.* splash, scatter, spray, shower, sprinkle, scatter, dot, speckle, dabble, spot.

spawn *v.* produce young, reproduce, bring forth, generate, engender, bear, give birth to, beget, *hatch, create.

spay *v.* sterilize.

spaz *n. Sl.* *nerd, *geek, oddball, *goofball, *goober.

speak *v.* **1.** UTTER talk, say, state, mouth, voice, vocalize, articulate, verbalize, communicate, express, enunciate, pronounce, babble, blurt, cry, shout, bellow, shriek, rant, rave, exclaim, mutter, mumble, whine, murmur, whisper, stutter, stammer. **2.** MAKE A SPEECH lecture, give a talk, discourse, orate, address, hold forth, preach, pontificate, deliver a sermon. **3.** CONVERSE talk, chat, *shoot the breeze, confabulate.

speaker *n.* talker, lecturer, orator, speechmaker, spokeswoman, spokesman, keynoter, spellbinder.

spear *n.* lance, javelin, dart, bolt, shaft, harpoon, pike, trident, leister.

spear *v.* pierce, stab, stick, run through, impale, lance, puncture, harpoon.

SPEARHEAD *v.* [SPEER hed] to start, pioneer or lead. *He spearheaded the environmental movement.* SYN. start, pioneer, lead, *blaze the trail, *get the ball rolling, launch, originate, initiate.

special *a.* **1.** PARTICULAR specific, specialized, appropriate. **2.** DISTINGUISHED exceptional, extraordinary, distinctive, different, unusual, unique, out-of-the-ordinary, singular, important, *red-letter, momentous, marked, select. ANT. *usual, ordinary, standard, normal.*

specialist *n.* expert, authority, master, professional, connoisseur, ace, virtuoso, scholar, devotee. ANT. *jack-of-all-trades, master of none, amateur.*

specialize *v.* concentrate on, practice, major in, devote oneself exclusively to.

specialty *n.* line, forte, area of expertise, specialization, metier, major, bailiwick, profession, skill, strength.

species *n.* variety, class, line, type, sort, breed, order, genus, division, stripe, genre.

specific *a.* specified, particular, express, designated, explicit, precise, exact, clear, defined, spelled-out, unequivocal, unambiguous, obvious, concrete. ANT. *vague, indefinite, ambiguous.*

specifically *adv.* particular, expressly, explicitly, precisely, specially, exactly, clearly, definitely, especially.

specification *n.* detail, particular, item, spec, feature, ingredient, stipulation, measurement, size.

specify *v.* be specific, detail, spell out, be precise, name, designate, itemize, define, express, explain.

specimen *n.* sample, sampling, example, instance, exemplar, cross section, model, representative, individual.

SPECIOUS *a.* [SPEE shus] plausible but invalid, having only the appearance of the truth. *Lawyers are adept at putting forth specious arguments.* SYN. plausible, sophistic, seeming, conceivable, possible, misleading, credible, unsound, ostensible, deceptive, fallacious. ANT. *true, valid, unquestionable, genuine.*

speck *n.* bit, spot, fleck, particle, grain, drop, iota, mite, jot, dot, atom, molecule, crumb.

spectacle *n.* sight, curiosity, display, exhibition, show, scene, *eyeful, sensation, marvel, wonder, pageant, exposition, extravaganza, performance, parade.

spectacles *n.* specs, lenses. SEE GLASSES

spectacular *a.* striking, sensational, breathtaking, extraordinary, exceptional, staggering, *eye-popping, stunning, impressive, dazzling, grand, wonderful, magnificent, awesome, marvelous, glorious. ANT. *mediocre, dull, boring, *nothing to write home about.*

spectator *n.* onlooker, watcher, observer, viewer, witness, passerby, bystander, *rubberneck.

specter *n.* ghost, spirit, apparition, *spook, phantom, phantasm, bogey, poltergeist, wraith, shadow.

spectral *a.* ghostly, phantom, phantasmal, eerie.

speculate *v.* **1.** THINK ABOUT meditate, ponder, reflect, deliberate, contemplate, cogitate, weigh, ruminate, muse, *chew over, deliberate, *turn over in one's mind, mull over. **2.** RISK invest, venture, *toss the dice, buy stocks, sell stocks, gamble, *play the market, trade.

speculation *n.* **1.** THINKING meditation, pondering, reflection, deliberation, contemplation, cogitation, rumination, musing, mulling, weighing. **2.** THEORY guess, guesswork, assumption, conjecture, forecast, presumption, suspicion. **3.** RISK OF CAPITAL investment, venture, *toss of the dice, playing the stock market, gambling, trading.

speculative *a.* theoretical, hypothetical, conjectural, presumptive, questionable, assumed, suppositional, experimental, unproven, iffy, risky, unpredictable. ANT. *certain, sure, guaranteed, unquestionable.*

speculator n. guesser, theorist, gambler, stock trader.

speech n. **1.** SPEAKING communication, verbalization, vocalization, talk, expression, articulation, utterance, pronunciation, elocution, conversation. "The index and mirror of the soul." — Thomas Robertson "Speech is power: speech is to persuade, to convert, to compel." — Ralph Waldo Emerson. **2.** LANGUAGE vocabulary, dialect, idiom, tongue, vernacular, parlance, lingo, patois. **3.** LECTURE talk, address, oration, discourse, keynote, sermon, salutation, dissertation, recitation, soliloquy, stem-winder, filibuster, tirade.

WORD FIND

aptness in expression: felicity
art of word usage: rhetoric, oratory
ecstatic: rhapsody
figure of: metaphor, simile, litotes, trope
fluency, expressiveness: eloquence
graduation: valedictory
impairment: dysphasia, speech impediment, dysphonia
incoherent: gibberish, glossolalia
incongruous figure of speech: oxymoron
individual dialect: idiolect
individual dialect quirk: idiologism
informal, conversational: colloquial
insertion of words like "um," "like," "you know," etc.: embolalia
long and tiresome: screed
loss for words, be at a: aporia
loss of: aphasia, muteness
lying, artful: mendaciloquence
modulation, change in tone: inflection
obscuring: obfuscation
pompous: bombast, fustian
pronounce clearly: enunciate
pronunciation, poor or improper: cacology
recall word, inability to: lethologica
showing off one's education through: pedantry
slip of the tongue: lapsus linguae, Freudian slip
speaking easily, fluently: voluble
Ssss or Shh sound in: sibilance
style of: elocution, locution
understatement for ironic effect: meiosis
unexpressive: inarticulate
word and sentence construction: syntax

speechless a. tongue-tied, at a loss for words, mute, struck dumb, inarticulate, aphonic, aphasic, voiceless, silent, *choked up. ANT. *loquacious, talkative, *motor-mouthed, voluble.*

speed n. swiftness, quickness, velocity, fleetness, rapidity, celerity, hustle, promptness, acceleration, rush, pace. ANT. *slowness, sluggishness.*

speed v. rush, hurry, fly, zoom, race, whiz, go like the wind, hustle, dash, tear, sprint, *go like lightning, run, hightail, *go like hell, *floor it, accelerate. ANT. *move in slow motion, crawl, drag, *move slower than a glacier.*

speedy a. fast, quick, rapid, fleet, *quicker than greased lightning, expeditious, hurried, nimble, prompt. ANT. *slow, sluggish, slothlike.*

spell n. **1.** INCANTATION charm, invocation, hex, jinx, voodoo, hoodoo, magic, enchantment, bewitchment, entrancement, sorcery, mesmerism, hypnotism, trance. **2.** TIME period, interval, *stretch, course, run, turn, tour, shift, bout, episode, fit.

spell v. relieve, give a break, take over, stand in for, cover for, take turns.

spellbind v. enchant, entrance, bewitch, mesmerize, hypnotize, charm, fascinate, hold, rivet, enthrall, transfix.

spellbound a. enchanted, entranced, bewitched, mesmerized, hypnotized, charmed, fascinated, held, riveted, enthralled, transfixed.

spelunker n. cave explorer. SEE CAVE

spend v. exhaust, disburse, squander, pay out, *blow, use up, expend, fritter, consume, dispense, outlay, splurge, *fork over, deplete. ANT. *save, conserve, hoard.*

spendthrift n. squanderer, *big spender, *free spender, prodigal, profligate, wastrel, high roller. ANT. *Scrooge, miser, tightwad, *penny-pincher.*

spent a. exhausted, consumed, burned out, worn out, used up, blown, depleted, expended, drained, prostrate, *beat, *pooped, fagged out. ANT. *refreshed, energized, invigorated.*

sperm n. seed, semen.

spew v. gush, flow, issue, spit, eject, vomit, throw up, disgorge, expel, *blow lunch, *ralph, *hurl, *puke.

sphere n. **1.** BALL globe, orb, spheroid, globule, moon, planet. **2.** PROVINCE range, domain, realm, scope, territory, field, bailiwick, department, turf.

spherical a. globular, spheroid, orbicular, round, oval, elliptical.

sphincter n. constrictor.

spice n. seasoning, flavoring, flavor, herb, condiment, piquancy, zest, *zing, pungency, sharpness, bite, relish, excitement, allspice, angelica, anise, basil, bay leaf, black pepper, bouquet garni, calamint, capers, caraway seed, celery seed, chervil, chicory, chili pepper, chili powder, chives, cilantro, cinnamon, cloves, coriander, cumin, curry, dill, fennel, flaxseed, garlic, ginger, lemon grass, licorice, mace, marjoram, mint, mustard, nutmeg, oregano, paprika, parsley, pepper, peppermint, poppy seed, rosemary, saffron, sage, sweet basil, tarragon, thyme, turmeric, white pepper.

spice v. season, flavor, enliven, enhance.

spick-and-span a. neat, clean, trim, fresh.

spicy a. 1. FLAVORFUL pungent, *zippy, tangy, sharp, hot, zesty, seasoned, savory, lively, piquant, biting, aromatic, fragrant. 2. RISQUÉ racy, bawdy, suggestive, off-color, *raunchy, obscene, titillating. ANT. 1. *bland, blah, dull, tasteless.* 2. *G-rated, clean, wholesome.*

spider n. arachnid, *daddy longlegs, black widow, tarantula, wolf spider, violin spider, trap-door spider.

WORD FIND

web-spinning appendage: spinneret

spiel n. Sl. sales pitch, speech, talk, *line, *song and dance, hard sell.

spiffy a. Sl. spruce, dapper, smart, neat, trim, sharp, well-dressed, natty. ANT. *disheveled, bedraggled, frumpy.*

spigot n. tap, faucet, valve, cock.

spike n. nail, bolt.

spill n. tumble, *header. SEE FALL

spill v. 1. SLOP overflow, slosh, dribble, pour, run over, brim over, splatter, splash. 2. DIVULGE *spill the beans, *let the cat out of the bag, disclose, make known, reveal, confess, *sing.

spin n. rotation, twirl, roll, twist, revolution, English.

spin v. 1. ROTATE twirl, roll, revolve, go 'round, whirl, gyrate, wheel, pivot, reel, pirouette. 2. TELL weave, fabricate, narrate, concoct.

spindle n. shaft, rod, pin, axis, axle.

spindly a. thin, slim, slender, scrawny, bony, long, tall, lanky, gangling, weak, frail. ANT. *fat, squat, stout.*

spindrift n. sea spray, foam, scud.

spine n. 1. BACKBONE vertebrae, spinal column. 2. NEEDLE thorn, prickle, barb, quill. 3. WILLPOWER intestinal fortitude, determination, courage, pluck, resolve. ANT. *spinelessness, ir-*resolution.

spineless a. 1. INVERTEBRATE 2. COWARDLY *wimpy, irresolute, *chicken, weak, weak-willed, timid, lily-livered, without backbone, *gutless, fainthearted. ANT. 2. *tough, determined, courageous, resolute.*

spin-off n. by-product, offshoot, outgrowth, offspring, derivative.

spinster n. old maid, widow, divorcee, femme sole, single woman.

spiny a. barbed, spiked, tined, pronged, bristly, hispid, thorny, prickly.

spiral n. helix, corkscrew, coil, gyre, curlicue, vortex, whirlpool, eddy, whorl.

spiral a. helical, coiled, winding, corkscrew, twisted, whorled, spiroid, turbinate, volute, curled, scrolled, cochleate.

spire n. steeple, belfry, tower, bell tower, fleche, campanile, minaret, shaft, peak, pinnacle.

spirit n. 1. SOUL consciousness, anima, life breath, mind, psyche, self, heart, ego. "The life of God within us."—Saint Teresa. "A vital breath of more ethereal air."—H.W. Longfellow. "An inward flame; a lamp the world blows upon but never puts out."—Margot Asquith. 2. GHOST phantom, phantasm, spook, apparition, specter, poltergeist, shadow, supernatural entity, wraith, presence. 3. MOOD disposition, frame of mind, attitude, humor, feeling, temper, morale, tone, outlook. 4. LIVELINESS vigor, vitality, vivacity, energy, animation, enthusiasm, eagerness, zeal, ardor, courage, bravery. 5. MEANING intention, intent, sense, aim, purpose.

spirited a. lively, energetic, dynamic, animated, vivacious, fiery, *charged, eager, enthusiastic, zealous, effervescent, spunky, perky. ANT. *dead, slothful, lifeless, dispirited.*

spiritless a. listless, *out of it, *dead, suffering from malaise, *down in the dumps, depressed, *bummed out, melancholy, indifferent, lifeless, slothful, sluggish, passionless. ANT. *spirited, *charged, lively.*

spiritual a. 1. OF THE SOUL incorporeal, immaterial, extramundane, unearthly, otherworldly, ethereal, metaphysical. 2. RELIGIOUS sacred, devotional, holy, divine, pious, godly, pure, righteous, heavenly. ANT. 1. *of the body, corporeal, of the flesh.* 2. *secular, worldly.*

spit n. 1. SALIVA spittle, drool, *loogie, sputum, slaver, expectoration, *clam. 2. SKEWER broach, rotisserie, pin.

spit v. expectorate, hawk, *hawk a loogie, *hawk up a clam, spray, drool, dribble.

spite *n.* malice, ill will, grudge, hard feelings, resentment, malevolence, maliciousness, vindictiveness, vengeance, hate, meanness. ANT. *goodwill, warmth, affection.*

spite *v.* hurt, injure, offend, get back at, harass, annoy, frustrate, be nasty. ANT. **give a hand, help, be nice to.*

spiteful *a.* malicious, viperous, venomous, vindictive, vengeful, nasty, resentful, mean, catty, hateful, malevolent, vicious, bitter. ANT. *sweet, nice, helpful.*

spitting image *n.* mirror image, twin, likeness.

spittle *n.* SEE SPIT

spittoon *n.* cuspidor.

splash *n.* **1.** SPLATTER squirt, jet, spurt, spray, sprinkle, slosh, slop, plop, *kerplunk. **2.** SMALL AMOUNT drop, touch. **3.** SPECTACLE display, sensation, show.

splash *v.* splatter, squirt, jet, spurt, spray, sprinkle, slosh, slop, plop, *kerplunk.

splatter *v.* splash, spray, sprinkle spatter, streak, stain.

splay *v.* spread, expand, extend.

spleen *n.* malice, spite, hatred, ill will, hard feelings, venom, resentment, malevolence, petulance, waspishness, grouchiness. ANT. *warmth, friendliness, affection, good humor.*

splendid *a.* **1.** LUSTROUS, MAGNIFICENT shining, brilliant, splendiferous, dazzling, gorgeous, luxurious, sumptuous, elegant, *ritzy, *posh. **2.** EXCELLENT exceptional, great, fabulous, fantastic, wonderful, outstanding, fine, superb, sterling. ANT. *1. drab, dull, poor. 2. poor, inferior, awful, lousy.*

splendor *n.* **1.** BRILLIANCE luster, brightness, shine, resplendence, radiance, glitter. **2.** MAGNIFICENCE glory, grandeur, pomp, show, spectacle.

splenetic *a.* irritable, grouchy, bad-tempered, nasty, waspish, petulant, crabby, grumpy, peevish, sour. ANT. *good-humored, easygoing.*

splice *v.* join, unite, wed, weave together, bind, connect, twine, braid.

splinter *n.* sliver, fragment, bit, shiver, shard.

splinter *v.* split, break, fragment, crack, separate.

split *n.* **1.** BREAK crack, tear, fragmenting, separation, splintering, rip, slash, gash, rupture, rift, cleft. **2.** DIVISION OR DIFFERENCE OF OPINION schism, dissension, fragmentation, disunion, breach, rift.

split *v.* **1.** BREAK splinter, separate, divide, sever, crack, tear, cleave, fragment, rip, slash, rupture, halve. **2.** BE AT ODDS be at opposite ends of the spectrum, polarize, fragment. **3.** DIVIDE

*divvy up, allocate, apportion, share, mete out, subdivide, distribute. ANT. *1. join, unite, bind. 2. unite.*

split up *v.* break up, separate, divorce, go separate ways, part company.

splotch *n.* spot, stain, blob, mark, splash, smudge.

splurge *v.* indulge, *spend like there's no tomorrow, *blow, squander, *spend like a drunken sailor, *go overboard, *go whole hog, be extravagant. ANT. *conserve, *tighten one's belt, *pinch pennies.*

splutter *v.* sputter, spit, hiss, spatter, *spray, stumble, stammer, stutter, *trip over one's words.

spoil *v.* **1.** DAMAGE ruin, destroy, injure, impair, wreck, harm, *mess up, *louse up, demolish, mar, blemish. **2.** OVERINDULGE pamper, coddle, mollycoddle, cosset, baby, wait on, cater to, *kill with kindness, overprotect, smother, lavish, shelter. **3.** DECAY rot, putrefy, go bad, decompose, sour, turn moldy, addle, deteriorate. ANT. *1. enhance, better, improve. 2. harden, be strict with, deprive.*

spoilage *n.* garbage, waste, refuse, damaged goods, rotten food, moldy food, putrid food.

spoiled *a.* **1.** DAMAGED ruined, destroyed, injured, impaired, wrecked, harmed, *messed up, *loused up, demolished, marred, blemished. **2.** OVERINDULGED pampered, coddled, mollycoddled, *bratty, cossetted, babied, overprotected, smothered. **3.** DECAYED rotten, putrid, gone bad, decomposed, sour, moldy, addled, deteriorated, rancid. ANT. *1. enhanced, improved. 2. disciplined, hardened, deprived. 3. fresh.*

spoils *n.* plunder, booty, property, pillage, loot, winnings, bounty, prize, reward.

spoilsport *n.* killjoy, *wet blanket, marplot, *party pooper.

spoken *a.* uttered, vocalized, said, articulated, voiced, expressed verbally, declared, pronounced, oral.

spokesman *n.* spokeswoman, prolocutor, *mouthpiece, *PR man/woman, voice, speaker, representative, deputy, intermediary, agent.

sponge *n.* *sponger, *moocher, *bum, *freeloader, beggar, *leech, parasite, *bloodsucker, *deadbeat.

sponge *v.* *mooch, beg, cadge, *bum, *freeload, scrounge.

sponger *n.* SEE SPONGE

spongy *a.* porous, absorbent, elastic, springy, mushy, boggy, marshy, moist, waterlogged.

sponsor n. underwriter, endorser, financier, supporter, backer, *angel, patron, guarantor, advertiser, advocate, champion, godfather, godmother.

spontaneous a. unrehearsed, off the cuff, extemporaneous, unprepared, spur of the moment, unplanned, impulsive, impromptu, *off the top of one's head, ad-lib, unpremeditated, reflexive, natural, instinctual. ANT. planned, premeditated, rehearsed, prepared, unnatural.

spoof n. parody, satire, *takeoff, *send-up, caricature, lampoon, burlesque, travesty, joke, comedy.

spoof v. satirize, parody, *send up, caricature, lampoon, burlesque, travesty.

spook n. ghost, specter, apparition, spirit, poltergeist, phantom, phantasm.

spooky a. ghostly, spectral, supernatural, eerie, weird, scary, unnerving, frightening, creepy.

spool n. bobbin, reel, cylinder.

spoon n. eating utensil, implement, silverware, ladle, scoop.

spoon-feed v. pamper, coddle, mollycoddle, baby, indulge, overindulge. SEE SPOIL

spoor n. trail, track, footprints, markings, droppings.

sporadic a. irregular, on and off, infrequent, intermittent, spotty, random, occasional, periodic, erratic, fitful, scattered. ANT. regular, steady, constant.

sport(s) n. **1.** ATHLETICS recreation, pastime, diversion, competitive activity, contest, competition, game, play, amusement, entertainment. "War minus the shooting." —George Orwell. "Nature's survival of the fittest organized and civilized." —Marc McCutcheon. SEE BASEBALL, BASKETBALL, BOWLING, BOXING, BULLFIGHT, FENCING, FOOTBALL, GOLF, MOUNTAINEERING, RACE, SKIN DIVING, SKATING, SKIING, SKYDIVING, SOCCER, TENNIS, VOLLEYBALL, WRESTLING. **2.** OBJECT OF TEASING butt, object of ridicule, laughingstock, *easy target, *fair game, *patsy, ridicule. **3.** JOKING AROUND fun, frolic, teasing, jollity, merriment, *jollies, antics, tomfoolery, skylarking, kidding, ridicule.

sporting a. fair, sportsmanlike, even, equitable, *on a level playing field, gentlemanly, honest. ANT. unfair, dishonest.

sportive a. playful, fun, romping, merry, joking, frisky, roguish, frolicsome, gamesome, jaunty. ANT. serious, grave, earnest.

sportscaster n. *play by play man/woman, color commentator, broadcaster.

sportsman n. hunter, fisherman, outdoorsman, adventurist.

sportsmanship n. integrity, honor, honesty, fairness, courtesy. ANT. dishonesty, cheating.

sportswear n. casual wear, informal wear.

sporty a. flashy, showy, loud, casual, informal. ANT. formal, conservative.

spot n. **1.** STAIN blot, speck, smudge, mark, splotch, discoloration, speckle, dot, patch, daub, smirch. **2.** LOCATION locale, position, point, place, site, area, section, setting, region, space. **3.** DILEMMA bind, *sticky situation, fix, mess, predicament, *pickle, jam.

spot v. **1.** STAIN blot, blemish, smudge, mark, discolor, speckle, daub, dirty, splash, sprinkle, fleck. **2.** SEE detect, recognize, make out, pinpoint, discern, spy, sight, catch sight of, find, identify.

spot-check n. random sampling.

spotless a. **1.** CLEAN immaculate, unstained, unblemished, untainted, laundered, washed, scrubbed, *squeaky clean, pristine, virgin. **2.** IRREPROACHABLE above reproach, pure, innocent, uncorrupted, above suspicion, *having clean hands, faultless, impeccable, virginal, chaste, *squeaky clean. ANT. **1.** dirty, filthy, spotty. **2.** faulty, defective, tarnished.

spotlight n. **1.** LAMP klieg light, *spot, floodlight, arc light, search light, pin spot, beam projector, *bon-bon, limelight, keg light, *ashcan. **2.** PROMINENCE recognition, notice, public scrutiny, *fishbowl existence, *public microscope, limelight, center stage.

spotlight v. light, illuminate, highlight, cast in the limelight, flood, focus on. ANT. obscure, conceal, veil.

spotted a. speckled, flecked, spotty, dotted, dappled, mottled, blotched, piebald, guttate.

spotty a. irregular, sporadic, inconsistent, intermittent, patchy, uneven, erratic, fitful, on again off again, *running hot and cold, variable. ANT. consistent, regular, even.

spouse n. mate, husband, wife, groom, bride, partner, companion, consort, *old man, *old lady, *better half.

spout n. nozzle, spile, spigot, faucet, lip, snout, mouth, tube, outlet, jet, discharge, spurt, geyser, squirt.

spout v. **1.** FLOW shoot, jet, discharge, spurt, squirt, gush, pour, surge, emit, spew, issue. **2.** RANT AND RAVE harangue, *shoot off one's mouth, *go on and on about, orate, gush.

sprain v. wrench, twist, strain, tear ligaments.

sprawl v. spread, stretch out, spread-eagle, loll, slouch, recline, lounge, slump, lie.

spray n. mist, drizzle, sprinkle, spritz, vapor, shower, *mizzle, spindrift, spume, jet, cloud.

spray v. atomize, drizzle, sprinkle, spritz, vaporize, shower, jet, mist, nebulize.

spread n. **1.** EXTENSION expansion, spreading, increase, mushrooming, growth, broadening, contagion, proliferation, diffusion, span, extent, range, scope, expanse. **2.** FEAST banquet, smorgasbord, meal, buffet.

spread v. **1.** UNFOLD open, unfurl, stretch out, stretch, sprawl, splay, uncoil, display. **2.** EXPAND extend, increase, mushroom, grow, broaden, proliferate, cover, disperse, pervade, permeate. **3.** SCATTER strew, distribute, disperse, sprinkle. **4.** DISSEMINATE broadcast, publicize, trumpet, circulate, publish, promulgate, advertise. **5.** APPLY slather, daub, smear, paint, plaster. ANT. *1. close, fold, curl, contract. 2. shrink, contract, recede. 3. gather, amass, pile. 4. censor, keep quiet.*

spree n. frolic, *field day, party, celebration, orgy, carousal, *binge, *tear, *bender, *drunk.

sprig n. twig, spray, nosegay, stem, slip, sprout.

sprightly a. lively, spirited, gay, energetic, brisk, vivacious, animated, playful, jaunty, chipper, blithe, cheerful, spry. ANT. *sluggish, lifeless, glum.*

spring n. **1.** LEAP jump, bound, vault, hop; bounce, resilience, elasticity, springiness, recoil. **2.** COIL shock absorber, spiral, helix, compression spring. **3.** WELL upwelling, gush, fountain, waterhole, *drink, pool, spa, baths. **4.** ORIGIN wellspring, source, fountain, fount, beginning, motive, impetus. **5.** SEASON March, April, May, *rebirth, *new beginning, blossoming time, mating season. "Nature's bait to mate."—Anon. "A true reconstructionist."—Henry Timrod. "Earth's annual facelift."—Anon. "An Audubonesque tableau of birds and flowers."—Anon.

spring v. **1.** LEAP jump, bound, vault, hop, hurdle, lunge, skip. **2.** SPRING BACK recoil, rebound. **3.** RISE *pop up, crop up, emerge, grow, emanate, stem, originate.

springy a. elastic, resilient, rubbery, spongy, bouncy, flexible.

sprinkle n. light rain, mist, drizzle, spit, spray, shower, dash, smattering, pinch, scattering, dusting. ANT. *deluge, flood.*

sprinkle v. rain lightly, mist, drizzle, spit, spray, shower, dash, sparge, scatter, dust.

sprint v. run, race, *go full out, dash, *run like hell, *beat feet, tear, rush, *hotfoot. SEE RUN

sprite n. fairy, elf, pixie, nymph, brownie,

gnome, goblin, hobgoblin, leprechaun.

sprout v. germinate, grow, shoot, bud, bloom, burgeon, develop, flower. ANT. *die, wither.*

spruce a. neat, trim, smart, natty, dapper, chic, well-groomed, sharp, *spiffy, *slick. ANT. *sloppy, bedraggled, frumpy, disheveled.*

spruce up v. clean up, neaten up, groom, *fix up, *doll up, *spit and polish, *gussy up, primp.

SPRY a. [SPRI] active and nimble, lively. *He was surprisingly spry for a ninety-year-old.* SYN. active, nimble, lively, vigorous, vital, hearty, *peppy, robust, brisk, quick, agile. ANT. *lifeless, lethargic, bedridden.*

spume n. foam, froth, fizz, cream, suds, lather, spindrift, scum.

spunk n. courage, heart, *guts, spirit, intestinal fortitude, pluck, backbone, mettle, nerve, *moxie, grit, *balls, mental toughness. ANT. *timidity, *wimpiness, cowardice.*

spunky a. courageous, brave, *gutsy, spirited, game, plucky, gritty, *ballsy, tough, nervy, lionhearted, red-blooded, resolute. ANT. *timid, *wimpy, cowardly.*

spur n. goad, impetus, incentive, motivation, *spark, *spark plug, stimulus, trigger, prod, jolt, *swift kick. ANT. *damper, discouragement.*

spur v. goad, instigate, provide an incentive, spark, stimulate, trigger, prod, jolt, *give a swift kick, prompt, incite, *goose. ANT. *put a damper on, discourage, slow.*

SPURIOUS a. [SPYOOR ee us] false, counterfeit. *The purported Jack the Ripper diary turned out to be spurious.* SYN. fake, ungenuine, bogus, phony, simulated, fraudulent, forged, sham, pseudo, mock, artificial, apocryphal. ANT. *genuine, authentic, real.*

spurn v. reject, refuse, decline, scorn, snub, *give the cold shoulder, *turn one's nose up at, *nix, *give a thumbs down, have no part of, rebuff, disdain, sneeze at. ANT. *embrace, accept, welcome.*

spurt n. **1.** SQUIRT jet, rush, gush, spray, spate, geyser, surge. **2.** BURST OF ACTIVITY rush, surge, flurry, flare-up, spell.

spurt v. squirt, jet, rush, gush, spray, surge, well up, spout, ejaculate.

sputter v. **1.** SPLUTTER *spray one's words, spit, stammer, stutter, *gibber-jabber, *trip over one's words, talk excitedly. **2.** SIZZLE spit, crackle, pop, snap.

sputum n. spittle, saliva, spit.

spy n. intelligence agent, secret agent, undercover agent, double agent, secret service agent, CIA agent, operative, snoop, investigator, *mole, *tail, informer, *private eye, scout. SEE SPYING

spy *v.* **1.** WATCH SURREPTITIOUSLY observe, stake out, keep under surveillance, shadow, *case, *tail, *check out, scout, reconnoiter, eavesdrop, *bug, snoop, investigate, pry, engage in espionage, infiltrate, gather intelligence. SEE SPYING **2.** CATCH SIGHT OF see, perceive, make out, detect, spot, sight, glimpse.

spying *n.* espionage, intelligence gathering, reconnaissance, infiltration, eavesdropping, bugging.

WORD FIND

agent who does not spy but works to confuse enemy: confusion agent

coded communication, science of: cryptology

code form, put information into: encrypt, encipher

concealed micropnone: *bug, listening device

decode: decrypt, decipher

decoding encrypted messages: cryptanalysis

expose as a spy: *blow one's cover, *burn

group: cell

infiltrator of enemy intelligence agency: mole, double agent

information, secret: classified information, top secret information

International Criminal Police Organization: Interpol

misleading or phony information: disinformation, counterintelligence

penetration into enemy's affairs: infiltration

safe haven or meeting house: safe house

secret code: cipher, password

traitorous work performed for enemy: collaboration

undercover, secret: covert

U.S. government agency: CIA, Central Intelligence Agency

squabble *n.* quarrel, dispute, argument, fight, tiff, disagreement, difference of opinion, controversy, row, wrangle. ANT. *agree, get along.*

squabble *v.* quarrel, dispute, argue, fight, have a tiff, disagree, have a difference of opinion, *lock horns, wrangle, contend. ANT. *agreement, harmony, accord.*

squad *n.* group, team, crew, company, unit, platoon, battalion, band, gang, *outfit.

squadron *n.* **1.** GROUP OF VESSELS convoy, unit, two divisions. **2.** FLIGHT FORMATION escadrille.

SQUALID *a.* [SKWALL id] filthy or run-down due to neglect. *A squalid row of tenement buildings.* SYN. filthy, dirty, foul, unclean, grungy, dingy, grimy, rat-infested, stinking, slummy, run-down, dilapidated, wretched, miserable, seedy, sordid. ANT. *clean, immaculate, well-kept.*

squall *n.* **1.** WINDSTORM gale, blow, gust, blast, tempest, downpour, cloudburst, shower, gale, blow, gust, tempest, storm, flurry. **2.** DISTURBANCE blow-up, furor, tumult, commotion, trouble, fuss. **3.** CRY scream, wail, shriek, bawling, yell, yowl, howl, outcry, outburst.

SQUALOR *n.* [SKWALL ur] filth and poverty, wretchedness. *Many in the inner cities live in squalor.* SYN. filth, poverty, dirtiness, foulness, grunginess, dinginess, slum conditions, seediness, wretchedness, misery, sordidness, *Dickensian poverty. ANT. *luxury, wealth, *bed of roses, *clover.*

SQUANDER *v.* [SKWAN dur] to waste. *She squandered the last of her inheritance.* SYN. waste, *blow, be extravagant, fritter away, throw away, *piss away, *spend like there was no tomorrow, lavish, play the profligate, dissipate. ANT. *save, conserve, be frugal.*

square *n.* **1.** QUADRATE quadrangle, rectangle, cube, box. **2.** PLAZA park, common, village green, piazza, quadrangle, quad.

square *v.* **1.** EVEN UP adjust, align, true, plumb, fix, rectify, straighten, fit, settle. **2.** SETTLE ONE'S ACCOUNTS pay off, clear, satisfy, discharge, balance, even up. **3.** AGREE correspond, match, dovetail, coincide, synchronize, coordinate, harmonize. ANT. 1. *misalign, skew.* 2. *go into debt, be in arrears.* 3. *disagree, contrast, contradict.*

square *a.* **1.** QUADRANGULAR four-sided, quadrate, boxy, equilateral, rectangular, cubelike. **2.** *Sl.* OLD-FASHIONED *straight, conservative, prudish, conformist, straitlaced, *uptight, prim. **3.** EVEN straight, level, true, accurate. **4.** HONEST straightforward, just, on the level, on the up and up, fair, equitable, ethical. ANT. 1. *round, circular, triangular.* 2. *hip, *cool, *with it, nonconforming.* 3. *uneven, inaccurate.* 4. *dishonest, unjust, unethical.*

squash *v.* **1.** SQUISH flatten, compress, press, smash, mash, crush, squeeze, compact, crowd, jam. **2.** QUASH bring to an end, stop, bring down, suppress, stifle, crush, squelch, *crack down on, *pull the plug on. ANT. 2. *fortify, strengthen, support.*

squat *v.* crouch, hunker down, sit on one's

heels, sit on one's haunches.

squat *a.* short, *built like a fireplug, stubby, stumpy, stocky, pudgy, dumpy, fubsy, thickset, tubby. ANT. *tall, gangling, lanky.*

squatter *n.* settler, claimant, applicant.

squawk *n.* **1.** CRY shriek, screech, call, scream, squeal, crowing, cackle, outcry, howl. **2.** *Sl.* COMPLAINT fuss, protest, objection, *bitch, gripe, shout, yell.

squawk *v.* **1.** CRY shriek, screech, call, scream, squeal, crow, cackle, outcry. **2.** COMPLAIN put up a fuss, protest, object, *bitch, *cry foul, yell, fume, gripe.

squeak *n.* cry, peep, cheep, whine, mew, squeal, creak, screech.

squeak *v.* cry, peep, cheep, whine, mew, squeal, creak, screech.

squeal *v.* **1.** CRY scream, whine, shriek, howl, wail, screech, yelp, squeak. **2.** INFORM *rat on, turn in, *drop a dime on, *snitch, tell, tattle, *sell down the river, *blow the whistle on, betray.

squeamish *a.* oversensitive, dainty, delicate, queasy, qualmish, prudish, prim, easily offended, easily shocked, having a weak stomach. ANT. *tough, *having a cast-iron stomach, thick-skinned.*

squeeze *n.* embrace, hug, clasp, *clinch, grip, compression.

squeeze *v.* **1.** PRESS compress, squash, squish, crush, contract, tighten, constrict, wring. **2.** HUG embrace, *bear hug, enfold, take in one's arms, clasp, *clinch. **3.** CRAM crowd, jam, pack, wedge, ram. **4.** EXTORT extract, wrest, blackmail.

squelch *v.* squash, suppress, silence, crush, put down, quash, extinguish, kill, smother, shoot down, stifle, defeat. ANT. *help, boost, strengthen.*

squib *n.* firecracker. SEE FIREWORKS

squint *v.* focus intently, peer at with half-closed eyes, look at narrowly, peer, peep, *screw up one's eyes, skew.

squire *n.* gentleman, landowner, proprietor, attendant, armor-bearer, servant, valet, escort, gallant, attendant, date, companion.

squirm *v.* wiggle, wriggle, writhe, twist, turn, twitch, contort, fidget, flounder.

squirt *n.* spritz, jet, spurt, spray, fountain, stream, gush.

squirt *v.* spritz, spray, spurt, shoot, spout, jet, stream, discharge, spew, gush, ejaculate.

squish *v.* compress, flatten. SEE SQUASH

stab *n.* **1.** PRICK, PAIN piercing, puncture, cut, gash, laceration, wound, sharp pain, shoot-

ing pain, twinge, pange, searing pain, ache. **2.** TRY shot, crack, attempt, effort, chance, *whirl, *go. SEE STAB IN THE BACK

stab *v.* pierce, prick, stick, slit, gash, puncture, run through, knife, cut, impale, penetrate, lance, plunge, thrust, gore. SEE KILL, MURDER

stability *n.* steadiness, sturdiness, firmness, solidity, equilibrium, balance, strength, soundness, permanence, constancy, dependability, reliability. ANT. *instability, shakiness, unsteadiness.*

stabilize *v.* steady, secure, firm, equalize, balance, strengthen, root, fix, ground, fortify, brace, set, support. ANT. *destabilize, weaken, undermine.*

stab in the back *n.* backstabbing, betrayal, treachery, *doublecross, Judas kiss.

stab in the back *v.* backstab, betray, *doublecross, backbite, sell out, sell down the river, give the Judas kiss, turn traitor.

stable *n.* barn, stall, shelter, pen, paddock.

stable *a.* **1.** STEADY secure, firm, sturdy, equalized, balanced, strong, solid, sound, rooted, fixed, grounded, fortified, braced, set, steadfast, immovable, permanent. **2.** MENTALLY SOUND sane, rational, compos mentis, sensible, of clear mind, composed, self-possessed, calm. ANT. *1. unstable, shaky, unsteady, unreliable. 2. unstable, crazy, insane, unbalanced.*

stack *n.* **1.** PILE heap, mass, mound, hill, load, assemblage, pack, bundle, sheaf, rick, cord, pyramid. **2.** SMOKESTACK chimney, flue.

stack *v.* pile, heap, amass, mound, load, assemble, stockpile, pyramid.

stacked *a.* *Sl.* built, curvaceous, full-figured, *top-heavy, *built like a brick shithouse, well-endowed.

stadium *n.* arena, bowl, sports complex, athletic field, football field, baseball field, ballpark, astrodome, circus, hippodrome, coliseum, ampitheater.

staff *n.* **1.** STICK rod, pole, shaft, walking stick, cane, alpenstock, crook, crosier, truncheon, shillelagh, mace, scepter. **2.** ASSISTANTS employees, work force, crew, team, personnel, help, cadre, cast, faculty.

stage *n.* **1.** PLATFORM rostrum, dais, *the boards, podium. **2.** THEATER show business, *show biz, footlights, set, limelight, spotlight, Broadway. SEE THEATER **3.** PERIOD phase, step, point in time, juncture, moment. **4.** LEVEL grade, rung, position, echelon, status.

stage *v.* present, exhibit, put on, perform, produce, arrange, engineer, mount, carry out.

stagecoach *n.* concord, coach, *mud wagon.

WORD FIND

escort who protected against robbers: shotgun rider, outrider

robber: road agent

section of road between relays of animals: stage

section of road comprised of several drives: division

section of road comprised of several stages: drive

trunk: boot

stagehand *n.* grip, callboy. SEE MOVIE

stagger *v.* **1.** TOTTER reel, sway, stumble, wobble, careen, weave, bob, lurch, falter, pitch. **2.** SHOCK bowl over, stun, *hit like a ton of bricks, take one's breath away, astonish, overwhelm, *blow away, jolt, take aback.

stagnant *a.* unmoving, still, standing, stationary, dormant, inert, dead, foul, stinking, stale, putrid, polluted, dirty. ANT. *fast-moving, flowing, fresh, clean.*

stagnate *v.* stand, idle, stop, be motionless, lie still, go stale, die, rot, decay, putrefy, deteriorate, stink. ANT. *move, flow, freshen.*

STAGNATION *n.* [stag NA shun] lack of motion or activity, decline, death. *The economy underwent a period of stagnation.* SYN. motionlessness, inactivity, decline, deterioration, death, stillness, quiet, inertia, dormancy. ANT. *activity, movement, growth.*

stagy *a.* theatrical, melodramatic, affected, *hammy, ostentatious, overdone, showy.

STAID *a.* [STAYD] sedate, restrained, serious. *He was a staid, bookish character who rarely laughed.* SYN. sedate, restrained, serious, sober, solemn, conservative, subdued, quiet, grave, dignified, proper, formal, decorous, settled. ANT. *wild, abandoned, jovial, frivolous.*

stain *n.* **1.** SPOT discoloration, streak, smudge, mark, blotch, speck, spatter, blemish, smirch. **2.** DISHONOR stigma, shame, guilt, taint, disgrace, *black eye, odium, infamy, blot.

stain *v.* **1.** SPOT discolor, streak, smudge, mark, blotch, speck, spatter, blemish, smirch. **2.** DISHONOR stigmatize, shame, taint, *drag one's name through the mud, disgrace, *give a black eye, tarnish, discredit.

stairs *n.* steps, stairway, staircase, flight, perron, spiral staircase, escalator, companionway.

stake *n.* **1.** POST stick, pale, picket, pole, stick, shaft, peg, upright, boundary marker. **2.** PRIZE pot, jackpot, purse, pool, winnings, bet, wager, ante.

stake *v.* **1.** MARK OFF demarcate, bound, limit,

delineate. **2.** BET wager, risk, venture, chance, gamble, pledge.

stale *a.* **1.** FLAT, TASTELESS flavorless, old, bad, musty, dry, hard, unfresh, moldy, bland, vapid, spoiled. **2.** UNORIGINAL old, overused, trite, hackneyed, clichéd, tired, threadbare, *old hat, stock, shopworn, dead, banal, vapid, insipid. ANT. *1. fresh, tasty. 2. fresh, original, new, imaginative.*

STALEMATE *n.* [STAYL mate] a deadlock or draw. *The negotiations ended in a disappointing stalemate.* SYN. deadlock, gridlock, standstill, *Catch 22, impasse, stop, standoff, check, draw, tie.

stalk *v.* hunt, pursue, sneak up on, follow, tail, trail stealthily, creep up on, shadow, track down, terrorize.

stall *n.* **1.** COMPARTMENT booth, stable, pen, shelter, cubicle, cell, cubby hole, stand, kiosk, enclosure, room, chamber. **2.** DELAYING TACTIC evasion, *footdragging, *stonewalling, ruse, subterfuge, ploy.

stall *v.* **1.** PLAY FOR TIME delay, *drag one's feet, *stonewall, slow down, postpone, filibuster, dillydally, procrastinate, waste time, hem and haw, put off, temporize. **2.** CONK OUT shut down, break down, run out of gas, *sputter and die. ANT. *1. rush, hurry, expedite.*

stallion *n.* stud, steed. SEE HORSE

stalwart *n.* supporter, staunch supporter, loyalist, upholder, mainstay.

STALWART *a.* [STALL wuht] strong, firm, brave, resolute. *A stalwart member of the Republican party.* SYN. strong, firm, robust, powerful, firm, hearty, vigorous, brave, courageous, tough, fearless, daring, valiant, heroic, resolute, determined, steadfast, staunch, unflinching, unwavering, tenacious. ANT. *weak, fearful, irresolute, halfhearted, spineless.*

stamina *n.* endurance, *wind, fitness, heart, strength, staying power, energy, vigor, aerobic power, *steam, conditioning, *legs, intestinal fortitude. ANT. *weakness, lack of fitness.*

stammer *v.* stutter, splutter, hem, trip over one's words, stumble over one's words, speak haltingly, falter.

stamp *n.* **1.** IMPRINT mark, seal, impression, symbol, brand, hallmark, emblem. **2.** CHARACTER kind, type, variety, sort, class.

stamp *v.* **1.** STOMP tramp, trample, step on, beat, pound. **2.** IMPRINT mark, seal, impress, brand, label, engrave, print, emboss. **3.** CHARACTER-

IZE brand, style, tag, distinguish, classify.

stampede *n.* rush, mad dash, flight, run, race, panic, scattering.

WORD FIND

slow or stop stampede by making cattle circle around: mill

stamping ground: n. stomping ground, haunt, hangout.

stamp out: v. extinguish, snuff out, crush, put out, squelch, stop, kill.

stance *n.* position, posture, standpoint, viewpoint, attitude, stand.

stanchion *n.* support, beam, post, upright, brace.

stand *n.* **1.** RESISTANCE defense, counter, repulsion, opposition. **2.** POSITION stance, view, viewpoint, standpoint, attitude, belief, point of view, policy. **3.** PLATFORM stage, dais, podium, rostrum, pulpit, lectern, witness box. **4.** GRANDSTAND bleachers, seats. **5.** KIOSK booth, stall, counter. **6.** TABLE holder, rack, shelf, cradle.

stand *v.* **1.** RISE TO ONE'S FEET, STAY ON ONE'S FEET be erect. **2.** ENDURE take, put up with, withstand, suffer, abide, tolerate, bear, weather, brave. ANT. *1. sit, recline. 2. *cave in, collapse, buckle.*

standard *n.* **1.** CRITERION guideline, norm, measure, model, ideal, rule, gauge, mean, median, specification, yardstick, principle, regulation. **2.** FLAG ensign, banner, pennant, streamer, Old Glory, Stars and Stripes, Union Jack.

standard *a.* regular, conventional, normal, stock, accepted, established, customary, classic, orthodox, usual, traditional, *run-of-the-mill, general, basic, *garden variety. ANT. *unconventional, unusual, out of the ordinary.*

standardize *v.* normalize, regulate, systematize, homogenize, equalize, regulate.

standby *n.* fill-in, substitute, backup, replacement, stand-in, understudy, pinch hitter.

stand for *v.* mean, represent, signify, denote, symbolize, indicate.

standing *n.* **1.** STATUS position, rank, stature, place, class, station, reputation, repute, place in the pecking order, prestige, eminence, importance. **2.** DURATION longevity, time, tenure.

standoff *n.* draw, tie, deadlock, gridlock, stalemate.

standoffish *a.* aloof, cool, cold, reserved, withdrawn, reticent, remote, distant, unsociable, antisocial, unfriendly, unapproachable, snooty, snobby, haughty. ANT. *friendly, warm, sociable.*

standout *n.* *phenom, winner, star, superstar, ace, *crackerjack, talent, *one for the books, *hit, *smash, *whiz kid. ANT. *secondstringer, *benchwarmer, *nothing to write home about, *just another brick in the wall.*

stand pat *v.* resist, resist change, stay put, *stick to one's guns, *stand one's ground, hold out, *die hard.

standpoint *n.* point of view, position, perspective, viewpoint, stance, outlook, belief, opinion, attitude.

standstill *n.* stop, halt, impasse, *dead end, cessation, deadlock, gridlock, *jam-up, *bottleneck, arrest, stalemate, draw. ANT. *progress, movement.*

stanza *n.* stave, quatrain, sextain, triolet, verses.

staple *n.* chief commodity, essential product, primary product, necessary product, basic, fundamental, essential, necessity.

staple *a.* principle, leading, main, basic, fundamental, chief, foremost, vital, important, necessary, essential. ANT. *secondary, minor, unnecessary.*

star *n.* **1.** sun, *flaming gasball, celestial body, heavenly body, burning orb, *cooling fires of creation, *candlelight of the gods, *heavenly beacon. "The forget-me-nots of the angels."—H.W. Longfellow.

WORD FIND

brightness measurement: magnitude

brightness, star with variable: variable star

bright star: Sirius, Polaris

chain of galaxies stretching across universe: Great Wall

chart of positions: ephemeris

closest: Proxima Centauri

cloudy, gassy birthplace of: nebula

collapsed star with massive gravity forces: black hole, neutron star, pulsar

concealment by another celestial body: occultation

constellation, group of stars not belonging to any: asterism

cool red star of massive proportions: red giant

double star that may appear as one: binary

effect that reveals whether star is approaching or receding: Doppler effect

erupting, brightening star: nova

exploding star: supernova

galactic-like superobject at ends of universe: quasar

galaxy, nearby: Andromeda

group of stars forming a distinctive configuration: constellation

group of stars in which earth is located: Milky Way galaxy

group of stars or island universe: galaxy, globular cluster

hazy group too distant to be seen with naked eye: stardust

mapping of: uranography

motion unrelated to earth's rotation: proper motion

referring to: stellar, astral

shooting star: SEE METEOR

tiny star with immense mass: white dwarf

twinkling of: scintillation

X-ray emitting: pulsar

SEE ASTRONOMY, COMET, CONSTELLATION, METEOR, MOON, PLANET, SPACE, SUN **2.** ASTERISK pentagram, pentacle, hexagram. **3.** CELEBRITY superstar, luminary, *name, *big-shot, *bigwig, *celeb, personage, leading lady, leading man, matinee idol, headliner. ANT. *nobody, unknown.*

star v. headline, be featured, lead.

star a. leading, prominent, outstanding, standout, celebrated, main, famous, renowned, illustrious. ANT. *unknown, secondary.*

starch n. **1.** STIFFNESS formality, rigidity, prudishness, decorum, manners, primness, propriety. **2.** ENERGY vigor, pep, vitality, drive, spirit. ANT. *1. casualness, informality, folksiness. 2. sluggishness, lethargy.*

starchy a. stiff, formal, rigid, prudish, decorous, mannered, prim, a model of propriety, stuffy, strict, conservative, puritanical. ANT. *casual, informal, relaxed.*

star-crossed a. doomed, unfortunate, unlucky, ill-destined, ill-fated, damned, cursed, condemned. ANT. *fortunate, lucky, blessed.*

stardom n. superstardom, notoriety, fame, acclaim, greatness, renown, celebrity status, prominence. ANT. *anonymity, oblivion.*

stare n. gaze, gawking, ogling, eyeballing, glare, withering stare, glower. SEE ANGRY

stare v. watch, gaze, gawk, gape, ogle, eyeball, glare, *rubberneck, peer, fix one's gaze on, *burn holes with one's eyes, *scorch with one's eyes, *regard saucer-eyed, stare down. SEE ANGRY

stargazing n. SEE ASTRONOMY

stark a. **1.** BARE desolate, unadorned, undecorated, plain, simple, spartan, austere, bald, naked, stripped, barren, bleak, empty, deserted. **2.** UTTER sheer, downright, outright, absolute, complete, unmitigated, out-and-out. ANT. *1. ornate, adorned, decorated. 2. partial, mitigated.*

starry-eyed a. unrealistic, impractical, romantic, optimistic, dreaming.

start n. **1.** BEGINNING commencement, opening, outset, onset, *blast-off, conception, inception, birth, origin, genesis, dawn. **2.** SHOCK fright, surprise, jump, startle, flinch, jolt, turn. **3.** HEAD START lead, advantage, *jump, handicap, allowance. ANT. *1. end, termination, finish, death.*

start v. begin, commence, open, *blast off, depart, *get the ball rolling, set off, get going, get under way, *dive in, initiate, conceive, give birth to, give rise to, found, pioneer, institute, create, introduce, invent; spring, arise, emerge. ANT. *end, stop, die, terminate.*

startle v. surprise, alarm, shock, frighten, scare, jolt, *give a turn, stun, unnerve, astonish, *scare the living daylights out of, *scare the pants off of.

starve v. go hungry, become emaciated, be malnourished, waste away, die of starvation, perish, succumb, be ravenous, be famished, fast, diet. ANT. *stuff oneself, gorge, *pig out.*

starved a. hungry, famished, starving, ravenous, *hungry enough to eat a horse, malnourished, emaciated, wasting away. ANT. *full, *stuffed, gorged.*

state n. **1.** CONDITION status, circumstances, form, shape, situation, mode, position, phase, stage, station, standing, footing, mood, frame of mind. **2.** NATION, STATE republic, union, commonwealth, country, people, land, government, kingdom. "Great engines moving slowly." — Frances Bacon. "A secular deity." — Georg Hegel. "Embodied morality." — Georg Hegel. "That cawing rookery of committees and subcommittees." — V.S. Pritchett.

WORD FIND STATE NICKNAMES

Alabama: Cotton State, Heart of Dixie

Alaska: Last Frontier

Arizona: Grand Canyon State

Arkansas: Land of Opportunity

California: Golden State

Colorado: Centennial State

Connecticut: Nutmeg State, Constitution State

Delaware: First State, Diamond State

Florida: Sunshine State

Georgia: Peach State, Empire State of the South

Hawaii: Aloha State

Idaho: Gem State
Illinois: Prairie State
Indiana: Hoosier State
Iowa: Hawkeye State
Kansas State: Sunflower State
Kentucky: Blue Grass State
Louisiana: Pelican State, Creole State
Maine: Pine Tree State
Maryland: Old Line State
Massachusetts: Bay State
Michigan: Wolverine State
Minnesota: Gopher State, North Star State
Mississippi: Magnolia State
Missouri: Show Me State
Montana: Treasure State
Nebraska: Cornhusker State
Nevada: Sagebrush State, Silver state
New Hampshire: Granite State
New Jersey: Garden State
New Mexico: Land of Enchantment
New York: Empire State
North Carolina: Tar Heel State, Old North State
North Dakota: Flickertail State, Sioux State
Ohio: Buckeye State
Oklahoma: Sooner State
Oregon: Beaver State
Pennsylvania: Keystone State
Rhode Island: Little Rhody
South Carolina: Palmetto State
South Dakota: Coyote State, Sunshine State
Tennessee: Volunteer State
Texas: Lone Star State
Utah: Beehive State
Vermont: Green Mountain State
Virginia: Old Dominion
Washington: Evergreen State
West Virginia: Mountain State
Wisconsin: Badger State
Wyoming: Equality State

state v. say, declare, assert, put forth, utter, voice, express, articulate, deliver, announce, speak, avow.

stately a. dignified, majestic, grand, august, imposing, distinguished, regal, royal, impressive, elegant, formal, palatial, ceremonial. ANT. *undignified, cheap, modest, poor.*

statement n. declaration, assertion, announcement, utterance, pronouncement, comment, remark, profession, proclamation, communication, verbalization, articulation, revelation, testimony, affidavit, deposition.

state of the art *cutting edge, *leading edge, *twenty-first century, advanced, new, modern, ultramodern, up-to-the-minute, trend-

setting. ANT. *antiquated, old-fashioned, outdated.*

statesman n. politician, diplomat, elder statesman, legislator, solon. "Somebody old enough to know his own mind and keep quiet about it."—Bernard Baruch.

static n. **1.** ELECTRICAL INTERFERENCE *atmospherics, discharges, noise. **2.** CRITICISM *flak, *grief.

STATIC a. [STAT ik] unmoving, stationary. *Electric batteries are a static power source.* SYN. unmoving, motionless, stationary, inactive, fixed, still, constant, inert, stagnant. ANT. *dynamic, active, moving.*

station n. **1.** DEPOT terminal, terminus, stop, end of the line, transfer station, substation. **2.** POST battle station, assigned area, department, position, location. **3.** HEADQUARTERS base, command post, nerve center, office. **4.** SOCIAL STANDING status, class, position, rank, caste, grade, footing.

stationary a. fixed, unmoving, immobile, motionless, static, anchored, rooted, at a standstill, stable, still, inert. ANT. *moving, mobile, on the move.*

stationery n. letterhead, writing papers, envelopes.

statistician n. statist, demographer, pollster, *number cruncher.

statistics n. facts, hard data, *stats, *numbers, percentages, *the book, track record, *dope. "The heart of democracy."—Simeon Strunsky. "Statistics are like a bikini. What they reveal is suggestive, but what they conceal is vital."—Aaron Levenstein.

statue n. statuette, sculpture, figure, figurine, colossus, bust, monument, icon, acrolith, rendering, carving. SEE SCULPTURE

statuesque a. tall, graceful, dignified, well-proportioned, beautiful, handsome, imposing, majestic, stately, like a Greek god.

statuette n. figurine, *Oscar.

stature n. **1.** HEIGHT tallness, size, length, measurement. **2.** STANDING status, rank, position, importance, eminence, station, development, growth, prestige.

status n. **1.** CONDITION state, shape. **2.** RANK position, standing, station, class, *place in the pecking order, *place on the corporate ladder, stature, grade, rating, prestige, distinction, eminence.

statute n. regulation, law, rule, ordinance, legislation, edict, act, bill.

staunch v. stanch, stop, close off, seal, lessen.

STAUNCH a. [STAWNCH] strong, steadfast, loyal. *Her father was a staunch republican.* SYN. strong, rock-solid, firm, steadfast, unwavering, resolute, faithful, tried-and-true, unflinching, devoted, stalwart, reliable, constant, red-blooded, dyed-in-the-wool. ANT. *weak, uncommitted, irresolute, unfaithful.*

stave off v. ward off, hold off, fend off, avoid, repel, block.

stay n. **1.** STOP stopover, holiday, visit, sojourn. **2.** POSTPONEMENT delay, suspension, deferment, reprieve.

stay v. **1.** STOP halt, freeze, remain, wait, abide, pause. **2.** VISIT stop over, sojourn, lodge, reside, live, dwell, reside. **3.** CONTINUE endure, last, persist, abide.

staying power n. endurance. SEE STAMINA.

STEADFAST a. [STED fast] constant, fixed, resolute. *He remained steadfast until the end.* SYN. constant, fixed, firm, resolute, resolved, steady, dedicated, devoted, loyal, faithful, settled, firm, persevering, stalwart. ANT. *irresolute, unfaithful, wavering.*

steady v. stabilize, secure, firm, balance.

steady a. **1.** SOLID fixed, stable, rock-solid, balanced, secure, anchored. **2.** CONSTANT unchanging, unwavering, continuous, incessant, unceasing, unremitting, nonstop, endless, perpetual, regular. **3.** FREQUENT regular, habitual, long-standing, loyal, faithful. **4.** CALM composed, controlled, cool, collected, levelheaded, self-possessed, poised. **5.** RELIABLE dependable, stable. ANT. *1. unstable, insecure, shaky, wobbly. 2. inconstant, irregular, broken. 3. rare, infrequent. 4. nervous, shaky, unstable, agitated.*

steak n. cut of beef, sirloin, T-bone, filet mignon, porterhouse.

steal v. **1.** TAKE burgle, burglarize, rob, filch, pocket, shoplift, thieve, *rip off, walk off with, swipe, pilfer, *pinch, purloin, misappropriate, lift, embezzle. **2.** SNEAK creep, prowl, skulk, slink, pussyfoot.

stealth n. secrecy, sneakiness, surreptitiousness, covertness, slyness, furtiveness, stealthiness.

stealthy a. secret, secretive, sneaky, surreptitious, covert, sly, furtive, clandestine, undercover, feline, quiet. ANT. *open, loud, public, conspicuous.*

steam n. **1.** VAPOR heat, condensation, moisture, cloud, mist, fog, fume, exhalation, gas. **2.** POWER energy, force, muscle, horsepower, drive, vigor, strength.

steamship n. paddlewheeler, sidewheeler, liner, river boat, *floating palace.

steed n. charger, stallion. SEE HORSE

steel v. harden, toughen, inure, brace, fortify, strengthen.

steely a. strong, tough, hard, hardened, severe.

steep v. soak, saturate, imbue, souse, douse, drench, sop, marinate, bathe, immerse, submerge.

steep a. **1.** PRECIPITOUS sheer, high, abrupt, vertical, vertiginous, dizzying, *steep enough to scare a mountain goat, sky-high, lofty. **2.** EXPENSIVE high, costly, exorbitant, unreasonable. ANT. *1. gradual, horizontal. 2. cheap, low-priced, reasonable.*

steeple n. spire, belfry, minaret, belfry. SEE TOWER

steer v. guide, direct, navigate, *man the helm, drive, pilot, take the wheel, skipper, captain, point, plot a course, *be in the driver's seat.

stein n. SEE MUG

stellar a. **1.** OF THE STARS astral, starry, galactic. **2.** OUTSTANDING excellent, shining, splendid, chief, leading.

stem n. stalk, branch, shoot, petiole, pedicel.

stem v. **1.** ARISE rise, originate, issue, spring, emanate, derive. **2.** STOP check, damn, plug, curb, end, arrest, slow down, staunch, block.

stench n. smell, odor, stink, reek, fetor, foulness, rankness, rottenness, malodor.

stentorian a. loud, booming, thunderous, powerful, resonant, deafening. ANT. *quiet, low.*

step n. **1.** FOOTSTEP footfall, stride, gait, pace, tread, walk, hobble, forward movement, footprint. **2.** DOORSTEP stair, tread, riser, rung. **3.** ACT action, maneuver, process, measure, phase, stage. **4.** LEVEL grade, degree, rung.

step v. stride, walk, shuffle, carry oneself, pad, tread, saunter, march, ambulate, traipse, trudge, plod, slog, hobble, limp, tiptoe. SEE RUN, WALK

step down v. resign, quit, abdicate, retire.

steppe n. plain, grassland, savanna, wasteland.

stereo a. binaural, stereophonic.

STEREOTYPE n. [STER ee uh tipe] a fixed idea, impression or characterization that ignores individuality, a habitual but often inaccurate characterization. SYN. preconceived notion, type, faulty characterization, classification, convention, mold, average, stock character, cliche. ANT. *individual.*

stereotype v. characterize, paint with a broad brush, tar with a broad brush, pigeonhole, typecast, generalize, brand, label, prejudge, categorize.

sterile a. **1.** UNPRODUCTIVE barren, fruitless,

childless, infertile, infecund, impotent, fallow, unprolific. **2.** GERM-FREE antiseptic, disinfected, pure, sanitary, aseptic, clean. **3.** DULL bland, uninteresting, lifeless, unstimulating. ANT. *1. productive, fruitful, fecund. 2. infected, unsanitary. 3. interesting, lively.*

sterilize *v.* **1.** DISINFECT purify, cleanse, decontaminate, sanitize, autoclave, fumigate, kill germs. **2.** GELD castrate, emasculate, spay, fix, alter, neuter. ANT. *1. infect, contaminate.*

sterling *a.* excellent, superb, A-1, first-rate, high-quality, superior, supreme, choice, select, the best, superlative, meritorious. ANT. *poor, inferior, second-rate.*

stern *n.* aft, rear, back.

stern *a.* **1.** HARD severe, strict, authoritarian, tough, rigid, harsh, frowning, hard-nosed, critical, demanding, dour, ironhanded, sober, grim, austere. **2.** FORBIDDING grim, black, dour, grave, cold, icy, frowning, hard, steely, stony. ANT. *1. soft, easygoing, permissive. 2. friendly, warm.*

stevedore *n.* loader, lumper, longshoreman, dockworker.

stew *n.* soup, mishmash, goulash, melange, hodgepodge, ragout, burgoo, chowder, beef stew, salmagundi, *mulligan stew.

stew *v.* **1.** SIMMER bubble, heat, seethe, boil. **2.** FRET fume, seethe, fuss over, worry over, brood.

steward *n.* major domo, seneschal, chamberlain, domestic manager, attendant, maitre d' hotel, butler, manager, administrator.

stewardess *n.* flight attendant, hostess, host.

stewed *a.* inebriated, intoxicated. SEE DRUNK

stick *n.* branch, twig, limb, stalk, bough, switch, cane, rod, pole staff, stake, stave, bat, club, billy club, truncheon, nightstick, cudgel, shillelagh, baton, wand.

stick *v.* **1.** ADHERE cling, hold, grip, hang on to, stay, cleave, bond, bind, fix, attach, fasten, paste, glue, tape, pin. **2.** PRICK stab, poke, jab, puncture, pierce, impale, penetrate, spear. **3.** PUT place, lay, set, position, deposit, drop. **4.** ENDURE persevere, persist, hold out, *keep on plugging, *stick to one's guns. ANT. *4. give up, quit.*

stick in the mud *n.* conservative, diehard, *fuddy-duddy.

stickler *n.* *nitpicker, *fussbudget, perfectionist, disciplinarian.

sticks, the *n.* *the boonies, boondocks, backwoods, country, *tall timbers.

stick-to-itiveness *n.* persistence, pertinacity. SEE PERSEVERANCE

stickup *n. Sl.* holdup, heist, mugging. SEE ROBBERY

sticky *a.* **1.** TACKY adhesive, viscid, viscous, gummy, gluey, gooey, glutinous, *clingy. **2.** HUMID muggy, steamy, sultry, close, clammy, hot. **3.** TROUBLESOME difficult, awkward, tricky, delicate, ticklish, thorny, painful. ANT. *2. dry, cool.*

stiff *a.* **1.** RIGID inflexible, unyielding, unbending, hard, firm, rock-solid, inelastic, impliable, tight, taut, *stiff as a board. **2.** TIGHT sore, not limber, cold, arthritic. **3.** THICK dense, solidified, firm, viscous. **4.** STRONG powerful, potent, intense, brisk, vigorous. **5.** HARSH severe, punitive, merciless, tough, stringent, extreme, sharp. **6.** FORMAL, AWKWARD wooden, forced, unnatural, labored, self-conscious, *uptight, constrained, prim. **7.** DIFFICULT formidable, hard, challenging, laborious, heavy, trying, complicated. ANT. *1. soft, flexible, yielding, pliable. 2. loose, limber, warmed-up. 3. thin, loose, watery. 4. gentle, mild. 5. soft, easy, merciful. 6. relaxed, *folksy, spontaneous, warm. 7. easy, simple, unchallenging.*

stiffen *v.* harden, firm, firm up, tighten, thicken, congeal, set, gel. ANT. *loosen, soften, liquefy.*

stifle *v.* **1.** SUFFOCATE smother, choke, asphyxiate, strangle, throttle. **2.** SUPPRESS repress, stop, check, curb, squelch, silence, shut up, still, quash, squash, put an end to, scotch.

STIGMA *n.* [STIG muh] something that brands one with a negative reputation, mark of disgrace or shame. *The stigma of mental illness.* SYN. mark of shame, disgrace, brand, blemish on one's reputation, blot, taint, scar, odium, dishonor, *black eye, reflection.

STIGMATIZE *v.* [STIG muh tize] to brand with a characterization that detracts from one's reputation. *It's easy to stigmatize the learning-disabled with negative labels.* SYN. brand, characterize, disgrace, ruin one's reputation, defame, *give a black eye, label, mark with shame.

stiletto *n.* knife, blade. SEE DAGGER

still *n.* silence, quiet, hush, peace, tranquility, serenity, calm, motionlessness. ANT. *racket, noise, bustle.*

still *v.* silence, hush, quiet, shut up, muzzle, subdue, calm, becalm, soften, tranquilize, pacify. ANT. *amplify, intensify, agitate.*

still *a.* **1.** SILENT quiet, hushed, noiseless, soundless, peaceful, tranquil, serene, *quiet as a mausoleum, *quiet as the grave, *silent as the vacuum of space, mute, subdued. **2.** MOTIONLESS becalmed, lifeless, static, unmoving, inert, dormant, idle, quiescent, dead. ANT. *1. noisy, uproarious, loud, deafening. 2. bustling, active, busy.*

stillness *n.* silence, quiet, hush, peace, tranquility, serenity, calm, motionlessness. ANT. *racket, din, noise.*

stilted *a.* pompous, overly dignified, affected, wooden, pretentious, bombastic, stiff, pedantic, grandiloquent, mannered, formal. ANT. *casual, natural, *folksy.*

stimulant *n.* excitant, *pick-me-up, energizer, jolt, *upper, bracer, *shot in the arm. ANT. *soporific, depressant, *downer.*

stimulate *v.* excite, rouse, energize, spark, stir, invigorate, initiate, prompt, *turn on, jolt, revive, incite, instigate, goad, prompt, *light a fire under, *fire up, *fan the flames, galvanize. ANT. *depress, *turn off, tranquilize.*

stimulating *a.* exciting, rousing, energizing, stirring, invigorating, bracing, exhilarating, heart-quickening, pulse-quickening, *adrenalizing, interesting, fascinating, thought-provoking, titillating, provocative, gripping, enthralling. ANT. *soporific, somnolent, boring.*

stimulus *n.* incentive, incitement, provocation, impetus, goad, spur, fillip, motive, push, spark, stimulant, impulse, *shot in the arm, *good swift kick, catalyst. ANT. *tranquilizer, soporific, depressant.*

sting *n.* **1.** INJURY INFLICTED BY INSECT OR ANIMAL bite, wound, venom, poison. **2.** PAIN burning, tingling, smarting, soreness, hurt, irritation, twinge, pang, painful sensation. **3.** POLICE ENTRAPMENT *sting operation, *come-on. **4.** SCAM swindle, *con, *flimflam, *grift, *suckering.

sting *v.* **1.** PRICK, BITE, WOUND envenom, injure, burn, stick, infect, urticate, nettle. **2.** HURT smart, burn, tingle. **3.** MAKE UNHAPPY distress, hurt, cut to the quick, insult, cut, grieve, offend.

stingy *a.* **1.** CHEAP tight, tightfisted, miserly, penny-pinching, niggardly, penurious, parsimonious, grudging, stinting, thrifty, frugal. **2.** SCANTY inadequate, insufficient, sparing, meager, skimpy, paltry, *measly, lean. ANT. *1. generous, charitable, giving. 2. generous, abundant, plentiful.*

stink *n.* stench, smell, odor, reek, foulness, malodor, fetor, *BO, putridness.

stink *v.* **1.** SMELL reek, fume, offend, *smell to high heaven. **2.** BE BAD *suck, *bite, *bite the big one, be lousy.

stinking *a.* smelly, reeking, offensive, malodorous, odiferous, fetid, foul, rank, noisome, spoiled, putrid.

stint *n.* task, duty, assignment, chore, job.

stint *v.* limit, restrict, scrimp, conserve.

stipend *n.* payment, allowance, wage, salary, fee, compensation, remuneration, honorarium, earnings.

STIPULATE *v.* [STIP yoo late] to specify a requirement, especially in a formal agreement or contract. *He stipulated in the contract that work would begin on the first of the month.* SYN. specify, lay out, require, spell out, detail, fix, set terms, contract, condition, designate.

stipulation *n.* specification, requirement, agreement, condition, obligation, article, demand, provision, proviso, item.

stir *n.* commotion, excitement, tumult, uproar, hullabaloo, ado, fuss, furor, pother, turmoil, bustle.

stir *v.* **1.** MIX mingle, mix, blend, commingle, churn, whip, beat. **2.** MOVE shake, wiggle, shift, budge, jiggle, flutter. **3.** EXCITE move, disturb, stimulate, rouse, electrify, spark, *work up, galvanize, prompt, awaken.

stirring *a.* rousing, moving, exciting, stimulating, electrifying, exhilarating, inspiring, *mind-blowing, dramatic, soul-stirring. ANT. *boring, soporific.*

stitch *v.* sew, fasten, thread, suture.

stock *n.* **1.** MERCHANDISE inventory, products, goods, supply, assortment, variety, array, range, stockpile, reserve, hoard. **2.** FARM ANIMALS livestock, herd, flock, horses, cows, pigs. **3.** ANCESTRY lineage, family, bloodline, pedigree, heritage, extraction. **4.** INVESTMENT shares, security, mutual fund. SEE STOCK MARKET **5.** RAW MATERIAL, MAIN INGREDIENTS makings, *fixings, essence, broth, foundation.

stock *v.* supply, provision, fill, provide, equip, stockpile, furnish, lay in.

stock *a.* common, in ready supply, in stock, *off the shelf, *run-of-the-mill, plain, garden variety, everyday, overused, tired, trite, hackneyed. ANT. *original, fresh, custom-made.*

stockade *n.* enclosure, fort, palisade, pen, prison, jail.

stocking *n.* sock, hose, nylon.

stock market *n.* stock exchange, stock brokerage, American Stock Exchange, Wall Street, New York Stock Exchange, NASDAQ.
WORD FIND
agent who buys, sells on behalf of another: broker
Amex: American Stock Exchange

average daily price of thirty blue chip companies: Dow-Jones Industrial Average

Big Blue: IBM, International Business Machines

Big Board: New York Stock Exchange

blue chip: common stock of a large, high-quality company

broker's frequent trading of client's stocks to generate more commissions: churning

buyer and seller: trader

buying from one market, selling to another at higher price: arbitrage

buying just before price drops, selling just before rise: whipsaw

buying strategy that is opposite from what most others do: contrarian

collapse of market: crash

collecting stock certificates as a hobby: scripophily

company's history, earnings, finances, circular of: prospectus

credit, buying securities on: buying on margin

corporate credit information, company that publishes: Dun and Bradstreet

declining market: bear market

diversified stock investment: mutual fund

dividends paid preferentially over common stock, stock with: preferred stock

dollar, stocks selling under a: penny stocks

earnings distribution: dividend

electronic display of trading activity: ticker

expert: analyst

Fed, the: Federal Reserve System, Federal Reserve Bank

51 percent of company's voting shares, owning: controlling interest

growing or rising market: bull market

high-quality, high-profile company's stock: blue chip

high-risk investing: speculating, taking a flyer

high-risk trader: speculator

holdings, investor's: portfolio

inexperienced investor: lamb

inflated market, downward trend that corrects: correction

investment services, ratings, index, company that offers: Standard and Poor's

load: service or sales charge

membership on an exchange: seat

moving assets to another investment: rollover

optimistic about economy: bullish

order to buy or sell at predetermined price: option, stop order

OTC: over the counter

overlooked stock with great potential: sleeper

pessimistic about economy: bearish

plunge dramatically, day on which stock prices: Black Friday, Black Monday

poorly performing stock: dog, turkey

private company offering shares for the first time: going public

privileged information, one who has access to: insider

privileged information, trading on: insider trading

purchase large volume of stock to control its price: corner, corner the market

reflects market as a whole, individual stock that: barometer, bellwether

skirt lengths, theory that market rises and falls with women's: hemline theory

speculating on a company takeover: arbitrage

stock owner: shareholder

stock's price divided by earnings per share: price-earnings ratio

takeover blackmail: greenmail

takeover of company with borrowed money: leveraged buyout

takeover, one who attempts a company: raider, shark

unstable: volatile

stockpile *n.* supply, reserve, hoard, store, amassment, nest egg, larder, cache, stash.

stockpile *v.* stock, hoard, store, reserve, amass, cache, stash, squirrel away, save, lay in. ANT. *expend, spend, deplete.*

stocky *a.* thickset, short, heavy, stout, sturdy, *built like a fireplug, stubby, pudgy, squat, husky. ANT. *skinny, tall, lean, lanky.*

stodgy *a.* uninteresting, drab, *blah, dull, tedious, *dull as dishwater, boring, wooden, dry, stuffy, formal, staid, old-fashioned. ANT. *exciting, lively, *hip, wild.*

STOIC *a.* [STOH ik] showing indifference toward pain, grief pleasure or any other emotion. *Although he was bleeding profusely, the accident victim remained stoic.* SYN. indifferent, impassive, cool, philosophical, stony, dispassionate, apathetic, uninterested, stolid, detached, resigned. ANT. *emotional, passionate, hysterical.*

stoke *v.* stir, turn the coals, tend, fill, refuel.

STOLID *a.* [STAW lid] showing little emotion, impassive. *The prisoner remained stolid throughout his sentencing.* SYN. emotionless, impassive, stoic, stoical, indifferent, apathetic, stony, disinterested, dull, phlegmatic, stupid, bovine. ANT. *hysterical, emotional, wild.*

stomach n. belly, abdomen, gut, midsection, intestinal cavity, digestive organ, bowels, viscera, esophagus, craw, rumen, *breadbasket, *spare tire, *beer belly, paunch. "The greatest of deities." — Euripides. "Nature's greatest slavedriver." — Anon "A portable stewpot." — Anon.

WORD FIND

backing up of food into esophagus, causing pain: reflux, pyrosis, heartburn

digestive chemical: gastrin, hydrochloric acid, pepsin

infant's stomachache: colic

inflammation: gastritis

lesion caused by too much acid: ulcer

muscular contractions that push food out of: peristalsis

rumbling: borborygmus

soupy mixture made from digested meal: chyme

tube leading to stomach: esophagus

upset: nausea, queasiness, indigestion, dyspepsia

stomp v. stamp, tramp, crush, squash, kill.

stone n. rock, boulder, pebble, granite, cobblestone, gravel, crag, jewel, gemstone, gem, precious stone, semiprecious gem, *ice, birthstone, bijou, diamond, emerald, sapphire, ruby, pearl, topaz, amethyst, tourmaline, onyx, garnet, zircon.

WORD FIND

bits and pieces: rubble, spall, grit

capstone on ancient monument: dolmen

cutter: mason

cutter, polisher, engraver: lapidary

cutting, polishing, engraving, art of: lapidary

excavation pit: quarry

fire-starting: flint

giant: boulder, megalith

globular stone with a crystal-lined center: geode

memorial pile or trailmarker: cairn

piles found on mountain slopes: scree, talus; cairn

polishing: pumice

sharpening: whetstone

stony: petrous, lithoid

transported far from native land by glacier: erratic, glacial erratic

turn to: petrify

SEE ROCK

Stone Age n. Paleolithic, Mesolithic, Neolithic, prehistoric times.

stoned a. Sl. 1. DRUNK intoxicated, inebriated, *buzzed, *drunker than a brewer's fart, *plastered, *bombed, *crocked, *drunker than a boiled owl, *drunk as a lord, *half in the bag, *three sheets to the wind, under the influence. 2. HIGH ON DRUGS *buzzed, *baked, drugged, *blitzed, *coked out, *doped up, *flying, *fried, *polluted, *spacey, *tripping, *wasted, under the influence. ANT. *sober, *stone-cold sober, clearheaded, lucid.*

stone-deaf a. *deaf as a post, hard of hearing, hearing-impaired.

stonewall v. impede, obstruct, be closemouthed, *clam up, stall, refuse to cooperate.

stony a. hard, cold, unfeeling, merciless, pitiless, indifferent, heartless, uncaring, callous, tough, harsh, severe, steely. ANT. *soft, warm, sympathetic, compassionate.*

stooge n. foil, dupe, pawn, flunky, victim, dummy, underling.

stool n. 1. SEAT footstool, ottoman, bar stool. 2. FECES excrement, dropping, waste, *crap.

stool pigeon n. informer, spy, *nark, decoy.

stoop n. porch, platform, portico, veranda.

stoop v. 1. BEND OVER bow, crook, crouch, lean forward, tilt, slouch, slump, nod. 2. LOWER ONESELF degrade oneself, sink, condescend, deign, demean oneself, resort.

stop n. 1. HALT cessation, termination, suspension, discontinuance, standstill, *freeze, letup, end, intermission, interlude. 2. STOPOVER destination, sojourn, visit, layover, depot, station, terminal. ANT. 1. *start, commencement, progression.*

stop v. 1. HALT cease, terminate, suspend, discontinue, stand still, *freeze, hold it, let up, end, arrest, turn off, shut down, quit, finish, break, stay. 2. STAUNCH stanch, plug up, stem the flow, seal, check, block, occlude, choke off. 3. OBSTRUCT impede, restrain, block. 4. DEFEAT put down, check, put an end to, crush, quash, silence. ANT. *1. go, proceed, continue. 2. open, unplug. 3. clear the way. 4. strengthen, fortify, help.*

stopgap a. makeshift, temporary, emergency, provisional, improvised, substitute, juryrigged, impermanent. ANT. *permanent.*

stoppage n. 1. STOP halt, close, ending, shutdown, layoff. 2. OBSTRUCTION blockage, impediment, check, hindrance, obstacle.

stopper n. cork, plug, bung, tap, tampion.

storage n. stowage, stockpile, storehouse, storeroom, cache, arsenal, depot, bin, silo, granary, repository.

store n. **1.** SHOP market, mart, retail outlet, *Mom and Pop operation, emporium, *five and dime, supermarket, department store, mall, factory outlet, boutique, convenience store, drugstore, thrift shop, business establishment, canteen, PX. **2.** SUPPLY stock, stockpile, reserve, savings, inventory, provisions, hoard, cache, *nest egg, stash.

store v. save, reserve, put away, stow, *squirrel away, stock, stockpile, lay in supplies, hoard, cache, warehouse, stash, provision, load up, *salt away. ANT. *spend*, *blow, deplete*.

storekeeper n. shopkeeper, grocer, proprietor, merchant.

storeroom n. repository, depository, cache, warehouse, depot, arsenal, silo, granary, buttery.

storm n. **1.** WEATHER DISTURBANCE cloudburst, thunderstorm, thundershower, *thunderboomer, electrical storm, deluge, downpour, *gullywasher, squall, tempest, gale, windstorm, hurricane, monsoon, tropical storm, typhoon, tornado, whirlwind, cyclone, *twister, snowstorm, northeaster, blizzard, hailstorm, blow, inclement weather.

WORD FIND

fair weather spot in center of storm: eye of the storm

line between clashing air masses: front

raising of shoreline water during storm: storm surge

sandstorm of North Africa, India, Middle East: Haboob

whirlwind over water that sucks up funnel of water: waterspout

SEE CLOUD, RAIN, PRECIPITATION, SNOW, WIND

2. UPROAR controversy, outburst, disturbance, brouhaha, furor, eruption, hubbub, attack, hysteria, outcry, squall.

storm v. **1.** RAIN, BLOW squall, rage, pour, thunder, boom, thunder and lightning, snow. **2.** CHARGE attack, assault, rush, blitz, blitzkrieg, assail, invade, besiege. **3.** RAGE blow up, lose one's temper, rant and rave, fume, *throw a fit, roar, bellow, *go on the rampage, *go ballistic.

stormy a. turbulent, wild, tempestuous, violent, rough, windy, squally, blustery, howling, pouring, raining, snowy, inclement. ANT. *calm, becalmed, balmy, mild*.

story n. **1.** NARRATIVE account, tale, chronicle, myth, legend, fable, yarn, fairy tale, short story, parable, allegory, folktale, saga, epic, drama, comedy, tragedy, romance, history, novel, novella, novelette, anecdote, plot.

WORD FIND

category of: genre

long, pointless story with anticlimactic ending: shaggy dog story

real-life feeling given to characters, setting: verisimilitude

warning, story given as a: cautionary tale

SEE NOVEL, BOOK

2. LIE fabrication, *tall tale, *fish story, falsehood, excuse, fib, canard, hoax. **3.** REPORT scoop, news, dispatch, rumor.

storyteller n. raconteur, author, writer, novelist, narrator, spinner of yarns, historian.

stout a. thickset, fat, big, obese, portly, stocky, husky, rugged, sturdy, corpulent, heavy, heavyset, strong, bull-like, brawny, hulking, hefty. ANT. *skinny, anorexic, bony, puny*.

stouthearted a. brave, courageous, daring, nervy, *ballsy, lionhearted, valiant, undaunted, fearless, *gutsy, bold. ANT. *cowardly, timid, *wimpy*.

stove n. range, oven, microwave, toaster oven, heater, wood stove, furnace.

stow v. pack, store away, put away, load, stash, deposit, save, stockpile, cram, wedge, stuff.

straddle v. **1.** BESTRIDE sit astride, split. **2.** TAKE BOTH SIDES OF AN ISSUE straddle the fence, hedge, waffle, *talk out of both sides of one's mouth. ANT. **2.** *be committed*.

strafe v. pepper, gun down, spray with bullets, bombard, fire on.

straggle v. stray, wander, ramble, meander, deviate, drift, range, rove.

straggler n. stray, wanderer, lagger, late arrival.

straight a. **1.** UNBENT undeviating, linear, direct, even, vertical, horizontal, in line, plumb, square, aligned. **2.** HONEST straightforward, frank, candid, upfront, forthright, trustworthy, reliable, sincere. **3.** UNDILUTED pure, whole, unmodified, unmixed, *neat. **4.** CONTINUOUS nonstop, unbroken, sustained, uninterrupted, consecutive, constant. **5.** ORDERLY in good order, neat, arranged. **6.** Sl. *SQUARE conventional, conformist, conservative. ANT. **1.** *bent, curving, wavy, deviating*. **2.** DISHONEST *unreliable, insincere*. **3.** *diluted, mixed, modified*. **4.** *interrupted, broken*. **5.** *messy, sloppy*. **6.** *HIP unconventional, *cool, wild*.

straightforward a. honest, frank, candid, upfront, forthright, direct, plain, explicit, aboveboard, unambiguous, open. ANT. *dis-*

honest, insincere, ambiguous.

strain *n.* **1.** STRESS tension, pressure, force, pull, tightness, exertion, effort. **2.** INJURY sprain, muscle pull, wrench, cramp, twist. **3.** ANCESTRY lineage, extraction, bloodline, stock, pedigree, family, descent, descendants, breed. **4.** TRACE hint, suggestion, streak, shade, touch, suspicion.

strain *v.* **1.** STRETCH tighten, draw tight, pull, exert, overexert, tax, force, struggle, labor. **2.** INJURE sprain, pull a muscle, wrench, cramp, twist. **3.** DISTORT stretch, exaggerate. **4.** FILTER sieve, screen, sift, refine, percolate.

strained *a.* labored, forced, unnatural, stiff, studied, affected, uneasy, tense. ANT. *relaxed, natural.*

strait *n.* narrow, channel, waterway, inlet. SEE STRAITS

straitjacket *v.* confine, immobilize. SEE RESTRAIN

straitlaced *a.* prudish, prim, strict, severe, upright, proper, puritanical, rigid, stiff, stuffy, priggish. ANT. *wild, immoral, *fast.*

straits *n.* difficulty, plight, emergency, predicament, dilemma, bind, hot water, mess, jam, hole.

strand *n.* thread, fiber, filament, line, string, cord, hair.

strand *v.* maroon, run ashore, run aground, beach, wreck, abandon, leave in the lurch.

strange *a.* **1.** FOREIGN alien, exotic, unfamiliar, otherworldly, new, novel, remote, outlandish. **2.** UNUSUAL weird, peculiar, odd, bizarre, uncommon, unconventional, singular, atypical, queer, outlandish, uncanny, extraordinary, curious, funny, eccentric, *far out. **3.** UNEASY ill, ill at ease, uncomfortable, odd, peculiar, disoriented, out of place, out of sorts. **4.** REMOTE reserved, distant, aloof, reclusive. ANT. **1.** *familiar, everyday, common, native.* **2.** *usual, typical, conventional.* **3.** *normal.* **4.** *friendly, gregarious, sociable.*

stranger *n.* unknown, outsider, foreigner, alien, *new kid in town, interloper, *just another face in the crowd. ANT. *friend, acquaintence.*

strangle *v.* **1.** CHOKE throttle, strangulate, asphyxiate, suffocate, *cut off one's wind, garrote, hang, smother. **2.** SUPPRESS stifle, repress, check, curb, restrict, stop, squelch, silence.

strap *n.* thong, cord, lash, band, rein, halter, leash, belt, strop.

strap *v.* tie, tie down, bind, lash, secure, truss, tether, fasten.

strapped *a.* penniless, *broke, destitute, impoverished, poverty-stricken, needy, *down to one's last dime. ANT. *wealthy, *rolling in dough.*

strapping *a.* well-built, tall, husky, athletic, brawny, muscular, sinewy, rugged, powerful, fit, healthy, hearty, robust. ANT. *anorexic, puny, sickly.*

stratagem *n.* trick, scheme, plan, ploy, subterfuge, maneuver, set-up, machination, artifice, deception, tactic, play.

strategic *a.* essential, crucial, critical, vital, important, key, decisive, significant, tactical. ANT. *unimportant, inconsequential.*

strategy *n.* plan, *game plan, design, procedure, blueprint, plot, scheme, approach, machination, tactic.

stratified *a.* layered, laminated, multileveled.

STRATUM *n.* [STRAT um] a layer or level, as that of sedimentary rock or a socioeconomic group. *He came from the upper stratum of society.* SYN. **1.** layer, level, grade, bed, stratification, seam, tier. **2.** class, station, standing, position, rank, echelon, *upper crust.

straw in the wind indication, indicator, sign, omen, portent, harbinger.

straw vote *n.* poll, opinion poll, unofficial vote.

stray *n.* wanderer, rover, waif, orphan, vagabond, lost pet, maverick.

stray *v.* **1.** WANDER roam, rove, drift, range, get lost, ramble, straggle, meander. **2.** GO WRONG deviate, digress, err, go astray, go off course, be in error.

streak *n.* **1.** STRIPE mottle, marking, bar, line, dash, smear, slash, stroke, ray, vein. **2.** TRAIT strain, nature, characteristic, idiosyncrasy, touch, trace, tendency, vein.

stream *n.* **1.** BROOK creek, river, tributary, branch, freshet, creek, rill, runnel, watercourse, waterway, beck.

WORD FIND

sound: murmur, purl, babble, gurgle, white noise

SEE RIVER

2. SERIES succession, steady flow, torrent, outpouring, flood, deluge.

stream *v.* flow, rush, pour, flood, run, gush, surge, course, surge, spill, overflow.

streamer *n.* flag, banner, pennant, ribbon, strip.

street *n.* road, avenue, lane, thoroughfare, boulevard, drive, *main drag, artery, highway, alley, dead end, route, pavement, rue, via.

streetcar *n.* tram, trolley, rail coach.

street people *n.* the homeless, transients, street Arabs, street urchins, gamins, vagrants, derelicts, *bag ladies.

street smart *a.* cunning, shrewd, experienced, seasoned, aware, worldly, savvy, *hip, *streetwise. ANT. *naive, inexperienced, unaware.*

streetwalker *n.* *hooker, whore, *pro, *hustler, independent business woman. SEE PROSTITUTE

strength *n.* **1.** POWER force, vigor, muscle, brawn, punch, *oomph, horsepower, might, energy, potency, drive. **2.** MENTAL TOUGHNESS stability, mental health, intestinal fortitude, courage, *guts, *nerve, character, endurance, durability, will, willpower, tenacity, backbone, grit. **3.** SOLIDITY impregnability, durability. **4.** INTENSITY concentration, potency, power, effectiveness, forcefulness. ANT. *1. weakness, impotency. 2. weakness, instability, cowardice, timidity. 3. flimsiness. 4. weakness, impotence.*

strengthen *v.* fortify, prop, beef up, reinforce, bolster, buttress, harden, temper, steel, shore up, intensify, heighten. ANT. *weaken, undermine, sap.*

strenuous *a.* vigorous, hard, arduous, demanding, difficult, laborious, backbreaking, *ballbusting, tough, Herculean, burdensome, taxing. ANT. *easy, simple, effortless.*

stress *n.* **1.** STRAIN tension, pressure, anxiety, nervousness, disquiet, fear, worry, dread, burden, intensity. "Nature's fight or flight mechanism overburdened by modern society's prohibition against fighting and fleeing."—Harmon Maxwell. "Nature's way of saying bite or run."—Anon. **2.** EMPHASIS accent, force, importance, weight. ANT. *1. relaxation, peace, tranquility.*

stress *v.* emphasize, accent, underscore, underline, accentuate, highlight, *spotlight, play up.

stress out *v.* fill with tension, tax one's nerves, unnerve, disquiet, agitate, overburden, frighten, worry, make anxious, *adrenalize. ANT. *relax, tranquilize, calm.*

stretch *n.* **1.** EXTENSION expansion, elongation, reach. **2.** EXPANSE area, run, spread, tract, space, distance, sweep, area, extent. **3.** DURATION spell, time, period, span, run, interval, tour of duty, term. **4.** EXAGGERATION. ANT. *1. contraction, retraction.*

stretch *v.* **1.** EXTEND expand, elongate, reach, protract, lengthen, span, traverse, inflate, prolong, drag out. **2.** STRAIN force. **3.** EXAGGERATE. ANT. *1. contract, retract.*

stretcher *n.* litter.

strew *v.* spread, scatter, sprinkle, disperse, broadcast, distribute, diffuse, sow. ANT. *gather, amass.*

stricken *a.* afflicted, affected, beset, struck, hit, wounded, injured, hurt, burdened, plagued.

strict *a.* **1.** EXACT, COMPLETE accurate, perfect, precise, faithful, meticulous, unerring, absolute. **2.** STRINGENT punctilious, exacting, particular, fussy. **3.** AUTHORITARIAN disciplinary, firm, stern, rigid, hard-nosed, tough, dour, demanding, rigorous, puritanical, no-nonsense. ANT. *1. inexact, loose, broad. 2. loose, easy, permissive.*

stricture *n.* censure, *slam. SEE CRITICISM

stride *n.* step, gait, pace, walk.

stride *v.* step, walk, swagger, strut, tread, trudge, pace, march, traipse. SEE WALK

strides *n.* progress, advancement, headway.

STRIDENT *a.* [STRI dunt] shrill, harsh. *His strident screaming got the governor's attention.* SYN. shrill, harsh, loud, noisy, vociferous, raucous, grating, piercing, stridulous, high-pitched. ANT. *silent, quiet, hushed, soft.*

strife *n.* conflict, discord, dissent, fighting, contention, controversy, struggle, squabbling, war, clash, contest, feud, unrest. ANT. *accord, peace, harmony.*

strike *n.* **1.** MILITARY ASSAULT attack, offensive, bombing, bombardment, air strike, onslaught, raid, invasion. **2.** LABOR DISPUTE walkout, protest, wage dispute, shutdown, lockout, sit-in, hunger strike. "A labor pain."—Leonard Levinson.

strike *v.* **1.** HIT deliver a blow, punch, pound, smack, knock, clobber, box, cuff, whack, pommel, crack, rap, slap, slug, thump, wallop, clout, smite. **2.** ATTACK assault, launch an offensive, bomb, raid, charge, invade, storm. **3.** BUMP crash, smash into, collide with. **4.** DISCOVER find, unearth, uncover, encounter. **5.** PROTEST go on strike, dispute one's labor contract, walk out, shut down, picket, demonstrate. **6.** DAWN ON register, *hit, impress. **7.** REMOVE delete, cross out, erase, cancel.

strikebreaker *n.* scab, goon, fink.

striking *a.* noticeable, outstanding, remarkable, conspicuous, impressive, extraordinary, out of the ordinary, arresting, awesome, prominent, astounding. ANT. *inconspicuous, unnoticeable.*

string *n.* **1.** CORD twine, rope, strand, thread, line, yarn, fiber, filament, gut. **2.** SERIES succession, row, chain, train, file, progression, procession.

STRINGENT *a.* [STRIN junt] strict, rigid,

tight. *The bar had stringent rules against rowdy behavior.* SYN. strict, rigid, tight, restrictive, rigorous, exacting, tough, harsh, stiff, severe, demanding. ANT. *loose, relaxed, casual, easy.*

stringy *a.* fibrous, ropy, long, thin, sinewy, wiry.

strip *n.* length, cutting, piece, swath, band, section, segment, ribbon.

strip *v.* **1.** UNDRESS disrobe, peel off, slip out of, shuck, bare, divest, remove one's clothing, doff, *drop one's drawers. **2.** REMOVE peel, decorticate, excoriate, pare, uncover. **3.** DEPRIVE dispossess, rob, plunder.

stripe *n.* **1.** BAND streak, line, bar, strip, stroke, slash, striation, mark, chevron. **2.** TYPE kind, sort, ilk, variety, style, breed, race, strain. **3.** WELT wheal, wale.

stripling *n.* sprig, youth, adolescent, young man, lad.

strive *v.* try, make an effort, struggle, labor, toil, apply oneself, *bust one's hump, *bust one's balls, *break one's back, drive oneself, *burn the midnight oil, *work one's fingers to the bone, go after, fight.

stroke *n.* **1.** BLOW impact, hit, punch, rap, knock, belt, whack, cuff, slap. **2.** CARESS pat, rub, massage. **3.** SEIZURE apoplexy, brain hemorrhage. **4.** ACCOMPLISHMENT feat, coup, coup de grace, blow, move.

stroke *v.* caress, fondle, pat, pet, rub, massage.

stroll *n.* walk, constitutional, amble, saunter, excursion, ramble, jaunt.

stroll *v.* walk leisurely, take one's constitutional, amble, saunter, ramble, meander, take in the scenery.

strong *a.* **1.** PHYSICALLY POWERFUL mighty, muscular, athletic, rugged, strapping, robust, fit, able-bodied, brawny, stalwart, Herculean, *strong as a bull, *strong as a locomotive, virile, fit, hale, healthy, hearty. **2.** HAVING STRENGTH OF CHARACTER moral, upright, ethical, secure, self-confident, courageous, plucky, tough, thick-skinned, independent, hardened, resilient. **3.** STRONG-WILLED determined, resolute, staunch, firm, tenacious, strong-minded, *having a mind of one's own. **4.** DURABLE well-constructed, well-built, solid, sturdy, heavy-duty, *built like a brick shithouse, tough, impregnable. **5.** FORMIDABLE powerful, mighty, challenging, tough, intense, *big-time, *major league. **6.** INTENSE potent, concentrated, severe, harsh, bright, deep, undiluted, acute, sharp. **7.** EARNEST fervent, zealous, rabid, *gungho. ANT. *1. weak, feeble, lame, out of shape, *atrophied. 2. immoral, unethical, insecure, cowardly, thin-skinned, dependent, needy. 3. irresolute, indecisive. 4. flimsy, jerry-built, weak. 5. weak, *lightweight, inconsequential, *bush-league. 6. mild, soft, diluted. 7. half-hearted, apathetic, impassive.*

strongarm *v.* twist one's arm, intimidate physically, beat, punch, coerce, force, lean on, squeeze.

strongbox *n.* safe, chest, lockbox, coffer, vault.

stronghold *n.* fortification, fort, fortress, defensive position, citadel, castle, bastion, bulwark, battlement, rampart. SEE CASTLE

strong-willed *a.* strong-minded. SEE STRONG

structure *n.* **1.** BUILDING construction, edifice, erection, skyscraper, high-rise, tower, bridge, dam. **2.** ORGANIZATION arrangement, makeup, framework, shape, form, configuration, construction, infrastructure, composition, fabric.

structure *v.* CONSTRUCT arrange, organize, frame, shape, form, compose, plan, put together, assemble.

struggle *n.* **1.** EFFORT exertion, strain, labor, toil, striving, work, grind, *long haul, *never ending battle, trial. **2.** CONFLICT fight, contention, battle, tug of war, strife, war, tussle, rivalry, combat. ANT. *1. a cakewalk, *a snap, a *breeze.*

struggle *v.* **1.** STRAIN exert, labor, toil, put in great effort, strive, work, *break one's back, *bust one's hump, *bust one's balls, *work like a dog, sweat, *plug away, *fight an uphill battle. **2.** CONFLICT contend, fight, battle, fight a tug of war, war, combat, vie, grapple, tussle, wrestle, wrangle. ANT. *1. hardly break a sweat, *breeze through, *coast through. 2. harmonize, reach accord, make peace, unite.*

strum *v.* thrum, stroke, pluck, pick.

strumpet *n.* harlot, whore, hussy, slut, tramp, trollop, *lady of the evening, *call girl, streetwalker. SEE PROSTITUTE

strut *n.* **1.** COCKY GAIT swagger, promenade, cakewalk, peacock walk, prance. **2.** BRACE support, upright, prop, bolster.

strut *v.* swagger, sashay, peacock, *strut one's stuff, show off, parade, promenade, cakewalk, *walk like a pompous ass.

stub *n.* end, butt, piece, remainder.

stubble *n.* whiskers, bristles, beard, *five o'clock shadow, growth. SEE BEARD

stubborn *a.* obstinate, unyielding, inflexible, uncompromising, strong-willed, muleheaded, pigheaded, tenacious, headstrong, dogged, intractable, bullheaded, resolute, unbending, fixed, willful, pertinacious. ANT.

yielding, compromising, reasonable, irresolute.

stubby *a.* short, thickset, stocky, squat, pudgy, *built like a fireplug, heavyset, stout. ANT. *tall, gangling, skinny.*

stucco *n.* plaster, cement.

stuck-up *a.* snobbish, haughty, arrogant, snooty, uppity, conceited, *carrying one's nose in the air, high hat, hoity-toity, snotty. ANT. *down to earth, folksy, modest, humble.*

stud *n.* stallion, Casanova, Don Juan, *makeout artist, *wolf, *studhammer, *skirtchaser, *tomcat, *buck, playboy.

student *n.* pupil, schoolgirl, schoolboy, freshman, sophomore, junior, senior, collegian, cadet, trainee, apprentice, disciple, apostle, follower.

studied *a.* calculated, practiced, rehearsed, prepared, affected, self-conscious, stiff, unnatural, forced, contrived, labored. ANT. *unstudied, natural, spontaneous.*

studio *n.* workshop, atelier, room, work room.

studious *a.* bookish, scholarly, academic, thoughtful, literary, well-read, hard-working, industrious, hard at it, plugging away, lettered. ANT. *illiterate, ignorant, unschooled, lazy.*

study *n.* reading, investigation, review, examination, research, scrutiny, inquiry, survey, analysis, instruction, edification, erudition, memorizing, book learning, schoolwork, academic work, training, course, subject, lesson. "The noblest exercise of the mind within doors, and most befitting a person of quality." William Ramsey.

study *v.* read, pore over, *bone up on, *crack the books, learn by rote, *cram, go over, *burn the midnight oil, scrutinize, review, examine, research, inquire, survey, analyze, instruct oneself, memorize, learn, train, weigh, consider, ponder, think about, concentrate on.

stuff *n.* **1.** MATERIAL raw material, substance, things, contents, *nuts and bolts, elements, makings, debris, *crap, cloth, fabric. **2.** BELONGINGS effects, things, possessions, *junk, gear, paraphernalia, goods, trappings, objects. **3.** ESSENCE substance, character, *the right stuff, heart, core. **4.** FOOLISHNESS rot, idiocy. SEE NONSENSE

stuff *v.* **1.** LOAD pack, cram, ram, jam-pack, fill, squeeze, wedge, crowd, press. **2.** GORGE gluttonize, glut, gormandize, *pig out, surfeit, sate, *stuff to the gills.

stuffed *a.* crammed, full, loaded, filled, jam-packed, full, replete.

stuffing *n.* fill, wadding, padding, innards.

stuffy *a.* **1.** STALE close, oppressive, poorly ventilated, stifling, airless, suffocating. **2.** STODGY prim, straitlaced, dull, conservative, staid, old-fogyish, stiff, starched, *square, old-fashioned, *button-down. ANT. *1. fresh, breezy. 2. wild, casual, fun-loving.*

stumble *v.* **1.** TRIP slip, fall, stagger, lose one's balance, totter, pitch, *take a spill, *take a header, tumble. **2.** TRIP OVER ONE'S WORDS slip, blunder, flub, bungle, trip over one's tongue, *get hung by the tongue. **3.** STUMBLE UPON chance upon, come upon, bump into, meet, hit.

stumbling block *n.* roadblock, impediment, hindrance, obstacle, barrier, obstruction, drawback, hurdle, bar, snag.

stump *n.* butt, stub.

stump *v.* baffle, perplex, puzzle, confound, bewilder, mystify, confuse, muddle.

stun *v.* daze, stupefy, shock, paralyze, *floor, lay flat, *blow away, *blow one's mind, *drop a bomb on, stagger, overwhelm, *bowl over, shake up.

stunned *a.* dazed, stupefied, shocked, paralyzed, dumbfounded, *bowled over, *floored, *blown away, *seeing stars, overwhelmed, astonished.

stunning *a.* **1.** STUPEFYING shocking, paralyzing, staggering, overwhelming, mind-blowing, astonishing, incredible, jolting. **2.** BEAUTIFUL attractive, lovely, dazzling, gorgeous, ravishing, striking. ANT. *1. *ho-hum, *blah, boring. 3. plain, homely.*

stunt *n.* feat, trick, *daredevilry, act, exploit, performance.

stunt *v.* check, dwarf, hinder, impede, restrain, shorten, slow, arrest, restrict.

stuntman *n.* daredevil, double, stunt double, acrobat.

stunted *a.* dwarf, dwarfed, pygmy, undersized, runty, short, miniature, stubby. ANT. *oversized, giant, towering.*

stupefied *a.* stunned, dazed, *out of it, staggered, knocked out, struck dumb, *stupid, benumbed, *floored, shocked, paralyzed, *seeing stars, astounded, amazed, astonished.

stupefy *v.* stun, daze, stagger, knock out, numb, *floor, shock, paralyze, astound, amaze, astonish.

stupendous *a.* great, gigantic, huge, prodigious, gargantuan, colossal, vast, titanic, immense, monstrous, massive, overwhelming, astonishing, breathtaking, spectacular, staggering, mind-boggling. ANT. *tiny, puny, modest, trivial, ordinary.*

stupid *a.* **1.** NOT INTELLIGENT dumb, dull, witless, retarded, intellectually challenged, thick, dense, ignorant, moronic, brainless, mindless, dim-witted, imbecilic, boneheaded, *having the IQ of a woodchuck, having the IQ of a provolone, *dense as a post, *chowderheaded, *dead from the neck up, *down a quart, *birdbrained, *pea-brained, *three bricks shy of a load. **2.** IRRATIONAL foolish, silly, brainless, idiotic, nonsensical, senseless, unwise, ridiculous, poorly conceived, half-baked. ANT. *1. brilliant, bright, smart, intelligent. 2. rational, thoughtful, wise.*

stupidity *n.* dumbness, witlessness, mental retardation, thickness, denseness, ignorance, brainlessness, mindlessness, dim-wittedness, imbecility, low IQ, idiocy, simple-mindedness. "Unconscious ignorance." — Josh Billings. "Not so much brain as ear-wax." — Shakespeare.

stupor *n.* shock, paralysis, numbness, stupefaction, insensibility, daze, bewilderment, trance, dreaminess, lethargy, torpor, dullness, apathy. ANT. *clearheadedness, sharpness, lucidity, alertness.*

sturdy *a.* **1.** WELL-CONSTRUCTED strong, solid, rock-solid, well-built, built to last, *built like a brick shithouse, rugged, tough, sound, stable, stout, muscular. **2.** FIRM resolute, unyielding, uncompromising, steadfast, staunch, determined, fixed, tenacious. **3.** PHYSICALLY STRONG hardy, vigorous, fit, healthy, strapping, robust, hale. ANT. *1. flimsy, rickety, jerry-built, unstable. 2. irresolute, indecisive. 3. weak, unhealthy, unfit.*

stutter *v.* stammer, splutter, *trip over one's own words, *get hung by the tongue, falter, hesitate, stumble.

style *n.* **1.** MANNER mode, design, way, type, form, sort, kind, variety, genre, method, cut, expression, execution. **2.** DISTINCTION flair, voice, technique, originality, character. "The dress of thoughts." — Lord Chesterfield. "A man's style is his mind's voice." — Ralph Waldo Emerson. "The creation of one's own language." — Roger Hemings. **3.** STYLISHNESS high fashion, fashion, vogue, rage, fad, craze, trend.

stylish *a.* fashionable, chic, smart, *hip, in vogue, *chichi, *riding the cutting edge, modish, trendy, modern, sharp, dapper. ANT. *passé, outmoded, antiquated, obsolete.*

STYMIE *v.* [STI mee] to impede or thwart.

Travel was stymied by a traffic jam. SYN. impede, thwart, obstruct, stop, block, check, foil, prevent, hinder, frustrate, throw up a stumbling block, get in one's way.

SUAVE *a.* [SWAHV] smooth in social interactions, gracious, tactful and diplomatic. *He made everyone feel at ease; he was very suave.* SYN. smooth, polished, refined, gracious, urbane, tactful, diplomatic, charming, cultured, worldly, polite, courtly, ingratiating. ANT. *coarse, unrefined, rude, clumsy, impolite.*

subconscious *a.* unconscious, unaware.

subdue *v.* **1.** CONQUER vanquish, overpower, crush, overthrow, overrun, put down, quell, silence, subjugate, *get the better of, tame. **2.** LESSEN reduce, diminish, soften, mellow, moderate, temper, tone down, allay, mollify, mitigate. ANT. *1. surrender, give in, *cave in. 2. increase, intensify.*

subject *n.* **1.** TOPIC issue, matter, theme, material, problem, question, point, affair, thesis, lesson, course, study. **2.** CITIZEN national, subordinate, follower.

subject *v.* put through, make vulnerable, expose.

subject *a.* **1.** BOUND BY answerable, governed, controlled, subordinate, owing, under, submissive, dependent, servile. **2.** LIABLE prone to, apt to. ANT. *1. ruling, dominating, controlling.*

SUBJECTIVE *a.* [sub JEK tiv] personal, as felt or seen through the eyes of one individual, not objective. *It was a subjective opinion, based only on personal observances.* SYN. personal, individual, biased, prejudiced, nonobjective, emotional, idiosyncratic, introspective. ANT. *objective, impersonal, impartial.*

SUBJUGATE *v.* [SUB juh GATE] to conquer, make subservient. *He was an old-fashioned man who believed in subjugating women.* SYN. conquer, vanquish, control, dominate, make subservient, overpower, enslave, crush, master, tyrannize, tame.

SUBLIMATE *v.* [SUB luh MATE] to refine or put into a socially acceptable form, as channeling one's anger or animal urges into constructive outlets. *He sublimated his rage by playing the drums.* SYN. channel, redirect, transfer, refine, make acceptable, suppress, repress.

SUBLIME *a.* [suh BLIME] exalted, grand, magnificent, majestic. *The ballet presented a sublime performance.* SYN. exalted, grand, magnificent, majestic, lofty, ennobled, high, awe-inspiring, superb, overwhelming, breathtaking, glorious, stately. ANT. *humdrum*, **blah*, **ho-hum*, *pedestrian, ordinary, low.*

submarine *n.* sub, U-boat, submersible, **steel shark, *pigboat.*

WORD FIND
body of: hull
crew member: submariner
exhaust and air intake: snorkel
hazard: mine, depth charge, shoal
locator: sonar, sonobuoy
miniature: submersible
missile: torpedo
nuclear-powered: Trident
observation tower: conning tower, bridge
propellor sound that gives presence away: cavitation
rudder that helps sub to submerge: hydroplane
safe haven: submarine sanctuary, submarine haven
scope: periscope
stabilizing rudder: sail plane
submarinelike observation vessel: bathyscaphe, submersible
water tanks that control submerging: ballast tanks

submerge *v.* sink, submerse, plunge, immerse, dip, dunk, descend, go down, dive, swamp, drown.

submersible *n.* SEE SUBMARINE

submission *n.* **1.** SURRENDER capitulation, submitting, compliance, giving in, **caving in, yielding, acquiescence, deference, subordination, subjugation, obedience, complaisance. **2.** REMITTANCE mailing in, handing in. ANT. *1. domination, resistance, rebellion.*

submissive *a.* nonresistant, nonresisting, yielding, docile, meek, tame, **broken, prostrate, compliant, obeisant, deferential, passive, servile, subservient, *bootlicking, *brownnosing.* ANT. *dominant, ruling, resistant, rebellious.*

submit *v.* **1.** SURRENDER capitulate, comply, give in, **cave in, yield, acquiesce, defer, *knuckle under, abide by, relinquish, *say uncle.* **2.** PRESENT offer, suggest, propose, put forth, remit, hand in, mail in. ANT. *1. dominate, rule, resist, disobey.*

subordinate *n.* inferior, junior, underling, second, attendant, servant, slave, dependent, subaltern, **flunky, *second fiddle, *low man on the totem pole.* ANT. *superior, senior, boss.*

subordinate *v.* subject, dominate, **keep under one's thumb, control, *boss around, order* around, **keep down, reduce.* ANT. *empower, raise.*

SUBORDINATE *a.* [suh BORD in et] inferior or secondary to another. *The subordinate members of the group had no power to vote.* SYN. inferior, secondary, below, under, junior, **under one's thumb, minor, lesser, second-class, submissive, subaltern, ancillary.* ANT. *superior, first-class, higher, major.*

suborn *v.* SEE BRIBE

SUBPOENA *n.* [suh PEE nuh] a written order to appear in court. *The witness was served a subpoena.* SYN. summons, written order, court order, writ, notice, notification, instruction, demand.

subpoena *v.* summon, serve a court order, serve notice, order to testify, instruct, demand.

subscribe *v.* support, favor, approve, agree to, consent to, believe in, accept, endorse, go along with, sanction. ANT. *reject, disapprove, oppose.*

subsequent *a.* following, succeeding, later, latter, ensuing, future, resultant, next. ANT. *previous, preceding, prior.*

subsequently *adv.* later, afterward.

SUBSERVIENT *a.* [sub SERV ee unt] submissive and compliant, servile, subordinate. *He divorced his wife because she wasn't subservient enough.* SYN. submissive, compliant, servile, subordinate, obsequious, submissive, deferential, fawning, sycophantic, groveling, cringing, **brownnosing, *bootlicking.* ANT. *dominant, dominating, ruling, controlling, rebellious, disobedient.*

subside *v.* sink, fall, lessen, abate, wane, ebb, decline, level off, settle, decrease, recede, die down, ease, diminish, let up, **peter out, fade.* ANT. *rise, increase, intensify.*

subsidiary *a.* secondary, supplementary, auxiliary, subordinate, supportive, in a supporting role, ancillary, accessory, lesser, inferior, minor. ANT. *main, major, primary, chief.*

subsidize *v.* aid, support, back, finance, fund, underwrite, sponsor, **pick up the tab, *foot the bill, bankroll.*

subsidy *n.* aid, support, grant, subvention, appropriation, money.

subsist *v.* exist, live, survive, get by, maintain, be sustained, **eke out a living, *make ends meet, persist, endure.* ANT. *die, perish, starve to death.*

subsistence *n.* livelihood, living, support, means of support, means of survival, sustenance, provisions, maintenance, upkeep, sustainment, daily bread, survival, existence, endurance.

substance n. 1. MATTER material, element, stuff, constituent, ingredient, something. 2. REALITY solidity, substantiality, concreteness. 3. ESSENCE meaning, gist, spirit, core, heart, meat, nucleus, thrust, sense, point, *bottom line, *sum total. 4. WEALTH resources, possessions, affluence, assets, worth, riches, property.

substandard a. inferior, poor, below average, below par, subpar, second-rate, below normal, lousy, shoddy. ANT. *superior, first-rate, above par.*

substantial a. 1. CONSIDERABLE large, ample, generous, sizable, great, big, healthy, significant, meaningful, goodly, hefty. 2. STRONG solid, firm, sound. 3. REAL concrete, actual, physical, material, bodily. 4. IMPORTANT valuable, fundamental, essential. 5. WEALTHY rich, affluent, well-to-do, well-off, prosperous. ANT. *1. tiny, paltry, insignificant. 2. weak, flimsy, fragile. 3. imaginary, abstract. 4. unimportant, inessential. 5. poor, impoverished, destitute.*

SUBSTANTIATE v. [sub STAN she ate] to prove to be true by showing evidence. *The detective tried to substantiate her story with circumstantial evidence.* SYN. prove, confirm, authenticate, verify, corroborate, support, validate, demonstrate, attest to, certify. ANT. *disprove, refute, discredit.*

substantive a. actual, solid, real, substantial.

substitute n. alternate, *fill-in, sub, backup, replacement, stand-in, understudy, *temp, double, *pinch hitter, *second-stringer, *bench warmer, surrogate, proxy.

substitute v. alternate, fill in for, sub, replace, switch, stand in, *temp, double, *pinch-hit, *come off the bench, spell, supplant, surrogate.

substitute a. alternate, alternative, backup, temporary, reserve, acting, stopgap. ANT. *primary.*

SUBTERFUGE n. [SUB tur fyooj] a trick or deception, a device used to conceal one's true purpose, actions, etc. *The spy used a clever subterfuge to get by the guard.* SYN. trick, deception, device, ruse, stratagem, artifice, scheme, evasion, maneuver, dodge, machination, Trojan horse, pretense.

subterranean a. underground, below ground, sunken, subsurface, buried, hidden, secret, concealed, under cover.

subtle a. 1. NOT OBVIOUS slight, delicate, faint, fine, suggestive, understated, quiet, inconspicuous, implied, inferred, indirect, insinuated, elusive. 2. THIN, TENUOUS rare, light, slight, airy, ethereal, rarefied. 3. KEEN sharp, acute, astute, discerning, shrewd. 4. CLEVER, SLY skillful, deft, smart, adroit, crafty, sly, cunning. ANT. *1. obvious, conspicuous, heavy, blatant, direct. 2. heavy, dense. 3. dull, stupid, undiscerning.*

subtract v. deduct, take away, detract, lessen, remove, withdraw.

suburb n. residential district, bedroom community, suburbia, *burbs, suburban district, hamlet, outskirt, neighborhood, development, division, subdivision. "The home of the middle class." — Louis Harris. "Where the developer bulldozes out the trees, then names the streets after them." — William Vaughan.

SUBVERSIVE a. [sub VURS iv] contributing to the overthrow or destruction of a government, institution, etc. *He was expelled for his subversive actions.* SYN. destructive, undermining, insurrectionary, seditious, insurgent, treasonous, traitorous, revolutionary.

subvert v. undermine, destroy, weaken, disrupt, ruin, corrupt, poison, upset, damage, overthrow, topple, destroy. ANT. *support, fortify, build.*

subway n. underground railway, *tube, rapid transit system, tunnel, metro.

succeed v. 1. ACCOMPLISH achieve, make good, win, triumph, *pull off, arrive, fulfill, *make it, prevail, work, score, *nail it, *pan out, *fly, *come through with flying colors, reach one's goals, realize, *make it big, *hit the jackpot, ace, *go over with a bang, *lay them in aisles, *knock 'em dead, *get off the ground, *set the world on fire. 2. COME AFTER follow, ensue, replace, supplant, take the place of, inherit. ANT. *1. fail, lose, *blow it, flop, *bomb, *lay an egg. 2. precede, antedate.*

succeeding a. successive, following, subsequent, ensuing, next, upcoming. ANT. *preceding, prior, former.*

success n. fulfillment, accomplishment, achievement, attainment, realization, reaching one's goals, arrival, triumph, win, victory, *big time, hit, *smash, *success d'estime, fame and fortune, winner, sensation, good fortune, prosperity, wealth, riches, *Easy Street, blockbuster. "Luck sweated out from one's own labors." — Anon. "Getting paid for what you love." — Anon. "The reward of toil." — Sophocles. "Not the result of spontaneous combustion. You must set yourself on fire." — Reginald Leach. "The degree to which other people envy you." — Anon. "The child of audacity." — Benjamin Disraeli. "The bitch-goddess." — William James. ANT. *failure, defeat, *bombing, *washout, nonfulfillment.*

successful *a.* winning, accomplished, triumphant, victorious, favorable, prosperous, well-off, well-to-do, achieving, thriving, booming, fortunate, lucky, *on top, *making it big, *on top of one's game, profitable, lucrative, meeting one's goals, *climbing the corporate ladder. ANT. *failing, losing, unfortunate, unsuccessful.*

succession *n.* **1.** SEQUENCE series, procession, progression, train, cycle, course, round. **2.** ACCESSION assumption, rise to power, taking over, crowning.

successive *a.* succeeding, consecutive, following, sequential, ensuing, continuous, one after the other.

SUCCINCT *a.* [suk SINKT] brief and to the point, concise. *The politicians were asked to keep their speeches succinct.* SYN. brief, to the point, concise, pithy, condensed, short, compact, terse, *in a nutshell, *boiled down to its essence, *short and sweet. ANT. *wordy, long-winded, prolix, verbose.*

succor *n.* help, aid, relief, assistance, helping hand.

succor *v.* help, aid, assist, relieve, give relief, give a helping hand.

succulent *a.* juicy, moist, fleshy, dripping, pulpy, mushy. ANT. *dry, dehydrated.*

succumb *v.* **1.** DIE perish, expire, pass away, *croak, *bite the dust, *kick the bucket, *cash in one's chips. SEE DIE. **2.** YIELD submit, give in, give way, surrender, capitulate, *knuckle under, acquiesce, defer to. ANT. **2.** *hold out, resist.*

suck *v.* draw, sip, inhale, slurp.

sucker *n.* **1.** DUPE *patsy, *chump, *sitting duck, *pushover, victim, fool, fair game, easy mark. **2.** LOLLIPOP

sudden *a.* abrupt, unexpected, unforeseen, quick, *out of the blue, fast, *in a heartbeat, *in a wink, instantaneous, meteoric, *precipitate, *like a flash. ANT. *gradual, eventual, slow.*

suddenly *adv.* abruptly, unexpectedly, without warning, quickly, *out of the blue, *in a heartbeat, *in a wink, instantly, meteorically, all of a sudden, all at once, like a flash. ANT. *gradually, eventually, slowly.*

suds *n.* foam, froth, bubbles, lather, soap.

sue *v.* bring court action, file a lawsuit, prosecute, bring to trial, bring civil action against, litigate against, petition the court.

suffer *v.* **1.** EXPERIENCE PAIN hurt, ache, agonize, be racked with pain, writhe in pain, endure, grieve. **2.** EXPERIENCE undergo, endure, bear, encounter, live with, *stick it out, *tough it out, tolerate, withstand. **3.** ALLOW tolerate, permit, admit, grant.

suffering *n.* pain, misery, agony, torture, torment, ache, distress, grief, depression, heartache, despair, anguish, ordeal, hell, discomfort, burden, *cross to bear. "A cleansing fire that clears away triviality and restlessness." — Louis E. Bisch. "A test of faith." — J. Messner. ANT. *comfort, pleasure, peace.*

suffice *v.* serve, do, satisfy, be enough, be adequate, be sufficient, answer, *fill the bill, *do the trick.

sufficient *a.* adequate, enough, plenty, satisfactory, ample, commensurate, passable, acceptable, tolerable, okay, all right. ANT. *insufficient, inadequate, unsatisfactory, short.*

suffocate *v.* smother, choke, stifle, cut off one's air, strangle, throttle, asphyxiate, burke, garrote, kill, silence.

suffrage *n.* right to vote, the vote, voice, franchise.

suffuse *v.* overspread, spread, bathe, infiltrate, permeate, pervade, fill, saturate, imbrue.

sugar *n.* sweetener, sucrose, saccharose, dextrose, fructose, cane sugar, brown sugar, maple sugar, saccharine, *Sweet and Low, *Equal.

sugarcoat *v.* sweeten, gloss over, make agreeable, make palatable, honey, candy. ANT. *poison.*

sugary *a.* **1.** SWEET-TASTING saccharine, candied, honeyed, confectionary. **2.** OVERLY NICE OR SENTIMENTAL mawkish, sickeningly sweet, flattering, oversweet, cloying. ANT. *sour, bitter, acid.*

suggest *v.* **1.** PUT FORTH propose, offer, submit, recommend, proffer, advance, *throw out, move, advise. **2.** BRING TO MIND imply, insinuate, hint, intimate, allude, evoke, infer.

suggestion *n.* **1.** PROPOSAL offering, submission, recommendation, idea, thought, proffer, proposition, presentation, tip, counsel. **2.** TRACE hint, intimation, insinuation, suspicion, allusion, inference, telltale, reminder, shade, tinge, touch.

suggestive *a.* **1.** INDECENT improper, risque, off-color, racy, bawdy, dirty, sexy, erotic, obscene, ribald, titillating, *raunchy. **2.** REMI-

NISCENT signifying, evocative, expressive.

suicidal *a.* **1.** SELF-DESTRUCTIVE *harboring a death wish, reckless, rash, clinically depressed, despondent. **2.** DEADLY lethal.

suicide *n.* self-destruction, self-murder, self-immolation. "A permanent solution to a temporary problem." — Anon. "The serverest form of self-criticism." — Leonard Levinson.

WORD FIND

agreement by two or more: suicide pact

Japanese dive-bombing in World War II: kamikaze

Japanese ritual of disembowelment: hari-kari, seppuku

one who commits: felo-de-se

suit *n.* **1.** SET group, series, ensemble. **2.** LAWSUIT case, litigation, trial, court action. **3.** SET OF CLOTHES WORN TOGETHER outfit, ensemble, costume, uniform, *threads, *getup, *Sunday go-to-meeting clothes, *Sunday best, *bib and tucker, formal evening wear, dress suit, leisure suit, sack suit, seersucker suit, sport suit, business suit, three-piece suit, tuxedo, zoot suit, jumpsuit. SEE COAT, DRESS, JACKET, PANTS, SHIRT, SKIRT

suit *v.* **1.** BEFIT satisfy, meet one's requirements, meet one's needs, *fill the bill, be appropriate, accommodate, please, conform, fit. **2.** ADAPT fit, adjust, tailor, change, proportion, modify.

suitable *a.* fitting, fit, befitting, appropriate, proper, right, correct, acceptable, apt, meet, becoming, seemly. ANT. *unsuitable, improper, unacceptable.*

suitcase *n.* valise, case, grip, travel case, carry-all, overnight bag.

suite *n.* **1.** SET OF ROOMS penthouse, apartment, flat. **2.** ATTENDANTS servants, retinue, entourage, train, company, cortege, court, escort, following, staff.

suitor *n.* courter, admirer, boyfriend, wooer, *beau, *flame, *steady, swain.

sulk *v.* mope, pout, wallow in self-pity, *have a pity party, brood, fret, be gloomy, be sullen, put on a long face. ANT. *rejoice, jump for joy.*

sulky *a.* sullen, gloomy, down in the mouth, moping, pouting, self-pitying, glum, morose, moody, depressed, withdrawn, resentful, dissatisfied. ANT. *happy, cheerful, elated.*

sullen *a.* withdrawn, morose, resentful, sulky, glum, moody, depressed, glowering, petulant, peevish, brooding. ANT. *happy, cheerful, jovial.*

sully *v.* soil, stain, dirty, blemish, smudge, blacken, taint, disgrace, dishonor, defile, corrupt, *drag through the mud. ANT. *cleanse, shine, honor.*

sultry *a.* **1.** HOT steamy, muggy, humid, sweltering, torrid, baking, tropical, sizzling, *roasting, suffocating, oppressive, fiery. **2.** PASSIONATE hot, inflamed, lustful, amorous, *horny, ardent, torrid, erotic, seductive. ANT. *1. cold, freezing, chilling. 2. turned-off, frigid, cold.*

sum *n.* **1.** AMOUNT money, cash, quantity. **2.** TOTAL aggregate, whole, entirety, lot, *whole shebang, *works, mass. **3.** GIST essence, point, content, crux.

summarize *v.* run down briefly, encapsulate, condense, outline, give main points, *recap, recapitulate, synopsize, review, abridge.

summary *n.* rundown, brief, gist, synopsis, outline, precis, *recap, recapitulation, condensation, compendium, abstract, short version, review, sketch, core.

summary *a.* prompt, expeditious, quick, swift, hasty, peremptory, brief, direct.

summer *n.* summer solstice, *dog days, school vacation, season, *lazy days. "Days dripping away like honey off a spoon." — Wallace Stegner.

summit *n.* top, peak, apex, high point, zenith, crown, height, pinnacle, crest, acme, vertex, head, cap, limit, climax. ANT. *bottom, depth, low.*

summon *v.* **1.** CALL FOR call in, beckon, request one's presence, invite, send for, subpoena, order to appear, page, muster, assemble, convene, rally. **2.** GATHER collect, rouse, call up, invoke, muster up.

summons *n.* subpoena, writ, warrant, call, order, court order, command, evocation, signal, alarm.

sump *n.* pool, cesspool, pit, well, cistern.

sumptuous *a.* lavish, extravagant, rich, costly, expensive, magnificent, luxurious, fancy, posh, deluxe, splendid, *ritzy, opulent. ANT. *cheap, poor, *ratty, plain.*

sum up *v.* close, finish, summarize, review, *recap, recapitulate.

sun *n.* *flaming gasball, star, fireball, flaming orb, sphere, luminary, heavenly body, Sol, Helios, Hyperion, Horus, Ra. "The fire that severs day from night." — Shakespeare. "The glorious lamp of heaven." — Dryden.

WORD FIND

dark spots: sunspots

gas: hydrogen, helium

massless particles produced by: neutrinos

mock optical illusion: parhelion, sundog, mock sun

obscuring of by moon: solar eclipse

orbit: ecliptic

outer atmosphere of: chromosphere, corona

plant's movement following: heliotaxis

plant that bends to follow sun: heliotrope

referring to: helio, solar

sunlight therapy: heliotherapy

sunspot cycle of eleven years: solar cycle

sunspot's dark, inner region: umbra

surface: photosphere

tongue of flame and gas, huge: solar flare, solar prominence

variable intensity, sun with: variable star

worship: heliolatry

SEE STAR

sunburned *a.* burned, red, *red as a cooked lobster, scarlet, crimson, blistering, peeling.

Sunday *n.* sabbath, the Lord's day. "The golden clasp that binds together the volume of the week."—H.W. Longfellow.

sunder *v.* separate, split, part, sever, break apart, cleave, divide, halve, quarter.

sundry *a.* miscellaneous, assorted, various, divers, diverse, diversified, many, myriad.

sunken *a.* hollow, depressed, caved in, fallen in, concave, indented, submerged, submersed, drowned, inundated. ANT. *raised, swollen, bulging, elevated.*

sunny *a.* **1.** CLEAR bright, radiant, brilliant, cloudless, dazzling, blazing, sunshiny, golden, *honeyed light, clement. **2.** HAPPY cheerful, cheery, beaming, smiling, optimistic, blithe, lighthearted, joyous, mirthful, buoyant. ANT. 1. *cloudy, gloomy, dark, overcast.* 2. *grim, gloomy, miserable, unhappy.*

sunrise *n.* dawn, daybreak, sunup, daylight, break of day, *the holy light of dawn, crack of dawn, cockcrow, twilight. "First scimitar of light slashing back the night."—Marc McCutcheon. "Daily proof that the earth is still turning."—Anon.

WORD FIND

goddess of dawn: Aurora

sunset *n.* sundown, dusk, nightfall, evening, gloaming, twilight, eventide. "Like the spreading of a peacock's tail."—John Ashberry.

sunshine *n.* sunlight, sunbeams, rays, radiance, brilliance, daylight. "Gold embroidery on the grass."—Paul Horgan. "A shower of gold."—Silvia Tennenbaum.

super *a.* excellent, superb, outstanding, extraordinary, great, terrific, sensational, fine, out of this world, *superhuman, superior. ANT. *terrible, awful, lousy, inferior.*

superabundance *n.* overabundance, surplus, excess, glut, plethora, flood, overflow, more than enough, surfeit, oversupply. ANT. *shortage, dearth, lack.*

superannuated *a.* old, worn out, *over the hill, *put out to pasture, past one's prime, antiquated, obsolete, old-fashioned, outdated. ANT. *young, fresh, new, modern, contemporary.*

superb *a.* excellent, great, superior, superlative, first-class, first-rate, select, choice, magnificent, grand, noble, splendid, super. ANT. *poor, inferior, awful.*

SUPERCILIOUS *a.* [soo pur SIL ee us] haughtily disdainful, proud, regarding with raised eyebrows. *He looked down on her superciliously.* SYN. haughty, proud, contemptuous, scornful, disdainful, lofty, condescending, imperious, arrogant, high and mighty, superior, snobbish. ANT. *down to earth, humble, modest.*

superficial *a.* **1.** SURFACE exterior, outer, external, outside, outward, peripheral, skin-deep, cosmetic. **2.** SHALLOW obvious, apparent, lacking depth, minimal, not profound. **3.** QUICK cursory, perfunctory, hasty, slapdash, hurried, slight. **4.** FRIVOLOUS shallow, featherbrained, unprofound, silly. ANT. *1. internal, inner, deep. 2. deep, profound. 3. thorough, careful, complete. 4. serious, deep, profound.*

SUPERFLUOUS *a.* [suh PUR floo us] unnecessary, more than what is needed. *They lightened their load by getting rid of all superfluous provisions.* SYN. unnecessary, extra, unneeded, excess, surplus, redundant, inessential, nonessential, spare, expendable, more than enough. ANT. *necessary, needed, indispensable, vital.*

superhighway *n.* freeway, autobahn. SEE HIGHWAY

superhuman *a.* supernatural, divine, omnipotent, godlike, preternatural, omniscient, otherworldly, extraterrestrial. ANT. *subhuman.*

superintend *v.* direct, manage, administer. SEE SUPERVISE

superintendent *n.* **1.** DIRECTOR supervisor, overseer, manager, chief, administrator, boss, head, foreman. **2.** CARETAKER custodian, janitor, super, maintenance man.

superior *n.* boss, head, senior, chief, leader, *head honcho, *biggest toad in the puddle, master, higher-up, supervisor, CEO, commander in chief, ranking officer, *big cheese. ANT. *inferior, junior, *low man on the totem pole, subordinate.*

superior *a.* **1.** HIGHER greater, above, better, supreme, superlative, first-class, first-rate, peerless, excellent, outstanding, *a cut above, *tops, unrivaled, predominant, preeminent, incomparable, *A-1, exceptional. **2.** HAUGHTY arrogant, snobbish, high and mighty, proud, supercilious, stuck-up, condescending, patronizing, pretentious. ANT. *1. inferior, lower, second-rate, poor. 2. down to earth, humble, modest.*

superlative *a.* superior, supreme, highest, greatest, best, first-class, first-rate, peerless, excellent, outstanding, *a cut above, *tops, unrivaled, nonpareil, paramount, preeminent. ANT. *poor, inferior, worst, lowest.*

supernal *a.* celestial, heavenly, divine, from the sky, ethereal, lofty.

supernatural *a.* superhuman, otherworldly, unearthly, not of this world, supranatural, metaphysical, transcendental, spiritual, paranormal, occult, psychic, heavenly, divine, breaking the laws of nature, miraculous, ghostly, mysterious, unfathomable, incomprehensible. ANT. *mundane, earthly, natural, normal.*

SUPERSEDE *v.* [soo pur SEED] take the place of, replace. *The automobile superseded the horse and buggy as a primary means of transportation.* SYN. take the place of, replace, succeed, displace, supplant, dethrone, oust, outmode.

supersensitive *a.* ultrasensitive, thin-skinned.

superstar *n.* *megastar, idol, celebrity. SEE STAR

superstition *n.* irrational fear, fallacy, old wives' tale, delusion, false belief. "Religion which has grown incongruous with intelligence."—John Tyndall. "The religion of feeble minds."—Edmund Burke.

superstitious *a.* fearful, naive, irrational, deluded, apprehensive, obsessed.

supervise *v.* oversee, manage, direct, superintend, look after, head, administer, run things, *call the shots, *call the plays, quarterback, command, boss, control, guide, regulate.

supervision *n.* management, control, direction, superintendence, running, administration, guidance, leadership, regulation.

supervisor *n.* boss, overseer, manager, director, superintendent, head, administrator, quarterback, commander, guide, regulator, *whip, *CEO, chief, foreman.

supine *a.* **1.** LYING DOWN flat on one's back, prone, recumbent, horizontal, laid out. **2.** SLUGGISH listless, inactive, lifeless, inert, motionless, *brain-dead, vegetative. ANT. *1.*

standing, upright. *2. lively, active.*

supper *n.* dinner, repast. SEE MEAL

supplant *v.* replace, take the place of, supersede, displace, succeed, oust, dethrone, unseat, bump.

supple *a.* **1.** FLEXIBLE bendable, pliable, pliant, resilient, malleable, elastic, plastic, springy, rubbery. **2.** LIMBER lithe, loose, lissom, agile, nimble, willowy. **3.** COMPLIANT yielding, non-resisting, passive, complaisant, acquiescent, easy. **4.** ADAPTABLE adjustable, flexible, resilient, elastic. ANT. *1. inflexible, hard, rigid, stiff. 2. tight, stiff, out of shape. 3. resistant, rebellious, unyielding. 4. rigid, unchangeable, inflexible.*

supplement *n.* addition, extension, attachment, amendment, addendum, appendix, augmentation, complement, rider, insert, postscript.

supplement *v.* add to, augment, complement, enlarge, increase, reinforce.

supplementary *a.* additional, augmenting, attached, appended, supportive, auxiliary, secondary, ancillary.

supplicant *n.* petitioner, solicitor, applicant, pleader, beggar.

supplicate *v.* request, pray for, petition, plead, appeal, beg, entreat, ask for, implore, beseech, adjure.

supplication *n.* request, prayer, petition, pleading, appeal, entreaty, solicitation, application, plea, cry, begging.

supplies *n.* provisions, stores, issues, rations, stock, necessities, essentials, equipment, victuals, food.

supply *n.* reserve, stock, stockpile, store, inventory, amount, quantity, provision, fund, hoard, cache, load, mass.

supply *v.* provide, furnish, stock, fund, provision, equip, outfit, cater, accommodate, contribute, give.

support *n.* **1.** BRACE, FOUNDATION buttress, prop, underpinning, substructure, bed, joist, beam, girder, stanchion, stay. **2.** BACKING, HELP aid, assistance, hand, lift, encouragement, advocacy, approval, promotion, comfort. **3.** SUBSISTENCE living, sustenance, livelihood, upkeep, provisions, necessities, food, money, child support, alimony.

support *v.* **1.** HOLD UP brace, buttress, prop, shoulder, carry, bear, bolster, sustain, shore up. **2.** BACK help, aid, assist, give a hand, give a lift, sustain, comfort, encourage, bolster, foster, advocate, approve, promote, endorse, subscribe. **3.** PROVIDE FOR maintain, pay one's way, finance, bankroll, subsidize, underwrite, *pick up the tab. **4.** CORROBORATE verify, substantiate, confirm, attest, validate, authenticate.

supporter *n.* backer, advocate, champion, defender, stalwart, helper, proponent, abettor, adherent, fan, benefactor, patron.

supportive *a.* bolstering, encouraging, helping, helpful, sympathetic, strengthening.

suppose *v.* assume, presume, figure, expect, think, guess, imagine, reckon, suspect, theorize, believe, conclude, understand.

supposed *a.* assumed, presumed, figured, expected, thought, guessed, imagined, reckoned, suspected, theorized, believed, understood.

supposition *n.* assumption, hypothesis, presumption, thought, guess, suspicion, theory, belief, conjecture, postulate.

suppress *v.* **1.** PUT DOWN stop, crush, quell, squelch, squash, crack down on, subdue, silence, extinguish, kill, put an end to. **2.** CENSOR keep quiet, withhold, stifle, keep in the dark, silence, shut up, hide, conceal, check, restrain, curb, *put a lid on, muzzle. ANT. *1. throw fuel on the fire, unleash, free up. 2. broadcast, amplify, publish.*

suppression *n.* crushing, quelling, squelching, squashing, silencing, extinguishing, censorship, smothering, stifling, muzzling, restraint.

suppurate *v.* fester, discharge, maturate, ooze.

supremacy *n.* dominance, preeminence, primacy, superiority, transcendence, predominance, rule, authority, mastery, sovereignty.

supreme *a.* greatest, superior, preeminent, dominant, leading, transcendent, highest, ultimate, paramount, crowning, predominant, first, superlative, finest, excellent, utmost, top, ranking, peerless, ruling, chief, sovereign, *eclipsing all others, *overshadowing all others, *standing head and shoulders above all others. ANT. *worst, lowest, poorest.*

sure *a.* **1.** CERTAIN definite, assured, doubtless, unquestionable, fixed, set, incontrovertible, positive, conclusive, proven, demonstrated, unmistakable, certified, beyond a shadow of a doubt. **2.** RELIABLE dependable, trustworthy, tried and true, trusty, faithful, steadfast. **3.** CONVINCED confident, certain, satisfied, positive. **4.** INEVITABLE assured, bound, unavoidable, guaranteed, inescapable, *iced. ANT. *1. uncertain, doubtful, questionable, unproven. 2. unreliable, undependable. 3. uncon-*

vinced, uncertain. 4. uncertain.*

surely *adv.* certainly, doubtless, undoubtedly, absolutely, positively, unquestionably, beyond a shadow of a doubt, definitely, indubitably.

sure thing *n.* safe bet, certainty, *shoo in, *cinch.

surety *n.* security, guarantee, bond, assurance, pledge.

surf *n.* waves, breakers, rollers, combers, spindrift, seaspray, swells, foam, swash, riptide.

WORD FIND
common wave with convex back: plunger
gray-crested waves: graybeards
hollow between waves: trough
series of waves: train
sound: rote, swash, crash, thunder, lap
SEE BEACH, OCEAN

surf *v.* ride the waves, *hang five, *hang ten.

WORD FIND
fall off: wipe out
ride under a breaking wave: *shoot the tube, *shoot the curl
shorts: baggies, jams
show off: *hotdog
surf without a board: body surf

surface *n.* exterior, outside, top, skin, shell, facade, face, crust, veneer, finish.

surface *v.* **1.** SMOOTH level, plane, even, pave, finish. **2.** ARISE emerge, break the surface, ascend. **3.** BECOME KNOWN materialize, come up, come to light.

SURFEIT *n.* [SUR fit] an excessive amount, fullness, overindulgence. *The baker made a surfeit of cookies for the party.* SYN. **1.** EXCESS surplus, overabundance, superabundance, too much, glut, overflow, flood, inundation, overkill, exorbitance, plethora. **2.** SATIETY fullness, satiation, overindulgence, sickness, nausea, disgust, discomfort. ANT. *1. dearth, shortage, lack. 2. hunger, craving, emptiness.*

surfeit *v.* overindulge, *stuff oneself, overfill, gorge, satiate, glut, *pig out, overdo, cloy, overeat.

surge *n.* **1.** SWELL wave, billow, flood, torrent, rush, heave, sweep, mass, storm surge, rise, gush, rising tide. **2.** INCREASE rise, escalation, skyrocketing, growth, expansion, explosion, jump, rise. ANT. *2. decline, drop, plunge.*

surge *v.* **1.** SWELL billow, flood, rush, heave, sweep, roll, amass, rise, gush, wash. **2.** INCREASE rise, escalate, skyrocket, grow, expand, explode, jump, rise.

surgeon *n.* medical professional, doctor, physician, specialist, *sawbones. "An eagle's eye, a lion's heart, a lady's hand." — John Ray. SEE OPERATION

surgery *n.* medical procedure, *the knife, excision, biopsy, bypass, mastectomy, transplant, angioplasty, neoplasty. SEE OPERATION

surgical *a.* accurate, precise, exacting, pinpoint, ticklish, delicate. SEE OPERATION

surly *a.* bad-tempered, sour, moody, rude, nasty, cross, sullen, brusque, dour, ugly, hostile, unfriendly, harsh, short, grouchy, grumpy, gruff. ANT. *friendly, cheery, cheerful, warm, good-humored.*

surmise *n.* guess, conjecture, deduction, assessment, hypothesis, *shot in the dark, assumption, hunch, supposition, idea, speculation, presumption.

surmise *v.* guess, conjecture, imagine, infer, *put two and two together, *hazard a guess, conclude, deduce, assess, hypothesize, *take a shot in the dark, assume, suppose, speculate, presume, reckon, opine.

surmount *v.* go over, climb over, mount, clear, prevail over, get the best of, overcome, conquer, vanquish, subdue, triumph over, master, top.

surname *n.* family name, last name, cognomen. For lists of ethnic surnames and given names SEE NAME.

surpass *v.* excel, beat, exceed, outdo, better, outdistance, eclipse, *leave the competition swirling in one's wake, *leave in the dust, *run circles around, overshadow, trump, put to shame, outperform, outrun, top, transcend, *blow one's doors off.

surplus *n.* excess, surfeit, glut, overabundance, overstock, overkill, extra, plethora, spate, oversupply, remainder, residue. ANT. *shortage, shortfall, deficiency.*

surplus *a.* extra, excess, spare, leftover, unused, superfluous, remaining, residual. ANT. *short, deficient.*

surprise *n.* **1.** SHOCK start, bombshell, thunderbolt, bolt from the blue, eye-opener, stunner, unforeseen turn of events. **2.** AMAZEMENT astonishment, astoundment, wonder, shock, incredulity.

surprise *v.* **1.** SHOCK give a start, startle, *drop a bombshell on, stun, open one's eyes, astonish, astound, amaze, take one's breath away, *blow away, *knock for a loop, flabbergast, daze, take aback, floor. **2.** CATCH OFF GUARD catch napping, take unawares, *catch flatfooted, ambush, *catch red-handed.

surprising *a.* unexpected, unforeseen, shocking, sudden, startling, stunning, eye-open-

ing, astonishing, astounding, amazing, breathtaking, *out of the blue. ANT. *expected, foreseen.*

SURREAL *a.* [sur RE ul] having the strange or bizarre quality of dreams or the unconscious mind. *Salvador Dali's paintings are known for their surreal quality.* SYN. strange, bizarre, fantastic, grotesque, weird, nightmarish, Kafkaesque, *far out, *reminiscent of the Twilight Zone, odd, queer, peculiar. ANT. *ordinary, everyday, normal.*

surrealistic *a.* strange, bizarre, fantastic, grotesque, weird, nightmarish, dreamlike, Kafkaesque, *far out, *reminiscent of the Twilight Zone, odd, queer, peculiar. ANT. *ordinary, everyday, normal.*

surrender *n.* yielding, submission, giving up, giving in, *crying Uncle, capitulation, *throwing in the towel, *white flag, relenting, prostration, acquiescence, resignation, relinquishment.

surrender *v.* yield, submit, give up, give in, *cry Uncle, capitulate, *throw in the towel, *raise the white flag, relent, *cave in, prostrate oneself, acquiesce, resign, relinquish, cede. ANT. *defy, *hang tough, *dig in, fight.*

SURREPTITIOUS *a.* [sur up TISH us] sneaky, secret. *He glanced surreptitiously at her wedding band.* SYN. sneaky, secret, stealthy, clandestine, furtive, covert, hidden, sly, undercover, *on the QT, underhanded, confidential. ANT. *open, public, overt, conspicuous.*

SURROGATE *n.* [SUR uh GIT] A substitute or stand-in. *She served as a surrogate until the boss recuperated.* SYN. substitute, stand-in, representative, *sub, agent, replacement, proxy, deputy, understudy.

surround *v.* envelop, encircle, enclose, encompass, circumscribe, ring, bound, hem in, fence in, confine, blockade.

surroundings *n.* environment, environs, setting, habitat, milieu, background, neighborhood, ambience.

surveillance *n.* observation, watch, spying, *stakeout, vigil, scrutiny, shadowing, *bugging, wiretapping, reconnaissance.

survey *n.* inspection, study, examination, appraisal, exploration, review, overview, scrutiny, inquiry, probe.

survey *v.* **1.** EXAMINE study, inspect, appraise, explore, review, scrutinize, inquire, probe, canvass, assess, measure. **2.** LOOK AT view, regard, scan, study, eyeball, *give a onceover, watch, observe.

survival n. living, subsistence, endurance, durability, continuity, lasting, toughing it out.

survive v. live, endure, continue, last, tough it out, remain, persist, hold one's ground, carry on, withstand, *weather the storm, *ride out the storm, *stay afloat, outlive, outlast.

susceptible a. vulnerable, exposed, sensitive, ultrasensitive, thin-skinned, prone, subject, liable, open. ANT. *invulnerable, hardened, resistant.*

suspect n. the accused, defendant, *shady character, supposed perpetrator.

suspect v. **1.** DISTRUST mistrust, *trust as far as one can spit, disbelieve, question, doubt, *smell a rat, *harbor suspicions. **2.** GUESS imagine, conjecture, surmise, suppose, think, believe, assume, presume, theorize, hypothesize, infer, gather. ANT. 1. *trust, believe.*

suspect a. suspicious, *fishy, suspected, unbelievable, questionable, doubted, mistrusted, *shady, dubious. ANT. *believable, reliable, trustworthy.*

suspend v. **1.** DEBAR exclude, dismiss, throw out, expel, evict, ban, blackball, shut out. **2.** STOP TEMPORARILY postpone, delay, defer, *put on the back burner, hold off, *put on hold, put off, discontinue. **3.** HANG dangle, sling, swing, pend.

suspenders n. garters, braces, galluses.

suspense n. tension, anxiety, uncertainty, anticipation, expectation, build-up, *white-knuckle anticipation, *cliffhanger.

suspension n. **1.** BARRING exclusion, dismissal, expulsion, eviction, ban, banishment, blackballing. **2.** TEMPORARY STOP postponement, delay, moratorium, stay, deferral, hold, discontinuance. **3.** HANGING dangling, slinging.

suspicion n. **1.** MISTRUST distrust, doubt, dubiousness, disbelief, *bad vibes, leeriness, wariness, *funny feeling, *gut feeling, sneaking hunch, suspicion, qualm, misgiving. **2.** TRACE touch, hint, suggestion, shadow, tinge, shade, inkling. ANT. 1. *trust, belief, confidence.*

suspicious a. **1.** SUSPECT questionable, *fishy, *funny, dubious, peculiar, *not kosher, doubtful, *doesn't have the ring of truth, shady. **2.** DISTRUSTING mistrusting, doubting, disbelieving, questioning, wary, leery, incredulous, skeptical, cynical. ANT. 1. *aboveboard, *kosher. 2. trusting, believing, confident.*

sustain v. **1.** KEEP UP maintain, continue, keep alive, prolong, protract, preserve, keep going. **2.** SUPPORT nourish, nurture, feed, provide for, aid, nurse. **3.** CARRY THE WEIGHT OF support, hold, prop, uphold, shoulder, bear. **4.** ENDURE withstand, tolerate, suffer, brook, stand, live with, abide, undergo.

sustenance n. livelihood, support, living, subsistence, upkeep, nourishment, food, daily bread, victuals, rations, provisions, bread and butter, nutriment, groceries, *grub.

suture n. sewing, stitching, joining. SEE OPERATION

SVELTE a. [SVELT] slender and lithe. *The svelte dancers moved as gracefully as cats.* SYN. slender, thin, lithe, graceful, lissome, willowy, thin, lanky, slight, trim, lean, slinky. ANT. *fat, obese, roly-poly, awkward.*

swab n. **1.** MOP **2.** COTTON, CLOTH sponge, wad.

swaddle v. wrap, bind, swathe, bundle up.

swag n. **1.** FESTOON decoration, valance, garland, loop, chain, ornament. **2.** LOOT plunder, stolen money, booty, *haul.

swagger n. strut, parade, bluster, pomp, *the air of one who thinks he's the cock of the walk, peacock walk, braggadocio, bravado, boastfulness, muscle-flexing.

swagger v. strut, parade, bluster, *act like the cock of the walk, *peacock, brag, boast, flex one's muscles, show off, flaunt, grandstand, vaunt, *blow one's own horn, stride pompously. ANT. *cringe, skulk.*

swaggerer n. strutter, *cock of the walk, blusterer, *blowhard, peacock, braggart, showoff, *grandstander, pompous ass, *horse's ass, swashbuckler.

swain n. lover, suitor, gallant, beau, boyfriend, flame, sweetheart, squire, country boy, rustic.

swallow v. **1.** GULP down, ingest, guzzle, eat, drink, *choke down, gobble, bolt, *wolf down, *chug-a-lug, quaff. **2.** ENGULF absorb, devour, overwhelm, envelop. **3.** PUT UP WITH tolerate, endure, suffer, bear, ignore. **4.** BELIEVE WITHOUT QUESTION *swallow hook, line and sinker; *buy, take on faith, accept, swallow whole, *fall for, be naive. ANT. 1. *regurgitate, vomit, throw up.* 4. *disbelieve, reject, mistrust.*

swami n. lord, master, fakir, teacher, mentor, guru.

swamp n. bog, marsh, slough, quagmire, fen, bayou, morass, everglade, swale, mire, wetland, muskeg.

WORD FIND

filling in of a lake by vegetation: eutrophication

floating island of decayed vegetation: battery

gas: methane
luminescence seen at night: foxfire
moss: sphagnum
tree islands: hammocks
SEE LAKE

swamp v. flood, overwhelm, submerge, sink, engulf, inundate, drown, deluge, wash over.

swap v. trade, exchange, switch, barter.

sward n. grass, turf, lawn, sod.

swank n. style, ostentation, stylishness, showiness, fashion, flashiness, flamboyance.

swanky a. stylish, ostentatious, showy, fashionable, flashy, chic, glamorous, snappy, smart, dapper, classy, *snazzy. ANT. *frumpy, unfashionable, out of style.*

swarm n. hive, cloud, flight, crowd, throng, multitude, mass, horde, shoal, school, assembly.

swarm v. mass together, crowd, throng, cluster, flock, gather together, herd, congregate, concentrate.

swarthy a. dark-complexioned, dark, dusky, black, brown, olive-skinned, coal-black, ebony, chocolate, tawny, nutbrown, obsidian, *dark as the Rio Grande, *dark as the Congo. ANT. *light, white, pale.*

swash v. splash, wash, dash, strike.

swashbuckler n. swaggerer, fighting man, adventurer, fencer, soldier of fortune, pirate, blusterer, daredevil.

swashbuckling a. swaggering, loud, boastful, strutting, adventurous, derring-do, daredevilry, blustering, fighting.

swat n. blow, hit, spank, smack, slap, whack, wallop, belt, slug.

swat v. hit, spank, smack, slap, whack, wallop, belt, slug, clout, smite.

swatch n. sample, piece, bit, scrap, specimen, example.

swath n. clearing, stripe, path, opening, cut, space, strip.

swathe v. wrap, bind, swaddle, bundle up, dress, bandage.

sway n. 1. SWINGING leaning, undulation, fluctuation. 2. INFLUENCE control, power, command, domination, rule, hand, reign, authority, mastery.

sway v. 1. MOVE FROM SIDE TO SIDE swing, move to and fro, move back and forth, waver, wobble, fluctuate, undulate, oscillate, rock, teeter, vacillate. 2. INFLUENCE persuade, talk into, divert, control, brainwash, prevail upon, move, convince, impress, win over, lead, guide, *sell on.

swaybacked a. sagging, broken-backed, caving in, slumping.

swear v. 1. PROMISE vow, pledge, take an oath, give one's word, warrant, avow, attest, declare. 2. CURSE cuss, use profanity, use dirty language, use four-letter words, *spit barnyard epithets, take the Lord's name in vain, use gutter language.

swear by v. have confidence in, recommend, believe in.

swearing n. cussing, cursing, foul language, bad language, four-letter words, obscenities, expletives, profanity, dirty words, *barnyard epithet, *cow pasture vulgarism, vulgarity, *henhouse epithet, X-rated language, gutter language. "The garlic in the salad of taste."—Cyril Connolly. ANT. *polite word, euphemism.*

swear off v. give up, abjure, renounce, forswear, forego, quit, turn one's back on.

sweat n. 1. PERSPIRATION sudoresis, excretion, moisture, lather, body odor, *BO. 2. HARD WORK toil, labor, drudgery, grind, backbreaking work, slavery. 3. ANXIETY apprehension, stress, tension.

sweat v. 1. PERSPIRE excrete, *glow, *work up a lather, *sweat bullets, swelter, ooze, exude. 2. GET NERVOUS *stress out, fret, worry, suffer anxiety, suffer distress. 3. TOIL labor, break one's back, strain, struggle, slave, drudge, work.

sweater n. pullover, turtleneck.

WORD FIND

coatlike: cardigan

coat sweater with school letter: letter sweater

deer or geometric pattern on front: jacquard

diamond-designed: argyle, Aran Isle sweater

goat hair: cashmere

Irish, water-repellant: fisherman's sweater

long: fanny sweater

natural-colored, with bands around neck: Icelandic

pullover with rounded neck: crew neck

pullover with wedge-shaped neck: V-neck

sleeveless pullover: shell

white, cable-knit pullover: tennis sweater

sweep n. 1. RANGE scope, reach, stretch, span, width, breadth, compass, extent. 2. SWIPE stroke, swing, cut. 3. COMPLETE VICTORY *skunk, *clean sweep.

sweep v. 1. WHISK take a broom to it, brush, clean up, tidy, clear. 2. CLEAR, DESTROY remove, strip, drive out. 3. RUSH hurry, race, fly, charge, zoom, *zip, glide, tear. 4. WIN IT ALL *skunk, *pull off a clean sweep.

sweeping *a.* extensive, broad, widespread, far-reaching, all-inclusive, blanket, general, across-the-board, comprehensive, thorough. ANT. *limited, partial.*

sweepstakes *n.* lottery, contest.

sweet *n.* candy, confection, dessert.

sweet *a.* **1.** SUGARY saccharine, honeyed, nectarous, candied, confectionary, tasty, luscious. **2.** PLEASANT agreeable, enjoyable, delightful. **3.** FRIENDLY kind, gentle, good, nice, charming, angelic, pleasant, agreeable, amiable, helpful. **4.** SWEET-SMELLING fragrant, fresh, perfumed, pure, aromatic. **5.** SWEET-SOUNDING dulcet, melodious, harmonious, euphonic. ANT. *1. sour, bitter, tart, acid. 2. unpleasant, awful, miserable. 3. unfriendly, sour, grouchy. 4. sour, rotten, spoiled. 5. harsh, discordant.*

sweeten *v.* **1.** ADD SUGAR sugarcoat, honey, candy, dulcify, mull. **2.** EASE soften, lighten, mollify, *take the edge off, alleviate, temper, mellow, moderate.

sweetener *n.* saccharine, sugar, *Sweet and Low, *Equal.

sweetheart *n.* darling, love, *sweetie, honey, *honeybunch, *honeybun, *honeybunny, dear, *sugar pie, lover, pet, girlfriend, boyfriend, flame, *steady, love of one's life, heartthrob, turtledove, *baby.

sweetmeat *n.* sweet, confection, delicacy, treat, cake, candy, preserve, nougat.

sweet-talk *v.* flatter, *butter up, cajole, softsoap, *lay it on with a trowel, *bullshit, *blarney.

swell *n.* **1.** BULGE wave, roller, surge, surf, rise, mound, hill, hump, protuberance, prominence, protrusion, distension, expansion, growth. **2.** SMART DRESSER dandy, clotheshorse, Beau Brummel, fop.

swell *v.* **1.** BULGE rise, billow, balloon, inflate, blow up, puff up, bloat, mound, form a hump, protrude, distend, dilate, expand, grow, surge, become turgid. **2.** PUFF UP FROM PRIDE swagger, strut, stick one's chest out, parade, show off, be pleased with oneself. ANT. *1. deflate, shrink, collapse. 2. be crestfallen, cringe, shrink.*

swell *a.* fine, excellent, great, first-rate.

swelling *n.* lump, bulge, distension, bump, growth, enlargement, edema, puffiness, inflammation, knob, welt, abcess.

swelter *v.* sweat, perspire, drip, *slow cook under the sun, *burn up under the sun, suffer heatstroke, roast.

sweltering *a.* hot, humid, roasting, scorching, torrid, sultry, stifling, baking, broiling, muggy, close, oppressive. ANT. *cold, frigid, chilling.*

swerve *v.* turn sharply, deviate, veer, diverge, dodge, sheer off, shift, careen.

swift *a.* **1.** FAST quick, rapid, speedy, hasty, fleet, express, *quick as lightning, *quicker than greased lightning, supersonic, hypersonic, faster than the speed of sound, swift as a gazelle, swift as a cheetah, prompt, brisk, winged, breakneck, meteoric, *on the double. **2.** SHORT-LASTING fleeting, brief, quick, transient, ephemeral, *passing in a heartbeat, *passing in the wink of an eye. **3.** QUICK-ACTING alert, *on one's toes, ready, prompt. ANT. *1. slow, *slower than a glacier, sluggish, *slower than the Second Coming. 2. long-lasting, permanent, eternal. 3. slow, *asleep, *out to lunch.*

swig *n.* mouthful, gulp, slug, *hit, drink, quaff, swill, draft.

swill *n.* garbage, table scraps, slop, hogwash, refuse, waste, remains.

swill *v.* swig, guzzle, gulp, wash down, *take a slug, *take a hit, quaff, *chug-a-lug, *knock off, drain.

swim *v.* **1.** *GO FOR A DIP breaststroke, crawl, backstroke, do the butterfly, dog-paddle, stroke, *skinnydip, tread water, float, bathe, paddle, snorkel, scuba dive, skin dive. **2.** BE SATURATED be soaked, be steeped in, float in.

swim *v.* be dizzy, be lightheaded, be off balance.

swimming *a.* dizzy, lightheaded, dopey, reeling, whirling, off-balance.

swimmingly *a.* easily, successfully, readily, effortlessly, beautifully, well, smoothly, *without a hitch, perfectly. ANT. *with great effort, with difficulty, unsuccessfully.*

swimsuit *n.* swim shorts, swimming trunks, bathing suit, *jams, bikini, T-back, swimwear.

swindle *n.* fraud, cheat, *rip-off, *con, skin game, trickery, scam, shell game, hustle, gyp.

swindle *v.* defraud, cheat, *rip off, *con, trick, *scam, hustle, gyp, dupe, rook, fleece, *chisel, *burn, bamboozle, *take to the cleaners, *screw, bilk, extort, *flimflam, *sell a bill of goods, *take for a ride.

swindler *n.* cheat, *con artist, *con man, fraud, *flimflam man, chiseler, *rip-off artist, crook, *bunco artist, *grifter, *sharper, *hustler, shark.

swine *n.* **1.** PIG hog, porker, piglet, sow, boar. **2.** A DESPICABLE PERSON *bastard, *SOB, creep, pig, animal, rogue, cad, scoundrel, *rat, *jerk.

swing n. **1.** OSCILLATION pendulation, sway, swaying, undulation, arc. **2.** PUNCH blow, stroke, uppercut, roundhouse left, hook. **3.** RHYTHM beat, cadence, meter, pulse, measure.

swing v. **1.** OSCILLATE pendulate, sway, rock, teeter, seesaw, waver, wobble, move back and forth. **2.** TURN pivot, come around, spin, wheel, rotate, whirl, swivel, pirouette. **3.** DELIVER A BLOW deliver a roundhouse right, punch. **4.** HAVE AN EXCITING RHYTHM *have a groove, *groove, rock. **5.** BE LIBERAL SEXUALLY *wife-swap, swap partners, *go both ways, *bed-hop.

swinish a. piggish, *like a hog, beastly, filthy, gross, disgusting, brutish, gluttonous, coarse. ANT. refined, cultured, delicate.

swipe n. blow, slap, smack, roundhouse, punch, swat, cuff, wallop, clip.

swipe v. Sl. steal, pilfer, pocket, take, shoplift, filch, pinch, appropriate, thieve.

swirl v. whirl, twirl, twist, eddy, form a whirlpool, revolve, circle, whorl, rotate, gyrate, spin, churn.

swish v. hiss, brush, whoosh, rustle.

swishy a. Sl. *faggy, effeminate, *queer, *limpwristed, campy.

switch n. **1.** CHANGE swap, exchange, reversal, about-face, 360 degree turn, *flip-flop, new tack, change of course. **2.** STICK rod, lash, whip, cane, branch.

swivel v. turn, rotate, swing, pivot, revolve, hinge, spin.

swollen a. enlarged, distended, bloated, puffy, puffed up, bulging, inflated, edemic, tumid, turgid. ANT. deflated, contracted, shrunken.

swoon v. faint, pass out, lose consciousness, collapse, go limp, keel over, feel lightheaded, suffer from syncope.

swoop v. **1.** DIVE plunge, plummet, drop down on, pounce on. **2.** SWEEP UP snatch, seize, scoop up.

sword n. weapon, blade, cutlass, saber, broadsword, rapier, samurai sword, scimitar, *cold killing steel.

WORD FIND

belt: baldric

dagger that is notched to catch and break sword: swordbreaker

fencing: foil, epee

handle: haft, hilt, pommel

Indian saber with curved blade: shamshir

legendary: Excalibur

Scottish Highlander's duel-edged broad-

sword: claymore

shaped like: ensiform, gladiate

sheath: scabbard

short: skean

side projections at hilt: quillons

smaller sword used as a backup: hanger, side-arm

swordplay: fencing, dueling

swordsman: fencer, blade

sworn a. pledged, promised, bound.

SYCOPHANT n. [SIK uh funt] one who flatters and kisses up to others to gain their favor. The boss had a retinue of sycophants and yes-men. SYN. toady, flatterer, *brownnose, *kissass, *asskisser, bootlicker, yes-man, fawner, groveler, *flunky, *apple-polisher, parasite.

syllabus n. summary, outline, synopsis, abstract, brief, condensation, digest, abridgement, epitome.

sylvan a. woodland, wooded, woody, forested, arboreal.

SYMBIOTIC a. [sim bee AW tik] referring to a relationship that is mutually beneficial. Bees and flowers enjoy a symbiotic relationship. SYN. mutually beneficial, mutually advantageous, give and take, commensalistic, parasitic.

symbol n. character, design, letter, emblem, figure, insignia, sign, trademark, representation, badge.

symbolic a. representative, illustrative, metaphorical, indicative, characteristic, symptomatic, emblematic, allegorical.

symbolize v. represent, stand for, signify, denote, express, epitomize, mean, connote, personify.

symmetrical a. balanced, even, uniform, corresponding, similar, matching, proportionate, harmonious, regular, parallel. ANT. asymmetrical, unbalanced, uneven.

SYMMETRY n. [SIM uh tree] similarity or correspondence in form, uniformity, balance. They evened out the forms to create a rough symmetry. SYN. similarity, correspondence, balance, parity, proportion, uniformity, evenness, congruity, harmony, grace. ANT. asymmetry, imbalance, unevenness.

sympathetic a. **1.** COMPASSIONATE concerned, commiserative, caring, feeling, solicitous, understanding, kind, sensitive, tender, pitying, humane, empathetic, charitable, *having a bleeding heart. **2.** CONGENIAL agreeable, like-minded, companionable, simpatico, having a good rapport with, *on the same wavelength, compatible, *en rapport, friendly. ANT. *1. uncaring, indifferent, cold, stony, unfeeling, insensitive. 2. disagreeable, clashing, incompatible.*

sympathize *v.* feel for, understand, have compassion for, pity, commiserate, care, empathize, condole, feel sorry for, *have one's heart go out to, *have one's heart bleed for, feel compassion for.

sympathy *n.* **1.** COMPASSION concern, commiseration, caring, feeling, solicitousness, understanding, kindness, sensitivity, tenderness, pity, humanity, empathy, charity, *bleeding heart. "A fellow-feeling."—Robert Burton. "Two hearts tugging at one load."—Charles Parkhurst. "Dissolved selfishness."—Ludwig Boerne. **2.** AFFINITY, AGREEMENT BETWEEN TWO PEOPLE harmony, like-mindedness, rapport, compatibility, *same wavelength, accord, congeniality, friendship, unity, mutual attraction. **3.** APPROVAL agreement, assent, consent, *okay, acceptance, acquiescence. ANT. *1. indifference, coldness, stoniness, insensitivity. 2. clash, conflict, discord. 3. disapproval, disagreement.*

symphony *n.* **1.** HARMONY OF SOUNDS euphony, polyphony, multiplicity of sound, chorus. **2.** MUSICAL COMPOSITION opus, piece, concerto, arrangement, suite, score. SEE MUSIC (SYMPHONIC TERMS). **3.** CONCERT performance. **4.** ORCHESTRA philharmonic. **5.** GENERAL HARMONY unity, correspondence, concord, agreement.

symposium *n.* conference, meeting, gathering, discussion, panel discussion, seminar, forum, round table, debate, assembly, congress.

symptom *n.* indication, sign, warning, warning sign, prodrome, dead giveaway, earmark, manifestation, tip-off, signal, evidence, telltale.

symptomatic *a.* indicative, suggestive, characteristic, peculiar, signaling.

synagogue *n.* place of worship, temple, shul. SEE CHURCH

synch *v. Sl.* SEE SYNCHRONIZE

synchronize *v.* coordinate, regulate, make simultaneous, *put in sync, harmonize, set.

synchronous *a.* simultaneous, *in sync, concurrent, parallel.

syndicate *n.* association, group, organization, cartel, joint concern, consortium, pool, company, conglomerate, partnership, coalition, trust, Mafia, mob.

syndrome *n.* disease, condition, group of symptoms, disorder, sickness, affliction, malady, spectrum of complaints.

synergy *n.* working together, collaboration, cooperative action, coordination, teamwork, joint action, pulling together, *hitching horses, symbiosis.

synod *n.* ecclesiastical council, conclave, meeting of bishops, convocation, assembly, council, session, meeting, tribunal.

SYNONYMOUS *a.* [si NAWN uh mus] having a similar meaning. *Cat is synonymous with feline.* SYN. similar, same, equivalent, parallel, comparable, corresponding, like, alike, interchangeable. ANT. *antonymous, opposite.*

synopsis *n.* summary, abridgement, outline, sketch, brief, epitome, abstract, precis, condensation, digest, rundown.

syntax *n.* word arrangement, sentence structure, word order, phrasing.

synthesis *n.* **1.** ASSEMBLY composition, combination, integration, mixing, blending. **2.** WHOLE FROM MANY PARTS conglomeration, mixture, compound, alloy, blend, amalgam, composite.

synthesize *v.* assemble, combine, integrate, mix, blend, conglomerate, compound, alloy, fuse, meld. ANT. *separate, divide, disassemble.*

synthesizer *n.* electronic keyboard, *sound machine. SEE MUSIC, MUSICAL INSTRUMENT

synthetic *a.* artificial, man-made, manufactured, unnatural, synthesized, imitation, ersatz, sham, fake. ANT. *natural, real, genuine.*

syphilis *n.* venereal disease, sexually transmitted disease (STD), lues, pox.

syrupy *a.* sickeningly sweet, cloyingly sweet, overly sentimental, *dripping with sweetness, *sweet enough to gag a maggot, mawkish, maudlin, *mushy.

system *n.* arrangement, organization, structure, scheme, set-up, method, plan, operation, procedure, course of action, approach, technique, standard operating procedure, program, way.

systematic *a.* orderly, regular, methodical, arranged, organized, ordered, routine, regulated. ANT. *disorderly, random, unarranged.*

systematize *v.* arrange, order, regulate, organize, methodize, standardize, coordinate, program.

T

tab n. **1.** FLAP strip, tongue, tag, projection, loop, ring. **2.** BILL check, cost, expenses, tally, account, record, reckoning, score.

tabernacle n. **1.** PLACE OF WORSHIP temple, shrine, sanctuary. **2.** TENT dwelling.

table n. **1.** FURNITURE board, counter, sideboard, stand, dining room table, drop-leaf table, coffee table, end table, parsons table, buffet, writing table, desk. **2.** LIST chart, graph, diagram, column, tabulation, index, register.

table v. postpone, delay, shelve, *put on the back burner, put aside, suspend, hold off, sideline, defer, pigeonhole, freeze.

tableau n. picture, scene, view, depiction, spectacle, illustration.

tableland n. karoo, mesa. SEE PLATEAU

tablet n. **1.** WRITING PAD pad of paper, notebook, scratch pad. **2.** SLAB piece, stone, plaque. **3.** PILL capsule, lozenge, troche.

tableware n. flatware, silverware, glassware, dishes.

tabloid n. scandal sheet, *rag, newspaper.

taboo n. prohibition, restriction, *no-no, *don't, *thou-shalt-not, proscription, ban, limitation, forbiddance, reservation.

taboo a. prohibited, restricted, proscribed, *frowned on, forbidden, banned, verboten, unacceptable, out-of-bounds, against social convention, anathema. ANT. accepted, *okay, allowed.

tabulate v. list, put in columns, graph, chart, inventory, index, formulate, figure, arrange, systematize.

TACIT a. [TASS it] implied but unspoken, unexpressed. They had a tacit agreement to stay sober while hunting. SYN. unspoken, unexpressed, silent, implied, implicit, understood, unsaid, unvoiced, inferred. ANT. spoken, expressed, explicit.

TACITURN a. [TAS i TURN] untalkative, uncommunicative, quiet by nature. He was a taciturn old farmer who rarely said anything more than an obligatory "nope" and "yep." SYN. untalkative, uncommunicative, quiet, closemouthed, reticent, reserved, speechless, withdrawn, tight-lipped, mute. ANT. talkative, loquacious, *motor-mouthed, voluble.

tack n. **1.** NAIL thumbtack, pushpin, brad, rivet, staple. **2.** COURSE heading, direction, way, route, path, approach, line, plan, zigzag.

tack v. nail, pin, attach, fasten, fix, affix, staple.

tackle n. gear, apparatus, equipment, outfit, riggings, paraphernalia, implements, trappings, rope and pulley.

tackle v. **1.** THROW DOWN knock down, sack, drop, down, seize, pounce on, grab, intercept, *collar, wrestle to the ground. **2.** UNDERTAKE take on, *take a shot at, endeavor, work at, *take a crack at, attack, deal with, try, set about, *give it the old college try.

tacky a. **1.** TASTELESS unstylish, cheap, *chintzy, unfashionable, in poor taste, gawdy, garish, *schlocky, loud, shabby, dowdy, frumpy, *grubby, frowzy. **2.** STICKY gummy, gluey, adhesive, viscid. ANT. **1.** tasteful, stylish, elegant.

tact n. diplomacy, grace, good manners, delicacy, sensitivity, savoir-faire, finesse, discretion, thoughtfulness, consideration, courtesy. "The unsaid part of what you think."—Henry Van Dyke. "Tongue in check."—Susan Dytri. "In the battle of existence, talent is the punch; tact is the clever footwork."—Wilson Mizner. "The art of making a point without making an enemy."—Howard Newton. "The ability to tell a man he's open-minded when he has a hole in his head."—F.G. Kernan. ANT. insensitivity, rudeness, bluntness.

tactful a. diplomatic, gracious, well-mannered, delicate, sensitive, discreet, thoughtful, considerate, courteous, polite, politic, civil. ANT. blunt, rude, insensitive.

tactical a. strategic, cunning, tricky, clever, skillful.

tactics n. strategy, *game plan, battle plan, strategics, stratagems, plans, scheme, ploys, moves, maneuvers, machinations, tricks, course of action.

tactile a. touchable, tangible.

tactless a. rude, blunt, insensitive, inconsiderate, boorish, indiscreet, thoughtless, rough, undiplomatic, disrespectful, frank, direct, gauche, sharp, offensive. ANT. tactful, diplomatic, gracious, sensitive.

tag n. label, card, ticket, *ID, identification, logo, stub, sticker, tab, slip, marker, trademark, emblem.

tag v. mark, identify, label, name, call, title, style, designate, earmark.

tail n. **1.** REAR rump, backside, buttocks, *butt, hind end, posterior, behind, derriere, *tush, *ass. **2.** APPENDAGE extremity, brush, whip, scut, coccyx.

tail v. follow, trail, shadow, dog, hound, stalk,

tag.

tailing *n.* waste, refuse, leavings, remains.

tailor *n.* garment maker, seamstress, clothier, designer.

tailor *v.* fit, suit, adapt, shape, adjust, modify, alter, cut, style, fine-tune.

tailor-made *a.* made to order, custom-made, custom-fit, tailored.

taint *n.* corruption, blot, blemish, disgrace, discredit, stigma, black mark, *black eye, contamination.

taint *v.* infect, corrupt, contaminate, pollute, affect, poison, blemish, blot, disgrace, discredit, stigmatize, *give a black eye, muddy, dirty, defile. ANT. *clean, purify, enhance.*

take *n.* proceeds, profit, yield, *haul, return, gate, net, income, gain.

take *v.* **1.** SEIZE, GATHER UP get, secure, grab, grasp, acquire, snatch, pocket, steal, appropriate, purloin, *nab, *swipe, borrow, help oneself to, pick up, obtain, carry off, pluck, reap. **2.** CHOOSE select, pick, *go with, opt for, single out, settle on, prefer, favor. **3.** CONVEY carry, bring, deliver, transport, haul, tote, lug, *schlep, usher, bear, drive. **4.** ENDURE stand, withstand, put up with, suffer, bear, abide, tolerate, weather, brave, stomach, *hack. **5.** REQUIRE demand, necessitate, call for, need. **6.** CHARM captivate, enchant, win over, bewitch, fascinate, dazzle. **7.** *Sl.* CHEAT trick, *ripoff, fleece. ANT. *1. give, leave, let go. 2. reject, pass over.*

take after *v.* emulate, imitate, copy, act like, be like, resemble, look like.

take back *v.* retract, recant, backpedal, disavow, *flip-flop, *eat one's words. ANT. *stand by.*

takeoff *n.* **1.** LAUNCH liftoff, departure, leaving. **2.** SATIRE parody, send-up, spoof, burlesque, caricature, lampoon, mockery, comedy.

take off *v.* leave, *split, *blow, *book, *beat feet, *scram, depart, skedaddle.

takeover *n.* overthrow, usurpation, coup, coup d'etat, vanquishment, conquest, subjugation, rout, dethronement, deposition.

tale *n.* story, narrative, account, fairy tale, fable, myth, legend, yarn, cautionary tale, drama, saga, chronicle.

talent *n.* gift, endowment, natural ability, innate ability, *God-given talent, genius, knack, flair, aptitude, facility, bent, capability, expertise, faculty. "Each man has his vocation. Talent is the call." — Ralph Waldo Emerson. "To do easily what is difficult for others." — Henry Amiel. "Like a grain of pearl sand shifting about in the creative mind. A valued tormentor." — Truman Capote.

talented *a.* gifted, naturally endowed, capable, having a knack, having a flair, having innate ability, having an aptitude for, *having the right stuff, proficient.

talisman *n.* amulet, charm, good luck charm, fetish, ring, stone.

talk *n.* **1.** SPEECH conversation, verbalization, words, communication, utterance, articulation, expression. **2.** DISCUSSION chat, dialogue, *confab, conference, tete-a-tete, *rap session, *powwow, consultation, argument, *gabfest, interview, *heart-to-heart. **3.** LECTURE address, discourse, oration, speech, sermon, recitation, allocution, tirade. **4.** GOSSIP rumor, scuttlebutt, *buzz, hearsay, word, *grapevine, blabbing, idle talk, *hot air, drivel.

talk *v.* **1.** SPEAK converse, verbalize, frame words, communicate, utter, articulate, express, voice, say, pronounce, enunciate, intone, chatter, babble, prattle, palaver, *shoot the breeze, *yak, *gab, *run off at the mouth, blurt, cry, fume, grumble, huff, rant, rave, shout, snap, sputter, exclaim, grunt, murmur, stammer, whisper. "To open and close the mouth rapidly while the bellows in the throat pumps out the gas in the brain." — Elbert Hubbard. **2.** DISCUSS chat, have a dialogue, confer, consult, *have a powwow, *rap, confabulate, *interface, *touch base, parley. **3.** DELIVER A SPEECH deliver a sermon, address, orate, give a talk. **4.** GOSSIP *fuel the rumor mill, blab. **5.** CONFESS *spill the beans, *let the cat out of the bag, divulge, disclose, *sing, reveal.

talkative *a.* loquacious, garrulous, voluble, *motor-mouthed, *long-winded, chatty, having the gift of gab, gabby, rambling, verbose, *bigmouthed. ANT. *taciturn, quiet, reserved, uncommunicative, *clammed up.*

talker *n.* *chatterbox, *motormouth, *windbag, *bigmouth, *magpie, gossip, mouthpiece, spokesman, spokeswoman.

tall *a.* **1.** TOWERING high, big, of great stature, lofty, sky-scraping, sky-high, soaring, elevated, *having two different weather systems. **2.** EXAGGERATED unbelievable, farfetched, hard to believe, outlandish, preposterous. ANT. *1. short, squat, groundhugging, low. 2. believable, credible.*

tally *n.* total, reckoning, account, score, count, sum, number, amount, *bottom line.

tally v. add up, total, reckon, account, score, count, sum up, register, enter, mark, list.

talon n. claw, nail.

tame a. **1.** TAMED docile, domesticated, broken, housebroken, trained, gentle, submissive, manageable, tractable, obedient, *busted. **2.** SPIRITLESS lifeless, half-hearted, boring, dull, tedious, uninteresting, *blah, bland, dry. ANT. **1.** wild, undomesticated, spirited. **2.** spirited, lively, wild.

tamp v. pack, pound down, push down.

tamper v. interfere, meddle, mess with, fiddle, fool with, monkey with, *doctor, alter, change, corrupt, bribe.

tan v. flog, thrash. SEE WHIP

tan a. tawny, brown, golden brown, bronze, copper, fawn, sand, leather, buff, beige.

tang n. **1.** SHARP FLAVOR OR SMELL scent, aroma, piquancy, bite, pungency, sharpness, punch, zest, zip. **2.** TOUCH OR TRACE suggestion, hint, tinge, dab.

tangent a. touching, contiguous.

tangential a. divergent, digressing, off on a tangent, straying, shifting, rambling, peripheral, barely related.

TANGIBLE a. [TAN juh bul] touchable, palpable, having physical form. *The tire tracks were tangible evidence that a motorbike had torn up the field.* SYN. touchable, palpable, solid, concrete, physical, hard, substantial, real, material, perceivable, tactile, corporeal, visible, actual, definite. ANT. *intangible, immaterial, imperceptible, imaginary.*

tangle n. knot, snarl, entanglement, mess, mass of confusion, snag, kink, *ball-up, ravel, web, mat, jumble, labyrinth, *bird's nest, trap, complication, mish-mash, mix-up.

tangle v. **1.** KNOT snarl, entangle, mess, become a mass of confusion, snag, kink, *ball up, ravel, web, mat, jumble, mix up, enmesh, entwine, trap, catch. **2.** FIGHT wrangle, quarrel, argue, bicker, *lock horns.

tangy a. sharp, flavorful, biting, piquant, zesty, tart, spicy, pungent. ANT. *dull, bland, mild.*

tank n. **1.** VAT receptacle, tub, container, vessel, cistern, boiler, holding tank, storage tank, reservoir. **2.** ARMORED MILITARY VEHICLE combat vehicle, Abrams M-1, Bradley M-2, Sherman tank, armored personnel carrier.

tankard n. cup, mug, stein, pottle.

tantalize v. tease, tempt, entice, bait, plague, make one's mouth water, titillate, *lead on, bewitch, frustrate, *give the Tantalus treatment.

TANTAMOUNT a. [TAN tuh MOUNT] equal, equivalent, same. *A prison sentence in some third world countries is tantamount to torture.* SYN. equal, equivalent, much the same, like, as good as, parallel, synonymous, comparable, identical. ANT. *different, opposite, unequal.*

tantrum n. rage, outburst, fit, fit of temper, *blowup, rampage, eruption, seizure, storm, temper tantrum, conniption, *hissy fit, *nutty, *freak-out, *piss hemorrhage.

tap n. faucet, spigot, spout, nozzle, valve, cock, stopper, bung, plug, cork, spile.

tap v. **1.** POKE hit, touch, rap, pat, drum, smack, strike. **2.** DRAIN draw, siphon, empty, bleed, milk, pump, broach, pierce. **3.** WIRETAP *bug, eavesdrop.

tap dance n. SEE DANCE

tape n. strip, band, binding, ribbon, roll, adhesive tape, masking tape, electrician's tape.

tape v. **1.** BIND fasten, band together, stick up, mend, close. **2.** RECORD put on tape.

taper v. diminish, decrease, dwindle, taper off, lessen, fade, wane, decline, thin out, contract, abate, die out. ANT. *grow, broaden, increase.*

tapestry n. wall hanging, decorative cover, dossal, Gobelin.

tar n. pitch, asphalt, bitumen.

tardy a. late, overdue, past due, delayed, slow, belated, behind, behind schedule, unpunctual, detained, held up, lagging. ANT. *early, on time, punctual.*

target n. **1.** OBJECTIVE aim, goal, bull's-eye, destination, mark, point, quarry. **2.** SCAPEGOAT butt, *mark, laughingstock, victim, *patsy, *easy mark.

target v. set one's sights on, *draw a bead on, aim for.

tariff n. tax, import tax, charge, toll, excise, assessment, fee, levy, duty, bill.

tarnish n. dullness, discoloration, oxidation, patina, stain, blemish, wax buildup, cloudiness, haziness, smudge.

tarnish v. **1.** DULL discolor, oxidize, fade, dim, smudge, stain, darken, remove luster, blacken. **2.** SULLY ONE'S REPUTATION spoil, ruin, taint, disgrace, dishonor, discredit, defame, degrade, damage, slander. ANT. **1.** shine, add luster, polish, brighten. **2.** honor, credit, clear one's name.

tarpaulin n. tarp, canvas, cover.

tarry v. loiter, stay, linger, remain, wait around, hang around, dilly-dally, lag, dawdle, procrastinate, stall.

tart n. **1.** FRUIT PIE pastry, flan, turnover, Danish.

2. SLUT prostitute, hussy, *easy lay, tramp, whore, strumpet, trollop.

tart *a.* sharp, sour, acid, *mouth-puckering, acidulous, acerbic, bitter, biting, piquant, tangy, pungent. ANT. *sweet, honeyed.*

task *n.* job, chore, assignment, duty, charge, work, responsibility, occupation, undertaking, stint, burden, mission, errand.

taskmaster *n.* overseer, *whip, slave driver, boss, commander, supervisor, superintendent, manager, disciplinarian, tyrant.

taste *n.* **1.** FLAVOR flavoring, savor, tang, sensation, bite, *kick, piquancy, zing, zip, aftertaste, saltiness, sweetness, sourness. **2.** SAMPLE spoonful, bite, mouthful, sip, bit, morsel, touch. **3.** PREFERENCE liking, leaning, fancy, predilection, penchant, love, affection, partiality. **4.** GOOD JUDGMENT fashion sense, discrimination, sense of style, discernment, cultivation, refinement, feeling, tastefulness, grace. "A fine judgment in discerning art." — Horace.

taste *v.* sample, savor, relish, discern, try, eat.

tasteful *n.* in good taste, stylish, smart, refined, cultured, restrained, decorous, aesthetically pleasing, elegant, discriminating, correct, fitting. ANT. *tasteless, in poor taste, tacky, ugly, loud, unrefined.*

tasteless *a.* **1.** WITHOUT FLAVOR flavorless, bland, insipid, flat, stale, watery, weak, thin, vapid. **2.** TACKY in poor taste, unrefined, cheap, graceless, vulgar, crude, garish, loud, flashy, gaudy, ostentatious, offensive. ANT. *tasteful, in good taste, refined.*

tasty *a.* good-tasting, delicious, mouth-watering, *yummy, *scrumptious, toothsome, delectable, savory, appetizing, flavorful, palatable. ANT. *disgusting, gross, nauseating.*

tatter *n.* shred, scrap, piece, torn piece, rip, ribbon.

tattered *a.* shredded, torn to pieces, ripped, ragged, cut to ribbons.

tattle *v.* **1.** TELL ON inform, blab, *squeal on, tattletale, *snitch, *rat on, divulge, reveal, betray, leak, give away, *spill the beans. **2.** CHATTER talk idly, gossip, *gab, chitchat, *yak, *run off at the mouth, prattle, babble.

tattletale *n.* informer, *squealer, *snitch, *rat, tattler, telltale, blabbermouth, *stool pigeon.

tatoo *n.* drum signal, bugle signal, call, summons.

taunt *n.* mocking, ridicule, jeer, sneer, sarcasm, *swipe, crack, provocation, teasing, jibe, barb, insult.

taunt *v.* jeer at, mock, reproach, ridicule, sneer at, *swipe at, provoke, tease, insult, harass, make fun of, *razz, *rag, ride.

taut *a.* **1.** TIGHT tense, strained, stressed, drawn, stiffened, rigid, firm. **2.** TRIM neat, tidy, efficient, shipshape, spruce, in good order.

tautology *n.* repetition, redundance, redundancy, reiteration, verbosity, prolixity, pleonasm.

tavern *n.* bar, saloon, pub, taproom, drinking establishment, ale house, roadhouse, inn, watering hole, cocktail lounge, public house, nightclub.

TAWDRY *a.* [TAW dree] cheap and gaudy, loud, showy. *She spent all her money on tawdry jewelry.* SYN. cheap, gaudy, loud, showy, flashy, sleazy, tacky, garish, meretricious, *chintzy, tasteless, raffish. ANT. *elegant, tasteful.*

tax *n.* **1.** LEVY toll, tariff, charge, assessment, duty, excise, surcharge, impost, *Uncle's Sam's share, *the Governor's share, *the federal treasury's share, the state treasury's share, custom, percentage, income tax, property tax, sales tax. "The sinews of the state." — Cicero. "Capital punishment." — Jeff Hayes. "The fine we pay for thriving." — Anon. **2.** BURDEN demand, onus, strain, weight, responsibility, *albatross, *millstone.

tax *v.* **1.** LEVY A CHARGE assess, charge, appraise, exact, demand payment, tithe. "Consists in so plucking the goose as to get the most feathers with the least hissing." — Jean Colbert. **2.** BURDEN weigh down, strain, stress, drain, encumber, saddle, load, push, drive, exhaust. **3.** ACCUSE charge, blame, indict.

taxi *n.* taxicab, cab, hack.

taxing *v.* draining, strenuous, sapping, exhausting, burdensome, wearing, heavy, demanding, backbreaking.

tea *n.* **1.** DRINK beverage, brew, decoction, green tea, black tea, oolong, pekoe, Lapsang, Darjeeling, herb tea, mint, sassafras, camomile tea. **2.** RECEPTION get-together, party, klatch.

teach *v.* educate, instruct, instill knowledge, school, enlighten, edify, tutor, indoctrinate, *show the ropes, train, drill, *beat into one's head, ground, explain, guide, coach, acquaint with, program. ANT. *learn, be enlightened.*

teacher *n.* educator, instructor, tutor, professor, mentor, trainer, preceptor, schoolmaster, schoolmarm, pedagogue, coach, guide, counselor, guru, don, faculty member. "The child's third parent."—Hyman Berston. "The mediocre teacher tells. The good teacher explains. The superior teacher demonstrates. The great teacher inspires."—William Arthur Ward.

teaching n. education, instruction, training, schooling, tutelage, pedagogy, inculcation, grounding, indoctrination, tuition. "To cultivate talent until it ripens for the public to reap its bounty."—Jascha Heifetz.

team n. squad, crew, band, company, troupe, corps, duo, trio, quartet, club, gang, string, unit, faction, partners.

teamwork n. collaboration, pulling together, tandem work, cooperation, synergy, synergism, concert, interaction, *logrolling.

tear n. **1.** TORN PLACE rip, opening, split, slash, slit. **2.** HURRY scramble. SEE RUSH **3.** Sl. SPREE *bender, *binge, carousal, *drunk, party, revelry. SEE TEARS

tear v. **1.** RIP cut, slash, slit, open, split, shred, fray, tatter, rend, rive, run, come apart at the seams, lacerate, mutilate. **2.** RUSH fly, bolt, run, dart, hurry, speed, shoot, hustle, *zip, *zoom, *go like lightning, *go like the wind.

tear down v. raze, level, flatten, bulldoze, demolish, dismantle, destroy, pull down, wreck.

tearful a. lachrymose, *weepy, *misty-eyed, teary, dewy-eyed, *brimming with tears, watery-eyed, sobbing, crying, sniveling, blubbering, wailing, sad, mournful, heartbroken, sorrowful.

tears n. teardrops, weeping, gushing. "The silent language of grief."—Voltaire. "Holy water"—Shakespeare. "Remorse code."—I. Masai. SEE CRY

tease v. **1.** MAKE FUN OF taunt, ridicule, ride, *razz, *josh, *give a hard time, *pick on, kid, *rib, harass, *pull one's leg, *roast, *get a rise out of, pester, mock, bedevil, tantalize. **2.** COMB brush, card, fluff, fluff up.

teat n. nipple, tit, mammilla.

technical a. mechanical, technological, *high-tech, scientific, professional, specialized, special, methodological.

technicality n. minor detail, minor point, specification, formality, *nitpicky rule.

technician n. specialist, expert, master, professional, authority, journeyman, *pro, *techie.

technique n. method, execution, style, approach, artistry, way, procedure, mode, manner, fashion, course, tack, craft, system.

tedious a. boring, tiresome, wearisome, dull, monotonous, uninteresting, *humdrum, prosaic, sleep-inducing, drawn out, long-winded, repetitious, bland, flat, dry. ANT. *stimulating, exciting, electrifying.*

tedium n. boredom, monotony, ennui, dullness, sameness, routine, rut, repetitiousness, flatness, deadness. ANT. *excitement, stimulation.*

teem v. abound, swarm, be full of, brim, burst, overflow, bristle with, be overrun with.

teeming a. abounding, swarming, full, brimming, packed, bursting, thick, overflowing, bristling with, overrun, crawling with, swimming with. ANT. *bare, empty, scanty.*

teenager n. adolescent, teen, juvenile, youth, minor, teenybopper, sophomore, *bobby soxer, *punk, high school kid.

teeny a. tiny, teentsy, *teensy-weensy, minute, microscopic, wee, Lilliputian, miniature, pint-sized. ANT. *huge, gigantic.*

teepee n. wigwam, wickiup, lodge, tent.

teeter v. seesaw, totter, oscillate, wobble, pivot, balance, rock, waver, vacillate.

teeth n. molars, bicuspids, incisors, canines, *grinders, fangs, *pearly whites.

WORD FIND

adolescence, last molars that erupt in late: wisdom teeth

baby or temporary teeth: deciduous teeth, milk teeth

cavities: caries

cut one's first teeth: teethe

eruption through gums: dentition

gum disease: periodontal disease, periodontitis, pyorrhea

gum inflammation: gingivitis

hard covering: enamel

false: denture

gnashing or grinding: bruxism

large teeth, condition of having: macrodontia

loss of: dedentition

meet, clench or align properly, failure of upper and lower to: malocclusion

pointy part: cusp

small teeth, condition of having: microdontia

sound of clicking: chatter

sticky film that forms on after eating: plaque

tipped over and pushing on adjacent tooth: impacted

yellowish concretion on: tartar

teetotaler n. nondrinker, abstainer, *dry.

teetotalism n. abstinence. SEE TEMPERANCE

telecast n. SEE BROADCAST

telegram n. wire, message, telegraph, cable, *telex, dispatch, transmission.

telegraph n. wire, Telex, cable, ticker, news ticker, signaling system.

WORD FIND

code of dots and dashes: Morse code

national service: Western Union

typed wire message and printer itself: Teletype

telepathy n. extrasensory perception, *ESP, clairvoyance, mindreading, sixth sense, thought transference, psychic power.

telephone n. phone, *horn, line, extension phone, car phone, cellular phone, transmitter, receiver, rotary phone, touchtone phone.

WORD FIND

beeper: pager

buzz: dial tone

conference held with speakerphones, closed circuit television: teleconference

connecting phone lines, apparatus for: switchboard

digits of phone number, first three: prefix

eavesdrop electronically on another's phone line: tap

hand instrument: handset

line kept open and accessible without dialing: hot line

long-distance service for companies: WATS (Wide Area Telecommunications Service)

loudspeaker, phone with: speakerphone

message system: voice mail

rest for handset: cradle

room-to-room or interoffice communication device: intercom, PBX (Private Branch Exchange)

science: telephonics, telephony

telescope n. optical instrument, scope, spy glass, binoculars, field glass, radio telescope.

telescope v. contract, condense, shorten, shrink, truncate, consolidate. ANT. extend, lengthen.

telethon n. pledge campaign, charity drive, appeal for funding.

televise v. broadcast, transmit, show.

television n. TV, *tube, *boob tube, video, *telly, *idiot box, console, set, entertainment center, *one-eyed monster. "Chewing gum for the eyes." — Frank Lloyd Wright. "An invention that permits you to be entertained in your livingroom by people you wouldn't have in your home." — David Frost. "The plug-in drug." — Anon. "A vast wasteland." — Anon.

WORD FIND

ABC: American Broadcasting Company

affiliated TV stations, collectively: network

audition for TV show, open: cattle call

award: Emmy

background scene slide: balop

BBC: British Broadcasting Corporation

brief clip of politician's or other newsmaker's remarks: soundbite

broadcast: air, telecast

broadcast on radio and TV at same time: simulcast

"brought to you by" opening of show: opening billboard

camera crane for moving, outdoor shots: cherry picker

camera crane operator: crane grip

camera dolly, one who pushes: dolly grip

camera elevating device: riser

camera shot, moving: crab shot, dolly shot, truck shot

card with performer's lines on it: cue card, idiot card, flip card

CBS: Columbia Broadcasting System

color test strip: color bar, colorburst

commercials, group of: pod

credits at end of show, moving: crawl

directing and engineering room: control room

distribution of TV shows to subscriber stations: syndication

distributor of TV shows: syndicate

8 PM to 11 PM: prime time

electrician head in studio: gaffer

goofs made by actors or crew edited out of tape: bloopers, outtakes

hand or assistant in studio: grip, hammer, set carpenter

high resolution TV: HDTV (High Definition TV)

identifying, introductory scenery of TV show: signature montage

light, studio: floodlight, klieg light, scoop, basher

local prohibition of program to attract bigger audience at live show: blackout

local station part of national network: affiliate

microphone boom, long: *fishpole

minimum standard fee for performer: scale

monitor console from which director chooses which camera shot will air: preview monitor

moral standards, department that assures program meets society's: standards and practices narrator's voice heard over program: voice-over

NBC: National Broadcasting System

network performers under contract: stable

optical effect: freeze-frame, superimposition, split screen

optical effect used to create a ghost: Pepper's ghost

optical transition device: wipe, dissolve, fade-in, fade-out, fade to black

performers in a show, collective term for: cast

portable TV news camera: minicam

prerecorded laughter: laughtrack

prerecorded material: canned

promo piece of upcoming show: trailer, teaser, preview

rails on which camera may ride in outdoor, moving shot: dolly tracks

ratings company: Arbitron, A.C. Nielson

ratings months: sweeps

read script from front of TV camera, device that allows actor to: prompter, Teleprompter

record a program: tape

recorded as it happened with no takeouts: live on tape

record in sound effects, music: dub, foley

red light on camera that lights during recording: tally light

regulating commission: FCC (Federal Communications Commission)

royalty paid to performer for reuse of their work: residual

satellite used for TV transmission: *bird

scrambling pay TV signals: encryption

show where performer or camera will stand or move: block

situation comedy: sitcom

sound effect: foley

sound effects, one who performs: foley artist

sound effects studio: foley studio, foley stage

studio scaffolding where lights are hung: catwalk

superimposed script read from TV camera's lens: prompter script

superimposed text on screen: legend

superimposes bulletins, news, weather on bottom of screen, apparatus that: flashcaster

superimpose text on screen: key

talk show, cancel a guest at the last minute on a: bump

talk show waiting room for guests: green room

tear down a set: strike

time off between show's taping: hiatus

trailer with dressing rooms for shooting on location: honey wagon

transmission of show from network to local station: feed

tryout episode of TV show: pilot

union for performers: AFTRA (American Federation of Television and Radio Artists)

videotape cutter, splicer, arranger: editor

"We'll be back after these messages' transitional device: bumper

unscrambling of pay TV signals: decryption

video disk jockey: veejay

SEE MOVIE

tell *v.* **1.** COMMUNICATE relate, state, say, declare, make known, speak, divulge, disclose, reveal, impart, voice, announce, utter, *spit it out, inform, mention, report, confess, assert, let slip, *spill the beans, *let the cat out of the bag, blab, admit, break the news. **2.** TATTLE *blow the whistle on, *squeal, *rat, betray. **3.** GIVE AN ACCOUNT narrate, chronicle, recount, relate, detail, describe, recite. **4.** DISCERN recognize, distinguish, discriminate, make out, detect, ascertain, determine, recognize, identify.

teller *n.* **1.** NARRATOR storyteller, chronicler, reporter, raconteur, recounter. **2.** CASHIER clerk.

telling *a.* **1.** REVEALING indicative, suggestive, expressive, telltale. **2.** FORCEFUL striking, effective, weighty, important, potent, influential, decisive, consequential, momentous. ANT. *2. ineffective, inconsequential, insignificant.*

tell off *v.* rebuke, reprimand, upbraid, berate, admonish, *ream out, *lambaste, *rake over the coals, *give one a piece of one's mind, *chew out, *bawl out, *call on the carpet, *dress down, *give hell, *jump down one's throat, *let have it with both barrels, *read the riot act, *rip into. ANT. *commend, give a pat on the back, praise.*

telltale *a.* revealing, indicative, demonstrative, giveaway, meaningful, betraying, illuminating, informative.

TEMERITY *n.* [tuh MER i tee] foolhardy boldness, recklessness. *I can't believe he had the temerity to scold the boss.* SYN. rashness, boldness, recklessness, foolhardiness, gall, carelessness, audacity, indiscretion, nerve, *balls, precipitateness, *chutzpah, impudence. ANT. *timidity, cautiousness, cowardice,* *judiciousness.*

temper *n.* **1.** FRAME OF MIND mood, disposition, temperament, spirits, humor, attitude, outlook, character. **2.** TENDENCY TO BECOME ANGRY *short fuse, *hairtrigger temper, *low boiling point, *low critical mass, *hot blood, *hot head, explosive personality, volatility, impatience, irritability, touchiness, petulence, *hypersensitivity, *type-A personality, *walking timebomb. **3.** ANGER rage, tantrum, outburst, fury, wrath, rampage, *blowup, storm. **4.** COMPOSURE calmness, equanimity, good humor, sang-froid, coolness. ANT. 2. *long fuse, *high boiling point, easygoing personality, cool head. 3. composure, calmness, tranquility.

temper *v.* **1.** MODERATE soften, lessen, tone down, ease, mollify, assuage, dilute, mitigate, relieve, pacify. **2.** TOUGHEN harden, strengthen, anneal. ANT. 1. intensify, harden, increase. 2. soften, weaken.

temperament *n.* nature, frame of mind, disposition, character, makeup, mood, mind-set, inclination, natural tendencies, humor, constitution, personality.

temperamental *a.* excitable, *hot-headed, *hot-blooded, moody, easily upset, volatile, touchy, irritable, unstable, tempestuous, high-strung, thin-skinned, *short-fused. ANT. even-tempered, easygoing, stable.

temperance *n.* moderation, abstemiousness, abstinent, self restrained, unindulgent, self-control, sobriety, soberness, forbearance, teetotalism. "The moderating of one's desires in obedience to reason." — Cicero. "The golden mean." — Horace. ANT. indulgence, abandon, immoderation.

TEMPERATE *a.* [TEM pur it] moderate, mild, restrained. *Hawaii is known for its temperate climate.* SYN. moderate, mild, restrained, agreeable, *middle-of-the-road, fair, clement, unextreme, medium, reasonable, conservative. ANT. intemperate, extreme, immoderate.

temperature *n.* hotness, coldness, heat, cold, degrees, body heat, fever.

tempest *n.* **1.** STORM blow, hurricane, typhoon, wind storm, squall, tornado, cyclone, *twister, blizzard. **2.** OUTBURST outbreak, tumult, disturbance, unrest, turmoil, ferment, eruption, uproar, upheaval, *tempest in a teapot. ANT. calm, tranquility, serenity, quiet.

tempestuous *a.* stormy, wild, violent, turbulent, raging, intense, furious, tumultuous, feverish, impassioned. ANT. calm, quiet, tranquil.

template *n.* pattern, guide, outline, prototype, gauge.

temple *n.* place of worship, house of worship, church, cathedral, synagogue, holy place, shrine, sanctuary, pagoda.

tempo *n.* speed, rate, pace, measure, velocity, time, meter, cadence, rhythm, pulse, beat.

temporal *a.* **1.** TEMPORARY transitory, fleeting, ephemeral, short-lived, momentary, passing, impermanent. **2.** WORLDLY mundane, earthly, mortal, of this world, terrestrial, material, nonspiritual, secular. ANT. 1. permanent, long-lasting, eternal. 2. spiritual, heavenly, godly.

temporary *a.* impermanent, transitory, short-term, passing, transient, fleeting, ephemeral, brief, pro tempore, stopgap, makeshift, make-do, provisional, interim. ANT. permanent, lasting, eternal, fixed.

temporize *v.* evade, parley, stall, procrastinate, delay, hem and haw, tarry, equivocate, fillibuster.

tempt *v.* lure, entice, bait, tantalize, seduce, attract, court, *suck in, *hold out a carrot, draw, captivate, bewitch. ANT. repulse, repel, turn off.

temptation *n.* lure, enticement, tantalization, seduction, attraction, courting, *carrot, captivation, bait, *come-on, draw, snare.

tempter *n.* enticer, temptress, tantalizer, seducer, seductress, teaser, Satan.

tempting *a.* alluring, enticing, tantalizing, seductive, attractive, magnetic, appetizing, mouth-watering, baiting. ANT. repulsive, repellant, sickening.

TENABLE *a.* [TEN uh bul] defensible, that can be argued for. *His alibi was entirely tenable.* SYN. defensible, defendable, indisputable, incontestable, ironclad, solid, maintainable, reasonable, credible, viable. ANT. untenable, indefensible, unjustifiable.

TENACIOUS *a.* [tuh NAY shus] persistent, tough, not giving up readily, holding fast, stubborn. *He clung tenaciously to his beliefs.* SYN. persistent, tough, stubborn, resolute, dogged, perseverant, strong, steadfast, unyielding, unwilling to let go, determined, unwavering, staunch. ANT. irresolute, weak-willed, yielding.

tenacity *n.* persistence, toughness, mental toughness, stubbornness, resolve, resolution, backbone, doggedness, perseverance, strength, *stick-to-itiveness, grit, endurance. ANT. weakness, weak will, spinelessness.

tenant n. renter, leaseholder, lessee, occupant, lodger, roomer, resident.

tend v. **1.** TAKE CARE OF care for, mind, minister to, attend, cater to, look after, wait on, manage, assist, aid. **2.** INCLINE be apt, be liable, lean, be likely, have a tendency, be disposed.

tendency n. inclination, disposition, leaning, bent, propensity, proclivity, proneness, penchant, predisposition, course, drift.

tender n. **1.** OFFER proffer, proposition, presentation. **2.** CARETAKER sitter, watcher, maintenance man.

tender v. offer, proffer, present, proposition, put forth, submit, advance, give.

tender a. **1.** SOFT delicate, fragile, frail, feeble, weak, feeble. **2.** GENTLE mild, light, soft, easy. **3.** YOUTHFUL immature, young, unseasoned, unhardened, soft, raw, vulnerable, *wet behind the ears. **4.** TENDERHEARTED loving, kind, compassionate, sympathetic, caring, warm, understanding, supportive, sweet, considerate. **5.** PAINFUL hurting, smarting, sore, raw, sensitive, inflamed. ANT. *1. hard, stony, tough. 2. rough, hard. 3. mature, seasoned, experienced, hardened. 4. uncaring, cold, indifferent, cruel.*

tenderfoot n. newcomer, beginner, novice, amateur, *greenhorn, *rookie, neophyte, tyro, raw recruit, new kid on the block.

tenderhearted a. tender, loving, kind, compassionate, sympathetic, caring, warm, understanding, supportive, sweet, considerate. ANT. *coldhearted, brutal, cruel, uncaring.*

tenderness n. tenderheartedness, love and kindness, compassion, sympathy, caring, warmth, understanding, support, sweetness, consideration, humanity, pity, mercy. ANT. *hardheartedness, brutality, cruelty.*

tendon n. sinew, connective tissue, muscle fiber, thew.

tenement n. apartment, flat, house, duplex, boarding house, *dump, *rat's nest, slum, rookery.

TENET n. [TEN it] a principle or belief. *She didn't agree with all the tenets of her church.* SYN. principle, belief, doctrine, dogma, conviction, creed, credo, canon, rule, teaching, maxim.

tennis n. racket sport, lawn tennis, game, sphairistike.

WORD FIND

boundary line marking end of service boxes: service line

championships held in England: Wimbledon

court area between net and service line: forecourt

court on which ball bounces, skids quickly: fast court

court rectangles in which ball must land when served: service court

diagonal shot: crosscourt shot

doubles player move into partner's court for surprise shot: poaching

drive the ball directly at opponent's body to throw off balance: jam

finesse player: touch player

40-40 tie situation: deuce

four players, game with: doubles

injury or inflammation of elbow tendons: tennis elbow

lines at ends of court: baseline

long back and forth exchange without a miss: rally

officials: baseline judge, linesman, net judge

original name: sphairstike

racket grip: Australian grip, continental grip, eastern, *shake hands grip

racket, middle of: sweet spot

return ball before it hits ground: volley

rotation imparted on ball: topspin, backspin

score of zero: love

scoring unit or point: fifteen

serve in two tries, failure to deliver a legal: double fault

serve on first try, failure to deliver a legal: fault

serve, stepping over baseline while making: foot fault

serve that nicks top of net and must be replayed: let

serve that opponent is unable to return: ace

showoff play to impress spectators: gallery play

spectator area, stands: gallery

stroke: forehand, backhand, lob, smash, drive, slice, chop, chip, dink, volley, punch volley

teams tournament, international: Davis Cup

tie-breaker game: sudden death

tournament open to amateurs as well as pros: open

win a game against the server: break, service break

winning best of three or more sets: match

winning point: game point

winning point in a set: set point

winning point in a set-winning game: game set

win of six games: set

wins a game against the server, point that:

break point

tenor *n.* **1.** ALTO falsetto. **2.** MEANING intent, sense, drift, purport, gist, tone.

tense *a.* **1.** TIGHT taut, stressed, strained, stretched, drawn, stiff. **2.** NERVOUS stressed, *uptight, *bundle of nerves, anxious, edgy, jittery, strained, restless, apprehensive, *having butterflies in stomach, keyed up, *sweating bullets, *on pins and needles, jumpy. ANT. *1. loose, slack, relaxed. 2. calm, composed, relaxed, tranquil.*

tense up *v.* stress out, *choke, *choke under pressure, *swallow the apple.

tension *n.* **1.** TIGHTNESS tautness, stress, strain, stiffness, rigidity, pressure, pull, stretching. **2.** NERVOUSNESS stress, anxiety, edginess, jitters, strain, restlessness, apprehension, *butterflies, *sweat, jumpiness, pressure. ANT. *1. looseness, slackness, relaxation. 2. relaxation, calm, tranquility.*

tent *n.* canvas shelter, pup tent, tepee, wigwam, wickiup, yurt, pavilion.

TENTATIVE *a.* [TEN tuh tiv] indefinite, not firmed up, as one's plans to do something, uncertain, conditional. Also, hesitant or timid. *They made tentative plans to hike the north face of the mountain.* SYN. uncertain, unsure, not firmed up, conditional, possible, proposed, contingent, indefinite, *not carved in stone, subject to change, unconfirmed, hesitant, timid, doubtful, cautious. ANT. *certain, firm, definite, confident.*

TENUOUS *a.* [TEN yoo us] thin, weak, flimsy, insubstantial, rare. *His excuse for being late was tenuous at best.* SYN. thin, weak, flimsy, insubstantial, rare, fragile, slight, light, negligible, fine, shaky. ANT. *solid, rock-solid, firm, substantial, strong.*

tenure *n.* **1.** TERM time, occupation, stay, residence, incumbency, reign. **2.** PERMANENCY permanent status, lifetime position, permanent seat, job security.

tepee *n.* wigwam, wickiup. SEE TENT

tepid *a.* **1.** LUKEWARM room temperature, barely warm. **2.** UNENTHUSIASTIC halfhearted, cool, apathetic, lukewarm, indifferent, mild, moderate, limp. ANT. *1. hot, boiling, scalding. 2. enthusiastic, passionate, fervent, wild.*

term *n.* **1.** PERIOD OF TIME duration, time, span, timespan, cycle, session, semester, quarter, spell, course, interval, stretch. **2.** PHRASE OR WORD description, designation, expression, name, denomination, terminology. **3.** CONCLUSION close, end, finish, completion, limit. limitation. **4.** SEE TERMS

term *v.* name, designate, call, label, title, dub, style.

terminal *n.* station, depot, junction, end of the line, terminus.

terminal *a.* ending, concluding, final, closing, last, final, concluding, extreme. ANT. *beginning, first.*

terminate *v.* **1.** STOP end, cease, discontinue, conclude, close, finish, cancel, eliminate, halt, desist, fire, dismiss, let go, abort. **2.** BOUND limit, demarcate, circumscribe. ANT. *start, begin, open.*

termination *n.* stoppage, end, cessation, discontinuance, conclusion, close, finish, cancellation, elimination, halt, firing, dismissal, aborting. ANT. *start, beginning, opening.*

terminology *n.* wording, phraseology, vocabulary, nomenclature, terms, language, *lingo, jargon, cant, argot.

terminus *n.* end, limit, boundary, extremity, margin, pale.

terms *n.* conditions, particulars, specifications, provisions, provisos, stipulations, *fine print, qualifications, points, agreement.

terrace *n.* **1.** PATIO OR VERANDA garden, lawn, gallery, colonnade, balcony, piazza. **2.** STAIR-STEPPING EARTH FORMATION berm, plateaus.

terra firma *n.* earth, solid ground.

terrain *n.* ground, topography, lay of the land, tract, landscape, land, turf, country, region, territory.

terrestrial *a.* earthly, worldly, terrene, tellurian, mundane. ANT. *extraterrestrial, spiritual, ethereal.*

terrible *a.* **1.** BAD awful, lousy, inferior, *crappy, horrible, appalling, objectionable, disagreeable, *rotten, revolting, atrocious, dreadful, poor. **2.** FRIGHTFUL terrifying, fearful, dreadful, harrowing, horrifying, horrific, distressing. **3.** EXTREME severe, intense, acute, fierce. ANT. *1. excellent, great, wonderful. 2. reassuring, encouraging, comforting. 3. mild, light, moderate.*

terribly *adv.* very, extremely, awfully, thoroughly, frightfully.

terrific *a.* **1.** GREAT fabulous, fantastic, excellent, wonderful, first-rate, superb, marvelous, good, sensational, *out of this world, superior, outstanding. **2.** TERRIFYING scary, frightful, fearful, dreadful, appalling, terrible, harrowing, horrifying, distressing. ANT. *1. bad, awful, lousy, terrible. 2. reassuring, comforting, encouraging.*

terrify *v.* frighten, scare, fill with terror, petrify, *curdle one's blood, *paralyze with fear, *put the fear of God into, alarm, *scare stiff, shock, startle, frighten out of one's wits, *make one's hair stand on end, *scare the bejesus out of, *make one's hair curl, panic, trigger one's fight or flight response. ANT. *reassure, comfort.*

territorial *a.* proprietary, defensive.

territory *n.* **1.** AREA region, district, province, land, country, terrain, locale, zone, vicinity, precinct, neighborhood, tract. **2.** DOMAIN sphere, realm, turf, area, field, bailiwick.

terror *n.* **1.** FEAR fright, panic, dread, horror, alarm, shock, awe, dismay, heart-pounding terror, paralysis, paroxysm of fear. **2.** UNRULY CHILD hellion, rascal, pest, nuisance, *holy terror, *hell on wheels, imp, troublemaker.

terrorism *n.* fear campaign, intimidation tactics, arm-twisting, bullying, extortion, coercion, firebombing, hostage-taking, bomb threats.

terrorist *n.* extortionist, vigilante, bully, arm-twister, radical, revolutionary, rebel, anarchist, subversive.

terrorize *v.* terrify, frighten, scare, fill with terror, intimidate, threaten, menace, bully, browbeat, arm-twist, strongarm, coerce.

TERSE *a.* [TURS] concise, to the point, brief. *He gave a suprisingly terse speech and left.* SYN. concise, succinct, brief, to the point, short, taut, pithy, condensed, trenchant, compact, sparing, laconic. ANT. *long-winded, verbose, wordy.*

test *n.* **1.** EXAMINATION exam, quiz, multiple choice, midterm, trial, evaluation, probe, assessment, questionnaire, inspection, inquest. **2.** TRIAL experiment, assay, try, dry run. **3.** STANDARD criterion, *acid test, *litmus test, measure, touchstone, proof.

test *v.* examine, quiz, try, evaluate, probe, assess, question, inspect, investigate, analyze, conduct a trial run, assay, check, *see which way the wind blows, sound.

TESTAMENT *n.* [TES tuh munt] that which testifies to the validity or truth of something. *That the number of highway fatalities have decreased is a testament to better safety regulations.* SYN. testimony, testimonial, affirmation, confirmation, proof, evidence, profession, statement.

tested *a.* tried, proven.

testicles *n.* testes, sex glands, gonads, *balls, *nuts, *family jewels.

testify *v.* **1.** PROVIDE TESTIMONY bear witness, give evidence, attest, affirm, vouch for, corroborate, swear to, declare, verify, uphold, support, substantiate. **2.** BE EVIDENCE OF prove, show, indicate, be a testament to, provide testimony for, demonstrate. ANT. **2.** *disprove, contradict.*

testimonial *n.* commendation, recommendation, *plug, tribute, compliment, affidavit, endorsement, certificate, letter of recommendation, letter of reference.

testimony *n.* **1.** DECLARATION profession, affirmation, attestation, proof, evidence, witness, corroboration, statement, sworn statement, affidavit, deposition, documentation, avowal, support. **2.** INDICATION evidence, attestation, confirmation, affirmation, demonstration.

testosterone *n.* hormone, male hormone, sex hormone, steroid.

testy *a.* irritable, touchy, grouchy, grumpy, cranky, petulant, *snappy, ornery, thin-skinned, *short-fused, quick-tempered, peevish. ANT. *good humored, easygoing, cheerful.*

tetched *a.* demented, neurotic, *not right in the head, *a little crazy, touched, *nuts. SEE CRAZY, INSANE, NEUROTIC

tete-a-tete *n.* heart-to-heart talk, conversation, intimate discussion, talk, discussion, confidential discussion, face-to-face chat.

tether *n.* rope, leash, chain, halter, restraint, cord, line.

text *n.* words, wording, main body, body, printed matter, written matter.

textbook *n.* text, schoolbook, reference book, manual.

textile *n.* fabric, cloth, woven material, fibrous material, cotton, wool, yarn, dry goods.

texture *n.* surface quality, feel, character, composition, grade, smoothness, roughness, coarseness, weave, grain, nap, pile, woof, wale.

thank *v.* acknowledge, show one's appreciation, show one's gratitude, bless.

thankful *a.* grateful, appreciative, obliged, indebted, beholden.

thankless *a.* **1.** UNGRATEFUL unappreciative, rude, inconsiderate. **2.** UNAPPRECIATED unrewarded, unnoticed, unrecognized, unacknowledged. ANT. **1.** *thankful, grateful.* **2.** *appreciated, rewarded.*

thatch *n.* mat, straw, rushes, palm leaves, roofing.

thaw *v.* **1.** MELT liquefy, soften, warm, defrost, dissolve. **2.** LOOSEN UP warm, relax. ANT. *1. freeze, harden, solidify. 2. become stiff and formal, cool.*

theater *n.* **1.** PLAYHOUSE opera house, auditorium, ampitheater, theater in the round, boards, odeum, dinner theater, hall, arena, movie house, cinema, drive-in. **2.** STAGE PERFORMANCE dramatic arts, drama, show business, the stage. "An escape from reality."—George Nathan. "A tradition of villains and heroes."—George Bernard Shaw. "A window open on the life of our fellow creatures."—Mario Fratti.

WORD FIND

above stage, walk or platform for lights: fly

actor's emergency fill-in: understudy

advertisement at front of theater: marquee

afternoon show: matinee

alcove in center of stage where prompter hides from audience: prompt box

allegorical drama illustrating Christian teaching: morality play

anxiety, performance: stage fright, *flop sweat

award: Tony

background scenery: backdrop, olio, ground row, cyclorama

backstage area: wings

box in front of balcony or mezzanine: loge

Broadway, play not produced on: off Broadway production

brochure of cast and description: program, playbill

comedy featuring wit: high comedy

comedy of exaggeration: farce

comedy on morbid subject: black comedy

comedy satirizing manners of fashionable society: comedy of manners

comedy, slapstick or physical: low comedy

comedy that spoofs: send-up, parody

company producing several shows with same performers: repertory company

company production of plays in summer: summer stock

cues a song, line of dialogue that: dakota

dim lighting used for effect: pool hall lighting

district of theaters: white light district, Great White Way, Broadway, Rialto

draw attention away from another actor: upstage, steal the show

dress rehearsal before an audience: audience dress

emotions are exaggerated, play in which: melodrama

exaggerated acting or overacting: histrionics

explosion or flash, device that creates: flashpot

falling in love with theater: stagestruck

financier, backer: angel

hit show: boffo

horrifying, macabre or gruesome drama: Grand Guignol

Japanese, all-male: Kabuki

large-scale act or musical number: production number

lights: footlights, limelight, *ace, *ashcan, baby spot, bon-bon, flood, house lights, *keg light, klieg light, pin spot

list of characters: dramatis personae

makeup: grease paint, pancake makeup

mark the stage to direct actors where to stand, move: block

musicals, theater that specializes in: lyric theater

musical with sketches: revue

musician's area: orchestra pit

narrator to audience: raisonneur

object used in show: prop

open audition: *cattle call

outfit a stage with scenery: dress

pack theater by distributing free tickets: paper the house

rehearsal, rough: walk-through

religious play centering around suffering of Christ: passion play

remember lines during show, helps actors: prompter

sad or heartbreaking play: tragedy

segment: act

serious performances as opposed to vaudeville: legitimate theater

set, take down a: strike

set that is real, as opposed to that of facades: practical set

skyline or horizon scenery piece: ground row, cyclorama

sound effects made from offstage: noises off

SRO: standing room only

stage, front of: proscenium, apron

stage props, functioning: practicals

talk with audience, actor's solo: soliloquy

top balcony for lowerclass patrons: peanut gallery

union for actors: Actors Equity Association

unsuccessful play: *flop, *bomb, *turkey, *dog

variety show, old time: vaudeville, burlesque

waiting room, performer's: green room, dressing room

wardrobe assistant: dresser

worker: stagehand

writer of plays: playwright

written music: score

SEE MOVIE, TELEVISION

theatrical *a.* **1.** SHOW BUSINESS staged, stagy, thespian, operatic, Broadway, off-Broadway. **2.** MELODRAMATIC dramatic, histrionic, *hammy, showy, campy, pretentious, affected, overacted, overwrought, *fake, *put on. ANT. *2. sincere, natural, real, understated.*

theft *n.* stealing, larceny, grand larceny, petty larceny, thievery, burglary, robbery, purse-snatching, *holdup, mugging, looting, pilferage, shoplifting.

theme *n.* topic, subject, idea, motif, leitmotif, matter, point, question, keynote, strain, recurrent pattern.

theme song *n.* signature song.

theologian *n.* student of religion, religious scholar, divine.

theology *n.* study of religion, divinity, study of God, theosophy, doctrine, dogma, Scripture, the Gospel. "Science of mind applied to God." — Henry Ward Beecher. "The rhetoric of morals." — Ralph Waldo Emerson.

theorem *n.* assumption, proposition, hypothesis, theory, postulate, principle, law, rule, formula, equation.

theoretical *a.* hypothetical, speculative, academic, conjectural, abstract, assumed, notional, untried, unproven, presumed, *on paper, untested. ANT. *practical, applied, proven.*

theorize *v.* hypothesize, speculate, conjecture, suppose, guess, presume, assume, imagine, formulate, posit, think.

theory *n.* hypothesis, speculation, conjecture, supposition, guess, presumption, assumption, formulation, idea, thesis, surmise, postulate, hunch. "A hunch with a college education." — J.A. Carter. "Something usually murdered by facts." — Anon.

therapeutic *a.* curative, remedial, healthful, healing, corrective, restorative, beneficial, medicinal, sanative, helpful. ANT. *harmful, unhealthy, detrimental.*

therapy *n.* treatment, regimen, regime, remedy, healing, curative, homeopathy, rehabilitation, *rehab, physical therapy, speech therapy, group therapy.

thereabouts *adv.* near, about, around, approximately, roughly.

thereafter *adv.* afterwards, after, later, subsequently, thenceforth, following.

therefore *adv.* consequently, thus, so, hence, ergo, for that reason, as a result, accordingly.

thermal *a.* warm, hot, heated, thermic.

thermos *n.* bottle, flask, insulated container.

thesaurus *n.* lexicon, word treasury, synonym finder, word book.

thesis *n.* **1.** PROPOSITION premise, assumption, belief, theory, hypothesis, argument, belief, opinion, belief, idea, theorem, position. **2.** DISSERTATION treatise, research paper, essay, study, investigation, monograph, composition.

thespian *n.* actor, actress, player, performer, *ham, tragedian. SEE MOVIE, TELEVISION, THEATER

thick *a.* **1.** DEEP extensive, fat, massive, thickset, obese, wide, large, solid, bulky. **2.** DENSE closely packed, concentrated, close, crowded, heavy, condensed, compact, impermeable, luxuriant, viscid, viscous, glutinous, congealed, caked. **3.** HAVING A GREAT NUMBER CLOSELY PACKED crowded, teeming, chockfull, bursting, numerous, great, swarming, replete, overflowing, *jam-packed, crammed. **4.** STUPID dense, retarded, dull, bovine, slow, dim-witted, obtuse, dumb, moronic, imbecilic, simple, *chowderheaded, *lamebrained, *dense as a post. ANT. *1. thin, slim, slight. 2. thin, sparse, scant, watery. 3. empty, rare, thin, scarce. 4. brilliant, smart, intelligent, sharp.*

thicken *v.* concentrate, condense, congeal, compact, solidify, harden, clot, coagulate, jell, curdle, set, cake. ANT. *thin, liquefy, dilute.*

thicket *n.* underbrush, shrubs, bushes, brush, scrub, brake, copse, bosket, tangle.

thickset *a.* stocky, stout, beefy, heavyset, big, chunky. ANT. *skinny, slim, slender.* SEE FAT

thick-skinned *a.* hardened, tough, insensitive, callous, hard-boiled, unfeeling, strong, stony. ANT. *thin-skinned, sensitive, ultrasensitive.*

thief *n.* *crook, robber, burglar, shoplifter, mugger, swindler, bandit, criminal, kleptomaniac, *klepto, cheat, *rip-off artist, *con artist, pickpocket, filcher, purse-snatcher, embezzler, larcener, rustler. "One who just has a habit of finding things before people lose them." — Joe E. Lewis.

thieve *v.* steal, rob, burglarize, *rip off, pilfer, filch, shoplift, snatch, *swipe, *walk off with, purloin, appropriate, *heist, embezzle, swindle, cheat.

thievery *n.* theft, robbery, larceny, grand larceny, petty larceny, burglary, stealing, pilfering, shoplifting, kleptomania, embezzlement, swindle.

thin *v.* dilute, cut, reduce, rarefy, water down, decrease, trim, weaken, attenuate, prune. ANT. *thicken, concentrate, condense.*

thin *a.* **1.** SLENDER slight, slim, skinny, lean, anorexic, emaciated, bony, spare, wispy, *thin as linguine, *thin enough to fall through a flute and not sound a note, skin and bones, half-starved, scrawny, gaunt, rawboned, spindly. **2.** SCANTY sparse, rare, few and far between, meager, skimpy, deficient. **3.** WATERY diluted, weak, runny, rarefied. **4.** SHEER transparent, airy, fine, diaphanous, delicate, translucent, wispy, flimsy. ANT. *1. fat, obese, heavy, *broad in the beam. 2. full, thick, teeming, swarming. 3. condensed, concentrated, thick. 4. opaque, heavy, dense.*

thing *n.* **1.** ARTICLE object, item, subject, element, substance, matter, entity, it, body, being, creature, organism. **2.** THINGAMAJIG gadget, device, contrivance, *doohickey, *thingamabob, contraption, apparatus, gizmo, widget, mechanism, *whatchamacallit, *dingus, *whatsit. **3.** DEED act, event, happening, action, feat, performance, accomplishment, exploit. **4.** MATTER affair, circumstance, happening, situation. **5.** SEE THINGS

thingamajig *n.* SEE THING 2

things *n.* belongings, possessions, stuff, personal effects, paraphernalia, outfit, equipment, trappings, accoutrements, gear.

think *v.* **1.** CONTEMPLATE meditate, cogitate, ponder, concentrate, focus on, study, analyze, intellectualize, turn over in one's mind, evaluate, reflect, deliberate, mull over, ruminate, consider, deduce, reason, conceive, imagine, picture, remember, marshal one's thoughts. **2.** BELIEVE judge, opine, suppose, assume, presume, surmise, gather, guess, imagine, understand, reckon, conclude, estimate.

thinkable *a.* conceivable, imaginable, comprehensible, feasible, possible. ANT. *unthinkable, inconceivable.*

thinker *n.* philosopher, deep thinker, sage, wise man, scholar.

thinking *n.* thought, brain power, contemplation, meditation, cogitation, concentration, study, analysis, evaluation, reflection, deliberation, reasoning, logic, deduction, speculation, *putting two and two together. "The magic of the mind." — Lord Byron. "The talking of the soul with itself." — Plato.

thin-skinned *a.* sensitive, oversensitive, ultrasensitive, hypersensitive, easily hurt, delicate, vulnerable, easily offended, touchy, irritable. ANT. *thick-skinned, hardened, callous, insensitive.*

third world *n.* undeveloped nations, emergent nations.

thirst *n.* craving, desire, want, longing, hunger, hankering, appetite, yen, lust, thirstiness.

thirst *v.* crave, desire, want, long for, hunger for, hanker for, have an appetite for, have a yen for, lust after.

thong *n.* strap, strip, leather, lace, whiplash, leash.

thorn *n.* **1.** PRICKLE needle, barb, spike, point, spine. **2.** THORN IN ONE'S SIDE irritation, trouble, nuisance, pain, plague, torment, affliction, curse.

thorny *a.* **1.** PRICKLY brambly, barbed, briery, spiny, spiked, bristly. **2.** DIFFICULT complicated, ticklish, delicate, troublesome, challenging, nettlesome, trying, touchy, sticky. ANT. *2. easy, simple, *child's play.*

thorough *a.* **1.** EXHAUSTIVE complete, total, comprehensive, thoroughgoing, in-depth, A to Z, all-out, all-inclusive, *whole hog, full, painstaking, *down to the last detail. **2.** ABSOLUTE out-and-out, utter, total, complete, entire, perfect, unmitigated, sheer. **3.** EXACT accurate, painstaking, precise, meticulous, careful, scrupulous. ANT. *1. partial, incomplete, superficial. 2. partial, qualified. 3. sloppy, slipshod, careless.*

thoroughbred *a.* **1.** PURE unmixed, full-blooded, pedigreed. **2.** EXCELLENT first-rate, first-class, trained, educated, cultured, refined, genteel, aristocratic. ANT. *1. half-breed, mongrel, crossbred, mixed breed. 2. second-class, second-rate, unrefined.*

thoroughfare *n.* street, road, passage, road, highway, avenue, boulevard, thruway, beltway, expressway, turnpike.

thoroughgoing *a.* **1.** THOROUGH exhaustive, painstaking, precise, in depth, *down to the last detail, precise, exact, meticulous. **2.** COMPLETE utter, absolute, unmitigated, out-and-out, unqualified, sheer. ANT. *1. superficial, partial, careless. 2. partial, incomplete, qualified.*

thoroughly *adv.* completely, utterly, entirely, totally, absolutely, downright, wholly, quite, exhaustively. ANT. *partially, superficially, incompletely.*

thought *n.* **1.** THINKING cogitation, intellection, cerebration, concentration, reflection, consideration, cognition, study, meditation, deliberation, contemplation, rumination, reflection, pondering, speculating, weighing, brown study, reasoning, rationalization, calculation, deduction, introspection. "Dreams till their effects be tried."—Shakespeare. "An electrochemical soup stirred by pleasure, pain and nervous impulses."—Jack E. French. "Feelings gone to seed."—John Burroughs. **2.** INTELLECT imagination, brain power, intelligence, reason, smarts, *gray matter. **3.** IDEA concept, notion, theory, hypothesis, *brainstorm, belief, assumption, conclusion, opinion, surmise. **4.** ATTENTION consideration, regard, study, notice.

thoughtful a. **1.** THINKING meditative, reflective, introspective, pondering, lost in thought, intellectual, meditative, pensive, abstracted. **2.** CONSIDERATE kind, mindful, attentive, solicitous, graceful, diplomatic, sensitive, unselfish, nice, sweet. ANT. *1. mindless, unthinking, brainless. 2. thoughtless, inconsiderate, inattentive.*

thoughtless a. inconsiderate, insensitive, unthinking, selfish, inattentive, careless, negligent, heedless, oblivious, rude, impolite, discourteous. ANT. *thoughtful, considerate, attentive.*

thrash v. **1.** FLOG whip, beat, lash, flail, strap, switch, cane, scourge, flagellate. **2.** DEFEAT SOUNDLY *skunk, *kill, *blow away, rout, drub, *kick butt, *whoop, *whip, trounce, shellac.

thread n. **1.** LINE filament, string, yarn, strand, cord, fiber. **2.** THEME motif, subject.

threadbare a. **1.** WORN ragged, tattered, moth-eaten, frayed, holey, raveled, *ratty, shabby. **2.** STALE overused, shopworn, commonplace, clichéd, banal, tired, stock, hackneyed, *old hat, *ho-hum. ANT. *1. new, plush, luxurious. 2. fresh, original, new.*

threat n. intimidation, scare, menace, danger, peril, hazard, jeopardy, dark cloud on the horizon, *sword of Damocles, portent, *sleeping giant.

threaten v. intimidate, scare, menace, *put the fear of God into, *scare the bejesus out of one, terrorize, frighten, alarm, bully, cow, put on alert, loom.

threatening a. intimidating, menacing, terrorizing, frightening, scary, sinister, ominous, impending, looming, foreboding. ANT. *encouraging, bright, reassuring.*

threesome n. menage a trois, trio.

thresh v. beat, flail, thrash.

threshold n. **1.** DOORSILL entrance. **2.** BEGINNING start, opening, entrance, brink, verge, dawn, starting point, debut, onset. ANT. *2. close, end.*

thrift n. thriftiness, frugality, economy, economizing, saving, conservation, parsimony, penny-pinching, scrimping, cheapness. ANT. *waste, improvidence, extravagance.*

thrifty a. frugal, economical, economizing, conserving, saving, parsimonious, penny-pinching, miserly, stingy, provident. ANT. *wasteful, improvident, extravagant.*

thrill n. **1.** EXCITEMENT *rush, *adrenalin rush, *head rush, kick, *spine-tingling experience, chills, blast, titillation, *charge, *mind-blower, *high, exhilaration, sensation, *heart-pounder, *hair-raiser. **2.** TREMOR quiver, fluttering, tingling, vibration.

thrill v. excite, stimulate, electrify, *adrenalize, *give a rush, exhilarate, titillate, *blow one's mind, stir, *turn on, *give a charge. ANT. *tranquilize, put to sleep.*

thrive v. flourish, prosper, grow, blossom, mushroom, burgeon, luxuriate, succeed, boom, progress, do well, be vigorous. ANT. *fail, die, wither, languish.*

throat n. neck, gullet, larynx, pharynx, trachea, Adam's apple.

throaty a. hoarse, guttural, husky, gravel-voiced, raspy, whiskey-voiced.

throb n. pulsation, pulse, throbbing, beat, tremor, palpitation, thump.

throb v. pulsate, pulse, beat, palpitate, thump, pound, flutter, vibrate, quiver, drum.

throes n. spasms, pangs, pains, convulsions, seizures, paroxysm.

throne n. seat of power, cathedral.

throng n. crowd, multitude, horde, bunch, congregation, swarm, mass, mob, flock, army, flood, pack, press, host.

throng v. crowd, gather, assemble, congregate, swarm, mass, mob, flock, flood, pack, press, stand cheek to jowl.

throttle n. accelerator, gas pedal, choke, butterfly valve.

throttle v. **1.** CHOKE strangle, garrote, suffocate, smother, stifle, asphyxiate, *cut off one's wind. **2.** SUPPRESS censor, shut up, silence, squelch, gag, inhibit.

through a. done, finished, completed, over, ended, concluded, terminated.

through prep. **1.** IN ONE SIDE AND OUT THE OTHER from one end to the other, from start to finish. **2.** BY WAY OF via, inside, in and out of.

throw n. pitch, lob, toss, pass, shot, delivery, hurl, cast, fling, heave, chuck.

throw v. pitch, lob, toss, pass, shoot, hurl, cast, fling, heave, chuck, deliver, propel, catapult, launch, peg, thrust.

throw out *v.* throw away, dispose of, dump, discard, scrap, cast off, dispense with, junk, jettison.

throw up *v.* vomit, regurgitate, upchuck, puke, disgorge, *spit up, *barf, *ralph, spew, hurl, *toss one's cookies, *blow lunch, retch, *have the dry heaves.

thrust *n.* **1.** PUSH shove, lunge, drive, advance, propulsion, stab, plunge, poke. **2.** ATTACK blitz, blitzkrieg, onslaught, offensive, charge, push, drive, raid, strike. **3.** ENERGY power, drive, horsepower, lift, pickup. **4.** POINT gist, force, meaning, essence, substance.

thrust *v.* **1.** PUSH shove, lunge, drive, force, advance, power, propel, throw, stab, plunge, poke. **2.** IMPOSE ONESELF intrude, force oneself into, inject.

thud *n.* thump, bump, bang, *whack, *clunk, rap, boom, crash, slam, clump, plunk, blow.

thug *n.* hoodlum, *hood, brute, gangster, mobster, mafioso, ruffian, hooligan, *roughneck, *goon, gunman, killer, murderer.

thumbnail *a.* brief, concise, small, minute.

thump *n.* SEE THUD

thump *v.* strike, hit, beat, pound, pommel, *slug, slam, drub, cudgel, bludgeon.

thunder *n.* thunderclap, boom, rumbling, crack, *whiplash, roll, crash, peal, explosion, roar, discharge, report, reverberation.

thunder *v.* **1.** BOOM rumble, crack, roll, crash, peal, explode, discharge, reverberate. **2.** FULMINATE roar, boom, shout, bellow, yell, growl, curse, bark, denounce.

thunderbolt *n.* lightning.

thunderstorm *n.* thundershower, thunder squall, *thunder-boomer, cloudburst, electrical storm.

WORD FIND

cloud: cumulonimbus, thunderhead

lightning: ball lightning, chain lightning, heat lightning

mythical creature of North American Indians thought to cause: thunderbird

SEE CLOUD, RAIN, STORM

thunderstruck *a.* shocked, floored, staggered, amazed, astonished, dumbstruck, dumbfounded, flabbergasted, *knocked for a loop, *bowled over.

thus *adv.* therefore, so, hence, ergo.

thwart *v.* obstruct, hinder, frustrate, slow, stop, roadblock, foil, defeat, check, inhibit, prevent, block, preclude, confound. ANT. *facilitate, help, assist, ease.*

tic *n.* spasm, contraction, nervous tic, twitch, jerk.

tick *n.* click, tap, beat, pulse, second.

ticket *n.* **1.** PASS admission, voucher, receipt, stub, token, coupon, *ducat, raincheck, certificate. **2.** LABEL tag, sticker, slip. **3.** BALLOT slate, roster.

WORD FIND

free ticket or pass: *Annie Oakley

resell tickets far above cost: scalp

traffic ticket: summons, citation, fine

tickle *v.* please, delight, thrill, excite, gratify, *tickle to death, *tickle pink, amuse, make one smile, make one laugh.

ticklish *a.* delicate, sensitive, prickly, dicey, touchy, risky, slippery, difficult, thorny, tricky, awkward.

ticky-tacky *a. Sl.* cheap, tacky, poor quality, dull, shoddy, shabby, *rinky-dink, *chintzy, *cheesy, tawdry.

tidal wave *n.* tsunami, tidal bore, eagre.

tidbit *n.* morsel, bit, mouthful, spoonful, piece, titbit.

tide *n.* flood, wash, ebb, neap, spring tide, rip tide, high tide, low tide. SEE BEACH, OCEAN

tidings *n.* news, information, report, word, communication, *scoop, *lowdown, *scuttlebutt.

tide over *v.* keep one's head above water, keep one going, help, assist, *bridge the gap.

tidy *v.* neaten, clean, order, unclutter, arrange, pick up, spruce up, fix up, straighten up, groom. ANT. *mess, clutter, disorder.*

tidy *a.* **1.** NEAT clean, shipshape, orderly, *spick-and-span, trim, well, ordered, spruce, uncluttered, *in apple pie order, organized. **2.** CONSIDERABLE large, substantial, generous, respectable, healthy, ample. ANT. *1. messy, sloppy, unkempt. 2. small, piddling*

tie *n.* **1.** FASTENING fastener, connection, knot, link, catch, clip, string, rope, strap, cord, cinch, sash, binding. **2.** NECKTIE ascot, string tie, cravat, bow tie. **3.** RELATIONSHIP association, bond, tie-in, connection, kinship, friendship, liaison, affiliation. **4.** DEADLOCK draw, standoff, *sudden death faceoff.

tie *v.* **1.** FASTEN connect, knot, bind, link, catch, clip, string up, strap, cinch, lash, interlace, moor, secure, tether, leash. **2.** RESTRICT limit, stop, hinder, inhibit, hobble, check, bind, fetter. **3.** MATCH UP be dead even, be neck and neck. ANT. *1. unfasten, untie, loose, release. 2. facilitate, free, liberate.*

tier *n.* row, line, file, rank, echelon, grade, level, story, floor.

tie-up *n.* snag, gridlock, bottleneck, logjam, traffic jam, *SNAFU, stoppage.

tiff n. quarrel, argument, spat, fight, altercation, squabble, wrangle, run-in, clash, disagreement, *words, *row. ANT. *peace, accord, *meeting of the minds.*

tiger n. predator, *big cat, carnivore, hunter, stalker, saber-toothed tiger, jaguar, leopard.

tight a. **1.** CLOSE snug, skintight, form-fitting, close-fitting, confined, cramped, taut, drawn. **2.** FIXED secured, secure, set, made fast, immovable, firm, locked. **3.** AIRTIGHT watertight, sealed, plugged, secure, sound, hermetically sealed, impervious, impermeable, nonporous, leakproof. **4.** RIGOROUS strict, stringent, severe, restraining, demanding. **5.** DIFFICULT trying, precarious, delicate, ticklish, tricky, perilous, tough, prickly. **6.** STINGY tightfisted, sparing, frugal, cheap, miserly, penurious, parsimonious, penny-pinching. ANT. 1. *loose, slack, baggy.* 2. *loose, unsecured, slack.* 3. *porous, holey.* 4. *undemanding, mild, easy.* 5. *easy, simple.* 6. *generous, charitable, giving.*

tighten a. firm up, close up, fix, secure, lock up, tauten, tense, stretch, contract, squeeze, constrict, screw. ANT. *loosen, slacken, unfasten.*

tightfisted a. cheap, stingy, miserly, sparing, frugal, penny-pinching, penurious, parsimonious, niggardly, greedy. ANT. *generous, charitable, giving.*

tight-lipped a. silent, mute, taciturn, reserved, reticent, quiet, close-mouthed, secretive, mum. ANT. *loquacious, talkative.*

tightwad n. miser, *cheapskate, *Scrooge, penny-pincher, *pinchpenny, *piker, *nickel-squeezer, niggard, *cheap bastard. ANT. *philanthropist, giver, free-spender, spendthrift.*

till n. cash box, cash drawer, cash tray, cash register.

till v. plow, harrow, cultivate, work, turn over, dig, hoe, spade, dress.

tilt n. incline, inclination, slant, slope, lean, pitch, grade, gradient, rake.

tilt v. tip, incline, slant, slope, lean, turn, upend, list, cant, angle.

timber n. **1.** WOOD beam, joist, girder, rafter, pile, board, spar, log, lumber. **2.** TREES forest, woods, woodland, timberland.

timberland n. woodland, forest, stumpage.

timbre n. tone, pitch, voice.

time n. **1.** DURATION span, stretch, spell, period, interval, term, age, epoch, era, juncture, point, second, instant, moment, hour, day, month, year, century, millennium, eon, infinity, continuance, chronology, fourth dimension, *tick of the clock, *water under the bridge, *sand through the hourglass. "A file that wears and makes no noise." — Henry G. Bohn. "A flowing river." — Christopher Morley. "A sandpile we run our fingers in." — Carl Sandburg. "The moving image of eternity." — Plato. "The great mainspring." — Anon. "A storm in which we are all lost." — William Carlos Williams. "Time like an ever-rolling stream bears all its sons away." — Isaac Watts. **2.** OCCASION opportunity, opening, chance, shot.

time-honored a. classic, vintage, time-tested, venerable, respected, traditional.

timeless a. eternal, neverending, everlasting, ageless, perpetual, immortal, immemorial, infinite, undying. ANT. *temporary, passing, ephemeral.*

timely a. opportune, well-timed, favorable, auspicious, convenient, fitting, propitious, seasonable. ANT. *untimely, unfavorable, inopportune.*

timepiece n. clock, watch, sundial, hourglass, horologe.

timid a. afraid, fearful, timorous, mousy, fainthearted, *wimpy, *lily-livered, *chicken, sheepish, cowardly, *candy-assed, *yellow, spineless, shy, bashful, nervous. ANT. *courageous, brave, bold, *ballsy, fearless.*

timorous a. SEE TIMID

tinderbox n. explosive situation, volatile situation, *hot spot, trouble spot, war zone, powder keg, time bomb, combustible situation.

tinge n. trace, touch, hint, suggestion, smattering, drop, tincture, shade, tint, color, coloring, tone, pigment.

tinge v. shade, color, tint, give a touch of, give a trace of, flavor, season.

tingle n. tickle, electrical sensation, sting, prickle, thrill.

tingle v. tickle, sting, prickle, crawl, creep, quiver.

tinker v. putter, fix, mend, doctor, fuss over, fiddle with, *monkey around with, *mess with, toy with, *diddle, fumble with.

tinkle n. ring, jingle, tingle, tinkling, ding, tintinnabulation, plink, chime.

tinkle v. ring, jingle, tingle, ding, jangle, tintinnabulate, plink, chime.

tinsel a. gaudy, showy, glittery, flashy, garish, ornate, tawdry, cheap.

tint n. hue, tinge, shade, tone, color, cast, tinge, tincture, pigmentation, complexion, touch, trace, hint.

tintinnabulation n. ringing, tinkling, jingling, jangling.

tiny a. small, diminutive, little, wee, puny, miniature, minute, miniscule, Lilliputian, dwarf, pygmy, *pint-sized, *pocket-sized, teeny, *itsy-bitsy, microscopic, infinitesimal. ANT. *huge, gigantic, gargantuan, towering, massive.*

tip n. **1.** INFORMATION *word to the wise, advice, *pointer, *hot tip, suggestion, helpful hint, clue, warning, tip-off, inkling. **2.** GRATUITY percentage, compensation, consideration. **3.** point, nib, head, top, peak, pinnacle, apex, summit, crown.

tip v. **1.** COMPENSATE *take care of, pay, reward for service. **2.** TILT incline, overturn, upend, capsize, upset, topple, slant, lean, turn over, cant.

tipsy a. intoxicated, inebriated, unsteady, *three sheets to the wind, woozy, *pickled, *loaded, *drunker than a brewer's fart, *crocked, under the influence. ANT. *sober, *stone sober.*

TIRADE n. [TYE rade] a long, scolding or condemning speech. *Before we knew it, he was launching into another tirade about faulty government policy.* SYN. harangue, diatribe, lecture, denunciation, condemnation, *jeremiad, invective, vituperation, censure, *tongue-lashing, outburst.

tire v. **1.** EXHAUST wear out, weary, fatigue, drain, *run out of juice, *run one's battery down, enervate, *bush, *poop out, burn out, flag, fail. **2.** GET SICK OF lose interest, be bored with, lose patience with, lose fascination with. ANT. *1. energize, invigorate, revive. 2. interest, be fascinated with, stimulate.*

tired a. **1.** EXHAUSTED worn out, weary, fatigued, drained, *out of juice, out of energy, *run down, enervated, sleepy, drowsy, *bushed, *pooped, burned out, *all in, *beat, spent, flagging, *dog-tired, *dead, *tuckered out. **2.** SICK OF bored with, *fed up with. ANT. *1. energized, invigorated, revived, refreshed. 2. fascinated by, stimulated by.*

tireless a. untiring, energetic, *high octane, unflagging, hyperactive, *supercharged, indefatigable, determined, persevering, industious, unremitting, slogging, plugging. ANT. *tiring, flagging, faltering, failing.*

tiresome a. wearisome, tiring, exhausting, fatiguing, arduous, demanding, wearing, strenuous, laborious, boring, dull, tedious, *humdrum, monotonous. ANT. *energizing, invigorating, stimulating.*

tit n. teat, nipple, breast, *boob, *hooter, *jug,

*knocker.

titan n. giant, colossus, deity, Zeus, Prometheus.

titanic a. gigantic, colossal, gargantuan, towering, huge, massive, immense, enormous, herculean, monstrous, Brobdingnagian. ANT. *tiny, microscopic, Lilliputian.*

tithe v. levy. SEE TAX

TITILLATE v. [TIT ul ate] to stimulate or arouse, excite. *Rock videos are often designed to titillate.* SYN. stimulate, arouse, excite, *turn on, thrill, *stir one's blood, provoke, tantalize, seduce, *tickle one's fancy.

title n. **1.** NAME appellation, epithet, designation, *moniker, nickname, *handle, cognomen, denomination. **2.** HEADING caption, legend, name, label, subtitle, inscription. **3.** CHAMPIONSHIP crown, claim, right. **4.** PROOF OF OWNERSHIP deed.

titter n. giggle, laugh, suppressed laugh, snicker, snigger, chuckle, cackle.

titter v. giggle, tee-hee, laugh under one's breath, snicker, snigger, chuckle, cackle.

tittle n. dot, particle, iota, speck, whit, jot, scintilla, mote, drop.

titular a. nominal, by name only, by title only, so-called, honorary, token, self-styled. ANT. *actual, real.*

toady n. sycophant, flatterer, *kiss-up, *brownnose, *ass-kisser, *yes-man, bootlicker, apple polisher, lickspittle, fawner, flunky, lackey, groveler, toadeater.

toady v. flatter, *kiss up, *brownnose, *kiss ass, fawn, grovel, kowtow, *apple polish, bootlick, curry favor, *suck up to, *fall all over, bow and scrape. ANT. *disrespect, defy, abuse.*

toast n. drink, salute, salutation, compliment, honor, *cheers, *to your health, *here's mud in your eye, *skoal, *salut, *salud, *mazel tov.

toast v. **1.** SALUTE drink to, honor, compliment, share a sentiment, raise one's glass to, hail. **2.** BROWN BREAD heat, warm.

toastmaster n. master of ceremonies, emcee, M.C., speaker, host, moderator.

tobacco n. weed, leaves, perique, caporal. "Pernicious weed." —William Cowper. "That hell fume in God's clean air." —Carry Nation. "A lone man's companion, a bachelor's friend, a hungry man's food, a sad man's cordial, a wakeful man's sleep, and a chilly man's fire." —Charles Kingsley.

WORD FIND

ash left in pipe after burning: dottle
box: humidor

chew: quid, plug

poor grade: shag

powder inhaled or chewed: snuff

smoke, aversion to the: misocapnia

smoke, one who has an aversion to the: misocapnist

stinky: mundungus

tocsin n. alarm, bell, warning.

to-do n. fuss, commotion, bother, uproar, *brouhaha, stir, *flap, *hoopla, ado, hubbub, furor, excitement, hurly-burly, *tempest in a teapot.

toddle v. falter, totter, be unsteady on one's feet.

toddler n. baby, tot, child, preschooler, *rug rat, *holy terror. SEE BABY

toehold n. foothold, footing, purchase.

toga n. robe, gown, garment, wrap.

WORD FIND

belt formed by the twisted folds of: baltaeus

dark toga for mourning: toga pulla

purple toga with gold embroidery, worn by emperors, consuls: toga picta

together adv. 1. AS ONE all at once, all at the same time, in unison, in concert, collectively, simultaneously, en masse, conjointly, concurrently, *in sync, in tandem. 2. IN SUCCESSION consecutively, in a row, succesively. ANT. 1. singly, alone, separately.

togs n. clothes, clothing, *duds, outfit, wear, apparel, *toggery, attire, dress, garb, gear, *threads.

toil n. labor, work, grind, drudgery, *sweat of one's brow, exertion, struggle, pains, *elbow grease, slavery. ANT. ease, leisure, relaxation.

toil v. work, labor, sweat, exert, struggle, slave, *break one's back, *bust one's hump, *bust one's balls, drudge, strain, *plug away, *knock oneself out, *drive oneself into the grave. ANT. relax, *take it easy, rest.

toilet n. 1. BATHROOM *john, rest room, wash room, *little boy's room, *little girl's room, head, latrine, *can, *privy, *loo, *throne room, outhouse, *shithouse, *potty, commode, flush, urinal, bidet. 2. GROOMING dressing, toilette, clean-up, bathing.

toilsome a. laborious, hard, arduous, difficult, backbreaking, strenuous, fatiguing, exhausting, wearing, demanding. ANT. easy, simple, effortless.

toke n. Sl. puff, *hit.

token n. 1. INDICATION sign, evidence, mark, expression, manifestation, testimony, testament, symbol. 2. KEEPSAKE souvenir, memento, reminder.

token a. superficial, symbolic, nominal, minimal, perfunctory, for show.

tolerable a. 1. ENDURABLE sufferable, bearable. 2. FAIR passable, acceptable, all right, okay, good enough, *so-so, *not bad, mediocre, middling, adequate, sufficient, satisfactory. ANT. 1. intolerable, unbearable. 2. excellent, first-rate, unacceptable, unsatisfactory.

tolerance a. 1. ACCEPTANCE understanding, open-mindedness, broad-mindedness, grace, sensitivity, liberal-mindedness, magnanimity, goodwill, lack of prejudice, sympathy, receptivity, indulgence. 2. ENDURANCE strength, mental toughness, stamina, stoicism, sufferance, grit, fortitude. ANT. 1. prejudice, bigotry, intolerance. 2. weakness.

tolerant a. accepting, understanding, open-minded, broad-minded, gracious, sensitive, liberal-minded, magnanimous, sympathetic, receptive, indulgent, unprejudiced. ANT. rejecting, prejudiced, bigoted, intolerant.

tolerate v. 1. ACCEPT understand, recognize, respect, be open-minded toward, be broad-minded toward, be sensitive toward, be liberal-minded toward, indulge. 2. ALLOW permit, put up with, look the other way, let go, condone, bear, stand for, be lenient, indulge. 3. ENDURE bear, suffer through, stand, put up with, take, *tough out, *stomach, *sit still for. ANT. 1. reject, be intolerant, disapprove. 2. prohibit, forbid, proscribe. 3. collapse, *cave in, *lose it.

toll n. tax, charge, fee, user fee, levy, tariff, assessment, duty, impost, dues.

toll v. ring, sound, strike, clang, chime, peal, knell, announce, summon, signal.

tomb n. vault, chamber, grave, crypt, mausoleum, sepulchre, catacomb, ossuary, cenotaph, monument. SEE CEMETERY

tomboy n. hoyden, gamine, *one of the boys.

tombstone n. gravestone, headstone, monument, stele, grave marker. SEE CEMETERY

tome n. book, volume, reference book, opus.

tomfoolery n. silliness, foolishness, childish behavior, nonsense, *monkeyshines, *shenanigans, antics, joking, jesting, *horseplay, high jinks. ANT. seriousness, gravity.

ton n. load, truckload, mass, huge amount, pile, two thousand pounds, short ton, long ton.

tone n. 1. PITCH intonation, sound, note, modulation, voice, frequency, timbre. 2. ATTITUDE spirit, quality, mood, tenor, air, mode, manner. 3. SHADE hue, color, tint, tinge, cast.

tone down v. quiet down, moderate, temper, soften, mute, dampen.

tongs n. pincers, clamp, forceps, *graspers.

tongue n. language, dialect, speech, talk, vernacular, idiom, lingo, parlance, native tongue, jargon, slang, argot, articulation. "A wild beast; once let loose it is difficult to chain." — Baltasar Gracian. "The only edged tool that grows keener with constant use." — Washington Irving.

tongue-in-cheek a. jokingly, kiddingly, in jest, in fun, ironic, insincere, facetiously. ANT. *sincere, serious.*

tongue-tied a. speechless, at a loss for words, dumbstruck, mute, inarticulate, shy, bashful, reticent, reserved, *hung by the tongue. ANT. *loquacious, verbose, long-winded, *motor-mouthed.*

tonic n. *pick-me-up, restorative, *shot in the arm, *bracer, stimulant, *upper, drug, medicine, beverage.

tony a. Sl. stylish, fashionable, luxurious, chic.

too adv. **1.** ALSO as well, additionally, likewise, to boot, furthermore, besides, moreover. **2.** EXCESSIVELY in excess, unduly, beyond, extremely, inordinately.

tool n. **1.** IMPLEMENT instrument, utensil, gadget, labor-saving device, apparatus, mechanism, machine, contraption, contrivance, *gizmo, *doohickey, *whatsit. SAWS band saw, bayonet, bucksaw, buzz saw, chain saw, circular saw, compass saw, coping saw.

WORD FIND

SAWS

hand, saw comprised of rotating, toothed: band saw

chained blade: chain saw

circular saw, stationary: buzz saw, bench saw

curve-cutting, electrical saw: jigsaw, saber saw

curve-cutting handsaw: compass saw, keyhole saw, coping saw

curving ornamentation, cuts: scroll saw

grain, cuts across: crosscut saw

grain, cuts with: ripsaw

hand-powered saw used with sawbuck: bucksaw

hole-cutting saw: dial saw

Japanese craftsman's hatchetlike saw for cutting dovetails: dozuki

Japanese craftsman's saw that cuts on the pull stroke: dozuki

Japanese craftsman's saw with dual-edged blade that cuts on the pull stroke: ryoba

metal-cutting: hacksaw

miter-cutting circular saw: miter saw

miter-cutting guide: miter box

shallow-cutting or veneer-cutting saw: veneer saw

stationary, electrical saw with mobile blade-holding arm: radial arm saw

two-person hand-powered saw for cutting timbers: whipsaw

wire coated with tungsten carbide, used by campers: pocket saw

KNIVES, PIERCERS, CARVERS, CUTTERS

axlike tool for trimming wood: adz

brush or sugar-cane cutter: machete

fabric-cutting shears: pinking shears

glass-cutting device: glass-cutter

grain-cutter with short, curving blade: sickle

grass-cutter with long, curving blade: scythe

hole-piercer, esp. for leather: awl

metal shears: tin snips, hawk's bill snips

pencillike precision knife for cutting light material: precision knife, *Xacto knife

pipe-cutting tool: pipe cutter

pole with hook on end, used by lumberjacks: pickaroon

retractable blade, hollow handle with multiple-uses: utility knife

wedgelike tool that is hammered: chisel

wire-cutting pliers: wire cutter

SHARPENERS, SHAVERS, SMOOTHERS

abrader: file, rasp

gouger: router

planing tool: bullnose plane, chamfering plane, planer, spokeshave

polisher: buffer

sander: belt sander, disk sander

stone for sharpening blades: whetstone

wood-turning machine used to cut, plane and shape: lathe

HAMMERS AND NAIL-PULLERS

automatic, mechanical nail-driver: nail gun

brad driver: brad pusher

clawed, nail-pulling hammer: claw hammer

claws, hammer with straight: rip hammer

hammer with rounded instead of clawed back: ball peen hammer, machinist's hammer

long or short-handled hammer with very heavy metal head: sledgehammer

mallet filled with shot to prevent rebounding: deadblow hammer

nail-pulling steel bar resembling crowbar: cat's paw

sledgehammer, small: engineer's hammer

sledgehammer, sometimes having one ax edge: maul

square or cylindrical head made of wood or rubber, hammer with: mallet tack driver, magnetized: tack hammer

WRENCHES AND PLIERS

adjustable jaws, pliers with: slip-joint pliers, tongue-and-groove pliers

adjustable jaws, steel wrench with: adjustable wrench, *crescent wrench

clamping pliers: locking pliers, *Vise-Grips

English term for wrench: spanner

L-shaped, hexagonal rod: allen wrench, hex key

lug nut tightener, loosener: lug wrench

needle-nosed pliers for manipulating wire: long-nose pliers

open jaws on one end and closed, toothed ring on the other, wrench with: combination wrench

oversized nuts, large-mouthed wrench used to turn: spud wrench

pipe-turning wrench equipped with power-assisting chain: chain wrench, pipe wrench

plumber's flat bar with varied openings down its length: faucet spanner

plumber's heavy, adjustable wrench: monkey wrench, pipe wrench

ratcheting wrench with variable socket fittings: socket wrench

screwdriverlike wrench for turning nuts and bolts in tight spaces: nut driver

toothed rings for tightening or loosening nuts, wrench with: box wrench

wire-manipulating pliers: lineman's pliers, electrician's pliers, long-nose pliers, fence pliers

SCREWDRIVERS

crisscross driving head, screwdriver with: Phillips head screwdriver

powered screwdriver: screw gun

ratcheting screwdriver turned by pushing down on handle: return spiral ratchet screwdriver, impact screwdriver

short screwdriver: *stubby

S-shaped tool that is cranked for use in tight spaces: offset screwdriver, cranked screwdriver

DRILL AND RELATED TOOLS

bit-holder: chuck

borer: auger, trepan, gimlet

drilling part, variable sized: bit

hand-cranked drill: eggbeater

hole enlarger: reamer

stationary power drill: drill press

2. PUPPET instrument, pawn, dupe, *stooge.

toot n. honk, whistle, crow, beep, blast.

toot v. honk, whistle, crow, beep, blow, blast.

tooth n. **1.** MOUTH GRINDER OR CUTTER molar, incisor, fang, bicuspid, tusk, *chopper. SEE TEETH **2.** TINE OR COG prong, projection, sprocket, snag, spur.

toothed a. notched, indented, serrated, dentate.

toothpaste n. dentrifice.

toothsome a. tasty, palatable, flavorful, good-tasting, delicious, *yummy, scrumptious, mouth-watering, savory, appetizing, *finger-licking good, delectable. ANT. disgusting, gross, *yucky, nauseating.

top n. **1.** HIGHEST POINT peak, pinnacle, summit, apex, zenith, height, roof, crown, crest, vertex, cap. **2.** LID cap, cover, stopper, cork. ANT. **1.** bottom, low point, foot.

top v. **1.** SURPASS best, beat, outdistance, outperform, outclass, eclipse, exceed, outshine, outdo, dominate, *leave the competition in one's wake, *blow away, *skunk. **2.** COVER cap, crown, put over. ANT. **1.** fail, lose, lag behind, trail.

top a. highest, uppermost, topmost, leading, chief, dominant, greatest, best, paramount, highest-ranking, capital, most important, supreme, foremost, preeminent. ANT. bottom, lowest, worst.

top-drawer a. first-rate, first-class, excellent, the best.

tophat n. gibus, stovepipe hat.

topic n. subject, subject matter, point of discussion, issue, question, material, theme, problem, text, business, thesis.

topical a. current, contemporary, in the news, up-to-the-minute, up-to-date, popular, local, provincial.

top-level a. high-echelon, top-ranking, ranking, chief, leading.

top-notch a. first-rate, first-class, top-drawer, excellent, the best, supreme, the greatest, A-1, *blue-chip. ANT. the worst, poor, low.

topple v. fall, totter, pitch, collapse, tip over, founder, overturn, tumble, knock over, upset, knock down, bring down, overthrow, vanquish, unseat, unhorse.

tops a. SEE TOP-NOTCH

topsy-turvy a. upside-down, upended, wrong side up, inside-out, mixed up, jumbled, confused, backwards, *bass-ackwards, *ass-backwards, helter-skelter, *pell-mell, chaotic. ANT. right-side up, orderly.

torch n. light, flambeau, taper, firebrand, beacon.

torment n. suffering, pain, torture, anguish, agony, distress, misery, hell, irritation, trouble, plague, rack, scourge.

torment *v.* torture, punish, hurt, agonize, abuse, distress, trouble, bother, pain, irritate, bully, hurt, persecute, harass, aggravate, *drive crazy, plague, hector.

torn *a.* **1.** RIPPED cut, slashed, slit, lacerated, ragged, rent, split. **2.** DIVIDED undecided, of two minds, *on the fence.

tornado *n.* whirlwind, twister, cyclone, windstorm, tempest.

torpid *a.* dormant, sluggish, slow, inert, motionless, hibernating, unmoving, slow, lethargic, languid, listless, phlegmatic, lazy, dull, apathetic. ANT. *active, lively, energetic.*

TORPOR *n.* [TOR pur] a state of inactivity or sluggishness. *The oppressive heat caused widespread torpor.* SYN. inactivity, dormancy, inertia, sluggishness, slothfulness, deadness, lifelessness, languor, listlessness, *the blahs, drowsiness, laziness, apathy. ANT. *liveliness, pep, vigor.*

torrent *n.* flood, rush, stream, deluge, gush, white water, rapids, waterfall, cataract, cascade, overflow, tsunami, outpouring, downpour, cloudburst, spate.

torrential *a.* flooding, rushing, streaming, gushing, cascading, overflowing, drowning, swamping, violent.

TORRID *a.* [TOR id] scorching hot. Also, highly passionate or ardent. *She was having a torrid love affair with her boss.* SYN. hot, *red hot, *white hot, scorching hot, blazing, blistering, parching, fiery, burning, flaming, sizzling, sweltering, boiling, broiling, passionate, *hot, ardent, lustful, amorous, sexually charged, sexual, erotic. ANT. *icy, cold, frigid, wintry.*

torsion *n.* twisting, turning, torque, stress, strain.

tortuous *a.* **1.** WINDING twisted, twisting, sinuous, crooked, serpentine, zigzagging, curvy, meandering, labyrinthine, involute, convoluted. **2.** DEVIOUS tricky, deceitful, deceptive, dishonest, misleading, indirect. ANT. *1. straight, direct. 2. straightforward, honest, forthright.*

torture *n.* agony, torment, suffering, pain, anguish, hell, crucifixion, persecution, excruciation, punishment, abuse, misery, distress, trial, tribulation, rack, third degree. SEE PUNISHMENT

torture *v.* torment, pain, hurt, put through hell, crucify, persecute, punish, abuse, distress, agonize, mistreat, afflict, excruciate, rack, *work over, *make one cry Uncle.

toss *n.* throw, pitch, lob, cast, chuck, fling, heave, flip, pass.

toss *v.* throw, pitch, lob, cast, chuck, fling, heave, flip, pass.

tot *n.* child, toddler, preschooler, baby, infant, *rugrat.

total *n.* whole, sum, entirety, totality, bulk, amount, aggregate.

total *v.* add up, tote, number, figure, sum up, count, compute, calculate, reckon.

total *a.* complete, whole, entire, thorough, comprehensive, A to Z, thoroughgoing, all-inclusive, combined, full, absolute, unconditional, unqualified, unmitigated, all-out. ANT. *partial, limited, incomplete, qualified.*

TOTALITARIAN *a.* [to TAL uh TAIR ee un] authoritarian, autocratic, controlled by only one party or group. *They suffered under a totalitarian regime.* SYN. authoritarian, autocratic, fascist, dictatorial, tyrannical, monolithic, despotic, undemocratic, Nazi. ANT. *democratic.*

totally *adv.* completely, entirely, wholly, comprehensively, fully, utterly, absolutely, thoroughly, unconditionally. ANT. *partially, slightly.*

tote *v.* carry, haul, lug, transfer, convey, *schlep, transport.

totter *v.* falter, rock, stagger, wobble, topple, lurch, shake, stumble, sway, waver, bob, reel.

touch *n.* **1.** CONTACT feel, stroke, pat, kiss, caress, tap, fingering. **2.** SENSE OF TOUCH feel, tactile sense, tactility, sensation. **3.** TEXTURE feel, grain, surface. **4.** SKILL technique, way, sensitivity, finesse, art, flair. **5.** TRACE hint, suggestion, slight amount, tinge. **6.** COMMUNICATION contact.

touch *v.* **1.** FEEL finger, handle, stroke, pat, caress, palpate, fondle, paw, palm, massage. **2.** BRING INTO CONTACT strike, brush, tap, hit, graze, bump into, come up against. **3.** ADJOIN border on, abut, join, meet, converge, impinge upon. **4.** AFFECT move, *pluck at one's heartstrings, *strike a chord, make an impression, influence, arouse, excite, stimulate, stir one's soul, *hit home, strike a nerve, disturb. **5.** REGARD bear upon, have to do with, involve, deal with, concern, pertain to. **6.** COMPARE WITH equal, rival, *hold a candle to, *be in the same league, match, *be on a par with.

touched *a.* **1.** MOVED affected, stirred, impressed, shaken, disturbed, softened. **2.** DEMENTED unbalanced, unstable, crazy, *nuts, insane, cuckoo, non compos mentis, mentally ill, mad, deranged.

touching *a.* moving, affecting, heartwarming, soul-stirring, *heavy, disturbing, heartbreaking, heartrending, poignant, tear-jerking, pitiful, pitiable, arousing emotions.

TOUCHSTONE *n.* [TUCH stone] any measure or test for worth or genuineness, a standard. *His masterpiece was the touchstone against which all others were judged.* SYN. measure, standard, yardstick, benchmark, gauge, criterion, test, acid test, ideal, model.

touchy *a.* **1.** IRRITABLE oversensitive, ultrasensitive, hypersensitive, easily offended, grouchy, testy, grumpy, cranky, petulant, moody, churlish, thin-skinned, temperamental. **2.** RISKY ticklish, delicate, prickly, precarious, sensitive, tricky, *dicey, touch-and-go. ANT. *1. easygoing, imperturbable, thick-skinned. 2. safe.*

tough *n.* *tough guy, bully, *roughneck, *punk, thug, hoodlum, ruffian, hooligan, *goon.

tough *a.* **1.** STRONG pliable, *tough as shoe leather, unbreakable, *tough as nails, rugged, hardened, durable, enduring, sound, firm, vigorous, solid, conditioned, fit, hardy, brawny, strapping, muscular, herculean, burly, robust. **2.** CHEWY uncooked, stringy, leathery, gristly, *touch as shoe leather, *tougher than a boiled owl. **3.** STUBBORN obstinate, unyielding, inflexible, *hard-nosed, headstrong, firm, adamant, unbending, resolute, strict, severe, rough, bullheaded. **4.** HARD demanding, difficult, troublesome, vigorous, laborious, toilsome, brutal, harsh, rough, trying, formidable, complicated, complex, violent. ANT. *1. weak, soft, fragile, breakable. 2. softened, tender, tenderized, cooked. 3. yielding, acquiescent, irresolute. 4. easy, undemanding, simple.*

toughen *v.* harden, temper, anneal, season, strengthen, inure, steel, fortify, acclimate. ANT. *weaken, enfeeble.*

tough-minded *a.* realistic, practical, unsentimental, *hard-nosed.

toupee *n.* wig, *rug, hairpiece, peruke.

tour *n.* **1.** SHIFT turn, stint, spell, stretch, period, cycle, round. **2.** TRIP sight seeing expedition, journey, cruise, voyage, excursion, junket, jaunt, expedition, itinerary, grand tour.

tour *v.* visit, sightsee, travel, journey, take a trip, go on the road, *globetrot, cruise, voyage, take a junket, go on an excursion, explore, *barnstorm.

TOUR DE FORCE *n.* [toor de FORS] a feat of exceptional skill, talent or strength, a spectacular achievement. *The critics called his latest book a tour de force.* SYN. spectacular achievement, feat of strength, feat of great skill, grand achievement, accomplishment, masterpiece, masterwork, chef d'oeuvre.

tourist *n.* traveler, visitor, sightseer, *globetrotter, wayfarer, day-tripper, jet-setter, *rubbernecker.

tournament *n.* contest, tourney, competition, duel, meet, match, sporting event, joust, tilt.

tousled *v.* mussed, messed up, disordered, disarranged, tangled, entangled, disheveled, rumpled, unkempt, uncombed, ungroomed.

tout *v.* **1.** RECOMMEND puff, ballyhoo, praise, *talk up, brag about, extol, *hype, idealize, exaggerate, *plug, acclaim, promote. **2.** SOLICIT peddle, *drum up business, hawk, vend, pitch. ANT. *1. condemn, denigrate, *badmouth.*

tout de suite *a.* at once, immediately, right away, pronto, without delay, now.

tow *v.* pull, drag, haul, lug, transport, yank, trawl.

towel *n.* wipe, hand cloth, wash cloth.

tower *n.* **1.** TALL BUILDING skyscraper, high-rise, spire, monolith, obelisk, belfry, steeple, minaret, belltower. **2.** FORTRESS castle, prison, dungeon, donjon, keep, bastille.

tower *v.* rise over, soar, overshadow, eclipse, loom, *stand head and shoulders above, ascend.

towering *a.* **1.** HIGH tall, skyscraping, *cloud-puncturing, *cloud-kissing, sky high, lofty, soaring, airy, titanic, gigantic. **2.** GREAT huge, intense, powerful, extraordinary, massive, extreme, tremendous, stupendous, unrivaled, unmatched, unequaled, *head and shoulders above. ANT. *1. low, short, stubby. 2. insignificant, small, trivial.*

town *n.* village, settlement, hamlet, community, township, whistlestop, municipality, city, burg. "Where there is no place to go where you shouldn't be." — Alexander Woollcott.

toxic *a.* poisonous, unhealthy, harmful, noxious, deadly, lethal, fatal, nocuous, venomous, virulent. ANT. *nontoxic, harmless, healthy.*

toxin *n.* poison, noxious substance, venom, virus, pathogen, contaminant, botulism, hemlock, arsenic, deadly nightshade.

toy *n.* plaything, game, doll, ball, teddy bear, bauble, trinket.

toy *v.* play with, entertain oneself with, trifle, dally.

toy *a.* miniature, dwarf, pygmy, small-scale.

trace *n.* touch, hint, tinge, suggestion, shade, suspicion, taste, whiff, vestige, evidence, pinch, breath, drop, speck.

trace *v.* **1.** TRAIL track, follow, search for, shadow. **2.** ASCERTAIN dig up, root out, investigate, discover, unearth. **3.** DRAW OVER duplicate, copy, sketch, delineate.

track *n.* **1.** PRINT footprint, tread, imprint, trail, spoor, mark. **2.** COURSE race course, roadway, railway, path, walkway, passage.

track record *n.* history, statistics, *stats, performance history.

tract *n.* **1.** EXPANSE stretch, acreage, parcel, lot, area, extent, real estate, plot, spread, land. **2.** PAMPHLET booklet, brochure, leaflet, study, sermon, propaganda.

tractable *a.* obedient, docile, manageable, compliant, controllable, tame, submissive, yielding, meek, pliant, malleable. ANT. *intractable, disobedient, wild, unmanageable.*

traction *n.* grip, adherence, adhesion, *bite, purchase, hold, pulling, drawing.

tractor-trailer *n.* truck, *semi, trailer truck, eighteen wheeler.

trade *n.* **1.** LINE OF WORK occupation, business, profession, vocation, job, metier, craft, skill, employment, calling. **2.** BUYING AND SELLING commerce, marketing, exchange, merchandising, mercantilism, barter, interchange, transaction. **3.** CUSTOMERS clientele, patrons.

trade *v.* **1.** SWAP exchange, barter, switch, interchange. **2.** DO BUSINESS WITH buy and sell, deal, transact, patronize, shop.

trademark *n.* symbol, brand, label, logo, logotype, identification, insignia, colophon.

trader *n.* merchant, monger, buyer and seller, dealer, retailer, trafficker, vendor, hawker, peddler, business person.

trade secret *n.* proprietary knowledge.

tradition *n.* custom, practice, convention, habit, unwritten law, institution, observance, ritual, belief, folklore, lore, *generational hand-me-down. "What you resort to when you don't have the time or the money to do it right." —Kurt Adler.

traditional *a.* customary, conventional, habitual, handed down, established, practiced, institutional, accustomed, fixed, classic, orthodox, time-honored, familial, historic. ANT. *new, untried, unconventional.*

traduce *v.* vilify, defame, slander, malign, slur, cast aspersions on, smear, libel, denigrate, *bad-mouth, calumniate, *drag one's name through the mud. ANT. *praise, extol, honor.*

traffic *n.* **1.** VEHICULAR MOVEMENT congestion, *bottleneck, jam, gridlock, *bumper-to-bumper traffic, rush hour, transportation, movement, commuters, travelers. **2.** BUYING AND SELLING trade, commerce, merchandising, marketing, exchange, business, barter, smuggling, black marketing, transactions.

traffic *v.* buy, sell, trade, merchandise, market, exchange, do business in, deal in, peddle, smuggle, sell on the black market, *bootleg.

tragedy *n.* **1.** MISFORTUNE disaster, catastrophe, adversity, calamity, blow, heartbreaker, bad luck, hardship, shock, reversal. "The difference between what is and what might have been." —Alfred North Whitehead. **2.** TRAGIC PLAY drama, melodrama. ANT. *1. blessing, good fortune, boon. 2. comedy.*

tragic *a.* disastrous, unfortunate, catastrophic, calamitous, sad, heartbreaking, unlucky, shocking, unhappy, crushing, dreadful, terrible, grievous, pitiful, wretched, lamentable, horrible. ANT. *1. blessed, good, wonderful, fortunate.*

trail *n.* **1.** PATH pathway, footpath, track, beaten track, footprints, bridle path, course, rut, trace. **2.** SPOOR scent, markings, telltale.

trail *v.* **1.** DRAG BEHIND haul, tow, pull, train. **2.** FOLLOW track, shadow, hunt down, *dog, stalk, sniff out. **3.** HANG dangle, depend. **4.** LAG BEHIND bring up the rear, fall back, drop behind. ANT. *4. lead, head.*

train *n.* **1.** RAILROAD TRANSPORT Amtrak, *choo-choo, steam train, locomotive, monorail, subway, el, maglev train, express. SEE RAILROAD **2.** PROCESSION caravan, line, cortege, retinue, following, cavalcade, parade, entourage, series, chain.

train *v.* **1.** PREPARE school, drill, educate, teach, coach, qualify, instruct, discipline, practice, condition, work out, get in shape. **2.** AIM draw a bead on, point, level, sight.

trainee *n.* apprentice, student, pupil, novitiate, learner.

trainer *n.* coach, instructor, teacher, mentor, manager, handler.

training *n.* preparation, schooling, drilling, education, teaching, coaching, qualification, instruction, discipline, practice, conditioning, workout, exercise.

traipse *v.* walk, wander, tramp, roam, gad, rove, ramble, meander, walk aimlessly.

trait *n.* characteristic, quality, attribute, distinguishing feature, idiosyncrasy, quirk, property, hallmark, trademark.

traitor *n.* betrayer, *backstabber, turncoat, Judas, renegade, *double-crosser, *Benedict

Arnold, *snake in the grass, one who commits treason, one who practices treachery, recreant, deserter, defector. ANT. *loyalist, patriot.*

traitorous *a.* disloyal, treacherous, treasonous, betraying, *backstabbing, *double-crossing, sneaky, untrue, Janus-faced, renegade, turncoat, recreant. ANT. *loyal, faithful, true.*

trajectory *n.* course, path, track, flight, arc, curve, orbit.

tram *n.* rail car, streetcar, trolley.

trammel *n.* restraint, shackle, constraint, impediment, hindrance, fetter, yoke.

trammel *v.* restrain, shackle, restrict, constrain, confine, impede, hinder, obstruct, fetter.

tramp *n.* **1.** HOBO vagrant, transient, *bum, vagabond, derelict, street person, homeless person, panhandler, beggar. **2.** *Sl.* SLUT whore, loose woman, hussy, bimbo, harlot, trollop. **3.** HIKE OR MARCH walk, trek, expedition, traipse.

tramp *v.* stamp, tread, trudge, plod, stump, slog, hike, march, wander, travel, ramble, trek, traipse.

trample *v.* stomp on, crush, walk on, tread on, tramp, flatten, run over, stamp, squash.

trance *n.* hypnotic state, altered state of consciousness, daze, stupor, spell, glaze, transfixed state, dream state, abstraction, reverie.

tranquil *a.* calm, peaceful, serene, quiet, still, relaxed, sedate, motionless, unmoving, halcyon, untroubled, restful. ANT. *wild, noisy, troubled, uproarious.*

tranquility *n.* serenity, calm, peace, peacefulness, quiet, stillness, relaxation, sedation, motionlessness, restfulness. ANT. *wildness, agitation, uproar.*

tranquilize *v.* sedate, calm, quiet, relax, hush, pacify, soothe, put to sleep, *settle one's nerves. ANT. *agitate, stir up, stress out.*

transact *v.* carry out, carry on, perform, make a deal, execute, accomplish, do, discharge, prosecute, take care of, handle.

transaction *n.* deal, agreement, bargaining, contract, buy, sale, business, arrangement, performance, operation, enterprise.

TRANSCEND *v.* [tran SEND] to exceed, surpass or go beyond. *The event transcended expectations.* SYN. exceed, surpass, go beyond, outdo, pass, go above and beyond, excel, eclipse, top, outshine, outdistance, outperform.

TRANSCENDENTAL *a.* [tran sen DENT ul] beyond human experience, supernatural, spiritual. Also, excelling, surpassing. *Deep meditation brings him transcendental experiences.* SYN. **1.** supernatural, spiritual, otherworldly, mystical, intangible, preternatural, metaphysical, abstract. **2.** excelling, surpassing, extraordinary, supreme, unsurpassed, unrivaled, unequalled, incomparable, superior. ANT. **1.** *worldly, earthly, physical, tangible.* **2.** *common, ordinary.*

transcribe *v.* write out, type out, type up, record, copy, transfer, translate, transliterate, decipher shorthand.

transcriber *n.* stenographer.

transcript *n.* copy, written copy, typed copy, printed copy, translation, transcription, recording, transliteration.

transcription *n.* SEE TRANSCRIPT

transfer *n.* transference, transferal, transposition, repositioning, relocation, move, transplant, displacement, transportation, conveyance.

transfer *v.* **1.** MOVE remove, relocate, convey, reposition, transplant, transpose, transport, send, deliver, forward, transmit. **2.** SIGN OVER deed, convey.

transferal *n.* transference, transfer, move, removal, relocation, conveyance, transportation, transplantation, transposition, displacement.

transfix *v.* **1.** HOLD ONE'S ATTENTION put in a trance, spellbind, hypnotize, mesmerize, fascinate, absorb, enchant, paralyze, rivet, freeze. **2.** IMPALE pierce, nail, spike, skewer, lance, spear.

transform *v.* change, convert, metamorphose, transmute, alter, remodel, *do a chameleon, transmogrify, mutate, switch, *change one's spots, reinvent.

transformation *n.* change, conversion, metamorphosis, transmutation, alteration, remodeling, *a chameleon, transmogrification, mutation, transfiguration, metastasis.

transfuse *v.* transfer, infuse, permeate, instill, imbue.

TRANSGRESS *v.* [trans GRESS] sin, break a law, overstep a limit or boundary. *A recidivist can be counted on to transgress again and again.* SYN. sin, break a law, break a commandment, overstep one's bounds, go beyond the limit, violate, trespass, disobey, infringe.

TRANSGRESSION *n.* [trans GRESH un] sin, a breaking of the law. *The courts will not forgive major transgressions.* SYN. sin, crime, offense, violation, felony, evil, disobedience, trespassing, infringement, infraction, misdemeanor, wrong, breach.

transient n. drifter, vagrant, vagabond, tramp, hobo, migrant worker, traveler.

TRANSIENT a. [TRAN shunt] temporary, passing quickly. *The blue moon is a transient phenomenon.* SYN. temporary, passing, fleeting, impermanent, short-lived, transitory, ephemeral, momentary, short-term, brief, evanescent. ANT. *permanent, long-term, lasting.*

transit n. passage, conveyance, transport, progress, transition, change. SEE TRANSITION

transition n. change, transformation, switch, shift, conversion, changeover, metamorphosis, passage, transmogrification, transmutation.

transitory a. transient, passing, temporary, fleeting, impermanent, short-lived, ephemeral, momentary, short-term, brief, evanescent. ANT. *permanent, long-term, lasting.*

translate v. 1. INTERPRET metaphrase, decipher, transcribe, transliterate, *put in English, render, spell out, clarify, decode, paraphrase, rephrase, reword. 2. CHANGE convert, transform, alter, transpose, metamorphose, transmogrify, turn.

translation n. interpretation, rendition, transcription, metaphrase, paraphrase, rewording, rephrasing, version, rendering, deciphering, decoding, decryption. "Not versions but perversions." —Saint Jerome. "Like viewing a piece of tapestry on the wrong side where though the figures are distinguishable yet there are so many ends and threads that the beauty and exactness of the work is obscured." —Miguel de Cervantes.

translator n. interpreter, linguist, polyglot.

translucent a. semitransparent, clear, pellucid, gauzy, diaphanous, see-through, transparent. ANT. *opaque.*

transmission n. 1. TRANSMITTING transference, passage, sending, conveyance, carrying. 2. BROADCAST telecast, relay, airing. 3. GEARBOX drive train.

transmit v. send, transfer, convey, conduct, dispatch, transport, forward, relay, impart, carry, communicate, broadcast, telecast, radio, air. ANT. *receive.*

transmitter n. conductor, transceiver, beacon, signal source.

transmogrify v. change, metamorphose, mutate, transmute. SEE TRANSFORM

transmute v. mutate, change, metamorphose, transmogrify. SEE TRANSFORM

transparent a. 1. CLEAR see-through, glassy, diaphanous, crystalline, sheer, translucent, gauzy, limpid, pellucid, lucid, invisible. 2. SIMPLE plain, obvious, understandable, apparent, self-explanatory, straightforward, evident, patent. 3. OPEN frank, honest, candid, open, forthright, ingenuous, direct, real. ANT. 1. *opaque, nebulous, cloudy.* 2. *complex, unclear, confusing, murky, *clear as mud.* 3. *dishonest, underhanded, disingenuous.*

transpire v. happen, come to pass, occur, come about, take place, materialize, befall, arise, evolve, ensue.

transplant n. graft, donor organ.

transplant v. 1. GRAFT transfer, relocate. 2. REPLANT repot, uproot, transfer, relocate. 3. MOVE resettle, relocate, transfer, remove.

transport n. 1. TRANSPORTATION transporting, conveyance, movement, carrying, transit, shipment, hauling, trucking, delivery. 2. JOY rapture, ecstasy, bliss, euphoria, seventh heaven, exaltation, *high, *rush, *cloud nine, happiness, nirvana. ANT. 2. *depression, misery, melancholy.*

transport v. 1. CARRY convey, move, ship, haul, truck, deliver, send, cart, transfer, run, lug, *tote, relay. 2. ENRAPTURE fill with joy, overjoy, carry away, make ecstatic, entrance, thrill, enthrall, make euphoric, bewitch, charm. ANT. 2. *depress, fill with melancholy.*

transportation n. transport, conveyance, carrying, carriage, transit, transferal, movement, shipment, hauling, trucking, flight, delivery.

transported a. enraptured, overjoyed, filled with joy, carried away, ecstatic, euphoric, blissful, entranced, enthralled, *in seventh heaven, *on cloud nine, experiencing nirvana. ANT. *depressed, melancholic, miserable.*

transpose v. interchange, reverse, exchange, switch, change places, swap places, *flip-flop, commute, transfer.

transsexual n. epicene, transvestite, cross-dresser, *he-she, *AC-DC, sexual deviant.

transverse a. crosswise, athwart, crossed, cross, horizontal, diagonal, oblique.

transvestite n. cross-dresser, *drag queen, fetishist, sexual deviant, transsexual.

trap n. snare, pitfall, deadfall, *booby trap, spring trap, net, ploy, trick, artifice, ambush, bait, lure, hook, deception, machination, stratagem, ruse, decoy, blind.

trap v. snare, catch, capture, nab, corner, corral, net, entrap, ambush, trick, take by surprise, hook, bait, lure, *suck in.

trappings n. articles, articles of clothing, adornments, outfit, gear, equipment, trimmings, accoutrements, attire, apparel, paraphernalia.

trash n. **1.** RUBBISH refuse, waste, garbage, junk, leavings, remains, litter, debris, *crap, scraps, dregs, rubble. **2.** NONSENSE foolishness, drivel, *bilge, *rubbish, *bunk, *crap, *hogwash, *malarkey, balderdash, tripe, *baloney. **3.** CHEAP LITERATURE yellow journalism, tabloid journalism, *crap, sensationalism, kitsch, dime novel. **4.** RIFFRAFF *bum, criminal, *dregs of the earth, scum, *good-for-nothing, scoundrel, rogue.

trash v. Sl. **1.** CRITICIZE pan, insult, knock, badmouth, *dump on, disparage, put down, slam, *rank out, lambaste. **2.** VANDALIZE destroy, wreck, ruin, demolish, tear apart.

trashy a. worthless, junky, *crappy, no good, cheap, *not worth the powder to blow it to hell, useless, *crummy, *cruddy, *tinhorn, *two-bit, *schlocky.

trauma n. shock, blow, injury, wound, jolt, bombshell, upset, *emotional minefield, ordeal, stress.

traumatic v. shocking, injurious, physically wounding, psychologically wounding, upsetting, disturbing, stressful, horrifying, deeply emotional, scarring, damaging.

traumatize v. shock, injure, wound, upset, disturb, *stress out, horrify, *put through hell, *put through an emotional minefield, scar, scar for life, *drop a bomb on, jolt.

travail n. **1.** WORK toil, labor, sweat of one's brow, strain, grind, exertion, drudgery, pains, slavery. **2.** PAIN agony, torture, anguish, torment, hurt, suffering, distress. ANT. 1. leisure, relaxation, recreation. 2. pleasure, joy.

travel n. traveling, journeying, touring, transit, voyaging, cruising, globe-trotting, sightseeing, day-tripping, riding, flying, passage, excursion, trek, jaunt. "A fool's paradise." — Ralph Waldo Emerson. "An experience we shall always remember, or an experience, which, alas, we shall never forget." — Julius Gordon.

travel v. **1.** JOURNEY take a trip, tour, voyage, cruise, globe-trot, sight-see, day-trip, ride, fly, see the world, go on an excursion, take a junket, *hit the road, go abroad, explore, ramble, roam. **2.** PROGRESS advance, move, go forward, pass. ANT. 1. *have an armchair adventure, stay put.

traveler n. tourist, journeyer, voyager, sailor, cruiser, globe-trotter, sightseer, day-tripper, rider, flyer, *frequent flyer, explorer, rambler, roamer, wayfarer, vagabond.

traverse v. **1.** CROSS pass over, go over, travel over, cut across, span, bridge, intersect, bisect. **2.** OPPOSE thwart, hinder, impede, obstruct, check, foil, frustrate.

TRAVESTY n. [TRAV is tee] a farce, an absurd caricature or imitation. The bungled murder trial was a travesty of justice. SYN. farce, imitation, poor imitation, caricature, mockery, parody, burlesque, spoof, mimicry, perversion.

travesty v. imitate, caricature, mock, parody, burlesque, mimic, lampoon, ridicule, pervert.

trawl n. net, dragnet, line.

tray n. holder, receptacle, platter, salver, server, serving plate.

treacherous a. **1.** DISLOYAL traitorous, backstabbing, untrue, unfaithful, duplicitous, double-dealing, two-faced, Janus-faced, perfidious, treasonous, *like a snake in the grass. **2.** UNRELIABLE untrustworthy, insecure, hazardous, slippery, undependable, precarious, dangerous, unsafe, unstable, shaky. ANT. 1. loyal, true, faithful. 2. safe, secure, reliable.

treachery n. disloyalty, betrayal, traitorous behavior, *stab in the back, backstabbing, perfidy, duplicity, double-dealing, treason, infidelity, *double-cross, *two-timing. ANT. loyalty, faithfulness, fidelity.

treacle n. syrup, molasses.

tread v. **1.** WALK OR WALK ON trod, trample, tramp, march, trudge, step on, plod, hoof, stride, stomp, stump, crush. **2.** OPPRESS subdue, crush, trample, suppress, *jackboot into submission, subjugate.

treason n. betrayal, sedition, subversion, disloyalty, treachery, stab in the back, insurrection, insubordination, rebellion, revolt. ANT. loyalty, patriotism, faithfulness.

treasonous a. betraying, traitorous, seditious, subversive, disloyal, treacherous, *backstabbing, insubordinate, rebellious, mutinous. ANT. loyal, patriotic, faithful.

treasure n. **1.** WEALTH riches, money and jewels, fortune, hoard, pirate's hoard, miser's hoard, *tidy bundle, treasure-trove, king's ransom. **2.** VALUABLE THING OR PERSON gem, jewel, pearl, rarity, prized possession, prize, *find, *pride and joy.

treasure v. cherish, prize, value, appreciate, adore, love, esteem, hold dear, regard highly. ANT. dislike, hold in contempt, disdain.

treasure-trove n. SEE TREASURE

treasurer n. bursar, purser, controller, banker, clerk.

treasury n. **1.** BANK vault, coffer, depository, repository, safe, strongbox, safe deposit box, thesaurus. **2.** FUNDS revenue, savings, assets, money, reserve.

treat n. rare pleasure, rare delight, special favor or gift TO ONESELF OR ANOTHER, a special joy, a welcome change, goody, tidbit, indulgence, extravagance. ANT. *same old same old, *the usual.

treat v. **1.** ACT OR BEHAVE TOWARD use, deal with, handle, look upon, manage, react toward, relate to. **2.** DOCTOR nurse, tend to, mend, fix, care for, minister, prescribe, remedy, heal, medicate, dress, bandage. **3.** DISCUSS cover, talk about, write about, examine, go over, consider, touch upon, review. **4.** PICK UP THE TAB FOR ANOTHER pay for, cover, *spring for, pick up the check, foot the bill.

treatise n. study, article, work, essay, discussion, dissertation, thesis, examination, treatment, composition, paper, book, monograph, tract.

treatment n. **1.** HANDLING behavior towards, dealing, usage, processing, management, conduct toward, manner toward. **2.** MEDICAL CARE doctoring, nursing, prescription, remedy, medication, cure, therapy, therapeutics, regimen.

treaty n. agreement, contract, pact, entente, covenant, compact, deal, alliance, arrangement, mutual understanding, suspension of hostilities, cease-fire.

treble a. high-pitched, shrill, soprano

tree n. hardwood tree, softwood tree, conifer, evergreen, shrub, sapling, timber, acacia, alder, apple, ash, aspen, balsam, banyan, bayberry, beech, birch, breadfruit, butternut, cacao, camphor tree, cashew, cedar, cherry, chestnut, chinaberry, cinnamon, clove, coconut, cottonwood, cypress, date palm, dogwood, ebony, elder, elm, eucalyptus, fig, fir, frankincense, gingko, grapefruit, guava, gum, hawthorn, hazelnut, hemlock, hickory, holly, hornbeam, ironwood, juniper, larch, laurel, lemon, lime, linden, locust, magnolia, mahogany, mango, mangrove, maple, mimosa, mountain ash, mulberry, nutmeg, oak, olive, orange, palm, papaw, papaya, peach, pear, pecan, persimmon, pine, pistachio, plum, pomegranate, poplar, redwood, rosewood, sandalwood, sassafras, satinwood, sequoia, spruce, sycamore, tamarack, tamarind, tangerine, teak, tulip oak, walnut, willow, witch hazel, yew.

WORD FIND

bristles growing out of leaves: beard

center of trunk: heartwood

covering: bark

cultivates, one who: arborculturist

cultivation of: arborculture

dwarfed or stunted, Japanese variety of: bonsai

fantastically shaped, as an animal, by pruning: topiary

flaky bark, such as birch: scurf

fungus sometimes growing out of side: conk

garden of: arboretum

giant: redwood, sequoia

growth rings to determine past climate, study of: dendrochronology

leaf-shedding: deciduous

pertaining to: arboreal

pitch hole: pitch pocket

region, trees of a: sylva

ring marking past location of branch, tough: knot

rings of trunk from which age can be determined: growth rings

root, central: taproot

rope and thread, inner bark used in: bast

rotting leaves and debris collected under a tree: litter

sap or resin, excretes: gland

secretion: resin, sap

shady recess created by boughs: bower

stub: stump

studies trees, one who: dendrologist

study of: dendrology

thicket of shrubby trees: chaparral, copse

thick with branches: ramose

top cut to stimulate growth, tree with: pollard

trunk: bole, stock

tumor in which insect lives: gall

twisted: gnarled

uppermost story of leaves: canopy, crown

walk, tree-bordered: alameda

wartlike protuberance: burl

wind, knocked over by or off by wind: windfall, windthrow

wind, line of trees planted to check: windbreak

wood between bark and heartwood: sapwood

SEE JUNGLE, FOREST

trek n. journey, trip, odyssey, walk, hike, expedition, peregrination, march, migration, exodus, voyage.

trek v. walk, hike, *hoof it, slog, plod, trudge, tramp, *beat feet, hobble along, journey, travel, migrate, roam, rove, range.

trellis *n.* lattice, latticework, espalier, pergola, grate, grid, arbor, bower.

tremble *v.* shake, shiver, quiver, shudder, quake, quaver, flutter, shake like a leaf, tremor, oscillate, throb.

tremendous *a.* **1.** ENORMOUS huge, gigantic, colossal, monumental, massive, titanic, whopping, great, grand, monstrous, gargantuan. **2.** WONDERFUL great, extraordinary, fantastic, fabulous, *super, excellent, marvelous, *out of this world. **3.** TERRIFYING horrifying, dreadful, unnerving, frightening, scary, *bloodcurdling, shocking, horrendous, monstrous. ANT. *1. tiny, miniscule, puny, microscopic, insignificant. 2. terrible, awful, rotten.*

tremor *n.* shaking, tremble, shiver, shudder, quaking, quaver, fluttering, throb, quiver, ripple, trepidation.

tremulous *a.* **1.** TREMBLING shaking, shaky, shivering, shuddering, fluttering, throbbing, quivering, quavering, rippling. **2.** FEARFUL scared, timid, timorous, cowardly, flinching, fainthearted, anxious, nervous. ANT. *1. steady, still. 2. fearless, calm, relaxed.*

trench *n.* ditch, furrow, hole, excavation, channel, gully, fosse, moat, arroyo, gutter, conduit, drain, cut.

TRENCHANT *a.* [TRENCH unt] sharp, scathing or penetrating. *He gave a trenchant critique of the movie.* SYN. sharp, scathing, cutting, biting, pointed, caustic, acerbic, sarcastic, penetrating, incisive, keen, strong, forceful. ANT. *mild, dull, weak, *watered-down.*

trend *n.* direction, course, drift, tendency, prevalence, drift, inclination, track, flow, fashion, style, *in thing, rage, craze, fad, vogue.

trend *v.* run, tend, course, flow, incline, go, lean, drift, gravitate, move.

trendy *a.* *Sl.* en vogue, fashionable, *in, stylish, current, *now, *mod, modern, *up-to-the-minute, *cutting edge, *with it, contemporary. ANT. *old-fashioned, outdated, obsolete, passé, *out of it, *out.*

TREPIDATION *n.* [trep uh DA shun] anxiety, fear, trembling. *We approached the haunted house with trepidation.* SYN. anxiety, fear, apprehension, uneasiness, nervousness, worry, dread, misgiving, cold sweat, fright, panic, terror, *butterflies, *cold feet, consternation. ANT. *calm, composure, *nerves of steel.*

trespass *n.* **1.** ENCROACHMENT overstepping of bounds, infringement, invasion, intrusion, incursion, *offsides. **2.** TRANSGRESSION offense, violation, wrong, sin, misdeed, crime, criminal act, felony.

trespass *v.* **1.** ENCROACH overstep one's bounds, enter unlawfully, invade, infringe, intrude, *gate-crash. **2.** VIOLATE offend, commit a wrong, commit a sin, sin, commit a crime, break the law, transgress, misbehave.

tress *n.* lock of hair, plait, braid, ringlet, hank.

triad *n.* trinity, trio, threesome.

trial *n.* **1.** TRYOUT test, try, run, dry run, check, experiment, venture, *shot, *crack, *go, examination, essay, trial balloon, road test, lab test, clinical trial, *double blind, qualifying run. **2.** HARDSHIP tribulation, test of one's mettle, trial by fire, ordeal, travail, torment, torture, trouble, difficulty, distress, adversity, misfortune, hard times, suffering, grief, *cross to bear. **3.** COURT PROCEEDING legal proceeding, hearing, inquisition, jury trial, court case, suit, lawsuit, litigation, action, examination, arraignment, prosecution.

trial *a.* testing, experimental, tryout, observational, exploratory, probationary, pilot, tentative, provisional, preliminary, *watch and see.

triathlon *n.* *iron man contest, marathon.

tribe *n.* clan, family, group, ethnic group, race, kin, stock, *blood brothers, dynasty, community.

tribulation *n.* misery, distress, suffering, anguish, woe, affliction, misfortune, pain, grief, hardship, trouble, adversity, tragedy, ordeal, burden. ANT. *pleasure, good fortune, joy.*

tribunal *n.* court, judiciary, forum, bench, bar.

tributary *n.* branch, fork, feeder, stream, brook.

tribute *n.* gift, testimonial, gift of praise, applause, eulogy, accolade, honor, respect, acclaim, recognition, acknowledgement.

trick *n.* **1.** DECEPTION artifice, dodge, ruse, *fast one, machination, device, ploy, subterfuge, hoax, fraud, evasion, feint, fake, cheat, con, decoy. **2.** PRANK joke, gag, practical joke, stunt, antic, *monkey business, *funny business, *shenanigan, caper. **3.** MAGIC STUNT sleight of hand, presdigitation, *fast shuffle, rabbit out of a hat, *smoke and mirrors, legerdemain, hocus-pocus, illusion, *mind-reading, *mentalism. **4.** TECHNIQUE method, skill, secret, art, knack.

trick *v.* deceive, fool, cheat, take in, *pull a fast one, hoodwink, hoax, delude, *pull the wool over one's eyes, *fake out, *sucker in, *rope in, decoy, defraud, swindle, *play for a fool.

trickery *n.* deception, deceit, subterfuge,

cheating, fraud, hoax, imposture, delusion, artifice, *razzle-dazzle, sleight of hand, *fast shuffle, ledgerdemain, hocus-pocus, *smoke and mirrors, chicanery, *funny business, skulduggery. ANT. *honesty, truthfulness, openness.*

trickle *n.* dribble, seepage, weeping, flow, sprinkle, leak, stream, running, percolation, drizzling.

trickle *v.* dribble, seep, weep, flow, sprinkle, leak, stream, run, percolate, drizzle.

tricky *a.* **1.** DECEPTIVE deceitful, artful, crafty, wily, sly, clever like a fox, cunning, underhanded, *crooked as a three-dollar bill, slippery, cagey, shrewd. **2.** COMPLICATED complex, intricate, delicate, ticklish, sticky, knotty, thorny, touch-and-go. ANT. 1. *honest, truthful, open, artless. 2. easy, simple, *a snap.*

tried and true tried, tested, proven, proved, trustworthy, dependable, reliable, standing the test of time, reputable, *okay.

trifle *n.* **1.** TRIVIAL THING triviality, insignificant matter, nothing, no big thing, *nothing to sweat about, *nothing to get worked up about, *tempest in a teapot, *molehill. **2.** SMALL AMOUNT paltry amount, pittance, plug nickel, little, speck, *thimbleful, drop, *tad, smidgen, mite. **3.** BAUBLE knickknack, gewgaw, trinket, gimcrack, bagatelle, toy. ANT. 1. *big deal, monumental matter, weighty matter, *mountain. 2. wealth, bonanza, deluge, mass.*

trifle *v.* treat lightly, make light of, play with, toy with, mock, fool with, dally, discount, shortchange, laugh off, pass over, *play games with, disrespect, *dis. ANT. *respect.*

trifling *a.* trivial, frivolous, unimportant, insignificant, nominal, inconsequential, petty, minor, worthless, miniscule, piddling, slight, small, negligible, *not worth a hill of beans, *not worth the powder to blow it to hell. ANT. *important, weighty, monumental, crucial.*

trigger *n.* impulse, spark, impetus, goad, spur.

trigger *v.* set off, initiate, spark, fire, goad, spur, touch off, cause, generate, launch, trip. ANT. *dampen, inhibit, stop.*

trill *n.* warble, vibrato, tremolo, quaver, chirr, tiralee. SEE BIRD

trill *v.* warble, quaver, pipe, chirr, tiralee.

trim *n.* **1.** CUTTING clipping, pruning, shaping. **2.** CONDITION order, shape, fitness. **3.** DECORATION ornamentation, trimming, adornment, border, edging.

trim *v.* **1.** CUT clip, prune, lop, shear off, snip, shave, crop, bob, pare down, sculpt, reduce,

boil down, edit. **2.** DECORATE ornament, adorn, bedeck, embellish, dress, garnish, festoon, *spruce up, edge, border.

trim *a.* **1.** WELL-PROPORTIONED shapely, fit, toned, wasp-waisted, having an hourglass figure, statuesque, slender, thin, svelte. **2.** NEAT orderly, tidy, shipshape, organized, *in apple-pie order, uncluttered, groomed. ANT. 1. *out of shape, fat, roly-poly, obese. 2. messy, sloppy, disarranged.*

trimming *n.* overwhelming defeat, loss, beating, thrashing, *skunk.

trimmings *n.* side dishes, extras, fixings, appetizers.

trinity *n.* triad, trio, threesome, unit. SEE TRIO

trinket *n.* bauble, trifle, ornament, toy, gimcrack, gewgaw, knickknack, bagatelle, token, souvenir, keepsake.

trio *n.* group of three, unit of three, triad, trinity, threesome, menage a trois, trilogy, triangle, triplets, troika, triumvirate.

trip *n.* **1.** JOURNEY voyage, cruise, excursion, trek, expedition, jaunt, junket, outing, hike, flight, run, drive, errand. **2.** STUMBLE misstep, fall, tumble, slip, loss of footing, *header, pratfall, flop, mistake, blunder, faux pas. **3.** *Sl.* MIND TRIP *rush, hallucination, euphoria, *psychedelic experience, altered state, consciousness raising, *head trip, *high, *buzz.

trip *v.* **1.** STUMBLE misstep, lose one's footing, fall, tumble, slip, *take a header, lose one's balance, go headlong, fall flat on one's face. **2.** MAKE A MISTAKE blunder, *screw up, slip, err, *blow it, *muff, *flub, commit a faux pas. **3.** *Sl.* GET HIGH FROM DRUGS *catch a buzz, *have a psychedelic experience, *fly, experience an altered state, hallucinate.

tripe *n. Sl.* nonsense, *baloney, *BS, *crap, *rot, rubbish, garbage, bilge, drivel, trash.

TRITE *a.* [TRITE] unoriginal, worn out, lacking freshness. *His writing is uninspired and trite.* SYN. unoriginal, stale, worn out, overused, hackneyed, lacking freshness, cliche, cliched, stock, threadbare, pedestrian, commonplace, uninspired, stereotyped, tired, shopworn, routine. ANT. *original, fresh, imaginative, new.*

triumph *n.* **1.** VICTORY success, win, achievement, accomplishment, hit, feat, conquest, score, *home run, *grand slam, *touchdown, *slam-dunk, coup, tour de force. **2.** CELEBRATION elation, rejoicing, happiness, jubilation, exultation, acclamation. ANT. 1. *failure, loss, flop, *goose egg. 2. humiliation, shame, dishonor.*

triumph v. **1.** BE VICTORIOUS win, best, master, defeat, beat, *blow away, conquest, prevail, *leave swirling in one's wake, succeed, achieve, accomplish, score, *hit a home run, *hit a grand slam, *throw a touchdown, *slam-dunk, *skunk. **2.** CELEBRATE rejoice, exult, be elated, bask in the glory, revel, gloat. ANT. *1.* lose, *blow it, *choke, flop. *2. mope, fret.*

triumphant a. **1.** VICTORIOUS winning, successful, masterful, undefeated, unbeaten, conquering, *on top, champion. **2.** REJOICING celebrating, exultant, elated, proud, basking in glory, gloating. ANT. *1. defeated, beaten, *blown away. 2. moping, fretting, humiliated, *taken down a peg, crestfallen.*

trivia n. **1.** INSIGNIFICANT MATTERS trivialities, trifles, minutiae. **2.** USELESS INFORMATION tidbits, fascinating facts, memorabilia.

trivial a. unimportant, insignificant, inconsequential, petty, trifling, slight, picayune, piddling, frivolous, worthless, meaningless, minor, slight, *rinky-dink, *penny-ante, paltry. ANT. *important, significant, weighty, monumental.*

triviality n. trifle, nothing, no big thing, *no big deal, *nothing to sweat about, *nothing to get worked up about, detail.

troglodyte n. caveman, cave-dweller, Neanderthal, anthropoid, brute, beast, animal, ape, recluse, hermit.

troika n. triumvirate, trinity, group of three. SEE TRIO

troll n. mythical beast, giant, goblin, hobgoblin, ogre, monster, imp, gnome, dwarf, troglodyte.

trolley n. streetcar, tram, cart.

trollop n. prostitute, whore, *hooker, slut, hussy, harlot, loose woman, slattern, hag, frump.

troop n. group, herd, flock, throng, crowd, band, gang, assembly, assemblage, bunch, swarm, host, multitude.

troop v. walk, pass, march, parade, file, swarm, tramp, hike.

troops n. soldiers, military, men, infantry, G.I.s, armed forces, army, marines, corps, squad, combatants, cannon fodder. SEE ARMY

trophy n. prize, award, cup, loving cup, medal, laurel, plaque, blue ribbon, recognition, honor, citation, memorial.

tropical a. hot, humid, sweltering, torrid, sultry, *like a steambath, steamy, sticky, damp, muggy, close, oppresive, equatorial. ANT. *frigid, icy, snowy, polar.*

trot n. jog, run, lope, gait, canter. SEE HORSE

trot v. jog, run, lope, canter, amble, hurry along, move along quickly, *clip-clop.

trot out v. show, display, exhibit, parade, show off.

troubador n. poet, songwriter, balladeer, lyricist, singer, minstrel.

trouble n. **1.** DIFFICULTY distress, problem, predicament, hardship, *hot water, *fix, mess, *scrape, *deep doodoo, spot, dire straits, bind, hole, jam, *pickle, *sticky wicket, adversity, bad news, misfortune, heavy weather, danger, calamity, tribulation, pain, suffering, misery, grief, woe. "The tools by which God fashions us for better things."— Henry Ward Beecher. "What you make it."—Edmund Cooke. **2.** DISTURBANCE agitation, turmoil, disorder, unrest, rebellion, discord, upset, discontent. **3.** BOTHER effort, pains, inconvenience, difficulty, headache, work, labor, stress, strain, exertion, *pain in the neck, *pain in the ass. **4.** TROUBLING PERSON OR THING *pain, *pain in the neck, *pain in the ass, *bad news, troublemaker, nuisance, nag. ANT. *1. ease, pleasure. 2. peace, tranquility, calm.*

trouble v. **1.** DISTURB bother, inconvenience, put out, discommode, *bug, impose upon, harass, burden, distress, perturb, pain, worry, upset, stress, agitate, fluster. **2.** MAKE AN EFFORT take pains, exert.

troublemaker n. agitator, mischief-maker, imp, devil, hellion, pest, rebel, agent provocateur, *pain in the neck, *pain in the ass, instigator, incendiary, firebrand, malcontent, enfant terrible. ANT. *pacifist, peacemaker, angel.*

troubleshooter n. repairman, repair person, maintenance person, technician, serviceman, *Mr. Fixit.

troublesome a. difficult, bothersome, distressful, stressful, hard, challenging, demanding, tough, taxing, trying, burdensome, tricky, complex, complicated, thorny, convoluted, vexing, irritating, irksome. ANT. *easy, simple, undemanding, untroubling, *a breeze.*

trough n. channel, gutter, hollow, trench, ditch, culvert, drain, sluice, moat.

trounce v. beat, thrash, whip, flog, *whoop, *whale on, defeat, *lick, *skunk, *kick butt, rout, drub, best, overwhelm, *walk all over, *kill, *shellac. ANT. *lose, *choke, fail, be beaten soundly.*

troupe n. troop, cast, company, band, group, performers, actors, thespians, stock company. SEE THEATER

trousers *n.* pants, slacks, breeches, *britches, pantaloons, jeans, dungarees, overalls, *Levis, corduroys, *cords. SEE PANTS

trousseau *n.* outfit, clothes, bundle.

truant *n.* absentee, malingerer, shirker, dodger, *goldbricker, idler, *goof-off, layabout, juvenile delinquent.

truant *a.* absent, *playing hooky, *cutting class, *skipping school, absent without leave AWOL

truce *n.* armistice, cease-fire, peace treaty, peace agreement, cessation of hostilities, suspension of hostilities, reconciliation, *white flag.

truck *n.* **1.** *BIG RIG eighteen wheeler, tractor-trailer, trailer truck, *semi, *Kenworth, *Peterbilt, *flatface, flatbed, dump truck, *pickup, van, panel truck, lorry. **2.** DEALINGS relationship, association, business, transactions, commerce, barter, trading, buying and selling.

WORD FIND

cab with sleeping department: sleeper
driver and passenger portion: cab

truck *v.* haul, transport, carry, ship, transfer, convey, run.

truckle *v.* cringe, toady, *kiss up, *brownnose, kowtow, bow before, bow and scrape, grovel, *fall all over, *suck up to, fawn, *bootlick, submit. ANT. *dominate, stand up to, resist.*

truculent *a.* fierce, mean, harsh, pugnacious, nasty, hostile, belligerent, combative, brutal, ferocious, savage, vicious, ruthless, murderous, cruel, rude. ANT. *pleasant, good-natured, good-humored, nice.*

trudge *n.* walk, tramp, slogging, plodding, hike, *schlepp.

trudge *v.* walk, tramp, slog, plod, hike, traipse, *schlepp, clomp, *drag one's feet, stump, hobble.

true *n.* **1.** FACTUAL, REAL actual, valid, legitimate, bona fide, accurate, correct, genuine, authentic, veracious, verified, proven, confirmed, straight, literal, beyond question, right. **2.** FAITHFUL loyal, allegiant, devoted, dedicated, trustworthy, steady, reliable, dependable, constant, staunch, pure, dutiful, patriotic, *true-blue. **3.** RIGHTFUL lawful, legitimate, legal. **4.** FITTED aligned, level, plumb. ANT. *1. untrue, false, fictional, imaginary. 2. disloyal, unfaithful, backstabbing. 3. illegal, illegitimate, unlawful. 4. misaligned, skewed.*

true *adv.* truly, truthfully, honestly, accurately,

correctly, precisely, exactly. ANT. *falsely, untruthfully.*

true-blue *a.* faithful, loyal, tried and true. SEE TRUE

truffle *n.* fungi, mushroom, delicacy.

truism *n.* platitude, cliche, bromide, saw, commonplace, axiom, fact, maxim, aphorism, truth, universal truth.

truly *adv.* truthfully, honestly, accurately, correctly, genuinely, unquestionably, really, sincerely, actually, literally. ANT. *falsely, questionably, inaccurately.*

trump *v.* surpass, outdo, outsmart, outwit, best, defeat, outperform, excel, beat, outscore, vanquish.

trumped up *a.* false, made up, fraudulent, concocted, invented, fabricated, devised, *cooked up.

trumpet *n.* **1.** HORN wind instrument, bugle, flugelhorn. SEE MUSICAL INSTRUMENT **2.** CLARION BLAST toot, trumpeting, fanfare, blare, honk.

trumpet *v.* proclaim, announce, herald, cry out.

truncate *v.* cut off, shorten, lop, clip, trim, prune, pare, dock, curtail, abbreviate.

truncheon *n.* baton, billy club, cudgel, stick, bat, blackjack, mace.

trundle *v.* roll along, wheel.

trunk *n.* chest, box, footlocker, coffer, container, case, *Saratoga trunk.

trunks *n.* shorts, swim shorts, breeches.

truss *n.* framework, bracing, girders, support.

truss *v.* **1.** TIE bind. **2.** SUPPORT hold up, prop, strengthen.

trust *n.* **1.** CONFIDENCE belief, faith, hope, store, reliance, assurance, certainty, conviction, security. **2.** CARE keeping, safekeeping, custody, responsibility, charge, guardianship, protection, watchful eye. **3.** CORPORATION monopoly, cartel, company, conglomeration. ANT. *1. distrust, doubt, reservations.*

trust *v.* **1.** BELIEVE IN have confidence in, have faith in, set store by, rely on, take stock in, depend on, bank on, count on, swear by. **2.** HOPE be optimistic, assume, anticipate. **3.** ENTRUST give for safekeeping, assign. ANT. *1. distrust, disbelieve, have reservations about.*

trustee *n.* warden, custodian, agent, executor, fiduciary.

trusting *a.* trustful, believing, credulous, gullible, unquestioning, unsuspecting, confident, naive, innocent, oblivious. ANT. *suspicious, wary, cynical, skeptical.*

trustworthy *a.* reliable, dependable, honest, honorable, tried and true, upright, ethical, responsible, truthful, loyal, faithful, principled, *okay. ANT. *dishonest, dishonorable, unreliable, irresponsible.*

trusty *a.* SEE TRUSTWORTHY

truth *n.* **1.** REALITY facts, factualness, actuality, veracity, verity, *gospel, *naked truth, *unvarnished truth, plain truth, truthfulness, accuracy. "The heart of morality." — Thomas Henry Huxley. "The strongest argument." — Sophocles. "A jewel which should not be painted over; but it may be set to advantage and shown in a good light." — George Santayana. **2.** FACT principle, rule, universal truth, certainty, truism, axiom, platitude. ANT. **1.** *fiction, imagination.* **2.** *lie, falsehood.*

truthful *a.* **1.** HONEST straight, candid, plainspoken, frank, *on the level, *from the heart, sincere, straightforward, forthright, veracious. **2.** ACCURATE precise, exact, literal, true, factual, real. ANT. **1.** *dishonest, insincere, deceitful.* **2.** *inaccurate, inexact, exaggerated.*

try *n.* attempt, *shot, *crack, *whirl, *go, *stab, effort, trial, turn, essay.

try *v.* **1.** ATTEMPT endeavor, *take a shot at, *take a crack at, *give it a whirl, *give it a go, *make a stab at, make an effort, take a turn, make a bid for, undertake, essay, venture, strive, *knock oneself out, struggle, do one's best, work hard, labor, vie for, *buckle down, *go all out, *give it the old college try. **2.** TEST experiment, try out, evaluate, examine, assay, *put to the test, *check out, appraise, prove, sample, taste. **3.** BRING A CASE TO COURT hear a case, adjudicate, judge, examine, decide. **4.** STRAIN stress, burden, tax, weary, trouble, sap.

trying *a.* stressful, taxing, exasperating, draining, irritating, annoying, irksome, tiresome, wearisome, burdensome, hard, troublesome, aggravating. ANT. *pleasurable, easy, relaxing.*

tryout *n.* audition, test, *cattle call, trial, demonstration, hearing, *shot, opportunity, *opportunity to strut one's stuff.

TRYST *n.* [TRIST] a secret rendezvous made by lovers, an appointment to meet. *The boss and his secretary had a tryst every Friday night after work.* SYN. rendezvous, meeting, appointment, date, engagement, assignation.

T-shirt *n.* tee-shirt, undershirt, pullover, *muscle shirt. SEE SHIRT

tsunami *n.* tidal wave, deluge, flood, tidal bore, eagre, surge, giant sea swell. SEE OCEAN

tub *n.* bathtub, bath, hot tub, washtub, vessel, vat, tank, cask, keg, barrel.

tuba *n.* helicon. SEE MUSICAL INSTRUMENT

tubby *a.* squat, chubby, chunky, fat, pudgy, dumpy.

tube *n.* cylinder, pipe, conduit, hose, duct, catheter, drain, conductor, line, inlet, outlet, shaft, tunnel, subway.

tubercle *n.* projection, growth, wart, nub, knob, node, nodule, protuberance, tumor.

tubular *a.* cylindrical.

tuck *n.* fold, pleat, crease, gather, pucker.

tuck *v.* **1.** FOLD OR STICK enfold, gather, pleat, insert, stuff, cram. **2.** WRAP enfold, cover, swaddle, swath, enwrap, blanket.

tuckered out *a.* tired, exhausted, worn out, weary, fatigued, *wiped out, spent, drained, *pooped, *dog tired.

tuft *n.* clump of hair, cluster, bunch, knot, wisp, thatch, lock, shock, cowlick, topknot, plume, tassel, tussock.

tug *n.* pull, yank, heave, tow, drag, haul, jerk, wrench.

tug *v.* pull, yank, heave, tow, drag, haul, jerk, wrench, draft, *lug, draw, wrestle, *muscle.

tuition *n.* schooling fee, charge, cost of education.

tumble *n.* **1.** ROLL OR FALL somersault, handspring, stumble, trip, *header, *pratfall, spill, flop, crash, slip, dive. **2.** DISORDER mess, confusion, jumble, disarray, chaos, heap.

tumble *v.* **1.** ROLL OR FALL somersault, handspring, stumble, trip, *take a header, *do a pratfall, spill, flop, crash, slip, dive, drop, pitch, topple, plunge, *lose one's footing, *go flying, collapse, plummet, nosedive.

tumbledown *a.* dilapidated, rickety, unstable, broken-down, shaky, unsteady, ramshackle, *ready to collapse at the word boo, crumbling, rundown, decrepit, condemned. ANT. *rock-solid, secure, stable, sturdy.*

tumescent *a.* swollen, distended, bloated, turgid, puffed up, enlarged, tumid, *ballooned out, bulging. ANT. *limp, flaccid, deflated.*

tummy *n.* abdomen, belly, gut. SEE STOMACH

tumor *n.* growth, mass, tissue mass, neoplasm, lump, carcinoma, sarcoma, cancer, melanoma, malignancy, cyst, polyp. SEE CANCER

tumult *n.* uproar, commotion, disturbance, hubbub, clamor, hullabaloo, pandemonium, upheaval, turmoil, furor, bedlam, ferment, *to-do, ado, riot. ANT. *peace, calm, tranquility.*

TUMULTUOUS *a.* [tuh MUL choo us] uproarious, loud, wild, turbulent. *The meeting turned tumultuous after it was announced that taxes would be raised.* SYN. uproarious, loud, noisy, wild, turbulent, clamorous, riotous, stormy, tempestuous, vociferous, raging, violent, raucous, out of control, rowdy, boisterous. ANT. *peaceful, calm, tranquil.*

tundra n. plain, wasteland.

tune n. **1.** MELODY song, *ditty, air, number, composition, piece, aria, strain, ballad.

WORD FIND

catchy part: hook, chorus

SEE OPERA, MUSIC, SONG

2. PITCH agreement, harmony, concord, conformity, calibration.

tune v. adjust, put in tune, pitch, harmonize, align, calibrate.

tuneful a. melodious, melodic, musical, harmonious, lyrical, euphonious, euphonic, symphonic, pleasing to the ear, *catchy. ANT. *cacophonous, discordant, jarring.*

tunic n. coat, toga, frock, jupon, gipon, garment, blouse, vestment.

tunnel n. subway, subterranean passage, tube, mine, mineshaft, *chunnel, underpass, burrow, hole. SEE CAVE

tunnel v. dig, burrow, excavate, cut, mine, blast out.

tunnel vision narrow outlook, shortsightedness, myopia.

turban n. headdress, head covering, hat, scarf, bandanna, tarboosh.

turbid a. muddy, cloudy, murky, unclear, dirty, filthy, opaque, thick, soupy, roily, agitated, stirred-up. ANT. *clear, crystal, transparent, limpid.*

turbine n. engine, motor, power source, *work horse, generator. SEE MOTOR

turbulence n. agitation, violence, swirling, commotion, instability, roughness, disturbance, turmoil, tumult, storminess, wildness, wind shear, gustiness. ANT. *calm, quiet, motionlessness.*

turbulent a. agitated, wild, violent, riled up, swirling, full of commotion, unstable, rough, disturbed, tumultuous, stormy, tempestuous, gusty, choppy. ANT. *peaceful, calm, tranquil, still, smooth.*

turf n. **1.** SOD earth, clod, clump, divot, sward, grass, patch. **2.** Sl. ONE'S TERRITORY neighborhood, ground, home ground, domain, *stomping grounds, backyard.

turgid a. **1.** SWOLLEN distended, bloated, puffed up, tumescent, tumid, inflated, *ballooned out. **2.** BOMBASTIC inflated, overblown, grandiose, grandiloquent, florid, pompous, orotund, flatulent. ANT. *1. flaccid, deflated. 2. concise, succinct.*

turkey n. Sl. **1.** FAILURE flop, *bomb, *dog, loser, *clunker, *clinker, *dud, *Edsel, *lemon, *washout. **2.** JERK loser, ass, *bozo, clown, *dildo, *creep, *dink, *dipshit, *dork, *drip, *dweeb, *goober, *ho-dad, *jerk-off, *lunkhead, *nerd, punk, *twerp, *weenie.

turmoil n. turbulence, commotion, tumult, uproar, disturbance, agitation, unrest, wildness, chaos, confusion, disorder, pandemonium, bedlam. ANT. *peace, calm, tranquility.*

turn n. **1.** REVOLUTION rotation, gyration, circle, curving, circuit, cycle, gyre, spin, twirl, eddy, whirl, roll, about-face, deviation, pivot, twist, shift, winding, convolution. **2.** CHANGE OF DIRECTION change of course, deviation, swerve, turnabout, reversal, divergence, shift, switch, curve, detour, fork, shunt, deflection. **3.** CURVE bend, hairpin turn, S-curve, zigzag, U-turn, arc, tack, dogleg, oxbow, hook. **4.** OPPORTUNITY *crack, *shot, try, move, time, chance, go, *whack, spell. **5.** SHOCK fright, start, scare. **6.** ACTION act, deed, favor, kindness, service.

turn v. **1.** REVOLVE rotate, go round, wheel, gyrate, circle, make a circuit, cycle, spin, twirl, eddy, whirl, roll, pivot, wind, crank, curve, swerve, veer. **2.** CHANGE DIRECTION change course, curve, swerve, veer, deviate, diverge, detour, sidetrack, shunt, *take a fork in the road, diverge, reverse, loop, do an about-face, make a U-turn, follow a serpentine path, zigzag. **3.** REVERSE invert, transpose, flip over, turn upside down, turn inside out. **4.** CHANGE transform, alter, metamorphose, convert, transmute, mutate, transmogrify, reconstruct, remodel. **5.** GO SOUR go bad, spoil, ferment, curdle, putrefy, rot, become tainted. **6.** SICKEN nauseate, unsettle. **7.** TWIST, AS AN ANKLE sprain, wrench, dislocate, throw out of joint.

turnabout n. about-face, reversal, shift, volte-face, turnaround, *switcheroo, *a 180, *flip-flop, backpedaling.

turncoat n. traitor, betrayer, renegade, Judas, Benedict Arnold, backstabber, *double-crosser, *two-timer, snake, *squealer, *fink.

turndown n. rejection, no, rebuff, *nix, *thumbs-down, refusal, declining, disapproval, *no-go, veto. ANT. *acceptance, approval, okay.*

turn down v. reject, say no to, rebuff, *give a thumbs-down, refuse, decline, disapprove, *nix, veto, *shoot down. ANT. *accept, okay, approve.*

turning point *n.* crossroads, pivotal moment, critical moment, crisis point, juncture, *zero hour, Rubicon, point of no return.

turn off *v. Sl.* bore, disinterest, *put to sleep, disgust, *make one sick, nauseate, sicken, *turn one's stomach. ANT. *turn on.*

turn on *v. Sl.* stimulate, excite, titillate, arouse, *get one's motor running, *charge one's battery, impassion, *make hot. ANT. *turn off, disgust, sicken.*

turnout *n.* **1.** GATHERING, NUMBER crowd, multitude, gathering, assemblage, gate, showing, collection, mob, bunch, swarm. **2.** OUTPUT production, productivity, yield, amount.

turn out *v.* make, produce, manufacture, fabricate, build, construct, put out.

turn over *v.* flip, overturn, upset, upend, capsize, tip, *turn turtle.

turnpike *n.* toll highway, toll road, interstate, expressway, superhighway, pike. SEE STREET

TURPITUDE *n.* [TUR pi TOOD] depravity, wickedness. *She divorced him because of his moral turpitude.* SYN. depravity, wickedness, immorality, corruption, vileness, baseness, evil, nastiness, sinfulness, vice, perversion. ANT. *morality, virtue, uprightness, goodness.*

turret *n.* tower, bartizan, watchtower, lookout, cupola, steeple. SEE TOWER

tush *n.* rump, *fanny, rear, gluteus maximus. SEE BUTTOCKS

turtle *n.* terrapin, chelonian, tortoise, snapping turtle, reptile.

WORD FIND

shell: carapace, plastron.

tusk *n.* tooth, fang, ivory.

tussle *n.* struggle, scuffle, fight, wrestling match, boxing match, *scrap, contest, combat, *tug-of-war, battle, conflict, fray, brawl, clash, *locking of horns, melee, donnybrook, *rumble.

tussle *v.* struggle, scuffle, fight, wrestle, box, *scrap, contest, combat, *have a tug-of-war, battle, conflict, brawl, clash, *lock horns, grapple.

tussock *n.* tuft, clump, thicket.

TUTELAGE *n.* [TOOT ul ij] teaching, instruction or care. *Under the tutelage of his current coach, he won three championships.* SYN. teaching, instruction, tutoring, schooling, training, coaching, guidance, direction, care, guardianship, supervision.

tutor *n.* teacher, private teacher, instructor, private instructor, coach, mentor, educator, trainer, guide, guru, master.

tutor *v.* teach, instruct, coach, educate, train,

enlighten, cram, *show the ropes, *drum into, drill.

TV *n.* *telly, video, *idiot box. SEE TELEVISION

twaddle *n.* nonsense, foolishness, balderdash, *rot, *rubbish, *crap, claptrap, drivel, prattle, tripe, blather, hogwash, *piffle.

tweak *n.* pinch, twist, turn, squeeze, nip, yank.

tweak *v.* pinch, twist, turn, squeeze, nip, yank.

tweet *n.* chirp, chip, cheep, chirrup, twitter. SEE BIRD

tweezers *n.* nippers, pincers, forceps, tongs.

twiddle *v.* twirl, tweak, twist, spin, finger, fiddle with, toy with, trifle with, fool with.

twig *n.* branch, limb, shoot, bough, stick, stem, sprig, offshoot.

twilight *n.* **1.** DUSK gloam, sundown, sunset, eventide, nightfall, evening, moonrise, *shank of the evening, *gauzy light of dawn, *premonition of dawn. **2.** DECLINE last days, *last gasp, swan song, ebb, *final curtain, passing, retirement.

twilight zone *n.* hallucinatory state, hypnogogic state, *dream world, nightmare world.

twin *n.* double, match, fellow, duplicate, mirror image, carbon copy, clone, counterpart, *dead ringer, match, mate, alter ego, brother, sister, identical twin, fraternal twin, Siamese twin.

twin *a.* dual, double, paired, duplicate, matching, same, corresponding, mirroring, identical, fellow.

twine *n.* **1.** STRING thread, cord, cordage, yarn, rope, hemp, braid, line, cable. **2.** TANGLE knot, snarl, twist.

twine *v.* intertwine, interlace, entwine, twist, plait, braid, knit, weave, coil, wreathe.

twinge *n.* **1.** PAIN pang, stab, stabbing, stitch, twitch, pinch, cramp, prick, spasm, shooting pain. **2.** REMORSE qualm, regret, pang of conscience, misgiving.

twinkle *n.* scintillation, flicker, flash, sparkle, glint, glimmer, flash, shimmering, gleam, glitter, spark, wink.

twinkle *v.* scintillate, flicker, flash, sparkle, glint, glimmer, shimmer, gleam, glitter, spark, wink.

twinkling *n.* instant, split second, wink, blink of an eye, heartbeat, flash, moment.

twirl *v.* spin, rotate, whirl, wheel, turn, pirouette, revolve, pivot, gyrate, twist.

twist *n.* **1.** KNOT turn, winding, twine, twining, braid, kink. **2.** ROTATION twirl, spin, revolution, torsion. **3.** SPRAIN wrench, turn. **4.** TURN IN THE ROAD curve, zigzag, S-curve, hairpin turn, bend, snake. **5.** QUIRK eccentricity, idiosyncrasy, peculiarity, oddity, abnormality, aberration. **6.** DISTORTION perversion, misrepresentation, misinterpretation, falsification, slant. **7.** UNEXPECTED DEVELOPMENT plot twist, surprise, invention.

twist v. **1.** KNOT turn, wind, twine, braid, kink, entwine, tangle, plait, braid. **2.** ROTATE turn, spin, twirl. **3.** SPRAIN wrench, turn. **4.** TURN IN THE ROAD curve, zigzag, bend, snake, follow a serpentine pattern. **5.** DISTORT pervert, misrepresent, misstate, misinterpret, falsify, slant, lie, misconstrue.

twisted a. **1.** KNOTTED wound up, balled up, entwined, full of kinks, tangled, plaited, braided, convoluted, crooked. **2.** DISTORTED wrong, inaccurate, mixed-up. **3.** PERVERTED eccentric, weird.

twister n. cyclone, whirlwind. SEE TORNADO

twit n. idiot, jerk. SEE MORON

twit v. reproach, tease, taunt, *dig, *razz, gibe, make fun of, kid, *rib, *rag on, disparage.

twitch n. jerk, spasm, tic, quiver, shiver, quaver, tremor, shake, throb.

twitch v. jerk, go into spasms, quiver, shiver, quaver, tremor, shake, throb, convulse, flutter, vellicate.

twitter n. chirping, singing, chirruping, whistling, tweeting, warbling, trilling. SEE BIRD

twitter v. chirp, sing, chirrup, vocalize, call, chatter, warble, trill, tweet, whistle. SEE BIRD

two-bit a. cheap, inferior, gaudy, *bush, *bush-league, dime-a-dozen, *one-horse, *tinhorn, small-time, piddling, second-rate. ANT. first-rate, superior, big-league.

two-faced a. Janus-faced, deceitful, insincere, double-dealing, treacherous, hypocritical, disingenuous, dishonest, backstabbing, disloyal. ANT. loyal, *real, honest, sincere.

two-time v. Sl. betray, cheat, deceive, backstab, stab in the back, be unfaithful, be disloyal.

tycoon n. industrialist, mogul, financier, magnate, capitalist, *big shot, bigwig, *big wheel, big-time operator, enterpriser, businessman.

tyke n. child, toddler, *little shaver, brat, imp.

type n. **1.** KIND sort, class, breed, order, species, variety, persuasion, cast, genre, form, classification, genus, family, stock. **2.** EXAMPLE model, archetype, pattern, standard, epitome, personification, essence, rule. **3.** CHARACTERS typeface, printing, font.

type v. **1.** CLASSIFY categorize, sort, stamp, class, grade, order. **2.** TYPEWRITE *hunt and peck, *touchtype, *bang out, key in, word process.

Type A n. hostile personality, *high octane personality, *hot reactor, aggressive personality.

typewriter n. word processor, office machine, portable.

typhoon n. tropical storm, cyclone, hurricane, rain storm, deluge.

typical a. normal, standard, average, common, regular, usual, conventional, expected, habitual, stock, par, ordinary, run-of-the-mill. ANT. atypical, unusual, extraordinary, unexpected.

typecast v. stereotype.

typify v. exemplify, represent, personify, epitomize, embody, characterize, stand for, denote, serve as an example.

typist n. word processor, secretary, clerk, office worker.

typo n. typographical error, spelling error.

tyrannical a. despotic, dictatorial, autocratic, ironhanded, authoritarian, high-handed, domineering, oppressive, cruel, harsh, unjust, arbitrary. ANT. democratic.

tyrannize v. dictate, rule with an iron hand, dominate, oppress, bully, order around, *jackboot into submission, *keep under one's thumb, step on, intimidate, subdue. ANT. rule democratically.

tyranny n. dictatorship, autocracy, totalitarianism, despotism, oppression, reign of terror, iron hand, *jackboot authority, iron rule, domination, authoritarianism, brutality, cruelty, severity. "Oppression, and Sword-law."—John Milton. "The worst of treasons."—Lord Byron.

tyrant n. dictator, despot, autocrat, authoritarian, *Hitler, fascist, bully, absolute ruler, oppressor, overlord. "Nothing but a slave turned inside-out."—Herbert Spencer.

tyro n. beginner, novice, amateur, *rookie, *greenhorn, neophyte, novitiate, raw recruit, *tenderfoot, trainee. ANT. expert, master, professional, *old hand.

U

UBIQUITOUS *a.* [yoo BIK wuh tus] present everywhere at the same time, or seemingly so, omnipresent. *The faithful believe God is ubiquitous.* SYN. everywhere, omnipresent, widespread, all-over, pervasive, universal, worldwide, far and wide, to the four corners of the earth.

U-boat *n.* *steel shark. SEE SUBMARINE

UFO *n.* unidentified flying object, flying saucer, *bogey, extraterrestrial spacecraft.

ugliness *n.* unattractiveness, repulsiveness, homeliness, grotesqueness, unsightliness, plainness, deformity, monstrousness, hideousness, eyesore. ANT. *beauty, attractiveness, loveliness.*

ugly *a.* **1.** UNATTRACTIVE repulsive, homely, hideous, unbecoming, grotesque, unsightly, plain, deformed, monstrous, revolting, *gross, misshapen, unappealing, *toadfaced, *rat-faced, *fish-faced, *not much on looks, *has a great personality, an eyesore. **2.** DISAGREEABLE, BAD offensive, objectionable, unpleasant, disgusting, nasty, repugnant, repellent, obnoxious, sickening, nauseating, vile, distasteful. **3.** THREATENING ominous, menacing, forbidding, portentious, dangerous, black, sinister, malevolent, malignant. **4.** CROSS ill-tempered, *mad, angry, *pissed, quarrelsome, bad-tempered, surly, mean, nasty, cantankerous. ANT. *1. attractive, beautiful, lovely, appealing. 2. agreeable, pleasant, good. 3. auspicious, harmless, promising. 4. good-natured, good-humored, easygoing.*

ulcer *n.* ulceration, sore, peptic ulcer, canker, abscess, festering, lesion.

ulcerous *a.* ulcerated, cankerous, cankered, festering, sore.

ULTERIOR *a.* [ul TEER ee er] undisclosed, hidden, beyond what is spoken. *John said he wanted to judge the beauty pageant for the money, but we suspected he had an ulterior motive.* SYN. undisclosed, hidden, unspoken, unexpressed, covert, remote, unrevealed, concealed, personal. ANT. *expressed, obvious, evident.*

ultimate *n.* greatest, highest, best, height, top, pinnacle, summit, peak, last word, ne plus ultra, culmination. ANT. *lowest, minimum.*

ultimate *a.* **1.** UTMOST maximum, highest, greatest, uppermost, supreme, paramount, extreme, best, superlative, preeminent. **2.** FINAL conclusive, last, concluding, ending, completing, finishing, terminal, terminating, closing, furthest, farthest, eventual. ANT. *1. lowest, minimum, worst. 2. beginning, initial, opening.*

ultimately *adv.* in the end, finally, eventually, sooner or later, at last, after all, after all is said and done.

ultimatum *n.* last offer, final proposal, demand, last chance, warning.

ultra *a.* extreme, beyond, excessive, radical, extravagant, inordinate, extraordinary, above and beyond, drastic.

ultramodern *a.* futuristic, advanced, ahead of its time, *cutting edge.

ululate *v.* howl, wail, lament.

umbrage *n.* offense, resentment, indignation, hurt, displeasure, grudge, pique, anger, huff. ANT. *pleasure.*

umbrella *n.* parasol, shade, sunshade, cover, canopy, bumbershoot. "A portable roof."— Leonard Levinson.

umpire *n.* judge, referee, arbiter, arbitrator, mediator, adjudicator, *ump.

unable *a.* incapable, not up to, helpless, powerless, incompetent, ineffectual, ineffective, impotent, unskilled, unfit, unschooled, unqualified, inoperative, *out of commission. ANT. *able, capable, effective.*

unabridged *a.* uncut, whole, complete, full-length, total, intact, unshortened. ANT. *abridged, cut, condensed.*

unacceptable *a.* unsatisfactory, unsuitable, not acceptable, improper, *not up to snuff, *below par, unfit.

unaccompanied *a.* alone, lone, solo, sole, solitary, unattended, single. ANT. *accompanied, paired, escorted.*

unaccustomed *a.* inexperienced, unseasoned, unused to, *green, raw, ignorant, unacquainted.

unadorned *a.* unembellished, undecorated, bare, bald, stark. SEE PLAIN

UNADULTERATED *a.* [un uh DULT uh rate ed] pure, unpolluted, undiluted, unmixed. *We found the national park still unadulterated and pristine.* SYN. pure, unmixed, undiluted, unpolluted, unalloyed, uncorrupted, untainted, uncontaminated, unspoiled. ANT. *adulterated, contaminated, impure.*

unaffected *a.* **1.** NATURAL real, sincere, down-to-earth, unstudied, *folksy, *down-home, unpretentious, genuine, plain, simple. **2.**

NOT AFFECTED unmoved, impassive, cool, hard, callous, *thick-skinned, unimpressed, unconcerned, unchanged. ANT *affected, phony, pretentious*.

unafraid *a.* fearless, brave, courageous, bold, *having nerves of steel, *having ice water in one's veins, dauntless, unflinching, *gutsy, *ballsy. ANT *cowardly, fearful, timid*.

unanimous *a.* undivided, universal, united, like-minded, of one mind, concordant, in accord, in concert, as one, solid. ANT *divided, split, disagreeing*.

unappetizing *a.* unappealing, nauseating, sickening, *stomach-turning, *gross, disgusting, unpalatable, unsavory, distasteful, *yucky. ANT *appetizing, mouth-watering, appealing*.

unapproachable *a.* **1.** ALOOF cold, distant, remote, standoffish, *snobby, snobbish, inaccesible, forbidding, unfriendly, unsociable. **2.** INCOMPARABLE unbeatable, unrivaled, unequaled, unparalleled, without equal, peerless. ANT *1. approachable, warm, friendly, open. 2. second-rate, mediocre, poor, average*.

unarmed *a.* defenseless, disarmed, weaponless, unprotected, vulnerable, exposed, weak, open to attack, assailable. ANT *armed, *bristling with arms, unassailable*.

unassailable *a.* undeniable, incontrovertible, indisputable, beyond argument, sound, certain, firm, rock-solid. ANT *assailable, open to attack, open to question, dubious*.

UNASSUMING *a.* [un uh SOO ming] modest and unpretentious. *They were surprised to find the famous actor to be shy and unassuming.* SYN. modest, unpretentious, humble, self-effacing, retiring, down-to-earth, unaffected, natural, quiet, diffident, shy, bashful. ANT *arrogant, loud, pretentious, conceited*.

unattached *a.* detached, unconnected, disconnected, apart, independent, separate, loose, unaffiliated, autonomous, single, on one's own. ANT *attached, connected, associated*.

unattractive *a.* repulsive, homely, plain, hideous. SEE UGLY

unauthorized *a.* unsanctioned, uncertified, illegal, unlawful, unapproved, unlicensed, not permitted, illegitimate, illicit, unofficial, criminal. ANT *authorized, sanctioned, legal*.

unavailing *a.* futile, ineffective, ineffectual, to no avail, vain, unsuccessful, unproductive, unprofitable, fruitless, worthless. ANT *fruitful, worthwhile, productive*.

unavoidable *a.* inevitable, inescapable, bound to happen, fated, unpreventable, inexorable, predestined, fixed, certain, *in the stars, required, obligatory, requisite, compulsory. ANT *avoidable, preventable, optional, elective*.

unaware *a.* unconscious, unknowing, ignorant, oblivious, unsuspecting, unwitting, blind, deaf, asleep, *out to lunch, *off in space. ANT *aware, conscious, knowing*.

unawares *adv.* unexpectedly, suddenly, by surprise, without warning, unknowingly, unwittingly, off guard, *flat-footed, *out of the blue.

unbalanced *a.* **1.** UNSTABLE OR ASYMMETRICAL off-balance, unsteady, uneven, lopsided, irregular, top-heavy, unequal. **2.** CRAZY *nuts, deranged, insane, mentally ill, psychotic, *psycho, erratic, irrational, eccentric, demented. ANT *1. balanced, stable, symmetrical, steady, even. 2. sane, rational, stable*.

unbearable *a.* intolerable, insufferable, unendurable, too much, unacceptable, more than one can stand, agonizing. ANT *bearable, tolerable, endurable*.

unbecoming *a.* unattractive, unappealing, inappropriate, unsuitable, improper, offensive, unseemly, indecent, tasteless, indecorous, ill-fitting, unladylike, ungentlemanly. ANT *proper, befitting, appropriate, ladylike, gentlemanly*.

unbelievable *a.* beyond belief, incredible, far-fetched, suspect, questionable, outlandish, inconceivable, impossible, implausible, doubtful, dubious, improbable, *fishy. ANT *believable, credible, conceivable, probable*.

unbeliever *n.* doubter, skeptic, *doubting Thomas, disbeliever, scoffer, nonbeliever, agnostic, atheist, infidel. ANT *believer, faithful, adherent*.

unbelieving *a.* skeptical, doubting, disbelieving, scoffing, questioning, suspicious, cynical, dubious, incredulous, agnostic, atheist. ANT *believing, faithful, *buying, *swallowing hook, line and sinker*.

unbending *a.* rigid, firm, stiff, resolute, inflexible, unyielding, uncompromising, *holding one's ground, *sticking to one's guns, determined, hellbent. ANT *flexible, compromising, yielding*.

unbiased *a.* fair, unprejudiced, impartial, objective, uninvolved, neutral, disinterested, evenhanded, equitable, nondiscriminatory. ANT *unfair, biased, prejudiced*.

unbidden *a.* uninvited, unasked, unrequested, unprompted, spontaneous.

unblemished *a.* perfect, flawless, spotless, unmarred, clean, stainless, immaculate, unmarked, undamaged. ANT *spotted, stained*, *flawed.*

unblushing *a.* shameless, with no sense of modesty.

unbounded *a.* boundless, unrestrained, unrestricted, unconfined, uncontrolled, unchecked, wild, free, loose.

unbridled *a.* unrestrained, wild, loose, unrestricted, uncontrolled, unconstrained, unchecked. ANT. *restrained, restricted.*

unburden *v.* unload, relieve, get rid of, *take a load off, disencumber, lighten one's load, *get off one's chest, confess, disclose, confide, *come clean. ANT. *burden, saddle, weigh down, encumber.*

uncalled-for *a.* unnecessary, needless, unwelcome, inappropriate, unwarranted, gratuitous, uninvited, unjustified, undeserved. ANT. *welcome, invited, wanted, needed.*

uncanny *a.* **1.** STRANGE, MYSTERIOUS weird, bizarre, queer, eerie, unfamiliar, unusual, spooky, creepy, scary, preternatural. **2.** REMARKABLE extraordinary, amazing, incredible, exceptional, astounding, astonishing, fantastic, unbelievable. ANT. *1. normal, usual, commonplace. 2. unexceptional, usual.*

uncaring *a.* indifferent, impassive, remote, uninvolved. SEE APATHETIC

unceasing *a.* incessant, continuous, endless, perpetual, unending, never ending, nonstop, unremitting, undying.

uncertain *a.* unsure, indefinite, questionable, hazy, indeterminate, unfixed, undecided, iffy, *up in the air, unpredictable, doubtful, unreliable, changeable, unsettled, unconfirmed, conjectural, vague. ANT. *certain, sure, doubtless, definite.*

uncertainty *n.* doubt, doubtfulness, question, indefiniteness, dubiety, ambiguity, unpredictability, guesswork, guess, speculation, conjecture, unknown. ANT. *certainty, assurance.*

uncharted *a.* unknown, unexplored, unmapped, mysterious.

uncivil *a.* rude, discourteous, coarse, uncivilized, barbarous, nasty, unrefined, boorish, impolite, indelicate, ungentlemanly, unladylike, ill-mannered, unfriendly. ANT. *civil, courteous, gentlemanly, ladylike.*

uncivilized *a.* **1.** BARBAROUS barbarian, barbaric, primitive, uncultured, savage, wild, brutish, crude, coarse, rude, discourteous, vulgar, animal-like. **2.** UNDEVELOPED wild, remote, unsettled, untamed. ANT. *1. civilized, civil, cultured, refined, courteous. 2. developed, civilized, settled.*

unclean *a.* dirty, filthy, soiled, befouled, tainted, grimy, polluted, nasty, impure, contaminated, vile, infected, germ-ridden. ANT. *clean, washed, antiseptic.*

unclear *a.* vague, ambiguous, hazy, fuzzy, blurred, veiled, cloudy, foggy, muddy, indistinct, obscure. ANT. *clear, distinct, obvious.*

uncomfortable *a.* **1.** PAINFUL agonizing, irritating, excruciating, awkward, harsh, cutting, pinching, biting, cramped, troublesome, bothersome. **2.** UNEASY ill-at-ease, self-conscious, nervous, anxious, distressed, on edge, tense, restless miserable, *on pins and needles, troubled, *sweating bullets. ANT. *1. comfortable, pleasurable, agreeable. 2. relaxed, comfortable, at ease.*

uncommitted *a.* undecided, neutral, not bound, free, unpledged, *sitting on the fence, nonaligned. ANT. *committed, pledged.*

uncommon *a.* **1.** RARE unusual, unique, exceptional, odd, freakish, infrequent, extraordinary, novel, unconventional, different, unheard of, singular, peculiar, queer, one-of-a-kind, scarce, few. **2.** REMARKABLE outstanding, exceptional, extraordinary, incomparable, superior, unique, distinctive, peerless, unequaled. ANT. *1. common, usual, ordinary. 2. average, typical, ordinary, mediocre.*

uncommunicative *a.* closemouthed, tight-lipped, secretive, silent, mute, reserved, reticent, shy, taciturn, *clammed up, quiet, guarded, speechless, aloof, distant, remote. ANT. *talkative, loquacious, *motor-mouthed.*

uncomplicated *a.* easy, *child's play, *a snap, *a breeze, uninvolved. SEE SIMPLE

uncompromising *a.* inflexible, rigid, *won't give an inch, stubborn, obstinate, unbending, single-minded, unyielding, set, immovable, hard-line, unrelenting. ANT. *flexible, yielding, open to compromise, conciliatory.*

unconcerned *a.* uncaring, careless, carefree, indifferent, apathetic, dispassionate, uninvolved, detached, cool, uninterested, disinterested, above it all, oblivious, distant, remote. ANT. *concerned, caring, interested, passionate.*

unconditional *a.* unrestricted, unqualified, complete, total, absolute, categorical, downright, outright, out-and-out, utter, unlimited. ANT. *restricted, qualified, limited.*

unconnected *a.* disconnected, detached, separate, unattached, divided.

unconscionable *a.* **1.** IMMORAL unethical, wicked, criminal, sinful, unscrupulous, antisocial, shameless, perverse, inhuman, beastly, barbaric, Satanic, uncaring. **2.** UN-REASONABLE outrageous, extreme, excessive, inordinate, unforgivable, extravagant. ANT. *1. moral, ethical, of good moral conscience. 2. reasonable, fair.*

unconscious *a.* **1.** IN A SLEEPLIKE STATE asleep, comatose, *out cold, *blacked out, *knocked out, insensient, *out like a light, *passed out, *dead to the world, oblivious, stunned, stupefied, anesthetized. **2.** UN-AWARE ignorant, unknowing, unwitting. **3.** UNDELIBERATE accidental, inadvertent, involuntary, unintentional, unpremeditated, unwitting, reflex, *gut, instinctual, subconscious. ANT. *1. awake, alert, conscious, aware. 2. aware, knowing. 3. deliberate, conscious, intentional, premeditated.*

unconstitutional *a.* unlawful, against the law. SEE ILLEGAL

uncontrollable *a.* ungovernable, wild, out of control, unmanageable, intractable, out of hand, carried away, unrestrainable, frenzied, beside oneself, rabid, *gone ballistic, riotous. ANT. *governable, manageable, tractable.*

unconventional *a.* unorthodox, unusual, uncommon, irregular, nonconforming, nonconformist, different, weird, unique, odd, out of the ordinary, eccentric, avant-garde, *off the beaten path, experimental. ANT. *conventional, orthodox, conforming, standard.*

unconvincing *a.* open to question, open to doubt, unproven, weak, *full of holes, flimsy, suspect. ANT. *convincing, incontrovertible.*

uncoordinated *a.* clumsy, *klutzy, bumbling, ungraceful, awkward, *can't walk and chew gum at the same time, *graceful as an ox, ungainly, blundering, *like a bull in a china shop, *all thumbs, uncouth, lumbering. ANT. *coordinated, graceful.*

uncouth *a.* boorish, crude, coarse, rude, vulgar, uncivil, uncivilized, ungentlemanly, unladylike, unrefined, uncultured, crass, *tacky, loutish. ANT. *refined, civilized, gentlemanly, ladylike.*

uncover *v.* reveal, expose, remove, lay bare, unwrap, open, unearth, unveil, unmask, disclose, divulge, make known. ANT. *cover, conceal, hide.*

uncovered *a.* exposed, bare, nude, unclothed, unprotected, open.

UNCTUOUS *a.* [UNGK choo us] overly slick or suave, insincere, oily. *The unctuous televangelist talked some of his followers into giving up their lifesavings.* SYN. slick, suave, oily, insincere, honey-tongued, smooth, ingratiat-

ing, slippery, sycophantic, mealy-mouthed, smug. ANT. *sincere, plainspoken, genuine, frank.*

undaunted *a.* intrepid, bold, *gutsy, fearless, determined, courageous, lionhearted, plucky, *having icewater in one's veins, *having nerves of steel, unshaken, unflinching. ANT. *fearful, frightened, cowed, intimidated.*

undecided *a.* **1.** UNSETTLED undetermined, uncertain, open, unsure, up in the air, unresolved, *a question mark, unknown, pending. **2.** INDECISIVE wavering, unsure, of two minds, ambivalent, vacillating, *torn, *betwixt and between, *on the fence, irresolute, *blowing hot and cold. ANT. *1. decided, determined, known. 2. decisive, resolute, sure.*

undecipherable *a.* illegible, unreadable, indistinct, incomprehensible, unclear. ANT. *legible, readable.*

undeniable *a.* indisputable, incontestable, incontrovertible, beyond argument, unquestionable, certain, beyond a shadow of a doubt, irrefutable, solid, sure, proven, established. ANT. *questionable, debatable, uncertain.*

undependable *a.* unreliable, irresponsible, careless, untrustworthy, *fly-by-night, unpredictable, fickle, capricious, unsafe, unsound, insecure. ANT. *dependable, reliable, responsible, sound.*

under *a.* inferior, lower, subordinate, lesser, junior, subsidiary, ancillary. ANT. *superior, higher.*

under *adv. prep.* beneath, underneath, below, on the bottom, lower, nether. ANT. *over, above.*

underachiever *n.* *late bloomer, slow learner, one with a learning deficit, *sleeper.

underage *a.* minor, juvenile, immature.

underbrush *n.* brush, bushes, shrubs, undergrowth, scrub, thicket.

undercover *a.* covert, secret, clandestine, underground, under wraps, concealed, private, hush-hush, *incognito, stealthy, surreptitious, sneaky, CIA, FBI, KGB. SEE SPY

undercurrent *n.* feeling, aura, *vibes, atmosphere, suggestion, hint, overtone, sense, latency.

undercut *v.* weaken, undersell. SEE UNDERMINE

underdog *n.* *long shot, *dark horse, loser, weakling, *low man on the totem pole, *benchwarmer, unlikely winner.

underdone *a.* rare, bloody, raw, uncooked.

underestimate *v.* *sell short, *shortchange, *discount, minimize, slight, underrate, *consider a lightweight, scoff at, belittle, *sneeze at. ANT. overestimate, *make a mountain out of a molehill.

undergarment n. slip, chemise. SEE UNDERWEAR

undergo v. experience, go through, endure, suffer, be subjected to, encounter, abide, stand, withstand, sustain, tolerate.

undergraduate n. sophomore, junior, *frosh, *plebe.

underground a. **1.** SUBTERRANEAN nether, buried, below ground, below the surface, underfoot, sunken, subterrestrial. **2.** SECRET covert, undercover, clandestine, under wraps, concealed, private, hush-hush, surreptitious, backdoor. ANT. 1. aboveground, aerial, surface. 2. public, open, overt.

underhanded a. deceitful, tricky, sneaky, dishonest, sly, secret, devious, crafty, dirty, crooked, treacherous, two-timing, scheming, cunning, unscrupulous. ANT. aboveboard, open, honest.

underline v. emphasize, stress. SEE UNDERSCORE

underling n. subordinate, inferior, flunky, lackey, *low man on the totem pole, *low man in the pecking order, junior, subaltern, *brownnose, *kiss-ass. ANT. superior, boss, chief.

underlying a. basic, fundamental, elementary, rudimentary, essential, primary, root.

undermine v. weaken, impair, cripple, undercut, debilitate, sabotage, subvert, disable, erode, wear away. ANT. help, reinforce, strengthen.

underneath adv. beneath, below, under, lower.

underpinning n. foundation, base, footing, support, framework, prop, undercarriage.

underprivileged a. disadvantaged, deprived, impoverished, poor, needy, poverty-stricken, indigent, destitute.

underscore v. underline, stress, emphasize, highlight, accent, play up, bring to the fore.

undersized a. stunted, dwarfed, puny, underdeveloped, tiny, little, pint-sized, midget, underweight, emaciated, anorexic.

understaffed a. shorthanded, undermanned.

understand v. **1.** COMPREHEND grasp, know, appreciate, figure out, *catch the drift, get it, *get the point, *get through one's head, see, recognize, master. **2.** THINK gather, believe, take it, reckon, perceive, hear, assume, interpret.

understanding n. **1.** COMPREHENSION knowledge, knowing, grasp, appreciation, recognition, mastering, intelligence, intellect, sense, perception, savvy, discernment, awareness.

"Hearing in retrospect." — Marcel Proust. **2.** INTERPRETATION inference, estimation, judgment, belief, thinking, reckoning, perception, sense, idea. **3.** MUTUAL AGREEMENT meeting of the minds, covenant, promise, deal, compromise. **4.** EMPATHY sympathy, compassion, commiseration. ANT. 1. denseness, stupidity, misunderstanding, ignorance, befuddlement.

understated a. restrained, subtle, downplayed, minimized, soft-pedaled, quiet, modest. ANT. loud, blatant.

understudy n. stand-in, substitute, fill-in, double, backup, alternate, apprentice.

undertake v. take on, enter into, assume, tackle, make a commitment, engage in, endeavor, venture, shoulder, promise, pledge, contract. ANT. avoid, shun, reject.

undertaker n. mortician, funeral director, embalmer.

undertaking n. project, endeavor, enterprise, venture, effort, job, commitment, affair, adventure, operation, task.

undertow n. riptide.

underwater a. submarine, submerged, submersed.

underwear n. undershorts, panties, *skivvies, shorts, *undies, briefs, boxers, jockstrap, slip, lingerie, chemise, teddy, *long johns, flannels, underclothes, unmentionables, T-shirt, bra, brassiere, corset, girdle, garter belt.

underweight a. anorexic, emaciated, undernourished, malnourished, underdeveloped, *skin and bones, boney, skeletal, *could slip through a flute and not sound a note. ANT. overweight, obese.

underworld n. **1.** NETHERWORLD nether regions, Hades, hell, Erebus, Sheol, Orcus. **2.** ORGANIZED CRIME Mafia, Cosa Nostra, the mob, syndicate, criminal element.

underwrite v. pay for, finance, fund, bankroll, sponsor, subsidize, back, support, endow, guarantee, insure, cover.

underwriter n. backer, financier, sponsor, *angel, supporter, insurer, insurance company.

undesirable a. unwanted, unpopular, objectionable, unwelcome, unappealing, unsatisfactory, offensive, unacceptable, unsuitable, disliked, rejected, scorned, disagreeable, nauseating, repellant. ANT. desirable, wanted, appealing.

undeveloped a. immature, unripe, unfinished, underdeveloped, latent. ANT. developed, mature, ripe.

undignified a. unseemly, beneath one's dignity, degrading, childish, juvenile, inelegant, tasteless, crude, rude, indecorous, ungentlemanly, unladylike, *goofy, out of character. ANT. *elegant, proper, decorous.*

undiluted a. pure, 100 percent, unadulterated, uncut, *unwatered down, unmixed. ANT. *thinned, watered down, weakened.*

undisciplined a. lazy, unregimented, self-indulgent, overindulgent, unrestrained, uncontrolled, inconsistent, unsteady, unreliable, undependable, irresolute, irresponsible. ANT. *disciplined, strict, regimented.*

undisguised a. unconcealed, open, overt, frank, candid, up front, glaring, blatant, loud, exposed. ANT. *disguised, secret, covert.*

undisputed a. indisputable, unquestionable, irrefutable, uncontested, clear-cut, accepted, unmistakable, recognized, undeniable, beyond question. ANT. *questionable, contested, disputable.*

undistinguished a. mediocre, *run of the mill, *same old same old, ordinary, average, typical, common, pedestrian, plain, so-so, *nothing to write home about, unexceptional, *nothing special. ANT. *distinguished, exceptional, extraordinary, rare.*

undivided n. whole, complete, total, unbroken, uncut, solid, in one piece, intact, in its entirety. ANT. *divided, split, fractured.*

undo v. **1.** UNFASTEN unhitch, unlock, untie, unbuckle, unbutton, loosen, free, detach, disconnect. **2.** REVERSE rescind, annul, cancel, nullify, void, make null and void, invalidate, offset, erase. ANT. **1.** *fasten, tighten, tie, knot, attach.* **2.** *uphold, strengthen.*

undoing n. ruin, ruination, destruction, downfall, defeat, collapse, overthrow, fall, bane, disgrace, shame.

undone a. unfinished, uncompleted, incomplete, unperformed, unrealized, unfulfilled, *half-baked, half-done.

undoubtedly a. without a doubt, doubtless, *beyond a shadow of a doubt, unquestionably, beyond certainty, surely, assuredly, indubitably, definitely.

undreamed-of a. unexpected, unimagined, inconceivable, unforeseen.

undress v. strip, disrobe, remove clothing, doff, peel off, shuck, unclothe, *strip to one's birthday suit, *strip to one's goosebumps, *strip to a growing state of deshabille, *do a striptease. ANT. *dress, put on, clothe.*

undue a. excessive, immoderate, extreme, extravagant unnecessary, unwarranted, unjust-

ified, uncalled-for, needless, undeserved. ANT. *due, appropriate, reasonable.*

undulate v. wave, ripple, swing, move sinuously, roll, billow, flap, sway, swell, heave, oscillate.

undulation n. wave, ripple, roll, billow, flap, sway, swell, heave, oscillation, pulsation, surge.

undying a. immortal, eternal, everlasting, never-ending, perpetual, unceasing, unending, endless, infinite. ANT. *mortal, finite, short-lived.*

unearned a. undeserved, unmerited, gratis, free.

unearth v. dig up, exhume, excavate, dredge up, uncover, bring to light, discover, find, root out, expose, reveal, disclose. ANT. *bury, cover, conceal, hide.*

unearthly a. otherworldly, extraterrestrial, alien, out of this world, ethereal, heavenly, supernatural, extramundane, spiritual, ghostly, weird, strange, nightmarish, mysterious. ANT. *earthly, mundane, terrestrial.*

uneasiness a. apprehension, anxiety, fear, insecurity, worry, troubled mind, edginess, restlessness, angst, qualm, misgiving, disquiet, unrest. ANT. *tranquility, serenity, relaxation.*

uneasy a. apprehensive, anxious, nervous, tense, fearful, insecure, worried, troubled, restive, fidgety, edgy, restless, *on pins and needles, having qualms, having misgivings, fretful. ANT. *relaxed, tranquil, serene, calm.*

uneducated a. unschooled, untrained, unenlightened, illiterate, ignorant, uncultured, unsophisticated, unrefined, stupid. ANT. *educated, schooled, literate, enlightened, scholarly.*

unemotional a. dispassionate, unresponsive, indifferent, apathetic, disinterested, remote, cold, *having ice water in one's veins, impassive, deadpan, phlegmatic, unexcitable, laid-back, stony, staid, reserved. ANT. *emotional, passionate, demonstrative, excitable.*

unemployed a. out of work, jobless, laid-off, fired, idle, free, off, available for hire, *on the breadline, *on welfare. ANT. *employed, working.*

unending a. everlasting, eternal, never ending, ceaseless, incessant, unceasing, immortal, infinite, continuous, perpetual, permanent. ANT. *temporary, finite, ending.*

unenlightened a. SEE UNEDUCATED

unequal a. **1.** UNEVEN disparate, different, dissimilar, unlike, mismatched, unmatched, diverse. **2.** UNBALANCED asymmetrical, lopsided, disproportionate, uneven, irregular. **3.**

UNFAIR unjust, not equitable, one-sided. ANT. *1. equal, same, alike. 2. balanced, symmetrical, regular. 3. fair, just.*

unequaled *a.* unparalleled, peerless, incomparable, unmatched, unrivaled, second to none, unsurpassed, supreme, preeminent.

UNEQUIVOCAL *a.* [un ee KWIV uh kul] clear and unambiguous. *For a change, the politician's answer was unequivocal.* SYN. clear, crystal-clear, unambiguous, plain, explicit, unmistakable, absolute, straight, direct, certain, definite. ANT. *equivocal, ambiguous, *clear as mud.*

unerring *a.* exact, precise, accurate, certain, sure, infallible, perfect, unfailing, flawless, faithful, true. ANT. *inaccurate, imprecise, faulty.*

unessential *a.* inessential, unneeded, needless, unnecessary, unimportant, dispensable, irrelevant, superfluous, extraneous, extra. ANT. *essential, necessary, needed, indispensable.*

unethical *a.* wrong, unfair, immoral, dishonest, dishonorable, illegal, *dirty, *shady, disreputable, underhanded, unprincipled, crooked, unprofessional, corrupt, criminal. ANT. *ethical, honest, upright, moral, reputable.*

uneven *a.* **1.** CROOKED bumpy, slanted, unbalanced, misaligned, not level, broken, rough, jagged, rugged, not smooth. **2.** UNEQUAL lopsided, one-sided, unmatched, different, asymmetrical, unbalanced. ANT. *1. even, smooth, planed, level. 2. equal, matching, symmetrical.*

uneventful *a.* quiet, peaceful, dull, monotonous, routine, *same old same old, boring, unvaried, tedious, unexciting. ANT. *eventful, exciting, momentous.*

unexceptional *a.* ordinary, mediocre, run-of-the-mill, garden variety, common, commonplace, usual, *same old same old, *nothing to write home about, *dime-a-dozen, undistinguished, *just another brick in the wall. ANT. *exceptional, extraordinary, out of the ordinary, remarkable.*

unexciting *a.* dull, boring, prosaic, humdrum, *blah, *dull as dishwater, *ho-hum, monotonous, uninteresting, dry, routine, tedious, tiresome. ANT. *exciting, thrilling, stimulating.*

unexpected *a.* unforeseen, unanticipated, surprising, shocking, stunning, unpredicted, unprepared for, *out of the blue. ANT. *expected, foreseen, anticipated.*

unexplainable *a.* inexplicable, beyond explanation, mystifying, puzzling, baffling, incomprehensible, unaccountable, bewildering, strange.

unexpressive *a.* inexpressive, expressionless, undemonstrative, deadpan, stony, wooden, *poker-faced, unresponsive, vacant, dead, bland. ANT. *expressive, demonstrative, responsive.*

unfailing *a.* never-failing, reliable, dependable, constant, steady, unflagging, inexhaustible, consistent, persistent, faithful. ANT. *unreliable, undependable.*

unfair *a.* unjust, partial, biased, prejudiced, one-sided, bigoted, inequitable, discriminatory, uneven, unethical, *not playing on a level field, unsportsmanlike, unsporting, *dirty, cheating. ANT. *fair, just, equitable, unprejudiced, *on a level playing field.*

unfaithful *a.* **1.** DISLOYAL faithless, untrue, treacherous, adulterous, *two-timing, cheating, backstabbing, false, fickle. **2.** INACCURATE imprecise, inexact, imperfect, incorrect, *off, faulty, erring. ANT. *1. loyal, faithful, true. 2. accurate, precise, true.*

unfamiliar *a.* **1.** UNACQUAINTED ignorant, unconversant, uninitiated, unversed in, inexperienced, unaccustomed, untrained, unschooled. **2.** UNKNOWN strange, alien, foreign, exotic, new, novel, unusual, outlandish, peculiar, rare. ANT. *1. familiar, acquainted, versed. 2. known, familiar, common, everyday.*

unfashionable *a.* unstylish, old-fashioned, outmoded, antiquated, passé, out of style, outdated, obsolete, frumpy, dumpy, *as fashionable as a freshly pressed burlap bag, *as fashionable as a potato sack, *tacky. ANT. *fashionable, chic, sharp, stylish, in vogue.*

unfasten *v.* unlatch, unbuckle, untie, unclasp, uncouple, undo, loosen, detach, unbutton, unzip, disengage. ANT. *fasten, tie, buckle, clasp.*

unfathomable *a.* incomprehensible, inscrutable, beyond comprehension, impenetrable, unknowable, deep, profound.

unfavorable *a.* adverse, poor, bad, negative, unpromising, contrary, hostile, unhappy, inadvisable, ill-advised, inauspicious, unlucky. ANT. *favorable, lucky, good, auspicious.*

unfeeling *a.* **1.** CALLOUS cold, apathetic, indifferent, unsympathetic, heartless, unemotional, stony, *having veins filled with ice water, cold-blooded, pitiless, merciless, hard. **2.** INSENSATE insensient, numb, paralyzed, unconscious, comatose, dead. ANT. *1. feeling, sympathetic, warmhearted, emotional. 2. sen-*

tient.

unfinished *a.* incomplete, uncompleted, half-done, *half-baked, unperfected, lacking, rough, wanting, crude, deficient, undeveloped. ANT. *finished, perfected, done.*

unfit *a.* **1.** UNSUITABLE inadequate, unacceptable, inappropriate, ill-equipped, useless, out of place, inexpedient, inapplicable. **2.** OUT OF SHAPE unhealthy, unconditioned, sickly, ailing, weak. ANT. *1. suitable, fit, adequate. 2. fit, healthy, conditioned.*

unflagging *a.* unfailing, inexhaustible, tireless, undying, unfaltering, indefatigable, constant, persistent, unremitting, unceasing. ANT. *failing, tiring, wearing.*

UNFLAPPABLE *a.* [un FLAP uh bul] calm, not excitable. *Even in the midst of the riots, the mayor was unflappable.* SYN. calm, unexcitable, imperturbable, cool, collected, composed, self-contained, unruffled, level-headed, self-possessed, nonchalant. ANT. excitable, *high-strung, temperamental, *hot-reacting.*

unfledged *a.* undeveloped. SEE IMMATURE

unflinching *a.* unblinking, unfaltering, steadfast, resolute, staunch, firm, unshrinking, unshaken, undaunted, unafraid. ANT. *shrinking, flinching, shaken.*

unfold *v.* **1.** SPREAD OUT unfurl, open, unroll, outstretch, unravel, undo, straighten out, fan out. **2.** MAKE KNOWN disclose, reveal, show, expose, describe, divulge, set forth, expand on. ANT. *1. fold, furl. 2. conceal, cover up.*

unforeseeable *a.* unknowable. SEE UNPREDICTABLE

unforeseen *a.* unexpected, unanticipated, not bargained for, not predicted, unplanned, surprising, *catching by surprise, unprepared for, *out of the blue. ANT. *foreseen, expected, anticipated.*

unforgettable *a.* memorable, *mind-blowing, indelible, meaningful, important, memory-making, powerful, notable, striking, historic. ANT. *forgettable, insignificant, trivial.*

unforgivable *a.* unpardonable, inexcusable, indefensible, unconscionable, shameful, despicable, contemptible, unjustifiable. ANT. *forgivable, pardonable, excusable.*

unfortunate *a.* unlucky, unfavorable, hapless, ill-fated, *jinxed, cursed, *star-crossed, untimely, ill-timed, inopportune, inauspicious, unhappy, sad, bad, deplorable, lamentable, adverse, regrettable, unsuccessful, pitiful, disastrous, tragic, grievous. ANT. *fortunate,*

lucky, blessed, timely, happy.

unfounded *a.* baseless, groundless, unproven, unsupported, unsubstantiated, fallacious, false, untrue, tenuous, speculative. ANT. *proven, true, substantiated.*

unfriendly *a.* cold, aloof, hostile, standoffish, distant, remote, unapproachable, snobbish, haughty, unsociable, inhospitable, nasty, mean, surly, not on speaking terms. ANT. *friendly, warm, approachable, nice.*

unfruitful *a.* unprofitable. SEE FRUITLESS

ungainly *a.* awkward, clumsy, oafish, *klutzy, cloddish, bumbling, lumbering, ungraceful, uncoordinated, gawky. ANT. *graceful.*

ungodly *a.* **1.** SINFUL wicked, evil, Satanic, devilish, hellish, criminal, villainous, immoral, impious, not religious, profane. **2.** OUTRAGEOUS dreadful, horrendous, god-awful, frightful, intolerable. ANT. *1. godly, pious, moral. 2. reasonable.*

ungovernable *a.* wild, unmanageable, uncontrollable, out of control, out of hand, unruly, intractable, rebellious, defiant. ANT. *docile, controllable, manageable.*

ungracious *a.* rude, discourteous, impolite, ill-mannered, uncivil, ungentlemanly, unladylike, insulting, boorish, rough. ANT. *gracious, courteous, polite.*

ungrateful *a.* unappreciative, unthankful, *looking a gift horse in the mouth, dissatisfied, *spoiled rotten, *biting the hand that feeds you. ANT. *appreciate, thankful.*

unguarded *a.* **1.** UNPROTECTED exposed, vulnerable, defenseless, unwatched, unpatrolled, assailable. **2.** OPEN honest, sincere, genuine, frank, candid, artless, aboveboard, straightforward, ingenuous. ANT. *1. protected, guarded, defended. 2. guarded, discreet, self-censored.*

unguent *n.* salve, ointment, balm, salve, lotion, liniment.

unhappy *a.* **1.** SAD depressed, melancholy, downhearted, miserable, *blue, *down in the mouth, *down in the dumps, low, grief-stricken, mournful, downhearted, heavy-hearted, gloomy, despondent, disconsolate, forlorn, long-faced, disheartened, desolate, cheerless, anguished, glum, *bummed out, wretched, somber, crestfallen. **2.** UNLUCKY unfortunate, inauspicious, hapless, cursed, star-crossed, ill-fated, jinxed, infelicitous. ANT. *1. happy, joyous, glad, beaming, elated, euphoric. 2. lucky, fortunate.*

unharmed *a.* unhurt, uninjured, unscathed, intact, okay, all right, safe. ANT. *wounded, in-*

jured.

unhealthy *a.* **1.** SICK sickly, ill, unwell, diseased, in poor health, unfit, weak, run-down, *under the weather, debilitated, bedridden, *in bad shape. **2.** BAD FOR YOU unwholesome, hazardous to one's health, unhealthful, detrimental, deleterious, noxious, toxic, virulent, harmful, malignant. ANT. *1. healthy, fit, in good shape, robust. 2. good for you, wholesome, healthful.*

unheard-of *a.* unprecedented, unknown, new, novel, outlandish, exceptional, unique, little-known, unusual, unbelievable, outrageous. ANT. *known, usual, ordinary.*

unhinge *v.* upset, confuse, unnerve, throw into a panic, make crazy, disorient, fluster, agitate, discompose. ANT. *calm, pacify.*

unhitch *v.* unfasten, detach, release, undo, untie.

unholy *a.* wicked, evil, sinful, ungodly, immoral, corrupt, sacrilegious, unhallowed, not sacred. ANT. *holy, sacred, godly, hallowed.*

unhorse *v.* overthrow, upset.

unhurt *a.* SEE UNHARMED

unhurried *a.* slow, leisurely, deliberate, snaillike, sluggish, *slower than molasses, nonchalant. ANT. *hurried, rushed, impatient.*

unidentified *a.* unknown, unrecognized, nameless, unnamed, anonymous, secret, mysterious, incognito, undercover. ANT. *known, recognized.*

unidentified flying object *n.* UFO, flying saucer, *bogey.

unified *a.* united, joined, one, together, combined, coupled, consolidated, amalgamated, combined, confederated. ANT. *separated, fractured.*

uniform *n.* outfit, costume, attire, dress, *getup, suit, livery, habit, vestment, work clothes.

uniform *a.* **1.** UNCHANGING unvarying, unvariable, the same, undeviating, consistent, even, constant, level, stable. **2.** CONFORMING the same, symmetrical, alike, identical, like, similar, comparable, correspondent, *like two peas in a pod. ANT. *1. changing, varying, uneven, inconsistent. 2. unconforming, different, dissimilar.*

unify *v.* unite, join, bring together as one, bring together, combine, couple, wed, consolidate, amalgamate, combine, confederate. ANT. *separate, fracture, divorce.*

unilateral *a.* one-sided.

unimaginable *a.* incomprehensible, beyond comprehension, *beyond one's wildest dreams, inconceivable, unheard-of, undreamed-of, *out of this world, fantastic, *mind-boggling, *mind-blowing, incredible. ANT. *imaginable, conceivable.*

unimaginative *a.* unoriginal, dull, trite, hackneyed, clichéd, mindless, tired, stock, stale, dry, bland, uninteresting, *same old same old, boring, pedestrian. ANT. *imaginative, original, creative, inventive.*

unimportant *a.* trivial, trifling, insignificant, petty, minor, *lightweight, frivolous, picayune, inconsequential, worthless, irrelevant, paltry, meaningless, *mickey mouse. ANT. *important, crucial, critical, vital.*

uninformed *a.* unaware, unenlightened, ignorant, unschooled, *in the dark, uneducated, unacquainted, uninitiated. ANT. *informed, *hip, enlightened.*

uninhibited *a.* free, open, unreserved, not self-conscious, relaxed, spontaneous, loose, extroverted, outgoing, unrestrained, informal. ANT. *inhibited, reserved, self-conscious.*

uninspired *a.* lifeless, spiritless, lacking creativity, dull, tired, trite, hackneyed, pedestrian, dull, bland, uninteresting, prosaic. ANT. *inspired, original, imaginative, creative.*

unintelligent *a.* dumb, moronic, imbecilic. SEE STUPID

unintelligible *a.* incomprehensible, incoherent, undecipherable, illegible, unreadable, unclear, muddled, meaningless, Greek, jumbled. ANT. *intelligible, legible, clear.*

unintentional *a.* unintended, inadvertent, unplanned, accidental, undesigned, unconscious, unwitting, unpremeditated, chance, haphazard. ANT. *intended, planned, designed.*

uninterested *a.* disinterested, indifferent, apathetic, uncaring, bored, uninvolved, blasé, incurious, remote, *turned off, cool, *above it all. ANT. *interested, fascinated, passionate, involved, riveted.*

uninteresting *a.* boring, dull, tiresome, monotonous, tedious, prosaic, *ho-hum, *blah, *as interesting as a plain brown wrapper, *dull as dishwater, unexciting, *humdrum, uneventful. ANT. *exciting, fascinating, riveting, heart-stopping.*

uninvited *a.* unwanted, unwelcome, undesired, uncalled for.

uninviting *a.* unattractive, unappealing, repellent, repulsive, repugnant, stomach-turning, nauseating, sickening, unappetizing. ANT. *appealing, attractive, desirable.*

union *n.* **1.** JOINING combination, unification, consolidation, marriage, merger, amalgamation, unity, fusion, incorporation, coupling, blend. **2.** GROUP WITH COMMON INTEREST alliance, coalition, league, confederation, guild, trade union, labor union, federation, association, association, partnership, cartel, syndicate. ANT. *1. separation, segregation, breakup.* SEE MARRIAGE

unique *a.* one of a kind, single, sole, unparalleled, lone, only, incomparable, distinctive, unprecedented, extraordinary, special, peculiar, strange, in a class by itself. ANT. *common, commonplace, run-of-the-mill, *common as a brick.*

unison *n.* harmony, agreement, concord, accord, concert, consonance, unity, togetherness. ANT. *disagreement, discord, dissonance.*

unit *n.* part, piece, quantity, member, element, section, segment, constituent, component.

unite *v.* combine, join, bring together, marry, couple, link, merge, connect, unify, blend, consolidate, incorporate, amalgamate, affiliate, confederate, cooperate, band together. ANT. *separate, disband, break up, divide.*

united *a.* combined, joined, brought together, married, coupled, linked, merged, connected, unified, blended, consolidated, incorporated, amalgamated, affiliated. ANT. *separated, disbanded, divided.*

United States *n.* U.S., U.S.A., America, land of opportunity, Uncle Sam, North America, Land of Liberty, Columbia, *the great melting pot. "Half-brother of the world. With something good and bad of every land." — Philip Bailey. "A nation of immigrants." — John F. Kennedy. "The largest shopping center in the world." — Richard Nixon. "A large, friendly dog in a very small room. Every time it wags its tail, it knocks over a chair." — Arnold Toynbee.

unity *n.* oneness, togetherness, wholeness, unification, union, agreement, harmony, accord, concord, solidarity, unanimity. ANT. *separation, division, discord.*

universal *a.* general, generic, common, catholic, all-inclusive, comprehensive, all-over, worldwide, planetary, intercontinental, pandemic, global, widespread, broad, prevalent, unlimited, unrestricted. ANT. *local, exclusive, limited, restricted.*

universe *n.* cosmos, space, outer space, *cooling fires of creation, creation, macrocosm, infinity. "One of God's thoughts." — Friedrich Schiller. "One vast symbol of God." — Thomas Carlyle. "A handful of dust which God enchants." — Theodore Parker. "A

great smelting pot." — Chuang-tzu. "God's tent." — Anon. SEE SPACE

university *n.* institution of higher learning, graduate school, college. "A place of light, of liberty, and of learning." — Benjamin Disraeli. "A thought-control center." — Joan Tepperman. "Sophistry and affectation." — Francis Bacon. SEE COLLEGE

unjust *a.* unfair, inequitable, wrong, unethical, unjustified, unwarranted, prejudiced, partial, biased, one-sided.

unjustifiable *a.* unwarranted, unpardonable, indefensible, inexcusable, unmerited. ANT. *justifiable, warranted.*

unkempt *a.* disheveled, messy, sloppy, bedraggled, rumpled, tousled, tangled, uncombed, ungroomed, shabby, shaggy, *grungy, grubby. ANT. *neat, groomed, sharp.*

unkind *a.* mean, cruel, brutal, unfeeling, unsympathetic, cold, harsh, unmerciful, heartless, inhumane, inhuman, vicious, coldblooded, insensitive, barbarous, nasty, venomous, insulting, cutting, offensive, rude, callous. ANT. *kind, nice, friendly, compassionate, merciful.*

unknowing *a.* unaware, unenlightened, ignorant, uninformed, unschooled, unwitting, oblivious, *out to lunch, *in the dark. ANT. *aware, enlightened, informed.*

unknown *a.* mysterious, undiscovered, hidden, secret, obscure, unrecognized, undetermined, unidentified, anonymous, unnamed, unexplored, uncharted, unfamiliar, unheard-of, strange, foreign, alien, dark. ANT. *known, famous, celebrated, familiar.*

unlawful *a.* illegal, illicit, prohibited, against the law, forbidden, criminal, illicit, banned, proscribed, felonious. ANT. *legal, lawful, legitimate.*

unleash *v.* release, let loose, free, untie, let go.

unlike *a.* different, dissimilar, opposite, unalike, disparate, contrasting, unrelated, *like night and day, *like comparing apples and oranges, clashing. ANT. *alike, similar, matching.*

unlikely *a.* improbable, implausible, hardly possible, doubtful, inconceivable, dubious, questionable, *as likely as snow in July, remote, *as likely as the sky falling, *as likely as pigs learning to fly, having an outside chance, *a longshot. ANT. *likely, probable, certain.*

unlimited *a.* limitless, unrestricted, boundless, endless, immeasurable, countless, infinite, vast, complete, total, unqualified, indefinite.

ANT. *limited, restricted, bounded.*

unload *v.* remove, unburden, disburden, lighten one's load, dump, disgorge.

unlock *v.* open, release, turn the combination, unlatch, unbar.

unlucky *a.* unfortunate, ill-fated, cursed, jinxed, hapless, star-crossed, *down on one's luck, inauspicious, unhappy, unfavorable. ANT. *lucky, fortunate, happy.*

unmanly *a.* effeminate, womanish, cowardly, weak, *wimpy, *candy-assed, timid, *afraid of one's own shadow, submissive, homosexual, *swishy, *limp-wristed. ANT. *manly, macho, virile.*

unmanageable *a.* ungovernable, intractable, wild, out of control, uncontrollable, indocile, rebellious, defiant, indomitable, stubborn. ANT. *manageable, governable, controllable.*

unmannerly *a.* rude, discourteous, impolite, uncivil, uncivilized, indelicate, unrefined, uncultivated, ungracious, ungentlemanly, unladylike. ANT. *polite, courteous, gracious.*

unmarried *a.* single, unwed, unattached, eligible, available, celibate, virgin, maiden. ANT. *married, wed, *spoken for.*

unmask *v.* reveal, expose, unveil, *blow one's cover, disclose, *come out of the closet, *out. ANT. *disguise, mask, cover.*

unmistakable *a.* clear, clear-cut, plain, obvious, evident, sure, definite, certain, beyond question, unambiguous, positive, patent, unequivocal, *plain as the nose on one's face, *beyond a shadow of a doubt, glaring, blatant. ANT. *unclear, ambiguous, questionable, hazy, fuzzy.*

UNMITIGATED *a.* [un MIT uh gate id] not lessened or weakened in any way, absolute, out-and-out. *He had the unmitigated gall to call the mayor a buffoon.* SYN. unlessened, unmoderated, unweakened, unwatered-down, unqualified, pure, downright, outright, out-and-out, absolute, complete, thoroughgoing, sheer. ANT. *weakened, watered-down, moderated, partial.*

unmotivated *a.* uninspired, indifferent, apathetic, impassive, lazy, goalless, unambitious, unenterprising. ANT. *motivated, inspired, *sparked.*

unnatural *a.* **1.** ARTIFICIAL imitation, synthetic, man-made, manufactured, fabricated, processed, ersatz. **2.** AFFECTED contrived, strained, forced, theatrical, put-on, not spontaneous, studied, stiff, labored. **3.** ABNORMAL strange, queer, monstrous, grotesque, freakish. ANT. *1. natural, organic, of the earth. 2. sincere, genuine, spontaneous, unstudied, unaffected. 3. normal, ordinary.*

unnecessary *a.* unneeded, inessential, needless, unrequired, noncompulsory, uncalled-for, gratuitous, superfluous, extraneous, redundant, surplus, expendable. ANT. *indispensable, essential, needed.*

unnerve *v.* *shake up, *fill with the fear of God, upset, disconcert, discourage, scare, frighten, daunt, intimidate, spook, demoralize. ANT. *encourage, embolden, fortify.*

unobtrusive *a.* unnoticed, unnoticeable, inconspicuous, low-key, quiet, *minding one's own business, retiring, unassertive, modest. ANT. *obtrusive, loud, conspicuous, noticeable.*

unoccupied *a.* empty, vacant, open, free.

unorganized *a.* disorderly, sloppy, disarranged, unarranged, haphazard, unsystematic, mixed-up, confused, jumbled, cluttered, scrambled, muddled, random. ANT. *organized, arranged.*

UNORTHODOX *a.* [un ORTH uh doks] unconventional, not standard or accepted. *He was slightly eccentric and had an unorthodox way of painting.* SYN. unconventional, nonstandard, abnormal, out of the norm, out of the ordinary, uncommon, deviant, nonconforming, unaccepted, unofficial, eccentric. ANT. *orthodox, conventional, standard.*

unparalleled *a.* unmatched, unequaled, incomparable, peerless, without rival, unrivaled, without equal, unprecedented, one-of-a-kind, unique, unheard-of. ANT. *equaled, rivaled, common.*

unperturbed *a.* calm, unruffled, cool, composed, unflappable, unflustered, tranquil, serene, placid, sedate. ANT. *unnerved, disturbed, flustered.*

unpleasant *a.* disagreeable, nasty, painful, unwelcome, irritating, annoying, aggravating, bothersome, irksome, repellent, repugnant, sickening, nauseating, offensive, bad, objectionable, negative. ANT. *pleasant, agreeable, nice, enjoyable.*

unprecedented *a.* a first, new, novel, unheard-of, unique, singular, original, unexampled, unparalleled, extraordinary, unusual, one of a kind, uncommon. ANT. *precedented, usual, common.*

unpredictable *a.* unforeseeable, *iffy, left to chance, impossible to predict, uncertain, unsure, *up in the air, random, changeable, erratic, *as capricious as the wind, fickle. ANT. *predictable, foreseeable, certain.*

unprejudiced *a.* unbiased, fair, equitable, evenhanded, unbigoted, impartial, nonpartisan, objective, neutral, just. ANT. *prejudiced, biased, bigoted.*

unpremeditated *a.* unplanned, unplotted, unintentional, spontaneous, *spur of the moment, *in the heat of passion, impulsive, impromptu, off the cuff, impetuous. ANT. *premeditated, thought out, planned.*

unprepared *a.* not ready, *caught off guard, *caught napping, *caught flat-footed, caught by surprise, ill-equipped. ANT. *prepared, ready.*

unpretentious *a.* humble, modest, down-to-earth, unassuming, unaffected, *folksy, simple, plain, natural. ANT. *pretentious, affected, arrogant.*

unprincipled *a.* immoral, unethical, unscrupulous, dishonest, dishonorable, corrupt, underhanded, crooked, devious, shady. ANT. *moral, ethical, principled.*

unproductive *a.* fruitless, nonproductive, worthless, unrewarding, unprofitable, vain, barren, useless, counterproductive, unavailing, to no avail, a losing proposition. ANT. *productive, fruitful, successful.*

unprofessional *a.* **1.** AMATEUR amateurish, sloppy, inexperienced, unskillful, inadequate, unschooled, untrained, second-rate, inferior, *bush-league, nonprofessional. **2.** UNETHICAL unprincipled, improper, indecorous, unseemly, unfitting. ANT. *1. professional, skilled, trained, experienced, expert. 2. ethical, principled, proper.*

unprotected *a.* undefended, vulnerable, open, assailable, unsafe, insecure, pregnable, exposed, unarmed. ANT. *protected, defended, armed, guarded.*

unqualified *a.* **1.** NOT MEETING REQUIREMENTS inadequate, unskilled, unschooled, ill-equipped, unequipped, not up to the job, unfit, incompetent. **2.** UNMODIFIED absolute, unmitigated, total, complete, downright, out-and-out, thorough, utter, sheer, categorical. ANT. *1. qualified, fit, competent. 2. modified, qualified, partial.*

unquestionable *a.* without question, without doubt, doubtless, certain, sure, incontrovertible, incontestable, indisputable, irrefutable, indubitable, definite, unmistakable. ANT. *open to question, doubtful, uncertain, dubious.*

unreadable *a.* illegible, undecipherable, incomprehensible.

unreal *a.* imaginary, fanciful, make-believe, visionary, hallucinatory, nonexistent.

unrealistic *a.* unreasonable, impractical, romantic, starry-eyed, *pie in the sky, *castles in Spain, *castles in the air, fanciful, idealistic, fantastic. ANT. *realistic, reasonable, practical.*

unreasonable *a.* **1.** EXTRAVAGANT outrageous, preposterous, extreme, immoderate, exorbitant, unjustifiable. **2.** IRRATIONAL nonsensical, illogical, senseless, stupid, foolish, unreasoning, unwise, witless, *without rhyme or reason. ANT. *1. reasonable, moderate. 2. rational, logical.*

unrefined *a.* rough, coarse, crude, unfinished, unpolished.

unrehearsed *a.* extemporaneous, spontaneous, off the cuff, impromptu, spur of the moment, unprepared, unplanned, ad-libbed, improvised, *off the top of one's head. ANT. *rehearsed, prepared, planned.*

unreliable *a.* undependable, irresponsible, untrustworthy, unstable, fickle, changeable, capricious, *blowing hot and cold. ANT. *reliable, dependable, trustworthy, steady.*

unremitting *a.* relentless, unrelenting, incessant, continual, constant, unending, unabating, perpetual, persistent. ANT. *ending, stopping, irregular.*

unreserved *a.* uninhibited, outspoken, bold, forthright, unrestrained, unabashed, blunt, frank, to the point, not shy, loquacious, extroverted, outgoing, *motor-mouthed. ANT. *reserved, reticent, inhibited, shy.*

unresolved *a.* unsettled, *up in the air, undetermined, undecided, pending, debatable, open to debate, unfinished, *hung jury. ANT. *resolved, settled, decided.*

unrest *n.* restlessness, agitation, disturbance, discontentment, trouble, uneasiness, disquiet, turbulence, rebellion, protest, upset. ANT. *peace, tranquility, serenity.*

unrestrained *a.* uninhibited, unrestricted, free, unhampered, unconfined, abandoned, unreserved, unbridled. ANT. *restrained, restricted, inhibited.*

unrestricted *a.* unrestricted, free, unbounded, unhampered, uninhibited, unlimited, unregulated, *no holds barred, unchecked. ANT. *restricted, limited, regulated.*

unripe *a.* green, immature, premature, unseasoned.

unrivaled *a.* peerless, matchless, unmatched, unequaled, unparalleled, supreme, superior, *number one, incomparable, unsurpassed. ANT. *equaled, mediocre, run-of-the-mill, average.*

unruly a. unmanageable, uncontrollable, ungovernable, intractable, rebellious, reckless, refractory, riotous, out of control, disorderly, insubordinate. ANT. *manageable, governable, controllable, docile.*

unsafe a. dangerous, hazardous, perilous, treacherous, threatening, insecure, unstable, precarious, life-threatening, *on thin ice, menacing, *dicey, *ticklish, *touch and go, *a tinderbox, *a powderkeg, explosive, risky. ANT. *safe, secure, protected, harmless.*

unsanitary a. unclean, dirty, unhealthy, unhygienic, filthy, contaminated, foul, polluted, germ-infested, tainted. ANT. *sanitary, clean, sterile, antiseptic.*

unsatisfactory a. inadequate, unfulfilling, unacceptable, deficient, insufficient, lacking, wanting, unworthy, *not up to par. ANT. *satisfactory, good enough, adequate.*

unsavory a. **1.** TASTELESS OR BAD-TASTING unappetizing, nauseating, sickening, stomach-turning, unpalatable, disagreeable, rotten, *yucky, *gross. **2.** OFFENSIVE, OBNOXIOUS nasty, objectionable, repugnant, repellant, revolting. ANT. *1. tasty, delicious, *yummy. 2. pleasant, good, agreeable.*

UNSCRUPULOUS a. [un SCROOP yoo lus] unprincipled, immoral, unethical. *He was unscrupulous enough to steal all of the church's money.* SYN. unprincipled, immoral, unethical, dishonest, dishonorable, without conscience, indifferent to right and wrong, corrupt, underhanded, criminal, antisocial. ANT. *principled, moral, ethical, scrupulous.*

unseat a. oust, remove from power, remove from office, unhorse, dislodge, dethrone, depose, overthrow. ANT. *install.*

unseemly a. improper, unbecoming, indecorous, in bad taste, undignified, unbefitting, out of place, inappropriate, indelicate, indecent, vulgar, crude. ANT. *seemly, proper, appropriate.*

unselfish a. giving, generous, selfless, other-directed, charitable, altruistic, philanthropic, openhanded, magnanimous, kind, bighearted, considerate, compassionate. ANT. *selfish, self-centered, greedy, *a taker, *thinking the world revolves around oneself.*

unsettle a. disturb, unnerve, upset, disconcert, trouble, agitate, bother, ruffle, rattle, disquiet, perturb, *shake up, discompose. ANT. *relax, calm, soothe.*

unsettled a. SEE UNRESOLVED

unsightly a. ugly, unattractive, *an eyesore, repulsive, repellent, *gross, hideous, grotesque, homely, revolting, repugnant. ANT. *attractive, beautiful, pretty.*

unskilled a. untrained, unschooled, inexpert, amateurish, inept, incompetent, incapable, unable, inexperienced, bumbling, *all thumbs. ANT. *skilled, proficient, trained, expert.*

unskillful a. SEE UNSKILLED

unsociable a. unfriendly, aloof, cold, remote, distant, hermitlike, antisocial, withdrawn, introverted, shy, *standoffish, *stuck-up, preferring one's own company. ANT. *extroverted, outgoing, gregarious, friendly.*

unsolicited a. unasked, unsought, unrequested, voluntary, spontaneous, free. ANT. *solicited, asked-for, sought.*

unsophisticated a. simple, naive, innocent, unworldly, childlike, inexperienced, green, *born yesterday, uncultured, unrefined, unpolished, *down-home, *folksy, *like a hick, *like a hayseed, artless, ingenuous. ANT. *sophisticated, worldly, experienced, *hip.*

unsound a. **1.** UNHEALTHY unwell, sickly, ill, ailing, infirm, afflicted, diseased, abnormal, insane, crazy, psychotic, *psycho. **2.** UNSAFE insecure, unstable, flimsy, shaky, unsteady, unreliable, dangerous, perilous, hazardous, rickety. **3.** INACCURATE unreliable, untruthful, erroneous, invalid, irrational, weak, groundless, illogical, fallacious. ANT. *1. healthy, fit, normal. 2. safe, solid, stable, secure. 3. accurate, valid, true, reliable.*

unsparing a. liberal, free, lavish, profuse, generous, giving.

unspeakable a. bad, horrible, terrible, beyond words, beyond description, unimaginable, evil, wicked, vile, horrendous, heinous, monstrous, atrocious. ANT. *good, wonderful.*

unspoiled a. fresh, pristine, untouched, unadulterated, unpolluted, perfect, whole, pure, unblemished, undamaged. ANT. *spoiled, ruined, rotten.*

unspoken a. unsaid, silent, tacit, understood, implicit, assumed. ANT. *spoken, expressed.*

unstable a. **1.** UNFIXED unsteady, unbalanced, variable, wobbling, shaky, rickety, teetering, unanchored. **2.** CHANGEABLE erratic, capricious, fickle, unpredictable, mercurial, vacillating, volatile. ANT. *1. fixed, rock-solid, anchored, secure. 2. constant, steady, unchanging.*

unsteady a. SEE UNSTABLE

unstudied a. natural, unaffected, spontaneous, unconscious, offhand, unlabored, impromptu, *off the cuff, extemporaneous.

ANT. *studied, affected, labored.*

unsubstantiated *a.* uncorroborated, unproven, unconfirmed, open to question, questionable, unauthenticated, uncertified. ANT. *corroborated, proven.*

unsuccessful *a.* a failure, a loser, *a turkey, *a dog, *a flop, *a bomb, unprofitable, fruitless, futile, vain, useless, abortive, ineffectual, unfortunate, unlucky, unhappy, ill-fated, doomed, disastrous, catastrophic. ANT. *successful, profitable, winning, fortunate.*

unsuitable *a.* inappropriate, unfit, wrong, improper, inadequate, unacceptable, unsatisfactory, unbefitting, inapt, out of place, ill-fitting. ANT. *appropriate, fit, right, acceptable.*

unsung *a.* unrecognized, unacclaimed, unapplauded.

unsure *a.* uncertain, doubtful, in doubt, questionable, *iffy, *up in the air, undecided, dubious, skeptical, not confident, insecure. ANT. *sure, certain, confident.*

unsurpassed *a.* supreme, superior, unrivaled, peerless, unparalleled, the best, incomparable, greatest, leading, preeminent. ANT. *second-rate, average, worst.*

unsuspecting *a.* trusting, naive, gullible, credulous, unknowing, unaware, innocent, unwary, inexperienced, believing, unsophisticated, oblivious. ANT. *wary, suspicious, questioning.*

unsympathetic *a.* cold, uncaring, indifferent, apathetic, heartless, lacking compassion, unfeeling, stony, unmoved, callous, mean, hard, 'hard as nails, *having ice water in one's veins, insensitive. ANT. *sympathetic, caring, compassionate, caring.*

untamed *a.* wild, unbroken, ungovernable, uncontrollable, unmanageable, spirited, undomesticated. ANT. *tamed, broken, domesticated.*

untangle *v.* disentangle, unravel, extricate, straighten out, unsnarl, untie. ANT. *tangle, snarl.*

untarnished *a.* stainless, spotless, clean, bright, unblemished, uncorrupted, innocent, pure. ANT. *tarnished, corrupted.*

untenable *a.* indefensible, insupportable, weak, flawed, *full of holes, groundless, unsound. ANT. *tenable, sound, secure.*

unthankful *a.* ungrateful, unappreciative.

unthinkable *a.* inconceivable, unimaginable, incomprehensible, beyond belief, unbelievable, incredible, out of the question.

untidy *a.* sloppy, messy, slovenly, disheveled, bedraggled, unkempt, disarranged, disorderly, cluttered, littered. ANT. *tidy, neat, orderly.*

untie *v.* unfasten, loosen, free, undo, unlace, unbind, loose.

untimely *a.* ill-timed, inconvenient, inopportune, inexpedient, premature, early, unseasonable, inappropriate, unfavorable, unfortunate, inauspicious. ANT. *timely, opportune, well-timed.*

untold *a.* innumerable, countless, incalculable, uncountable, myriad, *umpteen, immeasurable, infinite, limitless.

untoward *a.* inappropriate, unseemly, improper, indecorous, in bad taste, unbefitting, out of place, tactless, indelicate, ungentlemanly, unladylike. ANT. *proper, appropriate, seemly.*

untrained *a.* unschooled, uneducated, inexperienced, green, raw, unskilled, *not knowing the ropes, unqualified, incompetent, inexpert, ignorant. ANT. *trained, schooled, educated.*

untroubled *a.* unperturbed, unruffled, calm, cool, relaxed, worry-free, *unflappable, dispassionate, tranquil, placid. ANT. *agitated, troubled, worried, anxious.*

untrue *a.* false, wrong, incorrect, erroneous, inaccurate, not right, in error, fictitious, fallacious, specious, spurious, distorted. ANT. *true, factual, correct.*

untrustworthy *a.* undependable, unreliable, dishonest, deceitful, devious, false, disloyal, unfaithful, treacherous, disreputable. ANT. *trustworthy, dependable, honest, loyal.*

untruthful *a.* lying, dishonest, deceptive, deceitful, mendacious, lying, fraudulent, misleading, insincere. ANT. *truthful, honest.*

unusual *a.* out of the ordinary, odd, rare, atypical, unfamiliar, singular, uncommon, exceptional, unconventional, peculiar, queer, strange, bizarre, weird, extraordinary, unique, unheard-of, unprecedented, unparalleled, different, abnormal, distinguished, refreshing, *far-out, unexpected, unorthodox. ANT. *usual, ordinary, common, run-of-the-mill.*

unvarnished *a.* plain, straightforward, unembellished, unpolished, naked, raw.

unveil *v.* reveal, expose, show, uncover, disclose.

unwarranted *a.* uncalled-for, unjustified, inexcusable, indefensible, groundless, baseless, gratuitous. ANT. *warranted, justifiable.*

unwary *a.* incautious, heedless, unguarded, unthinking, careless, unsuspecting, rash, reckless, imprudent, unobservant, naive, ignorant. ANT. *wary, cautious, guarded.*

unwavering *a.* steady, firm, consistent, unfaltering, staunch, resolute, determined, single-minded, persistent, steadfast, unswerving. ANT. *wavering, faltering, unsteady.*

unwelcome *a.* unwanted, not wanted, undesirable, rejected, spurned, *shut out, *as welcome as the plague. ANT. *welcome, wanted, desired.*

unwell *a.* unhealthy, sick, sickly, ailing, ill, diseased, bedridden, *out of sorts, *under the weather, *green around the gills, run-down, *off one's feed. ANT. *well, healthy, fit.*

unwholesome *a.* harmful, unhealthy, deleterious, not good for one, unsound, detrimental, hurtful, noxious, pernicious, poisonous, insalubrious. ANT. *wholesome, healthy, good for one.*

unwieldy *a.* hard to handle, awkward, unmanageable, clumsy, cumbersome, bulky, hulking, massive, unhandy, ponderous, heavy. ANT. *handy, pocket-sized, lightweight.*

unwilling *a.* against, disagreeable, loath, opposed, reluctant, not in the mood, disinclined, unobliging, unenthusiastic, averse, unaccommodating, resistant, contrary, balky. ANT. *willing, enthusiastic, eager.*

unwind *v.* relax, take it easy, calm down, relieve one's tension, recreate, *loosen up, *kick back, wind down. ANT. *tense up, *get wound up, *make oneself a nervous wreck, *stress oneself out.*

unwise *a.* imprudent, injudicious, not smart, unintelligent, dumb, stupid, ill-advised, thoughtless, foolish, naive, moronic, brainless, irrational, illogical. ANT. *wise, smart, prudent, intelligent.*

unwitting *a.* unknowing, unaware, unconscious, oblivious, inadvertent, accidental, unplanned, chance, involuntary. ANT. *knowing, aware, planned.*

unwonted *a.* uncommon, unusual, rare, unaccustomed, unfamiliar.

unworldly *a.* **1.** UNSOPHISTICATED naive, inexperienced, innocent, *born yesterday, *like a babe in the woods, raw, unaffected. **2.** SPIRITUAL divine, religious, godly, ethereal, heavenly.

unworthy *a.* undeserving, unmerited, unearned, unqualified, ineligible, worthless, inferior, no good, unacceptable, disgraceful. ANT. *worthy, deserving.*

unyielding *a.* immovable, inflexible, firm, stubborn, obstinate, unbending, uncompromising, headstrong, resolute, determined, hard,

stiff. ANT. *flexible, compromising, yielding.*

up *a.* excited, *psyched.

up-and-coming *a.* rising, *climbing the ladder of success, *growing by leaps and bounds, succeeding, growing in status, promising.

upbeat *a.* positive, optimistic, bright, cheerful, rosy, sunny, happy, heartening, uplifting, encouraging. ANT. *down, negative, dark.*

UPBRAID *a.* [up BRADE] to reproach or scold. *The officer upbraided the motorist for driving drunk.* SYN. reproach, scold, rebuke, reprimand, chastise, *bawl out, *chew out, admonish, berate, reprove, censure, *give a tongue-lashing, *rake over the coals, *take to task. ANT. *commend, praise, approve.*

upbringing *n.* raising, rearing, breeding, grooming, training, nurturing, schooling.

upchuck *v.* vomit, throw up, *puke, spew, *hurl, *ralph, *toss one's cookies, regurgitate, *blow lunch, be sick.

update *v.* bring up to date, modernize, revise, renew, *bring into the twenty-first century, renovate.

upend *v.* invert, turn over, upset, topple.

upgrade *v.* raise, improve, promote, elevate, enhance, better, make better, advance, enrich. ANT. *degrade, downgrade, demote.*

upheaval *n.* eruption, blowup, explosion, earthquake, cataclysm, destruction, catastrophe, revolution, overthrow, change. ANT. *peace, quiet, tranquility.*

uphill *a.* laborious, arduous, hard, difficult, taxing, hard, strenuous, grueling, labor intensive, backbreaking, *ball-busting. ANT. *downhill, easy, effortless.*

uphold *v.* support, hold up, maintain, stand by, sustain, carry, back, champion.

upkeep *n.* maintenance, repair, running, costs, overhead, outlay, expenses, expenditure.

uplift *v.* raise, elevate, inspire, lift, improve, hearten. ANT. *bring down, depress.*

upper hand *n.* advantage, control, domination, *driver's seat, whip hand, catbird seat, supremacy, rule, a leg up.

uppermost *a.* highest, top, loftiest, foremost, greatest, superior, ultimate, chief, maximum, leading. ANT. *lowest.*

uppity *a.* arrogant, snobbish, haughty, stuck-up, *high-falutin, lofty, proud, uppish, *full of oneself, conceited, presumptuous. ANT. *folksy, down to earth, modest, humble.*

upright *a.* **1.** ERECT standing, vertical, perpendicular, on end, straight up. **2.** HONORABLE honest, moral, ethical, decent, good, righteous, upstanding, scrupulous, principled, virtuous, reputable. ANT. *1. prone, lying, horizontal. 2. dishonorable, disreputable, corrupt, dishonest.*

uprising *n.* rebellion, revolt, revolution, insurrection, insurgence, mutiny, riot, unrest, anarchy, outbreak of violence, overthrow, coup d'etat.

uproar *n.* stir, turmoil, ado, *to-do, clamor, *flap, furor, fuss, noise, riot, brouhaha, *blowup, *hoopla, outburst, *ruckus, disturbance, *big stink, hullabaloo. ANT. *peace, quiet, tranquility.*

uproarious *a.* **1.** NOISY loud, clamorous, tumultuous, boisterous, wild, riotous, deafening, earsplitting. **2.** HILARIOUS *a scream, sidesplitting, hysterical, *a laugh riot, rollicking. ANT. *1. quiet, peaceful, still. 2. somber, sober, grim.*

uproot *v.* root up, root out, extirpate, pull out, rip out, move, weed, remove, eradicate, destroy.

ups and downs *n.* peaks and valleys, highs and lows, feasts and famines, vicissitudes.

upset *n.* **1.** DISTURBANCE unhappiness, agitation, trouble, distress, worry, shake-up, perturbation, illness. **2.** DEFEAT overthrow, reversal, surprise loss. **3.** TURNOVER flip, tipping, toppling, capsizing.

upset *v.* **1.** DISTURB make unhappy, bother, agitate, trouble, distress, worry, disquiet, hurt, make angry, disconcert, perturb, unsettled, grieve, *stress out, make anxious. **2.** OVERTURN upend, turn upside-down, capsize, topple, tip, flip, turn over, knock over. **3.** DEFEAT overthrow, triumph over, beat, *get the better of. ANT. *1. make happy, fill with contentment, soothe. 2. turn upright, stand up. 3. lose, be defeated.*

upset *a.* **1.** DISTURBED unhappy, bothered, agitated, troubled, distressed, worried, disquieted, hurt, angry, disconcerted, perturbed, unsettled, grieved. **2.** OVERTURNED upended, upside-down, capsized, toppled, flipped. ANT. *1. contented, happy, blissful. 2. upright, standing.*

upshot *n.* outcome, result, conclusion, end result, end product, effect, payoff, eventuality, culmination, consequence, aftermath, consummation.

upside-down *a.* inverted, bottom-side up, topside down, reversed, wrong-side up, backward, *bassackwards, topsy-turvy.

upstage *v.* steal the spotlight, steal the show, draw attention to one's self, outshine.

upstanding *a.* upright, honorable, honest, rep-

utable, virtuous, moral, ethical, good, principled, uncorrupt, of sterling character. ANT. *corrupt, low, disreputable, immoral.*

upstart *n.* parvenue, nouveau riche, arriviste, pretender, status seeker, jackanapes, whippersnapper.

upswing *n.* advancement, expanding market, bull market, upsurge, improvement, rise, progress, recovery, uptick.

uptight *a.* Sl. nervous, tense, anxious, on edge, edgy, uneasy, troubled, restive, worried. ANT. *relaxed, calm, cool.*

up-to-date *a.* current, up-to-the-minute, contemporary, *cutting edge, *state of the art, new, modern, in vogue, *all the rage, au courant, fashionable, stylish, trendy, late, *now. ANT. *outdated, out-of-date, old-fashioned, antiquated, passé.*

upturn *n.* SEE UPSWING

upward *adv.* skyward, overhead, above, aloft, atop. ANT. *downward, below.*

upward mobility *n.* social climbing, climbing the corporate ladder, status seeking, *clawing one's way to the top.

urban *a.* city, citified, metropolitan, cosmopolitan, densely populated, municipal, civic. ANT. *rural, country, deep woods.*

URBANE *a.* [ur BANE] smoothly polite, suave, refined. *The tour guide was charming and urbane.* SYN. smooth, suave, polite, courteous, polished, refined, gracious, debonair, mannerly, elegant, poised, charming. ANT. *rude, coarse, impolite, offensive.*

urchin *n.* kid, boy, youngster, child, imp, *little devil, troublemaker, rogue, rascal, guttersnipe, brat, juvenile delinquent.

urge *n.* drive, yearning, desire, hunger, longing, impulse, craving, compulsion, yen, passion, hankering, stimulus, goad.

urge *v.* **1.** ENCOURAGE press, push for, implore, plead, exhort, beg, beseech, advocate, entreat, ask, solicit. **2.** STIMULATE provoke, incite, push, drive, force, spur, accelerate, speed.

urgency *n.* matter of life or death, emergency, crisis, extremity, exigency.

urgent *a.* a matter of life or death, pressing, crucial, critical, exigent, requiring immediate attention, imperative, first priority, paramount. ANT. *unimportant, insignificant, trivial.*

urinate *v.* micturate, *pee, *piss, relieve oneself, *wee-wee, tinkle, pass water, *take a leak.

urn *n.* vase, container, receptacle, jar, vessel, ossuary.

usage *n.* custom, habit, practice, tradition, convention, routine, way.

use *n.* **1.** SERVICE *mileage, usefulness, employment, worth, benefit. **2.** UTILIZATION application, employment, exercise. **3.** FUNCTION service, usefulness.

use *v.* **1.** UTILIZE employ, make use of, work, practice, operate, exercise, manipulate, ply. **2.** ABUSE take advantage of, exploit, *walk on, *play for a sucker, *bleed dry. **3.** EXPEND spend, consume, exhaust, deplete.

used *a.* secondhand, pre-owned, hand-me-down, passed down, recycled, old, castoff.

used to *adv.* familiar with, accustomed to, habituated, acclimated.

useful *a.* serviceable, helpful, valuable, practical, utilitarian, beneficial, handy, of use, functional. ANT. *useless, worthless, of no help.*

useless *a.* worthless, of no use, unavailing, unserviceable, ineffectual, ineffective, to no avail, unproductive, unprofitable, futile, vain. ANT. *useful, valuable, helpful.*

usher *n.* usherette, guide, escort, doorkeeper, attendant, page.

usher *v.* **1.** GUIDE escort, lead, conduct, show in, marshal, direct, accompany. **2.** PRECEDE herald, pave the way, introduce, inaugurate.

usual *a.* ordinary, customary, common, everyday, conventional, normal, standard, regular, habitual, routine, accustomed, traditional, stock, run-of-the-mill, average, typical. ANT. *unusual, uncommon, abnormal, irregular.*

USURP *v.* [yoo SURP] to take over a position of power by force, overthrow. *The rebels attempted to usurp the president's office.* SYN. take over, overthrow, depose, dethrone, oust, unseat, unhorse, commandeer, wrest, seize, expropriate.

utensil *n.* implement, tool, instrument, fork, knife, spoon.

UTILITARIAN *a.* [yoo TIL i TAIR ee un] useful, practical. *He chose a car that was utilitarian rather than showy.* SYN. useful, practical, functional, pragmatic, serviceable, efficient, down to earth, sensible. ANT. *impractical, romantic, fanciful.*

utility *n.* usefulness, practicality, service, function, benefit, adaptability.

utilize *v.* use, put to use, employ. SEE USE

utmost *a.* **1.** GREATEST highest, maximum, maximal, most, uppermost, supreme, preeminent, best. **2.** FARTHEST most distant, outermost, extreme, last, remotest. ANT. *1. lowest, smallest, worst. 2. closest, nearest.*

UTOPIA *n.* Shangri-la, paradise, Eden, best of all possible worlds, heaven on earth, perfect society, idealized society, land of milk and honey.

Utopian *a.* idealistic, ideal, visionary, perfect, fanciful, chimerical, grandiose, *pie in the sky, romantic, fictitious, make-believe, impractical, unfeasible. ANT. *realistic, down to earth.*

utter *v.* speak, say, vocalize, emit, articulate, enunciate, voice, state, verbalize, assert, declare, shout, come out with, mouth.

utter *a.* thorough, complete, absolute, outright, out-and-out, total, sheer, pure, perfect, unmitigated.

utterance *n.* vocalization, articulation, expression, speech, statement, verbalization, assertion, declaration, shout, sound, wording, mouthing.

utterly *adv.* completely, totally, entirely, thoroughly, wholly, absolutely, purely, perfectly, fully. ANT. *partially, partly.*

V

vacancy n. opening, space, emptiness, gap, room, void, vacuousness, hole, nothing, hollow.

vacant a. **1.** EMPTY open, unfilled, unoccupied, clear, bare, deserted, void, devoid, hollow, uninhabited, unused. **2.** MINDLESS stupid, blank, vacuous, oblivious, expressionless, dull, bovine, *bubbleheaded. ANT. *1. full, filled, occupied, used. 2. intelligent, thoughtful, alert.*

vacate v. leave, give up, leave behind, quit, desert, withdraw, depart, abandon. ANT. *fill, occupy.*

vacation n. holiday, time off, *R&R, rest and relaxation, recess, furlough, sabbatical, respite, hiatus, break, trip, cruise. "A semi-annual reminder that doing nothing is hard work."—Art Hinkle. ANT. *daily grind, hard labor.*

vaccination n. inoculation, *shot, immunity.

VACILLATE v. [VAS uh LATE] to waver or be indecisive. *He couldn't make up his mind and vacillated between choices all day.* SYN. waver, be indecisive, go back and forth, fluctuate, hesitate, shilly-shally, *blow hot and cold, be irresolute, *sit on the fence, hedge, equivocate, hem and haw.

vacuity n. **1.** EMPTINESS nothingness, vacuum, void, blankness. **2.** EMPTY-HEADEDNESS stupidity, ignorance, dullness, denseness, mindlessness, lack of intelligence, *bubbleheadedness, imbecility. ANT. *1. substance, matter, fullness. 2. intelligence, brains, *smarts.*

vacuous a. stupid, empty-headed, dumb, dense, unintelligent, ignorant, imbecilic, moronic, *bubbleheaded, blank, bovine. ANT. *intelligent, smart, bright, knowledgeable.*

vacuum n. emptiness, nothingness, void, blankness, vacuity.

vagabond n. vagrant, drifter, tramp, wanderer, transient, *bum, hobo, nomad, rambler, rover, floater, itinerant.

vagabond a. moving, wandering, drifting, traveling, roving, rambling, roaming, wayfaring, itinerant, homeless, shiftless, idle. ANT. *rooted, responsible.*

vagary n. caprice, whim, whimsy, impulse, notion, fancy, crotchet, idea, oddity, *flash.

vagina n. sex organ, private parts, genitals, genitalia, reproductive organ, labia, *pussy, *snatch, *bearded clam, *beaver, *quim, *twat.

vagrant n. wanderer, roamer, vagabond, nomad, rambler, rover, Bohemian, gypsy, tramp, hobo, *bum.

vagrant a. wandering, roaming, wayward, vagabond, nomadic, rambling, roving, aimless, Bohemian, gypsy.

vague a. indefinite, unclear, uncertain, obscure, fuzzy, hazy, foggy, nebulous, amorphous, indistinct, unspecific, imprecise, ambiguous, equivocal, questionable. ANT. *definite, clear, distinct, explicit.*

vain a. **1.** WORTHLESS, OF NO USE useless, empty, hollow, futile, unproductive, fruitless, pointless, unsuccessful, unavailing, idle. **2.** CONCEITED proud, vainglorious, *full of oneself, egotistical, self-important, arrogant, pompous, self-admiring, primping, preening, haughty, dandyish, foppish, swaggering, strutting, *in love with oneself. ANT. *1. productive, effective, worthwhile. 2. modest, humble, self-effacing.*

vainglorious a. proud, boasting, vain, singing one's own praises, bragging, *blowing one's own horn, *talking big, swaggering, strutting, arrogant, pompous, basking in one's own glory. ANT. *modest, humble, self-effacing.*

vainglory n. pride, boastfulness, vanity, pomp, ostentation, arrogance, bragging, swaggering, strutting, haughtiness. ANT. *modesty, humbleness, shyness.*

valance n. drapery, curtain.

vale n. dale, dell. SEE VALLEY

valedictory n. farewell speech, goodbye speech.

valedictory a. farewell, parting, goodbye, departing, last.

valet n. dresser, manservant, servant, groom, foot servant, attendant.

valiant a. brave, courageous, fearless, bold, heroic, unflinching, lionhearted, unafraid, intrepid, *gutsy, *ballsy, manly, *macho, virile, gallant, chivalrous. ANT. *cowardly, *chicken, timid, craven, *wimpy.*

valid a. **1.** LEGAL legitimate, authorized, certified, sanctioned, lawful, warranted, approved, authentic, genuine. **2.** SOUND well-grounded, well-founded, solid, validated, logical, substantiated, correct, accurate, unassailable. ANT. *1. illegal, illegitimate, unauthorized, invalid. 2. flimsy, unsound, unproven.*

validate v. **1.** MAKE LEGAL make legitimate, authorize, certify, sanction, warrant, approve. **2.** CONFIRM verify, prove, substantiate, corroborate, back up, support, authenticate, certify. ANT. *1. invalidate, cancel. 2. disprove, invalidate.*

validation *n.* **1.** LEGALIZATION legitimization, authorization, certification, sanctioning. **2.** CONFIRMATION verification, proof, substantiation, corroboration, support, authentication, certification. ANT. *invalidation.*

validity *n.* **1.** LEGALITY lawfulness, legitimacy, authority, sanction. **2.** SOUNDNESS solidity, correctness, accuracy, authenticity, genuineness.

valise *n.* suitcase, bag, travel bag, hand bag, carryall, luggage, case, grip.

valley *n.* dale, dell, vale, canyon, gorge, lowland, basin, gulch, chasm, hollow, glen. ANT. *mountain, highland.*

valor *n.* courage, bravery, boldness, fearlessness, *guts, *balls, nerve, heroism, daring, *derring-do, backbone, *moxie, stoutheartedness, bravado, confidence, manliness, gallantry, chivalry, heart. ANT. *cowardice, fear, *wimpiness, spinelessness.*

valorous *a.* courageous, brave, bold, fearless, *gutsy, *ballsy, nervy, heroic, daring, stouthearted, confident, manly, gallant, chivalrous, tough. ANT. *cowardly, fearful, *wimpy.*

valuable *a.* costly, priceless, precious, dear, expensive, high-priced, valued, prized, in demand, worthwhile, invaluable, important, useful, profitable, beneficial, helpful. ANT. *worthless, cheap, *not worth the powder to blow it to hell, unimportant.*

valuation *n.* appraisal, evaluation, estimate.

value *n.* **1.** WORTH market price, appraisal, assessment, equivalent, return, face value. **2.** WORTH, MERIT use, importance, weight, desirability, esteem, respect, benefit, profit, power, utility, marketability. ANT. *insignificance, uselessness, unimportance.*

value *v.* **1.** APPRAISE assess, evaluate, rate, valuate, estimate, put a price on. **2.** TREASURE prize, cherish, hold dear, respect, esteem, appreciate, consider important, love.

valued *a.* treasured, prized, cherished, dear, respected, esteemed, appreciated, highly regarded, admired, loved.

values *n.* principles, morals, ideals, standards, ethics, beliefs, mores, what's important.

valve *n.* stopper, shutoff, cock, gate, flap, plug, lid.

vamoose *v.* *skedaddle, go, *git. SEE LEAVE

vamp *n.* seductress, temptress, seducer, flirt, vampire, femme fatale, siren, enchantress.

vamp *v.* seduce, tempt, flirt, charm, beguile, lure with one's feminine charms.

vampire *n.* bloodsucker, Dracula, ghoul, bat.

van *n.* truck, wagon, lorry, trailer.

vandal *n.* despoiler, wrecker, destroyer, mutilator, graffiti artist, defacer, hoodlum, juvenile delinquent.

vandalism *n.* destruction, defacing, grafitti, *trashing, wrecking, smashing, breaking, disfigurement, tearing apart, spoiling.

vandalize *v.* destroy, deface, spray paint, *trash, wreck, smash, break, disfigure, tear apart, ruin, spoil.

VANGUARD *n.* [VAN gard] the leading or front members of an attacking army. Also, the leading or pioneering members of a movement, project, trend, etc. *He was among the vanguard of the new age artists.* SYN. front, forefront, fore, head, front line, advance guard, cutting edge, leading edge, leaders, trailblazers, pioneers, trendsetters, innovators, avant-garde, forerunners. ANT. *rear, back, followers, stragglers.*

vanish *v.* disappear, fade, evanesce, dissolve, dematerialize, pass from sight, vanish into thin air, vaporize, evaporate, leave no trace. ANT. *materialize, appear, come into view.*

vanity *n.* **1.** PRIDE vainglory, self-admiration, conceit, ego, *ego trip, egotism, narcissism, arrogance, boastfulness, self-importance, smugness. "[That which] keeps persons in favor with themselves who are out of favor with all others." —Shakespeare. "The greatest of all flatterers." —La Rochefoucauld. "An itch for the praise of fools." —Robert Browning. **2.** FUTILITY uselessness, worthlessness, emptiness, hollowness. ANT. *1. modesty, humility, humbleness, self-effacement. 2. worth, usefulness.*

vanquish *v.* conquer, defeat, overcome, beat, best, overpower, overthrow, master, subdue, crush, destroy, trample, prevail over, triumph over. ANT. *lose, be defeated, submit.*

vantage *n.* advantage, *leg up, leverage, superiority, high ground, edge, *inside track, *jump.

vantage point *n.* perspective. SEE POSITION

VAPID *a.* [VAP id] dull, flat, tasteless. *He watched one vapid television show after another and finally fell asleep.* SYN. dull, flat, boring, uninteresting, tiresome, tedious, tasteless, flavorless, colorless, insipid, inane, lifeless, bland, lame, unimaginative, *dull as dishwater, *blah. ANT. *interesting, stimulating, imaginative, exciting.*

vapor *n.* moisture, mist, fog, haze, steam, cloud,

spray, breath, exhalation, humidity, condensation, miasma, smog.

vaporize v. humidify, mist, steam, fume.

vaporous a. humid, misty, steamy, foggy, damp, clammy, muggy, moist, hazy, gaseous, fumy, murky. ANT. *dry.*

variable a. changeable, changing, unstable, fluctuating, irregular, inconstant, vacillating, wavering, *like a chameleon, on again off again, *blowing hot and cold, diverse, fickle, capricious, as variable as the wind. ANT. *unchangeable, invariable, fixed, steady, stable.*

variance n. **1.** DIFFERENCE discrepancy, divergence, deviation, disparity, departure. **2.** DISPUTE argument, quarrel, disagreement, altercation, division, contention, difference of opinion, conflict. **3.** PERMISSION pass, *okay, pass-through. ANT. *2. agreement, harmony, accord.*

variant n. different version, variation.

variation n. change, difference, alternative, departure, turn, fluctuation, break from the norm, aberration, variant, modification, variety. ANT. *sameness, uniformity.*

varied a. various, assorted, diverse, diversified, mixed, miscellaneous, different, motley, sundry, multifarious, heterogeneous, *a mixed bag. ANT. *the same, uniform, homogeneous.*

variegated a. particolored, varicolored, multicolored, polychromatic, streaked, mottled, dappled, spotted, striped, kaleidoscopic, *like a rainbow. ANT. *monochromatic, one-colored, uniform.*

variety n. **1.** VARIATION diversity, change, difference, heterogeneity. **2.** ASSORTMENT miscellany, *mixed bag, potpourri, mixture, hodgepodge, collection, melange. **3.** TYPE sort, kind, class, make, category, species, genus. ANT. *1. sameness, homogeneity.*

various a. **1.** VARIED different, diverse, assorted, sundry, manifold, mixed, motley. **2.** SEVERAL many, countless, numerous, abundant. ANT. *same, similar.*

varnish n. lacquer, shellac, enamel, stain, gloss, veneer, coat, finish, glaze, polish.

vary v. differ, alter, change, modify, deviate, diverge, diversify, depart.

varying a. variable, changing, alternating, differing, different, fluctuating, deviating, diverging, departing, *blowing hot and cold.

vase n. flower holder, pot, jar, vessel, pitcher, jug, amphora, tazza, potiche, urn.

vast a. huge, immense, enormous, extensive, boundless, colossal, astronomical, gigantic, titanic, massive, infinite, far-reaching, immeasurable, stupendous. ANT. *1. tiny, limited, small, microscopic.*

vat n. tub, container, tank, cauldron, cistern, cask, tun.

vault n. **1.** CHAMBER mausoleum, safe, security room, strongroom. **2.** JUMP leap, hop, bound, spring.

vault v. JUMP leap, hop, bound, spring, hurdle.

vaunt v. boast, brag, crow, *talk big, gloat, swagger, strut, *lay it on thick.

veer v. turn, swerve, curve, change direction, change course, wheel, deviate, shift, diverge, tack.

vegetable n. **1.** PLANT herb, root, produce, potato, tomato, carrot, cabbage, broccoli, turnip, lettuce, spinach, cucumber, onion, scallion, leek, beet, green bean, asparagus, artichoke, eggplant. **2.** NONFUNCTIONING HUMAN comatose patient, *brain-dead patient, imbecile, idiot, moron, blob.

vegetarian n. vegan.

vegetarian a. herbivorous, plant-eating.

vegetate v. wither and die, languish, stagnate, be brain-dead, be comatose.

vegetation n. plants, greenery, plant-life, flora, herbage.

vehemence n. intensity, passion, force, violence, fierceness, emotion, zeal, fire, fervor, ardor, fury, enthusiasm, power. ANT. *indifference, apathy, mildness.*

VEHEMENT a. [VEE uh munt] intense, passionate, fervent. *She denied her part in the crime vehemently.* SYN. intense, passionate, fervent, ardent, forceful, violent, fierce, emotional, zealous, fiery, furious, enthusiastic, powerful. ANT. *indifferent, apathetic, mild, passive.*

vehemently a. intensely, passionately, fervently, ardently, forcefully, violently, fiercely, emotionally, zealously, furiously, enthusiastically, powerfully. ANT. *indifferently, passively, mildly.*

vehicle n. **1.** TRANSPORT automobile, car, truck, tractor, van, wagon, *buggy, *heap, *shitbox, jalopy, motorcycle, wheels, *gas hog, *bucket of bolts, *clunker, *crate, *hunk-of-junk, *puddle jumper, boat, bus, train, carriage, coach.

WORD FIND

boxlike coach of 1800s: brougham

bus traveling regular route, small, passenger: jitney

cab, old-time: hackney, hansom cab

carriage, enclosed: coach

carriage, four-wheeled: landau, phaeton, surrey

carriage, two-wheeled: chaise, curricle, gig, sulky

carriage, Western, open, four-wheel: buckboard

funeral: hearse

Oriental cab pulled by one or two persons: ricksha, jinrickisha

parade: float

sledlike conveyance: sleigh, bob-sleigh, carriole, cutter, pung

stagecoach: Concord

streetcar: trolley, cable car

three-wheeled motorcycle for backwoods: ATV, all-terrain vehicle

wagon, covered: Conestoga, prairie schooner

SEE AIRPLANE, AUTOMOBILE, BOAT, MOTORCYCLE, SHIP, TRAIN

2. MEANS medium, instrument, tool, agent, channel, intermediary.

veil *n.* cover, covering, gauze, net, drapery, cloth, caul, shroud, curtain, screen, purdah, mask.

veil *v.* cover, shroud, curtain, screen, mask, disguise, hide, conceal, obscure, darken, cloak, shield.

veiled *a.* disguised, hidden, covered up, concealed, obscured, shrouded, screened, darkened, shielded. ANT. *exposed.*

vein *n.* **1.** BLOOD VESSEL capillary, artery. **2.** TONE quality, feeling, style, manner, mode, strain, mood, way, fashion. **3.** STREAK seam, load, line, layer, stratum.

velocity *n.* speed, rate of speed, pace, quickness, swiftness, fleetness, rapidity, celerity, miles per hour, revolutions per minute, rate.
WORD FIND
measuring device: tachometer

velvet *n.* velveteen, velour, silk.

VENAL *a.* [VEEN ul] easily corrupted or bribed, corrupt. *He was the most venal judge the courts had ever encountered.* SYN. corruptible, easily bribed, unscrupulous, greedy, buyable, unprincipled, immoral, unethical, mercenary. ANT. *scrupulous, principled, ethical, honest, incorruptible.*

vend *v.* sell, peddle, market, retail, hawk.

VENDETTA *n.* [ven DETT uh] a feud or family feud fueled by the need for vengeance. *He launched a personal vendetta against his sister's abuser.* SYN. feud, blood feud, family feud, retaliation, fight, quarrel, bad blood, war, vengeance campaign, vengeance-seeking, revenge.

vendor *n.* seller, salesman, peddler, retailer, hawker, dealer, monger, merchant, trader, merchandiser, huckster.

veneer *n.* **1.** SHOWY LAYER facade, facing, surface, overlay. **2.** FALSE FRONT front, facade, cover-up, show, pretense, guise.

VENERABLE *a.* [VEN ur uh bul] esteemed because of one's age or character. *The venerable judge.* SYN. respected, revered, esteemed, worthy, venerated, honored, time-honored, august, dignified, old. ANT. *disrespected, dishonorable, undignified.*

venerate *v.* [VEN ur ate] revere, look up to, worship. *Everyone venerated the local priest.* SYN. revere, look up to, respect, esteem, honor, worship, adore, idolize, *put on a pedestal, hallow. ANT. *disdain, scorn, regard with contempt, disrespect.*

veneration *n.* respect, reverence, esteem, worship, adoration, awe, idolization, regard, admiration, homage. ANT. *disrespect, disdain, contempt.*

vengeance *n.* revenge, retaliation, retribution, eye for an eye, tooth for a tooth, tit for tat, reprisal, requital, vendetta, settling the score. ANT. *forgiveness, turning the other cheek, letting bygones be bygones.*

vengeful *a.* vindictive, seeking revenge, revengeful, *launching a personal vendetta, retaliatory, avenging, unforgiving, spiteful, bitter, *out to settle the score, punitive. ANT. *forgiving, tolerant.*

venial *a.* forgivable, pardonable, excusable, tolerable, allowable, understandable, minor, *human. ANT. *unforgivable, inexcusable, intolerable, sinful.*

venom *n.* **1.** POISON toxin. **2.** NEGATIVE FEELINGS spite, malice, hatred, animosity, malevolence, malignance, resentment, ill will, bitterness, hostility, acrimony. ANT. 1. *antidote, antivenin, antitoxin.* 2. *love, goodwill, friendliness, warmth.*

venomous *a.* **1.** POISONOUS toxic, lethal, deadly, viperous, stinging. **2.** FULL OF NEGATIVE FEELINGS spiteful, malicious, hating, malevolent, malignant, resentful, bitter, hostile, acrimonious, caustic, antagonistic, vicious. ANT. 1. *harmless, nontoxic.* 2. *friendly, warm, full of goodwill.*

vent *n.* **1.** HOLE opening, outlet, aperture, orifice, mouth, passage, flue, exhaust duct, ventilating shaft. **2.** EXPRESSION release, voicing.

vent *v.* **1.** DISCHARGE release, let out, expel, give off. **2.** EXPRESS air, spout off, voice, verbalize, let out, tell, unburden oneself. ANT. 2. *hold it all in, pent up.*

ventilate *v.* **1.** BRING IN OR EXPEL AIR circulate, freshen, renew, air, air out, refresh, fan. **2.** BRING OUT INTO THE OPEN air, voice, discuss, verbalize.

venture *n.* undertaking, enterprise, adventure, business proposition, endeavor, project, investment, risk, gamble, *long shot, stake, speculation, experiment.

venture *v.* **1.** RISK take a chance, gamble, wager, dare, attempt, *take a shot, *lay it all on the line, *go out on a limb, *take a flier, speculate, endeavor, undertake. **2.** DARE SAY express, hazard an opinion.

venturesome *a.* daring, risky, chancy, brave, courageous, bold, *gutsy, *nervy, audacious, intrepid, enterprising, adventurous, speculative. ANT. *safe, cowardly, guaranteed.*

venue *n.* locale, locality, location, place, scene.

Venus *n.* goddess of love, goddess of beauty, Aphrodite.

veracious *a.* truthful, honest, true, factual, accurate, trustworthy, dependable, reliable, faithful, straightforward, *on the up and up, straight. ANT. *false, dishonest, untruthful, inaccurate.*

VERACITY *n.* [vu RAS uh tee] honesty, truthfulness, accuracy. *We never doubted the veracity of her statements.* SYN. honesty, truthfulness, accuracy, dependability, reliability, credibility, authenticity, reality, integrity, faithfulness. ANT. *dishonesty, deception, deceitfulness, inaccuracy.*

veranda *n.* porch, portico, gallery, deck, stoop, balcony.

verbal *a.* in words, oral, spoken, uttered, articulated, expressed, by mouth, voiced, informal, unwritten. ANT. *written, formal.*

verbalize *v.* speak, say, voice, utter, articulate, express, communicate, put forth, put into words, *spit out.

VERBATIM *adv.* [ver BAY tum] word for word. *She quoted passages of the book verbatim.* SYN. word for word, exactly, literally, precisely, as written, faithfully, to the letter, line for line. ANT. *by way of paraphrasing, roughly, inexactly.*

verbiage *n.* wordiness, long-windedness, prolixity, verbosity, logorrhea, repetition, redundancy, loquacity, tautology. ANT. *concision, conciseness, condensation, pithiness.*

verbose *a.* wordy, long-winded, prolix, tautological, loquacious, garrulous, talkative, repetitive, redundant, voluble, *motor-

mouthed. ANT. *concise, succinct, to the point, pithy.*

verbosity *n.* wordiness, long-windedness, prolixity, tautology, loquaciousness. "Shooting without aiming."—William Benham. "Superfluous breath."—Shakespeare.

verdant *a.* green, grassy, leafy, lush.

verdict *n.* finding, decision, judgment, ruling, conclusion, determination, adjudication, opinion, sentence.

verge *n.* edge, brink, border, margin, limit, threshold, boundary, extremity, fringe, skirt, rim, lip, outer limits.

verge *v.* incline, tend, lean toward, approach, come close, edge, neighbor, touch.

verification *n.* proof, authentication, certification, corroboration, substantiation, confirmation, affirmation, attestation, validation, evidence. ANT. *discredit, invalidation.*

verify *v.* prove, confirm, substantiate, authenticate, certify, corroborate, affirm, attest, validate, testify to, support, demonstrate. ANT. *shoot full of holes, discredit, debunk, invalidate.*

verily *a.* truly, in truth, certainly.

verisimilitude *n.* realism, appearance of reality, appearance of truth, truth, credibility, believability.

veritable *a.* actual, real, for real, true, bona fide, genuine, authentic. ANT. *false, questionable.*

verity *n.* truth, reality, actuality.

vermin *n.* **1.** PESTS varmints, bugs, flies, lice, fleas, cockroaches, rats. **2.** *CREEP *sleazebag, *scum of the earth, dregs, *scumbag, weasel, snake, riffraff.

VERNACULAR *n.* [vur NAK yoo lur] everyday language or idiom. *Even though he was a highly intellectual author, he always spoke in a relaxed vernacular.* SYN. native tongue, dialect, native language, conversational English, plain English, colloquial speech, slang, idiom, lingo, cant, argot, shoptalk. ANT. *formal English, formal language.*

vernacular *a.* native, regional, local, provincial, common, popular, vulgar, indigenous, informal, conversational.

vernal *a.* fresh, young, youthful, *spring-fresh. ANT. *old.*

versatile *a.* multitalented, multifaceted, *Jack of all trades, all-around, multipurpose, resourceful, ingenious, clever, multiskilled, handy, adaptable. ANT. *limited.*

verse *n.* line, stanza, poem, poetry, rhyme, composition, lyrics.

versed *a.* learned, acquainted, experienced,

trained, schooled, educated, practiced, familiar with, informed, conversant, skilled, proficient, *up on. ANT. *unschooled, untrained, ignorant.*

version n. rendition, rendering, interpretation, reading, depiction, account, story, paraphrase, form, translation.

vertex n. apex, summit, highest point, high point, pinnacle, peak, crown, zenith, acme, apogee.

vertical a. upright, up and down, perpendicular. ANT. *horizontal.*

vertiginous a. causing vertigo, dizzy, dizzying, *making one's head spin, whirling, reeling.

vertigo n. dizziness, unsteadyness, whirling, reeling sensation, loss of balance.

verve n. energy, spirit, liveliness, vivaciousness, enthusiasm, vitality, animation, vigor, passion, gusto, *pizzazz. ANT. *dullness, sleepiness, weariness.*

very a. **1.** COMPLETE absolute, total, entire, out-and-out, downright, unqualified, sheer. **2.** SAME identical, precise, exact, perfect, fitting, suitable, needed. ANT. *1. partial.*

very adv. **1.** EXTREMELY excessively, exceedingly, profoundly, unusually, highly, *terribly, *awfully, uncommonly, vastly, extraordinarily, deeply, richly, notably. **2.** EXACTLY precisely. ANT. *1. slightly, barely, hardly. 2. roughly.*

vespers n. evening prayer, canonical hour.

vessel n. **1.** BOAT craft, sailboat, trawler, ship, freighter, barge, tugboat, tanker, ocean liner, cruise ship, *tub. SEE BOAT, SHIP **2.** CONTAINER receptacle, holder, utensil, pot, pan, kettle, bottle, vase, jug, tub, vat, cistern, cask, keg, urn.

vest n. waistcoat.

vest v. place in control, invest, entrust, bestow, authorize, empower, assign, confer, grant.

vested a. fixed, absolute, set, inviolable, inalienable, guaranteed by law, protected by law, warranted.

vestibule n. entrance, entranceway, foyer, lobby, reception area, waiting room, antechamber.

vestige n. trace, ancestral remnant, relic, memento, surviving evidence, shadow, glimmer, token, remainder, *ancestral hand-me-down.

vestigial a. obsolete, ancestral, degenerate, atrophied, nonfunctional, rudimentary, remaining, passed-down.

vestment n. garment, robe, gown, alb, amice, cassock, surplice, tippet, cope.

veteran n. professional, pro, seasoned pro, *vet, experienced hand, *old hand, old-timer, past master, senior, authority, expert, trouper, *war horse, ex-soldier. ANT. *amateur, neophyte, beginner.*

veteran a. experienced, old, seasoned, professional, senior, practiced, hardened, masterly, battle-scarred, worldly-wise, weathered. ANT. *inexperienced, immature, young, untried, amateur.*

veterinarian n. vet, animal doctor.

veto n. prohibition, no, refusal, rejection, disapproval, *thumbs down, *nix, nay, stoppage, proscription, denial. ANT. *approval, yes, okay, acceptance, ratification.*

veto v. prohibit, refuse, reject, disapprove, *give a thumbs down, *give a no vote, *nix, stop, kill, proscribe, deny, bar. ANT. *accept, approve, ratify.*

vex v. irritate, annoy, aggravate, trouble, bother, *bug, irk, peeve, ruffle, *rattle one's cage, pester, plague, rile, harass, perturb, *get on one's nerves. ANT. *please, delight, soothe.*

vexation n. irritation, annoyance, aggravation, trouble, bother, *pain, *pain in the neck, *pain in the ass, *headache, *thorn in one's side, disturbance, affliction. ANT. *pleasure, delight, joy.*

vexatious a. irritating, annoying, aggravating, troubling, bothersome, irksome, nerve-racking, ruffling, disturbing, perturbing, nagging, nettling. ANT. *pleasing, delightful, joyful.*

via prep. by, by way of, through.

VIABLE a. [VI uh bul] able to live or survive, workable, doable. *We came up with a number of viable plans to make the company more profitable.* SYN. capable of surviving, workable, doable, practical, feasible, possible, within the realm of possibility. ANT. *likely to perish, impractical, unworkable.*

viaduct n. span. SEE BRIDGE

vial n. phial, bottle, ampule, vessel, test tube, syringe.

vibrant a. **1.** VIBRATING quivering, resonating, resonant, reverberating, reverberant, resounding, ringing, pulsing, throbbing. **2.** LIVELY alive, spirited, vigorous, energetic, animated, throbbing with life, vital, sparkling, radiant. ANT. *1. still. 2. dead, weak, sleepy, dull.*

VICARIOUS a. [vye KAIR ee us] experienced indirectly or imagined through the experiences of others. SYN. indirect, imagined, fantasized, secondhand, secondary, sympathetic, empathetic, surrogate. ANT. *direct, firsthand, personal.*

vice n. sin, evil, wickedness, depravity, wrong, indecency, debauchery, immorality, degeneracy, corruption, prostitution, bad habit, weakness, compulsion, failing, fault, flaw, shortcoming, wrong, crime. "Servility." — Karl Marx. "Instruments to plague." — Shakespeare.

vicinity n. proximity, neighborhood, area, *neck of the woods, region, surroundings, environs, vicinage.

vicious a. **1.** MEAN, NASTY bad, fierce, cruel, malicious, murderous, brutal, merciless, bloodthirsty, savage, ferocious, hateful, venomous, spiteful **2.** EVIL wicked, sinful, base, corrupt, depraved, immoral, debauched, villainous, degenerate, perverted, shameful, bad. ANT. *1. nice, kind, sweet, good. 2. moral, virtuous, righteous, Christian.*

VICISSITUDES n. [vi SIS i TOOD] changes, ups and downs, difficulties. *He learned to accept the vicissitudes of life.* SYN. changes, ups and downs, peaks and valleys, ebb and flow, changes in fortune, reversals, variations, mutability, uncertainty, difficulties.

victim n. **1.** SUFFERER fatality, casualty, injured party. **2.** DUPE target, *patsy, *fall guy, *sucker, *sitting duck, *easy mark, quarry, prey.

victimize v. prey on, attack, kill, destroy, abuse, torment, molest, sexually abuse, rape, mug, rob, wrong, injure, pick on, take advantage of, single out for abuse, *rip off, trick, *burn, fool, *sucker, con, swindle, *flimflam, defraud, *frame.

victor n. winner, champion, *champ, gold medalist, conqueror, vanquisher, *top dog, *number one, master. ANT. *loser, failure.*

Victorian a. respectable, prudish, proper, straitlaced, stuffy, puritanical, prim, priggish, antiquated, obsolete. ANT. *free-spirited, loose, fast, liberal.*

victorious a. winning, conquering, vanquishing, triumphant, successful, champion, on top, prevailing, dominant, undefeated. ANT. *failing, losing, defeated.*

victory n. success, win, triumph, superiority, mastery, sweep, upset, killing, *grand slam, *landslide, *wipe out, the gold medal, the silver medal, the bronze medal, defeat, vanquishing, overthrow, subduing. "A matter of staying power." — Elbert Hubbard. "That which must be bought with the lives of young men to retrieve the errors of the

old." — Gordon Munnoch. ANT. *loss, failure, flop, *choke.*

victuals n. food, foodstuffs, provisions, groceries, rations, *grub, *eats, *chow, *three squares, sustenance, nourishment, larder.

video n. TV, television, tape, videocassette, movie; picture transmission. SEE TELEVISION

videocassette n. video, tape, movie, *flick. SEE MOVIE

vie v. compete, contend, rival, match up against, struggle, contest, *lock horns, *fight tooth and nail, challenge, *jockey for position, *establish a pecking order.

view n. **1.** LOOKING seeing, observation, examination, inspection, scrutiny, scan, look-see, once-over. **2.** SIGHT vision, range. **3.** SCENE scenery, vista, panorama, outlook, prospect, landscape, seascape. **4.** OPINION judgment, perspective, thoughts, feeling, observation, point of view, belief, impression, conviction, attitude.

view v. **1.** LOOK AT see, behold, observe, examine, inspect, scrutinize, scan, check out, survey, *get a load of, regard, peep, eyeball. **2.** CONSIDER regard, judge, deem, think, look at.

viewpoint n. point of view, opinion, perspective, attitude, way of thinking, position, standpoint, feeling, vantage point, angle, slant.

vigil n. watch, standing-by, overnight watch, surveillance, lookout, observation, monitoring.

vigilance n. watchfulness, caution, alertness, wariness, attentiveness, circumspection, lookout, carefulness, heed. ANT. *carelessness, disregard, letting down one's guard.*

vigilant a. watchful, alert, on the lookout, cautious, wary, attentive, circumspect, careful, *on one's toes, on guard. ANT. *unwary, incautious, off guard, *flat-footed, asleep.*

vigilante n. member of a lynch mob, member of a vigilance committee, night rider.

vigilantism n. taking the law into one's own hands, mob law, mob rule, lynch law, lynching.

vignette n. sketch, scene, cameo, skit, bit, depiction

vigor n. **1.** STRENGTH AND VITALITY energy, zip, power, pep, fire, vim, liveliness, drive, force, potency, might, hardiness, heartiness, health, *get up and go, *punch. **2.** INTENSITY force, spirit, passion, enthusiasm, vehemence, fire, fervor. ANT. *1. weakness, feebleness, failing health. 2. feebleness, halfheartedness, weariness.*

vigorous *a.* strong, vital, energetic, *full of zip, powerful, peppy, *full of fire, lively, forceful, potent, mighty, hardy, hearty, healthy, robust, intense, spirited, passionate, enthusiastic, vehement, fervent. ANT. *weak, feeble, sickly, failing, impotent.*

viking *n.* pirate, sea rover, Norseman.

vile *a.* **1.** BASE immoral, wicked, evil, sinful, debased, bad, degenerate, venal, iniquitous, villainous, depraved, Satanic. **2.** OFFENSIVE disgusting, sickening, nauseating, stomach-turning, rotten, loathsome, despicable, monstrous, atrocious, obnoxious, contemptible. ANT. *1. moral, good, wholesome, virtuous. 2. pleasant, delightful, agreeable.*

VILIFY *v.* [VIL uh FYE] to defame, slander, put down. *He vilified nearly everyone in the organization.* SYN. defame, slander, put down, mudsling, libel, smear, criticize, abuse, denounce, *slam, malign, denigrate, revile, calumniate, vituperate, *bad-mouth, *drag one's name through the mud. ANT. *praise, compliment, commend.*

vilification *n.* defamation, slander, mudslinging, libel, smear, criticism, verbal abuse, denunciation, *slamming, maligning, denigration, calumny, character assassination, *bad-mouthing. ANT. *praising, commendation, acclaim.*

villa *n.* country house, country estate, summer house, *spread, vacation home, hacienda.

village *n.* municipality, hamlet, small town, crossroads, burg, community, settlement, township.

villain *n.* criminal, *bad guy, scoundrel, evil-doer, wretch, knave, antihero, *black hat, fiend, rogue, rascal, *weasel, *snake, *rat, *Simon Legree, dastard, cur, *the heavy, *bastard, *SOB, cad, *creep, *rotter, *stinker, *bad actor, *bad hombre. ANT. *hero, *good guy, good Samaritan, law-abiding citizen.*

villainous *a.* criminal, evil, wicked, sinful, unlawful, lawbreaking, mean, knavish, black, fiendish, dastardly, ignoble, blackhearted, antisocial, vile, low, felonious, shameful, reprehensible, immoral, diabolic. ANT. *heroic, good, kind, Christian.*

villainy *n.* crime, dirty deed, felony, evil, wickedness, sinfulness, knavery, meanness, delinquency, blackheartedness, antisocial behavior, antisocial act, vileness, immorality, heinous act. ANT. *heroism, goodness, kindness, Christianity.*

vim *n.* vitality, vigor, energy, strength, robust-ness, liveliness, *pep, *get up and go, *zip, potency, vivacity, spirit. ANT. *feebleness, weariness.*

VINDICATE *v.* [VIN duh KATE] to clear one of blame, charges or suspicion; to absolve. *The new evidence vindicated the accused and he was promptly released with apologies.* SYN. clear, clear one's name, exonerate, prove innocence, absolve, acquit, exculpate, excuse, pardon, uphold one's innocence, defend, support. ANT. *damn, implicate, convict.*

VINDICTIVE *a.* [vin DIK tiv] seeking revenge, seething with the desire for vengeance. *The divorce made both parties mean and vindictive.* SYN. vengeful, revengeful, retaliatory, retributive, spiteful, unforgiving, resentful, hostile, out for revenge, out to even the score, nasty. ANT. *forgiving, *turning the other cheek, accepting.*

vintage *n.* **1.** TIME PERIOD season, year, date, period, model. **2.** CROP harvest, yield. SEE WINE

vintage *a.* **1.** CHOICE the best, select, prize, excellent, superior, good, fine. **2.** HISTORICAL past, period, retro, old-time, old-fashioned, antiquated, antique, outdated. ANT. *1. the worst, poor, inferior. 2. future, modern, contemporary.*

vintner *n.* wine merchant, wine maker. SEE WINE

violate *v.* **1.** BREAK A LAW transgress, breach, disobey, trespass, defy, disregard the law, infringe, commit a felony, commit a crime, commit a misdemeanor. **2.** RAPE molest, sexually abuse, ravish, assault, deflower, take by force. **3.** DESECRATE profane, disrespect, dishonor, defile, blaspheme, degrade, corrupt. **4.** BREAK IN interrupt, invade one's space, invade one's privacy, disturb. ANT. *1. comply, observe, respect. 3. respect, honor, revere.*

violation *n.* **1.** BREAKING OF THE LAW transgression, breach, trespass, defiance, infringement, felony, crime, misdemeanor, nonobservance. **2.** RAPE molestation, sexual abuse, sexual assault, deflowering. **3.** DESECRATION disrespect, defiling, degradation. **4.** INVASION OF PRIVACY invasion of one's space, interruption, disturbance.

violence *n.* **1.** PHYSICAL ANGER AND DESTRUCTION brute force, manhandling, brutality, roughness, terrorism, bloodshed, killing, murder, destructiveness, barbarity, savagery, ferocity, fisticuffs, *rumble, rioting, physical abuse, *ass-kicking, pummeling, cruelty, torture, *when push comes to shove. "The state calls its own violence law, but that of the individual crime." — Max Stirner. "The physical manifestation of the sense of injustice."— Anon. "The beast in man let loose."— Anon. **2.** INTENSE FORCE OF NATURE energy, explosiveness, storminess, ferocity, fury, turbulence, wildness, intensity, fierceness, upheaval, cataclysm, eruption, blowup.

violent a. **1.** DESTRUCTIVE brutal, beastly, manhandling, rough, terrorizing, killing, murderous, barbarous, savage, ferocious, riotous, physically abusive, assaultive, cruel, bloodthirsty, homicidal, rabid, maniacal, berserk, rowdy, hurtful, crazed, out of control, vehement, furious. **2.** INTENSE powerful, strong, extreme, severe, acute, rough, explosive, turbulent, stormy, ferocious, wild, fierce, cataclysmic. ANT. *1. nonviolent, pacific, passive, peaceful. 2. mild, gentle, slight.*

violin n. string instrument, fiddle, Stradivarius. SEE MUSICAL INSTRUMENT

VIP n. very important person, dignitary, *big shot, *big enchilada, *brass hat, *top brass, celebrity, *high muckety-muk, nabob. ANT. *nobody, *lightweight, nobody special.*

viper n. *snake, *snake in the grass, scoundrel, rogue, villain, cur, *SOB, *bastard, cad, rat, *heel, worm, *rotter. ANT. *nice guy, choirboy, good Samaritan.*

viperous a. malicious, vicious, spiteful, nasty, venomous, malignant, mean, vindictive, Satanic, deadly. ANT. *nice, sweet, harmless.*

virago n. shrew, nag, scold, *bitch, witch, *battle-ax, spitfire, fishwife, *biddy, hag.

virgin n. maid, maiden, celibate, vestal.

Virgin n. Mary, Mother of Jesus, Madonna, the Virgin Mother, Queen of Saints, Blessed Virgin Mary.

virgin a. virginal, chaste, celibate, untouched, pure, immaculate, unused, innocent, pristine, unspoiled, inexperienced, without sin, maidenly, wholesome. ANT. *impure, tried, experienced, defiled.*

virginal a. SEE VIRGIN

virginity n. chastity, celibacy, purity, maidenhood, innocence, virtue, modesty, continence, abstinence. ANT. *promiscuity, experience, immodesty.* "A frozen asset."—Clare Boothe Luce. "Peevish, proud, idle, made of self-love, which is the most inhibited sin in the canon."—Shakespeare.

virile a. manly, masculine, male, *macho, strong, powerful, forceful, vigorous, potent, red-blooded, lusty, two-fisted, strapping, muscular, fearless, *gutsy, bold, *ballsy. ANT. *effeminate, *wimpy, weak, impotent.*

virility n. manliness, masculinity, maleness,

strength, power, forcefulness, vigor, potency, red-bloodedness, lustiness, muscularity, fearlessness, gutsiness, *ballsiness. ANT. *femininity, *wimpiness, weakness, impotency.*

virtual a. practical, in effect, just about, tantamount to, essential, equal to, implicit.

virtually a. practically, for all practical purposes, in effect, just about, tantamount to, essential, equal to, basically, essentially.

virtue n. **1.** MORALITY goodness, righteousness, uprightness, moral excellence, decency, character, integrity, incorruptibility, honor, Christian values, principle, ethic. "The fount whence honor springs."—Christopher Marlowe. "Forebearance."—F. Scott Fitzgerald. "Reason in practice."—Marie de Chenier. "A mean state between two vices, the one of excess and the other of deficiency."—Aristotle. "Blood is an inheritance, virtue an acquisition."—Miguel de Cervantes. "Virtue is insufficient temptation."—George Bernard Shaw. **2.** CHASTITY chasteness, purity, virginity, celibacy, innocence, modesty, abstinence, continence. **3.** EXCELLENCE merit, effectiveness, value. ANT. *1. immorality, evil, wickedness, sin. 2. promiscuity, immodesty, impurity. 3. inferiority, ineffectiveness.*

virtuosity n. skill, proficiency, greatness, mastery, expertise, command, artistry, craftsmanship, brilliance. ANT. *inexperience, incompetence, ineptness.*

virtuoso n. master, expert, artist, *whiz, craftsman, genius, prodigy, ace, professional, pro, *crackerjack, maestro, mavin. ANT. *amateur, beginner, bumbler, neophyte.*

virtuous a. **1.** MORAL AND EXEMPLARY good, righteous, upright, principled, decent, incorruptible, honorable, showing character, having integrity, having Christian values, ethical. **2.** CHASTE virginal, pure, untouched, innocent, celibate, continent, abstinent. ANT. *1. immoral, evil, sinful, wicked. 2. promiscuous, impure, immodest.*

virulence n. **1.** TOXICITY noxiousness, harmfulness, deadliness. **2.** ANIMOSITY venom, hostility, malevolence, rancor, malice, acrimony.

virulent a. **1.** POISONOUS noxious, toxic, venomous, harmful, unhealthy, lethal, deadly, fatal, malignant, deleterious. **2.** ANTAGONISTIC hostile, venomous, malevolent, rancorous, vicious, malicious, nasty, acrimonious, bitter, spiteful, vindictive. ANT. *1. nontoxic, harmless, benign. 2. friendly, nice, warm.*

virus n. *bug, germ, microorganism, microbe,

infection, pathogen, prokaryote, cold virus, flu virus.

visa *n.* endorsement, authorization, certification, passport stamp.

visage *n.* face, countenance, expression, appearance, aspect, look, cast, bearing.

vis-a-vis *a.* face to face, opposite.

viscera *n.* internal organs, intestines, guts, bowels, *innards, entrails.

VISCERAL *a.* [VIS ur ul] instinctive, intuitive, felt in one's gut. *The desire to hunt is largely visceral.* SYN. instinctive, intuitive, *gut, internal, natural, unconscious, subconscious, reflexive, emotional. ANT. *intellectual, cerebral.*

viscid *a.* SEE VISCOUS

viscosity *n.* cohesiveness, stickiness, tackiness, adhesion, viscidity, gumminess, pastiness.

viscount *n.* nobleman.

viscous *a.* cohesive, sticky, viscid, tacky, gluey, gummy, adhesive, syrupy, mucilaginous, pasty.

vise *n.* clamp, holder, grip, gripper.

visibility *n.* range of vision, clearness, clarity, cloudiness, cloud ceiling, fogginess, perceptibility.

visible *a.* seeable, perceptible, observable, perceivable, discernible, palpable, apparent, evident, obvious, conspicuous, dictinct, clear, plain, manifest. ANT. *invisible, concealed, hidden, imperceptible.*

vision *n.* **1.** EYESIGHT sense of sight, sight, seeing, perception, optical perception. SEE EYE **2.** DREAM hallucination, fantasy, daydream, illusion, mirage, apparition, ghost, specter, phantom, visitation, prophecy, prophetic vision, revelation. **3.** MENTAL PICTURE image, imagining, fantasy, concept, idea. **4.** FORESIGHT OR IMAGINATION astuteness, farsightedness, understanding, insight, wisdom, perspective, keenness, intuition.

visionary *n.* **1.** DREAMER daydreamer, idealist, romantic, Utopian, castle-builder, Don Quixote. **2.** PROPHET seer, mystic, fortune-teller, psychic.

visionary *a.* imaginary, fantasized, dreamed, fanciful, impractical, unrealistic, idealized, idealistic, starry-eyed, romantic, speculative; ghostly, spectral, prophetic. ANT. *realistic, down to earth, practical.*

visit *n.* social call, stopover, stay, sojourn, appointment, talk, chat.

visit *v.* **1.** DROP IN ON call on, stop in, stop over, stop by, see, look up, look in on, pay a call, stay over, sojourn. **2.** AFFLICT inflict, assail,

befall, wreak, smite, attack.

visitation *n.* affliction, punishment, plague, curse, blight, disaster, catastrophe, tragedy, calamity, reward, just reward.

visitor *n.* caller, guest, houseguest, company, drop-in company, sojourner, tourist, traveler.

vista *n.* view, outlook, scene, scenery, panorama, sight, prospect.

visual *a.* **1.** OPTICAL optic, ocular. **2.** VISIBLE seeable, observable, perceptible, discernible, perceivable. ANT. **2.** *invisible, imperceptible, auditory, olfactory.*

visualize *v.* picture, imagine, envision, conceive, fantasize, see in the mind's eye, envisage, conjure up, form a mental image.

vital *a.* **1.** LIVING live, life, animate, life-giving, life-supporting, life-sustaining. **2.** ESSENTIAL necessary, indispensable, critical, crucial, fundamental, basic, important, life or death, key. **3.** VIGOROUS energetic, lively, full of life, spirited, animated, vivacious, vibrant, dynamic, full of zest. ANT. **1.** *dead, lifeless, inanimate.* **2.** *inessential, unnecessary, dispensable.* **3.** *lifeless, sluggish, sickly, tired.*

vitality *n.* vigor, energy, liveliness, life, spirit, animation, vivacity, zest, vim, robustness, get up and go, power, strength. ANT. *weakness, sluggishness, lethagy, dullness.*

vitriol *n.* bitterness, sarcasm, nastiness, venom, acid, maliciousness, malevolence, hatefulness, contempt, disdain. ANT. *sweetness, kindness, pleasantness.*

VITRIOLIC *a.* [vi tree AWL ik] caustic, bitter or sarcastic. *His vitriolic speech drove many people out of the conference room.* SYN. caustic, bitter, sarcastic, nasty, venomous, acid, malicious, malevolent, hateful, biting, cutting, disdainful. ANT. *sweet, nice, pleasant.*

vittles *n.* victuals, food, edibles, *grub, *chow, eats, nourishment.

vituperate *v.* scold, berate, censure, verbally abuse, revile, reprove, reproach, rebuke, upbraid, chasten, disparage. ANT. *commend, praise, compliment.*

vituperation *n.* scolding, berating, verbal abuse, abusive language, castigation, *dressing down, condemnation, criticism, revilement, denunciation. ANT. *praise, compliments, commendation.*

VIVACIOUS *a.* [vi VAY shus] full of life. *She was bubbly and vivacious.* SYN. lively, bubbly, effervescent, spirited, animated, ebullient, vital, bouncy, cheerful. ANT. *lifeless, dead, dull, sluggish.*

vivacity *n.* life, liveliness, bubbliness, effervescence, spirit, animation, ebullience, vitality, bounciness, cheerfulness. ANT. *deadness, lifelessness, dullness.*

vivid *a.* **1.** BRIGHT brilliant, intense, striking, strong, rich, radiant, resplendent, glowing, brightly colored. **2.** CLEAR crystal-clear, strong, powerful, realistic, graphic, distinct, picturesque, sharp, loud, impressive. ANT. *1. dull, faded, faint, pale. 2. vague, dull, faint.*

vivify *v.* give life to, animate, vitalize, quicken.

vivisection *n.* animal dissection, animal research, medical research.

vixen *n.* shrew, *bitch, witch, *battle-ax, virago, fishwife, scold, hellcat, spitfire.

vocabulary *n.* lexicon, glossary, word stock, vernacular, language, slang, jargon, lingo, cant, tongue, terminology, phraseology, dictionary, thesaurus.

vocal *a.* **1.** SPOKEN oral, verbal, voiced, vocalized, uttered, articulated, expressed, put into words, sung. **2.** OUTSPOKEN expressive, articulate, vociferous, *not backward about coming forward, loud, noisy, blunt, forthright, making oneself heard. ANT. *1. mute, silent, written. 2. shy, reserved, reticent, quiet.*

vocalist *n.* singer, soloist, crooner, diva, prima donna, *songbird, song stylist, songstress, recording artist, pop star, minstrel.

vocalize *v.* verbalize, voice, put into words, articulate, express, speak, utter, say, communicate, phonate, sing.

vocation *n.* profession, occupation, trade, calling, line of work, career, livelihood, employment, job, line, metier, business, *racket, field, *bag.

vociferate *v.* shout, clamor, holler, bellow, rant, rave, thunder, fume, fuss, *raise a stink, raise one's voice, carry on vehemently. ANT. *whisper, speak softly.*

VOCIFEROUS *a.* [vo SIF ur us] loud, bellowing; making one's point in a noisy manner. *Both sides had become increasingly vociferous over the gun control issue.* SYN. loud, bellowing, shouting, hollering, clamorous, ranting, raving, thunderous, fuming, vehement, vocal, uproarious, loud-mouthed. ANT. *quiet, reserved, silent, shy.*

vogue *n.* mode, fashion, style, *fad, *rage, *craze, trend, latest thing, custom, dernier cri, *last word.

vogue *a.* in vogue, in fashion, fashionable, trendy, *in, current, stylish, *on the cutting edge. ANT. *old-fashioned, outdated, obsolete.*

voice *n.* **1.** SPEECH power of speech, vocal power, vocal cords, tongue. "An arrow for the heart." — Lord Byron. "A second face." — Gerard Bauer.

WORD FIND

descriptive: alto, baritone, bass, bellowing, booming, breathy, cackling, childish, cracking, croaking, cultured, deep, drawling, droning, falsetto, faltering, feeble, flat, fluting, gargling, gravel, guttural, harsh, hoarse, hollow, hushed, husky, inflectionless, lilting, lisping, monotone, nasal twang, powerful, ponderous, purring, quavering, rasping, reedy, resonant, robust, scabrous, sensuous, Shakespearian actor's, sharp, shrill, singsong, soothing, soprano, spluttering, squawking, squeaky, stentorian, strangled, subterranean, sultry, tenor, thick, thin, throaty, thunderous, tremulous, velvety, warbling, wheezing, whining, whiskey-voiced.

loss of: aphonia

loud: megalophonic, megalophonous

organ: larynx, vocal cords, voicebox

pertaining to: phonetic

pitch, variation in: modulation, inflection

quality: timbre

voiceless: mute

SEE SING, SPEECH

2. SAY vote, choice, opinion, *two cents worth, part to play, preference.

voice *v.* express, articulate, say, verbalize, state, announce, air, vocalize, utter, communicate, put into words, sound off, vent.

void *n.* emptiness, vacuum, empty space, vacuity, nothing, nothingness, hole, oblivion, blank.

void *v.* **1.** NULLIFY invalidate, cancel, annul, abolish, repeal, rescind, reverse, revoke, stop. **2.** DISCHARGE evacuate, empty, clear, eliminate, excrete, purge. ANT. *1. validate.*

void *a.* **1.** EMPTY vacant, devoid, vacuous, desolate, barren, unoccupied, bare, hollow, blank. **2.** INVALID null, ineffective, cancelled, ineffectual, not in force, annulled, worthless, meaningless. ANT. *1. full, occupied, filled. 2. valid, in force, binding.*

VOLATILE *a.* [VOL uh tul] unstable, liable to change quickly. Also, likely to explode due to instability. *Tensions between nations created a volatile situation.* SYN. unstable, changeable, rapidly changing, unpredictable, unsettled, erratic, explosive, tense, fickle, capricious, up and down, hot and cold, mercurial. ANT. *stable, steady, predictable.*

volcanic *a.* explosive, violent. SEE VOLCANO

volcano *n.* vent, mountain, crater, Pelee, Vesuvius, Etna, Mt. St. Helens.

WORD FIND

avalanche of hot gas and ash: pyroclastic flow, nuee ardente

blob of lava ejected from: bomb

cavern formed by lava flow: lava tube

cinderlike lava: scoria

crater that eventually fills with water to become lake: caldera

descriptive: devil's throne, hellish forge, festering boil

device that measures bulge in side of mountain: tiltmeter

device that measures vibration: seismograph

ejaculate: clastic, tephra

eruption: cataclysm, upheaval, paroxysm, belching

"fireworks" associated with: pyrotechnics

glass, volcanic: obsidian

god of fire, Roman: Vulcanus

inactive permanently: extinct

lava that hardens and stops up volcano throat: plug

molasses-like lava found in Hawaii: pahoehoe

molten rock after it is expelled: lava

molten rock before it is expelled: magma

mouth: crater

mud or ash flow, heated: lahar

rock, porous: pumice

rock produced by, dark igneous: basalt

reaction of lava when it meets water: base surge

science of: volcanology

scientist: volcanologist, vulcanist

sleeping, inactive: dormant

superheated gas and fire cloud: nuee ardente

vent, secondary: monticule, fumarole, blowhole, cinder cone

truncated cone left after eruption: basal wreck

SEE MOUNTAIN

VOLITION *n.* [vo LISH un] will, a conscious choice. *She went into the dangerous area of her own volition.* SYN. will, free will, willingness, choice, choosing, election, determination, desire. ANT. *coercion, arm-twisting.*

volley *n.* barrage, rain, shower, peppering, burst, salvo, fussilade, enfillade, discharge, wall of fire, bombardment.

volleyball *n.* sport.

WORD FIND

fake spike in which ball is tapped very lightly

over net: dink shot, off-speed spike

jump serve that hooks: *candy cane

powerful, driving shot into opponent's court: spike

save near the floor, underhand: dig

sets ball for spiker, one who: setter

soft serve easily returned: *lollipop

spike into opponent's face: *facial

spiking directly into opponent's armpits: *sizzling the pits

spin on the ball: English

touching net illegally: netting

transfer of serve to other team: side out

violation: fault, foul

voluble *a.* talkative, loquacious, garrulous, *motor-mouthed, long-winded, effusive, blabby, *having the gift of gab, fluent, rambling. ANT. *quiet, silent, reticent, taciturn.*

volume *n.* **1.** BOOK work, tome, opus, hardcover, paperback, album. **2.** CUBIC SPACE cubic feet, cubic inches, size, dimensions, capacity, mass, extent. **3.** LOUDNESS amplification, intensity, sound.

voluminous *a.* **1.** HUGE large, sizable, big, great, vast, extensive, bulky, full, expansive, capacious, spacious. **2.** FILLING VOLUMES prolific, comprehensive, profuse, abundant, abounding, plentiful. ANT. *small, tiny, slight.*

voluntarily *a.* of one's own free will, willingly, of one's own volition, volitionally, electively, freely. ANT. *by force, by coercion, unwillingly, against one's will.*

voluntary *a.* of one's own free will, willing, of one's own volition, volitional, elected, opted, unforced, gratuitous, free, optional, spontaneous. ANT. *forced, compulsory, coerced, against one's will.*

volunteer *v.* offer, sign up, donate one's services, step up, come forward, present, proffer, tender, contribute. ANT. *go kicking and screaming, resist, refuse.*

voluptuary *n.* sensualist, sybarite, hedonist, pleasure seeker.

voluptuous *a.* **1.** SENSUAL sensuous, pleasure-seeking, hedonistic, sybaritic, sexual, erotic, libidinal, erogenous, fleshly, lustful, lascivious, licentious. **2.** SEXUALLY ATTRACTIVE *built, shapely, *stacked, buxom, curvaceous, well-endowed, gorgeous, *hot, *foxy, good-looking. ANT. 1. *abstemious, puritanical, ascetic.* 2. *ugly, repulsive.*

volute *n.* spiral, twist, whorl.

vomit *v.* throw up, upchuck, puke, disgorge, *barf, regurgitate, spew, retch, *hurl, *ralph, *blow lunch, *toss one's cookies, *blow grits, *pray to the porcelain god, *talk to the seals, expel.

voodoo *n.* black magic, witchcraft, hoodoo, obeah, sorcery.

WORD FIND

animated corpse or snake deity: zombie

object thought to have magical power: fetish, charm

VORACIOUS *a.* [vo RAY shus] extremely hungry or greedy, insatiable. *He wolfed his food voraciously.* SYN. ravenous, gluttonous, edacious, greedy, hungry, starved, devouring, insatiable, unquenchable, wild, rabid, out of control. ANT. *moderate, dainty, satiated.*

vortex *n.* whirlpool, maelstrom, eddy, gyre, whirlwind, tornado, cyclone, *twister.

votary *n.* monk, nun, devotee, worshipper, disciple, follower, adherent, fan.

vote *n.* say, voice, choice, option, right to choose, suffrage, franchise, ballot, poll, referendum, show of hands, *yea, *nay. SEE ELECTION

vote *v.* cast one's ballot, choose, elect, decide on, opt for, *give thumbs up, *give thumbs down, *yea, *nay, go to the polls. SEE ELECTION

vouch *v.* affirm, back up, support, swear to, testify, attest, bear witness, substantiate, corroborate, guarantee, warrant, authenticate, certify.

voucher *n.* receipt, chit, debenture, note, IOU.

vouchsafe *v.* give, grant, confer, bestow, concede, allow, condescend.

vow *n.* promise, pledge, oath, word, solemn word, word of honor, troth, assurance.

vow *v.* promise, pledge, give one's word, give one's solemn word, give one's word of honor, swear to, solemnly swear, assure, *cross one's heart and hope to die, guarantee, warrant.

voyage *n.* cruise, pleasure cruise, ocean-crossing, sail, trip, passage, journey, tour, junket.

voyage *v.* cruise, cross the ocean, sail, take a trip, journey, tour, travel, go abroad.

voyeur *n.* *peeping Tom, pervert, spy, watcher.

vulgar *a.* **1.** COMMON popular, everyday, general, plebeian, folk, of the masses, proletarian, working class, colloquial. **2.** CRUDE coarse, unrefined, *gross, rough, boorish, uncultivated, ill-bred, ill-mannered, uncivilized, loutish, impolite. **3.** INDECENT obscene, tasteless, disgusting, *gross, dirty, offensive, X-rated, blue, ribald, off-color, smutty. ANT. *1. upper class, aristocratic. 2. refined, civilized, well-mannered, well-bred. 3. tasteful, decent, clean, G-rated.*

vulgarity *n.* **1.** CRUDENESS coarseness, lack of refinement, roughness, ill manners, bad manners, rudeness, boorishness, grossness, impoliteness. "The garlic in the salad of taste." — Cyril Connolly. **2.** OBSCENITY expletive, swear word, four-letter word, profanity, smut, pornography. ANT. *1. refinement, good manners, tact.*

vulnerable *a.* **1.** ASSAILABLE open to attack, defenseless, undefended, weak, helpless, *helpless as a baby, exposed, susceptible, unprotected, pregnable. **2.** SENSITIVE thin-skinned, easily hurt, ultrasensitive. ANT. *unassailable, strong, impregnable, invincible.*

vulture *n.* **1.** BIRD OF PREY raptor, condor, scavenger. **2.** RUTHLESS PERSON shark, con man, jackal, bloodsucker, parasite, user, opportunist, *golddigger.

W

wacko n. Sl. *nut, *fruitcake, oddball, *sicko, *psycho, psychotic, deranged person, unstable person, neurotic, *screwball, mentally unbalanced person.

wacky a. crazy, *loony, demented, deranged, *screwy, *psycho, psychotic, eccentric, irrational, *goofy, *buggy, *kooky, *zany, *off the wall. ANT. rational, sensible, reasonable, sober, sane.

wad n. mass, ball, lump, hunk, chunk, gob, clump, plug.

waddle v. toddle, wobble, walk like a duck, sway.

wade v. slog, slosh, plod, ford, bathe.

waders n. hip boots.

wafer n. cracker, cookie, snap, disk, biscuit.

WAFFLE v. [WAU ful] to speak or write vaguely or ambiguously, to equivocate. The senator waffled on the issue and told us to get back to him. SYN. equivocate, dodge, *dance around an issue, sidestep, hem and haw, duck, hedge, speak ambiguously, speak vaguely, tergiversate, evade, *beat around the bush. ANT. be decisive, come to the point, be straightforward, be direct, take a stand.

waft v. float, fly, sail, glide, drift, blow, puff, carry, propel.

wag n. shake, wiggle, wave, waggle, swing, sway, waver, jiggle, bob.

wag v. shake, wiggle, wave, waggle, swing, sway, jiggle, bob.

wage n. pay, wages, salary, income, earnings, stipend, compensation, remuneration, hire, *take-home, net, recompense.

wage v. engage in, carry on, maintain, conduct, undertake, make, prosecute.

wager n. bet, gamble, play, *long shot, *flier, speculation, *toss of the dice, stake, money.

wager v. bet, gamble, put money on, speculate, venture, risk, chance, hazard, stake.

waggish a. merry, playful, funny, comical, jesting, humorous, clowning, teasing, jovial, jolly. ANT. serious, grim, sober.

wagon n. cart, trailer, dray, Conestoga, prairie schooner, truck, carriage, buggy. SEE VEHICLE

waif n. orphan, homeless child, stray, foundling, street child, gamin, ragamuffin.

wail n. cry, outcry, lament, moan, whine, howl, sob, boohoo.

wail v. cry, cry out, cry out in mourning, bewail, weep, moan, whine, howl, sob, boohoo, bawl, whimper, lament, grieve, mourn.

wait n. delay, holdup, stop, halt, suspension, pause, layover.

wait v. hold up, hold, stop, halt, suspend, pause, delay, procrastinate, linger, abide, bide one's time, *sweat it out, dally, *hang back, *hold the phone, *freeze. ANT. go, proceed, start.

waiter n. waitress, server, steward, garcon, carhop, host, hostess, maitre d', servant.

wait on v. serve, attend to, tend to, minister to, be at one's beck and call, *wait on hand and foot, *gopher.

waitress n. SEE WAITER

waive v. 1. GIVE UP relinquish, surrender, forbear, forgo, renounce, dispense with, forsake, abandon. 2. POSTPONE defer, put off, table, *put on hold. ANT. 1. keep, retain, claim.

waiver n. relinquishment, disclaimer.

wake n. 1. WATCH vigil, funeral service, rites. 2. BACKWASH wash, trail, track, path, contrail.

wake v. 1. AWAKEN wake up, awake, get up, rouse, stir, *rise and shine, open one's eyes, *shake the cobwebs out, come around. 2. ACTIVATE animate, come out of dormancy, revive, stir. ANT. 1. sleep, nod off, doze. 2. quiet, deactivate.

wakeful a. awake, alert, wide-eyed, bright-eyed, wide-awake, restless, insomniac. ANT. sleepy, tired, dull.

walk n. 1. STROLL hike, tramp, amble, march, promenade, constitutional, perambulation, traipse, step, stride, gait, saunter, trek. 2. WALKWAY sidewalk, boardwalk, path, pathway, trail, lane, esplanade, promenade, mall, arcade.

walk v. stroll, hike, tramp, amble, pad, march, promenade, *beat feet, hoof it, tramp, traipse, wend one's way, go on foot, perambulate, shuffle, mosey, step, stride, waddle.

WORD FIND

angry: stalk out, storm out, stamp out, stomp out, catapult into the room

baby: toddle

backward: backpedal, double-back, retrace one's steps

brush, through: blaze, bushwhack, pick one's way, negotiate, weave

casual: walk with elaborate nonchalance, mosey, shuffle, pad, saunter, stroll

complicated path, through or around: pick one's way, negotiate, step nimbly around, thread one's way, edge along, inch forward, take mincing steps

crowd, through a: sidle, jostle, elbow, shoulder, jockey for position, bull one's way through, be borne along by

difficult or laborious: dodder, falter, hobble, limp, lumber, plod, shamble, shuffle, stagger, stumble, totter, trudge, slog, slosh

drunken: stagger, falter, blunder forward, careen, totter

fours, on all: crab

graceful: with feline grace, with the grace of a porteuse, with calculated grace

group: parade, march, file out, tramp, troop, swarm, flood, spill out, be borne along by the crowd

military march: goose-step

show off: stagger, strut, peacock

slide by the soles of one's feet: glissade

sneaky or cautious: creep, edge, inch, slip away, slink, steal, tiptoe, shrink, skulk, prowl, withdraw, lurk, shadow

wet or mud, through: slog, slosh, squelch, splash, wade

wind, against: lean into, battle forward
SEE RUN

walking papers n. dismissal, *pink slip, layoff, *the door, *the boot, firing, *sack, *heave-ho.

walk on v. walk all over, take advantage of, use, abuse, trample, dominate, exploit.

walk out on v. leave, turn one's back on, abandon, *leave high and dry, leave in the lurch, *dump, reject, jilt, depart, strike.

wall n. partition, divider, screen, bulkhead, load-bearing wall, non-load-bearing wall, panel, barrier, parapet.

wallop v. beat, thrash, pound, pummel, punch, slug, hit, bash, thump, sock, *drub, batter, cuff, *clean one's clock, coldcock, knock senseless, smack, *clobber, belt, bop, defeat, *beat the crap out of, *skunk, *blow away, *blow one's doors off, *leave swirling in one's wake, whip, lick, rout, *bury, *eat for breakfast, massacre.

wallow v. 1. ROLL AROUND lie in, lounge, slosh, splash. 2. INDULGE luxuriate, bask, relish, savor, take pleasure in, revel.

waltz n. valse. SEE DANCE

wan a. 1. PALE colorless, pallid, white, ghostly, pasty, blanched, anemic, ashen, cadaverous. 2. WEAK faint, feeble, sickly, tired, half-hearted, weary, sad, gaunt. ANT. 1. rosy, apple-cheeked, ruddy, flushed. 2. bright, strong, wholehearted.

wand n. stick, rod, staff, baton, scepter, switch.

wander v. 1. ROAM rove, range, wend, wind, go about aimlessly, ramble, drift, meander, trek, straggle, gallivant, gad, idle, stroll, lose one's way, stray, go off the beaten track. 2. DIGRESS get off the subject, deviate, get sidetracked, ramble, go off on a tangent. ANT. 1. make a beeline, go directly. 2. stick to the subject, stay on track.

wanderlust n. urge to travel, urge to explore, urge to wander, restlessness.

wane n. ebb, decline, fading, decrease, drop, recession, falling-off. ANT. increase, growth.

wane v. ebb, recede, decline, fade, decrease, drop, shrink, diminish, dwindle, abate, subside, lessen, fall, lapse, die out. ANT. increase, wax, grow.

wangle v. *finagle, machinate, make happen, *pull off, *pull strings, engineer, *swing, contrive, *wheel and deal.

want n. 1. DESIRE need, longing-for, wish, yearning, hunger, thirst, craving, appetite, hankering, requirement, demand. 2. LACK absence, need, dearth, shortage, scarcity, deficiency, paucity, privation. 3. POVERTY destitution, indigence, impoverishment.

want v. 1. DESIRE need, long for, wish for, yearn, hunger for, thirst for, crave, have an appetite for, have a hankering for, require, demand, covet. 2. LACK be deficient, be without, require, need.

wanting a. absent, lacking, missing, deficient, insufficient, inadequate, incomplete, bereft, short, substandard, subpar, poor. ANT. sufficient, adequate.

wanton a. 1. UNMANAGEABLE undisciplined, wild, intractable, unruly, wayward, refractory, unrestrained. 2. SEXUALLY UNRESTRAINED loose, libidinous, promiscuous, lustful, licentious, salacious, carnal, lewd, abandoned, fast. 3. UNPROVOKED groundless, uncalled-for, unnecessary, unjustifiable, senseless, needless, gratuitous, malicious, cruel, mean. 4. RECKLESS rash, unrestrained, careless, *devil-may-care. ANT. 1. manageable, disciplined, well-behaved. 2. chaste, celibate, prudish, puritanical. 3. provoked, necessary. 4. judicious, careful.

war n. warfare, hostilities, conflict, clash, strife, contest, struggle, battle, combat, military operation, confrontation, engagement, crusade. "Death's feast." —George Herbert. "A passion play performed by idiots." —William Corum. "A biological necessity of the first order." —Friedrich von Bernhardi. "That attractive rainbow that rises in showers of blood." — Abraham Lincoln. "The most successful of our cultural traditions." — Robert Ardrey. "Darwin's survival of the fittest on a grand scale." — Anon. "Only a cowardly escape from the problems of peace." — Thomas Mann. ANT. *peace, friendship, accord, harmony.*

WORD FIND

attack, intense, all-out: blitzkrieg, sweep
attack or action: offensive
ceasefire: armistice, truce, peace treaty
games: maneuvers
god of: Mars, Ares
holy: jihad, crusade
nuclear attck to prevent enemy nation's nuclear attack: preemptive strike
operation: campaign
presence of military force in control of another's nation: occupation
pretext for or provocation: casus belli, act of war
referring to: martial
ruining an area before returning it to the enemy: scorched earth policy
science of organization, procurement, deployment, etc.: logistics
surrender: capitulation, white flag
tensions between hostile nations: cold war
threatening another nation with: saber-rattling, gunboat diplomacy
victory won with extremely heavy losses: Pyrrhic victory
winnings: spoils
SEE AIR FORCE, AMMUNITION, ARMY, BOMB, BULLET, GUN, NAVY, NUCLEAR BOMB, SOLDIER, WEAPON

war *v.* conflict, contest, fight, battle, contend, struggle, *lock horns, take up arms, attack, cross swords, skirmish.

warble *v.* sing, trill, quaver, carol, yodel.

ward *n.* **1.** WING section, division, room, annex, pavilion. **2.** DISTRICT quarter, area, zone, precinct, borough, diocese. **3.** CHARGE foster child, dependent, minor, protege, incompetent.

warden *n.* keeper, guard, custodian, caretaker, superintendent, watchman, overseer, prison superintendent.

ward off *v.* fend off, deflect, avert, parry, turn aside, block, defend, *keep at bay, rebuff, check, repulse.

wardrobe *n.* **1.** CLOSET clothes closet, cabinet, armoire, locker, bureau, chest. **2.** CLOTHES COLLECTION clothes, clothing, apparel, attire, outfits, garments, costumes, garb, togs, duds,

*threads.

WORD FIND

bride's outfit: trousseau
ecclesiastical garments: vestments

warhead *n.* bomb, payload, explosive charge, *the business end. SEE MISSILE, NUCLEAR BOMB

warehouse *n.* storage facility, storehouse, stock house, stock room, depot, depository, repository, armory, arsenal, magazine, wholesale store.

wares *n.* merchandise, products, goods, stock, line, articles, stuff, commodities.

warfare *n.* SEE WAR

wariness *n.* caution, circumspection, alertness, guardedness, carefulness, watchfulness, mindfulness. ANT. *carelessness, inattentiveness, devil-may-care attitude.*

warlike *a.* combative, pugnacious, aggressive, militant, aggressive, bellicose, belligerent, hostile, hawkish, contentious, martial, *bristling with arms. ANT. *peaceful, pacifistic, nonviolent.*

warlock *n.* sorcerer, wizard, magician, conjurer, practicer of black magic, necromancer, shaman, witch doctor, male witch.

warlord *n.* tyrant, autocrat. SEE DICTATOR

warm *v.* **1.** RAISE TEMPERATURE heat, simmer, toast, cook, thaw. **2.** FILL WITH EXCITEMENT excite, stimulate, *turn on, *fire up, stir. **3.** GLADDEN make happy, fill with joy, delight, cheer, *melt one's heart, make smile. **4.** BECOME FRIENDLY *break the ice, thaw, become intimate, *loosen up. ANT. **1.** *lower temperature, cool, chill, freeze.* **2.** *bore, tire, *turn off.* **3.** *depress, *bum out.* **4.** *cool.*

warm *a.* **1.** HEATED thermal, lukewarm, body temperature, *toasty, room temperature, comfortable, tepid, sunny, hot, sultry, sweaty, roasting. SEE HOT **2.** FERVENT fervid, ardent, enthusiastic, passionate, eager, vehement, *hot, excited, spirited. **3.** GENIAL cordial, friendly, affectionate, nice, loving, heartfelt, amiable, warmhearted, hospitable, amorous. ANT. **1.** *cold, freezing, cool, chilled, frigid.* **2.** *indifferent, apathetic, lukewarm, cool.* **3.** *cold, unfriendly, cool, hostile.*

warmhearted *a.* warm, friendly, genial, cordial, affectionate, nice, loving, heartfelt, amiable, compassionate, sympathetic, understanding, hospitable, tender, amorous. ANT. *coldhearted, hard-hearted, mean, heartless, *veins filled with ice water.*

warmonger *n.* hawk, militarist, jingo.

warmth *n.* **1.** HEAT glow, temperature, *toastiness, room temperature, fever. **2.** EXCITE-

MENT enthusiasm, ardor, zeal, vigor, fervor, passion, intensity, vehemence. **3.** WARM-HEARTEDNESS friendliness, geniality, cordiality, affection, love, tenderness, compassion, sympathy, understanding, hospitality. ANT. *1. cold, chilliness, frigidity. 2. boredom, indifference, apathy. 3. coolness, coldness, unfriendliness.*

warn *v.* caution, advise, alert, signal, forewarn, admonish, exhort, apprise, give fair warning, notify, threaten, give a word to the wise, *put the fear of God into.

warning *n.* caution, advisory, alert, signal, forewarning, admonition, exhortation, apprisal, notification, threat, *word to the wise, *wake-up call, caveat, portent, sign of things to come, omen.

warp *v.* **1.** BEND OUT OF SHAPE distort, twist, deform, contort, curve, turn, misshape. **2.** PERVERT twist, bias, prejudice, jaundice.

warrant *n.* **1.** AUTHORIZATION authority, sanction, right, word, *OK, permission, license, permit, mandate, subpoena, summons, writ, order, justification. **2.** ASSURANCE guarantee, surety, security.

warrant *v.* **1.** AUTHORIZE sanction, give authority, give the right, *OK, permit, license, allow, invest, certify, empower. **2.** JUSTIFY give grounds for, account for, excuse, defend, provide a reason for. **3.** ASSURE guarantee, back, promise, pledge, vow, swear to, insure, vouch for, underwrite.

warranty *n.* guarantee, assurance of quality, assurance, contract, covenant, promise, pledge.

warrior *n.* fighter, soldier, combatant, commando, G.I., service man, infantryman, *grunt, *leatherneck, brave, samurai, gladiator. SEE ARMY, SOLDIER

warship *n.* man o'war, battleship, missile cruiser, destroyer, frigate, aircraft carrier, dreadnought, galleon. SEE NAVY, SHIP

wart *n.* growth, tumor, papilloma.

wary *a.* cautious, on one's guard, careful, watchful, circumspect, chary, vigilant, *on one's toes, leery, alert, on the lookout, suspicious. ANT. *careless, off guard, unsuspecting.*

wash *n.* **1.** CLEANING rinse, scrubbing, bath, soak, washing, shower, shampoo, laundering, ablution. **2.** SURGE rush, sweep, wave, gush, flow, swell, roll.

wash *v.* **1.** CLEAN rinse, scrub, bathe, soak, shower, shampoo, launder, hose down, freshen up. **2.** WET drench, moisten, rinse, soak, flood.

washed-out *a.* faded, pale, bleached-out, blanched, dull, wan, colorless, lackluster. ANT. *bright, vivid.*

washed-up *a.* finished, through, done, *done for, *shot, *kaput, *over the hill.

washout *n. Sl.* flop, failure, *bomb, *dud, *clinker, *loser, *turkey, fiasco.

washroom *n.* lavatory, restroom, bathroom.

washy *a.* watery, weak, pale.

WASP *n.* white Anglo-Saxon Protestant.

waspish *a.* bad-tempered, hot-tempered, irritable, petulant, testy, venomous, *ornery, touchy, peevish.

wassail *n.* celebration, carousal, party, *bash, *beer bash, spree, revelry, *shindig, gala, *binge, *bust, bacchanalia, drunk fest, toast, salute.

wassail *v.* celebrate, party, carouse, drink, get drunk, make merry, *whoop it up, revel, *cut loose, toast, make a toast, salute.

waste *n.* **1.** TRASH rubbish, garbage, refuse, junk, leavings, scrap, debris, rubble, *crap, hazardous waste, discharge. **2.** EXCREMENT feces, droppings, *crap, sewage. **3.** WASTEFULNESS squandering, extravagance, excessiveness, lavishness, *spending like there's no tomorrow, consumption, conspicuous consumption, misuse, dissipation. ANT. *3. conservation, frugality, economy, saving, thrift.*

waste *v.* **1.** SQUANDER lavish, fritter away, *blow, *piss away, *spend like there's no tomorrow, dissipate, misspend, mismanage, spend extravagantly, splurge, throw away, idle, loiter, fiddle and diddle, loaf, procrastinate. **2.** LOSE ONE'S HEALTH OR STRENGTH waste away, dwindle, fail, weaken, emaciate, atrophy, *circle the drain, wither, deteriorate, decay, decline, *go downhill. **3.** DESTROY ruin, devastate, wreck, demolish, lay waste, spoil, strip, ravage. ANT. *1. conserve, save, economize. 2. strengthen, grow, put on weight. 3. build up, repair.*

wasted *a.* **1.** GAUNT emaciated, wizened, atrophied, deathly, cadaverous, rawboned, withered, anorexic, deathly. **2.** *Sl.* *high, *buzzed, intoxicated, *baked, *fried, *flying, *loaded, *out of it, *polluted, *stoned, *tripping. ANT. *1. healthy, robust. 2. sober.*

wasteful *a.* prodigal, extravagant, lavish, spendthrift, improvident, excessive, immoderate, free-spending, overgenerous, penny-wise and pound-foolish. ANT. *thrifty, economical, frugal.*

wasteland *n.* waste, tundra, dust bowl, desert, badlands, *Devil's backyard, *Devil's garden, barrens, wilderness.

wastrel *n.* spendthrift, prodigal, waster, free-spender, good-for-nothing.

watch *n.* **1.** OBSERVATION lookout, surveillance, eye, sharp eye, weather eye, attention, observance, vigil, supervision, inspection, guarding, sentry. **2.** TIMEPIECE wristwatch, chronometer, horologue, *ticker, *Timex.

watch *v.* **1.** OBSERVE look at, eyeball, eye, pay attention to, inspect, scrutinize, gaze at, view, regard, keep one's eyes on, see, behold, examine. **2.** GUARD watch over, *baby-sit, protect, look after, oversee, keep an eye on, patrol.

watchdog *n.* guard dog, guard, sentry, patrol, sentinal, lookout, guardian.

watchful *a.* observant, alert, wide-eyed, on guard, attentive, vigilant, on the lookout, heedful, wide-awake, cautious, wary, circumspect, *on one's toes. ANT. *inattentive, *asleep at the wheel, *out to lunch, unobservant.*

watchman *n.* guard, security guard, sentry, sentinal, lookout, patrol, policeman, policewoman, police officer, warder.

watchtower *n.* lookout.

watchword *n.* **1.** PASSWORD countersign, shibboleth. **2.** SLOGAN cry, battle cry, catchphrase, rallying cry.

water *n.* H$_2$0, liquid, fluid, rain, aqua, *Perrier, mineral water, soda water, *Adam's ale. "The noblest of the elements." — Pindar. SEE LAKE, OCEAN, RIVER

water *v.* wet, soak, drench, dampen, irrigate, hose down, saturate, spray, wash, sprinkle.

waterfall *n.* falls, cascade, cataract, chute, whitewater, deluge.

WORD FIND

descriptive: falling like a bridal veil, stair-stepping.

SEE RIVER

waterlogged *a.* saturated, soaked, sopping, sodden, drenched, heavy, swampy.

WATERLOO *n.* [WAW tur loo] defeat. A metaphor coined after Napoleon's defeat in Waterloo, Belgium in 1815. *We were afraid that the match against the crosstown team would prove to be our Waterloo.* SYN. defeat, downfall, ruin, collapse, destruction, upset, rout, conquest, beating, vanquishment, massacre, comeuppance. ANT. *victory, win.*

watershed *n.* turning point, pivotal event, landmark, milestone, crucial event.

watertight *a.* airtight, solid.

watery *a.* diluted, thin, watered-down, weak, washy, bland, mild, tasteless, flavorless, anemic. ANT. *strong, intense, undiluted, concentrated, condensed.*

wattle *n.* weave, plait, intertwining, twigs, sticks.

wave *n.* **1.** SURGE OR SWELL surf, breaker, comber, plunger, spiller, bore, eagre, whitecap, billow, undulation, ripple, ridge.

WORD FIND

abnormally large wave in a train of smaller ones: rogue wave

concave-backed wave found offshore: spiller

convex-backed wave, common beach: plunger

frothy, gray-crested waves: graybeards

giant, formerly called tidal wave: tsunami

high dangerous wave caused by tidal surge: bore, eagre

high point: crest

hollow between: trough

marine vegetation washed ashore by: wrack

mounds of sand left by waves breaking at right angles: cusps

ripples in sand left by receding waves: swashmarks

roughness at sea: chop

series of: train

shallow sweep up a beach: swash, backwash

sound: lapping, crashing, booming, white noise, hiss

spray: spindrift

structure erected to prevent wave erosion: jetty, groin

tiny: wavelet

towering crests formed by opposing waves colliding: cross seas

upward heaving of ship caused by wave: scend

wind shore receiving smaller waves, low: lee shore

wind travel distance and its relationship to wave size: fetch

SEE BEACH, OCEAN

2. UPSURGE surge, rise, rash, flood, deluge, explosion, groundswell. **3.** CURL curve, roll, twist.

wave *v.* **1.** UNDULATE swing, sway, oscillate, ripple, flutter, flap, waggle, shake, move to and fro, move back and forth, rise and fall. **2.** SIGNAL gesture, gesticulate, *flag down, acknowledge.

waver *v.* **1.** VACILLATE go back and forth, blow hot and cold, *waffle, *see-saw, be irresolute, dilly-dally, flip-flop, fluctuate, equivocate, hem and haw, be indecisive. **2.** SWING sway, move to and fro, move back and forth, wobble, wave, shake, oscillate, flutter, flap. ANT. *1. make up one's mind, be resolute, decide one way or another.*

wavy *a.* rolling, curling, snaking, serpentine, sinuous, undulating, curved, curvilinear, rippling, winding. ANT. *level, flat.*

wax *v.* grow, enlarge, increase, expand, build, swell, develop, spread, intensify, magnify, strengthen, brighten. ANT. *wane, decrease, diminish.*

way *n.* **1.** METHOD mode, style, technique, form, practice, usage, approach, course, system, manner, procedure. **2.** DIRECTION route, course, path, tack, bearing, approach, course, passage, track, trail, road, lane, access, entry. **3.** NATURE personality, characteristic manner, behavior, custom, habit. **4.** WILL wish, desire, demand, choice.

wayfarer *n.* traveler, roamer, rover, hitchhiker, walker, wanderer, nomad, drifter, gadabout.

wayfaring *a.* hiking, hitchhiking, walking, traveling, roaming, roving, wandering, drifting, nomadic, on the move.

waylay *v.* ambush, attack, lie in wait, entrap, ensnare, surprise, take by surprise, ambuscade.

wayward *a.* **1.** DISOBEDIENT headstrong, rebellious, defiant, nonconforming, contrary, willful, delinquent, incorrigible, stubborn, obstinate, bullheaded, unmanageable, ungovernable, refractory. **2.** UNPREDICTABLE erratic, fickle, capricious, changeable, fickle, unstable, impulsive, unsteady. ANT. *1. obedient, compliant, deferential. 2. predictable, stable, steady.*

weak *a.* **1.** FEEBLE powerless, frail, enervated, impotent, limp, faint, flaccid, ineffectual, exhausted, anemic, worn out, spent, sickly, debilitated, unfit, out of shape, infirm, emasculated. **2.** MORALLY OR MENTALLY WEAK cowardly, fainthearted, faint of heart, spineless, mousy, wishy-washy, weak-kneed, irresolute, *wimpy, timid, *candy-assed, timorous. **3.** STUPID dim-witted, unintelligent, retarded, moronic, imbecilic, dense, dull. **4.** INSECURE unstable, easily broken, unfortified, vulnerable, delicate, fragile, rickety, flimsy, shaky, frail. **5.** FAINT soft, dim, mild, gentle, pale, thin, feeble, low, muted, diluted, watered-down. **6.** LACKING deficient, poor, inadequate, wanting, unsatisfactory, shaky, inept. ANT. *1. strong, powerful, fit, robust, effectual, muscle-bound. 2. strong, headstrong, courageous, bold, *gutsy, 3. smart, intelligent,*

sharp. *4. stable, fortified, rock-solid, unassailable. 5. strong, intense, powerful, undiluted. 6. adequate, satisfactory.*

weaken *v.* drain, sap, debilitate, cripple, exhaust, flag, impair, tire, enervate, enfeeble, droop, slow, run down, deplete, handicap, diminish, reduce, wane, ebb, fade, *lose one's charge, *run one's battery down, *run out of juice, dilute, water down. ANT. *strengthen, fortify, invigorate, energize.*

weakling *n.* *wimp, milquetoast, *pansy, pantywaist, sissy, coward, mouse, *lightweight, *pushover, namby-pamby, *mama's boy, *creampuff, crybaby. ANT. *Hercules, scrapper, hero, strongman, *iron man.*

weak-minded *a.* irresolute, indecisive, mealy-mouthed, wishy-washy, spineless, feeble-minded, dumb, stupid, weak in the head, retarded, moronic, slow, dense. ANT. *headstrong, resolute, decisive, intelligent, smart, bright.*

weakness *n.* **1.** LACK OF STRENGTH feebleness, exhaustion, depletion of energy, enervation, anemia, frailty, fragility. **2.** VULNERABILITY imperfection, flaw, weak spot, *Achilles heel, *chink in one's armor, deficiency, failing, soft underbelly, shortcoming. **3.** LIKING fondness, passion, penchant, taste, appreciation, soft spot, sweet tooth, propensity, inclination. ANT. *1. strength, vigor, energy, robustness. 2. strong point, strength. 3. aversion, dislike, hatred.*

weal *n.* ridge, welt, wale, line.

wealth *n.* money, riches, resources, plenty, fortune, security, affluence, opulence, prosperity, abundance, luxury, capital, property, assets, means, holdings, stocks and bonds. "The savings of many in the hands of one." — Eugene Debs. "Evidence of greatness." — Thomas Reed. "A contented mind." — Mohammed. ANT. *poverty, destitution, indigence, want, lack.*

wealthy *a.* rich, affluent, well-off, *rolling in dough, comfortable, prosperous, *well-heeled, *well-to-do, moneyed, opulent, *filthy rich, *on easy street, *loaded, financially secure. ANT. *poor, destitute, penniless.*

weapon *n.* arm, arms, armament, firearm, gun, rifle, pistol, knife, sword, defense, offensive weapon, weapon of mass destruction, spear, halberd, lance, pike, poleax, trident, bow and arrow. SEE ARMY, BOMB, BULLET, GUN, MISSILE, NAVY, NUCLEAR BOMB, SWORD

weaponry *n.* SEE WEAPON

wear *n.* **1.** CLOTHING clothes, dress, apparel,

garb, attire, formal wear, evening wear, sportswear. **2.** DETERIORATION decay, erosion, wear and tear, corrosion, decomposition.

wear *v.* **1.** DON put on, dress in, be clothed in, fit out, attire, slip on. **2.** DETERIORATE decay, erode, corrode, decompose, abrade, tatter, fall apart, degenerate, rub down, grow threadbare, weather, fray. **3.** DISPLAY show, put on, sport. **4.** TIRE exhaust, fatigue, sap, drain, overwork, tax.

wearing *a.* tiring, exhausting, fatiguing, taxing, draining, sapping, strenuous, laborious, arduous, wearisome, hard. ANT. *invigorating, energizing.*

wearisome *a.* tiring, tiresome, exhausting, fatiguing, taxing, draining, sapping, strenuous, laborious, arduous, hard, tedious, boring, monotonous, humdrum, *ho-hum. ANT. *invigorating, energizing, stimulating.*

weary *v.* tire, get sick of, burn out, exhaust, fatigue, tax, drain, sap, enervate, bore. ANT. *invigorate, energize, stimulate.*

weary *a.* **1.** TIRED worn out, exhausted, fatigued, taxed, drained, sapped, *wrung out, *trashed out, spent, *pooped, bushed, tuckered out, all in, *beat, *dead, burned out, *shot. **2.** SICK OF *had it, fed up, disgusted, bored, intolerant, jaded, burned out. **3.** TIRESOME tedious, boring, monotonous. ANT. **1.** *invigorated, refreshed, energized.* **2.** *fascinated, stimulated.* **3.** *stimulating, interesting.*

weasel *n.* sneak, snake, *snake in the grass, cheater, crook, snitch, *double-crosser, *rat, *squealer.

weasel *v.* avoid, evade, dodge, equivocate, waffle, hedge, duck, double-talk, *dance around an issue, skirt an issue, get out of, *worm one's way out of, renege.

weather *n.* climate, clime, atmospheric conditions, temperature, humidity. "A social invention to facilitate small talk." —Anon. SEE CLOUD, FOG, METEOROLOGY, PRECIPITATION, RAIN, SNOW, WIND

weather *v.* withstand, stand, endure, resist, be exposed to the elements, face, season, harden, survive, *tough out, *ride through. ANT. *die, succumb.*

weatherman *n.* meteorologist, forecaster, climatologist.

weave *v.* intertwine, interlace, entwine, intermingle, interweave, braid, plait, combine, mesh, piece together, blend, incorporate, merge, wattle.

web *n.* webbing, network, net, mesh, skein, lattice, tangle, trap, snare, gossamer.

wed *v.* **1.** MARRY join together in holy matrimony, *tie the knot, *get hitched, *say I do, become man and wife, espouse. **2.** UNITE join, marry, merge, fuse, link, combine, ally, connect, unify. ANT. **1.** *divorce, *split up, separate.* **2.** *separate, split, divide.*

wedding *n.* **1.** MARRIAGE vows, nuptials, matrimony, espousal, holy wedlock, ceremony. "When the blind lead the blind." —George Farquhar. SEE MARRIAGE **2.** UNIFICATION joining, marriage, merger, fusion, linking, connection. ANT. **1.** *separation, divorce.* **2.** *division, split, disconnection.*

wedge *n.* **1.** CHOCK cleat, shim, quoin. **2.** OPENING beginning, start, *foot in the door.

wedge *v.* split, force apart, force in, squeeze in, cram, open.

wedlock *n.* matrimony, union. SEE MARRIAGE

wee *a.* tiny, little, diminutive, pint-sized, pocket-sized, Lilliputian, microscopic, minuscule, miniature, *teeny-weeny. ANT. *giant, huge, Brobdingnagian.*

weed *n.* "A plant whose virtues have not yet been discovered." —Ralph Waldo Emerson.

weed *v.* remove, pull, yank, uproot, cull, get rid of, weed out.

weep *v.* cry, bawl, shed tears, sob, wail, blubber, boohoo, whimper, snivel, *break down, *lose it, lament, bewail, mourn, grieve, bemoan, get misty-eyed.

weepy *a.* tearful, teary-eyed. SEE SAD

weigh *v.* **1.** MEASURE WEIGHT put on the scales, tip the scales, heft, gauge. **2.** CONSIDER ponder, deliberate, think about, contemplate, consider the pros and cons, evaluate, mull over, study, examine, reflect on.

weigh down *v.* saddle, encumber, load. SEE BURDEN

weight *n.* **1.** HEAVINESS mass, pounds, tons, tonnage, burden, heft, gravity, g force, gs, density, volume. **2.** BURDEN responsibility, load, millstone, cross to bear, albatross, *ball and chain, encumbrance, saddle, handicap, onus, hardship. **3.** IMPORTANCE consequence, significance, seriousness, influence, value, import, clout, power, moment, magnitude.

weight *v.* weigh down, make heavy, load, burden.

weight lifting *n.* power lifting, working out, conditioning, weight training.

weighty *a.* **1.** HEAVY hefty, massive, ponderous, cumbersome, dense, hard to lift. **2.** BURDENSOME hard, difficult, oppressive, demanding, backbreaking, onerous, taxing. **3.** IMPOR-

TANT consequential, significant, serious, influential, valuable, important, powerful, momentous, crucial, critical, life or death. **4.** INFLUENTIAL powerful, forceful, persuasive, having clout. ANT. *1. light, airy, light as a feather. 2. easy, effortless, simple. 3. unimportant, insignificant, inconsequential. 4. powerless, unconvincing.*

weir n. dam, milldam, fence, fishtrap.

weird a. bizarre, strange, odd, fantastic, unearthly, otherworldly, alien, supernatural, mysterious, outlandish, nightmarish, surrealistic, Kafkaesque, peculiar, queer, grotesque, eerie, uncanny, *freaky, unusual. ANT. *ordinary, conventional, usual, normal.*

weirdo n. *Sl.* oddball, eccentric, character, *space case, *space cadet, *strange bird, *flake, *geek, freak, *kook, *queer duck, *screwball, *sicko, *wacko, nonconformist. ANT. *conformist, *Joe Average, *just another brick in the wall.*

welcome n. greeting, reception, salute, salutation, *red carpet treatment, hospitality, acceptance, hail. ANT. *rejection, snub.*

welcome v. greet, receive, receive with open arms, receive with a handshake, *roll out the red carpet, hail, salute. ANT. *reject, snub.*

welcome a. wanted, accepted warmly, pleasing, pleasant, agreeable, happily received, invited, delightful, esteemed, desirable. ANT. *unwelcome, unwanted, uninvited.*

weld v. fuse, unite, bond, join, solder.

welfare n. **1.** WELL-BEING health, happiness, good, benefit, profit, prosperity, success, interest, contentment, commonweal. **2.** PUBLIC ASSISTANCE relief, financial assistance, city aid, food stamps, the dole, Social Security.

well n. spring, wellspring, reservoir, shaft, chasm, pit, hole, fountain, water hole.

well a. **1.** HEALTHY fit, in good shape, strong, fine, hearty, vigorous, sound, in fine fettle, *fit as a fiddle, hale. **2.** GOOD fortunate, happy, lucky, proper, right. ANT. *1. unwell, sickly, in failing health. 2. bad, unlucky, unfortunate.*

well adv. **1.** SATISFACTORILY successfully, adequately, happily, nicely, splendidly, famously, capably, ably, in fine fashion. **2.** THOROUGHLY sufficiently, completely, properly, right, correctly, adequately, carefully, conscientiously, competently. ANT. *1. unsatisfactorily, poorly, badly. 2. insufficiently, poorly, *half-assed.*

well up v. flow, spring, gush, stream, run, trickle, spout, bubble, boil.

well-advised a. wise, smart, intelligent, prudent, judicious.

well-appointed a. well-equipped, well-furnished.

well-balanced a. sensible, reasonable, rational, prudent, intelligent, sound. ANT. *unreasonable, irrational.*

well-being n. welfare, health, happiness, prosperity, profit, good, comfort, contentment, benefit, success.

well-bred a. mannerly, cultivated, refined, polite, courteous, civil, gentlemanly, ladylike, polished, groomed, genteel, courtly, gracious, finished, sophisticated. ANT. *ill-bred, unrefined, coarse, vulgar, uncouth, beastly.*

well-defined a. clear, distinct, sharp, clearly delineated, graphic, clear-cut, unambiguous. ANT. *vague, hazy, nebulous.*

well-founded a. factual, based on hard facts, based on hard data, solid, rock-solid, proven, substantiated, authoritative, well-grounded. ANT. *unfounded, based on speculation, questionable.*

well-informed a. schooled, trained, au courant, conversant with, savvy, up to date, aware, versed, *with it, *hip. ANT. *ignorant, *in the dark.*

well-known a. famous, famed, prominent, celebrated, illustrious, infamous, notorious, notable, renowned, *on the map. ANT. *obscure, unknown.*

well-off a. rich, well-to-do. SEE WEALTHY

well-preserved a. youthful.

well-read a. widely read, bookish, literate, scholarly, educated, au courant, versed. ANT. *illiterate, ignorant.*

wellspring n. source, supply, reservoir. SEE WELL

well-to-do a. well-off, rich, prosperous. SEE WEALTHY

welsh v. *Sl.* cheat, swindle, *rip off, renege, dodge, *weasel out of.

welt n. ridge, wale, weal, mark, swelling.

welter n. turmoil, turbulence, confusion, tossing about, commotion, hubbub, disturbance, tumult, uproar, bedlam, to-do.

wench n. girl, young woman, young lady, maiden, lass.

wend v. go on one's way, make one's way, go, proceed, journey, travel, progress.

wet v. dampen, moisturize, water, drench, soak, sprinkle, wash, rinse, hose down, humidify, irrigate, submerge. ANT. *dry, dehydrate, desiccate.*

wet a. moist, damp, watery, liquefied, drenched, soaked, waterlogged, soggy, sodden, dripping, humid, clammy, dank, rainy, foggy. ANT. *dry*, **bone-dry, dehydrated*.

wet blanket *n.* killjoy, spoilsport, poor sport, *drag, *gloomy Gus, *pain in the ass, *drip, *grinch, *prophet of doom. ANT. *good sport, life of the party.*

wetland *n.* marsh, swamp, everglades, fen, quagmire.

wetness *n.* moisture, dampness, liquid, water, humidity, clamminess, mist, fog, rain. ANT. *dryness, aridity.*

whack *v.* strike, slap, hit, smack, punch, slug, *bop, belt, wallop, bash, rap, cuff, crack.

whale *n.* cetacean, leviathan, aquatic mammal, humpback whale, blue whale, finback, sperm whale, beluga, rorqual, gray whale.

WORD FIND
air hole: blowhole, spiracle
beaching of: stranding
biblical survivor of ingestion: Jonah
bone or tooth carvings: scrimshaw
carcass: kreng
comblike strainer in the mouth of some breeds: baleen
cut blubber off from: flense
diving: sounding
fat: blubber
fatty substance used in candles, ointments: spermaceti
female: cow
fictional hunter: Ahab
fin: dorsal fin
fins, tail: flukes
horned: narwhal
hunter's whale: right whale
killer whale: orca
leaping out of the water: breaching
male: bull
perfumes, waxy substance used in: ambergris
prehistoric: zeuglodon
school: pod, gam
slapping tail down hard on surface: lobtailing
sound location: sonar
study of: cetology
toothed whales, order of: odontoceti
toothless whales that feed on plankton: baleen whale, mysticeti
young: calf

whale *v.* whale on, beat, whip, pound, whack, thrash.

whammy *n. Sl.* jinx, evil eye, curse, spell, hex.

wharf *n.* dock, pier, marina, slip, landing, quay, berth, mooring, jetty.

whatchamacallit *n.* *thingamajig, *thingamabob, *doohickey, gadget, contraption, *din-

gus, *doodad, *gidget, *gizmo, *jigger, *whangdoodle, *whatsit, widget.

wheedle *v.* wangle, cajole, persuade, coax, inveigle, influence, flatter, charm, *charm the sox off of.

wheel *n.* tire, caster, roller.

wheel *v.* roll, revolve, rotate, spin, turn, trundle, whirl, twirl, pivot, swivel, gyrate, pirouette, reel.

wheeze *v.* rasp, gasp, whistle, puff, huff and puff, have an asthmatic attack.

whet *v.* **1.** SHARPEN hone, edge, grind, file, rasp, strop. **2.** STIMULATE make keen, arouse, excite, kindle, stir, awaken, *jumpstart, pique. ANT. **1.** *blunt, dull.* **2.** *dampen, inhibit.*

whiff *n.* **1.** PUFF OF AIR wind, gust, breath, breeze, waft. **2.** SMELL scent, aroma, odor, trace, hint, suspicion.

whim *n.* caprice, impulse, passing fancy, notion, crotchet, idea, *brainstorm.

whimper *v.* cry, sob, whine, snivel, *choke back tears, have a hitch in one's voice, moan, sniffle.

whimsical *a.* fanciful, odd, out of the ordinary, weird, peculiar, quaint, fantastic, unusual, capricious, amusing, playful.

whimsy *n.* SEE WHIM

whine *n.* pule, whimper, mewl, cry, sob, snivel, moan, complaint.

whine *v.* pule, whimper, mewl, cry, sob, snivel, moan, complain, fret, *bellyache, fuss.

whinny *v.* neigh.

whip *n.* bullwhip, horsewhip, *blacksnake, lash, switch, scourge, rawhide, quirt, thong, crop, cat-o'-nine-tails.

whip *v.* **1.** LASH flog, flagellate, flail, flay, horsewhip, hit, beat, scourge, whale, *take the strap to, *tan one's hide, *whallop, cane, spank, punish. **2.** JERK whip out, yank, pull out, whisk, snatch, grab. **3.** DEFEAT SOUNDLY *lick, beat, *cream, *skunk, *blow away, trounce, clobber, rout, *shellac, overpower, *get the better of, vanquish. **4.** BEAT mix, stir, whisk. **5.** AGITATE stir up, spark, kindle, spur, incite, instigate, foment, prompt.

whippersnapper *n.* upstart.

whipping *n.* thrashing, flogging, flagellation, horsewhipping, *whalloping, beating, spanking, pounding, punishment.

whipping boy *n.* *fall guy. SEE SCAPEGOAT

whip up *v.* SEE WHIP

whir *n.* buzz, hum, birr, vibration.

whirl *v.* spin, twirl, wheel, gyrate, reel, turn, rotate, revolve, swirl, pivot, pirouette.

whirlpool *n.* maelstrom, vortex, eddy, swirl,

whirl.

whirlwind n. tornado, cyclone, twister, hurricane, typhoon, *blow.

whisk v. **1.** BRUSH sweep, flick. **2.** BEAT whip. **3.** MOVE QUICKLY whip, dart, hurry, rush, hasten.

whiskers n. bristles, beard, sideburns, *five o'clock shadow, stubble, hair. SEE BEARD, MUSTACHE

whiskey n. liquor, alcohol, *hard stuff, spirits, *firewater, drink, booze, *moonshine, *rotgut, scotch, rye, bourbon, *sauce, *tarantula juice. "The devil'spring water." — Anon.

whisper n. **1.** HUSHED VOICE murmur, mutter, undertone, soft voice, mumble, sigh, confidential tone, conspiratorial tone. **2.** SECRET rumor, gossip, confidence, insinuation. **3.** SOFT NOISE sigh, sough, breath. ANT. 1. roar, bellow, shout.

whisper v. murmur, mutter, speak in an undertone, speak softly, mumble, speak confidentially, speak in a conspiratorial tone, breathe, intimate, confide. ANT. roar, bellow, shout.

whistle v. pipe, flute, trill, toot, blow.

whit n. bit, jot, iota, speck, grain, pinch, mite, atom, particle.

white a. **1.** LIGHT-COLORED alabaster, argent, blond, bone, chalk, columbine, dove, eggshell, ivory, milk, oyster, pearl, platinum, snow, snowy, hoary, albino. **2.** PALE blanched, bleached, wan, pallid, sickly, bloodless. **3.** CAUCASIAN light-skinned, fair. ANT. 1. black, dark, ebony. 2. rosy, ruddy, red.

whiten v. bleach, blanch, fade.

whitewash v. gloss over, cover up, smooth over, conceal, tone down, soft-pedal, palliate.

whittle v. carve, cut, shave, pare, slash, shape, sculpt, reduce, decrease.

whiz n. **1.** WHISTLE buzz, hum, whir, drone, hiss. **2.** Sl. EXPERT wizard, crackerjack, master, prodigy, ace, virtuoso, pro, *whiz kid, genius.

whiz v. buzz, hiss, hum, whir, drone.

whole n. total, sum total, aggregate, all, entirety.

whole a. complete, total, entire, full, undivided, intact, uncut, unbroken, perfect, in one piece. ANT. partial, incomplete, broken.

wholehearted a. earnest, all-out, sincere, enthusiastic, eager, complete, emphatic, dedicated, unqualified, fervent, ardent, hearty. ANT. halfhearted, lukewarm, reserved.

wholesale a. extensive, sweeping, massive, broad, comprehensive, far-reaching, large-scale, general. ANT. limited, small-scale.

wholesome a. healthful, healthy, good for you,

beneficial, helpful, hygienic, nutritious, nourishing, virtuous, moral, clean-cut, decent. ANT. unhealthy, harmful, bad for you.

wholly adv. totally, completely, entirely, utterly, fully, thoroughly. ANT. partially.

whoop n. yell, shout, cry, *holler, scream, shriek, hurrah, cheer, *yahoo, hoot.

whoop v. yell, shout, cry, *holler, scream, shriek, hurrah, cheer, *yahoo, hoot.

whopper n. **1.** GIANT *mother of all, colossus, titan, monster, Goliath, mammoth, behemoth, leviathan, *grandaddy of them all, jumbo. **2.** BIG LIE tall tale, *fish story, stretching of the truth. ANT. 1. midget, dwarf, shrimp.

whopping a. great, huge, large, gigantic, gargantuan, massive, colossal, extraordinary, enormous, prodigious, immense. ANT. tiny, insignificant, little.

whore n. prostitute, lady of the evening, *call girl, *streetwalker, *hooker, *working girl, woman of ill repute, tramp, hussy, slut, fille de joie, strumpet, adventuress, courtesan, escort, *floozy. "Social worker on the night shift." — Anon. SEE PROSTITUTE

whorl n. spiral, coil, convolution, volution.

wicked a. **1.** EVIL bad, immoral, depraved, sinful, villainous, fiendish, shameless, rotten, nasty, iniquitous, nefarious, blackhearted, unprincipled, low, lawless, criminal. **2.** NAUGHTY mischievous, devilish, rascally, impish, roguish, misbehaving, prankish. **3.** SEVERE bad, awful, nasty, fierce, intense, acute, harsh, horrible. ANT. 1. good, moral, virtuous. 2. well-behaved, well-mannered. 3. mild, gentle, easy, slight

wide a. **1.** BROAD roomy, extensive, ample, spread-out, spacious, expansive, capacious, commodious, vast. **2.** SWEEPING broad, comprehensive, all-inclusive, general, large. **3.** OPEN outstretched, extended. **4.** OFF TARGET off, off course, inaccurate. ANT. 1. narrow, cramped, restricted. 2. limited, specific. 3. closed, folded. 4. on target, accurate.

wide-awake a. alert, watchful, sharp, *on one's toes, *on the ball, vigilant, *bright-eyed and bushy-tailed, wary, wide-eyed, *saucer-eyed. ANT. asleep, sleepy, unobservant.

wide-eyed a. **1.** NAIVE inexperienced, innocent, green, childlike, unschooled, unsophisticated, *born yesterday. **2.** SURPRISED shocked, astonished, saucer-eyed, agog. ANT. 1. jaded, blasé, *ho-hum. 2. bored.

widen v. broaden, expand, extend, spread, enlarge, swell, distend, increase. ANT. narrow, restrict, taper.

widespread *a.* all over, far-reaching, far-flung, pervasive, extensive, nationwide, worldwide, universal, rife, rampant, common, prevalent, epidemic, pandemic. ANT. *confined, local, limited, rare.*

widget *n.* gadget, *gizmo, device, contraption, *thingamajig, *doohickey, *whatsit, *thingamabob, *whatchamacallit, *doodad.

widow *n.* widower, surviving spouse, dowager.

width *n.* breadth, wideness, broadness, girth, span, thickness, diameter, spread, extent.

wield *v.* **1.** HANDLE use, ply, manipulate, brandish, swing, hold. **2.** EXERCISE employ, control, command, hold, exert.

wife *n.* spouse, mate, bride, partner, companion, *better half, consort, squaw, soul mate. "A crown to her husband." — Bible. "A former sweetheart." — Henry Louis Mencken.

wig *n.* hairpiece, toupee, *rug, *fall, peruke, periwig.

wiggle *n.* jiggle, wriggle, wag, waggle, squirm, worming, writhing, shake, jerk, twitch, quiver.

wiggle *v.* jiggle, wriggle, wag, waggle, squirm, worm, writhe, shake, jerk, twitch, quiver.

wild *a.* **1.** NATURAL undomesticated, uncultivated, organic, untamed, feral, native, unbroken, uncivilized, primitive, primeval, primordial, untouched, pristine, uninhabited, overgrown, wooded, desert, godforsaken. **2.** SAVAGE barbarous, rough, beastly, brutish, primitive, ignorant, uncivilized. **3.** UNRESTRAINED, UNCONTROLLABLE out of control, unmanageable, intractable, rebellious, unruly, rough, rowdy, crazy, undisciplined, reckless, impulsive, lawless. **4.** MORALLY LOOSE unbridled, unrestrained, dissolute, profligate, wanton, debauched, immoral, orgiastic. **5.** STORMY rough, turbulent, tempestuous, turbulent, violent, explosive, gusting, windy, disturbed, wind-whipped. **6.** EXCITED frantic, frenzied, maniacal, hysterical, enthusiastic, eager. **7.** DISORDERED in disarray, confused, tangled, messy, tousled, unkempt. ANT. *1. unnatural, domesticated, tame, manmade, civilized, urbanized. 2. civilized, refined, polished. 3. restrained, polite, well-behaved. 4. moral, prudish, puritanical. 5. calm, mild, gentle, quiet. 6. calm, reserved, low-key. 7. neat, orderly.*

wilderness *n.* wilds, *howling wilderness, woods, forest, jungle, uncultivated area, wasteland, desert, badland, backcountry, outback.

wildlife *n.* animals, fauna, beasts, creatures, game.

wile *n.* artifice, artfulness, trick, trickery, cunning, stratagem, ruse, craftiness, machination, deception, fraud, ploy.

will *n.* **1.** POWER OF CHOICE choice, decision, desire, want, wish, determination, conviction, volition, prerogative, intention, mind, preference, discretion, command, decree. **2.** RESOLVE willpower, determination, single-mindedness, commitment. **3.** DOCUMENT DISPOSING OF WEALTH AFTER DEATH bequest, legacy, testament, last will and testament, dispensation.

will *v.* desire, wish, choose, want, determine, demand, command, direct.

willful *a.* **1.** DELIBERATE intentional, intended, planned, purposeful, volitional, premeditated, willing, conscious. **2.** SELF-WILLED stubborn, obstinate, headstrong, bullheaded, pigheaded, mulish, intractable, uncompromising, inflexible. ANT. *1. involuntary, unintentional, accidental. 2. flexible, compromising, acquiescent.*

willing *a.* agreeable, unreluctant, inclined, enthusiastic, eager, accommodating, obliging, ready, amenable, in favor, consenting, disposed, game. ANT. *unwilling, disinclined, averse.*

willowy *a.* slender, gracefully slender, slim, svelte, thin, skinny, twiggy, lithe, lissome, pliant, supple, limber. ANT. *obese, fat, inflexible.*

willpower *n.* self-control, will, firmness, drive, determination, resolve, strength, backbone, iron will, discipline, grit. ANT. *weakness, lack of control.*

wilt *v.* droop, wither, slump, slouch, sag, sink, shrivel, flag, wane, diminish, ebb, weaken, die.

WILY *a.* [WI lee] sly, crafty. *The wily coyote always manages to survive.* SYN. sly, crafty, cunning, tricky, sharp, designing, shrewd, *cagey, artful, sneaky, foxy, underhanded, astute, slippery, slick. ANT. *stupid, dull, dumb.*

win *n.* victory, triumph, conquest, success, sweep, gold medal, achievement, accomplishment, coup. ANT. *loss, defeat.*

win *v.* **1.** BE VICTORIOUS defeat, best, beat, triumph, succeed, vanquish, *take home the gold, sweep, clinch, prevail, come in first, *leave competitors swirling in one's wake, carry the day. **2.** ACHIEVE accomplish, gain, obtain, attain, get, earn. ANT. *1. lose, be defeated, fail, *choke. 2. fail.*

wince v. flinch, cringe, blink, recoil, draw back, shrink, cower, grimace, duck, quail, brace oneself.

wind n. **1.** BREEZE gust, draft, breath, waft, zephyr, air current, puff, blast, blow, gale, tempest, whirlwind, cyclone, tornado.

WORD FIND

aircraft hazard: windshear

Asian wind accompanied by heavy rain: monsoon

breeze that ripples water's surface: cat's paw

debris knocked down by: windfall

dry, desert wind of west coast of Africa: harmattan

dry: foehn

force source: Coriolis force

god of: Aeolus

Hawaii, light, consistent wind of: trade wind

high-speed, high-altitude wind: jet stream

hot wind of the Asiatic and African deserts: simoon

indicator, direction: anemoscope

indicator: sock, weather vane

measuring device: anemometer

Mediterranean, cold, northerly: mistral

Mexican, hurricane-borne wind: cordonazo

mountain, warm and dry wind descending leeward side of: chinook

North African: sirocco

pertaining to: eolian

recurring winds over the Mediterranean: etecians

scale: Beaufort

shifting: variable, veering, backing

sound: sough, moan, howl, whistle

squall of North American southwest coast: chubasco

sudden burst, accompanied by rain: squall

windless sea region: doldrums

2. BREATH air, expiration, inhalation, respiration. **3.** INFORMATION scent, smell, news, inkling, report, rumor. **4.** NONSENSE *hot air, pomposity, idle talk, bluster, empty talk, claptrap, balderdash.

wind v. turn, bend, coil, curl, crook, roll, twine, twist, furl, screw, corkscrew, twirl, reel, crank, meander, snake.

windbag n. *blowhard, *chatterbox, *motor-mouth, *big-mouth.

windfall n. fortune, stroke of luck, jackpot, godsend, manna from heaven, boon, lucky strike.

window n. opening, glass, portal, casement, dormer, bay window, oriel, skylight, roundel, deadlight.

windy a. blustery, gusting, breezy, tempestuous, stormy, blowing, windswept, wind-whipped, drafty. ANT. *still, calm, becalmed.*

wine n. fermented grape juice, alcohol, red wine, white wine, champagne, vintage, port, muscatel, brandy, Chablis, Chianti, Chardonnay, Zinfandel. "The blood of grapes." — Bible. "Bottled poetry." — Robert Louis Stevenson. "[That which] makes man mistake words for thoughts." — Samuel Johnson. "That ancient social lubricant." — Anon.

WORD FIND

addicted to: vinous

aftertaste: finish

American red grape: Catawba

California wine region: Napa Valley

California winery: Gallo, Inglenook

city of, French: Bordeaux

deposit: lees, dregs

distilled from: cognac, brandy

driest of champagnes: brut

flavor, crisp: flinty

flavor, dull: flat

flavor, having delicate: finesse

flavor intensity: body

flavor, lively and acidic: piquant

flavor, multiple: complex

flavor, poor: flabby

flavor, sharp: tart

flavor, soft and full: mellow

flavor that is rough: coarse

fragrance: bouquet

French red: Beaujolais, Cabernet Sauvignon, claret

French region: Burgundy

French white: Chablis

German white: Moselle, Rhine

god: Bacchus

inventor of champagne: Dom Perignon

Italian red: Bardolino, Barolo, Chianti, Tuscany

Italian white: Soave

lover: oenophilist

merchant: vintner

new: must

pink: rosé, blush

Portuguese: Madeira, port

pour: decant

pucker factor in red wine: astringency

rice wine: sake

shop: bistro, bodega

Spanish wine and brandy: sherry

steward or waiter: sommelier

storage: cellar

sweeten: mull

sweet, not: dry
vineyard, stone-walled: clos
white wine flavored with herbs: vermouth
year of grape's harvest: vintage

wing *n.* annex, addition, unit, arm, section, extension, part, flank, branch.

wing *v.* fly, soar, glide, zoom, hurry, speed.

wing it *v. Sl.* improvise, ad lib.

wink *v.* blink, bat an eyelid, nictitate.

winner *n.* victor, champion, *champ, medalist, gold medalist, *number one, titleholder, *top dog, conqueror, vanquisher. ANT. *loser, failure, *also-ran.*

winning *a.* charming, attractive, delightful, pleasing, enchanting, bewitching, captivating, disarming, charismatic, engaging, sweet, winsome. ANT. *repulsive, nasty, disgusting.*

winnow *v.* sift, separate, extract, cull, divide the good from the bad, screen, glean, weed out, differentiate, separate the wheat from the chaff.

wino *n. Sl.* drunk, drunkard, alcoholic.

winsome *a.* charming, sweet, attractive, nice, engaging, winning, delightful, pleasing, disarming, likable, lovable. ANT. *repellent, repulsive, disgusting.*

winter *n.* season, cold season, snow season. "A climatic gulag." — Anon. "Trees stooping under burdens of snow, windows filligreed with frost, shadows of drifting hummocks turning blue-cold as northerners mummify themselves in coats and scarves." — Henry Clayborne.

WORD FIND
of or like: hiemal, brumal, hibernal
SEE SNOW

wintry *a.* hiemal, hibernal, brumal, cold, frigid, bone-chilling, raw, biting, bitter, snowy, frost-patterned, filigreed with frost, stark, pristine, frozen, icy. ANT. *summery, hot, warm.*

wipe *v.* rub, brush, wash, sponge, clean, dust, towel, dry, remove, swab, polish.

wipeout *n. Sl.* fall, crash, collapse, spill, dive, tumble, nose-dive.

wipe out *v.* destroy, eradicate, annihilate, obliterate, exterminate, demolish, get rid of, kill, slaughter, abolish, decimate.

wiry *a.* lean, strong, tough, sinewy, muscular, strapping, athletic, agile, fit, trim, in shape, hardened. ANT. *fat, obese, out of shape, flabby.*

wisdom *n.* knowledge, experience, erudition, good judgment, insight, sagacity, common sense, *horse sense, intelligence, smarts, *brains, discernment, acumen, savvy, en-
lightenment, foresight. "A special knowledge in excess of all that is known." — Ambros Bierce. "The soul's natural food." — Jacob Anatoli. "[That which] comes by suffering." — Aeschylus. ANT. *ignorance, inexperience, stupidity, foolishness.*

wise *v.* **1.** KNOWLEDGEABLE experienced, erudite, prudent, judicious, insightful, sagacious, sage, informed, learned, sensible, intelligent, smart, *brainy, shrewd, astute, discerning, sharp, savvy, enlightened, understanding. **2.** *Sl.* FRESH smart-mouthed, impudent, *smartalecky, insolent, impertinent, *sassy, disrespectful, flippant, flip. ANT. *1. ignorant, inexperienced, stupid, uninformed, foolish. 2. respectful, polite, deferential.*

wiseacre *n.* *wise guy, *wiseass, *smart-ass, *smartaleck, know-it-all, *wisenheimer.

wisecrack *n.* joke, dig, gibe, flippant remark, quip, retort.

wise guy *n. Sl.* SEE WISEACRE

wish *n.* desire, want, pleasure, aspiration, hope, prayer, will, hunger, thirst, longing, yen.

wish *v.* desire, want, need, aspire, set one's heart on, fancy, hope for, pray for, hunger, thirst, crave, hanker, request, ask, order.

wishful *a.* desirous, longful, hopeful, aspiring, yearning, hankering, wistful, impractical, unrealistic, daydreaming.

wishy-washy *a.* indecisive, irresolute, undecided, blowing hot and cold, equivocating, vacillating, feeble, weak, spineless. ANT. *resolute, decisive, decided.*

wisp *n.* strand, shred, strip, trace, hint.

wispy *a.* slight, slender, thin, delicate, frail.

WISTFUL *a.* [WIST ful] longing sadly or with a troubled mind. *He looked back wistfully at his childhood.* SYN. longing, yearning, pining, desirous, wishful, heartsick, pensive, nostalgic, daydreaming, reflective, melancholy, forlorn, introspective.

wit *n.* **1.** INTELLECTUAL POWERS intelligence, reason, *brains, *brain power, intellect, sense, common sense, sagacity, understanding, judgment, acumen, perception, wisdom, comprehension. **2.** CLEVERNESS sense of humor, humor, drollery, satire, irony, repartee, banter, bon mot, jest, wordplay, wisecrack, pun, joke, witticism. "Educated insolence." — Aristotle. "The salt of conversation." — William Hazlitt. **3.** CLEVER HUMORIST comedian, satirist, jokester, comic, *wise guy, wiseacre, quipster, *cutup. ANT. *1. stupidity, dullness, slowness.*

witch *n.* sorceress, enchantress, magician, practitioner of the black arts, *spellcaster, hex, warlock, crone, hag, she-devil, ogress.

witchcraft n. sorcery, black magic, black arts, spellcasting, wizardry, magic, enchantment, diabolism, Satanism, necromancy, voodoo.

witch doctor n. shaman, medicine man.

withdraw v. **1.** TAKE BACK take out, remove, draw, extract. **2.** MOVE BACK retreat, shrink, recede, retire, leave, pull out, quit, evacuate. **3.** RETRACT recall, recant, take back, back down, do an about-face, backpedal, rescind. **4.** ISOLATE ONESELF *go into one's shell.

withdrawal n. **1.** REMOVAL extraction, retreat, shrinking, retirement, leaving, leave, exit, retraction, disavowal. **2.** CRAVING distress, longing, hunger.

withdrawn a. introverted, reserved, shy, bashful, reticent, introspective, retiring, aloof, unfriendly, distant, remote, reclusive, solitary. ANT. extroverted, outgoing, friendly, sociable.

wither v. shrivel, wilt, droop, dry up, decay, waste away, fade, wizen, shrink.

withhold v. **1.** HOLD BACK keep, detain, reserve, deduct, retain, restrain. **2.** REFUSE refrain. **3.** HIDE conceal, deny, cover up, keep from, keep secret.

withstand v. take, tolerate, bear, put up with, endure, stand up to, weather, brave, face, cope, *ride out. ANT. *cave in, collapse, give in.

witless a. foolish, nonsensical, stupid, mindless, dumb, imbecilic, moronic, idiotic, brainless, *birdbrained, *dumb as a post. ANT. intelligent, smart, *brainy.

witness n. **1.** EYEWITNESS observer, onlooker, bystander, spectator, corroborating witness. **2.** ATTESTING testimony, evidence, attestation, proof, corroboration.

witness v. **1.** SEE observe, watch, view, notice, behold. **2.** TESTIFY provide testimony, give evidence, attest, prove, corroborate, confirm, certify, verify.

witticism n. clever remark, witty remark, bon mot, quip, wisecrack, crack, *one-liner, joke, pun, retort, riposte.

witty a. clever, sharp, funny, comical, humorous, *saber-witted, *having a razor wit, droll, quick-witted, amusing, whimsical, entertaining, quick, *wise, sarcastic.

wizard n. **1.** CONJURER magician, sorcerer, witch, warlock, necromancer, Merlin, enchanter, diviner, practitioner of the black arts. **2.** *ACE *crackerjack, genius, prodigy, *whiz, *whiz kid, virtuoso, master.

wizardry n. **1.** MAGIC conjuring, sorcery, witchcraft, necromancy, black art, diabolism, Satanism. **2.** CLEVERNESS genius, magic.

wizened a. withered, dried up, shriveled, wilted, wrinkled, brown, shrunken, dry, dehydrated, wasted.

wobble v. shake, tremble, totter, teeter, seesaw, stagger, waggle, rock, oscillate, sway, reel, move unsteadily.

woe n. **1.** SORROW grief, anguish, sadness, misery, suffering, wretchedness, distress, pain, heartache, unhappiness, depression, melancholy. **2.** TROUBLE trial, tribulation, affliction, adversity, blow, burden, hardship, ordeal, misfortune. ANT. 1. happiness, joy, glee. 2. fortune, blessing.

woebegone a. sad, depressed, melancholy, miserable, mournful, grieving, unhappy, woeful, downhearted, heartbroken, wretched, desolate, disconsolate. ANT. happy, joyful, gleeful.

woeful a. SEE WOEBEGONE

wolfish a. predatory, carnivorous, rapacious, beastly, vicious, bloodthirsty, fierce, ferocious.

woman n. lady, female, girl, gal, lass, *broad, maid, maiden, *colleen, damsel, matron, miss, Ms., matriarch, mother. "A ministering angel." — Walter Scott. "A creature between man and the angels." — Honore de Balzac. "[One who] has to be twice as good as a man to go half as far." — Fannie Hurst.

womanizer n. Don Juan, Casanova, *skirt-chaser, lecher, *wolf, *ladies' man, stud, playboy, *make-out artist, Lothario, heartbreaker.

womanly a. womanish, feminine, matronly, ladylike, motherly, sisterly, soft, gentle, tender. ANT. manly, male.

wonder n. **1.** ASTONISHMENT amazement, wonderment, awe, fascination, enchantment, surprise. "The root of knowledge." — Abraham Heschel. "The seed of our science." — Ralph Waldo Emerson. **2.** MARVEL miracle, phenomenon, spectacle, curiosity, rarity, sight, *mind-blower, *mind-boggler, oddity, freak occurrence, freak of nature.

wonder v. **1.** MARVEL be awestruck, be fascinated, gawk, gape, stare saucer-eyed, disbelieve one's eyes, be amazed, be astonished, be stunned. **2.** TO BE CURIOUS question, ponder, think about, ponder, speculate, doubt, deliberate, puzzle over, meditate.

wonderful a. **1.** MARVELOUS amazing, astonishing, awesome, fascinating, unbelievable, miraculous, spectacular, curious, odd, *freaky.

2. EXCELLENT great, extraordinary, terrific, fantastic, fabulous, superb, sensational, first-rate, out of the ordinary, *out of this world. ANT. 1. *ho-hum, common, ordinary. 2. terrible, awful, lousy.

wonderment n. amazement, astonishment, fascination, curiosity, wonder, awe, surprise; spectacle, sensation, sight, rarity, marvel, *mind-blower, *mind-boggler.

woo v. court, seek, coax, pursue, persuade, cajole, urge, *curry favor, *butter up.

wood n. lumber, timber, board, plank, beam, firewood, kindling, slat.

woodcutter n. lumberjack, logger, sawyer.

wooden a. stiff, rigid, awkward, graceless, formal, tense, expressionless, blank, stony, dull, lifeless. ANT. loose, limber, relaxed, informal, expressive.

woodland n. woods, forest, timberland, bush, grove, thicket, wilderness, *howling wilderness. SEE FOREST, JUNGLE, TREE

woods n. SEE WOODLAND

woolgathering n. absentmindedness, daydreaming, dreaming, reverie, *castle-building, abstraction, preoccupation.

woozy a. Sl. dizzy, dazed, muddled, befuddled, unsteady, reeling, unclear, punch-drunk, *seeing stars. SEE DRUNK

word n. **1.** TERM noun, verb, adjective, pronoun, expression, name, lexeme, morpheme. "Words are loaded pistols." —Jean-Paul Sartre. "The soul's ambassadors." —James Howell. "The dress of thoughts; which should no more be presented in rags, tatters, and dirt, than your person should." —Lord Chesterfield.

WORD FIND

acceptable word used in place of socially unacceptable one: euphemism

antiquated word: archaism

arrangement, construction of words and sentences: syntax

baby words: lallation

backwards, reads the same: palindrome

book: lexicon, dictionary, thesaurus

characterizing: epithet

coiner: neologist

combining words or word parts to form new word: agglutination

confusion, transposition of letters: dyslexia

contradictory juxtaposition of: oxymoron

difficult to pronounce correctly: jawbreaker

disgust for certain words: logomasia

exact or appropriate word: mot juste

incorrect use of word confused with another: catachresis, malapropism

incorrect word that sounds like another: catchfool

individual word stock: ideolect

informal: colloquial, colloquialism

invention of new word: coinage

figurative: metaphor, simile, trope

foreign word sound English, make: Anglicize

forgotten word, obsession to remember: loganamnosis

humorous transposition of word sounds, such as "Hoobert Heever" for "Herbert Hoover": spoonerism

initials, word constructed of: acronym

local: localism

loss for words, at a: aporia

new: neologism

nonstandard use: barbarism, corruption

opposite in meaning: antonym

origin of: etymology

pronounce clearly: enunciate

pronunciation, poor: cacology

recall word on tip of one's tongue, inability to: lethologica

restate in different words: paraphrase

reversal of standard meaning, such as "bad" meaning "good": melioration

showing off one's knowledge of words: pedantry

similar in meaning: synonym

sounding like the thing it names: onomatopoeia

sounding the same but having different meanings: homonym, homophone

study of meanings: semantics

wrong title, wrong name: misnomer

2. NEWS report, communication, announcement, communique, dispatch, bulletin, intelligence, information. **3.** TALK chat, meeting, consultation, conversation, discussion. **4.** REMARK statement, comment. **5.** PROMISE pledge, solemn word, oath, word of honor, vow, assurance, guarantee.

word v. put into words, frame, phrase, rephrase, paraphrase.

wording n. phrasing, phraseology, language, syntax, terminology, choice of words, style.

wordy a. verbose, long-winded, windy, prolix, redundant, rambling, loquacious, garrulous, voluble, digressive, tautological. ANT. succinct, concise, to the point, terse.

work n. **1.** LABOR exertion, toil, effort, struggle, drudgery, *daily grind, *elbow grease, muscle, sweat, slavery, pains. **2.** JOB employment, occupation, *daily grind, livelihood, line, trade, profesion, vocation, business, calling. "A remedy against all ills." — Charles Baudelaire. "Paid struggle." — Max Gralnik. "The refuge of people who have nothing better to do." — Oscar Wilde. **3.** CHORE task, duty, assignment, charge, burden, responsibility. ANT. *idleness, sloth, leisure, play, relaxation.*

work *v.* **1.** LABOR exert, toil, put in effort, struggle, drudge, *apply elbow grease, *put muscle into it, sweat, slave, take pains, *bust one's hump, *bust one's balls, *break one's back, strain, *plug away, *keep one's nose to the grindstone, *burn the midnight oil, *work one's fingers to the bone, be employed, do business, earn one's living, *moonlight. **2.** OPERATE run, function, perform, tick, go. **3.** SUCCEED be effective, *fly, effect, fulfill, bring about, produce, create. **4.** HANDLE maneuver, run, use, drive. **5.** SHAPE manipulate, knead, mold. ANT. *1. relax, recreate, play, take it easy.*

workable *a.* doable, practical, practicable, feasible, viable, possible. ANT. *unworkable, impractical.*

worker *n.* employee, laborer, blue-collar worker, white-collar worker, hand, workman, wage earner, *working stiff, *nine-to-fiver, slave, *temp. "The wealth of a country." — Theodor Herzl. "Soldiers with different weapons but the same courage." — Winston Churchill.

workmanlike *a.* skilled, well-done, well-crafted, professional, meticulous, expert, competent, thorough. ANT. *incompetent, slack, amateurish.*

workmanship *n.* craftsmanship, skill, artistry, expertise, proficiency, handiwork, technique, style, mastery.

world *n.* **1.** EARTH planet, globe, Gaea, sphere, biosphere, terra, terra firma, orb, ocean world, heavenly body. "A great, wandering ark." — Anon. "A rip in the ocean of the universe." — Anon. "A small parenthesis in eternity." — Thomas Browne. "God's epistle to mankind — his thoughts are flashing upon us from every direction." — Plato. "The truth of the existence of God." — William Hocking. **2.** ALL CREATION universe, cosmos, macrocosm, nature. **3.** HUMANKIND humanity, human community, human race, mankind, civilization, society, people, men and women, everybody. "This great stage of fools." — Shakespeare. "A comedy to those who think, a tragedy to those who feel." — Horace Walpole. **4.** REALM domain, sphere, area, province, kingdom, field, group.

worldly *a.* **1.** EARTHLY terrestrial, mundane, material, human, fleshly, physical. **2.** SOPHISTICATED experienced, worldly-wise, knowing, learned, urbane, cosmopolitan, *wise in the ways of the world. ANT. *1. spiritual, heavenly, divine, godly. 2. inexperienced, unsophisticated, naive.*

worldly-wise *a.* SEE WORLDLY

worldwide *a.* global, international, multinational, universal, general, from the four corners of the earth, extensive, pandemic. ANT. *local, localized, limited, domestic.*

worn *a.* **1.** THREADBARE worn out, frayed, ragged, tattered, weathered, deteriorated, abraded, *shot. **2.** EXHAUSTED weary, tired, burned out, haggard, drained, *wrung out, *the worse for wear, drained. ANT. *1. new, fresh. 2. fresh, refreshed.*

worrisome *a.* troublesome, anxiety-provoking, disturbing, distressing, disquieting, unnerving. ANT. *reassuring, calming, relaxing.*

worried *a.* anxious, distressed, troubled, disturbed, apprehensive, uneasy, having misgivings, uncertain, concerned, sick with dread, *on pins and needles. ANT. *at peace, relaxed, reassured.*

worry *n.* anxiety, distress, troubled mind, disturbance, apprehension, uneasiness, misgiving, uncertainty, concern, disquiet, trepidation, care. "Interest paid on trouble before it becomes due." — William Inge. ANT. *peace of mind, reassurance, tranquility.*

worry *v.* distress, trouble, disturb, make apprehensive, make uneasy, concern, disquiet, fill with trepidation, gnaw at, perturb, fill with dread. ANT. *calm, soothe, reassure.*

worsen *v.* deteriorate, degenerate, take a turn for the worse, slip, decay, decline, lapse, *go downhill, *hit the skids, diminish. ANT. *improve, get better.*

worship *n.* homage, reverence, devotion, veneration, honoring, idolization, adoration, love, admiration, glorification, genuflection, exaltation, church service, rite. "Climbing the altar stairs to God." — Dwight Bradley.

worship *v.* pay homage, revere, show devotion, venerate, honor, idolize, adore, love, admire, glorify, look up to, put on a pedestal, exalt, adulate. ANT. *disdain, despise, disparage.*

worth *n.* **1.** VALUE merit, benefit, greatness, worthiness, importance, weight, desirability. **2.** AMOUNT quantity, price, cost, expense, appraisal, valuation, estimation. **3.** WEALTH riches, assets, possessions, holdings.

worthless *a.* valueless, useless, good-for-nothing, unproductive, unprofitable, profitless, vain, futile, impotent, ineffective, empty, *not worth the powder to blow it to hell, *not worth beans, *not worth a bucket of warm spit. ANT. *valuable, worthwhile, profitable, effective.*

worthwhile *a.* valuable, useful, profitable, lucrative, remunerative, gainful, beneficial, rewarding, worthy, worth the trouble, productive. ANT. *worthless, waste of time, unproductive.*

worthy *a.* meriting, deserving, meritorious, good enough, praiseworthy, creditable, estimable, worthwhile, commendable, exemplary, excellent, virtuous. ANT. *unworthy, worthless, undeserving.*

wound *n.* **1.** INJURY trauma, cut, laceration, lesion, gash, tear, scrape, scratch, abrasion, contusion, bruise, *black-and-blue mark, hurt, sore, tender area, bump. **2.** HURT FEELINGS offense, insult, anguish, pain, grief, heartache, blow to one's self-esteem.

wound *v.* **1.** INJURE cut, lacerate, gash, rip open, scrape, scratch, stick, stab, abrade, bruise, bump, traumatize. **2.** HURT ONE'S FEELINGS offend, insult, grieve, *touch a nerve, *break one's heart, affront, *cut to the quick, traumatize, mortify.

wow *v. Sl.* *bring an audience to their feet, *bowl over, fill with awe, stagger, electrify, make one's jaw drop, impress.

wrangle *n.* quarrel, dispute, argument, fight, altercation, tiff, disagreement, row, squabble, clash, spat.

wrangle *v.* quarrel, dispute, argue, fight, altercate, have a tiff, *lock horns, disagree, have a row, clash, *have words, *cross swords.

wrap *n.* covering, shawl, overcoat, jacket, cloak, cape, mantle.

wrap *v.* cover, envelop, package, bind, pack, bundle, giftwrap, swaddle, swathe, shroud, tuck.

wrath *n.* anger, rage, towering rage, spitting rage, fury, temper, passion, *hot blood, indignation, resentment, venom, virulence. ANT. *good humor, pleasure, cheerfulness.*

wreak *v.* inflict, cause, bring, vent, bring down on, unleash, execute.

wreath *n.* band, garland, decoration, festoon, chaplet, laurel, crown.

wreathe *v.* entwine, encircle, coil, twist, festoon.

wreck *n.* wreckage, destruction, devastation, ruin, debris, smashup, crash, accident, derelict, *heap, *junker, *hulk.

wreck *v.* destroy, ruin, tear apart, smash, devastate, demolish, raze, flatten, *total, sabotage, vandalize, *trash, spoil, shatter, break, gut, blow up, level, bulldoze. ANT. *fix, repair, protect.*

wreckage *n.* debris, flotsam and jetsam, rubble, detritus, bits and pieces, fragments, ruins, smoking remains.

wrench *n.* **1.** TOOL spanner, monkey wrench, pliers. SEE TOOL **2.** TWIST jerk, turn, pull, sprain.

wrench *v.* twist, pull, jerk, turn, wring, sprain, strain.

wrest *v.* twist away from, take, jerk, pull, wrestle, extract, wring, grab.

wrestle *v.* grapple, struggle, fight, combat, muscle, strong-arm, tussle, battle, contend, tangle, *lock horns, *put in a half-nelson, *body slam, *put in a headlock, *put in a hammerlock, *give a bear hug, throw, flip, *turk, *deliver a flying dropkick, clinch, pin.

wretch *n.* **1.** *MISERABLE SOUL *poor soul, *poor bastard, martyr, unfortunate, victim, outcast, *loser, *sorry sight. **2.** SCOUNDREL bastard, *SOB, *creep, *jerk, *rat, dog, cur, rogue, criminal, villain.

wretched *a.* **1.** MISERABLE unhappy, depressed, melancholic, sad, brokenhearted, downhearted, forlorn, dejected, disconsolate, *bummed out, pathetic, pitiable. **2.** *LOUSY awful, terrible, miserable, poor, inferior, *rotten, pathetic, bad, inferior, cheap. **3.** CONTEMPTIBLE despicable, *rotten, mean, low, shameless, detestable, beneath contempt. ANT. **1.** *happy, cheerful, joyous.* **2.** *good, superior, superb, excellent.* **3.** *admirable, commendable, good.*

wriggle *v.* wiggle, squirm, jiggle, waggle, worm, twist, writhe.

wring *v.* **1.** TWIST squeeze, press, compress, wrench, choke, throttle, strangle. **2.** EXTORT force, strong-arm, twist one's arm, make, exact, coerce.

wrinkle *n.* **1.** CRINKLE furrow, ridge, crease, crimp, pucker, line, rumple, fold, pleat, crow's foot, laugh line, frown line. **2.** IDEA trick, device, gimmick.

wrinkle *v.* crinkle, furrow, crease, crimp, pucker, line, rumple, fold, pleat, corrugate, scrunch up.

writ *n.* order, legal order, legal document, court order, warrant, injunction, summons, subpoena, command.

write *v.* pen, compose, print, jot, scrawl,

*scratch out, scribble, inscribe, *dash off, set down, draft, type, draw up, record, author, sign, autograph.

writer *n.* scribe, calligrapher, stenographer, author, wordsmith, poet, reporter, journalist, columnist, novelist, freelancer, hack, man of letters, playwright, screenwriter, ghostwriter. "Apprentices in a craft where no one ever becomes a master."—Hemingway. "A frustrated actor who recites his lines in the hidden auditorium of his skull."—Rod Serling.

writhe *v.* twist, contort, squirm, thrash, worm, wiggle, recoil in agony, flail.

writing *n.* **1.** HANDWRITING penmanship, longhand, calligraphy, printing, print. **2.** COMPOSITION work, publication, prose, fiction, novel, short story, poem, poetry, belles-lettres, nonfiction, letters, correspondence, article, editorial. "All writing is a process of elimination."—Martha Albrand. "The art of applying the seat of the pants to the seat of the chair."—Mary Vorse. "The art of torturing a blank sheet of paper and vice versa."—Mary McCutcheon.

wrong *n.* wrongdoing, sin, crime, offense, misdeed, injustice, evil, insult, wicked act, inequity, infraction, mistake, blunder, oversight.

wrong *v.* hurt, injure, insult, offend, commit a crime against, sin against, abuse, mistreat, exploit, use, aggrieve, transgress; malign, dishonor, defame, slur.

wrong *a.* **1.** INCORRECT inaccurate, imprecise, faulty, erroneous, false, mistaken, untrue, off, amiss, erring, unsound, *wide of the mark, *off base, *barking up the wrong tree, *all wet. **2.** IMMORAL bad, improper, unethical, sinful, illegal, criminal, corrupt, dishonest, crooked, wicked, naughty, felonious, dishonorable, reprehensible. **3.** INAPPROPRIATE unsuitable, inapt, improper, unfitting, unseemly, unbecoming, malapropos. **4.** OUT OF ORDER amiss, awry, out of kilter, *out of whack, *haywire. **5.** REVERSE back. ANT. *1. correct, accurate, exact, precise. 2. good, virtuous, righteous, moral. 3. appropriate, apropos, suitable.*

wrongdoer *n.* sinner, criminal, felon, offender, evildoer, perpetrator, miscreant, malefactor, transgressor, culprit, trespasser, *bad guy.

wrought *a.* formed, shaped, fashioned, made, built, constructed, crafted.

wry *a.* **1.** TWISTED distorted, turned to one side, lopsided, crooked, awry, askew. **2.** IRONIC distorted, sarcastic, sardonic, mocking, twisted, perverted. ANT. *1. straight.*

X

X-ray *n.* roentgenogram, roentgenograph, radiograph, radiogram, fluoroscope.

Y

yacht *n.* boat, cruiser, cabin cruiser, pleasure craft, vessel. SEE BOAT, SAILING

yahoo *n.* brute, *blithering idiot, barbarian, savage, Neanderthal, *redneck, *clod, *clodhopper, *dumb ox, *farmer, *jughead, hick, yokel, lummox, *nitwit, *brush ape, *Clem, hillbilly, *hayseed, *nose-picker, *party animal.

yak *v.* talk, chatter, gab, yap, babble, run on, jabber, prattle, blather, *blah blah blah.

yammer *v.* whine, complain, whimper, moan, gripe, grumble.

yank *n.* jerk, pull, tug, plucking, wrenching, extraction, grab.

yank *v.* jerk, pull, tug, pluck, wrench, extract, grab.

yard *n.* lawn, property, grounds, lot, plot, court, courtyard, gardens, patio, quad, garth, enclosure, compound.

yardstick *n.* measuring rod, measure, standard, test, gauge, guide, guideline, touchstone, benchmark, criterion.

yarn *n.* story, tale, fairy tale, fable, narrative, fiction, *fish story, adventure, myth, legend.

yaw *v.* swing, pitch, swerve, roll, veer, deviate, wheel, go off course.

yearn *v.* desire, long for, want, crave, hunger for, thirst for, pine for, hanker for, ache for, wish.

yearning *n.* desire, longing, want, need, craving, hunger, thirst, hankering, ache, wish, *yen, fancy.

years *n.* decades, generation, lifetime, centuries, millenium, eon, period, age, epoch.

yell *n.* shout, *holler, bellow, roar, thundering, howl, scream, shriek, bark, cry, whoop, yelp, hoot, *Stentorian bellow.

yell *v.* raise one's voice, shout, *holler, bellow, roar, thunder, howl, scream, shriek, bark, cry, whoop, yelp, hoot, cheer. ANT. *whisper, speak softly, murmur.*

yellow *a.* **1.** GOLDEN flaxen, straw, lemon, saffron, sunny, canary, amber, honey, butter. **2.** COWARDLY spineless, craven, fearful, *mousy, *wimpy, *lily-livered, *chicken, fainthearted, *afraid of one's own shadow. **2.** SENSATIONAL cheap, melodramatic, exaggerated, lurid, *keyhole-peeping. ANT. **2.** *brave, courageous, *gutsy.*

yelp *n.* cry, bark, yip, yap, squeal, howl, shout.

yelp *v.* cry, bark, yip, yap, squeal, howl, shout.

yen *n.* desire, longing, want, hunger, appetite, thirst, yearning, craving, hankering, urge, itch, passion. ANT. *aversion, revulsion.*

yes *adv.* yea, aye, *uh-huh, affirmative, *yeah, *yep, *ayuh, certainly, positively, doubtless, surely, *oui, *si, *da, *you bet. ANT. *no, nay, negative.*

yes man *n. Sl.* sycophant, toady, *brownnose, *kiss-up, *ass-kisser, *bootlicker, *apple-polisher, *ass-wiper, fawn, flatterer, underling, groveler, kowtower.

yield *n.* production, output, proceeds, harvest, crop, profit, return, gain, earnings.

yield *v.* **1.** PRODUCE furnish, generate, return, pay out, put out, give rise to, bear fruit. **2.** GIVE UP give in, surrender, back down, *cave in, submit, acquiesce, relinquish, accede, capitulate, *knuckle under, grant, concede. ANT. **2.** *resist, fight.*

yoga *n.* Hindu discipline, ascetic discipline, meditation, posturing.

WORD FIND

chant used during meditation: mantra
folded-legs position: lotus position
one who practices: yogi

yoke *n.* **1.** BOND harness, collar, coupling. **2.** BONDAGE servitude, subjection, enslavement.

yoke *v.* link, couple, bond, join, pair, unite, harness.

yokel *n.* country bumpkin, rustic, farmer, hick, hayseed, clodhopper, *Clem, *Okie, hillbilly, *sodbuster, yahoo, *one who just fell off the turnip truck.

yonder *a.* yon, faraway, away, beyond, distant, remote, further.

young *n.* children, offspring, litter, babies, progeny.

young *a.* immature, undeveloped, unfinished, growing, youthful, tender, fresh, newborn, infantile, fledgling, childish, juvenile, teenage, adolescent, pubescent, school-age, boyish, girlish, junior, new, untested, unpracticed, unseasoned, unhardened, inexperienced, naive. ANT. *mature, developed, old, experienced, adult, aged.*

youngster *n.* baby, infant, toddler, tot, child, boy, girl, schoolboy, schoolgirl, youth, kid, adolescent, teenager, minor.

youth *n.* **1.** CHILDHOOD infancy, preschool years, school years, young years, teens, adolescence, pubescence, puberty, minority, developing years. "Life's morning march." — Thomas Campbell. "The glad season of life." — Thomas Carlyle. "A feeling of eternity." — William Hazlitt. **2.** CHILD youngster, kid, boy, girl, teen, teenager, adolescent, minor, young man, young lady, juvenile, children, boys and girls, youngsters, teens, adolescents. ANT. *1. old age, adulthood, retirement years.*

youthful *a.* young, immature, unseasoned, growing, developing, fresh, new, maturing, juvenile, childish, rosy-cheeked, bright-eyed, full of life, vigorous, callow, naive, inexperienced, carefree. ANT. *old, aged, mature, experienced.*

yummy *a.* delicious, tasty, *scrumptious, mouth-watering, delectable, ambrosial, savory, good, heavenly, out of this world. ANT. *disgusting, nauseating, *gross.*

Z

zaftig *a. Sl.* full-figured, shapely, buxom, rounded, rotund.

zany *a.* foolish, crazy, silly, comical, ludicrous, *loony, hilarious, uproarious, *goofy, *nutty, slapstick, *madcap, funny.

ZEAL *n.* [ZEEL] great passion, enthusiasm. *His zeal for reform was contagious.* SYN. passion, enthusiasm, ardor, fervor, drive, fanaticism, zest, intensity, devotion, gusto, spirit, fire, earnestness. ANT. *indifference, apathy, disinterest.*

zealot *n.* fanatic, enthusiast, devotee, extremist, radical, *nut, champion, disciple, dogmatist, believer, crackpot.

ZEALOUS *a.* [ZEL us] enthusiastic, passionate. *He was a zealous supporter of gun control.* SYN. enthusiastic, passionate, devoted, fervent, fanatical, radical, eager, intense, rabid, impassioned, vehement, earnest, *gung-ho. ANT. *indifferent, apathetic, uncaring.*

Zen *n.* Buddhism, quest for enlightenment, meditation.

zenith *n.* high point, summit, pinnacle, top, peak, height, apex, acme, apogee, maximum, crown, culmination. ANT. *bottom, low point, nadir.*

zephyr *n.* gentle breeze, gentle wind, west wind.
SEE WIND

zeppelin *n.* dirigible, blimp.

zero *n.* nothing, naught, *goose egg, *zip, nothingness, *thin air, *zilch, blank, *nobody, nonentity.

zero hour *n.* crisis point, turning point, crossroads, pivotal moment, appointed hour, *D-day, climax, moment of truth, *crunch time.

zest *n.* **1.** FLAVOR relish, zing, piquancy, spice, zip, *pizzazz. **2.** GUSTO enjoyment, pleasure, *kick, spirit, liveliness, elation, excitement, eagerness. ANT. **2.** *boredom, apathy.*

zip *n.* **1.** HISS whiz, whistle, whine, hum. **2.** ENERGY vigor, *get-up-and-go, vitality, life, pep, strength, liveliness, drive, zest, spirit. **3.** *Sl.* NOTHING zero, *zilch.

zip *v.* speed, fly, zoom, rush, tear, bolt, dart, dash, hurry, jet.

zippy *a.* energetic, brisk, vigorous, full of life, lively, peppy.

zit *n. Sl.* pimple, pustule, papule, blemish.

zombie *n.* the living dead, walking dead, corpse, weirdo, oddball, *dope, dullard.

zone *n.* area, district, sector, section, region, quarter, tract, band, locality, territory, precinct, domain.

zonked *a. Sl.* drunk, intoxicated, inebriated, under the influence, high, *flying, *out of it, exhausted, unconscious.

zoo *n.* menagerie, animal park, animal conservation area, zoological garden, wildlife park.

zoom *v.* **1.** ZIP fly, shoot, rocket, whiz, speed, dive, streak, buzz, hum. **2.** RISE climb, skyrocket, surge.

More Great Books for Writers!

The Writer's Guide to Everyday Life in the Middle Ages — This time-travel companion will guide you through the medieval world of Northwestern Europe. Discover the facts on dining habits, clothing, armor, festivals, religious orders and much more — everything you need to paint an authentic picture of the time. *#10423/$17.99/256 pages*

Writing for Money — Discover where to look for writing opportunities — and how to make them pay off. You'll learn how to write for magazines, newspapers, radio and TV, newsletters, greeting cards and a dozen other hungry markets! *#10425/$17.99/256 pages*

Thesaurus of Alternatives to Worn Out Words and Phrases — Rid your work of trite clichés and hollow phrases for good! You'll learn how to vivify your work with alternative, lively and original words! *#10408/$17.99/304 pages*

Writing the Short Story — With Bickham's unique "workshop on paper" you'll plan, organize, write, revise and polish a short story. Clear instruction, helpful charts and practical exercises will lead you every step of the way! *#10421/$16.99/224 pages*

Writer's Digest Guide to Good Writing — Put the best advice and inspiration from the past 75 years of *Writer's Digest* magazine to work for you! You'll be inspired by authors like Vonnegut, Sinclair, Michener, Steinbeck, and over a dozen others! *#10391/$18.95/352 pages*

Beginning Writer's Answer Book — In this totally revised edition, you'll find what you need to know to get published — from how to generate great ideas, to the most up-to-date business advice and tax tips. *#10394/$16.99/336 pages*

Writing the Blockbuster Novel — You'll create the memorable characters, exotic settings, clashing conflicts and universal plots sure to make your novel a success. *#10393/$17.99/224 pages*

Magazine Writing That Sells — Discover the secrets to sensational queries, in-depth interviewing, reader-grabbing leads, solidly-written pieces and can't miss marketing strategies. *#10409/$16.95/240 pages*

20 Master Plots — Write great contemporary fiction from timeless plots. This guide outlines 20 plots from various genres and illustrates how to adapt them into your own fiction. *#10366/$17.99/240 pages*

The Writer's Digest Character Naming Sourcebook — Finally, you'll discover how to choose the perfect name to reflect your character's personality, ethnicity, and place in history. Here you'll find 20,000 first and last names (and their meanings) from around the world! *#10390/$18.95/352 pages*

Creating Characters — Learn how to build characters that jump off the page. In-depth instruction shows you how to infuse characters with emotion so powerful they will touch every reader. *#10417/$14.99/192 pages/paperback*

30 Steps to Becoming a Writer — This informational, inspirational guide helps you get started as a writer, develop your skills and style, and get your work ready for submission. *#10367/$16.99/176 pages*

Make Your Words Work — Loaded with samples and laced with exercises this guide will help you clean up your prose, refine your style, strengthen your descriptive powers, bring music to your words, and much more! *#10339/$14.95/304 pages/paperback*

Beginner's Guide to Getting Published — This comprehensive collection of articles will calm your worries, energize your work, and help you get published! You'll find in-depth, expertly written articles on idea generation, breaking into the business, moving up the ladder and much more! *#10418/$16.99/208 pages*

The Art & Craft of Novel Writing — With help from John Steinbeck, Joyce Carol Oates, Anton Chekhov, and many others, Hall shows you what works in novel writing and why. You'll gain inspiration along with instruction from this enlightening discussion of the elements of fiction. *#48002/$14.99/240 pages/paperback*

The Best Writing on Writing—This is the first in a series that will bring you the most provocative new articles, essays and lectures on fiction, nonfiction, poetry, playwriting, and the writing life. You'll enjoy this lively feast on the well-written word and how it is crafted. *#48001/$16.99/208 pages/paperback*

The Writer's Digest Guide to Manuscript Formats—Don't take chances with your hard work! Learn how to prepare and submit books, poems, scripts, stories and more with the professional look editors expect from a good writer. *#10025/$19.99/200 pages*

How To Write and Sell Children's Picture Books—If you yearn to put smiles on little faces, you need this charming guide. You'll discover how to put your picture book on paper and get it published—whether you're retelling a wonderful old tale, or spinning a splendid new yarn. *#10410/$16.95/192 pages*

Children's Writer's Word Book—Even the most original children's story won't get published if its language usage or sentence structure doesn't speak to young readers. You'll avoid these pitfalls with this fast-reference guide full of word lists, reading levels for synonyms, and more! *#10316/$19.99/352 pages*

The Craft of Writing Science Fiction That Sells—Discover how to fascinate audiences (and attract editors) with imaginative, well-told science fiction. *#10395/$16.95/224 pages*

The Writer's Complete Crime Reference Book—Now completely revised and updated! Incredible encyclopedia of hard-to-find facts about the ways of criminals and cops, prosecutors and defenders, victims and juries—everything the crime and mystery writer needs is at your fingertips. *#10371/$19.99/304 pages*

Police Procedural: A Writer's Guide to the Police and How They Work—Learn how police officers work, when they work, what they wear, who they report to, and how they go about controlling and investigating crime. *#10374/$16.99/272 pages/paperback*

Private Eyes: A Writer's Guide to Private Investigators—How do people become investigators? What procedures do they use? What tricks/tactics do they use? This guide gives you the "inside scoop" on the world of private eyes! *#10373/$15.99/208 pages/paperback*

Setting—Expert instruction on using sensual detail, vivid language and keen observation to help you create settings that provide the perfect backdrop to every story. *#10397/$14.99/176 pages*

Conflict, Action & Suspense—Discover how to grab your reader with an action packed beginning, build the suspense throughout your story, and bring it all to a fever pitch through powerful, gripping conflict. *#10396/$14.99/176 pages*

The Writer's Guide to Everyday Life in the 1800s—From clothes to food, social customs to furnishings, you'll find everything you need to write an accurate story about this century. Plus, the entries are dated so you don't invent something before its creation. *#10353/$18.99/320 pages*